# Everything

## Travel

# Dreams Become Reality
# With AAA Travel

EXPLORE THE MOUNTAINS, THE DESERTS, AND THE
CITIES - ANYWHERE, ANYTIME - WITH AAA,
THE MOST TRUSTED NAME IN TRAVEL.®
LET AAA TRAVEL TAKE CARE OF ALL YOUR TRAVEL NEEDS.
TO RECEIVE EXCLUSIVE AAA MEMBER BENEFITS, CALL
OR VISIT YOUR NEAREST AAA TRAVEL OFFICE, OR CLICK ON
www.aaa.com TODAY.

**AAA** Travel

*Travel With Someone You Trust.®*
www.aaa.com

# Maine, New Hampshire & Vermont

Are we meeting your travel needs?

Send written comments to:

AAA Member Comments
1000 AAA Drive, Box 61
Heathrow, FL 32746-5063

**Published by:**
AAA Publishing
1000 AAA Drive
Heathrow, FL 32746-5063
Copyright AAA 2004

**Advertising Rate and Circulation Information**
Call: (407) 444-8280

Printed in the USA by
Quebecor World, Buffalo, NY

*Photo Credit: (Cover & Title Page)*
*Portland Head Light, Cape Elizabeth*
*© Owaki - Kulla*
*Corbis*

 Printed on recyclable paper.
Please recycle whenever possible.

Stock #4615

# Maine,
# New Hampshire
# & Vermont

# ■ *Vermont*

## *Featured Information*

4

ALL I WANT IS...

a picture perfect moment and a real deal.

With 10% off our rates, isn't it time you got away? At Hampton's 1,100 locations, AAA members get 10% off the best available rates* when you book with your AAA card. Breakfast is complimentary and we give you both Hilton HHonors® points and airline miles. We'll make sure you feel 100% satisfied. Guaranteed. Call Hampton® at 1-800-456-7793 or visit hamptoninn.com.

The Hilton Family

*Rates vary by location. Black-out dates may apply. Hilton HHonors membership, earning of Points & Miles® and redemption of points are subject to HHonors Terms and Conditions. ©2003 Hilton Hospitality, Inc.

WE LOVE HAVING YOU HERE.™

When planning your next trip, check out the many time saving tools and member saving benefits on www.aaa.com to make your travels fun, easy and affordable. Highlights include:

**Internet TripTik®/Traveler.** Ranked #1 by the *Wall Street Journal*, ITT provides sightseeing and dining recommendations, online hotel reservations at great rates and, of course, AAA's famous maps, driving directions and custom routes!

**Online TourBook®.** Reserve rooms at great rates PLUS get AAA Diamond ratings for lodgings and restaurants and insider tips on attractions and local events!

**AAA Drive Trips.** Over 50 driving tours nationwide with precise directions and candid area overviews*

**Vacation Getaways.** Take to the skies, hit the high seas or select a tour and receive exclusive benefits from AAA's Preferred Travel Partners.

**Travel Accessories.** Order luggage, car games for the kids, accessories, and more to make travel easy.

**Travel Guides.** Get a 5% discount on AAA's famed travel guides and learn your destination inside out.

**Disney® Vacations.** Get exclusive benefits and savings on AAA Vacations® Disney vacation packages.

**Hertz Rental.** Up to 20 % discount from AAA's Exclusive Car Rental Partner.

**Show Your Card & Save.** Search for savings on lodging, travel, entertainment, retail, and e-Merchants in the database.

**AAA Travel Money.** Get no-fee travelers cheques, foreign currency and prepaid cards.

**AAA Map Gallery*.** Know the best way to go wherever you travel.

**Cash Back.** Get a 5% rebate every time you use your AAA credit card to gas up.

**AAA Approved Auto Repair.** Enter your zip code to get your car road-trip ready at the nearest AAR shop.

Click on www.aaa.com for numerous products and services that will make your next trip easy to plan, more enjoyable and full of value. **Travel to www.aaa.com TODAY for all your vacation planning needs!**

**www.aaa.com**

*Travel With Someone You Trust®*

Products and Services available through participating AAA and CAA Clubs.

8

# Drive
# See
# Stay
# Play

## DO IT ALL WITH AAA!

*Vacation planning, travel and destination information, AAA's famous maps and TripTiks®, TourBook® guides, air, cruise, tour, rail, and hotel reservations, attraction tickets and more! It's all part of the service for AAA members! Choose whatever method fits you best — online, in person, or by phone — to enjoy helpful services like these:*

- Online TourBook® guide featuring hotel information AAA Diamond ratings.
- Internet TripTik®/Traveler itinerary planner rated No. 1 by the *Wall Street Journal*.
- Travel accessories such as luggage, travel guides, car games for the kids, and more.

- Ready-to-go, 2- to 5-day AAA Drive Trips vacation* for major U.S. and Canadian travel destinations.
- Flights, cruises and tours and expert advice from AAA Travel professionals.
- AAA Travel money options including no fee Travelers Cheques.
- AAA Credit Cards featuring a 5% gas rebate.

With AAA's expert travel information and pricing power behind you, you'll enjoy better quality and value than you'll find anywhere else. And, with AAA's extensive range of products and services, you'll enjoy complete, hassle-free vacation planning from a single source you know and trust.

**Before your next vacation, visit www.aaa.com or your nearest AAA office. Discover the many ways AAA can help you drive more, see more, stay more and play more!**

*TRAVEL WITH SOMEONE YOU TRUST*®

**www.aaa.com**

*PRODUCTS AND SERVICES AVAILABLE THROUGH PARTICIPATING AAA AND CAA CLUBS.

# Trust
the AAA TourBook® guide for objective travel information. Follow the pages of the TourBook Navigator to thoroughly understand this unique member benefit.

## Making Your Way Through the AAA Listings

Attractions, lodgings and restaurants are listed on the basis of merit alone after careful evaluation, approval and rating by one of our full-time, professionally trained Tourism Editors. Annual evaluations are unannounced to ensure that our Tourism Editors see an establishment just as our members would see it.

Those lodgings and restaurants listed with an [fyi] icon have not gone through the same evaluation process as other rated properties. Individual listings will typically denote the reason why this icon appears. Bulleted recreational activity listings are not inspected but are included for member information.

An establishment's decision to advertise in the TourBook guide has no bearing on its evaluation or rating. Advertising for services or products does not imply AAA endorsement.

## How the TourBook is
# Organized

Geographic listing is used for accuracy and consistency. This means attractions, lodgings and restaurants are listed under the city in which they physically are located—or in some cases under the nearest recognized city. The Comprehensive City Index located in the back of the book contains an A-to-Z list of cities. Most listings are alphabetically organized by state, province, region or island; city; and establishment name. A color is assigned to each state or province so that you can match the color bars at the top of the page to switch from ❶ Points of Interest to ❷ Lodgings and Restaurants.

## Destination Cities and Destination Areas

The TourBook guide also groups information by destination city and destination area. If a city is grouped in a destination vicinity section, the city name will appear at its alphabetical location in the book, and a handy cross reference will give the exact page on which listings for that city begin. Maps are placed at the beginning of these sections to orient you to the destinations.

❸ **Destination cities,** established based on government models and local expertise, are comprised of metropolitan areas plus nearby vicinity cities.

**Destination areas** are regions with broad tourist appeal. Several cities will comprise the area.

---

**All information in this TourBook guide was reviewed for accuracy before publication. However, since changes inevitably occur between annual editions, we suggest you contact establishments directly to confirm prices and schedules.**

# Points of Interest Section

### Orientation maps

near the start of each Attractions section show only those places we call points of interest. Coordinates included with the city listings depict the locations of those cities on the map. A GEM symbol (♥) accents towns with "must see" points of interest which offer a *Great Experience for Members ®*. And the black ovals with white numerals (**22** for example) locate items listed in the nearby Recreation Areas chart.

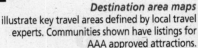

### Destination area maps

illustrate key travel areas defined by local travel experts. Communities shown have listings for AAA approved attractions.

### National park maps

represent the area in and around the park. Some campground sites and lodges spotted on the maps do not meet AAA/CAA criteria, but are shown for members who nevertheless wish to stay close to the park area.

### Walking or self-guiding tour maps

correspond to specific routes described in TourBook guide text.

### City maps

show areas where numerous points of interest are concentrated and indicate their location in relation to major roads, parks, airports and other landmarks.

# Lodgings & Restaurants Section

**Destination area maps**
illustrate key travel areas defined by
local travel experts. Communities
shown have listings for AAA-RATED®
lodgings and/or restaurants.

**Spotting maps**
show the location of lodgings and
restaurants. Lodgings are spotted with
a black background (**22** for example);
restaurants are spotted with a white
background (**23** for example). Spotting map indexes have
been placed immediately after each map to provide the user
with a convenient method to identify what an area has to
offer at a glance. The index references the map page number
where the property is spotted, indicates if a property is an
Official Appointment and contains an advertising reference
if applicable. It also lists the property's diamond rating, high
season rate range and listing page number.

**Downtown/city spotting maps**
are provided when spotted facilities are very concentrated.
GEM points of interest also appear on these maps.

**Vicinity spotting maps**
spot those properties that are outside the downtown or city area. Major
roads, landmarks, airports and GEM points of interest are shown on vicinity
spotting maps as well. The names of suburban communities that have
AAA-RATED® accommodations are
shown in magenta type.

# Featured Information Section

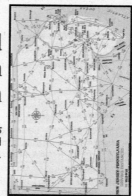

**Driving distance maps**
are intended to be used only for trip-distance and
driving-time planning.

# Sample Attraction Listing

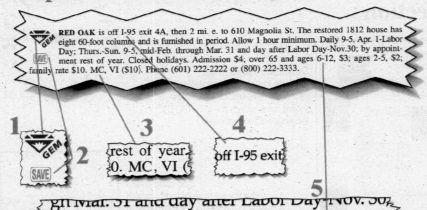

**RED OAK** is off I-95 exit 4A, then 2 mi. e. to 610 Magnolia St. The restored 1812 house has eight 60-foot columns and is furnished in period. Allow 1 hour minimum. Daily 9-5, Apr. 1-Labor Day; Thurs.-Sun. 9-5, mid-Feb. through Mar. 31 and day after Labor Day-Nov.30; by appointment rest of year. Closed holidays. Admission $4; over 65 and ages 6-12, $3; ages 2-5, $2; family rate $10. MC, VI ($10). Phone (601) 222-2222 or (800) 222-3333.

**1** — rest of year. 0. MC, VI (

**4** — off I-95 exit

**5** — Admission $4; over 65 and ages 6-12, $3; a

**1** This attraction is of exceptional interest and quality and therefore has been designated a AAA GEM—offering a *Great Experience for Members* ®.

**2** Participating attractions offer AAA/CAA, AAA MasterCard or AAA Visa cardholders a discount off the attraction's standard admission; members should inquire in advance concerning the validity of the discount for special rates. Present your card at the admission desk. A list of participating points of interest appears in the Indexes section of the book. The SAVE discount may not be used in conjunction with other discounts. Attractions that already provide a reduced senior or child rate may not honor the SAVE discount for those age groups. All offers are subject to change and may not apply during special events, particular days or seasons or for the entire validity period of the TourBook. Shopping establishments preceded by a SAVE icon also provide discounts and/or gift with purchase to AAA/CAA members; present your card at the mall's customer service center to receive your benefit.

**3**
| | | |
|---|---|---|
| AX = American Express | DS = Discover | MC = MasterCard |
| CB = Carte Blanche | JC = Japan Credit Bureau | VI = VISA |
| DC = Diners Club | | |

Minimum amounts that may be charged appear in parentheses when applicable.

**4** Unless otherwise specified, directions are given from the center of town, using the following highway designations: I (interstate highway), US (federal highway), Hwy. (Canadian or Caribbean highway), SR (state route), CR (county road), FM (farm to market road), FR (forest road), MM (mile marker), Mex. (Mexican highway).

**5** Admission prices are quoted without sales tax. Children under the lowest age specified are admitted free when accompanied by an adult. Days, months and age groups written with a hyphen are inclusive. Prices pertaining to points of interest in the United States are quoted in U.S. dollars; prices for Canadian province and territory points of interest are quoted in Canadian dollars; prices for points of interest in Mexico and the Caribbean are quoted as an approximate U.S. dollar equivalent.

**Bulleted Listings**: Casino gambling establishments are visited by AAA personnel to ensure safety; casinos within hotels are presented for member information regardless of whether the lodging is AAA approved. Recreational activities of a participatory nature (requiring physical exertion or special skills) are not inspected. Wineries are inspected by AAA Tourism Editors to ensure they meet listing requirements and offer tours. All are presented in a bulleted format for informational purposes.

These Show Your Card & Save® partners provide the listed member benefits. Admission tickets that offer greater discounts may be available for purchase at the local AAA/CAA club. A maximum of six tickets is available at the discount price.

# Attraction Partners

## SeaWorld/Busch Gardens

- SAVE Save $4 at SeaWorld and Busch Gardens
- SAVE Save $3 at Sesame Place, Water Country USA and Adventure Island
- SAVE Save 10% on select up-close dining. Reservations are required; visit Guest Relations for details

## Six Flags Theme Parks

- SAVE Save $4 on general admission at the gate
- SAVE Save $12 on general admission at the gate each Wednesday
- SAVE Save 10% on selected souvenirs and dining (check at main gate for details)

## Universal Orlando (www.aaa.com/Universal)

- SAVE Save $4 on a 2-day/2-park pass or $5 on a 3-day/2-park pass at Universal Orlando's theme parks (savings apply to tickets purchased at the gate)
- SAVE Save 10% on select dining and souvenirs at both Universal Orlando theme parks and at select Universal CityWalk Orlando restaurants (except Emeril's)

## Universal Studios Hollywood

- SAVE Save $3 on a 1-day Universal Hollywood pass (savings applies to tickets purchased at the gate)
- SAVE Save 10% on select dining and souvenirs at Universal Studios Hollywood and Universal CityWalk

## Gray Line

- SAVE Save 10% on sightseeing tours of 1 day or less

# Restaurant Partners

## Landry's Seafood House, The Crab House, Chart House, Muer Seafood Restaurants, Joe's Crab Shack

- SAVE Save 10% on food and non-alcoholic beverages at Landry's Seafood House, The Crab House, Chart House, Muer Seafood Restaurants and Joe's Crab Shack and 10% on merchandise at Joe's Crab Shack. Savings applicable to AAA/CAA members and up to six people

## Hard Rock Cafe

- SAVE Save 10% on food, beverage, and merchandise at all U.S., Canada, and select international locations. Members also save 10% at The Hard Rock Vault.

# Mexican Partners

- SAVE An alliance between AAA/CAA and AMA (Mexican Automobile Association) provides members visiting Mexico savings from Mexicana Airlines, Tony Roma restaurants and Six Flags of Mexico

---

**Visit aaa.com to discover all the great Show Your Card & Save® discounts in your area.**

# Sample Lodging Listing

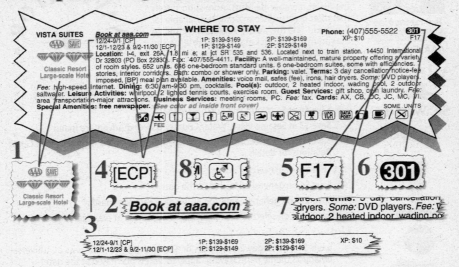

## 1

**⊕⊕** or **⊕⊕** indicates our Official Appointment (OA) lodgings. The OA program permits properties to display and advertise the **⊕⊕** or **⊕⊕** emblem. We highlight these properties with red diamonds and classification. Some OA listings include special amenities such as free continental breakfast; expanded continental breakfast or full breakfast; early check-in/late check-out; free room upgrade or preferred room, such as ocean view or poolside (subject to availability); free local phone calls; and free daily newspaper. This does not imply that only these properties offer these amenities. The **⊕⊕** or **⊕⊕** sign helps traveling members find accommodations that want member business.

**▼▼▼** or **▼▼▼▼** The number of diamonds—not the color—informs you of the overall level of quality in a lodging's amenities and service. More diamond details appear on page 16.

Classic Resort Large-scale Hotel or Classic Resort Large-scale Hotel: All diamond rated lodgings are classified using three key elements: style of operation, overall concept and service level. See pages 22-23 for details about our Lodging Classifications and Subclassifications.

## Member Values

**SAVE** Official Appointment properties guarantee members a minimum 10% discount off the standard room rates published in TourBook guides or the lowest public rate available at the time of booking for the dates of stay, for standard rooms.

**S/D** Establishments offer a minimum senior discount of 10% off the listed rates. This discount is available to members 60 or older.

**ASK** Many properties offer discounts to members even though the lodgings do not participate in a formal discount program. The **ASK** is another reminder to inquire about available discounts when making your reservations or at check-in.

Discounts normally offered at some lodgings may not apply during special events or holiday periods. Special rates and discounts may not apply to all room types. Some Member Values may not apply in Mexico or the Caribbean.

To obtain published rates or discounts, you must identify yourself as a AAA or CAA member, request AAA rates when making reservations and have written confirmation sent to you. The SAVE or senior discount may not be used in conjunction with other discounts. At registration, show your membership card and verify the room rate.

Discounts normally offered at some lodgings may not apply during special events or holiday periods. Special rates and discounts may not apply to all room types. Some Member Values may not apply in Mexico or the Caribbean.

The rates listed for approved properties are provided to AAA by each lodging and represent the regular (rack) rate for a standard room. Printed rates, based on rack rates and last room availability, are rounded to the nearest dollar. Rates do not include taxes and discounts. U.S., Mexican and Caribbean rates are in U.S. dollars; rates for Canadian lodgings are in Canadian dollars.

## 2  Book at aaa.com - Internet Reservations
Indicates AAA/CAA members can conveniently check room availability and make reservations in a secure online environment at aaa.com.

## 3  Rate Lines
Shown from left to right: dates the rates are effective; meal plan provided with rates (see Meal Plan Indicators-if no plan noted, rate includes room only); rates for 1 person or 2 persons; extra person charge (XP); and any applicable family plan indicator.

### Rates Guaranteed
AAA/CAA members are guaranteed that they will not be charged more than the maximum regular rate printed in each rate range for a standard room. Rates may vary within the range depending on season and room type. Listed rates are based on last standard room availability. Rates for properties operating as concessionaires for the U.S. National Park Service are not guaranteed due to governing regulations. Rates in the Mexico TourBook are not guaranteed and may fluctuate based on the exchange rate of the peso.

### Exceptions
Lodgings may temporarily increase room rates, not recognize discounts or modify pricing policies during special events. Examples of special events range from Mardi Gras and Kentucky Derby (including pre-Derby events) to college football games, holidays, holiday periods and state fairs. Although some special events are listed in AAA/CAA TourBook guides, it is always wise to check, in advance, with AAA travel professionals for specific dates.

### Discounts
Member discounts will apply to rates quoted, within the rate range, applicable at the time of booking. Special rates used in advertising, and special short-term, promotional rates lower than the lowest listed rate in the range, are not subject to additional member discounts.

## 4  Meal Plan Indicators
The following types of meal plans may be available in the listed room rate:
AP = American Plan of three meals daily
BP = Breakfast Plan of full hot breakfast
CP = Continental Plan of pastry, juice and another beverage
ECP = Expanded Continental Plan, which offers a wider variety of breakfast items
MAP = Modified American Plan of two meals daily
See individual listing "Terms" section for additional meal plans that are not included in the room rate.

Check-in times are shown in the listing only if they are after 3 p.m.; check-out times are shown only if they are before 10 a.m.

## 5  Family Plan Indicators
F = Children stay free
D = Discounts for children
F17 = Children 17 and under stay free (age displayed will reflect property's policy)
D17 = Discount for children 17 and under

## 6  Lodging Locators
Black ovals with white numbers are used to locate, or "spot," lodgings on maps we provide for larger cities.

## 7  Unit Types
Unit types, amenities and room features preceded by the word "Some" indicate the item is available on a limited basis, potentially within only one unit.

## 8  Lodging Icons
A row of icons is included with each lodging listing. These icons represent the member values, member services, and facilities offered by that lodging. See page 19 for an explanation of each icon.

# The Lodging Diamond Ratings

AAA Tourism Editors evaluate and rate each lodging based on the overall quality, the range of facilities and the level of services offered by a property. The size, age and overall appeal of an establishment are considered as well as regional architectural style and design.

While guest services are an important part of all diamond ratings, they are particularly critical at the four and five diamond levels. A property must provide a high level of service, on a consistent basis, to obtain and support the four and five diamond rating.

These establishments typically appeal to the budget-minded traveler. They provide essential, no-frills accommodations. They meet the basic requirements pertaining to comfort, cleanliness, and hospitality.

These establishments appeal to the traveler seeking more than the basic accommodations. There are modest enhancements to the overall physical attributes, design elements, and amenities of the facility typically at a modest price.

These establishments appeal to the traveler with comprehensive needs. Properties are multifaceted with a distinguished style, including marked upgrades in the quality of physical attributes, amenities and level of comfort provided.

These establishments are upscale in all areas. Accommodations are progressively more refined and stylish. The physical attributes reflect an obvious enhanced level of quality throughout. The fundamental hallmarks at this level include an extensive array of amenities combined with a high degree of hospitality, service, and attention to detail.

These establishments reflect the characteristics of the ultimate in luxury and sophistication. Accommodations are first-class. The physical attributes are extraordinary in every manner. The fundamental hallmarks at this level are to meticulously serve and exceed all guest expectations while maintaining an impeccable standard of excellence. Many personalized services and amenities enhance an unmatched level of comfort.

The lodging listings with **fyi** in place of diamonds are included as an "information only" service for members. The icon indicates that a property has not been rated for one or more of the following reasons: too new to rate; under construction; under major renovation; not evaluated; or may not meet all AAA requirements. Those properties not meeting all AAA requirements are included for either their member value or because it may be the only accommodation available in the area. Listing prose will give insight as to why the **fyi** designation was assigned.

# Guest Safety

### Room Security

In order to be approved for listing in AAA/CAA TourBook guides for the United States and Canada, all lodgings must comply with AAA's guest room security requirements.

In response to AAA/CAA members' concern about their safety at properties, AAA-RATED® accommodations must have dead-bolt locks on all guest room entry doors and connecting room doors.

If the area outside the guest room door is not visible from inside the room through a window or door panel, viewports must be installed on all guest room entry doors. Bed and breakfast properties and country inns are not required to have viewports. Ground floor and easily accessible sliding doors must be equipped with some other type of secondary security locks.

Tourism Editors view a percentage of rooms at each property since it is not feasible to evaluate every room in every lodging establishment. Therefore, AAA cannot guarantee that there are working locks on all doors and windows in all guest rooms.

### Fire Safety

Because of the highly specialized skills needed to conduct professional fire safety inspections, AAA/CAA Tourism Editors cannot assess fire safety.

Properties must meet all federal, state and local fire codes. Each guest unit in all U.S. and Canadian lodging properties must be equipped with an operational, single-station smoke detector. A AAA/CAA Tourism Editor has evaluated a sampling of the rooms to verify this equipment is in place.

**For additional fire safety information, read the page posted on the back of your guest room door, or write:**

**National Fire Protection Association**
**1 Batterymarch Park**
**P.O. Box 9101**
**Quincy, MA 02269-9101**

Requirements for some features, such as door locks and smoke detectors/sprinkler systems, differ in Mexico and the Caribbean. If a property met AAA's security requirements at the time of the evaluation, the phrase "Meets AAA guest room security requirements" appears in the listing.

# Access for Mature Travelers and Travelers with Disabilities

Qualified properties listed in this guide are shown with symbols indicating they meet the needs of the hearing-impaired or offer some accessible features for mature travelers or travelers with disabilities.

##  Hearing Impaired

Indicates a property has the following equipment available for hearing-impaired travelers: TDD at front desk or switchboard; visual notification of fire alarm, incoming telephone calls, door knock or bell; closed caption decoder; text telephone or TDD for guest room use; telephone amplification device, with shelf or electric outlet next to guest room telephone.

##  Accessible Features

Indicates a property has some accessible features meeting the needs of mature travelers and travelers with disabilities. Lodging establishments will provide at least one guest room meeting the designated criteria as well as accessible restrooms and parking facilities. Restaurants provide accessible parking, dining rooms and restrooms.

AAA/CAA strongly urges members to call the property directly to fully understand the property's exact accessibility features. Some properties do not fully comply with AAA/CAA's exacting accessibility standards but may offer some design standards that meet the needs of some guests with disabilities.

AAA/CAA does not evaluate recreational facilities, banquet rooms, or convention or meeting facilities for accessibility.

## Service Animals

No fees or deposits, even those normally charged for pets, may be charged for service animals. Service animals fulfill a critical need for their owners—they are *not* pets.

The Americans With Disabilities Act (ADA) prohibits U.S. businesses that serve the public from discriminating against persons with disabilities. Some businesses have mistakenly denied access to persons who use service animals. ADA, a federal mandate, has priority over all state and local laws, as well as a business owner's standard of business, which might bar animals from the premises. Businesses must permit entry to guests and their service animals, as well as allow service animals to accompany guests to all public areas of a property. A property is permitted to ask whether the animal is a service animal or a pet, and whether the guest has a disability. The property may not, however, ask questions about the nature of the disability, the service provided by the animal or require proof of a disability or certification that the animal is a service animal.

**Note:** These regulations may not apply in Canada, Mexico or the Caribbean.

# What The Lodging Icons Mean

*NAVIGATOR · Lodgings*

## Member Values
*(see p. 14)*

**AAA** or **AAA** Official Appointment

**SAVE** Offers minimum 10% discount or lowest public rate *(see p. 14)*

**ASK** May offer discount

**S/D** Offers senior discount

**fyi** Informational listing only

## Member Services

**✈** Airport transportation

**🐕** Pets allowed

**⫟** Restaurant on premises

**⫟+** Restaurant off premises (walking distance)

**24⫟** 24-hour room service

**Y** Cocktail lounge

**fi** Child care

## Accessibility Feature
*(see p. 18)*

**&M** Accessible features

**♿** Roll-in showers

**🔊** Hearing impaired

## Safety Features
*(Mexico and Caribbean only)*

**S** Sprinklers

**D** Smoke detectors

## Leisure Activities

**🎲** Full service casino

**≈** Pool

**💪** Health club on premises

**💪** Health club off premises

**⊗** Recreational activities

## In-Room Amenities

**⊠** Designated non-smoking rooms

**A/C** No air conditioning

**TV** No TV

**CTV** No cable TV

**VCR** VCR

**🎥** Movies

**DATA PORT** Data port/modem line

**☎** No telephones

**🔲** Refrigerator

**🔲** Microwave

**🔲** Coffee maker

# Availability and Additional Fees

If an in-room amenity is available only on a limited basis (in one or more rooms), the term "SOME UNITS" will appear above those icons. Fees may be charged for some of the services represented by the icons listed here. The word "FEE" will appear below each icon when an extra charge applies.

SOME UNITS

**&M** **🔊** **VCR** **🎥** **🔲** / **⊠** **DATA PORT** **🔲** /
          FEE   FEE                                              FEE

# Preferred Lodging Partners

**Show Your Card & Save**

**AAA. Every Day.**

**SAVINGS. SELECTION. SATISFACTION.** — When contacting one of the partners listed, you will be given AAA's best rates for your dates of stay. Your valid membership card must be presented at check-in.

**SATISFACTION GUARANTEE** — If you are not satisfied with any part of your stay, you must provide the property the opportunity to correct the situation during your stay. If the matter cannot be resolved, you will be entitled to recompense for a portion of, or your entire, stay. Satisfaction guarantee varies by chain.

**Select the chain you want and have your membership card available when making a reservation and checking in.**

| **Visit** Over 1,100 AAA Offices | **Click** aaa.com | **Call** 866-AAA-SAVE |

# Making Reservations

When making reservations, you must identify yourself as a AAA or CAA member. Give all pertinent information about your planned stay. Ask about the lodging's pet policy, or the availability of any other special feature that is important to your stay. Request written confirmation to guarantee: type of room, rate, dates of stay, and cancellation and refund policies. At registration, show your membership card. Note: Age restrictions may apply.

## Confirm Deposit, Refund and Cancellation Policies

Most establishments give full deposit refunds if they have been notified at least 48 hours before the normal check-in time. Listing prose will note if more than 48 hours notice is required for cancellation. However, when making reservations, confirm the property's deposit, cancellation and refund policies. Some properties may charge a cancellation or handling fee.

When this applies, "cancellation fee imposed" will appear in the listing. If you cancel too late, you have little recourse if a refund is denied.

When an establishment requires a full or partial payment in advance, and your trip is cut short, a refund may not be given.

When canceling reservations, phone the lodging immediately. Make a note of the date and time you called, the cancellation number if there is one, and the name of the person who handled the cancellation. If your AAA/CAA club made your reservation, allow them to make the cancellation for you as well so you will have proof of cancellation.

## Review Charges for Appropriate Rates

When you are charged more than the maximum rate listed in the TourBook guide for a standard room, question the additional charge. If management refuses to adhere to the published rate, pay for the room and submit your receipt and membership number to AAA/CAA within 30 days. Include all pertinent information: dates of stay, rate paid, itemized paid receipts, number of persons in your party, the room number you occupied, and list any extra room equipment used. A refund of the amount paid in excess of the stated maximum will be made if our investigation indicates that unjustified charging has occurred.

## Get the Room You Reserved

When you find your room is not as specified, and you have written confirmation of reservations for a certain type of accommodation, you should be given the option of choosing a different room or finding one elsewhere. Should you choose to go elsewhere and a refund is refused or resisted, submit the matter to AAA/CAA within 30 days along with complete documentation, including your reasons for refusing the room and copies of your written confirmation and any receipts or canceled checks associated with this problem.

## How to Get the Best Room Rates

You'll find the best room rate if you book your reservation in advance with the help of a travel professional or agent at your local AAA/CAA office.

If you're not yet ready to make firm vacation plans or if you prefer a more spontaneous trip, take advantage of the partnerships that preferred hotel chains have arranged with AAA. Phone the toll-free number 866-AAA-SAVE that has been set up exclusively for members for the purpose of reserving with these Show Your Card & Save® chain partners.

Even if you were unable to make a reservation, be sure to show your membership card at the desk and ask if you're being offered the lowest rate available for that time. Many lodgings offer reduced rates to members.

# Lodging Classifications

To ensure that your lodging needs/preferences are met, we recommend that you consider an establishment's classification when making your travel choices.

While the quality and comfort at properties with the same diamond rating should be consistent (regardless of the classification), there are differences in typical décor/theme elements, range of facilities and service levels. Please see the descriptions below.

### Large-scale Hotel

A multistory establishment with interior room entrances. A variety of guest unit styles is offered. Public areas are spacious and include a variety of facilities such as a restaurant, shops, fitness center, spa, business center, or meeting rooms.

Hotel Royal Plaza, Lake Buena Vista, FL

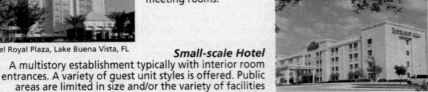

### Small-scale Hotel

A multistory establishment typically with interior room entrances. A variety of guest unit styles is offered. Public areas are limited in size and/or the variety of facilities available.

Baymont Inn, Dallas/Ft. Worth-Airport North, TX

### Motel

A one- to three-story establishment typically with exterior room entrances facilitating convenient access to parking. The standard guest units have one bedroom with a bathroom and are typically similar in décor and design throughout. Public areas are limited in size and/or the variety of facilities available.

Best Western Deltona Inn, Deltona, FL

### Country Inn

Similar in definition to a bed and breakfast, but usually larger in scale with spacious public areas and offers a dining facility that serves at least breakfast and dinner.

Greenville Inn, Greenville, ME

### Bed & Breakfast

Small-scale properties emphasizing a high degree of personal touches that provide guests an "at home" feeling. Guest units tend to be individually decorated. Rooms may not include some modern amenities such as televisions and telephones, and may have a shared bathroom. Usually owner-operated with a common room or parlor separate from the innkeeper's living quarters, where guests and operators can interact during evening and breakfast hours.

1884 Paxton House Inn, Thomasville, GA

Evening office closures are normal. A continental or full, hot breakfast is served and is included in the room rate.

### Condominium

Vacation-oriented or extended-stay, apartment-style accommodations that are routinely available for rent through a management company. Units vary in design and décor and often contain one or more bedrooms, living room, full kitchen, and an eating area. Studio-type models combine the sleeping and living areas into one room. Typically, basic cleaning supplies, kitchen utensils and complete bed and bath linens are supplied. The guest registration area may be located off-site.

Sands of Kahana, Kahana, Maui, HI

Desert Rose Inn, Bluff, UT

### Cabin/Cottage

Vacation-oriented, small-scale, freestanding houses or cabins. Units vary in design and décor and often contain one or more bedrooms, living room, kitchen, dining area, and bathroom. Studio-type models combine the sleeping and living areas into one room. Typically, basic cleaning supplies, kitchen utensils, and complete bed and bath linens are supplied. The guest registration area may be located off-site.

C Lazy U Ranch, Granby, CO

### Ranch

Typically a working ranch with an obvious rustic, Western theme. In general, equestrian-related activities are featured, but ranches may include other animals and activities as well. A variety of guest unit styles is offered in a family-oriented atmosphere.

### Vacation Home

Vacation-oriented or extended-stay, large-scale, freestanding houses that are routinely available for rent through a management company. Houses vary in design and décor and often contain two or more bedrooms, living room, full kitchen, dining room, and multiple bathrooms. Typically, basic cleaning supplies, kitchen utensils, and complete bed and bath linens are supplied. The guest registration area may be located off-site.

ResortQuest, Hilton Head Island, SC

# Lodging Subclassifications

The following are subclassifications that may appear along with the classifications listed above to provide a more specific description of the lodging.

### Casino

Extensive gambling facilities are available such as blackjack, craps, keno, and slot machines. **Note:** This subclassification will not appear beneath its diamond rating in the listing. It will be indicated by a dice icon and will be included in the row of icons immediately below the lodging listing.

### Classic

Renowned and landmark properties, older than 50 years, well-known for their unique style and ambience.

### Historic

These properties are typically over 75 years of age and exhibit many features of a historic nature with respect to architecture, design, furnishings, public record, or acclaim. Properties must meet one of the following criteria:

- Maintained the integrity of the historical nature
- Listed on the U.S. National Register of Historic Places
- Designated a U.S. National Historic Landmark
- Located in a U.S. National Register Historic District

Separate criteria designate historic properties in Canada, Mexico and the Caribbean.

### Resort

Recreation-oriented, geared to vacation travelers seeking a specific destination experience. Travel packages, meal plans, theme entertainment, and social and recreational programs are typically available. Recreational facilities are extensive and may include spa treatments, golf, tennis, skiing, fishing, or water sports, etc. Larger resorts may offer a variety of guest accommodations.

# Sample Restaurant Listing

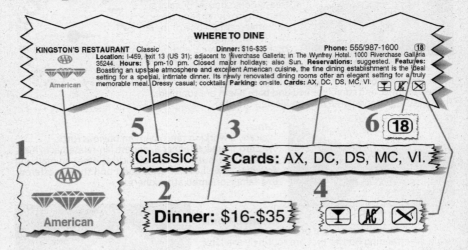

**WHERE TO DINE**

**KINGSTON'S RESTAURANT** Classic  **Dinner:** $16-$35  **Phone:** 555/987-1600 ⑱
**Location:** I-459, exit 13 (US 31); adjacent to Riverchase Galleria; in The Wynfrey Hotel. 1000 Riverchase Galleria 35244. **Hours:** 5 pm-10 pm. Closed major holidays; also Sun. **Reservations:** suggested. **Features:** Boasting an upscale atmosphere and excellent American cuisine, the fine dining establishment is the ideal setting for a special, intimate dinner. Its newly renovated dining rooms offer an elegant setting for a truly memorable meal. Dressy casual; cocktails. **Parking:** on-site. **Cards:** AX, DC, DS, MC, VI.

**5** Classic

**3** **Cards:** AX, DC, DS, MC, VI.

**6** ⑱

**2** **Dinner:** $16-$35

**1** American

**4**

---

**1** 🔺🔺🔺 or 🔺🔺 indicates our Official Appointment (OA) restaurants. The OA program permits properties to display and advertise the 🔺🔺🔺 or 🔺🔺 emblem. We highlight these properties with red diamonds and cuisine type. The 🔺🔺🔺 or 🔺🔺 sign helps traveling members find restaurants that want member business.

◆◆◆ or ◆◆◆◆◆ The number of diamonds—not the color—informs you of the overall level of quality for food and presentation, service and ambience. Menus for red Diamond restaurants can be viewed on <u>aaa.com.</u>

A cuisine type is assigned for each restaurant listing. AAA currently recognizes more than 90 different cuisine types.

**2** Prices represent the minimum and maximum entree cost per person. Exceptions may include one-of-a-kind or special market priced items.

**3** AX = American Express
CB = Carte Blanche  DS = Discover  MC = MasterCard
DC = Diners Club  JC = Japan Credit Bureau  VI = VISA

**4** These three icons are used in restaurant listings. When present, they indicate: the presence of a cocktail lounge, the lack of air conditioning, and/or that the restaurant has a designated non-smoking section or is entirely smoke-free.

**5** If applicable, restaurants may be further defined as:

**Classic**—renowned and landmark restaurant operations in business longer than 25 years, known for unique style and ambience.

**Historic**—properties must meet one of the following criteria:
- Listed on the U.S. National Register of Historic Places
- Designated a U.S. National Historic Landmark
- Located in a U.S. National Register Historic District

Separate criteria designate historic properties in Canada, Mexico and the Caribbean.

**6** These white ovals with black numbers serve as restaurant locators and are used to locate, or "spot," restaurants on maps we provide for larger cities.

# The Restaurant Diamond Ratings

AAA Tourism Editors are responsible for determining a restaurant's diamond rating based on established criteria.

These criteria were established with input from AAA trained professionals, members, and restaurant industry experts. They are purposely broad to capture what is typically seen throughout the restaurant industry at each diamond rating level.

These establishments appeal to a diner seeking good, wholesome, no-nonsense eating at an affordable price. They typically provide simple, familiar, and unadorned foods served in a sensible, casual or self-service style. Often quick service and family oriented.

Examples include coffee shops, diners, cafeterias, short order, and modest full service eateries.

These establishments provide for dining needs that are increasingly complex, but still reasonably priced. They typically exhibit noticeable efforts in rising above the ordinary in many aspects of food, service and decor. Service is typically functional yet ambitious, periodically combining informal style with limited self-service elements. Often well-suited to traditional, special occasion, and family dining.

Examples include a varied range of specific concept (theme) and multi-purpose establishments.

These establishments impart an increasingly refined and upscale, adult-oriented experience. This is the entry level into fine dining. Creative and complex menus offer a blend of traditional and trendy foods. The service level is typically semi-formal with knowledgeable and proficient staff. Routinely these restaurants appeal to the diner in search of an experience rather than just a meal.

Examples include high-caliber, chic, boutique, and conventional restaurants.

These establishments impart a luxurious and socially refined experience. This is consistent fine dining. Menus typically reflect a high degree of creativity and complexity, featuring elaborate presentations of market-driven or traditional dishes. A cultured, professional, and highly proficient staff consistently demonstrates a profound desire to meet or exceed guest expectations. Restaurants of this caliber are geared to individuals with an appetite for an elite, fine-dining experience.

Examples include dining rooms associated with luxury lodgings, or exclusive independent restaurants often found in metropolitan areas.

Often renowned, these establishments impart a world-class and opulent, adult-oriented experience. This is "haute cuisine" at its best. Menus are often cutting edge, with an obvious dedication to use of only the finest ingredients available. Even the classic dishes become extraordinary under the masterful direction of highly acclaimed chefs. Presentations are spectacular, reflecting impeccable artistry and awareness. An expert, formalized staff continuously anticipates and exceeds guest expectations. Staff members' unfailing attention to detail appears effortless, well-rehearsed and unobtrusive. Undoubtedly, these restaurants appeal to those in search of the ultimate dining experience.

Examples include renowned dining rooms associated with luxury lodgings, or exclusive independent restaurants often found in metropolitan areas.

The restaurants with **fyi** in place of diamonds are included as an "information only" service for members. These listings provide additional dining choices but have not yet been evaluated.

# YOU'RE READY...

# NOW YOU'RE READY FOR ANYTHING.

**Travelers Cheques**
Available in US Dollars, Canadian Dollars, Euros, and Pounds Sterling; AAA VISA® Travelers Cheques are accepted worldwide.

**Cash Passport Card**
With AAA Cash Passport you can withdraw cash in the local currency from any VISA® ATM in the world.

**Credit Card**
The AAA VISA® Credit Card is accepted in over 24 million locations around the world.

**Foreign Currency**
We supply over 100 different currencies and can advise which is the best for your destination.

## AAA TRAVEL MONEY
*Know Before You Go.*

**Visit** Participating AAA offices  **Click** aaa.com and go to Travel Money  **Call** 866-339-3378

# Savings for all Seasons

Hertz rents Fords and other fine cars. ® REG. U.S. PAT. OFF. © HERTZ SYSTEM INC., 1999/2000-99.

## No matter the season, Hertz offers AAA members exclusive discounts and benefits.

**O**perating in 150 countries at over 7,000 locations, Hertz makes traveling more convenient and efficient wherever and whenever you go. Hertz offers AAA members discounts up to 20% on car rentals worldwide.

**T**o receive your exclusive AAA member discounts and benefits, mention your AAA membership card at time of reservation and present it at time of rental. **In addition**, to receive a free one car class upgrade, in the United States mention PC# 929714, in Canada mention PC# 929725 and in Puerto Rico mention PC# 929736 at the time of reservation. Offer available through 12/31/04.

**F**or reservations and program details, call your AAA Travel office or the Hertz/AAA Desk at **1-800-654-3080**.

**Hertz** ®
exactly.

# AMERICA ON THE MOVE

## A NEW EXHIBITION ON TRANSPORTATION IN AMERICAN HISTORY

1903 Winton, First Car to Cross the Country

**National Museum of American History**

14th and Constitution Ave. NW ♦ Washington, D.C.

Open Daily: 10 a.m. - 5:30 p.m. (Except December 25)

americanhistory.si.edu/onthemove

Free Admission

 **Smithsonian**
*National Museum of American History*
*Behring Center*

 **AMERICA**
ON THE MOVE

# Maine

## From the Sea
Lobstering is a long-standing and delicious Maine tradition

## Guiding the Way
More than 60 lighthouses line Maine's rocky coast

## Seasonal Brilliance
Crisp fall days bring out nature's vibrant palette of scarlet, russet and bright yellow

## Savor the History
Quaint inns and cozy bed-and-breakfasts recall bygone eras

## Tranquil Inlets, Bays and Harbors
Picturesque coastal cities line Maine's Atlantic shore

Cape Neddick Light, York Harbor
© Bob & Suzanne Clemenz

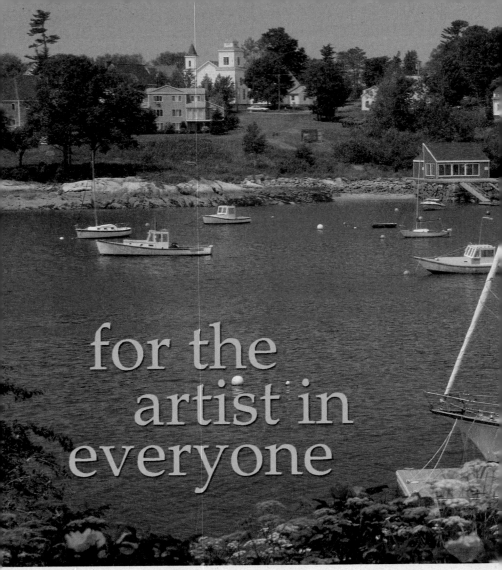

for the
artist in
everyone

Rockport / © David Forbert / SuperStock

A rocky coastline dotted with lighthouses and lobster boats. Sparkling lakes surrounded by evergreens and white pine. Mountains that run headlong into the ocean. Maine is a vigorous landscape frequently captured in literature, paintings and photographs. But the state has other sides waiting to be explored.

Ornate Victorian buildings in Portland's Old Port Exchange district contrast with the majestic headlands and beautiful coves of Monhegan Island. Frolicking summer fun at southern Maine's beaches blends into fall's statewide foliage display, which fades into the Moose River Valley's quiet, snow-covered expanses of wilderness.

From Winslow Homer's paintings
of the sea's endless fury to Edna St.
Vincent Millay's lyrical description of
the view from Mount Battie, artists
have portrayed the contrasting shades
of Maine.

But art cannot imitate life—the feel
of the spray when the ocean meets
the rocks in Acadia National Park,

the sound of the water
rushing over Moxie Falls,
the sight of wildlife along
the shoreline of Moosehead Lake.
Experiences like these can be recorded
with camera, pen or brush, but they'll
linger fondest in your memories.

Maine is a love affair between earth and water. Here, the two meet in an embrace to create some of the most beautiful coastal scenery in America. And like any relationship, the encounter between unlike partners can be stormy; whipped by marine winds and pounded by white-capped breakers, the rugged shore is a sight to behold.

## Land and Sea

No visit to Maine would be complete without an excursion to the crown jewel of its scenic coast: Acadia National Park. Consisting mostly of Mount Desert Island, Acadia is the second most visited national park in the country. The reason? An array of stunning landscapes range from sandy beaches—a rare sight along Maine's rocky northern coast—to Cadillac Mountain, the highest point on the eastern coastline of North America.

From a distance, the rounded granite humps of Acadia's mountains seem to materialize out of a purple haze hovering above the ocean. Two of the island's top draws: Thunder Hole, a cleft in the Otter Cliffs that produces a rumbling boom when the surf crashes through it, and Bar Harbor, a resort village of fine mansions, quaint inns and fishing wharves. Local marinas serve as a convenient departure point for sightseeing and whale-watch cruises.

Think of Maine and you'll likely picture a lighthouse looming over a rock-strewn, wave-washed shore. There's a reason: More than 60 such towers dot the coast here, including Pemaquid Point Lighthouse, one of the state's most picturesque. During storms, raging surf often engulfs the lighthouse's base, which is perched 79 feet above water. Even locals come to watch this spectacle.

In Portland's Fort Williams Park stands the Portland Head Light, one of the nation's most historic; it was constructed in 1791 under the authorization of George Washington.

A "stern and rockbound coast" isn't the only place where water and land meet to produce splendid scenery. Numerous lakes and mountains farther inland draw an increasing number of sightseers and outdoor sports enthusiasts.

More than 90 percent of Maine's land area is forested, which amply justifies its official nickname: The "Pine Tree State." The "Vacation State" is another equally deserved moniker, and vast areas of virtually uninhabited woodland offer plenty of room for vacationers to get away from it all. There's no

---

**S**amuel de Champlain sights Mount Desert Island, now the location of Acadia National Park.

**1604**

**A** trading post is begun by the Plymouth Colony at the present-day site of Augusta; John Alden and Capt. Miles Standish are among the original settlers.

**1628**

Library of Congress

**A**ugusta is named state capital.

**1827**

© Jeff Greenberg/Index Stock/PictureQuest

**1775**

**T**he first naval battle of the Revolutionary War is fought in Machias Bay; 40 colonists capture the English warship *Margaretta*.

# Maine Historical Timeline

**1820**

**M**aine enters the Union as a free state as part of the Missouri Compromise.

better time to make your escape than during Maine's fall foliage season, when the hills catch fire with autumn hues. The countryside around Augusta, the state capital, normally achieves its most brilliant russets and golds in mid-October.

The Appalachian Trail is always a good bet for gorgeous alpine scenery; the footpath follows the crest of the Appalachian Mountains from Mount Springer in Georgia to the foot of Mount Katahdin. A huge granite monolith rising 5,268 feet, this peak—Maine's highest—is just a stone's throw away from Moosehead Lake, an outdoor recreation magnet attracting campers, boaters and water skiers.

## Authors and Artists

For more than a century artists of all kinds have sought refuge and inspiration along the state's craggy shores and wooded hillsides.

One of the first to do so was poet Henry Wadsworth Longfellow, who referred to his childhood home of Portland as "the beautiful town that is seated by the sea." Mainers today seem to agree with Longfellow's sentiments: Roughly one-quarter of Vacation State residents live in the greater Portland metropolitan area. To explore the town, stop by the brick 1786 Wadsworth-Longfellow House, where the poet lived as a boy; to experience the sea, hop aboard one of the tour boats that cruise into Casco Bay among the picturesque Calendar Islands.

Maine has recharged the creative batteries of other authors as well. Harriet Beecher Stowe penned Uncle Tom's Cabin while living in Brunswick. Edna St. Vincent Millay was born in Rockland and began her career in Camden, where she is honored by a statue at the harbor's head. And various state locations have served as backdrops in the horror novels of Bangor resident Stephen King.

The dramatic, wind-swept coastline and hardy Down East fishermen kept painter Winslow Homer busy for many years of his career, while the town of Cushing inspired several of Andrew Wyeth's paintings.

Mix earth and water and you normally get mud. Yet these same ingredients combine in Maine to form everything from sea-sprayed cliffs to mountain-bordered lakes. Clearly there's something special about this recipe.

The University of Maine opens with 12 students and two teachers.
**1868**

The first Maine Lobster Fest is held in Rockland. Today, it attracts more than 70,000 revelers to the city, known as the "Lobster Capital of the World." **1947**

Maine native Edmund Muskie is the Democratic nominee for vice president of the United States.
**1968**

© Roger Ressmeyer/Corbis

**1842**
Maine's northeastern boundary with New Brunswick is finally settled by the Webster-Ashburton Treaty.

**1997**
Senator William Cohen is chosen by President Clinton to be Secretary of Defense.

**1962**
The main ground station for the nation's first communications satellite is installed in Andover.

© AFP/Corbis

## Recreation

Warm weather brings a migration of visitors to the powder-soft sand of southern Maine's shoreline. Despite the summer crowds, there still are some quiet beaches where you can enjoy the rush of water between your toes. But getting wet isn't necessary to enjoy the water; **windjammer cruises** in Penobscot Bay pass by historic lighthouses and nature preserves filled with dolphins, seals and bald eagles.

**Swimmers** will find the water somewhat warm July through August. Ogunquit, a historic seaside village, was named after the Abenaki Indian word for "the beautiful place by the sea." Its beach is a wide sandbar between the Ogunquit River and the Atlantic, allowing you to swim in either the river or the ocean.

Old Orchard Beach, with its amusement park, pier and arcades, is a center for summer fun. As a result, the beach around the pier can be a bit crowded late June through Labor Day. Try heading north up the shore if you need room for sand castles or sunning. **Horseback riding** along the beach is offered in the spring and fall by Horseback Riding Plus; phone (207) 883-6400.

Other water adventures lead you inland. The Forks—where two churning rivers meet to form the Kennebec—offers a 12-mile **rafting** run through a deep, tree-lined gorge. High water combines with few obstacles, creating raging foam and class IV drops. The rafting season starts with the spring runoff and continues through October.

The Allagash Wilderness Waterway is a **canoe** camper's dream. This 92-mile corridor of lakes and river flows from Telos Lake, west of Baxter State Park, to within a few miles of the St. John River. Wildlife is abundant and moose sightings are common. The area also is used extensively in the winter for **ice fishing.**

## Where Mountains Touch the Sea

Acadia National Park, Maine's premier outdoor destination, is a breathtaking combination of cobblestone beaches and glacier-carved mountains. More than 115 miles of **hiking** trails range from short beach walks to the steep Precipice Trail. Forty-five miles of broken-stone carriage roads are populated with hikers and **cyclists** in summer; they are groomed for **cross-country skiers** and **snowshoers** soon after the first snowfall.

Nearly all of Acadia is contained on Mount Desert Island. Park Loop Road, which passes jagged bluffs, glassy lakes and majestic Cadillac Mountain, is wide enough to offer a safe, scenic route for cyclists. In summer the road is full, but you'll have the island practically to yourself during the spring and fall. While Park Loop Road is closed to private vehicles in winter, it does offer access to **snowmobilers.**

Baxter State Park in north-central Maine is the northern terminus of the Appalachian Trail. Maine's highest peak, Mount Katahdin, is the main attraction here and draws a crowd; consider **climbing** one of the other 46 peaks and ridges in this 200,000-acre park. A popular winter **camping** area, Baxter is a top destination for snowshoeing and cross-country skiing.

## A Winter Wonderland

**Downhill skiing** takes on a new twist at Camden Snow Bowl. There's nowhere else in the East where you can sail down slopes while enjoying spectacular views of the Atlantic Ocean. The Snow Bowl also has Maine's only public **toboggan** chute. Other major ski areas include Sunday River, renowned for its snowmaking ability, and Sugarloaf/USA. Both resorts are within driving distance of Farmington, gateway to Maine's ski country.

The cold winds of October and November signal the peak of **hunting** season. It's the perfect opportunity to bag small game, waterfowl, deer, bears and moose (for those with the proper tags and permits, of course). Obtain fishing and hunting license information from the Department of Inland Fisheries and Wildlife.

No matter which outdoor activity you choose, you'll want to stay close to the action. Maine's camping facilities range from rustic lean-tos to resort cabins. Most campgrounds are open May through October.

## Recreational Activities

Throughout the TourBook, you may notice a Recreational Activities heading with bulleted listings of recreation-oriented establishments listed underneath. Similar operations also may be mentioned in Destination City recreation sections. Since normal AAA inspection criteria cannot be applied, these establishments are presented only for information. Age, height and weight restrictions may apply. Reservations often are recommended and sometimes are required. Addresses and/or phone numbers are provided so visitors can contact the attraction for additional information.

# Fast Facts

**POPULATION:** 1,274,923

**AREA:** 33,215 square miles; ranks 39th.

**CAPITAL:** Augusta.

**HIGHEST POINT:** 5,268 ft., Mount Katahdin.

**LOWEST POINT:** Sea level, Atlantic Ocean.

**TIME ZONE(S):** Eastern. DST.

**MINIMUM AGE FOR DRIVERS:** 16

**SEAT BELT/CHILD RESTRAINT LAWS:** Seat belts required for driver and all passengers over 8 and more than 55 inches; child restraints required for 40-80 pounds and under 8.

**HELMETS FOR MOTORCYCLISTS:** Required while operating under a learner's permit or for 1 year after being licensed, or for all passengers under 15.

**RADAR DETECTORS:** Permitted.

**FIREARMS LAWS:** Vary by state and/or county. Contact Maine State Police License Division, State House Station #164, Augusta, ME 04333; phone (207) 624-8775.

**HOLIDAYS:** Jan. 1; Martin Luther King Jr. Day, Jan. (3rd Mon.); Washington's Birthday, Feb. (3rd Mon.); Patriot's Day, Apr. (3rd Mon.); Memorial Day, May (4th Mon.); July 4; Labor Day, Sept. (1st Mon.); Columbus Day, Oct. (2nd Mon.); Veterans Day, Nov. 11; Thanksgiving; Dec. 25.

**TAXES:** Maine's statewide sales tax is 6 percent.

**STATE INFORMATION CENTERS:** are between I-95 and US 1 in Kittery; on US 2 in Bethel; between I-295 exit 17 and US 1 in Yarmouth; on US 302 in Fryeburg; at 7 Union St. in Calais; north at mile 169 on I-95N in North Hampden and at mile 172 on I-95S in South Hampden; and at jct. I-95 and US 1 in Houlton. All offices are open daily 9-5 except Fryeburg, which is open Wed.-Mon. 8-6, mid-July through Labor Day. The Kittery office is closed Thanksgiving and Dec. 25; the Hampden offices are closed Jan. 1, Easter, Thanksgiving and Dec. 25.

**FURTHER INFORMATION FOR VISITORS:**

Maine Publicity Bureau
P.O. Box 2300
Hallowell, ME 04347
(207) 623-0363 or (888) 624-6345

**FISHING AND HUNTING REGULATIONS:**

Department of Inland Fisheries and Wildlife
284 State St.
Augusta, ME 04333
(207) 287-8000

## Maine Temperature Averages
### Maximum / Minimum
From the records of the National Weather Service

| | JAN | FEB | MAR | APR | MAY | JUNE | JULY | AUG | SEPT | OCT | NOV | DEC |
|---|---|---|---|---|---|---|---|---|---|---|---|---|
| Caribou | 20 / 1 | 22 / 3 | 32 / 14 | 45 / 28 | 61 / 39 | 69 / 49 | 75 / 54 | 73 / 52 | 64 / 44 | 52 / 34 | 37 / 24 | 24 / 8 |
| Portland | 32 / 12 | 34 / 12 | 41 / 22 | 53 / 32 | 64 / 42 | 73 / 51 | 80 / 57 | 78 / 55 | 70 / 47 | 60 / 37 | 48 / 29 | 35 / 16 |

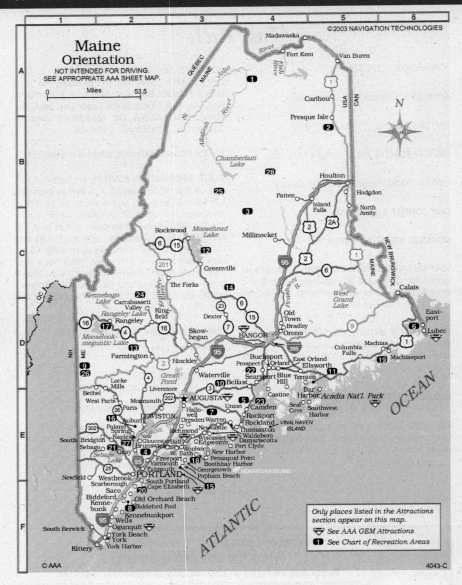

# Maine
## Orientation

NOT INTENDED FOR DRIVING.
SEE APPROPRIATE AAA SHEET MAP.

0        Miles        53.5

©2003 NAVIGATION TECHNOLOGIES

*Only places listed in the Attractions
section appear on this map.*

⬇ *See AAA GEM Attractions*

**1** *See Chart of Recreation Areas*

© AAA

4043-C

# Points of Interest Offering A Great Experience for Members®

## Acadia National Park (E-5)

ACADIA NATIONAL PARK—One of the most popular national parks, Acadia's natural beauty incorporates both ocean and mountain vistas. See p. 39.

## Augusta (E-3)

MAINE STATE MUSEUM—The state's natural, cultural and social history are examined in this museum in Maine's Statehouse Complex. See p. 41.

## Bangor (D-4)

COLE LAND TRANS-PORTATION MU-SEUM—The evolution of land transportation in Maine is depicted through more than  200 vehicles, including wagons, fire trucks, farm equipment and snowplows; an 1840s covered bridge helps carry out the theme. See p. 42.

## Bath (E-3)

MAINE MARITIME MUSEUM—On the banks of the Kennebec River, the museum relates Maine's seafaring history on the site of a 19th-century shipyard. See p. 45.

## Lubec (D-6)

ROOSEVELT CAMPOBELLO INTERNATIONAL PARK—Visit the 34-room summer home of Franklin D. Roosevelt and the coves, cliffs and beaches where he and his family once roamed. See p. 60.

## Ogunquit (F-2)

OGUNQUIT MU-SEUM OF AMERICAN ART—In a scenic meadow setting overlooking the Atlantic Ocean, the museum displays the works of prominent American artists. See p. 63.

## Portland (E-2)

PORTLAND MUSEUM OF ART—In a building designed by I.M. Pei & Partners, the museum features a collection of American and European  works dating from the 18th century to the present. See p. 68.

VICTORIA MANSION—Built 1858-60, the Italianate-style home is elaborately decorated with trompe l'oeil walls and ceilings, stained glass and Gustave Herter furnishings. See p. 69.

WADSWORTH-LONGFELLOW HOUSE—This first brick home in Portland was constructed 1785-86 by Henry Wadsworth Longfellow's grandfather; the poet lived here during his childhood. See p. 69.

## Wiscasset (E-3)

MUSICAL WONDER HOUSE—Antique mechanical musical instruments made in America, France, Germany and Switzerland are displayed and operated. See p. 78.

# RECREATION AREAS

| | MAP LOCATION | CAMPING | PICNICKING | HIKING TRAILS | BOATING | BOAT RAMP | BOAT RENTAL | FISHING | SWIMMING | PETS ON LEASH | BICYCLE TRAILS | WINTER SPORTS | VISITOR CENTER | LODGE/CABINS | FOOD SERVICE |
|---|---|---|---|---|---|---|---|---|---|---|---|---|---|---|---|
| **NATIONAL PARKS** *(See place listings)* | | | | | | | | | | | | | | | |
| **Acadia (E-5)** 47,633 acres. | | • | • | • | • | • | | • | • | • | • | • | • | | • |
| **STATE** | | | | | | | | | | | | | | | |
| **Allagash Wilderness Waterway (A-4)** River and lakes in northwestern Maine. | ❶ | • | | | • | • | | • | • | • | | • | | | |
| **Aroostook (B-5)** 577 acres 4 mi. s. of Presque Isle on US 1, then w. and s. via a park road. Scenic. Cross-country skiing, snowmobiling. *(See Presque Isle p. 70)* | ❷ | • | • | • | • | • | • | • | • | • | | • | | | |
| **Baxter (C-4)** 201,018 acres (10 separate areas) n. of Millinocket and w. of Patten in north-central Maine off SR 159. Canoeing; primitive camping. | ❸ | • | • | • | | | | • | • | | | • | | | |
| **Bradbury Mountain (E-2)** 272 acres w. of Freeport off US 95 on SR 136, then n. on SR 9. | ❹ | • | • | • | | | | | | • | | • | | | |
| **Camden Hills (E-4)** 5,474 acres 2 mi. n. of Camden on US 1. Scenic. *(See Camden p. 50)* | ❺ | • | • | • | | | | | | • | | • | | | |
| **Cobscook Bay (D-6)** 868 acres 2 mi. s.e. of Dennysville off US 1. | ❻ | • | • | • | • | • | | • | | • | | • | | | |
| **Damariscotta Lake (E-3)** 17 acres in Jefferson off SR 32. | ❼ | | • | | | | | • | • | • | | | | | |
| **Ferry Beach (F-2)** 117 acres in Saco on SR 9. Nature trails. *(See Saco p. 71)* | ❽ | | • | • | | | | | • | • | | | | | |
| **Grafton Notch (D-1)** 3,112 acres 14 mi. n. of Bethel on SR 26 between Upton and Newry. *(See Bethel p. 46)* | ❾ | | • | • | | | | • | | • | | | | | |
| **Lake St. George (D-3)** 360 acres 2 mi. w. of Liberty on SR 3. | ❿ | • | • | | • | • | • | • | • | • | | • | | | |
| **Lamoine Beach (D-5)** 55 acres 6.5 mi. s.e. of Ellsworth on SR 184. *(See Ellsworth p. 53)* | ⓫ | • | • | | • | • | | • | | • | | | | | |
| **Lily Bay (C-3)** 924 acres 8 mi. n.e. of Greenville on Lily Bay Rd. | ⓬ | • | • | | • | • | • | • | • | • | | • | • | | |
| **Mount Blue (D-2)** 1,273 acres (two areas) n. of Weld on a gravel road. | ⓭ | • | • | • | • | • | • | • | • | • | | • | | | |
| **Peaks-Kenny (C-3)** 839 acres 6 mi. n. of Dover-Foxcroft on SR 153. | ⓮ | • | • | • | | | | • | • | • | | | | | |
| **Popham Beach (F-3)** 529 acres w. of Popham Beach via SR 209. Windsurfing. *(See Popham Beach p. 65)* | ⓯ | | • | | | | | • | • | • | | | | | |
| **Range Ponds (E-2)** 750 acres in Poland off SR 122. | ⓰ | | | | • | • | • | • | • | • | | | | | |
| **Rangeley Lake (D-2)** 691 acres s.w. of Rangeley via SR 17 on the s. shore of Rangeley Lake. | ⓱ | • | • | | • | • | | • | • | • | | • | | | |
| **Reid (E-3)** 768 acres 2 mi. e. of Georgetown on SR 127. | ⓲ | | • | | | | | • | • | • | | | | | • |
| **Roque Bluffs (D-6)** 275 acres 7 mi. s. of Machias off US 1 on Roque Bluffs Rd. *(See Machias p. 60)* | ⓳ | | • | | | | | • | • | • | | | | | |
| **Scarborough Beach (F-2)** 5 acres 3 mi. s. of Scarborough off SR 207. | ⓴ | | • | | | | | | • | • | | | | | |
| **Sebago Lake (E-2)** 1,300 acres 3 mi. s. of Naples off US 302. Nature programs. *(See Sebago p. 73)* | ㉑ | • | • | | • | • | | • | • | • | | | • | | • |
| **Swan Lake (D-4)** 67 acres n. of Swanville off SR 141. | ㉒ | | • | | | | | • | • | • | | | | | |
| **Warren Island (E-4)** 70 acres in Penobscot Bay. | ㉓ | • | • | | | | | • | | • | | | | | |
| **OTHER** | | | | | | | | | | | | | | | |
| **Bigelow Preserve (C-2)** 29,000 acres n. of New Portland off SR 27. | ㉔ | • | • | • | • | | | • | • | • | | • | | | |
| **Gero Island (B-3)** 3,000 acres n.w. of Millinocket off SR 11. Ice fishing. | ㉕ | • | • | | • | • | | • | • | • | | | | | |
| **Mahoosucs (D-1)** 21,000 acres near Bethel off SR 26. | ㉖ | • | • | • | | | • | | | | | • | | | |
| **Outlet Beach (E-2)** on Outlet Rd. 1 mi. e. of SR 26 on shore of Sabbathday Lake near Poland Spring. *(See Poland Spring p. 65)* | ㉗ | | • | | • | • | • | • | • | | | | | • | |
| **Scraggly Lake (B-4)** 10,000 acres off Grand Lake Rd. n.w. of Mount Chase. | ㉘ | • | • | • | • | • | | • | • | • | | • | | | |

# Points of Interest

**ACADIA NATIONAL PARK (E-5) .**

Elevations in the park range from sea level at Sand Beach to 1,530 ft. at Cadillac Mountain. Refer to AAA maps for additional elevation information.

Southeast of Bangor, Acadia National Park possesses an unusual combination of ocean and mountain scenery. The park includes more than 50 square miles of Mount Desert Island, the largest rock-based island on the Atlantic coast.

Dominating the park are the ancient, rounded peaks of the Mount Desert Mountains, worn down by countless centuries of erosion. Great granite cliffs, undermined by the pounding surf at their bases, rise from the ocean. Nowhere along the Atlantic seaboard is the "stern and rockbound coast" more picturesque.

More than 15 peaks, mostly bare at their summits, are forested with spruce, fir, pine and northern

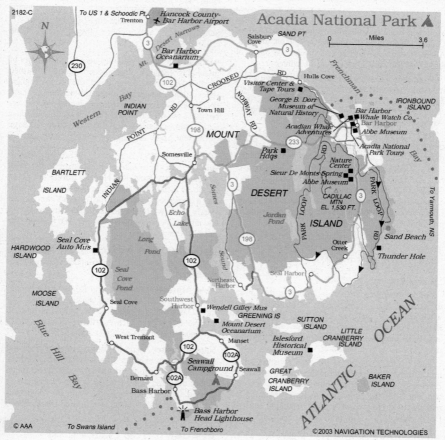

In January 2004 exit numbers on Maine's interstate highway system began shifting from sequential numbering to mileage-based numbering. Both new and old numbers will remain posted for one year. The exit numbers provided in the Points of Interest section reflect the new mileage-based system. Completion is expected in May 2004 (weather permitting).

hardwood trees. Some 500 types of wildflowers, including many Arctic species, grow in the park, and the area is a sanctuary for a variety of birds and other animals.

Samuel de Champlain sighted Mount Desert Island in 1604 and named it "L'Isle des Monts Deserts," which means island of barren mountains. It was the site of a short-lived settlement by French Jesuits in 1613, and for many years was part of the French province of Acadia, from which the park derives its name.

## General Information

The park is accessible all year. However, except for a 2-mile section along the ocean, the 27-mile Park Loop Road is closed in winter by snow, sleet or ice; state and town roads are kept open. Cadillac Mountain Road extends to the summit of 1,530-foot Cadillac Mountain—the highest point on the U.S. Atlantic seaboard—offering a spectacular view of the coast. The road is closed in the winter.

More than 115 miles of hiking trails reach every mountain summit and valley; maps are available. There also are 45 miles of graded carriage roads suitable for walking tours, bicycling, cross-country skiing and jogging.

Park ranger programs are usually offered from mid-May through Columbus Day. Programs include mountain hikes, campfire talks and natural history walks. Check the park's newspaper, the *Beaver Log*, for details. Park rangers also explain the area's geology, history, marine life and wildlife on cruises around Frenchman Bay and the Cranberry Islands. Check at the visitor center for a current listing of programs.

Park information is available from the park headquarters on SR 233, 3 miles west of Bar Harbor, which is open daily 8-4:30, Nov. 1 to mid-Apr.; Mon.-Fri. 8-4:30, rest of year. Closed Jan. 1, Thanksgiving and Dec. 24-25.

Private operators are available during the season to conduct daily sightseeing, deep-sea fishing, whale-watching and lobster-fishing cruises from Bar Harbor as well as from Northeast, Southwest and Bass harbors. *See Recreation Chart and the AAA Northeastern CampBook.*

Tape Tours, available at the park's visitor center near Hulls Cove and through Eastern National Bookstore, describe the geological origin, ecology and history of the park and contain instructions for making the drive around Acadia, beginning at Hulls Cove; phone (207) 288-4988 for the bookstore.

**ADMISSION** to the park is by 7-day pass, which costs $20 per private vehicle. Annual passes cost $40. A camping fee is charged. MC, VI.

**PETS** are permitted in the park if they are attended and physically restricted at all times; leashes may be up to 6 feet in length. Pets are not permitted on the swimming beaches or the four ladder hiking trails on mountain cliffs.

**ADDRESS** inquiries to Acadia National Park Information, P.O. Box 177, Bar Harbor, ME 04609; phone (207) 288-3338.

**HULLS COVE VISITOR CENTER** is 2.75 mi. n. of Bar Harbor on SR 3 at Hulls Cove. A 15-minute film about the island is shown on the half-hour. Daily 8-6, July-Aug.; 8-4:30, mid-April through June 30 and Sept.-Oct. Free. Phone (207) 288-3338.

## Points of Interest

**ISLESFORD HISTORICAL MUSEUM** is accessible via mailboat or tour boat from Northeast or Southwest Harbor to Little Cranberry Island. The exhibits focus on 19th-century living on the Cranberry Islands and include tools, harpoon guns and ship clocks. Allow 30 minutes minimum. Daily 10:30-noon and 12:30-4:30, mid-June through Sept. 31. Schedule may vary; phone ahead. Free. Phone (207) 288-3338.

**PARK LOOP ROAD** provides access to a number of interesting features: Sand Beach, partially formed of shell fragments; Great Head, one of the highest sheer Atlantic headlands in the United States; Thunder Hole, a wave-cut chasm producing loud reverberations when waves and tide are right; and Otter Cliffs, with a dense forest that extends to the edge of the sea. Allow 3 hours, 30 minutes minimum.

**SCHOODIC POINT** is at the tip of Schoodic Peninsula on the eastern side of Frenchman Bay—about an hour's drive from Bar Harbor. Beside the point, Schoodic Head rises more than 400 feet, commanding a sweeping view eastward toward the Bay of Fundy and westward toward the Mount Desert Mountains. A park road from SR 186 follows the coast of the peninsula.

**SIEUR DE MONTS SPRING,** near Bar Harbor, is a memorial to George B. Dorr, founder of Acadia National Park.

**Abbe Museum,** off Park Loop Rd. near the spring, contains regional artifacts of American Indian culture. Daily 9-5, July-Aug.; 10-4, late May-June 30 and Sept. 1 to mid-Oct. Admission $2; ages 6-15, $1; under 6 free. Phone (207) 288-3519.

**Nature Center,** near the spring, includes several natural history exhibits. The Acadia Wild Gardens, a living field guide to flowers and trees found within the park, is next to the center. Nature center open daily 9-5, June-Sept; Sat.-Sun. in May. Gardens open daily 24 hours, year-round. Free. Phone (207) 288-3338.

## AUBURN (E-2) pop. 23,203, elev. 183'

Auburn and its more populous neighbor Lewiston *(see place listing p. 59)* flank the Androscoggin River 30 miles inland from its mouth. With a rich heritage of textile and shoe production, and the more recent additions of electronics, plastics and other manufacturers, the two cities constitute what is often termed the "industrial heart" of Maine.

During the early 1840s the exploitation of water-power potential spurred swift manufacturing development in Auburn. The shoe industry, which had begun in the 1830s, grew despite the laborious hand methods of the time. Then, about 1850, the factory system and the first laborsaving machinery were introduced. By the 1870s two million pairs of shoes were leaving Auburn factories each year.

Although shoe production has declined significantly, new technological and entrepreneurial enterprises have combined with the growth of a large service and retail industry, and have successfully revitalized the city.

Opportunities exist for play as well as for work. Lake Auburn, 3 miles north, offers fishing at selected sites.

**Androscoggin County Chamber of Commerce:** 179 Lisbon St., P.O. Box 59, Lewiston, ME 04243-0059; phone (207) 783-2249.

**ANDROSCOGGIN HISTORICAL SOCIETY MUSEUM,** at 2 Turner St. in the County Building, presents exhibits tracing the history of the state and county. Displays include a bird collection, American Indian artifacts, Civil War memorabilia, military items, postcards, photographs, clothing, and farm and domestic tools. A library containing local, county and state history is available for research purposes. Allow 30 minutes minimum. Wed.-Fri. 9-noon and 1-5; closed holidays. Hours may vary; phone ahead. Donations. Phone (207) 784-0586.

## RECREATIONAL ACTIVITIES

### Skiing (cross-country)

- **Lost Valley Ski Area,** Youngs Corner Rd. Write P.O. Box 260, Auburn ME 04212-0260. Daily, Dec. 13-Mar. 16. Phone (207) 784-1561.

## AUGUSTA (E-3) pop. 18,560, elev. 47′

A trading post was founded in 1628 by the Plymouth Colony. John Alden and Capt. Miles Standish, immortalized by Henry Wadsworth Longfellow, were among the original settlers. In 1754 Fort Western was erected on the east bank of the Kennebec River. In 1797 the community chose Augusta as its name, presumably to honor the daughter of Gen. Henry Dearborn.

Capital of the state since 1827, Augusta is at the head of navigation on the Kennebec River. The city differs from most Maine communities that occupy both sides of a river in that it did not grow into twin cities. Augusta is the seat of many of Maine's governmental agencies and offices.

**Kennebec Valley Chamber of Commerce:** 21 University Dr., P.O. Box 676, Augusta, ME 04332; phone (207) 623-4559.

**AUGUSTA STATE PARK** (Capitol Park), between the Statehouse and the Kennebec River, contains 72 species of indigenous trees and 23 species of exotic trees as well as varieties of shrubs and ferns. The park also is the site of the Maine Vietnam Veterans Memorial, a unique triangular piece of art. Daily 24 hours. Free.

**CHILDREN'S DISCOVERY MUSEUM,** 265 Water St., presents children with different role-playing opportunities at a simulated diner, grocery store, post office, film studio and live stage. Other interactive exhibits can be found in a board game room and a literature room for toddlers. Mon.-Fri. 9-4, Sat. 10-4, Sun. 1-4. Hours may vary; phone ahead. Admission $4, under 1 free. MC, VI. Phone (207) 622-2209.

**MAINE STATE MUSEUM,** in the Library-Museum-Archives Building in the Statehouse Complex, contains exhibits depicting Maine's natural environment, prehistory, social history and manufacturing heritage. This Land Called Maine introduces five natural history scenes and a display of gems and minerals found in Maine, while 12,000 Years in Maine is an extensive exhibition about Maine's prehistoric cultures that highlights archeological materials.

Made In Maine is the museum's exhibit of 19th-century manufacturing technologies and products. Other exhibits examine the early economic activities of agriculture, fishing, granite quarrying, ice harvesting and lumbering. American Indian basketry, a collection of more than 500 glass objects and one of the oldest American-made locomotive engines also are displayed.

Allow 1 hour minimum. Tues.-Fri. 9-5, Sat. 10-4; closed holidays. Admission $2; ages 6-18, $1. Phone (207) 287-2301.

SAVE **OLD FORT WESTERN,** 16 Cony St., is said to be America's oldest surviving wooden fort. Costumed interpreters are available to answer questions about the fort's military, storekeeping and residential past spanning the years from the 1750s to the early 1800s. Allow 1 hour minimum. Mon.-Fri. 10-4, Sat.-Sun. 1-4, July 4-Labor Day; daily 1-4, Memorial Day weekend-July 3; Sat.-Sun. 1-4, day after Labor Day-Columbus Day; first Sun. of the month 1-3, Nov.-May. Admission $5; ages 6-16, $3. MC, VI. Phone (207) 626-2385.

**STATE HOUSE,** State and Capitol sts., was originally designed by Charles Bulfinch. Although many additions and changes have been made, the graceful portico has been left undisturbed. The 1829 building contains many portraits and an exhibit of battle flags. Interpretive wall plaques designate points of interest. Allow 30 minutes minimum. Mon.-Fri. 9-5; closed holidays. Guided tours Mon.-Thurs. 9-1, Fri. 9-noon. Reservations for guided tours are required. Free. Phone (207) 287-2301 for tour information.

## BANGOR (D-4) pop. 31,473, elev. 21′

Bangor, at the head of tidewater and navigation on the Penobscot River, is the principal retail, cultural and commercial center for eastern and northern Maine. Bangor area industries are based on papermaking, timber products, electronics, shoes and tourism. Several notable public and private colleges and universities are located here.

Bangor's survival was threatened by the War of 1812; blockade running and privateering became essential to maintain solvency. A resurgence in the timber trade following the war tripled Bangor's population during the 1830s. Within a few decades, the city became the leading lumber port of the world. Bangor's harbor became known as the Devil's Half-Acre due to the proliferation of drinking and gambling.

Of interest is the Paul Bunyan statue on Main Street, which is an appropriate 31 feet high and weighs about 1.5 tons. Blackbeard's Family Fun Park at 339 Odlin Rd. offers miniature golf courses, a go-cart track and a 10-cage batting facility. The Bangor Raceway features harness racing from late May through July.

**Note:** Policies concerning admittance of children to pari-mutuel betting facilities vary. Phone ahead for information.

**Bangor Region Chamber of Commerce:** 519 Main St., P.O. Box 1443, Bangor, ME 04402-1443; phone (207) 947-0307.

**Self-guiding tours:** Aspects of the city's history can be experienced through a self-guiding walking tour; maps are available from the historical society.

[SAVE] **BANGOR HISTORICAL SOCIETY MUSEUM** (Thomas A. Hill House), 159 Union St., is a Greek Revival house designed by Richard Upjohn and built in 1836. Three period rooms contain furnishings from the 19th century; there are portraits and landscapes by notable local artists. The Grand Army of the Republic Memorial Room of Civil War Artifacts also is featured. Allow 30 minutes minimum. Guided tours are offered Tues.-Sat. noon-4; closed major holidays. Admission $4, under 18 free. MC, VI. Phone (207) 942-5766.

[GEM] [SAVE] **COLE LAND TRANSPORTATION MUSEUM,** I-95 exit 182B following signs to the World War II Memorial at 405 Perry Rd., includes a 72-foot 1840s covered bridge and more than 200 vehicles illustrating the evolution of land transportation from wagons to automobiles to 18-wheelers. Among the items exhibited are antique recreational vehicles, motorcycles, a locomotive, a railroad station, farm equipment, horse-drawn logging sleds and logging trucks, snowplows and some 2,000 enlarged and captioned photographs of early life in Maine.

Also featured are hundreds of military artifacts from the Civil War to World War II, including fire, personnel and armored vehicles. The museum also is home to the Maine World War II Veterans Memorial, the Maine Vietnam Veterans Memorial and the Maine Military Order of the Purple Heart Memorial. Allow 1 hour minimum. Daily 9-5, May 1-Veterans Day. Admission $6; over 62, $4; under 19 free. Phone (207) 990-3600.

[SAVE] **MAINE DISCOVERY MUSEUM** is at 74 Main St. This museum comprises three floors of hands-on exhibits and activities for children including Nature Trails, which explores Maine's ecosystem; Passport, a display featuring world travel, mapping and geography; and Sounds Abound, which focuses on music. Picnicking is permitted. Allow 1 hour minimum. Tues.-Sat. 9:30-5, Sun. 11-5; closed Easter, Thanksgiving and Dec. 25. Admission $5.50. MC, VI. Phone (207) 262-7200.

## BAR HARBOR (E-4) pop. 2,680, elev. 240'
*See map page 39.*

Bar Harbor lies at the entrance to Acadia National Park on Mount Desert Island. The beauty of sea, mountain, lake and forest have made this region well-known as a resort. By the turn of the 20th century Bar Harbor had become the summer playground for America's wealthy; millionaires J.P. Morgan, Joseph Pulitzer and John D. Rockefeller were among those who owned "cottages."

However, newly instituted income taxes, World War I and the Great Depression nearly removed the leisure class from Bar Harbor by the 1930s. Many of the abandoned cottages, like their owners, succumbed to disaster and bad luck. Then a fire swept through Bar Harbor in 1947, ravaging 237 homes, including most of the estates, destroying 17,188 acres and leaving $23 million in charred ruins.

A network of motor highways, carriage roads and mountain trails preserves the striking scenery for visitors. The Great Meadow Loop Trail connects downtown Bar Harbor with Acadia National Park.

One of the best ways to explore the area is to hop on the Island Explorer, a free shuttle bus operating late June through early September. Rides to Northeast Harbor, Southwest Harbor, Brown Mountain, Acadia National Park, beaches, campgrounds and other destinations originate at the Bar Harbor Village Green. Shuttle passengers going to Acadia National Park should purchase a park entry permit at the Village Green prior to departing; phone (207) 288-4573.

Whale-watching cruises, sailing charters and working lobster boat excursions depart from Bar Harbor May through October.

Bay Ferries operates a high-speed catamaran providing car and passenger service from Bar Harbor to Yarmouth, Nova Scotia. The 3-hour ferry trip runs late May to late October; reservations are recommended. For schedules and rates phone (207) 288-3395 or (888) 249-7245. *See color ad p. 43.*

Jackson Laboratory, 1.5 miles south on SR 3, is a national genetics research center; phone (207) 288-6087 for information.

**Bar Harbor Chamber of Commerce:** 93 Cottage St., P.O. Box 158, Bar Harbor, ME 04609; phone (207) 288-5103 or (800) 288-5103.

# Drive The Coastal Discovery Trail

## Maine to Nova Scotia with The CAT™

Thanks to the all-new, state-of-the-art CAT, the wonders of The Coastal Discovery Trail — from Maine to Nova Scotia — are easier than ever to explore.

- Tour Maine's famous rockbound coast to Acadia National Park
- Take The CAT from Bar Harbor, Maine to Yarmouth, Nova Scotia
- Explore Nova Scotia and its 4,600 miles of magnificent coastline

## The CAT — The Ultimate Passenger Experience

The CAT is the only ferry in North America that can carry 900 passengers and up to 250 cars and 14 motor homes or tour buses across the ocean at highway speeds. It is like no car ferry you've ever seen:

Cabot Trail

- The CAT's incredible, wave-piercing catamaran technology whisks you from Maine to Nova Scotia in less than three hours — you save 600 driving miles and a full day behind the wheel
- On board, enjoy food & beverage, the casino and TV-movie lounge areas, duty-free shop and the spectacular views

**For more information on how you can explore the Coastal Discovery Trail with The CAT, call 1-888-249-SAIL or visit www.catferry.com. Get ready to experience one of the best driving vacations in North America.**

THE CAT

the high-speed catamaran from BAY ferries

1-888-249-SAIL
www.catferry.com

Acadia National Park

Lunenberg

Halifax Waterfront

Where the salt of the sea
meets the salt of the earth.

*This is* Nova Scotia.

Nova Scotia is the place where you'll always feel welcome. Where strangers are greeted with smiles. Where you'll experience all manner of delicious cuisine. Where music fills the air in our historic seacoast cities. **Nova Scotia - it's no place like home.**

**Tour the bustling waterfront in our seacoast city of Halifax.**

**Tantalize your taste-buds with delicious Digby scallops.**

**Explore our 4,600 miles of seacoast.**

**NOVA SCOTIA**
CANADA'S SEACOAST

Searching for a different kind of vacation destination? Then look no further than Nova Scotia. It's only a day's drive from Boston. And remember, your dollar goes a whole lot further in Canada.

*Discover our true nature*

For your free 400+ page guide to Canada's Seacoast, visit **novascotia.com**/scenery or call **1-800-565-0000**, op. 004

**ABBE MUSEUM** is downtown at 26 Mount Desert St. Permanent and changing exhibits devoted to Maine's American Indian heritage grace the galleries. Exhibits focus on the cultures, history and archeology of the Wabanaki people—members of the Passamaquoddy, Penobscot, Micmac and Maliseet tribes—who live in Maine today.

Allow 1 hour minimum. Daily 10-5, late May to mid-Oct. (also Thurs.-Sat. 5-9, July-Sept.); Thurs.-Sun. 10-5, mid-Oct. through Dec. 31 and Feb. 1-late May. Closed Thanksgiving and Dec. 25. Admission $4.50; ages 6-15, $2. MC, VI. Phone (207) 288-3519.

[SAVE] **ACADIA NATIONAL PARK TOURS**, 53 Main St., offers narrated 2.5-hour bus tours of Bar Harbor and Acadia National Park. The tour includes the mansions of Bar Harbor, Sand Beach, Thunder Hole and Cadillac Mountain. Tours depart daily at 10 and 2, mid-May through Oct. 31. Fare $20; under 13, $10. MC, VI. Phone (207) 288-0300.

**ACADIAN WHALE ADVENTURES** departs from the pier at the Harborside Hotel and Marina at 55 West St. A 2.5- to 3-hour tour aboard the 100-foot catamaran leads to humpback and giant finback whales. Dolphins, seals, puffins, sharks and giant tuna are common sights. Microphones and underwater cameras give visitors a better understanding of the active aquatic life.

Food is available. Allow 3 hours minimum. Departures daily at 8:30, 12:30 and 4, July-Aug.; at 8:30 and 12:30, Memorial Day-June 30 and Sept. 1-Columbus Day. Fare $37-$45; ages 8-15, $25-$30; under 8, $8. Schedule and fares may vary; phone ahead. AX, DC, DS, MC, VI. Phone (207) 288-9800 or (888) 533-9253.

**BAR HARBOR OCEANARIUM**, 8.5 mi. w. to 1351 SR 3, includes the Maine Lobster Museum and a lobster hatchery. The museum features trap-making demonstrations and a visit aboard a lobster boat; a licensed Maine lobsterman is on site to answer questions. At the hatchery, visitors can examine fry via a microscope linked to a television monitor. A 2-hour marsh walk is offered. Guided tours are available Memorial Day through Labor Day.

Allow 2 hours minimum. Mon.-Sat. 9-5, Memorial Day through mid-Oct.; 9-4, mid-May through day before Memorial Day. Admission $7.95; ages 4-12, $5.75. Combination ticket with the Mount Desert Oceanarium in Southwest Harbor *(see attraction listing p. 75)* $12; ages 4-12, $8.65. Phone (207) 288-5005.

**BAR HARBOR WHALE WATCH CO.** departs from the Town Pier at 1 West St. The company offers narrated, 3-hour whale-watching or 3.5-hour combination whale- and puffin-watching excursions aboard a 112-foot high-speed catamaran. The catamaran offers three decks for viewing and two heated cabins. Nature cruises and combination lobster- and seal-watching trips also are offered aboard other craft. Warm clothing is recommended.

Food is available. Whale-watching trips daily at 9, 10:30, 1 and 3, Sept. 7-Oct. 9; at 10:30, 1 and 3, Aug. 24-Sept. 6; at 1, June 10-Aug. 23; at noon, Oct. 10-25. Combination whale- and puffin-watching trips daily at 8:30, 10:30, 3 and 4:30, July 1-Aug. 23; at 9, 10:30 and 3, June 17-30; at 8:30 and 4:30, Aug. 24-Sept. 6; at noon, May 26-June 9; at 9, June 10-16. Whale-watching fare $39; ages 6-14, $25; under 6, $8. Combination whale- and puffin-watching fare $43; ages 6-14, $25; under 6, $8. DS, MC, VI. Phone (207) 288-2386 or (800) 942-5374.

[SAVE] **GEORGE B. DORR MUSEUM OF NATURAL HISTORY** is at 105 Eden St. on the College of the Atlantic campus. The museum displays mounted mammals and birds in lifelike scenes. Other exhibits depict natural aspects of maritime Maine, including a tidal pool. A changing interpretive program is offered daily July 1 through Labor Day. A natural history lecture series also is available.

Allow 30 minutes minimum. Museum open Mon.-Sat. 10-5, mid-June through Labor Day; Thurs.-Fri. and Sun. 1-4, Sat. 10-4, rest of year. Natural history lecture series Wed. at 7:30 p.m., July-Aug. Admission $3.50; over 59, $2.50; ages 13-19, $1.50; ages 3-12, $1. MC, VI. Phone (207) 288-5015.

# BATH (E-3) pop. 9,266, elev. 7′

Bath, on the west bank of the Kennebec River, has been an active center of shipbuilding since the early 1600s. Nuclear naval vessels and large merchant ships are now built at Bath Iron Works. Residential sections have a number of old mansions dating from Bath's days as a major port. The Chocolate Church Arts Center, 804 Washington St., offers year-round cultural events; phone (207) 442-8455.

**Bath/Brunswick Region Chamber of Commerce:** 45 Front St., Bath, ME 04530; phone (207) 443-9751.

**Self-guiding tours:** Brochures describing historic driving and walking tours are available from the chamber of commerce.

[GEM] **MAINE MARITIME MUSEUM**, at 243 Washington St., is a 20-acre site located on a 19th-century shipyard where large wooden sailing ships were constructed. The Maritime History Building contains paintings, ship models, displays of ship artifacts and interpretive exhibits of life at sea and maritime technology. Visiting vessels may be boarded when they are docked on the site.

The shipyard houses the Boat Shop; visitors can watch the building process and tour five of the original shipyard buildings. The exhibit Lobstering and the Maine Coast describes the development of one of the state's leading economic concerns. Tours of the shipyard are offered Memorial Day through Columbus Day. A children's play ship is on the premises; daily boat cruises are available for an additional fee from June through October.

Allow 1 hour minimum. Daily 9:30-5; closed Jan. 1, Thanksgiving and Dec. 25. Admission $9.75; over 65, $8.75; ages 7-17, $6.75; family rate $28. DS, MC, VI. Phone (207) 443-1316.

## BELFAST (D-3) pop. 6,381, elev. 103′

Formerly a prosperous shipbuilding center, Belfast is a community resplendent with restored Federal and early Victorian homes built by former sea merchants. The city, located on Penobscot Bay, is becoming a cultural center with artists, writers and craftspeople adding to the economic revival of Waldo County.

The Belfast Maskers, a local theater group, offers productions year-round. Belfast and Moosehead Lake Railroad, as well as local cruise and aviation companies, offers summer and fall foliage tours.

**Belfast Area Chamber of Commerce:** 17 Main St., P.O. Box 58, Belfast, ME 04915; phone (207) 338-5900.

**Self-guiding tours:** Walking tour brochures are available from the chamber of commerce.

## BETHEL (D-1) elev. 643′

Bethel lies along a quiet stretch of the Androscoggin River adjacent to the Mahoosuc mountain range that connects in the southwest to the White Mountains. Settled in 1774 as Sudbury-Canada, it is one of the oldest villages in northwestern Maine. The Revolutionary War so slowed growth that in 1781, when the village experienced the last New England raid by Indians from Canada, it had only 10 families.

Bethel, as the community was rechristened in 1796, grew into an important farming and lumbering center. Once the railroad linked it with Portland and Montréal, assuring its position in commerce, Bethel became a favorite spot for visitors to the White Mountains. Founded in 1836, Gould Academy on Church Street is one of the state's leading preparatory schools. A well-known resident was Dr. John Gehring, a neurologist for whom a ward of the New York Neurological Institute is named.

Swimming, camping, hiking, bicycling, canoeing, kayaking, fishing and rockhounding are favorite summer activities.

Grafton Notch State Park (see Recreation Chart), 14 miles north on SR 26, is at the end of the Mahoosuc Range between Newry and Upton. The park, which is open daily from mid-May to mid-October, contains such scenic points as Screw Auger Falls, Spruce Meadow, Mother Walker Falls and Moose Cave.

**Bethel Area Chamber of Commerce:** 8 Station Pl., P.O. Box 1247, Bethel, ME 04217; phone (207) 824-2282 or (800) 442-5826.

**Self-guiding tours:** Booklets detailing a self-guiding walking tour of the Broad Street Historic District and Bethel Hill Village as well as guides describing a self-guiding driving tour of historic homes are available at the Bethel Historical Society Regional History Center (see attraction listing) and the chamber of commerce. Information about scenic driving tours also is available from the chamber of commerce.

SAVE **BETHEL HISTORICAL SOCIETY REGIONAL HISTORY CENTER,** 10-14 Broad St., is the restored Federal-style home of Dr. Moses Mason, physician and U.S. congressman from Maine. The nine-room 1813 house is furnished in period. Of special interest are the Rufus Porter murals depicting seascapes and foliage. A research facility is available. The 1821 O'Neil Robinson House, at 10 Broad St., has changing exhibits as well as the offices of the historical society.

Allow 30 minutes minimum. Tues.-Sun. 1-4, July 1-Labor Day; Tues.-Fri. 1-4 and by appointment rest of year. Admission $3, children $1.50. Donations are accepted for use of the research library. MC, VI. Phone (207) 824-2908 or (800) 824-2910.

### RECREATIONAL ACTIVITIES

#### Skiing

- **Sunday River Ski Resort,** on US 2. Write P.O. Box 450, Bethel, ME 04217. Other activities are offered. Daily Oct.-Apr. Phone (207) 824-3000.

## BIDDEFORD (F-2) pop. 20,942, elev. 75′

In 1662 one of the region's first sawmills was erected in Biddeford. The lure of waterpower gradually built the city into an important manufacturing center. Biddeford's diverse economic base relies on boatbuilding and the production of plastic, machinery, electronics and baked goods.

Biddeford is closely bound economically and culturally to Saco (see place listing p. 71), its sister city across the river. This interdependency is evident in the cooperative efforts shown in the restoration of the 1895 opera house; the acoustically perfect theater is an outstanding example of late 19th-century ornamental architecture.

Both cities take advantage of the educational and cultural opportunities offered by the University College at Saco and the University of New England, 4 miles east on Pool Road overlooking the sea.

**Biddeford-Saco Chamber of Commerce & Industry:** 110 Main St., Suite 1202, Saco, ME 04072; phone (207) 282-1567.

## BIDDEFORD POOL (F-2) elev. 20′

**EAST POINT SANCTUARY,** 5 mi. s. on US 208 on Lester B. Orcutt Blvd. to end, encompasses 30 acres of rocky coastal headland considered to be one of the best sites for bird-watching in southern Maine. A shoreline trail offers views of such marine birds as gannets, red-throated loons, sea ducks and terns. Two rocky islands visible from the trail support large bird colonies. Daily dawn-dusk. Free. Phone (207) 781-2330.

# AMERICA ON THE MOVE
## A NEW EXHIBITION ON TRANSPORTATION IN AMERICAN HISTORY

1903 Winton, First Car to Cross the Country

**National Museum of American History**
14th and Constitution Ave. NW ✦ Washington, D.C.

Open Daily: 10 a.m. - 5:30 p.m. (Except December 25)

americanhistory.si.edu/onthemove

Free Admission

**Smithsonian**
*National Museum of American History*
*Behring Center*

AMERICA
ON THE MOVE

## BLUE HILL (D-4) elev. 40′

Since its 19th-century halcyon days as a shipbuilding, seafaring and lumbering town, Blue Hill has become a popular summer vacation and crafts center. It is especially noted for wheel-thrown pottery, some of which is produced from local clays; Rackliffe Pottery on Ellsworth Road and Rowantree Pottery on Union Street welcome visitors. A number of art galleries are in the area.

Craftsmanship is not new; in the early 1800s, Parson Jonathan Fisher designed and built his own house, made the paint that adorned it and created most of its furniture, paintings and woodcuts. Having invented machines to saw wood, split straws and dig stones, he then built a windmill to power them. The life of this unusual man was chronicled by Mary Ellen Chase, a novelist born in Blue Hill in 1887. The parson's house still stands on SR 15; phone (207) 374-2459.

The village is the namesake of a 934-foot hill that overlooks the town, situated at the head of Blue Hill Bay. The hill's blue appearance from a distance no doubt inspired the name. From its summit the view extends eastward to Mount Desert Island and Acadia National Park *(see place listing p. 39)* and westward to Camden Hills State Park *(see Recreation Chart)*.

An extensive and eclectic collection of sheet music is housed in Blue Hill's Bagaduce Music Lending Library. Organized according to the instrument for which each piece was written, the library's 620,000 titles include many rare items that might be difficult to find anywhere else. Throughout the summer young performers at the Kneisel Hall Summer Music Center present recitals and concerts.

## BOOTHBAY HARBOR (E-3)

pop. 1,237, elev. 20′

A picturesque seaport, Boothbay Harbor retains the atmosphere of an old New England village. Fishing craft lie alongside wharves that follow the quaint, winding village streets. Yachtsmen and artists began vacationing in the area in the early 1900s. Word soon spread of the region's natural beauty, and Boothbay Harbor began the slow transition from shipping center to resort area.

The Boothbay Harbor region's waterfront offers visitors a glimpse of seafaring history and an array of nautical activities on the Maine coast. With a strong shipbuilding and fishing heritage, the harbor shelters a wide variety of boats.

River cruises, ocean cruises, whale watches, sailing and deep-sea fishing trips leave local piers daily and vary in length from 1 hour to an entire day. The *Balmy Days II* makes day trips to Monhegan Island *(see place listing p. 61)* from Memorial Day weekend through mid-October. Ninety-minute trips depart Boothbay Harbor daily at 9:30 and leave Monhegan Island at 2:45. The fare is $30; ages 3-11, $18. Reservations are recommended. Phone (207) 633-2284 or (800) 298-2284.

Noteworthy events include the Fall Foliage Festival, with craft displays and train rides, held in mid-October. Also of interest is the Carousel Music Theatre, which presents musicals and variety shows mid-May to early fall.

**Boothbay Harbor Region Chamber of Commerce:** 192 Townsend Ave., P.O. Box 356, Boothbay Harbor, ME 04538; phone (207) 633-2353. *See color ad p. 197.*

**BOOTHBAY RAILWAY VILLAGE,** 3.5 mi. n. on SR 27 to 586 Wiscasset Rd., depicts a turn-of-the-20th-century Maine village containing railroad memorabilia, antique cars and trucks and includes such restored buildings as a blacksmith shop and general store as well as the 1847 Boothbay Town Hall and the Spruce Point Chapel. Visitors can ride on a narrow-gauge, coal-fired steam engine. A Halloween train runs in late October. Allow 2 hours minimum. Daily 9:30-5, June 5-Oct. 10. Trains depart hourly 10-4. Admission $8; under 16, $4. AX, MC, VI. Phone (207) 633-4727.

**CAP'N FISH'S WHALE WATCH AND SCENIC NATURE CRUISES,** downtown on the waterfront at Pier 1, offers a variety of sightseeing cruises along the Maine coast. Available cruises include a 3.5-hour whale-watch cruise, a 3-hour Kennebec River trip, a 2-hour harbor cruise and a 1.25-hour seal-watch cruise. Food is available. Cruises usually depart daily at 9:30, 10, 1, 2 and 3:30, June-Oct. Fare $14-$28; under 12, $7-$18. Reservations are recommended. AX, MC, VI. Phone (207) 633-3244 or (800) 636-3244.

**HENDRICKS HILL MUSEUM,** 4 mi. s. via SR 27 to 419 Hendricks Hill Rd., on the island of Southport, includes a restored early 19th-century house containing such artifacts as period household items, tools from the local fishing industry and navigation instruments and charts. A boat shop contains early fishing boats and woodworking tools from the ice harvesting industry. Allow 30 minutes minimum. Tues., Thurs. and Sat. 11-3, July 1-Labor Day; by appointment, day after Labor Day-Sept. 30. Donations. Phone (207) 633-2370.

**KENNETH E. STODDARD SHELL MUSEUM,** 4.5 mi. n. on SR 27 past the lighthouse parking lot, displays thousands of shells in wood-and-glass cases housed in a building inside a covered bridge. The mainly Pacific shells range in size from specimens smaller than a finger to large conch shells. Sand dollars and lobster claws also are exhibited. Allow 1 hour minimum. Daily 10-10, May 1-Sept. 15; by appointment rest of year. Donations. Phone (207) 633-4828.

## BRADLEY (D-4)

**LEONARD'S MILLS AND MAINE FOREST LOGGING MUSEUM,** n. on SR 9, n. on SR 178, then 1.25 mi. e. on a dirt road following signs, allows visitors a glimpse into the area's forestry and logging history. Entered by crossing Blackman Stream through a covered bridge on foot, the site contains a sawmill powered by a water wheel as well as a blacksmith shop, a stone dam and cabins. Site maps and information are available at the covered bridge. Picnicking is permitted. Daily 10-dusk, early Apr.-late Oct. Donations. Phone (207) 581-2871.

## BRUNSWICK (E-2) pop. 14,816, elev. 63′

Industry, recreation and education are important pursuits in Brunswick, the chief city of the eastern Casco Bay area. Industry began in the 1620s when an English trader's success with exporting sturgeon and salmon from the falls of the lower Androscoggin River induced his company to establish a post. From that time until about 1730 the settlement of Pejepscot rose and fell as warring American Indians destroyed it in 1690 and again in 1722.

Between disasters, during 1714-15, a group called the Pejepscot Proprietors bought the post, built Fort George and planned the spacious grid pattern of the streets. One thoroughfare was the Twelve Rod Road, now Maine Street; measuring 198 feet across, it is one of the widest streets in New England. By the late 1700s the settlement, renamed Brunswick, was an important lumbering, milling and shipbuilding center.

Bowdoin College, established in 1794, is the home of the Maine State Music Theater, where a professional cast performs Broadway musicals mid-June to late August. A chamber music concert series is presented on Friday evenings in the summer at the First Parish Church. Free open-air concerts are held on the Mall on Wednesday evenings July through August.

Harriet Beecher Stowe's inspiration for "Uncle Tom's Cabin" supposedly came from a sermon delivered at the First Parish Church on Maine Street, open for worship since 1717. Another celebrated local was Gov. Joshua Lawrence Chamberlain, noted for his defense at Gettysburg and for being the only Union general to receive a battlefield promotion from Gen. Ulysses S. Grant.

**Chamber of Commerce of the Brunswick-Bath Region:** 59 Pleasant St., Brunswick, ME 04011; phone (207) 725-8797.

**BOWDOIN COLLEGE** occupies a 110-acre campus at Maine, Bath and College sts. In addition to Nathaniel Hawthorne and Henry Wadsworth Longfellow, alumni include Arctic explorers Robert Peary and Donald MacMillan, and President Franklin Pierce. Tours depart from the Burton-Little House on College Street. Allow 1 hour minimum. Campus tours Mon.-Fri. at 9:30, 11:30 and 1:30; Sat. at 11:30. Free. Phone (207) 725-3000.

**Bowdoin College Museum of Art,** in the Walker Art Building, contains Colonial and Federal portraits, a fine collection of classical antiquities, old masters' drawings, a collection of more than 14,000 objects featuring notable Assyrian reliefs, contemporary art, works by European artists and changing exhibits. Guided tours are available by appointment.

**Note:** Renovations commence Dec. 2004. The museum is scheduled to reopen in fall 2006. During renovations, the ancient collection is the only artwork available for viewing. It is located in the Susan Dwight Bliss Room at Hubbard Hall. Allow 1 hour minimum. Tues.-Sat. 10-5, Sun. 2-5; closed major holidays. Free. Phone (207) 725-3275.

**Peary-MacMillan Arctic Museum,** in Hubbard Hall, has displays relating to the two explorers as well as life and the environment in the Arctic region. The collections include Arctic exploration gear, natural history specimens, and artifacts and drawings created by Inuit and Indians of North America. Allow 30 minutes minimum. Tues.-Sat. 10-5, Sun. 2-5; closed holidays. Donations. Phone (207) 725-3416.

SAVE **JOSHUA LAWRENCE CHAMBERLAIN MUSEUM,** 226 Maine St., is a partially restored Federal-style house with Victorian Gothic additions. The house once belonged to Joshua Lawrence Chamberlain, a Civil War hero, president of Bowdoin College and governor of Maine 1867-71. Guests Chamberlain entertained at the house include Gen. Ulysses S. Grant, Helen Keller, Henry Wadsworth Longfellow and Harriet Beecher Stowe.

Guided tours are given Tues.-Sat. 10-3:15, June 1 through mid-Oct.; closed holidays. Admission $5; ages 6-16, $2.50. Phone (207) 729-6606.

SAVE **PEJEPSCOT MUSEUM/SKOLFIELD-WHITTIER HOUSE,** 159-161 Park Row, is a brick Italianate semidetached house built by a shipmaster for his two sons in 1858. The adjoining house contains original furnishings and the personal belongings of three generations of Skolfields and Whittiers left perfectly intact in 1925. The collections reflect the families' involvement in seafaring, shipping, medicine and education. The history museum features changing exhibits.

Allow 1 hour minimum. Museum open Tues.-Fri. 9-5 (also Thurs. 5-8), Sat. 9-4, Memorial Day-Columbus Day; Tues.-Fri. 9-5 (also Thurs. 5-8), Sat. noon-4, rest of year. Closed holidays. Guided tours of the Skolfield-Whittier House depart Tues.-Sat. at 10, 11:30, 1 and 2:30, June 1 through mid-Oct. Museum by donations. Guided tours of house $5; ages 6-16, $2.50. Phone (207) 729-6606.

## BUCKSPORT (D-4) pop. 2,970, elev. 43′

**NORTHEAST HISTORIC FILM,** 85 Main St., is in a renovated 1916 cinema. The museum traces the history of northern New England moviegoing through films and movie artifacts. Every weekend, movie screenings are preceded by rare archival film clips. A silent film festival is held in summer. A study center with films, videos and books also is available for visitors.

Museum Mon.-Fri. 9-4. Screenings Fri.-Sat. at 6:30 p.m. and 8:30 p.m., Sun. at 2. Screening schedule may vary; phone ahead. Museum by donation. Screenings $6, over 61 and students with ID $5. MC, VI. Phone (207) 469-0924, or (207) 469-6910 for screening information.

## CALAIS (C-6) pop. 3,447, elev. 19'

Calais (KAL-is) is on the west bank of Passamaquoddy Bay at the mouth of the St. Croix River, a U.S.-Canadian boundary. Connected by the International Bridge to St. Stephen, New Brunswick, the city enjoys the distinction of being Maine's only international city.

Timber, fertile soil and an abundance of fish and game attracted the first settlers to the area in 1604. The town became an important lumbering and shipbuilding center. In 1809 the Massachusetts legislature named the settlement for the port of Calais, France, in acknowledgment of that country's assistance during the American Revolution.

The section of US 1 between Calais and Bar Harbor is a scenic drive from which visitors might see nesting eagles.

**Calais Regional Chamber of Commerce:** 16 Swan St., P.O. Box 368, Calais, ME 04619; phone (207) 454-2308.

**Shopping areas:** An Ammex Tax & Duty Free Shop is at 14 Main St.

**DR. HOLMES COTTAGE MUSEUM,** 245 Main St., is a two-story, Cape Cod-style structure built about 1804 and restored to its appearance of the mid-1800s. The cottage housed the practices of several physicians, and it now displays medical equipment and period furnishings. Allow 30 minutes minimum. Mon.-Fri. 1-4, July-Aug.; by appointment rest of year. Donations. Phone (207) 454-2604.

**MOOSEHORN NATIONAL WILDLIFE REFUGE** is divided into two areas, the Baring Unit. 3 mi. s.w. on Charlotte Rd., and the Edmunds Unit, about 2 mi. s.e. of Dennysville off US 1. The two sites constitute a migratory bird refuge totaling 24,390 acres. The Baring Unit encompasses 17,200 acres containing nature and hiking trails and a 4,700-acre wilderness area. The 7,190-acre Edmunds Unit, at Cobscook Bay State Park *(see Recreation Chart),* includes a 2,782-acre wilderness area offering nature trails and fishing opportunities. Allow 1 hour minimum. Daily dawn-dusk. Free. Phone (207) 454-7161.

## CAMDEN (E-4) pop. 3,934, elev. 33'

Camden's beauty has attracted many writers, painters and artisans, including Edna St. Vincent Millay, whose career began in this town. A statue at the head of the harbor honors the poet, and Millay memorabilia is housed in the Whitehall Inn. Shaded streets, white clapboard churches and flower gardens contribute to the tranquil atmosphere, which draws the annual return of the Summer Harp Colony of America.

As a year-round resort the seaside town also is popular with sports enthusiasts. Bicycling is a favorite pastime and sailing, kayaking and canoeing, on either the ocean or one of many lakes, prevails in the summer; ice skating and cross-country and

downhill skiing predominate in winter. The toboggan run at the Camden Snow Bowl is open to the public. Windjammer cruises and lobstering provide summer recreation, and coastal cruising via scenic US 1 is rewarding year-round.

Cultural enthusiasts can attend performances at the Camden Opera House or the Rockport Opera House. Summer highlights include a variety of events; schooner races, art shows, folk festivals, antique shows, church fairs and lobster festivals are all on the agenda. Occasional concerts as well as juried art shows in July and October are presented at Amphitheatre and Marine Park, on Atlantic Avenue at the waterfront.

Camden Hills State Park *(see Recreation Chart)* is 2 miles north on US 1. A 1-mile road that leads to the summit of Mount Battie offers scenic views of Camden village and harbor. On a clear day, Acadia National Park and Monhegan Island can be seen.

**Camden-Rockport-Lincolnville   Chamber   of Commerce:** P.O. Box 919, Camden, ME 04843; phone (207) 236-4404 or (800) 223-5459 to request a visitors' guide.

**Self-guiding tours:** Brochures and maps are available from the chamber of commerce, which is on the public landing.

**CONWAY HOMESTEAD-CRAMER MUSEUM** is 1 mi. s. via US 1. The Conway House is an 18th-century farmhouse with an herb garden and antique furnishings. The barn displays include sleighs and a spinning wheel. Other highlights include a blacksmith shop and an 1820 maple sugar house. The Mary Meeker Cramer Museum exhibits ship models, quilts, period clothing and other local memorabilia, including items from the USS *Conway.*

Allow 1 hour minimum. Mon.-Thurs. 10-4, July-Aug.; by appointment in June and Sept. Admission $5; senior citizens $4; ages 6-18, $2. Phone (207) 236-2257.

**MERRYSPRING NATURE PARK** is at 30 Conway Rd. The 66-acre nature park and horticultural center includes herb, rose and perennial gardens; the Kitty Todd Arboretum; three greenhouses; walking trails; and the Ross Center, which houses a library and visitor facilities. Allow 1 hour, 30 minutes minimum. Park open daily dawn-dusk. Ross Center open Tues.-Fri. 9-2. Free. Phone (207) 236-2239.

## CAPE ELIZABETH (F-2) elev. 27'

Cape Elizabeth was named by Capt. John Smith in 1615 for Princess Elizabeth, sister of Charles I of England. Early settlers managed to exist by fishing and farming, despite repeated raids by American Indians and pirates. Closely associated with Portland (then Falmouth) in its earliest days, the settlement was recognized as a separate district in 1765 and finally granted status as an incorporated town during the Revolutionary unrest of 1775.

Few farms remain, as "the Cape" has become primarily a residential center for the Greater Portland area. The diverse coastal landscape includes sandy beaches, craggy cliffs and saltwater marshes and is accessible through two state parks as well as one town-owned park.

Two Lights State Park, 3 miles south on SR 77, features walking areas, scenic views from a rocky headland and picnic facilities. The park is next to Two Lights Lighthouse, which marks the entrance to Casco Bay. Crescent Beach State Park, 1 mile south on SR 77, offers swimming, picnic facilities and views of Richmond Island.

**Greater Portland Convention and Visitors Bureau:** 245 Commercial St., Portland, ME 04101; phone (800) 306-4182.

**PORTLAND HEAD LIGHT** is at 1000 Shore Rd. in Fort Williams Park. First operated in 1791 under the authorization of President George Washington, it was the first light completed after the founding of the United States and is one of the oldest lighthouses in continuous use in the country. Highlights include a museum, several walking paths, picnic facilities and a view of Portland Harbor.

Park open daily dawn-dusk. Museum open daily 10-4, June-Oct.; Sat.-Sun. 10-4, Apr.-May and Nov.-Dec. Park free. Museum $2; ages 6-18, $1. AX, DS, MC, VI. Phone (207) 799-2661.

## CARIBOU (A-5) pop. 8,312, elev. 400´

Caribou is a business center for Aroostook County, source of 90 percent of the state's potato crop and one of the largest potato-shipping areas in the world. The Aroostook and Little Madawaska rivers, which offer excellent trout and salmon fishing, flow through town. The city offers a variety of recreational opportunities, including canoeing, fishing, camping, autumn foliage drives and winter sports.

Caribou was settled by soldiers who had been sent to the frontier during the 1838-39 Aroostook War and then stayed to log or farm. Development was slow, primarily because the town lacked the means to transport goods to market. The potato crop was unable to realize its commercial potential until the Bangor and Aroostook Railroad arrived in the early 1890s. As a major junction point, Caribou flourished.

Northwest of Caribou along SR 161, communities with such names as Sweden, New Sweden, Jemtland and Stockholm reveal the origins of those who settled the region in the 1870s.

**Caribou Chamber of Commerce:** 24 Sweden St., Suite 101, Caribou, ME 04736; phone (207) 498-6156 or (800) 722-7648.

**NYLANDER MUSEUM,** 657 Main St., contains the extensive collections of rocks, minerals, fossils, shells, marine specimens and American Indian artifacts of Swedish-born Olof Nylander. A self-taught naturalist, Nylander spent his life amassing and

classifying—an effort that gained him an honorary Master of Science degree from the University of Maine. Visitors may participate in nature walks and tours.

Allow 1 hour minimum. Tues.-Sat. 12:30-4:30, Memorial Day weekend-Labor Day; Mon.-Tues. and Thurs. 3-7, rest of year. Donations. Phone (207) 493-4209.

## CARRABASSETT VALLEY (D-2)

### RECREATIONAL ACTIVITIES
#### Skiing

- **Sugarloaf/USA**, off SR 27, R.R. 1, Box 5000, Carrabassett Valley, ME 04947-9799. Other activities are offered. Daily Nov.-Apr. Phone (800) 843-5623.

## CASTINE (E-4)

Coveted by world powers for its strategic port, Castine endured 2 centuries of disputes among the American Indians, French, British, Dutch and Americans. The French erected a fort in 1613, but the first permanent settlement was made by England in 1760. The British occupied the town during the Revolution, after handing the American Navy its most humiliating and devastating defeat in the largest amphibious operation of the Revolutionary War.

Although severely outnumbered, a handful of British sloops-of-war pummeled a Colonial fleet of some 40 ships sent to defend the harbor, which was used as a base for hit-and-run missions against His Majesty's navy. After securing the town the British built Fort George; it passed into American possession in 1783. Fort Madison was built in 1811. The British occupied both forts during the War of 1812.

Fort Madison was rebuilt during the Civil War; the earthworks and protective moat are still visible. Fort George, partially restored, is maintained as a memorial. Castine also is home to Maine Maritime Academy, founded in 1941, it prepares its students for careers in nautical and ocean sciences, engineering and management.

**THE T/V STATE OF MAINE,** berthed near Pleasant St. at the Maine Maritime Academy waterfront, is a 499-foot training ship for academy students. The ship, the former USNS *Tanner,* originally served as a Navy oceanographic research vessel. Guided 30-minute tours are given daily on the hour 10-noon and 1-3, early July-late Aug.; Sat.-Sun. 10-noon and 1-3, early Sept.-early May. Hours may vary; phone ahead. Free. Phone (207) 326-4311 or (207) 326-2420.

**WILSON MUSEUM,** 107 Perkins St., contains exhibits that include prehistoric artifacts from North and South America; and a range of displays depicting the advancement of man's ability to fabricate tools, from the early Paleolithic through the Neolithic, Bronze and Iron Ages. Also featured is the John Perkins House, a pre-Revolutionary War structure restored and furnished with period antiques.

Allow 1 hour minimum. Museum open Tues.-Sun. 2-5, Memorial Day-Sept. 30. Guided tours of the John Perkins House Wed. and Sun. 2-5, July-Aug. Museum free. John Perkins House $5. Phone (207) 326-8753.

## COLUMBIA FALLS (D-5) elev. 30'

Columbia Falls, a few miles up the Pleasant River from Pleasant Bay, was settled about 1780. Several fine old homes remain as testimony to the community's affluent days as a successful shipbuilding and lumbering center. With the passing of that era, the economy shifted to agriculture. Cranberry bogs, acres of blueberry fields and vast woodland lots offer seasonal crops that sustain the community economically.

**RUGGLES HOUSE**, .5 mi. off US 1 on Main St., was built 1818-20 for Judge Thomas Ruggles, a wealthy lumber dealer, merchant, postmaster and militia captain. The two-story Adams-style house is noted for its flying staircase that rises without lateral support and for its delicate interior and exterior woodcarvings, which were created by a craftsman using only a penknife. Many of the period furnishings are original. Mon.-Sat. 9:30-4:30, Sun. 11-4:30, June 1-Oct. 15. Admission $5; ages 6-12, $2. Phone (207) 483-4637.

## DAMARISCOTTA (E-3)

Although John Brown—recipient in 1625 of the first deed tendered within the present borders of Maine—lived in this area in the mid-1600s, permanent settlement did not take place until 1730. In that year, three Boston families sailed up the Damariscotta River to take up grants along its shore. Their village prospered with an economy based on lumbering, agriculture, shipping and brick making.

Its position at the head of navigation and the ready supply of timber made Damariscotta a natural place for shipbuilding. Among several noted vessels built in this town was the 1849 *Excelsior,* the first three-decked ship constructed in Maine. The builder's model is in the Information Bureau building at the head of Main Street.

Damariscotta is now a shopping and financial center for the nearby resort area that extends south to Christmas Cove and the Pemaquids *(see Pemaquid Point p. 64).* Much of the character of the Main Street business district stems from the brick structures erected after a fire in 1845. Houses dating from the Colonial and Federal periods are scattered throughout the community and south along SR 129/130.

**Damariscotta Region Chamber of Commerce:** P.O. Box 13, Damariscotta, ME 04543; phone (207) 563-8340.

**ROUND TOP CENTER FOR THE ARTS**, 1.5 mi. n. to 1316 US 1 Bus. Rte., is a community center for the visual and performing arts. The center offers classes, concerts, lectures and demonstrations. A gallery houses changing arts and crafts exhibits, and several local artists work on site. Admission is charged for classes, concerts and plays. Drama and music festivals are held year-round.

Allow 1 hour minimum. Center Mon.-Sat. 9-4, Sun. 1-4. Gallery Mon.-Fri. 11-4, Sat. noon-4 (also Sun. 1-4, June-Sept.). Closed major holidays. Donations. Phone (207) 563-1507.

## DEXTER (D-3) pop. 2,201, elev. 429'

**DEXTER HISTORICAL SOCIETY MUSEUM AND MILLER'S HOUSE**, downtown at 3 Water St., features an 1854 gristmill that was operational until 1966 and a restored one-room schoolhouse used 1845-1944. Other exhibits include an old-fashioned kitchen and agricultural implements. The Miller's House, behind the museum, contains business offices, but visitors are welcome to see the photograph gallery and Victorian-style parlor. Genealogical records are available.

Mon.-Fri. 10-4, Sat. 1-4, June 1 through mid-Sept. Genealogical archives by appointment year-round. Donations. Phone (207) 924-5721.

## DRESDEN (E-2)

**POWNALBOROUGH COURTHOUSE** is w. on SR 128. The only pre-Revolutionary courthouse remaining in the state, this three-story 1761 structure includes a furnished courtroom, judges' chambers, bedrooms, kitchen, tavern and parlor. President John Adams once tried a case at the courthouse. Displays of antique tools and machinery chronicle the area's history. A Revolutionary-era cemetery is on the grounds.

Guided tours and nature trails are available. Picnicking is permitted. Allow 30 minutes minimum. Tues.-Sat. 10-4, Sun. noon-4, July 1-Labor Day; Sat. 10-4, Sun. noon-4 in June and day after Labor Day-Sept. 30. Admission $4; ages 7-17, $2. Phone (207) 882-6817.

## EAST ORLAND (D-4)

**CRAIG BROOK NATIONAL FISH HATCHERY**, 1.25 mi. s.w. of US 1/SR 3 (Hatchery Rd.), is dedicated to the replenishment of the Atlantic salmon in Maine's waters. More than 3 million eggs are hatched here annually. A visitor center contains educational displays, and a display pool and a nature trail are on the grounds. The Friends of Craig Brook Atlantic Salmon Museum also is featured.

Visitor center daily 8-3:30. Museum Tues., Thurs. and Sun. noon-3, July 1-Labor Day. Hours may vary; phone ahead. Free. Phone (207) 469-2803.

## EASTPORT (D-6) pop. 1,640, elev. 41'

Eastport, on Moose Island in Passamaquoddy Bay, was first settled about 1780. In a roundabout way, the capture of Eastport by the British in 1814 put Gen. Andrew Jackson in the White House 15 years later. News of Eastport's fall during the War of 1812 halted peace negotiations and prolonged the fighting so that Jackson won the decisive Battle of New Orleans. It was the general's victory that ultimately led him to the presidency in 1829.

In Eastport, fishing, scallop harvesting and lumber shipping are principal concerns. A deepwater commercial port and a large aquaculture industry that specializes in raising trout and salmon characterize the waterfront.

The moorlike wilderness of Washington County, which is larger in area than Rhode Island and Delaware combined, yields some of the state's richest blueberry and cranberry harvests. The record tidal variation on the east coast of the United States is registered in the vicinity, with a rise and fall as great as 26 feet during some seasons.

Old Sow, which is said to be the second largest whirlpool in the world, can be seen 2 hours before high tide from Dog Island, reached by way of Water Street. Air and boat charters are available to view the region's scenic areas, whales and other marine life and such native birds as eagles and ospreys.

**Eastport Area Chamber of Commerce:** Water St., P.O. Box 254, Eastport, ME 04631; phone (207) 853-4644.

**WAPONAHKI MUSEUM AND RESOURCE CENTER,** 2.5 mi. n. on SR 190, exhibits artifacts, photographs and paintings that illustrate the history and culture of the Passamaquoddy Indians. Items on display include tools, weapons and an original 17-foot birch bark canoe. Many objects are more than 100 years old. The museum also contains books and tapes created to preserve the Passamaquoddy language. Allow 1 hour minimum. Mon.-Fri. 8-11 and 11:30-2; closed major holidays. Donations. Phone (207) 853-4001.

# EDGECOMB (E-3)

**FORT EDGECOMB STATE HISTORIC SITE** occupies 3 acres on the s. end of Davis Island, just s. off US 1. An 1808-09 octagonal wooden blockhouse built of hand-hewn timbers for the War of 1812 offers an interesting example of the construction methods of the period. Remains of the earthworks are evident. Informational panels are available. Picnicking is permitted. Allow 30 minutes minimum. Daily 9-5, Memorial Day-Labor Day. Admission $2; ages 5-11, $1. Phone (207) 882-7777.

# ELLSWORTH (D-4) pop. 6,456, elev. 112'

Ellsworth began as a lumbering and shipbuilding center in 1763 and moved into the industrial era via waterpower from the Union River. Lamoine Beach State Park (see Recreation Chart), 6.5 miles southeast of the southern terminus of SR 184, offers scenic views of Frenchman Bay and Mount Desert Island. Visitors can see eagles, ospreys, harbor seals and other wildlife at Ellsworth Marine Waterfront Park off Water Street.

Ellsworth also is surrounded by several lakes and streams that offer opportunities for boating, canoeing and fishing.

**Ellsworth Area Chamber of Commerce:** 163 High St., P.O. Box 267, Ellsworth, ME 04605; phone (207) 667-5584.

**STANWOOD HOMESTEAD MUSEUM AND WILDLIFE SANCTUARY (BIRDSACRE),** on SR 3 just s. of US 1, is the former home of Cordelia Stanwood, Maine's pioneer ornithologist. The museum, built in 1850, houses original furnishings. Also on exhibit at the Richmond Nature Center are collections of mounted birds, nests, eggs, paintings and prints. Birdsacre, a 170-acre wildlife preserve with nature trails and picnic facilities, is a sanctuary for more than 100 bird species.

Allow 1 hour minimum. Museum and nature center open daily 10-4, June 15-Oct. 15; otherwise by appointment. Sanctuary open daily dawn-dusk. Museum and sanctuary by donation. Phone (207) 667-8460.

SAVE  **WOODLAWN MUSEUM/BLACK HOUSE,** on SR 172 off US 1, is a Federal-style house built in the 1820s by Col. John. Black, who played a major role in developing Maine's lumber industry. With elegant woodwork and an elliptical flying staircase, the home is as it appeared during occupation by three generations of the Black family. Period furnishings reflect a privileged lifestyle. On the 180-acre grounds are gardens, hiking trails and a carriage house.

Allow 30 minutes minimum. Grounds daily dawn-dusk. House Tues.-Sat. 10-5, Sun. 1-4, June-Sept.; Tues.-Sun 1-4 in May and Oct. Tours are given on the hour. Admission $6; ages 5-12, $3. MC, VI. Phone (207) 667-8671.

# DID YOU KNOW

Social activist Dorothea Dix, director John Ford, author Stephen King, actor Judd Nelson and poet Edna St. Vincent Millay all hail from Maine.

## FALMOUTH (E-2) elev. 48'

Originally part of Portland, Falmouth became a separate community in 1786. Farming and fishing, the town's traditional industries, have enabled Falmouth to retain much of its rural charm. The Foreside area along SR 88 is the location of several waterfront estates as well as the Portland Yacht Club.

**Greater Portland Convention and Visitors Bureau:** 305 Commercial St., Portland, ME 04101; phone (207) 772-5800.

**GILSLAND FARM SANCTUARY & ENVIRONMENTAL CENTER,** 1.9 mi. n. off I-295N exit 9 on US 1 following signs, encompasses 65 acres of coastal lowlands along the Presumpscot River. Natural features include open meadows and orchards. Two miles of trails wind throughout the sanctuary. The refuge also is a seasonal haven for foxes, raccoons, Canada geese and bobolinks. The headquarters building has animal and bird exhibits and a teacher's research center.

Grounds and trails open daily dawn-dusk. Building open Mon.-Sat. 9-4:30, Sun. and holidays noon-5. Free. Phone (207) 781-2330.

## FARMINGTON (D-2) pop. 4,098, elev. 365'

Farmington is the shire town and a major commercial center for Franklin County, which ranges from rolling farms and apple orchards in the south to lakes and forested mountains in the north. The first settlers were recipients of land grants for service in the Revolutionary War in the area of Farmington Falls, a few miles down the Sandy River; soon families were scattered all along the valley.

With the opening of its first school in a log cabin home in 1788, Farmington began a long association with education. In 1841 the Abbott family opened a boys' school that gained fame as the "Little Blue School." Additionally, Jacob Abbott was author of the "Rollo" stories, children's sermons laced with history and science. The tradition continues: The University of Maine at Farmington is an outgrowth of the Farmington Academy, founded in the late 1860s.

Recreational opportunities include boat and canoe rentals at Clearwater Lake, 4 miles east on SR 43. Cross-country skiing and snowmobiling are favorite winter activities.

**Farmington-Wilton Chamber of Commerce:** 575 Wilton Rd., Farmington, ME 04938; phone (207) 778-4215.

**ART GALLERY AT THE UNIVERSITY OF MAINE-FARMINGTON,** 102 Main St., displays works by Maine artists. Rotating exhibits represent a variety of media. Tues.-Sat. noon-4, mid-Sept. to mid-May; closed holidays and university breaks. Free. Phone (207) 778-7001.

**NORDICA HOMESTEAD MUSEUM,** 1 mi. n. on SR 4, then .5 mi. e. to 116 Holley Rd., is the birthplace of opera singer Lillian Nordica, whose pure, strong coloratura brought her world renown. Displays present her costumes, stage jewelry, career mementos and original 19th-century furnishings. A library also is available. Allow 30 minutes minimum. Guided tours Tues.-Sat. and holidays 10-noon and 1-5, Sun. 1-5, June 1-Labor Day; by appointment, day after Labor Day-Oct. 15. Admission $2; ages 5-16, $1. Phone (207) 778-2042.

## THE FORKS (C-3)

The Forks is a tiny logging village in the heart of Maine's North Woods, on the Old Canada Road National Scenic Byway (US 201). Situated at the confluence of the Kennebec and Dead rivers, it is a popular white-water rafting area.

## RECREATIONAL ACTIVITIES

### White-water Rafting

- **Northern Outdoors,** 3.5 mi. s. on US 201. Write P.O. Box 100, The Forks, ME 04985. Other activities are offered. Trips depart daily, May-Oct. Phone (800) 765-7238.

- **Wilderness Expeditions,** on the shore of Moosehead Lake, P.O. Box 41-N, Rockwood, ME 04478. Trips depart daily, May-Oct. Reservations are required. Phone (800) 825-9453.

## FORT KENT (A-4) pop. 1,978, elev. 522′

Separated from Canada by the St. John River, Fort Kent was settled by French Acadians deported from Nova Scotia by the British in 1755. Incorporated in the 1820s, the territory became the issue of a boundary dispute between Great Britain and the United States. Troops were called in and a fort was built, but the Webster-Ashburton Treaty of 1842 averted bloodshed.

Fort Kent is the starting point of US 1, which runs along the eastern coast to Key West, Fla.; it also is the northern terminus for a scenic section of SR 11, which stretches south to Portage, as well as for the Allagash Waterway and canoe trips down the St. John River.

**Greater Fort Kent Area Chamber of Commerce:** 76 W. Main St., P.O. Box 430, Fort Kent, ME 04743-0430; phone (207) 834-5354.

**FORT KENT STATE HISTORIC SITE,** off US 1, features a blockhouse of hand-hewn timber. The fort was built in 1839 for defense during the bloodless Aroostook War. Allow 30 minutes minimum. Daily 9-dusk, Memorial Day-Labor Day. Free. Phone (207) 941-4014.

## FREEPORT (E-2) pop. 1,813, elev. 126′

Freeport is the acknowledged "Birthplace of Maine." Colonial legislators signed the paper that granted Maine separation from Massachusetts—and finally statehood in 1820. The town is best known as the home of the L.L. Bean sporting goods store, which is open daily 24 hours, 365 days a year. More than 130 other retail shops and name-brand outlets surround the village.

In addition to retail outlet merchandising, chief contributors to the economy are shoe manufacturing, tourism, crabbing and crabmeat packing. The 40-foot Big Indian statue, 1 mile north of I-295 exit 17, is a frequently photographed local landmark.

Wolfe's Neck Woods State Park, on Wolfe's Neck Road, offers several self-guiding nature trails that include views of Casco Bay and the Harraseeket River. The park, which is open Memorial Day through Labor Day, also presents educational and interpretive programs.

Harrington House, 45 Main St., features changing exhibits relating to the history of Freeport dating from the late 18th century to the present; phone (207) 865-3170. Pettengill Farm & Gardens, open by appointment only at 45 Main St., is a 19th-century saltwater farm that includes an 1810 saltbox house and 140 acres of gardens, fields and hiking trails; phone (207) 865-3170.

**Freeport Merchants Association:** 23 Depot St., P.O. Box 452, Freeport, ME 04032; phone (207) 865-1212, or (800) 865-1994 for the automated request line. *See color ad.*

**ATLANTIC SEAL CRUISES** depart from the Freeport wharf on Main St. for 3-hour sightseeing excursions to Eagle Island State Park, where passengers can visit the Robert E. Peary State Memorial. Also offered are 2-hour evening seal- and osprey-watching cruises on Casco Bay and 2.5-hour foliage trips along the coast. A 6-hour trip to Seguin Island, including a lighthouse tour, is available; phone for schedule and details about climbing requirements.

Sightseeing cruises depart daily at 9:30 and 1:30, May-Sept. Seal/osprey watches depart daily at 6, June-Aug. Foliage cruises depart Mon.-Fri. at 1:30, Sat.-Sun. at 9:30 and 1:30, late Sept.-late Oct. (weather permitting). Eagle Island fare $24; ages 1-12, $18. Seguin Island fare $45; ages 1-10, $30. Reservations are recommended. AX, MC, VI. Phone (207) 865-6112 or (877) 285-7325.

[SAVE] **DESERT OF MAINE,** I-295 exit 20 (Desert Rd.), then 2 mi. w. to 95 Desert Rd., is an area of sand dunes that has grown since the early 1900s. What was once the Tuttle Farm is now an area of moving sand dunes, some more than 70 feet high and covering trees and a small building. In 1897 the topsoil began to erode exposing the ancient glacial plain. Guided tours, nature trails and a museum are available.

Allow 30 minutes minimum. Daily 9-5, May 8-Oct. 15. Admission $7.75; ages 13-16, $5.25; ages 6-12, $4.25. AX, DS, MC, VI. Phone (207) 865-6962.

**MAST LANDING SANCTUARY** is 1 mi. e. on Bow St., then n. on Upper Mast Landing Rd. to entrance.

Situated at the tideway on the Harraseeket River, the site once served as a delivery point for Maine timbers. The sanctuary now encompasses 125 acres of open fields, apple orchards, alder lowlands and mature pine and hemlock forest. Porcupines, minks, deer and the ruins of a historic mill can be seen along 2.5 miles of marked trails. Picnicking is permitted. Daily dawn-dusk. Free. Phone (207) 781-2330.

## GEORGETOWN (E-3)

**JOSEPHINE NEWMAN SANCTUARY** is 9 mi. s. of jct. US 1 and SR 127. Owned and managed by the Maine Audubon Society, the sanctuary incorporates various habitats rich in animal life within its 119 acres, including tidal mud flats, marshes and forest. The sanctuary's 2 miles of walking trails meander through stands of hemlock, pine, oak and spruce. Visitors are warned that the area harbors an abundance of mosquitoes. Daily dawn-dusk. Free. Phone (207) 781-2330.

## GRAY (E-2) elev. 300'

Needing land upon which to raise their families, the original settlers of the area known as New Boston petitioned the General Court of Boston for the grant of a township. Although the pioneers were blessed with abundant stands of white pine and oak, American Indian raids caused repeated desertions of the buildings and land.

Incorporated as the town of Gray in 1778, the settlement prospered when several mills were erected, including what is said to be the first machine-powered woolen mill in the United States. Gray is known as the "Crossroads of Maine." Within its boundaries, Gray boasts four freshwater bodies and other natural resources that offer residents and visitors many outdoor recreational opportunities. Six major routes pass through the village.

**MAINE WILDLIFE PARK,** .25 mi. s. off I-95 exit 63 following signs, then 3 mi. n. on SR 26, houses wildlife native to Maine, including moose, deer and bears. Many of the animals cared for at the center are injured, orphaned or have become dependent upon man because they were raised in captivity. The visitor center has interactive displays about Maine's wildlife resources. A nature trail is available.

Picnicking is permitted. Allow 1 hour minimum. Daily 9:30-4, mid-Apr. through Veteran's Day (weather permitting). Admission $3.50; over 59, $2.50; ages 4-12, $2. Phone (207) 657-4977.

## GREENVILLE (C-3) pop. 1,319, elev. 1,034'

Greenville, at the south end of Moosehead Lake, is in an area noted for a variety of year-round recreational activities. Swimming, fishing, canoeing, hiking, mountain climbing, horseback riding, seaplane tours and white-water rafting are pursued in summer. Hunting for deer, bears and partridges is available in the fall; cross-country and alpine skiing and snowmobiling are enjoyed in winter. Several cruises and shuttle service are available to Mount Kineo, a historic American Indian gathering place in Moosehead Lake. Visitors to the peninsula can enjoy hiking trails and a pebble beach.

**Moosehead Lake Region Chamber of Commerce:** P.O. Box 581, Greenville, ME 04441; phone (207) 695-2702.

*KATAHDIN,* 12 Lily Bay Rd. at the center of town, is a restored 1914 lake steamboat. The vessel makes 3-hour sightseeing voyages on Moosehead Lake as well as a 6-hour cruise to Mount Kineo on Wednesdays; a galley is on board. Allow 3 hours minimum. Sightseeing cruises depart Tues. and Thurs. and Sat.-Sun. at 12:30, June 26-Columbus Day. Fare for sightseeing cruises $22; over 62, $20; ages 6-15, $14. Fare for Mount Kineo cruise $28; over 62, $26; ages 6-15, $17. MC, VI. Phone (207) 695-2716.

**Moosehead Marine Museum,** 12 Lily Bay Rd., comprises two rooms of area memorabilia, including a map collection and items pertaining to lake transportation and logging history. Allow 30 minutes minimum. Daily 10-2, June 1-Columbus Day. Donations. Phone (207) 695-2716.

## RECREATIONAL ACTIVITIES

### Skiing

- **Big Squaw Mountain Ski Area**, off SR 6/15. Write P.O. Box 430, Greenville, ME 04441. Other activities are available. Daily Thanksgiving weekend-late March. Phone (207) 695-1000, or (800) 754-6246 out of Maine.

## HALLOWELL (E-3) pop. 2,467, elev. 53′

Since the 1600s Hallowell's position on the Kennebec River has played a vital role in the city's history. At this site Abenaki Indians traded with Plymouth merchants for nearly 40 years. By the late 1700s Hallowell was a thriving international port, its streets crowded with horses and wagons carrying goods to the ships at the great wharves. Today, pleasure boats depart from the city's docks. Trails offer visitors opportunities for walking, bicycling or cross-country skiing.

**Hallowell City Hall:** 1 Winthrop St., Hallowell, ME 04347; phone (207) 623-4021.

## HINCKLEY (D-3) pop. 200, elev. 135′

SAVE **L.C. BATES MUSEUM**, 5 mi. n of I-95 exit 133 on US 201 is housed in a three-story Romanesque building constructed in 1903. Exhibits relate to Maine's natural history, archeology and ethnology. Additional highlights include a children's room and a turn-of-the-19th-century classroom. A top-floor gallery displays rotating art exhibits. The grounds feature an arboretum. Bird-watching tours and children's workshops are offered weekly.

Wed.-Sat. and holidays 10-4:30, Sun. 1-4:30, Apr. 15 through mid-Nov.; by appointment rest of year. Admission $2; ages 12-18, $1; under 12, 75c. Phone (207) 238-4250.

## HODGDON (B-5)

**LT. GORDON MANUEL WILDLIFE MANAGEMENT AREA,** at the Linneus and Cary Plantation, is a recreation area offering more than 6,000 acres of woodlands and wetlands ideal for fishing, canoeing, hiking, bird-watching and cross-country skiing. Two small boat launches on the Meduxnekeag River are available. In winter snowmobile trails are available.

Camping is not permitted. Daily 24 hours (weather permitting). Roads are not plowed Dec.-Mar. and are closed during mud season, Apr.-May. Free. Phone (207) 435-3231.

## HOULTON (B-5) pop. 5,270, elev. 357′

On the Meduxnekeag River, Houlton is the seat and one of the oldest communities of 6,453-square-mile Aroostook County, largest in the state and greater in area than Rhode Island and Connecticut combined. Houlton first prospered from lumber, but now the Aroostook potato dominates its economy, along with various light industries, and technological and educational ventures. As the shipping point for the products of this agriculturally rich region, Houlton is sometimes referred to as the "Garden of Maine."

The Aroostook Historical and Art Museum in the White Building at 109 Main St., displays tools, vintage clothing, historical artifacts and local archival materials. The museum is open Memorial Day-Labor Day; phone (207) 532-4216. In Pierce Park is a drinking fountain with an interesting 1916 cast-iron statue, "The Boy with the Leaking Boot." The sculptor is unknown; one theory is that the boy is bringing water to a wounded soldier. The statue is one of only 26 in the world.

**Greater Houlton Chamber of Commerce:** 109 Main St., Houlton, ME 04730; phone (207) 532-4216.

**Shopping areas:** An Ammex Tax & Duty Free Shop is at the junction of Airport Road and I-95.

## ISLAND FALLS (B-5) elev. 450′

**JOHN E. & WALTER D. WEBB MUSEUM OF VINTAGE FASHION,** off I-95 exit 276 in center of town on Sherman St., displays antique clothing in themed rooms ranging from an old-fashioned millinery shop to a men's haberdashery to a bridal salon. Housed in an 1894 residence, the museum's collection includes Edwardian and Victorian apparel as well as fashions from 1800-1950. Allow 1 hour minimum. Mon.-Thurs. 10-4, Fri.-Sun. by appointment, June 1-Oct. 4. Admission $3, senior citizens $2, children $1. Phone (207) 463-2404.

## KENNEBUNK (F-2) pop. 4,804, elev. 51′

The Kennebunks—Kennebunk, Kennebunkport *(see place listing)* and Kennebunk Beach—constitute one of Maine's most popular coastal resort areas. Kennebunk developed between the Mousam and Kennebunk rivers about 1650 and was originally part of the town of Wells *(see place listing p. 77).* By 1730 there were shipyards along the Mousam; these and a brisk West Indies trade supported Kennebunk until the Revolution, after which waterpowered industries assumed economic leadership.

In the first half of the 19th century Kennebunk, like Kennebunkport and nearly every other tidewater Maine settlement, caught shipbuilding fever. Between 1800 and 1850 more than 1,000 wooden schooners, clippers and cargo vessels emerged from the area's 50-odd shipyards.

Legacies of this period's wealth and skill are the beautifully detailed Colonial, Federal, Greek Revival and Victorian houses that grace Kennebunk's national historic district, which includes upper Main Street, Summer Street and a portion of US 1. First Parish Church on Main Street has a bell cast by Paul Revere's foundry in its Christopher Wren steeple.

**Kennebunk-Kennebunkport Chamber of Commerce:** 17 Western Ave. (SR 9), P.O. Box 740, Kennebunk, ME 04043; phone (207) 967-0857.

**THE BRICK STORE MUSEUM,** 117 Main St., occupies a dry goods store dating from 1825. Fine and decorative arts and exhibits pertain to local history. Allow 2 hours minimum. Tues.-Fri. 10-4:30, Sat. 10-1; closed holidays. Admission $3, under 6 free. MC, VI. Phone (207) 985-4802.

## KENNEBUNKPORT (F-2)
pop. 1,376, elev. 5′

A popular summer resort, Kennebunkport has long been a favorite among artists and writers who have found both its history and quaint setting conducive to creativity. Novelist Kenneth Roberts, born in Kennebunk, used the Kennebunkport area as a setting for his "Chronicles of Arundel," and author Booth Tarkington wrote at dockside in his schooner *Regina*. Many galleries and craft shops attest to Kennebunkport's continuing affinity with the arts.

Dock Square has restored structures housing boutiques and galleries. Parson's Way, a scenic public walkway, begins at Dock Square and continues past Walker's Point. Along the docks several boats offer chartered deep-sea fishing, sailing, whale-watching or lobstering excursions. Sightseeing cruises of the Kennebunk River and coastal islands also are available.

Beyond the village Ocean Avenue follows the rocky shore of Cape Arundel to Cape Porpoise, a year-round fishing village. From Cape Porpoise pier it is possible to view the lighthouse on Goat Island. This scenic drive is lined with fine old mansions that are now restaurants or lodgings.

A waterspout, produced by water forced by the incoming tide through such formations as the spouting rock and the blowing cave, can be seen at Cape Arundel near Walker's Point—summer home of former President George Bush. Parking is not permitted along Ocean Avenue, but it is available at nearby Womby Beach. Farther "down east" via SR 9 is picturesque Goose Rocks Beach.

The renovated boathouse of author Booth Tarkington houses the Kennebunkport Maritime Museum and Gallery, open June through August; phone (207) 967-3218.

The Kennebunkport Historical Society offers guided walking tours of the historic village; phone (207) 967-2751.

**Kennebunk-Kennebunkport Chamber of Commerce:** 17 Western Ave. (SR 9), P.O. Box 740, Kennebunk, ME 04043; phone (207) 967-0857.

**THE KENNEBUNKPORT HISTORICAL SOCIETY,** 125 North St., includes several historic buildings. The Henry H. Pasco Exhibit Center offers exhibits about Kennebunkport's past. Guide books for a self-guiding walking tour of the village are available. Guided tours are offered. Tues.-Fri. 10-4, Sat. 10-1, mid-June to mid-Oct.; Tues.-Fri. 10-4, rest of year. One-hour guided walking tours are given Thurs. at 1:30, Sat. at 11, July-Aug.; Thurs. at 1:30, mid-June through June 30 and in Sept. (weather permitting). Closed holidays. Admission $3, under 19 free. MC, VI. Phone (207) 967-2751.

**THE NOTT HOUSE,** 8 Maine St., is an 1853 Greek Revival-style house containing original Victorian furnishings, pictures and personal belongings from four generations of Perkins and Nott families. Allow 1 hour minimum. Tues.-Fri. 1-4, Sat. 10-1, mid-June to mid-Oct.; closed holidays. Admission $5, under 19 free. Phone (207) 967-2751.

[SAVE] **SEASHORE TROLLEY MUSEUM,** 3.2 mi. n. on Log Cabin Rd. via North St., has one of the world's largest collections of antique electric streetcars—more than 30. Visitors have an opportunity to experience public transportation from a bygone era by embarking on a 4-mile trolley ride. Allow 2 hours minimum. Museum open daily 10-5, Memorial Day weekend-Columbus Day; Sat.-Sun. 10-5, May 12-day before Memorial Day weekend. Admission $7.50; over 59, $5.50; ages 6-16, $5. AX, DS, MC, VI. Phone (207) 967-2800.

## KINGFIELD (D-2) elev. 570′

[SAVE] **THE STANLEY MUSEUM,** 40 School St., is a tribute to the creative efforts of the Stanley family, best known for the Stanley Steamer automobile. Photography by Chansonetta Stanley and other family artworks depict turn-of-the-20th-century rural Maine life. Other items created by family members also are displayed. In addition, the museum exhibits four steam-powered cars from 1905, 1909-1910 and 1916.

Allow 1 hour minimum. Tues.-Sun. 1-4, June-Oct.; Tues.-Fri. 1-4, rest of year. Admission $4; senior citizens $3; under 17, $2. Phone (207) 265-2729.

## KITTERY (F-1) pop. 5,884, elev. 34′

Settled in 1623, Kittery was an important shipbuilding, shipping and lumbering center. One of the oldest shipyards in the nation and among the first owned by the federal government, the Portsmouth Naval Shipyard on Seavey's Island was established in 1800. The *Ranger*, the first ship to fly the Stars and Stripes, was launched at Kittery under the command of John Paul Jones on May 10, 1777. In 1917 the first American submarine, the L-8, was launched.

Kittery is noted for its historic sites, rocky beaches and thriving outlet trade on US 1. Fort Foster, constructed soon after the Civil War, is situated on Gerrish Island in a park setting. The remains of the fort are open to the public, and visitors can enjoy views of Portsmouth Harbor, picnicking and nature trails.

**Shopping areas:** More than 120 outlet shops can be found at Kittery Outlets, off N. US 1, including Factory Stores of America Outlet Center, Manufacturer's Outlet, [SAVE] Tanger Factory Outlet and Tidewater Outlet Mall.

**FORT McCLARY STATE HISTORIC SITE** covers 27 acres about 2 mi. e. on SR 103. The initial fortifications were erected in the early 18th century; the current blockhouse was built about 1844 and modified in the 1860s. Picnicking is permitted. Allow 30 minutes minimum. Daily 9-8, Memorial Day-Labor Day; 9-6, day after Labor Day-Sept. 30. Admission $1.50, under 12 free. Phone (207) 384-5160.

SAVE **KITTERY HISTORICAL AND NAVAL MU-SEUM** is off I-95 exit 2; take SR 236S to 200 Rogers Rd. At the traffic circle follow signs to US 1N, then make the first right after the traffic circle onto Rogers Rd. Exhibits portray more than 350 years of Kittery's maritime and cultural heritage. Included are early shipbuilding tools; navigational instruments; ship models; a 14-foot replica of John Paul Jones' ship, the *Ranger;* photographs; and the lens from the Boon Island Lighthouse.

Allow 1 hour minimum. Tues.-Sat. 10-4, June 1-Columbus Day; Wed. and Sat. 10-4, day after Columbus Day through mid-Dec.; by appointment rest of year. Closed holidays. Admission $3; ages 7-15, $1.50; family rate $6. DS, MC, VI. Phone (207) 439-3080.

# LEWISTON (E-2) pop. 35,690, elev. 200′

The larger of the "Twin Cities of the Androscoggin" and the second largest city in the state, Lewiston occupies the river's east bank, across from Auburn (*see place listing p. 40*). Lewiston's early years gave little hint of what it would become. The first settler erected a log cabin within the present city limits in 1770, but subsequent growth was slow.

Although a woolen mill began operation in 1819, it was not until the waterpower of the Androscoggin River was harnessed about 1850 that Lewiston began developing into a major textile center. By the 1870s cottons and woolens were issuing from the mills of several large companies.

At the same time many French Canadians were recruited to work in the mills, leaving Lewiston with a rich Franco-American heritage. The city now is experiencing economic diversification, with strong service, retail and innovative technology sectors.

Another Lewiston tradition is Bates College, founded in 1864. A highlight of the 75-acre campus is rocky 340-foot Mount David. The view from its summit encompasses Lewiston, Auburn and the Androscoggin Valley and extends 50 miles west to the Presidential Range in New Hampshire. Lewiston Falls and Dam, which provided the city's industrial impetus, is best seen from Longley Bridge on US 202.

**Androscoggin County Chamber of Commerce:** 179 Lisbon St., P.O. Box 59, Lewiston, ME 04243-0059; phone (207) 783-2249.

**BATES COLLEGE MUSEUM OF ART** is 2 blks. e. of US 202 at 75 Russell St. in the Olin Arts Center located on the Bates College campus. The museum displays changing exhibits of 18th-, 19th- and 20th-century prints, contemporary art, watercolors and drawings. A permanent collection of works by Marsden Hartley, a Lewiston native and prominent 20th-century artist, also is featured. Allow 1 hour

minimum. Tues.-Sat. 10-5; closed major holidays. Free. Phone (207) 786-6158.

**THORNCRAG BIRD SANCTUARY**, .1 mi. e. at jct. Montello St. and Highland Spring Rd., encompasses more than 310 acres of forest, fields, ponds and hardwood stands. The sanctuary is a habitat for a wide variety of birds native to northern New England. There are 4 miles of marked hiking trails; maps are available at the gate. Hiking, picnicking, cross-country skiing and snowshoeing are permitted. Daily dawn-dusk. Free. Phone (207) 782-5238.

# LIVERMORE (E-2) elev. 344′

With a lake at its north edge and 1,207-foot Bear Mountain to the west, Livermore enjoys a pleasant setting. The community is a trading center for the farming, dairying and lumbering interests in the area.

SAVE **WASHBURN-NORLANDS LIVING HISTORY CENTER**, 1 mi. n. on SR 4, 1.2 mi. e. on SR 108, then 1.8 mi. n. on Norlands Rd., is a 19th-century farm and living-history center. On the 445-acre estate, which dates from 1870, are the restored Washburn family mansion, stone library, schoolhouse, farmer's cottage, church and barn. Sleigh and hayrides are offered seasonally. For further information contact the Norlands Foundation, 290 Norlands Rd., Livermore, ME 04253.

Allow 2 hours minimum. Guided tours Mon.-Fri. 10-4. Schedule may vary; phone to confirm. Admission $8; under 14, $5. The tour is not recommended for under age 5; phone for details. MC, VI. Phone (207) 897-4366.

# LOCKE MILLS (E-2) elev. 753′

## RECREATIONAL ACTIVITIES
### Skiing
• SAVE **Ski Mt. Abram**, 1.5 mi. w. of SR 26 on Howe Hill Rd. Write P.O. Box 240, Locke Mills, ME 04255. Thurs.-Sun. and holidays, Dec.-Mar. Phone (207) 875-5002.

# LUBEC (D-6) elev. 10′

Settled in 1780, Lubec is in the easternmost area of Maine. It holds the distinction of being the first spot where the sun rises in the continental United States. Situated on a peninsula, the community offers scenic ocean vistas and many opportunities to explore Maine's rugged coastline.

Planes and boats may be chartered to view the coastal scenery as well as whales, seals and birds. Machias Seal Island, one of only three islands in Maine that serve as home to the Atlantic puffin, also is accessible by boat. Lubec's sardine-packing heritage is preserved through the Sardine Village Museum just south of Lubec on SR 189. Some of the highest tides in the United States occur at Johnson Bay.

**Lubec Chamber of Commerce:** P.O. Box 123, Lubec, ME 04652; phone (207) 733-4522.

**CAMPOBELLO ISLAND,** New Brunswick, Canada, lies across Lubec Narrows and is connected to Lubec by the Franklin D. Roosevelt Memorial Bridge. From 1767 to 1881 the island belonged to William Owen and his family. The 1835 home of Adm. William F. Owen, who so loved the sea that he reputedly built a quarterdeck on which to pace, still stands at Deer Point.

James Roosevelt went to Campobello in 1883, when his son Franklin was 1 year old. From then until 1921, FDR spent most of his summers on the island.

**Roosevelt Campobello International Park,** on Campobello Island, is linked to the mainland by the Franklin D. Roosevelt Memorial Bridge at Lubec, Maine, and also can be reached by ferry from Deer Island in July and August. The centerpiece of the 2,741-acre memorial is a 34-room "cottage" occupied 1905-21 by the soon-to-be president. The house contains furniture, photographs, toys and other items belonging to the Roosevelt family. The surrounding area features scenic drives and walking trails along coves, bogs, beaches and cliffs. A 15-minute videotape is shown at the visitor center.

Picnicking is permitted. Visitor center daily 9-5 (EDT), late May-Oct. 31. Cottage daily 9-5 (EDT), late May-Columbus Day. Last admission is 15 minutes before closing. Nature areas and trails are open year-round. Donations. Phone (506) 752-2922.

**QUODDY HEAD STATE PARK,** s. of Lubec, consists of more than 500 acres. The West Quoddy Head Light, on West Quoddy Point, was built in 1808 and rebuilt in 1858. The lighthouse is closed to the public. The park features 4.5 miles of hiking trails, extensive forests, two bogs and diverse habitat for rare plants. A visitor center/museum in the lighthouse keeper's house is available.

Picnicking is permitted. Allow 1 hour minimum. Park open daily 9-dusk, May 15-Oct. 15. Visitor center/museum open daily 10-4. Admission $1.50. Phone (207) 733-0911 or (207) 941-4014.

**RIER'S OLD SARDINE VILLAGE MUSEUM** is 10.1 mi. e. on SR 189 from jct. US 1. This museum takes visitors through the process of sardine canning in the 19th and early 20th centuries and displays the tools and machinery used. A blacksmith's shop, sheet metal shop, general store, mustard mill and print shop are among 25 shops that have been reconstructed to depict typical 19th-century life. Nautical artifacts and a model boat collection are housed in the maritime shop.

Allow 1 hour minimum. Tues., Thurs. and Sun. 1-5, Sat. 1-4, June-Sept. Admission $5; senior citizens and ages 15-18, $4. Phone (207) 733-2822.

## MACHIAS (D-5) pop. 1,376, elev. 20'

Founded in 1763, Machias (ma-CHY-as) is Maine's oldest town east of the Penobscot River. The name means "bad little falls," in reference to the Machias River's plunge through a deep gorge that lies just behind Main Street. Machias is the center of commerce and government for Washington County; industries include blueberry processing, seafood harvesting and processing, and lumber and wood products. It also is a starting point for hunting and fishing trips into the interior lake country.

As the Revolution became inevitable, patriotic enthusiasm engulfed the citizens of Machias, especially the group who frequented Job Burnham's tavern. In June 1775, after learning that a British warship would arrive to requisition lumber for British barracks, Capt. Jeremiah O'Brien and his cohorts convened at the tavern to plan a Colonial response. The battle resulting from that meeting took place off Machiasport (*see place listing*) on June 12, 1775—5 days before Bunker Hill.

Roque Bluffs State Park, 7 miles south off US 1 on Roque Bluffs Road, contains Maine's easternmost sandy beach. *See Recreation Chart.*

**Machias Bay Area Chamber of Commerce:** C5-112 Dublin St., P.O. Box 606, Machias, ME 04654; phone (207) 255-4402.

**BURNHAM TAVERN MUSEUM,** Main and Free sts., contains articles from the Revolutionary period. Built in 1770, it is one of the oldest structures in eastern Maine and served as the meeting place where plans were formulated for the first naval battle of the Revolutionary War, which resulted in the capture of the *Margaretta*. Photographs, paintings, antique furniture and Civil War relics also are on display.

Allow 1 hour minimum. Mon.-Fri. 9-5, mid-June through Labor Day; by appointment rest of year. Admission $2.50; under 12, 25c. Phone (207) 255-4432.

## MACHIASPORT (D-6)

The first naval engagement of the American Revolution was fought in Machias Bay on June 12, 1775, when Capt. Jeremiah O'Brien and 40 ill-armed colonists aboard the small sloop *Unity* captured the English warship *Margaretta*. Among the casualties was the *Margaretta's* commander, who died in Machias the next day. The incident gave weight to the Revolutionary leaders' arguments for the establishment of a U.S. Navy.

Soon after the beginning of the Revolutionary War, Fort Machias was built on the bluffs overlooking the Machias River. Strengthened in 1777, the fort stood until 1814 when the British destroyed it. The present earthworks, which overlook Machias Bay, are the remnants of a fort erected on the spot in 1863; Fort O'Brien is now a state park and historic site that is open daily dawn to dusk Memorial Day through Labor Day.

Quieter now, Machiasport concentrates on such daily concerns as fishing, boatbuilding and pleasing its many summer visitors. Rockhounds can while away the hours seeking jasper pebbles at Jasper Beach, south near Bucks Harbor.

**GATES HOUSE**, on SR 92, is an 1807 Federal-style house. The marine room houses an extensive collection of photographs of sea captains, vessels and sardine carriers. The exhibits include ship models, caulking tools, stick barometers and navigational tools. Several rooms are restored and furnished in period. Visitors may utilize the genealogical library. Allow 1 hour minimum. Tues.-Sat. 12:30-4:30, July-Aug.; by appointment rest of year. Donations. Phone (207) 255-8461.

## MADAWASKA (A-4) pop. 3,326, elev. 500′

Madawaska, a Malecite Indian word meaning "porcupine," was settled by Acadian refugees from Nova Scotia in 1785. The Acadian Cross Historic Shrine off US 1 commemorates the first Acadian landing in the St. John Valley. On the site of the shrine is the Tante Blanche Historic Museum, which depicts the Acadians and the founding of the St. John Valley.

**Greater Madawaska Chamber of Commerce:** 363 Main St., Suite 101, Madawaska, ME 04756; phone (207) 728-7000.

**NEXFOR FRASER PAPERS INC.,** on Bridge Ave., makes paper from pulp produced across the river in Edmundston, New Brunswick, and sent by pipeline to Madawaska. The mill produces a variety of papers on eight paper machines and is one of the world's largest producers of Bible papers. Comfortable, close-toed shoes are recommended. Plant tours are given on the hour Mon.-Fri. 9-11 and 1-3. Hours may vary; phone ahead. Free. Cameras and under age 12 are not permitted. Reservations are recommended 24 hours in advance. Phone (207) 728-8200 for tour reservations.

## MILLINOCKET (C-4) pop. 5,190, elev. 359′

### RECREATIONAL ACTIVITIES
**White-water Rafting**

* **New England Outdoor Center**, Old Medway Rd., P.O. Box 669, Millinocket, ME 04462. Other activities are offered. Daily, May-Oct. Phone (800) 766-7238.

## MONHEGAN ISLAND (F-4)

Tiny Monhegan Island, 9 miles off the Maine coast, has the highest cliffs on the New England shore. Artists who flocked to the 1.5-mile-long island during the late 19th century are credited with popularizing it. Many working studios are open to the public.

Lobster and fishing boats, as well as pleasure craft, keep the harbor busy all year. A 1-day excursion from Boothbay Harbor (see place listing p. 48) and New Harbor (see place listing p. 62) also visits the island. Contrasting with the bustle of Monhegan's port is a wildlife sanctuary containing more than 600 varieties of wildflowers and some 200 kinds of birds, such as peregrine falcons, ospreys and marsh hawks.

Other peaceful retreats on the island include Cathedral Woods, an area of spruce trees that is a haven for deer, and the 160-foot cliffs Black Head and White Head. Several hiking trails lead to scenic points on the island. Maritime exhibits and flora, fauna and marine life collections are displayed at a museum on Lighthouse Hill. The lighthouse was built in 1824. Comfortable shoes are recommended, as some of the hiking trails are fairly rugged.

Regular passenger service between Monhegan Island and Port Clyde aboard the *Laura B.* and the *Elizabeth Ann* is offered daily May through October; the boats run Monday, Wednesday and Friday, rest of year. Sightseeing cruises also are offered. Phone for schedule. One-way fare $16; ages 2-12, $10. Round-trip fare $27; ages 2-12, $14. Reservations are required. Contact Monhegan-Thomaston Boat Line, P.O. Box 238, Port Clyde, ME 04855; phone (207) 372-8848.

A ferry service between Monhegan Island and New Harbor departs daily mid-May to mid-October. The ferry departs Monhegan Island at 10:15 and 3:15 and departs New Harbor at 9 and 2. One-way fare $13.50; under 12, $7.50. Round-trip fare $27; under 12, $15. Reservations are recommended. Contact Hardy Boat Cruises, P.O. Box 326, New Harbor, ME 04554; phone (207) 677-2026 or (800) 278-3346.

## MONMOUTH (E-2) elev. 265′

The Cochnewagon Indians were the first inhabitants of the Monmouth area, though by the 1800s they were virtually wiped out by the arrival of white settlers, disease and war. Incorporated in 1792, the town was named after the Battle of Monmouth, N.J., which involved one of its first citizens, Gen. Henry Dearborn.

Cumston Hall, on Main Street, is a beautiful Victorian opera house ornamented with frescoes and murals. It is home to the Theatre at Monmouth, a professional Shakespearean repertory theater that performs July through August; phone (207) 933-9999.

**MONMOUTH MUSEUM,** on Main St. in the center of town, is a complex of five buildings that recreates various aspects of 19th-century rural Maine. The structures include a stencil shop, blacksmith shop, carriage house and freight shed containing farm equipment and other artifacts. The five-room Blossom House is estimated to have been built in 1802. Also on site are genealogical records.

Guided tours Tues.-Sun. 1-4, Memorial Day-Labor Day; by appointment rest of year. Admission $3, children $1. Children must be accompanied by an adult. Phone (207) 933-2287.

## NAPLES (E-2) elev. 276′

On the northwestern edge of Sebago Lake, Naples, is the location of the Songo Lock, opened in 1830 for transportation along the 42-mile canal system to Portland. The lock now links the north end of Long Lake and Sebago Lake. The hand-operated gate is the only remnant of the old lock system connecting western Maine with the coast.

Such recreational opportunities as boating, windsurfing, seaplane rides and mail boat runs are popular in Naples, an area characterized by rolling hills and crystal-blue lakes. The causeway offers the opportunity for striking views of Mount Washington in the White Mountains of New Hampshire.

**Naples Business Association:** P.O. Box 412, Naples, ME 04055; phone (207) 693-3285.

*SONGO RIVER QUEEN II,* berthed at the causeway in the center of town on US 302, offers sightseeing cruises on an old-fashioned riverboat. The 2.5-hour Songo River Ride tours Long Lake, Brandy Pond and the Songo River, passing through the hand-operated Historic Songo Lock, in use since the 1830s. The Long Lake Cruise is an hour-long excursion on Long Lake.

Food is available. Songo River Ride departs daily at 9:45 and 3:45, July 1-Labor Day. Long Lake Cruise departs daily at 1, 2:30 and 7, July 1-Labor Day. Cruises also are offered by appointment in June and after Labor Day. Songo River Ride $8; under 12, $6. Long Lake Cruise $5; under 12, $4. Phone (207) 693-6861.

## NEWCASTLE (E-3) elev. 91′

**DODGE POINT PRESERVE,** 3.5 mi. s. on River Rd. to Fire Lane A31, preserves 506 acres of habitat along the Damariscotta River. Hiking and cross-country skiing trails wind through the property. An interpretive trail relates educational information about the local environment. This is a day-use area only; camping is not permitted. Exercise caution: Hunting is permitted on the property; hunters are not allowed to fire a weapon within 300 feet of a marked trail. Swimming, fishing and skating are permitted. Preserve open daily dawn-dusk. Free.

**ST. PATRICK'S CHURCH** is 2.5 mi. n. of US 1 on SR 215 (Academy Hill Rd.). Although the cemetery dates from 1760, the church itself was built in 1808 and is said to be the oldest surviving Catholic church in New England. Daily 8-dusk. Donations. Phone (207) 563-3240.

## NEWFIELD (E-1)

Apple orchards, farms and summer cottages adorn the gently rolling, pond-dotted terrain around Newfield. The township was settled in 1778 and known as Washington Plantation until its incorporation in 1794. The village flourished in the 19th century; many of the buildings from that time are incorporated in the Willowbrook restoration.

SAVE **WILLOWBROOK AT NEWFIELD,** off SR 11 on Elm St., is a 37-building restored 19th-century village depicting trades and crafts at two period homesteads. Particularly noteworthy are the restored carriages and sleighs. The Turn of the Century area includes gasoline engines and the equipment they powered. The Trades of Yesteryear Building includes a barbershop and bank. Also featured are a one-man print shop and a one-room schoolhouse.

Allow 3 hours minimum. Daily 10-5, May 15-Sept. 30. Admission $8.50; ages 6-17, $4. MC, VI. Phone (207) 793-2784.

## NEW GLOUCESTER (E-2)

SAVE **SABBATHDAY LAKE SHAKER VILLAGE,** at 707 Shaker Rd. (SR 26), is said to be the last active Shaker village; it dates from 1782. Most of the late 18th- and early 19th-century buildings are of singular Shaker design and contain Shaker furniture, ingenious inventions, handicrafts and workshops. Special events are held throughout the season. Shaker Sunday meetings also are open to visitors.

Allow 2 hours minimum. Mon.-Sat. 10-4:30, Memorial Day-Columbus Day. Guided tours are given at 10:30, 11:30, 12:30, 1:30, 2:30 and 3:15. Museum free. Guided tour $6.50; ages 6-12, $2. MC, VI. Phone (207) 926-4597.

## NEW HARBOR (E-3)

*HARDY III* **BOAT TOUR** departs from Shaw's Wharf on SR 32 for tours of the area's picturesque coastal waters. Offered are 1.5-hour puffin-watching cruises with a naturalist to Eastern Egg Rock, 1-hour narrated seal-watching cruises and 1-hour lighthouse cruises to Pemaquid Point. Fall foliage tours and a ferry service to Monhegan Island also are available.

Puffin watches depart daily at 5:30, early June to mid-Aug.; Wed. and Sat.-Sun. at 5:30, mid-May to early June. Seal watches depart daily at noon and lighthouse cruises depart daily at 7:30 p.m., late June-Labor Day. Puffin-watch fare $18; under 12, $11. Seal-watch and lighthouse cruise fares $10; under 12, $7. Reservations are recommended for all trips. MC, VI. Phone (207) 677-2026 or (800) 278-3346.

## NORTH AMITY (C-5) elev. 611′

**A.E. HOWELL WILDLIFE CONSERVATION CENTER AND SPRUCE ACRES REFUGE,** .5 mi. w. off US 1 on Lycette Rd., consists of more than 60 acres featuring a recreation area, trout pond and 5.5 miles of marked walking trails. Visitors may see a variety of wild animals. The refuge is home to a bull moose said to be the largest in captivity. Eagles, hawks and owls also may be sighted. Snowshoeing and cross-country skiing are available. An environmental learning center and a library also are offered.

Picnicking is permitted. Allow 1 hour minimum. Tues.-Sat. 10-4. Admission $5; over 60 and ages 13-18, $2. Under 12 must be with an adult when fishing. Reservations are required for rehabilitation refuge. Phone (207) 532-6880.

## OGUNQUIT (F-2) elev. 20′

Ogunquit was called "beautiful place by the sea" by the Abenaki Indians, who were early inhabitants of this region. The town is 15 miles north of the New Hampshire border, with a 3-mile sandy beach stretching northward and more than a mile of picturesque rocky shore to the south. The Ogunquit River, a 2-mile tidewater river, parallels the beach and is separated from it by sand dunes.

Shore Road leads to Bald Head Cliff, a perpendicular projection 100 feet high that extends 300 feet into the ocean. The sea pounding against the cliff sometimes sends spray 100 feet into the air. The "Marginal Way" is a mile-long footpath to Perkins Cove, a working harbor with a footbridge spanning its entrance. Perkins Cove offers specialty shops, waterfront restaurants and art galleries as well as fishing, lobstering and whale-watching opportunities.

Ogunquit is a popular summer resort, especially among artists. The Village Center has craft shops, theaters and parks lining its streets. The Ogunquit Playhouse, a half-mile south of town on US 1, has presented exceptional summer theater since the 1930s; phone (207) 646-5511. Art exhibits are held throughout the summer months at the Ogunquit Museum of American Art *(see attraction listing)* and the Ogunquit Arts Collaborative Gallery. Trolleys offer transportation around town from May to October.

**Ogunquit Chamber of Commerce:** P.O. Box 2289, Ogunquit, ME 03907; phone (207) 646-2939 or (207) 646-1279.

**FINESTKIND SCENIC CRUISES** depart from Barnacle Billy's Dock in Perkins Cove. A number of cruises are offered, including a lobster boat trip with a narrated lobstering demonstration, 1.5-hour lighthouse sightseeing trips and sailing cruises. Breakfast and evening cocktail cruises are offered in season.

Allow 1 hour minimum. Lighthouse cruises depart daily at 10, noon, 2 and 4, May 1 through mid-Oct. Lobstering cruises depart about every hour Mon.-Sat. 9:30-3, July 1-Labor Day; daily at 10, 11, 1 and 2, May-June and day after Labor Day through mid-Oct. Sailing cruises depart daily at 11, 2:30 and 4:30, May 1 through mid-Oct. Departure times may vary due to weather; phone ahead. Lighthouse cruise fare $16; ages 4-11, $10. Lobstering cruise fare $11; ages 4-11, $7. Sailing cruise fare $25. Phone (207) 646-5227.

**OGUNQUIT MUSEUM OF AMERICAN ART,** 543 Shore Rd., is in a meadow overlooking a cove and the Atlantic Ocean. The museum displays the works of such renowned American artists as Charles Burchfield, Marsden Hartley, Robert Henri, Edward Hopper, Rockwell Kent, Walt Kuhn, Gaston Lachaise, Reginald Marsh and William Zorach. Changing special exhibits feature other nationally known American artists.

Allow 1 hour minimum. Mon.-Sat. 10:30-5, Sun. 2-5, July 1 through mid-Oct.; closed Labor Day and during exhibit installations in mid-Aug. Hours may vary; phone ahead. Admission $5; over 60, $4; students with ID $3; under 12 free. Phone (207) 646-4909.

**THE *SILVERLINING*** departs from Perkins Cove, 1 mi. s. on Shore Rd. The 42-foot yacht, a 1939 Hinckley sloop, takes visitors on 1.5- and 2-hour excursions along the Ogunquit coastline. Allow 1 hour, 30 minutes minimum. Departures daily at 9:30, 11:30, 2, 4:30 and 6:30, Memorial Day weekend through mid-Sept. Fare for 1.5-hour cruise $30; 2-hour cruise $36. Reservations are recommended. Phone (207) 646-9800.

## OLD ORCHARD BEACH (F-2)
pop. 8,856, elev. 15′

Old Orchard Beach, one of the oldest seashore resorts in Maine, boasts a 7-mile strip of white sand coastline. The low surf makes the area a favorite spot for swimming. Recreational pastimes include golf, tennis and deep-sea fishing. There are amusement parks and arcades in town. Automobile races take place at nearby Beech Ridge Speedway, and there is harness racing in summer at Scarborough Downs, 7 miles north of town.

**Note:** Policies concerning admittance of children to pari-mutuel betting facilities vary. Phone for information.

**Old Orchard Beach Chamber of Commerce:** First St., P.O. Box 600, Old Orchard Beach, ME 04064; phone (207) 934-2500.

## OLD TOWN (D-4) pop. 8,130, elev. 94′

With the Penobscot River providing waterpower and transportation, Old Town grew into a busy sawmilling and iron-making center in the early 19th century. In 1836 it became the northern terminus of New England's first railroad—a 13-mile line between the Penobscot Ironworks and Bangor. The city spans several islands in the Penobscot River.

Diversified manufacturing continues to sustain the city; textiles, shoes, various wood products and metal goods are produced. The Old Town Canoe Co. makes canoes of fiberglass and other modern materials, but is best known as one of the last remaining producers of traditional canvas and wooden canoes. An audiovisual presentation at the visitor center, 130 Main St., details this process; phone (207) 827-1530.

The Penobscot Indian reservation occupies Indian Island at the north edge of the city and numerous uninhabited isles in the Penobscot River as far north as Mattawamkeag. Once the largest tribe of the Abenaki Confederacy, the Penobscots were excellent woodsmen and basket makers. A few Penobscot-made baskets can still be found in shops on the island.

**OLD TOWN MUSEUM,** at 353 S. Main St., offers rotating exhibits of historical objects in addition to displays depicting the lumber industry. Permanent exhibits include a birch bark canoe more than 200 years old, American Indian artifacts, a horse-drawn hearse used locally in the late 19th century and sculptures and paintings by Bernard Langlais, an Old Town native. Allow 30 minutes minimum. Wed.-Sun. 1-5, early June-Oct. 30. Donations. Phone (207) 827-7256.

## ORLAND (D-4) elev. 190′

Traditional handcrafting became a major industry in Orland with the 1970 establishment of H.O.M.E. (Home-workers Organized for More Employment). The cooperative, which began as an outlet for locally made products, has since expanded to include a chapel, museum, lumber mill, pottery and weaving shops and an extensive rural education program.

Various craft demonstrations can be seen at the H.O.M.E. compound, which is at the corner of US 1 and School House Road; for further information phone (207) 469-7961.

## ORONO (D-4) pop. 8,253, elev. 80′

Although small industries and farming contribute to Orono's economy, the main focus of this Penobscot Valley town is the University of Maine. Since its opening in 1868 with 12 students and two teachers, the land-grant institution, comprised of eight colleges, has grown to an enrollment of more than 11,000. The university is a center for teaching, research, public service and cultural activity.

The Maine Center for the Arts houses the 1,628-seat Hutchins Concert Hall. The Maynard F. Jordan Planetarium and Observatory offers multimedia astronomy programs and views of the heavens. Other university highlights are the ornamental gardens, art museum, dairy and sheep barns, modern athletic facilities and the largest library in the state. Brochures for a self-guiding walking tour are available at the visitor center near the Munson Road entrance. For information or university tours phone the visitor center at (207) 581-3740.

**HUDSON MUSEUM** is in the Maine Center for the Arts Building on the University of Maine campus. The museum's permanent exhibits include pre-Hispanic Mexican and Central American holdings; Native American collections from the Northwest Coast, Plains, Southwest, Maine and the Arctic as well as artifacts from Panama. Allow 1 hour minimum. Tues.-Fri. 9-4, Sat. 11-4; closed major holidays. Free. Phone (207) 581-1901.

## PARIS (E-2) elev. 780′

**HAMLIN MEMORIAL LIBRARY,** on Paris Hill Rd., is in a converted 1822 jailhouse. The library has a collection of papers, paintings and artifacts belonging to Hannibal Hamlin, vice president under Abraham Lincoln, and Hamlin's family. Also noteworthy are an original copy of the *Boston Gazette*

reporting the Boston Massacre and an early 1800s map of the Rangeley Lakes region hand drawn on birch bark. Tues.-Fri. noon-5, Sat. 10-2, Mar.-Dec. Free. Phone (207) 743-2980.

## PATTEN (B-4) elev. 546′

Since the 1830s the Shin Pond Road (SR 159) through Patten has been a major artery for the lumber industry. In the early days, horses pulled supply-laden wagons along the rough trace to remote lumber camps. There loggers with axes and handsaws cut millions of board feet of pine and spruce, then hauled it out with ox teams or drove it down the Penobscot River to Bangor.

Patten developed as a trading, supply and business center for the lumber interests. Its primary industry is the manufacture of plywood and other wood products. The community also caters to hunters and anglers bound for the deep woods and recreationists who follow SR 159 to Baxter State Park *(see Recreation Chart).*

SAVE  **LUMBERMEN'S MUSEUM,** .5 mi. w. on SR 159 to 61 Shin Pond Rd., at the n. entrance to Baxter State Park, has more than 4,000 exhibits in nine separate buildings—a legacy of the town's long-standing involvement with logging. Displays include carpenters', surveyors' and timber cruisers' tools; a blacksmith shop; a steam and a gas log hauler; pre-mechanized, horse-drawn equipment; photographs; and a full-scale replica of an 1820s lumber camp.

Picnicking is permitted. Tues.-Sun. 10-4, July-Aug.; Fri.-Sun. 10-4, Memorial Day weekend-June 30 and Sept. 1-Columbus Day. Admission $7; ages 6-11, $2. Phone (207) 528-2650.

## PEMAQUID POINT (E-3)

Pemaquid Point is on SR 30 at the end of a long peninsula jutting into the Atlantic. The first permanent settlement in Maine was made at the point 1625-26. The sea battle between the English brig *Boxer* and the American brig *Enterprise* was fought between the point and Monhegan Island in 1813. The 1827 Pemaquid Lighthouse is perched upon rugged granite ledges and is accessible by automobile.

**COLONIAL PEMAQUID STATE HISTORIC SITE AND FORT WILLIAM HENRY,** off SR 130 on Colonial Pemaquid Dr., is the site of an English settlement dating from the 17th century. A museum displays artifacts excavated from the area. The original Fort Charles was replaced by Fort William Henry in 1692; 4 years later the French captured and destroyed it. Fort Frederick was erected on the same site in 1729. A reproduction built on the original foundation contains historical material.

Allow 30 minutes minimum. Daily 9-5, Memorial Day-Labor Day. Excavation site free. Museum $1 (includes admission to Fort William Henry State Historic Site), over 64 and under 13 free. Phone (207) 677-2423.

**LIGHTHOUSE PARK,** s. on SR 130, covers 6 acres. A noteworthy feature of the park is the Pemaquid Point Lighthouse, commissioned by John Quincy Adams in 1827. Its 11,000-candlepower beam is visible up to 14 miles at sea. The lighthouse is closed to the public. Picnicking is permitted. Daily 9-5, Memorial Day-Columbus Day. Admission $1; over 54, 50c; under 12 free.

**Fishermen's Museum** contains exhibits chronicling the history of the local fishing industry. Charts of lighthouses along the Maine coast, a bronze buoy bell with an iron chain and a Lyle gun for shooting a lifeline to ships in distress are displayed. Other exhibits include tools used in lobstering, gear for several different sea harvesting methods, and working models of fishing boats.

Mon.-Sat. 10-5, Sun. 11-5, Memorial Day-Columbus Day; by appointment rest of year. Donations. Phone (207) 677-2494.

**Pemaquid Art Gallery** contains the works of local artists. Mon.-Sat. 10-5, Sun. 1-5, late May-Columbus Day. Donations. Phone (207) 677-2752.

## POLAND SPRING (E-2) elev. 322′

Poland Spring is one of the oldest and best known resorts in the East. The spring, which flows from the solid ledge of one of the region's highest hills, is the source of Poland Spring Water. The spring is owned by a commercial bottling company and is closed to visitors. Nearby Outlet Beach *(see Recreation Chart)* offers a variety of water-oriented activities.

**MAINE STATE BUILDING AND ALL SOULS CHAPEL** is off SR 26. Originally built to represent Maine at the 1893 Columbian Exposition in Chicago, the Maine State building was dismantled and brought to Poland Spring. It was reconstructed as a library and an art gallery. The solid granite chapel is a fine example of Victorian architecture with an oak ceiling and exquisite hand painted windows. Exhibits relate to Poland Spring Resort.

Tues.-Sat. 9-4, Sun. 9-1, May-Aug.; Thurs.-Sat. 9-4 in Apr. and Sept.-Nov. Admission to Maine State Building $2. Phone (207) 998-4142 or (207) 998-5182.

## POPHAM BEACH (E-3)

The first English attempt to colonize New England occurred at Popham Beach in 1607. In 1608 settlers constructed the *Virginia*, the first vessel built in America. Nearby Popham Beach State Park has a sand beach offering picnicking, swimming, windsurfing and fishing *(see Recreation Chart)*.

## PORT CLYDE (E-3) elev. 65′

Passenger service is available from Port Clyde to the getaway oasis of Monhegan Island *(see place listing p. 61)* courtesy of Monhegan-Thomaston Boat Line. The 5-mile excursion passes a lighthouse and offers the possibility of whale sightings;

the return trip provides a view of Seal Rock. For information and reservations phone (207) 372-8848.

**MARSHALL POINT LIGHTHOUSE MUSEUM,** 1 mi. from town center on Marshall Point Rd. off SR 131, is housed in the 1895 keepers house and displays exhibits about local history. The 1857 Marshall Point Lighthouse is nearby. Picnicking is permitted. Sun.-Fri. 1-5, Sat. 10-5, June-Sept.; Sat.-Sun. 1-5, in May and Oct. Donations. Phone (207) 372-6450.

## PORTLAND (E-2) pop. 64,249, elev. 34′

*See map page 66.*

"The beautiful town that is seated by the sea," wrote poet Henry Wadsworth Longfellow of his birthplace, Portland. Longfellow's town has become the largest city in Maine, the leading wholesale distributing point for northern New England and, with more than 175 manufacturing concerns, a major industrial center. Attractively restored 19th-century buildings, tree-lined streets and a fringe of parks readily evoke the grace that inspired the poet's tribute.

Although a few traders had inhabited the area earlier, 1632 is generally accepted as the year of the city's establishment. By 1675 Falmouth—the most recent in a series of names—had attained a degree of prosperity despite a maelstrom of land claims, counterclaims, speculation and power plays that made property and business ownership tenuous at best.

This relative stability was short-lived, however. In 1676 a series of American Indian raids culminated in an attack that sent residents fleeing to various bay islands or to Massachusetts and left the town in ruins. This was the first of three disasters that led to the city's adoption of the phoenix as its symbol and "Resurgam"—I Shall Rise Again—as its motto.

The second disaster occurred on Oct. 18, 1775, after the town's citizens refused to surrender their arms to the British. The British opened fire, and by the next morning more than 400 buildings had been reduced to rubble and 2,000 residents were homeless. In 1866 came the third disaster: fire leveled most of the city.

The Old Port Exchange on the waterfront was the heart of Portland's busy 19th-century commercial activities. After the fire the district was reconstructed in a classic Victorian style. The architecture, cobblestone streets and old gas street lamps recapture the flavor of the city's early seaport days. Many of the old warehouses, ship chandleries and merchant exchanges now serve as boutiques and restaurants. At the Maine State Pier on Commercial Street is the "Whaling Wall," a 950-foot mural depicting sea life found in the Gulf of Maine.

Culturally, Portland is Maine's showplace. The Portland Performing Arts Center, which opened in 1984, is home to the Portland Stage Company. Three centuries of art and architecture are on display at the Portland Museum of Art *(see attraction listing p. 68)*. The Portland Symphony Orchestra offers a wide spectrum of classical and contemporary music during its season, and ballet, repertory opera and a variety of musical performances are held throughout the year.

The Calendar Islands, so called because of their number, 365, are east of Portland in Casco Bay. Capt. John Smith first visited these islands in 1614. Crescent Beach and Two Lights state parks are nearby in Cape Elizabeth.

Excursions and charters for whale watching, deep-sea fishing, fall foliage viewing and tours to lighthouses and the Casco Bay islands are available. For information contact AAA Northern New England, 68 Marginal Way, Portland, ME 04101; phone (207) 780-6800.

**Greater Portland Convention and Visitors Bureau:** 245 Commercial St., Portland, ME 04101; phone (207) 772-5800.

**Self-guiding tours:** Brochures for a walking tour of the city's architectural highlights are available daily for $1.25 at the convention and visitors bureau. Each map outlines tours through the Old Port Exchange, Congress Street, State Street and the Western Promenade. A general walking tour map also is available.

**Shopping areas:** The Portland Public Market, between Preble and Elm streets on Cumberland Avenue, offers produce, cheeses, seafood, flowers and prepared foods in a 37,000-square-foot building in Portland's downtown.

**BAY VIEW CRUISES,** downtown on Fisherman's Wharf at 184 Commercial St., offers sightseeing tours around the Calendar Islands on the waterways of Casco Bay. Evening cruises are offered beginning in late June. Food is available. Allow 1.5 to 2 hours minimum. Tours depart daily 10:30-6:30, mid-June through Labor Day; otherwise varies. Fare $10; over 65, $9; under 12, $7. Phone (207) 761-0496.

SAVE **CASCO BAY LINES,** on the waterfront at Commercial and Franklin sts., provides year-round ferry service to the Calendar Islands of Casco Bay. A lifeline to the islands, the ferries also offer passengers a scenic tour of the bay as they

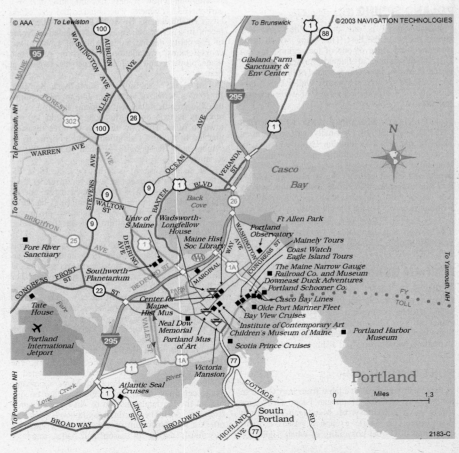

transport groceries, mail and residents to and from the islands. Several cruises are available in addition to the regular mail boat run. Mail boat run departs daily at 10 and 2:15, mid-June through Labor Day; at 10 and 2:45, rest of year. Fare $11-$18; over 64, $10.50; ages 5-9, $5-$8. Phone (207) 774-7871.

**CENTER FOR MAINE HISTORY MUSEUM, MAINE HISTORICAL SOCIETY,** 489 Congress St., displays changing exhibits from its extensive collection that includes paintings, costumes, military items, political memorabilia, archeological materials and manuscripts. Allow 1 hour minimum. Mon.-Sat. 10-5, Sun. noon-5, May-Oct.; closed holidays and between exhibitions. Schedule may vary; phone

ahead. Museum admission $4; over 65 and students with ID $3; ages 5-17, $2. Combination ticket with Wadsworth-Longfellow House $7. AX, DS, MC, VI. Phone (207) 774-1822.

SAVE **CHILDREN'S MUSEUM OF MAINE,** 142 Free St., is housed in a historic brick building and contains exhibits designed to interest children up to 10 years of age. Displays include a model space shuttle, a fire truck, a child-size grocery store, a farm exhibit and interactive science exhibits depicting the natural resources of Maine. Special events occur throughout the year.

Allow 1 hour minimum. Mon.-Sat. 10-5, Sun. noon-5, Memorial Day-Labor Day; Tues.-Sat. 10-5,

Sun. noon-5, rest of year. Admission $6, under 1 free. AX, DS, MC, VI. Phone (207) 828-1234.

**[SAVE] COAST WATCH EAGLE ISLAND TOURS** departs from Long Wharf. Offered are a variety of sightseeing cruises including a trip to Admiral Peary's summer home on Eagle Island and a 90-minute lighthouse and seal-watching cruise on Casco Bay. A combined boat and trolley tour also is available.

The Eagle Island cruise departs daily at 10, late June-Labor Day; Sat.-Sun. at 10, early June-late June and day after Labor Day through mid-Sept. Seal-watch and lighthouse cruise departs daily at 11:30, 1:30 and 3:45, late June-Labor Day; at 11:30 and 1:30, Memorial Day-late June and day after Labor Day-Columbus Day. Seal-watch and lighthouse fare $10; over 61, $9; ages 3-12, $7. Phone for Eagle Island cruise fare and the Land & Sea tour fare. Schedule and fares may vary; phone ahead. Reservations are recommended. AX, DS, MC, VI. Phone (207) 774-6498.

**DOWNEAST DUCK ADVENTURES** is at 94 Commercial St. An amphibious vehicle, the *Eider,* transports visitors on a narrated land and sea tour of Portland. The land cruise covers the historical landmarks of the city; the sea cruise allows visitors to view Casco Bay and the Calendar Islands. Allow 1 hour, 30 minutes minimum. Daily at 10, noon, 2 and 4, mid-Apr. to mid-Sept.; Thurs.-Sun. at 10, noon, 2 and 4, mid-Sept. to late Oct. Fare $20; over 64 and ages 6-11, $15. MC, VI. Phone (207) 774-3825.

**FORE RIVER SANCTUARY,** 1 mi. e. on Brighton Ave., then s. on Rowe Ave. to end, is an 85-acre preserve within the city of Portland that includes a 2.5-mile trail leading to the towpath of the historic Cumberland and Oxford Canal. The sanctuary includes salt marshes, forested ravines and Portland's only waterfall, Jewell Falls. Black ducks, cormorants and herring gulls nest in the area. Daily dawn-dusk. Free. Phone (207) 781-2330.

**INSTITUTE OF CONTEMPORARY ART** is at 522 Congress St., on the Maine College of Art campus. The institute features year-round exhibitions that showcase new perspectives and trends in contemporary art. Allow 30 minutes minimum. Wed.-Sun. 11-5 (also Thurs. 5-7 and first Fri. of the month 5-8). Free. Phone (207) 879-5742.

**THE MAINE NARROW GAUGE RAILROAD CO. AND MUSEUM,** off I-295 exit 7, .8 mi. s.e. on Franklin St., then .3 mi. e. to 58 Fore St. following signs, is dedicated to preserving Maine narrow gauge railroad equipment. Highlights of the museum include a Maine two-foot gauge parlor car, antique equipment, coaches, locomotives and rail cars. Rides aboard a train run along Casco Bay.

Allow 1 hour minimum. Museum daily 10-4. Trains depart on the hour daily 11-4, May 15-Oct. 11; Sat.-Sun. and holidays 11-4, mid-Feb. through May 14 and Oct. 12-late Nov.; Sat.-Sun. 11-3, late

Nov.-Dec. 20. Closed Thanksgiving. Museum free. Train rides $5; over 62, $4; ages 4-11, $3. MC, VI. Phone (207) 828-0814.

**MAINELY TOURS,** departing from 3 Moulton St., offers a 90-minute narrated trolley tour of Portland and the nearby coast, with a stop at Portland Head Light. A combination land/sea tour includes the trolley ride and a 90-minute narrated Lighthouse Lovers cruise on Casco Bay.

Trolley tour departs daily at 9:30, 11, 12:30, 2, 3:30 and 5, July-Aug.; at 9:30, 11, 12:30 and 2, Memorial Day weekend-June 30 and Sept. 1-day before Columbus Day; at 11 and 2, May 3-day before Memorial Day weekend and Columbus Day-Oct. 31. Trolley tour fare $14; over 64, $13; under 12, $7. Combination tour $22; over 64, $21; under 12, $13. AX, DS, MC, VI. Phone (207) 774-0808.

**NEAL DOW MEMORIAL,** 714 Congress St. is a Federal-style mansion built in 1829 for prominent Maine politician, abolitionist and prohibitionist Neal Dow, twice elected mayor of Portland. The family's original furniture, portraits, paintings and china are on display, as are memorabilia of Dow's military and political careers. There also is a library. Dow's death mask can be viewed upon special request. Guided tours Mon.-Fri. 11-4; closed major holidays. Donations. Phone (207) 773-7773.

**[SAVE] OLDE PORT MARINER FLEET,** departing from Long Wharf on Commercial St. (US 1A), offers narrated whale-watching, and lighthouse, seal and harbor cruises. Other tours and cruises also are available. Whale-watch cruises depart daily at 10, July-Aug.; Sat.-Sun. at 10, late May-June 30 and Sept.-Oct. Visitors must check-in 1 hour before departure. Fare $38; senior citizens $33; under 13, $28. Schedule and fares may vary; phone ahead. Reservations are required. Phone (207) 775-0727, or (800) 437-3270 out of Maine.

**PORTLAND HEAD LIGHT—**
*see Cape Elizabeth p. 51.*

**PORTLAND MUSEUM OF ART,** 7 Congress Sq. is in an award-winning building designed by I.M. Pei & Partners. It houses a collection of fine and decorative arts dating from the 18th century to the present. Displays include works by Winslow Homer, Rockwell Kent and Andrew Wyeth. The museum's European collection includes works by Edgar Degas, Claude Monet, and Pablo Picasso.

Food is available. Allow 1 hour minimum. Daily 10-5 (also Fri. 5-9), Memorial Day-Columbus Day; Tues.-Sun. 10-5 (also Fri. 5-9), rest of year. Admission $8; over 65 and students with ID $6; ages 6-17, $2. Phone (207) 775-6148.

**L.D.M. Sweat Memorial Galleries,** designed by prominent Maine architect John Calvin, were opened in 1911. The galleries house collections of 19th-century American art, including works by the acclaimed American artist Winslow Homer. Sculpture and decorative objects also are showcased. Picnicking is permitted. Allow 30 minutes minimum.

**McClellan House** reflects 19th-century architecture and design. Its interior is restored to the Federal period and includes vibrant wallpapers, carpeting and furniture. Three study centers, featuring interactive computers, allow visitors to learn more about former residents of the house as well as provide detailed information pertaining to the social, economic, political and artistic history of the era. Picnicking is permitted. Allow 30 minutes minimum.

**PORTLAND OBSERVATORY** is at 138 Congress St.; take I-295 exit 7 to jct. Congress and Franklin sts. Exhibits detail the history, architecture and preservation of what is said to be the last remaining maritime signal station in the United States. The observation station served Portland's bustling waterfront from 1807 to the early 20th century. Views of Portland, the White Mountains and Casco Bay are available from the 86-foot-high tower, reached by stairs.

Allow 1 hour minimum. Guided tours depart daily 10-5, Memorial Day-Columbus Day; closed July 4. Admission $4; ages 6-16, $2. Phone (207) 774-5561.

**PORTLAND SCHOONER CO.** departs Maine State Pier, Commercial St. Launched in 1924, the 72-foot schooner *Bagheera* is elegantly decorated in period with mahogany trim and brass oil lamps. The 2-hour trip on Casco Bay affords visitors an opportunity to experience the sounds of the ocean and the sights along the Maine coast. Tuesday's during July and August the schooner departs from Peaks Island.

Allow 2 hours minimum. Daily at 9:45, 12:30, 2:45 and 6, Memorial Day weekend-Columbus Day weekend. Schedule may vary in Sept., phone to confirm. Fare $25-$35; ages 2-12, $12-$35. MC, VI. Phone (207) 766-2500 or (877) 246-6637.

**SCOTIA PRINCE CRUISES,** 468 Commercial St. (at the International Marine Terminal), offers one-way and round-trip cruises between Portland and Yarmouth, Nova Scotia, aboard the *Scotia Prince*. The one-way trip takes 11 hours. Cabins and car ferry service aboard the ship are available.

Food is available. Cruises generally depart daily at 9 p.m., early May-late Oct. One-way fare late June to mid-Sept. $90; ages 5-14, $45. One-way fare early May-late June and mid-Sept. to late Oct. $70; ages 5-14, $35. Reservations are required. AX, DS, MC, VI. Phone (800) 341-7540. *See color ad p. 67.*

[SAVE] **SOUTHWORTH PLANETARIUM** is on the University of Southern Maine campus; take I-295 exit 6B, go 1 blk. w. on Forest Ave., then .5 blk. s. to 96 Falmouth St. It features a permanent exhibit of the solar system prepared by the National Geographic Society. Regularly changing astronomy shows, laser light shows and special programs are projected onto a 30-foot dome. Seating capacity is 60.

Allow 1 hour minimum. Exhibit area open Mon.-Fri. 9-4:30. Astronomy show Fri. at 7 p.m., Sat.-Sun. at 3 (also Sat. at 7 p.m.). Laser show Sat. at 8:30 p.m. Exhibit area free. Astronomy show $5; over 65 and ages 5-17, $4. Laser show $6; over 65 and ages 5-17, $5. Phone (207) 780-4249.

**TATE HOUSE** is 2 mi. w. on SR 22/9 at 1270 Westbrook St. in Stroudwater. In keeping with his importance as mast agent for the British Crown, George Tate built this Georgia house with indented gambrel roof in 1755. The house has a few unusual features. Eighteenth-century furnishings add to the London town house atmosphere. Wednesday afternoon tea is served in the 18th-century garden. Saturday afternoon architectural tours are offered.

Allow 1 hour minimum. Tues.-Sat. 10-4, Sun. 1-4, June 15-Sept. 30; Fri.-Sat. 10-4, Sun. 1-4, in Oct. Closed July 4. Admission $5; over 64, $4; ages 6-12, $1. Phone (207) 774-9781.

[GEM] [SAVE] **VICTORIA MANSION,** 109 Danforth St. between State and High sts., is an impressive Italianate villa representing Victorian-era style. Designed by the distinguished New Haven architect Henry Austin, the mansion was built 1858-60 and features a significant collection of furniture by interior designer Gustave Herter.

Original painted *trompe l'oeil* walls and ceilings, a stained-glass skylight, elaborate wood carvings, carpets, silver, glass and porcelain are some of the many treasures within. Special holiday festivities are offered in December.

Guided tours are available. Allow 1 hour minimum. Tues.-Sat. 10-4, Sun. 1-5, May-Oct.; closed July 4. Last tour begins at 3:45. Admission $10; over 62, $9; ages 6-17, $3. AX, MC, VI. Phone (207) 772-4841.

[GEM] **WADSWORTH-LONGFELLOW HOUSE,** 489 Congress St., was built 1785-86 by Gen. Peleg Wadsworth, maternal grandfather of poet Henry Wadsworth Longfellow, who lived in the house during his childhood. It was the first brick home in Portland, constructed of bricks barged from Philadelphia. The residence was originally a two-story structure; a third story was added in 1815.

Within are furniture, records and personal possessions of the Longfellow and Wadsworth families. The house has been restored to the 1850s period. Guided tours are available. Allow 1 hour minimum. Mon.-Sat. 10-4, Sun. noon-4, May-Oct. Special hours Nov.-Dec.; phone to confirm. Closed holidays. Admission $7; over 65 and students with ID $6; ages 5-17, $3. Price includes admission to the Center for Maine History Museum, Maine Historical Society. AX, MC, VI. Phone (207) 774-1822.

**Maine Historical Society Library** is at the rear of the grounds and is a research library containing a collection of more than 125,000 books and two million manuscript pages. Open Tues.-Sat. 10-4; closed holidays. First visit is free; subsequent visits are $2 per hour. Phone (207) 774-1822.

## PRESQUE ISLE (B-5) pop. 9,511, elev. 445'

When Maxie Anderson, Ben Abruzzo and Larry Newman climbed into the gondola of the *Double Eagle II* on Aug. 11, 1978, they began an adventure momentous in the history of aviation. Six days later they landed in a field in France, having completed the first successful transatlantic hot air balloon flight. A replica of the balloon, at Double Eagle II Park on Spragueville Road just beyond Echo Lake, indicates the starting point of the flight.

For the most part, however, Presque Isle's interests are more down to earth. The city is the chief industrial and commercial center of Aroostook County. Nearby, the University of Maine's 375-acre experiment station explores improved methods of growing and marketing potatoes as well as other crops. The university's Read Art Gallery, on the Main Street campus, serves as a cultural resource for the community and features works by local and regional artists.

Recreation is available all year at Aroostook State Park *(see Recreation Chart)*, 4 miles south on US 1, then west and south via a park road. In the winter snowmobile enthusiasts enjoy over 1,600 miles of groomed trails in the area.

**Presque Isle Area Chamber of Commerce:** 3 Houlton Rd., P.O. Box 672, Presque Isle, ME 04769; phone (207) 764-6561.

**Shopping areas:** The Aroostook Centre Mall, 830 Main St., offers more than 40 stores.

## PROSPECT (D-4)

From Prospect's eastern environs extends a broad view of the Penobscot River. The village lies just southeast of Mount Waldo, the site of major granite quarries. Mount Waldo granite is found not only at nearby Fort Knox but also in buildings in Boston, New York and Washington, D.C. Prospect is primarily a trading center for the surrounding farming and summer vacation area.

**FORT KNOX STATE HISTORIC SITE** is .2 mi. off US 1 from the s. end of the Waldo-Hancock Bridge. The pentagon-shaped fort was built on 125 acres overlooking the Penobscot River in the 1840s-60s as a deterrent to future British attempts to recapture Bangor and to control the river. The granite fort contains mounts for 64 cannons. Fort Knox garrisoned troops during the Civil and Spanish-American wars, yet the fort was never threatened. Periodic Civil War musters occur on the grounds.

Fort open daily 9-dusk, early May-late Oct. Guided tours are available Memorial Day-Labor Day. Grounds open daily 9-dusk, year-round. Admission $2; ages 5-11, 50c; over 65 free. Phone (207) 469-7719.

## RANGELEY (D-2)

**HUNTER COVE SANCTUARY,** 2.5 mi. w. on SR 4, offers 3 miles of trails that pass through the cedar swamps, woodland meadows, alder thickets and mature pine, spruce-fir and poplar forests bordering Rangeley Lake. Bears, coyotes, bobcats, deer and moose dwell in the area. Daily dawn-dusk. Free. Phone (207) 781-2330.

(SAVE) **THE WILHELM REICH MUSEUM,** 3.5 mi. w. off SR 4 on Dodge Pond Rd., is an imposing stone building filled with exhibits that reflect the life and work of the natural scientist Wilhelm Reich, a student of Freud. Guided tours of the museum begin with a biographical video presentation. The rooftop observatory affords visitors a panorama of the Rangeley Lakes Region. A nature program is offered in the summer. A hands-on discovery room for children is available.

Allow 1 hour minimum. Wed.-Sun. 1-5, July-Aug.; Sun. 1-5, in Sept. Last tour begins 1 hour before closing. Admission $5, under 12 free. AX, MC, VI. Phone (207) 864-3443.

## RECREATIONAL ACTIVITIES

### Skiing

- **Saddleback,** on Saddleback Rd., Box 490, Rangeley, ME 04970. Other activities are offered. Daily, late Nov.-Apr. 30. Phone (207) 864-5671.

## RICHMOND (E-3) pop. 1,864, elev. 76'

Located on the Kennebec River about 16 miles north of Brunswick on SR 24, this area was first explored by Pierre de Gaust and Samuel de Champlain in 1604. Permanent settlement began in 1719 with the erection of a frontier trading house that became Fort Richmond. Shortly after the American Revolution, Richmond grew as a farming community.

Shipbuilding and merchant activity built the wealth of the town, and in the late 19th century, shoemaking and river ice harvesting resulted in another period of prosperity that lasted for several decades. Several historic homes attest to the area's prosperity and the skill of its builders, and one of the finest collections of temple-style Greek Revival houses can be found in Richmond's historic district.

In the 1950s and '60s the town experienced an influx of Slavic immigrants escaping the spread of communism. The churches they established welcome visitors today.

**Town of Richmond:** 26 Gardiner St., P.O. Box 159, Richmond, ME 04357-0159; phone (207) 737-4305.

## ROCKLAND (E-4) pop. 7,609, elev. 35'

Rockland, one of Maine's largest fishing ports, is known as the "Lobster Capital of the World" and the "Schooner Capital of Maine"—ferries to several nearby islands are available along with schooners for daily and weeklong cruises. Shipbuilding, commercial fishing, granite quarrying and limekilns have contributed to area history and economy. The poet Edna St. Vincent Millay was born in Rockland.

A granite breakwater, extending seven-eighths of a mile across Penobscot Bay, leads to the Rockland Breakwater Lighthouse, built around 1888. The town's historic Main Street district is now a shopping area. Owls Head Light, 5 miles southeast, offers outstanding views of Penobscot Bay.

**Rockland-Thomaston Area Chamber of Commerce:** Harbor Park, P.O. Box 508, Rockland, ME 04841; phone (207) 596-0376 or (800) 562-2529.

**FARNSWORTH ART MUSEUM AND THE WYETH CENTER,** 16 Museum St., houses American art, with emphasis on artists with state ties: Winslow Homer; Fitz Hugh Lane; John Marin; Louise Nevelson; and Andrew, James and N.C. Wyeth. Works by the Wyeth family are in a former church on Union Street across from the Farnsworth Homestead. Changing exhibits feature important artists, current trends or historical themes.

Allow 1 hour, 30 minutes minimum. Daily 9-5 (also Wed. 5-7), Memorial Day-Columbus Day; Tues.-Sat. 10-5, Sun. 1-5, rest of year. Closed Jan. 1, Thanksgiving and Dec. 25. Admission Memorial Day-Columbus Day $9; over 64, $8; students over 17 with ID $5; free to all Wed. after 4. Admission rest of year $8; over 64, $7; students over 17 with ID $4. AX, MC, VI. Phone (207) 596-6457.

**Farnsworth Homestead,** next to the museum, is an example of Greek Revival architecture built in 1850; it contains many of the original family furnishings. Daily 10-5, Memorial Day weekend-Columbus Day. Admission included with museum.

**OWLS HEAD TRANSPORTATION MUSEUM,** 2 mi. s. on SR 73, has antique aircraft, automobiles, motorcycles, bicycles and carriages—all in operating condition. The collection includes World War I fighter planes, Stanley Steamers, limited-edition cars and pioneer vehicles. Demonstrations take place in the summer. Allow 1 hour minimum. Daily 10-5, Apr.-Oct.; 10-4, rest of year. Closed Thanksgiving and Dec. 25. Admission $6; ages 5-11, $4; family rate $16. Admission may vary for special events. DS, MC, VI. Phone (207) 594-4418.

**SHORE VILLAGE MUSEUM** is in G.A.R. Hall at 104 Limerock St. Also known as America's Lighthouse Museum, the facility contains a large collection of lighthouse equipment and exhibits of U.S. Coast Guard relics, including working lights, horns, bells and lifesaving devices. Also displayed are ship models, and postcards featuring lighthouses and lightships. Hands-on exhibits are offered. Daily 10-4, June 1-Oct. 15; by appointment rest of year. Donations. Phone (207) 594-0311.

## ROCKPORT (E-4)

Rockport was originally part of neighboring Camden; the towns officially split into two distinct communities in 1891. For many years Rockport was the summer sojourn of Andre, a harbor seal whose life was chronicled in the children's books "A Seal Called Andre" and "Andre."

The Vesper Hill Children's Chapel on Calderwood Lane offers views of Penobscot Bay and Rockport Harbor.

**Camden-Rockport-Lincolnville Chamber of Commerce:** Public Landing, P.O. Box 919, Camden, ME 04843; phone (207) 236-4404.

**CENTER FOR MAINE CONTEMPORARY ART,** 162 Russell Ave., offers changing exhibits of contemporary artwork by some of Maine's most talented artists. The gallery is housed in a large, renovated 19th-century livery stable. Allow 1 hour minimum. Tues.-Sat. 10-5, Sun. 1-5, June-Sept. Admission $3, students free. Phone (207) 236-2875.

**ROCKPORT MARINE PARK** is on Pascal Ave. next to the harbor. Highlights include a statue of Andre the seal and three restored limekilns dating to the early 1900s. A set of drawings next to the kilns describes their former purpose and function. Another highlight is a replica of the locomotives that were used to transport lime to waiting ships in the harbor. A public boat launch is available. Picnicking is permitted. Allow 30 minutes minimum. Daily dawn-dusk. Free. Phone (207) 236-0676.

## ROCKWOOD (C-3) elev. 1,047'

SAVE **MOOSEHEAD SAFARIS AND SCENIC CRUISES,** departing from the docks off SR 15, offers 3-hour sightseeing cruises on Moosehead Lake aboard a pontoon boat. In addition to scenic views of the lake and Mount Kineo, passengers are likely to see moose and peregrine falcons. Daily at 5, mid-May through July 31; at 4, Aug. 1-Oct. 5 (weather permitting). Fare $40; under 11, $20. AX, MC, VI. Phone (207) 695-4400.

## SACO (F-2) pop. 16,822, elev. 75'

Like its sister city Biddeford (see place listing p. 46), Saco (SAH-co) was settled in 1631 at a site first noted by Capt. John Smith in 1614; in 1762 the town was incorporated as Pepperellboro. Pepperellboro became Saco in 1805.

A few years later the first major industry, an ironworks, was established. Due to an abundance of readily available waterpower, Saco remained predominantly industrial until recently. The economy now has a broader base, with commerce taking the leading role.

Besides powering the city's industries, the Saco River provides opportunities for fishing, boating and swimming on its 4-mile run to the sea. Ferry Beach State Park (see Recreation Chart) occupies 117 acres on the east bank; a stand of tupelo trees, rare at this northern latitude, grows in the park.

Also nearby is one of the region's favorite seaside resorts, Old Orchard Beach (see place listing p. 63).

**Biddeford-Saco Chamber of Commerce & Industry:** 110 Main St., Suite 1202, Saco, ME 04072; phone (207) 282-1567.

[SAVE] **AQUABOGGAN WATER PARK,** 4 mi. n. on US 1, offers a wave pool, miniature race cars, a miniature golf course and a variety of water slides. Rides for small children are available. Picnicking is permitted. Daily 10-6, late June-Labor Day. Admission $14-$27. DS, MC, VI. Phone (207) 282-3112.

**DYER LIBRARY AND SACO MUSEUM** are in two buildings at 371 Main St. The Dyer Library, in the 19th-century Deering House, has changing exhibits and maintains a 500-volume collection on Maine history and more than 80,000 local manuscripts and city records. The Saco Museum was founded in 1866. The collection includes representative examples of Maine furniture and decorative arts. Special exhibits examine regional history and art.

Guided tours are available. Library Mon.-Fri. 9:30-5 (also Tues. and Thurs. 5-8), Sat. 9:30-12:30. Museum Mon.-Fri. noon-4 (also Thurs. 4-8). Admission $4, senior citizens $3, students $1, under 6 free; free to all Thurs. 4-8. Phone (207) 283-0958 or (207) 283-0684 for the museum, or (207) 283-3861 for the library.

**FUNTOWN/SPLASHTOWN USA,** 1 mi. n. on US 1, comprises two parks and offers an array of rides. Included within the water park are speed slides, a corkscrew slide, a two-tunnel slide and a fun lagoon, while bumper boats and cars, miniature golf and one of New England's longest and largest wooden roller coasters are among the attractions featured in the amusement park. Dragon's Descent offers an accelerated drop from a 200-foot tower.

Amusement and water park open daily at 10, mid-June through Labor Day. Amusement park open Sat.-Sun. at 11, mid-May to early June and at 10:30, early to mid-Sept.; closing times vary. Hours may vary; phone ahead. Admission $8 for non-participants. Funtown ride pass $23.50, under 48 inches tall $16. Splashtown pass $16.50, under 48 inches tall $13.50. Combination pass $30, under 48 inches tall $21.50. Under 11 must be with a paying adult. AX, DS, MC, VI. Phone (207) 284-5139.

## SCARBOROUGH (F-2) pop. 3,867

**SCARBOROUGH MARSH NATURE CENTER,** .5 mi. e. of jct. US 1 and SR 9 on Pine Point Rd., comprises more than 3,000 acres of tidal and fresh marsh, salt creeks and uplands. Wildlife can be observed along the Marsh Nature Trail. Exhibits, nature programs and a slide show are presented at the center. A bird-watching walk is offered weekday mornings in summer for a fee. Canoe tours and rentals are available. Full-moon canoe tours also are offered; phone for details.

Allow 1 hour, 30 minutes minimum. Daily 9:30-5:30, Memorial Day-Labor Day. Center free. DS, MC, VI. Phone (207) 883-5100 or (207) 781-2330.

## SEAL COVE (E-4)

**SEAL COVE AUTO MUSEUM,** 2.5 mi. n. on SR 102, houses more than 100 antique automobiles ranging from an 1899 DeDion Bouton to a 1934 Packard. The museum's diverse collection includes several rare models from the 1885-1915 "Brass Era." An assortment of antique motorcycles also is featured. Allow 1 hour minimum. Daily 10-5, June 1-Sept. 15. Admission $5; under 12, $2. Phone (207) 244-9242.

## SEARSPORT (D-4) pop. 1,102, elev. 60′

If shipping was the lifeblood of Maine from the late 1700s to the late 1800s, then Searsport was its heartbeat. During this time Searsport produced not only some 250 sailing vessels of substantial size but also more than 280 resident ship captains. In 1870 alone it was the home of 10 percent of the captains of the U.S. Merchant Marine.

Still a major Maine port, Searsport has since diversified. Its existing piers handle bulk cargoes for the manufacturing and agricultural industries throughout northern and eastern Maine. As part of Maine's maritime future, a new containerized cargo facility will replace the aging Bangor and Aroostook Pier. As the southern terminus of the Bangor and Aroostook Railroad, the new facility will have the potential to handle at least five vessels at one time.

A number of finely crafted mansions preside over the shaded streets of Searsport; some are part of the Penobscot Marine Museum (see attraction listing). A wealthy past carries into the present in the form of antiques; Searsport is one of the best known antique centers on Maine's mid-coast.

Those who prefer to experience seafaring on their own will find a municipal wharf and boat landing at their disposal. Just south of town off busy US 1, 183-acre Moose Point State Park offers picnic sites and an unobstructed view of Penobscot Bay. For exceptional sightseeing by car, the 46-mile drive on US 1 between Rockland and Verona runs through Searsport and along the ocean and bay.

[SAVE] **PENOBSCOT MARINE MUSEUM** is at jct. US 1 and Church St. Eight buildings—including an 1816 captain's home and the 1845 town hall—contain collections of paintings, navigational instruments, builders' half-models, shipbuilders' tools, and American and Oriental furnishings. Marine paintings by Thomas and James Buttersworth are on display. The museum also contains an art gallery and a research library.

Allow 2 hours minimum. Mon.-Sat. 10-5, Sun. noon-5, Memorial Day weekend-Oct. 19. Admission $8; over 65, $6; ages 7-15, $3. AX, MC, VI. Phone (207) 548-2529.

## SEBAGO (E-1) elev. 276'

The vacation village of Sebago lies among wooded hills a few miles from the west shore of Sebago Lake, Maine's second largest lake. Partly because of its proximity to Portland but mostly because of its lovely scenery and many recreational opportunities, the Sebago region is one of the most popular resort areas in the state.

There is fishing for trout and the indigenous landlocked salmon; local hatcheries keep lakes and streams supplied with both. Boating is especially good on Sebago Lake and the 42-mile waterway that links it with Long Lake by way of the historic Songo Lock. Sebago Lake State Park (see Recreation Chart), off US 302 between Naples and South Casco, embraces 1,300 acres on the north shore.

SAVE **JONES MUSEUM OF GLASS AND CERAM-ICS,** 1 mi. off SR 107 on Douglas Mountain, following signs, exhibits more than 10,000 pieces. The museum's collection spans the period from ancient Egypt to the present and represents glass and ceramic decorative arts of America, Great Britain, Europe and the Middle and Far East. There also are special exhibits, a lecture program and a reference library with more than 10,000 books and related items. Guided tours are available by appointment.

Allow 1 hour minimum. Tues.-Sat. 10-5, Sun. 1-5, mid-May to mid-Nov.; by appointment rest of year. Admission $5, senior citizens $3.75, students with ID $3, under 12 free. MC, VI. Phone (207) 787-3370.

## SKOWHEGAN (D-3) pop. 6,696, elev. 175'

The Abenaki Indians called this island in the Kennebec River *skowhegan*—"a place to watch"—as they looked for salmon in the depths below the falls. One still watches: A 62-foot Indian sculpted in wood by Bernard Langlais rises above town in honor of those who first watched from this spot.

In 1771 the island's second settlers arrived, drawn by timber and the river's plenty. Their village was brushed by Revolutionary history in 1775, when Col. Benedict Arnold's expedition crossed the island en route to Québec; a granite boulder marks the site.

Although Skowhegan gradually evolved into a predominantly manufacturing city, the colorful history of log driving on the Kennebec did not end until 1976. A paper pulp mill with an 800-ton daily capacity, 7 miles south on US 201, is further evidence of the area's continued interest in lumbering.

Lakewood Theater, on Lake Wesserunsett 6 miles north of Skowhegan on US 201, is Maine's state theater. Established in 1901, it is one of the oldest continuously operating summer stock theaters in the country. Matinee and evening performances run mid-May to late September; phone (207) 474-7176.

**Skowhegan Area Chamber of Commerce:** 23 Commercial St., Skowhegan, ME 04976; phone (207) 474-3621 or (888) 772-4392.

**HISTORY HOUSE,** 66 Elm St., is a well-preserved 1839 brick cottage that includes antique furniture, clothing, kitchen tools, dolls and china. Early town records, genealogical accounts, maps, newspapers, Civil War items and artwork are on display in the attached museum. Guided tours are available. Tues.-Fri. 1-5, mid-June to mid-Sept. Donations. Phone (207) 474-6632.

**MARGARET CHASE SMITH LIBRARY,** 56 Norridgewock Ave., offers displays about the life and career of Margaret Chase Smith, a prominent Maine politician who completed 32 years in the United States House of Representatives and Senate. A 20-minute videotape presentation introduces her. Mon.-Fri. 10-4; closed major holidays. Donations. Phone (207) 474-7133.

## SOUTH BERWICK (F-1) elev. 97'

South Berwick grew up around some of the earliest lumbering efforts in Maine. The region's straight white pines were prized as masts for the ships of the British navy, and a sawmill was in operation before 1640. Later successes in milling and shipping also contributed to the town's present-day appearance—a charming New England community with many Colonial houses set on spacious lawns.

A combination of manufacturing and farming sustains South Berwick as well as the neighboring communities of Berwick and North Berwick. Nearby Spring Hill Recreation Area on Knight's Pond Road offers summer and winter recreation.

**HAMILTON HOUSE** is reached via SR 236N off I-95, past jct. SR 91, w. on Brattle St., then s.w. on Vaughan's Ln. The Georgian mansion was built about 1785 by merchant Col. Jonathan Hamilton. He chose the site because it overlooked his warehouses and wharves on the Salmon Falls River. Later the house was the setting for Sarah Orne Jewett's book "The Tory Lover." It has lovely gardens, painted murals and simple country furnishings. Also featured is a garden cottage.

Tours on the hour Wed.-Sun. 11-5, June 1-Oct. 15. Last tour begins 1 hour before closing. Admission $5; over 65, $4.50; ages 6-12, $2.50. Phone (207) 384-2454.

**SARAH ORNE JEWETT HOUSE,** I-95 to SR 236N, then s. on S. Berwick to 5 Portland St., dates from 1774. In the early 19th century the stately Georgian house was occupied by the Jewett family; author Sarah Orne Jewett was born in 1849. The house museum is adorned with fine paneling, original 18th- and 19th-century wallpapers and period furnishings. Jewett's bedroom/study is arranged as she left it. Tours on the hour Wed.-Sun. 11-5, June 1-Oct. 15. Last tour begins 1 hour before closing. Admission $5; over 65, $4.50; ages 6-12, $2.50. Phone (207) 384-2454.

**VAUGHAN WOODS,** off SR 236 to 28 Old Field Rd. on the e. bank of Salmon Falls River, contains 165 wooded acres interspersed with 4.5 mi. of marked foot trails. According to legend, the *Pied*

*Cow* landed at Cow Cove in 1634, bringing the East Coast its first cows. Later that year the same ship brought the nation one of its first sawmills, which was erected nearby. Picnicking is permitted. Daily 9-8, Memorial Day-Labor Day; 9-6, day after Labor Day-Sept. 30. Admission $2; ages 5-11, $1. Phone (207) 384-5160.

## SOUTH BRIDGTON (E-2)

NARRAMISSIC is .5 mi. s. on SR 107 to Ingalles Rd., then w. following signs. Set in the foothills of the White Mountains, Narramissic is a converted farm. On the premises are a restored Georgian-style house built in 1797 by one of the area's first settlers, a barn and a blacksmith shop. Nature trails wind through the wooded grounds. Cabinetmakers and woodworkers periodically explain and demonstrate techniques of carpentry and restoration. Picnicking is permitted. Grounds Tues.-Sun. 9-5. Free. Admission is charged for demonstrations. Phone (207) 647-3699.

## SOUTH PORTLAND (F-2)
pop. 23,324, elev. 20'

SAVE **PORTLAND HARBOR MUSEUM** is on the Southern Marine Community College campus on Fort Rd.; from I-95 exit 44 take I-295N to exit 6A (SR 77), cross the Casco Bay Bridge, then go n.e. on Broadway to the college, following signs. The waterfront museum, housed in a former cannon repair building at historic Fort Preble, next to the Spring Point Ledge Lighthouse, features changing exhibits about various aspects of area history.

Highlights include permanent exhibits about the clipper ship *Snow Squall* and the Spring Point Ledge Lighthouse. Guided tours of Fort Preble are available.

Allow 1 hour minimum. Daily 10-4:30, Memorial Day-Columbus Day; Fri.-Sun. 10-4:30, Apr. 1-day before Memorial Day and day after Columbus Day-Nov. 30. Admission $4; ages 6-16, $2. Phone (207) 799-6337.

## SOUTHWEST HARBOR (E-5) elev. 468'

The fishing and boatbuilding center of Southwest Harbor shares Mount Desert Island with Acadia National Park *(see place listing p. 39)*. The town is located on the southwest side of Somes Sound and borders a natural fjord. With about 70 lobster fishermen operating from its wharves, it is the archetype of the New England coastal village. Bass Harbor Head Light, 3 miles south on SR 102A, is a favorite spot for photographers. Local conditions are ideal for boating, swimming and other water sports. Schooner cruises, deep-sea fishing excursions and canoe rentals are available.

**Southwest Harbor-Tremont Chamber of Commerce:** 204 Main St. (SR 102), P.O. Box 1143, Southwest Harbor, ME 04679; phone (207) 244-9264 or (800) 423-9264.

**MOUNT DESERT OCEANARIUM** is 1 mi. e. to 172 Clark Point Rd. The oceanographic learning center, in a former ship's chandlery, has unusual live coastal sea animals and exhibits about scallops, whales, tides, seawater, fishing gear and the weather. A touch tank contains horseshoe crabs, sea snails, sea cucumbers and starfish.

Allow 1 hour minimum. Mon.-Sat. 9-5, late May to mid-Oct. Admission $6.95; ages 4-12, $4.75. Combination ticket with Bar Harbor Oceanarium in Bar Harbor (see attraction listing p. 45) $12; ages 4-12, $8.65. Phone (207) 244-7330.

**WENDELL GILLEY MUSEUM**, Main St. and Herrick Rd., houses more than 200 bird models by the master woodcarver. In addition to the native and foreign species carved by Gilley, the museum offers audiovisual presentations about the life cycles of various bird species. A resident woodcarver demonstrates his skill. Special exhibits are presented throughout the year.

Allow 30 minutes minimum. Tues.-Sun. 10-5, July-Aug.; Tues.-Sun. 10-4 in June and Sept.-Oct.; Fri.-Sun. 10-4 in May and Nov.-Dec. Closed holidays. Admission $5; ages 5-12, $2. AX, MC, VI. Phone (207) 244-7555.

## THOMASTON (E-4) pop. 2,714, elev. 20'

In 1605 Capt. George Weymouth planted a cross on Allen's Island, off the mouth of the St. Georges River, making the first known claim of possession by an Englishman on New England soil. In 1630 a post for trading with the American Indians was established, and in 1736 settlers founded what is now Thomaston.

Village life soon centered on the busy harbor where some of America's finest sailing ships were built. Lime, quarried locally, was an important export. Boatbuilding, fishing, lobstering and clamming are still significant local industries. Many fine Colonial houses stand throughout the town, which also is the site of the Maine State Prison.

**Rockland-Thomaston Area Chamber of Commerce:** Harbor Park, P.O. Box 508, Rockland, ME 04841; phone (207) 596-0376 or (800) 562-2529.

SAVE **MONTPELIER-THE GENERAL HENRY KNOX MUSEUM**, 30 High St. near jct. US 1 and SR 131, is a replica of the home of Gen. Henry Knox, first U.S. secretary of war. The house contains many of Knox's original furnishings and possessions. Tours conducted by guides in period costumes are available. Tues.-Sat. 10-4, late May-late Sept.; by appointment rest of year. Last tour begins 1 hour before closing. Admission $6; over 65, $5; ages 5-14, $3; family rate $15. MC, VI. Phone (207) 354-8062.

## TRENTON (D-4) elev. 62'

**ACADIA ZOO**, 446 Bar Harbor Rd. (SR 3), is an educational facility housing rescued native and exotic animals in natural settings. Allow 1 hour minimum. Daily 9:30-dusk, early May-late Dec. Moose

demonstrations are given at 11, 2 and 5. Wolf demonstrations are given at 4. Admission $7.50; over 65 and ages 3-12, $6. MC, VI. Phone (207) 667-3244 to verify prices.

## UNION (E-3) elev. 97'

**MATTHEWS MUSEUM OF MAINE HERITAGE**, off SR 17 at the Union Fairground, displays memorabilia showing the ingenuity and craftsmanship of Maine's early settlers. Local artisans demonstrate a variety of handcrafts using antique tools. A one-room schoolhouse that operated 1864-1954 houses original furnishings and supplies. Allow 30 minutes minimum. Tues.-Sat. noon-5, July 1-Labor Day; by appointment in June and day after Labor Day-Sept. 30. Admission $2; over 64, $1; ages 8-16, 50c. Phone (207) 785-3281.

## VAN BUREN (A-5) pop. 2,369, elev. 496'

More than an international bridge links Van Buren to St. Léonard, New Brunswick, across the St. John River. Settled by displaced Acadians and French Canadians in 1789, Van Buren was incorporated in 1881 and named for the eighth president. Throughout the upper St. John Valley, to which Van Buren is the gateway, signs and citizens are mostly bilingual.

Van Buren's economy is based on potatoes and lumber. For recreation the surrounding woodlands offer hunting and fishing; there is a beach at Long Lake, about 10 miles west.

**Greater Van Buren Chamber of Commerce:** 65 Main St., Van Buren, ME 04785; phone (207) 868-5059.

SAVE **ACADIAN VILLAGE**, 5 mi. n. on US 1, includes 16 reconstructed buildings. Among them are dwellings and a general store, country schoolhouse, blacksmith shop and chapel, all of which depict the early 19th-century culture of the St. John Valley. A museum of local art has permanent and changing art exhibits. Allow 1 hour minimum. Daily noon-5, mid-June through Sept. 15. Admission $5; ages 5-15, $3. Phone (207) 868-5042.

## VINALHAVEN ISLAND (E-4) elev. 100'

Vinalhaven, 9 miles long and 6 miles wide, is the largest of Penobscot Bay's Fox Islands and the third largest along the Maine coast. This working island village is a popular day-trip destination with visitors and locals alike. The Maine State Ferry Service transports passengers, automobiles and trucks on a 1-hour, 15-minute cruise from Rockland to Carver's Harbor.

Incorporated in 1789, Vinalhaven at one time had numerous granite quarries that attracted settlers and provided a booming industry. Many buildings in Washington, D.C., and New York were made of Vinalhaven granite. Two abandoned spring-fed quarries are now town parks and popular swimming holes. Another abandoned site, Armbrust Hill, also is a town park.

The island is home to one of the most productive lobster-fishing fleets in the world. Parks, rocky beaches, hiking trails and natural areas offer a variety of recreational opportunities. Lane's Island, south of Vinalhaven and accessible by bridge, is a nature preserve.

**Vinalhaven Chamber of Commerce:** P.O. Box 703, Vinalhaven, ME 04863; phone (207) 863-4826.

**VINALHAVEN HISTORICAL SOCIETY MUSEUM,** High St., exhibits fishing and seafaring artifacts as well as tools and photographs from granite quarrying days. Allow 30 minutes minimum. Daily 11-3, June 12-Labor Day; by appointment rest of year. Donations. Phone (207) 863-4410.

## WALDOBORO (E-4) pop. 1,291, elev. 13′

During the 19th century Waldoboro was known for producing five-masted schooners. Shipbuilding has since given way to small industry, farming and other commercial activities. Situated at the headwaters of the Medomak River near Muscongus Bay, the community was settled largely by German families.

Clamming, lobstering and sauerkraut production are the primary industries. Several art galleries feature works by local artists. Waldoboro also is home to the renovated 1936 Waldo Theatre and the locally renowned Moody's Diner, a part of Maine lore and legend.

**WALDOBORO HISTORICAL SOCIETY MUSEUM,** .5 mi. s. on SR 220, comprises three buildings: the 19th-century Boggs Schoolhouse, the Hauck Building and The Barn. The Hauck Building contains ship models, fire engines and tools. The Barn features quilts and textiles. Also included are a 19th-century farm kitchen, a furnished Victorian bedroom and a country store. The town's shelter for stray farm animals also is on the property.

---

# DID YOU KNOW

**Maine native Joan Benoit Samuelson won the first women's Olympic marathon in the 1984 Summer Games in Los Angeles.**

---

Allow 30 minutes minimum. Daily 1-4:30, June 17-Labor Day; Sat.-Sun. 1-4:30, day after Labor Day-Sept. 30. Donations. Phone (207) 832-4713.

## WARREN (E-3)

**GEORGES RIVER CANAL SYSTEM,** in Payson Park on SR 90, 1 mi. e. of jct. US 1, is said to be the second oldest canal system in the country. The 28-mile canal was built in 1795. A bridge over the canal leads to hiking trails. Picnicking is permitted. Daily dawn-dusk. Free.

## WATERVILLE (D-3) pop. 15,605, elev. 112′

Abenaki Indians once met for tribal councils and summer encampments at the Kennebec River's Ticonic Falls, near the site of Waterville. The area is now a center for commerce and education.

The city of Waterville was established in 1802. The arrival of the steamship *Ticonic* in 1832 introduced Waterville's era as a prosperous freight and passenger port. By mid-century, as river traffic declined due to railroad advances, energies turned to new possibilities. A dam was erected at Ticonic Falls in 1868; 5 years later the first of many large factories was established. The city is an important industrial center for paper, biotechnology, health care and professional services.

Waterville also benefits from the presence of three colleges and several cultural organizations. Especially popular is the Waterville Theatre, a professional touring group whose presentations take place in the Waterville Opera House.

West of the city lies the Belgrade Lakes region, whose largest lake, Great Pond, inspired the play and movie "On Golden Pond."

**Mid-Maine Chamber of Commerce:** One Post Office Sq., Waterville, ME 04901; phone (207) 873-3315.

**COLBY COLLEGE** occupies a 714-acre campus on Mayflower Hill. The school, which was founded in 1813, is recognized as a national leader in research- and project-based undergraduate learning. Among the collections in the Miller Library are letters, manuscripts and memorabilia of Maine poet Edwin Arlington Robinson as well as the Thomas Hardy Collection. The campus also includes a 128-acre arboretum and bird sanctuary.

Allow 1 hour minimum. Campus tours are given year-round Mon.-Fri. and some Sat. Free. Phone (207) 872-3168 or (207) 872-3220.

**Museum of Art,** in Bixler Art and Music Center, features 18th-century American portraits, 19th-century landscapes and 20th-century contemporary American artwork. Among the American artists represented are watercolorist John Marin and contemporary artist Alex Katz. The museum's permanent collection also includes works by Mary Cassatt, John Singleton Copley and Winslow Homer. Changing exhibits also are displayed. Allow 2 hours minimum. Mon.-Sat. 10-4:30, Sun. 2-4:30; closed major holidays. Free. Phone (207) 872-3228.

**REDINGTON MUSEUM,** 62 Silver St., Unit A, contains displays about the early history of Waterville. Collections of furniture, household artifacts, toys and weapons are displayed in an elegant 1814 Federal-style home. A replica of a 19th-century apothecary shop in the museum annex contains an impressive set of matching mahogany, brass and glass cases filled with pharmaceutical artifacts and medicines. Allow 1 hour, 30 minutes minimum. Tours Tues.-Sat. at 10, 11, 1 and 2, Memorial Day-Labor Day. Admission $5; under 12, $3. Phone (207) 872-9439.

## WELLS (F-2) elev. 203′

Within a year of its settlement in 1640 Wells boasted a mill on the Webhannet River and showed signs of becoming a flourishing trading port. Although it ultimately fulfilled its potential, American Indian hostility made the village's first century precarious. Wells was one of only four English communities to survive the second French and Indian War, which occurred 1688-97.

Stubborn courage may have been at the heart of Wells' survival. For 2 days in 1692, 15 soldiers ensconced in the Joseph Storer House repulsed the attacks of 500 Indians and French. The house, south on US 1, still stands as a private home and business.

Wells remained primarily a fishing and farming center until the "discovery" of Wells Beach, Laudholm Beach and Drakes Island Beach by vacationers in the early 20th century. Since then visitors have thronged to the 7-mile-long strand to sun, swim and just relax. The town also is a popular shopping center with a variety of stores, shops and factory outlets.

**Wells Chamber of Commerce:** P.O. Box 356, Wells, ME 04090; phone (207) 646-2451.

**RACHEL CARSON NATIONAL WILDLIFE REFUGE,** n. on SR 9 to 321 Port Rd., is administered by the U.S. Fish and Wildlife Service. The refuge, embracing more than 5,000 acres of salt marshes and upland habitat between Kittery and Cape Elizabeth, is a haven for both migratory and resident wildlife. A mile-long interpretive nature trail overlooks marshes and barrier beaches; the trail begins at the refuge headquarters, which has exhibits and brochures about wildlife. Allow 30 minutes minimum. Grounds daily dawn-dusk. Visitor center Mon.-Fri. 8-4. Donations. Phone (207) 646-9226.

[SAVE] **WELLS AUTO MUSEUM,** on US 1, displays more than 80 antique and classic cars dating from the early 1900s to the 1960s, including models by Maxwell, Packard, Rolls Royce, Stanley and Stutz as well as a collection of nickelodeons, picture machines and other Americana. Allow 1 hour minimum. Daily 10-5, Memorial Day weekend-Columbus Day. Admission $5; ages 6-12, $2. Phone (207) 646-9064.

**WELLS NATIONAL ESTUARINE RESEARCH RESERVE** is off I-95 (Maine Tpke.) exit 19; go 1 mi. e. to US 1, 1.5 mi. n. to Laudholm Farm Rd., then .5 mi e. An educational, a research and recreational facility in a 19th-century saltwater farm with Greek Revival architecture, Laudholm Farm is set on a 1,600-acre preserve comprising beach, coastal marsh and scenic upland. The diverse habitats of the reserve house a wide variety of wildlife. Programs and tours are offered daily June through August. A visitor center is on site.

Allow 2 hours minimum. Reserve open daily dawn-dusk. Visitor center open Mon.-Sat. 10-4, Sun. noon-4, May-Oct.; Mon.-Fri. 10-4, rest of year. Closed mid-Dec. to mid-Jan. Admission $2 daily July-Aug.; Sat.-Sun. in June and Sept. Under 13 free. Phone (207) 646-1555.

## WEST BATH (E-2)

**HAMILTON SANCTUARY,** 4 mi. s. on Foster Point Rd. following signs, has 1.5 miles of trails that lead through fir, pine and spruce forests and open meadows. On a peninsula in the New Meadows River, the sanctuary offers views of the rugged Maine coastline. Visitors are likely see ospreys, great blue herons, king fishers and an array of other birds. Daily dawn-dusk. Free. Phone (207) 781-2330.

## WESTBROOK (E-2) pop. 16,142, elev. 30′

[SAVE] **SMILING HILL FARM** is at 781 County Rd. (SR 22). This 400-acre working dairy farm contains a barnyard petting zoo and more than 300 animals. Children may ride a pony or enjoy a hayride. Sleigh rides and cross-country skiing also are offered. Picnicking is permitted. Food is available. Allow 1 hour minimum. Barnyard daily 10-5, May-Oct. Hours may vary; phone ahead. Admission $5.50; over 60, $5; ages 1-14, $4.50. MC, VI. Phone (207) 775-4818.

## WEST PARIS (E-2) elev. 480′

In West Paris, as in many Oxford County communities, it is not the pleasant farm and woodland scenery but what lies beneath it that is of consuming interest. Oxford County is one of Maine's richest sources of minerals, harboring such gemstones as tourmaline, beryl, rose and smoky quartz, amethyst and aquamarine.

Many mines and quarries have been yielding their treasures since the late 1800s. Snow Falls Gorge, 2 miles south on SR 26, includes walkways around the scenic falls as well as picnic facilities.

**Oxford Hills Chamber of Commerce:** P.O. Box 167, South Paris, ME 04281; phone (207) 743-2281.

**PERHAM'S OF WEST PARIS,** at jct. SRs 26 and 219, displays jewelry, gems and minerals from Maine and around the world. Five quarries are open to the public for free mineral hunting; maps and equipment are available at the store. The Maine Mineral Museum has 500 exhibits of native minerals. Highlights are a model gem tourmaline pocket and a model feldspar quarry. Allow 30 minutes minimum. Daily 9-5, Apr.-Dec.; Tues.-Sun. 9-5, rest of year. Closed Thanksgiving and Dec. 25. Free. Phone (207) 674-2341.

## WISCASSET (E-3) pop. 1,203, elev. 11′

Wiscasset at one time was Maine's chief port. The Embargo Act of 1807 seriously crippled its prosperous sea trade, and the town never regained its stature as a seaport. However, the legacy of that era is evidenced by Wiscasset's mansions, built by ship owners and merchants in the 18th and early 19th centuries.

**CASTLE TUCKER HOUSE MUSEUM,** Lee and High sts., is an 1807 Federal-style mansion. Complementing the exterior are interior displays that include Federal and Victorian furniture, paintings and household items. A freestanding, elliptical staircase also is of note. Allow 30 minutes minimum. Tours on the hour Wed.-Sun. 11-5, June 1-Oct. 15. Last tour begins 1 hour before closing. Admission $5, senior citizens $4.50, children $2.50. Phone (207) 882-7169.

**FORT EDGECOMB STATE HISTORIC SITE—** *see Edgecomb p. 53.*

**MUSICAL WONDER HOUSE,** 18 High St., contains antique Swiss, German, French and American music boxes and grand player pianos, which are played and shown during presentations. A minimum of two people is required for presentations. Allow 1 hour minimum. Daily 10-5, June 1 through mid-Oct. Full presentations are available by appointment only. Three-hour presentation $35. One-hour presentation $18. Half-hour presentation $10. AX, DS, MC, VI. Phone (207) 882-7163 or (800) 336-3725.

**NICKELS-SORTWELL HOUSE,** at Main and Federal sts. on US 1, was the residence of prominent Maine shipmaster Capt. William Nickels. The 1807 house was later owned by Alvin Sortwell, a mayor of Cambridge, Mass. It contains Sortwell family furnishings. An elliptical staircase is illuminated by a third-floor skylight. Guided tours are available. Allow 30 minutes minimum. Wed.-Sun. 11-5, June 1-Oct. 15. Tours are given on the hour. Last tour begins 1 hour before closing. Admission $5; over 64, $4.50; ages 6-12, $2.50. Phone (207) 882-6218.

**OLD LINCOLN COUNTY JAIL AND MUSEUM,** 133 Federal St., is a fortresslike granite building used as a jail 1811-1913. Original graffiti from the 19th century still exists on cell walls. A brick jailer's home attached to the jail houses antiques and decorative arts as well as changing exhibits. Allow 30 minutes minimum. Tues.-Sat. 10-4, Sun. noon-4, July-Aug. Admission $4; ages 7-17, $2. Phone (207) 882-6817.

## WOOLWICH (E-3)

**WOOLWICH HISTORICAL SOCIETY RURAL MUSEUM,** at the corner of US 1 and Nequasset Rd., is housed in an early 19th-century home and features quilts, rugs, fabrics, home furnishings, farm equipment and tools from the 19th and early 20th centuries. Allow 30 minutes minimum. Tues.-Sat. 10:30-2:30, July-Aug. Admission $3, children $1. Phone (207) 443-4833.

## YARMOUTH (E-2) pop. 3,560, elev. 87′

Although Yarmouth was first settled in 1636, permanent habitation was not possible until 1713 due to repeated attacks by American Indians. Early residents took advantage of the power provided by four waterfalls on the Royal River, and the economy prospered due to fishing, lumbering, shipbuilding and farming.

Of interest is a 41-foot-high rotating globe dubbed EARTHA, on view in the lobby of DeLorme, a mapping company at Two DeLorme Dr. Exhibits describe data-gathering technology used to create the globe.

Yarmouth is known as a scenic coastal community. Picnicking, strolls on paved pathways and views of picturesque waterfalls are possible at Royal River Park, on Elm Street off SR 115.

**Yarmouth Chamber of Commerce:** 162 Main St., Yarmouth, ME 04096; phone (207) 846-3984.

**YARMOUTH HISTORICAL SOCIETY AND MUSEUM OF HISTORY,** 215 Main St., displays photographs, clothing, furnishings and other items reflecting the history of the area. Research materials include journals and documents. Allow 30 minutes minimum. Tues.-Fri. 1-5, Sat. 10-5, Sept.-June; Mon.-Fri. 1-5, July-Aug. Closed major holidays. Donations. Phone (207) 846-6259.

## YORK (F-2)

York is one of Maine's oldest, most historic places. First settled in 1624, it was called Agamenticus for the abandoned American Indian village on the site. Six years later an aristocratic group led by agents of Sir Ferdinando Gorges arrived; their plantation prospered, and they adopted the name of their home city of Bristol in 1638. In 1642 Gorges granted the settlement a city charter under the name of Gorgeana—making it the first chartered English city in America.

After Gorges' dream of a city in the wilderness ended with his death in 1647, the inhabitants formed a body politic with six other outposts and attempted self-rule. Plagued by contradictory land grants, threatened by American Indians and finally realizing the importance of a central government, they became freemen of Massachusetts in 1652. Massachusetts then promptly demoted the city of Gorgeana to a town and renamed it York.

One of the heaviest blows of the French and Indian Wars was struck at York in January 1692. In what became known as the Candlemas Massacre, some 500 Abenaki fell upon the village, killing 80 townspeople, capturing another 50 and burning most of the buildings. Snowshoe Rock, where the American Indians left their snowshoes before the attack, is 5 miles north on Chases Pond Road; a marker commemorates the disaster.

# Everything you need to travel. Including this handy bookmark.

Book in advance and as a AAA/CAA member you'll always save at Choice hotels.* Plus, it's easy to earn nights or flights with our reward programs at any of our over 3,000 locations across the U.S. Just visit your local AAA/CAA office or call 800.228.1AAA to book your next stay.

CHOICE HOTELS
INTERNATIONAL®

**choicehotels.com**
**800.228.1AAA**

The Power of Being There. **GO**®
CHOICE HOTELS INTERNATIONAL

Call us at 800.228.1AAA or visit us on the Web at choicehotels.com for more information and reservations.

 **TourBookMark**

## Lodging Listing Symbols

### Member Values
(see pg. 14)

- **AAA** Official Appointment
- **SAVE** Offers minimum 10% discount
- **SAVE** SYC&S chain partners
- **ASK** May offer discount
- **S$** Offers senior discount
- **fyi** Informational listing only

### Member Services

- Airport transportation
- Pets allowed
- Restaurant on premises
- Restaurant off premises (walking distance)
- 24-hour room service
- Cocktail lounge
- Child care

### Accessibility Features
(see pg. 18)

- Accessibility features
- Roll-in showers
- Hearing impaired

### Leisure Activities

- Full Service Casino
- Pool
- Health Club on premises
- Health Club off premises
- Recreational activities

### In-Room Amenities

- Non-smoking rooms
- No air conditioning
- No TV
- No Cable TV
- VCR
- Movies
- Data port/modem line
- No telephones
- Refrigerator
- Microwave
- Coffee maker

Call property for detailed information about fees & restrictions relating to the lodging listing symbols.

CHOICE HOTELS
INTERNATIONAL ®1

# Your trip across America starts here.

CHOICE HOTELS
INTERNATIONAL ®

**choicehotels.com**
**800.228.1AAA**

Reminders of York's past include residential areas dating from the 18th century, Colonial churches, farmhouses with large woodpiles of white birch, stone walls along tree-lined streets and an old burying ground where quaint epitaphs are favorites for stone rubbings. Ancient traditions are strong, but there also are new industries and plentiful facilities for recreation. The York River provides a setting for boating and swimming, and Agamenticus Mountain has facilities for picnicking, hiking and horseback riding.

**The Greater York Region Chamber of Commerce:** 1 Stonewall Ln., York, ME 03909; phone (207) 363-4422.

[SAVE] **OLD YORK HISTORICAL SOCIETY,** 207 York St., maintains eight restored historic house museums representing 4 centuries of life in the coastal village of York. Guided tours begin at Jefferds' Tavern. Each site open Mon.-Sat. 10-5, mid-June to mid-Oct. Combination ticket for all buildings $7; ages 6-16, $3; family rate $15. MC, VI. Phone (207) 363-4974.

**Elizabeth Perkins House** is on the banks of the York River at the s. end of Sewall's Bridge on Southside Rd. Furnishings reflect the eclectic tastes of a family of collectors from the Colonial Revival period. Restored gardens and landscaped grounds also are available. Allow 30 minutes minimum.

**Emerson-Wilcox House,** center of town on York St., has served as a tavern, general store, tailor shop, post office and private residence. The 1742 building contains a series of period rooms furnished with American antiques dating 1750-1850. Among the rare items is a complete set of crewelwork bedhangings made about 1750 by York resident Mary Bulman. Allow 30 minutes minimum.

**Jefferds' Tavern** is just off US 1A, on Lindsay Rd. facing the Old Burying Ground. The tavern is an education and information center where all tours begin. Built by Capt. Samuel Jefferds in 1750 in Wells, the structure was moved to York in 1939.

**John Hancock Warehouse,** on the York River on Lindsay Rd., was owned by John Hancock until 1794. One of the oldest surviving commercial buildings in Maine, it has exhibits that illustrate the maritime history of the Yorks.

**Old Gaol,** center of town on York St., is one of the oldest English public buildings in the United States and was used as a jail until 1860. The 1719 structure is furnished according to the inventory of William Emerson, gaoler in 1790. Dungeons and cells for felons and debtors and galleries of local historical artifacts are included. Allow 30 minutes minimum.

**Old Schoolhouse,** center of town on Lindsay Rd., dates from 1745 and is one of the oldest surviving one-room schoolhouses in the state.

## YORK BEACH (F-2)

**YORK'S WILD KINGDOM ZOO AND AMUSE-MENT PARK,** I-95 exit York Ogunquit, then 2 mi. n. on US 1, is home to some 200 animals, including bears, lions and a white Bengal tiger. Elephant shows and a petting zoo also are offered. An amusement park features 20 rides.

Picnicking is permitted. Allow 3 hours minimum. Zoo daily 10-6, July 1-Labor Day; 10-5, Memorial Day-June 30. Amusements daily noon-9, July 1-Labor Day; Sat.-Sun. noon-6, Memorial Day-June 30. Phone for schedule, day after Labor Day through mid-Sept. Zoo admission $12.50; ages 4-10, $8.25; under 4, $1. Combination zoo and rides $15.25; ages 4-10, $11.75; under 4, $3.50. AX, DS, MC, VI. Phone (207) 363-4911 or (800) 456-4911.

## YORK HARBOR (F-2) pop. 3,321, elev. 56′

The fashionable resort member of the Yorks, York Harbor has enjoyed this role since the Civil War. Well-to-do residents of Boston, Philadelphia and other large cities built rambling three-story "cottages" and grand hotels in which to while away their summers, cooled by the New England sea breezes. York Harbor's summer colony once rivaled those of Bar Harbor *(see place listing p. 42)* and Newport, R.I.

The harbor itself, with the town wharves and marina, remains as busy now as in the 18th century, when it was the Yorks' marketplace and the scene of lively market fairs. It is a favored stopover among yachtsmen and an equally popular starting point for deep-sea fishing trips.

One block south of SR 103 and US 1 a footpath leads to Wiggley Bridge, a restored suspension bridge spanning the York River. From York Harbor, Long Sands Beach extends northeastward past York Beach toward Cape Neddick Light, popularly known as the Nubble Light. One of the most photographed lighthouses in Maine, the Nubble extends a rocky thumb into the sea; from a tiny island just off its tip the Cape Neddick Light, built in 1879, once guided seamen.

The Sayward-Wheeler House at 9 Barrell Ln. Ext., open weekends, contains antique furniture and items brought back as booty from the expedition against the French at Louisburg in 1745; phone (207) 384-2454.

# New Hampshire

### Robust Reds
The coppers and scarlets of fall give way to rosy winter cheeks

### Wonderful Whites
White church steeples and snowcapped peaks reach to the clouds

### Brilliant Blues
Clear valley pools reflect indigo mountain shadows under a chambray sky

### Gorgeous Greens
Contrast the deep shades of the North Woods with the verdant hues of the Merrimack Valley

### Gleaming Golds
Scenic drives pass fields of sunflowers or the shimmering State House dome

Eaton Center
© F. Sieb
Robertstock

Waterloo / © G. Ahrens / Robertstock

Nature. Quiet. Peace. Such is the essence of New Hampshire. But don't mistake a subtle presence for an unimportant one.

The state holds a distinguished position in politics. Its residents cast the decisive vote in ratifying the Constitution, and the first presidential primary is held here each election year.

The most populous region, the Merrimack Valley, is culturally and historically rich. In addition to housing the State House and other structures associated with the state's governmental core, the area claims art galleries, stately residences and an established Shaker settlement.

Hillsborough boasts the homestead of 14th president Franklin Pierce.

# breath of fresh air

Education and art are at the heart of the laid-back Dartmouth-Lake Sunapee area. Dartmouth College flavors the Hanover atmosphere. Sculptor Augustus Saint-Gaudens left his lasting mark on the tiny township of Cornish.

However, nothing more aptly says "New Hampshire" than the great outdoors.

Rolling hills dominate the terrain around Lake Winnipesaukee. Lush, sprawling forests extend all the way to the summits of the White Mountains. And blazing colors bring the hills to life in the fall.

Live free or die.

To understand New Hampshire's blunt motto, it's necessary to take a close look at the state's feisty and pathfinding past.

Twenty years after English sea captain Martin Pring sailed up the lower Piscataqua River to explore the region, Europeans established the first white settlements at Odiorne's Point and Dover in 1623. Others followed in nearly a century of allegiance to the English crown.

When the colonists would have no more, New Hampshire declared independence from England, and in 1776 became the first colony to adopt a provisional constitution and government.

Durham was a hotbed of this Revolutionary activity. Led by native son Maj. Gen. John Sullivan, patriots took gunpowder from the British and stored it in a town meeting-house; a tablet marks the site. Several historic houses along the Portsmouth Harbor Trail owe their significance to the strife. A then-renowned haven for dissenters, Exeter now is home to the American Independence Museum.

Out of this epic struggle for freedom, a simple motto was born.

## Safety for the Shakers

In post-independence New Hampshire, the spirited maxim had even broader implications. It meant immunity from religious persecution to the Shakers, who built villages in Canterbury Center and Enfield.

The influence of the state's majestic backdrop of mountains, caves, lakes and wide open spaces encouraged creative figures to freely express themselves. Poet John Greenleaf Whittier wrote "Sunset on the Bearcamp" about the river of the same name. An ascent of Mount Monadnock inspired Ralph Waldo Emerson's poem "Monadnoc." Many writings of Robert Frost drew upon his life on a Derry farm.

Author Thomas Bailey Aldrich penned "The Story of a Bad Boy," which includes references to his Portsmouth boyhood home. Composer Edward MacDowell thrived in the woodland retreat of Peterborough, which he later introduced to scores of other artists.

Nearly everything about New Hampshire's environment has the ability to spur such imaginative genius. From the White Mountains to Lake Winnipesaukee, the largely pristine Granite State epitomizes much of what is amazing—and liberating—about nature.

English sea captain Martin Pring becomes the first European to visit New Hampshire.
**1603**

New Hampshire becomes the first colony to adopt a provisional constitution and government, declaring independence from England.
**1776**

New Hampshire is the ninth and deciding state to ratify the U.S. Constitution.
**1788**

**1622**
Captain John Mason is given a land grant to the area and names it after the English county of Hampshire.

# New Hampshire Historical Timeline

Library of Congress

**1842**
Orator Daniel Webster settles a border dispute between New Hampshire and Québec with the Webster-Ashburton Treaty.

Mountain roads like Kancamagus Highway (SR 112) wind through White Mountain National Forest, skirting breathtaking vistas of the peaks. In autumn the vivid hues of changing leaves are unmatched in their glory and beauty.

Railways and tramways climb to the top of Cannon Mountain, Loon Mountain and Mount Washington, the Northeast's tallest peak at 6,288 feet. Well-trodden hiking paths through the entire mountainous region often lead to tumbling waterfalls.

## At the Bottom, Looking Up

The low-level vantage points of mountain gaps give a different perspective. Impressive characteristics of Franconia Notch, which splits the Kinsman and Franconia ranges are The Flume, a lengthy chasm flanking Mount Liberty, The Lost River, which frequently disappears as it snakes through boulder caves and potholes in Kinsman Notch, and Dixville Notch, which boasts such striking sights as the Cathedral Spires and Table Rock.

Walk amid granite boulders and mineral formations in Plymouth's Polar Caves, six caves formed by glacial activity more than 20,000 years ago.

Climb aboard a steamship or boat in Portsmouth and cruise through Portsmouth Harbor to the Isles of Shoals. Navigate around Loon Island, Georges Mills Bay and Mount Kearsarge as you explore Lake Sunapee. Or try to keep your mouth from opening in awe as you marvel at Lake Winnipesaukee's natural spectacles—coves and islands set against an outline of mountain peaks; cruises depart from Weirs Beach and Wolfeboro.

Wildlife viewing is extraordinary. Head to Gorham to catch a glimpse of a moose. Trails at Moultonborough's Loon Center weave through areas where the nesting birds live. Nature centers in Hebron, Portsmouth and Seabrook are home to other native animals, such as great blue herons, harbor seals, ospreys and turkeys. Whale-watch expeditions depart from the harbor at Rye.

Kick back, shake off your encumbrances and live life to its fullest in New Hampshire. It's certainly the better of the motto's two options!

New Hampshire native Franklin Pierce is elected president of the United States.
**1852**

The state adopts the first legal lottery in the 20th-century United States.
**1963**

Christa McAuliffe, a Concord social studies teacher chosen to be the first civilian in space, is killed when the space shuttle *Challenger* explodes just after lift-off.
**1986**

© Bettmann/Corbis

**1944**
The Breton Woods Conference leads to the establishment of the International Monetary Fund and the International Bank of Reconstruction and Development.

**1952**
New Hampshire holds the first presidential primary.

**1999**
New Hampshire becomes the first state to have a female governor, Senate president and House speaker all at the same time.

## Recreation

If New Hampshire needs a recreation slogan, here's an idea: "Have skis, will travel."

The state sport is unrivaled in popularity.

Like it fast? Schuss down the slopes at one of 21 resorts. The White Mountain Region is the hot spot. You'll find more than 150 **downhill skiing** and **snowboarding** trails among the three largest resorts: Attitash Bear Peak in Bartlett, Waterville Valley and Loon Mountain in Lincoln.

**Tubing** parks are among the additional facilities at Cranmore Mountain Resort in North Conway, Gunstock in Gilford, King Pine Ski Area in East Madison, Pats Peak in Henniker and Whaleback in Lebanon.

If crowds cramp your style, head up north to The Balsams Wilderness in Dixville Notch.

If you prefer skiing on more level ground, there are 24 **cross-country** facilities that fit the bill. Lengthy trails and scenic vistas characterize Jackson X-C in Jackson and Franconia Village in Franconia.

Winter adventures don't end here.

Head to the state's northernmost quarter, where **snowmobiling** is sure to get your motor running. A 6,000-mile interconnecting trail system weaves through some of the state's most breathtaking scenery.

In addition to welcoming cross-country skiers and snowmobilers, 780,000-acre White Mountain National Forest teems with opportunities for **snowshoeing** and **ice climbing.**

## Shaking off the Snow

When the snow melts away, you'll warm to New Hampshire's more temperate pursuits.

**Bicycling** fanatics are in for a special treat when they pedal through the Granite State: endless vistas of dark green mountainsides and clear blue skies. The trail system is extensive, particularly along the Connecticut River, around Lake Winnipesaukee and in the Merrimack Valley region, from Concord to Nashua.

Many ski areas are open in the off-season for mountain biking. Take a lift to the top, and chart your course back down to the bottom. Bear Brook, Moose Brook, Pawtuckaway and Pisgah state parks—in Allenstown, Gorham, Nottingham and Chesterfield, respectively—also have challenging routes.

More than 1,200 miles of **hiking** trails traverse White Mountain National Forest. Short walks are suitable for families with young children, while more seasoned trekkers can ascend above the tree line.

The easy 1-mile hike up Blue Job Mountain, near Strafford, culminates in great views of Boston and Mount Washington. Table Rock, a prominent rock spire near Dixville Notch, is an interesting spectacle.

The terrain is rocky along parts of the 2.2-mile trail up Mount Kearsarge, in Wilmot. If you've got half a day, take on White Dot Trail on Mount Monadnock, one of the most climbed mountains in the world. A section of the Appalachian Trail links Hanover to the Maine state line, north of Shelburne.

## On the Mountain Face

If you've got nerves of steel, **rock climbing** options here are exhilarating. Cathedral Ledge, in Echo Lake State Park near Bartlett, and Franconia Notch State Park, near Franconia and Lincoln, are noteworthy locales.

The Swift River beckons to **white-water rafting** enthusiasts. For tamer paddling, try **canoeing** on the Connecticut or Merrimack rivers or on Lake Umbagog, where you can view bald eagles and loons. **Kayaking** is good on the Androscoggin River, which can be slightly rough upstream from Berlin.

Water sports also prevail along 18 miles of Atlantic frontage at such beaches as Great and Little Boars Head, Hampton, Rye, Seabrook and Wallis Sands.

To enjoy what the water has to offer without having to get wet, wait for a bite from a bass, walleye, salmon or trout while **fishing** in the state's lakes and rivers.

Strong winds over the surface of Lake Winnipesaukee make for excellent **sailing.** Weirs Beach, with an atmosphere suggesting an inland version of a seaside resort, brims with activity. For **boating** and **swimming,** check out Newfound, Squam and Sunapee lakes.

## Recreational Activities

Throughout the TourBook, you may notice a Recreational Activities heading with bulleted listings of recreation-oriented establishments listed underneath. Similar operations also may be mentioned in Destination City recreation sections. Since normal AAA inspection criteria cannot be applied, these establishments are presented for information only. Age, height and weight restrictions may apply. Reservations are often recommended and sometimes required. Visitors should phone or write the attraction for additional information, and the address and phone number are provided for this purpose.

# *Fast Facts*

**POPULATION:** 1,235,786.

**AREA:** 9,024 square miles; ranks 44th.

**CAPITAL:** Concord.

**HIGHEST POINT:** 6,288 ft., Mount Washington.

**LOWEST POINT:** Sea level, Atlantic Ocean.

**TIME ZONE(S):** Eastern. DST.

**MINIMUM AGE FOR DRIVERS:** 16 with driver's training, 18 without.

**SEAT BELT/CHILD RESTRAINT LAWS:** Seat belts required for under 18; child restraints are required for under 4.

**HELMETS FOR MOTORCYCLISTS:** Required for under 18.

**RADAR DETECTORS:** Permitted.

**FIREARMS LAWS:** Vary by state and/or county. Contact the New Hampshire State Police, 10 Hazen Dr., Concord, NH 03305; phone (603) 271-3575.

**HOLIDAYS:** Jan. 1; Washington's Birthday, Feb. (3rd Mon.); Easter; Memorial Day, May (last Mon.); July 4; Labor Day, Sept. (1st Mon.); Columbus Day, Oct. (2nd Mon.); Veterans Day, Nov. 11; Thanksgiving, Nov. (4th Thurs.); Dec. 25.

**TAXES:** New Hampshire does not have a statewide sales tax. There is an 8 percent Meals & Rooms Tax that includes beverages.

**STATE INFORMATION CENTERS:** Welcome centers that provide details about state attractions, accommodations, historic sites, parks and events are maintained year-round at Canterbury, I-93N between exits 18 and 19; Hooksett, I-93N and I-93S between exits 10 and 11; Lebanon, I-89S between exits 17 and 18; North Conway, US 16 and US 302; Salem, I-93N before exit 1; Sanbornton, I-93S between exits 20 and 22; Seabrook, I-95N before exit 1; Springfield, I-89N between exits 12A and 13; Littleton, I-93S before exit 44; and Sutton, I-89S between exits 9 and 10. Information centers are maintained Memorial Day to mid-October at Antrim, Colebrook, Epsom, Rumney and Shelburne.

**FURTHER INFORMATION FOR VISITORS:**

Office of Travel and Tourism
P.O. Box 1856
Concord, NH 03302
(603) 271-2665
(800) 386-4664

**FISHING AND HUNTING REGULATIONS:**

Fish and Game Department
2 Hazen Dr.
Concord, NH 03301
(603) 271-3421

**NATIONAL FOREST INFORMATION:**

White Mountain National Forest
719 Main St.
P.O. Box 638
Laconia, NH 03247
(603) 528-8721
(877) 444-6777 (reservations)

## New Hampshire Temperature Averages Maximum/Minimum
### From the records of the National Weather Service

|         | JAN | FEB | MAR | APR | MAY | JUNE | JULY | AUG | SEPT | OCT | NOV | DEC |
|---------|-----|-----|-----|-----|-----|------|------|-----|------|-----|-----|-----|
| Concord | 32  | 34  | 42  | 56  | 69  | 78   | 83   | 81  | 72   | 62  | 48  | 35  |
|         | 11  | 12  | 22  | 32  | 42  | 51   | 56   | 54  | 46   | 36  | 27  | 15  |

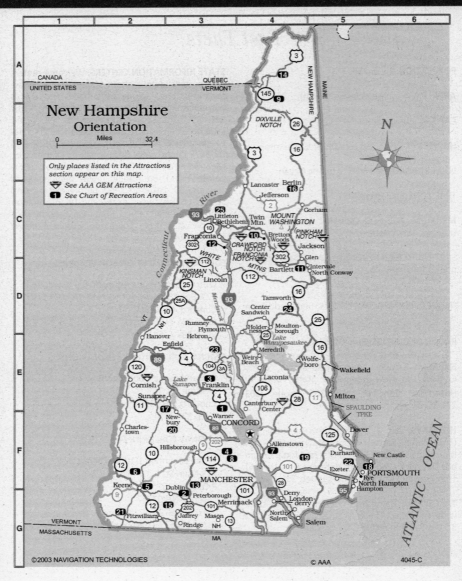

New Hampshire
Orientation

Only places listed in the Attractions section appear on this map.

See AAA GEM Attractions

See Chart of Recreation Areas

©2003 NAVIGATION TECHNOLOGIES

© AAA

4045-C

# Points of Interest Offering A
## *Great Experience for Members*®

### Bretton Woods (C-4)

**MOUNT WASHINGTON COG RAILWAY**—The old-fashioned steam train takes passengers on scenic trips to the top of Mount Washington, the highest peak in the northeast. See p. 92.

### Canterbury Center (E-4)

**CANTERBURY SHAKER VILLAGE**—The customs, inventions and values of the Shakers are demonstrated at this restored hilltop village. See p. 92.

### Cornish (E-2)

**SAINT-GAUDENS NATIONAL HISTORIC SITE**—The 18th-century house of renowned sculptor Augustus Saint-Gaudens is surrounded by terraced perennial gardens. See p. 94.

### Crawford Notch (C-4)

**CRAWFORD NOTCH**—This mountain pass captures the natural beauty of the Presidential Mountain Range with its many majestic waterfalls. See p. 94.

### Franconia Notch (D-4)

**CANNON MOUNTAIN AERIAL TRAMWAY**—A spectacular view of the Franconia Range awaits at Cannon's 4,040-foot summit. See p. 97.

**THE FLUME**—A scenic 2-mile boardwalk takes you through this 800-foot-long gorge, complete with glacial boulders and rushing waterfalls. See p. 97.

**FRANCONIA NOTCH**—Between the high peaks of the Kinsman and Franconia mountain ranges lies this haven for recreational opportunities. See p. 96.

### Kinsman Notch (D-3)

**LOST RIVER**—The river plays hide-and-seek between the boulders and glacial potholes of a beautifully carved gorge. See p. 101.

### Manchester (F-3)

**THE CURRIER MUSEUM OF ART**—Housed in a 1929 Beaux Arts building, the museum's collection ranges from American fine and decorative arts to European masterpieces. See p. 103.

### Pinkham Notch Scenic Area (C-4)

**PINKHAM NOTCH SCENIC AREA**—Framed by towering peaks, this area offers spectacular views of White Mountain National Forest. See p. 107.

# RECREATION AREAS

| | MAP LOCATION | CAMPING | PICNICKING | HIKING TRAILS | BOATING | BOAT RAMP | BOAT RENTAL | FISHING | SWIMMING | PETS ON LEASH | BICYCLE TRAILS | WINTER SPORTS | VISITOR CENTER | LODGE/CABINS | FOOD SERVICE |
|---|---|---|---|---|---|---|---|---|---|---|---|---|---|---|---|
| **NATIONAL FORESTS** *(See place listings)* | | | | | | | | | | | | | | | |
| White Mountain 770,000 acres. Northern New Hampshire. | | • | • | • | • | • | | • | • | • | • | • | • | | |
| **ARMY CORPS OF ENGINEERS** | | | | | | | | | | | | | | | |
| Blackwater Dam (E-3) 18 mi. n. of Concord off SR 127. | **1** | | | • | | | | • | | | | • | | | |
| Edward McDowell Lake (G-3) 1,198 acres 4 mi. w. of Peterborough off SR 101. | **2** | | • | | | • | | • | | | | • | | | |
| Franklin Falls Dam (E-3) 2,800 acres 15 mi. along Pemigewassett River, 2 mi. n. of Franklin off SR 127. | **3** | | | • | | | | • | | | | • | | | |
| Hopkinton-Everett Lake (F-3) 7,992 acres off I-89 exit 6, then 3 mi. w. on SR 127. Hunting; horse trails. | **4** | | • | • | • | • | | • | • | | | • | • | | |
| Otter Brook Lake (F-2) 458 acres 2 mi. e. of Keene off SR 101 on Branch Rd. | **5** | | • | • | | • | | • | • | | | • | | | |
| Surry Mountain Lake (F-2) 1,700 acres 6 mi. n. of Keene off SR 12A. Nature trails. | **6** | | • | • | • | • | | • | • | | | • | | | |
| **STATE** | | | | | | | | | | | | | | | |
| Bear Brook (F-4) 9,800 acres 2 mi. e. of Allenstown off SR 28. Museums. | **7** | • | • | • | | | • | • | • | • | | • | • | | • |
| Clough (F-3) 140 acres 5 mi. e. of Weare between SRs 114 and 13. | **8** | | • | | | | | • | • | • | | • | | | |
| Coleman (A-4) 1,605 acres 12 mi. e. of Colebrook off SR 26. | **9** | • | • | | • | • | | • | | • | | • | | | |
| Crawford Notch (C-4) 5,950 acres 12 mi. w. of Bartlett on US 302. *(See Crawford Notch p. 94)* | **10** | • | • | • | | | | • | | • | | | • | | • |
| Echo Lake (D-4) 396 acres 1.5 mi. w. of US 302 on Westside Rd. in North Conway. Scenic. *(See North Conway p. 106)* | **11** | | • | | | | | • | • | | | | | | |
| Franconia Notch (C-3) 6,440 acres 5 mi. n. of North Woodstock off US 3. | **12** | • | • | • | • | | | • | • | • | | • | • | | • |
| Greenfield (F-3) 401 acres 1 mi. w. of Greenfield off SR 136. Canoe rental. | **13** | • | • | • | • | • | | • | • | • | | • | | | |
| Lake Francis (A-4) 1,684 acres 7 mi. n. of Pittsburg off US 3. | **14** | • | • | | • | • | | • | | | | • | | | |
| Monadnock (G-3) 699 acres 4 mi. n.w. of Jaffrey off SR 124. | **15** | • | • | • | | | | | | | | • | • | | • |
| Moose Brook (C-4) 755 acres 2 mi. w. of Gorham off US 2. | **16** | • | • | | | | | • | • | • | | | | | |
| Mount Sunapee (E-3) 2,893 acres 3 mi. s. of Sunapee at jct. SRs 103 and 103B. *(See Sunapee p. 111)* | **17** | • | • | • | • | • | | • | • | • | | • | • | | • |
| Odiorne Point (F-5) 370 acres on SR 1A in Rye. | **18** | | • | | • | • | | • | | | • | • | • | | |
| Pawtuckaway (F-4) 5,500 acres 4 mi. n.e. of Raymond off SR 156. | **19** | • | • | • | • | • | | • | • | • | | • | | | • |
| Pillsbury (F-3) 3,702 acres 3.5 mi. n. of Washington on SR 31. | **20** | • | • | • | | | | • | | | | • | | | |
| Pisgah (G-2) 13,500 acres off SR 63 in Chesterfield. Hunting. | **21** | | • | • | | | | • | | | | • | | | |
| Rye Harbor (F-5) 63 acres 10 mi. s. of Portsmouth on SR 1A. Marina. | **22** | | • | | • | • | | • | | | | | | | |
| Wellington (E-3) 183 acres 4 mi. n. of Bristol off SR 3A. | **23** | | • | | • | • | | • | • | | | | | | • |
| White Lake (D-4) 603 acres 1 mi. n. of West Ossipee on SR 16. | **24** | • | • | | • | • | • | • | • | | | • | | | • |
| **OTHER** | | | | | | | | | | | | | | | |
| Moore Reservoir (C-3) 3,500 acres 8 mi. w. of Littleton off I-93 via SRs 18 and 135. *(See Littleton p. 102)* | **25** | | • | • | • | • | | • | • | • | | | • | | |

# Points of Interest

## ALLENSTOWN (F-4)

**MUSEUM OF FAMILY CAMPING,** 2 mi. e. off SR 28 in Bear Brook State Park, is dedicated to the history and enjoyment of family camping. Old camping gear, photographs, publications and trailers of the past are displayed. The museum also offers audiotape and videotape displays. Daily 10-4, Memorial Day weekend-Columbus Day. Donations. Phone (603) 485-3782, or (603) 239-4768 off-season.

## BARTLETT (D-4) elev. 2,630′

With Bear Mountain to the south, Mount Parker to the north and symmetrical Mount Carrigan rising at the western end of the valley, Bartlett is a year-round recreation center. The land along the Saco River east of its emergence from Crawford Notch was granted to William Stark and several others for their service in the French and Indian War; the village was incorporated in 1790.

From Bartlett a scenic road runs south through Bear Notch to the Kancamagus Highway (see White Mountains and White Mountain National Forest p. 112).

### RECREATIONAL ACTIVITIES
**Alpine Slide**

- **Attitash Bear Peak Alpine Slide** is on US 302. Write P.O. Box 308, Bartlett, NH 03812. Other activities are offered. Daily 10-6, mid-June through Labor Day; Sat.-Sun. 10-5, Memorial Day to mid-June and day after Labor Day-Columbus Day. Phone (603) 374-2368.

## BERLIN (C-4) pop. 10,331, elev. 1010′

**NORTHERN FOREST HERITAGE PARK & MUSEUM** is at 961 Main St. The museum houses interactive displays explaining the history of the local paper mill and the lifestyle of mill workers in the mid-19th century. The park offers heritage boat tours along the Androscoggin River with scenic views of the area. Moose tours give visitors a close-up look at these wild animals in their natural setting. Allow 1 hour minimum. Daily 10-7, June-Aug.; daily 10-6 in Sept.; Mon.-Fri. 10-5, rest of year. Closed major holidays. Museum free. Boat tour $10, children $5. Moose tour $20; under 13, $15. Phone (603) 752-7202.

**NORTHERN FOREST MOOSE TOUR,** departing from the Northern Forest Heritage Park at 961 Main St., provides educational guided tours with opportunities to view moose. An informative film also is included. Guided sunset tours daily, mid-June through Columbus Day. Hours vary; phone ahead. Fare $20; under 13, $15. Children under 5 must have a car seat. Reservations are recommended. MC, VI. Phone (800) 992-7480.

## BETHLEHEM (C-3)

**THE ROCKS** is off I-93 exit 49, then .5 mi. e. on US 302. The 1882 estate of Chicago businessman John Jacob Glessner, a founder of International Harvester, sits on the grounds. Scenic trails with wildlife viewing and hiking and skiing opportunities surround the 1,300-acres. Glessner's grandchildren donated the land to the Society for Protection of New Hampshire Forests in 1978. A Christmas tree farm with more than 50,000 trees is open to the public. Allow 2 hours minimum. Daily dawn-dusk. Free. Phone (603) 444-6228 or (800) 639-5373.

## BRETTON WOODS (C-4)

With the opening of the Mount Washington Hotel in July 1902, Bretton Woods became a well-known resort. Wealthy families spent pre-Depression summers at this lavish European-style spa. Some 50 trains arrived daily, and private railroad cars sat on a siding by the golf course, waiting to take passengers home.

A second surge of fame came in July 1944 when the World Monetary Fund Conference convened at the hotel, refurbished for the occasion by the federal government. This meeting set the gold standard at $35 an ounce, thereby stabilizing post-World War II currency and establishing the American dollar as the cornerstone of international financial exchange. The conference room is now a small museum. *See color ad p. 91.*

**Twin Mountain-Bretton Woods Chamber of Commerce:** P.O. Box 194, Twin Mountain, NH 03595.

**MOUNT WASHINGTON COG RAILWAY** is 6 mi. n.w. on SR 302, then 6 mi. n.e. on Base Rd. The old-fashioned steam-powered railway takes a scenic 3-hour round trip to the top of Mount Washington, the highest peak in the Northeast. A museum features artifacts, dioramas, historic displays and photographs.

Guided and self-guiding tours are available. Allow 3 hours minimum. Tours are given daily on the hour 9-4, mid-June through Aug. 2; 8-5, Aug. 3-Sept. 8; 9-3, Sept. 9-20 and early to mid-Oct. Schedule varies rest of year; phone ahead. Fare $49; over 65, $45; ages 6-12, $35. Advance ticket purchase is recommended; cancellations must be made 24 hours in advance. MC, VI. Phone (800) 922-8825. *See ad p. 91 & color ad starting on p. 370.*

**RECREATIONAL ACTIVITIES**

**Skiing**

• **Bretton Woods Mountain Resort** is on SR 302. Write P.O. Box 351, Bretton Woods, NH 03575. Daily 8:30-4, early Nov.-early May. Phone (800) 258-0330.

## CANTERBURY CENTER (E-4) elev. 375′

**CANTERBURY SHAKER VILLAGE,** off I-93 exit 18, following signs, was one of the nation's most important Shaker communities. Established in 1792, the village is now a museum and historic site. Members of this religious colony farmed and created fine tools, textiles, utensils and the graceful furniture for which they are known.

Visitors can tour the village where 25 of the original buildings have been restored. Narrated tours offer a glimpse into the simple Shaker lifestyle. Skilled artisans re-create the traditional Shaker crafts of broom making, dovetailing, oval box making and weaving. Nature trails wind along the herb gardens and millponds the Shakers designed to maximize water usage. The village plays host to several events throughout the year.

Food is available. Allow 3 hours minimum. Tours are given daily on the hour 10-5, May-Oct.; Sat.-Sun. 10-4 in Apr. and Nov.-Dec. Last tour begins 1 hour before closing. Admission $12; ages 6-15, $6; family rate $30. AX, MC, VI. Phone (603) 783-9511.

## CENTER SANDWICH (D-4)

Near the east end of Squam Lake and bordered on the north by the Sandwich Mountains, Center Sandwich is the principal village of the Sandwich region. Now a summer resort and craft center, the area was a favorite of poet John Greenleaf Whittier; his "Sunset on the Bearcamp" refers to the Bearcamp River, which lies between Center Sandwich and North Sandwich.

**SANDWICH HISTORICAL SOCIETY MUSEUMS,** 6 Maple St., house 18th-century to present-day Americana. An 1849 house is furnished with antiques; a wing contains changing exhibits, archives, a library, replicas of a country store and post office and a dugout canoe. Farm implements, tools and transportation vehicles are displayed in the Quimby Barn Museum. Allow 1 hour minimum. Wed.-Sat. 10-4, mid-June to early Oct. Donations. Phone (603) 284-6269.

## CHARLESTOWN (F-2) pop. 1,145, elev. 369′

The 12 families who lived in this northwestern outpost in 1744 found their position increasingly precarious as King George's War accelerated. In 1746 Abenaki Indian raids confined them to the fortified village, and that winter they abandoned the settlement. Capt. Phineas Stevens and 50 provincial soldiers returned in April. Their withstanding a 3-day siege by 700 French and Indians was celebrated in Boston.

Charlestown revived as settlers returned to the fertile Connecticut River Valley. During the Revolutionary War the town's wide main streets supposedly served as a training ground for the soldiers of Gen. John Stark, hero of the Battle of Bennington (*see Bennington, Vt., p. 127*). Main Street has buildings that date from the early 19th century.

**FORT AT NUMBER FOUR LIVING HISTORY MUSEUM** is on SR 11, .5 mi. e. of I-91 exit 7. This reconstruction of the 1744 fortified village of Charlestown follows detailed drawings made in 1746 and includes the Great Hall, stockade, watchtower, two barns and 12 other buildings. Furnishings and demonstrations depict 18th-century frontier life.

Events include Colonial musters, 18th-century festivals and musical programs. Picnicking is permitted. Allow 1 hour minimum. Daily 10-4:30, Apr.-Oct. Admission $8; over 55, $6; ages 6-12, $5; family rate $25. MC, VI. Phone (603) 826-5700 or (888) 367-8284.

## CONCORD (F-4) pop. 40,687, elev. 264′

The political and financial center of the state—and capital since 1808—Concord also is a major industrial, transportation and distribution point. At the root of its prosperity is easy accessibility. Historically, settlement and commerce followed the Merrimack River and later, a canal to Boston. Now a convergence of highways forms the city's busy lifelines.

A trading post operating as early as 1660, the locale gained notoriety in 1697 as the place where

Hannah Dustin, abducted by Penacook Indians in a raid on Haverhill, Mass., scalped her sleeping captors and escaped.

Settlement came somewhat more slowly. Not until 1725 did the group of citizens from Haverhill, who had petitioned for permission to make a new settlement at Penny Cook, take possession of their grant on the west bank of the crooked place *(penacook)* on the river. In 1765 the area was renamed Concord.

Because generally peaceful relations with the Penacook people had allowed Concord to grow, by the Revolutionary War it was a sturdy community able to send companies to fight at Lexington and Concord, Mass., Bunker Hill and other battle sites. A tablet at Walker and Bouton streets marks the site where New Hampshire ratified the Constitution on June 21, 1788.

Industry began to develop during the early 1800s. Wheelwright Lewis Downing and coach builder J. Stephens Abbot created a product that was instrumental in opening the frontier—the bouncing, high-wheeled Concord coach used by Wells Fargo and other stage lines throughout the West.

A few reminders of Concord's past stand along some of the town's wide, shaded streets. The Rev. Timothy Walker House, 276 N. Main St., dates from 1734; it is closed to the public. The structure at 205 N. Main St. once was the Eagle Hotel, a popular tavern 1814-40; it is occupied by the League of New Hampshire Craftsmen.

A community-wide effort resulted in the restoration of the Capitol Theatre, built in the neo-Egyptian style in 1927 to house vaudeville shows. The Capitol Center for the Arts, with the newly renamed Chubb Theatre as its centerpiece, presents stage plays, concerts by the Granite State Symphony Orchestra, entertainers and dance troupes. The 1,300-seat theater is at 44 S. Main St.; phone (603) 225-1111.

The city balances its governmental and business orientation with ample opportunities for recreation. Among several city parks offering both summer and winter sports are 20-acre White Park on Centre Street and 16-acre Merrill Park on Eastman Street.

**Greater Concord Chamber of Commerce:** 40 Commercial St., Concord, NH 03301; phone (603) 224-2508.

**Self-guiding tours:** Concord on Foot, a tour of downtown, includes historical and architecturally interesting buildings. The tour proceeds along the Coach and Eagle Trail beginning at Eagle Square Marketplace. Brochures are available at the chamber of commerce and at the Museum of New Hampshire History *(see attraction listing)* for $2.

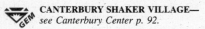 **CANTERBURY SHAKER VILLAGE—** *see Canterbury Center p. 92.*

**THE CHRISTA McAULIFFE PLANETARIUM,** I-393 exit 1, following signs, is a memorial dedicated to the teacher chosen to be the first civilian in space, who died in the 1986 space shuttle *Challenger* explosion. The planetarium offers a variety of shows, an interactive exhibit area and educational programs.

Allow 2 hours minimum. Mon.-Wed. 10-2, Thurs.-Sat. 10-5, Sun. noon-5. Show times vary; phone for schedule. Closed major holidays. Admission $8; over 61, college students with ID and ages 3-17, $5. Reservations are suggested; ticket sales are by telephone Mon.-Fri. 9-5 or at the sales desk during shows. MC, VI. Phone (603) 271-7827.

**CONSERVATION CENTER** is off I-93 exit 16, then s.e. on SR 132, following signs to 54 Portsmouth St. The center is a demonstration of passive solar and wood heating methods, including an envelope room, fiberglass water tubes and a wood-chip gasifier furnace. A 2-mile interpretive hiking trail explores native flora. A cross-country skiing trail is available. Self-guiding tours include a map and audiotape. Center open Mon.-Fri. 9-5; closed holidays. Trail open daily dawn-dusk. Free. Phone (603) 224-9945.

[SAVE] **MUSEUM OF NEW HAMPSHIRE HISTORY,** 6 Eagle Sq. off N. Main St. across from the State House, features an overview of the state's history. Exhibits highlight American Indian Chief Passaconaway, Revolutionary War Gen. John Stark, statesman Daniel Webster, poet Robert Frost and Cmdr. Alan B. Shepard Jr., the first American in space. Other displays include an early American Indian canoe, the original model of the Mount Washington Cog Railway and an original Concord coach.

Mon.-Sat. 9:30-5 (also Thurs. 5-8:30), Sun. noon-5, Feb.-May, July-Oct. and in Dec.; Tues.-Sat. 9:30-5 (also Thurs. 5-8:30), Sun. noon-5, rest of year. Admission $5.50; over 54, $4.50; ages 6-18, $3.50; free to all Thurs. 5-8:30; family rate $17. AX, DS, MC, VI. Phone (603) 228-6688.

**PIERCE MANSE,** 14 Horse Shoe Pond Rd., was the 1842-48 home of President Franklin Pierce. Moved from its original location on Montgomery Street, the restored house is furnished in mid-19th-century style with Pierce family furnishings and memorabilia as well as other period items. Allow 1 hour minimum. Mon.-Fri. 11-3, mid-June through Labor Day; otherwise by appointment. Closed holidays. Admission $5; over 55, $4; under 12, $1. Phone (603) 225-2068 or (603) 224-5954.

**STATE HOUSE,** on Main St., is said to be the country's oldest statehouse; the legislature continues to meet in the original chambers. Constructed of Concord granite and Vermont marble, the 1819 neoclassic structure is the focal point of the State House Plaza.

Within the statehouse are more than 180 portraits of the state's well-known residents as well as the Hall of Flags. Mon.-Fri. 8-4:30; closed holidays. Free. Phone (603) 271-2154.

## RECREATIONAL ACTIVITIES

**Canoeing**

- **Hannah's Paddles**, 15 Hannah Dustin Dr., Concord, NH 03301. Tues.-Sun. 8-2, May-Sept. Phone (603) 753-6695.

## CORNISH (E-2)

In the first decade of the 20th century this township on the Connecticut River gained fame as a major New England art colony. The central force behind the reputation was sculptor Augustus Saint-Gaudens, but Maxfield Parrish and other notables in arts and letters also found a haven in the village.

About 2 miles south of Saint-Gaudens National Historic Site *(see attraction listing)* on SR 12A is one of the longest covered bridges in the United States. Built in 1866 and 460 feet long, the bridge spans the Connecticut River and links New Hampshire to Windsor, Vt.

SAVE **CORNISH COLONY GALLERY & MUSEUM** is 1.5 mi. n. of Saint-Gaudens National Historic Site on SR 12A. The site includes Mastlands, the home of Augustus Saint-Gaudens' sister. Several works by Maxfield Parrish, as well as other artists' paintings and sculptures are displayed. Gardens are available for strolling. Food is available. Allow 2 hours minimum. Tues.-Sat. 10-5, Sun. noon-5; Memorial Day-Oct. 24. Admission $6, over 64 and students with ID $4. DS, MC, VI. Phone (603) 675-6000.

 **SAINT-GAUDENS NATIONAL HISTORIC SITE** is off SR 12A. The 1885-1907 home and studio of sculptor Augustus Saint-Gaudens originally was a country tavern built in the early 1800s. Complemented by formal gardens, the house retains Saint-Gaudens' furnishings.

Other buildings include the Little Studio, which contains bas-reliefs, portraits and monuments; the New Gallery, with casts of some of the sculptor's largest works, cameos and coin models; the Picture Gallery, where contemporary art exhibitions are displayed; and the stable, which features a collection of horse-drawn vehicles. Hiking trails wind through the 150-acre site. Concerts are held on Sundays from early July to mid-August.

Allow 2 hours minimum. Grounds open daily dawn-dusk. Buildings open daily 9-4:30, Memorial Day-Oct. 31. Admission $5, under 17 free. Phone (603) 675-2175.

 **CRAWFORD NOTCH** (C-4)

Created when the Pleistocene ice sheet pushed through a narrow preglacial pass, majestic Crawford Notch stretches from Bartlett on the south to Saco Lake on the north. The Saco River and US 302 wind along its floor between steep, wooded Webster and Willey mountains. Behind Mount Webster rises Mount Jackson, the southernmost peak of the Presidential Range.

The scars of many landslides mark the mountainsides. In 1826 a landslide thundered down Willey Mountain, killing the fleeing family whose name the peak bears, but sparing the family's home. The event is recounted in "The Ambitious Guest," one of Nathaniel Hawthorne's "Twice-Told Tales." Near the site of the Willey House is the headquarters for Crawford Notch State Park *(see Recreation Chart)*, which embraces much of the notch; phone (603) 374-2272.

The Willey Slide also disrupted the Tenth New Hampshire Turnpike, one of a series of roads that laced the notch following Timothy Nash's discovery of the gap during a 1771 hunting expedition. Spurred by the governor's promise of a land grant if Nash could bring a horse through the notch, the hunter and a companion hauled the animal up and down the rocks by ropes.

As improvements made the route passable for freight traffic, the turnpike became instrumental in the opening of New Hampshire's North Country. Promptly repaired after the 1826 landslide, the road served as a channel for commerce until the railroad crossed the notch in 1875.

**ARETHUSA FALLS**, 1.2 mi. n. of US 302, can be reached by a steep, marked trail. With a drop of 200 feet, it is one of the highest waterfalls in New Hampshire.

**SILVER AND FLUME CASCADES** are near US 302 at the n. end of the notch. The Silver Cascade shoots across smoothly sloping ledges and bounds over precipices in its 1,000-foot course down Mount Webster.

## DERRY (G-4) pop. 22,661, elev. 278′

Water power from nearby Beaver Brook and linen-making skills brought by 18th-century Scot-Irish immigrants combined to make Derry a prosperous linen manufacturing center. Its quality cloth was widely imitated; during the Revolution one local weaver earned $40 and a diamond ring by providing linen for George Washington and his officers.

The art of weaving sustained Derry well into the 20th century. When the textile industry moved to the Southern states, manufacturing shifted to shoes and palm leaf hats. The city's present economy is based mainly on services and such manufactured products as printed circuit boards and giftwares. Derry was the boyhood home of Cmdr. Alan B. Shepard Jr., the first American in space.

Four miles east on Island Pond Road from the junction of SR 28 and the SR 28 bypass is the Taylor Up-and-Down Sawmill, a mechanized version of the old two-man vertical pit saw. Last operated in 1865, the water-powered mill is demonstrated periodically during the summer; it can be viewed from the outside at other times.

**Greater Derry Chamber of Commerce:** 39 E. Broadway, Derry, NH 03038; phone (603) 432-8205.

**ROBERT FROST FARM,** on SR 28, 1.5 mi. s of jct. SR 102, is where renowned poet Robert Frost lived 1900-11. The farm was the source of inspiration for many of his published works. Restored to its turn-of-the-20th-century condition, the house contains original family pieces and period furniture. Displays in the barn pertain to Frost and his writings. Videotapes feature readings of his works and describe the restoration of the farm. A .5-mile poetry nature trail winds through the farm.

Allow 1 hour, 30 minutes minimum. Mon.-Sat. 10-5, Sun. noon-5, mid-June through day before Labor Day; Sat.-Sun. noon-6, mid-May to mid-June and Labor Day-Columbus Day. Admission $3, under 18 free. Phone (603) 432-3091, or (603) 271-3556 during the off-season.

## DIXVILLE NOTCH (B-4) elev. 1,600′

The northernmost and most dramatic of the White Mountain notches, rocky Dixville Notch is traversed by SR 26 between Colebrook and Errol. Among its scenic highlights are Lake Gloriette, the Cathedral Spires, Cascades and Table Rock. Much of the area is within Dixville Notch State Park.

## RECREATIONAL ACTIVITIES
### Skiing

- **The Balsams** is on US 26E. Write R.R. 1, P.O. Box 1000, Dixville Notch, NH 03576. Daily 8-4, mid-Dec. to late Mar. Phone (603) 255-3400 or (800) 255-0600.

## DOVER (F-5) pop. 26,884, elev. 77′

Considered the oldest permanent settlement in the state, Dover was founded in 1623 by fishermen and traders who plied the tidewaters of the Great Bay area and landed at Pomeroy Cove, now called Dover Point. By the late 1600s population growth necessitated moving the settlement from Dover Point, on SR 4 at the Piscataqua River, to its present location.

The harnessing of the Cocheco Falls' water power caused the shift from a fishing and farming economy to one based on industry. Sawmills and gristmills gave way to cotton mills when the embargoes imposed during the War of 1812 curtailed mercantile interests.

Renovations in the downtown area and along the riverfront feature a variety of architectural styles, especially Colonial and Victorian.

**Greater Dover Chamber of Commerce:** 299 Central Ave., Dover, NH 03820; phone (603) 742-2218.

**WOODMAN INSTITUTE,** 182-190 Central Ave., consists of three display buildings. The oldest is the hand-hewn 1675 Dame Garrison House, with Early American utensils, tools, clothing and furniture.

The 1818 Woodman House has exhibits about natural history and science, Civil War rooms as well as a collection of Penacook artifacts.

The 1813 Hale House was the home of abolitionist Sen. John P. Hale. It features the largest display of the institute's historical collection.

Wed.-Sun. 12:30-4:30, Apr.-Dec.; closed holidays. Admission $3; over 65, $2; ages 14-18, $1; under 14 free with adult. Phone (603) 742-1038.

## DUBLIN (F-3) elev. 1,845′

The name Dublin is a reminder of the group of Scot-Irish immigrants who attempted to settle this densely forested region in 1753. Permanent settlement did not occur for another decade, however, and Dublin was not incorporated until 1771. Its slow start and distance from major rivers discouraged industry and kept the community essentially rural.

In the 1800s this isolation began to be viewed as an advantage, and the town at the base of Mount Monadnock became a popular summer resort area.

Mount Monadnock is well known among both geology students and vacationers. Its name has become the term for the type of occurrence it exemplifies: a mountain or hill of resistant rock rising above a plain created by glacial or other erosive action. Monadnock State Park (see Recreation Chart and the AAA Northeastern CampBook) embraces much of the mountain.

**THE FRIENDLY FARM,** 2 mi. w. on SR 101, presents farm livestock and their young in a natural setting. Visitors can feed and touch most of the animals. Picnicking is permitted. Allow 1 hour minimum. Daily 10-5, mid-May through Labor Day (weather permitting); Sat.-Sun. 10-5, day after Labor Day to mid-Oct. Admission $5; under 13, $4.25. DS, MC, VI. Phone (603) 563-8444.

## DURHAM (F-5) pop. 9,024, elev. 81′

Settled in 1635 and separated from Dover in 1732, historic Durham was the home of Maj. Gen. John Sullivan, a Revolutionary War hero and three-time governor of New Hampshire.

A tablet marks the site of the old meetinghouse where, in 1774, Sullivan and his band of Durham patriots supposedly stored the gunpowder they had taken from the British at Fort William and Mary in New Castle (see place listing p. 105). Although the British attempted to retrieve the gunpowder, the shallow river halted their frigate at Portsmouth.

The ensuing century of rural and maritime activity ended in 1893. A bequest to the state removed the College of Agriculture and Mechanical Arts (which later became the University of New Hampshire) from Hanover, where it had been founded in association with Dartmouth College in 1866, to Durham. University and community quickly blended, and Durham assumed its role as a college town. The university's Paul Creative Arts Center is a focus for cultural activities.

## ENFIELD (E-3) pop. 1,698, elev. 760′

In 1782 two Shaker brothers from Mount Lebanon, N.Y., came to a village in the rolling woodlands near the eastern shore of Lake Mascoma.

With others they formed the society that led to the establishment of Enfield, one of 19 Shaker communities to flourish in the United States. In 1793 they moved to the west side of the lake, where a permanent settlement was built.

The Enfield Shakers numbered 330 in the 1850s, but entries into the celibate order declined steadily after the Civil War. The last 10 members moved to the Canterbury society *(see Canterbury Center p. 92)* in 1923.

**(SAVE) ENFIELD SHAKER MUSEUM,** off I-89 exit 17, e. on US 4, then s. on SR 4A following signs, is a restored 19th-century village dedicated to preserving the legacy of the Enfield Shakers. A self-guiding walking tour includes the herb and vegetable garden, cemetery, barn, church, mill, 1854 cow barn, stone dwelling and the laundry and dairy complex. A museum displays Shaker artifacts, and skilled artisans demonstrate crafts; workshops are offered.

Food is available. Allow 1 hour minimum. Mon.-Sat. 10-5, Sun. noon-5, June-Oct.; Sat. 10-4, Sun. noon-4, rest of year. Admission $7; over 60, $6; students with ID and ages 10-18, $3. MC, VI. Phone (603) 632-4346.

**LA SALETTE SHRINE AND CENTER** is 1.5 mi. w. on SR 4A. The shrine, a replica of the Marian Shrine of the Blessed Virgin Mary at La Salette, France, offers a Rosary Pond, a Peace Walk and outdoor Stations of the Cross. Grounds open daily dawn-dusk. Free. Phone (603) 632-7087.

## EXETER (F-5) pop. 9,759, elev. 58'

Behind the peaceful charm of Exeter at the falls of the Squamscott River lies a history of outspoken dissent. The settlement was begun in 1638 by the Rev. John Wheelwright, whose radical views and religious nonconformity led to his expulsion from Boston. Wheelwright's individualism seemed to set the tone for the community, for revolutionary attitudes and politics were characteristic from the outset.

Exeter citizenry defied Royal commands, flouted talk of liberty and burned in effigy British lords Bute and North. When the war began, it was natural that the capital was moved from Tory-controlled Portsmouth to this Patriot stronghold.

Exeter is a mixture of industry and academia; Phillips Exeter Academy, a distinguished preparatory school, was chartered in 1781 and has conducted classes since 1783. Another link to the town's past is its architectural heritage, which is preserved with pride.

**Exeter Area Chamber of Commerce:** 120 Water St., Exeter, NH 03833; phone (603) 772-2411.

**(SAVE) AMERICAN INDEPENDENCE MUSEUM,** 1 Governors Ln., is in the restored Ladd-Gilman House, built in the early 1700s. Formerly known as Cincinnati Hall, the house served as the state treasury during the American Revolution. John Taylor Gilman, an early governor of New Hampshire, lived there during his 14 gubernatorial terms. The museum complex also features the 1775 Folsom Tavern.

Guided tours are available. Allow 1 hour minimum. Wed.-Sat. 10-4, Sun. 11-4, May-Oct. Last tour begins 1 hour before closing. Admission $5; ages 6-18, $3. MC, VI. Phone (603) 772-2622.

## FITZWILLIAM (G-2) elev. 1,057'

Fitzwilliam is a classic New England community with a village green framed by a meetinghouse, historic houses, several antiques shops and a 1796 inn. Settled in the early 1760s, the town was incorporated in 1773. During its early years Fitzwilliam's manufacturers made the wheels on which much of the yarn for the textile industry was spun. Small woodworking operations now stabilize the economy.

**RHODODENDRON STATE PARK,** 2,500 acres 2.5 mi. w. off SR 124, is noted for its 16 acres of native rhododendron maximum, considered to be one of the largest stands of the hardy shrub north of the Alleghenies. The bushes, some of which exceed 20 feet in height, usually bloom in mid-July. A .6 mile path encircles the grove. The park offers views of Mount Monadnock and other mountains in the region. Picnic facilities are available. Pets are not permitted. Daily dawn-dusk. Admission $3, under 12 free. Phone (603) 239-8153.

## FRANCONIA (C-3) elev. 990'

**THE FROST PLACE,** I-93 exit 38 to SR 116, following signs, is the house that poet Robert Frost purchased after his 1915 return from England. Two rooms contain memorabilia, including signed first editions of each of his books. A narrated videotape, a self-guiding tour of the 1859 farmhouse and a .5-mile nature trail marked with many of the poet's works create a detailed impression of Frost. Each summer a resident poet writes verse and gives readings in the old barn.

Allow 1 hour minimum. Wed.-Mon. 1-5, July 1-Columbus Day; Sat.-Sun. 1-5, Memorial Day-June 30. Admission $3; over 65, $2; ages 6-12, $1.25. Phone (603) 823-5510.

**NEW ENGLAND SKI MUSEUM,** beside the Cannon Mountain Aerial Tramway at Parkway exit 2 *(see Franconia Notch),* details the history of nordic and alpine skiing through artworks, a videotape presentation, photographs and exhibits of clothing and equipment. Daily noon-5, late May to mid-Oct. and Dec.-Mar. Free. Phone (800) 639-4181.

## 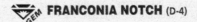 FRANCONIA NOTCH (D-4)

Franconia Notch is perhaps the most celebrated mountain gap in the East. A gap between the towering Kinsman and Franconia ranges, it has more scenic spots than any other White Mountain notch. It is crossed by US 3 from Echo Lake, southwest of Twin Mountain, to Lincoln.

The grandeur of the notch most likely was first seen by white settlers in the late 18th century. Its fame spread quickly, and by the mid-1800s it was a favorite tourist destination, with huge hotels to accommodate a plethora of visitors. Although the hotels no longer exist, throngs of visitors continue to enjoy the area's scenic and recreational aspects, many of which are within Franconia Notch State Park *(see Recreation Chart and Lincoln in the AAA Northeastern CampBook)*; phone (603) 823-5563.

**Franconia Notch Chamber of Commerce:** P.O. Box 780, Franconia, NH 03580; phone (603) 823-5661.

**THE BASIN,** reached by trail from US 3 n. of The Flume *(see attraction listing)*, is a deep glacial pothole at the base of a waterfall. Measuring 30 feet in diameter and 15 feet deep, its sides have been polished smooth by sand, stones and water. Below the basin the Pemigewasset River tumbles through the Baby Flume, a smaller version of the well-known gorge. Phone (603) 745-8391.

**CANNON MOUNTAIN AERIAL TRAMWAY** extends from Valley Station to the top of Cannon Mountain. The 80-passenger cars make the vertical 2,022-foot ascent in 7.5 minutes. From the Summit Observation Platform there is a spectacular view of mountains and valleys. Foot trails lead to other scenic points.

RV campsites are available. Food is available. Allow 1 hour minimum. Daily 9-5, mid-May to late Oct. Round trip $10; ages 6-12, $6. One-way trip $8. AX, DS, MC, VI. Phone (603) 823-5563. *See color ad starting on p. 370.*

**ECHO LAKE,** at the n. end of the notch, is bounded by mountains on three sides. Named for the acoustical phenomenon resulting from its setting, the lake is the largest body of water in the notch and offers boating, fishing and swimming. Beach admission $3. Phone (603) 823-5563.

**THE FLUME,** at the s. end of the notch, is a chasm extending nearly 800 feet along the flank of Mount Liberty. A mountain stream tumbles in a series of waterfalls and pools between its 60- to 90-foot-high granite walls. An optional shuttle bus takes visitors the first half-mile; it is then a 1.5-mile walk through the flume back to the visitor center. A well-constructed boardwalk leads through the gorge; there are, however, some steep grades. Within the flume are two covered bridges, waterfalls and cascades.

Allow 1 hour minimum. Daily 9-5:30, July-Aug.; 9-5, May-June and Sept. 1-late Oct. Admission $8; ages 6-12, $5. To confirm hours and admission phone (603) 745-8391. *See color ad starting on p. 370.*

**FRANKLIN (E-3) pop. 8,405, elev. 354′**

Upon separating from the town of Salisbury in 1828, citizens first thought to name their community after New Hampshire native Daniel Webster.

But the state already had a town called Webster, so Benjamin Franklin was honored instead.

Franklin flourished as a milling and industrial community, capitalizing on the water power made available by its location at the confluence of the Pemigewasset and Winnepesaukee rivers. At Central and Dearborn streets is a boulder with a depression created by a glacier and deepened through years of use by Penacook Indians and settlers for grinding corn. There also is a boulder imprinted with a carving of a shad, a fish that was plentiful in the Winnipesaukee River until the river's waters were dammed.

The 1820 Congregational Church, Franklin's first church, is another reminder of the past. A bust of Daniel Webster in front of the church is the work of Daniel Chester French, sculptor of the seated Abraham Lincoln in the Lincoln Memorial in Washington, D.C.

**Franklin Chamber of Commerce:** 337 Central St., Franklin, NH 03235; phone (603) 934-6909.

**DANIEL WEBSTER BIRTHPLACE** is off SR 127, 3.5 mi. s. via US 3. Webster was born in the two-room house in 1782. Now restored, the house contains period antiques and relics. Allow 30 minutes minimum. Sat.-Sun. 10:30-5:30, Memorial Day-Labor Day. Admission $3, over 65 and under 18 free. Phone (603) 934-5057.

**GLEN (D-5) elev. 544′**

An access point to both Franconia Notch *(see place listing p. 96)* and Pinkham Notch *(see place listing p. 107)*, Glen is an important link in the chain of communities in the Mount Washington Valley. Nearby ski areas include a large cross-country skiing center.

**HERITAGE-NEW HAMPSHIRE,** .5 mi. n. of US 302 on SR 16, uses audiovisual techniques to trace more than 350 years of New Hampshire history. The journey begins in 1634 with a voyage on a sailing ship to the New World. From there, visitors explore the countryside and its first English settlers, the Revolutionary War period and early industrial enterprises. A simulated steam train ride through Crawford Notch caps the experience.

Allow 2 hours minimum. Daily 9-5, mid-May through Columbus Day. Last admission 1 hour before closing. Admission $10; ages 4-12, $4.50. MC, VI. Phone (603) 383-4186. *See color ad starting on p. 370.*

**STORY LAND,** .5 mi. n. of US 302 on SR 16, is a family park with familiar fairy tale themes. Visitors can set sail on a pirate ship, experience Dr. Geyser's Remarkable Raft Ride, take an African safari or a journey on the Polar Coaster, visit the Oceans of Fun Sprayground or ride aboard a swan boat or pumpkin coach. Children can meet Cinderella and see how vegetables grow at the Farm Follies Theater.

Picnicking is permitted. Food is available. Allow a full day. Daily 9-6, mid-June through Labor Day;

Sat.-Sun. 10-5, day after Labor Day-Columbus Day. Last admission 45 minutes before closing. Schedule may vary; phone ahead. Admission $20, under 4 free. Free strollers and kennel service are available on a first-come, first-served basis. MC, VI. Phone (603) 383-4186. *See color ad starting on p. 370.*

## GORHAM (C-5) pop. 1,773, elev. 801'

A gateway to the Great North Woods, Gorham is home to several miles of scenic and challenging trails, including a section of the Appalachian Trail.

**Northern White Mountain Chamber of Commerce:** 164 Main St., Berlin, NH 03570; phone (603) 752-6060 or (800) 992-7480.

**MOUNT WASHINGTON AUTO ROAD—**
*see Mount Washington p. 104.*

### RECREATIONAL ACTIVITIES
**Winter Activities**

• **Great Glen Trails** is on SR 16 at Pinkham Notch, 8 mi. s. of jct. SR 16 and US 2. Write P.O. Box 300, Gorham, NH 03581. Other activities are offered. Daily 8:30-5, late Nov.-early Apr. Phone (603) 466-2333.

## HAMPTON (F-5) pop. 9,162, elev. 52'

One of New Hampshire's earliest towns, Hampton was settled in 1638. The town first was called Winnacunnet, meaning "beautiful place of pines." The first tax-supported public school was established in Winnacunnet in 1649 for the education of both boys and girls. The Tuck Memorial Museum on Meeting House Green depicts facets of Hampton's history. The Green itself is historic; it was established in 1638 and contains 42 stones representing the town's earliest families.

**Hampton Beach Area Chamber of Commerce:** 1 Park Ave., Suite 3G, Hampton, NH 03842; phone (603) 926-8717.

## HANOVER (E-2) pop. 8,162, elev. 603'

When Rev. Eleazar Wheelock arrived in Hanover to establish the school that was to be an experiment in spreading Christian education to the Abenaki Indians and other youth, he found a staid agricultural village of about 20 families. The community and Dartmouth College quickly established a symbiotic relationship that continues to the present, each growing and prospering with the other.

**Hanover Area Chamber of Commerce:** 216 Nugget Bldg., P.O. Box 5105, Hanover, NH 03755; phone (603) 643-3115.

**DARTMOUTH COLLEGE** is at 6016 N. Main St. Founded in 1769, Dartmouth is the ninth oldest college in the nation and the northernmost of the eight Ivy League institutions.

Notable Dartmouth Row consists of four classroom buildings, the oldest of which dates from 1784. The Thompson Arena and the Leverone Field House, designed by Pier Luigi Nervi, are examples of the modern use of architecture. Phone (603) 646-1110 or (603) 646-3278 for athletic information, or (603) 646-2466 for the ticket office.

**Baker Library** faces the n. end of the Green. This 1928 Georgian structure contains nearly two million volumes. Murals painted by Mexican artist José Clemente Orozco cover 3,000 square feet and depict the story of civilization on the American continents. Library and murals open daily 8 a.m.-midnight; library open 8-8, murals open 8-5, during campus holidays. Schedule may vary; phone ahead. Free. Phone (603) 646-2560.

**Hood Museum of Art** is connected to Hopkins Center and Wilson Hall on the s. side of the Green. Exhibitions include ancient Asian art, European paintings and sculptures, American paintings and silver, Oceanic and African art, and contemporary works by artists ranging from Pablo Picasso to Edward Ruscha. Ten galleries present changing exhibits. Public lectures and films are held year-round in Loew Auditorium. Tues.-Sat. 10-5 (also Wed. 5-9), Sun. noon-5; closed holidays. Free. Phone (603) 646-2808.

**Hopkins Center,** connected to Hood Museum on the s. side of the Green, was architect Wallace Harrison's prototype for his Metropolitan Opera House at Lincoln Center in New York City. Opened in 1962, Hopkins Center presents artists in music, dance and theatre, plus student performances, a film series and galleries with various works. Building open daily 7:30 a.m.-midnight; reduced hours during campus holidays. Box office open Mon.-Fri. 10-6, Sat. 1-6. Building free. Performances priced individually. Phone (603) 646-2422.

## HEBRON (E-3) pop. 400

**PARADISE POINT NATURE CENTER** is e. on N. Shore Rd., following signs. Owned by the Audubon Society, the center offers live animal exhibits, a day camp, evening programs and workshops. Three nature trails on 43 acres offer opportunities to view flora and fauna. The nature center borders Newfound Lake. Allow 1 hour, 30 minutes minimum. Daily 10-4, July-Aug. Donations. Phone (603) 744-3516.

## HILLSBOROUGH (F-3) pop. 1,842, elev. 580'

Hillsborough comprises several villages that feature Early American architecture, some of which is pre-Revolutionary. Stone arch bridges, built 1830-60 by Scottish stonemasons, are made from locally excavated granite. The town also was the home of the 14th president of the United States, Franklin Pierce.

Fox State Forest, on Center Road 2 miles north, covers 1,445 wooded acres. Its 20 miles of hiking paths become cross-country ski trails in winter; snowshoeing and snowmobiling also are available. Information about local plants and wildlife is available at headquarters; phone (603) 464-3453.

**Hillsborough Chamber of Commerce:** P.O. Box 541, Hillsborough, NH 03244; phone (603) 464-5858.

**FRANKLIN PIERCE HOMESTEAD NATIONAL HISTORIC LANDMARK,** n.w. near jct. SRs 9 and 31, was the boyhood home of the 14th president of the United States. The restored 1804 mansion, with its hand-stenciling and period furnishings, reflects the lifestyle of the affluent in the 19th century. Mon.-Sat. 10-4, Sun. 1-4; July 1-Labor Day; Sat. and holidays 10-4, Sun. 1-4, Memorial Day-June 30 and day after Labor Day-Sun. before Columbus Day. Admission $5, under 18 free. Phone (603) 478-3165.

## HOLDERNESS (D-4)

[SAVE] **SQUAM LAKES NATURAL SCIENCE CENTER,** jct. SRs 3 and 113, has nature trails featuring exhibits and live animal enclosures. Owls, bears, deer, bobcats, otters, birds of prey, mountain lions and other creatures are housed in settings that resemble their natural habitats. A native songbird exhibit contains an aviary. A children's activity center also is on the grounds. Daily programs are offered in July and August.

Daily 9:30-4:30, May-Oct. Admission $11; over 64, $10; ages 3-15, $8. MC, VI. Phone (603) 968-7194.

## INTERVALE (D-5) elev. 547'

[SAVE] **HARTMANN MODEL RAILROAD,** .2 mi. s. of jct. US 302 and SR 16, offers displays of domestic and foreign model trains, including a number of operating exhibits. Visitors may ride a small train through the surrounding woods. Food is available. Allow 1 hour minimum. Daily 10-5; closed Easter, Mother's Day, Thanksgiving and Dec. 25. Admission $6; over 60, $5; ages 5-12, $4. AX, DS, MC, VI. Phone (603) 356-9922.

## JACKSON (C-4)

The village of Jackson, nestled between several mountain peaks in the White Mountain National Forest *(see place listing p. 112)*, offers visitors numerous year-round recreational opportunities in a picturesque setting.

**Jackson Chamber of Commerce:** P.O. Box 304, Jackson, NH 03846; phone (603) 383-9356 or (800) 866-3334. *See color ad p. 341.*

**NESTLENOOK FARM,** jct. SRs 16 and 16A, then .2 mi. e. to Dinsmore Rd., following signs, offers year-round recreational activities on a picturesque 65-acre Victorian estate. Winter activities include snowshoeing, ice skating and horse-drawn sleigh rides. Fly fishing is offered during the summer. Visitors can feed the reindeer year-round; phone (603) 383-9443.

Sleigh rides Mon.-Fri. 4-8:30, Sat. noon-8:30, Sun. 11-3, Dec.-Mar. (weather permitting). Snowshoeing daily 9-4, Dec.-Mar. (weather permitting). Skating daily 9-8, Dec.-Mar. (weather permitting).

Farm admission free. Individual fees for sleigh rides, snowshoeing and skating. Phone (603) 383-0845.

## RECREATIONAL ACTIVITIES

### Skiing

- **Black Mountain** is n. on SR 16A to SR 16B. Write Black Mountain Rd., P.O. Box B, Jackson, NH 03846. Daily 8:30-4, Dec.-Mar. Phone (603) 383-4490.

- **Jackson Ski Touring Foundation** is n. on SR 16A. Write P.O. Box 216, Jackson, NH 03846. Daily 8-4:30, Dec.-Mar.; closed Dec. 25. Phone (603) 383-9355 or (800) 927-6697.

- **Wildcat Mountain** is n. on SR 16. Write P.O. Box R, Jackson, NH 03846. Other activities are available. Daily 9-4, Nov.-May. Phone (603) 466-3326 or (800) 255-6439.

## JAFFREY (G-3) pop. 2,802, elev. 1,000'

The Jaffrey area originally was part of a huge land grant owned by Capt. John Mason. Title to Mason's grant was later transferred to a group of men known as proprietors. At least one of these, George Jaffrey, left his mark on the wilderness when the area took its name in 1773.

In the 1840s the region became popular with summer visitors, including Ralph Waldo Emerson, who wrote the poem "Monadnoc" after climbing nearby Monadnock Mountain, reputedly one of the most climbed mountains in the United States. Several easy and intermediate hiking trails start from Monadnock State Park or from SR 124 *(see Recreation Chart)*.

Jaffrey is a quiet village surrounding the 1775 white clapboard Meeting House. The building is the site of the Amos Fortune Forum, an annual lecture series established in 1958. The forum honors Amos Fortune, a slave who was granted freedom and later became a prominent Jaffrey citizen.

**Jaffrey Chamber of Commerce:** 7 Main St., P.O. Box 2, Jaffrey, NH 03452; phone (603) 532-4549.

**SILVER RANCH & SILVER RANCH AIRPARK,** 1 mi. e. on SR 124, offers a variety of activities, including scenic airplane rides and horse-drawn carriage and sleigh rides. Allow 1 hour minimum. Open daily at 9. Plane rides $15 and up for groups of three. Sleigh and carriage rides $100 for up to 10 passengers. Reservations are suggested. MC, VI. Phone (603) 532-8870 for plane rides or (603) 532-7363 for stable activities.

## JEFFERSON (C-4) elev. 1,400'

Known locally as Jefferson Hill, Jefferson is primarily a summer resort community. From high on the flank of Mount Starr King, it commands a wide view of the Israel River Valley and the White Mountains southwest to the Franconias.

A marker just west on US 2 commemorates inventor and pioneer aeronaut Thaddeus S.C. Lowe, born nearby in 1823. During the Civil War Lowe organized and directed a Union balloon force; later he invented several important devices for use in atmospheric observation and metallurgical processing.

**Northern White Mountain Chamber of Commerce:** 164 Main St., P.O. Box 298, Berlin, NH 03570; phone (603) 752-6060 or (800) 992-7480.

**SANTA'S VILLAGE** is 1 mi. n.w. on US 2. This Christmas theme park, in a landscaped setting, features live entertainment and rides. Children can visit with Santa, feed his reindeer, play the Elfabet Game, become a helper at Santa's Workshop and enjoy live performances at the Polar Theater. Rides include Rudy's Rapid Transit Coaster, the Skyway Sleigh monorail and the Yule Log Flume.

Allow 3 hours minimum. Daily 9:30-6, June 16-Labor Day; Sat.-Sun. 9:30-5, day after Labor Day-Columbus Day. Last admission 1 hour before closing. Admission $19; over 62, $17; under 4 free. Those entering after 3 p.m. receive a pass to return any day throughout the season. MC, VI. Phone (603) 586-4445. *See color ad starting on p. 370.*

**SIX GUN CITY & FORT SPLASH WATER PARK**, .2 mi. w. of jct. SR 115 on US 2, offers 35 buildings in a frontier setting, including a church, schoolhouse and blacksmith shop. The Carriage and Sleigh Museum displays more than 100 horse-drawn vehicles and other antiques. Twelve rides are available, including a raft ride and two waterslides; there also is a wading area for children. Also included are a miniature horse show, a playground, cowboy shows, a miniature golf course and a frontier show.

Food is available. Allow 3 hours minimum. Daily 9-6, mid-June to Labor Day; Sat.-Sun. 10-5, Memorial Day weekend to mid-June. Admission $15.95; over 65, $10.95; under 4 free. MC, VI. Phone (603) 586-4592. *See color ad starting on p. 370.*

## KEENE (F-2) pop. 22,563, elev. 496′

The 1762 Wyman Tavern, 339 Main St., is one of Keene's important early buildings. In 1770 the well-known inn was the scene of the first meeting of the trustees of Dartmouth College; 5 years later Capt. Isaac Wyman led 29 Minutemen from the tavern to Lexington at the onset of the Revolutionary War.

Keene's industrial future was cast during the 19th century when the city became known for the production of glass and pottery. Henry Schoolcraft's flint glass bottles have become collectors' items, as has the white pottery made 1871-1926 by the Hampshire Pottery.

The Keene State College Arts Center on Wyman Way is the locale of plays, concerts and recitals during the academic year. "The Old Homestead" is held three nights in late July at Swanzey Center, 4 miles south on SR 32. This drama, an adaptation of the Prodigal Son story set in Swanzey during the 1880s, was first presented in 1886. The restored

Colonial Theatre at 95 Main St. features plays, concerts and opera as well as movies. In late October, the Pumpkin Festival along Main Street boasts a record-breaking tower of glowing jack-o'-lanterns.

Four covered bridges can be found on side roads off SR 10 between Keene and Winchester. Three of these bridges span the Ashuelot River: south of SR 119 at Ashuelot; east of SR 10 at West Swanzey; and a mile north of SR 32 at Swanzey Village. Still another covered bridge crosses the South Branch of the Ashuelot River east of SR 32, a half-mile south of Swanzey Village.

**Greater Keene Chamber of Commerce:** 48 Central Sq., Keene, NH 03431; phone (603) 352-1303.

**Shopping areas:** The Colony Mill Marketplace, 222 West St., is a restored woolen mill that contains a group of shops. The Center at Keene, 149 Emerald St., includes a collection of shops in a restored railroad repair depot.

**HORATIO COLONY HOUSE MUSEUM** is at 199 Main St.; parking is at the rear of St. Bernard's Church. The home was built in 1806 by Abel Blake, son of the first permanent settler of Upper Ashuelot. The house was later passed to Horatio Colony, grandson and namesake of Keene's first mayor. Colony had a flair for the unusual, mixing heirlooms with souvenirs of his world travels. Ornamental tin ceilings and decorative tiles enhance the decor of the house. Wed.-Sun. 11-4, June 1 to mid-Oct.; by appointment rest of year. Free. Phone (603) 352-0460.

**HORATIO COLONY WILDLIFE PRESERVE**, off SR 9, 1 mi. w. of jct. SRs 10, 12 and 101 on Daniels Hill Rd., is a 450-acre refuge for many species of birds and other animals as well as native plants. Nature trails wind through upland hardwood forest; hiking, cross-country skiing and snowshoeing are popular activities. Daily 24 hours. Free. Phone (603) 352-0460.

## KINSMAN NOTCH (D-3)

Rather than turn back when he found that he had taken the wrong road en route to a land grant at Landaff, pioneer Asa Kinsman, his wife and two Woodstock townsmen hacked their way through the rugged intervening miles to their destination. Thus was traversed—and named—Kinsman Notch, a pass between Mount Moosilauke and the Kinsman Range.

Kinsman, like the other White Mountain notches, was deepened and widened by the Pleistocene ice sheet. As the glaciers melted and frost weakened the fractures in the north face of the notch, huge blocks of granite plunged into Lost River Gorge to form the narrow passages among which the river gets lost.

**LOST RIVER,** 6 mi. w. of North Woodstock on SR 112, winds through a series of glacially formed boulder caves and potholes, the largest of which is 25 feet in diameter and 60 feet deep. Frequently disappearing altogether, the river emerges at the foot of the gorge to form Paradise Falls.

A self-guiding tour includes boardwalks, bridges and ladders, a tight squeeze through the Lemon Squeezer and the chance to stand under a rock formation called the Guillotine. Trips through the caverns are three-quarters of a mile long and last 45 minutes to an hour; walking shoes are advised. The caves can be bypassed.

Picnic facilities are available. Food is available. Allow 1 hour minimum. Daily 9-6, July-Aug.; 9-5, May-June and Sept.-Oct. Last admission 1 hour before closing. Admission $9.50; ages 4-12, $6.50. MC, VI. Phone (603) 745-8031.

**Lost River Nature Garden** includes 300 labeled varieties of native flowering plants, shrubs, ferns and mosses. Flowers bloom June through September. *See color ad starting on p. 370.*

## LACONIA (E-4) pop. 16,411, elev. 507'

A log cabin, the first structure on the site of Laconia, was probably erected in 1766. Before then the presence of Sachem Indians had prevented settlement, although the area had been granted as early as 1727. Growth was slow until the railroad reached the community—then called Meredith Bridge—in 1848. Thereafter mills and factories proliferated, and Laconia became a trading and manufacturing center.

Paugus Bay and lakes Winnisquam and Opechee extend into Laconia's city limits, bringing opportunities for water sports. About 5 miles north is Lake Winnipesaukee, the largest lake in the state and a major resort center *(see Weirs Beach p. 112)*. Sky Bright Inc. offers daily 20-minute sightseeing flights over the White Mountains and Lake Winnipesaukee; phone (603) 528-6818. The headquarters office of the White Mountain National Forest *(see White Mountains and White Mountain National Forest p. 112)* is in Laconia.

Cultural activities are presented at the Belknap Mill *(see attraction listing)*, a noted center for arts and humanities. Outdoor concerts are presented Thursday evenings at 6:30 July through August at the bandstand next to Belknap Mill.

**Greater Laconia-Weirs Beach Chamber of Commerce:** 11 Veterans Sq., Laconia, NH 03246; phone (603) 524-5531.

**Shopping areas:** Colony Mill Marketplace, 120 Laconia Rd. in nearby Tilton, offers more than 50 outlet stores including Brooks Brothers, Gap Outlet and Polo/Ralph Lauren.

**BELKNAP MILL** is at 25 Beacon St. E. Constructed in 1823, this building houses original looms, a renovated wheel house and a 1918 hydroelectric power plant. Live demonstrations explain the mechanics of knitting machines and looms used to make socks. An art gallery has changing exhibits and wooden crafts. Allow 1 hour minimum. Mon.-Fri. 9-5. Free. Phone (603) 524-8813.

## RECREATIONAL ACTIVITIES
### Recreational Complex

- **Gunstock** is 7 mi. e. on SR 11A. Write P.O. Box 1307, Laconia, NH 03247. Various activities are offered Apr.-Dec. Phone (603) 293-4341 or (800) 486-7862.

## LANCASTER (C-4) pop. 1,695, elev. 887'

Charming old houses create an atmosphere of the past in this busy trading center, settled in 1764 as the first town in northern New Hampshire. Its setting at the confluence of the Israel and Connecticut rivers is enhanced by the serrated Pilot Range to the northeast and the Presidential Range to the southeast. Abundant recreational activities are available, including hiking, biking, camping, fishing, hunting, skiing and snowmobiling.

**Lancaster Chamber of Commerce:** 25 Park St., P.O. Box 537, Lancaster, NH 03584; phone (603) 788-2530.

**WEEKS STATE PARK** consists of 430 acres 2 mi. s. on US 3. The park was the mountaintop summer estate of John Wingate Weeks, the one-time secretary of war and senator who wrote the legislation that established the Eastern national forests.

The fieldstone and stucco mansion contains exhibits and mementos of Senator Weeks' service during the Harding and Coolidge presidential administrations.

Nature and hiking trails as well as picnic facilities are available. Allow 1 hour minimum. Wed. 11-5, Thurs. noon-9, Fri.-Sun. 10-5, mid-June through Labor Day; Sat.-Sun. 10-5, day after Labor Day-Columbus Day. Admission $3, under 18 free. Phone (603) 788-4004, or (603) 323-2087 off-season.

## LINCOLN (D-3) elev. 808'

Lincoln is the western terminus of one of the state's most popular scenic drives, the Kancamagus Highway *(see White Mountains and White Mountain National Forest p. 112)*. With North Woodstock, its sister community across the Pemigewasset River, Lincoln serves those who visit the nearby recreational developments. The North Country Center for the Arts offers performing and visual art presentations during the summer; phone (603) 745-6032 for reservations.

**Lincoln-Woodstock Chamber of Commerce:** Rte. 112/Kancamagus Hwy., P.O. Box 358, Lincoln, NH 03251; phone (603) 745-6621 or (800) 227-4191.

**CLARK'S TRADING POST,** off I-93 exit 33, then 1 mi. s. on US 3, features North American black bear performances and rides on the White Mountain Central Railroad. The 1884 Pemigewasset Hook and Ladder Fire Station displays antique equipment; museum buildings feature early cameras, typewriters, guns and toys. Other attractions include Merlin's Mystical Mansion, Tuttle's Rustic House and water bumper boats.

Allow 2 hours, 30 minutes minimum. Daily 9:30-6, late June to mid-Aug. and Labor Day weekend; daily 10-5, mid- to late June and mid- to late Aug.; Sat.-Sun. 10-5, Memorial Day weekend to mid-June and early Sept. to mid-Oct. Last admission 1 hour before closing. Schedule may vary; phone ahead. Admission $12; over 64, $11; ages 3-5, $3. MC, VI. Phone (603) 745-8913. *See color ad starting on p. 370.*

[SAVE] **HOBO RAILROAD,** off I-93 exit 32 on SR 112, offers narrated 80-minute excursions in vintage, restored coaches along the Pemigewasset River. Specialty tours, including fall foliage trips, are offered. Food is available. Allow 1 hour, 30 minutes minimum. Trips depart daily at 11, 1 and 3, late June-Labor Day; schedule varies May 1-late June and day after Labor Day-late Oct. Fare $9; ages 3-11, $7. MC, VI. Phone (603) 745-2135.

[SAVE] **LOON MOUNTAIN RESORT** is off I-93 exit 32, then 2 mi. e. on the Kancamagus Hwy. A four-passenger gondola travels 7,000 feet from base to summit, offering sightseers a panorama of the White Mountain National Forest.

A four-story observation tower offers a panorama of the area, including Mount Washington. Children may enjoy pony rides and a mountaineer storyteller. Horseback riding, mountain bike trails and a climbing wall are offered.

Food is available. Park open daily 9-5:30, June-Oct. Gondola daily 9:30-5:30, June-Oct. Park free. Gondola fare $9.50; over 65, $8; ages 6-12, $5.50. Recreational activities are additional. Phone (603) 745-8111 or (800) 229-5666. *See color ad starting on p. 370.*

[SAVE] **THE WHALE'S TALE WATER PARK,** I-93 exit 33 to US 3, offers a wave pool with ocean-size breakers, a lazy river, a multi-passenger waterslide, two flume slides, two speed slides, a 310-foot tube slide and a children's area with a splash pool, slides, sand box, swings and more. Food is available. Allow 2 hours minimum. Daily 10-6, mid-June through Labor Day. Admission $25, over 65 and under 3 free. DS, MC, VI. Phone (603) 745-8810. *See color ad starting on p. 370.*

## LITTLETON (C-3) pop. 4,431, elev. 875'

Prior to the Civil War Littleton was a station on the branch of the Underground Railroad that led northward to Vermont and Canada. It is now better known as a resort center and stopover for travelers bound for the White Mountains.

The Ammonoosuc River's 235-foot descent through Littleton was the catalyst for the city's transformation into a manufacturing and commercial center. The job of energy production now falls

to Moore Station, a hydroelectric plant on the Connecticut River, 8 miles west on SR 18. One of New England's largest such projects, it impounds Moore Reservoir *(see Recreation Chart).* A visitor center receives guests Memorial Day-Columbus Day.

**Littleton Area Chamber of Commerce:** 120 Main St., P.O. Box 105, Littleton, NH 03561; phone (603) 444-6561.

**Self-guiding tours:** A free brochure describing a walking tour of 12 historic sites along Main Street is available from the chamber of commerce.

**LITTLETON GRIST MILL,** just s. of US 302 in the center of town at 18 Mill St., was built along the banks of the Ammonoosuc River in 1798. Restored to its original appearance, the mill produces stone-ground flours just as it did in the late 18th century. Food is available. Mon.-Fri. 10-5:30, Sat. 10-4, Sun. 11-3. Free. Phone (603) 444-7478 or (888) 284-7478.

## LONDONDERRY (G-4) pop. 11,417

**STONEYFIELD FARM YOGURT VISITORS CENTER** is off I-93 exit 5, 2.2 mi. n. on SR 28, following signs to 10 Burton Dr. A 12-minute videotape about yogurt manufacturing is followed by a guided tour of the plant. Visitors can view the entire yogurt making process, from the receipt of the milk through the incubation, chilling and packaging of the finished product. A free tasting is available upon completion of the tour.

Allow 30 minutes minimum. Guided tours are offered on the hour Mon.-Fri. 10-4. Visitor center Mon.-Sat. 9:30-5. Admission $1.50, under 5 free. Phone (603) 437-4040.

## MANCHESTER (F-3) pop. 107,006, elev. 210'

Logging helped to sustain early settlers in Manchester, and by 1810 the first cotton and woolen mills were in operation. The village was on its way to becoming the American counterpart of its British namesake, then the largest textile producing city in the world. In 1831 a group of Boston financiers bailed out a struggling cotton mill called the Amoskeag Cotton and Woolen Factory and reincorporated it as the Amoskeag Manufacturing Co.

Nearly 5 million yards of cloth were shipped each week from the brick mills, which employed thousands of workers and covered more than 8 million square feet. The mills thrived until the 1920s when a combination of stresses on the industry such as obsolete machinery, labor unrest and strong competition from the South, sapped its strength. In 1935 Amoskeag filed for bankruptcy and the mills fell silent.

But Manchester was not doomed to obscurity. A group of local businessmen pooled $5 million, purchased the mile-long ranks of mills and reactivated them with a diversified array of industries. Manchester is the state's industrial giant as well as its largest city and the home of nearly 10 percent of its population.

Just as the mills and the company houses have new tenants, so does the 1915 Palace Theatre at 80

Hanover St. The theater was known for its excellent acoustics and large stage. The fully restored Palace is now home to the New Hampshire Performing Arts Center. The New Hampshire Symphony and the Opera League of New Hampshire as well as national touring companies and various community groups perform at the theater.

Manchester also is noted for its association with Gen. John Stark, who was born in Derryfield—now Manchester—in 1728. Stark fought the Abenaki Indians with Maj. William Rogers and his Rogers' Rangers, a backwoods fighting team that is considered the forerunner of today's Army Rangers. Stark died in 1822, having outlived every Patriot general except Marquis de Lafayette. His childhood home stands at 2000 Elm St.; his grave is in Stark Park, off N. River Road overlooking the river.

**Greater Manchester Chamber of Commerce:** 889 Elm St., Manchester, NH 03101; phone (603) 666-6600.

**Shopping areas:** The Mall of New Hampshire, on S. Willow Street, features Filene's, JCPenney and Sears.

**THE CURRIER MUSEUM OF ART,** 201 Myrtle Way, is in a 1929 Beaux-Arts building reminiscent of an Italian Renaissance palace. Displayed are European and American paintings, sculpture and decorative arts from the 13th century to the present, including works by Winslow Homer, Henri Matisse, Claude Monet, Georgia O'Keeffe, Pablo Picasso and Andrew Wyeth. Also included are works by New Hampshire artists and craftsmen as well as a collection of American furniture.

Changing exhibitions, films, lectures and concerts are offered year-round. Food is available. Allow 1 hour, 30 minutes minimum. Sun.-Mon. and Wed.-Fri. 11-5 (also Thurs. 5-8), Sat. 10-5; closed major holidays. Admission $5, over 62 and students with ID $4, under 18 free, free to all Sat. 10-1. MC, VI. Phone (603) 669-6144.

**Zimmerman House** is reached by van from The Currier Museum of Art; parking is available at the museum. A tour of the house and grounds provides an introduction to one of Frank Lloyd Wright's Usonian houses. The house, designed for Isadore J. and Lucille Zimmerman in 1950, contains original built-in and free-standing furniture, textiles and landscaping designed by Wright. An extended tour includes an orientation to Manchester's architectural history.

Allow 1 hour, 30 minutes minimum. Tours are given Mon. and Thurs.-Fri. at 2, Sat. at 12:30, Sun. at 1, Apr.-Dec. Extended tours Sat.-Sun. at 2:30, Apr.-Dec. Closed major holidays. Schedule may vary; phone ahead. Admission (includes The Currier Museum of Art) $9; over 62 and students under 18, $6. Extended tour fare $15; over 62 and students under 18, $11. Under 7 are not permitted. Reservations are required. MC, VI. Phone (603) 626-4158

for reservations, or (603) 669-6144 for additional information.

**LAWRENCE L. LEE SCOUTING MUSEUM AND MAX I. SILBER LIBRARY,** off I-93 exit 5 to Camp Carpenter on Bodwell Rd., features a collection of Boy Scout memorabilia dating from the late 19th century. The Max I. Silber Library houses a collection of scouting periodicals, books and scouting handbooks, including Braille editions. Hiking and camping facilities are available. Picnicking is permitted. Allow 30 minutes minimum. Daily 10-4, July-Aug.; Sat. 10-4, rest of year. Free. Phone (603) 669-8919.

**MANCHESTER HISTORIC ASSOCIATION,** 129 Amherst St., features local history with permanent and changing exhibits. Among the museum's highlights are American Indian artifacts, 19th-century firefighting apparatus and images and articles illustrating Manchester's social and industrial history. The library contains the records of the Amoskeag Manufacturing Co. as well as regional maps, diaries, photographs and other documents. Allow 1 hour minimum. Tues.-Sat. 10-4, Sun. noon-4; closed holidays. **Note:** The association is closed for renovations; reopening is scheduled for late 2004. Free. Phone (603) 622-7531.

**NEW HAMPSHIRE INSTITUTE OF ART,** 148 Concord St. at Pine St., is an educational facility for fine arts, crafts and foreign languages. Changing exhibitions by local and nationally known artists are featured. The institute offers a film and concert series. Allow 30 minutes minimum. Mon.-Fri. 9-7:30, Sat. 9-5, Sun. 1-5; closed holidays. Free. Phone (603) 623-0313.

**SEE SCIENCE CENTER,** 200 Bedford St., has interactive exhibits that focus on a variety of topics including electricity, geology, aviation and reptiles. Allow 1 hour minimum. Mon.-Fri. 10-3, Sat.-Sun. noon-5; closed Easter, July 4, Thanksgiving and Dec. 25. Admission $4, under 1 free. MC, VI. Phone (603) 669-0400.

## MASON (G-3) elev. 760'

**PICKITY PLACE** is on Nutting Hill Rd. The site consists of themed gardens and the woods and cottage that inspired award-winning illustrator Elizabeth Orton Jones' drawings of the classic children's story "Little Red Riding Hood." Illustrations from the 1938 edition of the story are displayed. Workshops about herbs and gardening are offered. Food is available. Allow 1 hour, 30 minutes minimum. Daily 9-5, Apr.-Dec.; 9-4, rest of year. Closed Jan. 1, Easter, Thanksgiving and Dec. 25. Free. Phone (603) 878-1151.

## MEREDITH (E-4) pop. 1,739

**ANNALEE DOLL MUSEUM,** .5 mi. w. of jct. US 3 and Reservoir Rd. at 50 Reservoir Rd., displays a portion of the more than 500 dolls that make up the collection of the Annalee Doll Co. Dating from

1934, the soft sculpture, whimsical creations chronicle the life and career of artist Annalee Thorndike. The museum's Victorian facade is a reproduction of her childhood home in Concord. Allow 30 minutes minimum. Daily 9:30-5, Memorial Day-Oct. 31. Free. Phone (603) 279-3333.

**WINNIPESAUKEE SCENIC RAILROAD** departs Meredith and Weirs Beach stations. A 2-hour train ride takes visitors along the scenic shore of Lake Winnipesaukee. Picnicking is permitted. Food is available. Allow 2 hours minimum. Daily 10:30-4:30, late June-late Aug.; Sat.-Sun. 10:30-4:30, late May-late June. Fare $10, children $8. Reservations are recommended. MC, VI. Phone (603) 279-5253.

## MERRIMACK (G-3) elev. 122′

**ANHEUSER-BUSCH INC.** is e. off Everett Tpke. exit 10 at 221 Daniel Webster Hwy. Tours of the brewery, sampling room and Clydesdale stables are offered. Allow 1 hour, 30 minutes minimum. Daily 9:30-5, June-Aug.; 10-4 in May and Sept.-Dec.; Thurs.-Mon. 10-4, rest of year. Closed Jan. 1, Easter, Thanksgiving and Dec. 24-25 and 31. Free. Children must be with an adult. Phone (603) 595-1202.

## MILTON (E-5) elev. 440′

SAVE **NEW HAMPSHIRE FARM MUSEUM** is off SR 16 exit 18, then .7 mi. s. on SR 125. The museum, housed on Jones Farm, reflects New Hampshire's agricultural past through displays of antique farm implements. Jones Farm is considered the best preserved example of connected farm structures in the state. The structures extend 275 feet and offer examples of architectural styles that span 200 years. Workshops and demonstrations of early farm life are offered.

Guided tours are available. Allow 1 hour minimum. Wed.-Sun. 10-4, Memorial Day-late Oct. Admission $5; over 64, $4.50; ages 3-12, $1.50. Phone (603) 652-7840.

---

# DID YOU KNOW

## ?

New Hampshire
is the only state
without a
general sales tax or
a state income tax.

---

## MOULTONBOROUGH (D-4) elev. 808′

**CASTLE IN THE CLOUDS,** 3 mi. s. of jct. SRs 25 and 109, then 2 mi. e. on SR 171, is a turn-of-the-20th-century mansion set amid the Ossipee Mountains. A self-guiding tour provides visitors with an overview of the castle's history. Spectacular views of the surrounding area can be seen from virtually every room. Tours of the Castle Springs bottling plant and the Lucknow Brewery, as well as horseback riding, are available.

Food is available. Allow 1 hour, 30 minutes minimum. Daily 9-5, Memorial Day weekend-Labor Day; 9-4, day after Labor Day-Oct. 23. Admission $12; over 59, $10; ages 7-17, $8. DS, MC, VI. Phone (603) 476-2352 or (800) 729-2468.

**THE LOON CENTER,** jct. Blake Rd. and SR 25, 1 mi. s.w. on Blake Rd., then s. on Lee's Mills Rd., offers loon exhibits, videotape displays and a research library as well as hiking and nature trails that traverse an area indigenous to nesting loons, waterfowl, woodland birds and other wildlife. Allow 1 hour, 30 minutes minimum. Daily 9-5, July 4-Columbus Day; Mon.-Sat. 9-5, rest of year. Nature trails daily dawn-dusk. Donations. Phone (603) 476-5666.

## MOUNT WASHINGTON (C-5) elev. 6,288′

Mount Washington, in the Presidential Range of the White Mountains, is the Northeast's highest peak at 6,288 feet. The weather at its summit rivals that of Antarctica: the average annual temperature is below freezing. Fifteen feet of snow is the winter norm, and summer temperatures rarely exceed 72 F. The highest wind velocity ever recorded—231 mph—occurred in April 1934.

Conditions can change in minutes from balmy to subfreezing. Nevertheless, in clear weather, the summit rewards visitors with a panorama that includes the Atlantic Ocean, Maine, New Hampshire, Québec and Vermont.

**MOUNT WASHINGTON AUTO ROAD** is reached via SR 16 at Glen House, about 8 mi. s. of Gorham. The scenic trip requires 30 to 45 minutes each way; frequent turnouts provide emergency water needs. Low gear should be used both ways, and brakes, gas, water and the condition of the automobile should be checked before the drive. Because of steep grades and sharp curves, driving instructions are available at the toll house and should be heeded. For those who prefer not to drive, guided tours are available with a 30-minute stop at the summit.

Allow 2 hours minimum for the driving tour or 1 hour, 30 minutes for the guided tour. **Note:** For safety, towed trailers, motor homes, pickup campers, certain vehicles with full passenger loads and vehicles with a wheelbase longer than 161 inches are not permitted. Daily 7:30-6, mid-June through Labor Day; otherwise varies, mid-May to mid-June and day after Labor Day to mid-Oct. (weather permitting). Guided tours daily 8:30-5, mid-May to mid-Oct. (weather permitting). Driving tour (includes audio cassette) $16 for driver; passengers $6; ages 5-12, $4. Guided tour $22; over 61, $20; ages 5-12, $10. Phone (603) 466-3988. *See color ad starting on p. 370.*

 **MOUNT WASHINGTON COG RAILWAY**—*see Bretton Woods p. 91.*

**SHERMAN ADAMS SUMMIT BUILDING,** atop Mount Washington, offers a 360-degree view of the northern Presidential Range.

Visitors can see the restored 1853 Tip Top House, one of the oldest mountaintop buildings in the country and the first hotel on Mount Washington.

The summit building honors Sherman Adams, a former governor of New Hampshire and one of the state's best known political, civic and business leaders. An information desk, a glass-enclosed viewing area and the Mount Washington Summit Museum are in the building.

Food is available. Allow 1 hour minimum. Daily 8-8, Memorial Day-Columbus Day (weather permitting). Museum admission $2; ages 6-12, $1. Phone (603) 466-3347.

## NEWBURY (F-3)

SAVE **THE FELLS AT THE JOHN HAY NATIONAL WILDLIFE REFUGE** is 2.2 mi. n. on SR 103A. The Fells, which overlook Lake Sunapee, was the summer home of three generations of the Hay family. John M. Hay, a diplomat and writer, served as President Abraham Lincoln's private secretary and ambassador to Great Britain and secretary of state under presidents William McKinley and Theodore Roosevelt. Hiking trails and wildlife viewing are highlights.

Allow 1 hour minimum. Grounds open daily dawn-dusk. House open Tues.-Sun. and Mon. holidays 10-5, July-Aug.; Sat.-Sun. and Mon. holidays 10-5, Memorial Day-June 30 and Sept. 1-Columbus Day. Admission $5; ages 6-15, $2. MC, VI ($20). Phone (603) 763-4789.

## NEW CASTLE (F-6)

Narrow streets with old houses flush to the curbs lend a Colonial air to New Castle, founded as a fishing village on Great Island in the late 1600s. To the east of the square is a historic site containing the remnants of Fort Constitution, the site of the first overt acts of rebellion against the British Crown.

Originally Fort Constitution was the British stronghold Fort William and Mary. On Dec. 14, 1774, following a little-known warning ride by Paul Revere, Portsmouth's Sons of Liberty, accompanied by Durham and New Castle patriots, captured the fort and seized the British powder and arms. Stored in Durham *(see place listing p. 95)*, the munitions were used against the British 4 months later at the battle of Bunker Hill.

President Theodore Roosevelt won a Nobel Peace Prize for work done in New Castle. In 1905 he negotiated the Treaty of Portsmouth, which ended the Russo-Japanese War.

## NORTH CONWAY (D-5)

**pop. 2,069, elev. 546'**

So taken was he with the view of Mount Washington from North Conway's main street that artist Benjamin Champney set up his easel in the middle of the road in August 1850 and painted the scene. Subsequently he and other artists depicted Thompson's Falls and many other nearby spots. Champney supposedly sold several of his New Hampshire landscapes to a chromolithograph company that circulated reproductions.

As the commercial center of the Mount Washington Valley recreation area, the community thrives on a year-round throng of visitors who come not only for outdoor sports and sightseeing, but also for dining, shopping and nightlife. The arts scene is another attraction; the Mount Washington Valley Theatre Company offers a varied repertoire during July and August.

**Mount Washington Valley Chamber of Commerce:** P.O. Box 2300, North Conway, NH 03860; phone (603) 356-3171, or (800) 367-3364 out of N.H. *See color ad p. 378.*

**Shopping areas:** Bargain hunters enjoy Main Street, where the L.L. Bean Shopping Center, Red Barn Factory Stores, Settler's Green and Tanger Factory Outlet Center feature such stores as Anne Klein, Banana Republic, Calvin Klein, J. Crew, Liz Claiborne and Oneida.

**CONWAY SCENIC RAILROAD,** off SR 16 and US 302, offers nostalgic, narrated, round-trip train rides of varying duration through the countryside. A restored steam or early diesel locomotive pulls the train over track laid in the 1870s. Trains depart from the 1874 North Conway Station. The Valley Train runs to Conway and Bartlett, with dining service available on selected trips. The 5.5-hour Crawford Notch trip offers excellent views of fall foliage.

Allow 1 hour, 30 minutes minimum. Trains to Conway and Barlett depart mid-Apr. to late Dec. Crawford Notch train runs late June to mid-Oct. Schedules vary; phone ahead. Fares $10-$50. Reservations are recommended. MC, VI. Phone (603) 356-5251, or (800) 232-5251 out of N.H. *See color ad starting on p. 370.*

**ECHO LAKE STATE PARK,** 1.5 mi. w. of US 302 on Westside Rd., covers 396 acres. A scenic road near the top of Cathedral Ledge, 700 feet above the river valley, offers a view of the White Mountains and the Saco River Valley. Just south is Echo Lake, which offers swimming, picnicking, hiking and climbing opportunities, with White Horse Ledge providing a spectacular backdrop.

Allow 1 hour minimum. Daily 9-6, mid-June through Labor Day; Sat.-Sun. and holidays 9-7, mid-May to mid-June. Admission $3, New Hampshire residents, over 64 and under 12 free. Phone (603) 356-2672, or (603) 323-2087 in the off-season. *See Recreation Chart.*

## NORTH HAMPTON (F-5) elev. 77'

Its position on the seacoast about midway between Portland, Maine, and Boston prompted many of the wealthy from both cities to build summer homes in North Hampton in the late 19th and early 20th centuries. One such estate was Runnymede-by-the-Sea, belonging to former Massachusetts governor Alvan T. Fuller. Although the house no longer exists, the gardens remain as an attractive legacy of the era.

**FULLER GARDENS** occupies 2 acres off SR 1A at 10 Willow Ave. Designed in the early 1930s, the grounds are typical of Colonial Revival estate gardens. Early June brings spring bulbs, azaleas, rhododendrons and, in the Japanese garden, wisterias. Some 2,000 rose bushes bloom late June through October. Perennial and annual displays, statuary and fountains are interspersed throughout

the gardens, and a greenhouse contains tropical and desert plants.

Allow 30 minutes minimum. Daily 10-5:30, mid-May to mid-Oct.; closed Columbus Day. Admission $6; senior citizens $5; students with ID $3; under 12, $2. Phone (603) 964-5414.

## NORTH SALEM (G-4) elev. 147'

Low wooded hills and numerous ponds characterize the region around North Salem, a farming and residential community.

SAVE **AMERICA'S STONEHENGE,** 5 mi. e. of I-93 exit 3 on SR 111, then 1 mi. s. on Haverhill Rd., encompasses prehistoric stone structures proven by carbon dating to form the oldest known megalithic site on this continent. Continuing research indicates the site may be 4,000 years old; inscriptions deciphered offer possible evidence that Celt-Iberians used this site from about 800 to 300 B.C. Inscriptions are displayed and reading material is available.

Allow 1 hour minimum. Daily 9-7, late June-early Sept.; 9-5, Feb. 1 to late June and early Sept.-Oct. 31; 9-4, rest of year. Last admission 1 hour before closing. Admission $8.50; over 64, $7.50; ages 6-12, $5.50. AX, DS, MC, VI. Phone (603) 893-8300.

## PETERBOROUGH (G-3)
pop. 2,944, elev. 723'

Peterborough and the arts have been virtually synonymous since the late 19th century. In 1907 composer Edward MacDowell decided to share with other artists the peace and inspiration he had found at his nearby woodland retreat. Although he died the next year, the MacDowell Colony flourished. Pulitzer Prizes, Guggenheim Fellowships and many other international awards have been bestowed upon painters, sculptors, printmakers, filmmakers, writers and composers who have worked in Peterborough.

Because the colony closely guards the privacy of its resident artists, only Colony Hall, the library and MacDowell's gravesite are accessible to the public.

Nearly as venerable is the Peterborough Players, a professional summer theater company that began in a barn a few miles north of the MacDowell Colony in 1933. The players present several productions at the Hadley Barn on Hadley Road off Middle Hancock Road. For information contact the Peterborough Players, P.O. Box 118, Peterborough, NH 03458; phone (603) 924-7585.

**Greater Peterborough Chamber of Commerce:** 10 Wilton Rd., P.O. Box 401, Peterborough, NH 03458; phone (603) 924-7234.

**MILLER STATE PARK** covers 489 acres 3 mi. e. off SR 101. The state's oldest state park was founded in 1891 and offers a scenic drive and a foot trail to the 2,288-foot summit of Pack Monadnock Mountain. The Wapack Trail between North Pack Monadnock Mountain, 2 miles north, and Mount Watatic, in Massachusetts, also crosses the park. On clear days the view from the summit reaches from Mount Washington to Boston. Allow 1 hour, 30 minutes minimum. Daily dawn-dusk, mid-Apr. to mid-Nov. Admission $3, under 12 free. Phone (603) 924-3672.

**PETERBOROUGH HISTORICAL SOCIETY MUSEUM,** on Grove St. near Main St., has items pertaining to state and local history as well as a mill workers' home, a Victorian parlor, a country store and a Colonial kitchen. Changing exhibits include ceramics, pewter, textiles and toys. Guided tours are available. Allow 1 hour minimum. Mon.-Fri. 1-4. Admission $3; under 12 free. Phone (603) 924-3235.

**SHARON ARTS CENTER,** 30 Grove St., has two galleries featuring a permanent collection and changing exhibits. An arts library and an arts and crafts school are included. Mon.-Sat. 10-5, Sun. noon-5. Donations. Phone (603) 924-7676.

### ▼ GEM PINKHAM NOTCH SCENIC AREA (C-4)

Walled by the Presidential Range on the west and by Mount Moriah, North Carter Mountain, Carter Dome and other mountains on the east, Pinkham Notch is one of the easternmost of the New Hampshire White Mountain notches.

In 1790 Joseph Pinkham, whose name was bestowed on the notch, allegedly brought his possessions to his new home via pig-drawn sled. The rough trace that Pinkham and his companions followed has since evolved into scenic SR 16, which threads through the pass between Jackson and Gorham. On the south slope the road parallels the Ellis River and offers access to such spots as Glen Ellis Falls and Crystal Cascade along the Tuckerman Ravine Trail.

The ravine's sheer west wall challenges expert downhill skiers. The notch and its attractions are within the White Mountain National Forest (see White Mountains and White Mountain National Forest p. 112).

A visitor center on SR 16 between North Conway and Gorham is sponsored by the Appalachian Mountain Club. The center offers hikers and other travelers trail and weather information, food, educational displays about outdoor recreation in the White Mountains, free guided walks and evening lectures; phone (603) 466-2721.

### PLYMOUTH (D-3) pop. 3,528, elev. 514'

**POLAR CAVES PARK** is 5 mi. w. on SR 25 (Tenney Mountain Hwy.). The caves were formed by glacial action more than 20,000 years ago. Paths lead through a series of caves and passages featuring granite boulders as well as mineral formations of quartz, mica, garnet and beryl. The park also features peacocks, pheasants and European fallow deer. Nature trails offer educational plaques about native plants and natural history.

Picnic facilities are available. Allow 1 hour, 30 minutes minimum. Daily 9-5, mid-May to mid-Oct.

Admission $10, under 5 free. MC, VI. Phone (603) 536-1888. See color ad starting on p. 370.

## PORTSMOUTH (F-6) pop. 20,784, elev. 14'

To their delight, when the sea-weary travelers on the Pied Cow disembarked on the west bank of the Piscataqua River in 1630, they found the ground covered with wild strawberries. Thus was founded and named Strawbery Banke, the little settlement that took root around a tidal inlet and grew into the seaport of Portsmouth.

The passengers on the Pied Cow were not the first to settle in the area. In 1623 members of the Laconia Co. had come to the Piscataqua to establish a plantation and fishery. Part of the group continued upriver to Dover. The remainder settled at Odiorne Point, 2 miles east of Portsmouth, where they built the first house in New Hampshire. Odiorne Point is a state park that preserves an area little changed in the last 3 centuries.

Strawbery Banke, however, changed greatly. Fishing and farming sustained residents at first, but the ready supply of good timber and an excellent harbor soon engaged them in shipbuilding. Portsmouth—the name was changed in 1653—began attracting the merchant class in large numbers.

The community also served as the seat of the provincial government. As a center of political activity and a vital trade circuit that linked it with Great Britain and the West Indies, Portsmouth naturally was the focus of many Patriot vs. Tory confrontations prior to the Revolutionary War. British ammunition and stores taken from Fort William and Mary by Portsmouth patriots on Dec. 14, 1774, were used in the first battles of the revolution.

Private shipbuilding reached its apex in the early 19th century, producing many of the swift clipper ships that graced the sea. Two of America's first warships, the Ranger and the America, were built in Portsmouth Harbor under the direction of John Paul Jones. Thereafter, shipping and shipbuilding declined as steamships and the competing Massachusetts ports gained popularity.

In 1800 the historic U.S. Navy Yard on Seavey's Island (see Kittery, Maine, p. 58) became the impetus behind Portsmouth's economy, since augmented by diversified industry and a healthy summer resort trade.

Portsmouth's history is documented in many restored buildings and neighborhoods. Colonial structures as well as the finely detailed houses built by wealthy 19th-century sea captains line the narrow, winding streets of these sections.

The Old Harbor area at Bow and Ceres streets once was the focus of a thriving mercantile seaport; craft shops, restaurants and boutiques now occupy its chandleries and warehouses. Seacoast Repertory Theater, an all-year equity theater, is in a renovated brewery at 125 Bow St.; phone (603) 433-4472.

Similarly the 14 Federal and Georgian buildings of The Hill, at Deer and High streets, have been refurbished and now are used as offices. Seven of the structures were erected during or before the Revolutionary War. Across Mechanic Street from Prescott Park is the city's oldest cemetery, Point of Graves, which contains gravestones dating from 1682.

**Greater Portsmouth Chamber of Commerce:** 500 Market St., P.O. Box 239, Portsmouth, NH 03802; phone (603) 436-1118.

SAVE **CHILDREN'S MUSEUM OF PORTSMOUTH,** in the South Meeting House at 280 Marcy St., has hands-on exhibits for children. Youngsters can create a sculpture, play the drums and explore with shapes. A communication exhibit lets them experience electronic mail and teleconferences.

Allow 1 hour, 30 minutes minimum. Tues.-Sat. 10-5 (also Mon. 10-5 during summer and school vacations), Sun. 1-5. Admission $5, senior citizens $4, under 1 free. DS, MC, VI. Phone (603) 436-3853.

**ISLES OF SHOALS STEAMSHIP CO.,** Barker's Wharf at 315 Market St., offers trips to the historic Isles of Shoals and around Portsmouth Harbor aboard the late 19th-century steamship replica MV *Thomas Laighton* and the MV *Oceanic.* Sights along the cruise include forts, lighthouses, a naval prison and a shipyard. A stop at Star Island allows visitors to explore this exclusive island resort. Dinner cruises, fall foliage excursions and whale-watching expeditions also are available.

Two-and-a-half-hour trips depart daily at 10:55 and 2:25, mid-June through Labor Day. Fares $11-$55. Reservations are recommended. DS, MC, VI. Phone (603) 431-5500 or (800) 441-4620.

SAVE **PORTSMOUTH HARBOR CRUISES,** Ceres St. dock, travels around the 14 islands of Portsmouth Harbor to the Isles of Shoals and up the Piscataqua River as far as Dover and Great Bay via a 49-passenger vessel. Cruises lasting 1.5 and 2.5 hours are available. Trips depart daily May-Oct. (weather permitting). Hours vary; phone ahead. Fare $14-$18; over 55, $9.50-$17; ages 3-12, $7-$10. Reservations are recommended. DS, MC, VI. Phone (603) 436-8084 or (800) 776-0915.

**PORTSMOUTH HARBOR TRAIL,** beginning at Market Square, tours the waterfront, downtown and the south end and passes six historic houses. Guided tours Mon. and Thurs.-Sat. at 10:30 and 5:30, Sun. at 1:30, early July-Columbus Day. Admission $8. A 32-page guide with a map of the trail is available for $2 at the chamber of commerce and the downtown information kiosk. Phone (603) 436-1118.

**Governor John Langdon House,** 143 Pleasant St., was built in 1784 by John Langdon, a three-time governor of the state, signer of the Constitution and first president of the Senate. In 1789 George Washington described the Georgian mansion as "the finest house in Portsmouth." The main portion of the structure, with its balustrade and stately portico, retains its original appearance.

Allow 1 hour minimum. Guided tours are offered on the hour Wed.-Sun. 11-5, June 1 to mid-Oct. Last tour begins 1 hour before closing. Admission $6; over 65, $5.50; ages 6-12, $3. Phone (603) 436-3205.

SAVE **Moffatt-Ladd House** is at 154 Market St. Best known as the home of William Whipple, a signer of the Declaration of Independence, the house was built in 1763 by Whipple's father-in-law, John Moffatt, a wealthy sea merchant.

Paneled halls and chambers, an ornate staircase, original furniture and a museum room distinguish the house, which is set amid formal gardens with turf steps and raised beds. Allow 30 minutes minimum. Mon.-Sat. 11-5, Sun. 1-5, mid-June to late Oct. Admission $6; ages 7-12, $2.50. Phone (603) 436-8221.

SAVE **Portsmouth Historical Society Museum at the John Paul Jones House,** Middle and State sts., was built in 1758 by Capt. Gregory Purcell. After his death Purcell's widow operated the house as a genteel guesthouse. Most notable of her guests was Capt. John Paul Jones, who lived in the house while supervising the outfitting of the *Ranger* in 1777 and again in 1781 while the *America* was being built. China, silver, glass, portraits, costumes and a model of the *Ranger* are displayed. Tours are conducted by costumed guides.

Allow 30 minutes minimum. Tours on the hour Thurs.-Tues. 11-5, mid-May to mid-Oct. Admission $5; over 65, $4.50; ages 6-14, $2.50. Phone (603) 436-8420.

**Rundlet-May House,** 364 Middle St., is a three-story 1807 Federal mansion. Built by textile merchant James Rundlet, the house retains its original character while reflecting the varying lifestyles of successive generations of the family. Several pieces of furniture were made by noted Portsmouth craftsmen.

Allow 1 hour minimum. Tours are given on the hour Sat.-Sun. 11-5, June 1 to mid-Oct. Last tour begins 1 hour before closing. Admission $6; over 65, $5.50; ages 6-12, $3. Phone (603) 436-3205.

SAVE **Warner House,** Daniel and Chapel sts., is a noted example of Georgian architecture. The 1716 house has brick walls 18 inches thick, fine paneling and wall murals. The lightning rod on the west wall is said to have been installed in 1762 under the supervision of Benjamin Franklin, a frequent visitor. Allow 1 hour minimum. Mon.-Sat. 11-4, Sun. noon-4, early June-late Oct. Admission $5; ages 7-12, $2.50. Phone (603) 436-5909.

**Wentworth-Gardner House,** at Mechanic and Gardner sts., is said to rank among the finest Georgian-style buildings in the country. The restored blocked-front 1760 house is known for its doorway and woodcarvings. Allow 30 minutes minimum. Tues.-Sun. 1-4, early June to mid-Oct. Admission $5; under 10, $2. Phone (603) 436-4406.

**PRESCOTT PARK** is on Marcy St., between Strawbery Banke Museum *(see attraction listing)* and the riverfront. In addition to gardens, fountains and a fishing pier, the park contains two old warehouses. The 1705 Sheafe Warehouse, where John Paul Jones outfitted the *Ranger,* now houses changing art exhibits throughout the year. Allow 1 hour minimum. Daily 5 a.m.-midnight. Free. Phone (603) 431-8748.

**ST. JOHN'S CHURCH** is on Chapel St. Built in 1807, it is the successor to the 1732 Queen's Chapel. The church contains 17th- and 18th-century antiques, including a steeple bell that came from France to Nova Scotia in the mid-1700s. Colonial soldiers took the bell as a souvenir and presented it to Queen's Chapel in 1745. Damaged when the chapel burned in 1806, the bell was recast by Paul Revere.

Allow 30 minutes minimum. Daily 9-5, except during services. Phone (603) 436-8283.

**SEACOAST SCIENCE CENTER,** 3 mi. s. on SR 1A in Odiorne Point State Park, has cultural, marine and natural history exhibits as well as a tide pool touch tank. Interpretive programs are offered. Allow 1 hour minimum. Park open daily 8-dusk. Science center open daily 10-5. Closed Jan. 1, Thanksgiving and Dec. 25. Park admission $3, under 12 free. Science center $3; ages 3-12, $1. Phone (603) 436-7406 for the park, or (603) 436-8043 for the science center.

[SAVE] **STRAWBERY BANKE MUSEUM** is bounded by Marcy, Court, Washington and Hancock sts. The historic waterfront neighborhood offers more than 45 buildings covering 10 acres from the period 1695-1955, in various stages of restoration and adaptation.

The 1770 William Pitt Tavern, 1780 Wheelwright House, 1795 Drisco House, 1796 Walsh House, 1815 Chase House, 1830 Rider-Wood House, 1860 Goodwin Mansion and 1919 Shapiro House have been restored and furnished in different periods to show the changes in lifestyle and architectural fashion over 350 years.

Information about self-guiding tours, guided walking tours and holiday events is available at the ticket booth. Allow 1 hour, 30 minutes minimum. Mon.-Sat. 10-5, Sun. noon-5, May-Oct.; Thurs.-Sat. 10-2, Sun. noon-2, Nov.-Dec. and Feb.-Apr. Two-day admission May-Oct. $12; over 65, $11; ages 7-17, $8; family rate $28. Admission rest of year $6; over 65, $5; ages 7-17, $4; family rate $14. MC, VI. Phone (603) 433-1106. *See color ad.*

**URBAN FORESTRY CENTER** is 2 mi. s. on US 1 (Lafayette Rd.), then .1 mi. e. to 45 Elwyn Rd. Set on 170 acres of marshland, woods and meadows bordering Sagamore Creek, the center offers trails and gardens in a peaceful setting. Programs about forestry and natural resources are offered. Trails open daily 7-dusk. Office open Mon.-Fri. 8-4. Free. Phone (603) 431-6774.

**USS *ALBACORE*,** off I-95 exit 7, then .2 mi. e. off Market St. in Albacore Park and Memory Garden, was built in 1952 and served as an experimental prototype for modern submarines. The *Albacore's* radical hull design enabled it to set an underwater speed record.

From 1953-72 the *Albacore* was used to test innovations in sonar, dive brakes and controls. The Memorial Garden pays tribute to those killed in the line of duty in the submarine service. Allow 1 hour minimum. Daily 9:30-5; closed Jan. 1, Thanksgiving and Dec. 25. Hours may vary; phone ahead. Admission $5; over 62, $3.50; ages 7-17, $2; family rate $10. Phone (603) 436-3680.

**WATER COUNTRY,** 3 mi. s. on US 1, features a variety of water-related amusements, including a tube ride on a gentle river, a large wave pool, whitewater rapids, a bobsled run and 12 large waterslides. Food is available. Daily 10-6, mid-June through Labor Day. Admission $28.99, under 48 inches tall $18.99, under age 2 free. DS, MC, VI. Phone (603) 427-1111.

**WENTWORTH-COOLIDGE MANSION,** off Sagamore Rd. on Little Harbor Rd., was the official residence of Benning Wentworth, first royal governor 1741-66. The oldest part of the extensive structure is thought to have been built about 1720. Allow 1 hour minimum. Wed.-Sat. 10-3, Sun. 1-4,

mid-May through Labor Day; Sat. 10-3, Sun. 1-4, weekend after Labor Day to mid-Oct. Admission free. Guided tour $3, under 16 free. Phone (603) 436-6607.

## RINDGE (G-3)

Overlooking the rolling Monadnock Region from its hilltop location, the village of Rindge is the site of 1,000-acre Franklin Pierce College. Recreational activities are available year-round. Many nearby ponds and lakes offer boating and bass fishing.

**CATHEDRAL OF THE PINES**, 2 mi. n.e. off SR 119, is dedicated to all those killed in war. Sanderson Sloane, a B-17 bomber pilot, was lost over Germany Feb. 22, 1944; he had planned to build a home on this site.

The Memorial Bell Tower honors all American women who served in wartime. Hilltop House has state and foreign flags, war relics and art objects. Allow 1 hour minimum. Daily 9-5, May-Oct. Donations. Phone (603) 899-3300.

## RUMNEY (D-3) elev. 527'

A mountain, brook and lake near Rumney bear the name of David Stinson, a colleague of Gen. John Stark. The community, established in the 1760s near the confluence of Stinson Brook and the Baker River, serves summer travelers and the surrounding farming area.

**MARY BAKER EDDY HISTORIC HOUSE** is 1 mi. n. of SR 25 on Stinson Lake Rd. Mrs. Eddy, the founder of Christian Science, lived in the house 1860-62. Guide service is available to the home in nearby North Groton where she lived before moving to Rumney. Allow 30 minutes minimum. Tues.-Sat. 10-5, Sun. 2-5, May-Oct.; closed major holidays. Admission $3, over 64 and students with ID $1.50, under 12 free. Phone (603) 786-9943.

## RYE (F-5)

SAVE **GRANITE STATE WHALE WATCH**, on SR 1A (Ocean Blvd.), offers whale-watching expeditions and sightseeing cruises from Rye Harbor to the Isles of Shoals. Highlights of the Isles of Shoals cruise include a boat tour of nine islands and a local fireworks display. Whale-watch tours are conducted by research biologists. Write New Hampshire Seacoast Cruises, P.O. Box 232, Rye, NH 03870-0232.

Allow 3 hours minimum for island trips, 4 hours minimum for whale-watching trips. Whale-watching trips depart daily at 8:30 and 1:30, mid-June through Labor Day; Sat.-Sun. at 8:30, 9:30 and 1:30, Wed. and Fri. at 9:30, day after Labor Day-Columbus Day. Island trips depart Wed. at 7 p.m., late June-Labor Day. Schedule for island trips may vary. Whale-watching trip $22; over 60, $20; ages 4-17, $15. Island trip $15; over 60, $13; ages 4-17,

$12. Reservations are recommended. MC, VI. Phone (603) 964-5545 or (800) 964-5545.

## SALEM (G-5) elev. 147'

CANOBIE LAKE PARK is .2 mi. e., then 1 mi. n. of I-93 exit 2. The amusement park offers more than 85 rides, games and activities and features live entertainment. Highlights include four roller coasters, a Ferris wheel, an 1890s carousel with hand-carved horses, a lake cruise on a paddle wheeler, a replica of a Spanish galleon, two log flume water rides and a water coaster.

Allow 4 hours minimum. Daily noon-10, mid-June through Labor Day; hours vary Sat.-Sun., mid-Apr. to mid-June and day after Labor Day-late Sept. Admission (includes rides and shows) $24 ($15 after 5 p.m.), over age 60 and under 48 inches tall $16, under 2 free. MC, VI. Phone (603) 893-3506.

## SUNAPEE (E-2) elev. 914'

Sunapee is one of several resort communities that line many-lobed, 10-square-mile Lake Sunapee. A vacation spot since the mid-19th century, the area affords a variety of year-round outdoor recreation. The lake's name is derived from a Penacook Indian word believed to mean "wild goose water" or "flying geese." Boat cruises may be taken on the lake.

During the 1860s Sunapee seemed to attract residents with a flair for invention. In 1868 John Smith devised a machine that permitted the local clothespin factory—a major industry at the time—to produce 125 finished clothespins per minute.

The following year, after a decade of study, Enos Clough drove a horseless carriage throughout the area, but its tendency to terrify horses resulted in its being banned. Clough sold the contraption to a Newport man who ran it into a fence; the engine was finally installed in a boat.

New London-Lake Sunapee Region Chamber of Commerce: P.O. Box 532, New London, NH 03257; phone (603) 526-6575 or (877) 526-6575.

MV MT. SUNAPEE II, off SR 11 at Sunapee Harbor, offers 1.5-hour narrated cruises around Lake Sunapee. Loon Island, Georges Mills Bay, Fishers Bay and Mount Kearsarge are among the sights. Trips depart daily at 2, mid-June through Labor Day; Sat.-Sun. at 2, mid-May to mid-June and day after Labor Day to mid-Oct. Fare $14; ages 4-12, $8. AX, MC, VI. Phone (603) 763-4030.

MOUNT SUNAPEE STATE PARK is 3 mi. s. at jct. SRs 103 and 103B. This 2,893-acre recreation area includes a 200-acre network of trails for skiing and hiking. Chairlifts transport winter skiers (see Recreational Activities) and summer sightseers 1.2 miles to the 2,743-foot top of Mount Sunapee. The summit building has an observation platform. There is an exhibition trout pool near the base building. A beach with a bathhouse borders the lake.

Picnicking and swimming are permitted. Food is available. Park open daily dawn-8 p.m. Summer

chairlift operates daily 11-6, mid-June through Labor Day; Sat.-Sun. 9-5, Memorial Day to mid-June. Park free. Beach $3; under 12 free. Summer lift fare $5.50; ages 6-12, $2.50. Phone (603) 763-5561. See Recreation Chart.

## RECREATIONAL ACTIVITIES

### Skiing

- **Mount Sunapee** is on SR 103. Write P.O. Box 2021, Newbury, NH 03255. Other activities are offered. Mon.-Fri. 9-4, Sat.-Sun. and holidays 8-4, mid-Dec. to early Apr. Phone (603) 763-2356.

## TAMWORTH (D-4)

REMICK COUNTRY DOCTOR MUSEUM & FARM is at 58 Cleveland Hill Rd. The father of Dr. Edwin C. Remick began a successful medical practice in the village of Tamworth in 1894 and remained there until his death in 1993. The museum, which was once the home of the Remick family, pays homage to his work through multiple exhibits. A small petting and feeding farm also is on the grounds. Allow 1 hour minimum. Mon.-Sat. 10-4, July-Oct.; Mon.-Fri. 10-4, rest of year. Free. Phone (603) 323-7591 or (800) 686-6117.

## WAKEFIELD (E-5) elev. 681'

MUSEUM OF CHILDHOOD, .5 mi. e. of SR 16 following signs to Wakefield Corner, contains more than 3,000 dolls and toys dating from the mid-1800s, an 1890 one-room schoolhouse with original equipment and a sled collection featuring an original Flexible Flyer from the late 1800s. Allow 1 hour minimum. Mon. and Wed.-Sat. 11-4, Sun. 1-4, Memorial Day weekend-Labor Day. Admission $3; under 10, $1.25. Phone (603) 522-8073.

## WARNER (F-3) elev. 498'

A quiet agricultural village with a few structures dating from the late 1700s, Warner was the birthplace of three of New Hampshire's governors.

SAVE MT. KEARSARGE INDIAN MUSEUM, off I-89 exit 8N, 1 mi. e. on SR 103, then 1 mi. n. on Kearsarge Mountain Rd., depicts the culture and heritage of American Indians. A 10-minute videotape introduces visitors to the museum, followed by a 1-hour guided tour of dioramas and exhibits featuring baskets, canoes, quillwork and other artifacts. The adjacent Medicine Woods area offers a walking tour of 2 acres of plants, shrubs and trees used by various tribes for food, medicine and dyes.

Mon.-Sat. 10-5, Sun. noon-5, May-Oct.; Sat. 10-5, Sun. noon-5, Nov. 1-weekend before Dec. 25. Admission $7; over 61, $6; ages 6-12, $5; family rate $23. MC, VI. Phone (603) 456-2600.

ROLLINS STATE PARK is 5 mi. n. off SR 103. A scenic road winds 3.5 miles up the slope of Mount Kearsarge. A .5-mile trail continues to the 2,937-foot granite summit, with a view encompassing

Lake Sunapee, the White Mountains and mountains in Massachusetts and Vermont. Picnic facilities are available. Daily dawn-dusk, early May to mid-Nov. (weather permitting). Admission $3, under 12 free. Phone (603) 456-3808.

## WEIRS BEACH (E-4)

A boardwalk, waterslide, weekly fireworks displays, yachting, fishing, swimming and other water sports are among the diversions at Weirs Beach, New Hampshire's inland version of a seaside resort.

Weirs Beach lies on the shore of Lake Winnipesaukee. Its name is thought to mean "Smile of the Great Spirit." The title is apt, for island-studded Winnipesaukee is considered one of the most picturesque lakes in the state. It also is the largest; the many bays and deep coves create a 283-mile shoreline.

Endicott Rock, a large boulder, was marked by emissaries of Gov. John Endicott of Massachusetts Colony. Proceeding 3 miles north, they established the northern boundary of Massachusetts, a line that held until the separation of New Hampshire and Massachusetts in 1740.

**Greater Laconia-Weirs Beach Chamber of Commerce:** 11 Veterans Sq., Laconia, NH 03246; phone (603) 524-5531.

SAVE **MOUNT WASHINGTON CRUISES** depart from Weirs Beach docks. The MS *Mount Washington* has operated on Lake Winnipesaukee since 1872. The first boat burned in 1939 and was replaced by the present 1,250-passenger ship. The MV *Doris E.* offers 1- and 2-hour scenic and sunset cruises of the northern end of Lake Winnipesaukee. The MV *Sophie C.* is a U.S. mail boat that offers passengers a glimpse of quaint coves and waterfowl on 2-hour cruises.

MS *Mount Washington* scenic cruises daily at 10 and 12:30 (also at 3, July-Aug.), late May-late Oct.

---

# DID YOU KNOW

The 460-foot-long
Cornish-Windsor Bridge
is reputed to be
the longest covered bridge
in America.

---

MV *Sophie C.* cruises depart Mon.-Sat. at 11 and 2, mid-June to early Sept. MV *Doris E.* cruises daily, late June to Labor Day; phone for departure times. MS *Mount Washington* cruise fare $18; ages 4-12, $9. MV *Sophie C* fare $14; ages 4-12, $7. MV *Doris E.* fare $10; ages 4-12, $5. DC, MC, VI. Phone (603) 366-5531 or (888) 843-6686.

**SURF COASTER,** jct. of SRs 3N and 11B, offers 10 waterslides, a wave pool, and for children, a barefoot action lagoon and spray ground. Food is available. Daily 10-6, late June-Labor Day. Admission $24.95, under 48 inches $17.95, over age 70 and under 3 free. DS, MC, VI. Phone (603) 366-5600.

# WHITE MOUNTAINS AND WHITE MOUNTAIN NATIONAL FOREST

Elevations in the forest range from 440 ft. south of Deer Hill near Colton Brook to 6,228 ft. on Mount Washington. Refer to AAA maps for additional elevation information.

---

North of New Hampshire's central plateau, the White Mountains rise in dramatic relief, cloaked with forests and laced with streams. Among the ranges and ridges are the highest mountains in the Northeast, the Presidential Range, which culminate in the bare granite summit of 6,288-foot Mount Washington *(see place listing p. 104).* Mounts Adams, Jefferson, Monroe and Madison also exceed 5,000 feet in elevation.

Passes known as notches pierce the uplift; Crawford, Dixville, Franconia, Kinsman and Pinkham notches *(see place listings p. 94, 95, 96, 100 and 107)* provide some of the best scenic features in the state. Some 770,000 acres of the region lie within the White Mountain National Forest, which extends into Maine.

The names of several mountains in the southern section of the forest commemorate some of the state's best-known American Indians. Mount Passaconaway honors the chieftain who united 17 tribes into the Penacook Confederacy in the mid-17th century. Mount Kancamagus remembers Passaconaway's grandson Kancamagus, the last sagamore of the confederacy, who strove for peace with white settlers until he was provoked to attack Dover in 1689.

Because the White Mountains are as noted for outdoor recreation—particularly skiing and hiking—as for their beauty, they are one of the nation's most heavily used forest areas. Some of the ski resorts are world renowned. In summer anglers ply the rivers for several species of trout, and campers take advantage of the numerous campgrounds.

From spring through late fall the extensive network of trails, including the Appalachian Trail along the mountains' spine, lures hikers and backpackers. Many places, such as the Great Gulf Wilderness, are accessible only on foot. Only experienced back-country travelers thoroughly familiar with the terrain and weather should attempt the higher elevations—in any season.

There are visitor information centers at Lincoln and Campton and at the Saco Ranger Station at the east end of SR 112 near Conway; phone (603) 745-8720. Plymouth Information Center is open daily 8-4:30; phone (603) 536-1310.

For further information write to the Supervisor, White Mountain National Forest, 719 Main St., Laconia, NH 03246; phone (603) 528-8721, or TTY (603) 528-8722. *See Recreation Chart and the AAA Northeastern CampBook.*

**KANCAMAGUS HIGHWAY** (SR 112), traverses the forest between Conway and Lincoln. It follows the Swift River Valley, passing Rocky Gorge Scenic Area; old Passaconaway and Sabbaday Falls.

Self-guiding trails are near Covered Bridge Campground and at the Passaconaway Historic Site, 12 miles from Conway, near the junction with the Bear Notch road to Bartlett *(see place listing p. 91).* A trail along the Swift River is next to the house; phone the Saco Visitor Center at (603) 447-5448.

# WOLFEBORO (E-4) pop. 2,979, elev. 508'

Known as one of the oldest summer resorts in America, Wolfeboro attained this status in 1768 when Gov. John Wentworth of Massachusetts built the country's first summer home. A marker at the site, 6 miles east on SR 109, commemorates the estate. By the time the governor's manor house burned in 1820, it was no longer unique. Summer homes and resorts now line Lake Wentworth and the southeastern shore of Lake Winnipesaukee. Although it has an air of sedate venerability, modern Wolfeboro is a major lake port.

**Wolfeboro Chamber of Commerce:** P.O. Box 547-TA, Wolfeboro, NH 03894; phone (603) 569-2200.

[SAVE] **CLARK HOUSE MUSEUM COMPLEX,** across from Huggins Hospital on Main St., is a cluster of three historic buildings on the village green. Pleasant Valley School, an 1820 one-room schoolhouse, features 19th-century desks and the Wolfeboro Society Library. The Monitor Engine Co. Firehouse Museum is a replica of an 1862 firehouse with restored firefighting equipment, including a horse-drawn hose wagon and an 1872 steam pumper.

Allow 30 minutes minimum. Wed.-Fri. 10-4, Sat. 10-2, July-Aug. Admission $4, under 12 free. Phone (603) 569-4997.

[SAVE] **THE E. STANLEY WRIGHT MUSEUM,** n.w. of jct. SRs 109 and 28 at 77 Center St., displays memorabilia of the U.S. home front 1939-45. Exhibits illustrate details of American life as well as major events of World War II as they unfolded in Europe and the Pacific. An extensive collection of

vehicles, equipment, clothing and other relics is on permanent display and enhanced by music and news broadcasts of the period, film clips and vintage periodicals.

Allow 1 hour minimum. Mon.-Sat. 10-5, Sun. noon-4, May-Oct.; Sat. 10-4, Sun. noon-4, Nov. 1-22 and in Apr. Admission $6; veterans or over 55, $5; students with ID $3; under 8 free. Phone (603) 569-1212.

**HAMPSHIRE PEWTER COMPANY,** 1 blk. n. of Main St. at 43 Mill St., uses 16th-century techniques to produce quality hollowware and table accessories. It is said to be the only firm in the country to mix and use Queen's Metal, an alloy of tin, antimony, copper, bismuth and silver. A videotape presentation introduces the factory tours.

Allow 30 minutes minimum. Tours Mon.-Fri. at 10, 11, 1, 2 and 3, Memorial Day-Labor Day; Mon.-Fri. at 10, 11, 2 and 3, day after Labor Day-Columbus Day. Free. Phone (603) 569-4944.

**LIBBY MUSEUM** is 3.7 mi. n.w. on SR 109. Natural history and early life in Wolfeboro and the Lakes Region are depicted through collections of mounted animals and Abenaki Indian artifacts. Changing art exhibits, lectures and special programs are offered throughout the season, and children's nature classes are presented in July and August. Tues.-Sat. 10-4, Sun. noon-4, Memorial Day-Labor Day; Thurs.-Sat. 10-4, day after Labor Day-Sept. 30. Admission $2; under 12, $1. Phone (603) 569-1035.

# Vermont

### The Green Mountain State
Verdant mountains offer a wealth of recreational opportunities

### Pretty as a Picture
Pastoral towns provide a backdrop for Norman Rockwell's Americana paintings

### Seasons of Change
Scarlet-colored autumn leaves and winter's snowy peaks make Vermont a kaleidoscope of color

### Step Back in Time
Historic sites and quaint covered bridges take visitors back to yesteryear

### Sugar on Snow
Maple syrup harvests pay homage to the state's sweet staple

Waits River
© H.G. Ross
Robertstock

# a palette of greens

Craftsbury Common / © Gene Ahrens / SuperStock

amuel de Champlain, the French explorer who in 1609 visited what is now Vermont, called it *les verts mont*—"green mountains"— after the lush ridges that form the spine of the state.

The Green Mountains and Green Mountain National Forest in central Vermont certainly live up to their names: From a distance, peaks appear swathed in deep blue-green, the palette of balsam, hemlock and white pine trees.

Visit Vermont and you'll discover its namesake hue just about everywhere.

Maple trees adorned with emerald, five-fingered leaves contribute to the state's maple syrup production, while marble and granite quarries—said to be the world's largest—bolster the economy by increasing greenbacks.

Light green apples hang on orchard trees throughout the state in late summer, awaiting harvest. Fields of kelly green crops show off the state's green thumb.

Rainbow-colored hot air balloons float over dark green valleys and aqua lakes. And various shades of green can be found stitched or woven into quilts, baskets and other Vermont handicrafts.

Golfers aim for greens on more than 67 courses in the state, and hikers explore thickly-wooded terrain.

Consider Vermont your green light to fun and relaxation: Go!

In a cluttered attic, an elderly woman discovers a large book containing portraits of the "Green Mountain State."

Images fill her head as she recalls her childhood days in Vermont. Deciding to revisit a pleasant past, she carefully descends the stairs and fixes herself a cup of tea. Snuggling into an overstuffed chair, she dusts off the cover and cracks the binding.

## Vermont in Kodachrome

Page one: A stark white steeple pierces the deep blue sky. Lofty, green-leafed trees surround the church. A cranberry-colored barn and a lemon-yellow house with white shutters are in the foreground.

It's summer in Stowe, and Mount Mansfield, the state's tallest peak, keeps watch over the town. The outline of the mountain resembles a face, so much so that it's easy to make out the formations locals call the Forehead, Nose and Chin. From the summit, international views are possible; on a clear day you can see the Québec countryside.

The woman sips her tea and flips to page 11: A light blue truck is parked under a red covered bridge. Bands of soft light filter through the wooden lattice on one side wall,

and the outlines of two lip-locked lovers can be seen in the glow of the setting sun.

Page 14: Light from a full moon cloaked in clouds casts a violet glow over a field quilted in white. Squares of snow cling to barn roofs, and pine branches weigh heavy under cold icing. Oak skeletons stretch their spindly arms into the still night air.

She clutches the afghan around her shoulders and turns to page 25. A young girl brushes the shiny, chocolate-brown coat of a Morgan horse, Vermont's state animal and said to be the country's first equine breed. Beyond a white rail fence, a road meanders through grass-covered hills until it meets the sky.

On page 40, buckets are crookedly attached to the trunks of sugar maple trees, tapped to catch oozing sap in spring. Page 41 shows beige, gallon-sized jugs filled with the sugary stuff lining a shelf in an old-fashioned country store. The woman recalls that Vermont produces more maple syrup than any other state; groves and mills in Barton, Cabot, Montpelier, St. Johnsbury and Woodstock contribute to this sweet distinction.

Flames of fall color dominate pages 55 and 56. She can easily distinguish the softwoods from the hardwoods in a photograph

---

French explorer Samuel de Champlain discovers the Green Mountains and the lake that now bears his name.
**1609**

© Bettmann/Corbis

The nation's first marble quarry is begun in East Dorset by Isaac Underhill.
**1785**

Confederate soldiers raid St. Albans in the northernmost land battle of the Civil War.
**1864**

**1775**
Ethan Allen, the Green Mountain Boys and Benedict Arnold capture Fort Ticonderoga from the British.

Library of Congress

**1881**
Native son Chester Arthur is appointed the 21st president of the United States.

# Vermont Historical Timeline

of Green Mountains National Forest. Softwoods remain a deep green, while the leaves on oak, maple, beech, ash and cherry trees display the same crayon-splashed hues as school buses, blackberries, pumpkins and rosy lips.

## How Now, Brown Cow

She laughs as she finds herself on page 68. Cars are at a standstill on a dusty country road, waiting for a herd of brown-splotched dairy cows to cross. One cow has "mooved" closer to observe the humans who consume the cheddar and cottage cheese and the whipped and sour cream she helps to create.

Page 72: Even in a picture, the brilliant glow of the sun shining upon the gilded dome of the capitol—the Vermont State House—is enough to make her squint. Couple that with the six bright-white columns that adorn the Doric-style building and it proves a stately home base for the legislature.

Next, a father searches for the perfect pick off an apple tree while his son slyly taste-tests those already in the bucket. The flush of the boy's cheeks matches the red of the apples, and the scene mimics a Norman Rockwell painting—the artist lived in Arlington 1939-53 and used many townsfolk as models.

She flips to page 93: the granite spire of the Bennington Battle Monument reaches 306 feet into the cloudless sky; a statue of Col. Seth Warner, sword held firmly in hand, fronts the tower.

The monument honors the defeat of the British forces at this site by the Green Mountain boys, a Vermont militia group led by Warner. With the help of Benedict Arnold, they later captured Fort Ticonderoga, N.Y., which contributed to the British surrender at Saratoga in 1777.

Turning to the last page, she is greeted by the gap-toothed grins of two young girls. Their fingers are covered with dripping ice cream, their faces a sticky delight. The sugar cone wrappers display "Ben & Jerry's" in trademark bubble letters, and one of the girls' shirts reads "I loVERMONT."

As she slowly closes the book, she can't think of a reason *not* to love Vermont.

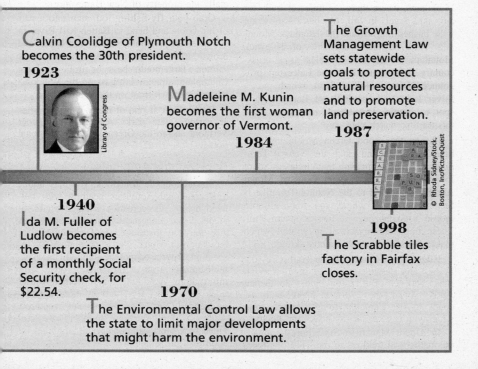

Calvin Coolidge of Plymouth Notch becomes the 30th president.
**1923**

Library of Congress

Madeleine M. Kunin becomes the first woman governor of Vermont.
**1984**

The Growth Management Law sets statewide goals to protect natural resources and to promote land preservation.
**1987**

© Rhoda Sidney/Stock, Boston, Inc/PictureQuest

**1940**
Ida M. Fuller of Ludlow becomes the first recipient of a monthly Social Security check, for $22.54.

**1970**
The Environmental Control Law allows the state to limit major developments that might harm the environment.

**1998**
The Scrabble tiles factory in Fairfax closes.

## Recreation

Question: What are the top three favorite things to do in Vermont? Answer: **Skiing,** skiing and skiing.

Mogul maniacs hit the slopes at Killington/Pico (the "Beast of the East"); Mount Snow; Stratton, the birthplace of **snowboarding;** Bromley in Manchester Center; Okemo in Ludlow; Sugarbush in Warren; Mad River Glen in Waitsfield; Stowe; Smugglers' Notch in Jeffersonville; Burke Mountain in East Burke; and Bolton Valley.

**Snowmobiling** on more than 1,800 miles of well-marked "corridor" throughout the state heats up winter chills. **Cross-country skiing** trails are at Hildene in Manchester Village; Prospect Mountain; and Viking and Wild Wings, both near Arlington.

But Vermont is versatile. **Hiking** and **biking** trails also accommodate cross-country skiers and snowmobilers; **fishing** and **boating** become **icefishing** and **iceboating** in winter; and ski slopes run **alpine slides** in summer. In fall, catch the blast of fiery color from the air while **ballooning** in Quechee.

## Thrills on a Blueberry Hill

Biking is best in central Vermont's Green Mountains, where there are miles of trails for any skill level. In fall, blueberries grow on wild bushes that crowd the Hogback Mountain Trail on the south side of Hogback Mountain, which also doubles as a cross-country skiing path. Ride the Leicester (pronounced Lester) Hollow Trail, which passes Silver Lake and the Falls of Lana, a good spot to **picnic. Horseback riders** also use this trail, so watch your step.

For another good Green Mountains ride, head to Ripton and catch the Natural Turnpike, an 11-mile dirt path that circles to South Lincoln and offers a great view of Mount Abraham. Linking to the Natural Turnpike is Steammill Road, where you may glimpse moose relaxing near a former steam mill. These trails are unplowed in winter, which makes for smooth cross-country skiing.

Hikers love Camel's Hump Trail. Crossing brooks and passing stands of birch trees, it runs between Burlington and Montpelier. Aptly named, the 270-mile Long Trail ascends to the Camel's Hump summit, from which you can see nearby peaks and ponds.

In Mount Mansfield State Forest, numerous paths lead trekkers to the Chin of Mount Mansfield for a spectacular 360-degree panorama. Elephant's Head Trail passes the peregrine falcon habitat (the area is inaccessible during nesting season, February to mid-July). Smugglers' Notch is a pretty passageway between Mount Mansfield and Sterling Peak; access to this trail is just south of Stowe.

The famed Appalachian Trail meanders along the Green Mountains' crown; continue south at Sherbern Pass to intersect with the lower portion of the Long Trail.

## Whatever Floats Your Boat

Put the wind in your sails on expansive Lake Champlain; its shoreline is a picturesque setting for **sailing** and boating. More than 400 other freshwater lakes—especially Lake Seymour, Lake Willoughby, and Caspian and Crystal lakes in the north—are good places to row a boat.

**Rafters** and **canoeists** put in and paddle the waters of the Connecticut, Batten Kill and White rivers. Otter Creek, the longest river in the state, provides a good view of the Green Mountains. The Winooski River starts at Montpelier and runs 58 miles through deep Winooski Gorge, around dams and eventually to Lake Champlain. Or make a splash in an **inner tube** on the Connecticut River (officially the property of New Hampshire).

Grab your **fly-fishing** rod, step into a pair of hip boots and head to Batten Kill River in southwestern Vermont, where wild brook and brown trout swim in clear water. Hook salmon, largemouth bass or trout in Lake Champlain; smallmouth bass on the Winooski River; or brown trout on the White River.

Pitch a tent at one of many **camping** sites at various state parks scattered throughout Vermont and in the Green Mountain National Forest.

## Recreational Activities

Throughout the TourBook, you may notice a Recreational Activities heading with bulleted listings of recreation-oriented establishments listed underneath. Similar operations also may be mentioned in Destination City recreation sections. Since normal AAA inspection criteria cannot be applied, these establishments are presented only for information. Age, height and weight restrictions may apply. Reservations often are recommended and sometimes are required. Addresses and/or phone numbers are provided so visitors can contact the attraction for additional information.

# Fast Facts

**POPULATION:** 608,827.

**AREA:** 9,609 square miles; ranks 43rd.

**CAPITAL:** Montpelier.

**HIGHEST POINT:** 4,395 ft., Mount Mansfield.

**LOWEST POINT:** 95 ft., Lake Champlain.

**TIME ZONE(S):** Eastern. DST.

**MINIMUM AGE FOR DRIVERS:** 18; junior license, 16.

**SEAT BELT/CHILD RESTRAINT LAWS:** Seat belts required for driver and all passengers; child restraints required for under 5.

**HELMETS FOR MOTORCYCLISTS:** Required.

**RADAR DETECTORS:** Permitted.

**FIREARMS LAWS:** Vary by state and/or county. Contact the Vermont State Police Headquarters, Waterbury State Office Complex, Waterbury, VT 05676; phone (802) 244-6941.

**HOLIDAYS:** Jan. 1; Martin Luther King Jr. Day, Jan. (3rd Mon.); Lincoln's Birthday, Feb. 12; Washington's Birthday, Feb. (3rd Mon.); Town Meeting Day, Mar. (1st Tues.); Memorial Day; July 4; Bennington Battle Day, Aug. 16; Labor Day; Columbus Day, Oct. (2nd Mon.); Election Day; Veterans Day, Nov. 11; Thanksgiving; Dec. 25.

**TAXES:** Vermont's statewide sales tax is 5 percent; the town of Williston imposes an additional 1 percent sales tax. The state's Meals and Rooms Tax assesses a tax of 8 percent on lodgings and food and 10 percent on alcoholic beverages.

**STATE INFORMATION CENTERS:** Information booths, open during the summer, are in Alburg, Barre, Bellows Falls, Bennington, Brandon, Brattleboro, Bristol, Burlington, Castleton, Chester, Hardwick, Island Pond, Jeffersonville, Killington, Ludlow, Manchester, Middlebury, Montpelier, Quechee, Randolph, Rutland, St. Albans, St. Johnsbury, Swanton, Vergennes, Waitsfield, Wells River, Wilmington and Woodstock. Year-round welcome centers are open in Montpelier (Mon.-Fri. 8-4:30) and on I-91 at Guilford, on SR 4A at Fair Haven, on I-89 at Highgate Springs and on I-93 at Lower Waterford.

**FURTHER INFORMATION FOR VISITORS:**

Vermont Department of Tourism and Marketing
134 State St.
Montpelier, VT 05602
(800) 837-6668

**RECREATION INFORMATION:**

State of Vermont
Department of Forests, Parks and Recreation
103 S. Main St.
Building 10 South
Waterbury, VT 05671
(802) 241-3655

**FISHING AND HUNTING REGULATIONS:**

Vermont Department of Fish and Wildlife
Agency of Natural Resources
103 S. Main St.
Building 10 South
Waterbury, VT 05671
(802) 241-3700

**NATIONAL FOREST INFORMATION:**

Forest Supervisor
Green Mountain National Forest
231 N. Main St.
Rutland, VT 05701
(802) 747-6700
(877) 444-6777

## Vermont Temperature Averages
### Maximum / Minimum
#### From the records of the National Weather Service

| | JAN | FEB | MAR | APR | MAY | JUNE | JULY | AUG | SEPT | OCT | NOV | DEC |
|---|---|---|---|---|---|---|---|---|---|---|---|---|
| Burlington | 27 | 29 | 38 | 53 | 67 | 77 | 82 | 80 | 71 | 57 | 44 | 31 |
| | 9 | 10 | 20 | 33 | 44 | 54 | 59 | 57 | 49 | 39 | 29 | 15 |

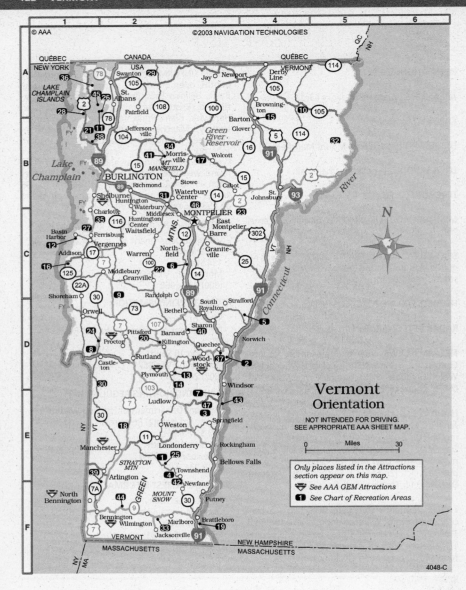

© AAA ©2003 NAVIGATION TECHNOLOGIES

QUÉBEC
CANADA
QUÉBEC
NEW YORK
USA
VERMONT
QC
NH

**A**

QUÉBEC
NEW YORK
LAKE
CHAMPLAIN
ISLANDS
Swanton
St. Albans
Fairfield
Jay
Newport
Derby
Line
Browning-
ton
Barton
Glover
114

**B**

Jefferson-
ville
Green
River
Reservoir
Morris-
ville
Wolcott
MT MANSFIELD
BURLINGTON
Richmond
Stowe
Cabot

Lake
Champlain

**C**

Shelburne
Huntington
Charlotte
Waterbury
Middlesex
Huntington
Center
Waltsfield
Basin
Harbor
Ferrisburg
Vergennes
Addison
Warren
North-
field
Granite-
ville
Waterbury
Center
MONTPELIER
East
Montpelier
Barre

**D**

Shoreham
Middlebury
Granville
Orwell
Pittsford
Proctor
Barnard
Killington
Wood-
stock
Castle-
ton
Rutland
Plymouth
Randolph
Bethel
Sharon
South
Royalton
Strafford
Quechee
Norwich
Windsor

**E**

Manchester
Arlington
North
Bennington
Ludlow
Weston
Londonderry
Townshend
Newfane
Rockingham
Bellows Falls
Springfield

Vermont
Orientation
NOT INTENDED FOR DRIVING.
SEE APPROPRIATE AAA SHEET MAP.

Miles
0        30

Only places listed in the Attractions
section appear on this map.
See AAA GEM Attractions
See Chart of Recreation Areas

**F**

STRATTON
MTN
GREEN
MOUNT
SNOW
Bennington
Wilmington
Marlboro
Jacksonville
Putney
Brattleboro

VERMONT
MASSACHUSETTS
NEW HAMPSHIRE
MASSACHUSETTS

N

4048-C

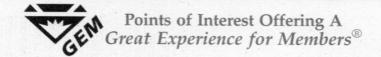

## Points of Interest Offering A
### *Great Experience for Members*®

### Bennington (F-2)

**BENNINGTON BATTLE MONUMENT**—The tallest structure in the state, this 306-foot-tall monument offers a view of three states. See p. 127.

**BENNINGTON MUSEUM**—In addition to regional history displays, this museum contains one of the largest collections of works by folk artist Grandma Moses. See p. 128.

### Manchester (E-1)

**HILDENE**—This 24-room Georgian Revival house was the home of Abraham Lincoln's son Robert Todd Lincoln; their descendants lived here until 1975. See p. 133.

### North Bennington (F-1)

**PARK-McCULLOUGH HOUSE**—When built, this 1865, 35-room Victorian "summer home" had innovative features such as a central heating system. See p. 136.

### Norwich (D-4)

**MONTSHIRE MUSEUM OF SCIENCE**—Lose yourself in science for an afternoon. See p. 137.

### Plymouth (D-2)

**PRESIDENT CALVIN COOLIDGE STATE HISTORIC SITE AT PLYMOUTH NOTCH**—The birthplace and boyhood home of Calvin Coolidge, this site also contains his grave. See p. 137.

### Proctor (D-2)

**WILSON CASTLE**—This 115-acre estate features European and Far Eastern furnishings set in 32 rooms of the 1867 castle. See p. 138.

### Shelburne (B-2)

**SHELBURNE MUSEUM**—Spread over 45 acres, 37 restored historic structures depict early New England life. See p. 140.

### Woodstock (D-3)

**BILLINGS FARM AND MUSEUM**—Visit this modern working dairy farm and learn more about Vermont farm life at the museum. See p. 145.

# RECREATION AREAS

| | MAP LOCATION | CAMPING | PICNICKING | HIKING TRAILS | BOATING | BOAT RAMP | BOAT RENTAL | FISHING | SWIMMING | PETS ON LEASH | BICYCLE TRAILS | WINTER SPORTS | VISITOR CENTER | LODGE/CABINS | FOOD SERVICE |
|---|---|---|---|---|---|---|---|---|---|---|---|---|---|---|---|
| **NATIONAL FOREST** *(See place listing)* | | | | | | | | | | | | | | | |
| **Green Mountain** 350,000 acres. South-central Vermont. | | • | • | • | • | | | • | • | • | | • | | | |
| **ARMY CORPS OF ENGINEERS** | | | | | | | | | | | | | | | |
| **Ball Mountain Dam (E-2)** 2 mi. n.e. of Rawsonville off SR 100. | ❶ | | • | | | | | • | • | | | | | | |
| **North Hartland Dam (D-4)** 1 mi. n. of North Hartland off US 5. | ❷ | • | • | | • | | | • | • | | | | | | |
| **North Springfield (E-3)** .5 mi. n.e. of North Springfield off SR 106. Hunting. | ❸ | | • | | • | | | • | • | | | | | | |
| **Townshend (E-2)** 6 mi. n. of Townshend on SR 30. Hunting. | ❹ | | • | • | | | | • | • | | | | | | |
| **Union Village Dam (D-4)** 5 mi. s. of Thetford Center on SR 132. Hunting. | ❺ | | • | • | | | | • | • | | | | | | |
| **STATE** | | | | | | | | | | | | | | | |
| **Allis (C-2)** 487 acres 5 mi. s. of Northfield on SR 65 off SR 12. Scenic. Hunting. | ❻ | • | • | • | | | | | | • | | | | | |
| **Ascutney (E-3)** 2,506 acres 3 mi. n.w. of Ascutney on SR 44 off US 5. Snowmobiling. | ❼ | • | • | • | | | | | | • | | • | | | |
| **Bomoseen (D-1)** 3,576 acres (two areas) .5 mi. n. of West Castleton. Nature center, nature trails. | ❽ | • | • | • | • | • | • | • | • | • | | • | | | • |
| **Branbury (C-2)** 64 acres 3 mi. e. of Salisbury off US 7 on SR 53. Nature center, nature trails. | ❾ | • | • | • | • | | | • | • | • | | | | • | • |
| **Brighton (A-4)** 610 acres 2 mi. e. of Island Pond off SR 105. Nature center, nature trails. | ❿ | • | • | • | • | • | • | • | • | • | | • | | | |
| **Burton Island (B-2)** 253 acres in Lake Champlain; access by boat only from Kill Kare State Park. Marina, nature center, nature trails. | ⓫ | • | • | • | • | • | | • | • | • | | | | | • |
| **Button Bay (C-1)** 236 acres 7 mi. w. of Vergennes. Nature center, nature trails. | ⓬ | • | • | • | • | • | • | • | • | • | | • | | | |
| **Calvin Coolidge Forest (D-3)** 21,416 acres 2 mi. n. of Plymouth via SR 100A. Snowmobiling. | ⓭ | • | • | • | | | | • | | • | | • | | | |
| **Camp Plymouth (D-3)** 295 acres off SR 100 n. of Ludlow. | ⓮ | | • | • | • | | • | • | • | | | • | | • | • |
| **Crystal Lake (B-4)** 16 acres in Barton on SR 16. | ⓯ | | • | • | | | | • | • | | | | | • | • |
| **DAR (C-1)** 95 acres 1 mi. n. of Chimney Point on SR 17. | ⓰ | • | • | | • | | | • | • | • | | | | | |
| **Elmore (B-3)** 939 acres at Elmore on SR 12. | ⓱ | • | • | • | • | | • | • | • | • | | | | | • |
| **Emerald Lake (E-2)** 720 acres at North Dorset on US 7. Nature center, nature trails. | ⓲ | • | • | • | | | • | • | • | • | | • | | | • |
| **Fort Dummer (F-3)** 217 acres 2 mi. s. of Brattleboro off I-91 exit 1 on Old Guilford Rd. Playground. | ⓳ | • | • | • | | | | | | • | | | | | |
| **Gifford Woods (D-2)** 114 acres 2 mi. n. of Killington on SR 100. | ⓴ | • | • | • | | | | | • | • | | | | | |
| **Grand Isle (B-1)** 226 acres 5 mi. n. of South Hero off US 2. | ㉑ | • | | | • | • | • | • | • | • | | • | • | | |
| **Granville Gulf (C-2)** 1,171 acres. Cross-country skiing. *(See Warren p. 143)* | ㉒ | | • | • | | | | | • | | | • | | | |
| **Groton Forest (C-3)** 26,175 acres (nine areas) midway between Montpelier and St. Johnsbury. Snowmobiling; nature center, nature trails. | ㉓ | • | • | • | • | • | • | • | • | • | | • | | • | • |

# RECREATION AREAS

| | MAP LOCATION | CAMPING | PICNICKING | HIKING TRAILS | BOATING | BOAT RAMP | BOAT RENTAL | FISHING | SWIMMING | PETS ON LEASH | BICYCLE TRAILS | WINTER SPORTS | VISITOR CENTER | LODGE/CABINS | FOOD SERVICE |
|---|---|---|---|---|---|---|---|---|---|---|---|---|---|---|---|
| **Half Moon Pond (D-1)** 50 acres 10 mi. n.w. of Castleton off SR 30. Nature programs. Nature trails. | 24 | • | • | • | | | • | • | • | • | | • | | • | |
| **Jamaica (E-3)** 758 acres 1 mi. e. of Jamaica on SR 30. | 25 | • | • | • | | | | • | • | • | | • | | | |
| **Kill Kare (A-2)** 17.75 acres 4 mi. w. of St. Albans on SR 36, then 3.5 mi. s.w. on Point Rd. | 26 | | • | | • | • | • | • | • | | | | | | |
| **Kingsland Bay (C-1)** 286 acres 4.5 mi. n.w. of Ferrisburg. | 27 | | • | • | • | | | • | • | | | • | | | |
| **Knight Point (A-1)** 54 acres 3 mi. s. of North Hero off US 2. | 28 | | • | | • | | | • | • | | | • | | | |
| **Lake Carmi (A-2)** 588 acres 3 mi. s. of East Franklin on SR 236. Nature trails. | 29 | • | • | • | • | • | • | • | • | • | | • | | • | • |
| **Lake St. Catherine (D-1)** 128 acres 3 mi. s. of Poultney on SR 30. Nature center, nature trails. | 30 | • | • | | • | • | • | • | • | • | | • | | | • |
| **Little River (B-2)** 60 acres 1.5 mi. w. of Waterbury on US 2, then 3.5 mi. n. on Little River Rd. | 31 | • | | • | • | • | • | • | • | • | | | | | |
| **Maidstone State Forest (B-5)** 469 acres 5 mi. s. of Bloomfield on SR 102 then 5 mi. s.w. on State Forest Hwy. Nature trails. | 32 | • | • | • | • | • | | • | • | • | | • | | | |
| **Molly Stark (F-2)** 168 acres 15 mi. w. of Brattleboro off SR 9. | 33 | • | • | • | | | | | | • | | | | | |
| **Mount Mansfield Forest (B-2)** 39,765 acres. Cross-country skiing, downhill skiing, snowmobiling. *(See Mount Mansfield p. 135)* | 34 | • | • | • | • | • | • | • | • | • | | • | | • | |
| **Mount Philo (C-1)** 163 acres 14 mi. s. of Burlington off US 7. Scenic. | 35 | • | • | • | | | | | | • | | • | | | |
| **North Hero (A-1)** 400 acres 8 mi. n. of North Hero off US 2. Nature trails. | 36 | • | • | | • | • | • | • | • | • | | • | | | |
| **Quechee Gorge (D-3)** 688 acres 7 mi. w. of White River Junction off US 4. | 37 | • | • | • | | | | • | | • | | | | | |
| **Sand Bar (B-2)** 20 acres n.w. of Burlington using I-89, exit 17 (Champlain Islands) then 4 mi n on U.S. 2. | 38 | | • | | • | • | • | • | | | | | | | • |
| **Shaftsbury (E-1)** 101 acres 10 mi. n. of Bennington via US 7A. Nature trail. | 39 | | • | | • | | • | • | • | | | | | | • |
| **Silver Lake (D-3)** 34 acres .5mi. e. of Barnard off SR 12. | 40 | • | • | | • | | • | • | • | • | | | | | • |
| **Smuggler's Notch (B-2)** 32 acres 8 mi. w. of Stowe on SR 108. | 41 | • | • | • | | | | • | | • | | | | | |
| **Townshend Forest (F-3)** 1,095 acres 17 mi. n.w. of Brattleboro via SR 30. | 42 | • | • | • | | | | • | | • | | | | | |
| **Wilgus (E-3)** 89 acres 1 mi. s. of Ascutney on US 5. Nature trails. | 43 | • | • | • | | | | • | | • | | | | | |
| **Woodford (F-2)** 400 acres 10 mi. e. of Bennington on SR 9. Nature trails. | 44 | • | • | • | • | | • | • | • | • | | | | | |
| **Woods Island (A-1)** 122 acres 4 mi. n. of Burton Island State Park in Lake Champlain. Permit camping only. | 45 | | • | | • | | | • | • | • | | | | | |
| **Wrightsville Dam (B-3)** 4 mi. n. of Montpelier off SR 12. | 46 | | • | | • | • | | • | • | | | | | | |
| **OTHER** | | | | | | | | | | | | | | | |
| **Stoughton Pond (E-3)** .5 mi. n.e. of Perkinsville off SR 106. | 47 | | • | | • | | | • | • | | | | | | |

# Points of Interest

## ADDISON (C-1)

A small crossroads town, Addison is bounded on the west by sweeping plains that lead to Lake Champlain. At Chimney Point, 8 miles west, a bridge spans the lake to connect Vermont with New York. It is said that Samuel de Champlain stood at Chimney Point on July 30, 1609, and gave his name to the huge body of water that lay before him.

**CHIMNEY POINT STATE HISTORIC SITE,** 8 mi. w. at jct. SRs 17 and 125 at the Champlain Bridge, is a late 18th-century tavern with displays and artifacts relating to this region's history, including the Native American and French heritage in Vermont. Wed.-Sun. 9:30-5, Memorial Day weekend-Columbus Day. Admission $2.50, under 15 free. Phone (802) 759-2412.

**THE DAR JOHN STRONG MANSION MUSEUM** is 1 mi. n. of Crown Point Bridge at 6656 SR 17W. Built in 1785, the mansion is a restored two-story brick house with period furnishings and accented by Colonial herb and perennial gardens. Allow 1 hour minimum. Guided tours Sat.-Sun. 10-6, Memorial Day weekend-Labor Day; by appointment, day after Labor Day-late Sept. and 2 weeks before Memorial Day. Last tour 1 hour before closing. Admission $3; over 59, $2; students with ID $1; family rate $6. Phone (802) 759-2309.

## ARLINGTON (E-2) pop. 1,199, elev. 689′

Founded in 1763 by Jehiel Hawley, a Loyalist, and settled initially by those of like mind, Arlington first was known as Tory Hollow. Because the Green Mountain Boys were active in the area during the Revolution, the Tory town clerk, Isaac Bisco, destroyed all records under his care and fled to Canada.

While visiting Arlington, a British officer reputedly carved the landscape that he saw from his window onto his horn drinking cup. Later the state seal was designed from his endeavor. Further testimony to this period in the town's history is St. James Church Cemetery, dating from 1830, where some old headstones bear interesting inscriptions. SR 7A offers 11 miles of scenic driving for those going north to Manchester Center.

**NORMAN ROCKWELL EXHIBIT,** 3772 SR 7A, occupies a 19th-century church in the artist's hometown 1939-53. Many local residents who modeled for his illustrations serve as hosts May through October. Hundreds of Rockwell's *Saturday Evening Post* covers, illustrations, advertisements and prints are displayed. A 15-minute videotape about Rockwell's life and work is shown regularly.

Allow 1 hour minimum. Daily 9-5, May-Oct.; 10-4, Nov.-Dec. and Feb.-Apr. Closed major holidays. Admission May-Oct. $2. Admission rest of year by donation. Phone (802) 375-6423.

## BARNARD (D-3)

A town of summer cottages and winter hideaways, Barnard was home to some of the state's elite. Journalist Dorothy Thompson and her husband, novelist Sinclair Lewis, lived at their picturesque white frame house, Twin Farms, during the 1930s. Thompson was one of the few female correspondents during World War II and the first woman to address the New York State Chamber of Commerce. She is buried in Village Cemetery on North Road.

## BARRE (C-3) pop. 9,291, elev. 515′

Barre (BARE-ie), often called the granite center of the world, has been the largest granite-producing district in the country since 1900. At the beginning of the 19th century many highly skilled Italian and Scottish stonecutters came to ply their trade. Barre granite, known for its almost flawless texture, comes in two shades, white and blue-gray.

Many large plants produce granite sculpture for use in monuments and tombstones. The Robert Burns Monument at 60 Washington St. was cut by local artisans and is considered one of the finest pieces of granite sculpture in the world. The 24-foot sculpture includes four panels depicting three of his poems, and a 9-foot statue of Burns.

**Central Vermont Chamber of Commerce:** Paine Tpke. and Stewart Rd., P.O. Box 336, Barre, VT 05641; phone (802) 229-5711 or (802) 229-4619.

**ROCK OF AGES—***see Graniteville p. 131.*

## BARTON (B-4) pop. 742, elev. 945′

Originally named Providence, this mill town reputedly had its name changed after a founder—of the same name—so decreed. Crystal Lake State Beach *(see Recreation Chart)* is popular with water enthusiasts.

**Barton Chamber of Commerce:** Box 403, Barton, VT 05822; phone (802) 525-1137.

**THE SUGARMILL FARM,** off I-91 exit 25, then .2 mi. s. on SR 16S to 1296 Glover Rd., offers self-guiding tours of its maple syrup-making facilities. Between mid-February and mid-April, visitors can view syrup production, grading, storage and packaging techniques. The grounds include a maple museum with a 15-minute videotape presentation about the history of maple syrup, a travel information plaza and a fish farm.

Picnicking is permitted. Allow 1 hour minimum. Daily 9-5, May-Oct.; Mon.-Fri. 10-4, rest of year. Phone to confirm off-season schedule. Self-guiding tours and museum free. Phone (802) 525-3701, (802) 525-4746 or (800) 688-7978.

## BASIN HARBOR (C-1)

SAVE **LAKE CHAMPLAIN MARITIME MUSEUM,** on the eastern shore of Lake Champlain at 4472 Basin Harbor Rd., chronicles the history of Lake Champlain. Visitors can watch conservators preserve artifacts. A boathouse displays more than 50 boats of different varieties. Also on the grounds is the *Philadelphia II*, a full-size working replica of Benedict Arnold's gunboat, and a reproduction of an 18th-century blacksmith's shop.

Picnicking is permitted. Daily 10-5, early May to mid-Oct. Admission $10; ages 5-17, $5; under 5 free with a paying adult. Phone (802) 475-2022.

## BELLOWS FALLS (E-3)
pop. 3,165, elev. 298′

Bellows Falls' namesake. and most prominent feature is the falls. Once called the Great Falls, they now are reduced frequently to a trickle because of the power demands of industry. A canal was constructed nearby 1792-1802 for navigation on the Connecticut River from Long Island Sound to Barnet. Its nine locks raised small steamers and barges over the falls until the 1840s when railroads took over the role of transportation.

Notoriety came to Bellows Falls in the person of Hetty Green, the Witch of Wall Street. Her house, now a bank, was at School and Westminster streets. Proclaimed the richest woman in the world in the 1870s, Green was known nationwide for her fabled money management as well as for her eccentricities. According to fellow Vermonters, she liked to "sit on the floor of a bank vault, shuffling her stocks and bonds."

The Connecticut River Valley Byways Center provides visitor information ranging from special events to the popular local fish ladder.

**Great Falls Regional Chamber of Commerce:** The Square, P.O. Box 554, Bellows Falls, VT 05101; phone (802) 463-4280.

SAVE **GREEN MOUNTAIN FLYER,** which departs from Union Railroad Station at 54 Depot St., offers sightseeing trips aboard a 1930s diesel train. Allow 2 hours minimum. Trips depart daily at 11 and 2, mid-Sept. through mid-Oct.; Tues.-Sat. at 11 and 2, late June-Aug. 31. Phone to verify schedule and prices, and for Easter Bunny Express and Santa Express information.

Regular fare $12; ages 3-12, $8; under 3 free when held and not occupying a seat; a senior citizen discount is offered Fri. Easter Bunny and Santa expresses $15; ages 3-12, $12; under 3, $4 when held and not occupying a seat. Fares for special trips vary. Reservations are required for Easter Bunny and Santa expresses and other special trips. Phone (802) 463-3069 or (800) 707-3530.

## BENNINGTON (F-2) pop. 9,168, elev. 728′

Bennington is set in a valley between Mount Anthony, part of the Taconic Range, and the foothills of the Green Mountains *(see place listing p. 131)*. In the Battle of Bennington on Aug. 16, 1777, the Americans under Gen. John Stark defeated a British expedition sent by Gen. John Burgoyne. The conflict is commemorated each year in mid-August on Bennington Battle Day Weekend.

Bennington's three covered bridges are reminders of times gone by. The Silk Road Bridge, Papermill Village Bridge and Bert Henry Bridge all are easily accessible from off SR 67A on Murphy Road; the third bridge also is off SR 67A. US 7A north to Manchester and SR 9 east to Brattleboro provide scenic drives.

Plays and exhibits are presented April through October, while concerts are offered the rest of the year in Bennington Center for the Arts on SR 9. Phone (802) 442-7158 for concert and exhibition information, or (802) 447-0564 for play information.

Hemmings Sunoco Filling Station and Exhibits displays vintage automobiles and automobile memorabilia in an old-fashioned, full-service gas station at 216 Main St.; phone (802) 753-3007.

Ten miles north at 121 Historic SR 7A in Shaftsbury is the Robert Frost Stone House Museum, in which the Pulitzer-Prize-winning poet lived 1920-29. The museum is open Tues.-Sun. 10-5, May-Dec. Phone (802) 447-6200.

Recreational activities possible in the area include downhill and cross-country skiing, snowmobiling, hiking and fishing. Favorite sites are Lake Paran and Lake Shaftsbury State Park *(see Recreation Chart)*.

**Bennington Area Chamber of Commerce:** 100 Veterans Memorial Dr., Bennington, VT 05201; phone (802) 447-3311 or (800) 229-0252.

**Self-guiding tours:** Maps of two walking tours of historic buildings, houses and streets are available from the chamber of commerce as well as a bike tour map and a driving tour map that features covered bridges.

**Shopping areas:** Bennington Potters Gift Shop and Factory Outlet, 324 County Street, offers free tours of the pottery works which produce fine and decorative art pottery for the home. Works in other media are offered in galleries throughout the town.

GEM **BENNINGTON BATTLE MONUMENT,** .5 mi. w. jct. SR 9 and US 7, then n. to the end of Monument Ave. to 15 Monument Cir., was the tallest battle monument in the world when completed in 1891; at 306 feet, it is still the tallest structure in Vermont. From the upper lookout chamber, reached by elevator, three states can be seen. A diorama and exhibit illustrate the battle and the monument. Events are scheduled throughout the season.

Allow 30 minutes minimum. Daily 9-5, second weekend in Apr. through Oct. 31. Admission $2; ages 6-14, $1. Phone (802) 447-0550.

**BENNINGTON MUSEUM** is 1 mi. w. of jct. SRs 7 and 9 on W. Main St. A large collection of paintings by folk artist Grandma Moses is displayed, as are her worktable, equipment and awards. The Grandma Moses Schoolhouse, which the artist attended as a youth, displays her personal belongings, photographs and family memorabilia.

Exhibits include the Bennington Flag, one of the oldest Stars and Stripes flags in existence; firearms; tools; an extensive array of American glass from the 19th to the early 20th century; American paintings and sculpture; and American furniture from the 18th and 19th centuries.

The Bennington Pottery Gallery showcases a renowned collection of 19th-century ceramics produced by local companies. Another gallery features the Wasp, a 1925 luxury touring car. A genealogy library is open to the public.

Allow 1 hour minimum. Daily 9-6, June-Oct.; 9-5, rest of year. Closed Jan. 1, Thanksgiving and Dec. 25. Admission $7, over 61 and students with ID $6, under 12 free. Phone (802) 447-1571.

**OLD FIRST CHURCH** (Congregational) is at 1 Monument Cir. in Old Bennington Village. The church organization, dating from 1762, is among the oldest in Vermont. Built 1805-06, the church is regarded as one of the more beautiful in New England. The restored building features vaulted ceilings of plaster and wood as well as historic box pews. Mon.-Sat. 10-noon and 1-4, Sun. 1-4, July 1-Columbus Day; Sat. 10-noon and 1-4, Sun. 1-4, Memorial Day weekend-June 30. Donations. Phone (802) 447-1223.

**Old Burying Ground** contains the graves of the founders of Bennington, soldiers killed in the Battle of Bennington, six Vermont governors and the poet Robert Frost, whose epitaph is "I had a lover's quarrel with the world."

## BETHEL (D-3) elev. 569′

According to Biblical lore, Jacob once slept in a field with only a stone for a pillow. Upon awakening, he set up the stone, saying that the name of the place would be Bethel. When a grantee dreamed of this passage, Bethel was thusly named. In order to fulfill Biblical prophecy, every stone on the ground of the site of the Church at Bethel Gilead, located on SR 12 between Bethel and Randolph, was incorporated into the foundation.

**WHITE RIVER NATIONAL FISH HATCHERY, 2** mi. w. on SR 107, following signs, has a visitor center with displays depicting the hatchery's work of restoring Atlantic salmon to the Connecticut River. The fish once thrived in New England rivers and streams, but by the mid-1800s dam construction and overfishing had drastically reduced their population. At the outdoor aquaculture pond, visitors can view fish at various developmental stages. Picnicking is permitted. Allow 30 minutes minimum. Daily 8-3. Free. Phone (802) 234-5241.

## BRATTLEBORO (F-3) pop. 8,289, elev. 226′

"Where Vermont Begins," is the adopted slogan of Brattleboro; it was here that the state's first permanent European settlement, Fort Dummer, was established in 1724.

Rudyard Kipling built a house for his bride north of Brattleboro in Dummerston. He wrote "Captains Courageous," "Just So Stories" and the two "Jungle Book" stories during his residence there; the house is not open to the public. Also of interest is Brooks Memorial Library, which has changing art and photography exhibits and a children's floor; phone (802) 254-5290.

Running west to Bennington is scenic SR 9, which offers spectacular views at Hogback Mountain.

**Brattleboro Area Chamber of Commerce:** 180 Main St., Brattleboro, VT 05301; phone (802) 254-4565.

**THE *BELLE OF BRATTLEBORO*** departs from the marina off I-91 exit 3, then s. 1.5 mi. on US 5 (Putney Rd.). This flat-bottom, 49-passenger wooden vessel provides 75-minute scenic cruises on the Connecticut River. Passengers hear historical anecdotes and have the opportunity to see the area's abundant wildlife.

Allow 1 hour minimum. Departures Wed.-Fri. at noon and 4, Sat.-Sun. at noon, 3:30 and 7, June 1 through mid-Oct. Phone to verify schedule. Fare $10-$12; senior citizens and students with ID $8-$10; ages 5-16, $5-$6. MC, VI. Phone (802) 254-1263.

**BRATTLEBORO MUSEUM AND ART CENTER,** off I-91 via SR 5 to Main and Vernon sts., is in the former Union Railroad Station. Four galleries present changing exhibits about traditional and contemporary visual arts and history. A fifth gallery houses a permanent collection about the history of Estey Organ Co. Allow 1 hour minimum. Tues.-Sun. noon-6, mid-May through mid-Dec.; closed holidays. Admission $3, over 61 and students with ID $2. Phone (802) 257-0124.

## BROWNINGTON (A-4)

[SAVE] **OLD STONE HOUSE MUSEUM,** off Hinman Rd., 2.5 mi. n. of Orleans, is in a four-story granite structure known as Athenian Hall. Built by Alexander Twilight, the country's first African-American college graduate, and completed in 1836, it served as a dormitory for schoolchildren. Displays include the collections of Orleans County Historical Society, Early American furniture, decorative arts, rural antiques and other artifacts.

Allow 1 hour minimum. Wed.-Sun. 11-5, May 15-Oct. 15. Admission $5, students with ID $2. Phone (802) 754-2022.

# BURLINGTON (B-2) pop. 38,889, elev. 112'

Built on the terraced slopes of Lake Champlain, Burlington is the largest city in Vermont and is an important industrial, retail and educational center. It is the headquarters of navigation on the lake and a principal port of air entry on the United States-Canada border.

The area first was settled in 1775, but most of its inhabitants left with the onset of the American Revolution, and settlement did not resume until after the war. Revolutionist Ethan Allen tended a farm north of the city and is buried in Greenmount Cemetery.

The city's oldest section is along Battery Street near the lakefront. Other historic areas are Pearl, South Willard and Church streets, the University Green and City Hall Park. Church Street Marketplace, a four-block pedestrian mall, is in the historic district.

On the upper level of town is the University of Vermont, founded in 1791. The Vermont Mozart Festival, held early July to early August, offers chamber-music concerts.

Burlington is at the end of the scenic portion of two highways: I-89, which runs 95 miles southeast to White River Junction, and SR 7, which runs south to Middlebury.

**Lake Champlain Regional Chamber of Commerce:** 60 Main St., Suite 100, Burlington, VT 05401; phone (802) 863-3489.

**Shopping areas:** Burlington Square Mall, I-89 exit 14W, features more than 40 stores. Champlain Mill, off I-89 in Winooski, is a renovated late 19th-century woolen mill that contains specialty shops and restaurants. Downtown, Church Street Marketplace provides shops, services and restaurants in a festive atmosphere that includes street musicians and sidewalk cafes. Mall 189, 516 Shelburne Rd., caters to bargain hunters. The University Mall on Dorest St. is home to more than 75 stores.

**BATTERY PARK,** downtown at the foot of Pearl St., was the 1812 scene of an engagement between U.S. land batteries and British vessels on Lake Champlain. The park affords scenic views and free summer concerts Thursday and Sunday. Daily dawn-dusk. Free.

**ETHAN ALLEN HOMESTEAD,** 1 mi. n. on SR 127 (the Beltline), take the North Ave. Beaches exit, then right at the small brown sign, was once the home of Ethan Allen. The homestead encompasses a timber frame house and several acres of land traversed by hiking trails. Guided tours include the restored farmstead, a multimedia show and the museum exhibits.

Picnicking is permitted. Allow 1 hour minimum. Mon.-Sat. 10-5, Sun. 1-5, May-Oct.; Sat 10-4, rest of year. Phone to verify schedule. Admission $5; over 65, $4; ages 5-17, $2.50; family rate $14. Phone (802) 865-4556.

**ETHAN ALLEN PARK,** 2.5 mi. n. on North Ave. to the w. end of College St., includes part of the farm once owned by Ethan Allen. A tower offers good views of Lake Champlain and the Adirondack Mountains. Recreational paths, a seasonal ferry and scenic boat cruises are available. Wed.-Sun. and holidays noon-8, Memorial Day weekend-Labor Day. Free.

**LAKE CHAMPLAIN FERRIES—**
*see Lake Champlain p. 132.*

**ROBERT HULL FLEMING MUSEUM,** 61 Colchester Ave. on the University of Vermont campus, opened in 1931. Displays of European, American, African, ancient Egyptian and Middle Eastern art, as well as paintings by 20th-century Vermont artists are featured. Rotating exhibits are shown periodically.

Tues.-Fri. 9-4, Sat.-Sun. 1-5, day after Labor Day through Apr. 30; Tues.-Fri. noon-4, Sat.-Sun. 1-5, rest of year. Closed major-holiday weekends. Admission $3; over 59 and ages 7-17, $2; family rate $5 (two adults and all minor children). Phone (802) 656-0750.

**SHELBURNE MUSEUM—**
*see Shelburne p. 140.*

*SPIRIT OF ETHAN ALLEN III* departs from Burlington Boat House at the bottom of College St. The 500-passenger, triple-deck cruise ship

offers sightseeing cruises on Lake Champlain; an audiotape provides information about Revolutionary War battles and local history. Brunch, lunch, nightly dinner and murder mystery cruises also are offered; reservations are required for dinner cruises.

Food is available. Ninety-minute sightseeing cruises depart every 2 hours daily 10-4, mid-May to mid-Oct. Sightseeing fare $9.95; ages 3-11, $3.95. AX, DS, MC, VI. Phone (802) 862-8300.

## CABOT (B-3) pop. 239

The town was named in honor of settler Lyman Hitchcock's bride, Miss Cabot of Connecticut. The first settlement in the area was on Cabot Plains, also known as Hazen Road.

Cabot was the birthplace of Zerah Colburn, a mathematical genius who, before he could read or write, could multiply two six-digit numbers in his head, calculating the correct answer in seconds. Born in 1804, Colburn was hailed as a boy wonder throughout America and Europe. He later became a teacher and clergyman at Norwich University (see Northfield).

**CABOT CREAMERY,** 2870 Main St., is a working creamery where the processing cheddar cheeses and cultured packaging can be viewed through observation windows. Thirty-minute guided tours include a videotape presentation. Free cheddar samples are offered. Tours daily every half-hour 9-5, June through Oct.; Mon.-Sat. 10-4, rest of year. Last tour begins 30 minutes before closing. Phone ahead for cheese-making schedule. Tour $1, under 12 free. Phone (802) 563-3393 or (800) 837-4261.

**GOODRICH'S MAPLE FARM,** 2427 US 2 half way between Marshfield and West Danville, offers tours that outline the production process for maple syrup, from the tree to the table. Displayed is one of the world's largest maple sap evaporators. Visitors can talk with the people who do the sugaring. Antique implements used in this family business begun in 1840 can be seen. Free syrup samples is available. Mon.-Sat. 9-5; closed holidays. Free. Phone (802) 426-3388 or (800) 639-1854.

## CASTLETON (D-2) elev. 441′

A resort area around Lake Bomoseen, Castleton is a town of historic significance and architectural charm. It was at Zadock Remington's tavern that the Green Mountain Boys, led by Ethan Allen and Seth Warner, planned their successful attack on Fort Ticonderoga during the Revolutionary War.

Marked by Ionic and Corinthian columns, porticoes, archways and Palladian motifs, many houses represent the style of architect Thomas Dake, who became a town resident around 1807. These well-preserved houses delight photographers and sightseers. Another pleasant diversion for sightseers is a scenic drive along SR 30 south to Manchester Center.

**HUBBARDTON BATTLEFIELD STATE HISTORIC SITE,** 7 mi. n. of US 4 on Monument Rd. at Hubbardton, is the site of the only Revolutionary War battle fought on Vermont soil. On July 7, 1777, Colonial troops in retreat from Fort Ticonderoga and Mount Independence delayed the pursuing British and Hessian forces. A diorama, interpretive display and relief map depict the battle.

Allow 1 hour minimum. Wed.-Sun. 9:30-5, Memorial Day weekend-Columbus Day. Admission $2; ages 6-24, $1.50. Phone (802) 273-2282, or (802) 759-2412 in the off season.

## CHARLOTTE (C-2) elev. 176′

Established in the late 18th century on the stagecoach route between Burlington and Troy, Charlotte (char-LOT) rivaled nearby Burlington in size during the early 1800s. The historic district east of SR 7 has many notable buildings dating from the town's early days. Charlotte also boasts three covered bridges: one spans Holmes Creek on a town road north of the Charlotte ferry; two others cross Lewis Creek in East Charlotte.

**LAKE CHAMPLAIN FERRIES—** see Lake Champlain p. 132.

SAVE   **VERMONT WILDFLOWER FARM,** on US 7, has 5 acres of public display gardens. Interpretive markers along a self-guiding trail explain the legends and practical uses of the hundreds of species in the gardens. Allow 1 hour minimum. Daily 9-6, Mar.-Dec. Admission $3. MC, VI. Phone (802) 425-3641.

## DERBY LINE (A-4) pop. 776, elev. 1,042′

**HASKELL FREE LIBRARY AND OPERA HOUSE** (La Bibliothèque Haskell et la Salle d'Opéra) lies directly on the international boundary. The stage sits in Canada and most of the 400 seats are in the United States. Guided opera house tours are available. Library open Tues.-Wed. and Fri.-Sat. 10-5, Thurs. 10-8. Opera House tours Tues.-Wed. and Fri.-Sat. 10-5, Thurs. 10-8, May-Oct. Library free. Opera house tour $2. Phone (802) 873-3022, or (819) 876-2471 in Québec.

## EAST MONTPELIER (C-3)

**BRAGG FARM SUGAR HOUSE,** 1005 SR 14N, is a fifth-generation family-operated maple sugar house offering educational tours which describe the history and practices of the maple sugar process. Visitors can hike through 30 acres of maple trees. Free tastings are offered. Daily 8:30-8, June-Aug.; 8-7, Sept.-Oct.; 8:30-6, rest of year. Closed Jan. 1, Thanksgiving and Dec. 25. Free. Phone (802) 223-5757 or (800) 376-5757.

## FAIRFIELD (A-2) elev. 356′

**PRESIDENT CHESTER A. ARTHUR STATE HISTORIC SITE** is 5 mi. n.e. on SR 36, following signs. The replica of the Arthur house contains an interpretive exhibit about the life of the 21st president of the United States, who was born in Fairfield in 1829. The brick church where Arthur's father preached stands nearby and features an exhibit about meetinghouse and church architecture in Vermont.

Allow 1 hour minimum. Wed.-Sun. 11-5, Memorial Day weekend-Columbus Day. Donations. Phone (802) 828-3051.

## FERRISBURG (C-2) elev. 176′

SAVE **ROKEBY MUSEUM**, 4334 US 7, was the home of the late-19th-century author, illustrator and naturalist Rowland E. Robinson; it looks much as it did at the end of the 19th century. Eight rooms contain furnishings and personal items spanning the Robinson family's occupancy from the 1790s to the 1960s. Eight outbuildings are on the grounds, a documented stop of the Underground Railroad.

Allow 1 hour minimum. Guided tours are given Thurs.-Sun. at 11, 12:30 and 2, mid-May to mid-Oct. Admission $6; over 64 and students with ID $4; under 12, $2. Phone (802) 877-3406.

## GLOVER (B-4) elev. 946′

**BREAD AND PUPPET MUSEUM**, .5 mi. s. on SR 16 to 753 Heights Rd./SR 122, is housed in a transformed 19th-century barn that contains a large collection of some of the biggest puppets in the United States, as well as masks and graphics of Bread and Puppet Theater. The theater presents traveling puppet shows which range from theater pieces presented by members of the company to extensive outdoor pageants.

Allow 1 hour minimum. Daily 10-6, June-Oct.; by appointment rest of year. Donations. Phone (802) 525-3031 or (802) 525-6972.

## GRANITEVILLE (C-3)

SAVE **ROCK OF AGES** is at 560 Graniteville Rd., following signs; from I-89 take exit 6. Guided tours of the 1880 quarry show the drilling, blasting and removal of stone from the 550-foot-deep, 50-acre hole carved out of the hillside over the last century. The Manufacturing Division is one of the largest granite plants in the world. The observation deck overlooks cutting, polishing and rubber-cutting operations.

Allow 1 hour minimum. Visitor center open Mon.-Sat. 8:30-5, Sun. noon-5, May-Oct. Manufacturing Division open Mon.-Fri. 8-3:30. A 30-minute shuttle tour of the active quarry departs about every 45 minutes Mon.-Fri. 9:15-3, June 1 to mid-Oct. (weather permitting). Visitor center closed July 4. Admission free. Shuttle fare $4; over 62, $3.50; ages 6-12, $1.50. AX, DS, MC, VI. Phone (802) 476-3119.

## GRANVILLE (C-2) elev. 1,013′

**GRANVILLE MANUFACTURING COMPANY** is on SR 100, 4.3 mi. n. jct. SR 125. Guided tours offer visitors insights into the art and tradition of the manufacture of one-piece wooden bowls and

quarter-sawn clapboard siding. Allow 1 hour minimum. Tours depart Mon.-Fri. 7-2:45. Bowl Barn open daily 9-5. Closed major holidays. Tours free. Phone (802) 767-4747 or (800) 828-1005.

## GREEN MOUNTAINS AND GREEN MOUNTAIN NATIONAL FOREST

Elevations in the forest range from 878 ft. near Rochester to 4,083 ft. Mount Ellen in Warren. Refer to AAA maps for additional elevation information.

Extending the length of the Vermont, the Green Mountains comprise several distinct ranges. The highest peaks lie in the north; several—including Mount Mansfield (see place listing p. 135), the highest mountain in Vermont—exceed 4,000 feet.

The 370,000-acre Green Mountain National Forest extends nearly two-thirds the length of Vermont along the main range of the Green Mountains. The forest is divided into two sections. The southern half stretches from the Vermont-Massachusetts border to SR 140 near Wallingford; the northern half extends from US 4 northeast of Rutland to SR 17 near Bristol.

Six wilderness areas as well as White Rocks National Recreation Area south of Wallingford are encompassed by the forest. The forest headquarters is in Rutland with district offices in Manchester Center, Middlebury and Rochester.

The forest's natural resources play an important role in the economy of Vermont and the Northeast. The scenic beauty of the region and a broad range of recreational opportunities attract thousands to the area. More than 500 miles of trails, including the Appalachian/Long Trail and the Robert Frost National Recreation Trail, traverse the gentle peaks and lush forests.

Developed campgrounds and picnic sites are available as well. For more information write the Forest Supervisor, Green Mountain National Forest, 231 N. Main St., Rutland, VT 05701; phone (802) 747-6700. See Recreation Chart and the AAA Northeastern CampBook.

## HUNTINGTON (B-2)

Green Mountain Audubon Center is a 255-acre sanctuary of fields, thickets, ponds, streams, a forest, a swamp and a river. Many types of wildlife are protected. A visitor center has exhibits; 5 miles of trails lead through the various habitats. A rope-guided sensory trail for the visually-impaired has signs in Braille. Phone (802) 434-3068.

SAVE **BIRDS OF VERMONT MUSEUM**, 1 mi. w. at 900 Sherman Hollow Rd., contains 175 exhibits, including 442 life-size carvings of birds. Each display includes a male and a female of the species as well as the nest, eggs and vegetation typical of their habitat. A bird observation area with live sound is available. Allow 1 hour minimum. Daily 10-4, May-Oct.; by appointment rest of year.

Admission $5; over 60, $4; ages 3-11, $2.50. Phone (802) 434-2167.

## HUNTINGTON CENTER (C-2)

**CAMEL'S HUMP STATE PARK,** 16,654 acres, encompasses 4,083-foot Camel's Hump and several areas of virgin spruce. Called "Le Lion Couchant" (the sleeping lion) by French explorers, Camel's Hump is one of the few undeveloped peaks among the highest mountains in Vermont. Scenic trails lead to the summit, where fragile alpine vegetation grows. The Long Trail, which extends the length of the state along the Green Mountains, traverses the park. Daily 24 hours. Free. Phone (802) 241-3655.

## JACKSONVILLE (F-3) pop. 237, elev. 1,334'

### WINERIES

- **North River Winery,** on SR 112. Daily 10-5; closed Jan. 1, Thanksgiving and Dec. 25. Phone (802) 368-7557.

## JAY (A-3)

Near the Canadian border in the shadow of Jay Peak, Jay is named after the statesman John Jay. Known for its winter sports facilities, the town offers access to year-round recreation in Jay Peak State Forest.

**Jay Peak Area Association:** P.O. Box 177, Troy, VT 05868; phone (802) 988-2259.

### RECREATIONAL ACTIVITIES

#### Skiing

- **Jay Peak Ski Resort,** off SR 242 in Jay State Forest. Write P.O. Box 152, Jay, VT 05859. Other activities are offered. Daily week before Thanksgiving-Apr. 30 (weather permitting). Phone (802) 988-2611 or (800) 451-4449.

## JEFFERSONVILLE (B-3) pop. 568, elev. 460'

**MARY BRYAN MEMORIAL ART GALLERY,** 180 Main St., displays works of local and regional artists. Paintings range from watercolor to oil and are of traditional New England scenery. Daily 11-5, June 1-late Oct. Free. Phone (802) 644-5100.

## KILLINGTON (D-3)

On the summit of Killington Peak, the Rev. Samuel Peters, a Connecticut clergyman, claimed to have named the state "Verdmont," "in token that her mountains and hills shall be ever green, and shall never die."

Though well-intentioned, the remark suggests that perhaps the reverend was not a skier. With its long snow season and challenging peaks, today's Killington is home to one of the largest ski resorts in the East. Other popular winter recreational activities include snowmobiling, snowshoeing and cross-country skiing. When green returns to the

mountains, the area provides abundant opportunities for hiking, mountain biking, tennis and golf.

**Killington Chamber of Commerce:** P.O. Box 114, US 4, Killington, VT 05751; phone (802) 773-4181 or (800) 337-1928.

### RECREATIONAL ACTIVITIES

#### Skiing

- **Killington Resort,** w. via US 4 in Calvin Coolidge State Forest. Write 4763 Killington Rd., Killington, VT 05751. Other activities are available. Mon.-Fri. 9-4, Sat.-Sun. and holidays 8-4, mid-Oct. through early June. Phone (802) 422-6200 or (800) 621-6867.

## LAKE CHAMPLAIN (B-1)

Extending from Canada southward for 120 miles, Lake Champlain varies from a quarter of a mile to 12 miles wide. Two-thirds of its area lies in Vermont; the rest, except for a small Canadian portion, is in New York. Lake Champlain—with its Hudson River connector, the Champlain Canal—accommodates large vessels to make navigation possible from New York City to Montréal and the Great Lakes. Lake Champlain briefly enjoyed the federal designation of the sixth Great Lake; after 2 months that designation was removed.

Legends of Lake Champlain's own version of the Loch Ness Monster have persisted since Samuel de Champlain sighted what he described as a serpentine creature 20 feet long, as thick as a barrel and with a head like a horse. Occasional sightings of the elusive creature, affectionately named "Champ," still occur, but whether a distant cousin of the legendary Scottish sea serpent really resides in the lake remains a matter of speculation.

**LAKE CHAMPLAIN FERRIES** offers scenic links between Vermont and New York via three crossings: Burlington to Port Kent, N.Y. (crossing time 1 hour); Charlotte to Essex, N.Y. (crossing time 20 minutes); Grand Isle to Plattsburgh, N.Y. (crossing time 12 minutes). AAA clubs have schedules and fares. Contact the Lake Champlain Transportation Co., King Street Dock, Burlington, VT 05401; phone (802) 864-9804.

## LAKE CHAMPLAIN ISLANDS (A-1)

Lake Champlain Islands is a picturesque summer resort area, affording a broad expanse of inland sea with the Adirondack Mountains on the west and the Green Mountains on the east. US 2 off I-89 connects the islands with the Vermont mainland, New York and Canada.

St. Anne's Shrine on Isle La Motte is on the site of Fort Ste. Anne, the first European settlement in Vermont. The shrine contains a statue of Samuel de Champlain that was sculpted at Expo '67 in Montréal.

Herrmann's Royal Lipizzan Stallions spend the summer in nearby North Hero. The barn is open to the public when performances are not being held. Shows are offered four times per week. Contact the chamber for information.

**Lake Champlain Islands Chamber of Commerce:** P.O. Box 213, North Hero, VT 05474; phone (802) 372-8400.

**HYDE LOG CABIN** is on US 2 in Grand Isle. Built in 1783 and considered the oldest existing log cabin in the nation, it is furnished with domestic items depicting rural life. Allow 30 minutes minimum. Thurs.-Mon. 11-5, Memorial Day weekend-Columbus Day. Admission $1. Phone (802) 828-3051.

## LONDONDERRY (E-3) elev. 1,115′

**Londonderry Area Chamber of Commerce:** P.O. Box 58, Londonderry, VT 05148; phone (802) 824-8178.

## RECREATIONAL ACTIVITIES
### Skiing

• **Magic Mountain**, on Magic Mountain Access Rd. off SR 11. Write P.O. Box 524, Londonderry, VT 05148. Daily 8:30-4, late Nov.-early Apr. Phone (802) 824-5645.

## LUDLOW (E-2) pop. 958, elev. 1,064′

Situated on SR 100/103 along the Black River, Ludlow offers views of mountain ranges, lakes and fertile farmland. Ludlow pioneered the manufacture of reworked wool to combat cloth shortages after the Civil War.

Ludlow is home to the 600-acre campus of the Fletcher Farm School for the Arts and Crafts, 611 Route 103 South, where artisans and craftspersons have been teaching the general public traditional techniques and exploring new media and methods since 1947. Classes generally last from 2 to 5 days. In the summer a shop features items made by members of the Society of Vermont Craftsmen. Phone (802) 228-8770 for class information and shop schedule.

**Okemo Valley Regional Chamber of Commerce:** P.O. Box 333, Ludlow, VT 05149; phone (802) 228-5830.

**BLACK RIVER ACADEMY MUSEUM** is at 14 High St. The academy opened in 1885 and drew students from all over New England until it closed in 1938; the facilities now house a fiber textile school. Manuscripts, photographs, tools and other items illustrate late 19th-century life in rural Ludlow and the Black River Valley. An exhibit is dedicated to President Calvin Coolidge, an 1890 graduate.

Allow 30 minutes minimum. Tues.-Sat. noon-4, Memorial Day weekend-Labor Day; Fri.-Sat. noon-4, day after Labor Day-Columbus Day; by appointment rest of year. Admission $2, students with ID $1. Phone (802) 228-5050.

## MANCHESTER (E-1) pop. 602, elev. 695′

Manchester, a year-round resort area guarded by Mount Equinox to the west, encompasses the communities of Manchester, Manchester Depot and Manchester Center. Elm-lined streets and marble sidewalks characterize Manchester, which is primarily residential; Manchester Center is more of a business area.

**Manchester & The Mountains Chamber of Commerce:** 5046 Main St., Suite 1, Manchester Center, VT 05255; phone (802) 362-2100 or (800) 362-4144.

**Shopping areas:** Highridge Plaza, Manchester Square on SR 7A and Manchester Commons & Manchester Marketplace on SR 11/30 all house factory outlets.

**HILDENE**, 1.5 mi. s. on US 7A to 1005 Hildene Rd., is a 24-room Georgian Revival mansion built as the summer home of Robert Todd Lincoln, Abraham Lincoln's only son to live to maturity. Lincoln descendants lived in the house until 1975. The house contains original furnishings, an Aeolian 1,000-pipe organ and family memorabilia. The formal gardens offer a panoramic view of the mountains.

Allow 1 hour, 30 minutes minimum. Guided tours are given daily on the half-hour 9:30-3, mid-May through Oct. 31; Sat.-Sun. 10-3, Thanksgiving Day weekend-Dec. 31. Cross-country skiing is available mid-Dec. to early Mar. for a fee; equipment rentals are available. Guided house tours $10; ages 6-14, $5. Grounds only $5; ages 6-14, $2. Phone for skiing fee. AX, DS, MC, VI. Phone (802) 362-1788.

**MOUNT EQUINOX**, on US 7A, 5 mi. s. of jct. SRs 11 and 30, is owned by a Carthusian Monastery. At 3,835 feet, the mountain is the highest peak in the Taconic Range. The view from the summit encompasses parts of New York, New Hampshire, Massachusetts and Québec. The summit is reached by a 5-mile paved road with guardrails, steep grades and sharp curves.

**Note:** Vehicles larger than a 7-passenger minivan, a full-size pickup truck, or a small camper are not permitted. Motorhomes are prohibited.

Hiking trails and picnic facilities are available at the summit. Daily 9-dusk, May-Oct. (weather permitting). Toll $6 per private vehicle and driver ($2 per passenger over age 12), $5 per motorcycle and driver ($2 per passenger over age 12). Phone (802) 362-1115.

**SOUTHERN VERMONT ARTS CENTER** is off US 7A, following signs to 930 Southern Vermont Arts Center Dr., on the slope of Mount Equinox. On a 740-acre campus, the center includes the Elizabeth de C. Wilson Museum of paintings and sculptures; the 400-seat Louise Arkell Pavilion; Yester House crafts galleries; a sculpture garden; and botany and hiking trails.

## Maple Syrup

American Indians taught Colonial settlers how to boil down the "sweet water" from maple trees into syrup by dropping hot stones into hollowed logs filled with sap. Though methods have since evolved, the principle behind making syrup has remained unchanged for centuries.

The trees—primarily sugar maples— are tapped during late winter and early spring, when a cycle of freezing and thawing causes the sap to rise. Elaborate arrays of plastic tubing that channel the sap to storage tanks and centralized evaporator plants have largely replaced collecting buckets and individual sugar-

Digital Archives

houses. Colorless and low in sugar, the sap must be boiled to concentrate the sugar and obtain the characteristic color and flavor of maple syrup. A mature maple tree yields about 8 gallons of sap; a single gallon of syrup requires 30 to 50 gallons of sap.

Maple syrup ranges from grade A (fancy), a translucent amber syrup with a delicate flavor, through B and C, which are progressively darker, heavier and stronger in taste. Grade C is used primarily in cooking.

With its extensive stand of sugar maples and ideal weather and soil, northeastern North America remains the only area where maple syrup is produced. The largest producers in order of rank are Québec, Vermont, New York, Ontario, Wisconsin, Ohio, Michigan, New Hampshire, Pennsylvania, Massachusetts and Maine.

Food is available 11:30-2, mid-May to late Oct. Allow two hours minimum. Tues.-Sat. 10-5, Sun. noon-5, mid-May to late Oct.; Mon.-Sat. 10-5, Dec.-Mar. Admission $6, students with ID $3, under 13 free. MC, VI. Phone (802) 362-1405.

### RECREATIONAL ACTIVITIES

#### Skiing

• **Bromley,** 6 mi. e. of Manchester Center on SR 11 on Bromley Mountain. Write P.O. Box 1130, Manchester Center, VT 05255. Other activities are available. Mon.-Fri. 9-4, Sat.-Sun. 8:30-4, Thanksgiving weekend through mid-Apr. Phone (802) 824-5522.

## MARLBORO (F-3) elev. 1,736'

Marlboro was settled in 1763 by two families who separately endured the hardships of pioneer life for more than a year before discovering they were neighbors. Today the town is the site of Marlboro College, with an enrollment of nearly 300, and a summer music school founded by pianist Rudolf Serkin.

## MIDDLEBURY (C-2) pop. 6,252, elev. 366'

Midway between Salisbury and New Haven, Middlebury was founded in 1761. Middlebury College was chartered in 1800; present enrollment exceeds 2,000. The campus includes Painter Hall, Vermont's oldest college building, built in 1816. Emma Hart Willard, a pioneer in American women's education, began her work in 1807 when she became the principal of Middlebury Female Academy.

Centered on the Common, this college town also is a summer and winter resort. The school plays host to the Bread Loaf Writers' Conference in August. A ranger district office provides maps and guides for hiking in nearby Green Mountain National Forest (see place listing p. 131).

**Addison County Chamber of Commerce:** 2 Court St., Middlebury, VT 05753; phone (802) 388-7951.

**Self-guiding tours:** Walking-tour maps are available from the chamber of commerce.

**HENRY SHELDON MUSEUM OF VERMONT HISTORY,** 1 Park St., is housed in the 1829 Judd-Harris House and depicts 19th-century Vermont life. The Walter Cerf Gallery presents changing exhibits related to art and history. The Stewart-Swift Research Center preserves a collection of 19th-century books, letters, newspapers and genealogical records.

Allow 30 minutes minimum. Museum and gallery open Tues.-Sat. 10-5 (also Mon. 10-5, late May to mid-Oct.). Research center open Tues.-Wed. 1-5, Thurs. 1-8, Fri. 1-5; closed major holidays. Museum and research center closed holidays and in Jan. Phone to verify schedule. Admission $5; over 59, $4.50; students with ID $4; ages 6-18, $3; family rate $12. MC, VI. Phone (802) 388-2117.

**UVM MORGAN HORSE FARM** is n.w. of US 7 off SR 23, following signs for 2.5 mi. The Morgan horse, state animal of Vermont, is said to be America's first breed of horse. After a guided tour and videotape presentation about the history and lineage of the Morgan horse, visitors can view a working horse farm. Comfortable shoes are recommended.

Picnicking is permitted. Allow 1 hour minimum. Tours are given daily on the hour 9-4, May-Oct. Fee $5; ages 13-19, $4; ages 5-12, $2. Phone (802) 388-2011.

## MIDDLESEX (C-2)

**CAMP MEADE VICTORY MUSEUM,** just e. on US 10 from I-89 exit 9, offers self-guiding tours through 25 indoor and outdoor exhibits detailing the years spanning the Great Depression through World War II. Camp Meade is a former Civilian Conservation Corps (CCC) camp where men thrown out of work by the Great Depression were trained and boarded while they worked on flood-prevention construction projects.

Picnicking is permitted. Allow 1 hour, 30 minutes minimum. Mon.-Sat. 9-4, mid-May to mid-Oct. Admission $5; over 61, $4.50; ages 7-11, $2.50; family rate (five person maximum) $12. MC, VI. Phone (802) 223-5537.

## MONTPELIER (C-3) pop. 8,035, elev. 484′

Capital of the state, Montpelier is a center for the insurance and granite-quarrying industries. The city was the birthplace of Adm. George Dewey, hero of Manila Bay during the Spanish-American War. Hubbard Park, 110 acres on a hill behind the Capitol, offers a good view of the Worcester Mountains and Winooski River Valley.

Also of architectural interest is the Supreme Court Building, built of Barre granite, at 111 State Street. The State Office Building, directly across from the Capitol, is a fine example of modern architecture. It is built of reinforced concrete with Vermont marble facing on the exterior and polished and matched marble in the lobby.

**MORSE FARM SUGARWORKS,** 2.7 mi. n. on Main St. to 1168 County Rd., following signs, shows a videotape about the sugaring process. A sample of maple syrup is included. Guided tours are available; check upon arrival for tour schedule. Tours show processing techniques as well as the history of syrup making. Also on the premises is the Outdoor Museum of Folk Art.

Allow 30 minutes minimum. Daily 8-8, June 15-Labor Day; 8-6:30, day after Labor Day-Oct. 15; 9-5, rest of year. Free. Phone (802) 223-2740.

**STATE CAPITOL,** 115 State St., is built of Barre granite in an impressive Doric style. The gilded dome is surmounted by a statue of Ceres, goddess of agriculture. Inside the portico stands a marble statue of Ethan Allen and a brass cannon captured from Hessians in the 1777 Battle of Bennington. Open Mon.-Fri. 8-4 (also Sat. 11-2:30, July 1 to mid-Oct.). Thirty-minute tours are given Mon.-Fri. 10-3:30, Sat. 11-2:30, July 1 to mid-Oct. Donations. Phone (802) 828-2228.

**T.W. WOOD GALLERY AND ART CENTER,** at Vermont College of the Union Institute and University campus on College St., presents changing exhibitions featuring works by New England artists. Permanent exhibitions include the work of Wood and other American artists of the 19th and early 20th centuries. Allow 30 minutes minimum. Tues.-Sun. noon-4; closed holidays and between exhibitions. Phone to verify that an exhibition is being presented. Donations. Phone (802) 828-8743.

**VERMONT HISTORICAL SOCIETY MUSEUM,** in the Pavilion Building at 109 State St., collects, preserves and interprets works of art, artifacts, books, documents, manuscripts and photographs that illustrate the history of Vermont. **Note:** The museum was scheduled to be closed for renovation until March 2004. Allow 30 minutes minimum. Tues.-Fri. 9-4:30, Sat. 9-4, Sun. noon-4. Phone to verify schedule. Admission $3, over 62 and students with ID $2. Phone to verify prices. Phone (802) 828-2291.

## MORRISVILLE (B-3) pop. 2,009, elev. 646′

Morrisville, like Vermont's other mountain-bound towns, grew rapidly when railroad service reached the area. Visible reminders of that event remain on Portland Street, where structures more closely resemble those of a Western boomtown than those of a New England village.

**Lamoille Valley Chamber of Commerce:** Tegu Bldg., 43 Portland St., P.O. Box 445, Morrisville, VT 05661; phone (802) 888-7607.

**MORRISVILLE NOYES HOUSE HISTORICAL MUSEUM,** 122 Lower Main St., is a two-story brick mansion built in the early 19th century. Miniature pitchers and articles related to early New England life are displayed. Wed.-Sat. 1-5, Memorial Day weekend-Labor Day. Donations. Phone (802) 888-7617.

## MOUNT MANSFIELD (B-2)

The loftiest peak in the Green Mountains and the highest point in Vermont, Mount Mansfield is 4,393 feet high and 5 miles long. Covering 27,613 acres of the mountain is Mount Mansfield State Forest *(see Recreation Chart)*. The forest can be reached by roads from Stowe through Smugglers' Notch or from Underhill Center.

The profile of Mount Mansfield is said to resemble a human face. The Long Trail and other trails lead to scenic spots and picnic areas. Campgrounds are available. The east side is a game refuge; hunting is permitted on the west side.

**MOUNT MANSFIELD AND STOWE AUTO ROAD**—*see Stowe p. 141.*

## MOUNT SNOW (F-2)

In southern Vermont's Green Mountains, Mount Snow is a year-round resort. Recreational activities include alpine skiing from early November to early May and golf, tennis, swimming, boating, fishing and mountain biking the rest of the year.

### RECREATIONAL ACTIVITIES

#### Skiing

- **Mount Snow Resort**, SR 100N. Write Mount Snow, VT 05356. Other activities are available. Mon.-Fri. 9-4, Sat.-Sun. and holidays 8-4, mid-Nov. through early May. Phone (802) 464-3333 or (800) 245-7669.

## NEWFANE (F-3) pop. 116, elev. 536′

**WINDHAM COUNTY HISTORICAL SOCIETY MUSEUM,** just s. of the village green on SR 30, offers items illustrating the history of the county. Displays include early portraits, Vermont furniture from the 18th and 19th centuries, clothing and textiles and Civil War artifacts. Exhibits change annually. Allow 30 minutes minimum. Wed.-Sun. noon-5, late May through mid-Oct. Free. Phone (802) 365-4148.

## NEWPORT (A-3) pop. 5,005

"The Border City," Newport is a gateway between New England and Canada. The city lies on the southern shore of Lake Memphremagog, whose name is derived from an Abenaki Indian word meaning "beautiful waters." On the western side of the 32-mile-long lake rises Owl's Head, named after an American Indian chief. Its 3,360-foot summit offers impressive views.

On Prospect Hill, the granite towers of St. Mary's Star of the Sea Church rise above the city; phone (802) 334-5066.

# DID YOU KNOW

Vermont
is the largest
producer
of maple syrup
in the country.

**Vermont's North Country Chamber of Commerce:** The Causeway, Newport, VT 05855-1701; phone (802) 334-7782 or (800) 635-4643.

## NORTH BENNINGTON (F-1)
pop. 1,428, elev. 287′

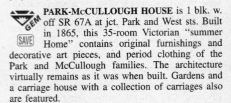
**PARK-McCULLOUGH HOUSE** is 1 blk. w. off SR 67A at jct. Park and West sts. Built in 1865, this 35-room Victorian "summer Home" contains original furnishings and decorative art pieces, and period clothing of the Park and McCullough families. The architecture virtually remains as it was when built. Gardens and a carriage house with a collection of carriages also are featured.

Picnicking is permitted. Allow 1 hour minimum. Guided tours are given daily on the hour 10-3, mid-May to mid-Oct.; phone for winter holiday schedule. Admission $8; over 59 and ages 12-17, $5. Phone (802) 442-5441.

## NORTHFIELD (C-3) pop. 3,208, elev. 732′

Norwich University was founded in 1819 by Capt. Alden Partridge, a former superintendent at West Point, and is considered the country's oldest private military college. It was one of the first universities to institute military programs, which later formed the basis for the Reserve Officer Training Corps (ROTC). Current enrollment is about 950 cadets and 750 civilian students.

Norwich University Museum in White Memorial Chapel has exhibits about the history of the university and the achievements of its alumni, including Adm. George Dewey, Maj. Gen. Grenville Dodge and Gen. I.D. White. Other collections include Norwich uniforms, flags, weapons and military equipment. Phone (802) 485-2379.

Guided tours of the Norwich University campus can be arranged at the admissions office in Roberts Hall near the north entrance; phone (802) 485-2001. The Corps of Cadets parades Friday at 1, September through mid-May. In late July the 1-day Russian School Slavic Festival presents Russian and Ukrainian folk songs and dances.

Also of interest in Northfield are five covered bridges, three on Cox Brook Road, one on Stony Brook Road and one on Slaughterhouse Road.

## NORWICH (D-4) elev. 398′

The King Arthur Flour Baking Education Center, Bakery and Store at 133 SR 5S is draws visitors from all over the United States and Canada. The store is staffed with experienced bakers who delight in answering technical baking questions and are quick to provide demonstrations and samples. The Baking education center offers registrants the chance to work side-by-side with some of the nation's finest master bakers. Classes range from half-day to week-long, and subjects range from chocolate to pita to pasta. Phone or (802) 649-3881 or (800) 827- 6836.

**MONTSHIRE MUSEUM OF SCIENCE,** I-91 exit 13 to 1 Montshire Rd. off SR 10A, features exhibits about science, natural history and technology. Permanent displays include freshwater and saltwater aquariums; live animals and mounted specimens from New England and around the world; and hands-on exhibits. There also are changing exhibits.

The museum is on 110 acres of woodland along the Connecticut River. Nature trails are available. Picnicking is permitted on the grounds. Allow 4 hours minimum. Daily 10-5; closed Jan. 1, Thanksgiving and Dec. 25. Admission $7; ages 3-17, $7. MC, VI. Phone (802) 649-2200.

## ORWELL (D-1) pop. 1,100, elev. 385'

Settled shortly before the Revolution by Scotsman John Charter from Montréal, Orwell lies near the southern end of Lake Champlain. The town is a sheep-raising center in the Champlain Valley.

**MOUNT INDEPENDENCE STATE HISTORIC SITE** is 6 mi. w. of jct. SR 22A and SR 73. The site also is accessible by taking the MV *Carillon* from Shoreham *(see attraction listing p. 141).* The site of the Revolutionary War's largest military fortifications, the remains include the foundation of a stockade, blockhouses, gun batteries and a hospital. A visitor center/museum traces the history of the site, displays archeological artifacts and shows a 12-minute orientation videotape. Trails with views of Lake Champlain traverse 300 acres of woodland and pasture.

Allow 2 hours minimum. Site and visitor center open daily 9:30-5, Memorial Day weekend-Columbus Day; trails accessible year-round. Admission $5, under 14 free. Phone (802) 948-2000, or (802) 759-2412 in the off season.

## PITTSFORD (D-2) elev. 370'

Counted among the many communities named for William Pitt, Pittsford is home to four covered bridges. The first U.S. patent was granted in the town. It was given to Samuel Hopkins for devising a way to create potash and pearl ash out of wood ash for making soap.

**NEW ENGLAND MAPLE MUSEUM,** n. on US 7, offers self-guiding tours describing the maple sugaring process since American Indian times. Dioramas, antiques and a slide show tell the history of "sweet water." Demonstrations are conducted, and visitors can sample different grades of maple syrup.

Picnicking is permitted. Allow 30 minutes minimum. Daily 8:30-5:30, Fri. before Memorial Day-Oct. 31; 10-4, Nov. 1-Dec. 23 and mid-Mar. through Thurs. before Memorial Day. Closed Easter and Thanksgiving. Admission 2.50; over 61, $2; ages 6-12, 75c. AX, DS, MC, VI. Phone (802) 483-9414 or (800) 639-4280.

**PITTSFORD NATIONAL FISH HATCHERY,** 4 mi. n.e. off US 7 at 4 Holden Rd., raises landlocked Atlantic salmon for restocking Lake Champlain, Atlantic salmon for the Connecticut River restoration program, and lake sturgeon for population recovery in New York state. Visitors can feed adult salmon in a display pool. Picnicking is permitted. Daily 7:30-3:30. Free. Phone (802) 483-6618.

## PLYMOUTH (D-2)

The small Green Mountain town of Plymouth was the birthplace of Calvin Coolidge. Coolidge was at home Aug. 3, 1923, when he heard the news of President Warren G. Harding's death. His father, a notary public, administered the oath of office to him in the parlor by the light of a kerosene lamp.

**PRESIDENT CALVIN COOLIDGE STATE HISTORIC SITE AT PLYMOUTH NOTCH,** off SR 100A, includes the birthplace, boyhood home and grave of Calvin Coolidge, the 30th president of the United States. The birthplace and homestead have original furnishings.

Other buildings include the visitor center, with an exhibit about Coolidge's career and changing displays of gifts presented to the president while in office; Wilder House, the childhood home of Coolidge's mother, which now serves as a restaurant; Wilder Barn, with a collection of 19th-century farm implements; Plymouth Cheese Factory, built in 1890 by Coolidge's father; the 1850s General Store; the office of the 1924 summer White House; and Union Christian Church, an 1840 meeting house still used. The Aldrich House contains exhibits pertaining to the village and to Coolidge.

Allow 2 hours minimum. Entire site open daily 9:30-5, Memorial Day weekend-Sun. after Columbus Day. Admission $6.50; ages 6-14, $2. Phone (802) 672-3773.

## PROCTOR (D-2) elev. 477'

In the narrow Otter Creek Valley, Proctor was named for Redfield Proctor, governor of the state 1878-80 and founder of Vermont Marble Co., an international corporation. The town appropriately is adorned with marble sidewalks and public buildings. Sutherland Falls, near the center of town, is a major source of Proctor's power supply.

**VERMONT MARBLE MUSEUM** is at 52 Main St. One of the largest exhibits of its kind in the country, it illustrates the origin, quarrying and finishing of marble. Displays include marble from Vermont and around the world. The Hall of Presidents displays statuary white marble relief carvings of all past United States presidents.

The 11-minute videotape "The Legacy of Vermont Marble" is shown continuously. Allow 1 hour minimum. Daily 9-5, mid-May through Oct. 31. Admission $6; over 61, $4; ages 15-18, $3. DS, MC, VI. Phone (802) 459-2300 or (800) 427-1396.

**WILSON CASTLE,** 3.5 mi. s. on W. Proctor Rd., was built in 1867 on a 115-acre estate. Eleven open proscenium arches overlooked by a towering turret, parapet and balcony dominate the elaborate facade of English brick and marble. The castle's 32 rooms feature 84 stained-glass windows and 13 fireplaces finished with domestic tiles and bronze; not all rooms are included in the tour.

Furnishings include European and Far Eastern antiques and museum pieces, along with statuary, Chinese scrolls and Oriental rugs. Paintings, sculpture and photographs are displayed in an art gallery. Cattle barns, stables and a carriage house are on the grounds.

Guided tours of two of the three floors depart continuously daily 9-5:30, late May through mid-Oct. Phone for winter holiday schedule. Admission $8; over 61, $7.50; ages 6-12, $4. Phone (802) 773-3284.

## PUTNEY (F-3) elev. 251′

Conservative Putney was catapulted into the realm of the avant-garde in 1838 when John Humphrey Noyes set up his experimental society based on perfectionism. One of the principal practices of the group was "complex marriage" or free love. Shortly after their founding, the Perfectionists were booted out of Putney. After all, it was not until the early 1960s that Putney even allowed summer residents to wear shorts.

SAVE SANTA'S LAND, off I-91 exit 4, then 4.5 mi. n. on US 5 to 655 Bellows Falls Rd., is a Christmas village which includes Santa's house, a walk through a deer park, a carousel and a petting zoo. A 5-minute train ride through the Christmas tunnel is provided.

Food is available. Picnicking is permitted. Allow 2 hours minimum. Daily 10-5, July 2-Labor Day; Sat.-Sun. 10-5, Memorial Day weekend-July 1 and day after Labor Day-Dec. 31. Closed Thanksgiving and Dec. 25. Ages 3-12, $15; adults $12; over 55, $10. AX, CB, DS, MC, VI. Phone (802) 387-5550 or (800) 726-8299.

## QUECHEE (D-3)

A scenic portion of Quechee Gorge (see Recreation Chart), Vermont's Little Grand Canyon, lies west of Quechee. The bridge on US 4 that spans the gorge 162 feet above the Ottauquechee River provides a good view of this natural spectacle. A covered bridge leads into the small village known in the 19th century for its busy woolen mills.

**Hartford Area Chamber of Commerce:** 1856 Quechee Main St., P.O. Box 106, Quechee, VT 05059; phone (802) 295-7900 or (800) 295-5451.

**Shopping areas:** Quechee Gorge Village, at Quechee Gorge, offers antiques, arts and crafts, miniature steam train rides and an antique carousel. In town is The Mill, a complex of shops including Simon Pearce Glass, where visitors can observe the glass-blowing process. The Dewey Barn Complex, on US 4 just before Quechee Gorge, houses specialty shops and the Ottauquechee Valley Winery, where the vintages visitors can sample include apple, pear, blueberry and rhubarb, but no grape.

## RANDOLPH (D-3)

SAVE PORTER MUSIC BOX MUSEUM is on US 66; from I-89 take exit 4 then go 2 mi. w. on US 66 to the parking lot and then up the wooden stairs. This is the only U.S. manufacturer of large-disk music boxes. A 15-minute videotape about the history and construction of the large music boxes precedes the guided tour of the museum. Note: Phone for directions to parking for the physically impaired.

Picnicking is permitted. Allow 1 hour minimum. Mon.-Sat. 9:30-5 (also Sun. noon-4, mid-Aug. through mid-Oct.), May-Oct.; Mon.-Sat. 10-4, Nov.-Dec. Closed major holidays. Last tour leaves 90 minutes before closing. Admission $5; ages 3-12, $3. Phone (802) 728-9694 or (800) 811-7087.

## RICHMOND (B-2) elev. 321′

THE OLD ROUND CHURCH NATIONAL HISTORIC LANDMARK, I-89 exit 11, 2 mi. e. on US 2, then .5 mi. s. on Bridge St., is a 16-sided polygon built 1812-13 as a place of worship for five different denominations. The building was renovated in 1981 and is now used for events, concerts, weddings and public gatherings.

Daily 10-4, July 4-Labor Day and during fall foliage season; Sat.-Sun. 10-4, Memorial Day-July 3 and day after Labor Day-Columbus Day. May be closed weekends for weddings. Phone to verify schedule. Donations. Phone (802) 434-2556 for guided tour information, or (802) 434-3480 for weddings information.

## RECREATIONAL ACTIVITIES

### Skiing

• **Cochran's Ski Area**, on Cochran Rd. 1 mi. s.e. of Round Church. Write 910 Cochran Rd., Richmond, VT 05477. Tues. and Thurs.-Fri. 2:30-5, Sat.-Sun. 9-4 (also Mon.-Fri. 9-4, Christmas and February vacations), mid-Dec. to late Mar. Phone (802) 434-2479 to verify schedule.

## ROCKINGHAM (E-3) elev. 357′

**Shopping areas:** Those who shop catalogues will enjoy visiting the Vermont Country Store with offerings ranging from candy and clothing, to a wooden canoe.

**THE OLD ROCKINGHAM MEETING HOUSE**, on SR 103 at 11 Meeting House Rd., 2 mi. n.w. jct. I-91 and SR 103, is a barn-like, severe Georgian building with a high pulpit and "pigpen-style" pews. Adjoining the 1787 church is a graveyard with interesting headstones. Views from this hilltop site are excellent. Allow 30 minutes minimum. Daily 10-4, Memorial Day weekend-Columbus Day. Admission 50c, under 12 free. Phone (802) 463-3964.

## RUTLAND (D-2) pop. 17,292, elev. 562′

The immense quarrying and finishing industries in Rutland are responsible for the community's reputation as the "Marble City." An industrial center in the Otter Creek Valley, Rutland is protected by the Taconic Mountains to the west and three striking Green Mountain peaks—Killington, Pico and Shrewsbury—to the east.

Rutland is the closest city to the recreational community of Killington *(see place listing p. 132)* and is headquarters for the Green Mountain National Forest *(see place listing p. 131)*. The state's oldest continuously published newspaper, the *Rutland Herald,* was founded in 1794. The Chaffee Center for the Visual Arts is in an elegant Victorian-era mansion and offers 10 galleries displaying works by Vermont artists.

**Rutland Region Chamber of Commerce:** 256 N. Main St., Rutland, VT 05701; phone (802) 773-2747.

SAVE **NORMAN ROCKWELL MUSEUM**, 2 mi. e. of jct. US 7 at 654 US 4 E, contains a large collection of Rockwell's work. The more than 2,500 reproductions displayed include illustrations for children's books, advertisements, and covers for the *Saturday Evening Post, Literary Digest, Life, Country Gentleman* and other magazines.

Allow 1 hour minimum. Daily 9-4; closed Jan. 1, Easter, Thanksgiving and Dec. 25. Admission $4.50; over 62, $4; ages 5-15, $2.50. MC, VI. Phone (802) 773-6095.

## ST. ALBANS (A-2) pop. 7,650, elev. 383′

Nestled between Lake Champlain and the Green Mountains, the town once described by Henry Ward Beecher as "a place in the midst of a greater variety of scenic beauty than any other I can remember in America" had anything but a placid history to match its serene setting. St. Albans was a notorious center for smuggling operations on Lake Champlain in the early 1800s and was an important link on the Underground Railroad.

Its rowdy days behind it, St. Albans is headquarters for the New England Central Railway, a production and distribution center for dairy products and a manufacturing center whose products include maple sugar, sugar-making equipment, medical-technology equipment, batteries and ice cream.

**St. Albans Area Chamber of Commerce:** 2 N. Main St., Suite 101, St. Albans, VT 05478; phone (802) 524-2444.

**ST. ALBANS HISTORICAL MUSEUM**, 9 Church St., is in a renovated 1861 brick schoolhouse. The museum exhibits quilts, clothing, china, glass, dolls, maps, photographs and Revolutionary and Civil War relics. Other collections feature railroad memorabilia and medical antiques. An interactive, narrated diorama depicts the history of St. Albans and the Lake Champlain region.

Allow 1 hour minimum. Mon.-Fri. 1-4, June 15-Sept. 30; by appointment rest of year. Admission $3, under 15 free. Phone (802) 527-7933.

## ST. JOHNSBURY (B-4)
pop. 6,319, elev. 556′

The converging valleys of the Moose, Passumpsic and Sleeper's rivers create a striking play of elevations upon which St. Johnsbury lies. The town was named after the French consul in New York, Saint Jean de Crèvecoeur, a friend of Ethan Allen and author of "Letters of an American Farmer." De Crèvecoeur suggested the addition of "bury" to the town's name to distinguish it from the many towns named St. John.

Much of St. Johnsbury's history and growth centered on Thaddeus Fairbanks' invention of the platform scale in 1830 and George Cary's idea of flavoring plug tobacco with maple sugar. The town prospered with the success of the Fairbanks Scale and maple-sugar industries, which continue to play a major role in its economy. It is now the industrial, retail and cultural center of the area of Vermont known as the Northeast Kingdom.

**Northeast Kingdom Chamber of Commerce and Welcome Center:** 51 Depot Rd., St. Johnsbury, VT 05819; phone (802) 748-3678 or (800) 639-6379.

**SAVE FAIRBANKS MUSEUM AND PLANETARIUM,** 1302 Main St., houses a large collection that includes more than 4,500 mounted birds and mammals, art and antiques, and village and crafts tools. The museum also is home to the Northern New England Weather Center and the Children's Nature Corner, which is open July through late August.

Allow 1 hour, 30 minutes minimum. Mon.-Sat. 9-5, Sun. 1-5; closed Jan. 1, Easter, Thanksgiving and Dec. 25. Planetarium shows daily at 11 and 1:30, July-Aug.; Sat.-Sun. at 1:30, rest of year. Museum $5; over 59, $4; ages 5-17, $3; family rate (two adults and their minor children) $12. Planetarium $3. MC, VI. Phone (802) 748-2372.

**MAPLE GROVE MAPLE MUSEUM,** 1 mi. e. on US 2, has maple exhibits and a videotape showing the sugaring process. The Old Sugar House demonstrates the process of boiling down maple sap. Allow 1 hour minimum. Museum open daily 8-5. Tours of Maple Grove Candy Factory are given Mon.-Fri. 8-4, May-Oct.; no tours on holidays. Museum free. Factory tour $1, under 12 free. Phone (802) 748-5141.

**ST. JOHNSBURY ATHENAEUM AND ART GALLERY,** 1171 Main St., contains paintings by 19th-century artists, emphasizing the Hudson River School. The collection includes Albert Bierstadt's monumental painting, "The Domes of the Yosemite." The gallery is housed in an ornate, architecturally superb library donated to the town by Horace Fairbanks in 1871.

Allow 30 minutes minimum. Mon.-Fri. 10-5:30 (also Mon. and Wed. 5:30-8), Sat. 9:30-4; closed major holidays. Donations. Phone (802) 748-8291.

## SHARON (D-3) elev. 500′

In the White River Valley and bordered by mountains on three sides, Sharon is the birthplace of Joseph Smith, founder of the Mormon faith. Born in 1805, Smith lived in the area until he was 11, when his family moved to New York.

**JOSEPH SMITH BIRTHPLACE MEMORIAL** is 350 acres 2 mi. off SR 14 between Sharon and Royalton. A solid granite monument, surrounded by landscaped grounds, hiking trails and a picnic area, marks the site of the Mormon prophet's birth. In the visitor center are pictures, paintings and a theater. Christmas decorations feature more than 100,000 lights and can be seen the night after Thanksgiving through Jan. 1.

Tours are given Mon.-Sat. 9-7, Sun. 1:30-7, May-Oct.; Mon.-Sat. 9-5, Sun. 1:30-5, rest of year. Free. Phone (802) 763-7742.

## SHELBURNE (B-2) elev. 159′

Shelburne, with the Adirondack Mountains to the west and the Green Mountains to the east, was settled in 1768 by two German lumbermen and later named for an English earl. Many downtown shops occupy renovated farm buildings dating from the 1700s.

**SHELBURNE FARMS,** 1.5 mi. w. on Bay and Harbor rds., is a 1,400-acre working farm and environmental center developed in the 1880s as a model farm. Demonstrators make cheese and furniture. The Children's Farmyard includes a hayride, cows, chickens and goats. The landscape was created by Frederick Law Olmsted, designer of New York City's Central Park. Some 8 miles of hiking trails are available (weather permitting).

Food is available. Allow 2 hours minimum. Open daily 8:30-5:30, guided 90-minute property tours at 9, 11, 1 and 3, mid-May to mid-Oct.; grounds and welcome center open 10-5, rest of year. Closed Thanksgiving and Dec. 25. Admission $6; over 62, $5; ages 3-14, $4. Guided property tour $10; over 62 and ages 3-14, $9. Phone (802) 985-8686.

**SHELBURNE MUSEUM,** on US 7, consists of 39 galleries and historic structures. Spread over 45 acres, the buildings house **SAVE** collections of art and artifacts depicting early New England life. Attractions include a railroad depot, private car and locomotive, a two-lane covered bridge, a round barn, a hand-crafted model circus parade more than 500 feet long and the sidewheeler *Ticonderoga*.

Americana displayed include a sizable group of wooden cigar-store figures; fine, folk and decorative art; tools; coaches, carriages and wagons; and firefighting and agricultural equipment. Electra Havemeyer Webb Memorial houses European furnishings, sculpture and paintings. Webb Gallery of American Art contains works by 18th-, 19th- and 20th-century artists. Formal gardens, ornamental trees and shrubs, roses and lilacs adorn the grounds.

Picnicking is permitted. Allow 4 hours minimum. Daily 10-5, May-Oct. Admission $17.50; students with ID and ages 6-18, $8.75. AX, MC, VI. Phone (802) 985-3346 to verify schedule and to obtain event information. *See color ad p. 129.*

**VERMONT TEDDY BEAR CO.,** 6655 Shelburne Rd. (US 7), offers a glimpse of the step-by-step creative process required to make these jointed Teddy bears. Visitors may design and create personalized bears in the Make A Friend for Life factory.

Guided 30-minute tours depart every half-hour Mon.-Sat. 10-4, Sun. 11-4; closed Jan. 1, Easter, Thanksgiving and Dec. 25. Phone for extended summer hours. Admission $2, under 12 free. A fee is charged for making a Teddy bear. Phone (802) 985-3001 or (800) 829-2327.

**VERMONT WILDFLOWER FARM—**
*see Charlotte p. 130.*

## SHOREHAM (C-1) elev. 333′

Twenty years after Shoreham's 1755 founding, Ethan Allen and his troops, including volunteer Benedict Arnold, captured Fort Ticonderoga from the British. The town is the birthplace of Levi Morton, vice president to Benjamin Harrison.

Shorewell Ferries Inc. provides 7-minute Lake Champlain crossings to Ticonderoga, N.Y., from early May to late October; phone (802) 897-7999.

**MV *CARILLON*,** departing from Teachout's Wharf on SR 74W at Larrabees Point, provides a cruise along unspoiled southern Lake Champlain with a historical narrative about Revolutionary War sites. The boat docks at Mount Independence State Historic Site *(see attraction listing p. 137),* allowing an opportunity for a self-guiding tour of the fortification remains as well as to explore a visitor center and walking trails.

Allow 2 hours minimum. Some departures require a minimum of six persons. Cruises depart Shoreham Wed.-Sat. at 1, July-Aug. Fare $8.50; ages 3-13, $4.50. Phone (802) 897-5331.

## SPRINGFIELD (E-3) pop. 3,938

The Black River powered a variety of Springfield mills in the 18th and early 19th centuries. Though some mills still exist along the river, none uses waterpower. An information center is in the restored Eureka Schoolhouse on SR 11. Built in 1785, the one-room schoolhouse is one of the few remaining 18th-century state public buildings. It stands next to a 37-foot-long covered bridge that was built in 1870.

**Springfield Chamber of Commerce:** 14 Clinton St., Suite 6, Springfield, VT 05156; phone (802) 885-2779.

**PRECISION VALLEY CORVETTE MUSEUM** is at 363 River St., behind the diner. This small museum houses eight Corvettes and authentic automotive memorabilia such as gasoline pumps. Allow 1 hour minimum. Daily 11-7; closed Dec. 25. Free. Phone (802) 886-1400.

## STOWE (B-3)

In the Green Mountains, Stowe offers year-round recreational activities. The area is known especially for its winter sports facilities, most notably the 47 slopes and trails that include some of the best runs in New England. Stowe also is on the scenic portion of SR 100 that runs from Wilmington to Troy.

**Stowe Area Association:** Main St., P.O. Box 1320, Stowe, VT 05672; phone (802) 253-7321 or (800) 247-8693. *See color ad p. 471.*

**THE HELEN DAY ART CENTER,** n. on Main St. then e. 1 blk. on School St., is in an 1860 Greek Revival building. The center offers changing exhibitions of the works of well-known local, national and international visual artists.

Allow 30 minutes minimum. Tues.-Sun. noon-5, June 22-Oct. 12; Tues.-Sat. noon-5, rest of year. Closed holidays. Admission $3; over 64, $1; ages 5-12, 50c. Phone (802) 253-8358.

**MOUNT MANSFIELD,** rising to 4,395 feet n.w. of town, is Vermont's highest peak. From the summit visibility averages 50 to 70 miles, encompassing

parts of Vermont, New Hampshire, New York and Québec.

**Stowe Auto Toll Road,** entered from SR 108, 6 mi. n.w., is a 4.3-mile gravel road traversing heavily forested slopes to about the 3,600-foot level; a long and difficult hiking trail continues to the summit. Parking, a visitor center and food are available at the end of the road.

**Note:** The winding road has some sharp, steep curves and is not recommended for novice drivers or for vehicles longer than a pickup truck. The vehicle should be in good condition; brakes, radiator and transmission should be checked.

Daily 9-4, Memorial Day-Columbus Day. Toll $16 per private vehicle (more than six passengers additional $4 per person), $8 per motorcycle. AX, CB, DC, DS, MC, VI. Phone (802) 253-3000 or (800) 253-4754.

**STOWE ALPINE SLIDE** is 7.5 mi. n.w. on SR 108 to 5781 Mountain Rd. The Alpine Chairlift at Spruce Peak climbs about 3,600 feet upward to the top of the slide in about 10 minutes. Riders descend the mountain on sleds and control their speed of descent, which takes 2 to 3 minutes.

Food is available. Picnicking is permitted. Children under age 6 or under 48 inches tall may not ride alone. Daily 10-5, mid-June through Labor Day; Sat.-Sun. and holidays 10-5, day after Labor Day to mid-Oct. (weather permitting). Single ride $11; ages 6-12, $7. AX, DS, MC, VI. Phone (802) 253-3000 or (800) 253-4754.

**STOWE LAUNCH ZONE** is 7.5 mi. n.w. on SR 108 to 5781 Mountain Rd. The park offers pipes and ramps for skateboarders, in-line skaters and mountain bikers. Helmets, knee pads, elbow pads and wrist guards—all required in the park—can be rented. Daily 10-5, mid-June through Labor Day; Sat.-Sun. 10-5, day after Labor Day to mid-Oct. All-day admission $15; ages 6-12, $12. Half-day $8; ages 6-12, $6.50. AX, CB, DC, DS, MC, VI. Phone (802) 253-3000 or (800) 253-4754.

**STOWE RECREATION PATH,** starting in Stowe Center, is a 5-mile scenic pathway that follows a mountain stream north toward Mount Mansfield, past cornfields, woodlands, pastures and swimming holes. This was the first such path where land was donated by individual owners rather than purchased by a government. Parking areas provide access along the route. Use is restricted to pedestrians and unmotorized conveyances.

Daily 24 hours. Free. Phone (802) 253-7321, or (800) 247-8693 out of Vt. and Canada.

**VERMONT SKI MUSEUM** is at jct. SR 100 and SR 108, in the Old Town Hall at 1 S. Main St. This museum uses permanent and changing exhibits to relate Vermont's skiing history—from handcrafted 8-foot-long skis to lost ski areas to the story of the 10th Mountain Division to Vermont Olympians. Allow 1 hour minimum. Generally open Wed.-Mon. noon-5; closed Thanksgiving and Dec. 25. Phone to verify schedule. Admission $3, family rate $5. AX, MC, VI. Phone (802) 253-9911.

## RECREATIONAL ACTIVITIES
### Skiing

- **Stowe Mountain Resort**, 7.5 mi. n.w. on SR 108 to 5781 Mountain Rd. Stowe, VT 05672. Other activities are offered. Sun.-Wed. 8-4, Thurs.-Sat. 8-4 and 5-9, mid-Nov. to late Apr. (weather permitting). Phone (802) 253-3000 · or (800) 253-4754.

## STRAFFORD (C-4) elev. 500′

**JUSTIN SMITH MORRILL STATE HISTORIC SITE,** on Justin Smith Morrill Hwy. in the center of Strafford Village, is a furnished Gothic Revival house built 1848-51 by Sen. Morrill, author of the Morrill Land Grant College Acts of 1862 and 1890. Exhibits featuring the Land Grant College Act and the Gothic Revival movement in 19th-century America are displayed in the carriage barn. Seven outbuildings also are on the grounds as well as period gardens and plantings.

Allow 1 hour, 30 minutes minimum. Tours are given Wed.-Sun. on the hour 11-4, Memorial Day weekend-Columbus Day. Admission $4, under 14 free. Phone (802) 828-3051.

## STRATTON MOUNTAIN (E-2) elev. 3,859′

## RECREATIONAL ACTIVITIES
### Skiing

- **Stratton Resort**, 17 miles east of Manchester off SR 30 on Stratton Mountain Rd. Write RR1 Box 145, Stratton Mountain, VT 05155. Other activities are offered. Daily 10-3:30 or 4, mid-Nov. to late Apr. (weather permitting). Phone (802) 297-2200 or (800) 787-2886.

## SWANTON (A-2) pop. 2,548, elev. 148′

In the past, smuggling was one of Swanton's more lucrative businesses. The town near the Vermont-Québec border was the scene of controversy when enterprising Vermonters drove cattle across the border into Canada, where the livestock was sold to British soldiers during the War of 1812. Twentieth-century smugglers followed in their predecessors' footsteps during Prohibition when they ran liquor into the state by automobile.

Before 1700, the St. Francis Indians, guided by French Jesuits, built the first chapel in the Vermont territory at Swanton. After France lost the land to the English, the Indians moved the chapel stone by stone to St. Hyacinthe, Québec.

Missisquoi National Wildlife Refuge, 2.5 miles west off SR 78, covers 5,651 acres along the Missisquoi River delta and Lake Champlain. Waterfowl and other wildlife can be seen along a 1.5-mile interpretive trail. Hunting is allowed in season with a permit.

## TOWNSHEND (E-3)

Townshend is the site of Scott Covered Bridge, built in 1870 over the West River. The first Vermont covered bridge to be marked for preservation, it has a 166-foot single span, one of the longest in the state. The total length of the three spans is 276 feet.

**MARY MEYER MUSEUM OF STUFFED TOYS** is in the Big Black Bear Shop 1 mi. n. of the town common on SR 30. Permanent and seasonal exhibits relate the story of the Mary Meyer's creation of her stuffed-toy business in the 1930s, and the production process of the early days. Exhibits include some of her more popular designs. Allow 1 hour, 30 minutes minimum. Daily 9:30-5 May 1-Dec. 23; Mon.-Fri. 9:30-4:30, rest of year. Closed Jan. 1, Easter, Thanksgiving and Dec. 24-26. Free. Phone (802) 365-4160 or (888) 758-2327.

## VERGENNES (C-2) pop. 2,741, elev. 176′

Settled in 1766 and incorporated in 1788, Vergennes is one of America's oldest incorporated cities and one of the smallest, at 1 square mile. During the War of 1812, 177 tons of cannon balls were cast in the city. The restored, 350-seat 1897 Vergennes Opera House, 120 Main St., is open weekdays for self-guiding tours; phone (802) 877-6737.

Bixby Memorial Library displays a collection of Abenaki Indian artifacts and items from other American Indian tribes; phone (802) 877-2211.

**Shopping areas:** Kennedy Brothers Factory Marketplace is in a two-story renovated creamery. The country store and more than 200 shops and booths in this red-brick building at 11 Main St. offer woodenware, crafts pieces, toys, food products and antiques. An ice cream shop, a bakery and a delicatessen also are on the premises. The marketplace is open daily 9:30-5:30.

## WAITSFIELD (C-2)

In the region known as Mad River Valley, which comprises Waitsfield, Warren and Fayston, Gen. Benjamin Wait founded a settlement in 1789. An old covered bridge marks the center of this former dairying and lumbering town that is now in the heart of a premier winter sports region. Polo is often played at the polo field on · weekends May through October. Hunting, fishing, canoeing and downhill and cross-country skiing are other popular activities.

**Sugarbush Chamber of Commerce:** 4061 Main St., P.O. Box 173, Waitsfield, VT 05673; phone (802) 496-3409 or (800) 828-4748.

## RECREATIONAL ACTIVITIES
### Skiing

- **Mad River Glen**, on SR 17 off SR 100. Write P.O. Box 1089, Waitsfield, VT 05673. Mon.-Fri.

9-4, Sat.-Sun. and holidays 8:30-4, Dec. 15-Apr. 15. Phone (802) 496-3551.

## WARREN (C-2)

Named for physician and general Joseph Warren who died in action at Bunker Hill, Warren is one of the trio of Mad River Valley communities.

**GRANVILLE GULF STATE PARK,** covering 1,200 acres between Warren and Granville, lies along the eastern boundary of the Green Mountain National Forest *(see place listing p. 131)*. The Mad River cuts through the park, creating picturesque Moss Glen Falls. The park offers a 6-mile scenic drive and the Puddledock Ski Touring Trail. Daily 24 hours. Free. *See Recreation Chart.*

**RECREATIONAL ACTIVITIES**
**Skiing**

- **Sugarbush Ski Resort**, 2405 Sugarbush Access Rd. off SR 100, Warren, VT 05674. Mon.-Fri. 9-4, Sat.-Sun. and holidays 8:30-4, early Nov.-late Apr. Phone (802) 583-6300.

## WATERBURY (B-3) pop. 1,706, elev. 427′

**BEN & JERRY'S ICE CREAM FACTORY TOURS,** off I-89 exit 10, then 1 mi. n. on SR 100, provides guided 30-minute tours of an ice cream factory detailing each step in making ice cream. Samples are given after the tour. **Note:** There is no ice cream production on Saturdays, Sundays and holidays; a videotape of the process is shown on these days. Cow Over the Moon Theater features a 7-minute multimedia presentation about the company's founders and its history.

Food is available mid-June through mid-October. Picnicking is permitted. Daily 9-8, July 1-late Aug.; 9-6, late Aug.-Oct. 31; 9-5 in June; 10-5, rest of year. Guided tours every 10 minutes daily 9-8, July 1-late Aug.; every 15 minutes 9-6, late Aug.-Oct. 31; every 20 minutes 9-5 in June; every 30 minutes 10-5, rest of year. Closed Jan. 1, Thanksgiving and Dec. 25. Admission $3; over 60, $2; under 12 free. MC, VI. Phone (802) 882-1240 ext. 2285 or (866) 258-6877.

## WATERBURY CENTER (B-3)

**COLD HOLLOW CIDER MILL,** off I-89 exit 10, 3.5 mi. n on SR 100, produces approximately a million gallons of cider each year. Self-guiding tours let visitors view many aspects of the mill's cider production. An 8-minute videotape explains the process from apple harvesting to cider bottling.

Picnicking is permitted. Allow 30 minutes minimum. Daily 8-7, first Sun. in July to late Oct.; 8-6, rest of year. Closed Thanksgiving and Dec. 25. Free. Phone (802) 244-8771 or (800) 327-7537.

## WESTON (E-3) elev. 1,300′

Weston is on a hilltop at the north end of the West River Valley. The many restored houses and

attractions preserve the atmosphere of a 19th-century Vermont village. Those who shop catalogues will enjoy visiting the Vermont Country Store with offerings ranging from candy and clothing, to a wooden canoe.

The Weston Priory, 3 miles north of the village, is a Benedictine monastery that welcomes the public; phone (802) 824-5409.

**WESTON PLAYHOUSE,** on the village green, initially was housed in a converted Congregational church renovated in 1935. Although the building burned in 1962, the reconstructed playhouse offers the fully restored Greek Revival facade of the original. Performing five or six musicals or plays, the summer theater company also offers an after-theater cabaret. Other performances are produced in late October and in December.

Performances are offered Tues.-Sat. at 8 p.m. (also Wed. and Sat. at 3), Sun. at 7 p.m., late June to early Sept. Admission $28-$35; ages 6-16, $14-$17. MC, VI. Phone (802) 824-5288.

## WILMINGTON (F-2)

[SAVE] **ADAMS FARM** is 3 mi. n. on SR 100 to 15 Higley Hill Rd. This working farm produces maple syrup, hand-spun woolens and garden products. Seasonal activities include feeding and interacting with farm animals, hands-on farm activities and demonstrations such as goat milking, pumpkin picking and maple syrup making. Evening hay rides are offered in the summer and fall, and sleigh rides are available in winter.

Picnicking is permitted. Food is available. Allow 2 hours minimum. Entire complex open Wed.-Mon. 10-5, July 1-Labor Day; Thurs.-Mon. 10-5, day after Labor Day-Oct. 31; livestock barn open Wed. and Fri.-Sun. 10-5, Dec. 1 through mid-June; otherwise varies. Phone for hay and sleigh ride schedules. Admission $6.50; senior citizens, $6; ages

## DID YOU KNOW

Vermont was
the first territory
to become
a state after the
original 13 colonies.

3-12, $5.50. Phone for ride fares. MC, VI. Phone (802) 464-3762.

## WINDSOR (D-3) elev. 321'

"The Birthplace of Vermont," Windsor is where, after a 6-day convention, the constitution of Vermont was adopted July 8, 1777. The general assembly often met in Windsor until 1805, when Montpelier became the permanent capital. The city was an invention center during the 19th century, spawning such products as firearms, the hydraulic pump, the coffee percolator and the sewing machine.

An 1866 covered bridge, one of the longest in the nation, spans the Connecticut River between Windsor and Cornish, N.H. Vermont State Craft Gallery, in the Windsor House at 54 Main St., exhibits works by some 150 Vermont and New Hampshire artisans; phone (802) 674-6729.

SAVE **AMERICAN PRECISION MUSEUM,** 196 Main St. at jct. Maple St., is housed in the Robbins and Lawrence Armory and Machine Shop built in 1846. Highlights include a collection of historic precision machine tools, guns, working scale models and special exhibits detailing the story of America's industrial past. Daily 10-5, Memorial Day weekend-last Sun. in Oct. Admission $6; over 65, $4; students with ID $3; family rate $18. MC, VI. Phone (802) 674-5781.

**HARPOON BREWERY,** SR 5/Ruth Carney Dr. in the Windsor Industrial Park, offers guided tours outlining the New England craft-brewing process and its history. Harpoon brews several signature ales and seasonal beers that can be sampled after the tour. Food is available. Allow 1 hour minimum. Daily 10-6. Tours are given at 11 and 3. Free. Phone (802) 674-5491.

**OLD CONSTITUTION HOUSE** is at 16 N. Main St. The constitution of the Free and Independent Republic of Vermont was written and signed in this former tavern in 1777. The building is now a museum devoted to Vermont history. Exhibits feature the Republic of Vermont, events leading to its statehood, and its constitution. Allow 30 minutes minimum. Wed.-Sun. 11-5, Memorial Day weekend-Columbus Day. Admission $2.50, under 14 free. Phone (802) 828-3051.

## WOLCOTT (B-3)

Wolcott is the home of Fisher Bridge, the last covered railroad bridge still in use in Vermont. It also is one of the few left in the United States, and the only one with a full-length cupola, which lets smoke escape. Built in 1908, the bridge spans the Lamoille River. So that the bridge could remain in use, heavy steel beams were placed beneath it in 1968. An information booth is located at the bridge.

## WOODSTOCK (D-3) pop. 977, elev. 700'

A resort and residential community, Woodstock is noted for its well-preserved old houses and charming village green. Five local church bells were cast in Boston by either Paul Revere or a member of his family.

On scenic US 4, three covered bridges—at the center of town, 4 miles east at Taftsville and 3 miles west—span the Ottauquechee River. Although it is most famous for skiing, Woodstock also offers summer recreation, including water sports, golf, tennis, riding and hiking.

**Woodstock Area Chamber of Commerce:** 18 Central St., P.O. Box 486, Woodstock, VT 05091; phone (802) 457-3555 or (888) 496-6378.

**BILLINGS FARM AND MUSEUM**, .5 mi. n. on SR 12 across the Elm Street Bridge, encompasses both a modern working dairy farm and a museum of Vermont farm life in the 1890s. Frederick Billings, a Vermont native, lawyer, railroad president and philanthropist, established the farm in 1871. The restored farm house is a living-history center offering a look at the Billings farm as it was in the 1890s.

The museum, housed in four renovated 19th-century barns, portrays daily chores such as butter-making and cheesemaking, as well as the cycle of seasonal experiences such as ice cutting and sugaring. Tools, home furnishings, machinery and a re-created workshop, kitchen and country store are displayed. Visitors also can observe the daily activities of the modern dairy operation and participate in livestock programs and traditional activities.

Guided tours of the farm house are available. Allow 2 hours minimum. Daily 10-5, May-Oct.; Sat.-Sun. 10-4, Thanksgiving-Dec. 24; daily 10-4, Dec. 26-Dec. 31. Phone to verify winter holiday schedule Admission $9; over 64, $8; ages 13-17, $7.50; ages 5-12, $4.50; ages 3-4, $2. MC, VI. Phone (802) 457-2355.

**SUGARBUSH FARM**, 3 mi. e. on US 4, n. over the covered bridge at Taftsville, n. on Quechee Main St. to Hillside Rd., following signs, produces maple syrup and cheeses. Exhibits, a videotape presentation, demonstrations of the production processes and free samples are provided.

Allow 1 hour minimum. Mon.-Fri. 8-5, Sat.-Sun. and holidays 9-5, May 1-Dec. 23; otherwise varies. Closed Thanksgiving and Dec. 25. Phone for winter hours and road conditions. Free. Phone (802) 457-1757 or (800) 281-1757.

**WOODSTOCK HISTORICAL SOCIETY**, n. of jct. SR 12 and US 4 at 26 Elm St., is in an 1807 house museum. Exhibits include paintings, decorative arts pieces, textiles, costumes, antique toys, dolls, dollhouses, furniture and other local items. Furnishings date 1740-1900. Guided tours are available. The Woodstock Works exhibit details the economic history of Woodstock since 1740.

Allow 1 hour minimum. Mon.-Sat. 10-4, Memorial Day-Columbus Day; Fri.-Sat. 10-4, Sun. noon-4, day after Thanksgiving-first three weekends in Dec. (also Mon.-Fri. 2 weeks prior to Dec. 25). Tours are given on the hour. Last tour begins 1 hour before closing. Fee $5. Phone (802) 457-1822.

# AMERICA ON THE MOVE
## A New Exhibition on Transportation in American History

Smithsonian
*National Museum of American History*
*Behring Center*

# Maine

Cape Neddick Light,
York Harbor

© Bob & Suzanne
Clemenz

In January 2004, exit numbers on Maine's interstate highway system began shifting from sequential numbering to mileage-based numbering. Both new and old numbers will remain posted for one year. The exit numbers reflected in the individual property listings reflect the new mileage-based numbering.

# ARUNDEL

## ——— WHERE TO STAY ———

**ARUNDEL MEADOWS INN**  Phone: (207)985-3770

| | | |
|---|---|---|
| 5/28-10/11 [BP] | 2P: $100-$160 | XP: $20 |
| 5/1-5/27 [BP] | 2P: $95-$150 | XP: $20 |
| 10/12-4/30 [BP] | 2P: $70-$125 | XP: $20 |

Historic Bed & Breakfast  **Location:** I-95 (Maine Tpke), exit 25, 2 mi e on SR 35, 1 mi n on US 1. 1024 Portland Rd 04046 (PO Box 1129, KENNEBUNK, 04043). Fax: 207/985-3770. **Facility:** Convenient to Kennebunkport and its attractions, this renovated early-1800s farmhouse is furnished with many original paintings and antiques. Smoke free premises. 7 units. 6 one-bedroom standard units. 1 two-bedroom suite. 2 stories (no elevator), interior/exterior corridors. *Bath:* combo or shower only. **Parking:** on-site. **Terms:** 2 night minimum stay - 5/31-10/11, 14 day cancellation notice-fee imposed, weekly rates available, no pets allowed (owner's pet on premises). **Leisure Activities:** whirlpool. **Cards:** MC, VI.

SOME UNITS
✕ ☎ / Ⓦ VCR /

## ——— WHERE TO DINE ———

*The following restaurant has not been evaluated by AAA but is listed for your information only.*

**SEAFOOD CENTER**  Phone: 207/985-7391

[fyi]   Not evaluated. **Location:** US Rt 1 04043. **Features:** Open all year, the restaurant enables guests to savor traditional lobster pound offerings without going to the ocean's edge.

# AUBURN pop. 23,203

## ——— WHERE TO STAY ———

**A FIRESIDE INN & SUITES**  Phone: (207)777-1777

| | | | |
|---|---|---|---|
| 6/21-9/6 [ECP] | 1P: $105-$120 | 2P: $105-$120 | XP: $10  F12 |
| 5/1-6/20 [ECP] | 1P: $80-$110 | 2P: $80-$110 | XP: $10  F12 |
| 9/7-11/1 [ECP] | 1P: $85-$100 | 2P: $85-$100 | XP: $10  F12 |
| 11/2-4/30 [ECP] | 1P: $80-$90 | 2P: $80-$90 | XP: $10  F12 |

Small-scale Hotel  **Location:** I-95 (Maine Tpke), exit 75, 5 mi s on US 202, SR 4 and 100. 1777 Washington St 04210. Fax: 207/777-1777. **Facility:** 100 units. 84 one-bedroom standard units. 16 one-bedroom suites ($80-$155) with efficiencies, some with whirlpools. 2 stories (no elevator), interior/exterior corridors. *Bath:* combo or shower only. **Parking:** on-site. **Terms:** 3 day cancellation notice, package plans. **Amenities:** irons, hair dryers. **Pool(s):** outdoor. **Guest Services:** valet and coin laundry. **Business Services:** meeting rooms. **Cards:** AX, CB, DC, DS, MC, VI. *(See color ad p 244)*

SOME UNITS
(ASK) (S⊘) 🐾 🍴 ⊅ DATA PORT / ✕ VCR 🛗 🖥 🖳 /
FEE  FEE

**EXECUTIVE INN**  Phone: (207)784-1331

(AAA) (SAVE)   All Year [ECP]   1P: $49-$120   2P: $59-$140   XP: $10  F10
  **Location:** North side on SR 4. 170 Center St 04210. Fax: 207/786-2286. **Facility:** 72 one-bedroom standard units. 2 stories (no elevator), interior/exterior corridors. **Parking:** on-site. **Terms:** cancellation fee imposed. **Amenities:** hair dryers. **Guest Services:** valet and coin laundry. **Business Services:** meeting rooms.
Small-scale Hotel  **Cards:** AX, DS, MC, VI. **Special Amenities:** free expanded continental breakfast and free local telephone calls. *(See color ad below)*

SOME UNITS
(S⊘) 🍴 📺 DATA PORT 🖳 / ✕ 🛗 🖥 /
FEE  FEE

——— The following lodging was either not evaluated or did not ———
meet AAA rating requirements but is listed for your information only.

**HILTON GARDEN INN AUBURN RIVERWATCH**  **Phone:** 207/784-4433
(fyi)  All Year  1P: $89-$179  2P: $89-$179  XP: $10  F18
Small-scale Hotel  Too new to rate. **Location:** SR 4, just e on Hampshire St; center. 14 Great Falls Plaza 04210. Fax: 207/777-7328.
**Amenities:** 108 units, restaurant, coffeemakers, microwaves, refrigerators, pool. **Cards:** AX, DC, DS, MC, VI.

——— **WHERE TO DINE** ———

**MAC'S GRILL**  **Lunch:** $5-$20  **Dinner:** $8-$20  **Phone:** 207/783-6885
◇◇ ◇◇  **Location:** Jct US 202, 2 mi sw on SR 121. 1052 Minot Ave 04210. **Hours:** 11:30 am-9:30 pm, Fri & Sat-10:30
Steak House  pm. Closed: 11/25, 12/25. **Features:** Rustic decor, including a moosehead wall mount, enhances the genuine log cabin. The restaurant's lively and casual atmosphere makes it a popular destination for locals and visitors alike. Although Black Angus steak is the main attraction, chicken and seafood also are available. Various sauces and ribs have hearty flavors. Casual dress; cocktails. **Parking:** on-site. **Cards:** AX, DS, MC, VI.

**ROLANDEAU'S**  **Lunch:** $6-$13  **Dinner:** $14-$22  **Phone:** 207/784-2110
◇◇ ◇◇  **Location:** 2.5 mi w on US 202 and SR 4, follow sign; I-95 (Maine Tpke), exit 75, e on US 202 to Auburn. 775
American  Washington St 04210. **Hours:** 11 am-2:30 & 5-10 pm, Sat from 5 pm; hours may vary in winter. Closed: 1/1, 12/25; also Sun & for dinner 12/24. **Reservations:** suggested, weekends. **Features:** The varied menu at Rolandeau's includes a good variety of French dishes as well as prime rib, rack of lamb, veal, fresh lobster and dessert, including cheesecake terrine and peach Melba. This fine restaurant has been serving guests for 30 years. Casual dress; cocktails. **Parking:** on-site. **Cards:** AX, DS, MC, VI.

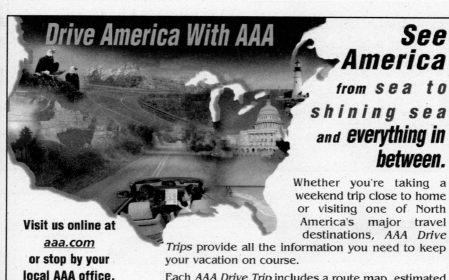

# AUGUSTA pop. 18,560

─── WHERE TO STAY ───

**BEST INN**    *Book at aaa.com*                                          Phone: (207)622-3776

(AAA) (SAVE)

|  |  |  |  |
|---|---|---|---|
| 7/1-8/31 [ECP] | 1P: $79-$119 | 2P: $79-$119 | |
| 9/1-10/31 [ECP] | 1P: $69-$119 | 2P: $69-$119 | |
| 5/1-6/30 [ECP] | 1P: $69-$109 | 2P: $69-$109 | |
| 11/1-4/30 [ECP] | 1P: $59-$79 | 2P: $59-$79 | XP: $10    F16 |

Motel    **Location:** I-95, exit 109 (Augusta-Winthrop) northbound; exit 109A southbound, west fork to Winthrop, s at light. Located in a commercial area. 65 Whitten Rd 04330. Fax: 207/622-3778. **Facility:** 58 one-bedroom standard units. 2 stories (no elevator), exterior corridors. **Parking:** on-site. **Amenities:** irons, hair dryers. **Pool(s):** outdoor. **Leisure Activities:** exercise room. **Guest Services:** valet and coin laundry. **Cards:** AX, CB, DC, DS, JC, MC, VI. **Special Amenities:** free expanded continental breakfast and free local telephone calls. *(See color ad below)*

SOME UNITS

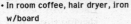
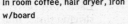

## BEST WESTERN SENATOR INN & SPA

**(AAA) (SAVE)**
**Book at aaa.com**

Phone: (207)622-5804

| | | | | |
|---|---|---|---|---|
| 7/1-8/31 [BP] | 1P: $109-$239 | 2P: $119-$259 | XP: $10 | F17 |
| 5/1-6/30 & 9/1-10/31 [BP] | 1P: $99-$189 | 2P: $109-$209 | XP: $10 | F17 |
| 11/1-4/30 [BP] | 1P: $89-$159 | 2P: $99-$179 | XP: $10 | F17 |

Small-scale Hotel
**Location:** I-95, exit 109 (Augusta-Winthrop) northbound; exit 109A southbound on US 202, SR 11 and 100. 284 Western Ave 04330. Fax: 04330. **Facility:** 103 one-bedroom standard units. 22 one-bedroom suites, some with whirlpools. 2 stories, interior/exterior corridors. **Parking:** on-site. **Terms:** pets ($50 deposit, $9 extra charge). **Amenities:** voice mail, irons, hair dryers. *Some:* CD players, dual phone lines. **Dining:** The Senator Restaurant, see separate listing. **Pool(s):** heated outdoor, heated indoor. **Leisure Activities:** sauna, whirlpool, exercise room, spa. **Guest Services:** valet and coin laundry. **Business Services:** meeting rooms. **Cards:** AX, CB, DC, DS, MC, VI. **Special Amenities: free full breakfast and free local telephone calls.** *(See color ad p 154)*

SOME UNITS

## COMFORT INN   Book at aaa.com

Phone: (207)623-1000

| | | | |
|---|---|---|---|
| 7/1-8/31 | 1P: $114-$189 | 2P: $114-$189 | XP: $10 | F18 |
| 5/1-6/30 & 9/1-4/30 | 1P: $94-$149 | 2P: $94-$149 | XP: $10 | F18 |

Small-scale Hotel
**Location:** I-95, exit 112B northbound; exit 112 southbound. 281 Civic Center Dr 04330. Fax: 207/623-3505. **Facility:** 99 one-bedroom standard units, some with whirlpools. 3 stories, interior corridors. **Parking:** on-site. **Terms:** 3 day cancellation notice. **Amenities:** voice mail, irons, hair dryers. **Pool(s):** heated indoor. **Leisure Activities:** whirlpool, exercise room. **Guest Services:** valet laundry. **Cards:** AX, CB, DC, DS, JC, MC, VI.

SOME UNITS

## ECONO LODGE INN & SUITES   Book at aaa.com

**(AAA) (SAVE)**

Phone: (207)622-6371

| | | | |
|---|---|---|---|
| 7/1-10/11 | 1P: $79-$109 | 2P: $89-$119 | XP: $10 | F |
| 5/1-6/30 & 10/12-4/30 | 1P: $69-$89 | 2P: $79-$99 | XP: $10 | F |

Small-scale Hotel
**Location:** I-95, exit 109 (Augusta-Winthrop) northbound; exit 109B southbound on US 202, SR 11 and 100. 390 Western Ave 04330. Fax: 207/621-0349. **Facility:** 128 units. 127 one-bedroom standard units. 1 one-bedroom suite. 2 stories (no elevator), exterior corridors. **Parking:** on-site. **Terms:** [CP] meal plan available. **Amenities:** irons, hair dryers. **Dining:** 4 pm-10 pm, cocktails. **Pool(s):** outdoor, wading. **Leisure Activities:** playground. **Guest Services:** valet and coin laundry. **Business Services:** meeting rooms. **Cards:** AX, DC, DS, MC, VI. **Special Amenities: free expanded continental breakfast and free local telephone calls.** *(See color ad p 154)*

SOME UNITS

## HOLIDAY INN   Book at aaa.com

Phone: (207)622-4751

| | | | |
|---|---|---|---|
| 7/1-8/31 | 1P: $114-$169 | 2P: $114-$169 | XP: $10 | F19 |
| 5/1-6/30 & 9/1-4/30 | 1P: $94-$129 | 2P: $94-$129 | XP: $10 | F19 |

Small-scale Hotel
**Location:** I-95, exit 112A northbound; exit 112 southbound, just s on SR 8, 11 and 27. Located adjacent to Augusta Civic Center. 110 Community Dr 04330. Fax: 207/622-3108. **Facility:** 102 one-bedroom standard units. 2 stories (no elevator), interior corridors. **Bath:** combo or shower only. **Parking:** on-site. **Terms:** 3 day cancellation notice. **Amenities:** dual phone lines, voice mail, irons, hair dryers. **Pool(s):** outdoor. **Leisure Activities:** exercise room. **Guest Services:** valet laundry. **Business Services:** meeting rooms. **Cards:** AX, CB, DC, DS, JC, MC, VI.

SOME UNITS

## SUPER 8 MOTEL   Book at aaa.com

Phone: (207)626-2888

| | | | |
|---|---|---|---|
| All Year [CP] | 1P: $48-$85 | 2P: $50-$105 | XP: $10 | F12 |

Small-scale Hotel
**Location:** I-95, exit 109 (Augusta-Winthrop) northbound; exit 109A southbound on US 202 and SR 11. 395 Western Ave 04330. Fax: 207/623-8468. **Facility:** 50 one-bedroom standard units. 2 stories (no elevator), interior corridors. **Parking:** on-site. **Guest Services:** valet and coin laundry. **Cards:** AX, CB, DC, DS, JC, MC, VI.

SOME UNITS

------ WHERE TO DINE ------

## BEALE ST BBQ

Barbecue

**Lunch:** $6-$18        **Dinner:** $6-$18        Phone: 207/622-8899
**Location:** Downtown. 300 Water St 04330. **Hours:** 11 am-9 pm. **Closed:** 11/25, 12/25. **Features:** Popular with locals and tourists alike, the restaurant serves Memphis-style barbecue, which is made on the premises. Guests also can sample such dishes as jambalaya, shrimp Louisianne and Santa Fe chicken. Casual dress; cocktails. **Parking:** street. **Cards:** MC, VI.

## THE SENATOR RESTAURANT

American

**Lunch:** $7-$14        **Dinner:** $14-$28        Phone: 207/622-0320
**Location:** I-95, exit 109 (Augusta-Winthrop) northbound; exit 109A southbound on US 202, SR 11 and 100; in Best Western Senator Inn & Spa. 284 Western Ave 04330. **Hours:** 6:30 am-10 pm. **Closed:** 12/25. **Reservations:** accepted. **Features:** Don't let the formal decor fool you into thinking the atmosphere is stuffy. You will see everything from jeans to business suits. The menu features fresh Maine seafood as well as pasta, vegetarian items, an oyster bar and Yankee dinners. Be sure to ask for the dessert cart as it looks good enough to add calories at a glance. Casual dress; cocktails. **Parking:** on-site. **Cards:** AX, CB, DC, DS, MC, VI. *(See color ad p 154)*

# BAILEY ISLAND

------ WHERE TO STAY ------

## LOG CABIN AN ISLAND INN

Country Inn

Phone: 207/833-5546

| | | |
|---|---|---|
| 5/1-10/30 & 4/2-4/30 | 2P: $109-$299 | XP: $20 |

**Location:** Cross Bailey Island Bridge, 0.5 mi s on SR 24. 5 Log Cabin Ln 04003 (PO Box 410). Fax: 207/833-7858. **Facility:** The inn overlooks Casco Bay and has an upscale log cabin ambience throughout; guest rooms have contemporary decor and most have a deck. Smoke free premises. 9 units. 7 one-bedroom standard units, some with kitchens and/or whirlpools. 2 one-bedroom suites with kitchens, some with whirlpools. 2 stories (no elevator), interior/exterior corridors. **Bath:** combo or shower only. **Parking:** on-site. **Terms:** open 5/1-10/30 & 4/2-4/30, 21 day cancellation notice-fee imposed. **Amenities:** video library, hair dryers. **Pool(s):** heated outdoor. **Guest Services:** gift shop. **Cards:** AX, DS, MC, VI.

SOME UNITS

## BANGOR pop. 31,473

──── WHERE TO STAY ────

**BANGOR MOTOR INN**
AAA SAVE
Small-scale Hotel

| | | | Phone: (207)947-0355 | |
|---|---|---|---|---|
| 7/1-10/31 [CP] | 1P: $68-$78 | 2P: $78-$88 | XP: $8 | F |
| 5/1-6/30 & 11/1-4/30 [CP] | 1P: $52-$62 | 2P: $62-$72 | XP: $6 | F |

**Location:** I-95, exit 187 (Hogan Rd), 0.3 mi w. Located next to a mall. 701 Hogan Rd 04401. Fax: 207/947-0350. **Facility:** 103 units. 93 one-bedroom standard units. 10 one-bedroom suites ($125-$145). 2 stories (no elevator), interior corridors. **Bath:** combo or shower only. **Parking:** on-site. **Amenities:** video library (fee). *Some:* hair dryers. **Guest Services:** valet laundry, area transportation-mall & hospital. **Business Services:** conference facilities. **Cards:** AX, CB, DC, MC, VI. **Special Amenities:** free continental breakfast and free local telephone calls.

SOME UNITS
[icons] SOME UNITS

---

**BEST INN**   *Book at aaa.com*
Small-scale Hotel

| | | | Phone: (207)942-1234 | |
|---|---|---|---|---|
| 7/1-9/4 [ECP] | 1P: $95-$110 | 2P: $95-$110 | XP: $10 | F18 |
| 6/30 & 9/5-10/31 [ECP] | 1P: $85-$95 | 2P: $85-$95 | XP: $10 | F18 |
| 11/1-4/30 [ECP] | 1P: $75-$85 | 2P: $75-$85 | XP: $10 | F18 |

**Location:** Jct I-395. 570 Main St 04401. Fax: 207/942-1234. **Facility:** 51 units. 50 one-bedroom standard units. 1 two-bedroom suite ($165-$195) with kitchen. 2 stories (no elevator), interior corridors. **Parking:** on-site. **Amenities:** video library (fee), hair dryers. **Guest Services:** valet laundry. **Business Services:** meeting rooms. **Cards:** AX, CB, DC, MC, VI.

SOME UNITS
[icons] FEE   FEE

---

**BEST WESTERN WHITE HOUSE**   *Book at aaa.com*
Small-scale Hotel

| | | | Phone: (207)862-3737 | |
|---|---|---|---|---|
| 7/1-9/6 [ECP] | 1P: $113-$123 | 2P: $113-$123 | XP: $10 | F12 |
| 9/7-10/31 [ECP] | 1P: $90-$100 | 2P: $90-$100 | XP: $10 | F12 |
| 5/1-6/30 [ECP] | 1P: $73-$83 | 2P: $73-$83 | XP: $10 | F12 |
| 11/1-4/30 [ECP] | 1P: $60-$70 | 2P: $60-$70 | XP: $10 | F12 |

**Location:** I-95, exit 180 (Coldbrook Rd), 5.5 mi s of downtown. Located in a rural area. 155 Littlefield Ave 04401. Fax: 207/862-3737. **Facility:** 65 one-bedroom standard units. 3 stories, interior/exterior corridors. **Parking:** on-site. **Terms:** package plans - seasonal & weekends. **Amenities:** irons, hair dryers. **Pool(s):** heated outdoor. **Leisure Activities:** sauna, volleyball. **Guest Services:** valet and coin laundry. **Cards:** AX, CB, DC, DS, MC, VI. *(See ad below)*

SOME UNITS
[icons] FEE

---

**COMFORT INN**   *Book at aaa.com*
Small-scale Hotel

| | | | Phone: (207)942-7899 |
|---|---|---|---|
| 7/1-10/19 [ECP] | 1P: $79-$89 | 2P: $89-$109 | |
| 10/20-4/30 [ECP] | 1P: $59-$69 | 2P: $69-$79 | |
| 5/1-6/30 [ECP] | 1P: $59-$69 | 2P: $59-$79 | XP: $6   F18 |

**Location:** I-95, exit 187 (Hogan Rd), 0.5 mi w. Located adjacent to a shopping mall. 750 Hogan Rd 04401. Fax: 207/942-6463. **Facility:** 96 one-bedroom standard units. 2 stories, interior corridors. **Parking:** on-site. **Terms:** small pets only ($6 extra charge). **Amenities:** hair dryers. *Fee:* video games, safes. *Some:* irons. **Pool(s):** small outdoor. **Leisure Activities:** exercise room, game room. **Guest Services:** valet laundry. **Business Services:** meeting rooms. **Cards:** AX, DC, DS, MC, VI.

SOME UNITS
[icons] FEE

---

**DAYS INN**   *Book at aaa.com*
Small-scale Hotel

| | | | Phone: (207)942-8272 | |
|---|---|---|---|---|
| 7/1-10/31 | 1P: $69-$89 | 2P: $79-$99 | XP: $6 | F17 |
| 5/1-6/30 & 11/1-4/30 | 1P: $49-$69 | 2P: $59-$79 | XP: $6 | F17 |

**Location:** I-95, exit 182B, 0.3 mi e on US 2 and SR 100. Located in a commercial area, next to entertainment complex. 250 Odlin Rd 04401. Fax: 207/942-1382. **Facility:** 101 one-bedroom standard units. 2 stories (no elevator), interior corridors. **Parking:** on-site. **Terms:** [ECP] meal plan available, pets ($6 extra charge). **Amenities:** video games, safes (fee), hair dryers. **Pool(s):** heated indoor. **Leisure Activities:** game room. **Guest Services:** valet laundry. **Cards:** AX, CB, DC, DS, JC, MC, VI.

SOME UNITS
[icons] FEE   FEE

---

**ECONO LODGE** *Book at aaa.com*

Motel

| |  |  |
|---|---|---|
| 7/1-8/31 | 1P: $69-$89 | 2P: $79-$99 |
| 9/1-10/20 | 1P: $59-$79 | 2P: $69-$89 |
| 5/1-6/30 | 1P: $49-$69 | 2P: $59-$79 |
| 10/21-4/30 | 1P: $40-$50 | 2P: $50-$60 |

**Phone:** 207/945-0111

**Location:** I-95, exit 182B, just e on US 2 and SR 100. Located next to a theme park. 327 Odlin Rd 04401. **Fax:** 207/942-8856. **Facility:** 128 one-bedroom standard units. 4 stories, interior corridors. **Parking:** on-site, winter plug-ins. **Terms:** pets ($6 fee). **Amenities:** video games (fee). **Guest Services:** valet and coin laundry. **Cards:** AX, DC, DS, MC, VI.

---

**FAIRFIELD INN BY MARRIOTT** *Book at aaa.com*

Small-scale Hotel

| |  |  |
|---|---|---|
| 7/7-8/31 [CP] | 1P: $89-$109 | 2P: $89-$109 |
| 5/1-7/6 & 9/1-4/30 [CP] | 1P: $69-$99 | 2P: $69-$99 |

**Phone:** 207/990-0001

**Location:** I-95, exit 182B, just e on US 2 and SR 100. Located in a commercial area. 300 Odlin Rd 04401. **Fax:** 207/990-0917. **Facility:** 153 one-bedroom standard units. 3 stories, interior corridors. **Parking:** on-site. **Amenities:** irons. **Pool(s):** heated indoor. **Leisure Activities:** sauna, whirlpool, exercise room. **Guest Services:** valet and coin laundry. **Cards:** AX, DC, DS, MC, VI. *(See ad below)*

---

**FOUR POINTS BY SHERATON BANGOR** *Book at aaa.com*

Small-scale Hotel

| |  |  |  | |
|---|---|---|---|---|
| 7/6-10/18 | 1P: $127-$159 | 2P: $127-$159 | XP: $10 | F17 |
| 5/1-7/5 & 4/1-4/30 | 1P: $111-$139 | 2P: $111-$139 | XP: $10 | F17 |
| 10/19-3/31 | 1P: $103-$129 | 2P: $103-$129 | XP: $10 | F17 |

**Phone:** (207)947-6721

**Location:** At Bangor International Airport. 308 Godfrey Blvd 04401. **Fax:** 207/941-9761. **Facility:** 102 one-bedroom standard units. 9 stories, interior corridors. **Parking:** on-site. **Terms:** pets ($20 extra charge). **Amenities:** voice mail, irons, hair dryers. **Pool(s):** outdoor. **Leisure Activities:** exercise room. **Fee:** game room. **Guest Services:** valet laundry. **Business Services:** meeting rooms. **Cards:** AX, DC, DS, MC, VI. *(See color ad p 5)*

---

**HAMPTON INN-BANGOR** *Book at aaa.com*

Small-scale Hotel

| |  |  |
|---|---|---|
| 7/25-10/23 | 1P: $109-$139 | 2P: $109-$139 |
| 6/6-7/24 | 1P: $89-$119 | 2P: $89-$119 |
| 5/1-6/5 & 10/24-4/30 | 1P: $79-$109 | 2P: $79-$109 |

**Phone:** (207)990-4400

**Location:** I-95, exit 187 (Hogan Rd). 10 Bangor Mall Blvd 04401. **Fax:** 207/990-0577. **Facility:** 119 one-bedroom standard units. 3 stories, interior corridors. *Bath:* combo or shower only. **Parking:** on-site. **Terms:** [ECP] meal plan available. **Amenities:** voice mail, irons, hair dryers. **Guest Services:** valet laundry. **Business Services:** meeting rooms. **Cards:** AX, CB, DC, DS, MC, VI.

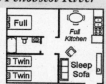

**HOLIDAY INN-BANGOR**    *Book at aaa.com*
Phone: 207/947-0101

| | 9/1-11/1 | 1P: $121 | 2P: $131 | XP: $10 | F17 |
| | 5/1-8/31 | 1P: $129 | 2P: $129 | XP: $10 | F17 |
| | 11/2-4/30 | 1P: $111 | 2P: $121 | XP: $10 | F17 |

Small-scale Hotel **Location:** I-95, exit 182B at jct Odlin Rd and I-395. 404 Odlin Rd 04401. Fax: 207/947-7619. **Facility:** 207 one-bedroom standard units. 3 stories, interior corridors. **Parking:** on-site. **Terms:** [AP], [BP], [CP] & [ECP] meal plans available, $2 service charge, pets (in smoking units). **Amenities:** video games (fee), voice mail, irons, hair dryers. *Some:* dual phone lines. **Pool(s):** outdoor, heated indoor. **Leisure Activities:** whirlpool. **Guest Services:** valet and coin laundry, area transportation. **Business Services:** meeting rooms. **Cards:** AX, MC, VI.

SOME UNITS
(ASK) ⊞ ⊠ ♿ ⛵ 🍴 ⛲ 📷 [DATA PORT] 🖥 / ⊠ 🛢 🖼 /
FEE FEE

---

**HOLIDAY INN BANGOR-CIVIC CENTER**    *Book at aaa.com*
Phone: (207)947-8651

| | All Year | 1P: $63-$119 | 2P: $63-$119 | F18 |

Small-scale Hotel **Location:** Center. 500 Main St 04401. Fax: 207/942-2848. **Facility:** 121 one-bedroom standard units. 2-4 stories, interior corridors. **Parking:** on-site. **Terms:** [BP] meal plan available. **Amenities:** video games (fee), irons, hair dryers. **Pool(s):** outdoor. **Leisure Activities:** exercise room. **Guest Services:** valet and coin laundry. **Business Services:** meeting rooms. **Cards:** AX, CB, DC, DS, JC, MC, VI.

SOME UNITS
(ASK) (SD) ⊠ 🍴 ⛲ 🛟 📷 [DATA PORT] 🖥 / ⊠ 🛢 /
FEE

---

**HOWARD JOHNSON INN**    *Book at aaa.com*
Phone: (207)942-5251

| | All Year | 1P: $59-$79 | 2P: $69-$99 |

(AAA) (SAVE) **Location:** I-95, exit 182B at jct Odlin Rd and I-395. Located in a commercial area. 336 Odlin Rd 04401. Fax: 207/942-4227. **Facility:** 58 one-bedroom standard units. 2 stories (no elevator), interior corridors. **Parking:** on-site. **Terms:** 30 day cancellation notice, pets ($10 extra charge). **Amenities:** safes (fee). Small-scale Hotel **Dining:** 6 am-11 pm, Fri & Sat-12:30 am, cocktails. **Pool(s):** heated outdoor. **Guest Services:** valet laundry. **Business Services:** meeting rooms. **Cards:** AX, CB, DC, DS, MC, VI. **Special Amenities:** free local telephone calls and free newspaper.

SOME UNITS
(SD) ⊠ 🍴 ⛲ 🛟 📷 [DATA PORT] 🖥 / ⊠ 🛢 🖼 /
FEE

---

**MAIN STREET INN**
Phone: (207)942-5282

| | 6/1-10/31 | 1P: $49 | 2P: $59 | XP: $5 | F17 |
| | 5/1-5/31 & 1/1-4/30 | 1P: $47 | 2P: $52 | XP: $5 | F17 |
| | 11/1-12/31 | 1P: $45 | 2P: $49 | XP: $5 | F17 |

Motel **Location:** I-95, exit 182A to jct I-395, exit 3B. 480 Main St 04401. Fax: 207/947-8733. **Facility:** 64 units. 63 one- and 1 two-bedroom standard units. 2 stories (no elevator), interior/exterior corridors. **Bath:** combo or shower only. **Parking:** on-site. **Terms:** [CP] meal plan available, small pets only (in smoking units). **Cards:** AX, DC, DS, MC, VI. **Special Amenities:** free continental breakfast.

SOME UNITS
(SD) ⊠ / ⊠ /

---

**RAMADA INN**    *Book at aaa.com*
Phone: (207)947-6961

| | All Year | 1P: $69-$139 | 2P: $79-$139 | XP: $10 | F16 |

Small-scale Hotel **Location:** I-95, exit 182B at jct Odlin Rd and I-395. 357 Odlin Rd 04401. Fax: 207/945-9428. **Facility:** 115 units. 113 one-bedroom standard units. 2 one-bedroom suites. 2 stories (no elevator), interior corridors. **Parking:** on-site. **Terms:** cancellation fee imposed, [AP] & [BP] meal plans available. **Amenities:** voice mail, irons, hair dryers. **Pool(s):** heated indoor. **Leisure Activities:** exercise room. *Fee:* game room. **Guest Services:** valet laundry. **Business Services:** meeting rooms, business center. **Cards:** AX, DC, DS, MC, VI.

SOME UNITS
(ASK) (SD) ⊞ ⊠ 🍴 ⛲ 🛟 📷 [DATA PORT] 🖥 / ⊠ 🛢 🖼 /
FEE

---

**RIVERSIDE INN**
Phone: 207/973-4100

| | All Year | 1P: $79-$129 | 2P: $79-$129 | XP: $10 | F10 |

Small-scale Hotel **Location:** Adjacent to Eastern Maine Medical Center. 495 State St 04401. Fax: 207/973-4110. **Facility:** Designated smoking area. 50 units. 41 one-bedroom standard units, some with whirlpools. 9 one-bedroom suites. 5 stories, interior corridors. **Parking:** on-site. **Terms:** small pets only ($5 extra charge). **Amenities:** video library (fee), voice mail, hair dryers. *Some:* dual phone lines. **Guest Services:** valet and coin laundry. **Cards:** AX, DS, MC, VI.

SOME UNITS
⊠ ⊠ (VCR) [DATA PORT] 🖥 / 🛢 🖼 /
FEE FEE

---

**SUPER 8 MOTEL**
Phone: (207)945-5681

| | All Year [ECP] | 1P: $44-$69 | 2P: $54-$79 | XP: $5 | F18 |

(AAA) (SAVE) **Location:** I-95, exit 182B. 462 Odlin Rd 04401. Fax: 207/945-5682. **Facility:** 77 one-bedroom standard units. 2 stories (no elevator), interior corridors. **Parking:** on-site. **Business Services:** meeting rooms. **Cards:** AX, DC, DS, MC, VI. **Special Amenities:** free expanded continental breakfast and free local telephone Small-scale Hotel calls.

SOME UNITS
(SD) ⊞ 🍴 🛟 (♿) 📷 [DATA PORT] 🖥 / ⊠ (VCR) /

---

**TRAVELODGE**    *Book at aaa.com*
Phone: (207)942-6301

| | 7/1-10/15 [CP] | 1P: $55-$95 | 2P: $65-$105 | XP: $10 | F12 |
| | 5/1-6/30 & 10/16-4/30 [CP] | 1P: $45-$85 | 2P: $55-$95 | XP: $10 | F12 |

Motel **Location:** I-95, exit 182B, just left. 482 Odlin Rd 04401. Fax: 207/941-0949. **Facility:** 98 one-bedroom standard units. 2 stories (no elevator), exterior corridors. **Parking:** on-site. **Terms:** small pets only ($10 extra charge). **Amenities:** hair dryers. **Guest Services:** valet laundry. **Cards:** AX, DS, MC, VI.

SOME UNITS
(ASK) (SD) ⊞ ⊠ 📷 [DATA PORT] 🖥 / ⊠ 🛢 /
FEE

## ——— WHERE TO DINE ———

**ATLANTIC SEAFOOD & GRILL**  **Lunch:** $7-$18  **Dinner:** $9-$20  **Phone:** 207/262-0097
**Location:** I-95, exit 187 (Hogan Rd). 8 Bangor Mall Blvd 04401. **Hours:** 11 am-9 pm. Closed: Mon 11/1-3/15.
**Features:** Close to Bangor Mall, the eatery has seafood shipped in fresh daily from the coast. The menu
Seafood   also includes items for landlubbers, such as steaks, chicken, pasta, sandwiches and soup. Casual dress;
cocktails. **Parking:** on-site. **Cards:** AX, DC, DS, MC, VI.

**BUGABOO CREEK STEAK HOUSE**  **Lunch:** $6-$12  **Dinner:** $10-$17  **Phone:** 207/945-5515
**Location:** I-95, exit 187 (Hogan Rd), 0.3 mi w, then 0.3 mi s. 24 Bangor Mall Blvd 04401. **Hours:** 11:30 am-10 pm,
Fri & Sat-10:30 pm, Sun noon-9 pm. Closed: 11/25, 12/25. **Reservations:** accepted, Mon-Thurs.
**Features:** The fun, lively restaurant has a North Woods theme. Although the menu centers on steak, it
Steak House   also lists jambalaya, chicken and seafood dishes. Homemade desserts are a special temptation. Casual
dress; cocktails. **Parking:** on-site. **Cards:** AX, DS, MC, VI.

**CAPTAIN NICK'S FAMILY RESTAURANT**  **Lunch:** $5-$10  **Dinner:** $12-$19  **Phone:** 207/942-6444
**Location:** Center. 1165 Union St 04401. **Hours:** 11 am-9:30 pm, Fri & Sat-10 pm, Sun-9 pm. Closed: 11/25,
12/25. **Reservations:** suggested, weekends. **Features:** Maine lobster, prime rib and fresh strawberry pie
Steak & Seafood   (in the summer) are the delicious specialties at Captain Nick's. This family-style restaurant across from the
Bangor International Airport has several dining areas, including a room within a railroad dining car. Casual
dress; cocktails. **Parking:** on-site. **Cards:** AX, DS, MC, VI.

**GUINNESS & PORCELLI'S**  **Dinner:** $8-$24  **Phone:** 207/947-2300
**Location:** I-395, exit 3B, just s. 735 Main St 04401. **Hours:** 5 pm-9 pm; closing time may vary. Closed: Sun.
**Reservations:** accepted. **Features:** In a renovated, historic sea captain's home, the restaurant offers
seating in several elegant dining rooms and in a sunny atrium. The seasonally changing menu centers on
traditional dishes, including hand-rolled pasta, chicken, lamb, fish and veal. Ingredients are local whenever
Italian   possible. Service is attentive. Casual dress; cocktails. **Parking:** on-site. **Cards:** AX, MC, VI.

**ICHIBAN**  **Lunch:** $6-$10  **Dinner:** $8-$16  **Phone:** 207/262-9308
**Location:** Jct US 2/SR 100 and 222. 226 Third & Union St 04401. **Hours:** 11 am-2:30 & 4:30-9 pm, Thurs-Sat to
10 pm, Sun 4 pm-9 pm. **Reservations:** not accepted. **Features:** The family-friendly restaurant features
fresh sushi selections, as well as tempura, teriyaki and combination lunches and dinners, and other
Japanese   traditional dishes. The atmosphere is casual. Casual dress; beer & wine only. **Parking:** on-site. **Cards:** AX,
MC, VI.

**MILLER'S RESTAURANT**  **Lunch:** $6-$10  **Dinner:** $11-$18  **Phone:** 207/942-6361
**Location:** US 1A, 202, SR 9 and 100. 427 Main St 04401. **Hours:** 11 am-10 pm, Sun 10:30 am-9 pm. Closed:
12/25. **Reservations:** accepted. **Features:** Miller's features good, family-style fare in its offerings. The
menu specializes in prime rib, wood-grilled steak, fresh seafood and chicken dishes. The casual
atmosphere is comfortable and relaxed; the serving staff is prompt, friendly and attentive. Casual dress;
American   cocktails. **Parking:** on-site. **Cards:** AX, DS, MC, VI.

**ORIENTAL JADE RESTAURANT**  **Lunch:** $4-$8  **Dinner:** $8-$17  **Phone:** 207/947-6969
**Location:** I-95, exit 187 (Hogan Rd), 0.3 mi w; behind Bangor Mall. 555 Stillwater Ave 04401. **Hours:** 11 am-9:30
pm, Fri & Sat-10:30 pm. Closed: 11/25. **Reservations:** accepted. **Features:** The world-class buffet at
Oriental Jade features Polynesian, Cantonese and Szechuan specialties, as well as several American
Chinese   dishes. Four different dining rooms display a comfortable and contemporary Oriental decor that's warm and
cozy. They have a gift shop too. Casual dress; cocktails. **Parking:** on-site. **Cards:** AX, DS, MC, VI.

**PEPINO'S MEXICAN RESTAURANT**  **Lunch:** $7-$11  **Dinner:** $8-$16  **Phone:** 207/947-1233
**Location:** I-95, exit 187 (Hogan Rd), 0.5 mi w. 570 Stillwater Ave 04401. **Hours:** 11 am-9 pm, Fri & Sat-10 pm.
Closed major holidays. **Features:** You'll enjoy the open and airy dining room at Pepino's. The restaurant
offers a plentiful menu selection, fine cocktail and beer list including a couple of Mexican beers, and a
Mexican   good wine list with a few by-the-glass offerings. Service is friendly. Casual dress; cocktails. **Parking:**
on-site. **Cards:** AX, DS, MC, VI.

**SEA DOG BREWING CO RESTAURANT**  **Lunch:** $7-$9  **Dinner:** $7-$18  **Phone:** 207/947-8004
**Location:** Center. 26 Front St 04401. **Hours:** 11 am-1 am. Closed: 11/25, 12/25. **Features:** A bustling
atmosphere and good food draw patrons to the nautically decorated restaurant/microbrewery, which affords
a good view of the Penobscot River. Included on the menu is a fine variety of seafood, vegetarian and
American   beef entrees. Deck seating can be requested in season. Casual dress; cocktails. **Parking:** on-site.
**Cards:** AX, DS, MC, VI.

**THISTLES RESTAURANT**  **Lunch:** $5-$12  **Dinner:** $16-$25  **Phone:** 207/945-5480
**Location:** Center; in Maliseet Plaza. 175 Exchange St 04401. **Hours:** 11 am-2:30 & 4:30-9 pm. Closed major
holidays; also Sun. **Reservations:** suggested. **Features:** In a business center, the restaurant sustains a
pleasant ambience with fine piano music and a friendly staff. The menu lists various seafood, meat and
International   pasta dishes and desserts made on the premises. Casual dress; cocktails. **Parking:** on-site. **Cards:** AX,
MC, VI.

——— *The following restaurant has not been evaluated by AAA* ———
*but is listed for your information only.*

**PAUL'S RESTAURANT & SPEAKEASY**  **Phone:** 207/942-6726
[fyi]   Not evaluated. **Location:** I-95, exit 187 (Hogan Rd), just w. 605 Hogan Rd 04401. **Features:** Pictures of stars
from the 1930s and '40s contribute to the mood of the popular eatery.

# BAR HARBOR pop. 2,680

──────── **WHERE TO STAY** ────────

### ACADIA INN

**Phone:** 207/288-3500

AAA SAVE

| | | | |
|---|---|---|---|
| 6/18-10/17 [ECP] | 1P: $125-$179 | 2P: $125-$179 | XP: $20 | F5 |
| 5/1-6/17 [ECP] | 1P: $75-$125 | 2P: $75-$125 | XP: $20 | F5 |
| 10/18-11/14 [ECP] | 1P: $75-$85 | 2P: $75-$85 | XP: $20 | F5 |
| 4/8-4/30 [ECP] | 1P: $69-$85 | 2P: $69-$85 | XP: $20 | F5 |

Small-scale Hotel **Location:** 1 mi w on SR 3. 98 Eden St 04609. Fax: 207/288-8424. **Facility:** 95 one-bedroom standard units. 3 stories, interior corridors. **Parking:** on-site. **Terms:** open 5/1-11/14 & 4/8-4/30, cancellation fee imposed, package plans. **Amenities:** irons, hair dryers. **Pool(s):** heated outdoor. **Leisure Activities:** whirlpool, playground. **Guest Services:** gift shop, coin laundry. **Cards:** AX, DS, MC, VI. **Special Amenities:** free expanded continental breakfast.
*(See color ad p 163)*

SOME UNITS

⊠ FEE

### ANCHORAGE MOTEL

**Phone:** 207/288-3959

AAA SAVE

| | | | |
|---|---|---|---|
| 7/13-8/31 | 1P: $89-$129 | 2P: $89-$129 | XP: $10 | F10 |
| 9/1-10/30 | 1P: $54-$99 | 2P: $54-$99 | XP: $10 | F10 |
| 6/26-7/12 | 1P: $69-$89 | 2P: $69-$89 | XP: $10 | F10 |
| 5/10-6/25 | 1P: $54-$69 | 2P: $54-$69 | XP: $10 | F10 |

Motel    **Location:** In town on SR 3. 51 Mt Desert St 04609. Fax: 419/828-4759. **Facility:** 46 one-bedroom standard units. 2 stories (no elevator), exterior corridors. **Parking:** on-site. **Terms:** open 5/10-10/30, 3 day cancellation notice-fee imposed, pets ($15 extra charge, in limited units). **Cards:** AX, CB, DC, DS, MC, VI. *(See color ad below)*

SOME UNITS

FEE    FEE  FEE  FEE

### ANNE'S WHITE COLUMNS INN

**Phone:** 207/288-5357

| | | | |
|---|---|---|---|
| 6/19-9/6 | 1P: $105-$150 | 2P: $105-$150 | XP: $15 | F5 |
| 9/7-10/11 | 1P: $95-$135 | 2P: $95-$135 | XP: $15 | F5 |
| 5/1-6/18 & 10/12-11/15 | 1P: $75-$100 | 2P: $75-$100 | XP: $15 | F5 |

Bed & Breakfast **Location:** Center. 57 Mt Desert St 04609. **Facility:** Designated smoking area. 10 one-bedroom standard units. 2 stories (no elevator), interior corridors. **Parking:** on-site. **Terms:** open 5/1-11/15, 7 day cancellation notice-fee imposed, [BP] meal plan available, no pets allowed (owner's pet on premises). **Cards:** AX, DS, MC, VI.

### THE ATLANTEAN INN

**Phone:** (207)288-5703

AAA SAVE

| | | | |
|---|---|---|---|
| 6/22-8/23 [BP] | 1P: $165-$285 | 2P: $165-$285 | XP: $20 | |
| 8/24-10/21 [BP] | 1P: $145-$275 | 2P: $145-$275 | XP: $20 | |
| 6/5-6/21 [BP] | 1P: $122-$185 | 2P: $122-$185 | XP: $20 | |
| 5/21-6/4 [BP] | 1P: $95-$185 | 2P: $95-$185 | XP: $20 | |

Historic Bed & Breakfast **Location:** Center. Located in a residential area. 11 Atlantic Ave 04609 (69 Mt Desert St). Fax: 207/288-3115. **Facility:** This 1903 Tudor-style building is furnished with many antiques. Smoke free premises. 8 units. 6 one-bedroom standard units, some with whirlpools. 2 two-bedroom suites with whirlpools. 3 stories (no elevator), interior corridors. *Bath:* combo or shower only. **Parking:** on-site. **Terms:** open 5/21-10/21, 2 night minimum stay, 10 day cancellation notice-fee imposed, package plans - seasonal, no pets allowed (owner's pet on premises). **Amenities:** video library, voice mail, irons, hair dryers. *Some:* CD players. **Cards:** AX, DS, MC, VI. **Special Amenities:** free full breakfast and free local telephone calls.

SOME UNITS

## ATLANTIC EYRIE LODGE

| | | | | |
|---|---|---|---|---|
| **AAA** SAVE | 7/1-9/5 | 1P: $110-$199 | 2P: $110-$199 | XP: $10 | F6 |
| | 9/6-10/17 | 1P: $85-$160 | 2P: $85-$160 | XP: $10 | F6 |
| ◇◇◇◇ | 6/15-6/30 | 1P: $69-$140 | 2P: $69-$140 | XP: $10 | F6 |
| | 5/20-6/14 | 1P: $56-$112 | 2P: $56-$112 | XP: $10 | F6 |

**Phone: 207/288-9786**

**Small-scale Hotel Location:** 1 mi w on SR 3 to Highbrook Rd. 6 Norman Rd 04609. Fax: 207/288-8500. **Facility:** 58 units. 57 one-bedroom standard units, some with efficiencies. 1 one-bedroom suite ($112-$199) with efficiency. 4 stories, exterior corridors. **Parking:** on-site. **Terms:** open 5/20-10/17, check-in 4 pm, 7 day cancellation notice-fee imposed, [CP] meal plan available. **Amenities:** hair dryers. **Pool(s):** heated outdoor. **Guest Services:** coin laundry. **Business Services:** meeting rooms. **Cards:** AX, DS, MC, VI. **Special Amenities:** free local telephone calls and free newspaper. (See color ad p 167)

SOME UNITS

⊠ / ⊠ 🛏 🖨 🖵 /

## ATLANTIC OAKES BY-THE-SEA

| | | | | |
|---|---|---|---|---|
| **AAA** SAVE | 7/1-9/5 | 1P: $159-$195 | 2P: $159-$195 | XP: $10 | F5 |
| | 9/6-10/20 | 1P: $143-$175 | 2P: $143-$175 | XP: $10 | F5 |
| ◇◇◇◇ | 5/1-6/30 | 1P: $91-$155 | 2P: $91-$155 | XP: $10 | F5 |
| | 10/21-4/30 | 1P: $62-$99 | 2P: $62-$99 | XP: $10 | F5 |

**Phone: (207)288-5801**

**Small-scale Hotel Location:** 1.8 mi w on SR 3. Located adjacent to the ferry landing. 119 Eden St 04609 (PO Box 3). Fax: 207/288-8402. **Facility:** 151 units. 149 one-bedroom standard units, some with efficiencies. 1 two- and 1 three-bedroom suites with kitchens. 2-4 stories, interior/exterior corridors. **Parking:** on-site. **Terms:** 7 day cancellation notice-fee imposed, package plans - seasonal. **Amenities:** voice mail, irons, hair dryers. **Pool(s):** heated outdoor, heated indoor. **Leisure Activities:** whirlpool, boat dock. *Fee:* 4 tennis courts (2 lighted). **Guest Services:** coin laundry. **Business Services:** conference facilities. **Cards:** AX, DS, MC, VI. **Special Amenities:** free local telephone calls and free newspaper. (See color ad p 166)

SOME UNITS

⊠ ⊠ DATA PORT 🛏 🖵 / ⊠ 🖵 /

## AURORA INN

| | | | | |
|---|---|---|---|---|
| **AAA** SAVE | 6/26-9/5 | 1P: $109-$149 | 2P: $109-$149 | XP: $10 | F18 |
| | 9/6-10/16 | 1P: $109-$139 | 2P: $109-$139 | XP: $10 | F18 |
| ◇◇ | 5/1-6/25 | 1P: $69-$109 | 2P: $69-$109 | XP: $10 | F18 |
| Motel | 10/17-4/30 | 1P: $69-$99 | 2P: $69-$99 | XP: $10 | F18 |

**Phone: (207)288-3771**

**Location:** Center. 51 Holland Ave 04609. Fax: 207/288-1214. **Facility:** 10 one-bedroom standard units. 1 story, exterior corridors. **Parking:** on-site. **Terms:** office hours 8 am-10 pm, 3 day cancellation notice. **Amenities:** hair dryers. **Cards:** AX, DS, MC, VI. **Special Amenities:** free local telephone calls. (See color ad p 165)

S🄳 🍴 ⊠ 🎬 🛏 🖵 🖵

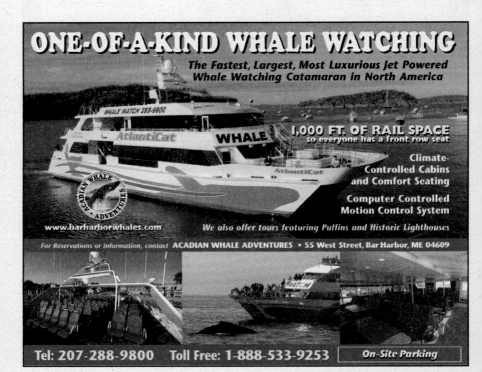

A WONDER VIEW INN & SUITES

Small-scale Hotel

| | | Phone: 207/288-3358 |
|---|---|---|
| 7/2-9/5 | 1P: $104-$230 | XP: $10 — F12 |
| 9/6-10/10 | 1P: $84-$200 | XP: $10 — F12 |
| 5/1-7/1 | 1P: $49-$160 | XP: $10 — F12 |
| 10/11-10/31 | 1P: $49-$155 | XP: $10 — F12 |

**Location:** 0.5 mi w on SR 3. Located in a quiet, secluded area. 50 Eden St 04609 (PO Box 25). Fax: 207/288-2005. **Facility:** 79 units. 74 one- and 5 two-bedroom standard units. 1-2 stories (no elevator), exterior corridors. **Parking:** on-site. **Terms:** open 5/1-10/31, 3 day cancellation notice-fee imposed, pets ($15 extra charge). **Amenities:** *Some:* irons, hair dryers. **Pool(s):** heated outdoor. **Guest Services:** coin laundry. **Cards:** AX, DS, MC, VI. *(See color ad p 164)*

SOME UNITS

GOLD AWARD WINNER

## BAR HARBOR

*Quality...Comfort...*
*Location, we have it all!*

**800-282-5403**
**or 207-288-5403**

Rte. 3 and Mt. Desert St.
Bar Harbor, ME 04609

**MAILING ADDRESS:**
40 Kebo Street
Bar Harbor, ME 04609

- Walk to shops & waterfront
- **Smoke-free** rooms
- Air-conditioned, RCCTV
- In-room coffee, free *USA Today*
- Free internet access in lobby
- Heated outdoor pool & hot tub
- Picnic area
- Coin-op laundry
- Bunny's Downeast Restaurant
- Acadia Nat'l Park—1 mile
- Ferry Terminal—1 mile

**www.barharborqualityinn.com**
(See our VIRTUAL TOUR)

**Email: qualityinn@adelphia.net**

## Bargain Packages

**$89** ppdo 4/30–5/27
10/18–10/29

**$109** ppdo 5/31–6/19

2 nights lodging
2 full breakfasts
1 lobster dinner (pp)

Tax and gratuities not included
**Inquire about other dates**

---

*A quaint little gem in the heart of Bar Harbor*

**Reservations 800-841-8925**

Walk to town ✦ 1 mile to Acadia
National Park ✦ Free local calls
Smoke-free rooms ✦ Micro fridges
Hairdryers ✦ HBO/Cable ✦ AC
In-room coffee ✦ (Pool and hot tub
privileges at nearby Quality Inn)

Open Year Round

AURORA INN

VACANCY

www.aurorainn.com ✦ Email: aurorainn@islandweb.com
Aurora Inn – 51 Holland Ave Bar Harbor, Me 04609 - 207 288 3771

**BALANCE ROCK INN 1903**                                                  **Phone:** (207)288-2610

| | | | |
|---|---|---|---|
| 7/1-8/31 | 1P: $225-$625 | 2P: $225-$625 | XP: $50 |
| 9/1-10/18 | 1P: $195-$595 | 2P: $195-$595 | XP: $50 |
| 10/19-10/23 | 1P: $125-$595 | 2P: $125-$595 | XP: $50 |
| 5/7-6/30 | 1P: $115-$595 | 2P: $115-$595 | XP: $50 |

**Historic Bed & Breakfast** · **Location:** S on Main St, just e; center. Located in a residential area. 21 Albert Meadow 04609. Fax: 207/288-5534. **Facility:** This turn-of-the-20th-century oceanfront mansion borders a shore path; many rooms feature decks, fireplaces and whirlpool baths. 16 units. 13 one-bedroom standard units, some with whirlpools. 1 one- and 2 two-bedroom suites, some with whirlpools. 3 stories, interior/exterior corridors. **Bath:** combo or shower only. **Parking:** on-site. **Terms:** open 5/7-10/23, 14 day cancellation notice-fee imposed, [ECP] meal plan available, package plans - seasonal, pets ($30 extra charge). **Amenities:** video library, DVD players, irons, hair dryers. **Pool(s):** heated outdoor. **Leisure Activities:** exercise room. **Guest Services:** valet laundry. **Cards:** AX, DS, MC, VI. **Special Amenities:** free expanded continental breakfast and free newspaper. *(See color ad p 168)*

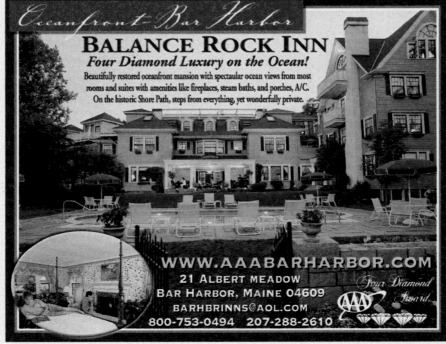

## BAR HARBOR GRAND HOTEL

Phone: 207/288-5226

AAA (SAVE)

| | | | | |
|---|---|---|---|---|
| 6/18-10/17 [ECP] | 1P: $149-$195 | 2P: $149-$195 | XP: $25 | F5 |
| 5/1-6/17 [ECP] | 1P: $95-$125 | 2P: $95-$125 | XP: $25 | F5 |
| 10/18-11/13 [ECP] | 1P: $79-$99 | 2P: $79-$99 | XP: $25 | F5 |
| 4/8-4/30 [ECP] | 1P: $99 | 2P: $99 | XP: $25 | F5 |

Small-scale Hotel **Location:** Downtown. 269 Main St 04609 (PO Box 7). Fax: 207/288-8548. **Facility:** Designated smoking area. 70 units. 66 one- and 4 two-bedroom standard units. 4 stories, interior corridors. *Bath:* combo or shower only. **Parking:** on-site. **Terms:** open 5/1-11/13 & 4/8-4/30, office hours 6 am-midnight, cancellation fee imposed, package plans. **Amenities:** DVD players, voice mail, irons, hair dryers. **Pool(s):** heated outdoor. **Guest Services:** gift shop, coin laundry. **Cards:** AX, DS, MC, VI. **Special Amenities: free expanded continental breakfast and free local telephone calls.** *(See color ad p 164)*

## BAR HARBOR HOTEL-BLUENOSE INN

Phone: 207/288-3348

AAA (SAVE)

| | | | | |
|---|---|---|---|---|
| 6/18-10/10 | 1P: $145-$339 | 2P: $145-$339 | XP: $25 | F14 |
| 5/28-6/17 | 1P: $109-$229 | 2P: $109-$229 | XP: $20 | F14 |
| 10/11-10/31 | 1P: $85-$215 | 2P: $85-$215 | XP: $20 | F14 |
| 5/1-5/27 | 1P: $75-$165 | 2P: $75-$165 | XP: $20 | F14 |

Small-scale Hotel **Location:** 1 mi w. 90 Eden St 04609. Fax: 207/288-2183. **Facility:** This inn overlooking Frenchman's Bay offers spacious suites and guest rooms in two lodging buildings. Smoke free premises. 98 units. 97 one-bedroom standard units. 1 two-bedroom suite ($190-$599) with kitchen. 3-4 stories, interior/exterior corridors. *Bath:* combo or shower only. **Parking:** on-site. **Terms:** open 5/1-10/31, 10 day cancellation notice-fee imposed, [MAP] meal plan available, package plans. **Amenities:** DVD players, CD players, high-speed Internet, voice mail, irons, hair dryers. *Some:* safes. **Dining:** The Rose Garden, see separate listing, entertainment. **Pool(s):** heated outdoor, heated indoor. **Leisure Activities:** whirlpool, exercise room. **Guest Services:** gift shop, valet and coin laundry. **Business Services:** meeting rooms. **Cards:** AX, DC, DS, MC, VI. **Special Amenities: free local telephone calls and free newspaper.** *(See color ad p 161)*

## BAR HARBOR INN

Phone: 207/288-3351

| | | | | |
|---|---|---|---|---|
| 6/18-8/28 [ECP] | 1P: $185-$369 | 2P: $185-$369 | XP: $25 | F5 |
| 8/29-11/28 [ECP] | 1P: $95-$325 | 2P: $95-$325 | XP: $25 | F5 |
| 5/1-6/17 [ECP] | 1P: $99-$285 | 2P: $99-$285 | XP: $25 | F5 |
| 3/25-4/30 [ECP] | 1P: $79-$159 | 2P: $79-$159 | XP: $25 | F5 |

Small-scale Hotel **Location:** Center. Located on the waterfront by town pier. Newport Dr 04609 (PO Box 7). Fax: 207/288-5296. **Facility:** 153 units. 142 one-bedroom standard units. 8 one- and 3 two-bedroom suites ($159-$589). 2 stories, interior/exterior corridors. *Bath:* combo or shower only. **Parking:** on-site. **Terms:** open 5/1-11/28 & 3/25-4/30, 10 day cancellation notice-fee imposed, [MAP] meal plan available, package plans. **Amenities:** video library (fee), voice mail, safes, irons, hair dryers. **Dining:** The Reading Room Restaurant at the Bar Harbor Inn, see separate listing. **Pool(s):** heated outdoor. **Leisure Activities:** whirlpool, exercise room. *Fee:* charter fishing. **Guest Services:** gift shop, valet laundry. **Business Services:** meeting rooms. **Cards:** AX, CB, DC, DS, MC, VI. **(See color ad p 163)**

**BAR HARBOR MANOR**                                                                                          Phone: 207/288-3829

| | | | | |
|---|---|---|---|---|
| 7/1-8/21 | 1P: $95-$175 | 2P: $95-$175 | XP: $25 |
| 8/22-10/31 | 1P: $75-$175 | 2P: $75-$175 | XP: $25 |
| 5/28-6/30 | 1P: $65-$145 | 2P: $65-$145 | XP: $25 |
| 5/1-5/27 | 1P: $55-$125 | 2P: $55-$125 | XP: $25 |

Small-scale Hotel **Location:** Center. 47 Holland Ave 04609. **Facility:** Designated smoking area. 24 units. 15 one-bedroom standard units. 6 one- and 3 two-bedroom suites ($75-$295), some with kitchens and/or whirlpools. 2-3 stories (no elevator), exterior corridors. *Bath:* combo or shower only. **Parking:** on-site. **Terms:** open 5/1-10/31, office hours 7 am-10 pm, 10 day cancellation notice-fee imposed, package plans. **Amenities:** irons, hair dryers. **Cards:** DS, MC, VI. **Special Amenities: free local telephone calls.** *(See color ad below)*

SOME UNITS

## Look For Savings

When you pick up a AAA TourBook® guide, look for establishments that display a bright red AAA logo, [SAVE] icon, and  Diamond rating in their listing. These AAA Official Appointment establishments place a high value on the patronage they receive from AAA members. And, by offering members great room rates*, they are  willing to go the extra mile to get your business.

So, when you turn to the AAA TourBook guide to make your travel plans, look for the establishments that will give you the special treatment you deserve.

*See TourBook Navigator section, page 14, for complete details.*

## BAR HARBOR MOTEL

Phone: 207/288-3453

AAA [SAVE]
WWW

| | | | |
|---|---|---|---|
| 7/1-8/28 | 1P: $126-$136 | 2P: $126-$136 | XP: $10  F12 |
| 6/11-6/30 & 8/29-10/24 | 1P: $98-$108 | 2P: $98-$108 | XP: $10  F12 |
| 5/6-6/10 | 1P: $58-$80 | 2P: $58-$80 | XP: $10  F12 |

Small-scale Hotel **Location:** 1.8 mi n on SR 3. 100 Eden St 04609. Fax: 207/288-3598. **Facility:** 78 units. 54 one- and 24 two-bedroom standard units. 1 story, exterior corridors. **Parking:** on-site. **Terms:** open 5/6-10/24, office hours 6 am-11 pm, 7 day cancellation notice-fee imposed. **Amenities:** voice mail, irons, hair dryers. **Pool(s):** heated outdoor. **Leisure Activities:** bike storage, hiking trails, playground. **Guest Services:** coin laundry. **Cards:** DS, MC, VI. **Special Amenities:** free local telephone calls. *(See color ad below)*

## BAR HARBOR QUALITY INN     *Book at aaa.com*

Phone: (207)288-5403

AAA [SAVE]
WWW

| | | | |
|---|---|---|---|
| 6/26-9/5 | 1P: $139-$189 | 2P: $139-$189 | XP: $10  F18 |
| 9/6-10/16 | 1P: $119-$159 | 2P: $119-$159 | XP: $10  F18 |
| 5/1-6/25 | 1P: $69-$129 | 2P: $69-$129 | XP: $10  F18 |
| 10/17-10/31 | 1P: $69-$99 | 2P: $69-$99 | XP: $10  F18 |

Small-scale Hotel **Location:** Jct SR 3 and 233; center. 40 Kebo St 04609. Fax: 207/288-5473. **Facility:** 77 units. 76 one- and 1 two-bedroom standard units, some with efficiencies. 2 stories (no elevator), exterior corridors. *Bath:* combo or shower only. **Parking:** on-site. **Terms:** open 5/1-10/31, 3 day cancellation notice, package plans - off season. **Amenities:** hair dryers. *Some:* irons. **Dining:** 6:30 am-10:30 & 4:30-9 pm, cocktails. **Pool(s):** heated outdoor. **Leisure Activities:** whirlpool. **Guest Services:** coin laundry. **Cards:** AX, DC, DS, MC, VI. **Special Amenities:** free local telephone calls and free newspaper. *(See color ad p 165)*

SOME UNITS

## BAR HARBOR REGENCY HOLIDAY INN     *Book at aaa.com*

Phone: 207/288-9723

AAA [SAVE]
WWW

| | |
|---|---|
| 8/2-9/1 | 1P: $109-$300 |
| 6/15-8/1 | 1P: $139-$275 |
| 9/2-10/31 | 1P: $109-$275 |
| 5/10-6/14 | 1P: $99-$175 |

Large-scale Hotel **Location:** 1 mi w on SR 3. Located adjacent to ferry terminal. 123 Eden St 04609. Fax: 207/288-3089. **Facility:** 221 one-bedroom standard units. 3-4 stories, interior corridors. *Bath:* combo or shower only. **Parking:** on-site. **Terms:** open 5/10-10/31, check-in 4 pm, cancellation fee imposed, [AP] meal plan available. **Amenities:** voice mail, irons, hair dryers. **Dining:** 6:30 am-11 & 5-10 pm, cocktails, also, Stewman's Lobster Pound, see separate listing. **Pool(s):** heated outdoor. **Leisure Activities:** sauna, putting green, 2 lighted tennis courts, exercise room. *Fee:* boat dock. **Guest Services:** gift shop, coin laundry. **Business Services:** meeting rooms. **Cards:** AX, DC, DS, MC, VI. *(See color ad p 172)*

SOME UNITS

## BAR HARBOR TIDES BED & BREAKFAST

**Historic Bed & Breakfast**

5/14-10/17 [BP]       1P: $225-$395       2P: $225-$395
5/1-5/13 & 10/18-4/30 [BP]    1P: $225-$275       2P: $225-$275

**Phone:** 207/288-4968

**Location:** Center. 119 West St 04609. Fax: 207/288-2997. **Facility:** This 1887 Greek Revival home overlooks the bay; its airy rooms are tastefully decorated with reproduction furniture and antiques. Smoke free premises. 4 units. 1 one-bedroom standard unit. 3 one-bedroom suites. 3 stories (no elevator), interior corridors. **Bath:** combo or shower only. **Parking:** on-site. **Terms:** 2 night minimum stay, age restrictions may apply, 25 day cancellation notice-fee imposed. **Amenities:** video library, hair dryers. **Cards:** AX, DC, MC, VI.

SOME UNITS

## THE BAYVIEW

AAA [SAVE]

| | | Phone: (207)288-5861 |
|---|---|---|
| 7/1-9/5 [ECP] | 2P: $270-$460 | XP: $20 F12 |
| 6/14-6/30 [ECP] | 2P: $210-$410 | XP: $20 F12 |
| 9/6-10/24 [ECP] | 2P: $170-$410 | XP: $20 F12 |
| 5/21-6/13 [ECP] | 2P: $145-$295 | XP: $20 F12 |

Small-scale Hotel **Location:** 1 mi w on SR 3. 111 Eden St 04609. Fax: 207/288-3173. **Facility:** Designated smoking area. 33 units. 26 one-bedroom standard units. 4 two- and 2 three-bedroom suites. 1 vacation home ($200-$410). 2-3 stories (no elevator), interior corridors. **Parking:** on-site. **Terms:** open 5/21-10/24, 2 night minimum stay - 10 day cancellation notice-fee imposed, package plans. **Amenities:** irons, hair dryers. **Pool(s):** small heated outdoor. **Leisure Activities:** tennis privileges, exercise room. **Guest Services:** valet laundry. **Business Services:** meeting rooms. **Cards:** AX, CB, DC, MC, VI. **Special Amenities:** free expanded continental breakfast and free newspaper. *(See color ad p 167)*

SOME UNITS

ⓢⒹ Ⓨ 🏊 ✕ 📶 📠 🖥 / 📼 🛄 📷 /

## BEST WESTERN INN    *Book at aaa.com*

AAA [SAVE]

| | | | Phone: (207)288-5823 |
|---|---|---|---|
| 7/1-10/31 | 1P: $115-$140 | 2P: $115-$140 | XP: $10 F12 |
| 5/1-6/30 | 1P: $74-$100 | 2P: $74-$100 | XP: $10 F12 |

Small-scale Hotel **Location:** 4.8 mi w. Located in rural area. 452 State Hwy 3 04609. Fax: 207/288-9827. **Facility:** 94 one-bedroom standard units. 1 story, exterior corridors. *Bath:* combo or shower only. **Parking:** on-site. **Terms:** open 5/1-10/31, [CP] meal plan available, small pets only. **Amenities:** irons, hair dryers. **Pool(s):** heated outdoor. **Guest Services:** gift shop, coin laundry. **Cards:** AX, DC, DS, MC, VI. **Special Amenities:** free continental breakfast and free local telephone calls.

SOME UNITS

ⓢⒹ 🐾 🏊 📶 📠 🖥 / ✕ 🛄 /

## BLACK FRIAR INN

| | | | Phone: 207/288-5091 |
|---|---|---|---|
| 6/11-10/18 [BP] | 1P: $110-$160 | 2P: $110-$160 | XP: $50 |
| 5/1-6/10 & 10/19-11/30 [BP] | 1P: $90-$130 | 2P: $90-$130 | XP: $50 |

Bed & Breakfast **Location:** Center. 10 Summer St 04609. Fax: 207/288-4197. **Facility:** A notable collection of family crests is displayed at this restored Victorian home on limited grounds. Smoke free premises. 7 units. 6 one-bedroom standard units. 1 one-bedroom suite. 3 stories (no elevator), interior corridors. *Bath:* combo or shower only. **Parking:** on-site. **Terms:** open 5/11-11/30, check-in 4 pm, 2 night minimum stay - mid June-mid Oct, age restrictions may apply, cancellation fee imposed. **Amenities:** hair dryers. *Some:* CD players. **Guest Services:** TV in common area. **Cards:** MC, VI.

🛗 ✕ 🅦 🆔

## BRIARFIELD INN BED & BREAKFAST

| | | | Phone: 207/288-5297 |
|---|---|---|---|
| 6/14-9/7 [BP] | 1P: $95-$180 | 2P: $95-$180 | XP: $25 |
| 9/8-10/20 [BP] | 1P: $90-$170 | 2P: $90-$170 | XP: $20 |
| 10/21-4/30 [BP] | 1P: $110-$135 | 2P: $110-$135 | |
| 5/1-6/13 [BP] | 1P: $105-$135 | 2P: $105-$135 | XP: $20 |

Historic Bed & Breakfast **Location:** Center. Located in the business district. 60 Cottage St 04609. Fax: 207/288-4057. **Facility:** A saltwater aquarium stands out among this B&B's comfortable period furnishings; lace curtains and floral wallcoverings accent guest rooms. Smoke free premises. 14 one-bedroom standard units. 3 stories (no elevator), interior corridors. *Bath:* combo or shower only. **Parking:** on-site. **Terms:** 2 night minimum stay, age restrictions may apply, 15 day cancellation notice-fee imposed, no pets allowed (owner's pet on premises). **Amenities:** hair dryers. **Cards:** AX, DS, MC, VI.

SOME UNITS

✕ 📠 / 📼 /

**CADILLAC MOTOR INN**
Phone: (207)288-3831

AAA SAVE
Motel

| | 7/1-9/1 | 1P: $84-$109 | 2P: $84-$109 | XP: $20 | F12 |
| | 5/14-6/30 & 9/2-10/23 | 1P: $74-$94 | 2P: $74-$94 | XP: $20 | F12 |

**Location:** 0.5 mi s on SR 3. 336 Main St 04609. Fax: 207/288-9370. **Facility:** 48 units. 45 one-bedroom standard units, some with efficiencies or kitchens. 3 two-bedroom suites ($109-$210) with kitchens. 2 stories (no elevator), interior/exterior corridors. *Bath:* combo or shower only. **Parking:** on-site. **Terms:** open 5/14-10/23, office hours 7 am-11 pm, 7 day cancellation notice-fee imposed. **Guest Services:** coin laundry. **Cards:** AX, DS, MC, VI. **Special Amenities:** free local telephone calls and preferred room (subject to availability with advanced reservations).** *(See color ad p 173)*

SOME UNITS

**CASTLEMAINE INN**
Phone: 207/288-4563

AAA SAVE
Historic Bed
& Breakfast

| | 6/25-8/26 | 1P: $109-$210 | 2P: $109-$210 | XP: $25 |
| | 8/27-10/12 | 1P: $89-$210 | 2P: $89-$210 | XP: $25 |
| | 5/5-6/24 | 1P: $62-$177 | 2P: $62-$177 | XP: $25 |
| | 10/13-10/25 | 1P: $62-$139 | 2P: $62-$139 | XP: $25 |

**Location:** Center. Located in a quiet, residential area. 39 Holland Ave 04609. Fax: 207/288-4525. **Facility:** Rooms are tastefully decorated and vary in style and shape at this elegantly appointed, renovated 1886 home. Smoke free premises. 17 units. 13 one-bedroom standard units, some with whirlpools. 4 one-bedroom suites, some with whirlpools. 3 stories (no elevator), interior/exterior corridors. *Bath:* combo or shower only. **Parking:** on-site. **Terms:** open 5/5-10/25, 15 day cancellation notice-fee imposed, [ECP] meal plan available. **Amenities:** video library (fee). **Cards:** MC, VI. **Special Amenities:** free expanded continental breakfast and free local telephone calls. *(See color ad below)*

**CLEFTSTONE MANOR**
Phone: 207/288-8086

Historic Bed
& Breakfast

| | 6/19-10/10 | 1P: $105-$225 | 2P: $105-$225 | XP: $20 |
| | 5/1-6/18 & 10/11-10/30 | 1P: $75-$145 | 2P: $75-$145 | XP: $20 |

**Location:** 1 mi w on SR 3. 92 Eden St 04609. Fax: 207/288-2089. **Facility:** This 19th-century Victorian-style country mansion includes some antique furnishings and features some guest rooms with fireplaces. Smoke free premises. 16 one-bedroom standard units. 3 stories (no elevator), interior corridors. *Bath:* combo or shower only. **Parking:** on-site. **Terms:** open 5/1-10/30, 2 night minimum stay - seasonal, age restrictions may apply, 14 day cancellation notice-fee imposed, [BP] meal plan available. **Amenities:** *Some:* hair dryers. **Cards:** DS, MC, VI.

SOME UNITS

**CROMWELL HARBOR MOTEL**

| | | | Phone: 207/288-3201 |
|---|---|---|---|
| AAA SAVE | 7/1-9/5 | 1P: $105-$150 | 2P: $105-$150 | XP: $15 |
| ▼▼▼ | 9/6-10/17 | 1P: $80-$110 | 2P: $80-$110 | XP: $10 |
| | 5/1-6/30 | 1P: $60-$99 | 2P: $60-$99 | XP: $10 |
| Motel | 10/18-4/30 | 1P: $60-$78 | 2P: $60-$78 | XP: $10 |

**Location:** 0.5 mi e on SR 3. 359 Main St 04609. Fax: 207/288-9282. **Facility:** 26 one-bedroom standard units, some with kitchens. 1-2 stories (no elevator), exterior corridors. **Parking:** on-site. **Terms:** office hours 7 am-11 pm, 5 day cancellation notice-fee imposed, package plans. **Amenities:** voice mail. **Pool(s):** heated outdoor. **Cards:** AX, DS, MC, VI. **Special Amenities: free local telephone calls and preferred room (subject to availability with advanced reservations).**

SOME UNITS

🏊 📷 📠 💻 / ✕ 🛏 🖥 /

---

**DAYS INN** *Book at aaa.com*

Phone: 207/288-3321

| ▼▼▼ ▼▼▼ | 6/15-8/1 | 1P: $129-$209 |
|---|---|---|
| Motel | 9/2-10/31 | 1P: $99-$209 |
| | 8/2-9/1 | 1P: $135-$199 |
| | 5/10-6/14 | 1P: $89-$149 |

**Location:** 1 mi w on SR 3. Located opposite the ferry terminal. 120 Eden St 04609. Fax: 207/288-5079. **Facility:** 66 one-bedroom standard units. 2 stories (no elevator), exterior corridors. **Parking:** on-site. **Terms:** open 5/10-10/31, cancellation fee imposed, [CP] meal plan available. **Amenities:** hair dryers. **Cards:** AX, DC, DS, MC, VI. *(See ad below)*

SOME UNITS

ASK 🔊 🛏 / ✕ 🛏 🖥 /

## DREAMWOOD PINES MOTEL

Phone: 207/288-9717

AAA SAVE ◆◆ ◆◆
Motel

| | | |
|---|---|---|
| 8/1-8/28 | 1P: $124-$144 | 2P: $124-$144 | XP: $12 |
| 7/1-7/31 | 1P: $110-$138 | 2P: $110-$138 | XP: $12 |
| 8/29-10/31 | 1P: $86-$118 | 2P: $86-$118 | XP: $12 |
| 5/1-6/30 | 1P: $68-$98 | 2P: $68-$98 | XP: $12 |

**Location:** 4.5 mi w. 389 State Hwy 3 04609. Fax: 207/288-4194. **Facility:** 22 units. 20 one- and 2 two-bedroom standard units, some with efficiencies. 1 story, exterior corridors. **Parking:** on-site. **Terms:** open 5/1-10/31, office hours 8 am-10 pm, 3 night minimum stay, 7 day cancellation notice. **Amenities:** hair dryers. **Pool(s):** heated outdoor. **Cards:** MC, VI. **Special Amenities:** free local telephone calls and preferred room (subject to availability with advanced reservations).

SOME UNITS
🏊 📷 🛏 📺 / 📠 /

## EDENBROOK MOTEL

Phone: 207/288-4975

AAA SAVE ◆◆ ◆◆
Motel

| | | |
|---|---|---|
| 7/1-8/31 | 1P: $70-$95 | 2P: $70-$95 | XP: $5 |
| 9/1-10/16 | 1P: $45-$75 | 2P: $45-$75 | XP: $5 |
| 5/15-6/30 | 1P: $36-$65 | 2P: $36-$65 | XP: $5 |

**Location:** 1 mi w on SR 3. 96 Eden St 04609. **Facility:** 47 units. 46 one- and 1 two-bedroom standard units. 1-2 stories (no elevator), exterior corridors. **Parking:** on-site. **Terms:** open 5/15-10/16, office hours 7 am-11 pm, 3 day cancellation notice. **Cards:** AX, DS, MC, VI. *(See color ad p 175)*

SOME UNITS
✕ / 🛏 /

## FAIRFIELD INN BY MARRIOTT

*Book at aaa.com*

Phone: 207/288-8983

◆◆ ◆◆
Small-scale Hotel

| | |
|---|---|
| 8/2-9/1 | 1P: $155-$245 |
| 6/15-8/1 | 1P: $155-$205 |
| 9/2-10/31 | 1P: $109-$205 |
| 5/10-6/14 | 1P: $99-$149 |

**Location:** 1 mi w on SR 3. Located adjacent to ferry terminal. 125 Eden St 04609. Fax: 207/288-8983. **Facility:** 59 one-bedroom standard units. 4 stories, interior corridors. *Bath:* combo or shower only. **Parking:** on-site. **Terms:** open 5/10-10/31, [CP] meal plan available. **Amenities:** irons, hair dryers. **Leisure Activities:** exercise room privileges. **Cards:** AX, DC, DS, MC, VI. *(See ad below)*

SOME UNITS
ASK 🔊 🍴 📷 DATA PORT 🛏 📺 / ✕ /

## GRAYCOTE INN

Phone: 207/288-3044

◆◆ ◆◆ ◆◆
Historic Bed & Breakfast

| | | |
|---|---|---|
| 6/17-10/10 [BP] | 1P: $105-$165 | 2P: $110-$175 | XP: $20 |
| 5/28-6/16 [BP] | 1P: $90-$125 | 2P: $95-$135 | XP: $20 |
| 5/1-5/27 & 10/11-4/30 [BP] | 1P: $75-$100 | 2P: $80-$110 | XP: $20 |

**Location:** Center. 40 Holland Ave 04609. Fax: 207/288-2719. **Facility:** This 19th-century home has been renovated to reflect the era's style. Smoke free premises. 12 units. 7 one-bedroom standard units. 3 one- and 2 two-bedroom suites ($110-$240). 2-3 stories (no elevator), interior/exterior corridors. *Bath:* combo or shower only. **Parking:** on-site. **Terms:** 2-3 night minimum stay - in season, 14 day cancellation notice-fee imposed, package plans, no pets allowed (owner's pet on premises). **Amenities:** hair dryers. **Cards:** AX, DS, MC, VI.

SOME UNITS
✕ 🐾 / ✕ 🐾 /

## THE HEARTHSIDE BED & BREAKFAST

Phone: 207/288-4533

◆◆ ◆◆ ◆◆
Bed & Breakfast

| | | |
|---|---|---|
| 6/18-10/16 [BP] | 1P: $100-$150 | 2P: $100-$150 | |
| 5/1-6/17 & 10/17-10/31 [BP] | 1P: $70-$100 | 2P: $70-$100 | |

**Location:** Center. Located in a residential area. 7 High St 04609. Fax: 207/288-9818. **Facility:** This property was built around the turn of the 20th-century. Smoke free premises. 9 one-bedroom standard units, some with whirlpools. 3 stories (no elevator), interior corridors. *Bath:* combo or shower only. **Parking:** on-site. **Terms:** open 5/1-10/31, 2 night minimum stay - 6/18-10/16, 14 day cancellation notice-fee imposed. **Amenities:** CD players, hair dryers. **Cards:** DS, MC, VI.

✕ 🐾 🐾

## HIGHBROOK MOTEL

Phone: 207/288-3591

AAA SAVE ◆◆ ◆◆
Motel

| | | |
|---|---|---|
| 7/1-8/28 | 1P: $78-$138 | 2P: $78-$138 | XP: $15 |
| 8/29-10/18 | 1P: $58-$108 | 2P: $58-$108 | XP: $15 |
| 5/17-6/30 | 1P: $48-$98 | 2P: $48-$98 | XP: $15 |

**Location:** 1 mi w on SR 3. 94 Eden St 04609. Fax: 207/288-9982. **Facility:** Smoke free premises. 26 one-bedroom standard units. 1 story, exterior corridors. **Parking:** on-site. **Terms:** open 5/17-10/18, office hours 7 am-10 pm, 3 day cancellation notice-fee imposed. **Cards:** AX, DS, MC, VI. **Special Amenities:** free local telephone calls. *(See color ad p 177)*

SOME UNITS
✕ DATA PORT 📺 / 🛏 /

## HIGH SEAS MOTEL

Phone: 207/288-5836

| |  |  |  | |
|---|---|---|---|---|
| 7/21-9/3 | 1P: $70-$135 | 2P: $70-$135 | XP: $10 | F11 |
| 6/30-7/20 | 1P: $60-$105 | 2P: $60-$105 | XP: $10 | F11 |
| 9/4-10/15 | 1P: $45-$105 | 2P: $45-$105 | XP: $10 | F11 |
| 5/15-6/29 | 1P: $35-$70 | 2P: $35-$78 | XP: $10 | F11 |

AAA SAVE ◆◆ ◆◆ Motel

**Location:** 4 mi w. 339 State Hwy 3 04609. **Facility:** 39 one-bedroom standard units. 1 story, exterior corridors. *Bath:* combo or shower only. **Parking:** on-site. **Terms:** open 5/15-10/15, office hours 7:30 am-11 pm, 3 day cancellation notice-fee imposed. **Amenities:** *Some:* hair dryers. **Pool(s):** heated outdoor. **Leisure Activities:** playground. **Cards:** DS, MC, VI.

SOME UNITS

---

**HOLBROOK HOUSE**
Phone: 207/288-4970

*(diamond diamond diamond diamond rating symbols)*

Historic Bed & Breakfast

| | | |
|---|---|---|
| 6/18-10/17 | 1P: $130-$180 | 2P: $130-$180 |
| 5/7-6/17 & 10/18-11/1 | 1P: $95-$135 | 2P: $95-$135 |

**Location:** Center. Located in a semi-commercial area. 74 Mt Desert St 04609. Fax: 207/288-4994. **Facility:** A large front porch with comfortable seating accents this handsome 1876 Victorian home, which also offers a bright and airy sun room. Designated smoking area. 12 units. 10 one- and 2 two-bedroom standard units. 2 stories (no elevator), interior/exterior corridors. *Bath:* combo or shower only. **Parking:** on-site. **Terms:** open 5/7-11/1, 2 night minimum stay, 14 day cancellation notice, no pets allowed (owner's pet on premises). **Amenities:** hair dryers. *Some:* CD players. **Cards:** MC, VI.

SOME UNITS
(icons)

---

**THE HOLLAND INN**
Phone: 207/288-4804

*(diamond diamond rating symbols)*

Bed & Breakfast

| | | |
|---|---|---|
| 6/13-9/7 [BP] | 1P: $85-$135 | 2P: $95-$145 |
| 9/8-11/2 [BP] | 1P: $75-$120 | 2P: $85-$130 |
| 5/1-6/12 [BP] | 1P: $65-$120 | 2P: $75-$130 |

**Location:** Center. 35 Holland Ave 04609. **Facility:** Smoke free premises. 9 units. 7 one-bedroom standard units. 2 one-bedroom suites. 2 stories (no elevator), interior corridors. *Bath:* combo or shower only. **Parking:** on-site. **Terms:** open 5/1-11/2, 10 day cancellation notice-fee imposed. **Cards:** MC, VI.

(icons)

---

**HUTCHINS MOUNTAIN VIEW COTTAGES**
Phone: 207/288-4833

*(diamond rating symbol)*

Cottage

| | | | |
|---|---|---|---|
| 7/1-9/6 | 1P: $64-$86 | 2P: $68-$96 | XP: $6 |
| 9/7-10/11 | 1P: $42-$70 | 2P: $44-$86 | XP: $6 |
| 6/14-6/30 | 1P: $42-$70 | 2P: $42-$86 | XP: $6 |

**Location:** 4 mi w. 286 State Rt 3 04609. Fax: 207/288-9272. **Facility:** 20 units. 4 one-bedroom standard units. 16 cottages ($78-$150). 1 story, exterior corridors. *Bath:* combo or shower only. **Parking:** on-site. **Terms:** open 6/14-10/11, office hours 9 am-9 pm, 14 day cancellation notice-fee imposed. **Pool(s):** heated outdoor. **Cards:** MC, VI. *(See color ad below)*

SOME UNITS
(icons)

---

**IVY MANOR INN**
Phone: 207/288-2138

*(AAA)* *(SAVE)*
*(diamond diamond diamond rating symbols)*

Country Inn

| | | | |
|---|---|---|---|
| 6/15-10/15 [BP] | 1P: $200-$350 | 2P: $200-$350 | XP: $50 F |
| 10/16-11/15 [BP] | 1P: $150-$250 | 2P: $150-$250 | XP: $50 F |
| 5/1-6/14 [BP] | 1P: $150 | 2P: $150 | XP: $50 F |

**Location:** Center. 194 Main St 04609. Fax: 207/288-0038. **Facility:** This 1940 Tudor is in town close to restaurants and shops; antiques furnish the guest rooms, which vary in size and include some fireplaces. Smoke free premises. 8 units. 7 one- and 1 two-bedroom standard units. 2 stories (no elevator), interior corridors. *Bath:* combo or shower only. **Parking:** on-site. **Terms:** open 5/1-11/15, 2-3 night minimum stay - weekends, 14 day cancellation notice-fee imposed, weekly rates available, package plans. **Amenities:** hair dryers. **Dining:** Michelle's Fine Dining, see separate listing. **Cards:** AX, DC, MC, VI. **Special Amenities: free full breakfast and free local telephone calls.**

(icons)

---

**THE KEDGE BED & BREAKFAST**
Phone: 207/288-5180

*(diamond diamond diamond rating symbols)*

Historic Bed & Breakfast

| | | |
|---|---|---|
| 6/21-8/28 [BP] | 1P: $95-$185 | 2P: $95-$185 | XP: $25 |
| 8/29-10/19 [BP] | 1P: $79-$159 | 2P: $79-$159 | XP: $25 |
| 5/1-6/20 [BP] | 1P: $65-$135 | 2P: $65-$135 | XP: $25 |
| 10/20-4/30 [BP] | 1P: $55-$125 | 2P: $55-$125 | XP: $25 |

**Location:** Center. 112 West St 04609. Fax: 207/288-5180. **Facility:** This 1870 home offers a variety of individually decorated rooms, one with a private deck and two with fireplaces. Smoke free premises. 4 units. 3 one- and 1 two-bedroom standard units. 2 stories (no elevator), interior corridors. **Parking:** on-site. **Terms:** age restrictions may apply, cancellation fee imposed, weekly rates available. **Cards:** DS, MC, VI.

SOME UNITS
(icons)

---

## THE LEDGELAWN INN

**Phone:** (207)288-4596

(AAA) (SAVE)
▽▽▽▽▽
Historic Bed & Breakfast

| | | | |
|---|---|---|---|
| 7/1-10/16 | 1P: $95-$325 | 2P: $95-$325 | XP: $30 |
| 10/17-10/23 | 1P: $85-$255 | 2P: $85-$255 | XP: $30 |
| 5/20-6/30 | 1P: $70-$245 | 2P: $70-$245 | XP: $30 |

**Location:** Center. Located in a semi-commercial area. 66 Mt Desert St 04609. **Fax:** 207/288-9968. **Facility:** An exterior painted vanilla and brilliant red distinguishes this 1904 mansion; its spacious parlor and pub have an Old World ambience. 33 units. 32 one-bedroom standard units, some with whirlpools. 1 one-bedroom suite. 3 stories (no elevator), interior/exterior corridors. *Bath:* combo or shower only. **Parking:** on-site. **Terms:** open 5/20-10/23, 14 day cancellation notice-fee imposed, [ECP] meal plan available, package plans - seasonal, pets ($15 extra charge). **Pool(s):** outdoor. **Cards:** AX, DS, MC, VI. **Special Amenities: free expanded continental breakfast.**
*(See color ad p 168)*

SOME UNITS
🛏️ 🕹️ / ⊠ VCR /
FEE

## MAINE STREET MOTEL

**Phone:** 207/288-3188

(AAA) (SAVE)
▽▽▽
Motel

| | | | |
|---|---|---|---|
| 6/18-10/16 | 1P: $95-$139 | 2P: $95-$139 | XP: $10 | F15 |
| 5/1-6/17 & 4/22-4/30 | 1P: $59-$75 | 2P: $59-$75 | XP: $10 | F15 |
| 10/17-10/31 | 1P: $68 | 2P: $68 | XP: $10 | F15 |

**Location:** 0.3 mi e on SR 3; downtown. 315 Main St 04609. **Fax:** 207/288-2317. **Facility:** 44 one-bedroom standard units. 2 stories (no elevator), exterior corridors. **Parking:** on-site. **Terms:** open 5/1-10/31 & 4/22-4/30, office hours 6 am-11 pm, 7 day cancellation notice-fee imposed. **Cards:** DS, MC, VI. **Special Amenities: free local telephone calls.** *(See color ad p 163)*

SOME UNITS
🍴 🕹️ / ⊠ 🛢️ /
FEE

## MANOR HOUSE INN

**Phone:** 207/288-3759

(AAA) (SAVE)
▽▽▽▽
Historic Bed & Breakfast

| | | | |
|---|---|---|---|
| 6/20-10/16 | 1P: $125-$250 | 2P: $125-$250 | XP: $20 |
| 5/1-6/19 & 10/17-11/15 | 1P: $75-$175 | 2P: $75-$175 | XP: $20 |

**Location:** Center. Located in a commercial area. 106 West St 04609. **Fax:** 207/288 2974. **Facility:** Tastefully decorated guest rooms are offered at this 1887 Victorian inn and carriage house; also available are deluxe cottages and new suites. Smoke free premises. 18 units. 9 one- and 1 two-bedroom standard units, some with whirlpools. 6 one-bedroom suites, some with whirlpools. 2 cottages. 1-3 stories (no elevator), interior/exterior corridors. *Bath:* combo or shower only. **Parking:** on-site. **Terms:** open 5/1-11/15, 14 day cancellation notice-fee imposed, [BP] meal plan available. **Amenities:** hair dryers. *Some:* irons. **Cards:** AX, DS, MC, VI. **Special Amenities: free full breakfast and free local telephone calls.**

SOME UNITS
⊠ / 🕹️ 🅩 🛢️ 🖥️ /

## THE MAPLES INN

**Phone: 207/288-3443**

Historic Bed & Breakfast

| | 6/18-10/30 | 1P: $110-$160 | 2P: $110-$160 |
| | 5/1-6/17 | 1P: $70-$110 | 2P: $70-$110 |

**Location:** Center. Located in a residential area. 16 Roberts Ave 04609. Fax: 207/288-0356. **Facility:** This is a quaint 1903 Victorian home; the guest rooms are tastefully decorated. Smoke free premises. 6 units. 5 one-bedroom standard units. 1 one-bedroom suite. 3 stories (no elevator), interior corridors. *Bath:* shower only. **Parking:** on-site. **Terms:** open 5/1-10/30, 2 night minimum stay, 14 day cancellation notice-fee imposed. **Cards:** DS, MC, VI.

## MIRA MONTE INN & SUITES

**Phone: (207)288-4263**

Historic Bed & Breakfast

| | 6/22-8/23 [BP] | 1P: $165-$285 | 2P: $165-$285 | XP: $20 |
| | 8/24-10/31 [BP] | 1P: $122-$265 | 2P: $122-$265 | XP: $20 |
| | 6/5-6/21 [BP] | 1P: $122-$204 | 2P: $122-$204 | XP: $20 |
| | 5/7-6/4 [BP] | 1P: $95-$200 | 2P: $95-$200 | XP: $20 |

**Location:** On SR 3; center. Located in a commercial area. 69 Mt Desert St 04609. Fax: 207/288-3115. **Facility:** Manicured grounds enhance this 1864 mansion; rooms vary in size and some have balconies and fireplaces. Smoke free premises. 13 units. 13 one-bedroom standard units, some with whirlpools. 2 one- and 1 two-bedroom suites, some with efficiencies, kitchens and/or whirlpools. 2 stories (no elevator), interior corridors. *Bath:* combo or shower only. **Parking:** on-site. **Terms:** open 5/7-10/31, 2 night minimum stay, 10 day cancellation notice-fee imposed, package plans - seasonal, no pets allowed (owner's pet on premises). **Amenities:** CD players, voice mail, irons, hair dryers. **Leisure Activities:** bicycle storage. **Cards:** AX, DS, MC, VI. **Special Amenities:** free full breakfast and free local telephone calls.

## PRIMROSE INN BED AND BREAKFAST

**Phone: 207/288-4031**

Historic Bed & Breakfast

| | 6/18-10/17 [BP] | 1P: $110-$215 | 2P: $110-$215 | XP: $30 |
| | 5/15-6/17 [BP] | 1P: $85-$160 | 2P: $85-$160 | XP: $30 |

**Location:** Center. Located in a commercial area. 73 Mt Desert St 04609. **Facility:** Afternoon tea is offered at this striking Victorian inn furnished with antiques and reproductions; some units with fireplace. The property is in town. Smoke free premises. 15 units. 11 one-bedroom standard units, some with whirlpools. 3 one- and 1 two-bedroom suites ($700-$1300), some with efficiencies or kitchens. 2 stories (no elevator), interior corridors. *Bath:* combo or shower only. **Terms:** open 5/15-10/17, check-in 4 pm, 2 night minimum stay, age restrictions may apply, 14 day cancellation notice-fee imposed, pets ($75 fee, dogs only, in designated unit). **Amenities:** hair dryers. **Cards:** DS, MC, VI. *(See color ad below)*

## QUIMBY HOUSE INN

**Phone: 207/288-5811**

Small-scale Hotel

| | 7/1-9/6 | 1P: $95-$175 | 2P: $95-$175 | XP: $10 | F |
| | 9/7-10/24 | 1P: $85-$150 | 2P: $85-$150 | XP: $10 | F |
| | 5/1-6/30 | 1P: $65-$125 | 2P: $65-$125 | XP: $10 | F |
| | 10/25-4/30 | 1P: $55-$100 | 2P: $55-$100 | XP: $10 | F |

**Location:** Center. 109 Cottage St 04609. Fax: 207/288-5811. **Facility:** Smoke free premises. 22 units. 15 one-bedroom standard units. 7 one-bedroom suites, some with efficiencies or kitchens. 2-3 stories (no elevator), interior/exterior corridors. *Bath:* combo or shower only. **Parking:** on-site. **Terms:** 10 day cancellation notice-fee imposed. **Amenities:** voice mail. **Cards:** AX, DS, MC, VI. **Special Amenities:** free local telephone calls and early check-in/late check-out. *(See color ad p 181)*

## THE RIDGEWAY INN

**Phone: 207/288-9682**

Historic Bed & Breakfast

| | 6/16-10/15 | 1P: $100-$160 | 2P: $100-$160 | XP: $15 |
| | 5/1-6/15 & 10/16-12/31 | 1P: $70-$110 | 2P: $70-$110 | XP: $15 |
| | 1/1-4/30 | 1P: $50-$90 | 2P: $50-$90 | XP: $15 |

**Location:** Center. Located in a residential area. 11 High St 04609. **Facility:** Guest rooms are tastefully decorated and vary in size at this 1894 Victorian inn, which is close to downtown. Smoke free premises. 5 units. 4 one-bedroom standard units, some with whirlpools. 1 one-bedroom suite ($90-$160). 3 stories (no elevator), interior corridors. *Bath:* combo or shower only. **Parking:** on-site. **Terms:** 2 night minimum stay - 7/1-8/31, age restrictions may apply, 14 day cancellation notice-fee imposed. **Cards:** DS, MC, VI.

**SEA BREEZE MOTEL**

Phone: 207/288-3565

| | 7/19-8/23 | 2P: $109-$169 | XP: $10 | F6 |
|---|---|---|---|---|
| (AAA) (SAVE) | 6/28-7/18 | 2P: $94-$139 | XP: $10 | F6 |
| ♦♦♦ | 8/24-10/25 | 2P: $74-$114 | XP: $5 | F6 |
| | 5/7-6/27 | 2P: $49-$114 | XP: $5 | F6 |

Small-scale Hotel **Location:** On SR 3, 4 mi w. Located in a quiet area. 323 State Hwy 3 04609. Fax: 207/288-9587. **Facility:** 32 one-bedroom standard units. 1-2 stories (no elevator), exterior corridors. *Bath:* combo or shower only. **Parking:** on-site. **Terms:** open 5/7-10/25, office hours 8 am-9 pm, 7 day cancellation notice-fee imposed. **Amenities:** voice mail. **Pool(s):** heated outdoor. **Leisure Activities:** whirlpool. **Cards:** AX, DS, MC, VI. **Special Amenities:** free local telephone calls and early check-in/late check-out. *(See color ad below)*

**SEACROFT INN**

Phone: 207/288-4669

| | 6/18-9/6 [CP] | 1P: $99-$129 | 2P: $99-$129 | XP: $10 |
|---|---|---|---|---|
| ♦♦ | 9/7-11/30 [CP] | 1P: $89-$119 | 2P: $89-$119 | XP: $10 |
| | 5/1-6/17 [CP] | 1P: $69-$89 | 2P: $69-$89 | XP: $10 |
| Bed & Breakfast | 4/1-4/30 | 1P: $39-$59 | 2P: $39-$59 | XP: $5 |

**Location:** Center. 18 Albert Meadow 04609. **Facility:** Smoke free premises. 7 units. 6 one- and 1 two-bedroom standard units, some with kitchens. 2 stories (no elevator), interior/exterior corridors. **Parking:** on-site. **Terms:** open 5/1-11/30 & 4/1-4/30, cancellation fee imposed, no pets allowed (owner's pet on premises). **Cards:** MC, VI.

SOME UNITS

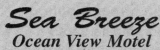

## SUNNYSIDE MOTEL & COTTAGES
**Phone:** 207/288-3602

| | | | |
|---|---|---|---|
| 7/24-8/23 | 1P: $75-$85 | 2P: $85-$105 | XP: $10 | F |
| 6/24-7/23 | 1P: $60-$65 | 2P: $60-$85 | XP: $10 | F |
| 8/24-10/19 | 1P: $45-$55 | 2P: $50-$60 | XP: $10 | F |
| 5/1-6/23 | 1P: $35-$50 | 2P: $40-$50 | XP: $10 | F |

Cottage   **Location:** 9 mi w. 1441 State Hwy 3 04609. **Facility:** 20 units. 10 one-bedroom standard units. 10 cottages ($45-$110). 1 story, exterior corridors. *Bath:* combo or shower only. **Parking:** on-site. **Terms:** open 5/1-10/19, cancellation fee imposed. **Pool(s):** outdoor. **Guest Services:** coin laundry. **Cards:** MC, VI.

SOME UNITS
🏊 ⊗ 🖥 / 🍴 📶 🖨 /

## TOWN MOTEL & MOSELEY COTTAGE INN
**Phone:** (207)288-5548

| | | | |
|---|---|---|---|
| 7/1-8/31 [BP] | | 2P: $120-$185 | XP: $10 | F12 |
| 9/1-10/25 [BP] | | 2P: $92-$150 | XP: $10 | F12 |
| 6/1-6/30 [BP] | | 2P: $86-$120 | XP: $10 | F12 |
| 5/1-5/31 [BP] | | 2P: $68-$100 | XP: $10 | F12 |

Small-scale Hotel   **Location:** Center. 12 Atlantic Ave 04609. Fax: 207/288-9406. **Facility:** Smoke free premises. 18 one-bedroom standard units. 1-3 stories (no elevator), interior/exterior corridors. *Bath:* combo or shower only. **Parking:** on-site. **Terms:** open 5/1-10/25, office hours 8 am-10 pm, 10 day cancellation notice-fee imposed. **Amenities:** hair dryers. **Cards:** AX, DS, MC, VI. **Special Amenities:** free full breakfast and free local telephone calls. *(See color ad below)*

SOME UNITS
⊗ 🎥 / 🍴 📶 🖥 /

## THE VILLAGER MOTEL
**Phone:** 207/288-3211

| | | | |
|---|---|---|---|
| 7/1-8/25 | 1P: $69-$148 | 2P: $79-$148 | XP: $10 | F5 |
| 8/26-10/11 | 1P: $69-$109 | 2P: $69-$109 | XP: $10 | F5 |
| 5/13-6/30 | 1P: $60-$99 | 2P: $60-$99 | XP: $10 | F5 |
| 10/12-10/31 | 1P: $59-$79 | 2P: $59-$79 | XP: $10 | F5 |

Motel   **Location:** Center. 207 Main St 04609. Fax: 207/288-2270. **Facility:** 52 one-bedroom standard units. 2 stories (no elevator), exterior corridors. **Parking:** on-site. **Terms:** open 5/13-10/31, office hours 6:30 am-2 am, cancellation fee imposed. **Pool(s):** heated outdoor. **Cards:** AX, MC, VI. *(See color ad below)*

SOME UNITS
🍴 🏊 / ⊗ /

# LOOK FOR THE RED

Next time you pore over a AAA TourBook® guide in search of a lodging establishment, take note of the vibrant red AAA logo, SAVE icon, and Diamond rating just under a select group of property names! These Official Appointment properties place a high value on the business they receive from dedicated AAA travelers and offer members great room rates*.

*See TourBook Navigator section, page 14, for complete details.*

——— *The following lodging was either not evaluated or did not* ———
*meet AAA rating requirements but is listed for your information only.*

**HARBORSIDE HOTEL AND MARINA**　　　　　　　　　　　　　**Phone:** 207/288-5033
　[fyi]　　　6/15-8/1　　　　　　　　　　1P: $159-$375
　　　　　9/2-10/31　　　　　　　　　1P: $109-$325
　Motel　　5/10-6/14　　　　　　　　1P: $99-$325
　　　　　8/2-9/1　　　　　　　　　　1P: $165-$295
Too new to rate, opening scheduled for June 2004. **Location:** Center. Located on the waterfront. 5 West St 04609. Fax: 207/288-3089. **Amenities:** 185 units, restaurant, coffeemakers, refrigerators, pool. **Terms:** open 5/10-10/31, cancellation fee imposed. **Cards:** AX, DC, DS, MC, VI. *(See color ad p 177)*

——— **WHERE TO DINE** ———

**124 COTTAGE STREET RESTAURANT**　　**Lunch:** $12-$25　　**Dinner:** $12-$25　　**Phone:** 207/288-4383
　　[AAA]　　**Location:** Center. 124 Cottage St 04609. **Hours:** Open 5/30-10/31 & 12/1-2/28; 7 am-noon & 5 to close; from
　　　　　5 pm 5/30-10/31. **Reservations:** accepted. **Features:** This restaurant's trademark is a large gourmet salad
　▽▽▽　bar included with all entrees. They have fresh swordfish, salmon, super stuffed shrimp, lobster, homemade
　　　　　dessert and bread. The decor includes a covered front porch, garden room and a new lounge. Casual
　American　dress; cocktails. **Parking:** street. **Cards:** MC, VI.　　　　　　　　　　　　　　　[Y] [X]

**ANTHONY'S CUCINA ITALIANA**　　　　　　**Dinner:** $15-$30　　　　　　　**Phone:** 207/288-3377
　▽▽▽　**Location:** Center. 191 Main St 04609. **Hours:** 5 pm-close. Closed major holidays. **Reservations:** accepted.
　　　　　**Features:** The authentic cuisine at Anthony's offers a wide range of creative entrees with an emphasis on
　Italian　fresh seafood dishes including seafood primavera, lobster fra diavlo, mussels marinara, lobster asiago,
MC, VI.　crabcakes and great chowder. Patio dining is available in season. Cocktails. **Parking:** street. **Cards:** DS,
　　　　　　　　　　　　　　　　　　　　　　　　　　　　　　　　　　　　　　　　　　　[X]

**CAFE BLUEFISH**　　　　　　　　　　　　**Dinner:** $15-$23　　　　　　　　**Phone:** 207/288-3696
　▽▽ ▽▽　**Location:** Center. 122 Cottage St 04609. **Hours:** 5:30 pm-9:30 pm; closing hours vary. Closed major holidays.
　　　　　**Reservations:** required. **Features:** An eclectic cuisine is featured at Cafe Bluefish, which offers fresh local
　Seafood　seafood and vegetables as well as several chicken entrees prepared with a Russian flavor and fine
　　　　　homemade dessert. The cafe's atmosphere is cozy and relaxed. Casual dress; cocktails. **Parking:** street.
**Cards:** AX, MC, VI.　　　　　　　　　　　　　　　　　　　　　　　　　　　　　　　[X]

**THE CHART ROOM RESTAURANT**　　　　**Lunch:** $5-$12　　　**Dinner:** $10-$25　　**Phone:** 207/288-9740
　　[AAA]　　**Location:** 2.5 mi w. SR 3 04644. **Hours:** Open 5/8-10/20; 11:30 am-9 pm. **Reservations:** suggested.
　　　　　**Features:** This restaurant serves only the freshest seafood and certified Angus beef. Located at the
　▽▽ ▽▽　entrance to Acadia National Park, this restaurant features a pleasant seaside setting with patio dining in
　　　　　season. The menu offers 35 steak and seafood entrees. Casual dress; cocktails. **Parking:** on-site.
　American　**Cards:** AX, DS, MC, VI.　　　　　　　　　　　　　　　　　　　　　　　　　　[X]

**COTTAGE STREET BAKERY & DELI**　　　　**Lunch:** $5-$11　　　**Dinner:** $5-$11　　**Phone:** 207/288-3010
　▽▽▽　**Location:** Center. 59 Cottage St 04609. **Hours:** Open 5/15-10/30; 6:30 am-10 pm; to 5 pm off season.
　　　　　**Features:** This restaurant is a self-serve operation with a fine selection of burgers, sandwiches, salad,
　American　excellent dessert and pastry and delicious homemade jam and jelly. The staff will also prepare a full picnic
　　　　　lunch for you. Patio dining in season. Casual dress. **Parking:** street. **Cards:** DS, MC, VI.　　[X]

**FREDDIE'S ROUTE 66 RESTAURANT**　　　**Lunch:** $6-$9　　　**Dinner:** $8-$20　　**Phone:** 207/288-3708
　▽▽▽　**Location:** Center. 21 Cottage St 04609. **Hours:** Open 5/12-10/15; 11 am-2:30 & 4:30-10 pm.
　　　　　**Reservations:** accepted. **Features:** The varied menu at Freddie's features a wide variety of meat and
　American　tasty fresh seafood dishes served in a lively and upbeat atmosphere that has a great nostalgic theme from
　　　　　the 50s and includes two levels filled with memorabilia. Casual dress; cocktails. **Parking:** street.
**Cards:** AX, DS, MC, VI.　　　　　　　　　　　　　　　　　　　　　　　　　　　　　[X]

**GALYN'S RESTAURANT**　　　　　　　　　**Lunch:** $6-$9　　　**Dinner:** $10-$22　　**Phone:** 207/288-9706
　▽▽▽　**Location:** Center. 17 Main St 04609. **Hours:** Open 5/1-11/30 & 3/1-4/30; 11:30 am-2 & 4-10 pm; hours vary
　　　　　off season. **Reservations:** accepted. **Features:** Flavorful fresh fish and slow-roasted prime rib are the
　American　house specialties at Galyn's. All desserts, including the chocolate truffle mousse cake, are made from
　　　　　scratch on the premises. You'll also enjoy the 1880s decor with original pressed-tin ceilings. Casual dress;
cocktails. **Parking:** street. **Cards:** AX, DS, MC, VI.　　　　　　　　　　　　　　　　[Y] [X]

**GEDDY'S PUB**　　　　　　　　　　**Lunch:** $5-$10　　　　**Dinner:** $8-$15　　　**Phone:** 207/288-5077
　▽▽ ▽▽　**Location:** Center. 19 Main St 04609. **Hours:** 11 am-10 pm; hours vary off season. Closed: 11/25, 12/25.
　　　　　**Features:** This upbeat, bustling pub offers live entertainment, friendly casual service and a varied menu
　American　offering ample portions. Casual dress; cocktails; entertainment. **Parking:** street. **Cards:** AX, DS, MC, VI.
　　　　　　　　　　　　　　　　　　　　　　　　　　　　　　　　　　　　　　　[A/C] [X]

**GEORGE'S RESTAURANT**　　　　　　　　　　**Dinner:** $25　　　　　　　　**Phone:** 207/288-4505
　▽▽▽　**Location:** Center; behind First National Bank. 7 Stephens Ln 04609. **Hours:** Open 5/31-10/31; 5:30 pm-10 pm; 6
　　　　　pm-9:30 pm off season. **Reservations:** suggested. **Features:** George's features a warm, intimate and
　Continental　sophisticated atmosphere. The cuisine offers wonderfully flavorful duck, lamb tenderloin, lobster strudel,
　　　　　mustard shrimp, grilled fish, steak and veal dishes. An extensive wine list enhances the excellent meals.
Casual dress; cocktails. **Parking:** on-site. **Cards:** AX, CB, DC, DS, MC, VI.　　　　　　[A/C] [X]

## HAVANA RESTAURANT

**Dinner:** $16-$32     **Phone:** 207/288-2822

American

**Location:** Center. 318 Main St 04609. **Hours:** Open 5/1-12/31 & 3/15-4/30; 5:30 pm-10 pm. **Reservations:** accepted. **Features:** You'll appreciate the creativity of Havana's cuisine flavored with Latin touches and its festive, relaxed atmosphere. The creative menu features fresh local seafood and prime steak, enhanced by a large and eclectic wine selection and delightful dessert. Casual dress; cocktails. **Parking:** street. **Cards:** AX, DC, DS, MC, VI.

## ISLAND CHOWDER HOUSE

**Lunch:** $4-$9    **Dinner:** $9-$20    **Phone:** 207/288-4905

Seafood

**Location:** Center. 38 Cottage St 04609. **Hours:** Open 5/1-10/31; 11 am-close. **Reservations:** suggested. **Features:** The Island Chowder House is a family-friendly restaurant with a model train running on a track circling the dining room! They serve lobster many different ways and have won several contests with their chowder recipe. The blueberry pie is sensational too. Casual dress; cocktails. **Parking:** street. **Cards:** AX, DS, MC, VI.

## LOG CABIN RESTAURANT

**Lunch:** $6-$12    **Dinner:** $9-$19    **Phone:** 207/288-3910

American

**Location:** 4 mi w. Rt 3 04609. **Hours:** Open 5/20-10/17; 7 am-9 pm. **Features:** Enjoy friendly attentive table service at this country-style restaurant with its high post beam construction, comfortable booth and table seating, plus the convenience of a 100-space parking area. Menu selection is vast with portions to match, seafood is fried or broiled, if meat is your choice they have prime rib and New York Angus steak. Casual dress; cocktails. **Parking:** on-site. **Cards:** AX, DS, MC, VI.

## LOMPOC CAFE

**Lunch:** $6-$12    **Dinner:** $13-$19    **Phone:** 207/288-9392

International

**Location:** Center. 36 Rodick St 04609. **Hours:** Open 5/1-10/20; 11:30 am-11 pm; hours vary seasonally. **Reservations:** not accepted. **Features:** Lompoc Cafe has an eclectic menu with seafood and vegetarian creations as well as a variety of microbrewed beers. Dining is available in the shady courtyard where one can enjoy a game of bocci. Live entertainment is featured on the weekends. Casual dress; cocktails. **Parking:** street. **Cards:** MC, VI.

## MAGGIES RESTAURANT

**Dinner:** $16-$24     **Phone:** 207/288-9007

Seafood

**Location:** Corner of Summer and Bridge sts. 6 Summer St 04609. **Hours:** Open 6/15-10/16; 5 pm-9:30 pm. Closed: Sun. **Reservations:** suggested. **Features:** Maggie's features an outstanding cuisine prepared with organic farm-raised vegetables, meat, fresh local seafood as well as home-baked bread and dessert. The candlelit atmosphere is charming and intimate, and the servers are friendly and attentive. Casual dress; cocktails. **Parking:** on-site. **Cards:** MC, VI.

## MAMA DIMATTEO'S

**Dinner:** $9-$24     **Phone:** 207/288-3666

Italian

**Location:** Center. 34 Kennebec Place 04609. **Hours:** 5 pm-close. Closed: 12/25, 12/26. **Reservations:** accepted. **Features:** The small, intimate eatery's menu emphasizes pasta and seafood. The staff is friendly. Casual dress; cocktails. **Parking:** street. **Cards:** AX, DS, MC, VI.

## MICHELLE'S FINE DINING   Country Inn

**Dinner:** $23-$40     **Phone:** 207/288-0038

French

**Location:** Center; in Ivy Manor Inn. 194 Main St 04609. **Hours:** Open 5/1-10/31; 8:30 am-10 & 5-10 pm, Sun-1 pm. **Reservations:** suggested. **Features:** Exquisite dining rooms enhance the restaurant's intimate ambience. Traditional French cuisine with a New England flair is prepared with fresh local ingredients, some imported. Presentations of marvelous and flavorful desserts show a creative flair. The wine list is extensive. Dressy casual; cocktails. **Parking:** on-site. **Cards:** AX, DS, MC, VI.

## MIGUEL'S MEXICAN RESTAURANT

**Dinner:** $8-$16     **Phone:** 207/288-5117

Mexican

**Location:** Top of Rodick St. 51 Rodick St 04609. **Hours:** Open 5/1-10/31 & 2/1-4/30; 5 pm-10 pm. Closed: Sun 3/1-5/24 & 9/6-10/31. **Features:** The locally popular Miguel's has a colorful, hacienda-style decor and a laid-back, yet bustling atmosphere. The menu offers a wide variety of authentic fare made with fresh ingredients including tacos, enchiladas and fajitas served in ample portions. Casual dress; cocktails. **Parking:** on-site. **Cards:** MC, VI.

## PARKSIDE RESTAURANT

**Lunch:** $6-$14    **Dinner:** $11-$25    **Phone:** 207/288-3700

American

**Location:** Center. 185 Main St 04609. **Hours:** Open 5/7-10/29; 11 am-3 & 5-10 pm. **Reservations:** suggested, for dinner. **Features:** This is an ideal location for people watching as it is located on a busy corner across from the village green. Atmosphere can be bustling during peak meal times, however service remains friendly and attentive. The menu features a fine array of fresh local seafood and meat entrees such as gulf shrimp scampi, bouillabaisse, lobster, Black Angus sirloin and rack of lamb to name but a few. Casual dress; cocktails. **Parking:** street. **Cards:** AX, DS, MC, VI.

## POOR BOYS GOURMET RESTAURANT

**Dinner:** $9-$17     **Phone:** 207/288-4148

American

**Location:** Downtown. 300 Main St 04609. **Hours:** Open 5/5-10/23; 4:30 pm-close. **Reservations:** accepted. **Features:** In a two-story house, the popular restaurant offers seating in the lounge, as well as on the patio and enclosed verandah. The varied menu lists fresh seafood and pasta dishes, which are served in generous portions and accompanied by selections from a good wine list. Service is attentive. On-site parking is limited. Casual dress; cocktails. **Parking:** on-site. **Cards:** AX, DS, MC, VI.

## QUARTERDECK RESTAURANT

**Lunch:** $7-$14    **Dinner:** $14-$25    **Phone:** 207/288-5292

Seafood

**Location:** Center. 1 Main St 04609. **Hours:** Open 5/15-10/30; 11 am-10 pm. **Reservations:** accepted. **Features:** You'll appreciate the great harbor view from Quarterdeck's upper floor and outside deck. The fresh local seafood offerings include lobster, scallops, salmon, halibut, tasty chowders, and some meat entrees. The serving staff is prompt and attentive. Casual dress; cocktails. **Parking:** street. **Cards:** AX, DS, MC, VI.

**THE READING ROOM RESTAURANT AT THE BAR HARBOR INN**   **Dinner:** $19-$30   **Phone:** 207/288-3351
**Location:** Center; in Bar Harbor Inn. Newport Dr 04609. **Hours:** Open 5/1-11/10 & 4/18-4/30; 7 am-10:30 & 5:30-9:30 pm; hours vary off season. **Reservations:** suggested. **Features:** The popular and busy restaurant used to be an 1887 social club. The lovely oceanfront setting and outdoor terrace afford splendid harbor views. On the menu are flavorful fresh seafood and pasta dishes, which match with a good wine list. Blueberry pie is excellent. Dressy casual; cocktails; entertainment. **Parking:** on-site. **Cards:** AX, DC, DS, MC, VI.

American

**THE ROSE GARDEN**   **Dinner:** $59   **Phone:** 207/288-3348
**Location:** 1 mi w; in Bar Harbor Hotel-Bluenose Inn. 90 Eden St 04609. **Hours:** Open 5/8-10/30; 7 am-10:30 & 5:30-9:30 pm. **Reservations:** suggested. **Features:** The wonderfully decorated room is ideal for classic dining in an upscale ambience. Creative, flavorful dishes of fresh seafood and wild game display superb preparation and presentation methods. Dressy casual; cocktails. **Parking:** on-site. **Cards:** AX, DC, DS, MC, VI. *(See color ad p 161)*

Regional
American

**RUPUNUNI-AN AMERICAN BAR & GRILL**   **Lunch:** $5-$11   **Dinner:** $9-$18   **Phone:** 207/288-2886
**Location:** Center. 119 Main St 04609. **Hours:** Open 5/1-10/31; 11 am-1 am. **Reservations:** accepted. **Features:** This restaurant features a varied menu of seafood and salad, patio dining, upbeat atmosphere, and excellent selection of fine liquor, wine, local and imported beer. Pleasant service. Casual dress; cocktails. **Parking:** street. **Cards:** AX, DC, DS, MC, VI.

American

**STEWMAN'S LOBSTER POUND**   **Lunch:** $7-$24   **Dinner:** $8-$26   **Phone:** 207/288-9723
**Location:** 1 mi w on SR 3; in Bar Harbor Regency Holiday Inn. 123 Eden St 04609. **Hours:** Open 5/15-10/11; noon-9:30 pm; hours vary off season. **Features:** The only waterfront lobster pound in the town proper, Stewman's has the feel of a traditional lobster pound. Some nontraditional seafood dishes complement mostly tried-and-true favorites. Casual dress; cocktails. **Parking:** on-site. **Cards:** AX, DC, DS, MC, VI.

Seafood
**(See color ads p 172)**

**TAHINIS BISTRO**   **Lunch:** $3-$7   **Dinner:** $15-$25   **Phone:** 207/288-0222
**Location:** Center. 116 Cottage St 04609. **Hours:** 11 am-2:30 & 5:30-10 pm; hours vary seasonally. Closed: 11/25, 12/25; also Mon. **Reservations:** suggested. **Features:** The small and colorful downtown bistro's carefully chosen wine list complements the Mediterranean cuisine. Dressy casual; beer & wine only. **Parking:** street. **Cards:** DS, MC, VI.

Mediterranean

**TESTA'S RESTAURANT**   **Lunch:** $6-$14   **Dinner:** $13-$20   **Phone:** 207/288-3327
**Location:** Center. 53 Main St 04609. **Hours:** Open 6/10-10/31; 8 am-11 pm. **Reservations:** suggested. **Features:** Testa's is a popular dining spot featuring seafood, steak, veal, chicken and Italian specialties, plus sandwiches, salad, soup, fresh dessert and berry pie, cappuccino and espresso. The casual pub-style environment displays antiques and memorabilia. Casual dress; cocktails. **Parking:** street. **Cards:** AX, DC, DS, MC, VI.

American

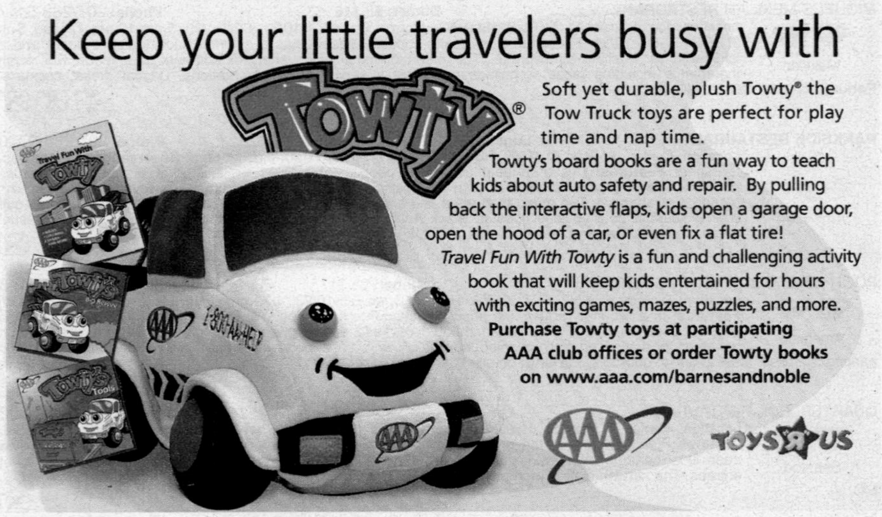

**BATH** pop. 9,266

——— WHERE TO STAY ———

**THE GALEN C MOSES HOUSE**   *Book at aaa.com*                       **Phone:** (207)442-8771

  Ⓐ SAVE   5/15-10/31 [BP]          1P: $109-$179       2P: $119-$189

  ▽▽◇▽▽   5/1-5/14 & 11/1-4/30 [BP]   1P: $99-$159       2P: $109-$169

                **Location:** US 1, exit historic district, 0.5 mi n; downtown. 1009 Washington St 04530. **Facility:** This striking 1874 Victorian mansion still has the original moldings and woodwork in the common areas. Smoke free premises. 4

Bed & Breakfast  one-bedroom standard units. 2 stories (no elevator), interior corridors. *Bath:* combo or shower only. **Parking:** on-site. **Terms:** 2 night minimum stay - weekends & 6/1-10/31, age restrictions may apply, 7 day cancellation notice-fee imposed, package plans, no pets allowed (owner's pet on premises). **Guest Services:** TV in common area. **Cards:** AX, DS, MC, VI. **Special Amenities:** free full breakfast and free local telephone calls.

                                                                                           ⊠ Ⓦ ☎

**HOLIDAY INN BATH/BRUNSWICK**   *Book at aaa.com*                  **Phone:** (207)443-9741

  ▽▽◇▽▽   6/16-10/31              1P: $89-$169       2P: $99-$179

           5/1-6/15 & 11/1-4/30   1P: $79-$129       2P: $89-$139

Small-scale Hotel  **Location:** 0.3 mi s on US 1. 139 Richardson St 04530. Fax: 207/442-8281. **Facility:** 141 one-bedroom standard units. 4 stories, interior corridors. *Bath:* combo or shower only. **Parking:** on-site. **Terms:** 1-2 night minimum stay - seasonal. **Amenities:** dual phone lines, voice mail, irons, hair dryers. **Pool(s):** heated outdoor. **Leisure Activities:** sauna, whirlpool, exercise room. **Guest Services:** valet and coin laundry. **Business Services:** meeting rooms. **Cards:** AX, CB, DC, DS, JC, MC, VI. *(See color ad below)*

                                                                    SOME UNITS

ASK S☉ 🛏 ♨ ⑪ 🖬 🐾 ⊠ 🎥 DATA PORT 🖬 🖾 🖳 /⊠/

# SAVE Yourself From Paying Full Room Rates

W hen selecting a AAA Approved lodging, look for the SAVE in TourBook® guide listings, and save money on your travel expenses. These properties actively solicit AAA business and offer members great room rates. See the TourBook Navigator section, pages 14 and 20, for details.

## ——— WHERE TO DINE ———

**BEALE STREET BARBEQUE & GRILL**
♦♦♦ ♦♦♦
Barbecue

**Lunch:** $6-$18 **Dinner:** $6-$18 **Phone:** 207/442-9514
**Location:** Center. 215 Water St 04530. **Hours:** 11 am-9 pm; to 10 pm 7/1-8/31. Closed: 11/25, 12/25. **Features:** Popular with locals and tourists alike, the restaurant makes Memphis-style barbecue on the premises. Guests also can sample such dishes as jambalaya, shrimp Louisiane and Santa Fe chicken. Casual dress; cocktails. **Parking:** street. **Cards:** MC, VI. ⊠

**J R MAXWELL & CO**
♦♦♦ ♦♦♦
Steak & Seafood

**Lunch:** $4-$9 **Dinner:** $8-$18 **Phone:** 207/443-2014
**Location:** Center. 122 Front St 04530. **Hours:** 11:30 am-2:30 & 5-9 pm, Fri & Sat-10 pm, Sun noon-9 pm. Closed: 11/25, 12/25. **Reservations:** suggested, weekends. **Features:** The restored 1840 building details the shipbuilding tradition of the historic city of Bath. Residents, businesspeople and visitors appreciate the casual atmosphere and traditional American cuisine. The menu lists poultry, seafood, lobster, steak and veal entrees, including the favorite prime rib, which is available Friday and Saturday. Casual dress; cocktails. **Parking:** street. **Cards:** AX, DS, MC, VI. ⊡ ⊠

**KENNEBEC TAVERN**
♦♦♦ ♦♦♦
American

**Lunch:** $4-$14 **Dinner:** $11-$24 **Phone:** 207/442-9636
**Location:** Center. 119 Commercial St 04530. **Hours:** 11 am-10 pm, Fri & Sat-11 pm. Closed: 12/25. **Reservations:** accepted. **Features:** The dining room offers views of the river and a marina. Menu items feature fresh local ingredients, with an emphasis on Maine seafood. Among other offerings are pasta, prime rib and vegetarian fare. Desserts are homemade. Casual dress; cocktails. **Parking:** on-site. **Cards:** AX, DC, DS, MC, VI. ⊾M ⊡ ⊠

**KRISTINA'S RESTAURANT & BAKERY**
♦♦♦ ♦♦♦
American

**Lunch:** $6-$9 **Dinner:** $10-$17 **Phone:** 207/442-8577
**Location:** Corner of High and Centre sts; center. 160 Centre St 04530. **Hours:** Open 5/1-12/31 & 2/1-4/30; 8 am-8 pm, Fri & Sat-9 pm, Sun 9 am-2 pm. Closed: Mon. **Reservations:** suggested. **Features:** Simple decor with a friendly and casual atmosphere. Eclectic cuisine with menu items primarily seafood and beef but made from scratch with fresh local foods whenever available. Brunch is offered on Saturday as well. Please note the parking lot is small but street parking is also available. Patio dining can be enjoyed seasonally. Casual dress; cocktails. **Parking:** on-site. **Cards:** DS, MC, VI. ⊾M ⊠

——— The following restaurant has not been evaluated by AAA ———
but is listed for your information only.

**MARYELLENZ CAFE**
[fyi]

**Phone:** 207/442-0960
Not evaluated. **Location:** 99 Commercial St 04530. **Features:** This small bistro features Italian cuisine and is located in the downtown waterfront area.

# BELFAST pop. 6,381

## ——— WHERE TO STAY ———

**BELFAST BAY MEADOWS INN** *Book at aaa.com*
♦♦♦ SAVE
♦♦♦ ♦♦♦
Bed & Breakfast

**Phone:** (207)338-5715

| | 1P:$90-$165 | 2P:$90-$165 | XP:$15 | F10 |
| 6/1-10/31 | | | | |
| 5/1-5/31 & 11/1-4/30 | 1P:$75-$115 | 2P:$75-$115 | XP:$15 | F10 |

**Location:** US 1, 2 mi s from jct SR 3. 192 Northport Ave (US 1) 04915. Fax: 207/338-5715. **Facility:** With grounds extending to Penobscot Bay, the inn offers two sections of rooms, some of which are modern while others are more traditional. Smoke free premises. 19 one-bedroom standard units, some with whirlpools. 2 stories (no elevator), interior/exterior corridors. *Bath:* combo or shower only. **Parking:** on-site. **Terms:** 2 night minimum stay - weekends 7/1-8/31, 14 day cancellation notice-fee imposed, pets ($15 extra charge, in annex building, with prior approval). **Dining:** 5:30 pm-9 pm, wine/beer only. **Leisure Activities:** cross country skiing, playground. **Cards:** AX, DC, DS, MC, VI. **Special Amenities:** free full breakfast and free local telephone calls.

SOME UNITS
[S⊘] [D] [⊟] [¶¶] [⊠] / [⊟] / FEE

**BELFAST HARBOR INN** *Book at aaa.com*
♦♦♦ SAVE
♦♦♦ ♦♦♦
Small-scale Hotel

*(See color ad p 189)*

**Phone:** (207)338-2740

| 6/25-10/10 [ECP] | 1P:$69-$129 | 2P:$69-$129 | XP:$10 |
| 5/1-6/24 & 10/11-4/30 [ECP] | 1P:$49-$89 | 2P:$49-$89 | XP:$10 |

**Location:** On US 1, 1.2 mi n from jct SR 3. 91 Searsport Ave 04915. Fax: 207/338-5205. **Facility:** 61 one-bedroom standard units. 2 stories (no elevator), interior/exterior corridors. **Parking:** on-site. **Terms:** pets ($10 fee). **Pool(s):** heated outdoor. **Business Services:** meeting rooms. **Cards:** AX, DS, MC, VI. **Special Amenities:** free expanded continental breakfast and free local telephone calls.

SOME UNITS
[S⊘] [D] [⊟] [⊸] / [⊠] [DATA PORT] FEE

**COMFORT INN OCEAN'S EDGE** *Book at aaa.com*
♦♦♦ ♦♦♦
Small-scale Hotel

**Phone:** (207)338-2090

| 7/2-8/28 [ECP] | 1P:$129-$179 | 2P:$129-$179 | XP:$10 | F17 |
| 8/29-10/23 [ECP] | 1P:$109-$159 | 2P:$109-$159 | XP:$10 | F17 |
| 5/1-7/1 & 10/24-4/30 [ECP] | 1P:$79-$109 | 2P:$79-$109 | XP:$10 | F17 |

**Location:** On US 1, 2 mi n from jct SR 3. 159 Searsport Ave 04915. Fax: 207/338-2528. **Facility:** 83 units. 76 one-bedroom standard units. 7 one-bedroom suites ($109-$350), some with efficiencies and/or whirlpools. 3 stories, interior corridors. *Bath:* combo or shower only. **Parking:** on-site. **Terms:** pets ($10 extra charge). **Amenities:** voice mail, irons, hair dryers. *Some:* CD players. **Pool(s):** heated indoor. **Leisure Activities:** sauna, whirlpool. *Fee:* game room. **Guest Services:** coin laundry. **Cards:** AX, DC, DS, JC, MC, VI. *(See color ad p 189)*

SOME UNITS
[ASK] [S⊘] [D] [⊟] [¶¶] [⊾M] [⊡] [⊘] [⊸] [⊠] [DATA PORT] [▦] / [⊠] [VCR] [⊟] / FEE FEE

## GULL MOTEL

**Phone:** (207)338-4030

| | | | |
|---|---|---|---|
| 6/25-10/17 | 2P: $69-$89 | XP: $10 | D12 |
| 5/1-6/24 | 2P: $41-$69 | XP: $10 | D12 |
| 10/18-4/30 | 2P: $39-$59 | XP: $10 | D12 |

(AAA) [SAVE]

▽▽▽▽

Motel

**Location:** On US 1, 3 mi n from jct SR 3. US Route 1 04915 (196 Searsport Ave). **Facility:** 14 one-bedroom standard units. 1-2 stories (no elevator), exterior corridors. *Bath:* combo or shower only. **Parking:** on-site. **Terms:** 3 day cancellation notice, weekly rates available, pets ($10 extra charge). **Cards:** AX, MC, VI.
**Special Amenities:** free local telephone calls and preferred room (subject to availability with advanced reservations).

SOME UNITS
[🛏]/[⊠][🖥][▣]/
FEE

## THE JEWELED TURRET INN

**Phone:** (207)338-2304

(AAA) [SAVE]

▽▽▽▽▽▽

Historic Bed
& Breakfast

All Year [BP]          1P: $100-$145          2P: $105-$150          XP: $25
**Location:** Center. 40 Pearl St 04915. **Facility:** Afternoon refreshments are served to guests of this 1898 Victorian home, which is enhanced by a large veranda. Smoke free premises. 7 one-bedroom standard units, some with whirlpools. 2 stories (no elevator), interior corridors. *Bath:* combo or shower only. **Parking:** on-site. **Terms:** age restrictions may apply, 14 day cancellation notice-fee imposed. **Guest Services:** TV in common area. **Cards:** MC, VI. **Special Amenities:** free full breakfast and preferred room (subject to availability with advanced reservations).

SOME UNITS
[S/D][⊠][W][Z]/[K]/

## SEASCAPE MOTEL & COTTAGES

**Phone:** (207)338-2130

(AAA) [SAVE]

▽▽▽▽

Motel

| | |
|---|---|
| 6/25-8/21 [CP] | 2P: $99-$123 |
| 8/22-10/17 [CP] | 2P: $73-$84 |
| 5/1-6/24 [CP] | 2P: $49-$69 |

**Location:** On US 1, 3 mi n from jct SR 3. 202 Searsport Ave 04915. Fax: 207/338-2130. **Facility:** 15 units. 12 one-and 1 two-bedroom standard units, some with kitchens. 2 cottages ($75-$159). 1 story, exterior corridors. *Bath:* combo or shower only. **Parking:** on-site. **Terms:** open 5/1-10/17, office hours 7:30 am-10 pm, 3 day cancellation notice-fee imposed, weekly rates available, package plans, small pets only ($10 extra charge, in cottages). **Amenities:** *Some:* hair dryers. **Pool(s):** heated outdoor. **Leisure Activities:** hot tub. **Cards:** MC, VI. **Special Amenities:** free continental breakfast and free local telephone calls.

SOME UNITS
[S/D][🛏][🏊][⊠][DATA PORT]/[VCR][🖥]/
FEE                    FEE

---

## ───── WHERE TO DINE ─────

## DARBY'S RESTAURANT & PUB

**Lunch:** $6-$9          **Dinner:** $11-$20          **Phone:** 207/338-2339

(AAA)

▽▽▽▽

International

**Location:** Center. 155 High St 04915. **Hours:** 11:30 am-3:30 & 5-9 pm, Fri & Sat-9:30 pm. Closed: 1/1, 3/27, 12/24, 12/25. **Reservations:** required. **Features:** A bar or restaurant has been at this location since it was built in 1865. Patrons will appreciate the antique bar, tin ceiling and colorful decor. The cuisine is an eclectic mix that includes a bit of everything, from Grandma Dublinsky's potato latkes to enchiladas, Pad Thai, spare ribs and BLTs. Casual dress; cocktails. **Parking:** street. **Cards:** AX, DC, DS, MC, VI.          [⊠]

## JED'S RESTAURANT

**Lunch:** $5-$15          **Dinner:** $7-$15          **Phone:** 207/338-3241

▽▽▽ ▽▽

Seafood

**Location:** US 1, 1.5 mi n. Searsport Ave 04915. **Hours:** 11 am-9 pm, Sun from 7 am; 11 am-8 pm 11/1-3/1. **Features:** The family-friendly restaurant prepares fresh local seafood and some meat dishes. Casual dress; cocktails. **Parking:** on-site. **Cards:** DS, MC, VI.          [⊠]

## THE MAINE CHOWDER STEAK HOUSE

**Lunch:** $5-$14          **Dinner:** $10-$28          **Phone:** 207/338-5225

(AAA)

▽▽▽▽

Steak & Seafood

**Location:** US 1, 2 mi n. 139 Searsport Ave 04915. **Hours:** 11 am-8 pm; to 9 pm 7/4-9/6; hours may vary in winter. Closed: 12/25. **Reservations:** accepted. **Features:** On the ridge overlooking Penobscot Bay, the restaurant employs a rustic decor in its large dining rooms. The menu features fresh lobster, mussels, crab and fish cakes, tasty chowder and some meat entrees. Patio dining is available in season. Casual dress; cocktails. **Parking:** on-site. **Cards:** AX, DS, MC, VI.          [&M][⊠]

## WEATHERVANE RESTAURANT

**Lunch:** $6-$8          **Dinner:** $6-$16          **Phone:** 207/338-1774

▽▽▽

Seafood

**Location:** At public landing; center. 3 Main St 04915. **Hours:** 11 am-9:30 pm; to 9 pm 10/15-5/31. Closed: 11/25, 12/24, 12/25. **Features:** At the public landing, the large and bustling restaurant features a good menu variety, including lobster, fried clams and crisp, Cape Cod apple-cranberry cobbler. Flavorful dishes are served in large portions. Casual dress; cocktails. **Parking:** on-site. **Cards:** AX, MC, VI.          [&M][Y][⊠]

## YOUNG'S LOBSTER POUND

**Lunch:** $12-$27          **Dinner:** $12-$27          **Phone:** 207/338-1160

▽▽▽

Seafood

**Location:** Jct SR 3, 1.5 mi n on US 1, then just e on Mitchell Ave, follow signs. 2 Fairview St 04915. **Hours:** 7:30 am-8 pm; hours vary seasonally. **Features:** The authentic lobster pound is on a working dock overlooking Penobscot Bay. Patrons can dine inside on the upper deck or outside on the dock. The menu lines up shore dinners, lobster rolls, chowders, freshly caught lobster, scallops, mussels clams and crabs. Guests can pick their own lobster from the aquarium. Casual dress. **Parking:** on-site. **Cards:** MC, VI.          [K][⊠]

# BETHEL

─── **WHERE TO STAY** ───

### BRIAR LEA INN & RESTAURANT

**Phone: (207)824-4717**

| | | | |
|---|---|---|---|
| 12/23-4/30 | 1P: $69-$89 | 2P: $79-$119 | XP: $15 | F3 |
| 7/2-10/18 | 1P: $69-$89 | 2P: $79-$109 | XP: $15 | F3 |
| 5/1-7/1 & 10/19-12/22 | 1P: $59-$79 | 2P: $69-$99 | XP: $10 | F3 |

Historic Country Inn **Location:** 1 mi n of jct US 2, SR 5 and 26. 150 Mayville Rd (US 2) 04217. Fax: 207/824-7121. **Facility:** Close to ski facilities, this renovated 1855 farmhouse is decorated with country-themed antiques; guest rooms have original hardwood floors. Smoke free premises. 6 one-bedroom standard units. 3 stories (no elevator), interior corridors. *Bath:* combo or shower only. **Parking:** on-site. **Terms:** check-in 4 pm, cancellation fee imposed, pets ($10 extra charge). **Dining:** restaurant, see separate listing. **Leisure Activities:** cross country skiing. **Cards:** AX, DS, MC, VI.

(ASK) (SD) (🛏) (🍴) (✕)
FEE

### GRAND SUMMIT RESORT HOTEL & CONFERENCE CENTER SUNDAY RIVER    *Book at aaa.com*

**Phone: (207)824-3500**

| | | | |
|---|---|---|---|
| 12/26-2/10 | 1P: $140-$340 | 2P: $140-$340 | XP: $15 | F12 |
| 2/11-4/30 | 1P: $130-$320 | 2P: $130-$320 | XP: $15 | F12 |
| 11/1-12/25 | 1P: $130-$170 | 2P: $130-$170 | XP: $15 | F12 |
| 5/1-10/31 | 1P: $120 | 2P: $120 | XP: $15 | F12 |

Resort Large-scale Hotel **Location:** Jct US 2, 3 mi n, follow signs. Sunday River Rd 04217 (PO Box 450). Fax: 207/824-3993. **Facility:** This mountainside hotel offers direct access to Sunday River ski facilities. 230 units. 180 one-bedroom standard units, some with efficiencies. 47 one-, 2 two- and 1 three-bedroom suites ($135-$530) with kitchens. 5 stories, interior corridors. *Bath:* combo or shower only. **Parking:** on-site and valet. **Terms:** check-in 6 pm, 2 night minimum stay - weekends 1/7-4/2, 14 day cancellation notice-fee imposed, weekly rates available, package plans. **Amenities:** video games (fee), CD players, voice mail, irons, hair dryers. **Pool(s):** heated outdoor. **Leisure Activities:** sauna, whirlpool, steamroom, 3 lighted tennis courts, ice skating, recreation programs, hiking trails, playground. *Fee:* downhill skiing, bicycles, massage, game room. **Guest Services:** gift shop, coin laundry, area transportation. **Business Services:** conference facilities. **Cards:** AX, DS, MC, VI. *(See color ad below)*

SOME UNITS
(🍴) (♿M) (♿) (🏊) (📶) (✕) (🎦) (DATA PORT) (💻) / (✕) (VCR) (📶) (📠) /

### THE INN AT THE ROSTAY

**Phone: 207/824-3111**

| | | | |
|---|---|---|---|
| All Year | 1P: $48-$120 | 2P: $48-$120 | XP: $10 | F3 |

Motel **Location:** On US 2, 2 mi e. 186 Mayville Rd (US 2) 04217. Fax: 207/824-0482. **Facility:** Designated smoking area. 18 one-bedroom standard units. 1 story, exterior corridors. *Bath:* combo or shower only. **Parking:** on-site. **Terms:** office hours 7 am-11 pm, 2 night minimum stay - weekends, 14 day cancellation notice-fee imposed, [BP] meal plan available, pets ($10 fee). **Amenities:** video library. **Pool(s):** heated outdoor. **Leisure Activities:** whirlpool. **Guest Services:** coin laundry. **Cards:** AX, DS, MC, VI.

SOME UNITS
(ASK) (SD) (🛏) (🍴) (📶) (✕) (VCR) (DATA PORT) (📠) / (📶) /
FEE

### JORDAN GRAND RESORT HOTEL & CONFERENCE CENTER    *Book at aaa.com*

**Phone: (207)824-5000**

| | | | |
|---|---|---|---|
| 12/26-2/10 | 1P: $140-$340 | 2P: $140-$340 | XP: $15 | F12 |
| 2/11-4/30 | 1P: $130-$320 | 2P: $130-$320 | XP: $15 | F12 |
| 11/1-12/25 | 1P: $130-$170 | 2P: $130-$170 | XP: $15 | F12 |
| 5/1-10/31 | 1P: $120 | 2P: $120 | XP: $15 | F12 |

Large-scale Hotel **Location:** US 2 E to Sunday River Rd, just n, follow signs. 1 Grand Cir 04217 (PO Box 450). Fax: 207/824-5399. **Facility:** Smoke free premises. 186 units. 166 one-bedroom standard units, some with kitchens. 15 one- and 5 two-bedroom suites ($135-$530) with kitchens, some with whirlpools. 3 stories, interior corridors. **Parking:** on-site and valet. **Terms:** check-in 4:30 pm, 2 night minimum stay - weekends 1/7-4/2, 14 day cancellation notice-fee imposed, weekly rates available, package plans. **Amenities:** video library (fee), voice mail. *Some:* CD players, irons, hair dryers. **Pool(s):** heated outdoor. **Leisure Activities:** sauna, whirlpools, steamroom, recreation programs in season, hiking trails. *Fee:* downhill skiing, bicycles, massage. **Guest Services:** gift shop, coin laundry. **Business Services:** conference facilities. **Cards:** AX, DS, MC, VI. *(See color ad below)*

SOME UNITS
(🍴) (🏋) (♿M) (🏊) (📶) (✕) (✕) (VCR) (🎦) (DATA PORT) / (📠) (📠) (💻) /

## L'AUBERGE COUNTRY INN & BISTRO

**Phone: 207/824-2774**

(AAA) [SAVE]

▽▽▽ ▽▽▽

Historic Country Inn

All Year            2P: $99-$189

**Location:** Center of village. Located adjacent to Village Common. 22 Mill Hill Rd 04217 (PO Box 21). Fax: 207/824-0806. **Facility:** This attractive mid-19th-century country inn, set on five acres, offers mountain views. Smoke free premises. 7 units. 6 one- and 1 two-bedroom standard units. 2 stories (no elevator), interior corridors. **Parking:** on-site. **Terms:** 14 day cancellation notice, [BP] meal plan available, pets (with prior approval). **Dining:** 5:30 pm-9 pm, Fri & Sat-9:30 pm, cocktails. **Guest Services:** TV in common area. **Cards:** AX, DS, MC, VI. **Special Amenities:** free full breakfast and early check-in/late check-out.

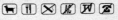

## NORSEMAN INN & MOTEL

**Phone: (207)824-2002**

▽▽▽ ▽▽▽

Motel

| | | | | |
|---|---|---|---|---|
| 11/24-4/30 [ECP] | 1P: $69-$119 | 2P: $79-$169 | XP: $10 | D4 |
| 6/16-10/22 [ECP] | 1P: $49-$89 | 2P: $59-$129 | XP: $10 | D4 |
| 5/1-6/15 & 10/23-11/23 | 1P: $49-$69 | 2P: $59-$79 | XP: $10 | D4 |

**Location:** On US 2, 2 mi e. 134 Mayville Rd (US 2) 04217 (PO Box 934). Fax: 207/824-0640. **Facility:** 29 units. 28 one-bedroom standard units. 1 one-bedroom suite ($99-$169). 2 stories (no elevator), interior/exterior corridors. *Bath:* combo or shower only. **Parking:** on-site. **Terms:** 14 day cancellation notice-fee imposed, [ECP] meal plan available. **Amenities:** *Some:* CD players. **Leisure Activities:** cross country skiing, hiking trails. *Fee:* game room. **Guest Services:** coin laundry. **Cards:** AX, DS, MC, VI.

SOME UNITS

## THE RIVER VIEW RESORT

**Phone: (207)824-2808**

(AAA) [SAVE]

▽▽▽ ▽▽▽ ▽▽▽

Condominium

| | | |
|---|---|---|
| 12/15-4/30 | 2P: $113-$337 | XP: $20 |
| 9/16-10/15 | 2P: $113-$160 | XP: $10 |
| 5/1-9/15 & 10/16-12/14 | 2P: $93-$120 | XP: $10 |

**Location:** 1.5 mi e on US 2, from jct SR 26. 357 Mayville Rd 04217. Fax: 207/824-6808. **Facility:** A walking path along the river is featured at this resort which offers two-bedroom housekeeping suites. 32 two-bedroom suites with kitchens. 2 stories (no elevator), exterior corridors. **Parking:** on-site. **Terms:** cancellation fee imposed. **Amenities:** voice mail. *Some:* irons. **Pool(s):** heated indoor. **Leisure Activities:** sauna, whirlpool, fishing, tennis court. **Guest Services:** coin laundry. **Cards:** AX, DS, MC, VI.

SOME UNITS

——— WHERE TO DINE ———

## BRIAR LEA INN & RESTAURANT   Country Inn

**Dinner: $10-$21**      **Phone: 207/824-4717**

▽▽▽ ▽▽▽

American

**Location:** 1 mi n of jct US 2, SR 5 and 26; in Briar Lea Inn & Restaurant. 150 Mayville Rd 04217. **Hours:** 8 am-11 & 5-8:30 pm; from 5 pm, Sat 8 am-11 & 5-8:30 pm, Sun 8 am-11 am 4/1-6/15 & 10/15-12/15. Closed: Tues, also Mon 4/1-6/15 & 10/15-12/15. **Reservations:** suggested. **Features:** Close to Sunday River Ski Resort, the restaurant occupies a renovated 1855 farmhouse inn. Menu items are prepared to order, and individual requests can be accommodated. Among standard entrees are filet mignon, chicken pot pie and Hampton haddock. Other dishes, such as tofu Parmesan, are prepared with an interesting twist. Breakfasts at the inn are hearty and include omelets, Belgian waffles and moose biscuit Benedict. Casual dress; cocktails. **Parking:** on-site. **Cards:** AX, DS, MC, VI.

## THE SUDBURY INN   Historic

**Dinner: $13-$24**      **Phone: 207/824-2174**

(AAA)

▽▽▽ ▽▽▽

American

**Location:** Center. 151 Main St 04217. **Hours:** 5:30 pm-9 pm. Closed: Sun-Thurs 4/1-5/31. **Reservations:** suggested. **Features:** The country inn's comfortable, informal dining room occupies a late 1800s home in the center of a village in the White Mountains foothills. The atmosphere is casually elegant, and servers are prompt and knowledgeable. Cocktails. **Parking:** on-site. **Cards:** AX, DC, DS, MC, VI.

## SUNDAY RIVER BREWING CO

**Lunch: $5-$15**    **Dinner: $5-$15**    **Phone: 207/824-4253**

▽▽▽▽ ▽▽▽▽

American

**Location:** Jct US 2. 1 Sunday River Rd 04217. **Hours:** 11:30 am-11 pm, Fri & Sat-1 am. **Features:** On the road to the Sunday River ski area, the popular brew pub presents a menu of burgers, pasta, sandwiches, salads and appetizers. Portions are generous. Casual dress; cocktails. **Parking:** on-site. **Cards:** AX, CB, DS, MC, VI.

# BIDDEFORD pop. 20,942

——— WHERE TO STAY ———

## BIDDEFORD MOTEL

**Phone: (207)284-8924**

▽▽▽▽ ▽▽▽▽

Motel

| | | | | |
|---|---|---|---|---|
| 6/20-9/5 | 1P: $59-$69 | 2P: $69-$79 | XP: $5 | F12 |
| 9/6-10/19 | 1P: $40-$49 | 2P: $49-$59 | XP: $5 | F12 |
| 10/20-4/30 | 1P: $40-$45 | 2P: $45-$49 | XP: $5 | F12 |
| 5/1-6/19 | 1P: $35-$45 | 2P: $45-$49 | XP: $5 | F12 |

**Location:** I-95 (Maine Tpke), exit 32 (SR 111), 1 mi e to US 1 S, then just s. 560 Elm St (US 1) S 04005. Fax: 207/282-8802. **Facility:** 17 one-bedroom standard units. 1 story, exterior corridors. *Bath:* combo or shower only. **Parking:** on-site. **Cards:** AX, DS, MC, VI.

SOME UNITS

**COMFORT SUITES-BIDDEFORD**   *Book at aaa.com*   Phone: (207)294-6464

| | | | |
|---|---|---|---|
| 7/1-10/19 | 1P: $99-$189 | 2P: $99-$189 | XP: $10  F18 |
| 5/1-6/30 & 10/20-4/30 | 1P: $99-$149 | 2P: $99-$149 | XP: $10  F18 |

Small-scale Hotel   **Location:** I-95 (Maine Tpke), exit 32 (SR 111), 0.4 mi e. Located in Thatcher Brook Business Park. 45 Barra Rd 04005. **Facility:** 70 one-bedroom standard units, some with whirlpools. 3 stories, interior corridors. *Bath:* combo or shower only. **Parking:** on-site. **Terms:** [ECP] meal plan available. **Amenities:** high-speed Internet, voice mail, irons, hair dryers. **Pool(s):** heated indoor. **Leisure Activities:** exercise room. **Guest Services:** coin laundry. **Business Services:** meeting rooms. **Cards:** AX, DC, DS, MC, VI.

SOME UNITS

**MOTEL ONE ELEVEN**   Phone: (207)284-2440

| | | | |
|---|---|---|---|
| 6/25-9/6 | 1P: $55-$74 | 2P: $65-$89 | XP: $5  F12 |
| 5/1-6/24 & 9/7-10/31 | 1P: $39-$47 | 2P: $49-$55 | XP: $5  F12 |
| 11/1-4/30 | 1P: $39-$44 | 2P: $44-$49 | XP: $5  F12 |

Motel   **Location:** I-95 (Maine Tpke), exit 32 (SR 111), 0.5 mi e. 2 Pomerleau St 04005. Fax: 207/286-2769. **Facility:** 19 one-bedroom standard units. 2 stories (no elevator), exterior corridors. **Parking:** on-site. **Terms:** office hours 7 am-10:30 pm, cancellation fee imposed. **Cards:** AX, DS, MC, VI. **Special Amenities:** free local telephone calls and preferred room (subject to availability with advanced reservations).

SOME UNITS

# BLUE HILL

## ———— WHERE TO STAY ————

**HERITAGE MOTOR INN**   Phone: 207/374-5646

| | | | |
|---|---|---|---|
| 7/1-9/6 | 1P: $95-$108 | 2P: $95-$108 | XP: $8 |
| 9/7-10/31 | 1P: $73-$78 | 2P: $80-$85 | XP: $8 |
| 5/1-6/30 | 1P: $67-$78 | 2P: $74-$85 | XP: $8 |
| 11/1-4/30 | 1P: $58-$78 | 2P: $65-$85 | XP: $8 |

Motel   **Location:** 0.5 mi n on SR 172. 60 Ellsworth Rd 04614 (PO Box 453). **Facility:** Smoke free premises. 22 units. 20 one-bedroom standard units. 2 one-bedroom suites with kitchens. 2 stories (no elevator), exterior corridors. **Parking:** on-site. **Terms:** office hours 8 am-10 pm. **Cards:** MC, VI.

SOME UNITS

# BOOTHBAY —*See also EAST BOOTHBAY.*

## ———— WHERE TO STAY ————

**HILLSIDE ACRES CABINS & MOTEL**   Phone: 207/633-3411

| | | | |
|---|---|---|---|
| 6/17-9/15 [CP] | 1P: $62-$85 | 2P: $62-$85 | |
| 5/1-6/16 & 9/16-4/30 | 1P: $50-$65 | 2P: $50-$65 | |

Small-scale Hotel   **Location:** US 1, 9 mi s on SR 27, then just w. 301 Adams Pond Rd 04537 (PO Box 300). **Facility:** 14 units. 8 one- and 2 two-bedroom standard units, some with efficiencies or kitchens. 1 one-bedroom suite with kitchen. 3 cottages. 1-2 stories (no elevator), interior/exterior corridors. *Bath:* some shared or private, combo or shower only. **Parking:** on-site. **Terms:** office hours 8 am-11 pm, 2 night minimum stay - weekends in season, package plans, pets (in cabins). **Pool(s):** outdoor. **Cards:** MC, VI.

SOME UNITS

**KENNISTON HILL INN**   Phone: (207)633-2159

| | | | |
|---|---|---|---|
| 6/29-10/20 | | 2P: $85-$135 | XP: $25  F10 |
| 5/1-6/28 & 10/21-4/30 | | 2P: $75-$105 | XP: $15  F10 |

Historic Bed & Breakfast   **Location:** US 1 to SR 27, 10 mi s. 988 Wiscasset Rd 04537 (PO Box 125). Fax: 207/633-2159. **Facility:** This Federal-style homestead dates from 1786 and is decorated in keeping with the period; in a country setting, it is removed from the bustle of town. Smoke free premises. 10 one-bedroom standard units. 1-2 stories (no elevator), interior/exterior corridors. *Bath:* combo or shower only. **Parking:** on-site. **Terms:** 14 day cancellation notice-fee imposed, package plans, pets (with prior approval). **Guest Services:** TV in common area. **Cards:** AX, DS, MC, VI.

**WHITE ANCHOR INN**   Phone: 207/633-3788

| | | | |
|---|---|---|---|
| 6/21-9/5 [CP] | 1P: $65-$79 | 2P: $65-$79 | XP: $8  F12 |
| 5/1-6/20 & 9/6-10/10 [CP] | 1P: $50-$59 | 2P: $50-$59 | XP: $8  F12 |
| 10/11-4/30 | 1P: $45-$49 | 2P: $45-$49 | XP: $8  F12 |

Motel   **Location:** US 1 to SR 27, 7.5 mi s. 609 Wiscasset Rd 04537. Fax: 207/633-3788. **Facility:** 29 one-bedroom standard units. 1-2 stories (no elevator), interior/exterior corridors. **Parking:** on-site. **Terms:** pets (with prior approval). **Cards:** AX, DS, MC, VI. **Special Amenities:** free continental breakfast and free local telephone calls.

SOME UNITS

## ———— WHERE TO DINE ————

### ———— *The following restaurant has not been evaluated by AAA but is listed for your information only.* ————

**MACNAB'S TEA ROOM**   Phone: 207/633-7222

[fyi]   Not evaluated. **Location:** 5 Lu Yu Tea Ln 04537. **Features:** Scones and lemon tarts accompany either afternoon or high tea, for which reservations are required.

# BOOTHBAY HARBOR pop. 1,237

———— WHERE TO STAY ————

### ADMIRAL'S QUARTERS INN

**Phone:** 207/633-2474

▽▽▽ 6/15-10/15 [BP]    1P: $165-$195    2P: $165-$195    XP: $20
5/1-6/14 & 10/16-4/30 [BP]    1P: $95-$135    2P: $95-$135    XP: $20

Bed & Breakfast   **Location:** Downtown harborfront; close to Pier 1 on the waterfront. 71 Commercial St 04538. Fax: 207/633-5904. **Facility:** A fireplace warms the glassed-in porch/breakfast room at this service-oriented inn, which offers good harbor views. Smoke free premises. 7 units. 2 one-bedroom standard units. 5 one-bedroom suites ($115-$195). 3 stories (no elevator), interior/exterior corridors. *Bath:* combo or shower only. **Parking:** on-site. **Terms:** age restrictions may apply, 14 day cancellation notice. **Amenities:** hair dryers. **Guest Services:** gift shop, complimentary laundry. **Cards:** AX, DS, MC, VI.

### ANCHOR WATCH BED & BREAKFAST

**Phone:** (207)633-7565

▽▽▽ 5/28-10/24    1P: $155-$175    2P: $155-$175    XP: $30
5/1-5/27 & 10/25-11/21    1P: $99-$110    2P: $99-$110    XP: $30

Bed & Breakfast   **Location:** 0.5 mi sw off Commercial St. 9 Eames Rd 04538. Fax: 207/633-7958. **Facility:** This converted home, on a hill bordering the harbor, is decorated in a seaside-cottage style and offers some rooms with water views and balconies. Smoke free premises. 5 one-bedroom standard units. 3 stories (no elevator), interior/exterior corridors. *Bath:* combo or shower only. **Parking:** on-site. **Terms:** open 5/1-11/21, 2 night minimum stay - weekends, age restrictions may apply, 14 day cancellation notice-fee imposed, [BP] meal plan available. **Amenities:** hair dryers. *Some:* irons. **Leisure Activities:** boat dock. **Guest Services:** complimentary laundry. **Cards:** MC, VI.

SOME UNITS

### ATLANTIC ARK INN

**Phone:** 207/633-5690

▽▽▽ 6/15-10/16    1P: $105-$185    2P: $105-$185
5/21-6/14 [BP]    1P: $95-$179    2P: $95-$179    XP: $25
10/17-10/31    1P: $95-$169    2P: $95-$169

Bed & Breakfast   **Location:** 0.3 mi se off SR 27, on east side of Boothbay Harbor. 62 Atlantic Ave 04538. **Facility:** This inn is characterized by a simple elegance, it offers well-appointed rooms. Smoke free premises. 6 one-bedroom standard units, some with whirlpools. 3 stories (no elevator), interior/exterior corridors. *Bath:* combo or shower only. **Parking:** on-site. **Terms:** open 5/21-10/31, age restrictions may apply, 14 day cancellation notice-fee imposed. **Amenities:** hair dryers. *Some:* DVD players, CD players. **Cards:** AX, MC, VI.

SOME UNITS

"I have been back to Brown's Wharf often enough to become part of the family...and it's a nice family to be a part of."

*Charles Kuralt's America*

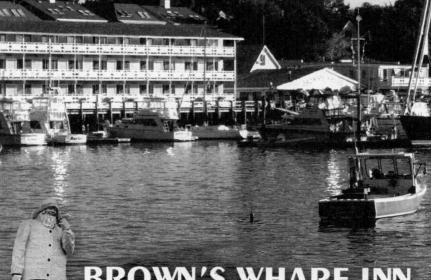

# BROWN'S WHARF INN
## www.brownswharfinn.com
### 121 Atlantic Ave., Boothbay Harbor, ME 04538
### 800-334-8110 · 207-633-5440

## BLUE HERON SEASIDE INN
**Phone:** 207/633-7020

▼▼▼▼
| | | |
|---|---|---|
| 6/18-11/15 [ECP] | 2P: $150-$215 | XP: $25 |
| 5/1-6/17 & 4/15-4/30 [ECP] | 2P: $135-$175 | XP: $25 |

**Bed & Breakfast** **Location:** Center. 65 Townsend Ave 04538. **Facility:** This nineteenth century renovated home is located in downtown with rooms styled in Victorian, Colonial and nautical themes and decks with harbor views. Smoke free premises. 6 units. 5 one- and 1 two-bedroom standard units, some with whirlpools. 3 stories (no elevator), interior/exterior corridors. *Bath:* combo or shower only. **Parking:** on-site. **Terms:** open 5/1-11/15 & 4/15-4/30, 2 night minimum stay - weekends, 14 day cancellation notice-fee imposed. **Amenities:** hair dryers. **Leisure Activities:** boating, canoeing, boat dock. **Business Services:** meeting rooms. **Cards:** AX, DS, MC, VI.

SOME UNITS
⊠ ⊠ [DATA PORT] 🖥 🖨 / [VCR] /

## BOOTHBAY HARBOR INN
**Phone:** 207/633-6302

(AAA) [SAVE]
▼▼▼▼
| | | | |
|---|---|---|---|
| 6/22-9/5 | 1P: $129-$210 | 2P: $129-$210 | XP: $14  F18 |
| 9/6-10/10 | 1P: $119-$180 | 2P: $119-$180 | XP: $14  F18 |
| 5/1-6/21 & 10/11-10/31 | 1P: $86-$160 | 2P: $86-$160 | XP: $14  F18 |

**Small-scale Hotel** **Location:** 0.3 mi e of SR 27, on east side of Boothbay Harbor. 31 Atlantic Ave 04538. Fax: 207/633-6704. **Facility:** Smoke free premises. 60 one-bedroom standard units. 2 stories (no elevator), interior/exterior corridors. *Bath:* combo or shower only. **Parking:** on-site. **Terms:** open 5/1-10/31, 2 night minimum stay - weekends, cancellation fee imposed, [MAP] meal plan available, package plans. **Amenities:** hair dryers. *Some:* irons. **Dining:** 7 am-10 & 5:30-9 pm, cocktails. **Cards:** AX, DS, MC, VI. **Special Amenities:** free newspaper. *(See color ad p 194)*

SOME UNITS
🍽 🍸 ⟨⟩ ⊹ ⊠ 🖥 / 🖨 /
FEE

## BROWN'S WHARF INN
**Phone:** 207/633-5440

(AAA) [SAVE]
▼▼▼▼
| | | | |
|---|---|---|---|
| 6/18-9/5 | 1P: $139-$169 | 2P: $139-$169 | XP: $15  F5 |
| 9/6-10/23 | 1P: $119-$149 | 2P: $119-$149 | XP: $15  F5 |
| 5/21-6/17 | 1P: $109-$129 | 2P: $109-$129 | XP: $15  F5 |
| 5/1-5/20 | 1P: $89-$109 | 2P: $89-$109 | XP: $15  F5 |

**Small-scale Hotel** **Location:** East side of Boothbay Harbor. 121 Atlantic Ave 04538 (PO Box 460). Fax: 207/633-5440. **Facility:** Smoke free premises. 70 units. 68 one-bedroom standard units, some with efficiencies. 2 one-bedroom suites with kitchens. 3 stories (no elevator), exterior corridors. **Parking:** on-site. **Terms:** open 5/1-10/23, 2 night minimum stay - weekends, 3 day cancellation notice-fee imposed. **Amenities:** hair dryers. **Dining:** restaurant, see separate listing. **Leisure Activities:** fishing. *Fee:* marina. **Guest Services:** coin laundry. **Cards:** AX, DS, MC, VI. **Special Amenities:** free newspaper. *(See color ad p 195)*

SOME UNITS
🍽 ⟨⟩ ⊠ 🖥 / [VCR] 🖨 🖵 /

## CAP'N FISH'S MOTEL & MARINA
**Phone:** 207/633-6605

▼▼ ▼▼
| | | | |
|---|---|---|---|
| 6/18-9/5 | 1P: $89-$140 | 2P: $89-$140 | XP: $10  F12 |
| 9/6-10/11 | 1P: $65-$120 | 2P: $65-$120 | XP: $10  F12 |
| 5/21-6/17 | 1P: $55-$120 | 2P: $55-$120 | XP: $10  F12 |

**Small-scale Hotel** **Location:** 0.3 mi se off SR 27, on east side of Boothbay Harbor. 65 Atlantic Ave 04538 (PO Box 660). **Facility:** 54 one-bedroom standard units. 2 stories (no elevator), exterior corridors. *Bath:* combo or shower only. **Parking:** on-site. **Terms:** open 5/21-10/11, office hours 7 am-10 pm, 2 night minimum stay - weekends, 7 day cancellation notice, package plans. **Amenities:** hair dryers. *Some:* irons. **Leisure Activities:** Fee: marina. **Guest Services:** gift shop. **Cards:** AX, MC, VI.

SOME UNITS
[🛏] / ⊠ 🖥 🖨 /

## FLAGSHIP INN
*Book at aaa.com*
**Phone:** (207)633-5094

(AAA) [SAVE]
▼▼ ▼▼
| | | | |
|---|---|---|---|
| 6/18-9/5 | 1P: $75-$105 | 2P: $75-$105 | XP: $10  F6 |
| 9/6-10/10 | 1P: $59-$85 | 2P: $59-$85 | XP: $10  F6 |
| 5/1-6/17 | 1P: $49-$75 | 2P: $49-$75 | XP: $10  F6 |
| 10/11-4/30 | 1P: $49-$69 | 2P: $49-$69 | XP: $10  F6 |

**Motel** **Location:** On SR 27, just n of jct SR 98. 200 Townsend Ave 04538. Fax: 207/633-7055. **Facility:** 82 one-bedroom standard units. 2 stories (no elevator), exterior corridors. *Bath:* combo or shower only. **Parking:** on-site. **Pool(s):** heated outdoor. **Cards:** AX, DS, MC, VI. **Special Amenities:** free local telephone calls and free newspaper. *(See color ad p 197)*

SOME UNITS
[🏊] 🌊 / ⊠ 🖥 🖨 /

## HARBORAGE INN ON THE EDGE OF THE BAY
**Phone:** 207/633-4640

▼▼▼ ▼▼
| | | | |
|---|---|---|---|
| 6/11-9/7 [CP] | 1P: $100-$185 | 2P: $100-$185 | XP: $25  D12 |
| 9/8-10/17 [CP] | 1P: $95-$165 | 2P: $95-$165 | XP: $25  D12 |
| 5/1-6/10 [CP] | 1P: $70-$120 | 2P: $70-$120 | XP: $25  D12 |
| 10/18-12/15 [CP] | 1P: $80-$100 | 2P: $85-$105 | XP: $25  D12 |

**Small-scale Hotel** **Location:** Center. 75 Townsend Ave 04538. **Facility:** Smoke free premises. 9 units. 8 one- and 1 two-bedroom standard units, some with efficiencies. 3 stories (no elevator), interior/exterior corridors. *Bath:* shower only. **Parking:** on-site. **Terms:** open 5/1-12/15, 2-3 night minimum stay - weekends in season, 14 day cancellation notice-fee imposed, weekly rates available, package plans - off season. **Amenities:** *Some:* irons, hair dryers. **Cards:** MC, VI.

SOME UNITS
⊠ 📷 / 🖥 🖨 /

## HOWARD HOUSE LODGE BED & BREAKFAST
**Phone:** (207)633-3933

▼▼ ▼▼
| | | | |
|---|---|---|---|
| 7/2-10/17 | 1P: $79-$96 | 2P: $79-$96 | XP: $15 |
| 5/27-7/1 | 1P: $59-$76 | 2P: $79-$96 | XP: $15 |

**Small-scale Hotel** **Location:** 12 mi s on SR 27 from US 1. 347 Townsend Ave 04538. **Facility:** Smoke free premises. 14 one-bedroom standard units. 2 stories (no elevator), exterior corridors. **Parking:** on-site. **Terms:** open 5/27-10/17, office hours 8 am-10 pm, 7 day cancellation notice-fee imposed, [BP] meal plan available, package plans.

⊠ [K] [Z]

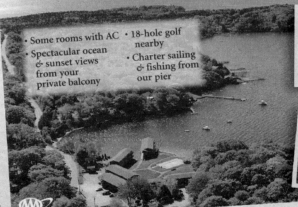

**THE PINES MOTEL**                                              Phone: (207)633-4555

AAA SAVE

| 7/1-9/4 | 1P: $85-$95 | 2P: $85-$95 | XP: $10 | F12 |
| 6/1-6/30 & 9/5-10/20 | 1P: $60-$70 | 2P: $60-$70 | XP: $10 | F12 |
| 5/7-5/31 | 1P: $50-$60 | 2P: $50-$60 | XP: $10 | F12 |

Motel

**Location:** 1 mi e of SR 27 via Atlantic Ave, on the east side of Boothbay Harbor. Located in a quiet area. 30 Sunset Rd 04538 (PO Box 693). **Facility:** 30 one-bedroom standard units. 1 story, exterior corridors. **Parking:** on-site. **Terms:** open 5/7-10/20, office hours 8 am-9 pm, cancellation fee imposed, [CP] meal plan available, pets (with prior approval). **Pool(s):** heated outdoor. **Leisure Activities:** tennis court, playground. **Cards:** DS, MC, VI. **Special Amenities:** free local telephone calls and preferred room (subject to availability with advanced reservations).

SOME UNITS

**ROCKTIDE INN**                                                Phone: (207)633-4455

AAA SAVE

| 6/21-8/29 [BP] | 1P: $119-$164 | 2P: $129-$184 | XP: $16 | F5 |
| 8/30-10/11 [BP] | 1P: $96-$154 | 2P: $106-$174 | XP: $16 | F5 |
| 6/10-6/20 [BP] | 1P: $89-$134 | 2P: $99-$154 | XP: $16 | F5 |

Small-scale Hotel  **Facility:** Designated smoking area. 97 one-bedroom standard units. 2 stories (no elevator), interior/exterior corridors. *Bath:* combo or shower only. **Parking:** on-site. **Terms:** open 6/10-10/11, 3 day cancellation notice, [MAP] meal plan available. **Dining:** restaurant, see separate listing. **Pool(s):** heated indoor. **Leisure Activities:** boat dock. **Cards:** DC, MC, VI. **Special Amenities:** free full breakfast and free newspaper. *(See color ad p 199)*

**SEAGATE MOTEL**                                              Phone: 207/633-3900

AAA SAVE

| 6/19-9/6 [CP] | 1P: $95-$115 | 2P: $115-$125 | XP: $10 | F12 |
| 4/22-4/30 [CP] | 1P: $85-$105 | 2P: $85-$115 | XP: $10 | F12 |
| 5/1-6/18 [CP] | 1P: $75-$95 | 2P: $75-$115 | XP: $10 | F12 |
| 9/7-10/17 [CP] | 1P: $85-$105 | 2P: $95-$105 | XP: $10 | F12 |

Motel

**Location:** On SR 27; center. 138 Townsend Ave 04538. Fax: 207/633-3998. **Facility:** 25 one-bedroom standard units, some with efficiencies. 1 story, exterior corridors. *Bath:* combo or shower only. **Parking:** on-site. **Terms:** open 5/1-10/17 & 4/22-4/30, office hours 8 am-10 pm, 5 day cancellation notice-fee imposed. **Pool(s):** heated outdoor. **Cards:** AX, DS, MC, VI. **Special Amenities:** free continental breakfast and free local telephone calls.

SOME UNITS

## TUGBOAT INN

AAA SAVE ◆◆◆

**Phone:** 207/633-4434

| | | | |
|---|---|---|---|
| 6/18-9/5 [CP] | 1P: $145-$195 | 2P: $145-$195 | XP: $15 F11 |
| 9/6-10/16 [CP] | 1P: $125-$175 | 2P: $125-$175 | XP: $15 F11 |
| 5/1-6/17 [CP] | 1P: $80-$150 | 2P: $80-$150 | XP: $15 F11 |
| 10/17-11/28 [CP] | 1P: $75-$135 | 2P: $75-$135 | XP: $15 F11 |

Small-scale Hotel **Location:** Downtown; waterfront area. 80 Commercial St 04538 (PO Box 267). **Facility:** 64 units. 61 one- and 1 two-bedroom standard units. 2 one-bedroom suites ($165-$215) with kitchens, some with whirlpools. 2-3 stories (no elevator), exterior corridors. *Bath:* combo or shower only. **Parking:** on-site. **Terms:** open 5/1-11/28, office hours 7 am-11 pm, 2 night minimum stay - with Saturday stayover 6/18-10/16, cancellation fee imposed, package plans. **Amenities:** hair dryers. *Some:* irons. **Dining:** restaurant, see separate listing. **Leisure Activities:** boat slips and mooring rentals. *Fee:* marina. **Guest Services:** coin laundry. **Cards:** AX, DS, MC, VI. **Special Amenities:** free continental breakfast. *(See color ad below)*

SOME UNITS
🍽 🍷 🅿 💻 / ✕ 🎆 🎆
FEE FEE

## WELCH HOUSE INN

AAA SAVE ◆◆◆

**Phone:** 207/633-3431

| | | |
|---|---|---|
| 5/28-10/11 [BP] | 2P: $125-$185 | XP: $20 F6 |
| 5/1-5/27 [BP] | 2P: $75-$135 | XP: $20 F6 |
| 10/12-4/30 [BP] | 2P: $75-$125 | XP: $20 F6 |

Bed & Breakfast **Location:** Center. 56 McKown St 04538. Fax: 207/633-3752. **Facility:** On a hill with views of the harbor, the inn is close to the center of town; rooms are decorated with antiques, fine furniture and art objects. Designated smoking area. 14 one-bedroom standard units. 3 stories (no elevator), interior/exterior corridors. *Bath:* combo or shower only. **Parking:** on-site. **Terms:** 2 night minimum stay - weekends 7/1-8/31, age restrictions may apply, 14 day cancellation notice, pets (with prior approval). **Amenities:** video library. **Cards:** MC, VI. **Special Amenities:** free full breakfast and free local telephone calls.

SOME UNITS
🛏 ✕ 📼 / 🅰 /

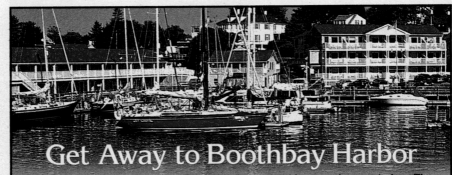

## ——— WHERE TO DINE ———

**BLUE MOON CAFE**
American
Cards: MC, VI.

**Lunch:** $4-$10    **Phone:** 207/633-2349
**Location:** Center. 54 Commercial St 04538. **Hours:** Open 5/1-11/11 & 4/1-4/30; 7:30 am-2:30 pm; to 2 pm off season. **Features:** This small cafe has counter service and is located harborside. It has an eclectic menu of soups, salads, sandwiches, vegetarian choices as well as full breakfasts. All are made on premises with fresh ingredients obtained locally. Deck dining is available seasonally. Casual dress. **Parking:** street.

---

**BROWN'S WHARF RESTAURANT**
△△△
Seafood

**Dinner:** $14-$23    **Phone:** 207/633-5440
**Location:** East side of Boothbay Harbor; in Brown's Wharf Inn. 121 Atlantic Ave 04538. **Hours:** Open 8 am-10 & 5:30-8:30 pm. Closed: Tues. **Reservations:** suggested, in season. **Features:** An area fixture since 1944, the family-owned restaurant provides a panoramic view of Boothbay Harbor. On the menu is a good selection of fresh seafood, steak, lamb and pasta dishes, plus prime rib on the weekends. Casual dress; cocktails. **Parking:** on-site. **Cards:** AX, DS, MC, VI. *(See color ad p 195)*

---

**CHINA BY THE SEA**
Chinese

**Lunch:** $4-$18    **Dinner:** $4-$18    **Phone:** 207/633-4449
**Location:** Center. 96 Townsend Ave 04538. **Hours:** 11 am-10 pm. Closed: 11/25. **Features:** Chinese cuisine is on the menu, as are lighter fare and some American offerings. The computer lounge has proven to be popular. Casual dress; cocktails. **Parking:** on-site. **Cards:** AX, DS, MC, VI.

---

**CHRISTOPHER'S BOATHOUSE**
Regional American

**Dinner:** $15-$25    **Phone:** 207/633-6565
**Location:** Corner of Pear and Union sts; center. 25 Union St 04538. **Hours:** 5:30 pm-9 pm; hours vary off season. Closed: 12/25; also Mon-Wed 11/1-1/31. **Reservations:** suggested. **Features:** Christopher's offers distinctive harborside dining. The New World cuisine features excellent regional offerings prepared in the open-style kitchen with a wood-fired grill. Sophisticated diners enjoy the exhibition cooking and warm, casual environment. Casual dress; cocktails. **Parking:** on-site. **Cards:** DS, MC, VI.

---

**THE LOBSTER DOCK**
Steak & Seafood

**Lunch:** $4-$25    **Dinner:** $4-$25    **Phone:** 207/633-7120
**Location:** 0.4 mi e of SR 27, on east side of Boothbay Harbor. 49 Atlantic Ave 04538. **Hours:** Open 5/31-10/11; 11:30 am-8:30 pm. **Reservations:** not accepted. **Features:** While the wonderful harbor views are enough to make the trip worthwhile, the restaurant's fresh local seafood make a visit all the more appealing. Hot lobster rolls are a local favorite. Casual dress; beer & wine only. **Parking:** on-site. **Cards:** MC, VI.

---

**LOBSTERMEN'S CO-OP**
Seafood

**Lunch:** $7-$13    **Dinner:** $7-$13    **Phone:** 207/633-4900
**Location:** 0.4 mi e of SR 27, on the east side of Boothbay Harbor. 97 Atlantic Ave 04538. **Hours:** Open 5/31-10/11; 11:30 am-8:30 pm; hours vary seasonally. **Features:** Guests can dine indoors or out at the dockside restaurant. Lobstermen dock nearby to unload their catch, which is on the menu shortly thereafter. Casual dress; beer & wine only. **Parking:** on-site. **Cards:** DS, MC, VI.

---

**ROCKTIDE RESTAURANT**
Seafood
Cards: DS, MC, VI.

**Dinner:** $12-$25    **Phone:** 207/633-4455
**Location:** 0.3 mi off SR 27, on east side of Boothbay Harbor; in Rocktide Inn. 35 Atlantic Ave 04538. **Hours:** Open 6/10-10/11; 7:30 am-9:30 & 5:30-9 pm; to 8:30 pm 9/4-10/11. **Reservations:** suggested. **Features:** Overlooking the harbor, the restaurant features such excellent dishes as jumbo popovers, filet mignon, prime roast beef, duck, salmon, swordfish, haddock and lobster. Homemade desserts are delicious. Semi-formal attire is expected in the dockside and harborside rooms. Casual dress; cocktails. **Parking:** valet.

---

**SPRUCE POINT INN DINING ROOM**
American
on-site. Cards: AX, DC, DS, MC, VI.

**Dinner:** $16-$30    **Phone:** 207/633-4152
**Location:** 2.5 mi s on Atlantic Ave. 88 Grand View Ave 04538. **Hours:** Open 5/18-10/26; 8 am-10 & 6-9 pm. **Reservations:** required. **Features:** This inn's restaurant offers an attractive oceanside setting for formal or casual dining. The fine cuisine features a good variety of fresh local seafood dishes and meat entrees such as veal medallions. The serving staff provides excellent attentiveness. Dressy casual; cocktails. **Parking:**

---

**TUGBOAT RESTAURANT**
American

**Lunch:** $8-$18    **Dinner:** $14-$28    **Phone:** 207/633-4434
**Location:** Downtown; waterfront area; in Tugboat Inn. 80 Commercial St 04538. **Hours:** Open 5/1-11/29 & 4/11-4/30; 11:30 am-2:30 & 5:30-9 pm; hours vary off season. **Features:** This popular restaurant lives up to its name—it's a converted tugboat! Its setting on the water gives a good view of the harbor. The menu features an excellent steak and lobster combination, wonderful seafood fettuccine and tugboat applejack crisp. Casual dress; cocktails. **Parking:** on-site. **Cards:** AX, DS, MC, VI.

# BREWER pop. 8,987

## ———— WHERE TO STAY ————

**BREWER MOTOR INN**

Phone: (207)989-4476

(AAA) (SAVE)

| | | | |
|---|---|---|---|
| 6/1-10/31 | 1P: $49 | 2P: $59 | XP: $5 | F17 |
| 5/1-5/31 & 1/1-4/30 | 1P: $47 | 2P: $52 | XP: $5 | F17 |
| 11/1-12/31 | 1P: $45 | 2P: $49 | XP: $5 | F17 |

Small-scale Hotel **Location:** I-95, exit 182A to I-395, exit 4, n on SR 15 to US 1A, then 0.7 mi e. Located in a commercial area. 359 Wilson St 04412. **Facility:** 30 units. 29 one- and 1 two-bedroom standard units, some with efficiencies (no utensils). 2 stories (no elevator), interior/exterior corridors. *Bath:* combo or shower only. **Parking:** on-site. **Terms:** [CP] meal plan available, small pets only (in smoking units). **Dining:** 11:30 am-11 pm, cocktails. **Cards:** AX, DC, DS, MC, VI.

SOME UNITS

[S/D] [🐾] [🍴] / [✕] /

## ———— WHERE TO DINE ————

**MUDDY RUDDER RESTAURANT**    Lunch: $9-$16    Dinner: $9-$20    Phone: 207/989-5389

Seafood

**Location:** Center. 5 S Main St 04412. **Hours:** 11 am-midnight. Closed: 12/25. **Reservations:** accepted. **Features:** Soup, stew, salad, lobster pie, steak and seafood dinners are among choices at the warm and inviting restaurant, which affords good views of the Penobscot River and city skyline. The downeast clambake is also popular. Tables display area maps from the 1800s. Casual dress; cocktails. **Parking:** on-site. **Cards:** AX, DC, DS, MC, VI.

[Y] [✕]

**WEATHERVANE RESTAURANT**    Lunch: $5-$9    Dinner: $8-$13    Phone: 207/989-4232

Seafood

**Location:** 2.5 mi e on US 1A. 710 Wilson St 04412. **Hours:** 11 am-9:30 pm; to 9 pm 10/12-5/31. Closed: 11/25, 12/25. **Features:** On the edge of town, the large, popular restaurant serves a good selection of fresh seafood, including boiled lobster and raw bar offerings. The staff is friendly and attentive. Casual dress; cocktails. **Parking:** on-site. **Cards:** AX, MC, VI.

[✕]

# BRIDGTON pop. 2,359

## ———— WHERE TO STAY ————

**HIGHLAND LAKE RESORT**

Phone: (207)647-5301

| | | | |
|---|---|---|---|
| 7/1-9/5 | 1P: $95-$115 | 2P: $95-$115 | XP: $10 | F11 |
| 9/6-10/23 | 1P: $75-$115 | 2P: $75-$115 | XP: $10 | F11 |
| 5/1-6/30 & 10/24-4/30 | 1P: $75-$105 | 2P: $75-$105 | XP: $10 | F11 |

Motel

**Location:** Jct US 302 and SR 117, 1.2 mi w on US 302. 115 N High St 04009. Fax: 207/647-2543. **Facility:** 23 units. 21 one-bedroom standard units, some with efficiencies. 1 one- and 1 two-bedroom suites ($130-$190) with kitchens, some with whirlpools. 1 story, exterior corridors. *Bath:* combo or shower only. **Parking:** on-site. **Terms:** 2 night minimum stay - in season, 8 day cancellation notice-fee imposed. **Amenities:** voice mail. *Some:* hair dryers. **Leisure Activities:** boating, canoeing, paddleboats, boat dock, fishing, tennis court, cross country skiing, snowmobiling, playground, exercise room, horseshoes, volleyball, game room. *Fee:* massage. **Guest Services:** coin laundry. **Business Services:** meeting rooms. **Cards:** AX, DS, MC, VI.

SOME UNITS

[ASK] [&M] [✕] [✕] [📹] [DATA PORT] [▣] / [VCR] [🔋] [📷] /
FEE

**PLEASANT MOUNTAIN INN**    *Book at aaa.com*

Phone: 207/647-4505

(AAA) (SAVE)

| | | | |
|---|---|---|---|
| All Year | | 2P: $55-$130 | XP: $10 | F12 |

Motel

**Location:** On US 302, 3 mi w of center. N High St 04009 (PO Box 246). Fax: 207/647-4540. **Facility:** 22 one-bedroom standard units, some with efficiencies or kitchens. 1 story, exterior corridors. **Parking:** on-site. **Terms:** office hours 8 am-4 pm, pets ($10 extra charge, with prior approval). **Dining:** 4 pm-9 pm, Sat & Sun from 8 am; closed Mon. **Cards:** DS, MC, VI. **Special Amenities:** free local telephone calls and early check-in/late check-out.

SOME UNITS

[S/D] [🐾] [🍴] [📹] [▣] / [✕] [🔋] [📷] /
FEE

## ———— WHERE TO DINE ————

**THE BLACK HORSE TAVERN**    Lunch: $5-$9    Dinner: $7-$19    Phone: 207/647-5300

American

**Location:** On US 302; center. 8 Portland St 04009. **Hours:** 11 am-9 pm, Sun 9 am-3 & 4-9 pm; hours vary seasonally. Closed: 11/25, 12/25; also Super Bowl Sun. **Features:** The tavern's motto is "casual dining in an equestrian atmosphere," which aptly describes the experience. The dining room resembles an old stable, with riding gear on the walls and old saddles on the "stall" walls between tables. On the menu are homemade soups, burgers, pasta, seafood and chicken. Prime rib is a specialty. Casual dress; cocktails. **Parking:** on-site. **Cards:** DS, MC, VI.

[Y] [✕]

# BRUNSWICK pop. 14,816

## ———— WHERE TO STAY ————

**CAPTAIN DANIEL STONE INN**    *Book at aaa.com*

Phone: (207)725-9898

(AAA) (SAVE)

| | | | |
|---|---|---|---|
| 7/1-10/31 [ECP] | 1P: $170-$245 | 2P: $180-$255 | XP: $15 | F16 |
| 11/1-4/30 [ECP] | 1P: $140-$230 | 2P: $150-$240 | XP: $15 | F16 |
| 5/1-6/30 [ECP] | 1P: $130-$220 | 2P: $140-$230 | XP: $15 | F16 |

Small-scale Hotel **Location:** Just n of center. 10 Water St 04011. Fax: 207/725-5663. **Facility:** 34 units. 30 one-bedroom standard units, some with whirlpools. 4 one-bedroom suites ($190-$255) with whirlpools. 3 stories, interior corridors. *Bath:* combo or shower only. **Parking:** on-site. **Terms:** check-in 4 pm, 3 day cancellation notice. **Amenities:** video library, dual phone lines, voice mail, irons, hair dryers. **Dining:** Narcissa Stone Restaurant, see separate listing. **Guest Services:** valet laundry. **Business Services:** meeting rooms. **Cards:** AX, DC, DS, MC, VI. **Special Amenities:** free expanded continental breakfast and early check-in/late check-out. *(See color ad p 203)*

SOME UNITS

[S/D] [🍴] [Y] [VCR] [DATA PORT] [▣] / [✕] [🔋] /

COMFORT INN    *Book at aaa.com*                                                              Phone: 207/729-1129
▽▽▽▽    6/29-10/1                                    2P: $123-$133            XP: $10         F17
            10/2-4/30                                    2P: $75-$99              XP: $10         F17
Small-scale Hotel    5/23-6/28                           2P: $99                 XP: $10         F17
            5/1-5/22                                     2P: $90-$96             XP: $10         F17
**Location:** 1.3 mi s on US 1. 199 Pleasant St 04011. Fax: 207/725-8310. **Facility:** 80 one-bedroom standard units. 2 stories, interior corridors. **Parking:** on-site. **Terms:** [CP] meal plan available. **Amenities:** voice mail, irons, hair dryers. **Guest Services:** valet laundry. **Business Services:** meeting rooms. **Cards:** AX, DC, DS, MC, VI.

SOME UNITS
(ASK) (S/D) (⊞+) (▦) (DATA PORT) / (✕) (▢) /

INTERSTATE OASIS ECONO LODGE    *Book at aaa.com*                                            Phone: (207)729-9991
▽▽▽    5/1-10/31 [CP]                  1P: $55-$105          2P: $55-$115          XP: $5          F18
            11/1-4/30 [CP]                 1P: $39-$59           2P: $44-$59           XP: $5          F18
Motel    **Location:** I-295, exit 28, 0.5 mi n on US 1. 215 Pleasant St 04011. Fax: 207/721-0413. **Facility:** 29 one-bedroom standard units. 1-2 stories (no elevator), exterior corridors. *Bath:* combo or shower only. **Parking:** on-site.
**Terms:** weekly rates available. **Pool(s):** outdoor. **Guest Services:** coin laundry. **Cards:** AX, CB, DC, DS, MC, VI.

SOME UNITS
(ASK) (S/D) (⇌) (DATA PORT) (▢) / (✕) (▯) /

MAINELINE MOTEL                                                                              Phone: (207)725-8761
(AAA) (SAVE)    7/1-8/31 [CP]                  1P: $49-$79           2P: $59-$99           XP: $5          F12
            9/1-10/31 [CP]                 1P: $44-$64           2P: $49-$84           XP: $5          F12
▽▽▽    5/1-6/30 [CP]                  1P: $44-$64           2P: $49-$74           XP: $5          F12
Motel    11/1-4/30 [CP]                 1P: $39-$44           2P: $44-$54           XP: $5          F12
**Location:** I-295, exit 28, 1 mi n on US 1. 133 Pleasant St 04011. Fax: 207/725-8300. **Facility:** 53 units. 52 one-bedroom standard units, some with efficiencies. 1 two-bedroom suite with efficiency. 2 stories (no elevator), exterior corridors. *Bath:* combo or shower only. **Parking:** on-site. **Terms:** office hours 7 am-11 pm, cancellation fee imposed. **Amenities:** *Some:* hair dryers. **Pool(s):** outdoor. **Guest Services:** coin laundry. **Cards:** AX, DS, MC, VI.

SOME UNITS
(S/D) (⇌) / (✕) (▯) (▣) /

## THE PARKWOOD INN

*Book at aaa.com*

Phone: (207)725-5251

| | 1P: $149-$229 | 2P: $149-$229 | XP: $10 | F17 |
| 8/1-10/31 [ECP] | 1P: $149-$229 | 2P: $149-$229 | XP: $10 | F17 |
| 7/1-7/31 [ECP] | 1P: $139-$229 | 2P: $139-$229 | XP: $10 | F17 |
| 5/1-6/30 [ECP] | 1P: $129-$229 | 2P: $129-$229 | XP: $10 | F17 |
| 11/1-4/30 [ECP] | 1P: $99-$199 | 2P: $99-$199 | XP: $10 | F17 |

Small-scale Hotel **Location:** US 1, exit Cooks Corner, 0.7 mi s on SR 24. 71 Gurnet 04011 (PO Box 92). **Fax:** 207/798-5867. **Facility:** Smoke free premises. 68 units. 62 one-bedroom standard units, some with whirlpools. 6 one-bedroom suites ($119-$229), some with whirlpools. 3 stories, interior corridors. **Bath:** combo or shower only. **Parking:** on-site. **Amenities:** irons, hair dryers. **Guest Services:** valet laundry. **Business Services:** meeting rooms. **Cards:** AX, CB, DC, DS, JC, MC, VI. **Special Amenities:** free expanded continental breakfast and free local telephone calls.

SOME UNITS

## SUPER 8 MOTEL

Phone: (207)725-8883

| 5/30-9/6 | 1P: $79-$95 | 2P: $84-$99 | XP: $8 | F17 |
| 5/1-5/29 | 1P: $64-$95 | 2P: $69-$99 | XP: $8 | F17 |
| 9/7-4/30 | 1P: $64-$79 | 2P: $69-$84 | XP: $8 | F17 |

Small-scale Hotel **Location:** US 1, exit Cooks Corner, left on Bath Rd, then 0.3 mi w. 224 Bath Rd 04011. **Fax:** 207/729-8766. **Facility:** 71 units. 70 one-bedroom standard units. 1 one-bedroom suite. 2 stories (no elevator), interior corridors. **Parking:** on-site. **Amenities:** hair dryers. **Cards:** AX, DC, MC, VI.

SOME UNITS

## TRAVELERS INN

Phone: (207)729-3364

| 7/1-8/31 [CP] | 1P: $55-$70 | 2P: $60-$99 | XP: $5 | F12 |
| 9/1-10/31 [CP] | 1P: $50-$60 | 2P: $55-$85 | XP: $5 | F12 |
| 5/1-6/30 [CP] | 1P: $45-$65 | 2P: $50-$80 | XP: $5 | F12 |
| 11/1-4/30 [CP] | 1P: $40-$50 | 2P: $45-$55 | XP: $5 | F12 |

Motel **Location:** On US 1, 0.5 mi s; center. 130 Pleasant St 04011. **Fax:** 207/721-8128. **Facility:** 37 units. 35 one- and 2 two-bedroom standard units. 2 stories (no elevator), exterior corridors. **Parking:** on-site. **Terms:** office hours 7 am-11 pm, cancellation fee imposed. **Guest Services:** coin laundry. **Cards:** AX, DS, MC, VI. **Special Amenities:** free continental breakfast and free local telephone calls.

SOME UNITS

## VIKING MOTOR INN

Phone: (207)729-6661

| 7/1-9/2 | 1P: $79-$129 | 2P: $89-$129 | XP: $10 | F12 |
| 9/3-10/31 | 1P: $69-$119 | 2P: $79-$119 | XP: $10 | F12 |
| 5/1-6/30 | 1P: $59-$119 | 2P: $69-$119 | XP: $10 | F12 |
| 11/1-4/30 | 1P: $49-$94 | 2P: $59-$94 | XP: $10 | F12 |

Motel **Location:** US 1, exit Cooks Corner, left on Bath Rd, then 1 mi w. 287 Bath Rd 04011. **Fax:** 207/729-6661. **Facility:** 38 one-bedroom standard units, some with efficiencies or kitchens. 1 story, interior/exterior corridors. **Bath:** combo or shower only. **Parking:** on-site. **Terms:** 2 night minimum stay - seasonal weekends, pets ($10 extra charge). **Amenities:** *Some:* voice mail. **Leisure Activities:** above ground pool with deck, volleyball. **Cards:** AX, DC, DS, MC, VI. **Special Amenities:** free local telephone calls and early check-in/late check-out. *(See color ad p 203)*

SOME UNITS

## ─── WHERE TO DINE ───

## BOMBAY MAHAL RESTAURANT

**Lunch:** $6-$8    **Dinner:** $9-$19    Phone: 207/729-5260

Ethnic **Location:** Center. 99 Maine St 04011. **Hours:** 11 am-10 pm. Closed: 1/1, 11/25, 12/25. **Reservations:** suggested, for dinner. **Features:** You'll appreciate the wide variety of authentic and very well-prepared dishes at this restaurant, which has a pleasant storefront setting on the main street of this college town. The menu specializes in lamb, chicken, vegetarian delights and Thai dishes. Casual dress; beer & wine only. **Parking:** street. **Cards:** AX, DS, MC, VI.

## GREAT IMPASTA

**Lunch:** $5-$8    **Dinner:** $10-$15    Phone: 207/729-5858

Italian **Location:** Center. 42 Maine St 04011. **Hours:** 11 am-9 pm, Fri & Sat-10 pm. Closed: 11/25, 12/25; also Sun. **Features:** This popular restaurant claims they serve the best-tasting garlic bread in the world! The menu also features nicely prepared pasta dishes combined with seafood, chicken and vegetables. They also have delicious homemade dessert and friendly servers. Casual dress; cocktails. **Parking:** on-site. **Cards:** AX, DS, MC, VI.

## MACMILLAN & CO

**Lunch:** $6-$9    **Dinner:** $8-$28    Phone: 207/721-9662

American **Location:** Center. 94 Maine St 04011. **Hours:** 11:30 am-2:30 & 5-9 pm, Fri & Sat-10 pm, Sun noon-9 pm. Closed: 11/25, 12/25. **Reservations:** accepted. **Features:** In the downtown area, the brick storefront restaurant celebrates arctic exploration. Residents, businesspeople and visitors appreciate the casual atmosphere and traditional American cuisine. The menu lists poultry, seafood, steak and veal entrees, including the favorite prime rib, which is available only Friday and Saturday. Smoking is permitted in the pub and game room. Casual dress; cocktails. **Parking:** street. **Cards:** AX, DS, MC, VI.

## NARCISSA STONE RESTAURANT

▼▼▼ ▼▼▼

Regional American

**Lunch:** $5-$10   **Dinner:** $13-$22   **Phone:** 207/725-9898
**Location:** Just n of center; in Captain Daniel Stone Inn. 10 Water St 04011. **Hours:** 11:30 am-2 & 5-9 pm. **Reservations:** accepted. **Features:** Guests peruse a creative menu in the well-appointed dining room. Among offerings are baked stuffed haddock, lobster fettuccine, broiled seafood sampler and a variety of tasty desserts. Sunday brunch is popular with locals and tourists alike. The double-hearth brick fireplace is a focal point of the decor. Service is friendly. Casual dress; cocktails. **Parking:** on-site. **Cards:** AX, DC, DS, MC, VI. ⓨ ☒

## RICHARD'S RESTAURANT

▼▼▼ ▼▼▼

German

**Lunch:** $5-$11   **Dinner:** $12-$18   **Phone:** 207/729-9673
**Location:** Center. 115 Main St 04011. **Hours:** 11 am-2 & 5-9 pm, Thurs-Sat to 9:30 pm. Closed: 1/1, 12/25; also Sun. **Features:** This restaurant exudes an Old World ambience. The extensive menu lists German entrees, as well as a page of American dishes, such as black Angus steaks. Casual dress; cocktails. **Parking:** on-site. **Cards:** MC, VI.
ⓨ ☒

## SCARLET BEGONIAS

▼

Mediterranean

**Lunch:** $8-$10   **Dinner:** $8-$10   **Phone:** 207/721-0403
**Location:** Center. 212B Maine St 04011. **Hours:** 11 am-8 pm, Thurs-8:30 pm, Fri-9:30 pm, Sat noon-9:30 pm. Closed major holidays; also Sun. **Features:** This is an unpretentious storefront bistro with simple decor and a casual family atmosphere. The cuisine is eclectic with a Mediterranean influence. Menu selections include soups, salads, sandwiches, pasta and personal pizzas, which are served all day. All of the reasonably priced offerings are delicious, healthy and made from fresh, interesting ingredients. Casual dress. **Parking:** street.
☒

## STAR FISH GRILL

▼▼▼ ▼▼▼

Seafood

**Dinner:** $15-$21   **Phone:** 207/725-7828
**Location:** 0.8 mi s on US 1. 100 Pleasant St 04011. **Hours:** 5 pm-9 pm. Closed: Mon. **Reservations:** suggested. **Features:** An open kitchen in the rear and a fish theme characterize this small, bistro-style restaurant. The atmosphere is casual, and the dress code varies from jeans to business attire. The menu centers on fresh seafood, which is prepared using many cooking traditions and fresh local seasonal ingredients, whenever possible. Menu items can be adapted to please both vegetarians and children. Don't pass up the lobster paella for two or the crab cake entrees. Cocktails. **Parking:** on-site. **Cards:** AX, DS, MC, VI. ☒

# BRYANT POND

## ──────── WHERE TO STAY ────────

### MOLLYOCKETT MOTEL & SWIM SPA

▼

Motel

**Phone:** 207/674-2345

| | | |
|---|---|---|
| 11/16-4/30 | 1P: $80-$95 | 2P: $80-$95 |
| 5/1-11/15 | 1P: $70-$85 | 2P: $70-$85 |

**Location:** 1.3 mi n on SR 26, from jct SR 219. 1132 S Main St 04219 (PO Box 58, WEST PARIS, 04289). Fax: 207/674-3985. **Facility:** 20 one-bedroom standard units, some with efficiencies. 2 stories (no elevator), interior/exterior corridors. **Parking:** on-site. **Amenities:** high-speed Internet. **Pool(s):** heated indoor. **Leisure Activities:** sauna, whirlpool, snowmobiling, playground. **Cards:** AX, CB, DC, DS, MC, VI.

SOME UNITS
(ASK) ☞ ⟲ ☒ 🖵 / ☒ 🖬 🖨 /

# BUCKSPORT pop. 2,970

## ──────── WHERE TO STAY ────────

### BEST WESTERN JED PROUTY MOTOR INN

▼▼▼ ▼▼▼

Small-scale Hotel

**Phone:** 207/469-3113

| | | | |
|---|---|---|---|
| 7/1-8/31 | 1P: $89-$159 | 2P: $89-$159 | XP: $10 | F12 |
| 9/1-10/31 | 1P: $99-$149 | 2P: $99-$149 | XP: $10 | F12 |
| 5/1-6/30 & 11/1-4/30 | 1P: $69-$109 | 2P: $69-$109 | XP: $10 | F12 |

**Location:** On SR 15; center. 64 Main St 04416 (PO Box 826). Fax: 207/469-3113. **Facility:** 40 one-bedroom standard units. 4 stories, interior corridors. **Parking:** on-site. **Amenities:** irons, hair dryers. **Cards:** AX, CB, DC, DS, MC, VI.

SOME UNITS
(ASK) (S/D) (☏) (DATA PORT) 🖵 / ☒ 🖬 🖨 /

## ──────── WHERE TO DINE ────────

### MACLEOD'S RESTAURANT

ⓐⓐⓐ
▼▼▼ ▼▼▼

Steak House

**Dinner:** $10-$18   **Phone:** 207/469-3963
**Location:** Corner of Main and Central sts; center. **Hours:** 4:30 pm-9 pm; to 8 pm in winter. Closed major holidays. **Reservations:** suggested. **Features:** Popular restaurant offering a wide range of entrees from fresh seafood to barbecued ribs, steak, burgers and sandwiches. All homemade baking with their hallmark dessert - silk pie. Casual dress; cocktails. **Parking:** street. **Cards:** AX, DS, MC, VI. ⓨ ☒

# CALAIS pop. 3,447

## ──────── WHERE TO STAY ────────

### CALAIS MOTOR INN

ⓐⓐⓐ (SAVE)
▼▼▼ ▼▼▼

Small-scale Hotel

**Phone:** 207/454-7111

| | | | |
|---|---|---|---|
| 7/1-9/30 | 1P: $84-$94 | 2P: $94-$104 | XP: $10 | F12 |
| 5/1-6/30 & 10/1-12/31 | 1P: $54-$64 | 2P: $64-$74 | XP: $10 | F12 |
| 1/1-4/30 | 1P: $44-$54 | 2P: $54-$64 | XP: $10 | F12 |

**Location:** 0.5 mi s on US 1. 633 Main St 04619. Fax: 207/454-8017. **Facility:** 70 one-bedroom standard units. 2 stories (no elevator), interior/exterior corridors. **Bath:** combo or shower only. **Parking:** on-site. **Terms:** [AP] meal plan available, package plans - weekends, pets ($10 extra charge). **Dining:** restaurant, see separate listing. **Pool(s):** heated indoor. **Leisure Activities:** whirlpool, exercise room. **Guest Services:** coin laundry. **Cards:** AX, CB, DC, DS, MC, VI. **Special Amenities:** free local telephone calls and early check-in/late check-out.

SOME UNITS
(S/D) ☞ (☏) ⓨ ⟲ (DATA PORT) / ☒ 🖬 🖨 /
FEE

## INTERNATIONAL MOTEL

**Phone:** (207)454-7515

(AAA) (SAVE)

Motel

| | 6/1-10/15 | 1P: $50-$70 | 2P: $60-$80 | XP: $5 | F10 |
| | 5/1-5/31 & 10/16-4/30 | 1P: $45-$60 | 2P: $50-$70 | XP: $5 | F10 |

**Location:** 0.5 mi s on US 1. 626 Main St 04619. Fax: 207/454-3396. **Facility:** 61 units. 60 one-bedroom standard units. 1 one-bedroom suite with whirlpool. 1-2 stories (no elevator), exterior corridors. *Bath:* combo or shower only. **Parking:** on-site. **Terms:** weekly rates available, small pets only. **Amenities:** *Some:* hair dryers. **Cards:** AX, CB, DC, DS, MC, VI. **Special Amenities:** free local telephone calls and early check-in/late check-out.

SOME UNITS

---

## ——— WHERE TO DINE ———

## BERNARDINI'S

**Lunch:** $6-$9 **Dinner:** $10-$14 **Phone:** 207/454-2237

(AAA)

Italian

**Location:** Center. 257 Main St 04619. **Hours:** 11 am-8 pm; hours vary seasonally. Closed major holidays; also Sun. **Reservations:** accepted. **Features:** Veal Marsala, chicken asigao and wonderful tiramisu are the specialties at Bernardini's, which is a 44-seat cafe. The restaurant's small and intimate setting has a casual, family-dining atmosphere. The serving staff is attentive and knowledgeable. Casual dress; cocktails. **Parking:** street. **Cards:** MC, VI.

---

## CALAIS MOTOR INN RESTAURANT

**Lunch:** $6-$10 **Dinner:** $9-$16 **Phone:** 207/454-7111

American

**Location:** 0.5 mi s on US 1; in Calais Motor Inn. 293 Main St 04619. **Hours:** 6:30 am-2 & 5-9 pm. Closed: 12/25. **Reservations:** accepted. **Features:** This large, elegant and airy restaurant has a family-style feel that's quite comfortable. Steak and seafood dishes are the featured attractions, and the homemade pie and pastry are also popular offerings. The serving staff is prompt and pleasant. Casual dress; cocktails. **Parking:** on-site. **Cards:** AX, CB, DC, DS, MC, VI.

---

## THE TOWNHOUSE RESTAURANT

**Dinner:** $9-$15 **Phone:** 207/454-8021

(AAA)

American

**Location:** Center. 234 Main St 04619. **Hours:** Open 5/1-11/15 & 4/15-4/30; 4 pm-9 pm. **Features:** The locally popular restaurant offers a good view of the St. Croix River from its downtown location. Lobster, shrimp, haddock, scallops and clams are offered, as well as prime rib, steak, chicken and pasta dishes. Patio dining in season. Casual dress; cocktails. **Parking:** street. **Cards:** AX, DS, MC, VI.

---

# CAMDEN pop. 3,934

## ——— WHERE TO STAY ———

## ABIGAIL'S BED & BREAKFAST INN

**Phone:** 207/236-2501

Historic Bed & Breakfast

| | 5/15-11/1 [BP] | 1P: $95-$165 | 2P: $125-$225 | XP: $35 |

**Location:** Just n on US 1; downtown. Located in a residential area. 8 High St 04843. Fax: 207/230-0657. **Facility:** Close to the center of town, this attractive Federal-style 1847 home has spacious rear grounds; one guest room includes a fireplace and a whirlpool. Smoke free premises. 4 one-bedroom standard units, some with whirlpools. 2 stories (no elevator), interior/exterior corridors. *Bath:* combo or shower only. **Parking:** on-site. **Terms:** open 5/15-11/1, 2 night minimum stay - weekends, age restrictions may apply, 30 day cancellation notice-fee imposed. **Amenities:** hair dryers. **Cards:** MC, VI.

SOME UNITS

---

## THE BELMONT INN

**Phone:** (207)236-8053

Historic Bed & Breakfast

| | 6/11-10/31 | 1P: $120-$175 | 2P: $120-$175 |
| | 5/1-6/10 & 11/1-4/30 | 1P: $85-$120 | 2P: $85-$120 |

**Location:** Center. Located in a residential area. 6 Belmont Ave 04843. Fax: 207/236-9872. **Facility:** This attractive 1892 Edwardian-style inn offers a pleasant sun porch, seasonal gardens and varied rooms. Smoke free premises. 6 one-bedroom standard units. 3 stories (no elevator), interior corridors. *Bath:* combo or shower only. **Parking:** on-site. **Terms:** 14 day cancellation notice-fee imposed, [BP] meal plan available. **Amenities:** CD players, hair dryers. **Guest Services:** TV in common area. **Cards:** AX, DS, MC, VI.

---

## BIRCHWOOD MOTEL

**Phone:** (207)236-4204

(AAA) (SAVE)

Motel

| | 7/1-9/6 [CP] | | 2P: $77-$83 | XP: $10 | F12 |
| | 9/7-10/31 [CP] | | 2P: $70-$77 | XP: $10 | F12 |
| | 5/10-6/30 [CP] | | 2P: $60-$65 | XP: $10 | F12 |

**Location:** 3 mi on US 1. 530 Belfast Rd 04843. **Facility:** 15 units. 14 one-bedroom standard units. 1 cottage ($95-$110). 1 story, exterior corridors. *Bath:* combo or shower only. **Parking:** on-site. **Terms:** open 5/10-10/31. **Cards:** AX, DS, MC, VI. **Special Amenities:** free continental breakfast and free local telephone calls.

SOME UNITS

---

## BLUE HARBOR HOUSE, A VILLAGE INN

**Phone:** 207/236-3196

Country Inn

| | 5/15-11/15 [BP] | 1P: $125-$205 | 2P: $125-$205 |

**Location:** On US 1; center. 67 Elm St 04843. Fax: 207/236-6523. **Facility:** This restored 1810 inn has a large lawn and garden and offers rooms that vary in size and decor; some bathrooms have antique claw-foot tubs. Smoke free premises. 11 units. 10 one-bedroom standard units, some with whirlpools. 1 one-bedroom suite ($175-$205). 2 stories (no elevator), interior/exterior corridors. *Bath:* combo or shower only. **Parking:** on-site. **Terms:** open 5/15-11/15, 2 night minimum stay - weekends, age restrictions may apply, 14 day cancellation notice-fee imposed, pets ($25 fee). **Amenities:** video library, hair dryers. **Cards:** AX, DS, MC, VI.

FEE

## CAMDEN HARBOUR INN

**Phone:** 207/236-4200

Property failed to provide current rates

*Historic Bed & Breakfast*

**Location:** Off US 1, 0.3 mi e; center. 83 Bayview St 04843. Fax: 207/236-7063. **Facility:** Some guest rooms at this 1874 inn include fireplaces; all are tastefully decorated and offer views of the bay or surrounding hills. 22 units. 21 one-bedroom standard units. 1 one-bedroom suite. 3 stories (no elevator), interior corridors. **Parking:** on-site. **Terms:** open 5/2-12/7, age restrictions may apply, small pets only ($20 fee, dogs only).
**Amenities:** voice mail, hair dryers.

SOME UNITS

🐄 🍸 🛗 DATA PORT / ⊠ /
FEE

## THE CAMDEN RIVERHOUSE HOTEL & INNS

**Phone:** (207)236-0500

| | 1P: $179-$219 | 2P: $179-$219 | XP: $20 | F16 |
| 5/24-10/31 [ECP] | | | | |
| 5/1-5/23 & 11/1-4/30 [ECP] | 1P: $99-$139 | 2P: $99-$139 | XP: $20 | F16 |

*Small-scale Hotel*

**Location:** Center. Located in a commercial area. 11 Tannery Ln 04843. Fax: 207/236-4711. **Facility:** 35 one-bedroom standard units, some with whirlpools. 4 stories, interior corridors. **Amenities:** voice mail, irons, hair dryers. **Pool(s):** small heated indoor. **Leisure Activities:** whirlpool, exercise room. **Guest Services:** coin laundry. **Business Services:** meeting rooms. **Cards:** AX, CB, DC, DS, MC, VI.

SOME UNITS

ASK SD 🍽 🏊 📽 DATA PORT 🖥 / ⊠ 📠 🖼 /

## THE CAMDEN WINDWARD HOUSE CIRCA 1854

**Phone:** 207/236-9656

ⒶⒶⒶ SAVE

| 6/20-10/31 [BP] | 1P: $190-$280 | 2P: $190-$280 | XP: $40 |
| 5/1-6/19 [BP] | 1P: $160-$240 | 2P: $160-$240 | XP: $40 |
| 11/1-1/3 [BP] | 1P: $140-$220 | 2P: $140-$220 | XP: $40 |
| 1/4-4/30 [BP] | 1P: $120-$200 | 2P: $120-$200 | XP: $40 |

*Historic Bed & Breakfast*

**Location:** Center. 6 High St 04843. Fax: 207/230-0433. **Facility:** Formerly the home of a shipbuilder, this 1854 house offers spacious rear grounds and well-decorated guest rooms and common areas. Smoke free premises. 8 units. 5 one-bedroom standard units, some with whirlpools. 2 one- and 1 two-bedroom suites, some with whirlpools. 3 stories (no elevator), interior/exterior corridors. *Bath:* combo or shower only. **Parking:** on-site. **Terms:** 2-3 night minimum stay - weekends, age restrictions may apply, 14 day cancellation notice-fee imposed. **Amenities:** video library, CD players, hair dryers. **Business Services:** fax. **Cards:** AX, DS, MC, VI. **Special Amenities:** free full breakfast and free local telephone calls.

SOME UNITS

🍽 ⊠ 📽 DATA PORT / VCR /

## CAPTAIN SWIFT INN

**Phone:** (207)236-8113

| 5/1-10/31 [BP] | 1P: $95-$139 | 2P: $99-$155 | XP: $35 |
| 11/1-4/30 [BP] | 1P: $89-$109 | 2P: $89-$109 | XP: $35 |

*Historic Bed & Breakfast*

**Location:** Center. 72 Elm St 04843. Fax: 207/236-0464. **Facility:** Dating from 1810, this Federal-style home has been restored and offers rooms of varying size and decor; colorful gardens surround the house in season. Smoke free premises. 4 one-bedroom standard units. 2 stories (no elevator), interior/exterior corridors. *Bath:* shower only. **Parking:** on-site. **Terms:** 2 night minimum stay - 8/1-8/31 & weekends 5/1-11/30, age restrictions may apply, 14 day cancellation notice-fee imposed. **Amenities:** hair dryers. **Guest Services:** TV in common area. **Cards:** MC, VI.

♿M ⊠ 🅦 🅩

**CEDAR CREST MOTEL**                                                    Phone: (207)236-4839

| | | | |
|---|---|---|---|
| 7/2-9/5 | 1P: $119-$139 | 2P: $119-$139 | XP: $10    F5 |
| 9/6-10/30 | 1P: $106-$119 | 2P: $106-$119 | XP: $10    F5 |
| 5/28-7/1 | 1P: $82-$96 | 2P: $82-$96 | XP: $10    F5 |
| 5/7-5/27 | 1P: $68-$76 | 2P: $68-$76 | XP: $10    F5 |

Small-scale Hotel **Location:** 0.8 mi s on US 1. 115 Elm St 04843. Fax: 207/236-6719. **Facility:** 37 one-bedroom standard units. 2 stories (no elevator), exterior corridors. **Parking:** on-site. **Terms:** open 5/7-10/30, office hours 7 am-11 pm, 3 day cancellation notice. **Amenities:** hair dryers. **Dining:** 6:30 am-4 pm, cocktails. **Pool(s):** heated outdoor. **Leisure Activities:** playground. **Guest Services:** coin laundry. **Cards:** AX, DS, MC, VI. **Special Amenities:** free local telephone calls and free newspaper. *(See color ad below)*

SOME UNITS

**ELMS BED & BREAKFAST AT BLACKBERRY COMMON**                           Phone: 207/236-6250

| | | | |
|---|---|---|---|
| 5/28-10/28 | 1P: $129-$199 | 2P: $129-$199 | XP: $35    D12 |
| 5/1-5/27 & 10/29-4/30 | 1P: $105-$169 | 2P: $105-$169 | XP: $35    D12 |

Historic Bed **Location:** Center. 84 Elm St 04843. **Facility:** Originally a sea captain's home, this house dating from 1806 of-& Breakfast fers pleasant common areas and guest rooms, including one with a fireplace. Smoke free premises. 7 one-bedroom standard units, some with whirlpools. 3 stories (no elevator), interior/exterior corridors. *Bath:* combo or shower only. **Parking:** on-site. **Terms:** 2 night minimum stay - weekends, 14 day cancellation notice-fee imposed, [BP] meal plan available. **Amenities:** hair dryers. *Some:* CD players, irons. **Cards:** DS, MC, VI.

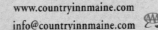

# GLENMOOR

## ~Oceanfront Resort & Cottages~

## Exceptional Accommodations & Service

Swimming & Tennis          The Grounds          Rooms, Suites, Cottages

Glenmoor is the Camden Area's intimate oceanfront resort.
Enjoy nearly 15 acres of property with outstanding Rooms, Suites, and Cottages.

*Please contact Reservations or view our Website to see how you can base
your entire Maine Vacation from Glenmoor!*

Enjoy the classic Maine shorefront, tennis, swimming, acres of lawn, and
exceptional service whether you stay with us for a day or a week...all at Glenmoor.
Camden Hills State Park, lakes, world-class museums, shopping, dining,
sailing, lighthouses, and much more are just minutes away.

**Reservations 1-800-439-3541   Tel. 1-207-236-3466**
*Located just 4 miles north of Camden Harbor on Coastal Rt. 1*

# www.glenmoorbythesea.com

*Please see our listing with rates under Lincolnville or go to our website for more detail*

**HAWTHORN INN**

**Phone:** 207/236-8842

5/1-11/14    1P: $125-$280    2P: $125-$280    XP: $40
11/15-4/30    1P: $90-$185    2P: $90-$185    XP: $40

Historic Bed & Breakfast

**Location:** 0.3 mi n on US 1. Located in a residential area. 9 High St 04843. **Fax:** 207/236-6181. **Facility:** Some of the rooms at this restored 1894 Victorian home and carriage house offer harbor views, and a few feature decks and gas fireplaces. Smoke free premises. 10 units. 8 one-bedroom standard units, some with whirl-pools. 2 one-bedroom suites. 3 stories (no elevator), interior corridors. *Bath:* combo or shower only. **Parking:** on-site. **Terms:** 2 night minimum stay - 6/1-10/31, age restrictions may apply, 21 day cancellation notice-fee imposed, [BP] meal plan available, package plans - seasonal, no pets allowed (owner's pet on premises). **Amenities:** hair dryers. *Some:* CD players. **Cards:** DS, MC, VI.

SOME UNITS

⊠ / ⓐⒸ ⓟⓥ ⓋⒸⓇ /

**THE LODGE & COTTAGES AT CAMDEN HILLS**

Phone: (207)236-8478

All Year      1P: $125-$225      2P: $125-$225      XP: $15      D18

Cottage

**Location:** 1.2 mi n on US 1. 186 Belfast Rd 04843 (PO Box 794). Fax: 207/236-7163. **Facility:** Well back from the highway in a village-type setting, the property offers some guest rooms and cottages with fireplaces and efficiency kitchens. Designated smoking area. 14 units. 6 one-bedroom standard units, some with efficiencies. 4 one-bedroom suites ($160-$189) with efficiencies. 4 cottages ($125-$225) with whirlpools. 1 story, exterior corridors. *Bath:* combo or shower only. **Parking:** on-site. **Terms:** office hours 8 am-8 pm, 10 day cancellation notice-fee imposed, weekly rates available, package plans. **Amenities:** voice mail, hair dryers. **Cards:** AX, CB, DC, DS, MC, VI.

SOME UNITS

🛗 ⊠ 📠 🗄 🖥 / 📼 📺 /

**LORD CAMDEN INN**

Phone: (207)236-4325

AAA SAVE

5/25-10/31 [BP]      2P: $160-$220      XP: $20      F12

5/1-5/24 & 11/1-4/30 [BP]      2P: $90-$140      XP: $20      F12

Historic Bed & Breakfast

**Location:** Center. 24 Main St 04843. Fax: 207/236-7141. **Facility:** The inn is in the center of town and offers rooms of varying size and shape, some with harbor or river views or private balconies. 31 units. 27 one-bedroom standard units. 4 one-bedroom suites. 4 stories, interior corridors. **Parking:** on-site. **Terms:** 7 day cancellation notice-fee imposed. **Business Services:** meeting rooms. **Cards:** MC, VI. **Special Amenities: free full breakfast and free local telephone calls.** *(See color ad below)*

SOME UNITS

📶 🔌 🛏 🛗 🖥 / ⊠ 🗄 📺 /

## A stay worth remembering

IN THE HEART OF DOWNTOWN CAMDEN, coastal Maine's most scenic and charming Harbor Village, sits an extraordinary and historic inn – the Lord Camden Inn. Enjoy our warm and inviting rooms, magnificent ocean views, complimentary full breakfast, village location and our gracious hospitality.

### www.lordcamdeninn.com
### (800) 336-4325

• Specials & Packages   • Online Reservations   • Full Breakfast   • AAA & Senior Discounts   • Cable TV

## Schooner Bay Motor Inn

Located between Camden and Rockland on Coastal Route 1 in Rockport, Maine

**Quality lodging without a high price tag**

Each of Schooner Bay's 23 *non-smoking rooms* has its own full bath and private entrance with:

• Complimentary Continental Breakfast
• All Rooms with AC, Cable TV, In-Room Phone
• King, Queen, or Double Beds

*See Our Listing Under Rockport*

### 207-236-2205

For Reservations
### 1-888-308-8855

www.
sbaymotorinn.com

## *Private cottages nestled in the pines with views of Penobscot Bay & the Islands*

1 & 2 bedrooms w/queen beds • private baths • full kitchens
cable TV w/remote • in-room phones • heat/AC • private decks
BBQs • sandy beach nearby • moderately priced

### *Pine Grove Cottages*

Please see our listing under Lincolnville

## 207-236-2929 • 800-530-5265

2076 Atlantic Highway • Lincolnville, ME 04849
www.pinegrovecamden.com
*Just 4 miles north from village of Camden on U.S. 1*

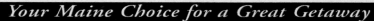

**WHITEHALL INN**

Historic Country Inn

7/1-10/17    1P: $80-$100    2P: $85-$170    XP: $30
5/28-6/30    1P: $65-$80    2P: $75-$125    XP: $20

**Phone: 207/236-3391**

**Location:** 0.5 mi n on US 1. 52 High St 04843. Fax: 207/236-4427. **Facility:** Though expanded in 1901 and 1910, this inn on manicured grounds features an original structure which dates from 1834. 49 units. 47 one- and 2 two-bedroom standard units. 3 stories (no elevator), interior corridors. **Bath:** some shared or private, combo or shower only. **Parking:** on-site. **Terms:** open 5/28-10/17, 2-3 night minimum stay - some weekends & 8/1-8/31, 22 day cancellation notice-fee imposed, [BP] meal plan available. **Leisure Activities:** tennis court, recreation programs, shuffleboard. **Guest Services:** TV in common area. **Business Services:** meeting rooms. **Cards:** AX, MC, VI.

SOME UNITS

⊞ ⊤ ⊠ ⊠ ⊠ ⊠ / ☎ /

---

## ──── WHERE TO DINE ────

**ATLANTICA RESTAURANT**

American

Lunch: $8-$14    Dinner: $19-$26    **Phone: 207/236-6011**

**Location:** Center. 1 Bayview Landing 04843. **Hours:** 11:30 am-2 & 5:30-9 pm; hours vary in winter. Closed major holidays. **Reservations:** required. **Features:** Upscale contemporary American cuisine shows an emphasis on seafood. The harborside restaurant's dishes are made to order, and fresh locally grown ingredients are used whenever possible. Casual dress; cocktails. **Parking:** on-site. **Cards:** AX, MC, VI.

⊠ ⊠

---

**CAPPY'S CHOWDER HOUSE**

American

Lunch: $6-$15    Dinner: $10-$17    **Phone: 207/236-2254**

**Location:** Center. 1 Main St 04843. **Hours:** 11 am-midnight; hours vary in winter. Closed: 11/25, 12/25. **Features:** This lively restaurant has a pub-style atmosphere with a menu that focuses on fresh seafood, but also includes a selection of meat entrees such as burgers and steak. A bakery and coffee bar is on the lower floor, with a pleasant garden terrace in back. Casual dress; cocktails. **Parking:** street. **Cards:** MC, VI.

⊠ ⊠

---

**CORK RESTAURANT**

International

Dinner: $20-$24    **Phone: 207/230-0533**

**Location:** Center. 51 Bayview St 04843. **Hours:** Open 5/1-2/28 & 4/1-4/30; 5:30 pm-close; hours vary seasonally. Closed: 11/25, 12/25. **Reservations:** suggested. **Features:** The second floor of the bi-level dining area affords a lovely view of Mount Battie. Nightly changing gourmet menus might include Chateaubriand with bearnaise sauce, herbed lamb chops, Asian-style tuna and breast of pheasant. Also available is a tasting menu that enables diners to sample many temptations. The friendly staff helps to create a relaxed, unhurried experience. Reservations are strongly recommended. Dressy casual; cocktails. **Parking:** street. **Cards:** AX, DC, DS, MC, VI.

⊠

---

**FROGWATER CAFE & BAKERY**

American

Lunch: $5-$22    Dinner: $5-$22    **Phone: 207/236-8998**

**Location:** Center. 31 Elm St 04843. **Hours:** 11 am-10 pm. Closed: 1/1, 12/25; also Wed & Sun 10/15-6/1. **Reservations:** accepted. **Features:** Garlic chicken ziti and sweet potato cakes are flavorful examples of the restaurant's creative fare, which includes seafood and meat entrees and fine desserts. Lighter fare, such as flat-bread pizzas and sandwiches, also is on the menu. Casual dress; beer & wine only. **Parking:** street. **Cards:** MC, VI.

⊠

---

**LOTUS CHINESE RESTAURANT**

Chinese

Lunch: $5-$7    Dinner: $7-$16    **Phone: 207/236-2133**

**Location:** On US 1; center. 133 Elm St 04843. **Hours:** 11 am-9 pm, Sun noon-8 pm. Closed: 11/25. **Reservations:** accepted. **Features:** This popular restaurant has ample variety on its menu of traditional Szechuan cuisine, seafood specials, tasty soups and good egg rolls—all made on-site with fresh ingredients. A daily buffet is offered for lunch. Service is prompt, pleasant and friendly. Casual dress; cocktails. **Parking:** on-site. **Cards:** AX, DS, MC, VI.

⊤ ⊠

---

**PETER OTTS RESTAURANT**

Steak & Seafood

Dinner: $12-$23    **Phone: 207/236-4032**

**Location:** Center. 16 Bayview St 04843. **Hours:** 5:30 pm-9:30 pm; hours vary off season. Closed: 11/25, 12/24, 12/25. **Reservations:** accepted. **Features:** The spacious restaurant has a casual pub atmosphere and offers a fine selection of meats and seafood entrees. Works from local artists adorn the walls. Casual dress; cocktails. **Parking:** street. **Cards:** AX, MC, VI.

⊤ ⊠

---

**QUARTERDECK BAR AND GRILL**

American

Lunch: $5-$12    Dinner: $7-$21    **Phone: 207/236-3272**

**Location:** Center. 21 Bayview St 04843. **Hours:** 11 am-1 am. **Features:** Although the menu shows an emphasis on seafood, it also incorporates burgers, ribs, pasta dishes and pizzas made in a brick oven. Casual dress; cocktails. **Parking:** street. **Cards:** MC, VI.

⊤ ⊠

---

**THE WATERFRONT RESTAURANT**

American

Lunch: $7-$10    Dinner: $12-$18    **Phone: 207/236-3747**

**Location:** Center. 40 Bayview St 04843. **Hours:** 11:30 am-2:30 & 5-9 pm. Closed: 11/25, 12/25. **Features:** Bordering Camden Harbor, the pleasant restaurant is decorated with a nautical theme. Some sections offer a nice harbor view. Patio seating is available in season. The menu varies from burgers to fresh seafood to steak, and food is plated in ample portions. Raw bar items are served daily from 2:30 pm to 5 pm in the bar. Casual dress; cocktails. **Parking:** on-site. **Cards:** AX, MC, VI.

⊠ ⊤ ⊠ ⊠

---

**ZADDIK'S**

Italian

Dinner: $8-$12    **Phone: 207/236-6540**

**Location:** Center. 20 Washington St 04843. **Hours:** 5 pm-10 pm; hours vary seasonally. Closed: Mon. **Features:** The menu for the lively family restaurant includes pasta, pizza, calzones, salads, quesadillas and more. Casual dress; beer & wine only. **Parking:** street. **Cards:** MC, VI.

⊠

——— *The following restaurant has not been evaluated by AAA* ———
*but is listed for your information only.*

**THE CAMDEN DELI**                                                              Phone: 207/236-8343
[fyi]   Not evaluated. **Location:** Center. 37 Main St 04843. **Features:** Eat in or take out—both are options at the
popular delicatessen in the center of town.

# CAPE ELIZABETH

——— **WHERE TO STAY** ———

**INN BY THE SEA**                                                              Phone: (207)799-3134
AAA [SAVE]      6/25-9/30             1P: $319-$639        2P: $319-$639        XP: $19        F12
5/1-6/24 & 10/1-10/31        1P: $229-$479        2P: $229-$479        XP: $19        F12
▽▽▽▽     11/1-4/30             1P: $179-$409        2P: $179-$409        XP: $19        F12
Small-scale Hotel  **Location:** On SR 77, 7 mi s. 40 Bowery Beach Rd (SR 77) 04107. Fax: 207/799-4779. **Facility:** Ocean views and
manicured grounds and gardens enhance this Crescent Beach Shingle-style inn, which features some rooms
with gas fireplaces. Smoke free premises. 43 units. 25 one- and 18 two-bedroom suites with efficiencies. 2
stories, interior/exterior corridors. **Parking:** on-site. **Terms:** check-in 4 pm, 2 night minimum stay - weekends, 14 day cancellation notice-fee imposed, package plans - 11/1-4/30, pets (with prior approval). **Amenities:** video library (fee), high-speed Internet,
dual phone lines, voice mail, irons, hair dryers. *Some:* CD players. **Dining:** Audubon Room at Inn by the Sea, see separate
listing. **Pool(s):** heated outdoor. **Leisure Activities:** golf privileges, lighted tennis court, croquet, jogging, shuffleboard, volleyball.
**Guest Services:** valet laundry. **Business Services:** meeting rooms. **Cards:** AX, DS, MC, VI. **Special Amenities:** free local
telephone calls and free newspaper. *(See ad p 275)*

[S] [🛏] [🍴] [👤M] [⛱] [♿] [✕] [✕] [🎵] [VCR] [DATA PORT] [🔌] [🖥] [🖨]

——— **WHERE TO DINE** ———

**AUDUBON ROOM AT INN BY THE SEA**       **Lunch:** $8-$15       **Dinner:** $21-$28       Phone: 207/767-0888
▽▽▽▽   **Location:** On SR 77, 7 mi s; in Inn By The Sea. 40 Bowery Beach Rd 04107. **Hours:** 7 am-11, noon-2 & 6-9 pm.
**Closed:** 12/25; also for dinner 12/24. **Reservations:** suggested. **Features:** The Audubon Room has an
American     elegant dining room with lovely ocean views. JJ Audubon engravings hanging on the walls give the dining
room its name. The restaurant specializes in New American cuisine, combining classical and contemporary
elements. Ingredients include fresh local seasonal produce and fresh seafood. Attire is country club casual. Cocktails.
**Parking:** on-site. **Cards:** AX, DS, MC, VI.                                                        [✕]

**TWO LIGHTS LOBSTER SHACK RESTAURANT**       **Lunch:** $4-$11       **Dinner:** $7-$17       Phone: 207/799-1677
▽   **Location:** On SR 77, 2 mi e. 225 Two Lights Rd 04107. **Hours:** Open 5/1-10/19 & 4/1-4/30; 11 am-8 pm; to
8:30 pm 7/1-8/31. **Features:** Popular with locals and tourists alike, the oceanfront lobster house offers
Seafood     excellent seafood and great views of the lighthouse. Specialties include clam chowder and lobster stew as
well as lobster dinners. Desserts are made on the premises. Casual dress. **Parking:** on-site.
**Cards:** MC, VI.                                                                              [🎵] [✕]

# CARIBOU pop. 8,312

——— **WHERE TO STAY** ———

**CARIBOU INN & CONVENTION CENTER**                                             Phone: (207)498-3733
AAA [SAVE]      All Year              1P: $68-$128         2P: $68-$128         XP: $8         F13
▽▽▽   **Location:** 3 mi s on US 1. 19 Main St 04736. Fax: 207/498-3149. **Facility:** 73 units. 70 one-bedroom standard
units. 3 one-bedroom suites ($112-$158) with efficiencies and whirlpools. 2 stories (no elevator), interior cor-
Small-scale Hotel  ridors. **Parking:** on-site. **Terms:** 14 day cancellation notice-fee imposed, package plans - seasonal.
**Amenities:** irons, hair dryers. **Dining:** The Greenhouse Restaurant, see separate listing. **Pool(s):** heated in-
door. **Leisure Activities:** sauna, whirlpool. **Guest Services:** gift shop, valet and coin laundry. **Business
Services:** meeting rooms. **Cards:** AX, CB, DC, DS, MC, VI. **Special Amenities:** free local telephone calls and free news-
paper.

SOME UNITS
[S] [🛏] [🍴] [♦] [⛱] [♿] [🐾] [DATA PORT] [🔌] [🖥] / [✕] [🖨] /

**CROWN PARK INN**                                                             Phone: 207/493-3311
▽▽   All Year [CP]          1P: $58-$68          2P: $58-$68          XP: $10        F17
**Location:** On SR 89, 0.4 mi e of jct US 1. 30 Access Hwy 04736 (PO Box 662). Fax: 207/498-3990. **Facility:** 60
Small-scale Hotel  units. 59 one-bedroom standard units, some with efficiencies. 1 one-bedroom suite with efficiency. 2 stories
(no elevator), interior corridors. **Parking:** on-site. **Leisure Activities:** game room. **Guest Services:** coin
laundry. **Business Services:** meeting rooms. **Cards:** AX, DC, DS, MC, VI.

SOME UNITS
[ASK] [S] [DATA PORT] [🔌] / [✕] /

——— **WHERE TO DINE** ———

**THE GREENHOUSE RESTAURANT**       **Lunch:** $5-$10       **Dinner:** $8-$42       Phone: 207/498-3733
AAA   **Location:** 3 mi s on US 1; in Caribou Inn & Convention Center. 19 Main St 04736. **Hours:** 6 am-2 & 5-9 pm, Sat
from 7 am, Sun 7 am-2 & 4-8 pm. **Closed:** 12/25; also for lunch & dinner 7/4, 11/25 & 12/24.
▽▽   **Reservations:** accepted. **Features:** The menu at the Greenhouse features different meat and seafood
American     entrees each night and offers a large variety of dessert. Travelers especially enjoy the warm, cozy
environment with a bright and airy feeling. This place is suitable for all occasions. Casual dress; cocktails.
**Parking:** on-site. **Cards:** AX, CB, DC, DS, MC, VI.                                          [♦] [✕]

# CARRABASSETT VALLEY

## ──── WHERE TO STAY ────

**GRAND SUMMIT RESORT HOTEL**

All Year [BP]                     1P: $118-$285          2P: $130-$310          **Phone:** (207)237-2222

Large-scale Hotel

**Location:** Off SR 27, 1 mi w up Sugarloaf Mountain access road. (RR 1, Box 2299). Fax: 207/237-2874. **Facility:** 119 units. 98 one-bedroom standard units, some with kitchens. 17 one-, 2 two- and 2 three-bedroom suites ($160-$385), some with kitchens and/or whirlpools. 6 stories, interior/exterior corridors. **Parking:** on-site. **Terms:** check-in 4 pm, 2 night minimum stay - in season, 21 day cancellation notice-fee imposed. **Amenities:** high-speed Internet, voice mail, irons, hair dryers. *Fee:* video library, video games. **Leisure Activities:** sauna, whirlpool, steamroom, cross country skiing, ice skating, exercise room. **Fee:** golf-18 holes, downhill skiing, massage. **Guest Services:** gift shop, coin laundry. **Business Services:** meeting rooms. **Cards:** AX, DC, DS, MC, VI. *(See color ad p 191 & below)*

SOME UNITS

# CASTINE

## ——— WHERE TO STAY ———

**THE CASTINE INN**

Phone: 207/326-4365

*Historic Country Inn*

Property failed to provide current rates
**Location:** Center. 33 Main St 04421 (PO Box 41). Fax: 207/326-4570. **Facility:** Operating since 1898, the Castine Inn has lovely landscaped gardens and modest to superior rooms, some with a harbor view. Smoke free premises. 19 units. 15 one-bedroom standard units. 4 one-bedroom suites. 3 stories (no elevator), interior corridors. *Bath:* combo or shower only. **Parking:** on-site. **Terms:** open 5/1-10/25. **Amenities:** *Some:* hair dryers. **Dining:** dining room, see separate listing. **Leisure Activities:** sauna.

[icons]

**PENTAGOET INN**

Phone: 207/326-8616

*Historic Country Inn*

5/1-11/1 [BP]          1P: $85-$195          2P: $95-$205
**Location:** Center. 26 Main St 04421 (PO Box 4). Fax: 207/326-9382. **Facility:** An 1894 Victorian Inn and adjacent Colonial-style building house guest rooms at this in-town property. Smoke free premises. 16 units. 15 one-bedroom standard units. 1 one-bedroom suite. 3 stories (no elevator), interior corridors. *Bath:* combo, shower or tub only. **Parking:** street. **Terms:** open 5/1-11/1, age restrictions may apply, 14 day cancellation notice, pets (in limited units). **Dining:** dining room, see separate listing. **Leisure Activities:** bicycles. **Cards:** MC, VI.

[icons]

## ——— WHERE TO DINE ———

**THE CASTINE INN**   Country Inn

Dinner: $65          Phone: 207/326-4365

*Seafood*

**Location:** Center; in The Castine Inn. 33 Main St 04421. **Hours:** Open 5/1-10/31; 6 pm-9 pm. Closed: Tues. **Reservations:** suggested. **Features:** The Castine Inn's owner/chef creates memorable and flavorful entrees, using only the best in locally produced seasonal foods. A tasting menu is available. The inviting dining room displays hand-painted murals of Castine. Pleasant terrace dining is available in season. Dressy casual; cocktails. **Parking:** on-site. **Cards:** MC, VI.

[icons]

*——— The following restaurant has not been evaluated by AAA but is listed for your information only. ———*

**PENTAGOET INN**

Phone: 207/326-8616

[fyi]

Not evaluated. **Location:** Center. 26 Main St 04421. **Features:** Fresh local seafood and other New England specialties are on the menu at The Pentegoet Inn.

# CORNISH

## ——— WHERE TO STAY ———

**THE CORNISH INN**

Phone: (207)625-8501

*Bed & Breakfast*

| | | | | |
|---|---|---|---|---|
| 7/1-10/13 [ECP] | 1P: $75-$105 | 2P: $75-$105 | XP: $15 | F6 |
| 5/1-6/30 & 10/14-11/30 [ECP] | 1P: $65-$95 | 2P: $65-$95 | XP: $15 | F6 |
| 12/1-4/30 [ECP] | 1P: $50-$75 | 2P: $50-$75 | XP: $15 | F6 |

**Location:** Jct SR 5 and 25, just n. 2 High St 04020 (PO Box 266). Fax: 207/625-0992. **Facility:** Smoke free premises. 16 one-bedroom standard units. 3 stories (no elevator), interior corridors. *Bath:* combo or shower only. **Parking:** on-site. **Terms:** 14 day cancellation notice. **Guest Services:** TV in common area. **Cards:** AX, MC, VI.

[icons]

**MIDWAY MOTEL**

Phone: (207)625-8835

*Motel*

| | | | | |
|---|---|---|---|---|
| 5/21-10/16 | 1P: $64-$79 | 2P: $64-$79 | XP: $10 | F12 |
| 5/1-5/20, 10/17-12/31 & 2/1-4/30 | 1P: $49-$59 | 2P: $49-$59 | XP: $10 | F12 |

**Location:** 0.7 mi w on SR 25, just past jct SR 25. 712 S Hiram Rd 04020. Fax: 207/625-4580. **Facility:** Smoke free premises. 12 one-bedroom standard units, some with whirlpools. 1-2 stories (no elevator), interior/exterior corridors. **Parking:** on-site. **Terms:** open 5/1-12/31 & 2/1-4/30, office hours 8 am-9 pm, 7 day cancellation notice, pets ($5 extra charge, small dogs only). **Amenities:** *Some:* voice mail, hair dryers. **Cards:** AX, DS, MC, VI.

SOME UNITS
[icons] FEE / (VCR) /

# DAMARISCOTTA

## ——— WHERE TO DINE ———

**SALT BAY CAFE**

Lunch: $4-$13          Dinner: $11-$17          Phone: 207/563-3302

*American*

**Location:** Center. Main St 04543. **Hours:** 7:30 am-10:30 & 11-9 pm; hours vary off season. Closed: 11/25; also Sun. **Reservations:** accepted. **Features:** With decor reminiscent of a library, the local favorite offers a good selection of seafood and meat entrees, as well as an extensive list of vegetarian items. Among homemade desserts is a superb strawberry shortcake. The staff is friendly and attentive. Casual dress; cocktails. **Parking:** on-site. **Cards:** MC, VI.

[icon]

**SCHOONER LANDING RESTAURANT & MARINA**

Lunch: $7-$16          Dinner: $7-$16          Phone: 207/563-7447

*Seafood*

**Location:** Center; on the waterfront. Main St 04543. **Hours:** Open 5/1-10/31 & 4/1-4/30; 11:30 am-8:30 pm. **Reservations:** accepted. **Features:** Although the emphasis is on fresh seafood, the menu also lists chicken and beef dishes, wraps and quesadillas. The dining room overlooks the water, and boaters often sail up and come in. The dining patio opens seasonally. Casual dress; cocktails. **Parking:** on-site. **Cards:** DS, MC, VI.

[icons]

# DURHAM

### ——— WHERE TO STAY ———

**THE BAGLEY HOUSE BED & BREAKFAST**
**Phone:** (207)865-6566

Historic Bed & Breakfast

All Year [BP]       1P: $85-$130       2P: $110-$175       XP: $25
**Location:** I-295, exit 22, 6 mi n on SR 136. 1290 Royalsborough Rd 04222. Fax: 207/353-5878. **Facility:** Elegant simplicity characterizes the decor of this 1722 farmhouse; a new carriage house offers modern conveniences and country decor. Smoke free premises. 8 one-bedroom standard units. 2 stories (no elevator), interior corridors. *Bath:* combo or shower only. **Parking:** on-site. **Terms:** 2 night minimum stay - weekends 8/1-8/31, 14 day cancellation notice-fee imposed, no pets allowed (owner's pet on premises). **Guest Services:** complimentary laundry. **Cards:** AX, CB, DC, DS, JC, MC, VI.

# EAGLE LAKE

### ——— WHERE TO STAY ———

**OVERLOOK MOTEL & LAKESIDE CABINS**
**Phone:** 207/444-4535

Motel

All Year       1P: $46-$150       2P: $46-$150       XP: $6       F10
**Location:** On SR 11; center. 3232 Aroostook Rd 04739 (PO Box 347). Fax: 207/444-6133. **Facility:** 16 units. 11 one-bedroom standard units, some with whirlpools. 1 two- and 1 three-bedroom suites ($82) with kitchens. 3 cabins ($104-$150). 1-2 stories (no elevator), interior/exterior corridors. **Parking:** on-site, winter plug-ins. **Terms:** office hours 7 am-10 pm, weekly rates available, [CP] meal plan available, small pets only. **Leisure Activities:** rental boats, canoeing, paddleboats. **Guest Services:** coin laundry, tanning facility. **Cards:** AX, DC, MC, VI.

# EAST BOOTHBAY —*See also BOOTHBAY.*

### ——— WHERE TO STAY ———

**FIVE GABLES INN**
**Phone:** (207)633-4551

Historic Bed & Breakfast

5/28-10/24       1P: $130-$195       2P: $130-$195       XP: $25
**Location:** Jct SR 27 and 96, 2.5 mi e. Located in a semi-residential area. 107 Murray Hill Rd 04544 (PO Box 335). **Facility:** Built in 1886, the inn is on a hill overlooking Linekin Bay; its spacious parlor, dining room and many guest rooms have ocean views. Smoke free premises. 16 one-bedroom standard units. 3 stories (no elevator), interior corridors. *Bath:* combo or shower only. **Parking:** on-site. **Terms:** open 5/28-10/24, 5 day cancellation notice, [BP] meal plan available. **Amenities:** hair dryers. **Cards:** MC, VI.

**LINEKIN BAY BED & BREAKFAST**
**Phone:** (207)633-9900

Historic Bed & Breakfast

5/28-10/31 [BP]       1P: $125-$175       2P: $125-$175       XP: $15
5/1-5/27 & 11/1-4/30 [BP]       1P: $90-$110       2P: $90-$110       XP: $15
**Location:** Jct SR 27, 3.9 mi e on SR 96. Located in a semi-residential area. 531 Ocean Point Rd 04544. **Facility:** Wraparound porches distinguish the exterior of this charming 1850s farmhouse, which offers good ocean views. Smoke free premises. 4 units. 2 one-bedroom standard units. 2 one-bedroom suites ($100-$175). 2 stories (no elevator), interior/exterior corridors. *Bath:* combo or shower only. **Parking:** on-site. **Terms:** age restrictions may apply, 14 day cancellation notice, package plans - seasonal. **Amenities:** CD players, hair dryers. **Cards:** MC, VI.

**OCEAN POINT INN**
**Phone:** 207/633-4200

Small-scale Hotel

6/18-9/5       1P: $120-$190       2P: $120-$190       XP: $20       D12
5/28-6/17 & 9/6-10/11       1P: $97-$151       2P: $97-$151       XP: $20       D12
**Location:** 3 mi e on SR 96, 0.6 mi on Middle Rd. Shore Rd 04544-0409 (PO Box 409). Fax: 207/633-6040. **Facility:** 61 units. 49 one- and 1 two-bedroom standard units, some with kitchens. 9 one- and 1 two-bedroom suites ($119-$201), some with kitchens. 1 cottage ($119-$201). 1-2 stories (no elevator), interior/exterior corridors. *Bath:* combo or shower only. **Parking:** on-site. **Terms:** open 5/28-10/11, office hours 7:30 am-11 pm, 2 night minimum stay - weekends, 10 day cancellation notice-fee imposed, package plans. **Dining:** 7:30 am-10 & 6-9 pm 7/2-9/5; from 6 pm 5/16-6/26 & 9/6-10/13, cocktails. **Pool(s):** heated outdoor. **Leisure Activities:** whirlpool, fishing, tennis privileges. **Business Services:** meeting rooms. **Cards:** AX, DS, MC, VI. **Special Amenities:** free local telephone calls and early check-in/late check-out. *(See color ad p 197)*

**SMUGGLER'S COVE MOTOR INN**
**Phone:** (207)633-2800

Small-scale Hotel

7/1-9/6       1P: $109-$229       2P: $109-$229       XP: $15       F12
9/7-10/10       1P: $69-$169       2P: $69-$169       XP: $15       F12
6/11-6/30       1P: $69-$159       2P: $69-$159       XP: $15       F12
**Location:** Jct SR 27, 4.5 mi e on SR 96. 727 Ocean Point Rd 04544-9406. Fax: 207/633-5926. **Facility:** 60 one-bedroom standard units, some with efficiencies. 2 stories (no elevator), exterior corridors. *Bath:* combo or shower only. **Parking:** on-site. **Terms:** open 6/11-10/10, 1-2 night minimum stay, cancellation fee imposed, pets ($10 fee, $50 deposit). **Dining:** 8 am-10 & 6-9 pm; closed Sun & Mon, cocktails. **Pool(s):** heated outdoor. **Leisure Activities:** boating, boat dock, fishing, charter sailing. **Cards:** AX, DS, MC, VI. **Special Amenities:** free local telephone calls and free newspaper. *(See color ad p 197)*

## ——— WHERE TO DINE ———

**CARRIAGE HOUSE RESTAURANT**　　　　**Dinner:** $9-$27　　　　　**Phone:** 207/633-6025
⬧⬧⬧
▽▽ ▽▽
Seafood

**Location:** Jct SR 27, 4.5 mi s. 388 Ocean Point Rd 04544. **Hours:** 5 pm-9 pm. Closed: 1/1, 11/25, 12/25. **Features:** The interior of the Carriage House displays swinging doors from a 1935 freighter, one bar made out of a boat, a second bar of mahogany from an old shipyard, and a third of maple and cherry. The menu features seafood and steak. Casual dress; cocktails. **Parking:** on-site. **Cards:** AX, DS, MC, VI.　📺 ✕

**LOBSTERMAN'S WHARF RESTAURANT**　　**Lunch:** $5-$17　　**Dinner:** $14-$22　　**Phone:** 207/633-3443
⬧⬧⬧
▽▽ ▽▽
Seafood

**Location:** Jct SR 27 and 96, 2.5 mi e. SR 96 04544. **Hours:** Open 5/7-10/10; 11:30 am-10 pm. Closed: Mon. **Features:** Beside a boatyard, the restaurant offers waterside tables, nautical decor and lots of seafood, such as lobster stew and crab cakes. Also on the menu are burgers, pasta and good wines. Popular with locals, this place is ideal for escaping the crowds. Casual dress; cocktails. **Parking:** on-site. **Cards:** DS, MC, VI.　🍸 🎘 ✕

# EASTPORT pop. 1,640

## ——— WHERE TO STAY ———

**THE MOTEL EAST**　　　　　　　　　　　　　　　　　　　　　**Phone:** (207)853-4747
▽▽▽▽▽
Motel

All Year　　　　　　　1P: $80-$95　　　　　　　　　　　　　XP: $10　　　　F16
**Location:** Center. 23A Water St 04631. Fax: 207/853-4747. **Facility:** 14 one-bedroom standard units. 2 stories (no elevator), exterior corridors. **Bath:** combo or shower only. **Parking:** on-site. **Cards:** AX, CB, DC, DS, MC, VI.

SOME UNITS
📶 🎘 🛢 🖥 / ✕ 🖵 /

# EDGECOMB

## ——— WHERE TO STAY ———

**COD COVE INN**　　　　　　　　　　　　　　　　　　　　　　**Phone:** (207)882-9586
⬧⬧⬧ [SAVE]
▽▽ ▽▽
Motel

All Year　　　　　1P: $109-$249　　　2P: $109-$249　　　XP: $20　　　F18
**Location:** Jct US 1 and SR 27, 1 mi n on US 1. 22 Cross Rd (PO Box 117). Fax: 207/882-9294. **Facility:** Designated smoking area. 30 units. 29 one-bedroom standard units. 1 one-bedroom suite ($199-$249) with whirlpool. 2 stories (no elevator), exterior corridors. **Bath:** combo or shower only. **Parking:** on-site. **Terms:** office hours 7 am-11 pm, 2 night minimum stay - weekends, 3 day cancellation notice-fee imposed, [ECP] meal plan available. **Amenities:** irons, hair dryers. **Pool(s):** heated outdoor. **Leisure Activities:** whirlpool.
**Cards:** AX, DS, MC, VI.

SOME UNITS
🆂🅳 🏊 ✕ DATA/PORT 🛢 🖵 / 🖵 /

**SHEEPSCOT RIVER INN**　　　　　　　　　　　　　　　　　　**Phone:** (207)882-6343
▽▽ ▽▽
Small-scale Hotel

7/1-9/2 [CP]　　　　　　1P: $89-$149　　　2P: $89-$149　　　XP: $10　　　F20
5/1-6/30 & 9/3-10/13 [CP]　1P: $89-$119　　　2P: $89-$119　　　XP: $10　　　F20
10/14-4/30 [CP]　　　　1P: $79-$99　　　　2P: $79-$99　　　XP: $10　　　F20
**Location:** 1 mi w on US 1; on east side of Davies Bridge, 1 mi e of Wiscasset. 306 Eddy Rd 04556. Fax: 207/443-1738. **Facility:** 40 units. 25 one-bedroom standard units. 15 one-bedroom suites ($89-$149) with kitchens. 1-2 stories (no elevator), interior/exterior corridors. **Bath:** combo or shower only. **Parking:** on-site. **Terms:** office hours 7 am-10 pm, weekly rates available, package plans, pets ($10 extra charge). **Dining:** Sheepscot River Inn and Restaurant, see separate listing. **Leisure Activities:** tennis court, cross country skiing, horseshoes. **Business Services:** meeting rooms. **Cards:** AX, DC, DS, MC, VI.

SOME UNITS
(ASK) 🆂🅳 🐾 🍴 ✕ 📹 / ✕ 🎘 VCR DATA/PORT 🛢 🖵 /
　　　　FEE　　　　　　　　　　　　　FEE

## ——— WHERE TO DINE ———

**SHEEPSCOT RIVER INN AND RESTAURANT**　　**Lunch:** $7-$14　　**Dinner:** $11-$19　　**Phone:** 207/882-7748
▽▽ ▽▽
American

**Location:** 1 mi w on US 1; on east side of Davies Bridge, 1 mi e of Wiscasset; in Sheepscot River Inn. 306 Eddy Rd 04556. **Hours:** Open 5/1-11/4; 11 am-9 pm. **Reservations:** suggested, summer/holidays. **Features:** You'll appreciate this restaurant's great view of the Sheepscot River, cozy and contemporary atmosphere, friendly service and creative cuisine. The fruit d'amier, seared rack of lamb and homemade dessert is exquisite. Live entertainment too. Casual dress; cocktails; entertainment. **Parking:** on-site. **Cards:** AX, CB, DC, DS, MC, VI.

🅼 🍸 ✕

# ELIOT

## ——— WHERE TO STAY ———

**HIGH MEADOWS BED & BREAKFAST**　　　　　　　　　　　　**Phone:** 207/439-0590
▽▽▽▽▽
Historic Bed
& Breakfast

5/1-11/1 [BP]　　　　1P: $80-$110　　　2P: $90-$120　　　XP: $20
**Location:** I-95, exit 3, n on US 1 to SR 101, then 4.5 mi w. Located in a quiet, rural area. 2 Brixham Rd 03903. Fax: 207/439-6343. **Facility:** Built in 1736, this B&B has the low ceilings and wide-planked hardwood floors characteristic of the era. Smoke free premises. 4 one-bedroom standard units. 2 stories (no elevator), interior corridors. **Bath:** shower only. **Parking:** on-site. **Terms:** open 5/1-11/1, age restrictions may apply, 7 day cancellation notice. **Leisure Activities:** hiking trails. **Guest Services:** TV in common area. **Cards:** MC, VI.

✕ 🎘 📺 🖵

# ELLSWORTH pop. 6,456

## ──── WHERE TO STAY ────

### COLONIAL INN
▼▼ ▼▼

|  |  |  |  |
|---|---|---|---|
| 7/1-10/15 [CP] | 1P: $90-$159 | 2P: $90-$159 | XP: $6   F17 |
| 5/1-6/30 & 10/16-4/30 [CP] | 1P: $58-$98 | 2P: $58-$98 | XP: $6   F17 |

Small-scale Hotel    **Location:** 1.3 mi e on SR 3. 321 High St 04605. Fax: 207/664-0527. **Facility:** 67 units. 66 one- and 1 two-bedroom standard units, some with kitchens. 1-2 stories (no elevator); interior/exterior corridors. **Parking:** on-site. **Terms:** small pets only. **Pool(s):** heated indoor. **Leisure Activities:** whirlpool. **Cards:** AX, DS, MC, VI.

Phone: (207)667-5548

### COMFORT INN    *Book at aaa.com*
▼▼▼ ▼▼▼

|  |  |  |  |
|---|---|---|---|
| All Year | 1P: $59-$139 | 2P: $59-$139 | XP: $10   F16 |

Small-scale Hotel    **Location:** Center. Located in a commercial area. 130 High St 04605. Fax: 207/667-1345. **Facility:** 63 one-bedroom standard units. 2 stories (no elevator); interior corridors. **Bath:** combo or shower only. **Parking:** on-site. **Terms:** [CP] & [ECP] meal plans available, pets ($5 extra charge). **Amenities:** safes (fee). *Some:* irons, hair dryers. **Leisure Activities:** exercise room. **Business Services:** meeting rooms. **Cards:** AX, DC, DS, MC, VI.

Phone: 207/667-1345

### THE EAGLE'S LODGE
▼▼

|  |  |  |  |
|---|---|---|---|
| 7/1-8/31 | 1P: $64-$74 | 2P: $74-$98 | XP: $10   F12 |
| 9/1-4/30 | 1P: $42-$70 | 2P: $48-$74 | XP: $10   F12 |
| 5/1-6/30 | 1P: $40-$58 | 2P: $48-$64 | XP: $10   F12 |

Motel    **Location:** Jct US 1 and 1A. 1.3 mi e on SR 3. 278 High St 04605. Fax: 207/667-9334. **Facility:** 44 one-bedroom standard units, some with efficiencies. 2 stories (no elevator); interior corridors. **Parking:** on-site. **Pool(s):** heated outdoor. **Cards:** DS, MC, VI.

Phone: 207/667-3311

### ELLSWORTH MOTEL
AAA SAVE
▼▼

|  |  |  |  |
|---|---|---|---|
| 11/1-4/30 Wkly | 1P: $150-$200 | 2P: $150-$200 |  |
| 5/1-10/31 Dly | 1P: $50-$75 | 2P: $60-$85 | XP: $10 |

Motel    **Location:** US 1 and SR 3; near jct US 1A. 24 High St 04605. Fax: 207/667-6942. **Facility:** 16 one-bedroom standard units. 1-2 stories (no elevator); exterior corridors. *Bath:* combo or shower only. **Parking:** on-site. **Terms:** office hours 8 am-10 pm. **Pool(s):** outdoor. **Cards:** MC, VI.

Phone: 207/667-4424

### HOLIDAY INN    *Book at aaa.com*
▼▼▼▼

|  |  |  |
|---|---|---|
| 6/28-8/21 | 1P: $123-$170 | 2P: $123-$170 |
| 8/22-10/11 | 1P: $93-$110 | 2P: $93-$110 |
| 5/1-6/27 | 1P: $76-$90 | 2P: $76-$90 |
| 10/12-4/30 | 1P: $65-$90 | 2P: $65-$90 |

Small-scale Hotel    **Location:** Jct US 1, 1A and SR 3. Located next to a shopping plaza. 215 High St 04605. Fax: 207/667-7294. **Facility:** 102 one-bedroom standard units, some with efficiencies. 2 stories (no elevator); interior corridors. **Parking:** on-site. **Terms:** pets (in smoking units). **Amenities:** video games (fee), voice mail, irons, hair dryers. **Pool(s):** heated indoor. **Leisure Activities:** sauna, whirlpool, exercise room. **Fee:** 2 indoor tennis courts. **Guest Services:** valet and coin laundry. **Fee:** tanning facility. **Business Services:** meeting rooms. **Cards:** AX, CB, DC, DS, JC, MC, VI.

Phone: (207)667-9341

### JASPER'S MOTEL
AAA SAVE
▼▼▼ ▼▼▼

|  |  |  |  |
|---|---|---|---|
| 6/16-9/7 [CP] | 1P: $71 | 2P: $81-$99 | XP: $8   F12 |
| 9/8-11/2 [CP] | 1P: $66 | 2P: $76-$86 | XP: $8   F12 |
| 5/1-6/15 & 11/3-4/30 [CP] | 1P: $49 | 2P: $49-$79 | XP: $8   F12 |

Small-scale Hotel    **Location:** 1 mi e on US 1 and SR 3. Located opposite the mall. 200 High St 04605. Fax: 207/667-5288. **Facility:** 33 units. 30 one- and 2 two-bedroom standard units. 1 one-bedroom suite ($79-$99). 1-2 stories (no elevator); exterior corridors. **Parking:** on-site. **Terms:** office hours 6 am-10 pm, 3 day cancellation notice, pets ($10 extra charge). **Dining:** Jasper's Restaurant, see separate listing. **Cards:** AX, DS, MC, VI. **Special Amenities:** free continental breakfast and free local telephone calls.

Phone: (207)667-5318

### TWILITE MOTEL
AAA SAVE
▼▼▼ ▼▼▼

|  |  |  |  |
|---|---|---|---|
| 6/25-9/6 [CP] | 1P: $79-$94 | 2P: $79-$94 | XP: $8   F13 |
| 9/7-10/17 [CP] | 1P: $69-$79 | 2P: $69-$79 | XP: $8   F13 |
| 5/1-6/24 [CP] | 1P: $56-$66 | 2P: $56-$66 | XP: $8   F13 |
| 10/18-4/30 | 1P: $56-$66 | 2P: $56-$66 | XP: $8   F13 |

Motel    **Location:** Jct US 1A. 1.5 mi w on US 1/SR 3. 147 Bucksport Rd 04605 (PO Box 633). Fax: 207/667-0289. **Facility:** 22 one-bedroom standard units. 1 story, exterior corridors. *Bath:* combo or shower only. **Parking:** on-site. **Terms:** 3 day cancellation notice-fee imposed, pets ($10 extra charge). **Amenities:** *Some:* hair dryers. **Leisure Activities:** horseshoes. **Guest Services:** gift shop, coin laundry. **Cards:** AX, DC, DS, MC, VI. **Special Amenities:** free continental breakfast and free local telephone calls.

Phone: (207)667-8165

THE WHITE BIRCHES
Phone: 207/667-3621
All Year
1P: $49-$99
XP: $6
F10
▼▼
**Location:** US 1, 1.5 mi n of jct SR 3. Rt 1 04605 (PO Box 743). **Fax:** 207/667-3480. **Facility:** 67 units. 65 one-bedroom standard units, some with efficiencies (no utensils). 2 one-bedroom suites ($119-$199) with whirl-pools. 1 story, exterior corridors. **Parking:** on-site. **Terms:** office hours 7 am-10 pm, [MAP] meal plan available. **Amenities:** *Some:* hair dryers. **Dining:** Crazy Gils, see separate listing. **Leisure Activities:** Fee: golf-18 holes. **Business Services:** meeting rooms. **Cards:** AX, CB, DC, DS, MC, VI.
Small-scale Hotel

SOME UNITS

(ASK) [icons] / [X] [DATA PORT] [icons] /

## ———— WHERE TO DINE ————

CHINA HILL RESTAURANT
**Lunch:** $5-$10
**Dinner:** $8-$15
Phone: 207/667-5308
▼▼▼
**Location:** Center. 301 High St 04605. **Hours:** 11 am-9 pm, Fri & Sat-10 pm. Closed: 7/4; also Mon. **Reservations:** accepted. **Features:** This restaurant has four dining areas. The menu features Cantonese dishes and has a great variety of very good soup, tasty egg rolls, generous entrees and many combination specials. The serving staff is pleasant and attentive. Casual dress; cocktails. **Parking:** on-site. **Cards:** AX, DS, MC, VI.
Chinese

[Y] [X]

CLEONICE MEDITERRANEAN BISTRO
**Lunch:** $5-$10
**Dinner:** $16-$20
Phone: 207/664-7554
▼▼
**Location:** Center. 112 Main St 04605. **Hours:** 11:30 am-2:30 & 5-8 pm; hours vary seasonally. Closed major holidays; also 12/24; Sun, Mon in winter. **Features:** "Local ingredients, international flavor" is how the restaurant characterizes offerings on its menu. Lunch and dinner could include such items as paella, moussaka, spanakopita, hummus or baba ghanoush. Ingredients are organic, whenever possible. Casual dress; cocktails. **Parking:** street. **Cards:** MC, VI.
Mediterranean

[X]

CRAZY GILS
**Dinner:** $8-$16
Phone: 207/667-3621
▼▼▼
**Location:** US 1, 1.5 mi n of jct SR 3; in The White Birches. **Hours:** 8 am-11 & 4-9 pm; hours vary seasonally. Closed: Mon-Thurs 11/1-5/15. **Reservations:** suggested. **Features:** The finest in Down East Maine seafood is offered at this restaurant, which offers lobster, clams, shrimp and haddock dishes. This pleasant, family-style eatery overlooks the golf course and has great views of the sunset. Good cocktails and dessert too. Casual dress; cocktails. **Parking:** on-site. **Cards:** AX, DC, DS, MC, VI.
American

[Y] [X]

HELEN'S RESTAURANT
**Lunch:** $6-$11
**Dinner:** $7-$16
Phone: 207/667-2433
(AAA)
**Location:** 0.5 mi n on US 1. 55 Downeast Hwy 04605. **Hours:** 11 am-9 pm; to 8 pm off season. Closed: 7/4, 11/25, 12/25. **Features:** Memorabilia from the '30s decorates this country-style family restaurant. On the menu is a variety of entrees—from fried or broiled seafood to steak, chicken and burgers. Boiled lobster is a favorite, as are the homemade desserts that satisfy a sweet tooth. Casual dress; beer & wine only. **Parking:** on-site. **Cards:** AX, DS, MC, VI.
▼▼
American

[X]

JASPER'S RESTAURANT
**Lunch:** $4-$8
**Dinner:** $7-$22
Phone: 207/667-5318
(AAA)
**Location:** 1 mi e on US 1 and SR 3; in Jasper's Motel. 200 High St 04605. **Hours:** 11 am-9 pm; to 8 pm in winter. Closed: 12/25. **Features:** This is a popular restaurant with a congenial atmosphere and a varied menu that includes lobster prepared ten different ways, daily blue-plate and fish-of-the-day specials, chargrilled steak and dessert made from scratch. Prime rib is featured on the weekend. Families and seniors like the good service here too. Casual dress; cocktails. **Parking:** on-site. **Cards:** AX, DS, MC, VI.
▼▼
Steak & Seafood

[X]

THE MEX
**Lunch:** $6-$10
**Dinner:** $7-$16
Phone: 207/667-4494
▼▼▼
**Location:** On US 1; center. 191 Main St 04605. **Hours:** 11 am-9 pm. Closed: 11/25, 12/25. **Reservations:** accepted. **Features:** The menu features Mexican cuisine with a Maine twist: seafood. Offerings are made to order and desserts are made on the premises. Try the chicken lime soup. Casual dress; cocktails. **Parking:** street. **Cards:** AX, DS, MC, VI.
Mexican

[X]

TURRIGLIO'S RESTAURANT ITALIANO
**Dinner:** $10-$21
Phone: 207/667-0202
▼▼▼
**Location:** Center. 59 Franklin St 04605. **Hours:** 5 pm-close. Closed: 3/27, 11/25, 12/25; also Sun & Mon. **Reservations:** suggested. **Features:** Turriglio's menu offers many Italian favorites using fresh local ingredients whenever possible. The dining rooms are perfect for a romantic evening for two. Casual dress; cocktails. **Parking:** street. **Cards:** MC, VI.
Italian

UNION RIVER LOBSTER POT RESTAURANT
**Lunch:** $7-$11
**Dinner:** $12-$21
Phone: 207/667-5077
▼▼▼
**Location:** Center; just s of bridge. 8 South St 04605. **Hours:** Open 6/15-9/21; 11:30 am-9 pm. **Features:** In a pleasant location on the river, the restaurant serves fresh seafood, including the specialty boiled lobster. A good selection of beer is on tap. This place is popular with local residents. Outdoor picnic-table dining is available in season. Service is friendly. Casual dress; beer & wine only. **Parking:** on-site. **Cards:** MC, VI.
Seafood

[X]

# EUSTIS

## ———— WHERE TO DINE ————

THE PORTER HOUSE RESTAURANT
**Dinner:** $12-$19
Phone: 207/246-7932
▼▼▼
**Location:** 4 mi n of jct SR 16. SR 27 04936. **Hours:** 5 pm-9 pm. Closed: 12/25; also Mon & Tues. **Reservations:** suggested. **Features:** The Porter House is a 1908 residence transformed into a delightful restaurant serving homemade bread and dessert, roast duck, steak, seafood, chicken and vegetarian entrees. Located on the Benedict Arnold Trail. Warm, Attentive Service. Terrific wine list. Casual dress; cocktails. **Parking:** on-site. **Cards:** MC, VI.
American

[X]

# FALMOUTH

## ——— WHERE TO STAY ———

### FALMOUTH INN

AAA [SAVE]

▽▽ ▽▽

Motel

| | | | | |
|---|---|---|---|---|
| 7/1-10/31 | 1P: $82-$108 | 2P: $90-$120 | XP: $10 | F12 |
| 6/1-6/30 | 1P: $59-$87 | 2P: $64-$94 | XP: $10 | F12 |
| 5/1-5/31 | 1P: $50-$80 | 2P: $57-$87 | XP: $10 | F12 |
| 11/1-4/30 | 1P: $45-$73 | 2P: $52-$80 | XP: $10 | F12 |

**Phone: 207/781-2120**

**Location:** I-295, exit 10, just e on Buckman Rd, then just s. 209 US 1 04105. Fax: 207/781-8286. **Facility:** 33 units. 27 one-bedroom standard units. 6 one-bedroom suites ($73-$130). 1 story, exterior corridors. *Bath:* combo or shower only. **Parking:** on-site. **Terms:** office hours 8 am-10 pm, cancellation fee imposed. **Guest Services:** coin laundry. **Cards:** AX, DC, MC, VI.

SOME UNITS
[📶] [DATA PORT] / [✕] [🛏] [💻] /

## ——— WHERE TO DINE ———

### FALMOUTH SEA GRILL

▽▽ ▽▽

Seafood

**Lunch:** $7-$15      **Dinner:** $16-$22      **Phone: 207/781-5658**

**Location:** On SR 88. 215 Foreside Rd 04105. **Hours:** Open 5/1-1/4 & 2/4-4/30; 11:30 am-9 pm, Fri & Sat-10 pm. Closed: 11/25, 12/24, 12/25. **Reservations:** suggested. **Features:** Fresh seafood is creatively prepared in this beautiful setting near the town landing. Casual dress; cocktails. **Parking:** on-site. **Cards:** AX, DS, MC, VI.

[📺] [🍴] [✕]

### FRENCH MEMORY CAFE

▽▽ ▽▽

American

**Lunch:** $5-$9      **Dinner:** $8-$18      **Phone: 207/347-5631**

**Location:** I-295, exit 10, just e on Buckman Rd, then 0.4 mi s. 190 US Rt 1 04105. **Hours:** 8 am-2 & 5-8 pm, Sun & Tues-2 pm. Closed: Mon. **Reservations:** accepted. **Features:** The small, charmingly decorated bistro serves all-day brunch, salads, sandwiches, soups and burgers. In the evening, the menu includes dinner crepes, salads, dinner tarts, chicken and fish prepared with a French flair. Casual dress; cocktails. **Parking:** on-site. **Cards:** AX, DS, MC, VI.

[⌖M] [✕]

### MOOSE CROSSING RESTAURANT

AAA

▽▽ ▽▽

American

**Dinner:** $10-$20      **Phone: 207/781-4771**

**Location:** I-295, exit 10, 0.3 mi e on Bucknam Rd; 0.3 mi n on US 1 from I-95, exit 9 to exit 15A, just n. 270 Rt 1 04105. **Hours:** 5 pm-9:30 pm, Sun 4 pm-9 pm. Closed: 7/4, 11/25, 12/25. **Features:** With a cabin like atmosphere, the pine walls, camping gear and antlers displayed promote a casual family atmosphere. Old photos of Moosehead Lake from the collections of the Maine Historical Society and the University of Maine are displayed. The menu features beef, chicken, chops, fresh seafood and fish dinners, including trout. They are known for their slow cooked prime rib and mesquite cooked salmon. Casual dress; cocktails. **Parking:** on-site. **Cards:** AX, MC, VI.

[📺] [✕]

### O'NATURAL'S

▽▽ ▽▽

Natural/Organic

**Lunch:** $5-$8      **Dinner:** $5-$8      **Phone: 207/781-8889**

**Location:** Center. 240 US Rt 1 04105. **Hours:** 10:30 am-8 pm, Fri & Sat-9 pm. Closed: 3/27, 11/25, 12/25. **Features:** The menu of natural and organic fast food comprises sandwiches, soups, salads and Asian noodles. Casual dress; beer & wine only. **Parking:** on-site. **Cards:** AX, DS, MC, VI.

[⌖M] [✕]

### RICETTA'S BRICK OVEN PIZZERIA

▽▽ ▽▽

Pizza

**Lunch:** $6-$10      **Dinner:** $10-$13      **Phone: 207/781-3100**

**Location:** Center. 240 US Rt 1 04105. **Hours:** 11:30 am-10 pm, Fri & Sat-11 pm. Closed major holidays. **Features:** A great place to bring the kids for a meal, this place is known for its creative, award-winning pizzas. Patrons can watch pizza being made at the open area with the brick oven. Also on the menu are original pasta dishes and calzones. At lunch is an all-you-can-eat buffet. Casual dress; cocktails. **Parking:** on-site. **Cards:** AX, DS, MC, VI.

[⌖M] [✕]

# FARMINGTON pop. 4,098

## ——— WHERE TO STAY ———

### COLONIAL VALLEY MOTEL

AAA [SAVE]

▽▽

Motel

| | | | |
|---|---|---|---|
| All Year | 1P: $50-$58 | 2P: $54-$62 | XP: $12   F12 |

**Phone: (207)778-3391**

**Location:** 2.5 mi w on US 2 and SR 4. 593 Wilton Rd 04938 (PO Box 32). Fax: 207/778-5475. **Facility:** 30 one-bedroom standard units, some with efficiencies. 1 story, exterior corridors. **Parking:** on-site. **Terms:** office hours 7 am-10 pm, weekly rates available. **Cards:** AX, DS, MC, VI.

SOME UNITS
[💲🛏] [📶] / [✕] [🛏] [📼] /

### FARMINGTON MOTEL

AAA [SAVE]

▽▽

Motel

| | | | |
|---|---|---|---|
| All Year | 1P: $50 | 2P: $60 | XP: $6 |

**Phone: 207/778-4680**

**Location:** 2 mi e on US 2. Located in a rural area. 489 Farmington Falls Rd 04938 (PO Box 447). **Facility:** 39 units. 38 one- and 1 two-bedroom standard units. 1 story, exterior corridors. **Parking:** on-site. **Terms:** office hours 7 am-10 pm, 30 day cancellation notice. **Leisure Activities:** fishing. **Cards:** AX, DC, DS, MC, VI.

SOME UNITS
/ [✕] /

### MOUNT BLUE MOTEL

AAA [SAVE]

▽▽

Motel

| | | | |
|---|---|---|---|
| All Year | 1P: $44-$60 | 2P: $48-$60 | XP: $5 |

**Phone: 207/778-6004**

**Location:** 2 mi w on US 2 and SR 4. 454 Wilton Rd 04938. **Facility:** 18 one-bedroom standard units. 1 story, exterior corridors. *Bath:* combo or shower only. **Parking:** on-site. **Terms:** office hours 8 am-11 pm, weekly rates available, package plans, pets ($7 fee). **Cards:** AX, DS, MC, VI. **Special Amenities:** free local telephone calls and early check-in/late check-out.

SOME UNITS
[💲🛏] [🐾]    / [✕] [🛏] /
FEE                          FEE

## WHERE TO DINE

**THE HOMESTEAD BAKERY & RESTAURANT**    **Lunch:** $4-$8    **Dinner:** $7-$15    **Phone:** 207/778-6162

American
**Location:** Center. 186 Broadway St 04938. **Hours:** 7 am-9 pm, Sun & Mon-3 pm. **Closed:** 11/25, 12/25.
**Reservations:** accepted. **Features:** Popular local restaurant. Unpretentious decor, hearty portions of down home style cooking. Fine selection of desserts in on premises bakery. Casual dress; cocktails. **Parking:** street. **Cards:** AX, DS, MC, VI.

## FREEPORT pop. 1,813

## WHERE TO STAY

**BEST WESTERN FREEPORT INN**    *Book at aaa.com*    **Phone:** (207)865-3106

| | | | |
|---|---|---|---|
| 7/16-9/5 | 1P: $120-$150 | 2P: $120-$150 | XP: $10    F18 |
| 5/1-7/15 & 9/6-10/23 | 1P: $100-$130 | 2P: $100-$130 | XP: $10    F18 |
| 10/24-4/30 | 1P: $75-$105 | 2P: $75-$105 | XP: $10    F18 |

Small-scale Hotel
**Location:** I-295, exit 17, 1 mi n. 31 US 1 S 04032. Fax: 207/865-6364. **Facility:** 80 one-bedroom standard units. 3 stories (no elevator), interior/exterior corridors. **Parking:** on-site. **Terms:** package plans - seasonal, pets (with prior approval). **Amenities:** voice mail, irons, hair dryers. **Dining:** 6 am-9 pm; to 8 pm 10/16-5/14. **Pool(s):** outdoor. **Leisure Activities:** rental canoes, playground. **Guest Services:** valet laundry. **Cards:** AX, DC, DS, MC, VI. **Special Amenities:** free local telephone calls and free newspaper. *(See color ad below)*                    SOME UNITS

# THE WORLD'S LARGEST HOTEL CHAIN®

- 3 miles from LL Bean & 120 Outlets
- Enjoy golfing, sight seeing & unique dining
- Rooms include: cable TV, iron/ board, dataports & more
- Children 18 & under stay free
- Canoe rental & playground
- Outdoor pool
- Ideal for families, business, or a quiet getaway

www.freeportinn.com

**Best Western Freeport Inn**
Each Best Western hotel is independently owned and operated.

31 US Rt 1 • Freeport, Maine 04032
Phone: 207-865-3106 • Fax: 207-865-6364
For reservations call: 800.99.Value

# Casco Bay Inn

45 NEW Large Kings &
Double Queens,
Continental Breakfast,
Reading Lounge & Fireplace,
Family Operated,
HIGH Speed Internet,
Near L.L. Bean, Freeport Shops
& Mid Coast Maine

107 U.S. Route 1
Freeport
1-207-865-4925

AAA Approved

**1-800-570-4970**
wwww.cascobayinn.com
## The INN Place for value in Freeport

**BREWSTER HOUSE BED & BREAKFAST**
▼▼◇◇▼ 5/16-12/31 [BP]        1P: $130-$250       2P: $130-$350
        5/1-5/15 [BP]        1P: $95-$140       2P: $95-$250
Bed & Breakfast  1/1-4/30 [BP]        1P: $90-$140       2P: $90-$140
**Phone: 207/865-4121**
**Location:** Just n. 180 Main St 04032. Fax: 207/865-4221. **Facility:** Tin ceilings, carved moldings and large guest rooms furnished with antiques set the stage at this restored Queen Anne home, which dates from 1888. Smoke free premises. 7 units. 5 one- and 2 two-bedroom standard units. 3 stories (no elevator), interior corridors. *Bath:* combo or shower only. **Parking:** on-site. **Terms:** age restrictions may apply, 14 day cancellation notice. **Guest Services:** TV in common area. **Cards:** DS, MC, VI.

**CAPTAIN BRIGGS HOUSE B & B**
▼▼◇◇▼ 5/17-11/1
        5/1-5/16 & 11/2-4/30          2P: $100-$150      XP: $15
                                     2P: $85-$130      XP: $15
**Phone: 207/865-1868**
Bed & Breakfast  **Location:** Just n of downtown, then just w. 8 Maple Ave 04032. Fax: 207/865-6083. **Facility:** A charming Federal-style home with a variety of accommodations available, this B&B is convenient to shopping. Smoke free premises. 6 one-bedroom standard units. 2 stories (no elevator), interior corridors. *Bath:* combo or shower only. **Parking:** on-site. **Terms:** age restrictions may apply, 7 day cancellation notice-fee imposed, [BP] meal plan available. **Cards:** AX, DS, MC, VI.

SOME UNITS

**CASCO BAY INN**
◇◇◇ (SAVE)  7/2-10/23 [ECP]      1P: $88-$114      2P: $98-$124      XP: $10      F12
        5/1-7/1 [ECP]       1P: $54-$88       2P: $64-$98       XP: $10      F12
▼▼◇◇▼ 10/24-4/30 [ECP]     1P: $54-$83       2P: $64-$93       XP: $10      F12
**Phone: (207)865-4925**
Small-scale Hotel  **Location:** I-295, exit 17 northbound, 1 mi n; exit 20 southbound, 1.5 mi s. 107 US Rt 1 04032. **Facility:** Smoke free premises. 45 one-bedroom standard units. 2 stories (no elevator), interior corridors. **Parking:** on-site. **Terms:** office hours 7 am-11 pm, no pets allowed (owner's pet on premises). **Amenities:** irons, hair dryers. **Cards:** AX, DS, MC, VI. **Special Amenities: free expanded continental breakfast and free local telephone calls.** *(See color ad p 222)*

SOME UNITS

FEE    FEE

**COASTLINE INN**
◇◇◇◇  5/1-10/24         1P: $50-$140      2P: $60-$150      XP: $10      F16
        10/25-4/30        1P: $40-$60       2P: $50-$70       XP: $10      F16
Motel  **Location:** I-295, exit 20, 0.3 mi s. 537 US Rt 1 04032. Fax: 207/865-4678. **Facility:** 108 one-bedroom standard units. 2 stories (no elevator), exterior corridors. **Parking:** on-site. **Terms:** check-in 4 pm, [ECP] meal plan available, small pets only. **Amenities:** *Some:* hair dryers. **Guest Services:** coin laundry. **Cards:** AX, DS, MC, VI.
**Phone: 207/865-3777**

SOME UNITS

**COMFORT SUITES**  *Book at aaa.com*
◇◇◇ (SAVE)  7/30-10/16 [ECP]    1P: $129-$199     2P: $129-$199     XP: $15      F18
        5/22-7/29 [ECP]    1P: $109-$199     2P: $109-$199     XP: $15      F18
▼▼◇◇▼ 5/1-5/21 [ECP]     1P: $89-$150      2P: $89-$150      XP: $15      F18
        10/17-4/30 [ECP]    1P: $89-$149      2P: $89-$149      XP: $15      F18
**Phone: (207)865-9300**
Small-scale Hotel  **Location:** I-295, exit 20, just s. 500 US Rt 1 04032. Fax: 207/865-9414. **Facility:** 78 units. 76 one-bedroom standard units, some with whirlpools. 2 one-bedroom suites, some with whirlpools. 3 stories, interior corridors. *Bath:* combo or shower only. **Parking:** on-site. **Amenities:** voice mail, irons, hair dryers. **Pool(s):** heated indoor. **Leisure Activities:** whirlpool, exercise room. **Guest Services:** valet laundry. **Business Services:** meeting rooms. **Cards:** AX, CB, DC, DS, JC, MC, VI. **Special Amenities: free expanded continental breakfast and free local telephone calls.** *(See ad below)*

SOME UNITS

**HAMPTON INN**

Small-scale Hotel

Phone: (207)865-1400

| | | | |
|---|---|---|---|
| 6/11-8/28 [ECP] | 1P: $159-$169 | 2P: $169-$179 |
| 8/29-10/16 [ECP] | 1P: $139-$149 | 2P: $149-$159 |
| 5/1-6/10 [ECP] | 1P: $99-$139 | 2P: $109-$149 |
| 10/17-4/30 [ECP] | 1P: $99-$109 | 2P: $109-$119 |

**Location:** I-295, exit 20, just n on US 1. 194 Lower Main St 04032. Fax: 207/865-4249. **Facility:** 77 one-bedroom standard units. 3 stories, interior corridors. *Bath:* combo or shower only. **Parking:** on-site. **Amenities:** video games (fee), voice mail, irons, hair dryers. **Pool(s):** heated indoor. **Leisure Activities:** exercise room. **Guest Services:** valet and coin laundry. **Business Services:** meeting rooms. **Cards:** AX, CB, DC, DS, MC, VI.

## HARRASEEKET INN  *Book at aaa.com*

**Phone:** (207)865-9377

(AAA) (SAVE)

| | 1P: $195-$275 | 2P: $195-$275 | XP: $25 | F12 |
| 7/1-10/23 [BP] | | | | |
| 5/1-6/30 [BP] | 1P: $140-$245 | 2P: $140-$245 | XP: $25 | F12 |
| 10/24-4/30 [BP] | 1P: $110-$245 | 2P: $110-$245 | XP: $25 | F12 |

Country Inn **Location:** I-295, exit 22, 0.5 mi e. 162 Main St 04032. Fax: 207/865-1684. **Facility:** Outlet shops are within walking distance of this Colonial-style inn; many rooms have fireplaces or whirlpools. Smoke free premises. 84 units. 82 one-bedroom standard units, some with whirlpools. 2 one-bedroom suites ($215-$275) with whirlpools. 4 stories, interior corridors. **Parking:** on-site. **Terms:** 3 day cancellation notice, [MAP] meal plan available, package plans - seasonal, pets ($25 extra charge, in limited units). **Amenities:** high-speed Internet, voice mail, irons, hair dryers. **Dining:** Maine Dining Room, Broad Arrow Tavern, see separate listings. **Pool(s):** heated indoor. **Guest Services:** gift shop, valet laundry. **Business Services:** meeting rooms. **Cards:** AX, DC, DS, MC, VI. **Special Amenities:** free full breakfast. *(See color ad p 224)*

SOME UNITS
FEE ... / VCR ...

### THE JAMES PLACE INN

**Phone:** 207/865-4486

| All Year [BP] | 1P: $100-$140 | 2P: $110-$155 | XP: $15 |

Bed & Breakfast **Location:** Just off US 2 (Main St), s of LL Bean; center. Located in a quiet area. 11 Holbrook St 04032. **Facility:** A residential ambience enhances this cottage-style inn, which is close to shopping. Smoke free premises. 6 one-bedroom standard units, some with whirlpools. 2 stories (no elevator), interior corridors. *Bath:* combo or shower only. **Parking:** on-site. **Terms:** 2 night minimum stay - weekends 6/1-12/31, age restrictions may apply, 3 day cancellation notice, no pets allowed (owner's pet on premises). **Amenities:** hair dryers. **Cards:** AX, DS, MC, VI.

SOME UNITS
... / VCR ...

### KENDALL TAVERN BED & BREAKFAST

**Phone:** 207/865-1338

| All Year | 2P: $95-$165 | XP: $20 |

Historic Bed & Breakfast **Location:** Just n of the downtown. 213 Main St 04032. Fax: 207/865-9213. **Facility:** Dating from the 1800s, this B&B has been renovated to appeal to modern tastes; it offers comfortable common areas and well-appointed guest rooms. Smoke free premises. 7 one-bedroom standard units. 3 stories (no elevator), interior corridors. *Bath:* shower only. **Parking:** on-site. **Terms:** age restrictions may apply, 7 day cancellation notice, [BP] meal plan available. **Guest Services:** TV in common area. **Cards:** MC, VI.

### SUPER 8 MOTEL

**Phone:** (207)865-1408

| 6/25-10/9 | 1P: $69-$118 | 2P: $79-$149 | XP: $10 | F12 |
| 5/14-6/24 | 1P: $69-$89 | 2P: $69-$99 | XP: $10 | F12 |
| 10/10-4/30 | 1P: $49-$69 | 2P: $59-$89 | XP: $10 | F12 |
| 5/1-5/13 | 1P: $39-$69 | 2P: $49-$79 | XP: $10 | F12 |

Small-scale Hotel **Location:** I-95, exit 20, 0.3 mi s. 506 US Rt 1 04032. Fax: 207/865-1417. **Facility:** 73 one-bedroom standard units. 1 story, interior corridors. **Parking:** on-site. **Terms:** [CP] meal plan available. **Amenities:** hair dryers. **Cards:** AX, DC, DS, MC, VI.

SOME UNITS

### WHITE CEDAR INN

**Phone:** 207/865-9099

| 5/20-10/31 [BP] | 1P: $108-$122 | 2P: $120-$135 | XP: $20 |
| 5/1-5/19 & 11/1-4/30 [BP] | 1P: $81-$103 | 2P: $90-$115 | XP: $20 |

Historic Bed & Breakfast **Location:** Just n. 178 Main St 04032. Fax: 207/865-6636. **Facility:** A century-old converted Victorian, this inn is within walking distance of outlet shops and is decorated with antiques; some rooms have fireplaces. Smoke free premises. 7 one-bedroom standard units. 2 stories (no elevator), interior/exterior corridors. *Bath:* combo or shower only. **Parking:** on-site. **Terms:** age restrictions may apply, 14 day cancellation notice-fee imposed. **Cards:** AX, MC, VI.

SOME UNITS

---

## ——— WHERE TO DINE ———

### AZURE ITALIAN CAFE

**Lunch:** $5-$10    **Dinner:** $12-$23    **Phone:** 207/865-1237

Italian **Location:** On US 1; center. 123 Main St 04032. **Hours:** 11 am-9 pm, Fri & Sat-10 pm. Closed: Tues 1/1-4/1. **Reservations:** accepted. **Features:** Azure's patio is the place to be to observe the happenings on Main Street. The intimate dining room has a colorful bistro feel and includes a Gulf of Maine fish tank. The menu features authentic Italtian cuisine. Casual dress; beer & wine only. **Parking:** on-site. **Cards:** MC, VI.

### BROAD ARROW TAVERN    Country Inn

**Lunch:** $9-$15    **Dinner:** $10-$25    **Phone:** 207/865-9377

Regional American **Location:** I-295, exit 22, 0.5 mi e; in Harraseeket Inn. 162 Main St 04032. **Hours:** 11:30 am-10:30 pm. **Features:** This popular restaurant, has a Maine backwoods hunting lodge feel with a moose head and canoe on the walls as well as a border with colorful Christmas lights. The wood fired oven and grill produce menu items, wiht all local organic ingredients, from pizza to filet mignon. Dining is casual and portions are hearty. Casual dress; cocktails. **Parking:** on-site. **Cards:** AX, DC, DS, MC, VI.

### CONUNDRUM

**Dinner:** $8-$14    **Phone:** 207/865-0303

American **Location:** I-295, exit 17 northbound, 1 mi n; exit 20 southbound, 1.5 mi s. 117 US Rt 1 04032. **Hours:** 4:30 pm-10 pm. Closed: 7/4, 11/25, 12/25; also Sun & Mon. **Features:** A local favorite, Conundrum has an extensive list of martinis and wine by the glass. The menu includes a number of cheeses, appetizers, salads as well as several pates to complement the beverage selection. Casual dress; cocktails. **Parking:** on-site. **Cards:** AX, DS, MC, VI.

### THE CORSICAN RESTAURANT

**Lunch:** $5-$15    **Dinner:** $10-$16    **Phone:** 207/865-9421

American **Location:** Center. 9 Mechanic St 04032. **Hours:** 11 am-9 pm; to 8 pm 10/1-4/30. Closed: 3/27, 11/25, 12/25. **Features:** In business since 1986, the casual eatery offers customers a choice of pizza, pasta, soups, sandwiches and vegetarian and seafood entrees. Breads and desserts are homemade. Casual dress; beer & wine only. **Parking:** street. **Cards:** DC, DS, MC, VI.

**CRICKETS RESTAURANT**                  **Dinner:** $9-$19                        Phone: 207/865-4005
▼▼▼        **Location:** On US 1, 0.7 mi s of center. 175 Lower Main St 04032. **Hours:** 11:30 am-8 pm, Fri & Sat-9 pm.
           Closed: 11/25, 12/25. **Features:** The restaurant offers "Maine lobsters served 10 ways," but that's not all
American   that's on the menu. Patrons also can sample pasta, ribs, fajitas, chicken, specialty sandwiches and fresh
           seafood. Casual dress; cocktails. **Parking:** on-site. **Cards:** MC, VI.                    ⓂⒺ ✕

**JAMESON TAVERN** Historic           **Lunch:** $7-$16         **Dinner:** $14-$28          Phone: 207/865-4196
▼▼ ▼▼      **Location:** Center. 115 Main St 04032. **Hours:** 11:30 am-close. Closed: 12/25. **Reservations:** suggested, for
           dinner. **Features:** In the heart of the downtown outlet district, this restaurant was built in 1779 as a private
Steak & Seafood  residence. The final papers of separation of the state of Maine from the Commonwealth of Massachusetts
           were signed here in 1820. The menu features American fare with fresh seafood and steak. The lighter all
day pub menu is available in the dining room at lunch. Casual dress; cocktails. **Parking:** on-site. **Cards:** AX, DC, DS, MC, VI.
                                                                                                        Ⓨ ✕

**THE LOBSTER COOKER RESTAURANT**        **Lunch:** $4-$17         **Dinner:** $4-$17          Phone: 207/865-4349
▼▼        **Location:** Center. 39 Main St 04032. **Hours:** 11 am-7 pm; to 9 pm 5/15-9/1. Closed: 11/25, 12/25.
           **Features:** In the heart of the downtown outlet district, this restaurant features simple decor in an 1860 barn
Seafood    with a lovely garden patio that is available seasonally. The menu features award-winning chowder as well
           as fresh seafood, sandwiches and salads. Counter service is fast and friendly, and the atmosphere is
casual. Be sure to try a delicious lobster roll. Casual dress; beer & wine only. **Parking:** on-site.   Ⓚ ✕

**MIYAKO**                            **Lunch:** $7-$12         **Dinner:** $11-$17          Phone: 207/865-6888
▼▼ ▼▼      **Location:** Center. 23 Main St 04032. **Hours:** 11 am-10 pm, Fri & Sat-11 pm; 11 am-2:30 & 5-9:30 pm, Fri &
           Sat-10 pm 10/19-4/19. Closed: 11/25. **Reservations:** accepted. **Features:** In the heart of town, the popular
Japanese   restaurant features sushi selections, as well as tempura, teriyaki and combination lunches and dinners and
           other traditional dishes. Presentations are attractive, and the ethnically attired serving staff is prompt,
friendly and helpful. Casual dress; cocktails. **Parking:** on-site. **Cards:** AX, DS, MC, VI.          ✕

**SCHOOL STREET CAFE**                **Lunch:** $6-$11         **Dinner:** $9-$22          Phone: 207/865-0100
▼▼▼        **Location:** Just e of US 1; center. 10 School St 04032. **Hours:** 11 am-9 pm, Fri & Sat-10 pm. Closed: 12/25.
           **Reservations:** suggested. **Features:** School Street Cafe's offers an upscale bistro cuisine utilizing fresh,
American   local ingredients. In fact herbs and microgreens are grown in their own gardens and all menu items are
           made on the premises. Casual dress; cocktails. **Parking:** on-site. **Cards:** AX, MC, VI.   Ⓨ ✕

───────── *The following restaurants have not been evaluated by AAA* ─────────
*but are listed for your information only.*

**MAINE DINING ROOM**                                                                          Phone: 207/865-9377
[fyi]      Not evaluated. **Location:** I-295, exit 22, 0.5 mi e; in Harraseeket Inn. 162 Main St 04032. **Features:** This upscale
           country inn serves a wide variety of regional American entrees, including tastefully prepared meats and
seafood. Among specialties are chateaubriand and rack of lamb. Seasonal produce is obtained from local suppliers. Diners are
urged to try one of the flaming tableside desserts. *(See color ad p 224)*                                Ⓨ

**OLD WORLD GOURMET DELI & WINE SHOP**                                                         Phone: 207/865-4477
[fyi]      Not evaluated. **Location:** 117 US Rt 1 04032. **Features:** A popular lunch and breakfast spot, the delicatessen
           is a showcase for the products of local producers. Sandwiches, soups, salads, pastries and fresh breads
are just some of the items on the menu. Desserts are made from scratch on the premises. Take-out dinners are also available.

# FRYEBURG pop. 1,549

───────── **WHERE TO STAY** ─────────

**ADMIRAL PEARY HOUSE**                                                                        Phone: (207)935-3365
▼▼▼▼       7/1-10/31 [BP]          1P: $125-$165          2P: $125-$165          XP: $25          D16
           12/23-4/30 [BP]         1P: $120-$155          2P: $120-$155          XP: $25          D16
           11/1-12/22 [BP]         1P: $110-$135          2P: $110-$135          XP: $25          D16
Bed & Breakfast  5/1-6/30 [BP]     1P: $105-$135          2P: $105-$135          XP: $25          D16
**Location:** Just s Elm St, off US 302; center of village. Located in a residential area. 9 Elm St 04037. Fax: 207/935-7765. **Facility:** Perennial gardens surround this 19th-century farmhouse on 10 acres; period antiques and reproductions set the tone inside. Smoke
free premises. 6 one-bedroom standard units. 2 stories (no elevator), interior corridors. *Bath:* shower only. **Parking:** on-site.
**Terms:** check-in 4 pm, 2 night minimum stay - seasonal, 14 day cancellation notice-fee imposed, package plans - seasonal &
some weekends. **Leisure Activities:** whirlpool, cross country skiing, bicycles. **Guest Services:** TV in common area. **Cards:** AX,
DS, MC, VI.                                                                          ⒶⓈⓀ Ⓢ⒟ ✕ ✕ Ⓦ Ⓩ

**ONE THIRTY THREE MAIN STREET BED & BREAKFAST**                                               Phone: (207)935-7171
🔺🔺🔺 SAVE   All Year             1P: $79-$179           2P: $89-$179           XP: $15          D
▼▼▼▼       **Location:** US 302, just e of jct SR 113; center of village. 133 Main St 04037. Fax: 207/935-7172. **Facility:** This fed-
           eralist era home has been renovated and refurnished; it offers good mountain views. Smoke free premises.
Bed & Breakfast  4 one-bedroom standard units, some with whirlpools. 2 stories (no elevator), interior corridors. *Bath:* some
           shared or private, combo or shower only. **Parking:** on-site. **Terms:** check-in 4 pm, 2 night minimum stay -
some weekends, 10 day cancellation notice, weekly rates available, no pets allowed (owner's pet on premises). **Leisure Activities:** cross country skiing, snowmobiling. **Guest Services:** TV in common area. **Cards:** MC, VI.
**Special Amenities:** free full breakfast and free local telephone calls.                          ✕ Ⓦ Ⓩ

**THE OXFORD HOUSE INN**                                                                        Phone: (207)935-3442
🔺🔺🔺 SAVE   All Year [BP]         1P: $75-$145           2P: $110-$145          XP: $15          D12
▼▼▼▼       **Location:** US 302, just w of jct SR 113; center of village. 105 Main St 04037. Fax: 207/935-7046. **Facility:** Fine
           woodwork distinguishes this Edwardian-style house, which offers nicely appointed guest rooms and is con-
Historic   venient to the fairgrounds. Smoke free premises. 4 units. 3 one-bedroom standard units. 1 one-bedroom
Country Inn  suite. 2 stories (no elevator), interior corridors. *Bath:* combo or shower only. **Parking:** on-site. **Terms:** 10 day
           cancellation notice-fee imposed, no pets allowed (owner's pet on premises). **Dining:** restaurant, see sepa-
rate listing. **Cards:** AX, DC, DS, MC, VI. **Special Amenities:** free full breakfast and preferred room (subject to availability with advanced reservations).                                          Ⓢ⒟ Ⓨ✕ ✕ ✕

------ **WHERE TO DINE** ------

THE OXFORD HOUSE INN  Country Inn                    Dinner: $22-$28                    Phone: 207/935-3442

▼▼▼▼

American

**Location:** US 302, just w of jct SR 113; center of village; in The Oxford House Inn. 105 Main St 04037. **Hours:** 6 pm-9 pm. Closed: Mon-Wed 11/1-7/1. **Reservations:** suggested. **Features:** This restaurant, which is very popular with locals and visitors alike, is in a handsome Edwardian-period inn offering wonderful mountain views. The very creative menu features a contemporary country cuisine using fresh Maine products. Attentive service. Casual dress; cocktails. **Parking:** on-site. **Cards:** AX, DC, DS, MC, VI.

# GEORGETOWN

------ **WHERE TO STAY** ------

COVESIDE BED & BREAKFAST                                              Phone: 207/371-2807

AAA  [SAVE]

▼▼▼▼

Bed & Breakfast

5/28-10/17 [BP]                1P: $110-$175            2P: $110-$175            XP: $10

**Location:** US 1 from Bath, 13 mi s on SR 127, follow signs. Located in a quiet area. 6 Gotts Cove Ln 04548. Fax: 207/371-2952. **Facility:** Wide water views and an open floor plan enhance this renovated B&B; its five-acre grounds extend to the cove and river. Smoke free premises. 7 one-bedroom standard units, some with whirlpools. 2 stories (no elevator), interior/exterior corridors. *Bath:* combo or shower only. **Parking:** on-site. **Terms:** open 5/28-10/17, age restrictions may apply, 14 day cancellation notice, no pets allowed (owner's pet on premises). **Amenities:** irons, hair dryers. **Leisure Activities:** canoeing, boat dock, bicycles. **Cards:** AX, DC, MC, VI. **Special Amenities:** free full breakfast and free local telephone calls.

------ **WHERE TO DINE** ------

ROBINHOOD FREE MEETING HOUSE  Historic              Dinner: $20-$27          Phone: 207/371-2188

▼▼▼▼

American

**Location:** US 1, in Woolwich just across the bridge from Bath, 6 mi s on SR 127, then 1 mi e. 210 Robinhood Rd 04548. **Hours:** 5:30 pm-9 pm. Closed: Sun-Wed 10/15-5/15. **Reservations:** suggested. **Features:** This fine-dining restaurant is in a beautifully restored 1855 post-and-beam building originally constructed by local craftsmen. The extensive menu offers an eclectic mix of classical American and fusion cuisine. The atmosphere is upscale casual. Cocktails. **Parking:** on-site. **Cards:** AX, DS, MC, VI.

# GORHAM pop. 4,164

------ **WHERE TO STAY** ------

PINE CREST BED & BREAKFAST                                            Phone: 207/839-5843

▼▼▼▼

Bed & Breakfast

| | | | |
|---|---|---|---|
| 5/1-10/31 [ECP] | 1P: $99-$139 | 2P: $99-$139 | XP: $10  F10 |
| 11/1-4/30 [ECP] | 1P: $89-$119 | 2P: $89-$119 | XP: $10  F10 |

**Location:** Jct SR 25, 0.5 mi s on SR 114. Located in a residential area. 91 South St 04038. **Facility:** A porch with white wicker furniture overlooks perennial gardens at this inn; the sunny guest rooms have hardwood floors and country-cottage decor. Smoke free premises. 5 units. 4 one-bedroom standard units. 1 one-bedroom suite. 3 stories (no elevator), interior corridors. *Bath:* combo or shower only. **Parking:** on-site. **Terms:** 2 night minimum stay - 7/1-8/31, 10 day cancellation notice, [BP] meal plan available. **Cards:** MC, VI.

------ **WHERE TO DINE** ------

SEBAGO BREWING COMPANY              Lunch: $10-$18              Dinner: $10-$18          Phone: 207/839-2337

▼▼

American

**Location:** Just e of US 202/SR 25; center. 29 Elm St 04083. **Hours:** 11 am-midnight, Sun-9 pm. Closed: 7/4, 11/25, 12/24, 12/25. **Features:** The stylish brew pub sustains a friendly, informal atmosphere. Self-described "American pub" cuisine includes delicious pasta, chicken, seafood and steak entrees, as well as tasty salads, burgers and sandwiches. The latter are available all day. The resident pastry chef prepares desserts on the premises each day. Casual dress; cocktails. **Parking:** on-site. **Cards:** AX, MC, VI.

# GOULDSBORO

------ **WHERE TO STAY** ------

THE BLUFF HOUSE                                                      Phone: 207/963-7805

▼▼

Country Inn

| | | | |
|---|---|---|---|
| 6/1-10/31 [ECP] | 1P: $69-$105 | 2P: $69-$105 | XP: $10  F12 |
| 5/1-5/31 & 11/1-4/30 [ECP] | 1P: $49-$78 | 2P: $49-$78 | XP: $10  F12 |

**Location:** 2.8 mi s on SR 186. 57 Bluff House Rd 04607 (PO Box 249). **Facility:** Smoke free premises. 9 units. 8 one-bedroom standard units. 1 two-bedroom suite with kitchen. 2 stories (no elevator), interior corridors. *Bath:* combo or shower only. **Parking:** on-site. **Terms:** 10 day cancellation notice, no pets allowed (owner's pet on premises). **Leisure Activities:** cross country skiing, hiking trails. **Cards:** AX, DS, MC, VI.

SOME UNITS

# GRAND LAKE STREAM

------ **WHERE TO STAY** ------

LEEN'S LODGE                                                        Phone: (207)796-2929

▼▼

Cabin

5/1-10/31                1P: $125                2P: $100

**Location:** 10 mi w off US 1, 2 mi n on gravel entry road. Located in a quiet, secluded area. 368 Bonney Brook Rd 04637 (PO Box 40). **Facility:** 10 cabins. 1 story, exterior corridors. **Parking:** on-site. **Terms:** open 5/1-10/31, 21 day cancellation notice-fee imposed, weekly rates available, [MAP] meal plan available, package plans, 15% service charge. **Leisure Activities:** rental canoes, rental paddleboats, boat dock, fishing. **Guest Services:** TV in common area. **Cards:** AX, MC, VI.

SOME UNITS

## WEATHERBY'S-THE FISHERMAN'S RESORT

**Phone: (207)796-5558**

*Classic Historic Cottage*

5/1-10/31                    1P: $108-$140
**Location:** 10 mi w off US 1. 1 Church St 04637 (PO Box 69). **Facility:** One- to five- bedroom rustic log cottages with screened porches are offered at this wooded fishing camp. 15 cottages. 1 story, exterior corridors. *Bath:* combo or shower only. **Parking:** on-site. **Terms:** open 5/1-10/31, 21 day cancellation notice-fee imposed, weekly rates available, [MAP] meal plan available, 15% service charge. **Leisure Activities:** rental boats, rental canoes. *Fee:* massage. **Cards:** DS, MC, VI.

# GRAY pop. 6,820

## ─── WHERE TO DINE ───

### COLE FARMS

**Lunch: $2-$9**          **Dinner: $2-$9**          **Phone: 207/657-4714**

*American*

**Location:** I-95 (Maine Tpke), exit 63, 1.3 mi e on US 202. 64 Lewiston Rd 04039. **Hours:** 5 am-9 pm, Sat & Sun from 6 am. **Closed:** 11/25, 12/25. **Features:** In business since 1952, the family restaurant prepares made-to-order home-style dishes. Casual dress. **Parking:** on-site.

### JULIEN'S FAMILY DINING

**Lunch: $4-$18**          **Dinner: $4-$10**          **Phone: 207/428-4300**

*American*

**Location:** I-95 (Maine Tpke), exit 63, 3.9 mi w on US 202/SR 115. 322 W Gray Rd 04039. **Hours:** 11 am-9 pm, Fri-10 pm, Sat 8:30 am-10 pm, Sun from 8:30 am-8 pm. **Features:** The menu includes fresh seafood, beef, pasta and vegetarian entrees, as well as 35 dessert items. Parents appreciate the children's menu. The dining rooms provide a relaxed atmosphere for lunch or dinner. Casual dress; cocktails. **Parking:** on-site. **Cards:** AX, DC, DS, MC, VI.

# GREENVILLE pop. 1,319

## ─── WHERE TO STAY ───

### CHALET MOOSEHEAD LAKEFRONT MOTEL

**Phone: (207)695-2950**

*Motel*

| | | | | |
|---|---|---|---|---|
| 6/4-9/11 | 1P: $83-$125 | 2P: $83-$125 | XP: $10 | F5 |
| 5/1-6/3 & 9/12-4/30 | 1P: $62-$125 | 2P: $62-$125 | XP: $10 | F5 |

**Location:** 1.5 mi w on SR 15. N Birch St 04442 (PO Box 327). **Facility:** 27 units. 19 one- and 8 two-bedroom standard units, some with efficiencies and/or whirlpools. 2 stories (no elevator), exterior corridors. *Bath:* combo or shower only. **Parking:** on-site. **Terms:** office hours 7 am-10 pm, pets ($10 extra charge, in designated units). **Amenities:** *Some:* hair dryers. **Leisure Activities:** canoeing, paddleboats, boat dock. **Cards:** DS, MC, VI.

SOME UNITS

### EVERGREEN LODGE AT MOOSEHEAD

**Phone: (207)695-3241**

*Bed & Breakfast*

All Year [BP]                1P: $110-$150          2P: $110-$150          XP: $20
**Location:** 5.5 mi s on SR 15. Located in a quiet, rural area. 182 Greenville Rd 04441. Fax: 207/695-3084. **Facility:** A casual ambience characterizes this property, which offers some guest rooms with fireplaces and others with balconies overlooking gardens. Designated smoking area. 6 one-bedroom standard units. 2 stories (no elevator), interior corridors. *Bath:* combo or shower only. **Parking:** on-site. **Terms:** 2 night minimum stay - weekends, 14 day cancellation notice-fee imposed, weekly rates available, package plans - seasonal. **Amenities:** hair dryers. **Leisure Activities:** whirlpool, cross country skiing, snowmobiling. **Guest Services:** TV in common area. **Cards:** MC, VI.

### GREENVILLE INN

**Phone: 207/695-2206**

*Country Inn*

All Year                                   2P: $140-$200          XP: $20
**Location:** On Norris St, 0.3 mi s. 40 Norris St 04441 (PO Box 1194). Fax: 207/695-0335. **Facility:** A country mansion dating from 1885 centers this property, which also features six modern cottages with decks; some rooms have lake views. Smoke free premises. 12 units. 4 one-bedroom standard units. 2 one-bedroom suites ($190-$275). 6 cottages ($180-$200). 2 stories (no elevator), interior/exterior corridors. *Bath:* combo, shower or tub only. **Parking:** on-site. **Terms:** 14 day cancellation notice-fee imposed, package plans, no pets allowed (owner's pet on premises). **Amenities:** hair dryers. *Some:* irons. **Dining:** dining room, see separate listing. **Cards:** AX, MC, VI.

SOME UNITS

### INDIAN HILL MOTEL

**Phone: 207/695-2623**

*Motel*

| | | | | |
|---|---|---|---|---|
| 5/1-6/3 & 10/12-12/22 | 1P: $44-$70 | 2P: $50-$70 | XP: $20 | F5 |
| 6/4-10/11 & 12/23-4/30 | 1P: $70 | 2P: $70 | XP: $20 | F5 |

**Location:** 0.5 mi s on SR 15. 127 Moosehead Lake Rd 04442 (PO Box 327). **Facility:** 15 one-bedroom standard units. 1 story, exterior corridors. **Parking:** on-site. **Terms:** office hours 7 am-10 pm. **Cards:** DS, MC, VI.

SOME UNITS

### KINEO VIEW MOTOR LODGE

**Phone: 207/695-4470**

*Motel* — AAA SAVE

| | | | | |
|---|---|---|---|---|
| 7/1-10/20 [CP] | 1P: $79-$89 | 2P: $89-$99 | XP: $10 | F12 |
| 12/23-4/30 | 1P: $59-$69 | 2P: $69-$79 | XP: $10 | F12 |
| 5/1-6/30 | 1P: $55-$65 | 2P: $69-$79 | XP: $10 | F12 |
| 10/21-12/22 | 1P: $59-$69 | 2P: $59-$69 | XP: $10 | F12 |

**Location:** 2.5 mi s on SR 15. Overlook Dr 04441 (PO Box 514). Fax: 207/695-4655. **Facility:** 13 units. 11 one-bedroom standard units. 1 one- and 1 two-bedroom suites ($149-$189), some with kitchens. 2 stories (no elevator), exterior corridors. **Parking:** on-site. **Terms:** office hours 7 am-9 pm, pets ($10 extra charge, in designated units). **Leisure Activities:** whirlpool. **Cards:** AX, MC, VI. **Special Amenities:** free local telephone calls and early check-in/late check-out.

SOME UNITS

## THE LODGE AT MOOSEHEAD LAKE

Phone: 207/695-4400

(AAA) (SAVE)

▼▼▼ ▼▼▼
Bed & Breakfast

All Year [BP]  1P: $250-$475  2P: $250-$475  XP: $35
**Location:** 2.5 mi n. 368 Lily Bay Rd 04441 (PO Box 1167). Fax: 207/695-2281. **Facility:** On a hill, the lodge overlooks Moosehead Lake; guest rooms are tastefully decorated in Maine themes. Smoke free premises. 8 one-bedroom standard units with whirlpools. 2 stories (no elevator), interior corridors. **Parking:** on-site. **Terms:** age restrictions may apply, 21 day cancellation notice-fee imposed, package plans - seasonal, no pets allowed (owner's pets on premises). **Amenities:** video library, CD players, irons, hair dryers. **Leisure Activities:** Fee: game room. **Business Services:** meeting rooms. **Cards:** AX, DS, MC, VI. **Special Amenities:** free full breakfast and free local telephone calls.

(X) (VCR) (☎) (▭)

----- WHERE TO DINE -----

## THE BLACK FROG

**Lunch:** $5-$12  **Dinner:** $7-$20  Phone: 207/695-1100

▼▼▼ ▼▼▼
American

**Location:** On SR 15; center. Pritham Ave 04441. **Hours:** 11:30 am-10 pm; hours may vary off season. Closed: 11/25, 12/25. **Reservations:** accepted. **Features:** On the shores of Moosehead Lake, the restaurant is a scenic spot in which to enjoy selections of mostly seafood and cooked-to-order steak. For the best views, diners should try to reserve a window table. Outdoor dining on a floating dock is available in season. Casual dress; cocktails. **Parking:** street. **Cards:** AX, DS, MC, VI.

(☎) (X)

## GREENVILLE INN  Country Inn

**Dinner:** $20-$24  Phone: 207/695-2206

▼▼▼ ▼▼▼
American

**Location:** On Norris St, 0.3 mi s; in Greenville Inn. 40 Norris St 04441. **Hours:** Open 5/18-10/27; 6 pm-8:30 pm; hours may vary off season. Closed: Sun; days may vary off season. **Reservations:** suggested. **Features:** Some of the cozy restaurant's tastefully decorated dining areas overlook Moosehead Lake. The menu features fresh seafood, steak and some game meat, all creatively prepared and well matched with selections from the fine wine list. The homemade desserts are wonderful. Dressy casual; cocktails. **Parking:** on-site. **Cards:** DS, MC, VI.

(☎) (K) (X)

## KELLY'S LANDING RESTAURANT

**Lunch:** $5-$20  **Dinner:** $8-$20  Phone: 207/695-4438

▼▼▼ ▼▼▼
American

**Location:** 1.5 mi w on SR 6 and 15. Rt 15 04442. **Hours:** 7 am-9 pm; hours vary off season. Closed: 12/25. **Reservations:** accepted. **Features:** Kelly's Landing offers a delightful view of Moosehead Lake; the deck is right on the water. The menu filled with home-style cooking features prime rib, seafood, chicken, pork, beef and veal entrees as well as sandwiches, soup and homemade dessert. Casual dress; cocktails. **Parking:** on-site. **Cards:** MC, VI.

(X)

# HALLOWELL pop. 2,467

----- WHERE TO STAY -----

## MAPLE HILL FARM B & B INN

Phone: (207)622-2708

▼▼▼ ▼▼▼
Historic Bed
& Breakfast

6/18-9/5 [BP]  1P: $85-$170  2P: $95-$185  XP: $20
5/1-6/17 & 9/6-10/23 [BP]  1P: $80-$155  2P: $90-$170  XP: $20
10/24-4/30 [BP]  1P: $70-$135  2P: $80-$145  XP: $20
**Location:** I-95 (Maine Tpke) exit 109 on SR 202 westbound then immediate left, s on Whitten Rd, then just nw on Winthrop St to Town Farm Rd, follow signs. Located in a quiet, rural area. Outlet Rd 04347 (RR 1, Box 1145). Fax: 207/622-0655. **Facility:** A converted barn houses meeting facilities at this inn, built circa 1890, on a 62-acre working farm. 8 one-bedroom standard units, some with whirlpools. 2 stories (no elevator), interior corridors. *Bath:* combo or shower only. **Parking:** on-site. **Terms:** 2-3 night minimum stay - weekends 7/1-8/31, 14 day cancellation notice, weekly rates available, no pets allowed (owner's pet on premises). **Amenities:** video library, irons, hair dryers. **Leisure Activities:** cross country skiing, hiking trails, horseshoes, volleyball. **Business Services:** meeting rooms. **Cards:** AX, CB, DC, DS, MC, VI.

(&M) (X) (X) (CTV) (VCR) (DATA PORT)

----- WHERE TO DINE -----

## THE LIBERAL CUP

**Lunch:** $5-$9  **Dinner:** $5-$14  Phone: 207/623-2739

▼▼ ▼▼
English

**Location:** Center. 115 Water St 04347. **Hours:** 11:30 am-9 pm, Fri & Sat-10 pm, Sun noon-9 pm. Closed major holidays. **Features:** Not far from the State Capitol, the eatery lets patrons match English-style pub fare with the hand-crafted beers made on the premises. Casual dress; cocktails. **Parking:** street. **Cards:** AX, DS, MC, VI.

(☎) (X)

## SLATES

**Lunch:** $5-$13  **Dinner:** $9-$18  Phone: 207/622-9575

▼▼▼ ▼▼▼
International

**Location:** Opposite river, 2 mi s of Augusta Rotary on SR 27 and 201; center. 167 Water St 04347. **Hours:** 7:30-11 am, 11:30-2:30 & 5:30-9 pm, Sat 9 am-2:30 & 5:30-9:30 pm, Sun 9:30 am-2 pm, Mon 5:30 pm-8 pm. Closed: 7/4, 11/25, 12/25. **Features:** This restaurant is located in an older storefront building with a brick interior and the works of local artists on the walls. It includes a cafe-deli as well as the dining room and has a relaxed and informal atmosphere. They describe their cuisine as eclectic, including South American, Thai, African, Italian, vegetarian and pasta entrees, all prepared to order. Desserts are prepared at their own bakery. The Monday night concert series includes Folk and Jazz artists. Cocktails. **Parking:** street. **Cards:** DS, MC, VI.

(X)

# HANCOCK

----- WHERE TO STAY -----

## LE DOMAINE INN

Phone: 207/422-3395

▼▼▼ ▼▼▼
Country Inn

6/6-10/23  2P: $200
**Location:** On US 1, 9 mi e of Ellsworth; center. US Rt 1, #1513 04640. Fax: 207/422-2316. **Facility:** This charming French-style inn is offers lovely gardens and guest rooms decorated with a taste of Provence, fireplaces and a deck. Smoke free premises. 5 units. 3 one-bedroom suites ($285). 2 stories (no elevator), exterior corridors. **Parking:** on-site. **Terms:** open 6/6-10/23, 14 day cancellation notice-fee imposed. **Amenities:** irons, hair dryers. *Some:* CD players. **Dining:** Le Domaine Restaurant Francais, see separate listing. **Leisure Activities:** hiking trails. **Cards:** AX, DC, MC, VI.

(❢❢) (X) (W) (DATA PORT)

──────── WHERE TO DINE ────────

**LE DOMAINE RESTAURANT FRANCAIS**  Country Inn    **Dinner:** $29    **Phone:** 207/422-3395
▼▼▼▼    **Location:** On US 1, 9 mi e of Ellsworth; center; le Domaine Inn. US Rt 1, #1513 04640. **Hours:** Open 6/4-10/16;
Regional French    6 pm-9 pm. Closed: Mon. **Reservations:** suggested. **Features:** The charming restaurant offers a delightful
French country theme and a large, open-hearth fireplace reflecting on polished wooden floors. Patrons can
relax with a beverage in the lounge before savoring the owner/chef's creative delights. Specialties include
French-cut hanger steaks pan seared with green peppercorn demi-glace sauce, quail roasted with juniper berries and grilled
veal with mushrooms. Desserts are exquisite. The vast wine list comprises more than 5,000 bottles. Casual dress; cocktails.
**Parking:** on-site. **Cards:** AX, DS, MC, VI.                   ⛾ ⊠

# HARPSWELL pop. 5,239

──────── WHERE TO DINE ────────

**DOLPHIN CHOWDER HOUSE**    **Lunch:** $8-$20    **Dinner:** $8-$20    **Phone:** 207/833-6000
▼▼ ▼▼    **Location:** From Brunswick jct SR 24, 12 mi s on SR 123, then follow signs 2.5 mi. 515 Basin Pt 04079.
Seafood    **Hours:** Open 5/1-11/1; 11 am-8 pm. **Features:** Owned by the same family for 37 years, the restaurant is
known for its clam chowder and lobster stew. Customers can come by land, by sea or sometimes by air to
enjoy fresh local seafood and water views. Casual dress; beer & wine only. **Parking:** on-site.
**Cards:** MC, VI.                                                  ⊠

# HOULTON pop. 5,270

──────── WHERE TO STAY ────────

**IVEY'S MOTOR LODGE**                                    **Phone:** 207/532-4206
AAA SAVE    5/1-10/31    1P: $64-$74    2P: $72-$80    XP: $10    F6
▼▼▼    11/1-4/30    1P: $60-$68    2P: $70-$78    XP: $10    F6
Motel    **Location:** I-95, exit 302. North St 04730 (PO Box 637). Fax: 207/532-4206. **Facility:** 24 one-bedroom standard
units. 1 story, interior corridors. **Parking:** on-site, winter plug-ins. **Terms:** cancellation fee imposed.
**Cards:** AX, DC, DS, MC, VI. **Special Amenities:** free local telephone calls.    SOME UNITS
[⧉] [⊪] [⛾] [⌘] [▪] / [⊠] [DATA PORT] /

**SCOTTISH INNS**    *Book at aaa.com*    **Phone:** (207)532-2236
AAA SAVE    5/1-10/31 & 4/1-4/30    1P: $50-$55    2P: $65-$75    XP: $10    F10
▼    11/1-3/31    1P: $45-$46    2P: $50-$55    XP: $5    F10
Motel    **Location:** I-95, exit 302, 1 mi s on US 1, then 1 mi sw on US 2A. 239 Bangor St 04730. Fax: 207/532-9893.
**Facility:** 40 units. 38 one- and 2 two-bedroom standard units. 1 story, interior/exterior corridors. *Bath:* combo
or shower only. **Parking:** on-site, winter plug-ins. **Terms:** office hours 7 am-11 pm, cancellation fee imposed,
package plans - weekends, pets ($6 extra charge). **Cards:** AX, DS, MC, VI. **Special Amenities:** free local
telephone calls and early check-in/late check-out.    SOME UNITS
[⧉] [⌂] [⊪] [⛾] [⌘] / [⊠] [▪] [▭] /
FEE

**SHIRETOWN MOTOR INN**                                    **Phone:** (207)532-9421
AAA SAVE    All Year    1P: $79-$99    2P: $79-$99    XP: $10    F17
▼▼ ▼▼    **Location:** I-95, exit 302, 0.3 mi n on US 1. 282 North St 04730. Fax: 207/532-3390. **Facility:** 51 one-bedroom stan-
dard units. 1 story, interior/exterior corridors. *Bath:* combo or shower only. **Parking:** on-site, winter plug-ins.
Small-scale Hotel    **Terms:** 3 day cancellation notice-fee imposed. **Dining:** The Atrium, see separate listing. **Pool(s):** heated in-
door. **Leisure Activities:** 2 tennis courts, exercise room. **Guest Services:** coin laundry. **Cards:** AX, DC, DS,
MC, VI. **Special Amenities:** free local telephone calls.    SOME UNITS
[⧉] [⊪] [⛾] [⤢] [⌘] [▪] / [⊠] [▭] /

──────── WHERE TO DINE ────────

**THE ATRIUM**    **Dinner:** $8-$20    **Phone:** 207/532-9421
▼    **Location:** I-95, exit 302, 0.3 mi n on US 1; in Shiretown Motor Inn. 282 North St 04730. **Hours:** 5 pm-9 pm, Fri &
American    Sat-9:30 pm. Closed: Sun & Mon. **Reservations:** accepted. **Features:** The family restaurant's
widely varied menu includes everything from burgers to steak to seafood. Casual dress; cocktails.
**Parking:** on-site. **Cards:** AX, CB, DC, DS, MC, VI.                   ⛾ ⊠

**ELM TREE DINER**    **Lunch:** $4-$8    **Dinner:** $5-$12    **Phone:** 207/532-3181
AAA    **Location:** I-95, exit 302, 1 mi s on US 1, 1 mi sw on US 2A. 146 Bangor St 04730. **Hours:** Open 5/1-11/30; open
▼    to 8 pm. **Features:** The popular restaurant has served diners since 1947. Examples of good,
home-style-cooking include boneless fried chicken, steak, clams, scallops, sandwiches and a terrific
American    selection of homemade pies and pastries. Breakfast is served all day. A friendly atmosphere and fast,
cordial servers enhance the experience. Casual dress. **Parking:** on-site. **Cards:** MC, VI.                   ⊠

# ISLESFORD

———— WHERE TO DINE ————

———— *The following restaurant has not been evaluated by AAA* ————
*but is listed for your information only.*

THE ISLEFORD DOCK                                                                                    **Phone:** 207/244-7494
(fyi)        Not evaluated. **Location:** On Little Cranberry Island. **Features:** Open seasonally for lunch and dinner, the
             restaurant is right on Islesford Dock. Fresh seafood makes up the menu.

# JACKMAN

———— WHERE TO STAY ————

**BISHOP'S COUNTRY INN MOTEL**                                                                **Phone:** (207)668-3231

| | | | | |
|---|---|---|---|---|
| (AAA) (SAVE) | 12/18-4/30 [ECP] | 1P: $80-$90 | 2P: $80-$90 | XP: $10 | F14 |
| | 5/1-10/23 [ECP] | 1P: $75-$85 | 2P: $75-$85 | XP: $10 | F14 |
| ▼▼▼ | 10/24-12/17 [ECP] | 1P: $60-$70 | 2P: $60-$70 | XP: $10 | F14 |

Motel        **Location:** Center. 461 Main St 04945 (PO Box 158). Fax: 207/668-9289. **Facility:** 23 units. 22 one- and 1 two-
             bedroom standard units, some with efficiencies. 2 stories (no elevator), exterior corridors. **Parking:** on-site,
             winter plug-ins. **Terms:** office hours 7 am-11 pm, cancellation fee imposed. **Amenities:** hair dryers. **Leisure
Activities:** Fee: game room. **Guest Services:** coin laundry. **Cards:** AX, DS, MC, VI. **Special Amenities:** free expanded continental breakfast and free local telephone calls.

SOME UNITS

[S/D] [&M] [📷] [🖥] / [✕] [VCR] /
                                                                                                FEE

———— WHERE TO DINE ————

**MOOSE POINT TAVERN**                              **Dinner:** $12-$21                     **Phone:** 207/668-4012
(AAA)        **Location:** On US 201; center. 16 Henderson Rd 04945. **Hours:** Open 5/27-3/31; 5 pm-9 pm, Fri & Sat-9:30 pm;
             hours vary seasonally. **Closed:** 11/25, 12/25; also Tues & Wed 9/1-6/30, 10/14-11/1, 11/28-12/25.
▼▼           **Features:** This restaurant has a marvelous setting that borders Big Wood Lake. The menu features fresh
             seafood and meat entrees and flavorful homemade desserts. The attractive rustic dining rooms include
American      patio dining in season. Locals say the food is fantastic. Casual dress; cocktails. **Parking:** on-site.
             **Cards:** AX, DS, MC, VI.

[AC] [✕]

## KENNEBUNK pop. 4,804

─────── **WHERE TO STAY** ───────

**THE KENNEBUNK GALLERY MOTEL & COTTAGES**    *Book at aaa.com*    Phone: (207)985-4543

AAA SAVE

| | | | | |
|---|---|---|---|---|
| 6/18-9/5 | 1P: $84-$114 | 2P: $84-$114 | XP: $10 | F12 |
| 5/14-6/17 & 9/6-10/17 | 1P: $60-$90 | 2P: $60-$90 | XP: $10 | F12 |

Cottage

**Location:** 0.5 mi s of center on US 1. 65 York St 04043. Fax: 207/985-4543. **Facility:** Smoke free premises. 19 units. 5 one-bedroom standard units. 2 two-bedroom suites with kitchens. 12 cottages ($65-$160). 1 story, exterior corridors. *Bath:* combo or shower only. **Parking:** on-site. **Terms:** open 5/14-10/17, office hours 7:30 am-10:30 pm, 3 day cancellation notice-fee imposed. **Pool(s):** outdoor. **Leisure Activities:** playground, basketball, horseshoes, volleyball. **Cards:** AX, DS, MC, VI. **Special Amenities:** free local telephone calls and free room upgrade **(subject to availability with advanced reservations).**

SOME UNITS

**KING'S PORT INN**    Phone: (207)967-4340

AAA SAVE

| | | | | |
|---|---|---|---|---|
| 6/21-9/1 | 1P: $159-$349 | 2P: $159-$349 | XP: $15 | F11 |
| 9/2-4/30 | 1P: $129-$349 | 2P: $129-$349 | XP: $15 | F11 |
| 5/1-6/20 | 1P: $79-$349 | 2P: $79-$349 | XP: $15 | F11 |

Small-scale Hotel

**Location:** Jct SR 35 and 9. 18 Western Ave 04043. Fax: 207/967-4810. **Facility:** 33 units. 32 one-bedroom standard units, some with whirlpools. 1 one-bedroom suite with kitchen and whirlpool. 2 stories (no elevator), interior/exterior corridors. **Parking:** on-site. **Terms:** office hours 7 am-11 pm; 2 night minimum stay - weekends 7/1-8/31, 14 day cancellation notice-fee imposed, [ECP] meal plan available, package plans - seasonal. **Amenities:** voice mail, hair dryers. **Guest Services:** valet laundry. **Business Services:** meeting rooms. **Cards:** AX, DS, MC, VI. **Special Amenities:** free continental breakfast and free local telephone calls. *(See color ad p 236)*

## THE LODGE AT KENNEBUNK

**Phone:** (207)985-9010

| | | | |
|---|---|---|---|
| 6/21-9/6 | 1P: $89 | 2P: $89 | XP: $10 F12 |
| 5/1-6/20 & 9/7-4/30 | 1P: $55 | 2P: $55 | XP: $10 F12 |

AAA SAVE

Motel

**Location:** I-95 (Maine Tpke), exit 25 (Kennebunk), just n on SR 35. 95 Alewive Rd 04043. **Fax:** 207/985-9259. **Facility:** 41 units. 38 one- and 2 two-bedroom standard units, some with whirlpools. 1 two-bedroom suite ($105-$145). 1 story, exterior corridors. *Bath:* some combo or shower only. **Parking:** on-site. **Terms:** 3 day cancellation notice-fee imposed, [CP] & [ECP] meal plans available, package plans, pets ($15 extra charge, in designated unit). **Pool(s):** heated outdoor. **Leisure Activities:** barbecue grills, picnic tables, playground, horseshoes, shuffleboard, volleyball. *Fee:* game room. **Cards:** AX, DS, MC, VI. **Special Amenities:** free expanded continental breakfast and free local telephone calls. *(See color ad p 232)*

SOME UNITS

## THE SEASONS INN OF THE KENNEBUNKS

**Phone:** (207)985-6100

| | | | |
|---|---|---|---|
| All Year | 1P: $59-$169 | 2P: $59-$169 | XP: $10 F8 |

AAA SAVE

Motel

**Location:** I-95 (Maine Tpke), exit 25 (Kennebunk), 2 mi e on SR 35 to jct US 1, then 0.9 mi s. 55 York St 04043 (PO Box 669, WELLS, 04090). **Fax:** 207/985-4031. **Facility:** Smoke free premises. 46 units. 45 one-bedroom standard units. 1 one-bedroom suite. 2 stories (no elevator), exterior corridors. **Parking:** on-site. **Terms:** [CP] meal plan available. **Amenities:** hair dryers. *Some:* irons. **Pool(s):** outdoor. **Cards:** AX, CB, DC, DS, MC, VI. *(See color ad p 232)*

SOME UNITS

## TURNPIKE MOTEL

**Phone:** 207/985-4404

| | | | |
|---|---|---|---|
| 7/1-9/6 | 1P: $80 | 2P: $80 | XP: $5 |
| 9/7-10/31 | 1P: $63 | 2P: $63 | XP: $5 |
| 5/1-6/30 | 1P: $55 | 2P: $55 | XP: $5 |
| 11/1-4/30 | 1P: $49 | 2P: $49 | XP: $5 |

AAA SAVE

Motel

**Location:** I-95 (Maine Tpke), exit 25 (Kennebunk). 77 Old Alewive Rd 04043. **Facility:** 24 one-bedroom standard units. 2 stories (no elevator), interior/exterior corridors. *Bath:* combo or shower only. **Parking:** on-site. **Terms:** office hours 8 am-10 pm, 7 day cancellation notice-fee imposed. **Cards:** MC, VI. **Special Amenities:** free local telephone calls.

SOME UNITS

## WALDO EMERSON INN

**Phone:** (207)985-4250

| | | |
|---|---|---|
| 5/1-10/30 [BP] | 2P: $125-$140 | XP: $15 |
| 10/31-4/30 [BP] | 2P: $95-$115 | XP: $15 |

Historic Bed & Breakfast

**Location:** Jct US 1/SR 35, 1 mi e. Located adjacent to Wedding Cake House. 108 Summer St 04043. **Fax:** 207/985-4250. **Facility:** This restored inn dating from 1753 offers pleasant public areas and handsomely appointed guest rooms. Smoke free premises. 4 one-bedroom standard units. 3 stories (no elevator), interior corridors. *Bath:* combo or shower only. **Parking:** on-site. **Terms:** age restrictions may apply, no pets allowed (owner's pet on premises). **Guest Services:** TV in common area, gift shop, complimentary evening beverages. **Cards:** AX, DC, MC, VI.

------- **WHERE TO DINE** -------

## FEDERAL JACK'S RESTAURANT & BREWPUB

**Lunch:** $6-$17    **Dinner:** $6-$17    **Phone:** 207/967-4322

American

**Location:** Jct SR 35 and 9, just e; before bridge to Dock Square. 8 Western Ave 04043. **Hours:** 11:30 am-10 pm. Closed: 11/25, 12/24, 12/25. **Features:** On the site of a former shipyard, the restaurant affords wonderful views of the Kennebunk River. Diners can tour the brewery or sample one of the many hand-crafted beers. The menu includes a variety of salads, sandwiches, wraps and burgers, as well as pasta, seafood, lamb, steak and chicken entrees. Seafood paella is outstanding. Casual dress; cocktails. **Parking:** on-site. **Cards:** AX, DS, MC, VI.

## GRISSINI ITALIAN BISTRO

**Dinner:** $16-$22    **Phone:** 207/967-2211

Italian

**Location:** US 1, 4 mi e on SR 35 and 9A; from Dock Square, 0.4 mi w on SR 35 and 9A. 27 Western Ave 04043. **Hours:** 5:30 pm-9 pm, Fri-9:30 pm, Sat 5 pm-9:30 pm; hours vary off season. Closed: 11/25. **Reservations:** suggested. **Features:** An elegant bistro featuring a flavorful array of dishes such as osso buco, linguine Bolognese, wood-grilled pizza and baked chicken stuffed with herb cream cheese. The very good staff can help you choose from their fine selection of wines. Casual dress; cocktails. **Parking:** on-site. **Cards:** AX, MC, VI. *(See color ad p 240)*

## KENNEBUNK INN DINING ROOM   Historic

**Dinner:** $16-$23    **Phone:** 207/985-3351

American

**Location:** On US 1; center of village. 45 Main St 04043. **Hours:** 5 pm-9 pm. Closed: 12/25. **Reservations:** suggested. **Features:** Enjoy pleasant country inn decor in this historic 1799 building. Smoking is permitted only in the lounge. A pub menu is available for light fare. Cocktails. **Parking:** on-site. **Cards:** AX, DS, MC, VI.

## MEKHONG THAI RESTAURANT

**Lunch:** $5-$8    **Dinner:** $7-$13    **Phone:** 207/967-8827

Ethnic

**Location:** Just w of jct SR 9 and 35; in Lower Village Shopping Center, 0.5 mi w of Dock Square Kennebunkport. 37 Western Ave #2 04043. **Hours:** 11 am-9 pm, Sat & Sun-9:30 pm; Fri & Sat-10 pm in summer. Closed: Mon 10/9-3/31. **Features:** This restaurant features a good menu variety of well-prepared seafood, chicken, stir-fry, curry and ginger dishes. The warm and homey atmosphere offers table or floor-cushion seating for guests. The staff is friendly, prompt and knowledgeable. Casual dress; cocktails. **Parking:** on-site. **Cards:** AX, MC, VI.

## ON THE MARSH RESTAURANT

**Dinner:** $18-$29    **Phone:** 207/967-2299

Continental

**Location:** Jct US 1, 5 mi e on SR 9. 46 Western Ave 04043. **Hours:** Open 5/1-1/1 & 1/24-4/30; 5:30 pm-close. Closed: 12/25. **Reservations:** suggested. **Features:** The lovely setting overlooks the salt marshes and colorful perennial gardens. In an 1800 converted barn, the restaurant features a romantic ambience, upscale rustic decor and attractive table settings. The menu centers on European classic country cuisine with excellent flavors. Sushi on the balcony. The wine list is award-winning. Casual dress; cocktails; entertainment. **Parking:** on-site. **Cards:** AX, MC, VI.

**WINDOWS ON THE WATER**

AAA

American

| | | |
|---|---|---|
| Lunch: $7-$38 | Dinner: $20-$39 | Phone: 207/967-3313 |

**Location:** Jct SR 35 and 9, just e on SR 9 to Chase. 12 Chase Hill Rd 04043. **Hours:** 11:45 am-2:30 & 5:30-9:30 pm, Fri & Sat-10:30 pm; Fri-Sun to 9:30 pm 10/21-6/19. Closed: 12/25. **Reservations:** suggested. **Features:** This small, cozy restaurant overlooks Kennebunkport harbor and river. Their signature dish is the thick and creamy lobster bisque. The California-style lobster ravioli, roasted rack of lamb and creme brulee are excellent also. Professional service. Casual dress; cocktails. **Parking:** on-site. **Cards:** AX, DC, DS, MC, VI.

---

# KENNEBUNK BEACH

## ——— WHERE TO STAY ———

**THE BEACH HOUSE INN**

AAA SAVE

Historic Bed & Breakfast

**Phone:** (207)967-3850

| | | |
|---|---|---|
| 7/2-9/5 [ECP] | 1P: $255-$445 | 2P: $255-$445 |
| 5/1-7/1 [ECP] | 1P: $185-$395 | 2P: $185-$395 |
| 9/6-10/30 [ECP] | 1P: $185-$390 | 2P: $185-$390 |
| 10/31-4/30 [ECP] | 1P: $155-$345 | 2P: $155-$345 |

**Location:** On the ocean. 211 Beach Ave 04043 (PO Box 560C, KENNEBUNKPORT, 04046). Fax: 207/967-4719. **Facility:** The inn offers several rooms with ocean views and others with a partial view of the water. Smoke free premises. 34 one-bedroom standard units, some with whirlpools. 4 stories, interior corridors. **Parking:** on-site. **Terms:** 2 night minimum stay - weekends, 30 day cancellation notice-fee imposed, package plans - seasonal. **Amenities:** video library, CD players, voice mail, irons, hair dryers. **Cards:** AX, MC, VI. *(See color ad p 240)*

**THE WHITE BARN INN**

AAA SAVE

Historic Country Inn

**Phone:** (207)967-2321

| | | |
|---|---|---|
| 9/1-10/31 [MAP] | | 2P: $510-$926 |
| 6/15-8/31 [ECP] | 1P: $335-$750 | 2P: $335-$750 |
| 11/1-4/30 [ECP] | 1P: $305-$740 | 2P: $305-$740 |
| 5/1-6/14 [ECP] | 1P: $315-$700 | 2P: $315-$700 |

**Location:** I-95 (Maine Tpke), exit 25 (Kennebunk), 7 mi e on SR 35. 37 Beach Ave 04043 (PO Box 560C, KENNEBUNK-PORT, 04046). Fax: 207/967-1100. **Facility:** This handsome 19th-century country inn features well-designed public rooms and lodgings as well as elegant cottages. Designated smoking area. 28 units. 25 one-bedroom standard units, some with whirlpools. 3 cottages. 3 stories (no elevator), interior/exterior corridors. **Parking:** on-site and valet. **Terms:** 2 night minimum stay - weekends, age restrictions may apply, 30 day cancellation notice-fee imposed, package plans - seasonal. **Amenities:** CD players, voice mail, irons, hair dryers. **Dining:** restaurant, see separate listing. **Pool(s):** heated outdoor. **Leisure Activities:** bicycles, in-room spa service. *Fee:* boats, charter fishing, tennis & golf privileges. **Guest Services:** valet laundry. **Business Services:** meeting rooms, business center. **Cards:** AX, MC, VI. *(See color ad p 239)*

## ——— WHERE TO DINE ———

**THE WHITE BARN INN** Country Inn

AAA

American

| | |
|---|---|
| Dinner: $83 | Phone: 207/967-2321 |

**Location:** I-95 (Maine Tpke), exit 25 (Kennebunk), 7 mi e on SR 35; in The White Barn Inn. 37 Beach Ave 04043. **Hours:** Open 5/1-1/3 & 1/18-4/30; 6 pm-9:15 pm, Fri-Sun from 5:30 pm. Closed: Mon & Tues 1/18-4/1. **Reservations:** suggested. **Features:** Rustic, elegant country decor in a beautifully renovated barn. The menu, which varies weekly, features outstanding American cuisine with emphasis on New England. While the atmosphere is formal-jackets are required for gentlemen-it is still relaxed. Floor-length table linens, formally attired staff, and a grand piano contrast wonderfully with the rustic nature of the barn, the memorabilia in the hayloft, old silverware table sculptures, and the shiny copper bar top. Service is first class. Semi-formal attire; cocktails; entertainment. **Parking:** on-site and valet. **Cards:** AX, MC, VI. *(See color ad p 239)*

---

# KENNEBUNKPORT pop. 1,376

## ——— WHERE TO STAY ———

**1802 HOUSE BED & BREAKFAST INN**

AAA SAVE

Bed & Breakfast

**Phone:** (207)967-5632

| | | |
|---|---|---|
| 6/18-11/1 | 1P: $169-$369 | 2P: $169-$369 |
| 11/2-4/30 | 1P: $139-$339 | 2P: $139-$339 |
| 5/1-6/17 | 1P: $139-$299 | 2P: $139-$299 |

**Location:** Dock Square; 0.3 mi e on SR 9 to stop sign, nw on Maine St/North St to Locke St, then just w. 15 Locke St 04046 (PO Box 646-A, 04046-1646). Fax: 207/967-0780. **Facility:** A secluded setting, attractive common rooms and well-furnished accommodations characterize this B&B; a golf course is adjacent. Smoke free premises. 6 units. 5 one-bedroom standard units, some with whirlpools. 1 one-bedroom suite ($259-$379) with whirlpool. 2 stories (no elevator), interior corridors. *Bath:* combo or shower only. **Parking:** on-site. **Terms:** 2 night minimum stay - weekends, age restrictions may apply, 14 day cancellation notice-fee imposed, [BP] meal plan available. **Amenities:** video library, CD players, hair dryers. **Cards:** AX, DS, MC, VI. **Special Amenities:** free full breakfast and free room upgrade (subject to availability with advanced reservations).

SOME UNITS

**CAPTAIN FAIRFIELD INN**

AAA SAVE

Historic Bed & Breakfast

**Phone:** 207/967-4454

| | | |
|---|---|---|
| 6/18-10/23 [BP] | 2P: $150-$295 | XP: $25 |
| 5/1-6/17 & 10/24-4/30 [BP] | 2P: $110-$250 | XP: $25 |

**Location:** Dock Square; 0.3 mi e on Ocean Ave, just n; corner of Green and Pleasant sts. Located in a quiet area. 8 Pleasant St 04046 (PO Box 2690). Fax: 207/967-8537. **Facility:** A four-course breakfast is served at this 1813 sea captain's home, which is set in a quiet area and furnished with antiques and period pieces. Smoke free premises. 9 one-bedroom standard units, some with whirlpools. 2 stories (no elevator), interior corridors. *Bath:* combo or shower only. **Parking:** on-site. **Terms:** 2 night minimum stay - weekends, 14 day cancellation notice-fee imposed. **Amenities:** hair dryers. **Cards:** AX, DC, DS, MC, VI. **Special Amenities:** free full breakfast and free local telephone calls.

SOME UNITS

## THE CAPTAIN JEFFERDS INN

**Phone:** (207)967-2311

AAA SAVE

Bed & Breakfast

| | | | |
|---|---|---|---|
| 5/1-10/31 [BP] | 1P: $165-$340 | 2P: $165-$340 | XP: $40 |
| 11/1-4/30 [BP] | 1P: $110-$340 | 2P: $110-$340 | XP: $40 |

**Location:** Dock Square; 0.3 mi e on Maine St, just s; corner of Pearl and Pleasant sts. 5 Pearl St 04046 (PO Box 691). **Fax:** 207/967-0721. **Facility:** 1804 Federal-style mansion offers a variety of room styles, color schemes and intangibles that make this inn a special place. 15 units. 14 one-bedroom standard units, some with whirlpools. 1 one-bedroom suite. 3 stories (no elevator), interior/exterior corridors. *Bath:* combo or shower only. **Parking:** on-site. **Terms:** 2-3 night minimum stay - weekends, 14 day cancellation notice-fee imposed, small pets only ($30 extra charge). **Amenities:** CD players, hair dryers. **Cards:** AX, MC, VI. **Special Amenities:** free full breakfast and free local telephone calls.

SOME UNITS
🛏 ✕ / 📺 VCR 📞 /
FEE

## CAPTAIN LORD MANSION

**Phone:** 207/967-3141

AAA SAVE

Historic Bed & Breakfast

| | | | |
|---|---|---|---|
| 7/1-10/31 [BP] | 1P: $204-$399 | 2P: $204-$399 | XP: $75 |
| 11/1-4/30 [BP] | 1P: $169-$349 | 2P: $169-$349 | XP: $50 |
| 5/1-6/30 [BP] | 1P: $149-$329 | 2P: $149-$329 | XP: $50 |

**Location:** Dock Square; 0.3 mi on Ocean Ave, left turn at sign. 6 Pleasant St 04046-0800 (PO Box 800). **Fax:** 207/967-3172. **Facility:** Guest rooms in this restored Federalist-style home feature fine furnishings and decor that is well coordinated. Smoke free premises. 16 one-bedroom standard units. 1 three-bedroom suite. 3 stories (no elevator), interior corridors. *Bath:* combo or shower only. **Parking:** on-site. **Terms:** 2 night minimum stay - weekends, 15 day cancellation notice-fee imposed. **Amenities:** CD players, voice mail, hair dryers. **Guest Services:** gift shop. **Business Services:** meeting rooms. **Cards:** AX, CB, DC, DS, MC, VI. **Special Amenities:** free full breakfast and free local telephone calls.

SOME UNITS
✕ DATA PORT / 📺 VCR 📞 /

## THE COLONY HOTEL    *Book at aaa.com*

**Phone:** 207/967-3331

AAA SAVE

Historic Small-scale Hotel

| | | | |
|---|---|---|---|
| 6/28-9/7 [BP] | 1P: $190-$435 | 2P: $190-$435 | XP: $25 |
| 9/8-10/24 [BP] | 1P: $145-$270 | 2P: $145-$270 | XP: $25 |
| 5/14-6/27 [BP] | 1P: $135-$260 | 2P: $135-$260 | XP: $25 |

**Location:** Dock Square; 1 mi s. 140 Ocean Ave 04046 (PO Box 511). **Fax:** 207/967-8738. **Facility:** Well-manicured grounds surround this classic turn-of-the-twentieth-century hotel overlooking the ocean. Designated smoking area. 124 units. 111 one- and 12 two-bedroom standard units. 1 three-bedroom suite. 2-3 stories, interior corridors. **Parking:** on-site. **Terms:** open 5/14-10/24, check-in 4 pm, 2 night minimum stay - weekends, 3 night 7/1-8/31, 3 day cancellation notice, $5 service charge, pets ($25 extra charge). **Amenities:** voice mail, irons, hair dryers. **Dining:** 7:30 am-9 & 6-9 pm; noon-2 pm 7/1-8/31, cocktails. **Leisure Activities:** putting green, recreation programs, badminton, bocci, croquet, shuffleboard. *Fee:* bicycles. **Guest Services:** gift shop. **Business Services:** meeting rooms. **Cards:** AX, MC, VI.

SOME UNITS
🛏 🍴 🍽 🏊 ✕ ✕ 🅰 DATA PORT / 📺 📞 🖥 /
FEE

## THE INN AT GOOSE ROCKS

**Phone:** (207)967-5425

Country Inn

| | | | | |
|---|---|---|---|---|
| 6/18-9/23 | 1P: $125-$175 | 2P: $125-$175 | XP: $10 | F15 |
| 9/24-10/24 | 1P: $85-$155 | 2P: $85-$155 | XP: $10 | F15 |
| 5/1-6/17 & 10/25-4/30 | 1P: $65-$155 | 2P: $65-$155 | XP: $10 | F15 |

**Location:** I-95 (Maine Tpke), exit 25, 5 mi e on SR 35 to SR 9, 6 mi e to Dyke Rd, then just s on road toward Goose Rocks Beach (Dyke Rd). 71 Dyke Rd 04046. **Fax:** 207/967-0204. **Facility:** On a wooded knoll above a salt marsh, the inn is decorated with Colonial-style furnishings and is within walking distance of Goose Rocks Beach. Smoke free premises. 32 one-bedroom standard units. 2 stories (no elevator), interior corridors. **Parking:** on-site. **Terms:** 2-3 night minimum stay - seasonal weekends, cancellation fee imposed, no pets allowed (owner's pet on premises). **Dining:** Goose Fare Dining Room, see separate listing. **Pool(s):** outdoor. **Leisure Activities:** whirlpools. **Guest Services:** gift shop. **Business Services:** meeting rooms. **Cards:** AX, DS, MC, VI.

SOME UNITS
🍴 🏊 ✕ 🖥 / VCR 📞
FEE

## THE INN ON SOUTH STREET

**Phone:** (207)967-5151

AAA SAVE

Bed & Breakfast

| | | | |
|---|---|---|---|
| 5/1-5/31 & 11/1-4/30 [BP] | 1P: $135-$185 | 2P: $135-$185 | |
| 6/1-10/31 [BP] | 1P: $185 | 2P: $185 | |

**Location:** Dock Square; 0.4 mi e on Maine St, then s. 5 South St 04046 (PO Box 529A). **Fax:** 207/967-4385. **Facility:** This 19th-century Federal-style inn has modern amenities with the feeling of yesteryear. Designated smoking area. 4 units. 3 one-bedroom standard units. 1 one-bedroom suite ($195-$275) with kitchen and whirlpool. 3 stories (no elevator), interior/exterior corridors. *Bath:* combo or shower only. **Parking:** on-site. **Terms:** 2 night minimum stay - seasonal, age restrictions may apply, 14 day cancellation notice. **Amenities:** CD players, irons, hair dryers. **Cards:** MC, VI. **Special Amenities:** free full breakfast and free local telephone calls.

✕ 📞

## THE KENNEBUNKPORT INN    *Book at aaa.com*

**Phone:** 207/967-2621

Country Inn

| | | | | |
|---|---|---|---|---|
| 6/25-10/14 | 1P: $179-$299 | 2P: $179-$299 | XP: $20 | F12 |
| 5/1-6/24 | 1P: $139-$299 | 2P: $139-$299 | XP: $20 | F12 |
| 10/15-4/30 | 1P: $89-$299 | 2P: $89-$299 | XP: $20 | F12 |

**Location:** Just up hill from Dock Square; center of downtown. 1 Dock Square 04046 (PO Box 111). **Fax:** 207/967-3705. **Facility:** Some luxury accommodations are offered at this 1890s sea captain's home and annex, which are in the heart of the village. Smoke free premises. 35 units. 34 one- and 1 two-bedroom standard units, some with kitchens and/or whirlpools. 3 stories (no elevator), interior corridors. *Bath:* combo or shower only. **Parking:** on-site. **Terms:** 2-3 night minimum stay - seasonal, 14 day cancellation notice-fee imposed, [BP] & [CP] meal plans available. **Amenities:** voice mail, irons, hair dryers. **Dining:** dining room, see separate listing. **Pool(s):** outdoor. **Cards:** AX, MC, VI.

SOME UNITS
🍴 🍽 🏊 ✕ DATA PORT / 📞 🖥 🖥 /

**KILBURN HOUSE**

Bed & Breakfast

| | 5/1-10/31 [BP] | 1P: $145-$195 | 2P: $145-$195 |
| | 11/1-4/30 [BP] | 1P: $99-$165 | 2P: $99-$165 |

**Phone:** 207/967-4762
XP: $50
XP: $50

**Location:** Just e of Dock Square; just off Ocean Ave. 6 Chestnut St 04046 (PO Box 424). Fax: 207/967-1065. **Facility:** In the center of a village, this 1890s Victorian inn has modern amenities and offers sunny rooms with attractive decor. Smoke free premises. 4 units. 3 one-bedroom standard units. 1 two-bedroom suite ($210-$395). 3 stories (no elevator), interior corridors. *Bath:* combo or shower only. **Parking:** on-site. **Terms:** check-in 4 pm, 2 night minimum stay - weekends, 6-10 nights seasonal, age restrictions may apply, 14 day cancellation notice-fee imposed, package plans - 11/1-5/31, no pets allowed (owner's pet on premises). **Amenities:** hair dryers. **Cards:** MC, VI.

SOME UNITS

## LODGE AT TURBAT'S CREEK

[AAA] [SAVE]
[diamonds]

Motel

| | | | | |
|---|---|---|---|---|
| 6/16-10/22 [ECP] | 1P: $99-$169 | 2P: $99-$169 | XP: $15 | F11 |
| 5/1-6/15 & 10/23-12/6 [ECP] | 1P: $79-$169 | 2P: $79-$169 | XP: $15 | F11 |

Phone: (207)967-8700

**Location:** Dock Square; 0.5 mi e on Maine St, 0.6 mi ne on Wildes, then just se. 7 Turbat's Creek Rd 04046 (PO Box 2722). Fax: 207/967-0528. **Facility:** 26 one-bedroom standard units. 2 stories (no elevator), exterior corridors. **Parking:** on-site. **Terms:** open 5/1-12/6, office hours 8 am-11 pm, 14 day cancellation notice-fee imposed, pets (in limited units, with prior approval). **Amenities:** voice mail, hair dryers. **Pool(s):** heated outdoor. **Leisure Activities:** bicycles. **Guest Services:** valet laundry. **Business Services:** fax. **Cards:** AX, DS, MC, VI. **Special Amenities:** free expanded continental breakfast and free newspaper. *(See color ad p 236)*

[SD] [pets] [wheelchair] [swim] [X] [film] [DATA PORT] [icon]

## MAINE STAY INN & COTTAGES AT THE MELVILLE WALKER HOUSE

[AAA] [SAVE]
[diamonds]

Bed & Breakfast

| | | | |
|---|---|---|---|
| 6/6-10/19 [BP] | | 2P: $139-$259 | XP: $25 | D12 |
| 1/1-4/30 [BP] | | 2P: $119-$239 | XP: $25 | D12 |
| 5/1-6/5 & 10/20-12/31 [BP] | | 2P: $109-$229 | XP: $25 | D12 |

Phone: (207)967-2117

**Location:** Dock Square; just e on SR 9 to Maine St, then just s. 34 Maine St 04046 (PO Box 500A). Fax: 207/967-8757. **Facility:** Dating from the 1860s, the inn offers rooms and suites of various sizes in the main inn as well as one-bedroom cottages with kitchens. Smoke free premises. 17 units. 14 one-bedroom standard units, some with kitchens and/or whirlpools. 2 one- and 1 two-bedroom suites, some with kitchens and/or whirlpools. 2 stories (no elevator), interior/exterior corridors. *Bath:* combo or shower only. **Parking:** on-site. **Terms:** 14 day cancellation notice-fee imposed, package plans - weekends off season. **Amenities:** video library, hair dryers. **Cards:** DS, MC, VI.

SOME UNITS

[X] [VCR] [film] [Z] / [icon] [icon] [icon] /

## THE NONANTUM RESORT

[AAA] [SAVE]
[diamonds]

Small-scale Hotel

| | | | |
|---|---|---|---|
| 6/19-9/5 [BP] | 1P: $199-$309 | 2P: $199-$309 | XP: $25 | F12 |
| 9/6-10/16 [BP] | 1P: $139-$299 | 2P: $139-$299 | XP: $25 | F12 |
| 5/1-6/18 [BP] | 1P: $139-$259 | 2P: $139-$259 | XP: $25 | F12 |
| 10/17-11/14 [BP] | 1P: $139-$199 | 2P: $139-$199 | XP: $25 | F12 |

Phone: (207)967-4050

**Location:** Dock Square; 0.6 mi e; center. 95 Ocean Ave 04046 (PO Box 2626). Fax: 207/967-8451. **Facility:** 115 units. 106 one- and 7 two-bedroom standard units, some with efficiencies and/or whirlpools. 2 one-bedroom suites ($199-$329), some with efficiencies. 3-4 stories, interior corridors. *Bath:* combo or shower only. **Parking:** on-site. **Terms:** open 5/1-11/14, 2 night minimum stay - weekends, cancellation fee imposed, package plans - weekdays. **Amenities:** *Some:* irons, hair dryers. **Dining:** 7:30 am-10 & 5:30-9 pm, cocktails. **Pool(s):** heated outdoor. **Leisure Activities:** whirlpool, fishing. *Fee:* sailing & scenic cruises. **Business Services:** meeting rooms. **Cards:** CB, DC, DS, MC, VI. **Special Amenities:** free full breakfast and free newspaper. *(See color ad p 238 & below)*

SOME UNITS

[SD] [fork] [swim] [X] [X] [DATA PORT] / [icon] [icon] [icon] /

## OLD FORT INN

Phone: (207)967-5353

AAA SAVE
Historic Bed & Breakfast

| | | | |
|---|---|---|---|
| 6/18-12/6 | 1P: $155-$275 | 2P: $175-$425 | XP: $50 |
| 5/1-6/17 | 1P: $99-$175 | 2P: $125-$375 | XP: $50 |

**Location:** Dock Square; 1 mi s on Ocean Ave, 0.3 mi se via Kings Hwy. Located in a quiet area. 8 Old Fort Ave 04046 (PO Box M). Fax: 207/967-4547. **Facility:** Antiques and country-inn decor enhance this converted 1900s carriage house; the property is within walking distance of the ocean. Smoke free premises. 16 units. 14 one-bedroom standard units, some with whirlpools. 1 one- and 1 two-bedroom suites with whirlpools: 2 stories (no elevator), interior corridors. *Bath:* combo or shower only. **Parking:** on-site. **Terms:** open 5/1-12/6, 2 night minimum stay - weekends, age restrictions may apply, 15 day cancellation notice, [BP] meal plan available. **Amenities:** honor bars, irons, hair dryers. **Pool(s):** heated outdoor. **Leisure Activities:** tennis court, horseshoes. **Guest Services:** gift shop, coin laundry. **Cards:** AX, DC, DS, MC, VI. **Special Amenities:** free full breakfast and free local telephone calls.

SOME UNITS

## RHUMB LINE MOTOR LODGE

Phone: (207)967-5457

Small-scale Hotel

| | | | | |
|---|---|---|---|---|
| 6/11-9/5 | 1P: $139-$175 | 2P: $149-$175 | XP: $10 | F12 |
| 9/6-12/30 | 1P: $79-$129 | 2P: $89-$135 | XP: $10 | F12 |
| 5/1-6/10 | 1P: $99-$129 | 2P: $89-$129 | XP: $10 | F12 |
| 2/4-4/30 | 1P: $79-$129 | 2P: $89-$129 | XP: $10 | F12 |

**Location:** 3 mi e. Located in a residential area. Ocean Ave 04046 (PO Box 3067). Fax: 207/967-4418. **Facility:** 59 one-bedroom standard units, some with efficiencies or kitchens. 2 stories (no elevator), interior/exterior corridors. **Parking:** on-site. **Terms:** open 5/1-12/30 & 2/4-4/30, office hours 8 am-10 pm, 2 night minimum stay - weekends in season, 7 day cancellation notice, [CP] meal plan available, package plans, $3 service charge. **Amenities:** voice mail, irons, hair dryers. **Pool(s):** heated outdoor, heated indoor. **Leisure Activities:** sauna, whirlpools, exercise room. **Business Services:** meeting rooms. **Cards:** AX, DS, MC, VI. *(See color ad below)*

SOME UNITS

## SCHOONERS INN

Phone: (207)967-5333

AAA SAVE
Small-scale Hotel

| | | | |
|---|---|---|---|
| 6/20-10/17 [ECP] | 1P: $245-$345 | 2P: $245-$345 | |
| 5/24-6/19 [ECP] | 1P: $275-$310 | 2P: $275-$310 | |
| 5/1-5/23 [ECP] | 1P: $195-$275 | 2P: $195-$275 | |
| 10/18-4/30 [ECP] | 1P: $150-$225 | 2P: $150-$225 | |

**Location:** 1 mi e from Dock Square on Ocean Ave; close to the mouth of the Kennebunk River. 127 Ocean Ave 04046 (PO Box 560C). Fax: 207/967-2040. **Facility:** Smoke free premises. 17 one-bedroom standard units, some with whirlpools. 3 stories, interior corridors. **Parking:** on-site. **Terms:** office hours 7 am-8 pm, 2 night minimum stay - some weekends, 30 day cancellation notice-fee imposed, package plans - seasonal. **Amenities:** CD players, voice mail, irons, hair dryers. **Dining:** Stripers Fish Shack, see separate listing. **Leisure Activities:** bicycles. *Fee:* charter fishing, golf privileges, tennis privileges. **Business Services:** meeting rooms. **Cards:** AX, MC, VI. *(See color ad on p 239)*

## VILLAGE COVE INN

Phone: (207)967-3993

Small-scale Hotel

| | | | |
|---|---|---|---|
| 6/18-9/5 [BP] | 1P: $119-$209 | 2P: $129-$219 | XP: $25 | F12 |
| 9/6-12/12 [BP] | 1P: $99-$169 | 2P: $109-$189 | XP: $25 | F12 |
| 5/1-6/17 & 2/4-4/30 [BP] | 1P: $89-$149 | 2P: $99-$179 | XP: $25 | F12 |

**Location:** Dock Square; 0.3 mi e on SR 9, straight at turn-off, follow signs. 29 S Main St 04046 (PO Box 650). Fax: 207/967-3164. **Facility:** 33 units. 32 one-bedroom standard units, some with whirlpools. 1 two-bedroom suite with kitchen. 1-2 stories (no elevator), interior/exterior corridors. *Bath:* combo or shower only. **Parking:** on-site. **Terms:** open 5/1-12/12 & 2/4-4/30, 2 night minimum stay - weekends, 14 day cancellation notice-fee imposed, [CP] meal plan available, package plans, $6 service charge. **Amenities:** hair dryers. **Pool(s):** heated outdoor, heated indoor. **Leisure Activities:** exercise room. **Business Services:** meeting rooms. **Cards:** AX, DS, MC, VI. *(See color ad below & p 239)*

SOME UNITS

# Stay on the Water...
## Dine in TUSCANY

### THE BEACH HOUSE

A romantic Victorian inn on the ocean furnished with period antiques. Hearty continental breakfast and afternoon tea served daily from the famed White Barn Inn kitchen. Canoes and bikes available. Great seasonal packages

211 Beach Avenue
P.O. Box 560C
Kennebunkport, Maine 04046
207-967-3850
email:innkeeper@beachhseinn.com
www.beachhseinn.com

### GRISSINI RESTAURANT

An Italian bistro with expansive stone hearth welcomes diners to enjoy authentic Tuscan food cooked in wood burning ovens. Breads and pastries baked on the premises. Open Nightly.

27 Western Avenue
Kennebunk, Maine 04043
207-967-2211
email:info@restaurantgrissini.com
www.restaurantgrissini.com

### THE YACHTSMAN LODGE

Luxurious rooms with private patios at the water's edge. Enjoy our abundant continental breakfast and afternoon tea overlooking the marina. Canoes and bikes available. Open from April – December.

Ocean Avenue
P.O. Box 560C
Kennebunkport, Maine 04046
207-967-2511
email:innkeeper@yachtsmanlodge.com
www.yachtsmanlodge.com

## THE YACHTSMAN LODGE & MARINA

AAA SAVE

WWW WWW

Motel

| | | |
|---|---|---|
| 6/14-10/11 [ECP] | 1P: $299-$314 | 2P: $299-$314 |
| 5/1-6/13 [ECP] | 1P: $189-$209 | 2P: $189-$209 |
| 10/12-12/5 [ECP] | 1P: $159-$189 | 2P: $159-$189 |

Phone: (207)967-2511

**Location:** Dock Square; 0.3 mi e. 57 Ocean Ave 04046 (PO Box 560C). Fax: 207/967-5056. **Facility:** Within walking distance of Dock Square, the Yachtsman overlooks the marina and Kennebunk River and has a private riverside patio. 30 one-bedroom standard units. 1 story, exterior corridors. **Parking:** on-site. **Terms:** open 5/1-12/5, 2 night minimum stay - weekends, 30 day cancellation notice-fee imposed, package plans - seasonal, pets ($19 extra charge). **Amenities:** CD players, voice mail, irons, hair dryers. **Leisure Activities:** canoeing, bicycles. *Fee:* marina, fishing, golf privileges, massage. **Guest Services:** valet laundry. **Cards:** AX, MC, VI. *(See color ad p 240)*

FEE

--------- WHERE TO DINE ---------

## ALISSON'S RESTAURANT

WWW WWW

Seafood

**Lunch:** $5-$14    **Dinner:** $11-$20    Phone: 207/967-4841

**Location:** Center. 11 Dock Square 04046. **Hours:** 11 am-10 pm, Fri & Sat-11 pm; Fri & Sat-9 pm off season. Closed: 11/25, 12/24, 12/25. **Features:** A favorite with both residents and visitors, this is the place to see and be seen in Kennebunkport. The casual, family-friendly restaurant specializes in seafood, but the menu also includes other selections, such as burgers, sandwiches, pasta, chicken and steak. There are two "can't misses"—the delicious lobster rolls and the flavorful chowder. Casual dress; cocktails. **Parking:** street. **Cards:** AX, DS, MC, VI.

## ARUNDEL WHARF RESTAURANT

AAA

WWWWW

American

**Lunch:** $4-$24    **Dinner:** $14-$30    Phone: 207/967-3444

**Location:** Just e of Dock Square. 43 Ocean Ave 04046. **Hours:** Open 5/1-10/31 & 4/15-4/30; 11:30 am-9:30 pm. **Reservations:** suggested. **Features:** This attractive harborfront restaurant features well-prepared fresh local seafood. Lighter fare is offered at lunch. The casual atmosphere displays a nautical decor that's comfortable and relaxed. Dining on the deck is offered, weather permitting. Cocktails. **Parking:** on-site. **Cards:** AX, DC, DS, MC, VI.

## CAPE ARUNDEL INN

WWWW

American

**Dinner:** $20-$44    Phone: 207/967-2125

**Location:** Dock Square; 2 mi e on Ocean Ave, corner of Ocean and Summit aves. 208 Ocean Ave 04046. **Hours:** Open 5/1-1/1 & 3/1-4/30; 5:30 pm-9 pm. Closed: 12/24, 12/25. **Reservations:** suggested. **Features:** This is a shingle-style Oceanside "cottage-turned-country-inn" with lovely views of the ocean as well as Walker's Point. The menu features American cuisine including seafood, beef and game, along with desserts made on the premises. Upscale, casual attire is the norm. Casual dress; cocktails. **Parking:** on-site. **Cards:** AX, DS, MC, VI.

## GOOSE FARE DINING ROOM

WWW

American

**Dinner:** $14-$25    Phone: 207/967-5425

**Location:** I-95 (Maine Tpke), exit 25 (Kennebunk), 5 mi e on SR 35 to SR 9, 6 mi e to Dyke Rd, then just s on road toward Goose Rocks Beach (Dyke Rd); in The Inn at Goose Rocks. 71 Dyke Rd 04046. **Hours:** 8 am-10 & 5:30-9 pm, Sat & Sun 8 am-11 & 5:30-9 pm. Closed: for dinner Tues & Sun; for dinner Sun-Wed 9/6-6/30. **Reservations:** suggested. **Features:** The Goose Fare is a traditional New England inn with a family atmosphere. The regional cuisine offers seafood, chicken and beef dishes and includes fresh seasonal produce and herbs grown on the premises. Windows overlook the beautiful wooded landscape. Casual dress; cocktails. **Parking:** on-site. **Cards:** AX, DS, MC, VI.

## HURRICANE RESTAURANT

WWWW

American

**Lunch:** $7-$15    **Dinner:** $17-$39    Phone: 207/967-9111

**Location:** Center. 29 Dock Square 04046. **Hours:** Open 5/1-12/9 & 2/12-4/30; 11:30 am-10:30 pm; to 9:30 pm Sun-Thurs 2/12-5/15. **Reservations:** suggested. **Features:** Located on Dock Square, this upscale eatery is open for lunch and dinner. Casual dress; cocktails. **Parking:** on-site (fee). **Cards:** AX, DC, DS, MC, VI.

## MABEL'S LOBSTER CLAW

WWWW

Seafood

**Lunch:** $8-$16    **Dinner:** $14-$28    Phone: 207/967-2562

**Location:** Dock Square; 1 mi e on Ocean Ave; close to mouth of Kennebunk River. 124 Ocean Ave 04046. **Hours:** Open 5/1-10/30 & 4/1-4/30; 11:30 am-3 & 5-9 pm. **Reservations:** suggested. **Features:** This popular restaurant has an excellent location close to the water. The decor features knotty-pine walls and local artwork on display. The dishes of local seafood, lobster and chowder and the pie made fresh each day are excellent. Couples like this place. Casual dress; cocktails. **Parking:** street. **Cards:** AX, DS, MC, VI.

## PORT TAVERN & GRILLE  Country Inn

WWW SAVE

Steak House

**Dinner:** $17-$27    Phone: 207/967-2621

**Location:** Just up hill from Dock Square; center of downtown; in The Kennebunkport Inn. 1 Dock Square 04046. **Hours:** 7 am-10:30 & 6-9 pm; Mon-Thurs from 6 pm 10/26-5/15. Closed: Sun-Tues 10/29-6/19, Christmas week. **Reservations:** suggested. **Features:** When you come here, you'll be dining in a sea captain's home of the 1890s. The romantic atmosphere features a piano bar in the comfortable lounge. The New England cuisine displays a French accent. Dressy casual attire is suggested. Patio dining is available, weather permitting. Cocktails. **Parking:** on-site. **Cards:** AX, MC, VI.

## STRIPERS FISH SHACK

WWW

Seafood

**Lunch:** $5-$20    **Dinner:** $12-$30    Phone: 207/967-3625

**Location:** 1 mi e from Dock Square on Ocean Ave; close to the mouth of the Kennebunk River; in Schooners Inn. 127 Ocean Ave 04046. **Hours:** Open 5/16-10/30; noon-3 & 6-9:30 pm. **Reservations:** suggested. **Features:** Fresh seafood, simply prepared, is the hallmark of the not-so-typical fish shack. Fish and chips has proved to be a popular choice with regulars, who also enjoy wonderful views of the Kennebunk River. Casual dress; cocktails. **Parking:** on-site. **Cards:** AX, MC, VI.

**TIDES INN BY THE SEA-THE BELVIDERE ROOM** Historic      **Dinner:** $15-$29      **Phone:** 207/967-3757
**Location:** I-95 (Maine Tpke), exit 25 (Kennebunk), just e on SR 35 to SR 9; through Dock Square, 5.5 mi e to Dyke Rd, follow Dyke Rd just e to end, 0.3 mi n along Beachfront Rd. 252 Kings Hwy Goose Rocks Beach 04046. **Hours:** Open 5/15-10/11; 5:30 pm-9 pm. Closed: Tues. **Reservations:** suggested. **Features:** You'll find a wonderful gourmet cuisine here. This restaurant's rustic room gives a good view of Goose Rocks Beach. The innovative menu features excellent lamb, halibut, filet mignon and crab cakes, homemade dessert and an exceptional wine list. Casual dress; cocktails. **Parking:** on-site. **Cards:** AX, MC, VI.

Regional American

# KINGFIELD

## ──── WHERE TO DINE ────

**LONGFELLOW'S RESTAURANT**      **Lunch:** $3-$7      **Dinner:** $7-$14      **Phone:** 207/265-4394
**Location:** Center. Main St 04947. **Hours:** 11 am-9 pm. Closed: 11/25, 12/25. **Reservations:** accepted. **Features:** Great for budget-conscious patrons, the popular restaurant offers a good view of the Carrabasset River. The setting is a 19th-century building with a pub, open-beam dining room and upstairs area with an outdoor deck. Good soups, crepes and sandwiches contribute to the menu. Casual dress; cocktails. **Parking:** on-site. **Cards:** MC, VI.

American

# KITTERY pop. 5,884

## ──── WHERE TO STAY ────

**THE COACHMAN INN**    *Book at aaa.com*      **Phone:** (207)439-4434

| | | | |
|---|---|---|---|
| 7/2-9/5 [ECP] | 1P: $116-$126 | 2P: $119-$129 | XP: $13 | F14 |
| 9/6-10/30 [ECP] | 1P: $91-$101 | 2P: $118-$128 | XP: $11 | F14 |
| 5/1-7/1 [ECP] | 1P: $78-$88 | 2P: $78-$88 | XP: $10 | F14 |
| 10/31-4/30 [ECP] | 1P: $63-$73 | 2P: $66-$76 | XP: $6 | F14 |

Small-scale Hotel   **Location:** I-95, exit 2 (Kittery), 1 mi n. 380 Rt 1 03904. Fax: 207/439-6757. **Facility:** 43 units. 40 one- and 3 two-bedroom standard units, some with whirlpools. 2 stories (no elevator), interior/exterior corridors. **Parking:** on-site. **Amenities:** hair dryers. **Pool(s):** outdoor. **Cards:** AX, DS, MC, VI. **Special Amenities:** free expanded continental breakfast and free room upgrade (subject to availability with advanced reservations). *(See color ad below)*

SOME UNITS

## ENCHANTED NIGHTS BED & BREAKFAST

Phone: 207/439-1489

| | | | | |
|---|---|---|---|---|
| 7/1-10/31 [BP] | 1P: $70-$300 | 2P: $80-$328 | XP: $25 | D17 |
| 11/1-12/31 [BP] | 1P: $52-$300 | 2P: $61-$328 | XP: $25 | D17 |
| 5/1-6/30 [BP] | 1P: $47-$300 | 2P: $56-$328 | XP: $25 | D17 |
| 1/1-4/30 [BP] | 1P: $35-$300 | 2P: $47-$328 | XP: $25 | D17 |

Bed & Breakfast

**Location:** I-95, exit 2 (Kittery), 1 mi s on SR 236, just w on SR 103. 29 Wentworth St 03904. **Facility:** Smoke free premises. 9 units. 7 one- and 1 two-bedroom standard units, some with whirlpools. 1 one-bedroom suite with kitchen. 3 stories (no elevator), interior/exterior corridors. **Bath:** some shared or private, combo, shower or tub only. **Parking:** on-site. **Terms:** check-in 3:30 pm, 2 night minimum stay - weekends 7/1-10/31, 15 day cancellation notice-fee imposed, pets ($10-$25 extra charge). **Amenities:** Some: irons. **Cards:** AX, CB, DC, DS, MC, VI.

SOME UNITS

## PORTSMOUTH HARBOR INN & SPA

Phone: 207/439-4040

| | | | |
|---|---|---|---|
| 5/1-10/31 [BP] | 1P: $139-$225 | 2P: $139-$225 | XP: $25 |
| 11/1-4/30 [BP] | 1P: $109-$199 | 2P: $109-$199 | XP: $25 |

Bed & Breakfast

**Location:** I-95, exit 2 (Kittery), 0.3 mi on SR 236 to Kittery Traffic Circle, just s on US 1; at base of Memorial Bridge. 6 Water St 03904. **Fax:** 207/438-9286. **Facility:** Displayed in guest rooms at this red-brick Victorian home are period antiques, watercolors and items from the owners' travels. Smoke free premises. 5 one-bedroom standard units. 3 stories (no elevator), interior corridors. **Parking:** on-site. **Terms:** check-in 4 pm, 2 night minimum stay - seasonal weekends, age restrictions may apply, 14 day cancellation notice-fee imposed, package plans. **Amenities:** voice mail, hair dryers. **Leisure Activities:** spa. **Cards:** MC, VI.

SOME UNITS

---

### ——— WHERE TO DINE ———

## CAP'N SIMEON'S GALLERY

Lunch: $7-$11     Dinner: $7-$15     Phone: 207/439-3655

Seafood

**Location:** In Kittery Point; jct US 1 and SR 103, 3 mi e on SR 103. 90 Pepperell Rd 03905. **Hours:** 11:30 am-9 pm; Sunday brunch 10 am-2 pm. Closed: 11/25, 12/25; also Tues 10/12-6/1. **Features:** This restaurant offers fabulous views of the cove and Portsmouth Harbor. Seafood is the specialty, but you can get anything from a grilled cheese sandwich to a New York sirloin steak. The atmosphere is warm and cozy. Service is friendly and helpful. Casual dress; cocktails. **Parking:** on-site. **Cards:** AX, DS, JC, MC, VI.

## QUARTER DECK RESTAURANT

Lunch: $5-$10     Dinner: $10-$15     Phone: 207/439-5198

Seafood

**Location:** Center. 326 US Rt 1 03904. **Hours:** 11 am-9 pm, Sun from 8 am. Closed: 11/25, 12/25. **Features:** Fish displays decorate the nautically themed restaurant, which overlooks the tidal estuary from its location in the heart of the city's outlet district. Although the menu lists primarily seafood, it also includes pasta and steak. Locally obtained seafood is fresh, as is other produce. Noteworthy chowders are made on the premises. Cocktails. **Parking:** on-site. **Cards:** AX, DS, MC, VI.

## WARREN'S LOBSTER HOUSE

Lunch: $5-$11     Dinner: $10-$15     Phone: 207/439-1630

Seafood

**Location:** I-95, exit 2 (Kittery), 0.3 mi e on SR 236 to Kittery Traffic Circle just s on US 1; at base of Memorial Bridge. 11 Water St 03904. **Hours:** 11:30 am-8:30 pm, Fri & Sat-9 pm; hours may vary in winter. Closed: 1/1, 11/24, 12/25. **Features:** A landmark from the 1940s, Warren's has a knotty-pine dining room overlooking the Piscataqua River. The salad bar has more than 50 selections. The specialty is lobster (priced daily), but the varied menu also has several beef dishes and plenty of seafood. Casual dress; cocktails. **Parking:** on-site. **Cards:** AX, MC, VI.

## WEATHERVANE

Lunch: $6-$17     Dinner: $6-$17     Phone: 207/439-0330

Seafood

**Location:** I-95, exit 2, 0.5 mi n. 306 US 1 03904. **Hours:** 11 am-9 pm; to 9:30 pm 5/27-10/14. Closed: 11/25, 12/24, 12/25. **Features:** Conveniently located near Kittery Outlet, this large and bustling restaurant features a very good menu variety that includes lobster, fried clams and crisp, Cape Cod apple-cranberry cobbler. The flavorful dishes are served in large portions. Casual dress; cocktails. **Parking:** on-site. **Cards:** AX, MC, VI.

# LEWISTON pop. 35,690

## ——— WHERE TO STAY ———

**CHALET MOTEL**
AAA SAVE
Small-scale Hotel

**Phone: 207/784-0600**
All Year      1P: $50-$55      2P: $60-$65      XP: $5      F18
**Location:** I-95 (Maine Tpke), exit 80. 1243 Lisbon St 04240. **Fax:** 207/786-4214. **Facility:** 72 units. 71 one- and 1 two-bedroom standard units, some with whirlpools. 2-3 stories (no elevator), interior/exterior corridors. **Parking:** on-site. **Terms:** weekly rates available, pets (with prior approval). **Dining:** 6 am-10:30 & 4-9 pm, Fri-11 pm, Sat & Sun 7 am-11:30 & 4-11 pm, cocktails. **Pool(s):** heated indoor. **Leisure Activities:** sauna, whirlpool, exercise room, game room. **Guest Services:** coin laundry. **Cards:** AX, DS, MC, VI.

SOME UNITS

---

**MOTEL 6 - 1223**
Small-scale Hotel

*Book at aaa.com*

**Phone: 207/782-6558**
6/10-9/5      1P: $43-$55      2P: $49-$61      XP: $3      F17
5/1-6/9 & 9/6-4/30      1P: $39-$49      2P: $45-$55      XP: $3      F17
**Location:** I-95 (Maine Tpke), exit 80, follow sign for Lisbon, just w. 516 Pleasant St 04240. **Fax:** 207/783-5270. **Facility:** 66 one-bedroom standard units. 2 stories (no elevator), interior/exterior corridors. *Bath:* combo or shower only. **Parking:** on-site. **Terms:** office hours 7 am-11 pm, small pets only. **Guest Services:** coin laundry. **Cards:** AX, CB, DC, DS, MO, VI.

SOME UNITS

---

**RAMADA CONFERENCE CENTER**
Small-scale Hotel

*Book at aaa.com*

**Phone: (207)784-2331**
All Year [BP]      1P: $95-$105      2P: $109-$129      XP: $10      F17
**Location:** I-95 (Maine Tpke), exit 80, right turn on Fach St, follow signs. 490 Pleasant St 04240. **Fax:** 207/784-2332. **Facility:** Smoke free premises. 117 one-bedroom standard units. 2 stories (no elevator), interior corridors. **Parking:** on-site. **Amenities:** voice mail, irons, hair dryers. *Fee:* video games, high-speed Internet. **Pool(s):** heated indoor. **Leisure Activities:** sauna, whirlpool, exercise room. **Guest Services:** gift shop, valet and coin laundry. **Business Services:** conference facilities, business center. **Cards:** AX, CB, DC, DS, MC, VI.

SOME UNITS

---

**SUPER 8 MOTEL LEWISTON MOTEL**
Small-scale Hotel

*Book at aaa.com*

**Phone: (207)784-8882**
5/1-8/31      1P: $56-$100      2P: $60-$100      XP: $7      F12
9/1-10/31      1P: $56-$70      2P: $58-$80      XP: $7      F12
1/1-4/30      1P: $50-$58      2P: $58-$66      XP: $7      F12
11/1-12/31      1P: $46-$56      2P: $50-$60      XP: $7      F12
**Location:** I-95 (Maine Tkpe), exit 80, just e on SR 196. 1440 Lisbon St 04240 (PO Box 2631, WOBURN, MA, 01888). **Fax:** 207/784-1778. **Facility:** 49 one-bedroom standard units. 2 stories (no elevator), interior corridors. **Parking:** on-site. **Terms:** cancellation fee imposed, [CP] meal plan available. **Cards:** AX, DC, MC, VI.

SOME UNITS

## ——— WHERE TO DINE ———

**DAVINCI'S**
Italian

**Lunch:** $6-$10      **Dinner:** $9-$17      **Phone:** 507/782-2088
**Location:** Center; in Bates Mill Complex. 35 Canal St 04240. **Hours:** 11 am-9 pm, Fri & Sat-10 pm. **Closed:** 12/25; also Sun. **Reservations:** accepted. **Features:** Located in the historic Bates Mill Complex, the locally popuar DaVinci's dining room features original features of the mill such as brick walls. The menu features Italian favorites. Casual dress; cocktails. **Parking:** on-site. **Cards:** AX, DS, MC, VI.

**MARCO'S RESTAURANT**
Italian

**Lunch:** $4-$10      **Dinner:** $8-$16      **Phone:** 207/783-0336
**Location:** In the downtown area. 177 Lisbon St 04240. **Hours:** 11 am-9 pm. **Closed:** 9/6, 12/25. **Reservations:** accepted. **Features:** The menu for this downtown restaurant offers pasta, chicken, veal and seafood dishes as well as calzones. Casual dress; cocktails. **Parking:** street. **Cards:** AX, DC, DS, MC, VI.

# LIMERICK

──────── WHERE TO STAY ────────

**JEREMIAH MASON HOUSE BED & BREAKFAST**
**Phone:** (207)793-4858
All Year [BP]          1P: $55          2P: $75          XP: $15          F3
**Location:** Center of village. 40 Main St 04048. **Facility:** Smoke free premises. 10 one-bedroom standard units.
Bed & Breakfast    3 stories (no elevator), interior corridors. *Bath:* some shared or private, shower or tub only. **Parking:** on-site.
**Cards:** MC, VI.

ASK S⊘ X ☎ / ⓀⓂ Ⓨ VCR /    SOME UNITS

# LINCOLNVILLE

──────── WHERE TO STAY ────────

**ABBINGTONS SEAVIEW MOTEL & COTTAGES**
**Phone:** 207-236-3471
5/21-10/17          1P: $60-$130          2P: $60-$130          XP: $10          F
**Location:** US 1, 4 mi n of downtown Camden; 1.5 mi s of Lincolnville Beach. Atlantic Hwy 04849 (PO Box 1385,
Motel    CAMDEN, 04843). Fax: 207-236-0017. **Facility:** 14 units. 11 one- and 2 two-bedroom standard units, some
with efficiencies. 1 one-bedroom suite ($130). 1-2 stories (no elevator), exterior corridors. *Bath:* combo or
shower only. **Parking:** on-site. **Terms:** open 5/21-10/17, office hours 3 pm-9 pm, 3 day cancellation notice-fee imposed, weekly
rates available, pets ($10 extra charge, in limited units). **Pool(s):** outdoor. **Leisure Activities:** horseshoes, volleyball. **Cards:** AX,
DS, MC, VI.

ASK 🛏 🐾 X / Ⓚ ☎ 🛢 🖥 🖳 /    SOME UNITS
FEE

**BLACK HORSE INN**
**Phone:** 207-236-6800
6/16-10/15 [CP]          1P: $89-$99          2P: $89-$99          XP: $10          F12
5/1-6/15 & 10/16-4/30 [CP]          1P: $65-$70          2P: $65-$70          XP: $10          F12
Small-scale Hotel    **Location:** 1 mi s on US 1. Located in a rural area. 2254 Atlantic Hwy 04843 (PO Box 1093, CAMDEN).
Fax: 207-236-6509. **Facility:** Smoke free premises. 21 one-bedroom standard units, some with whirlpools. 2
stories (no elevator), interior corridors. **Parking:** on-site. **Terms:** office hours 7 am-11 pm, 7 day cancellation notice-fee imposed.
**Leisure Activities:** cross country skiing, hiking trails. **Cards:** AX, DS, MC, VI.

Ⓨ X / 🛢 /    SOME UNITS

**CEDARHOLM GARDEN BAY INN**
**Phone:** 207-236-3886
5/1-12/15 [ECP]          1P: $159-$350          2P: $159-$350
**Location:** 2 mi s on US 1, 4 mi n of Camden. 2159 Atlantic Hwy 04849. **Facility:** These contemporary cottages offer
privacy and well-tended perennial gardens and are either oceanfront or offer ocean views. Smoke free prem-
Cottage    ises. 6 cottages. 1 story, exterior corridors. **Parking:** on-site. **Terms:** open 5/1-12/15, office hours 7 am-10
pm, 30 day cancellation notice-fee imposed. **Amenities:** irons, hair dryers. **Cards:** MC, VI.
**Special Amenities: free expanded continental breakfast.**

X 🛢 🖥 / Ⓚ ☎ 🖳 /    SOME UNITS

**GLENMOOR BY THE SEA RESORT & COTTAGES**
**Phone:** (207)236-3466
7/1-8/22 [CP]          2P: $109-$169          XP: $10          F18
5/26-6/30 & 8/23-10/31 [CP]          2P: $79-$129          XP: $10          F18
**Location:** 2 mi s on US 1, 4 mi n of Camden. 2133 Atlantic Hwy 04849 (PO Box 1389, CAMDEN, 04843).
Cottage    Fax: 207-236-7043. **Facility:** In a parklike setting, Glenmoor offers rooms, suites and cottages, all with decks,
some with fireplaces and some bordering the water. Smoke free premises. 35 units. 12 one- and 1 two-
bedroom standard units. 1 one- and 1 two-bedroom suites ($129-$325). 20 cottages ($109-$325). 1-2 stories
(no elevator), exterior corridors. **Parking:** on-site. **Pool(s):** 2 heated outdoor. **Leisure Activities:** tennis court, horseshoes, volleyball.
**Guest Services:** gift shop. **Business Services:** meeting rooms. **Cards:** AX, MC, VI. **Special Amenities: free continental
breakfast and free newspaper.** *(See color ad p 209)*

🐾 X X 📹 DATA PORT / VCR 🛢 🖳 🖥 /    SOME UNITS

**INN AT OCEANS EDGE**
**Phone:** (207)236-0945
6/25-10/23          1P: $195-$295          2P: $195-$295
5/1-6/24, 10/24-12/4 & 2/4-4/30          1P: $159-$265          2P: $159-$265
**Location:** 1.4 mi s on US 1, 4.3 mi n of Camden. Located in a quiet area. Atlantic Hwy 04849 (PO Box 704, CAMDEN,
04843). Fax: 207-236-0609. **Facility:** Picturesque gardens and ocean breezes give this property a retreatlike
Bed & Breakfast    ambience; rooms are well appointed and have gas fireplaces. Smoke free premises. 27 one-bedroom standard units with whirlpools. 3 stories, interior corridors. **Parking:** on-site. **Terms:** open 5/1-12/4 & 2/4-4/30,
age restrictions may apply, 14 day cancellation notice-fee imposed, [BP] meal plan available. **Amenities:** video library, irons, hair
dryers. **Dining:** guest pantry. **Leisure Activities:** exercise room. **Business Services:** meeting rooms. **Cards:** MC, VI.
**Special Amenities: free full breakfast and free local telephone calls.** *(See color ad p 210)*

Ⓨ 🅼 X VCR DATA PORT / 🛢 🖳 /    SOME UNITS

**THE INN AT SUNRISE POINT**
**Phone:** (207)236-7716
All Year [BP]          1P: $200-$470          2P: $200-$470          XP: $60
**Location:** 2 mi s on US 1, 4 mi n of Camden. Located in a quiet area. Sunrise Point Rd 04849 (PO Box 1344, CAMDEN,
04843). Fax: 207-236-0820. **Facility:** This secluded inn has large picture windows overlooking the bay. Some
Bed & Breakfast    guest units have whirlpools, private decks and natural wood burning fireplaces. Smoke free premises. 9 units.
8 one-bedroom standard units, some with whirlpools. 1 one-bedroom suite ($320-$440). 1-2 stories (no elevator), interior/exterior corridors. *Bath:* combo or shower only. **Parking:** on-site. **Terms:** 30 day cancellation
notice-fee imposed, package plans - seasonal. **Amenities:** video library, irons, hair dryers. **Guest Services:** complimentary
evening beverages. **Cards:** MC, VI.

X Ⓚ VCR DATA PORT / 🛢 🖥 🖳 /    SOME UNITS

## MT. BATTIE B&B

AAA SAVE

Motel

| | | | |
|---|---|---|---|
| 6/20-9/6 | | 2P: $89-$120 | XP: $15 |
| 9/7-10/14 | | 2P: $69-$99 | XP: $15 |
| 5/1-6/19 & 10/15-11/7 | | 2P: $59-$89 | XP: $15 |

**Phone:** 207/236-3870

**Location:** 2 mi s on US 1; 3 mi n of Camden. 2158 Atlantic Hwy 04849. Fax: 207/230-0068. **Facility:** 21 units. 19 one- and 1 two-bedroom standard units. 1 two-bedroom suite. 1 story, exterior corridors. *Bath:* combo or shower only. **Parking:** on-site. **Terms:** open 5/1-11/7, office hours 7 am-10 pm, 7 day cancellation notice-fee imposed, [ECP] meal plan available. **Amenities:** irons, hair dryers. **Cards:** AX, MC, VI. **Special Amenities:** free full breakfast and free local telephone calls. *(See color ad p 212)*

SOME UNITS

⊠ DATA PORT 🛄 💻 / 📠 /

---

## PINE GROVE COTTAGES

Cottage

| | | | |
|---|---|---|---|
| 6/20-9/7 | | 2P: $65-$150 | XP: $15 | D10 |
| 9/8-10/25 | | 2P: $65-$125 | XP: $15 | D10 |
| 5/1-6/19 | | 2P: $50-$100 | XP: $15 | D10 |

**Phone:** 207/236-2929

**Location:** 2 mi s on US 1. 2076 Atlantic Hwy 04849. **Facility:** 9 units. 3 one-bedroom standard units with kitchens, some with whirlpools. 6 cottages. 1 story, exterior corridors. *Bath:* combo or shower only. **Parking:** on-site. **Terms:** open 5/1-10/25, office hours 9 am-9 pm, 15 day cancellation notice-fee imposed, pets ($7 extra charge). **Cards:** DC, MC, VI. *(See color ad p 211)*

🏠 ⊠ 🛄 💻
FEE

---

## SNOW HILL LODGE

AAA SAVE

Motel

| | | | |
|---|---|---|---|
| 6/24-9/5 [ECP] | 1P: $65-$85 | 2P: $65-$85 | XP: $10 |
| 5/1-6/23 & 9/6-4/30 [ECP] | 1P: $49-$79 | 2P: $49-$79 | XP: $10 |

**Phone:** 207/236-3452

**Location:** 1 mi s on US 1, 4.8 mi n of Camden. 2298 Atlantic Hwy 04849. Fax: 207/236-8052. **Facility:** 30 one-bedroom standard units. 1-2 stories (no elevator), exterior corridors. *Bath:* combo or shower only. **Parking:** on-site. **Terms:** office hours 7 am-midnight, 7 day cancellation notice-fee imposed. **Cards:** AX, DS, MC, VI. **Special Amenities:** free expanded continental breakfast and free local telephone calls.

S_D ⊠ 🐾

---

## THE VICTORIAN BY THE SEA

Historic Bed & Breakfast

| | | | |
|---|---|---|---|
| 7/2-10/17 [BP] | 1P: $160-$235 | 2P: $160-$235 | |
| 5/28-7/1 [BP] | 1P: $135-$205 | 2P: $135-$205 | |
| 5/1-5/27 & 10/18-4/30 [BP] | 1P: $105-$155 | 2P: $105-$155 | |

**Phone:** 207/236-3785

**Location:** 2 mi s. Rt 1, Seaview Dr 04849 (PO Box 1385, CAMDEN, 04843). Fax: 207/236-0017. **Facility:** A pleasant porch dresses the front of this Victorian home dating from 1889; six guest rooms feature fireplaces and some have water views. Smoke free premises. 7 units. 5 one-bedroom standard units. 2 one-bedroom suites ($155-$235). 3 stories (no elevator), interior corridors. *Bath:* combo or shower only. **Parking:** on-site. **Terms:** 2 night minimum stay - seasonal, age restrictions may apply, 14 day cancellation notice-fee imposed. **Amenities:** hair dryers. **Cards:** AX, MC, VI.

SOME UNITS

ASK ⊠ 🐾 / 🅦 /

---

## YOUNGTOWN INN & RESTAURANT

Historic Country Inn

| | | | |
|---|---|---|---|
| 5/21-10/31 | 1P: $125-$160 | 2P: $125-$160 | XP: $40 | D12 |
| 5/1-5/20 & 11/1-4/30 | 1P: $110-$150 | 2P: $110-$150 | XP: $40 | D12 |

**Phone:** 207/763-4290

**Location:** 2 mi s on SR 52; 4 mi n of Camden. Located in a quiet, rural area. 581 Youngtown Rd 04849. Fax: 207/763-4078. **Facility:** A large dining room and cozy guest rooms, including two with fireplaces, are featured at this Federal-style farmhouse dating from 1810. Smoke free premises. 6 one-bedroom standard units. 3 stories (no elevator), interior corridors. *Bath:* combo or shower only. **Parking:** on-site. **Terms:** 2 night minimum stay - weekends, 14 day cancellation notice-fee imposed, [BP] meal plan available. **Amenities:** hair dryers. **Dining:** dining room, see separate listing. **Cards:** AX, MC, VI.

SOME UNITS

🍴 🍸 ⊠ / VCR /

---

### ———— WHERE TO DINE ————

## LOBSTER POUND RESTAURANT

AAA

Seafood

**Lunch:** $5-$19          **Dinner:** $12-$36          **Phone:** 207/789-5550

**Location:** Center. Rt 1 04849. **Hours:** Open 5/5-10/20; 11:30 am-9 pm; to 8 pm off season. **Reservations:** accepted. **Features:** This ever-popular place is a mecca for lobster lovers. The menu also offers other seafood, clams, roast turkey, ham, steak and chicken. This is a family-style restaurant and has picnic tables near a sandy beach and a take-out window. Casual dress; cocktails. **Parking:** on-site. **Cards:** AX, DC, DS, MC, VI.

Ⓛ,M ⊠

---

## YOUNGTOWN INN & RESTAURANT   Historic

French

**Dinner:** $19-$30          **Phone:** 207/763-4290

**Location:** 2 mi s on SR 52; 4 mi n of Camden; in The Youngtown Inn & Restaurant. 581 Youngtown Rd 04849. **Hours:** 6 pm-9 pm. **Reservations:** suggested. **Features:** Fireplaces warm the casually elegant dining rooms, and the French chef/owner creates a selection of well-prepared entrees and excellent homemade desserts. Veal chops, rack of lamb, souffles and salmon en croute are a few choices. Expect a fine wine list. Dressy casual; cocktails. **Parking:** on-site. **Cards:** AX, MC, VI.

🍸 ⊠

---

# LUBEC

### ———— WHERE TO STAY ————

## BETSY ROSS HOUSE

Small-scale Hotel

| | | | |
|---|---|---|---|
| 7/1-8/31 [CP] | 1P: $95 | 2P: $95 | XP: $10 |
| 5/1-6/30 & 9/1-11/30 [CP] | 1P: $65 | 2P: $65 | XP: $10 |

**Phone:** 207/733-8942

**Location:** SR 189, just s on Washington St, then just e; center. 61 Water St 04652. Fax: 207/733-8907. **Facility:** Smoke free premises. 4 one-bedroom standard units. 3 stories (no elevator), interior corridors. *Bath:* combo or shower only. **Parking:** on-site. **Terms:** open 5/1-11/30, 14 day cancellation notice-fee imposed, weekly rates available. **Cards:** MC, VI.

ASK ⊠ 🐾 Ⓩ

## THE EASTLAND MOTEL

**Phone:** (207)733-5501

| | | | |
|---|---|---|---|
| 5/15-10/15 | 1P: $49-$59 | 2P: $59-$69 | XP: $5 | D16 |
| 5/1-5/14 & 10/16-4/30 | 1P: $39-$49 | 2P: $49-$59 | XP: $5 | D16 |

**Location:** Jct US 1 and SR 189, 8.4 mi e on SR 189. 395 County Rd 04652. Fax: 207/733-2932. **Facility:** 19 one-bedroom standard units. 1 story, interior/exterior corridors. *Bath:* combo or shower only. **Parking:** on-site. **Terms:** office hours 7:30 am-10 pm, [CP] meal plan available, small pets only ($10 extra charge, in limited units). **Cards:** AX, DS, MC, VI. **Special Amenities: free continental breakfast and free local telephone calls.**

Motel

SOME UNITS

## THE HOME PORT INN

**Phone:** 207/733-2077

| | | | |
|---|---|---|---|
| 5/1-10/31 [ECP] | 1P: $85-$99 | 2P: $85-$99 | XP: $10 | F10 |

**Location:** Center. 45 Main St 04652 (PO Box 50). Fax: 207/733-2950. **Facility:** This Colonial-style country inn, which dates from 1880, offers quaint guest rooms and a homey parlor with a large fireplace. Smoke free premises. 7 units. 5 one-bedroom standard units. 2 stories (no elevator), interior corridors. *Bath:* combo or shower only. **Parking:** on-site. **Terms:** open 5/1-10/31, 7 day cancellation notice, no pets allowed (owner's pet on premises). **Amenities:** *Some:* hair dryers. **Dining:** dining room, see separate listing. **Cards:** AX, DS, MC, VI. **Special Amenities: free expanded continental breakfast.**

Historic
Country Inn

SOME UNITS

## PEACOCK HOUSE

**Phone:** 207/733-2403

| | | | |
|---|---|---|---|
| 5/1-10/31 | 1P: $85-$125 | 2P: $85-$125 | XP: $15 | |

**Location:** Center. 27 Summer St 04652. **Facility:** Comfortable, well-appointed common areas and accommodations are offered at of this house built in 1860. Smoke free premises. 7 units. 5 one-bedroom standard units. 2 one-bedroom suites. 3 stories (no elevator), interior corridors. *Bath:* combo or shower only. **Parking:** street. **Terms:** open 5/1-10/31, 7 day cancellation notice-fee imposed, [BP] meal plan available. **Amenities:** video library. **Cards:** MC, VI.

Historic Bed
& Breakfast

SOME UNITS

------ WHERE TO DINE ------

## THE HOME PORT INN DINING ROOM

**Dinner:** $12-$20    **Phone:** 207/733-2077

**Location:** Center; in The Home Port Inn. 45 Main St 04652. **Hours:** Open 5/28-10/12; 5 pm-8 pm. **Reservations:** suggested. **Features:** The pleasant, sunken dining room is cozy and attractive. Down east scampi and fresh poached salmon are good choices from the varied menu of reasonably priced food. The wine list is good. Casual dress; beer & wine only. **Parking:** street. **Cards:** AX, DS, MC, VI.

American

# LUCERNE IN MAINE

------ WHERE TO STAY ------

## THE LUCERNE INN

**Phone:** (207)843-5123

| | | |
|---|---|---|
| 7/1-10/31 | 2P: $99-$199 | |
| 5/1-6/30 | 2P: $79-$179 | |
| 11/1-4/30 | 2P: $59-$159 | |

**Location:** On US 1A. Rt 1A 04429 (Box 540, EAST HOLDEN). Fax: 207/843-6138. **Facility:** A lake and hills are the backdrop for this 1814 inn offering tastefully decorated rooms equipped with modern amenities. 31 units. 30 one-bedroom standard units. 1 one-bedroom suite with kitchen. 3 stories (no elevator), interior corridors. **Parking:** on-site. **Terms:** [ECP] & [MAP] meal plans available. **Amenities:** hair dryers. *Some:* irons. **Dining:** dining room, see separate listing. **Pool(s):** heated outdoor. **Leisure Activities:** golf course adjacent. **Business Services:** meeting rooms. **Cards:** AX, DS, MC, VI.

Country Inn

SOME UNITS

------ WHERE TO DINE ------

## THE LUCERNE INN DINING ROOM    Country Inn

**Dinner:** $10-$25    **Phone:** 207/843-5123

**Location:** On US 1A; in The Lucerne Inn. RR 3 04429. **Hours:** 5 pm-9 pm. **Closed:** 12/25. **Reservations:** suggested. **Features:** Pleasant dining rooms in the grand old mansion afford terrific views of Phillips Lake. Sunday brunch is popular, as are such specialties as roast duckling and Atlantic salmon. Daily specials and homemade desserts are offered. Casual dress; cocktails. **Parking:** on-site. **Cards:** AX, DS, MC, VI.

American

# MACHIAS pop. 1,376

------ WHERE TO STAY ------

## THE BLUEBIRD MOTEL

**Phone:** (207)255-3332

| | | | |
|---|---|---|---|
| 6/15-10/14 | 1P: $54 | 2P: $60-$64 | XP: $5 | F12 |
| 5/1-6/14 & 10/15-4/30 | 1P: $48 | 2P: $52-$56 | XP: $5 | F12 |

**Location:** On US 1, 1 mi s. Located in a rural area. Dublin St 04654 (US 1, Box 45, 04654-9710). **Facility:** 40 one-bedroom standard units. 1 story, exterior corridors. **Parking:** on-site. **Terms:** office hours 7 am-11 pm, 3 day cancellation notice. **Cards:** AX, MC, VI. **Special Amenities: free local telephone calls and preferred room (subject to availability with advanced reservations).**

Motel

SOME UNITS

## MACHIAS MOTOR INN

Phone: 207/255-4861

| | | | |
|---|---|---|---|
| 6/15-9/20 | 1P: $66-$75 | 2P: $72-$80 | XP: $10    F14 |
| 5/1-6/14 | 1P: $60-$70 | 2P: $64-$75 | XP: $10    F14 |
| 9/21-4/30 | 1P: $58-$65 | 2P: $64-$75 | XP: $5    F14 |

Motel

**Location:** 0.5 mi e on US 1. 26 E Main St 04654. Fax: 207/255-4863. **Facility:** 35 units. 34 one-bedroom standard units, some with kitchens. 1 two-bedroom suite ($80-$110) with kitchen. 2 stories (no elevator), exterior corridors. *Bath:* combo or shower only. **Parking:** on-site. **Terms:** pets ($5 extra charge, dogs only). **Business Services:** meeting rooms. **Cards:** AX, DS, MC, VI. **Special Amenities:** free local telephone calls.

SOME UNITS

FEE

─────── WHERE TO DINE ───────

## THE BLUEBIRD RANCH RESTAURANT

**Lunch:** $5-$11    **Dinner:** $7-$14    Phone: 207/255-3351

Seafood

**Location:** On US 1; center. 3 E Main St 04654. **Hours:** 6 am-9 pm; to 8 pm off season. Closed: 11/25, 12/25. **Features:** The large and casual family-style restaurant centers its menu on hearty home-style cooking, including daily specials. Tasty pastries are freshly baked. Service is friendly. Casual dress; cocktails. **Parking:** on-site. **Cards:** AX, DS, MC, VI.

## HELEN'S RESTAURANT

**Lunch:** $5-$8    **Dinner:** $7-$15    Phone: 207/255-8423

American

**Location:** 0.5 mi e on US 1. 28 E Main St 04654. **Hours:** 6 am-8 pm. Closed: 11/25, 12/25. **Features:** Helen's features generous servings and a wide choice of seafood, meat entrees, salad, fish stews, sandwiches, deep-fried items and down-home country cooking. Their specialty is homemade pie made with real whipped cream, such as strawberry and banana cream. Casual dress; beer & wine only. **Parking:** on-site.

**Cards:** AX, DS, MC, VI.

# MEDWAY

─────── WHERE TO STAY ───────

## KATAHDIN SHADOWS MOTEL

Phone: 207/746-5162

| | | | |
|---|---|---|---|
| All Year | 1P: $44 | 2P: $49 | XP: $10    F16 |

Motel

**Location:** I-95, exit 244, 1.5 mi w on SR 157. (PO Box 45). Fax: 207/746-5948. **Facility:** 10 one-bedroom standard units. 1 story, exterior corridors. **Parking:** on-site. **Terms:** office hours 7 am-10 pm. **Pool(s):** heated outdoor. **Leisure Activities:** whirlpool, boat dock, fishing. **Cards:** MC, VI.

SOME UNITS

## MILFORD pop. 2,197

——— WHERE TO STAY ———

**MILFORD MOTEL ON THE RIVER**

Motel

| | | | | |
|---|---|---|---|---|
| 5/1-10/31 | 1P: $59-$89 | 2P: $64-$89 | XP: $7 | F13 |
| 11/1-4/30 | 1P: $49-$74 | 2P: $54-$74 | XP: $7 | F13 |

Phone: 207/827-3200

**Location:** 0.5 mi n on US 2. 154 Main Rd 04461 (PO Box 850). **Facility:** 22 units. 12 one-bedroom standard units with efficiencies. 2 one- and 8 two-bedroom suites ($74-$89), some with efficiencies or kitchens. 2 stories (no elevator), interior/exterior corridors. *Bath:* combo or shower only. **Parking:** on-site. **Guest Services:** coin laundry. **Cards:** AX, DS, MC, VI. *(See color ad p 157)*

SOME UNITS

## MILLINOCKET pop. 5,190

——— WHERE TO STAY ———

**BEST WESTERN HERITAGE MOTOR INN**
Small-scale Hotel

| | | | | |
|---|---|---|---|---|
| 7/1-10/31 | 1P: $89-$119 | 2P: $89-$119 | XP: $10 | F12 |
| 5/16-6/30 | 1P: $79-$109 | 2P: $79-$109 | XP: $10 | F12 |
| 5/1-5/15 & 11/1-4/30 | 1P: $69-$99 | 2P: $69-$99 | XP: $10 | F12 |

Phone: 207-723-9777

**Location:** 0.8 mi e on SR 11 and 157. Located in a commercial area. 935 Central St 04462. **Facility:** 49 one-bedroom standard units, some with whirlpools. 2 stories (no elevator), interior corridors. **Parking:** on-site. **Terms:** [CP] meal plan available. **Amenities:** irons, hair dryers. **Leisure Activities:** whirlpools. **Business Services:** meeting rooms. **Cards:** AX, CB, DC, DS, MC, VI.

SOME UNITS

**THE KATAHDIN INN**    *Book at aaa.com*
Small-scale Hotel

| | | |
|---|---|---|
| All Year | 1P: $69-$99 | 2P: $69-$99  F13 |

Phone: 207-723-4555

**Location:** On SR 157; center. 740 Central St 04462. Fax: 207-723-6480. **Facility:** 82 units. 72 one-bedroom standard units, some with whirlpools. 10 one-bedroom suites ($99-$109). 3 stories, interior corridors. **Parking:** on-site. **Terms:** check-in 4 pm, 3 day cancellation notice-fee imposed, [CP] meal plan available. **Amenities:** video library (fee), voice mail. *Some:* irons, hair dryers. **Pool(s):** heated indoor, wading. **Leisure Activities:** whirlpool, exercise room. *Fee:* massage. **Guest Services:** coin laundry. **Cards:** AX, DS, MC, VI. *(See color ad below)*

SOME UNITS

FEE

——— WHERE TO DINE ———

**HANG WONG RESTAURANT**
Chinese

**Lunch:** $4-$7    **Dinner:** $8-$14    Phone: 207-723-6084

**Location:** I-95, exit 244 (Millinocket); center; in Pamola Motor Lodge. 973 Central St 04462. **Hours:** 11 am-9 pm, Fri & Sat-10 pm. Closed: 11/25, 12/25. **Features:** A selection of American dishes complements the well-prepared traditional dishes at the Man Chow Garden. The menu has a good selection that includes General Tso's chicken and several of the chef's specialties. A buffet is offered for lunch. Casual dress; cocktails. **Parking:** on-site. **Cards:** AX, DS, MC, VI.

**RIVER DRIVERS RESTAURANT**
Regional American

**Dinner:** $17-$26    Phone: 207-723-8475

**Location:** I-95, exit 244, 8 mi w on SR 11 and 157, then 1.2 mi s. Old Medway Rd 04462. **Hours:** 5 pm-9 pm. Closed: Sun off season. **Reservations:** suggested. **Features:** In the New England Outdoor Center, the restaurant has a casual atmosphere and rustic decor. The often-changing menu lists fish, chicken, meat and vegetarian entrees. All dishes are made to order with fresh local ingredients. Casual dress; cocktails. **Parking:** on-site. **Cards:** AX, DS, MC, VI.

# NAPLES

## ——— WHERE TO STAY ———

### AUGUSTUS BOVE HOUSE

**Phone:** (207)693-6365

(AAA) (SAVE)

| | | | |
|---|---|---|---|
| 5/1-9/1 | 1P: $99-$175 | 2P: $125-$200 | XP: $25 | D10 |
| 9/2-12/1 & 4/1-4/30 | 1P: $69-$150 | 2P: $99-$175 | XP: $20 | D10 |

Historic Bed & Breakfast

**Location:** Corner of SR 302 and 114. 11 Sebago Rd 04055. **Facility:** The inn is across the street from Long Lake and features rooms decorated in a mix of antiques and Victorian-style reproductions. Smoke free premises. 10 units. 8 one-bedroom standard units. 2 one-bedroom suites. 3 stories (no elevator), interior corridors. *Bath:* some shared or private, shower only. **Parking:** on-site. **Terms:** open 5/1-12/1 & 4/1-4/30, 2 night minimum stay - weekends, 14 day cancellation notice, 30 days in season-fee imposed, [BP] meal plan available. **Amenities:** hair dryers. *Some:* irons. **Leisure Activities:** whirlpool. **Guest Services:** valet laundry. **Cards:** AX, DC, DS, MC, VI.

SOME UNITS

### INN AT LONG LAKE

**Phone:** (207)693-6226

(AAA) (SAVE)

| | | | |
|---|---|---|---|
| 7/1-8/31 [BP] | | 2P: $160-$200 | XP: $40 | D |
| 5/1-6/30 [BP] | | 2P: $120-$170 | XP: $40 | D |
| 9/1-10/31 [BP] | | 2P: $120-$160 | XP: $40 | D |
| 11/1-4/30 [BP] | | 2P: $99-$125 | XP: $40 | D |

Bed & Breakfast

**Location:** Just w off SR 302; center. Lake House Rd 04055 (PO Box 806). Fax: 207/693-6226. **Facility:** A front porch and elegantly furnished parlor are featured at this turn-of-the-20th-century country inn just up a hill from a lake. Designated smoking area. 16 units. 14 one-bedroom standard units. 2 one-bedroom suites ($125-$200). 4 stories (no elevator), interior corridors. *Bath:* combo or shower only. **Parking:** on-site. **Terms:** 2-3 night minimum stay - 7/1-10/31, 7 day cancellation notice-fee imposed. **Cards:** MC, VI. **Special Amenities:** free full breakfast.

SOME UNITS

## ——— WHERE TO DINE ———

### RICK'S CAFE

**Lunch:** $8-$20    **Dinner:** $8-$20    **Phone:** 207/693-3759

American

**Location:** Center. Rt 302 04055. **Hours:** Open 5/28-9/6; 11:30 am-close. **Features:** Those who can't vacation in the tropics instead can visit the cafe, which sustains a tropical feel via palm trees and reggae music. On the menu are south-of-the-border favorites, as well as burgers, seafood and sandwiches. Patio seating affords views of the activity on Long Lake. Casual dress; cocktails. **Parking:** street. **Cards:** MC, VI.

# NEWCASTLE

## ——— WHERE TO STAY ———

### THE NEWCASTLE INN

**Phone:** 207-563-5685

| | | | |
|---|---|---|---|
| 5/1-10/31 [BP] | 1P: $155-$295 | 2P: $155-$295 | XP: $40 | |
| 11/1-4/30 [BP] | 1P: $125-$225 | 2P: $125-$225 | XP: $40 | |

Country Inn

**Location:** US 1 northbound, 0.5 mi right. 60 River Rd 04553. Fax: 207/563-6877. **Facility:** This property dates from 1840 and has been in operation as an inn since 1920; many rooms have views of the river. Smoke free premises. 15 units. 13 one-bedroom standard units. 2 one-bedroom suites with whirlpools, some with kitchens. 3 stories (no elevator), interior/exterior corridors. *Bath:* combo or shower only. **Parking:** on-site. **Terms:** 14 day cancellation notice-fee imposed, package plans - seasonal. **Amenities:** hair dryers. **Dining:** Lupines at The Newcastle Inn, see separate listing. **Cards:** AX, MC, VI.

SOME UNITS

## ——— WHERE TO DINE ———

### LUPINES AT THE NEWCASTLE INN    Historic

**Dinner:** $46    **Phone:** 207/563-5685

Regional American

**Location:** US 1 northbound, 0.5 mi right; in The Newcastle Inn. 60 River Rd 04553. **Hours:** 7 pm seating. Closed: Mon; Sun-Thurs 11/1-5/30. **Reservations:** required. **Features:** This restaurant's creative regional cuisine displays a real French flair and fine presentation in its four-course, fixed-price menu. The very attractive country inn circa 1840 features a charming decor with a fireplace. Service is very good. Cocktails. **Parking:** on-site. **Cards:** AX, MC, VI.

# NEW HARBOR

## ——— WHERE TO STAY ———

### THE BRADLEY INN AT PEMAQUID POINT

**Phone:** (207)677-2105

(AAA) (SAVE)

| | | | |
|---|---|---|---|
| 5/21-10/31 | 1P: $155-$285 | 2P: $155-$285 | XP: $35 | |
| 5/1-5/20 & 11/1-1/1 | 1P: $125-$225 | 2P: $125-$225 | XP: $35 | |

Historic Country Inn

**Location:** Jct US 1/129/130, 15 mi s on US 130. Located in a residential area. 3063 Bristol Rd 04554. Fax: 207/677-3367. **Facility:** A gazebo and perennial gardens beautify the grounds of the property, which offers accommodations in a main inn, a carriage house and a garden cottage. Smoke free premises. 16 units. 14 one-bedroom standard units. 1 one- and 1 two-bedroom suites, some with kitchens. 3 stories (no elevator), interior corridors. *Bath:* combo or shower only. **Parking:** on-site. **Terms:** open 5/1-1/1, 14 day cancellation notice. **Amenities:** irons, hair dryers. **Dining:** The Bradley Inn Dining Room, see separate listing. **Leisure Activities:** bicycles. **Guest Services:** gift shop. **Cards:** AX, JC, MC.

SOME UNITS

——— WHERE TO DINE ———

THE BRADLEY INN DINING ROOM **Dinner: $21-$28** **Phone:** 207/677-2105
▽▽▽ **Location:** Jct US 1/129/130, 15 mi s on US 130; in The Bradley Inn at Pemaquid Point. 3063 Bristol Rd 04554.
**Hours:** Open 5/1-12/31 & 4/1-4/30; 6 pm-9 pm. Closed: 12/24, 12/25. **Reservations:** suggested.
American **Features:** The upscale dining room and nautical pub feature fine art and antiques. The restaurant pairs its
award-winning wine list with New American cuisine that mingles fresh Maine products, including organic
ingredients whenever possible. Casual dress; cocktails. **Parking:** on-site. **Cards:** AX, MC, VI.

SHAW'S FISH & LOBSTER WHARF RESTAURANT **Lunch: $4-$10** **Dinner: $8-$20** **Phone:** 207/677-2200
▽▽ **Location:** Jct US 130 and 32, 0.5 mi ne on US 32. Shaw's Wharf 04554. **Hours:** Open 5/6-10/17; 11 am-9 pm; to
8 pm, Fri & Sat-9 pm 5/6-6/15 & 9/2-10/9. **Features:** You'll be right on top of a working harbor at this
Seafood popular, picturesque dockside restaurant that serves lobster (of course), steamed clams, scallops and
shrimp as well as meatloaf, fish cakes, stews, roast turkey and sandwiches. Outdoor deck dining is also
available. Casual dress; cocktails. **Parking:** on-site. **Cards:** MC, VI.

# NEWPORT pop. 1,754

——— WHERE TO DINE ———

SCOTTY'S RESTAURANT **Lunch: $5-$10** **Dinner: $7-$17** **Phone:** 207/368-9333
▽▽ ▽▽ **Location:** I-95, exit 157, in Triangle Plaza. Rt 2 04953. **Hours:** 11:30 am-8 pm; Fri & Sat-9 pm 5/31-10/11.
Closed: 1/1, 12/25; also Mon. **Reservations:** accepted. **Features:** Relax in a pleasant dining room with
American booth and table seating. The menu offers a wide variety of meat, seafood and pasta dishes. Specials are
featured daily. Casual dress; cocktails. **Parking:** on-site. **Cards:** AX, DS, MC, VI.

# NORTHEAST HARBOR

——— WHERE TO STAY ———

ASTICOU INN **Book at aaa.com** **Phone:** (207)276-3344
▽▽▽▽

| | 1P: $220-$300 | 2P: $270-$350 | XP: $35 | F3 |
| 8/1-8/31 | 1P: $190-$265 | 2P: $225-$300 | XP: $35 | F3 |
| 7/1-7/31 | 1P: $120-$195 | 2P: $155-$230 | XP: $35 | F3 |
| 9/1-10/11 | 1P: $95-$165 | 2P: $130-$200 | XP: $35 | F3 |
| 5/28-6/30 | | | | |

Historic
Country Inn

**Location:** Jct SR 3 and Peabody Dr; center. 15 Peabody Dr 04662. Fax: 207/276-3373. **Facility:** This property includes a main inn built in 1885 and three annex buildings; a deck on the manicured grounds overlooks the harbor. 48 units. 33
one-bedroom standard units. 15 one-bedroom suites, some with efficiencies. 2-4 stories, interior corridors. **Parking:** on-site.
**Terms:** open 5/28-10/11, 2 night minimum stay, 31 day cancellation notice, 3% service charge. **Amenities:** voice mail, irons.
**Pool(s):** heated outdoor. **Leisure Activities:** tennis court. **Guest Services:** TV in common area. **Business Services:** meeting
rooms. **Cards:** MC, VI.

SOME UNITS

KIMBALL TERRACE INN **Phone:** 207/276-3383
AAA SAVE

| 7/1-9/5 | 1P: $158-$180 | 2P: $158-$180 | XP: $10 | F5 |
| 9/6-10/23 | 1P: $95-$110 | 2P: $95-$110 | XP: $10 | F5 |
| 5/1-6/30 & 4/20-4/30 | 1P: $68-$87 | 2P: $68-$87 | XP: $10 | F5 |

▽▽▽▽ **Location:** Overlooking Municipal Pier. 10 Huntington Rd 04662. Fax: 207/276-4102. **Facility:** 70 one-bedroom
Small-scale Hotel standard units. 2-3 stories, exterior corridors. **Parking:** on-site. **Terms:** open 5/1-10/23 & 4/20-4/30, 3 day
cancellation notice. **Amenities:** voice mail. **Dining:** Main Sail Restaurant, see separate listing. **Pool(s):** outdoor. **Guest Services:** gift shop. **Business Services:** meeting rooms. **Cards:** AX, DS, MC, VI.

SOME UNITS

——— WHERE TO DINE ———

MAIN SAIL RESTAURANT **Lunch: $6-$10** **Dinner: $10-$18** **Phone:** 276-5857
AAA **Location:** Overlooking Municipal Pier; in Kimball Terrace Inn. 10 Huntington Rd 04662. **Hours:** Open 5/1-10/23; 7
am-9 pm. **Reservations:** suggested. **Features:** The Main Sail offers family dining in an open and spacious
▽▽ ▽▽ room overlooking the marina and harbor. In season, choose the patio for a terrific view. The menu's variety
American of seafood, beef and homestyle dishes are prepared with creativity and skill. Cocktails. **Parking:** on-site.
**Cards:** AX, DS, MC, VI.

# NORTHPORT

——— WHERE TO STAY ———

NORTHPORT MOTEL & COTTAGE **Phone:** 207/338-3018
AAA SAVE

| 7/1-10/15 [CP] | 1P: $55-$79 | 2P: $55-$79 | XP: $10 | F12 |
| 5/15-6/30 [CP] | 1P: $49-$65 | 2P: $49-$65 | XP: $10 | F12 |

▽▽ ▽▽ **Location:** On US 1; center. 561 Atlantic Hwy 04849. **Facility:** Smoke free premises. 8 units. 7 one-bedroom stan-
Motel dard units. 1 cottage ($85-$129). 1 story, exterior corridors. *Bath:* shower only. **Parking:** on-site. **Terms:** open
5/15-10/15, office hours 7:30 am-9:30 pm, 14 day cancellation notice-fee imposed. **Cards:** MC, VI.
**Special Amenities:** free continental breakfast and free local telephone calls.

SOME UNITS

# NORWAY pop. 2,623

------ **WHERE TO STAY** ------

**INN TOWN MOTEL**
**Phone:** (207)743-7706

AAA SAVE

All Year — 1P: $52-$95 — 2P: $52-$95
**Location:** Jct SR 117 and 26. 58 Paris St 04268. **Fax:** 207/743-5849. **Facility:** 29 one-bedroom standard units. 1 story, exterior corridors. **Parking:** on-site. **Terms:** office hours 7 am-10 pm, cancellation fee imposed. **Amenities:** hair dryers. **Cards:** AX, DS, MC, VI. **Special Amenities:** free local telephone calls and early check-in/late check-out.

Motel

SOME UNITS

# OCEAN PARK

------ **WHERE TO STAY** ------

**BILLOWHOUSE OCEANFRONT MOTEL & GUESTHOUSE B&B**
**Phone:** 207/934-2333

6/19-9/6 — 1P: $100-$195 — 2P: $100-$195
5/1-6/18 & 9/7-12/31 — 1P: $75-$135 — 2P: $75-$135

Historic
Small-scale Hotel

**Location:** I-95 (Maine Tpke), exit 36, e on I-195 and SR 5, 1.5 mi to where SR 5 turns n; continue straight 1 mi to end. 2 Temple Ave 04063-7543 (PO Box 7543, 04063). **Fax:** 207/934-1510. **Facility:** This oceanfront property includes a Victorian-era inn as well as a motel. Smoke free premises. 13 units. 10 one-bedroom standard units, some with efficiencies. 3 one-bedroom suites ($135-$195), some with efficiencies, kitchens and/or whirlpools. 4 stories (no elevator), interior/exterior corridors. *Bath:* combo or shower only. **Parking:** on-site. **Terms:** open 5/1-12/31, 90 day cancellation notice-fee imposed, weekly rates available, [ECP] meal plan available. **Amenities:** video library, irons, hair dryers. *Some:* CD players. **Cards:** MC, VI.

SOME UNITS

# OGUNQUIT

------ **WHERE TO STAY** ------

**THE ANCHORAGE BY THE SEA**
**Phone:** 207/646-9384

6/18-9/5 — 2P: $154-$245 — XP: $20
5/1-6/17 — 2P: $74-$205 — XP: $15
9/6-10/16 — 2P: $95-$200 — XP: $15
10/17-4/30 — 2P: $69-$155 — XP: $15

Small-scale Hotel

**Location:** 0.5 mi s of US 1. 125 Shore Rd 03907 (PO Box 2406). **Fax:** 207/646-6256. **Facility:** Smoke free premises. 242 one-bedroom standard units, some with whirlpools. 2-3 stories, interior/exterior corridors. **Parking:** on-site. **Terms:** 2-7 night minimum stay - in season & weekends off season, 10 day cancellation notice-fee imposed, package plans - off season. **Amenities:** *Some:* irons. **Pool(s):** heated outdoor, heated indoor, wading. **Leisure Activities:** sauna, whirlpools. **Business Services:** meeting rooms, fax. **Cards:** DS, MC, VI. *(See color ad below)*

SOME UNITS

# ogunquit.com
## ON-LINE RESERVATIONS

*from a* *family* outing *to a getaway* package

we have *your* perfect *vacation* *choice!*

**GORGES GRANT HOTEL**

Oversized guest rooms~fitness center
heated indoor/outdoor pools~jacuzzi
Raspberri's for breakfast~walk to beaches
golf privileges~smoke free~Year Round

**449 Main Street ~ Ogunquit 03907
800.646.5001 ~ 207.646.7003**

**JUNIPER HILL INN** the

Hickory lined path just minutes to beach~
heated indoor & 2 outdoor pools~sunning
decks~jacuzzis~fitness center~sauna
golf privileges~smoke free~Year Round

**336 Main Street ~ Ogunquit 03907
800.646.4544 ~ 207.646.4501**

**the MILESTONE**

Short walk to Footbridge Beach~heated
outdoor pool & jacuzzi~fitness center~
most rooms accessible from ground level
golf privileges~smoke free~April-October

**687 Main Street ~ Ogunquit 03907
800.646.6453 ~ 207.646.4562**

SAMPLE LOCAL CUISINE WITH OUR
OFF SEASON DINNER PACKAGES

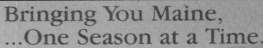

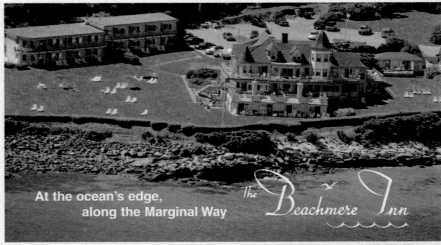

## THE BEACHMERE INN

**Phone:** (207)646-2021

<AAA> [SAVE]
WWW

| | | | |
|---|---|---|---|
| 6/12-10/17 [CP] | 1P: $95-$175 | 2P: $140-$240 | XP: $10 |
| 5/1-6/11 [CP] | 1P: $75-$130 | 2P: $80-$175 | XP: $10 |
| 10/18-12/12 & 3/25-4/30 [CP] | 1P: $65-$95 | 2P: $75-$140. | XP: $10 |

**Small-scale Hotel** **Location:** Jct US 1, just se on Shore Rd, then e. 62 Beachmere Pl 03907. Fax: 207/646-2231. **Facility:** Smoke free premises. 52 units. 43 one-bedroom standard units with efficiencies. 7 one-bedroom suites ($100-$250) with efficiencies. 1 vacation home ($185-$360) and 1 cottage ($115-$230). 2-3 stories (no elevator), interior/exterior corridors. *Bath:* combo or shower only. **Parking:** on-site. **Terms:** open 5/1-12/12 & 3/25-4/30, office hours 8:15 am-11 pm, 3-7 night minimum stay - seasonal, 21 day cancellation notice-fee imposed, package plans. **Amenities:** voice mail. *Some:* hair dryers. **Leisure Activities:** fishing, golf privileges. **Cards:** AX, CB, DC, DS, JC, MC, VI. **Special Amenities: free continental breakfast.** *(See color ad p 254)*

SOME UNITS

    / [VCR] /

## COLONIAL VILLAGE RESORT

**Phone:** (207)646-2794

<AAA> [SAVE]
WWW

| | | | |
|---|---|---|---|
| 6/25-9/5 | 1P: $129-$159 | 2P: $129-$159 | XP: $15 |
| 5/1-6/24 | 1P: $49-$139 | 2P: $49-$139 | XP: $10 |
| 9/6-10/10 | 1P: $58-$129 | 2P: $58-$129 | XP: $10 |
| 10/11-4/30 | 1P: $39-$65 | 2P: $39-$65 | XP: $10 |

**Small-scale Hotel** **Location:** 0.8 mi n on US 1. 548 Main St 03907 (PO Box 836). Fax: 207/646-2463. **Facility:** 67 units. 41 one-bedroom standard units, some with efficiencies and/or whirlpools. 4 one-, 17 two- and 1 three-bedroom suites ($82-$222) with efficiencies. 4 cottages ($650-$1600). 2 stories (no elevator), exterior corridors. **Parking:** on-site. **Terms:** office hours 7 am-11 pm, 3 night minimum stay, 7 day cancellation notice-fee imposed, [CP] meal plan available. **Amenities:** video library (fee). *Some:* hair dryers. **Pool(s):** outdoor, heated indoor. **Leisure Activities:** whirlpool, boating, tennis court. *Fee:* game room. **Guest Services:** coin laundry. **Cards:** DS, MC, VI. **Special Amenities: free continental breakfast and free local telephone calls.** *(See color ad below)*

SOME UNITS

[symbols] / [symbols] [VCR] [symbols]
FEE

## THE DUNES ON THE WATERFRONT

*Book at aaa.com*

Phone: (207)646-2612

AAA SAVE ♦♦♦

| | 6/18-9/12 | 1P: $95-$285 | 2P: $95-$285 | XP: $12 |
| | 5/27-6/17 | 1P: $80-$225 | 2P: $80-$225 | XP: $12 |
| | 9/13-11/1 | 1P: $70-$225 | 2P: $70-$225 | XP: $12 |
| | 5/1-5/26 | 1P: $70-$205 | 2P: $70-$205 | XP: $12 |

Cottage
**Location:** 0.8 mi n. 518 Main St 03907 (PO Box 917). Fax: 207/646-5292. **Facility:** Bordering the Ogunquit Tidal River, the Dunes has spacious grounds and includes some motel-style units and a number of cottages. 36 units. 15 one- and 1 two-bedroom standard units. 1 one-bedroom suite. 19 cottages ($125-$285). 1-2 stories (no elevator), exterior corridors. *Bath:* combo or shower only. **Parking:** on-site. **Terms:** open 5/1-11/1, office hours 7 am-10 pm, check-in 4 pm, 3-14 night minimum stay - seasonal, 30 day cancellation notice-fee imposed. **Amenities:** dual phone lines, voice mail. **Pool(s):** heated outdoor. **Leisure Activities:** boating, boat dock, shuffleboard. *Fee:* golf privileges. **Cards:** MC, VI.
*(See color ad p 255)*

SOME UNITS
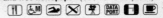

## GORGES GRANT HOTEL

Phone: 207/646-7003

AAA SAVE ♦♦♦

| | 6/18-9/5 | 1P: $139-$219 | 2P: $139-$219 | XP: $15 |
| | 9/6-10/23 | 1P: $99-$149 | 2P: $99-$149 | XP: $15 |
| | 5/1-6/17 | 1P: $64-$139 | 2P: $84-$139 | XP: $15 |
| | 10/24-4/30 | 1P: $69-$124 | 2P: $89-$124 | XP: $15 |

Small-scale Hotel **Location:** 0.3 mi n. 449 Main St 03907 (PO Box 2240). Fax: 207/646-0660. **Facility:** Designated smoking area. 81 one-bedroom standard units. 2 stories (no elevator), interior corridors. **Parking:** on-site. **Terms:** [BP] meal plan available, package plans - off season. **Amenities:** voice mail, irons, hair dryers. **Dining:** 7-11 am, Sat & Sun-noon. **Pool(s):** heated outdoor, heated indoor. **Leisure Activities:** whirlpool, golf privileges, exercise room. **Guest Services:** coin laundry. **Cards:** AX, CB, DC, DS, MC, VI. **Special Amenities:** free local telephone calls and free newspaper. *(See color ad p 253)*

## THE GRAND

Phone: 207/646-1231

♦♦♦

| | 7/6-9/5 [ECP] | | 2P: $125-$250 | XP: $20 |
| | 5/1-7/5 [ECP] | | 2P: $70-$250 | XP: $20 |
| | 9/6-12/12 [ECP] | | 2P: $70-$215 | XP: $20 |
| | 3/19-4/30 [ECP] | | 2P: $70-$180 | XP: $20 |

Small-scale Hotel
**Location:** Jct US 1, 0.7 mi se. 276 Shore Rd 03907 (PO Box 1526). Fax: 207/646-1231. **Facility:** Smoke free premises. 28 one-bedroom suites. 3 stories, interior corridors. **Parking:** on-site. **Terms:** open 5/1-12/12 & 3/19-4/30, office hours 8 am-10 pm, 2-4 night minimum stay - seasonal & weekends, 10 day cancellation notice-fee imposed, package plans - seasonal. **Amenities:** video library (fee), irons, hair dryers. **Pool(s):** heated indoor. **Leisure Activities:** whirlpool. **Cards:** AX, DS, MC, VI. *(See color ad below)*

## JUNIPER HILL INN

Phone: 207/646-4501

AAA SAVE ♦♦♦

| | 6/18-9/5 | 1P: $129-$219 | 2P: $129-$219 | XP: $15 |
| | 9/6-10/23 | 1P: $89-$144 | 2P: $89-$144 | XP: $15 |
| | 5/1-6/17 | 1P: $64-$134 | 2P: $74-$134 | XP: $15 |
| | 10/24-4/30 | 1P: $64-$119 | 2P: $74-$119 | XP: $15 |

Small-scale Hotel **Location:** 0.3 mi n on US 1. 336 Main St 03907 (PO Box 2190). Fax: 207/646-4595. **Facility:** Designated smoking area. 101 one-bedroom standard units. 2 stories (no elevator), interior/exterior corridors. **Parking:** on-site. **Terms:** office hours 6 am-midnight, package plans - off season. **Amenities:** voice mail, irons, hair dryers. **Pool(s):** 2 heated outdoor, heated indoor. **Leisure Activities:** sauna, whirlpools, golf privileges, exercise room. **Guest Services:** coin laundry. **Cards:** AX, CB, DC, DS, MC, VI. **Special Amenities:** free local telephone calls and free newspaper. *(See color ad p 253)*

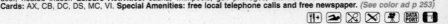

## MARINER RESORT MOTEL
**Phone: 207/646-5931**

| | | | |
|---|---|---|---|
| 6/25-9/6 | | 2P: $89-$195 | XP: $15 | F10 |
| 5/28-6/24 & 9/7-10/30 | | 2P: $49-$129 | XP: $10 | F10 |
| 5/1-5/27 | | 2P: $49-$79 | XP: $10 | F10 |

Small-scale Hotel   **Location:** 1.3 mi n on US 1. 734 Main St 03907 (PO Box 2056). Fax: 207/646-5931. **Facility:** 55 units. 51 one- and 4 two-bedroom standard units. 2 stories (no elevator), exterior corridors. *Bath:* combo or shower only. **Parking:** on-site. **Terms:** open 5/1-10/30, 2 night minimum stay - with Saturday stayover, 7 day cancellation notice-fee imposed. **Amenities:** hair dryers. **Pool(s):** outdoor, heated indoor. **Leisure Activities:** whirlpool. **Cards:** AX, DS, MC, VI.

SOME UNITS

## MEADOWMERE RESORT
**Phone: 207/646-9661**

| | | | | |
|---|---|---|---|---|
| 7/1-8/31 | 1P: $99-$269 | 2P: $99-$269 | XP: $12 | F5 |
| 11/10-4/30 | 1P: $44-$259 | 2P: $44-$259 | XP: $12 | F5 |
| 5/1-6/30 | 1P: $55-$249 | 2P: $55-$249 | XP: $12 | F5 |
| 9/1-11/9 | 1P: $59-$239 | 2P: $59-$239 | XP: $12 | F5 |

Small-scale Hotel   **Location:** 0.5 mi s. 74 Main St 03907 (PO Box 2347). Fax: 207/646-6952. **Facility:** Smoke free premises. 145 units. 141 one- and 1 two-bedroom standard units, some with efficiencies and/or whirlpools. 2 one- and 1 two-bedroom suites, some with kitchens and/or whirlpools. 3 stories, interior/exterior corridors. *Bath:* combo or shower only. **Parking:** on-site. **Terms:** 2 night minimum stay - weekends, 7 day cancellation notice-fee imposed, [ECP] meal plan available, package plans - seasonal & weekends. **Amenities:** *Some:* irons, hair dryers. **Dining:** 6:30 am-10:30 & noon-9 pm; hours vary seasonally. **Pool(s):** outdoor, heated indoor. **Leisure Activities:** saunas, whirlpool, steamrooms, Roman tub, spa. **Fee:** golf privileges, game room. **Guest Services:** coin laundry. **Business Services:** meeting rooms. **Cards:** AX, DS, MC, VI. **Special Amenities:** free expanded continental breakfast and free local telephone calls. *(See color ad p 254)*

SOME UNITS

## THE MILESTONE
**Phone: 207/646-4562**

| | | | |
|---|---|---|---|
| 6/18-9/5 | 1P: $109-$199 | 2P: $109-$199 | XP: $15 |
| 9/6-10/31 | 1P: $59-$124 | 2P: $59-$124 | XP: $15 |
| 5/1-6/17 | 1P: $49-$99 | 2P: $59-$99 | XP: $15 |
| 4/8-4/30 | 1P: $49-$69 | 2P: $59-$69 | XP: $15 |

Small-scale Hotel   **Location:** On US 1, 1 mi n. 687 Main St (US 1) 03907 (PO Box 2010). Fax: 207/646-1739. **Facility:** Designated smoking area. 70 one-bedroom standard units. 2 stories (no elevator), exterior corridors. **Parking:** on-site. **Terms:** open 5/1-10/31 & 4/8-4/30, office hours 7 am-11 pm, package plans - off season. **Amenities:** voice mail, irons, hair dryers. **Pool(s):** heated outdoor. **Leisure Activities:** whirlpool, golf priviliges, exercise room, shuffleboard. **Guest Services:** coin laundry. **Cards:** AX, CB, DC, DS, MC, VI. **Special Amenities:** free local telephone calls and free newspaper. *(See color ad p 253)*

## NELLIE LITTLEFIELD HOUSE
**Phone: 207/646-1692**

| | |
|---|---|
| 7/1-9/6 [BP] | 2P: $165-$220 |
| 5/1-6/30 & 9/7-10/11 [BP] | 2P: $100-$170 |
| 10/12-10/30 [BP] | 2P: $90-$140 |

Historic Bed & Breakfast   **Location:** Jct US 1, just se. 27 Shore Rd 03907 (PO Box 1599). **Facility:** A porch dresses the exterior of this house dating from 1889; shops, galleries and the beach are nearby. Smoke free premises. 8 units. 6 one-bedroom standard units. 2 two-bedroom suites, some with whirlpools. 3 stories, interior corridors. *Bath:* combo or shower only. **Parking:** on-site. **Terms:** open 5/1-10/30, 2 night minimum stay - weekends, age restrictions may apply, 14 day cancellation notice-fee imposed. **Amenities:** hair dryers. **Cards:** DS, MC, VI. **Special Amenities:** free full breakfast and free local telephone calls.

## OGUNQUIT RESORT MOTEL
**Phone: 207/646-8336**

| | | | | |
|---|---|---|---|---|
| 7/16-9/5 [CP] | 1P: $139-$199 | 2P: $139-$199 | XP: $15 | F12 |
| 6/18-7/15 [CP] | 1P: $119-$169 | 2P: $119-$169 | XP: $15 | F12 |
| 5/1-6/17 & 9/6-4/30 [CP] | 1P: $49-$119 | 2P: $49-$119 | XP: $10 | F12 |

Motel   **Location:** 1.3 mi n. 719 Main St 03907 (PO Box 656). Fax: 207/646-5481. **Facility:** 77 units. 70 one- and 3 two-bedroom standard units, some with whirlpools. 1 one- and 3 two-bedroom suites ($79-$269). 2 stories (no elevator), interior/exterior corridors. **Parking:** on-site. **Terms:** office hours 8 am-11 pm, 7-8 night minimum stay - seasonal & weekends, 7 day cancellation notice-fee imposed, package plans - off season. **Amenities:** voice mail, irons, hair dryers. **Pool(s):** heated outdoor. **Leisure Activities:** whirlpool, exercise room. **Cards:** AX, DC, MC, VI. **Special Amenities:** free continental breakfast and free local telephone calls. *(See color ad below)*

SOME UNITS

**THE PINE HILL INN**

**Phone:** 207/361-1004

Historic Bed & Breakfast

| | |
|---|---|
| 7/1-9/6 [BP] | 2P: $145-$185 |
| 9/7-10/11 [BP] | 2P: $130-$165 |
| 5/1-6/30 [BP] | 2P: $115-$165 |
| 10/12-4/30 [BP] | 2P: $115-$150 |

**Location:** I-95, exit 7 (York Ogunquit), 4.5 mi n on US 1 to Pine Hill Rd, 2 mi n, then just e. Located in a residential area. 14 Pine Hill Rd S 03907 (PO Box 2336). Fax: 207/361-1815. **Facility:** This Victorian summer house with a detached cottage is in a peaceful setting within walking distance of the Perkins Cove shopping district. 6 units. 5 one-bedroom standard units. 1 cottage ($900). 2 stories (no elevator), interior/exterior corridors. *Bath:* combo or shower only. **Parking:** on-site. **Terms:** check-in 4 pm, 2-3 night minimum stay - seasonal, age restrictions may apply, 7 day cancellation notice-fee imposed. **Amenities:** hair dryers. *Some:* irons. **Guest Services:** TV in common area. **Cards:** DC, DS, MC, VI.

SOME UNITS

## PINK BLOSSOMS RESORTS

Phone: 207/646-7397

AAA [SAVE]

| | | | |
|---|---|---|---|
| 6/18-9/5 | 2P: $110-$200 | XP: $20 | F5 |
| 5/20-6/17 | 2P: $70-$120 | XP: $10 | F5 |
| 9/6-10/18 | 2P: $70-$105 | XP: $10 | F5 |
| 5/1-5/19 | 2P: $53-$82 | XP: $10 | F5 |

**Small-scale Hotel** **Location:** Jct US 1, 0.6 mi se. 154 Shore Rd 03907 (PO Box 763). Fax: 207/646-2549. **Facility:** 57 units. 16 one-bedroom standard units with efficiencies. 31 one- and 10 two-bedroom suites ($82-$350), some with efficiencies or kitchens. 2-3 stories (no elevator), interior/exterior corridors. *Bath:* combo or shower only. **Parking:** on-site. **Terms:** open 5/1-10/18, 3-7 night minimum stay - some weekends & in season, 14 day cancellation notice, 30 day for two-bedroom units-fee imposed. **Amenities:** voice mail, hair dryers. *Some:* irons. **Pool(s):** heated outdoor, heated indoor. **Leisure Activities:** tennis court, exercise room. **Guest Services:** coin laundry. **Business Services:** meeting rooms. **Cards:** MC, VI. **Special Amenities:** free local telephone calls. *(See color ad p 258)*

SOME UNITS

## RIVERSIDE MOTEL

Phone: (207)646-2741

| | | | | |
|---|---|---|---|---|
| 6/25-9/5 | 1P: $135-$175 | 2P: $135-$175 | XP: $15 | F6 |
| 9/6-10/17 | 1P: $95-$150 | 2P: $95-$150 | XP: $15 | F6 |
| 5/28-6/24 | 1P: $95-$130 | 2P: $95-$130 | XP: $15 | F6 |
| 5/7-5/27 | 1P: $65-$95 | 2P: $65-$95 | XP: $15 | F6 |

Motel

**Location:** Jct US 1, 1.3 mi se on Shore Rd, then just e. 50 Riverside Ln 03907 (PO Box 2244). Fax: 207/646-0216. **Facility:** 38 one-bedroom standard units. 1 story, exterior corridors. **Parking:** on-site. **Terms:** open 5/7-10/17, office hours 8 am-10 pm, 2-3 night minimum stay - weekends, 7 day cancellation notice-fee imposed, [CP] meal plan available. **Amenities:** irons, hair dryers. **Cards:** MC, VI.

## SEA CHAMBERS

Phone: 207/646-9311

| | | | |
|---|---|---|---|
| 6/18-9/5 [CP] | 2P: $145-$205 | XP: $20 | F3 |
| 9/6-12/12 [CP] | 2P: $45-$155 | XP: $10 | F3 |
| 5/7-6/17 [CP] | 2P: $69-$148 | XP: $10 | F3 |
| 5/1-5/6 [CP] | 2P: $48-$98 | XP: $10 | F3 |

Small-scale Hotel

**Location:** Jct US 1, just se. 67 Shore Rd 03907 (PO Box 916). Fax: 207/646-0938. **Facility:** 46 units. 45 one-bedroom standard units, some with efficiencies and/or whirlpools. 1 one-bedroom suite with kitchen and whirlpool. 2 stories (no elevator), exterior corridors. *Bath:* combo or shower only. **Parking:** on-site. **Terms:** open 5/1-12/12, office hours 8 am-10:30 pm, 4 night minimum stay - 6/18-9/6, 7 day cancellation notice-fee imposed, package plans - seasonal. **Amenities:** video library (fee), voice mail. *Some:* high-speed Internet, hair dryers. **Pool(s):** heated outdoor. **Leisure Activities:** fishing, tennis court. **Guest Services:** coin laundry. **Cards:** AX, DS, MC, VI.

SOME UNITS

FEE

## SEAFARER MOTEL

Phone: 207/646-4040

AAA [SAVE]

| | | | | |
|---|---|---|---|---|
| 7/9-9/9 | 1P: $129-$229 | 2P: $129-$229 | XP: $20 | F7 |
| 6/18-7/8 | 1P: $89-$189 | 2P: $89-$189 | XP: $15 | F7 |
| 9/10-10/24 | 1P: $79-$149 | 2P: $79-$149 | XP: $15 | F7 |
| 5/1-6/17 | 1P: $69-$129 | 2P: $69-$129 | XP: $15 | F7 |

**Small-scale Hotel** **Location:** 0.5 mi s on US 1. 35 Main St 03907 (PO Box 2099). Fax: 207/646-7142. **Facility:** 78 units. 73 one-bedroom standard units, some with efficiencies. 5 one-bedroom suites ($129-$229) with efficiencies. 2 stories (no elevator), exterior corridors. **Parking:** on-site. **Terms:** open 5/1-10/24, office hours 8 am-10 pm, 2-4 night minimum stay - weekends & in suites, 7 day cancellation notice. **Amenities:** voice mail. **Pool(s):** outdoor, heated indoor. **Leisure Activities:** sauna, whirlpool. **Guest Services:** coin laundry. **Cards:** AX, DC, MC, VI. **Special Amenities:** free continental breakfast and free local telephone calls. *(See color ad below)*

SOME UNITS

## SEA VIEW MOTEL

**Phone:** 207/646-7064

| | | | | |
|---|---|---|---|---|
| 6/18-9/6 | 1P: $89-$189 | 2P: $89-$189 | XP: $12 | F3 |
| 5/1-6/17 & 9/7-12/12 | 1P: $54-$109 | 2P: $54-$109 | XP: $12 | F3 |
| 3/4-4/30 | 1P: $59-$99 | 2P: $59-$99 | XP: $12 | F3 |

Small-scale Hotel

**Location:** 0.3 mi n on US 1. 417 Main St 03907 (PO Box 2460). Fax: 207/646-7064. **Facility:** 42 units. 40 one-bedroom standard units. 1 one-bedroom suite with whirlpool. 1 vacation home. 3 stories (no elevator), exterior corridors. **Parking:** on-site. **Terms:** open 5/1-12/12 & 3/4-4/30, office hours 8 am-11 pm, 14 day cancellation notice, in season-fee imposed. **Pool(s):** heated outdoor. **Leisure Activities:** whirlpool. **Guest Services:** area transportation-beach & village. **Cards:** AX, DS, MC, VI. **Special Amenities:** free local telephone calls and preferred room **(subject to availability with advanced reservations).** *(See color ad below)*

SOME UNITS

## SPARHAWK RESORT MOTEL

**Phone:** 207/646-5562

| | | | | |
|---|---|---|---|---|
| 6/25-9/5 [ECP] | 1P: $170-$195 | 2P: $170-$195 | XP: $15 | |
| 5/1-6/24 [ECP] | 1P: $90-$165 | 2P: $90-$165 | XP: $10 | |
| 9/6-10/31 [ECP] | 1P: $90-$140 | 2P: $90-$140 | XP: $10 | |
| 4/14-4/30 [ECP] | 1P: $100-$125 | 2P: $100-$125 | XP: $15 | |

Small-scale Hotel

**Location:** Jct US 1, just se. 85 Shore Rd 03907 (PO Box 936C). Fax: 207/646-9143. **Facility:** 87 units. 79 one-bedroom standard units. 5 one- and 2 two-bedroom suites ($105-$305), some with efficiencies and/or whirlpools. 1 cottage ($210-$300). 2-3 stories (no elevator), interior/exterior corridors. **Parking:** on-site. **Terms:** open 5/1-10/31 & 4/14-4/30, office hours 6:45 am-10:45 pm, 14 day minimum stay - weekends, 7 night 7/1-8/15, 14 day cancellation notice-fee imposed. **Amenities:** voice mail, hair dryers. *Some:* irons. **Pool(s):** heated outdoor. **Leisure Activities:** tennis court. **Cards:** MC, VI.

SOME UNITS

## STAGE RUN MOTEL

**Phone:** 207/646-4823

| | | | | |
|---|---|---|---|---|
| 6/25-9/5 | 1P: $109-$159 | 2P: $109-$159 | XP: $10 | F3 |
| 6/4-6/24 | 1P: $59-$109 | 2P: $59-$109 | XP: $10 | F3 |
| 5/1-6/3 & 9/6-10/31 | 1P: $49-$89 | 2P: $49-$89 | XP: $10 | F3 |

Motel

**Location:** US 1, 0.6 mi n of center of the village. 2 Kingfield Ave 03907 (PO Box 1215). Fax: 207/641-2884. **Facility:** 24 one-bedroom standard units. 2 stories (no elevator), exterior corridors. **Parking:** on-site. **Terms:** open 5/1-10/31, office hours 8 am-10 pm, 5 day cancellation notice-fee imposed. **Amenities:** hair dryers. **Pool(s):** heated outdoor. **Cards:** DS, MC, VI. **Special Amenities:** free local telephone calls and preferred room (subject to availability with advanced reservations).

SOME UNITS
FEE

## STUDIO EAST MOTOR INN

**Phone:** (207)646-7297

| | | | | |
|---|---|---|---|---|
| 7/1-9/6 | 1P: $99-$159 | 2P: $99-$159 | XP: $10 | F6 |
| 6/11-6/30 | 1P: $79-$129 | 2P: $79-$129 | XP: $10 | F6 |
| 5/1-6/10 & 9/7-12/20 | 1P: $59-$99 | 2P: $59-$99 | XP: $10 | F6 |

Motel

**Location:** On US 1; center. 267 Main St 03907 (PO Box 1827). Fax: 207/646-5567. **Facility:** 30 one-bedroom standard units. 2 stories (no elevator). **Parking:** on-site. **Terms:** open 5/1-12/20, office hours 7 am-11 pm, 10 day cancellation notice-fee imposed, pets ($10 extra charge). **Amenities:** hair dryers. *Some:* irons. **Leisure Activities:** whirlpool. **Cards:** AX, DS, MC, VI.

SOME UNITS
FEE

## TERRACE BY THE SEA

**Phone:** 207/646-3232

AAA (SAVE)

| | | | |
|---|---|---|---|
| 6/25-9/30 [ECP] | | 2P: $88-$235 | XP: $20 |
| 5/28-6/24 [ECP] | | 2P: $75-$199 | XP: $20 |
| 10/1-12/12 [ECP] | | 2P: $59-$172 | XP: $20 |
| 5/1-5/27 [ECP] | | 2P: $58-$140 | XP: $15 |

Small-scale Hotel **Location:** Jct US 1, 1.1 mi se on Shore Rd, then just e. 23 Wharf Ln 03907 (PO Box 831). Fax: 207/646-0742. **Facility:** 36 one-bedroom standard units, some with efficiencies. 2 stories (no elevator), interior/exterior corridors. *Bath:* combo or shower only. **Parking:** on-site. **Terms:** open 5/1-12/12, office hours 8 am-9 pm, 2 night minimum stay - weekends, 4 nights 7/1-8/31, 14 day cancellation notice-fee imposed, package plans. **Pool(s):** heated outdoor. **Special Amenities:** free expanded continental breakfast and free newspaper.

SOME UNITS

## TOWNE LYNE MOTEL

**Phone:** 207/646-2955

| | | | | |
|---|---|---|---|---|
| 6/25-9/1 | 1P: $115-$125 | 2P: $115-$125 | XP: $15 | F8 |
| 6/4-6/24 | 1P: $65-$85 | 2P: $65-$85 | XP: $10 | F8 |
| 9/2-10/31 | 1P: $65-$70 | 2P: $65-$70 | XP: $10 | F8 |
| 5/1-6/3 | 1P: $55-$65 | 2P: $55-$65 | XP: $10 | F8 |

Motel

**Location:** 1.2 mi n on US 1. 747 Main St 03907 (PO Box 833). Fax: 207/646-1812. **Facility:** 20 one-bedroom standard units, some with efficiencies. 1 story, exterior corridors. *Bath:* combo or shower only. **Parking:** on-site. **Terms:** open 5/1-10/31, office hours 7 am-10 pm, 2 night minimum stay - weekends, 14 day cancellation notice-fee imposed. **Cards:** MC, VI.

SOME UNITS

## WHITE ROSE INN

**Phone:** 207/646-3432

AAA (SAVE)

| | | | | |
|---|---|---|---|---|
| 6/18-9/6 [BP] | 1P: $125-$280 | 2P: $125-$280 | XP: $35 | D9 |
| 5/1-6/17 [BP] | 1P: $89-$250 | 2P: $89-$250 | XP: $35 | D9 |
| 9/7-4/30 [BP] | 1P: $84-$250 | 2P: $84-$250 | XP: $35 | D9 |

Bed & Breakfast **Location:** Just s on US 1. 95 Main St 03907-2227 (PO Box 2227, 03907). Fax: 207/646-3432. **Facility:** Close to the village, the inn is surrounded by picturesque landscaping and offers guest rooms with updated decor in a main inn and a carriage house. Smoke free premises. 8 one-bedroom standard units, some with efficiencies. 2 stories (no elevator), interior/exterior corridors. *Bath:* combo or shower only. **Parking:** on-site. **Terms:** 2-3 night minimum stay, 15 day cancellation notice-fee imposed, no pets allowed (owner's pet on premises). **Amenities:** hair dryers. **Leisure Activities:** whirlpool. **Cards:** DS, MC, VI. **Special Amenities:** free full breakfast and free local telephone calls.

SOME UNITS

## YARDARM VILLAGE INN

**Phone:** 207/646-7006

| | | | |
|---|---|---|---|
| 5/28-9/30 | 1P: $99-$120 | 2P: $99-$120 | XP: $20 |
| 10/1-10/31 | 1P: $79-$120 | 2P: $79-$120 | XP: $20 |
| 5/1-5/27 | 1P: $69-$109 | 2P: $69-$109 | XP: $20 |

Bed & Breakfast **Location:** 1.1 mi s on Shore Rd, just s of entrance to Perkins Cove; center of the village. 406 Shore Rd 03907 (PO Box 773). Fax: 207/646-9034. **Facility:** 8 units. 5 one-bedroom standard units. 3 one-bedroom suites ($89-$120). 3 stories (no elevator), interior corridors. *Bath:* shower only. **Parking:** on-site. **Terms:** open 5/1-10/31, 14 day cancellation notice-fee imposed, [CP] meal plan available. **Amenities:** hair dryers. **Guest Services:** gift shop.

--------- WHERE TO DINE ---------

## ARROWS RESTAURANT Historic

**Dinner:** $40-$42 **Phone:** 207/361-1100

American

**Location:** 1.8 mi w of jct US 1. Berwick Rd 03907. **Hours:** Open 5/1-12/13 & 4/18-4/30; 6 pm-9:30 pm seatings Fri-Sun 11/5-5/31; hours and days may vary seasonally. Closed: Mon. **Reservations:** required. **Features:** This 18th-century country home now the setting of a memorable dining pleasure. An incredible changing menu, filled with unusual delectables and always freshly prepared. Alaskan king salmon, grilled loin of venison, or sauteed Maryland soft-shelled crabs are just a smattering of possible offerings. The attentive and friendly wait staff is eager to assist with entree and wine selections. Homemade pastry and dessert are always memorable. Semi-formal attire; cocktails. **Parking:** on-site. **Cards:** AX, MC, VI.

## BARNACLE BILLY'S

**Lunch:** $6-$20 **Dinner:** $10-$25 **Phone:** 207/646-5575

Seafood

**Location:** Jct US 1 and Shore Rd, 1 mi se on Shore Rd; in Perkins Cove. 50 Oarweed Cove Rd 03907. **Hours:** Open 5/1-10/18 & 4/12-4/30; 11 am-9 pm. **Features:** The deck at Barnacle Billy's gives a great view of Perkins Cove, and the stone fireplace offers a cozy, comfortable ambience. Fresh boiled lobster, steamed clams, grilled chicken, chowder and salad are a few of the selections on the varied menu. Casual dress; cocktails. **Parking:** valet. **Cards:** AX, MC, VI.

## BARNACLE BILLY'S ETC.

**Lunch:** $6-$20 **Dinner:** $6-$25 **Phone:** 207/646-4711

Seafood

**Location:** Jct US 1 and Shore Rd, 1 mi s; in Perkins Cove. 70 Perkins Cove Rd 03907. **Hours:** Open 5/1-10/31; noon-9 pm. **Features:** When there's a chill in the air, they stoke up the fireplaces at Barnacle Billy's, where you're sure to enjoy the "luxury" lobster. This place has served diners since 1961. The outdoor deck overlooks the harbor, and the garden is at the waters edge. Casual dress; cocktails. **Parking:** valet. **Cards:** AX, MC, VI.

## BINTLIFF'S OGUNQUIT

**Lunch:** $9-$18 **Dinner:** $18-$30 **Phone:** 207/646-3111

AAA

American

**Location:** Just n of center on US 1. 335 Main St 03907. **Hours:** 7 am-2 & 5-12:30 am. Closed: 11/25, 12/25. **Features:** The popular bistro-style restaurant lists more than 110 items on its specialty brunch menu, which is presented all day. On the dinner menu are varied chicken, seafood and steak favorites. Casual dress; cocktails. **Parking:** on-site. **Cards:** AX, MC, VI.

**BLUE STAR GRILLE**
♥♥ ♥♥
Regional American

**Lunch:** $4-$8          **Dinner:** $6-$20          **Phone:** 207/641-2200
**Location:** Just n of center on US 1. 355 Main St 03907. **Hours:** Open 5/4-11/15 & 3/1-4/30; 11:30 am-9 pm, Fri & Sat-10 pm; Fri & Sat only 3/1-5/1 & 10/15-11/15. **Features:** Located close to the center of Ogunquit, Blue Star is a popular family restaurant which is open for breakfast lunch & dinner. The menu features seafood, steak and lighter fare as well. Casual dress; cocktails. **Parking:** on-site. **Cards:** MC, VI.

**FIVE-O**
♥♥♥♥♥♥
American
MC, VI.

**Dinner:** $15-$25          **Phone:** 207/646-6365
**Location:** Jct US 1, just se. 50 Shore Rd 03907. **Hours:** 5 pm-10 pm; hours vary seasonally. **Reservations:** accepted. **Features:** Specialties of regional, American inspired cuisine include broiled haddock in white wine served with lemon butter and braised duck breast with eggplant and mushrooms in fresh sage sauce over grilled Parmesan polenta. Casual dress; cocktails. **Parking:** on-site. **Cards:** AX, DS,

**GYPSY SWEETHEARTS RESTAURANT**
♥♥♥♥♥♥
International

**Dinner:** $15-$25          **Phone:** 207/646-7021
**Location:** Jct US 1, just se. 30 Shore Rd 03907. **Hours:** Open 5/1-11/11 & 4/15-4/30; 5:30 pm-9 pm. Closed: Mon. **Reservations:** suggested. **Features:** The menu specialties by chef/owner Judy Clayton include East Coast crabcakes, fresh raspberry salad, shrimp margarita, Cuban Adobo pork and shelled native lobster. Enjoy a fine dining experience in a charming old house with a porch overlooking Shore Road. Dining is offered in the upstairs lounge. The wine list is wonderful. Casual dress; cocktails. **Parking:** on-site. **Cards:** AX, DS, MC, VI.

**HURRICANE RESTAURANT**
AAA
♥♥♥♥♥♥
American

**Lunch:** $7-$14          **Dinner:** $14-$26          **Phone:** 207/646-6348
**Location:** Jct US 1, 1 mi se on Shore Rd to Perkins Cove. 111 Perkins Cove Rd 03907. **Hours:** 11:30 am-9:30 pm, Fri & Sat-10:30 pm; to 10:30 pm 5/24-10/10. **Reservations:** required. **Features:** Offering spectacular ocean views, the popular restaurant presents a menu with such selections as soups, salads, grilled wild boar sausage pizza, deviled lobster cakes with salsa, roasted zucchini with wild-rice stuffing and mile-high or berry cheesecake. A "jazzy" brunch lures a good crowd on Sunday. Casual dress; cocktails; name entertainment. **Parking:** street. **Cards:** AX, DC, DS, MC, VI.

**IMPASTABLE DREAM**
♥♥ ♥♥
Italian
**Cards:** AX, DS, MC, VI.

**Dinner:** $9-$17          **Phone:** 207/646-3011
**Location:** Jct US 1, 0.7 mi se. 261 Shore Rd 03907. **Hours:** 5 pm-9 pm; closing hours may vary. Closed: 11/25, 12/25; also Tues & Wed. **Features:** You'll enjoy this restaurant featuring fresh vegetables, capers, olives, cheese, fish and beef with a variety of pasta and sauce. Portions are very generous! The informal atmosphere is very comfortable, and the serving staff is friendly and attentive. Cocktails. **Parking:** on-site.

**JONATHAN'S RESTAURANT**
AAA
♥♥♥♥♥♥
Continental

**Dinner:** $17-$30          **Phone:** 207/646-4777
**Location:** 0.5 mi s on US 1, just e. 2 Bourne Ln 03907. **Hours:** 5 pm-9 pm, Fri & Sat-9:30 pm; Fri & Sat-10 pm 10/15-5/28. Closed: 12/24, 12/25; also Tues 11/1-3/31. **Reservations:** suggested. **Features:** Specialties at Jonathan's include the caramelized, pan-seared salmon dusted with sugar and dill, and the lobster ravioli, each presented in attractive surroundings. They have a fine collection of American paintings and very pretty gardens. Casual dress; cocktails. **Parking:** on-site. **Cards:** AX, DC, DS, MC, VI.

**NINETY EIGHT PROVENCE**
♥♥♥♥♥♥
Regional French

**Dinner:** $25-$32          **Phone:** 207/646-9898
**Location:** Jct US 1, 0.7 mi se. 262 Shore Rd 03907. **Hours:** Open 5/1-12/12 & 4/1-4/30; 5:30 pm-9 pm. Closed: Tues; Mon 11/1-11/30, Wed 10/1-11/30 & 4/1-5/31. **Reservations:** suggested. **Features:** Intimate candlelight dining is the specialty at this restaurant. The menu is changed daily and features fine Provencal cuisine. Dishes include soupe de pecheur with mussels, shrimp, clams and scallops, and pan-seared Maine venison. Casual dress; cocktails. **Parking:** on-site. **Cards:** AX, MC, VI.

**THE OLD VILLAGE INN**   Historic
♥♥♥♥♥♥
Continental

**Dinner:** $15-$22          **Phone:** 207/646-7088
**Location:** On US 1; center of the village. 250 Main St 03907. **Hours:** Open 5/1-12/31 & 2/6-4/30; 5:30 pm-9 pm, Fri & Sat-9:30 pm; to 9:30 pm 6/15-9/7. **Reservations:** suggested. **Features:** This restaurant includes charming Victorian dining rooms and English pub-style bar, with a warm decor and paintings by local artists. The nicely prepared regional dishes of pasta, stir-fries, rack of lamb, filet mignon and lobster use local ingredients. Cocktails. **Parking:** on-site. **Cards:** AX, DS, MC, VI.

**POOR RICHARD'S TAVERN**
♥♥ ♥♥
Regional American

**Dinner:** $12-$26          **Phone:** 207/646-4722
**Location:** Jct US 1, 1 mi se, just s of entrance to Perkins Cove. 331 Shore Rd 03907. **Hours:** Open 5/1-12/31 & 4/15-4/30; 5:30 pm-9:30 pm. Closed: Sun, except holiday weekends. **Reservations:** suggested. **Features:** Poor Richard's is a local landmark in a charming old house near Perkins Cove. Chef/owner Richard Perkins creates a wonderful menu of delicious lobster stew and fabulous lobster pie. Meatloaf and charbroiled salmon filets are also among the offerings. Cocktails. **Parking:** valet. **Cards:** AX, DS, MC, VI.

**ROBERTO'S RESTAURANT**
AAA
♥♥♥♥
Italian

**Dinner:** $11-$25          **Phone:** 207/646-8130
**Location:** Jct US 1, 0.5 mi se. 200 Shore Rd 03907. **Hours:** 5 pm-9:30 pm; hours vary off season. Closed: 11/25, 12/25. **Reservations:** suggested. **Features:** The flavorful seafood dishes at Roberto's display the use of fresh local ingredients and an Italian flair. The informal and friendly atmosphere is complemented by the attractive grounds and landscaping. The bistro-style restaurant has a small, cozy bar. Casual dress; cocktails. **Parking:** on-site. **Cards:** AX, MC, VI.

**VINNY'S EAST COAST GRILLE**
**Dinner:** $8-$18
**Phone:** 207/646-5115

American

**Location:** 1.2 mi n on US 1. 696 Main St 03907. **Hours:** Open 5/1-11/1 & 4/1-4/30; 5 pm-11 pm. Closed: 3/27. **Reservations:** accepted. **Features:** In operation since 1980, Vinny's has something for everyone including a children's menu and dining room, sports bar, a seasonal terrace and a child free dining room. The cuisine includes, pasta, saefood, sandwiches, wraps, burgers, pizza, chicken and steak. Casual dress; cocktails. **Parking:** on-site. **Cards:** MC, VI.

# OLD ORCHARD BEACH pop. 8,856

———— **WHERE TO STAY** ————

**THE AQUARIUS MOTEL**
**Phone:** 207/934-2626

AAA [SAVE]

Motel

| | | |
|---|---|---|
| 6/25-9/5 | 1P: $119-$149 | 2P: $119-$179 |
| 6/8-6/24 | 1P: $80-$105 | 2P: $80-$125 |
| 9/6-10/15 | 1P: $65-$79 | 2P: $65-$99 |
| 5/1-6/7 | 1P: $54-$69 | 2P: $54-$89 |

**Location:** Just e on SR 9 (E Grand Ave), oceanfront at end of street. 1 Brown St 04064 (PO Box 768). Fax: 207/934-0046. **Facility:** 14 units. 9 one-bedroom standard units, some with efficiencies. 5 one-bedroom suites with efficiencies. 2 stories (no elevator), exterior corridors. **Parking:** on-site. **Terms:** open 5/1-10/15, 3 night minimum stay - 7/1-8/31, 21 day cancellation notice-fee imposed, weekly rates available. **Leisure Activities:** gas grills. **Cards:** DS, MC, VI. **Special Amenities:** free local telephone calls and free newspaper.

SOME UNITS

**ATLANTIC BIRCHES INN**     *Book at aaa.com*
**Phone:** 207/934-5295

Bed & Breakfast

| | | | | |
|---|---|---|---|---|
| 6/28-9/6 | 1P: $89-$135 | 2P: $89-$135 | XP: $10 | F5 |
| 6/11-6/27 | 1P: $79-$115 | 2P: $79-$115 | XP: $10 | F5 |
| 9/7-4/30 | 1P: $69-$115 | 2P: $69-$115 | XP: $10 | F5 |
| 5/1-6/10 | 1P: $69-$95 | 2P: $69-$95 | XP: $10 | F5 |

**Location:** Jct SR 5 and 98, just w on SR 98. Located in a residential area. 20 Portland Ave 04064. Fax: 207/934-3781. **Facility:** This pleasant Victorian inn and carriage house is not far from the beach. Smoke free premises. 10 units. 8 one-bedroom standard units. 2 one-bedroom suites ($94-$114) with efficiencies. 3 stories (no elevator); interior/exterior corridors. *Bath:* combo or shower only. **Parking:** on-site. **Terms:** 2 night minimum stay - 6/11-10/11, 14 day cancellation notice-fee imposed, [CP] meal plan available, package plans - 6/11-10/11, no pets allowed (owner's pet on premises). **Pool(s):** heated outdoor. **Cards:** AX, DS, MC, VI. *(See color ad below)*

SOME UNITS

**BEACHFRONT CONDOTELS**
**Phone:** (207)934-7434

Motel

| | | | | |
|---|---|---|---|---|
| 6/28-9/7 | 1P: $129-$189 | 2P: $129-$189 | XP: $10 | F16 |
| 6/11-6/27 | 1P: $84-$139 | 2P: $84-$139 | XP: $10 | F16 |
| 5/1-6/10 & 9/8-4/30 | 1P: $69-$104 | 2P: $69-$104 | XP: $10 | F16 |

**Location:** 0.4 mi e on SR 9 (E Grand Ave), just s. 1 Walnut St 04064 (PO Box 710). Fax: 207/934-0456. **Facility:** 22 units. 20 one-bedroom standard units with efficiencies, some with whirlpools. 2 two-bedroom suites with efficiencies. 2 stories (no elevator), exterior corridors. *Bath:* shower only. **Parking:** on-site. **Terms:** 3 day cancellation notice-fee imposed, package plans. **Amenities:** video library (fee). **Leisure Activities:** whirlpool. **Guest Services:** coin laundry. **Cards:** AX, DC, MC, VI.

SOME UNITS

**BEACH WALK-WIND SONG MOTEL**
**Phone:** 207/934-2381

Small-scale Hotel

| | | | | |
|---|---|---|---|---|
| 6/29-9/2 | 1P: $75-$200 | 2P: $75-$200 | XP: $15 | F7 |
| 5/1-6/28 & 9/3-9/21 | 1P: $60-$130 | 2P: $60-$130 | XP: $15 | F7 |

**Location:** 1 mi e on SR 9 (E Grand Ave), just e on Morrison St. 109 E Grand Ave 04064. Fax: 207/934-0396. **Facility:** 40 units. 27 one- and 8 two-bedroom standard units, some with efficiencies. 4 two-bedroom suites ($700-$1200) with kitchens. 1 cottage ($750-$1350). 1-3 stories (no elevator), interior/exterior corridors. *Bath:* combo or shower only. **Parking:** on-site. **Terms:** open 5/1-9/21, office hours 8 am-9 pm, 30 day cancellation notice-fee imposed, package plans. **Pool(s):** heated outdoor. **Cards:** AX, DC, MC, VI.

SOME UNITS

**BEAU RIVAGE MOTEL**

Motel

|  | 6/18-9/6 | 1P: $114-$199 | 2P: $114-$199 | XP: $10 | F12 |
|--|----------|---------------|---------------|---------|-----|
|  | 5/1-6/17, 9/7-11/15 & 4/15-4/30 | 1P: $49-$139 | 2P: $49-$139 | XP: $10 | F12 |

Phone: (207)934-4668

**Location:** 0.3 mi e of Old Orchard St. 54 E Grand Ave 04064 (PO Box 650). Fax: 207/934-7527. **Facility:** 65 units. 64 one- and 1 two-bedroom standard units, some with efficiencies, kitchens and/or whirlpools. 2 stories (no elevator), exterior corridors. *Bath:* combo or shower only. **Parking:** on-site. **Terms:** open 5/1-11/15 & 4/15-4/30, 2-3 night minimum stay - in summer, 14 day cancellation notice-fee imposed, small pets only ($25 deposit, $10 extra charge, in limited units). **Pool(s):** heated outdoor. **Leisure Activities:** sauna, whirlpool. **Cards:** AX, DS, MC, VI.

SOME UNITS

---

**THE CREST MOTEL**

Motel

|  | 6/25-9/6 | 1P: $155-$249 | 2P: $155-$249 | XP: $10 | F12 |
|--|----------|---------------|---------------|---------|-----|
|  | 6/4-6/24 | 1P: $125-$183 | 2P: $125-$183 | XP: $10 | F12 |
|  | 9/7-4/30 | 1P: $89-$150 | 2P: $89-$150 | XP: $10 | F12 |
|  | 5/1-6/3 | 1P: $79-$150 | 2P: $79-$150 | XP: $10 | F12 |

Phone: (207)934-4060

**Location:** Just e of Old Orchard St. 35 E Grand Ave 04064. Fax: 207/934-0456. **Facility:** 27 units. 24 one-bedroom standard units, some with whirlpools. 3 one-bedroom suites with efficiencies. 2 stories (no elevator), exterior corridors. *Bath:* combo or shower only. **Parking:** on-site. **Terms:** office hours 8 am-11 pm, 2-3 night minimum stay - weekends, 7 day cancellation notice-fee imposed. **Pool(s):** heated indoor. **Leisure Activities:** sauna, whirlpool, playground. **Cards:** DS, MC, VI.

SOME UNITS

**THE EDGEWATER**
◈◈ ◈◈
Motel

Phone: 207/934-2221

| | | | | |
|---|---|---|---|---|
| 6/18-9/6 | 1P: $149-$229 | 2P: $149-$229 | XP: $10 | F12 |
| 5/1-6/17 & 9/7-10/31 | 1P: $69-$169 | 2P: $69-$169 | XP: $10 | F12 |
| 11/1-4/30 | 1P: $69-$129 | 2P: $69-$129 | XP: $10 | F12 |

**Location:** 0.5 mi w on SR 9 (W Grand Ave). 57 W Grand Ave 04064. **Fax:** 207/934-3731. **Facility:** 36 units. 33 one-bedroom standard units, some with efficiencies. 2 one- and 1 two-bedroom suites with efficiencies. 2 stories (no elevator), exterior corridors. **Parking:** on-site. **Terms:** office hours 8 am-11 pm, 3 night minimum stay - 7/1-9/6, 7 day cancellation notice-fee imposed. **Pool(s):** heated outdoor. **Business Services:** meeting rooms. **Cards:** AX, DS, MC, VI. *(See color ad p 264)*

SOME UNITS

**EXECUTIVE MOTEL**
◈◈ ◈◈
Motel

Phone: 207/934-4637

| | | | | |
|---|---|---|---|---|
| 7/1-9/15 | 1P: $120-$140 | 2P: $125-$150 | XP: $15 | F11 |
| 6/7-6/30 | 1P: $85-$125 | 2P: $85-$125 | XP: $15 | F11 |
| 5/15-6/6 | 1P: $70-$95 | 2P: $70-$95 | XP: $15 | F11 |

**Location:** On SR 9 (E Grand Ave), just e. 38 E Grand Ave 04064. **Fax:** 207/934-9178. **Facility:** 24 one-bedroom standard units. 1 story, exterior corridors. *Bath:* combo or shower only. **Parking:** on-site. **Terms:** open 5/15-9/15, office hours 7 am-10 pm, 2-3 night minimum stay, 3 day cancellation notice-fee imposed. **Pool(s):** heated outdoor. **Cards:** AX, CB, DC, DS, MC.

SOME UNITS

**FRIENDSHIP MOTOR INN**
◈◈ ◈◈
Small-scale Hotel

Phone: 207/934-4644

| | | | |
|---|---|---|---|
| 6/18-9/6 | 1P: $119-$199 | 2P: $119-$199 | XP: $10 |
| 9/7-10/31 | 1P: $69-$129 | 2P: $69-$129 | XP: $10 |
| 5/1-6/17 & 4/22-4/30 | 1P: $69-$109 | 2P: $69-$109 | XP: $10 |

**Location:** 1 mi e on SR 9 (E Grand Ave). 167 E Grand Ave 04064. **Fax:** 207/934-7592. **Facility:** 71 one-bedroom suites, some with efficiencies. 2 stories (no elevator), exterior corridors. *Bath:* shower only. **Parking:** on-site. **Terms:** open 5/1-10/31 & 4/22-4/30, office hours 8 am-9 pm, 10 day cancellation notice-fee imposed. **Amenities:** video library (fee). **Pool(s):** heated outdoor. **Leisure Activities:** fishing. **Guest Services:** coin laundry. **Cards:** AX, DS, MC, VI. *(See color ad p 264)*

SOME UNITS

**GRAND BEACH INN**
(AAA) [SAVE]
◈◈ ◈◈
Small-scale Hotel

Phone: (207)934-4621

| | | | | |
|---|---|---|---|---|
| 6/26-9/7 | 1P: $139-$199 | 2P: $139-$199 | XP: $10 | F13 |
| 5/1-6/25 & 9/8-4/30 | 1P: $69-$109 | 2P: $69-$109 | XP: $5 | F13 |

**Location:** On SR 9 (E Grand Ave); center. Located close to railroad tracks. 198 E Grand Ave 04064. **Fax:** 207/934-4621. **Facility:** 86 units. 79 one-bedroom standard units, some with efficiencies or kitchens. 7 one-bedroom suites ($89-$200) with kitchens. 3 stories (no elevator), exterior corridors. **Parking:** on-site. **Terms:** office hours 8 am-10 pm, 2 night minimum stay - 7/1-9/1, 3 day cancellation notice, [BP] meal plan available, package plans - off season 9/1-6/25. **Dining:** 7-11 am. **Pool(s):** heated outdoor. **Guest Services:** coin laundry. **Cards:** AX, DS, MC, VI. *(See color ad below)*

SOME UNITS

**THE GULL MOTEL**
◈◈ ◈◈
Motel

Phone: 207/934-4321

| | | | | |
|---|---|---|---|---|
| 6/20-9/6 | 1P: $65 | 2P: $145 | XP: $10 | F5 |
| 5/1-6/19 & 9/7-10/11 | 1P: $55 | 2P: $75 | XP: $10 | F5 |

**Location:** 0.5 mi w on SR 9 (W Grand Ave). 89 W Grand Ave 04064. **Fax:** 207/934-1742. **Facility:** 21 one-bedroom standard units with efficiencies. 2 stories (no elevator), exterior corridors. *Bath:* combo or shower only. **Parking:** on-site. **Terms:** open 5/1-10/11, 3 night minimum stay - seasonal, 10 day cancellation notice-fee imposed. **Pool(s):** heated outdoor. **Cards:** DS, MC, VI.

SOME UNITS

**HORIZON MOTEL**
**Phone:** 207/934-2323

Motel

| | 1P: $120-$130 | 2P: $120-$130 | XP: $15 |
| 7/1-8/22 | 1P: $120-$130 | 2P: $120-$130 | XP: $15 |
| 8/23-10/11 | 1P: $65-$110 | 2P: $65-$110 | XP: $15 |
| 5/1-6/30 | 1P: $65-$75 | 2P: $65-$75 | XP: $15 |

**Location:** 0.5 mi w on SR 9 (W Grand Ave), just left. 2 Atlantic Ave 04064. Fax: 207/934-3215. **Facility:** 14 one-bedroom suites with efficiencies. 3 stories (no elevator), exterior corridors. **Parking:** on-site. **Terms:** open 5/1-10/11, office hours 8 am-10 pm, 7 day cancellation notice-fee imposed. **Guest Services:** complimentary laundry. **Cards:** AX, MC, VI.

**KEBEK 3 MOTEL**
**Phone:** 207/934-5253

Motel

| 7/1-9/6 | 1P: $120-$145 | 2P: $120-$145 | XP: $10 | F12 |
| 6/19-6/30 | 1P: $90-$110 | 2P: $90-$110 | XP: $10 | F12 |
| 5/6-6/18 & 9/7-10/12 | 1P: $65-$80 | 2P: $65-$80 | XP: $10 | F12 |

**Location:** 0.5 mi e on SR 9 (W Grand Ave). 53 W Grand Ave 04064. Fax: 207/934-3220. **Facility:** 35 units. 21 one-bedroom standard units with efficiencies. 14 one-bedroom suites with efficiencies. 2 stories (no elevator), exterior corridors. *Bath:* combo or shower only. **Parking:** on-site. **Terms:** open 5/6-10/12, office hours 9 am-9 pm, 3 night minimum stay, 14 day cancellation notice-fee imposed, weekly rates available. **Cards:** DC, MC, VI.

**OCEAN WALK HOTEL**
**Phone:** 207/934-1716

Motel

| 6/18-9/5 | 1P: $150-$230 | 2P: $150-$230 | XP: $20 |
| 5/1-6/17, 9/6-10/25 & 4/1-4/30 | 1P: $79-$160 | 2P: $79-$160 | XP: $20 |

**Location:** On SR 9 (E Grand Ave), 1.3 mi e. 197 E Grand Ave 04064. Fax: 207/934-2835. **Facility:** 44 units. 38 one-bedroom standard units with efficiencies. 6 one-bedroom suites ($160-$285) with efficiencies. 2 stories (no elevator), exterior corridors. **Parking:** on-site. **Terms:** open 5/1-10/25 & 4/1-4/30, 1-3 night minimum stay - weekends, 10 day cancellation notice-fee imposed. **Amenities:** video library (fee). **Pool(s):** heated indoor. **Guest Services:** coin laundry. **Cards:** AX, DC, DS, MC, VI. **Special Amenities:** free local telephone calls and free newspaper. *(See color ad below)*

SOME UNITS

## OLD COLONIAL MOTEL

| | | | | |
|---|---|---|---|---|
| | 7/2-9/5 | 1P: $130-$220 | 2P: $130-$220 | XP: $25 F6 |
| | 6/11-7/1 | 1P: $95-$180 | 2P: $95-$180 | XP: $15 F6 |
| | 9/6-10/31 | 1P: $80-$150 | 2P: $80-$150 | XP: $15 F6 |
| Motel | 5/1-6/10 | 1P: $70-$140 | 2P: $70-$140 | XP: $15 F6 |

**Phone:** (207)934-9862

**Location:** On SR 9 (W Grand Ave), 0.5 mi w. 61 W Grand Ave 04064. Fax: 207/934-3740. **Facility:** 30 units. 23 one-bedroom standard units, some with efficiencies. 7 one-bedroom suites. 2 stories (no elevator), exterior corridors. *Bath:* combo or shower only. **Parking:** on-site. **Terms:** open 5/1-10/31, office hours 8 am-11 pm, 14 day cancellation notice-fee imposed, package plans, pets ($5 extra charge). **Amenities:** video library (fee), DVD players. **Pool(s):** heated outdoor. **Leisure Activities:** sauna, whirlpool, limited exercise equipment. **Cards:** AX, DS, MC, VI. **Special Amenities:** free local telephone calls and free newspaper. *(See color ad below)*

SOME UNITS

## OLD ORCHARD BEACH INN

| | | | | |
|---|---|---|---|---|
| | 6/18-9/6 [CP] | 1P: $110-$185 | 2P: $110-$185 | XP: $20 D12 |
| | 5/1-6/17 & 9/7-10/17 [CP] | 1P: $70-$140 | 2P: $70-$140 | XP: $20 D12 |
| Bed & Breakfast | 10/18-4/30 [CP] | 1P: $70-$135 | 2P: $70-$135 | XP: $20 D12 |

**Phone:** 207/934-5834

**Location:** Center. 6 Portland Ave 04064 (PO Box 720). Fax: 207/934-0782. **Facility:** Period antiques, patchwork quilts and many original hardwood floors set the decor theme at this inn built in 1730. Smoke free premises. 18 units. 17 one-bedroom standard units. 1 two-bedroom suite ($150-$400) with kitchen. 3 stories (no elevator), interior corridors. *Bath:* combo or shower only. **Parking:** on-site. **Terms:** 15 day cancellation notice-fee imposed. **Cards:** AX, DS, MC, VI. **Special Amenities:** free continental breakfast and free local telephone calls. *(See color ad p 263)*

SOME UNITS

## ROYAL ANCHOR RESORT

**Phone:** 207/934-4521

(AAA) (SAVE)

| | | | |
|---|---|---|---|
| 6/18-9/6 [ECP] | | 2P: $129-$179 | XP: $15 |
| 9/7-10/17 [ECP] | | 2P: $69-$119 | XP: $15 |
| 5/1-6/17 & 4/23-4/30 [ECP] | | 2P: $69-$109 | XP: $15 |

Small-scale Hotel **Location:** 1.3 mi e on SR 9 (E Grand Ave). Located in a quiet area. 203 E Grand Ave 04064. Fax: 207/934-4521. **Facility:** 40 one-bedroom standard units. 3 stories (no elevator), exterior corridors. **Parking:** on-site. **Terms:** open 5/1-10/17 & 4/23-4/30, office hours 7 am-10 pm, 10 day cancellation notice-fee imposed. **Amenities:** voice mail. **Pool(s):** heated outdoor. **Leisure Activities:** fishing, tennis court, children's play area, basketball, shuffleboard, volleyball. **Guest Services:** coin laundry. **Cards:** AX, DS, MC, VI. **Special Amenities:** free expanded continental breakfast and preferred room (subject to availability with advanced reservations). *(See color ad below)*

SOME UNITS

## SEA VIEW MOTEL

**Phone:** 207/934-4180

(AAA) (SAVE)

| | | | | |
|---|---|---|---|---|
| 6/11-9/5 | | 2P: $80-$230 | XP: $20 | F10 |
| 5/25-6/10 | | 2P: $60-$175 | XP: $10 | F10 |
| 9/6-10/31 | | 2P: $50-$160 | XP: $10 | F10 |
| 5/1-5/24 | | 2P: $50-$130 | XP: $10 | F10 |

Small-scale Hotel **Location:** 0.5 mi w on SR 9 (W Grand Ave). 65 W Grand Ave 04064 (PO Box 677). **Facility:** 45 units. 39 one- and 1 two-bedroom standard units, some with efficiencies. 1 one- and 4 two-bedroom suites ($190-$290) with efficiencies. 3 stories (no elevator), exterior corridors. *Bath:* combo or shower only. **Parking:** on-site. **Terms:** open 5/1-10/31, 5 night minimum stay - in suites in summer, 3 day cancellation notice-fee imposed, package plans - seasonal, pets ($100 deposit, off season). **Amenities:** *Some:* irons, hair dryers. **Pool(s):** heated outdoor. **Cards:** AX, DS, MC, VI. **Special Amenities:** free local telephone calls and free newspaper. *(See color ad below)*

SOME UNITS

FEE

## WAVES OCEANFRONT RESORT

◆◆◆ ◆◆◆
Small-scale Hotel

**Phone: (207)934-4949**

| |  |  |  | |
|---|---|---|---|---|
| 7/1-9/5 | 1P: $140-$210 | 2P: $140-$210 | XP: $20 | D18 |
| 5/1-6/30 | 1P: $70-$180 | 2P: $70-$180 | XP: $10 | D18 |
| 9/6-10/31 & 4/15-4/30 | 1P: $70-$120 | 2P: $70-$120 | XP: $10 | D18 |

**Location:** 0.5 mi w on SR 9 (W Grand Ave). 87 W Grand Ave 04064. Fax: 207/934-5983. **Facility:** 143 units. 139 one-bedroom standard units with efficiencies. 4 cottages. 1-2 stories (no elevator), exterior corridors. **Parking:** on-site. **Terms:** open 5/1-10/31 & 4/15-4/30, 1-4 night minimum stay - seasonal, 3 day cancellation notice-fee imposed, pets ($10 extra charge, with prior approval). **Pool(s):** outdoor. **Guest Services:** coin laundry. **Cards:** AX, DS, MC, VI. *(See color ad below)*

SOME UNITS

🛏️ 🍽️ 🐾 📶 📺 / ✕ 🅺 🆆 🖥️ /
FEE

## WHITE CAP VILLAGE

◆◆◆ ◆◆
Small-scale Hotel

**Phone: 207/934-2553**

| |  |  |  | |
|---|---|---|---|---|
| 6/12-9/6 | 1P: $79-$120 | 2P: $79-$120 | XP: $8 | F12 |
| 9/7-10/11 | 1P: $47-$82 | 2P: $47-$82 | XP: $8 | F12 |
| 5/5-6/11 | 1P: $47-$60 | 2P: $47-$60 | XP: $8 | F12 |

**Location:** 0.6 mi w on SR 9 (W Grand Ave), just e. 5 Bay Ave 04064. Fax: 207/934-2553. **Facility:** 31 units. 12 one- and 7 two-bedroom standard units, some with kitchens. 2 one-, 7 two- and 3 three-bedroom suites ($70-$175) with kitchens. 3 stories (no elevator), exterior corridors. *Bath:* combo or shower only. **Parking:** on-site. **Terms:** open 5/5-10/11, office hours 8 am-9 pm, 30 day cancellation notice-fee imposed, weekly rates available, package plans. **Amenities:** video library (fee). **Pool(s):** heated outdoor. **Leisure Activities:** playground. **Cards:** MC, VI.

🐾 🆅🅲🆁 📶 🖥️ 📺

## THE WHITE LAMB COTTAGES

◆◆◆
Cottage

**Phone: 207/934-2231**

| |  |  |  | |
|---|---|---|---|---|
| 6/18-9/6 | 1P: $149-$229 | 2P: $149-$229 | XP: $10 | F12 |
| 5/20-6/17 & 9/7-10/11 | 1P: $99-$169 | 2P: $99-$169 | XP: $10 | F12 |

**Location:** 0.8 mi w on SR 9 (W Grand Ave), just e. Located in a quiet area. 3 Odessa Ave 04064. Fax: 207/937-3731. **Facility:** In a quiet section of town, these duplex cottages with New England-style decor are a few steps from the beach; check-in is at the Edgewater. 8 cottages. 1 story, exterior corridors. **Parking:** on-site. **Terms:** open 5/20-10/11, off-site registration, 3 night minimum stay - 7/1-9/6, 7 day cancellation notice-fee imposed, [CP] meal plan available. **Amenities:** hair dryers. **Leisure Activities:** whirlpool. **Cards:** AX, DC, MC, VI.

📶 🖥️

──── **WHERE TO DINE** ────

**BAREFOOT BOY RESTAURANT**               **Lunch:** $6-$15          **Dinner:** $9-$25          **Phone:** 207/934-0185
▼▼ ▼▼         **Location:** 0.5 mi n of center on SR 9 (E Grand Ave). 45 E Grand Ave 04064. **Hours:** Open 5/28-10/9; 7 am-noon
               & 5-9:30 pm, Fri-Sun to 2 pm. **Reservations:** accepted. **Features:** Steaks, seafood and chicken are the
Steak & Seafood   featured items at this restaurant, which is a block from the beach. The baked stuffed lobster is a flavorful
               specialty. For breakfast, try the delicious blueberry pancakes. The atmosphere has a tropical summer
theme. Casual dress; cocktails. **Parking:** street. **Cards:** DS, MC, VI.                                ✕

**THE CAPTIAN'S GALLEY RESTAURANT**       **Lunch:** $5-$10          **Dinner:** $8-$19          **Phone:** 207/934-1336
▼▼ ▼▼         **Location:** I-95 (Maine Tpke), exit 36, 3 mi e on I-195 and SR 5. 168 Saco Ave 04064. **Hours:** 7 am-8:30 pm; hours
               may vary seasonally. **Closed:** 1/1, 11/25, 12/25. **Features:** Seafood, especially the fresh variety, makes up
Seafood        much of the menu at the friendly family restaurant. Locals also favor the prime rib. Casual dress; cocktails.
               **Parking:** on-site. **Cards:** AX, DS, MC, VI.                                          ⓂⓂ ✕

**JOSEPH'S BY-THE-SEA**                              **Dinner:** $16-$28                         **Phone:** 207/934-5044
▼▼▼         **Location:** 0.5 mi e on SR 9 (W Grand Ave). 55 W Grand Ave 04064. **Hours:** Open 5/1-12/15 & 4/1-4/30; 7 am-11
               & 5-9 pm; hours vary seasonally. **Closed:** Mon-Wed & Sun evening 4/1-5/15 & 11/1-12/25.
Continental    **Reservations:** accepted. **Features:** This popular oceanside restaurant is family-operated and has an airy
               decor. The skillfully prepared entrees include tasty baked stuffed lobster and pepper-crusted filet mignon.
There's terrace dining in season. A 15% service charge is applied for dinner. Casual dress; cocktails. **Parking:** on-site.
**Cards:** AX, MC, VI.                                                                                   🍸 ✕

**THE VILLAGE INN**                       **Lunch:** $6-$15          **Dinner:** $6-$15          **Phone:** 207/934-7370
▼▼ ▼▼         **Location:** I-95 (Maine Tpke), exit 36, 1.5 mi e on I-195 and SR 5. 213 Saco Ave 04064. **Hours:** 11:30 am-9 pm, Fri
               & Sat-10 pm. **Closed:** 11/25, 12/24, 12/25; also 4/1-4/30. **Features:** A casual family style restaurant
American       conveniently located to area attractions. With an emphasis on seafood, the menu also includes pasta,
               prime rib, steak, chicken, veal and pork entrees. Be sure to try the lobster stew! Microbrewery also on
premises. Cocktails. **Parking:** on-site. **Cards:** AX, DS, MC, VI.                                    🍸 ✕

## OLD TOWN pop. 8,130

──── **WHERE TO DINE** ────

**CHOCOLATE GRILLE**                      **Lunch:** $6-$12          **Dinner:** $9-$18          **Phone:** 207/827-8971
▼▼ ▼▼         **Location:** On SR 43, just n of jct US 2. 301 N Main St 04468. **Hours:** 11 am-12:30 pm, Sun-10 pm. **Closed:** 7/4,
               12/25. **Features:** While the grill is not chocolate, a love of the sweet confection is reflected in the dessert
American       menu, as well as in coffees and cocktails. Soups, salads, sandwiches, burgers and pizza share menu
               space with pasta and seafood preparations. The patio is open seasonally. Casual dress; cocktails.
**Parking:** on-site. **Cards:** AX, DS, MC, VI.                                                    ⓂⓂ 🍸 ✕

## ORLAND

──── **WHERE TO STAY** ────

**ALAMOOSOOK LODGE BED & BREAKFAST**                                                   **Phone:** (207)469-6393
(AAA) SAVE   6/16-10/15 [BP]              1P: $75-$95          2P: $90-$115          XP: $10
             5/1-6/15 & 10/16-11/30 [BP]  1P: $60-$75          2P: $70-$90          XP: $10
▼▼▼▼     12/1-4/30 [BP]              1P: $60               2P: $70               XP: $10
Bed & Breakfast   **Location:** US 1, 2.5 mi n on Upper Falls Rd, follow signs, 3 mi e of Bucksport. Located in a quiet area. 229 Soper Rd
             04472 (PO Box 16). Fax: 207/469-2528. **Facility:** In a setting bordering Alamoosook Lake, this B&B offers cozy
             guest rooms and a pleasant common area. Smoke free premises. 6 one-bedroom standard units. 1 story, in-
terior corridors. **Parking:** on-site. **Terms:** 14 day cancellation notice, package plans - seasonal. **Amenities:** hair dryers. **Leisure
Activities:** canoeing, boat dock, fishing, kayaks. **Guest Services:** TV in common area. **Cards:** AX, DS, MC, VI.
**Special Amenities: free full breakfast and free local telephone calls.**              ✕ ✕ 🅚 🄿 ☎

## ORONO pop. 8,253

──── **WHERE TO STAY** ────

**BEST WESTERN BLACK BEAR INN & CONFERENCE CENTER**    *Book at aaa.com*        **Phone:** (207)866-7120
▼▼▼     7/1-10/31 [ECP]            1P: $89-$109         2P: $99-$129         XP: $5          F12
             11/1-4/30 [ECP]            1P: $79-$99          2P: $89-$119         XP: $5          F12
Small-scale Hotel   5/1-6/30 [ECP]             1P: $79-$89          2P: $89-$99          XP: $5          F12
             **Location:** I-95, exit 193 (Stillwater Ave). 4 Godfrey Dr 04473. Fax: 207/866-7433. **Facility:** 68 one-bedroom stan-
dard units, some with whirlpools. 3 stories, interior corridors. **Parking:** on-site. **Terms:** pets ($3 extra charge). **Amenities:** irons,
hair dryers. **Leisure Activities:** sauna, exercise room. **Guest Services:** coin laundry. **Business Services:** meeting rooms.
**Cards:** AX, DC, DS, MC, VI.
                                                                              SOME UNITS
                                        (ASK) 🛒 ⓂⓂ 🄳🄰🅃🄰 💻 / ✕ 🛡 🖥 /

**UNIVERSITY INN ACADEMIC SUITES**                                                    **Phone:** 207/866-4921
(AAA) SAVE   5/1-10/31               1P: $59-$69          2P: $69-$79          XP: $10         F12
             11/1-4/30               1P: $52-$62          2P: $62-$72
▼▼ ▼▼     **Location:** I-95, exit 191, 0.4 mi n on US 2, 8 mi n of Bangor. 5 College Ave 04473. Fax: 207/866-4550. **Facility:** 48
             one-bedroom standard units. 2 stories (no elevator), interior corridors. **Parking:** on-site. **Terms:** weekly rates
Small-scale Hotel   available, small pets only (on ground floor smoking units). **Amenities:** video library (fee), hair dryers.
             **Pool(s):** outdoor. **Business Services:** meeting rooms. **Cards:** AX, DS, MC, VI. **Special Amenities: free ex-
panded continental breakfast.**
                                                                              SOME UNITS
                                        🛏 🍸 🏊 / ✕ 🆅🅲🆁 🄳🄰🅃🄰 🛡 🖥 💻 /

**PORTLAND** pop. 64,249—*See also SOUTH PORTLAND.*

———— WHERE TO STAY ————

**DOUBLETREE HOTEL** *Book at aaa.com* Phone: (207)774-5611
| | 5/1-10/15 | 1P: $119-$189 | 2P: $119-$189 | XP: $10 | F16 |
| | 10/16-4/30 | 1P: $85-$159 | 2P: $85-$159 | XP: $10 | F16 |

Large-scale Hotel **Location:** I-295, exit 5 northbound, w on SR 22; exit 5B southbound. 1230 Congress St 04102. Fax: 207/761-1560. **Facility:** 149 units. 147 one-bedroom standard units. 2 one-bedroom suites ($159-$229). 6 stories, interior corridors. *Bath:* combo or shower only. **Parking:** on-site. **Terms:** check-in 4 pm, cancellation fee imposed, package plans - seasonal, pets ($50 extra charge). **Amenities:** video games (fee), dual phone lines, voice mail, irons, hair dryers. **Pool(s):** heated indoor. **Leisure Activities:** whirlpool, exercise room. **Guest Services:** gift shop, valet laundry, area transportation. **Business Services:** meeting rooms. **Cards:** AX, CB, DC, DS, MC, VI.

SOME UNITS

**EASTLAND PARK HOTEL** *Book at aaa.com* Phone: (207)775-5411
| | 7/1-10/20 | 1P: $149-$229 | 2P: $149-$229 | XP: $15 | F18 |
| | 5/1-6/30 | 1P: $139-$219 | 2P: $139-$219 | XP: $15 | F18 |
| | 10/21-4/30 | 1P: $129-$199 | 2P: $129-$199 | XP: $15 | F18 |

**Location:** At Congress Square; center. 157 High St 04101. Fax: 207/775-2872. **Facility:** 202 units. 184 one-bedroom standard units. 17 one- and 1 two-bedroom suites. 13 stories, interior corridors. *Bath:* combo or Large-scale Hotel shower only. **Parking:** valet. **Terms:** pets ($25 fee). **Amenities:** video games (fee), dual phone lines, voice mail, irons, hair dryers. **Dining:** 7-10:30 am, 11:30-2 & 5-10 pm, cocktails. **Leisure Activities:** exercise room. *Fee:* YWCA pool pass, massage. **Guest Services:** gift shop, valet and coin laundry. **Business Services:** meeting rooms. **Cards:** AX, CB, DC, DS, MC, VI. **Special Amenities:** free newspaper and free room upgrade (subject to availability with advanced reservations).** *(See color ad p 272)*

SOME UNITS

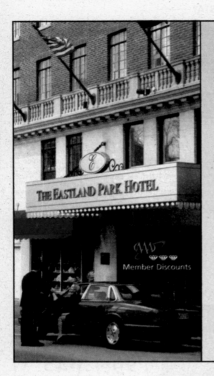

**EMBASSY SUITES HOTEL** *Book at aaa.com*     Phone: (207)775-2200

AAA SAVE

| | 7/1-10/31 [BP] | 1P: $179-$279 | 2P: $179-$279 | XP: $10 | F17 |
| | 5/1-6/30 [BP] | 1P: $139-$189 | 2P: $139-$189 | XP: $10 | F17 |
| | 11/1-4/30 [BP] | 1P: $129-$169 | 2P: $129-$169 | XP: $10 | F17 |

**Location:** At the Portland International Jetport. 1050 Westbrook St 04102. Fax: 207/775-4052. **Facility:** 120 units.
Large-scale Hotel 115 one- and 5 two-bedroom suites. 6 stories, interior corridors. **Parking:** on-site. **Terms:** 3 day cancellation notice-fee imposed, [AP] meal plan available, pets ($75 deposit). **Amenities:** video games (fee), dual phone lines, voice mail, irons, hair dryers. **Dining:** 6:30-10 am, 11:30-2 & 4-9:30 pm, Sat & Sun from 7 am, cocktails. **Pool(s):** heated indoor. **Leisure Activities:** saunas, whirlpool, exercise room, basketball. **Guest Services:** gift shop, valet and coin laundry, area transportation. **Business Services:** meeting rooms, fax. **Cards:** AX, MC, VI. **Special Amenities: free full breakfast and free newspaper.** *(See color ad p 272)*

SOME UNITS

---

**FAIRFIELD INN BY MARRIOTT-PORTLAND AIRPORT** *Book at aaa.com*     Phone: (207)871-0611

| | All Year [ECP] | 1P: $79-$159 | 2P: $79-$159 | XP: $10 | F17 |

**Location:** I-295, exit 5 on SR 22. 340 Park Ave 04102. Fax: 207/871-8243. **Facility:** 105 one-bedroom standard
Small-scale Hotel units. 4 stories, interior corridors. *Bath:* combo or shower only. **Parking:** on-site. **Amenities:** voice mail, irons.
**Pool(s):** outdoor. **Guest Services:** valet and coin laundry, area transportation. **Cards:** AX, CB, DC, DS, JC, MC, VI. *(See ad below)*

SOME UNITS

---

**HILTON GARDEN INN PORTLAND AIRPORT** *Book at aaa.com*     Phone: (207)828-1117

AAA SAVE

| | 6/16-10/31 | 1P: $170-$189 | 2P: $170-$189 | XP: $10 | F |
| | 5/1-6/15 | 1P: $141-$160 | 2P: $141-$160 | XP: $10 | F |
| | 11/1-4/30 | 1P: $132-$145 | 2P: $132-$145 | XP: $10 | F |

**Location:** At the Portland International Jetport. 145 Jetport Blvd 04102. Fax: 207/828-1118. **Facility:** 88 one-
Small-scale Hotel bedroom standard units. 3 stories, interior corridors. *Bath:* combo or shower only. **Parking:** on-site.
**Amenities:** video games (fee), dual phone lines, voice mail, irons, hair dryers. **Dining:** 6 am-10 & 5-10 pm,
cocktails. **Pool(s):** heated indoor. **Leisure Activities:** whirlpool, exercise room. **Guest Services:** valet and coin laundry, airport transportation-Portland International Jetport. **Business Services:** meeting rooms, business center. **Cards:** AX, CB, DC, DS, MC, VI.

SOME UNITS

---

**HILTON GARDEN INN PORTLAND DOWNTOWN WATERFRONT** *Book at aaa.com*     Phone: (207)780-0780

| | All Year | 1P: $239 | 2P: $249 | XP: $10 | F12 |

**Location:** In the Old Port; across from the Casco Bay ferry terminal. 65 Commercial St 04101. Fax: 207/780-0781.
Small-scale Hotel **Facility:** 120 units. 118 one-bedroom standard units. 2 one-bedroom suites ($259-$279). 6 stories, interior
corridors. **Parking:** valet. **Terms:** check-in 4 pm, cancellation fee imposed. **Amenities:** video games, high-speed Internet, dual phone lines, voice mail, irons, hair dryers. **Leisure Activities:** whirlpool, exercise room. **Guest Services:** valet and coin laundry. **Business Services:** meeting rooms, business center. **Cards:** AX, DC, DS, JC, MC, VI.

SOME UNITS

---

**HOLIDAY INN BY THE BAY** *Book at aaa.com*     Phone: (207)775-2311

AAA SAVE

| | 6/7-10/31 | 1P: $162-$172 | 2P: $172-$182 | XP: $10 | F19 |
| | 11/1-4/30 | 1P: $131-$141 | 2P: $141-$151 | XP: $10 | F19 |
| | 5/1-6/6 | 1P: $125-$135 | 2P: $135-$145 | XP: $10 | F19 |

**Location:** Center. 88 Spring St 04101. Fax: 207/761-8224. **Facility:** 239 one-bedroom standard units. 11 stories,
Large-scale Hotel interior corridors. *Bath:* combo or shower only. **Parking:** on-site. **Terms:** check-in 4 pm. **Amenities:** video games (fee), dual phone lines, voice mail, irons, hair dryers. **Dining:** 6 am-2 & 5:30-10 pm, cocktails. **Pool(s):** heated indoor. **Leisure Activities:** saunas, exercise room. **Guest Services:** gift shop, valet and coin laundry. **Business Services:** conference facilities, business center. **Cards:** AX, CB, DC, DS, JC, MC, VI. *(See color ad p 274)*

SOME UNITS

## HOLIDAY INN-WEST  *Book at aaa.com*

**Phone:** (207)774-5601

| | | |
|---|---|---|
| 6/20-10/23 | 1P: $150-$190 | 2P: $150-$190 |
| 5/1-6/19 | 1P: $123-$139 | 2P: $123-$139 |
| 10/24-4/30 | 1P: $110-$120 | 2P: $110-$120 |

AAA [SAVE] ▽▽▽▽

Small-scale Hotel

**Location:** I-95 (Maine Tpke), exit 48. 81 Riverside St 4103. Fax: 207/774-2103. **Facility:** 200 one-bedroom standard units. 2 stories (no elevator), interior corridors. *Bath:* combo or shower only. **Parking:** on-site. **Terms:** [BP] meal plan available, small pets only (in smoking units). **Amenities:** video games, voice mail, irons, hair dryers. **Dining:** 6 am-2 & 5-10 pm, cocktails, entertainment. **Pool(s):** heated outdoor, heated indoor. **Leisure Activities:** sauna, whirlpool, exercise room. **Guest Services:** valet and coin laundry. **Business Services:** meeting rooms. **Cards:** AX, CB, DC, DS, JC, MC, VI. **Special Amenities:** free local telephone calls. *(See color ad below)*

SOME UNITS

[icons] / FEE

## HOWARD JOHNSON PLAZA HOTEL  *Book at aaa.com*

**Phone:** (207)774-5861

| | | | |
|---|---|---|---|
| 7/1-10/31 | 1P: $115-$165 | 2P: $125-$175 | XP: $10  F17 |
| 5/1-6/30 | 1P: $75-$120 | 2P: $85-$130 | XP: $10  F17 |
| 11/1-4/30 | 1P: $75-$105 | 2P: $80-$115 | |

AAA [SAVE] ▽▽▽▽

Small-scale Hotel

**Location:** I-95 (Maine Tpke), exit 48, jct SR 25. 155 Riverside St 04103. Fax: 207/774-5861. **Facility:** 120 units. 119 one-bedroom standard units, some with whirlpools. 1 one-bedroom suite. 3 stories, interior corridors. **Parking:** on-site. **Terms:** pets ($50 deposit). **Amenities:** voice mail, irons, hair dryers. **Dining:** 2 restaurants, 6 am-11 pm, cocktails. **Pool(s):** heated indoor. **Leisure Activities:** whirlpool, exercise room. **Guest Services:** valet and coin laundry. **Business Services:** meeting rooms. **Cards:** AX, CB, DC, DS, MC, VI. **Special Amenities:** free local telephone calls and free newspaper.

SOME UNITS

[icons] / FEE

**INN ON CARLETON**
Phone: (207)775-1910

Historic Bed & Breakfast

| |  |  |  | |
|---|---|---|---|---|
| 6/16-10/28 [BP] | 1P: $155-$229 | 2P: $155-$229 | XP: $25 | D9 |
| 10/29-1/3 [BP] | 1P: $125-$189 | 2P: $125-$189 | XP: $25 | D9 |
| 5/1-6/15 [BP] | 1P: $125-$180 | 2P: $125-$180 | XP: $25 | D9 |
| 1/4-4/30 [BP] | 1P: $119-$149 | 2P: $119-$149 | XP: $25 | D9 |

**Location:** I-295, exit 6A (Forest Ave), s to SR 77 S (State St), just past Longfellow Monument, s on Pine St to West St, then just w. Located in Western Promenade Historic District. 46 Carleton St 04102. Fax: 207/761-0956. **Facility:** A restored 1869 Victorian townhouse, this inn is close to downtown. Smoke free premises. 6 one-bedroom standard units. 3 stories (no elevator), interior corridors. *Bath:* combo or shower only. **Parking:** on-site. **Terms:** check-in 4 pm, age restrictions may apply, no pets allowed (owner's pet on premises). **Amenities:** irons, hair dryers. *Some:* CD players. **Guest Services:** TV in common area. **Cards:** DS, MC, VI.

**PORTLAND HARBOR HOTEL**    *Book at aaa.com*
Phone: (207)775-9090

Small-scale Hotel

| |  |
|---|---|
| 7/1-10/23 | 1P: $259-$299 |
| 10/24-4/30 | 1P: $189-$219 |
| 5/1-6/30 | 1P: $179-$209 |

**Location:** In the Old Port. 468 Fore St 04101. Fax: 207/775-9990. **Facility:** Having the feel of the 19th-century, the hotel appeals to both the business and vacation traveler with luxurious rooms and lots of amenities. 100 units. 97 one-bedroom standard units, some with whirlpools. 3 one-bedroom suites ($279-$379). 5 stories, interior corridors. *Bath:* combo or shower only. **Parking:** valet. **Terms:** pets ($25 extra charge). **Amenities:** high-speed Internet, dual phone lines, voice mail, irons, hair dryers. **Dining:** 6:30 am-2 & 5:30-9:30 pm, Fri & Sat-10 pm, cocktails. **Leisure Activities:** exercise room. **Guest Services:** valet laundry. **Business Services:** meeting rooms. **Cards:** AX, CB, DC, DS, MC, VI.
*(See color ad below)*

SOME UNITS

## PORTLAND REGENCY HOTEL

**Phone:** (207)774-4200

| | 7/6-10/30 | 1P: $199-$239 | 2P: $209-$249 | XP: $20 |
| | 5/1-7/5 | 1P: $199-$229 | 2P: $199-$239 | XP: $20 |
| | 10/31-12/31 | 1P: $169-$209 | 2P: $169-$219 | XP: $20 |
| | 1/1-4/30 | 1P: $179-$209 | 2P: $179-$209 | XP: $20 |

Historic
Large-scale Hotel

**Location:** In the Old Port; between Market and Silver sts; downtown. 20 Milk St 04101. **Fax:** 207/775-2150. **Facility:** In a converted nineteenth-century armory, this hotel offers modern amenities with the feel of yester-year. 95 one-bedroom standard units, some with whirlpools. 5 stories, interior corridors. **Parking:** valet. **Amenities:** high-speed Internet, voice mail, honor bars, irons, hair dryers. *Some:* CD players. **Dining:** 6:30-11 am, 11:30-2 & 5:30-9:30 pm, Fri & Sat-10 pm, cocktails. **Leisure Activities:** saunas, whirlpool, steamrooms, exercise room, spa. **Guest Services:** valet laundry. **Business Services:** meeting rooms, business center. **Cards:** AX, CB, DC, DS, MC, VI. **Special Amenities:** free local telephone calls and free newspaper. *(See color ad below)*

SOME UNITS

⑤ᴅ ╋ ⅋ ⛾ 🕹 ✕ 🗚 DATA PORT / ✕ VCR / FEE

## WEST END INN

**Phone:** (207)772-1377

| | 5/1-10/31 | 1P: $129-$199 | 2P: $139-$209 | XP: $30 |
| | 11/1-4/30 | 1P: $89-$159 | 2P: $99-$169 | XP: $30 |

Bed & Breakfast

**Location:** I-295, exit 6A (Forest Ave S), s to SR 77 (S State St), just past Longfellow Monument, then just s. Located in the Western Promenade Historic District. 146 Pine St 04102. **Fax:** 207/828-0984. **Facility:** In-room telephone access is available on request at this 1871 Victorian inn. Smoke free premises. 6 one-bedroom standard units. 3 stories (no elevator), interior corridors. *Bath:* combo or shower only. **Parking:** on-site. **Terms:** check-in 3:30 pm, 2 night minimum stay - some weekends, age restrictions may apply, 14 day cancellation notice-fee imposed, [BP] meal plan available. **Amenities:** hair dryers. **Cards:** AX, MC, VI. **Special Amenities:** free full breakfast and free local telephone calls.

⑤ᴅ ✕ ☎

# Portland's Premier Hotel

---

**The following lodging was either not evaluated or did not meet AAA rating requirements but is listed for your information only.**

---

**DIAMOND COVE**
[fyi]

**Phone: 207/766-3005**

Not evaluated. **Location:** On Great Diamond Island; in Caso Bay. Facilities, services, and decor characterize a mid-range property.

---

## ——— WHERE TO DINE ———

**AURORA PROVISIONS**
American
MC, VI.

**Lunch:** $4-$6     **Dinner:** $6-$8     **Phone:** 207/871-9060

**Location:** Just w on Pine from jct with State St. 64 Pine St 04102. **Hours:** 8 am-6:30 pm. Closed major holidays; also Sun. **Features:** Gourmet sandwiches are prepared at this self-serve bistro-style, specialty food store with a small cafe. You may also choose from their selection of cakes, cookies and other desserts—all made on-site. Juices, soda, beer and wine are also offered. Casual dress. **Parking:** on-site. **Cards:** AX,

---

**BACK BAY GRILL**
American

**Dinner:** $19-$33     **Phone:** 207/772-8833

**Location:** I-295, exit 6A (Forest Ave), just e to Portland St, then just n; past main Post Office. 65 Portland St 04101. **Hours:** 5:30 pm-9:30 pm, Fri & Sat-10 pm; 5 pm-9 pm, Fri & Sat-9:30 pm in fall & winter. Closed: 1/1, 11/25, 12/24, 12/25; also Sun. **Reservations:** suggested. **Features:** As seasons change, so does the menu at Back Bay Grill. The extensive wine list is spectacular, the colorful murals add a lively feel, and the creme brulee is always special! Casual dress; cocktails. **Parking:** street. **Cards:** AX, DC, DS, MC, VI.

---

**BELLA CUCINA**
Italian

**Dinner:** $11-$17     **Phone:** 207/828-4033

**Location:** In the Arts District. 653 Congress St 04101. **Hours:** 5 pm-9 pm, Fri & Sat-10 pm. Closed: 7/4, 11/25, 12/25; also Mon. **Features:** Metal fish sculpture on the walls enhances the colorful bistro's atmosphere. Intimate tables have hand-painted tops. The cuisine has been described as country Italian, prepared with an Italian sensibility. However, not all entrees are strictly Italian. Although the emphasis is on fish, meat and vegetarian entrees also are on the menu. Casual dress; beer & wine only. **Parking:** on-site. **Cards:** AX, DC, DS, MC, VI.

---

**BINTLIFF'S AMERICAN CAFE**
American

**Lunch:** $6-$9     **Phone:** 207/774-0005

**Location:** Jct Portland St and Forest Ave, just n; across from main Post Office. 98 Portland St 04101. **Hours:** 7 am-2 pm. Closed: 12/25. **Features:** More than 110 items line the specialty all-day brunch menu. The popular bistro-style restaurant occupies a Greek revival building. Casual dress; cocktails. **Parking:** street. **Cards:** AX, DS, MC, VI.

---

**BLACK TIE CAFE**
American

**Lunch:** $7-$12     **Phone:** 207/761-6665

**Location:** In the Old Port; entrance off Exchange St. 188 Middle St 04101. **Hours:** 11:30 am-2 pm; to 3 pm in summer. Closed major holidays. **Features:** Set away from the hustle and bustle of the Old Port, the cafe is accessed through a courtyard off busy Exchange Street. All menu items are made from scratch on the premises from fresh, natural ingredients. The owner describes the cuisine as "comfort food at comfort prices.". Casual dress. **Parking:** street. **Cards:** AX, MC, VI.

---

**CINQUE TERRE**
Northern
Italian

**Dinner:** $8-$26     **Phone:** 207/347-6154

**Location:** In the Old Port. 36 Wharf St 04101. **Hours:** 6 pm-10 pm, Fri & Sat from 5 pm. Closed: 1/1, 11/25, 12/25. **Reservations:** accepted. **Features:** Food is prepared in the style of the Ligurian region of Northern Italy. Many small courses are made with fresh, local and organic ingredients, whenever possible. The stylish dining room occupies two levels. Casual dress; cocktails. **Parking:** street. **Cards:** AX, MC, VI.

---

**DAVID'S**
American

**Lunch:** $5-$11     **Dinner:** $9-$22     **Phone:** 207/773-4340

**Location:** In the Arts District. 22 Monument Sq 04101. **Hours:** 11:30 am-4 & 5-9 pm, Fri-10 pm, Sat 5 pm-10 pm, Sun 5 pm-9 pm. Closed major holidays. **Features:** The restaurant serves creative American cuisine, such as the signature pepper-crusted rare tuna, and more simply prepared items. The open kitchen, small tables, mosaic tile floors and long bar create a casual, intimate atmosphere. Casual dress; cocktails. **Parking:** no self-parking. **Cards:** AX, DS, MC, VI.

---

**DI'MILLO'S FLOATING RESTAURANT**
American

**Lunch:** $5-$9     **Dinner:** $11-$20     **Phone:** 207/772-2216

**Location:** Downtown waterfront. 25 Long Wharf 04101. **Hours:** 11 am-10 pm, Fri & Sat-11 pm. Closed: 11/25, 12/25. **Features:** A former car ferry on the city's waterfront, the family-owned restaurant presents a menu of lobster, other seafood, steaks and Italian dishes. Tourists frequent this place for its views and nautical atmosphere. Casual dress; cocktails. **Parking:** on-site. **Cards:** AX, DC, DS, MC, VI.

---

**FLATBREAD COMPANY**
Pizza

**Lunch:** $7-$19     **Dinner:** $7-$19     **Phone:** 207/772-8777

**Location:** In the Old Port. 72 Commercial St 04101. **Hours:** 11:30 am-close. Closed: 1/1, 11/25, 12/25. **Features:** In a great waterfront location, the restaurant serves flatbread pizzas made with organic, seasonal ingredients from local producers. All are cooked in a wood-fired clay oven open to the dining room. Casual dress; beer & wine only. **Parking:** street. **Cards:** AX, MC, VI.

---

**FORE STREET**
American

**Dinner:** $13-$28     **Phone:** 207/775-2717

**Location:** In the Old Port; downtown. 288 Fore St 04101. **Hours:** 5:30 pm-10 pm, Fri & Sat-10:30 pm; Sun-9:30 pm in winter. Closed: 11/25, 12/25. **Reservations:** suggested. **Features:** This very popular downtown restaurant, in a converted factory, features fantastic New England specialties. The wood-fired oven and rotisserie grill enhance the old-brick and polished-wood atmosphere. The friendly and attentive service is excellent. Casual dress; cocktails. **Parking:** on-site. **Cards:** AX, MC, VI.

**FUJI**
*Japanese*

**Lunch:** $7-$13  **Dinner:** $11-$19  **Phone:** 207/773-2900
**Location:** In the Old Port. 29 Exchange St 04101. **Hours:** 11:30 am-10 pm, Fri & Sat-11 pm, Sun noon-10 pm.
**Features:** Located in the heart of the Old Port, Fuji's has a menu which includes Japanese, Korean, and Thai cuisine. The dining rooms include a sushi bar, hibatchi tables and a traditional tatami roon. Validated parking is available for the Fore Street garage. Casual dress; cocktails. **Parking:** street. **Cards:** MC, VI.

**GRITTY MCDUFF'S**
*American*

**Lunch:** $5-$14  **Dinner:** $5-$14  **Phone:** 207/772-2739
**Location:** In the Old Port. 396 Fore St 04101. **Hours:** 11:30 am-10 pm, Fri & Sat-11 pm. Closed: 12/24, 12/25.
**Features:** The Old Port favorite was the city's first brew pub since Prohibition. The on-premises brewery's English-style brewing process produces small batches of ales without preservatives or additives. The menu lists American and English pub fare. Patio seating is available seasonally. Casual dress; cocktails.
**Parking:** street. **Cards:** AX, DS, MC, VI.

**HUGO'S RESTAURANT**
*Regional American*

**Dinner:** $35-$42  **Phone:** 207/774-8538
**Location:** Just ne of Franklin St, close to the Old Port. 88 Middle St 04101. **Hours:** 5:30 pm-9 pm, Fri & Sat-9:30 pm. Closed: 11/25, 12/25; also Sun & Mon. **Reservations:** required. **Features:** Near the Old Port District, the small restaurant nurtures a warm, comfortable atmosphere. Frequently changing menus center on French- and Italian-influenced Maine cuisine. Ingredients are local, fresh and organic whenever possible. Patrons can opt for two- or three-course prix fixe meals, a chef's menu or tapas. Casual dress; cocktails. **Parking:** on-site.
**Cards:** AX, MC, VI.

**LUCAYA**
*Caribbean*

**Lunch:** $7-$14  **Dinner:** $10-$25  **Phone:** 207/773-2215
**Location:** In the Old Port. 205 Commercial St 04101. **Hours:** 11 am-3 & 6-10 pm, Sat from 9 am, Sun 9 am-3 pm, Mon 11 am-3 pm. Closed: 7/4, 11/25, 12/25. **Reservations:** suggested, for dinner. **Features:** In an operating bakery, the unpretentious, European, country-style bistro has only nine tables. Focusing on Mediterranean cuisine, the menu includes salads, sandwiches, seafood, pasta, chicken and vegetarian entrees, all made from scratch on the premises. Tasty offerings are healthy and prepared from fresh, interesting ingredients. Delicious soups are the restaurant's signature. Two seasonal decks offer nice views of the water. Casual dress; cocktails. **Parking:** street. **Cards:** MC, VI.

**MESA VERDE**
*Mexican*

**Lunch:** $5-$17  **Dinner:** $9-$14  **Phone:** 207/774-6089
**Location:** In the Arts District. 618 Congress St 04101. **Hours:** 11:30 am-9 pm, Fri & Sat-9:30 pm, Sun-8:30 pm. Closed major holidays; also Mon. **Features:** This restaurant is known for its food and for the variety of juices and smoothies available at the juice bar. Casual dress; cocktails. **Parking:** no self-parking.
**Cards:** DC, MC, VI.

**MOLLY'S STEAKHOUSE & IRISH PUB**
*American*

**Dinner:** $11-$25  **Phone:** 207/761-4094
**Location:** In the Old Port. 46 Market St 04101. **Hours:** 4 pm-10 pm, Fri & Sat-11 pm, Sun 9 am-3 pm. Closed: 11/25, 12/24, 12/25; also Tues & Wed. **Reservations:** accepted. **Features:** Near Portland Regency Hotel, the storefront restaurant has an Irish pub downstairs and an informal dining room on the first floor. It specializes in steak and also offers many Irish and American favorites. Casual dress; cocktails. **Parking:** street. **Cards:** AX, DS, MC, VI.

**NATASHA'S**
*New World*

**Lunch:** $5-$12  **Dinner:** $11-$28  **Phone:** 207/774-4004
**Location:** In the Old Port. 82 Exchange St 04101. **Hours:** 11 am-3 & 5-10 pm, Mon & Sat from 5 pm. Closed: 1/1, 11/25, 12/25; also Sun. **Reservations:** accepted. **Features:** New World cuisine encompasses a good variety of pasta, seafood, grilled meat and vegetarian dishes. Examples of superb offerings on the changing menu include chicken breast with spicy coconut peanut sauce, rosemary chicken and linguine cioppino. Casual dress; cocktails. **Parking:** street. **Cards:** AX, DC, DS, MC, VI.

**NORM'S BAR & GRILL**
*American*

**Lunch:** $6-$10  **Dinner:** $11-$16  **Phone:** 207/828-9944
**Location:** Just s of jct Congress and State sts; center. 617 Congress St 04101. **Hours:** 11:30 am-10 pm, Sun from 4 pm. Closed major holidays. **Features:** In the Arts District, the restaurant is known for its frequently changing tapas menu, as well as for fresh seafood and a variety of locally brewed beers. The red brick dining room and bar has a lively atmosphere. Casual dress; cocktails. **Parking:** street. **Cards:** AX, DS, MC, VI.

**NORM'S EAST END GRILL**
*Barbecue*

**Lunch:** $5-$9  **Dinner:** $8-$15  **Phone:** 207/253-1700
**Location:** Just ne of Franklin St, close to the Old Port. 47 Middle St 04101. **Hours:** 11:30 am-4 & 4:30-10 pm, Sat from 4 pm, Sun 4 pm-9 pm. Closed major holidays. **Features:** This popular eatery specializes in barbecue. The red brick dining rooms are on two floors and the bar has a variety of locally brewed beers. Casual dress; cocktails. **Parking:** street. **Cards:** AX, MC, VI.

**OLD PORT SEA GRILL AND RAW BAR**
*Seafood*

**Dinner:** $17-$25  **Phone:** 207/879-6100
**Location:** In the Old Port. 93 Commercial St 04101. **Hours:** 11:30 am-10 pm, Fri & Sat-11 pm. Closed: 11/25, 12/25. **Features:** Stylish urban decor sets the scene for the dining experience. To ensure product quality, the restaurant obtains ingredients from local producers and fishermen. On the menu are wood-grilled seafood and meats, lobster, fried seafood, chicken and pork chops. Casual dress; cocktails. **Parking:** street. **Cards:** AX, DS, MC, VI.

**O'NATURAL'S**
*Natural/Organic*

**Lunch:** $5-$8  **Dinner:** $5-$8  **Phone:** 207/321-2050
**Location:** In the Old Port. 83 Exchange St 04101. **Hours:** 10:30 am-8 pm, Fri & Sat-9 pm. Closed major holidays. **Features:** O'Natural's provides natural and organic fast food consisting of sandwiches, soups, salads and Asian noodles. Their delicious flatbread is made in house. Food made prepared in small batches throughout the day. Menu items are free of additives & preservatives. Meats are range grown. Options are available for vegan, wheat free and dairy free needs. The dining room is light airy using recycled materials. Casual dress; beer & wine only. **Parking:** street. **Cards:** AX, DS, MC, VI.

## PEPPERCLUB

Ethnic

**Dinner:** $8-$15     **Phone:** 207/772-0531

**Location:** Jst ne of Franklin St, close to the Old Port. 78 Middle St 04101. **Hours:** 5 pm-9 pm, Fri & Sat-10 pm. Closed major holidays. **Reservations:** accepted. **Features:** Featured is a creative international cuisine with many vegetarian dishes. The colorful and funky decor enhances the comfortable atmosphere. The Caribbean jerk chicken with brown and wild rice and mixed vegetables is a delicious selection. Casual dress; beer & wine only. **Parking:** on-site. **Cards:** AX, DS, MC, VI.

## PERFETTO
Italian

**Lunch:** $8-$12     **Dinner:** $15-$26     **Phone:** 207/828-0001

**Location:** In the Old Port; center. 28 Exchange St 04101. **Hours:** 11:30 am-2:30 & 5-9 pm, Sun from 5 pm. Closed: 11/25, 12/25; also Mon. **Reservations:** suggested. **Features:** This restaurant is a converted brick storefront with a bistro atmosphere, oak floors and an open kitchen in the rear. Casual and a little noisy, it attracts an eclectic clientele. Cuisine is Mediterranean with international influences. The bread is delicious. Be sure to try the homemade dessert. Cocktails. **Parking:** street. **Cards:** AX, MC, VI.

## PORTLAND LOBSTER CO

Seafood

**Lunch:** $6-$17     **Dinner:** $6-$17     **Phone:** 207/775-2112

**Location:** In the Old Port. 180 Commercial St 04103. **Hours:** Open 5/15-10/15; 11 am-9 pm. **Features:** Patrons can order any number of fresh seafood entrees and enjoy them either inside or outdoors on the waterfront dock. Casual dress; beer & wine only. **Parking:** no self-parking. **Cards:** AX, MC, VI.

## RESTAURANT SAPPORO
Japanese

**Lunch:** $4-$9     **Dinner:** $7-$19     **Phone:** 207/772-1233

**Location:** In the Old Port; in Union wharf on the waterfront. 230 Commercial St 04112. **Hours:** 11:30 am-2 & 5-9:30 pm, Fri & Sat 4 pm-10 pm, Sun 4 pm-9 pm. Closed: 11/25, 12/25. **Reservations:** suggested, weekends. **Features:** This locally popular restaurant features sushi selections as well as tempura, teriyaki, combination lunches and dinners, and other traditional Japanese dishes. Presentations are attractive, and the serving staff is prompt, friendly and helpful. Casual dress; cocktails. **Parking:** street. **Cards:** AX, DS, MC, VI.

## RIBOLLITA

Regional
Italian

**Dinner:** $11-$18     **Phone:** 207/774-2972

**Location:** Just ne of Franklin St, close to the Old Port. 41 Middle St 04101. **Hours:** 5 pm-9 pm, Fri & Sat-10 pm. Closed major holidays; also Sun & Mon. **Reservations:** suggested. **Features:** The menu centers on hearty country Italian cuisine, including pasta, seafood and vegetarian entrees. Cozy dining rooms are simply decorated but create a romantic ambience. Casual dress; cocktails. **Parking:** on-site. **Cards:** AX, MC, VI.

## RI RA

American

**Lunch:** $7-$10     **Dinner:** $15-$26     **Phone:** 207/761-4446

**Location:** In the Old Port. 72 Commercial St 04101. **Hours:** 11:30 am-10 pm, Fri & Sat-11 pm. Closed: 11/25, 12/25. **Features:** The waterfront restaurant's menu reflects both Irish favorites and many American dishes, as well. Parts of the restaurant were imported from pubs in Ireland. Casual dress; cocktails. **Parking:** street. **Cards:** AX, DC, MC, VI.

## THE ROMA CAFE   Historic
Italian

**Lunch:** $5-$11     **Dinner:** $12-$22     **Phone:** 207/773-9873

**Location:** Downtown; close to Maine Medical Center. 769 Congress St 04102. **Hours:** 11:30 am-2 & 5-9 pm, Sun 5 pm-8 pm. Closed major holidays; also Sun 1/2-5/31. **Reservations:** suggested. **Features:** In a brick Victorian mansion on the West End, the cafe provides elegant dining in a romantic atmosphere. The menu lists traditional Italian cuisine, with a large selection of fresh seafood and lobster entrees. Fresh ingredients, including seasonal vegetables, are used in made-to-order dishes. Casual dress; cocktails. **Parking:** on-site. **Cards:** AX, DS, MC, VI.

## SEBAGO BREWING COMPANY

American

**Lunch:** $6-$10     **Dinner:** $9-$17     **Phone:** 207/775-2337

**Location:** In the Old Port. 164 Middle St 04101. **Hours:** 11 am-1 am. Closed: 3/27, 11/25, 12/24, 12/25. **Features:** This stylish brew pub has an informal friendly atmosphere. Self described "American Pub" cuisine includes delicious pasta, chicken, seafood and steak entrees as well as tasty salads, burgers and sandwiches. The latter are available all day. Desserts are prepared on the premises each day by their pastry chef. Casual dress; cocktails. **Parking:** street. **Cards:** AX, MC, VI.

## SOFFRITTO

Italian

**Lunch:** $5-$13     **Dinner:** $13-$19     **Phone:** 207/253-8001

**Location:** In the Old Port. 29 Wharf St 04101. **Hours:** 11:30 am-10 pm, Fri & Sat-2 am. **Reservations:** required, weekends. **Features:** The casual, family-friendly restaurant has a warm and colorful atmosphere evocative of the North End of Boston. All offerings incorporate fresh ingredients and are made to order. Portions are generous. Casual dress; beer & wine only. **Parking:** street. **Cards:** AX, DS, MC, VI.

## STREET & COMPANY
Mediterranean

**Dinner:** $14-$27     **Phone:** 207/775-0887

**Location:** In the Old Port; between Dana and Union sts. 33 Wharf St 04101. **Hours:** 11:30 am-9:30 pm, Fri & Sat-10 pm, Sun-9 pm. Closed: 11/25, 12/24, 12/25. **Reservations:** suggested. **Features:** This is a small bistro with an open kitchen at the entrance and a casual but lively atmosphere. Mediterranean seafood is on the menu, perfectly prepared and seasoned and presented in a variety of styles. Produce and seafood is fresh and local products are often utilized. Be sure to try the Lobster Diablo. Casual dress; cocktails. **Parking:** on-site (fee). **Cards:** AX, MC, VI.

## TANDOOR

Indian

**Lunch:** $7     **Dinner:** $10-$15     **Phone:** 207/775-4259

**Location:** In the Old Port. 88 Exchange St 04101. **Hours:** 11 am-3 & 4-10 pm, Fri & Sat-10:30 pm. Closed: 12/25. **Reservations:** suggested, weekends. **Features:** Indian music, artwork and colorful walls enhance the atmosphere of the colorful Indian restaurant. Food is cooked over charcoal in a traditional tandoor, a cylindrical clay oven. Casual dress; beer & wine only. **Parking:** street. **Cards:** AX, DS, MC, VI.

**TORTILLA FLAT**

Mexican

**Lunch:** $5-$13          **Dinner:** $5-$13          **Phone:** 207/797-8729
**Location:** US 302, 1.5 mi w of jct SR 100. 1871 Forest Ave 04103. **Hours:** 11:30 am-9 pm, Fri & Sat-11 pm, Sun noon-9 pm. Closed: 11/25, 12/25. **Features:** Dining rooms are decorated in the Mexican style—stucco, wall murals, stained glass and hanging plants—making for a fun, casual atmosphere. The menu is extensive, with many traditional favorites as well as a number of house specialties that provide an interesting twist on classic fare. Menu items are reasonably priced and portions are generous. Cocktails. **Parking:** on-site. **Cards:** AX, DS, MC, VI.

**THE VILLAGE CAFE**

Italian

**Lunch:** $5-$9          **Dinner:** $6-$23          **Phone:** 207/772-5320
**Location:** Just above Old Port; jct Franklin and Newbury sts, just n; downtown. 112 Newbury St 04101. **Hours:** 11 am-10 pm, Fri & Sat-11 pm, Sun 11:30 am-8 pm; to 9:30 pm 7/1-8/31. Closed: 11/25, 12/25. **Features:** Established in 1936, the restaurant is family operated. A homemade wine press built by the founder and used to produce wine sits in the lobby. Traditional style Italian restaurant is well designed for family and group dining. The menu features Italian cuisine as well as steak, seafood and lobster entrees. Casual dress; cocktails. **Parking:** on-site. **Cards:** AX, DS, MC, VI.

**WALTER'S CAFE**

American

**Lunch:** $7-$10          **Dinner:** $15-$23          **Phone:** 207/871-9258
**Location:** In the Old Port. 15 Exchange St 04101. **Hours:** 11 am-3 & 5-9 pm, Fri & Sat-10 pm. Closed: 11/25, 12/25; also for lunch Sun. **Features:** This very attractive California-style cafe in historic Old Port features a creative menu, friendly informal service and a relaxed atmosphere. The menu is changed daily and offers artistic presentation of New American dishes prepared in the open kitchen. Casual dress; cocktails.
**Parking:** street. **Cards:** AX, MC, VI.

**THE WINE BAR & RESTAURANT**

American

**Dinner:** $12-$19          **Phone:** 207/773-6667
**Location:** In the Old Port. 38 Wharf St 04101. **Hours:** 5 pm-10 pm. Closed: 12/25; also Sun-Tues 1/1-4/15. **Reservations:** suggested. **Features:** On a cobblestone street, the restaurant and wine bar has a casual bistro atmosphere. The menu features fresh local seafood, choice meats and vegetarian dishes. A nice selection of wines complements dinner. Casual dress; cocktails. **Parking:** on-site (fee). **Cards:** AX, MC, VI.

——— *The following restaurants have not been evaluated by AAA* ———
*but are listed for your information only.*

**BECKY'S DINER**
[fyi]
**Phone:** 207/773-7070
Not evaluated. **Location:** In the waterfront area. 390 Commercial St 04112. **Features:** A nice spot for families, the classic diner is open for breakfast, lunch and dinner.

**BIBO'S MADD APPLE CAFE**
[fyi]
**Phone:** 207/774-9698
Not evaluated. **Location:** 23 Forrest Ave 04101. **Features:** This colorful bistro is located in the Arts District.

**LOCAL 188**
[fyi]
**Phone:** 207/761-7909
Not evaluated. **Location:** 188 State St 04101. **Features:** Local 188 is the only Spanish tapas restaurant in Portland. It is located on Longfellow Square.

**UFFA!**
[fyi]
**Phone:** 207/775-3380
Not evaluated. **Location:** In Longfellow Square. 190 State St 04101. **Features:** The funky dining room is an interesting place in which to try reasonably priced seafood.

# PRESQUE ISLE pop. 9,511

——— WHERE TO STAY ———

**THE BUDGET TRAVELER MOTOR LODGE**

Motel

All Year [CP]          1P: $40          2P: $46          **Phone:** 207/769-0111
**Location:** 1.3 mi s on US 1. 71 Main St 04769. Fax: 207/764-6836. **Facility:** 53 one-bedroom standard units, some with whirlpools. 2 stories (no elevator), interior corridors. **Parking:** on-site. **Terms:** weekly rates available. **Amenities:** video library. **Guest Services:** coin laundry. **Cards:** AX, DC, DS, MC, VI.

SOME UNITS

**NORTHERN LIGHTS MOTEL**

Motel

All Year          1P: $38-$58          2P: $46-$68          XP: $7          F10
**Location:** 2 mi s on US 1. 72 Houlton Rd 04769. Fax: 207/764-6931. **Facility:** 13 one-bedroom standard units. 1 story, exterior corridors. *Bath:* shower only. **Parking:** on-site. **Terms:** office hours 7 am-10 pm, [CP] meal plan available. **Cards:** AX, DS, MC, VI. **Special Amenities:** free continental breakfast and free local telephone calls.

SOME UNITS

**PRESQUE ISLE INN & CONVENTION CENTER**

Small-scale Hotel

All Year          1P: $68-$128          2P: $68-$128          XP: $8          F13
**Location:** 1 mi s on US 1. 116 Main St 04769 (19 Main St, CARIBOU, 04736). Fax: 207/764-5167. **Facility:** 142 units. 138 one-bedroom standard units, some with whirlpools. 4 one-bedroom suites ($102-$150) with kitchens. 3 stories (no elevator), interior corridors. **Parking:** on-site. **Terms:** 14 day cancellation notice-fee imposed, package plans - seasonal. **Amenities:** irons, hair dryers. **Dining:** Gram Russo's Italian Restaurant, see separate listing. **Pool(s):** heated indoor. **Leisure Activities:** sauna. **Guest Services:** gift shop, coin laundry. **Business Services:** meeting rooms. **Cards:** AX, CB, DC, DS, MC, VI. **Special Amenities:** free local telephone calls and free newspaper.

SOME UNITS

--------- **WHERE TO DINE** ---------

**GOVERNOR'S RESTAURANT**            **Lunch:** $4-$9        **Dinner:** $6-$12        Phone: 207/769-2274
▼▼▼ ▼▼▼       **Location:** Center. 350 Main St 04769. **Hours:** 6:30 am-9 pm, Fri & Sat-10 pm, Sun from 7 am. Closed: 12/25.
              **Features:** The 12-page menu at Governor's features wonderful seafood dishes. A fish fry is scheduled
American      every Friday, and the homemade desserts are always popular. The atmosphere displays a casual,
              family-style feeling that's quite bustling on the weekends. Casual dress; beer & wine only. **Parking:** on-site.
**Cards:** AX, DC, DS, MC, VI.

**GRAM RUSSO'S ITALIAN RESTAURANT**      **Lunch:** $5-$8        **Dinner:** $8-$18        Phone: 207/764-3321
ⒶⒶⒶ          **Location:** 1 mi s on US 1; in Presque Isle Inn & Convention Center. 116 Main St 04769. **Hours:** 6 am-2 & 5-9 pm,
              Sat from 7 am, Sun 7 am-2 & 4-8 pm. **Reservations:** accepted. **Features:** The menu has a variety of
▼▼▼ ▼▼▼      popular Italian entrees in generous portions. The atrium dining room offers an outdoor feeling to its guests.
Italian       Casual dress; cocktails. **Parking:** on-site. **Cards:** AX, CB, DC, DS, MC, VI.

**MAI TAI RESTAURANT**              **Lunch:** $5-$8        **Dinner:** $8-$14        Phone: 207/764-4426
▼▼▼ ▼▼▼       **Location:** Center. 449 Main St 04769. **Hours:** 11 am-9 pm, Fri & Sat-10 pm. Closed: 7/4.
              **Reservations:** accepted. **Features:** The comfortable family restaurant offers an extensive menu that
Chinese       includes options for family dinners, combination plates and the buffet. Portion sizes are ample.
              Well-prepared menu selections also mingle with some American choices. Casual dress; cocktails. **Parking:**
on-site. **Cards:** AX, DS, MC, VI.

# PROUTS NECK

--------- **WHERE TO STAY** ---------

--------- *The following lodging was either not evaluated or did not* ---------
*meet AAA rating requirements but is listed for your information only.*

**BLACK POINT INN**                                          Phone: 207/883-2500
[fyi]         Not evaluated; management refused evaluation on 06/12/2003. **Location:** 5 mi e of US 1; on SR 207. 510 Black
              Point Rd 04074 (510 Black Point Rd, SCARBOROUGH). Facilities, services, and decor characterize a mid-range
              property.

# RANGELEY

--------- **WHERE TO STAY** ---------

**COUNTRY CLUB INN**                                          Phone: (207)864-3831
▼▼▼ ▼▼▼       5/15-10/20 & 12/26-3/31 [BP]      1P: $75          2P: $114          XP: $15          F
              **Location:** 2.5 mi w on SR 4 and 16, 0.8 mi s, follow signs. Country Club Dr 04970 (PO Box 680). **Fax:** 207/864-3831.
Country Inn   **Facility:** 19 one-bedroom standard units. 1 story, interior/exterior corridors. **Parking:** on-site. **Terms:**
              5/15-10/20 & 12/26-3/31, 7 day cancellation notice, [MAP] meal plan available. **Pool(s):** outdoor. **Leisure**
**Activities:** cross country skiing. *Fee:* golf-18 holes. **Guest Services:** TV in common area. **Business Services:** meeting rooms.
**Cards:** AX, MC, VI.
                                                             SOME UNITS
                            (ASK) (SD) (TI) (Y) (☇) (🏋) (W) (Z) / (X) /

**RANGELEY INN & MOTOR LODGE**                                Phone: (207)864-3341
ⒶⒶⒶ (SAVE)     5/1-10/31 & 12/26-4/1      1P: $78-$140      2P: $84-$140      XP: $10
              11/1-12/25 & 4/2-4/30        1P: $60-$140      2P: $65-$140      XP: $10
▼▼▼ ▼▼▼      **Location:** Center. 51 Main St 04970 (PO Box 160). **Fax:** 207/864-3634. **Facility:** 52 units. 50 one- and 2 two-
              bedroom standard units, some with efficiencies, kitchens and/or whirlpools. 2 stories (no elevator),
Small-scale Hotel  interior/exterior corridors. *Bath:* combo or shower only. **Parking:** on-site. **Terms:** 2 night minimum stay -
              weekends in winter, 15 day cancellation notice-fee imposed. **Amenities:** video library (fee). **Dining:** 2 res-
taurants, 8 am-11 & 5-9 pm, cocktails, dining room, see separate listing. **Leisure Activities:** rental canoes. **Business Services:**
meeting rooms. **Cards:** AX, DS, MC, VI. **Special Amenities:** free local telephone calls.
                                                             SOME UNITS
                            (SD) (TI) (Y) (X) (🏋) / (VCR) (DATA PORT) (Z) (📠) /
                                                        FEE

--------- **WHERE TO DINE** ---------

**THE RANGELEY INN DINING ROOM**            **Dinner:** $10-$24                Phone: 207/864-3341
▼▼▼ ▼▼▼       **Location:** Center; in Rangeley Inn & Motor Lodge. 51 Main St 04970. **Hours:** 7:30 am-10 & 5-9 pm, Sun 7:30
              am-11 & 5-9 pm. Closed: 12/25. **Reservations:** suggested. **Features:** An attractive turn-of-the-century
American      decor will make you feel right at home at this restaurant, which has a friendly pub adjacent to it. The menu
              features a nicely prepared regional cuisine of rack of lamb, cedar-plank salmon and filet mignon. Casual
dress; cocktails. **Parking:** on-site. **Cards:** AX, DS, MC, VI.
                                                             (Y) (🏋) (X)

# ROBBINSTON

--------- **WHERE TO STAY** ---------

**REDCLYFFE SHORE MOTOR INN**                                Phone: (207)454-3270
ⒶⒶⒶ (SAVE)     5/10-10/31      1P: $62          2P: $73          XP: $5          F12
              **Location:** Center; 12 mi s of Calais. Rt 1 04671 (PO Box 53). **Fax:** 207/454-8723. **Facility:** 16 one-bedroom stan-
▼▼▼ ▼▼▼      dard units. 1 story, interior/exterior corridors. **Parking:** on-site. **Terms:** open 5/10-10/31, 7 day cancellation
              notice-fee imposed. **Amenities:** hair dryers. **Dining:** dining room, see separate listing. **Cards:** AX, DS,
Small-scale Hotel  MC, VI. **Special Amenities:** free local telephone calls and free newspaper.
                                                             SOME UNITS
                            (SD) (TI) (🏋) (📠) / (X) /

—— WHERE TO DINE ——

**REDCLYFFE SHORE DINING ROOM**          **Dinner:** $12-$18          **Phone:** 207/454-3270
▽▽▽          **Location:** Center; 12 mi s of Calais; in Redclyffe Shore Motor Inn. Rt 1 04671. **Hours:** Open 5/10-1/7; 5 pm-9 pm.
American          **Reservations:** suggested. **Features:** The popular restaurant offers lovely views of the ocean and
          shoreline. On the menu are fresh local seafood dishes, varied beef and chicken entrees and homemade
MC, VI.          desserts. Service is friendly and attentive. Casual dress; cocktails. **Parking:** on-site. **Cards:** AX, DS,

## ROCKLAND pop. 7,609

—— WHERE TO STAY ——

**BERRY MANOR INN**          *Book at aaa.com*          **Phone:** 207/596-7696
 [SAVE]          6/21-10/24 [BP]          1P: $150-$260          2P: $150-$260          XP: $35
          5/1-6/20 & 10/25-4/30 [BP]          1P: $105-$175          2P: $105-$175          XP: $35
▽▽▽ ▽▽▽          **Location:** Center. Located in a residential area. 81 Talbot Ave 04841 (PO Box 1117). Fax: 207/596-9958. **Facility:** A
Historic Bed          front porch, pleasant parlors and guest rooms with fireplaces distinguish this 1898 Victorian mansion. Smoke
& Breakfast          free premises. 12 one-bedroom standard units, some with whirlpools. 3 stories (no elevator), interior corri-
          dors. *Bath:* combo or shower only. **Parking:** on-site. **Terms:** age restrictions may apply, 10 day cancellation
          notice-fee imposed, no pets allowed (owner's pet on premises). **Amenities:** hair dryers. *Some:* CD players,
high-speed Internet, irons. **Guest Services:** complimentary evening beverages. **Business Services:** fax. **Cards:** AX, MC, VI.
**Special Amenities:** free full breakfast and free local telephone calls.

SOME UNITS
[X] [DATA PORT] / [TV] [VCR] /

**CAPTAIN LINDSEY HOUSE INN**          **Phone:** (207)596-7950
▽▽▽          6/1-10/15 [ECP]          1P: $130-$190          2P: $130-$190          XP: $35
          10/16-4/30 [ECP]          1P: $85-$125          2P: $85-$125          XP: $35
Historic Bed          5/1-5/31 [ECP]          1P: $80-$120          2P: $80-$120          XP: $35
& Breakfast          **Location:** Center. 5 Lindsey St 04841. Fax: 207/596-2758. **Facility:** A common parlor area is featured at this
          1837 former sea captain's residence in the heart of town. Smoke free premises. 9 one-bedroom standard
units. 3 stories (no elevator), interior corridors. *Bath:* combo or shower only. **Parking:** on-site. **Terms:** age restrictions may apply,
10 day cancellation notice-fee imposed, package plans - seasonal. **Amenities:** hair dryers. **Cards:** AX, DS, MC, VI.

[ASK] [♦] [X] [DATA PORT]

**LAKESHORE INN**          **Phone:** (207)594-4209
▽▽▽          7/1-10/14 [BP]          1P: $135-$155          2P: $135-$155          XP: $25
          5/1-6/30 & 10/15-4/30 [BP]          1P: $105-$125          2P: $105-$125          XP: $25
Historic Bed          **Location:** 2 mi n on US 17. 184 Lakeview Dr 04841. Fax: 207/596-6407. **Facility:** This farmhouse built in 1767 is
& Breakfast          on a hill overlooking a lake and offers four tastefully decorated guest rooms with water views. Smoke free
          premises. 4 one-bedroom standard units. 2 stories (no elevator), interior corridors. *Bath:* combo or shower
only. **Parking:** on-site. **Terms:** 2-3 night minimum stay - seasonal, age restrictions may apply, 14 day cancellation notice-fee imposed. **Amenities:** hair dryers. **Leisure Activities:** whirlpool. **Guest Services:** TV in common area. **Cards:** MC, VI.

[SD] [X] [TV] [DATA PORT]

**NAVIGATOR MOTOR INN**          **Phone:** 207/594-2131
 [SAVE]          6/18-9/6          1P: $79-$115          2P: $79-$115          XP: $10          F16
          9/7-10/16          1P: $69-$99          2P: $69-$99          XP: $10          F16
▽▽▽          5/1-6/17          1P: $69-$89          2P: $69-$89          XP: $10          F16
          10/17-4/30          1P: $59-$79          2P: $59-$79          XP: $10          F16
Small-scale Hotel **Location:** On US 1. 520 Main St 04841. Fax: 207/594-7763. **Facility:** 81 one-bedroom standard units, some with
          efficiencies (utensil deposit required). 5 stories, exterior corridors. **Parking:** on-site. **Terms:** cancellation fee
imposed, small pets only (in smoking units). **Dining:** 6:30 am-2 & 5-9:30 pm, cocktails. **Guest Services:** coin laundry. **Business
Services:** meeting rooms. **Cards:** AX, DS, MC, VI. **Special Amenities:** free local telephone calls and free newspaper.

SOME UNITS
[SD] [🐾] [🍴] [DATA PORT] [🖥] / [X] [📷] /

**TRADE WINDS MOTOR INN**          **Phone:** (207)596-6661
 [SAVE]          6/25-9/5          1P: $79-$149          2P: $79-$149          XP: $10          F16
          9/6-10/10          1P: $69-$129          2P: $69-$129          XP: $10          F16
▽▽▽          5/1-6/24          1P: $65-$109          2P: $65-$109          XP: $10          F16
          10/11-4/30          1P: $55-$89          2P: $55-$89          XP: $10          F16
Small-scale Hotel **Location:** On US 1; center. 2 Park Dr 04841. Fax: 207/596-6492. **Facility:** 142 one-bedroom standard units,
          some with whirlpools. 3-5 stories, interior/exterior corridors. *Bath:* combo or shower only. **Parking:** on-site.
**Terms:** small pets only. **Dining:** 7 am-9 & 5-9 pm; hours vary off season, cocktails. **Pool(s):** heated indoor. **Leisure Activi-
ties:** sauna, whirlpool. **Fee:** exercise room. **Guest Services:** gift shop, coin laundry. **Business Services:** meeting rooms.
**Cards:** AX, DS, MC, VI. **Special Amenities:** free local telephone calls.

SOME UNITS
[SD] [🐾] [🍴] [Y] [🏊] [X] [DATA PORT] / [X] [🖥] [📷] /

—— WHERE TO DINE ——

**AMALFI**          **Dinner:** $14-$21          **Phone:** 207/596-0012
▽▽▽          **Location:** Center. 421 Main St 04841. **Hours:** 5 pm-9 pm, Sun-8 pm. Closed: 11/25, 12/25; also Mon.
Mediterranean          **Reservations:** suggested. **Features:** Chef Cooke's emphasis is on fresh, local ingredients, which are used
          whenever possible, and Mediterranean flavors, especially those of Italy and Spain. Diners are urged to try
          the paella. Casual dress; cocktails. **Parking:** on-site. **Cards:** MC, VI.
[X]

**CAFE' MIRANDA**
Italian

**Dinner:** $13-$18    **Phone:** 207/594-2034
**Location:** Center. 15 Oak St 04804. **Hours:** 5:30 pm-9:30 pm; to 8 pm 10/31-3/31. Closed: 12/25; also Mon. **Reservations:** suggested. **Features:** A diverse selection of entrees—from fresh pasta to seafood to Thai dishes—is available at this cozy, bistro-style restaurant. Well-prepared food is served in ample portions. The atmosphere is upbeat, and service is casual and friendly. Casual dress; beer & wine only. **Parking:** on-site. **Cards:** AX, MC, VI.

**GRAPES RESTAURANT**
Italian

**Lunch:** $5-$9    **Dinner:** $9-$17    **Phone:** 207/594-9050
**Location:** 1 mi s on US 1. 227 Park St 04841. **Hours:** 11:30 am-2 & 4:30-9 pm; hours vary off season. Closed major holidays. **Reservations:** accepted. **Features:** The innovative menu at this locally popular restaurant features a wide variety of steak and seafood as well as pasta and pizza. The atmosphere is relaxed and homey, and the serving staff is friendly, prompt and attentive. Local artwork is displayed here. Casual dress; cocktails. **Parking:** on-site. **Cards:** MC, VI.

**KATE'S SEAFOOD RESTUARANT**
Seafood

**Lunch:** $8-$16    **Dinner:** $8-$16    **Phone:** 207/594-2626
**Location:** On US 1, 1 mi s. 1 Payne Ave 04841. **Hours:** Open 5/1-10/15; 11:30 am-8 pm; hours vary seasonally. Closed: Mon. **Features:** This restaurant presents a menu loaded with plenty of fresh seafood dishes. Casual dress; beer & wine only. **Parking:** on-site. **Cards:** DS, MC, VI.

**LIL PIGGY'S BARBEQUE**
Barbecue

**Lunch:** $3-$11    **Dinner:** $3-$11    **Phone:** 207/594-4485
**Location:** On US 1, just n of center. 743-745 Main St 04841. **Hours:** 11 am-6 pm; hours may vary in winter. Closed: Sun-Thurs. **Features:** Barbecue grounds the menu at the small take-out restaurant, which uses regional sauces and rubs made on the premises. Meats are slow-cooked on hickory and mesquite. The menu lists many specialty sandwiches and barbecued meats. Casual dress. **Parking:** on-site. **Cards:** MC, VI.

**OH! BENTO**
Japanese

**Lunch:** $4-$7    **Dinner:** $13-$14    **Phone:** 207/593-9216
**Location:** Center. 10 Leland St 04841. **Hours:** 11 am-2:30 & 5:30-8:30 pm; to 9 pm in summer. Closed: 11/25, 12/25; also Sun & Mon. **Reservations:** accepted. **Features:** The small, casual eatery presents an array of sushi selections, as well as tempura, teriyaki and combination lunches and dinners and other traditional dishes. Beer & wine only. **Parking:** on-site. **Cards:** AX, MC, VI.

**PRIMO**
American

**Dinner:** $20-$32    **Phone:** 207/596-0770
**Location:** 1 mi s on SR 73. 2 S Main St 04841. **Hours:** 5:30 pm-9:30 pm. Closed: 1/1, 11/25, 12/25; also Tues & Wed. **Reservations:** suggested. **Features:** Fresh, local ingredients mingle in sophisticated preparations that reflect Mediterranean influences. Casual dress; cocktails. **Parking:** on-site. **Cards:** AX, DC, DS, MC, VI.

**ROCKLAND CAFE**
American

**Lunch:** $5-$9    **Dinner:** $8-$15    **Phone:** 207/596-7556
**Location:** Center. 441 Main St 04841. **Hours:** 6 am-8:30 pm, Fri & Sat-9:30 pm. Closed: 12/25. **Features:** Popular with local residents, this family cafe presents a menu with a nice selection of shrimp and haddock platters, as well as sublime carrot cake, lemon meringue pie and giant muffins, which are prepared on the premises. All-you-can-eat seafood is a draw. Casual dress; cocktails. **Parking:** on-site. **Cards:** AX, DS, MC, VI.

# ROCKPORT

------ **WHERE TO STAY** ------

**THE CLADDAGH MOTEL & SUITES**
Motel

**Phone:** 207/594-8479

| | 1P: | 2P: | XP: | |
|---|---|---|---|---|
| 7/15-8/21 [ECP] | 1P: $84-$119 | 2P: $84-$119 | XP: $10 | F16 |
| 5/1-7/14 [ECP] | 1P: $49-$105 | 2P: $49-$105 | XP: $10 | F16 |
| 8/22-10/23 [ECP] | 1P: $59-$96 | 2P: $59-$96 | XP: $10 | F16 |
| 10/24-4/30 | 1P: $45-$79 | 2P: $45-$79 | XP: $10 | F16 |

**Location:** 3 mi s on US 1. 1038 Commercial St (Rt 1) 04856 (PO Box 988). Fax: 207/594-4201. **Facility:** Smoke free premises. 19 units. 12 one- and 2 two-bedroom standard units, some with efficiencies or kitchens. 2 one- and 3 two-bedroom suites ($99-$179), some with efficiencies or kitchens. 1 story, interior/exterior corridors. *Bath:* combo or shower only. **Parking:** on-site. **Terms:** 3 day cancellation notice, up to 10 day in season-fee imposed. **Pool(s):** heated outdoor. **Cards:** AX, DS, MC, VI. *(See color ad p 207)*

SOME UNITS

**THE COUNTRY INN AT CAMDEN-ROCKPORT**
Small-scale Hotel

**Phone:** (207)236-2725

| | 1P: | 2P: | XP: | |
|---|---|---|---|---|
| 7/2-9/5 [ECP] | 1P: $159-$200 | 2P: $169-$200 | XP: $10 | F5 |
| 9/6-10/16 [ECP] | 1P: $129-$165 | 2P: $139-$165 | XP: $10 | F5 |
| 5/1-7/1 [ECP] | 1P: $105-$140 | 2P: $115-$140 | XP: $10 | F5 |
| 10/17-4/30 [ECP] | 1P: $89-$130 | 2P: $89-$130 | XP: $10 | F5 |

**Location:** Jct SR 90, 0.9 mi n on US 1. 40 Commercial St 04858 (PO Box 277, CAMDEN, 04843). Fax: 207/236-7344. **Facility:** 47 units. 12 one-bedroom standard units, some with whirlpools. 35 one-bedroom suites, some with whirlpools. 1-2 stories, interior/exterior corridors. **Parking:** on-site. **Terms:** 3 day cancellation notice. **Amenities:** irons, hair dryers. **Pool(s):** heated indoor. **Leisure Activities:** sauna, whirlpool, playground, exercise room. **Guest Services:** valet and coin laundry. **Business Services:** meeting rooms. **Cards:** AX, DS, MC, VI. **Special Amenities:** free expanded continental breakfast and free local telephone calls. *(See color ad p 208)*

SOME UNITS

## GLEN COVE MOTEL
**Phone: 207/594-4062**

**AAA SAVE**
♦♦♦

Small-scale Hotel

| | | | |
|---|---|---|---|
| 7/1-9/11 | 1P: $129-$229 | 2P: $129-$229 | XP: $10 | F16 |
| 9/12-10/12 | 1P: $89-$179 | 2P: $89-$179 | XP: $10 | F16 |
| 5/7-6/30 | 1P: $79-$169 | 2P: $79-$169 | XP: $10 | F16 |

**Location:** Jct SR 90, 3 mi s on US 1. 866 Commercial St 04856 (PO Box 35, GLEN COVE, 04846). Fax: 207/594-9434. **Facility:** 33 units. 30 one- and 3 two-bedroom standard units. 1 story, exterior corridors. *Bath:* combo or shower only. **Parking:** on-site. **Terms:** open 5/7-10/12, office hours 6:30 am-10:30 pm, cancellation fee imposed. **Amenities:** hair dryers. **Pool(s):** heated outdoor. **Cards:** AX, DS, MC, VI. **Special Amenities:** free local telephone calls and free newspaper. *(See color ad p 210)*

S/D  ⇆  ✕  🛈

## ISLAND VIEW INN
**Phone: 207/596-0040**

**AAA SAVE**
♦♦♦

Small-scale Hotel

| | | | |
|---|---|---|---|
| 7/16-8/21 | 1P: $139-$199 | 2P: $139-$199 | XP: $15 |
| 6/18-7/15 | 1P: $99-$149 | 2P: $99-$149 | XP: $15 |
| 8/22-4/30 | 1P: $69-$119 | 2P: $69-$119 | XP: $15 |
| 5/1-6/17 | 1P: $69-$99 | 2P: $69-$99 | XP: $15 |

**Location:** On US 1, 3.4 mi s of jct SR 90. 904 Commercial St 04856. Fax: 207/596-5953. **Facility:** Designated smoking area. 15 one-bedroom standard units. 2 stories (no elevator), interior/exterior corridors. *Bath:* combo or shower only. **Parking:** on-site. **Terms:** office hours 7 am-10 pm, 3 day cancellation notice-fee imposed. **Amenities:** voice mail, hair dryers. **Pool(s):** heated outdoor. **Cards:** AX, DS, MC, VI. *(See color ad p 212)*

♿M  ♿  ⊇  ✕  📷  DATA PORT  🛈

## SAMOSET RESORT    *Book at aaa.com*
**Phone: (207)594-2511**

**AAA SAVE**
♦♦♦  ♦♦♦

Resort
Large-scale Hotel

| | | | |
|---|---|---|---|
| 8/22-10/10 | 1P: $199-$389 | 2P: $199-$389 | XP: $20 | F18 |
| 7/9-8/21 | 1P: $258-$339 | 2P: $258-$339 | XP: $20 | F18 |
| 5/1-7/8 | 1P: $178-$319 | 2P: $178-$319 | XP: $20 | F18 |
| 10/11-4/30 | 1P: $130-$249 | 2P: $130-$249 | XP: $20 | F18 |

**Location:** 3.5 mi s on US 1, then 0.5 mi e on Waldo Rd. 220 Warrenton St 04856. Fax: 207/594-0722. **Facility:** The resort offers good recreational facilities and guest rooms with patios or balconies; many rooms overlook the ocean or a golf course. 178 units. 156 one-bedroom standard units. 18 one- and 4 two-bedroom suites ($299-$549). 4 stories, interior corridors. *Bath:* combo or shower only. **Parking:** on-site and valet. **Terms:** 3 day cancellation notice-fee imposed, package plans. **Amenities:** voice mail, irons, hair dryers. **Dining:** 7 am-9 pm, cocktails, also, Marcel's, see separate listing. **Pool(s):** outdoor, heated indoor. **Leisure Activities:** saunas, whirlpools, fishing, 4 tennis courts (2 lighted), recreation programs, video golf, playground, sports court, basketball, horseshoes, shuffleboard, volleyball. *Fee:* golf-18 holes, massage, game room. **Guest Services:** gift shop, valet laundry. **Business Services:** conference facilities, business center. **Cards:** AX, CB, DC, DS, JC, MC, VI. **Special Amenities:** free local telephone calls and free newspaper. *(See color ad p 212)*

SOME UNITS

S/D  ✈  🍴  🍸  ♿M  ♿  🌀  ⊇  🏋  ✕  📷  DATA PORT  🖥  / ✕  VCR  🛈  /

## SCHOONER BAY MOTOR INN
**Phone: 207/236-2205**

♦♦♦

Small-scale Hotel

| | | | |
|---|---|---|---|
| 7/2-8/29 [CP] | 1P: $75-$104 | 2P: $75-$104 | XP: $5 | F15 |
| 8/30-10/31 [CP] | 1P: $68-$88 | 2P: $68-$88 | XP: $5 | F15 |
| 5/1-7/1 & 4/15-4/30 [CP] | 1P: $69-$75 | 2P: $59-$75 | XP: $5 | F15 |

**Location:** Jct SR 90, 0.5 mi s on US 1. 337 Commercial St 04856 (PO Box 544). **Facility:** Smoke free premises. 23 one-bedroom standard units. 2 stories (no elevator), exterior corridors. **Parking:** on-site. **Terms:** open 5/1-10/31 & 4/15-4/30, office hours 7:30 am-10 pm, 3 day cancellation notice. **Amenities:** *Some:* hair dryers. **Cards:** AX, DS, MC, VI.
*(See color ad p 211)*

✕  DATA PORT

## STRAWBERRY HILL SEASIDE INN
**Phone: 207/594-5462**

**AAA SAVE**
♦♦♦

Small-scale Hotel

| | | | |
|---|---|---|---|
| 7/16-8/21 | 1P: $139-$179 | 2P: $139-$179 | XP: $15 |
| 6/18-7/15 | 1P: $99-$129 | 2P: $99-$129 | XP: $15 |
| 8/22-4/30 | 1P: $69-$119 | 2P: $69-$119 | XP: $10 |
| 5/1-6/17 | 1P: $69-$99 | 2P: $69-$99 | XP: $10 |

**Location:** Jct SR 90, 3 mi s on US 1. 886 Commercial St 04856. Fax: 207/596-6191. **Facility:** Smoke free premises. 21 one-bedroom standard units. 3 stories (no elevator), interior corridors. **Parking:** on-site. **Terms:** 3 day cancellation notice-fee imposed. **Amenities:** hair dryers. **Pool(s):** heated outdoor. **Cards:** AX, DS, MC, VI. **Special Amenities:** free local telephone calls and preferred room (subject to availability with advanced reservations). *(See color ad p 212)*

SOME UNITS

⊇  ✕  DATA PORT  🛈  / VCR /
FEE

─────── **WHERE TO DINE** ───────

## INGRAHAM'S ON RICHARDS HILL
**Dinner: $14-$21**     **Phone: 207/236-3227**

♦♦♦♦

American

**Location:** 1 mi s on US 1. 417 Commercial St 04856. **Hours:** 5 pm-9 pm. Closed major holidays. **Reservations:** suggested. **Features:** The restaurant nurtures a cozy country-inn atmosphere. The creative menu features fresh seafood, including several lobster dishes, as well as poultry and beef. Portions are ample. Casual dress; cocktails. **Parking:** on-site. **Cards:** AX, DS, MC, VI.

✕

## MARCEL'S
**Dinner: $17-$31**     **Phone: 207/593-1529**

**AAA**
♦♦♦  ♦♦♦

Continental

**Location:** 3.5 mi s on US 1, then 0.5 mi e on Waldo Rd; in Samoset Resort. 220 Warrenton St 04856. **Hours:** 7 am-10:30 & 6-9 pm, Fri-Sun to 10 pm; hours may vary seasonally. **Reservations:** suggested. **Features:** This spacious dining room offers a great view of the golf course and ocean. The menu features a wide variety of fresh lobster and other seafood dishes, beef and some tableside preparation. Fine dessert and a superb selection of wines are also offered. Dressy casual; cocktails. **Parking:** on-site. **Cards:** AX, DC, DS, MC, VI.

🍸  ✕

## MCMAHON'S ROCKPORT GRILLE
**Lunch: $6-$14**     **Dinner: $12-$26**     **Phone: 207/236-4431**

♦♦

American

**Location:** On US 1, 0.8 mi s of jct with SR 90. 399 Commercial St 04856. **Hours:** 11 am-9 pm; hours may vary seasonally. Closed: 7/4, 11/25, 12/25. **Reservations:** not accepted. **Features:** At Farmhouse Conference Center, the restaurant nurtures a casual atmosphere in a barnlike setting. The menu lists soups, salad-bar items, sandwiches, pasta and seafood. Dancing is encouraged when the nightly entertainment is on stage. Casual dress; cocktails. **Parking:** on-site. **Cards:** AX, DS, MC, VI.

✕

# ROUND POND

--------- WHERE TO DINE ---------

**MUSCONGUS BAY LOBSTER CO**     **Lunch:** $9-$23     **Dinner:** $9-$23     **Phone:** 207/529-5528
▼▼
Seafood
**Location:** SR 32, just e, follow signs. 28 Landing Rd 04564. **Hours:** Open 5/9-10/11; 11 am-8:30 pm; hours vary seasonally. **Features:** Priceless views of Muscongus Bay are among draws of the basic lobster pound. On the menu are cooked lobster, clams, oysters, lobster and crabmeat rolls and corn on the cob. Patrons should plan to bring their own beverage and utensils. Casual dress. **Parking:** on-site. **Cards:** MC, VI.

🍽️ ✕️

# RUMFORD pop. 4,795

--------- WHERE TO STAY ---------

**LINNELL MOTEL & RESTINN CONFERENCE CENTER**     **Phone:** (207)364-4511
(AAA) (SAVE)
▼▼▼ ▼▼▼
Small-scale Hotel
| | | | |
|---|---|---|---|
| All Year | 1P: $55-$70 | 2P: $60-$75 | XP: $10   F10 |

**Location:** 2 mi w, just off US 2. 986 Prospect Ave 04276. **Fax:** 207/369-0800. **Facility:** 50 one-bedroom standard units, some with efficiencies. 1-2 stories (no elevator), interior/exterior corridors. *Bath:* combo or shower only. **Parking:** on-site. **Terms:** [CP] meal plan available, pets ($5 extra charge). **Amenities:** *Some:* hair dryers. **Guest Services:** coin laundry. **Business Services:** meeting rooms. **Cards:** AX, CB, DC, DS, MC, VI. **Special Amenities:** free continental breakfast and free local telephone calls.

SOME UNITS
🆂🅳 🐾 🍴➤ / ✕️ 🖥️ 📶 /
FEE

**THE MADISON MOTOR INN**     **Phone:** (207)364-7973
▼▼▼ ▼▼▼
Small-scale Hotel
| | | | |
|---|---|---|---|
| All Year | 1P: $79-$139 | 2P: $79-$139 | |

**Location:** 4 mi w. 1257 US Rt 2 04276 (PO Box 398). **Fax:** 207/369-0341. **Facility:** 38 units. 36 one-bedroom standard units. 2 one-bedroom suites with kitchens. 2 stories (no elevator), exterior corridors. *Bath:* combo or shower only. **Parking:** on-site. **Terms:** 14 day cancellation notice, [AP] meal plan available, package plans, restaurant, see separate listing. **Pool(s):** outdoor. **Leisure Activities:** sauna, canoeing, fishing, jogging, exercise room. **Cards:** AX, CB, DC, DS, JC, MC, VI.

SOME UNITS
🅰🆂🅺 🆂🅳 🐾 🍴 🏊 ✕️ 📶 🖥️ / ✕️ 🖥️ /

# RUMFORD CENTER

--------- WHERE TO STAY ---------

**BLUE IRIS MOTOR INN**     **Phone:** 207/364-4495
▼▼▼ ▼▼▼
Motel
| | | | |
|---|---|---|---|
| All Year | 1P: $40-$60 | 2P: $45-$80 | XP: $10   F12 |

**Location:** 4.5 mi w on US 2 from town of Rumford. 1405 US Rt 2 04278 (PO Box 127). **Facility:** 14 units. 12 one-bedroom standard units, some with efficiencies. 2 one-bedroom suites ($65-$100) with efficiencies. 1 story, exterior corridors. *Bath:* combo or shower only. **Parking:** on-site. **Terms:** office hours 8 am-10 pm, 7 day cancellation notice. **Pool(s):** outdoor. **Leisure Activities:** fishing, cross country skiing. **Cards:** AX, DS, MC, VI.

SOME UNITS
🏊 / ✕️ 📶 🖥️ 🖥️ /

# SACO pop. 16,822

--------- WHERE TO STAY ---------

**EASTVIEW MOTEL**     **Phone:** 207/282-2362
▼▼ ▼▼
Motel
| | | | |
|---|---|---|---|
| 6/21-9/5 | 1P: $59-$69 | 2P: $79-$89 | XP: $5   F12 |
| 5/1-6/20 | 1P: $45-$55 | 2P: $59-$69 | XP: $5   F12 |
| 9/6-4/30 | 1P: $39-$49 | 2P: $55-$65 | XP: $5   F12 |

**Location:** I-95 (Maine Tpke), exit 36, 3 mi n on US 1. 924 Portland (US 1) Rd 04072. **Fax:** 207/282-2362. **Facility:** 22 one-bedroom standard units. 1 story, exterior corridors. *Bath:* combo or shower only. **Parking:** on-site. **Terms:** office hours 8 am-10 pm, 3 day cancellation notice. **Amenities:** voice mail. **Pool(s):** outdoor. **Leisure Activities:** playground, basketball, shuffleboard. **Cards:** AX, DC, MC, VI.

SOME UNITS
🅰🆂🅺 🆂🅳 🍴➤ 🏊 ✕️ 📶 / ✕️ 🖥️ 🖥️ /

**HAMPTON INN**     *Book at aaa.com*     **Phone:** (207)282-7222
(AAA) (SAVE)
▼▼▼ ▼▼▼
Small-scale Hotel
| | | | |
|---|---|---|---|
| 7/1-10/11 | 1P: $89-$139 | 2P: $89-$139 | XP: $10   F |
| 5/1-6/30 & 10/12-4/30 | 1P: $69-$99 | 2P: $69-$99 | XP: $10   F |

**Location:** I-95 (Maine Tpke), exit 36; I-195, exit 1. 48 Industrial Park Rd 04072. **Fax:** 207/282-7333. **Facility:** 100 units. 96 one-bedroom standard units. 4 one-bedroom suites ($99-$169). 5 stories, interior corridors. *Bath:* combo or shower only. **Parking:** on-site. **Terms:** [ECP] meal plan available, pets (with prior approval). **Amenities:** dual phone lines, voice mail, irons, hair dryers. **Pool(s):** heated outdoor. **Leisure Activities:** exercise room. **Guest Services:** valet and coin laundry. **Business Services:** meeting rooms. **Cards:** AX, CB, DC, DS, MC, VI. **Special Amenities:** free expanded continental breakfast and free local telephone calls.

SOME UNITS
🆂🅳 🐾 🅼 🏊 🎥 📶 🖥️ / ✕️ 📶 🖥️ /

**HOLIDAY INN EXPRESS HOTEL & SUITES**     *Book at aaa.com*     **Phone:** (207)286-9600
▼▼▼ ▼▼▼
Small-scale Hotel
| | | | |
|---|---|---|---|
| 6/26-8/28 [ECP] | 1P: $130-$160 | 2P: $130-$160 | XP: $10   F18 |
| 8/29-10/16 [ECP] | 1P: $105-$160 | 2P: $105-$160 | XP: $10   F18 |
| 5/1-6/25 [ECP] | 1P: $80-$125 | 2P: $80-$125 | XP: $10   F18 |
| 10/17-4/30 [ECP] | 1P: $75-$95 | 2P: $75-$95 | XP: $10   F18 |

**Location:** I-95 (Maine Tpke), access ramp at mile marker 35; exit 36 southbound; I-195, exit 1, follow signs. 352 North St 04072. **Fax:** 207/286-9696. **Facility:** 88 units. 85 one-bedroom standard units. 3 one-bedroom suites ($105-$250). 4 stories, interior corridors. *Bath:* combo or shower only. **Parking:** on-site. **Terms:** cancellation fee imposed. **Amenities:** high-speed Internet, dual phone lines, voice mail, irons, hair dryers. **Pool(s):** heated outdoor. **Guest Services:** valet laundry, area transportation. **Business Services:** meeting rooms. **Cards:** AX, CB, DC, DS, JC, MC, VI.

SOME UNITS
🅰🆂🅺 🆂🅳 ♿ 🅼 🏊 🍴➤ 🎥 📶 🖥️ / ✕️ 📶 🖥️ /

## SACO INN & SUITES

**Phone:** (207)284-4074

AAA SAVE

Motel

| | | | | |
|---|---|---|---|---|
| 6/24-9/14 | 1P: $75-$80 | 2P: $85-$95 | XP: $10 | F5 |
| 5/16-6/23 | 1P: $60-$65 | 2P: $65-$75 | XP: $10 | F5 |
| 5/1-5/15 & 9/15-4/30 | 1P: $45-$50 | 2P: $50-$60 | XP: $10 | F5 |

**Location:** 1.8 mi n on US 1. 720 Portland Rd 04072. Fax: 207/934-0321. **Facility:** 12 one-bedroom standard units. 1 story, exterior corridors. *Bath:* combo or shower only. **Parking:** on-site. **Terms:** office hours 8 am-10 pm, 1-2 night minimum stay, 3 day cancellation notice-fee imposed. **Pool(s):** indoor. **Cards:** AX, DS, MC, VI.
**Special Amenities:** free local telephone calls and early check-in/late check-out.

SOME UNITS

---

## SACO MOTEL

**Phone:** (207)284-6952

Motel

| | | | | |
|---|---|---|---|---|
| 7/2-9/6 | 1P: $60-$75 | 2P: $65-$80 | XP: $5 | F17 |
| 5/1-7/1 & 9/7-10/13 | 1P: $35-$45 | 2P: $40-$50 | XP: $5 | F17 |

**Location:** I-95 (Maine Tpke), exit 36, 0.5 mi s on US 1. 473 Main St 04072. **Facility:** 26 one-bedroom standard units. 1 story, exterior corridors. *Bath:* shower only. **Parking:** on-site. **Terms:** open 5/1-10/13, office hours 7 am-11 pm, 3 day cancellation notice, pets ($5 extra charge). **Pool(s):** outdoor. **Cards:** AX, DS, MC, VI.

SOME UNITS

---

## WAGON WHEEL MOTEL

**Phone:** (207)284-6387

Motel

| | | | | |
|---|---|---|---|---|
| 7/1-9/30 | 1P: $75-$85 | 2P: $85-$95 | XP: $5 | F12 |
| 5/1-6/30 | 1P: $48-$60 | 2P: $55-$75 | XP: $5 | F12 |
| 10/1-4/30 | 1P: $40-$55 | 2P: $48-$65 | XP: $5 | F12 |

**Location:** 1.8 mi n on US 1; 0.8 mi n of jct I-95, exit 36. 726 Portland Rd 04072. **Facility:** 11 one-bedroom standard units. 2 stories (no elevator), exterior corridors. **Parking:** on-site. **Terms:** office hours 8 am-11 pm, 2 night minimum stay - weekends, 3 day cancellation notice-fee imposed. **Amenities:** video library (fee). *Some:* irons, hair dryers. **Pool(s):** outdoor.
**Cards:** AX, MC, VI.

SOME UNITS

---

## —— WHERE TO DINE ——

## CASCADE FAMILY RESTAURANT

**Lunch:** $4-$8    **Dinner:** $7-$16    **Phone:** 207/283-3271

AAA

American

**Location:** Jct SR 98, 3 mi n. 941 Portland Rd (US 1) 04072. **Hours:** 11 am-8 pm, Sun from 9 am; seasonal hours may vary. Closed: 12/24, 12/25. **Reservations:** suggested, weekends. **Features:** A short drive to Old Orchard Beach, this restaurant has a simple traditional decor and a family atmosphere. The menu features American cuisine with an emphasis on seafood, especially lobster, as well as beef, poultry and pasta items. Portions are large. The luncheon menu has smaller portions. Be sure to try the brownie a la mode, a time tested favorite. Casual dress; cocktails. **Parking:** on-site. **Cards:** DS, MC, VI.

---

# SANFORD pop. 10,133

## —— WHERE TO STAY ——

## SANFORD INN

**Phone:** (207)324-4662

AAA SAVE

Motel

| | | | | |
|---|---|---|---|---|
| 6/21-9/9 | 1P: $59-$89 | 2P: $69-$99 | XP: $10 | F8 |
| 5/1-6/20 & 9/10-4/30 | 1P: $55-$59 | 2P: $59-$69 | XP: $10 | F8 |

**Location:** I-95 (Maine Tpke), exit 19, 8 mi w on SR 109. 1591 Main St 04073. Fax: 207/490-6999. **Facility:** 40 one-bedroom standard units. 1 story, exterior corridors. *Bath:* combo or shower only. **Parking:** on-site. **Terms:** office hours 7:30 am-10 pm, [CP] meal plan available. **Pool(s):** outdoor. **Cards:** AX, DS, MC, VI.
**Special Amenities:** free continental breakfast and free local telephone calls.

SOME UNITS

---

## SUPER 8 MOTEL

*Book at aaa.com*

**Phone:** (207)324-8823

Small-scale Hotel

| | | | | |
|---|---|---|---|---|
| 7/1-10/15 | 1P: $68-$81 | 2P: $81-$95 | XP: $7 | F12 |
| 10/16-11/15 | 1P: $53-$68 | 2P: $60-$70 | XP: $7 | F12 |
| 5/1-6/30 & 11/16-4/30 | 1P: $50-$53 | 2P: $57-$60 | XP: $7 | F12 |

**Location:** I-95 (Maine Tpke), exit 19, 7 mi w. Located adjacent to Sanford Airport. 1892 Main St (Rt 109) 04073. Fax: 207/324-8782. **Facility:** 49 one-bedroom standard units. 2 stories (no elevator), interior corridors. *Bath:* combo or shower only. **Parking:** on-site. **Terms:** cancellation fee imposed, pets ($15 extra charge). **Cards:** AX, DC, DS, MC, VI.

SOME UNITS

---

## —— WHERE TO DINE ——

## WEATHERVANE

**Lunch:** $4-$16    **Dinner:** $4-$16    **Phone:** 207/324-0084

Seafood

**Location:** 1 mi s on SR 109; close to Sanford Airport. 1601 Main St 04073. **Hours:** 11 am-9 pm; to 9:30 pm 6/1-10/15. Closed: 11/25, 12/24, 12/25. **Features:** This large and bustling family-style restaurant features a very good menu variety that includes lobster, fried clams and crisp, Cape Cod apple cranberry cobbler. The flavorful dishes are served in large portions. Friendly and attentive service. Casual dress; cocktails.
**Parking:** on-site. **Cards:** AX, MC, VI.

# SCARBOROUGH pop. 3,867

## ——— WHERE TO STAY ———

### FAIRFIELD INN
**Book at aaa.com**

Small-scale Hotel

| |  |  |
|---|---|---|
| 7/1-10/31 [ECP] | 1P: $132-$152 | 2P: $132-$152 |
| 5/1-6/30 [ECP] | 1P: $79-$109 | 2P: $109 |
| 11/1-4/30 [ECP] | 1P: $66-$85 | 2P: $66-$85 |

Phone: (207)883-0300

**Location:** I-95 (Maine Tpke), exit 45, follow signs for Maine Mall Rd, left on Payne Rd, then 0.5 mi s. 2 Cummings Rd 04074. Fax: 207/883-0572. **Facility:** 120 one-bedroom standard units. 3 stories, interior corridors. **Parking:** on-site. **Terms:** cancellation fee imposed. **Amenities:** voice mail, irons, hair dryers. **Pool(s):** heated outdoor. **Guest Services:** valet laundry. **Cards:** AX, CB, DC, DS, JC, MC, VI.

SOME UNITS

### LIGHTHOUSE INN AT PINE POINT
**Book at aaa.com**

Motel

| | 1P | 2P | XP |
|---|---|---|---|
| 7/1-9/6 | 1P: $125-$225 | 2P: $125-$225 | XP: $15 |
| 9/7-10/12 | 1P: $75-$150 | 2P: $75-$150 | XP: $15 |
| 5/28-6/30 | 1P: $75-$135 | 2P: $75-$135 | XP: $15 |

Phone: (207)883-3213

**Location:** I-95 (Maine Tpke), exit 42 to US 1, 2 mi s on US 1 to SR 9, then 3 mi e to Pine Point Beach. 366 Pine Point Rd 04074. **Facility:** 22 one-bedroom standard units. 2 stories (no elevator), exterior corridors. **Parking:** on-site. **Terms:** open 5/28-10/12, office hours 8 am-10 pm, 2 night minimum stay - weekends, 10 day cancellation notice-fee imposed. **Amenities:** hair dryers. **Cards:** AX, DS, MC, VI.

### MILLBROOK MOTEL

Motel

| | 1P | 2P | XP | |
|---|---|---|---|---|
| 6/18-9/12 | 1P: $80-$90 | 2P: $85-$95 | XP: $8 | F6 |
| 5/1-6/17 & 9/13-10/31 | 1P: $55-$65 | 2P: $65-$75 | XP: $8 | F6 |
| 11/1-4/30 | 1P: $48-$58 | 2P: $53-$65 | XP: $8 | F6 |

Phone: 207/883-6004

**Location:** I-95 (Maine Tpke), exit 42, continue 1.5 mi through toll gate to US 1, turn left, then 0.5 mi n. 321 US 1 04074. **Facility:** 18 one-bedroom standard units. 2 stories (no elevator), exterior corridors. *Bath:* combo or shower only. **Parking:** on-site. **Terms:** office hours 8 am-10 pm, 7 day cancellation notice-fee imposed, [CP] meal plan available. **Cards:** DS, MC, VI.

SOME UNITS

### PRIDE MOTEL & COTTAGES

Cottage

| | 1P | 2P | XP | |
|---|---|---|---|---|
| 6/21-9/6 | 1P: $70-$115 | 2P: $70-$115 | XP: $5 | F |
| 9/7-10/11 | 1P: $55-$85 | 2P: $55-$85 | XP: $5 | F |
| 5/1-6/20 | 1P: $45-$85 | 2P: $45-$85 | XP: $5 | F |
| 10/12-4/30 | 1P: $45-$60 | 2P: $45-$60 | XP: $5 | F |

Phone: 207/883-4816

**Location:** I-95 (Maine Tpke), exit 36, 0.5 mi e to US 1, then 4.5 mi n. 677 US 1 04070-2070 (PO Box 2070). Fax: 419/858-2619. **Facility:** 17 units. 7 one-bedroom standard units, some with efficiencies. 10 cottages. 1 story, exterior corridors. *Bath:* combo or shower only. **Parking:** on-site. **Terms:** office hours 8 am-10 pm, 2 night minimum stay - with Saturday stayover in summer, pets ($5 extra charge). **Pool(s):** heated outdoor. **Leisure Activities:** playground, volleyball. *Fee:* game room. **Guest Services:** coin laundry. **Cards:** AX, DS, MC, VI.

SOME UNITS
FEE

### RESIDENCE INN BY MARRIOTT
**Book at aaa.com**

Small-scale Hotel

All Year    1P: $109-$219

Phone: (207)883-0400

**Location:** I-95 (Maine Tpke), exit 42, 1.5 mi n on Payne Rd. 800 Roundwood Dr 04074. Fax: 207/883-6352. **Facility:** 78 units. 24 one-bedroom standard units with efficiencies. 42 one- and 12 two-bedroom suites, some with efficiencies or kitchens. 3 stories, interior corridors. *Bath:* combo or shower only. **Parking:** on-site. **Terms:** check-in 4 pm, 2 night minimum stay - seasonal, cancellation fee imposed, package plans, pets ($100 fee, $6 extra charge). **Amenities:** video games (fee), voice mail, irons, hair dryers. **Pool(s):** heated indoor. **Leisure Activities:** whirlpool, exercise room, sports court. **Guest Services:** valet and coin laundry. **Business Services:** meeting rooms. **Cards:** AX, CB, DC, DS, JC, MC, VI.

SOME UNITS
FEE    FEE

### SEA-WARD ON OCEANFRONT GUEST HOUSE

Motel

| |  |  | |
|---|---|---|---|
| 6/19-9/7 | 2P: $95-$137 | XP: $12 | F5 |
| 9/8-10/11 | 2P: $67-$120 | XP: $12 | F5 |
| 5/28-6/18 | 2P: $67-$99 | XP: $12 | F5 |

Phone: (207)883-6666

**Location:** I-95 (Maine Tpke), exit 42, 1.5 mi to US 1, 1.5 mi s to SR 9 (Pine Point Rd), 3 mi e, just s on E Grand Ave, then just e. 7 Bliss St, Pine Point 04074. **Facility:** Smoke free premises. 9 one-bedroom standard units, some with kitchens. 2 stories (no elevator), interior/exterior corridors. *Bath:* combo or shower only. **Parking:** on-site. **Terms:** open 5/28-10/11, 2 night minimum stay, 14 day cancellation notice. **Cards:** MC, VI.

### TOWNEPLACE SUITES BY MARRIOTT
**Book at aaa.com**

Small-scale Hotel

| |  |  |
|---|---|---|
| 6/15-10/19 [CP] | 1P: $149-$169 | 2P: $199-$219 |
| 5/1-6/14 [CP] | 1P: $109-$129 | 2P: $149-$169 |
| 10/20-4/30 [CP] | 1P: $79-$99 | 2P: $109-$129 |

Phone: (207)883-6800

**Location:** I-95 (Maine Tpke), exit 42, 1.5 mi n on Payne Rd. 700 Roundwood Dr 04074. Fax: 207/883-6866. **Facility:** 95 units. 69 one-bedroom standard units with kitchens. 4 one- and 22 two-bedroom suites with kitchens. 3 stories, interior corridors. *Bath:* combo or shower only. **Parking:** on-site. **Terms:** pets ($20 extra charge). **Amenities:** dual phone lines, voice mail, irons, hair dryers. **Pool(s):** heated outdoor. **Leisure Activities:** exercise room. **Guest Services:** valet and coin laundry. **Business Services:** business center. **Cards:** AX, CB, DC, DS, JC, MC, VI.

SOME UNITS
FEE

## WHERE TO DINE

**AMERICAN CAFE & LOUNGE**          **Lunch:** $5-$9          **Dinner:** $10-$17          **Phone:** 207/885-1523

American

**Location:** I-95 (Maine Tpke), exit 42, 0.5 mi e to US 1, then just n. US 1 04074. **Hours:** 8 am-3 & 4-9 pm, Sun-3 pm; hours may vary seasonally. Closed: 9/6, 11/25; also Mon. **Features:** The cafe's interior, with a mahogany bar and paneling, might remind patrons of an upscale diner. Items from the specialty brunch menu are served all day. Dinner shows an emphasis on fresh seafood mixed with local produce. Casual dress; cocktails. **Parking:** on-site. **Cards:** AX, DS, MC, VI.

**BAYLEY'S SEAFOOD RESTAURANT**          **Lunch:** $9-$17          **Dinner:** $9-$17          **Phone:** 207/885-9754

Seafood

**Location:** Jct US 1, 1 mi e on SR 9. 165 Pine Point Rd 04074. **Hours:** 11 am-9 pm; hours vary seasonally. Closed: 12/25; also Mon-Thurs 11/1-3/31. **Features:** Guests can order one of a variety of fresh seafood items at the counter. Favorite offerings include fresh onion rings and homemade chowders. Casual dress; cocktails. **Parking:** on-site. **Cards:** DS, MC, VI.

**DIMITRI'S RESTAURANT**          **Lunch:** $4-$8          **Dinner:** $12-$20          **Phone:** 207/883-9800

Greek

**Location:** Just n on SR 114. 185 US Rt 1 04074. **Hours:** 11:30 am-2:30 & 5-9 pm, Fri & Sat-10 pm, Sun 5 pm-9 pm. **Features:** Traditional recipes are used to create the offerings, many of which are cooked in a brick oven. The light and airy dining room has a Greek feel, in part due to Greek music and pictures of the Greek Isles. Casual dress; cocktails. **Parking:** on-site. **Cards:** AX, DS, MC, VI.

**KEN'S PLACE**          **Lunch:** $5-$23          **Dinner:** $5-$23          **Phone:** 207/883-6611

Seafood

**Location:** Jct US 1, 1.8 mi s on SR 9 W. Pine Point Rd 04074. **Hours:** Open 5/1-10/24 & 4/1-4/30; 11 am-9 pm; hours vary off season. **Features:** A popular restaurant since 1929, this spot focuses its menu on fresh local seafood, including raw bar offerings. Casual dress; cocktails. **Parking:** on-site. **Cards:** DS, MC, VI.

# SEAL HARBOR

## WHERE TO DINE

**JORDAN POND HOUSE**          **Lunch:** $10-$18          **Dinner:** $15-$22          **Phone:** 207/276-3316

Seafood

**Location:** In Acadia National Park; on Park Loop Rd 1.8 mi n of jct SR 3, Stanley Brook entrance. Acadia National Park 04675. **Hours:** Open 5/14-10/24; 11:30 am-9 pm; hours vary seasonally. **Reservations:** suggested. **Features:** An idyllic setting overlooking lovely Jordan Pond and the hills known as the Bubbles. You can choose to dine inside or if weather permits outside on the lawn and enjoy the breeze off the pond. Folks come for the popovers and homemade jams but can also sample the fresh Maine seafood, poultry and beef selections, try and save room for the homemade ice cream. Casual dress; cocktails. **Parking:** on-site. **Cards:** AX, DS, MC, VI.

# SEARSPORT pop. 1,102

## WHERE TO STAY

**BRASS LANTERN INN**          **Phone:** 207/548-0150

Historic Bed & Breakfast

Property failed to provide current rates

**Location:** 0.3 mi s on US 1. 81 W Main St 04974. Fax: 207/548-0304. **Facility:** This attractive 1850s Victorian home, formerly a sea captain's residence, has cozy parlors decorated with items from the owners' travels. Smoke free premises. 5 one-bedroom standard units. 2 stories (no elevator), interior corridors. *Bath:* combo or shower only. **Parking:** on-site. **Terms:** check-in 4 pm, age restrictions may apply. **Amenities:** *Some:* hair dryers. **Guest Services:** TV in common area.

**THE YARDARM MOTEL**          **Phone:** 207/548-2404

Motel

| | | | | |
|---|---|---|---|---|
| 6/19-8/24 | 1P: $68-$100 | 2P: $68-$100 | XP: $6 | F |
| 5/14-6/18 | 1P: $53-$95 | 2P: $53-$95 | XP: $6 | F |
| 8/25-10/17 | 1P: $60-$90 | 2P: $60-$90 | XP: $6 | F |

**Location:** 0.5 mi n on US 1. 172 E Main St 04974 (PO Box 246). **Facility:** 18 one-bedroom standard units. 1 story, exterior corridors. *Bath:* combo or shower only. **Parking:** on-site. **Terms:** open 5/14-10/17, office hours 9 am-9 pm, 3 day cancellation notice, [CP] meal plan available, small pets only (in limited units). **Cards:** MC; VI. **Special Amenities: free continental breakfast and free local telephone calls.**

SOME UNITS

## WHERE TO DINE

**ANGLER'S FAMILY SEAFOOD RESTAURANT**          **Lunch:** $4-$9          **Dinner:** $6-$16          **Phone:** 207/548-2405

Seafood

**Location:** 1.5 mi n on US 1. 215 E Main St 04974. **Hours:** 11 am-8 pm. Closed: 11/25, 12/24, 12/25. **Features:** Although the menu emphasizes seafood, it also lists chicken, steak, prime rib and roast pork. The restaurant caters to families. Casual dress; cocktails. **Parking:** on-site. **Cards:** DS, MC, VI.

**CHOCOLATE GRILLE**          **Lunch:** $6-$12          **Dinner:** $7-$19          **Phone:** 207/548-2555

American

**Location:** Center. 1 E Main St 04974. **Hours:** 11 am-11 pm, Fri & Sat-12:30 am, Sun-10 pm. **Reservations:** accepted. **Features:** While the grill here is nice, a love of chocolate is reflected in the restaurant's dessert menu, as well as in its coffees and cocktails. Soups, salads, sandwiches, burgers and pizza share menu space with pasta and seafood choices. The patio opens seasonally. Casual dress; cocktails. **Parking:** on-site. **Cards:** AX, DS, MC, VI.

# SEBASCO ESTATES

──────── WHERE TO STAY ────────

──────── *The following lodging was either not evaluated or did not* ────────
*meet AAA rating requirements but is listed for your information only.*

**SEBASCO HARBOR RESORT**        Phone: 207/389-1161
(fyi)    Not evaluated. **Location:** 1.3 mi se on SR 217, from jct SR 209. Rt 217 04565 (PO Box 75). Facilities, services, and decor characterize a mid-range property.

# SKOWHEGAN pop. 6,696

──────── WHERE TO STAY ────────

**BELMONT MOTEL**        Phone: (207)474-8315
(AAA) (SAVE)    6/15-10/15      1P: $60-$80      2P: $65-$85      XP: $6
10/16-4/30      1P: $55-$65      2P: $60-$70      XP: $6
◈◈◈◈    5/1-6/14      1P: $50-$60      2P: $55-$65      XP: $6
Motel    **Location:** 1 mi n on US 201. 273 Madison Ave 04976. Fax: 207/474-8315. **Facility:** 36 one-bedroom standard units. 1 story. **Parking:** on-site, winter plug-ins. **Terms:** office hours 7 am-10 pm, 3 day cancellation notice. **Pool(s):** outdoor. **Leisure Activities:** shuffleboard. **Cards:** AX, DC, DS, MC, VI. **Special Amenities: free local telephone calls and free newspaper.**

SOME UNITS
(&M) (≈) (📹) (DATA PORT) / (✕) (🛄)
FEE

**BREEZY ACRES MOTEL**        Phone: (207)474-2703
(AAA) (SAVE)    5/1-10/20      1P: $40-$48      2P: $58-$68      XP: $5      F12
◈◈◈    **Location:** 1.5 mi s on US 201. Located in a rural area. 315 Waterville Rd 04976. Fax: 207/474-2703. **Facility:** 13 units. 12 one- and 1 two-bedroom standard units. 1 story, exterior corridors. *Bath:* combo or shower only.
Motel    **Parking:** on-site. **Terms:** open 5/1-10/20, office hours 7:30 am-11 pm, weekly rates available, [CP] meal plan available, pets (with prior approval). **Pool(s):** outdoor. **Leisure Activities:** paddleboats, fishing, Bell Golf mini course. **Cards:** AX, MC, VI. **Special Amenities: free continental breakfast and free local telephone calls.**

SOME UNITS
(S/D) (🐾) (≈) (📹) (🛄) (💻) / (✕) /

**TOWNE MOTEL**        Phone: (207)474-5151
(AAA) (SAVE)    7/1-9/5                  2P: $68-$90      XP: $7      F14
9/6-10/23            2P: $61-$81      XP: $7      F14
◈◈◈◈    5/1-6/30            2P: $60-$79      XP: $7      F14
Motel    10/24-4/30         2P: $50-$67      XP: $7      F14
**Location:** 0.5 mi n on US 201. 172 Madison Ave 04976. Fax: 207/474-6407. **Facility:** 33 units. 26 one-bedroom standard units. 7 one-bedroom suites with efficiencies. 2 stories (no elevator), exterior corridors. *Bath:* combo or shower only. **Parking:** on-site, winter plug-ins. **Terms:** office hours 7 am-11 pm. **Amenities:** hair dryers. **Pool(s):** outdoor. **Guest Services:** coin laundry. **Cards:** AX, DS, MC, VI. **Special Amenities: free continental breakfast and free newspaper.**

SOME UNITS
(S/D) (≈) (📹) / (✕) /

──────── WHERE TO DINE ────────

**CHARRIER'S STEAK & SEAFOOD**    **Lunch:** $5-$9      **Dinner:** $9-$15      Phone: 207/474-9864
◈◈ ◈◈    **Location:** Center. 123 Madison Ave 04976. **Hours:** 7 am-8 pm, Fri & Sat-8:30 pm. Closed: 12/25.
**Features:** This spacious restaurant offers two dining sections, a casual restaurant in front with coffee
Steak & Seafood    counter and finer dining area in back. The menu is expansive and offers everything from burgers to seafood and steak. Home-style cooking serving ample portions. Casual dress; cocktails. **Parking:** on-site.
**Cards:** AX, DS, MC, VI.      (✕)

**HERITAGE HOUSE RESTAURANT**    **Lunch:** $4-$8      **Dinner:** $8-$15      Phone: 207/474-5100
◈◈ ◈◈    **Location:** 0.5 mi n on US 201. 260 Madison Ave 04976. **Hours:** 11:30 am-2 & 5-9 pm, Fri & Sat-10 pm. Closed:
9/6, 11/25, 12/25; also Sun 12/1-3/31. **Reservations:** accepted. **Features:** You'll enjoy the small and
American    intimate Heritage House and its 18th-century renovated Victorian-home setting. The cuisine features seafood, steak, chicken and spirits. The chocolate mousse and almond cheesecake are two of their excellent desserts. Casual dress; cocktails. **Parking:** on-site. **Cards:** AX, MC, VI.      (✕)

# SOUTH CASCO

──────── WHERE TO STAY ────────

**MIGIS LODGE**        Phone: 207/655-4524
◈◈◈◈    6/15-9/5 [AP]      1P: $250-$300
9/6-10/15 [AP]      1P: $200-$250
Resort    **Location:** 0.5 mi w of US 302, follow sign. Located in a quiet, secluded area, on Sebago Lake. Migis Lodge Rd 04077
Small-scale Hotel    (PO Box 40). Fax: 207/655-2054. **Facility:** Nestled in a forest setting, the lodge features handsomely furnished cottages and good recreational facilities. 39 units. 12 one-bedroom standard units. 16 one-, 3 two- and 8 three-bedroom suites. 1-2 stories, interior/exterior corridors. *Bath:* combo or shower only. **Parking:** on-site. **Terms:** open 6/15-10/15, 30 day cancellation notice. **Amenities:** irons, hair dryers. *Some:* DVD players (fee). **Leisure Activities:** sauna, boating, canoeing, paddleboats, sailboats, windsurfing, boat dock, waterskiing, fishing, 3 tennis courts, recreation programs. **Guest Services:** gift shop, valet laundry. **Business Services:** meeting rooms.

SOME UNITS
(🍽) (🛗) (&) (✚) (✕) (🅏) (🛄) / (🍴) (VCR)
FEE

# SOUTHPORT

―――――― **WHERE TO STAY** ――――――

**THE LAWNMERE INN**                                  **Phone:** (207)633-2544

(AAA) (SAVE)

| | | | | |
|---|---|---|---|---|
| 7/2-9/5 | 1P: $109-$199 | 2P: $109-$199 | XP: $15 | F6 |
| 5/15-7/1 & 9/6-10/11 | 1P: $89-$149 | 2P: $89-$149 | XP: $15 | F6 |

Country Inn
**Location:** 2 mi s of Boothbay Harbor on SR 27, just s of bridge to Southport Island. 65 Hendricks Hill Rd 04576 (PO Box 29, NEWAGEN). **Facility:** Smoke free premises. 30 units. 28 one-bedroom standard units. 2 one-bedroom suites. 3 stories (no elevator), interior/exterior corridors. *Bath:* some combo or shower only. **Parking:** on-site. **Terms:** open 5/15-10/11, 14 day cancellation notice-fee imposed, weekly rates available, [MAP] meal plan available, small pets only ($15 extra charge). **Amenities:** hair dryers. **Dining:** 7:30 am-10 & 6-9 pm, cocktails. **Leisure Activities:** boat dock. **Cards:** AX, MC, VI.

SOME UNITS

**OCEAN GATE INN**    *Book at aaa.com*                                     **Phone:** (207)633-3321

(AAA) (SAVE)

| | | | | |
|---|---|---|---|---|
| 7/16-8/29 [BP] | 1P: $129-$169 | 2P: $129-$169 | XP: $15 | F11 |
| 6/18-7/15 [BP] | 1P: $119-$159 | 2P: $119-$159 | XP: $15 | F11 |
| 8/30-10/10 [BP] | 1P: $89-$129 | 2P: $89-$129 | XP: $15 | F11 |
| 5/28-6/17 [BP] | 1P: $79-$109 | 2P: $79-$109 | XP: $15 | F11 |

Small-scale Hotel **Location:** SR 27, 2.5 mi s of Boothbay Harbor, 0.5 mi s of bridge to Southport Island. Located in a quiet, secluded area. 70 Oceangate Rd 04576 (PO Box 240). Fax: 207/633-2900. **Facility:** Designated smoking area. 66 units. 60 one- and 2 two-bedroom standard units, some with efficiencies or kitchens. 2 one-bedroom suites ($149-$329), some with efficiencies. 2 cottages ($239-$329). 1-2 stories (no elevator), exterior corridors. **Parking:** on-site. **Terms:** open 5/28-10/10, office hours 7 am-11 pm, 3 day cancellation notice-fee imposed. **Amenities:** irons, hair dryers. **Pool(s):** heated outdoor. **Leisure Activities:** whirlpool, canoeing, boat dock, fishing, private pond, kayaks, barbecue & picnic area, outdoor games, playground, exercise room, basketball. *Fee:* sailing instructions, massage. **Guest Services:** coin laundry. **Cards:** MC, VI. **Special Amenities: free full breakfast and free local telephone calls.** *(See color ad p 198)*

SOME UNITS

―――――― **WHERE TO DINE** ――――――

**ROBINSON'S WHARF**    **Lunch:** $2-$20        **Dinner:** $2-$20        **Phone:** 207/633-3830

Seafood
**Location:** 2 mi s of Boothbay Harbor on SR 27, just across bridge to Southport Island. Rt 27 04575. **Hours:** Open 6/15-9/3; 11:30 am-7:45 pm. **Features:** In a scenic cove offering a great view of boats and docks, Robinson's Wharf features their specialty—generously sized lobster rolls. The menu also features fried seafood and sandwiches served in a charming down-east, no-frills atmosphere. Casual dress; beer & wine only. **Parking:** on-site. **Cards:** DS, MC, VI.

# SOUTH PORTLAND pop. 23,324—*See also PORTLAND.*

―――――― **WHERE TO STAY** ――――――

**AMERISUITES (PORTLAND/MAINE MALL)**    *Book at aaa.com*       **Phone:** 207/775-3900

(AAA) (SAVE)

| | | | | |
|---|---|---|---|---|
| 7/16-10/21 | 1P: $149-$229 | 2P: $149-$229 | XP: $10 | F17 |
| 5/1-7/15 | 1P: $119-$159 | 2P: $119-$159 | XP: $10 | F17 |
| 10/22-4/30 | 1P: $99-$139 | 2P: $99-$139 | XP: $10 | F17 |

Small-scale Hotel **Location:** I-95 (Maine Tpke), exit 45, just n on Maine Mall Rd, then just w on Running Hill Rd. 303 Sable Oaks Dr 04106. Fax: 207/775-3993. **Facility:** 130 one-bedroom standard units. 6 stories, interior corridors. *Bath:* combo or shower only. **Parking:** on-site. **Terms:** cancellation fee imposed, [ECP] meal plan available, pets ($20 fee). **Amenities:** video games (fee), voice mail, irons, hair dryers. *Some:* dual phone lines. **Pool(s):** heated indoor. **Leisure Activities:** exercise room. **Guest Services:** valet and coin laundry, area transportation-within 2 mi. **Business Services:** meeting rooms, business center. **Cards:** AX, DC, DS, MC, VI. **Special Amenities: free expanded continental breakfast and free newspaper.** *(See color ad p 271)*

SOME UNITS

**BEST WESTERN MERRY MANOR INN**    *Book at aaa.com*           **Phone:** (207)774-6151

| | | | | |
|---|---|---|---|---|
| 9/1-10/31 | 1P: $140-$160 | 2P: $140-$160 | XP: $10 | F13 |
| 11/1-4/30 | 1P: $120-$140 | 2P: $120-$140 | XP: $10 | F13 |
| 6/19-8/31 | 1P: $100-$120 | 2P: $100-$120 | XP: $10 | F13 |
| 5/1-6/18 | 1P: $90-$110 | 2P: $90-$110 | XP: $10 | F13 |

Small-scale Hotel **Location:** I-95 (Maine Tpke), exit 45, 3 mi e on spur road to US 1, exit 7 spur road and US 1. 700 Main St 04106. Fax: 207/871-0537. **Facility:** 151 one-bedroom standard units. 2 stories, interior/exterior corridors. *Bath:* combo or shower only. **Parking:** on-site. **Amenities:** irons, hair dryers. *Some:* DVD players (fee). **Pool(s):** heated outdoor, wading. **Leisure Activities:** whirlpool. **Guest Services:** valet and coin laundry. **Business Services:** meeting rooms. **Cards:** AX, CB, DC, DS, JC, MC, VI.

SOME UNITS

**COASTLINE INN**                                        **Phone:** (207)772-3838

Motel

| | | | |
|---|---|---|---|
| 7/1-10/31 [ECP] | 1P: $100-$120 | 2P: $109-$130 | |
| 5/1-6/30 [ECP] | 1P: $60-$80 | 2P: $70-$90 | |
| 3/1-4/30 [ECP] | 1P: $60-$70 | 2P: $70-$80 | |
| 11/1-2/28 [ECP] | 1P: $50-$60 | 2P: $70-$80 | |

**Location:** I-95 (Maine Tpke), exit 45 to Maine Mall Rd, right turn, continue to Philbrook Ave; corner of Philbrook Ave and John Roberts Rd. 80 John Roberts Rd 04106. Fax: 207/772-4238. **Facility:** 54 one-bedroom standard units. 2 stories (no elevator), exterior corridors. **Parking:** on-site. **Terms:** cancellation fee imposed. **Guest Services:** valet laundry. **Cards:** AX, DS, MC, VI.

SOME UNITS

**COMFORT INN**
△△△ [SAVE]
▽▽▽
Small-scale Hotel

*Book at aaa.com*

**Phone:** (207)775-0409

| | | | |
|---|---|---|---|
| All Year | 1P: $80-$170 | 2P: $80-$170 | XP: $10  F18 |

**Location:** I-95 (Maine Tpke), exit 45, 1 mi n. 90 Maine Mall Rd 04106. **Fax:** 207/775-1755. **Facility:** 127 one-bedroom standard units. 3 stories, interior corridors. *Bath:* combo or shower only. **Parking:** on-site. **Terms:** [ECP] meal plan available. **Amenities:** voice mail, irons, hair dryers. **Pool(s):** heated outdoor. **Guest Services:** valet and coin laundry. **Cards:** AX, CB, DC, DS, MC, VI. **Special Amenities:** free continental breakfast. *(See color ad p 271)*

SOME UNITS

---

**DAYS INN PORTLAND-SOUTH PORTLAND**   *Book at aaa.com*

**Phone:** (207)772-3450

△△△ [SAVE]
▽▽▽
Small-scale Hotel

| | | | |
|---|---|---|---|
| 7/1-10/31 [ECP] | 1P: $109-$179 | 2P: $119-$189 | XP: $10  F17 |
| 5/1-6/30 [ECP] | 1P: $79-$159 | 2P: $89-$169 | XP: $10  F17 |
| 11/1-12/31 [ECP] | 1P: $69-$139 | 2P: $79-$149 | XP: $10  F17 |
| 1/1-4/30 [ECP] | 1P: $59-$139 | 2P: $69-$149 | XP: $10  F17 |

**Location:** I-95 (Maine Tpke), exit 45. 461 Maine Mall Rd 04106. **Fax:** 207/780-9748. **Facility:** 149 one-bedroom standard units. 2 stories (no elevator), interior corridors. **Parking:** on-site. **Terms:** 30 day cancellation notice. **Amenities:** irons, hair dryers. **Guest Services:** valet laundry. **Business Services:** meeting rooms. **Cards:** AX, CB, DC, DS, JC, MC, VI. **Special Amenities:** free expanded continental breakfast and free local telephone calls.

SOME UNITS

---

**HAMPTON INN HOTEL**   *Book at aaa.com*

**Phone:** (207)773-4400

▽▽▽
Small-scale Hotel

| | | |
|---|---|---|
| 7/4-10/19 | 1P: $149-$179 | 2P: $159-$189 |
| 6/2-7/3 | 1P: $99-$119 | 2P: $109-$129 |
| 5/1-6/1 [CP] | 1P: $89-$119 | 2P: $99-$129 |
| 10/20-4/30 | 1P: $89-$99 | 2P: $99-$109 |

**Location:** I-95 (Maine Tpke), exit 45. Located opposite Maine Mall. 171 Philbrook Ave. **Fax:** 207/773-6786. **Facility:** 117 one-bedroom standard units. 4 stories, interior corridors. **Parking:** on-site. **Terms:** [CP] meal plan available. **Amenities:** video games (fee), voice mail, irons, hair dryers. **Leisure Activities:** exercise room. **Guest Services:** valet laundry. **Cards:** AX, CB, DC, DS, MC, VI.

SOME UNITS

---

**HOWARD JOHNSON HOTEL**   *Book at aaa.com*

**Phone:** (207)775-5343

△△△ [SAVE]
▽▽▽
Small-scale Hotel

| | | | |
|---|---|---|---|
| 7/1-8/31 | 1P: $114-$154 | 2P: $124-$164 | XP: $10  F17 |
| 9/1-10/18 | 1P: $104-$124 | 2P: $114-$134 | XP: $10  F17 |
| 10/19-4/30 | 1P: $79-$109 | 2P: $89-$119 | XP: $10  F17 |
| 5/1-6/30 | 1P: $84-$104 | 2P: $94-$114 | XP: $10  F17 |

**Location:** I-95 (Maine Tpke), exit 45, 3 mi e on spur road to US 1, just n. 675 Main St 04106. **Fax:** 207/772-8789. **Facility:** 121 one-bedroom standard units. 4 stories, interior corridors. **Parking:** pets (with prior approval). **Amenities:** voice mail, irons, hair dryers. *Some:* dual phone lines. **Dining:** 7 am-9 pm; hours may vary seasonally, cocktails. **Pool(s):** heated indoor. **Leisure Activities:** exercise room. **Guest Services:** valet laundry, area transportation-bus station & Amtrak. **Business Services:** meeting rooms. **Cards:** AX, CB, DC, DS, MC, VI. **Special Amenities:** free local telephone calls and free newspaper. *(See color ad p 274)*

SOME UNITS
FEE FEE

---

**PORTLAND MARRIOTT HOTEL & GOLF RESORT**   *Book at aaa.com*

**Phone:** (207)871-8000

▽▽▽
Large-scale Hotel

| | |
|---|---|
| 7/12-10/17 | 1P: $188-$219 |
| 5/1-7/11 | 1P: $143-$189 |
| 10/18-4/30 | 1P: $99-$169 |

**Location:** I-95 (Maine Tpke), exit 45, just n on Maine Mall Rd, then just w on Running Hill Rd. 200 Sable Oaks Dr 04106. **Fax:** 207/871-7971. **Facility:** 227 units. 222 one-bedroom standard units. 5 one-bedroom suites, some with whirlpools. 6 stories, interior corridors. **Parking:** on-site. **Terms:** cancellation fee imposed, small pets only ($20 extra charge). **Amenities:** dual phone lines, voice mail, irons, hair dryers. **Pool(s):** heated indoor. **Leisure Activities:** saunas, whirlpool, exercise room. *Fee:* golf-18 holes. **Guest Services:** gift shop, valet and coin laundry, area transportation. **Business Services:** meeting rooms, business center. **Cards:** AX, CB, DC, DS, MC, VI.

SOME UNITS
FEE

---

**SHERATON SOUTH PORTLAND**   *Book at aaa.com*

**Phone:** (207)775-6161

▽▽▽
Large-scale Hotel

| | | | |
|---|---|---|---|
| 5/30-10/30 | 1P: $199 | 2P: $199 | XP: $10  F16 |
| 1/1-4/30 | 1P: $119-$139 | 2P: $119-$139 | XP: $10  F16 |
| 5/1-5/29 | 1P: $139 | 2P: $139 | XP: $10  F16 |
| 10/31-12/31 | 1P: $119 | 2P: $119 | XP: $10  F16 |

**Location:** I-95 (Maine Tpke), exit 45. Located opposite Maine Mall. 363 Maine Mall Rd 04106. **Fax:** 207/775-0196. **Facility:** 219 one-bedroom standard units. 7-9 stories, interior corridors. *Bath:* combo or shower only. **Parking:** on-site. **Terms:** cancellation fee imposed, small pets only ($50 deposit). **Amenities:** video games (fee), dual phone lines, voice mail, irons, hair dryers. *Some:* fax. **Pool(s):** heated indoor. **Leisure Activities:** saunas, whirlpool. **Guest Services:** valet laundry. **Business Services:** meeting rooms, fax. **Cards:** AX, CB, DC, DS, JC, MC, VI. *(See color ad p 5)*

SOME UNITS
FEE FEE FEE FEE

—— **WHERE TO DINE** ——

**BEALE STREET BARBEQUE**
**Lunch:** $7-$18     **Dinner:** $7-$18     **Phone:** 207/767-0130
▽▽ ▽▽
**Location:** At Mill Creek. 90 Waterman Dr 04106. **Hours:** 11:30 am-10 pm. **Closed:** 11/25, 12/25.
**Features:** Popular with locals and tourists alike, the restaurant makes Memphis-style barbecue on the premises. Guests also can sample such dishes as jambalaya, shrimp Louisiane and Santa Fe chicken.
Barbecue    Casual dress; cocktails. **Parking:** on-site. **Cards:** MC, VI.

**EGGSPECTATIONS**
**Lunch:** $8-$19     **Dinner:** $8-$19     **Phone:** 207/871-7000
▽▽ ▽▽
**Location:** I-295, exit Western Ave, just w. 125 Western Ave 04106. **Hours:** 6 am-10 pm, Fri & Sat-11 pm, Sun 7 am-9 pm. Closed major holidays. **Features:** Open breakfast, lunch and dinner, Eggspectations has an
American    upscale contemporary decor with an open kitchen in the back.The menu featues alarge variety of specialty egg dishes for breakfast and lunch as well as more traditional pasta, chicken, fish, pasta and steak dishes.
Casual dress; cocktails. **Parking:** on-site. **Cards:** AX, MC, VI.

**IMPERIAL CHINA**
**Lunch:** $5-$15     **Dinner:** $8-$15     **Phone:** 207/774-4292
▽▽ ▽▽
**Location:** I-95 (Maine Tpke), exit 45, 1 mi n on Maine Mall Rd, then just e; opposite the Maine Mall. 220 Maine Mall Rd 04106. **Hours:** 11 am-10 pm, Fri & Sat-11 pm, Sun noon-10 pm. **Closed:** 11/25. **Features:** The
Chinese    well-regarded restaurant presents a menu of Hunan and Szechuan offerings. Casual dress; cocktails.
**Parking:** on-site. **Cards:** AX, DS, MC, VI.

**JOE'S BOATHOUSE**
**Lunch:** $7-$10     **Dinner:** $11-$19     **Phone:** 207/741-2780
▽▽ ▽▽
**Location:** At Spring Point Marina. 1 Spring Point Dr 04106. **Hours:** 11 am-3 & 5-9:30 pm, Fri & Sat-10 pm, Sun 9 am-3 pm; seasonal hours may vary. **Closed:** 11/25, 12/24, 12/25. **Features:** Lovely views of Casco Bay
American    and the busy marina attract a large following to this restaurant. The menu featuring, New American cuisine with a number of pasta and seafood items, keeps them coming back. The decor is bright and
contemporary with a casual atmosphere. Patio dining is available seasonally. Cocktails. **Parking:** on-site. **Cards:** AX, MC, VI.

**NEWICK'S SEAFOOD RESTAURANT**
**Lunch:** $6-$19     **Dinner:** $6-$19     **Phone:** 207/799-3090
ⒶⒶⒶ
**Location:** I-95 (Maine Tpke), exit 45, 4 mi e. 740 Broadway 04106. **Hours:** 11:30 am-8:30 pm, Fri & Sat-9 pm.
▽▽
Closed: 11/25, 12/25; also Mon 10/1-5/15. **Features:** This very casual, family restaurant is always busy. They serve thick and creamy clam chowder, broiled or fried seafood platters, pasta and strawberry
Seafood    shortcake. A gift shop and fresh fish department are part of the operation. Casual dress; cocktails.
**Parking:** on-site. **Cards:** AX, DS, MC, VI.

**RICETTA'S BRICK OVEN PIZZERIA**
**Lunch:** $5-$8     **Dinner:** $7-$13     **Phone:** 207/775-7400
▽▽ ▽▽
**Location:** I-295, just w. 29 Western Ave 04106. **Hours:** 11:30 am-10 pm, Fri & Sat-11 pm. Closed major holidays. **Features:** A great place to bring the kids for a meal. Known for their award winning and creative
Pizza    pizza, you can see pizza being made at the open area with the brick oven. Also on the menu are original pasta and calzones. At lunch is an all-you-can-eat buffet. A casual restaurant which is also popular with
local residents. Casual dress; beer & wine only. **Parking:** on-site. **Cards:** AX, DS, MC, VI.

**SALTWATER GRILLE**
**Lunch:** $7-$13     **Dinner:** $15-$22     **Phone:** 207/799-5400
▽▽ ▽▽▽
**Location:** In Ferry Village, on the waterfront. 231 Front St 04106. **Hours:** 11 am-3 & 5-9 pm. **Closed:** 11/25, 12/24, 12/25. **Reservations:** accepted. **Features:** On the harbor, the marina-side restaurant offers
Regional American    wonderful sunset views of the city skyline. The menu centers on innovative cuisine, including preparations of Maine seafood, steak, pasta and vegetarian fare. Deck seating is available seasonally. Casual dress;
cocktails. **Parking:** on-site. **Cards:** AX, MC, VI.

**SEBAGO BREWING COMPANY**
**Lunch:** $7-$16     **Dinner:** $7-$16     **Phone:** 207/879-2537
▽▽ ▽▽
**Location:** Near the Maine Mall. 150 Philbrook Ave 04106. **Hours:** 11 am-1 am. **Closed:** 11/25, 12/25.
**Features:** The stylish brew pub has an informal, friendly atmosphere. Self-described "American pub" food
American    includes delicious pasta, chicken, seafood and steak entrees, as well as tasty salads, burgers and sandwiches. The latter are available all day. The pastry chef prepares desserts on the premises each day.
Casual dress; cocktails. **Parking:** on-site. **Cards:** AX, MC, VI.

**SNOW SQUALL RESTAURANT**
**Lunch:** $5-$12     **Dinner:** $10-$23     **Phone:** 207/799-2232
▽▽ ▽▽
**Location:** Corner of A and Ocean sts; center. 18 Ocean St 04106. **Hours:** 11:30 am-10 pm. **Closed:** 12/25.
**Reservations:** suggested. **Features:** Overlooking Portland Harbor, the restaurant's contemporary decor does promote a casual but upbeat atmosphere. The menu, featuring truly American cuisine, includes fresh
American    seafood, steak, poultry, lamb and venison items. The smoked crab cakes are a perennial favorite. You will be tempted by the yummy dessert cart. A favorite luncheon and dinner choice for both the local residents and tourists alike.
Casual dress; cocktails. **Parking:** on-site. **Cards:** AX, DC, DS, MC, VI.

**WEATHERVANE**
**Lunch:** $6-$16     **Dinner:** $6-$16     **Phone:** 207/772-3856
▽▽ ▽▽
**Location:** At the Maine Mall. 380 Gorham Rd 04106. **Hours:** 11 am-9:30 pm, Fri & Sat-10 pm; hours may vary off season. **Closed:** 11/25, 12/25. **Reservations:** accepted. **Features:** The large, bustling, family-oriented
Seafood    restaurant features good menu variety. Among offerings are lobster, fried clams and crisp, Cape Cod apple-cranberry cobbler. Flavorful dishes are served in large portions. Service is friendly and attentive.
Casual dress; cocktails. **Parking:** on-site. **Cards:** AX, MC, VI.

# SOUTH THOMASTON

——— **WHERE TO DINE** ———

——— *The following restaurant has not been evaluated by AAA* ———
*but is listed for your information only.*

**WATERMAN'S BEACH LOBSTER**
[fyi]    Not evaluated. **Location:** Waterman's Beach Rd 04861. **Features:** The award-winning restaurant overlooks the ocean. The menu lists lobster and clam dinners.

---

# SOUTHWEST HARBOR

——— **WHERE TO STAY** ———

**ACADIA CABINS**                                          Phone: 207/244-5388
▼▼ ▼▼     6/19-10/11                    1P: $79-$99        2P: $79-$99
Cabin    **Location:** Just s on SR 102. 410 Main St 04679 (PO Box 1214). **Facility:** 11 units. 8 one-bedroom standard units
with efficiencies. 3 cabins ($526-$659). 1 story, exterior corridors. *Bath:* combo or shower only. **Parking:** on-
site. **Terms:** open 6/19-10/11, 21 day cancellation notice-fee imposed, weekly rates available.
**Amenities:** voice mail. **Pool(s):** heated outdoor. **Guest Services:** coin-laundry. **Cards:** DS, MC, VI.

**CLARK POINT INN**                                        Phone: 207/244-9828
▼▼▲▼▼     5/1-9/15 [BP]                 1P: $105-$155       2P: $115-$165      XP: $10
         5/1-6/14 & 9/16-4/30 [BP]      1P: $65-$125        2P: $75-$135       XP: $10
Bed & Breakfast   **Location:** SR 102, just w. 109 Clark Point Rd 04679 (PO Box 826). Fax: 207/244-9924. **Facility:** Decorated in a
mix of bright contemporary styling and antiques, the inn is located within a short distance to the center of
town and it's activities. Smoke free premises. 5 one-bedroom standard units. 3 stories (no elevator), interior/exterior corridors.
*Bath:* combo or shower only. **Parking:** on-site. **Terms:** 2 night minimum stay - seasonal, cancellation fee imposed, no pets allowed (owner's pet on premises). **Amenities:** video library, hair dryers. **Cards:** MC, VI.
SOME UNITS

**THE INN AT SOUTHWEST**                                   Phone: 207/244-3835
▼▼▲▼▼     6/16-10/15 [BP]                                  2P: $110-$185      XP: $20
         5/1-6/15 & 10/16-10/31 [BP]                       2P: $75-$135       XP: $20
Historic Bed   **Location:** Center. 371 Main St 04679 (PO Box 593). Fax: 207/244-9879. **Facility:** This 1884 Victorian's varied
& Breakfast    guest rooms are named after historic lighthouses; some rooms have gas-log stoves. Smoke free premises.
7 units. 5 one-bedroom standard units. 2 one-bedroom suites. 3 stories (no elevator), interior corridors. *Bath:*
combo or shower only. **Parking:** on-site. **Terms:** open 5/1-10/31, 14 day cancellation notice-fee imposed. **Amenities:** hair dryers.
**Cards:** MC, VI.

**THE KINGSLEIGH INN**                                     Phone: 207/244-5302
▼▼▲▼▼     6/16-10/15 [BP]               1P: $110-$240       2P: $110-$240      XP: $25
         5/1-6/15 & 10/16-4/30 [BP]     1P: $75-$155        2P: $75-$155       XP: $25
Historic Bed   **Location:** On SR 102; center. 373 Main St 04679 (PO Box 1426). Fax: 207/244-7691. **Facility:** Turrets add archi-
& Breakfast    tectural interest to this turn-of-the-20th-century home; some rooms have harbor views and private balconies.
Smoke free premises. 8 units. 7 one-bedroom standard units. 1 one-bedroom suite ($155-$240). 3 stories
(no elevator), interior corridors. *Bath:* combo or shower only. **Parking:** on-site. **Terms:** 14 day cancellation notice-fee imposed.
**Amenities:** hair dryers. **Some:** irons. **Cards:** MC, VI.
SOME UNITS

**THE LINDENWOOD INN**                                     Phone: 207/244-5335
▼▼▲▼▼     5/1-11/1                      1P: $85-$255        2P: $95-$275       XP: $25
Bed & Breakfast   **Location:** SR 102, 1 mi e. 118 Clark Point Rd 04679. Fax: 207/244-3643. **Facility:** This inn, consisting of three
converted homes and cottages, offers a variety of tastefully decorated rooms, some with decks and gas fireplaces. Designated smoking area. 9 units. 7 one-bedroom standard units. 2 one-bedroom suites, some with
efficiencies. 1-3 stories (no elevator), interior/exterior corridors. **Parking:** on-site. **Terms:** open 5/1-11/1, 14 day cancellation
notice-fee imposed, [BP] meal plan available. **Pool(s):** heated outdoor. **Leisure Activities:** whirlpool. **Cards:** AX, DS, MC, VI.
SOME UNITS

——— **WHERE TO DINE** ———

**CAFE 2/EAT-A-PITA**          Lunch: $5-$9        Dinner: $12-$22     Phone: 207/244-4344
▼▼▲▼▼     **Location:** Center. 326 Main St 04679. **Hours:** Open 5/24-10/19; 8 am-9 pm. Closed: Mon evening.
American   **Reservations:** accepted. **Features:** For breakfast, Eat-a-Pita offerings include three-egg omelets,
blueberry pancakes and the signature blueberry-stuffed French toast. During the day, it serves a delicious
variety of salads and sandwiches. In the evening, the restaurant is transformed into Chef Marc, a more
upscale eatery, where the cuisine is American with a European flair. Casual dress; beer & wine only. **Parking:** street.
**Cards:** AX, MC, VI.

**CAFE DRY DOCK**              Lunch: $6-$11       Dinner: $10-$22     Phone: 207/244-5842
▼▼▲▼ ▼▼     **Location:** Center. 357 Main St 04679. **Hours:** Open 5/21-10/31; 11 am-10 pm; hours vary off season.
American   **Reservations:** accepted. **Features:** Located outside the hustle and bustle of Bar Harbor, this restaurant on
Main Street features very good burgers, great clam chowder, nicely prepared fresh seafood and
sandwiches. The serving staff is pleasant and professional. Deck dining is available. Casual dress;
cocktails. **Parking:** street. **Cards:** MC, VI.

# SPRUCE HEAD

## —— WHERE TO STAY ——

**CRAIGNAIR INN**                                                                      Phone: (207)594-7644

(AAA) (SAVE)   6/21-10/30 [ECP]            1P: $65-$145       2P: $97-$145      XP: $25       F5
             10/31-11/15 & 4/1-4/30 [ECP]  1P: $45-$122       2P: $60-$122      XP: $25       F5
▼▼▼▼         5/1-6/20 [ECP]               1P: $55-$105       2P: $68-$105      XP: $25       F5

**Location:** 2.5 mi w on SR 73, 1.5 mi s on Clark Island Rd; 10 mi s of Rockland. Located in a rural area. 5 Third St 04859.
Historic   **Fax:** 207/596-7124. **Facility:** Built in 1930, this oceanfront former quarrymen's boardinghouse overlooks
Country Inn   Clark Island and offers rooms of varying styles, some with an oceanview. Smoke free premises. 19 one-
bedroom standard units. 2-3 stories (no elevator). interior/exterior corridors. *Bath:* some shared or private,
combo or shower only. **Parking:** on-site. **Terms:** open 5/1-11/15 & 4/1-4/30, 14 day cancellation notice-fee imposed, pets ($10
extra charge, with prior approval, in selected units). **Dining:** restaurant, see separate listing. **Leisure Activities:** old rock quarry
on Clark Island. **Cards:** MC, VI. **Special Amenities: free expanded continental breakfast and free local telephone calls.**

## —— WHERE TO DINE ——

**CRAIGNAIR INN RESTAURANT**          **Dinner:** $13-$25        Phone: 207/594-7644
▼▼▼▼         **Location:** 2.5 mi w on SR 73, 1.5 mi s on Clark Island Rd; 10 mi s of Rockland; in Craignair Inn. 5 Third St 04859.
             **Hours:** Open 5/1-10/10; 5:30 pm-9 pm; to 8 pm, Fri & Sat-8:30 pm 9/6-10/10. Closed: Sun 9/1-6/30 &
American     Mon-Wed 5/1-5/31. **Reservations:** suggested. **Features:** Craignair's house specialties are wonderful
lobster Newburg, delicious crab cakes and flavorful homemade dessert. The restaurant has a country
kitchen feel and features outstanding views of the ocean and Clark Cove. Casual dress; cocktails. **Parking:** on-site.
**Cards:** DS, MC, VI.

# SURRY

## —— WHERE TO DINE ——

**SURRY INN DINING ROOM**   Country Inn          **Dinner:** $13-$20        Phone: 207/667-5091
▼▼▼         **Location:** Jct US 1, 4 mi s on SR 172. Surry Rd 04684. **Hours:** Open 5/1-1/15 & 3/15-4/30; 5:30 pm-9 pm;
             hours vary seasonally. Closed: 12/24-12/26. **Reservations:** suggested. **Features:** The owner/chef of this
French       restaurant is quite creative when preparing meals and uses only the freshest ingredients available. The
comfortable country-inn setting overlooks Contention Cove. Fireside dining is offered in the fall and winter
months. Casual dress; cocktails. **Parking:** on-site. **Cards:** DS, MC, VI.

# TOPSHAM pop. 6,271

## —— WHERE TO DINE ——

**SEA DOG BREWING CO**          **Lunch:** $7-$9        **Dinner:** $7-$18       Phone: 207/725-0162
▼▼▼ ▼▼▼         **Location:** On SR 24 and 201 at Bath Bridge. 1 Main St 04086. **Hours:** 11:30 am-10 pm; hours vary seasonally.
             Closed: 1/1, 11/25, 12/25. **Features:** The converted mill, a bustling atmosphere and good food draw
American     patrons to the nautically decorated restaurant and microbrewery, which affords a lovely view of the
Androscoggin River falls. Included on the menu is a fine variety of seafood, vegetarian and beef entrees.
Casual dress; cocktails. **Parking:** on-site. **Cards:** AX, DS, MC, VI.

# WATERVILLE pop. 15,605

## —— WHERE TO STAY ——

**BEST WESTERN WATERVILLE**   *Book at aaa.com*                Phone: (207)873-3335

(AAA) (SAVE)   7/1-10/31 [ECP]            1P: $99-$150       2P: $99-$150      XP: $10       F17
             5/1-6/30 & 11/1-4/30 [ECP]  1P: $89-$130       2P: $89-$130      XP: $10       F17

**Location:** I-95, exit 130 (Main St). 356 Main St 04901. Fax: 207/873-3335. **Facility:** 86 one-bedroom standard
Small-scale Hotel   units. 2 stories (no elevator), interior corridors. *Bath:* combo or shower only. **Parking:** on-site.
**Amenities:** video library, irons, hair dryers. *Some:* CD players. **Dining:** 6 am-10 pm; to 11 pm weekends,
cocktails. **Pool(s):** outdoor. **Leisure Activities:** whirlpool. **Guest Services:** valet laundry. **Business Serv-**
ices: meeting rooms. **Cards:** AX, CB, DC, DS, MC, VI. **Special Amenities: free expanded continental breakfast and free
local telephone calls.**

**BUDGET HOST AIRPORT INN**                                              Phone: (207)873-3366

(AAA) (SAVE)   7/1-8/31              1P: $50-$99        2P: $60-$110      XP: $5        F12
             9/1-10/31             1P: $45-$65        2P: $50-$75       XP: $5        F12
▼▼▼ ▼        5/1-6/30              1P: $40-$60        2P: $45-$70       XP: $5        F12
             11/1-4/30             1P: $35-$60        2P: $40-$65       XP: $5        F12

Small-scale Hotel   **Location:** I-95, exit 127, 0.3 mi e on SR 11 (Kennedy Memorial Dr). 400 Kennedy Memorial Dr 04901.
Fax: 207/873-3366. **Facility:** 45 one-bedroom standard units. 1 story, interior/exterior corridors. *Bath:* combo
or shower only. **Parking:** on-site. **Terms:** cancellation fee imposed, weekly rates available, [CP] meal plan available, pets ($5
fee). **Amenities:** video library. **Cards:** AX, DS, MC, VI. **Special Amenities: free continental breakfast and free local telephone calls.**

## COMFORT INN & SUITES   *Book at aaa.com*

(AAA) (SAVE)

◆◆◆ Small-scale Hotel

Phone: (207)873-2777

| | 1P | 2P | XP | |
|---|---|---|---|---|
| 5/1-6/30 [BP] | 1P: $79-$189 | 2P: $89-$199 | XP: $10 | F18 |
| 7/1-8/31 [BP] | 1P: $89-$149 | 2P: $99-$159 | XP: $10 | F18 |
| 9/1-10/31 [BP] | 1P: $79-$129 | 2P: $89-$139 | XP: $10 | F18 |
| 11/1-4/30 [BP] | 1P: $69-$119 | 2P: $79-$129 | XP: $10 | F18 |

**Location:** I-95, exit 130 (Main St), 0.4 mi e on SR 104. 332 Main St 04901. Fax: 207/872-2838. **Facility:** 101 units. 76 one-bedroom standard units. 22 one- and 3 two-bedroom suites ($159-$339) with kitchens, some with whirlpools. 4 stories, interior corridors. *Bath:* combo or shower only. **Parking:** on-site. **Amenities:** voice mail, irons, hair dryers. *Some:* dual phone lines. **Pool(s):** heated indoor. **Leisure Activities:** exercise room. **Guest Services:** valet and coin laundry. **Cards:** AX, CB, DC, DS, MC, VI. **Special Amenities:** free full breakfast and free local telephone calls.

SOME UNITS

## ECONO LODGE   *Book at aaa.com*

(AAA) (SAVE)

◆◆◆ Small-scale Hotel

Phone: (207)872-5577

| | 1P | 2P | XP | |
|---|---|---|---|---|
| 7/1-9/15 | 1P: $75-$85 | 2P: $85-$95 | XP: $5 | F18 |
| 5/1-6/30 & 9/16-10/31 | 1P: $60-$65 | 2P: $70-$75 | XP: $5 | F18 |
| 11/1-4/30 | 1P: $40-$45 | 2P: $50-$65 | XP: $5 | F18 |

**Fax:** 207/861-8019. **Facility:** 50 one-bedroom standard units. 2 stories (no elevator), interior/exterior corridors. **Parking:** on-site. **Terms:** pets ($5 extra charge). **Pool(s):** outdoor. **Cards:** AX, DC, DS, MC, VI. **Special Amenities:** free local telephone calls and early check-in/late check-out.

SOME UNITS

## HAMPTON INN WATERVILLE/AUGUSTA   *Book at aaa.com*

◆◆◆ Small-scale Hotel

Phone: 207/873-0400

| |  |  |
|---|---|---|
| 5/1-10/31 [ECP] | 1P: $89-$109 | 2P: $99-$119 |
| 11/1-4/30 [ECP] | 1P: $79-$99 | 2P: $89-$109 |

**Location:** I-95, exit 127, just e. 425 Kennedy Memorial Dr 04901. Fax: 207/873-5486. **Facility:** 81 units. 77 one-bedroom standard units. 4 one-bedroom suites. 4 stories, interior corridors. *Bath:* combo or shower only. **Parking:** on-site. **Amenities:** video games (fee), voice mail, irons, hair dryers. **Pool(s):** heated indoor. **Leisure Activities:** exercise room. **Guest Services:** valet and coin laundry. **Business Services:** meeting rooms. **Cards:** AX, CB, DC, DS, MC, VI.

SOME UNITS

## HOLIDAY INN   *Book at aaa.com*

◆◆◆ Small-scale Hotel

Phone: (207)873-0111

| |  |  | |
|---|---|---|---|
| 11/1-4/30 | 1P: $140-$150 | XP: $10 | F |
| 7/1-10/31 | 1P: $130-$140 | XP: $10 | F |
| 5/1-6/30 | 1P: $119-$129 | XP: $10 | F |

**Location:** I-95, exit 130 (Main St) on SR 104. 375 Main St 04901. Fax: 207/872-2310. **Facility:** 138 units. 137 one-bedroom standard units. 1 one-bedroom suite. 3 stories, interior corridors. *Bath:* combo or shower only. **Parking:** on-site. **Amenities:** video games (fee), voice mail, irons, hair dryers. **Pool(s):** heated indoor. **Leisure Activities:** sauna, whirlpool, exercise room. **Guest Services:** valet and coin laundry. **Business Services:** meeting rooms. **Cards:** AX, DC, DS, MC, VI.

SOME UNITS

———— WHERE TO DINE ————

## BREAD BOX CAFE'

◆◆ American

Lunch: $6-$10   Dinner: $14-$18   Phone: 207/873-4090

**Location:** Center. 137 Main St 04901. **Hours:** 11 am-9:30 pm. Closed major holidays; also Sun. **Features:** The menu at the small bistro centers on eclectic American cuisine made from local ingredients whenever possible. Delicious salads are complemented by homemade dressings. Jazz brunches are featured on Saturday and Tuesday nights are popular for the tapas menu. Casual dress; cocktails. **Parking:** street. **Cards:** AX, DC, MC, VI.

## JOHN MARTIN'S MANOR RESTAURANT

◆◆ American

Lunch: $5-$7   Dinner: $8-$12   Phone: 207/873-5676

**Location:** 0.5 mi n on US 201. 54 College Ave 04901. **Hours:** 11 am-9 pm, Sun 11:30 am-8 pm. Closed: 12/25. **Reservations:** suggested. **Features:** The restaurant has a pleasant, large dining room. Diners can choose from extensive selections on the all-you-can-eat buffet. Friendly table service is an option for steak and seafood preparations. Casual dress; cocktails. **Parking:** on-site. **Cards:** AX, DC, DS, MC, VI.

## THE LAST UNICORN

◆◆ American

Lunch: $6   Dinner: $12-$19   Phone: 207/873-6378

**Location:** Center. 8 Silver St 04901. **Hours:** 11 am-9 pm; to 10 pm in summer. Closed major holidays. **Features:** Creative American cuisine is on the menu of the popular downtown dining spot. Desserts, sauces and soups are made daily on the premises. Casual dress; cocktails. **Parking:** street. **Cards:** AX, MC, VI.

## SILVER STREET TAVERN

◆◆ American

Lunch: $5-$9   Dinner: $11-$17   Phone: 207/877-8323

**Location:** Center. 2 Silver St 04901. **Hours:** 11 am-9 pm. Closed: 11/25, 12/25; also Sun & Mon; for dinner 12/24. **Features:** The downtown restaurant's menu emphasizes fresh seafood but also lists such items as filet mignon and chicken Divan. A jazz duo performs on Friday and Saturday evenings. Casual dress; cocktails. **Parking:** street. **Cards:** MC, VI.

## WEATHERVANE RESTAURANT

◆ Seafood

Lunch: $4-$8   Dinner: $6-$12   Phone: 207/873-4522

**Location:** I-95, exit 127 on SR 11 (Kennedy Memorial Dr) at Waterville-Oakland. 470 Kennedy Memorial Dr 04901. **Hours:** 11 am-9:35 pm; to 9 pm 10/12-5/31. Closed: 11/25, 12/24, 12/25. **Features:** Conveniently located, this bustling restaurant features a very good menu variety that includes lobster, fried clams and crisp, Cape Cod apple cranberry cobbler. The flavorful dishes are served in large portions. Very friendly service. Casual dress; cocktails. **Parking:** on-site. **Cards:** AX, MC, VI.

----------- *The following restaurant has not been evaluated by AAA* -----------
*but is listed for your information only.*

FREEDOM CAFE                                                                    Phone: 207/859-8742
[fyi]     Not evaluated. **Location:** 21 Silver St 04901. **Features:** The charming bistro's menu reflects an eclectic mix
          of Caribbean, Cajun, Creole and traditional Southern entrees.

# WELLS

----------- **WHERE TO STAY** -----------

**CARRIAGE HOUSE MOTEL, COTTAGES & SUITES**                                     Phone: (207)646-2159

| | | | |
|---|---|---|---|
| 6/18-9/5 | 1P: $89-$140 | 2P: $99-$160 | XP: $10 |
| 5/1-6/17 & 4/1-4/30 | 1P: $49-$89 | 2P: $59-$140 | XP: $10 |
| 9/6-11/9 | 1P: $49-$79 | 2P: $59-$109 | XP: $10 |

Motel
**Location:** I-95 (Maine Tpke), exit 19 (Wells), 1 mi e on SR 109, 0.3 mi s on US 1. 1404 Post Rd 04090 (PO Box 988).
Fax: 207/646-2159. **Facility:** 27 units. 17 one-bedroom standard units, some with efficiencies. 1 two-bedroom suite ($69-$180)
with kitchen. 9 cottages ($413-$1015). 1-2 stories (no elevator), interior/exterior corridors. *Bath:* some combo or shower only.
**Parking:** on-site. **Terms:** open 5/1-11/9 & 4/1-4/30, office hours 7:30 am-10 pm, 2 night minimum stay - weekends, 15 day can-
cellation notice-fee imposed, weekly rates available, package plans - off season. **Amenities:** hair dryers. **Pool(s):** outdoor.
**Leisure Activities:** basketball, horseshoes, shuffleboard. **Cards:** AX, DS, MC, VI.

SOME UNITS

(ASK) (S/D) 🏊 ✕ (DATA PORT) 📶 📺 💻 / ✕ (VCR) /
FEE

**ELMWOOD RESORT HOTEL**                                                        Phone: 207/646-1038

| | | | |
|---|---|---|---|
| 6/18-9/6 | 1P: $145-$155 | 2P: $145-$155 | XP: $10 F17 |
| 9/7-10/30 | 1P: $90-$95 | 2P: $90-$95 | XP: $10 F17 |
| 5/1-6/17 & 10/31-4/30 | 1P: $85-$90 | 2P: $85-$90 | XP: $10 F17 |

(AAA) (SAVE)

Condominium
**Location:** Jct SR 109, 0.4 mi s on US 1. 1351 Post Rd 04090-1530 (PO Box 1530, 04090). Fax: 207/646-7751.
**Facility:** The hotel's office hours are limited; phone ahead. 50 units. 25 one-, 24 two- and 1 three-bedroom
suites ($95-$220) with kitchens, some with whirlpools. 2 stories (no elevator), exterior corridors. **Parking:**
on-site. **Terms:** office hours 8 am-9 pm, 2-7 night minimum stay, 10 day cancellation notice-fee imposed, package plans - seasonal. **Amenities:** video library (fee), voice mail, irons, hair dryers. **Pool(s):** heated outdoor, heated indoor. **Leisure Activities:** sauna, gas grills in picnic areas, playground. **Guest Services:** coin laundry. **Cards:** AX, DC, DS, MC, VI.

SOME UNITS

(S/D) 🏊 🏋 ✕ (VCR) (DATA PORT) 📶 📺 💻 / ✕ /

**GARRISON SUITES**                                                            Phone: 207/646-3497

| | | | |
|---|---|---|---|
| 7/2-8/28 | 1P: $110-$190 | 2P: $110-$190 | XP: $10 F7 |
| 6/17-7/1 | 1P: $75-$150 | 2P: $75-$150 | XP: $10 F7 |
| 8/29-10/16 | 1P: $59-$128 | 2P: $59-$128 | XP: $10 F7 |
| 5/1-6/16 | 1P: $49-$128 | 2P: $49-$128 | XP: $10 F7 |

(AAA) (SAVE)

Small-scale Hotel
**Location:** I-95 (Maine Tpke), exit 19 (Wells), 1.6 mi e on SR 109, then 0.9 mi s on US 1. 1099 Post Rd 04090.
**Facility:** Smoke free premises. 47 units. 16 one-bedroom standard units, some with efficiencies. 20 one-
bedroom suites with kitchens. 11 cottages ($795-$895). 1-2 stories (no elevator), exterior corridors. **Parking:** on-site.
**Terms:** open 5/1-10/16, office hours 7:30 am-11 pm, 3 night minimum stay - in suites in season, 10 day cancellation notice-fee
imposed, weekly rates available, package plans - seasonal. **Amenities:** irons, hair dryers. *Some:* DVD players. **Pool(s):** heated
outdoor. **Leisure Activities:** whirlpool, badminton, horseshoes, volleyball. **Cards:** DS, MC, VI. **Special Amenities:** free local
telephone calls and free newspaper. *(See color ad below)*

SOME UNITS

(🍴) 🏊 🏋 ✕ ✕ 🎥 📶 📺 💻 / (VCR) (Z) /

HOLIDAY HOUSE MOTEL AND COTTAGES                                               Phone: 207/646-5020

| | | |
|---|---|---|
| 6/10-9/9 | 2P: $95-$165 | XP: $10 |
| 5/1-6/9 | 2P: $65-$95 | XP: $10 |
| 9/10-10/15 | 2P: $65-$75 | XP: $10 |

Motel
**Location:** I-95 (Maine Tpke), exit 19 (Wells), 1 mi e on SR 109, then 3.5 mi s on US 1. 76 Post Rd 03907 (PO Box 714,
OGUNQUIT). **Facility:** 13 units. 6 one-bedroom standard units, some with efficiencies. 7 cottages ($845-$1500). 1-2 stories (no
elevator), exterior corridors. *Bath:* combo or shower only. **Parking:** on-site. **Terms:** open 5/1-10/15, office hours 9 am-11 pm, 2-4
night minimum stay, 30 day cancellation notice-fee imposed, weekly rates available. **Pool(s):** outdoor. **Cards:** DC, DS, MC, VI.

SOME UNITS

🏊 ✕ 📶 📺 💻 / (X) (Z) /

## NE'R BEACH MOTEL

| | | | |
|---|---|---|---|
| ▼▼▼ ▼▼▼ | 6/25-9/5 | 2P: $69-$109 | XP: $10 | F12 |
| | 6/4-6/24 | 2P: $49-$59 | XP: $10 | F12 |
| Motel | 5/1-6/3 | 2P: $44-$54 | XP: $10 | F12 |
| | 9/6-11/1 | 2P: $44-$49 | XP: $10 | F12 |

Phone: (207)646-2636

**Location:** US 1, 0.8 mi s of jct SR 9B. 395 Post Rd (Rt 1) 04090. Fax: 207/641-0968. **Facility:** 43 units. 35 one-bedroom standard units, some with efficiencies. 8 one-bedroom suites ($55-$119) with efficiencies. 1-2 stories (no elevator), exterior corridors. *Bath:* combo or shower only. **Parking:** on-site. **Terms:** open 5/1-11/1, office hours 8 am-10 pm, 2 night minimum stay - weekends in season, 7 day cancellation notice-fee imposed, weekly rates available, small pets only ($10 fee). **Amenities:** *Some:* irons. **Pool(s):** heated outdoor. **Leisure Activities:** seasonal healthclub privileges. **Cards:** DS, MC, VI.

SOME UNITS

🛏️ 🎦 📶 🏊 🎥 🍴 / ✕ 🖥️ /
FEE

## OGUNQUIT RIVER PLANTATION

| | | | | |
|---|---|---|---|---|
| AAA SAVE | 6/25-10/11 [CP] | 1P: $75-$215 | 2P: $75-$215 | XP: $20 | F9 |
| | 5/1-6/24 [CP] | 1P: $55-$175 | 2P: $55-$175 | XP: $10 | F9 |
| ▼▼◆◆◆ | 4/15-4/30 [CP] | 1P: $55-$155 | 2P: $55-$155 | XP: $10 | F9 |
| | 10/12-11/14 [CP] | 1P: $55-$100 | 2P: $55-$100 | XP: $10 | F9 |

Phone: (207)646-9611

Small-scale Hotel **Location:** 1.3 mi n of center on US 1; on the Wells-Ogunquit town line. 17 Post Rd 04054 (PO Box 1876, OGUNQUIT, 03907). Fax: 207/646-4640. **Facility:** Designated smoking area. 80 one-bedroom standard units. 4 stories (no elevator), interior/exterior corridors. **Parking:** on-site. **Terms:** open 5/1-11/14 & 4/15-4/30, 7 day cancellation notice-fee imposed. **Amenities:** *Some:* irons, hair dryers. **Pool(s):** heated outdoor. **Leisure Activities:** whirlpool. *Fee:* kayaking. **Guest Services:** area transportation-beach and village. **Business Services:** meeting rooms. **Cards:** AX, DS, MC, VI. **Special Amenities:** free continental breakfast and free local telephone calls. *(See color ad p 258)*

SOME UNITS

🆂 🏊 📶 ✕ 🍴 / 🖥️ 🖳 /

## SEACOAST MOTEL

| | | | |
|---|---|---|---|
| ▼▼▼ ◆◆ | 7/1-9/30 | 1P: $79-$149 | 2P: $79-$149 | XP: $10 |
| | 5/16-6/30 | 1P: $59-$99 | 2P: $59-$99 | XP: $10 |
| Motel | 10/1-12/31 | 1P: $39-$69 | 2P: $39-$69 | XP: $10 |
| | 5/1-5/15 | 1P: $39-$59 | 2P: $39-$59 | XP: $10 |

Phone: 207/646-2187

**Location:** US 1, 2.5 mi n of Ogunquit, 3 mi s of Wells. 40 Post Rd 04054 (PO Box 1794, OGUNQUIT, 03907). Fax: 207/646-6064. **Facility:** 15 one-bedroom standard units. 2 stories (no elevator), exterior corridors. **Parking:** on-site. **Terms:** open 5/1-12/31, office hours 9 am-11 pm, 10 day cancellation notice-fee imposed. **Pool(s):** outdoor. **Cards:** AX, MC, VI.

SOME UNITS

📶 🏊 🍴 / ✕ /

## THE SEAGULL INN

| | | | |
|---|---|---|---|
| AAA SAVE | 6/26-9/6 | 1P: $105 | 2P: $105 | XP: $14 | F6 |
| | 9/7-10/11 | 1P: $70-$90 | 2P: $70-$90 | XP: $14 | F6 |
| ▼▼◆◆◆ | 5/1-6/25 | 1P: $58-$90 | 2P: $58-$90 | XP: $14 | F6 |
| Motel | 10/12-10/31 | 1P: $50 | 2P: $50 | XP: $14 | F6 |

Phone: 207/646-5164

**Location:** I-95 (Maine Tpke), exit 19 (Wells), 1 mi e on SR 109, then 0.3 mi s. 1413 Post Rd (US 1) 04090 (PO Box 338). Fax: 207/641-8301. **Facility:** Smoke free premises. 48 units. 36 one-bedroom standard units, some with efficiencies. 12 cottages ($400-$1200). 1 story, exterior corridors. *Bath:* combo or shower only. **Parking:** on-site. **Terms:** open 5/1-10/31, office hours 8 am-10 pm, 2 night minimum stay - weekends, 14 day cancellation notice. **Pool(s):** heated outdoor. **Leisure Activities:** whirlpool, playground. **Cards:** MC, VI. **Special Amenities:** free local telephone calls.

SOME UNITS

🏊 ✕ 🍴 / 🎥 🖥️ /

**USA INN**
Phone: 207/646-9313

Motel

| | | | | |
|---|---|---|---|---|
| 6/19-9/5 | 1P: $60-$95 | 2P: $60-$95 | XP: $15 | |
| 5/1-6/18, 9/6-11/6 & 4/7-4/30 | 1P: $30-$60 | 2P: $30-$60 | XP: $10 | |

**Location:** 0.8 mi n of jct SR 9B. 1017 Post Rd (US 1) 04090. **Facility:** 42 one-bedroom standard units. 2-3 stories (no elevator), exterior corridors. **Parking:** on-site. **Terms:** open 5/1-11/6 & 4/7-4/30, office hours 7 am-10 pm, 10 day cancellation notice-fee imposed. **Guest Services:** coin laundry. **Cards:** AX, DS, MC, VI.

SOME UNITS

**VILLAGE GREEN MOTEL**
Phone: 207/646-3285

(AAA) [SAVE]

Motel

| | | | | |
|---|---|---|---|---|
| 5/2-10/15 | 1P: $58-$90 | 2P: $78-$120 | XP: $15 | |

**Location:** US 1, 2 mi s from jct SR 109, 0.3 mi n from jct SR 9B. 773 Post Rd (US Rt 1) 04090 (PO Box 146). Fax: 207/646-4889. **Facility:** 18 units. 10 one-bedroom standard units, some with efficiencies. 1 one-bedroom suite ($75-$160) with efficiency. 7 cottages ($60 - $150). 1-2 stories (no elevator), exterior corridors. *Bath:* combo or shower only. **Parking:** on-site. **Terms:** open 5/2-10/15, office hours 8 am-10 pm, 2-3 night minimum stay - in cottages & condos, 28 day cancellation notice-fee imposed, weekly rates available. **Pool(s):** heated outdoor. **Leisure Activities:** shuffleboard. **Cards:** MC, VI. **Special Amenities:** free local telephone calls and free newspaper. *(See color ad p 297)*

SOME UNITS

**WELLS-MOODY MOTEL**
Phone: 207/646-5601

Motel

| | | | | |
|---|---|---|---|---|
| 6/18-9/5 | 1P: $79-$139 | 2P: $79-$139 | XP: $10 | D12 |
| 5/1-6/17, 9/6-10/27 & 4/1-4/30 | 1P: $49-$69 | 2P: $49-$69 | XP: $10 | D12 |

**Location:** US 1, 2.5 mi n of Ogunquit, 3 mi s of Wells. 119 Post Rd (US 1) 04054 (PO Box 371, MOODY). **Facility:** 24 one-bedroom standard units. 1 story, exterior corridors. *Bath:* combo or shower only. **Parking:** on-site. **Terms:** open 5/1-10/27 & 4/1-4/30, office hours 8 am-9 pm, 10 day cancellation notice-fee imposed. **Pool(s):** outdoor. **Cards:** AX, DS, MC, VI.

SOME UNITS

---

## ——— WHERE TO DINE ———

**BILLY'S CHOWDER HOUSE**
Lunch: $9-$20     Dinner: $9-$20     Phone: 207/646-7558

Seafood

**Location:** 1 mi s on US 1, 0.5 mi e on Mile Rd toward Wells Beach; center. 216 Mile Rd 04090. **Hours:** Open 5/1-12/8 & 1/30-4/30; 11:30 am-9 pm; to 9:30 pm 7/1-9/2. Closed: 11/25. **Features:** This is an informal restaurant with rustic decor. It provides excellent views of the tidal river and salt marsh. The menu features fresh seafood as well as chicken and steak. They are famous for chowder but the lobster stew is their signature dish. Be sure to try the strawberry shortcake, which is available most of the year. Casual dress; cocktails. **Parking:** on-site. **Cards:** AX, DS, MC, VI.

**THE CAPTAINS TABLE RESTAURANT**
Lunch: $4-$12     Dinner: $9-$27     Phone: 207/646-3785

(AAA)

American

**Location:** Just n of jct SR 109/9 on US 1. 1677 Post Rd 04090. **Hours:** Open 5/4-10/15; 7 am-2 & 5-9:30 pm. **Reservations:** accepted. **Features:** Patrons can unwind in a comfortable, relaxing atmosphere while sampling compilations of seasonal seafood. Also offered are prime rib, steak, chicken and pasta entrees prepared with fresh produce. The decadent chocolate cake is worth a splurge. Breakfast is a good time to visit. Casual dress; cocktails. **Parking:** on-site. **Cards:** AX, DS, MC, VI.

**THE GREY GULL INN**   Country Inn
Dinner: $14-$28     Phone: 207/646-7501

Regional American

**Location:** I-95 (Maine Tpke), exit 19 (Wells),1 mi e to US 1, 1 mi s to Mile Rd, 1 mi e to Wells Beach, then 1 mi s along ocean. 475 Webhannet Dr 04090. **Hours:** 5:30 pm-8:30 pm, Fri & Sat-9 pm. Closed: Mon-Wed 12/15-3/15. **Reservations:** suggested. **Features:** Spectacular ocean views are a featured attraction at the Grey Gull, where the meals are outstanding and the atmosphere is pleasant and comfortable. The staff's teamwork provides very good service. Entrees offered include veal, chicken, beef and seafood. Casual dress; cocktails. **Parking:** on-site and valet. **Cards:** AX, DS, MC, VI.

**THE HAYLOFT**
Lunch: $5-$10     Dinner: $7-$20     Phone: 207/646-4400

(AAA)

American

**Location:** 3 mi s of jct US 1 and SR 109 in Wells; 2.5 mi n of center of Ogunquit. 124 Post Rd 04054. **Hours:** 8 am-9:30 pm, Sat 7 am-10 pm, Sun 7 am-9 pm. Closed: 12/24, 12/25. **Features:** Broasted chicken and certified Angus beef are the house specialties at the Hayloft, which also serves a variety of fresh seafood dishes and blueberry banana puff pastry. The casual atmosphere is warm and cozy; the staff is attentive and friendly. Casual dress; cocktails. **Parking:** on-site. **Cards:** AX, DS, MC, VI.

**MAINE DINER**
Lunch: $4-$16     Dinner: $4-$16     Phone: 207/646-4441

(AAA)

American

**Location:** 1.8 mi n. 2265 Post Rd (US 1) 04090. **Hours:** 7 am-9:30 pm; to 8 pm, Fri & Sat to 9 pm 11/1-5/15. Closed: 11/25, 12/25. **Features:** The Maine Diner is very popular with local residents and visitors. The menu features a variety of good seafood dishes including their signature lobster pie, as well as breakfast items served all day. The staff is friendly, prompt and attentive. Casual dress; beer & wine only. **Parking:** on-site. **Cards:** DS, MC, VI.

**MAINIAX RESTAURANT**
Lunch: $5-$8     Dinner: $9-$17     Phone: 207/646-0808

(AAA)

Steak & Seafood

**Location:** 1.2 mi s on US 1. 526 Post Rd 04090. **Hours:** 11:30 am-9:30 pm; to 8:30 pm, Fri & Sat-9 pm 10/11-5/30. Closed major holidays; also 12/24. **Features:** Families visit to enjoy the great woods theme of the dining rooms and the lunch and dinner preparations of seafood, pasta, steak and chicken. Casual dress; cocktails. **Parking:** on-site. **Cards:** MC, VI.

**MIKE'S CLAM SHACK**
▼▼▼ ▼▼▼
Seafood
**Lunch:** $8-$18        **Dinner:** $8-$18        **Phone:** 207/646-5999
**Location:** I-95 (Maine Tpke), exit 19 (Wells), 1 mi e on SR 109, then 0.8 mi s on US 1. 1150 Post Rd 04090.
**Hours:** Open 5/1-12/15 & 2/1-4/30; 9. am-9 pm; to 9:30 pm 7/1-8/31. Closed: Tues 9/1-6/30.
**Features:** The eatery started out as a clam shack in 1948 but has grown into a popular sit-down restaurant. Seafood is at the heart of the menu. A take-out window is still available seasonally. Casual dress; cocktails. **Parking:** on-site. **Cards:** AX, DS, MC, VI.

**THE STEAKHOUSE**
▼▼▼ ▼▼▼
Steak & Seafood
**Dinner:** $10-$22        **Phone:** 207/646-4200
**Location:** Jct SR 109 and US 1, 1 mi s on US 1; center. 1205 US 1 04090. **Hours:** Open 5/1-12/15 & 4/1-4/30; 4:30 pm-9 pm, Sun 3:30 pm-8 pm. Closed: 11/25; also Mon. **Features:** The Steakhouse's strawberry shortcake is a mouthwatering treat! Located in a turn-of-the-century barn, this popular restaurant has a rustic setting in which to serve its very well-prepared beef, seafood and chicken dishes—all served in large portions. Casual dress; cocktails. **Parking:** on-site. **Cards:** MC, VI.

----

*The following restaurant has not been evaluated by AAA but is listed for your information only.*

----

**JAKE'S SEAFOOD**
(fyi)
**Phone:** 207/646-6771
Not evaluated. **Location:** 127 Post Rd (US 1) 04054. **Features:** Jake's Seafood restaurant is a popular lunch and breakfast spot with the locals.

# WELLS BEACH

---- **WHERE TO STAY** ----

**ATLANTIC MOTOR INN**
AAA SAVE
▼▼▼ ◆◆
Motel
**Phone:** 207/646-7061

| | | | |
|---|---|---|---|
| 6/25-9/5 | 1P: $139-$219 | 2P: $139-$219 | XP: $15 |
| 5/1-6/24 | 1P: $49-$159 | 2P: $49-$159 | XP: $15 |
| 9/6-10/30 | 1P: $49-$149 | 2P: $49-$149 | XP: $15 |
| 4/1-4/30 | 1P: $49-$99 | 2P: $49-$99 | XP: $15 |

**Location:** US 1, 1 mi e on Mile Rd, just n. 37 Atlantic Ave 04090 (PO Box 386). Fax: 207/641-0607. **Facility:** 35 one-bedroom standard units. 3 stories (no elevator), exterior corridors. **Parking:** on-site. **Terms:** open 5/1-10/30 & 4/1-4/30, office hours 8 am-10 pm, 3 night minimum stay - in season, 10 day cancellation notice-fee imposed. **Amenities:** hair dryers. **Pool(s):** heated outdoor. **Cards:** AX, DS, MC, VI. **Special Amenities:** free local telephone calls.
*(See color ad below)*

SOME UNITS

**LAFAYETTE'S OCEAN FRONT RESORT AT WELLS BEACH**
▼▼▼ ◆◆
Small-scale Hotel
**Phone:** 207/646-2831

| | | | | |
|---|---|---|---|---|
| 5/1-9/5 | 1P: $95-$250 | 2P: $95-$250 | XP: $25 | D17 |
| 9/6-10/30 | 1P: $90-$160 | 2P: $90-$160 | XP: $10 | D17 |
| 4/15-4/30 | 1P: $70-$130 | 2P: $70-$130 | XP: $10 | D17 |
| 10/31-4/14 | 1P: $50-$100 | 2P: $50-$100 | XP: $10 | D17 |

**Location:** Jct US 1, 1 mi e. 393 Mile Rd 04090 (PO Box 639, WELLS). Fax: 207/646-6770. **Facility:** 149 one-bedroom standard units, some with efficiencies. 2-3 stories (no elevator), interior/exterior corridors. *Bath:* combo or shower only. **Parking:** on-site. **Terms:** 14 day cancellation notice-fee imposed. **Amenities:** irons, hair dryers. **Pool(s):** heated indoor. **Leisure Activities:** whirlpool. **Guest Services:** coin laundry. **Business Services:** meeting rooms. **Cards:** AX, CB, DC, DS, MC, VI.

SOME UNITS

## WESTBROOK pop. 16,142

―――――― WHERE TO STAY ――――――

**SUPER 8 MOTEL**                                                                       Phone: (207)854-1881

| | | | |
|---|---|---|---|
| AAA SAVE | 6/1-9/30 [CP] | 1P: $65-$115 | 2P: $65-$115 | XP: $6 | F14 |
| | 5/1-5/31 [CP] | 1P: $57-$77 | 2P: $65-$95 | XP: $6 | F14 |
| | 1/1-4/30 [CP] | 1P: $57-$70 | 2P: $57-$70 | XP: $6 | F14 |
| | 10/1-12/31 [CP] | 1P: $50-$70 | 2P: $50-$70 | XP: $6 | F14 |

Small-scale Hotel  **Location:** I-95 (Maine Tpke), exit 48. 208 Larrabee Rd 04092. Fax: 207/854-0078. **Facility:** 104 one-bedroom standard units, some with kitchens. 2 stories (no elevator), interior corridors. **Parking:** on-site. **Pool(s):** heated indoor. **Leisure Activities:** whirlpool. **Cards:** AX, DC, MC, VI. **Special Amenities:** free continental breakfast and free local telephone calls.

SOME UNITS

## WEST FORKS pop. 47

―――――― WHERE TO STAY ――――――

**INN BY THE RIVER**                                                                     Phone: 207/663-2181

| | | | |
|---|---|---|---|
| | 6/16-8/31 [BP] | 1P: $85-$200 | 2P: $85-$200 | XP: $25 | F6 |
| | 5/1-6/15 & 9/1-4/30 [BP] | 1P: $75-$160 | 2P: $75-$160 | XP: $25 | F6 |

Country Inn  **Location:** Center. US Rt 201 04985 (Box 24). Fax: 207/663-2207. **Facility:** Smoke free premises. 10 one-bedroom standard units, some with whirlpools. 2 stories (no elevator), interior corridors. **Parking:** on-site. **Terms:** 2 night minimum stay - seasonal weekends, 30 day cancellation notice-fee imposed. **Amenities:** Some: hair dryers. **Leisure Activities:** rental canoes, fishing, hiking trails. Fee: snowmobiling. **Guest Services:** TV in common area, complimentary laundry. **Cards:** MC, VI.

## WESTPORT

―――――― WHERE TO STAY ――――――

**THE SQUIRE TARBOX INN**                                                               Phone: 207/882-7693

| | | | |
|---|---|---|---|
| | 7/16-10/30 | 1P: $145-$190 | 2P: $145-$190 | | |
| | 5/1-7/15, 10/31-1/1 & 4/1-4/30 | 1P: $122-$167 | 2P: $122-$167 | | |

Historic Country Inn  **Location:** Jct US 1 and SR 144; in Wiscasset; 8.5 mi s on SR 144, follow signs. Located in a quiet, rural area. 1181 Main Rd 04578. Fax: 207/882-7107. **Facility:** Built in 1763, the inn reflects the ambience of the era with Colonial-style decor; phone for seasonal availability. Smoke free premises. 11 one-bedroom standard units. 2 stories (no elevator), interior/exterior corridors. Bath: shower only. **Parking:** on-site. **Terms:** open 5/1-1/1 & 4/1-4/30, 2 night minimum stay - weekends, 14 day cancellation notice-fee imposed, [BP] meal plan available, pets (with prior approval). **Amenities:** hair dryers. **Leisure Activities:** boating, boat dock, bicycles. **Guest Services:** TV in common area. **Cards:** AX, MC, VI.

SOME UNITS

## WILTON pop. 2,290

―――――― WHERE TO STAY ――――――

**WHISPERING PINES MOTEL**                                                              Phone: (207)645-3721

| | | | |
|---|---|---|---|
| AAA SAVE | 6/15-10/15 | 1P: $57-$99 | 2P: $63-$105 | XP: $6 | F12 |
| | 5/1-6/14 & 10/16-4/30 | 1P: $51-$92 | 2P: $57-$98 | XP: $6 | F12 |

Motel  **Location:** SR 2, 1 mi w of jct SR 4. 183 Lake Rd 04294 (PO Box 649). Fax: 207/645-4868. **Facility:** 31 units. 27 one-bedroom standard units, some with efficiencies. 1 one- and 3 two-bedroom suites with efficiencies. 2 stories (no elevator), exterior corridors. Bath: combo or shower only. **Parking:** on-site. **Terms:** office hours 7 am-10 pm, 3 day cancellation notice, pets ($3 extra charge, in designated units). **Amenities:** Some: DVD players (fee). **Leisure Activities:** boating, canoeing, boat dock, fishing, playground, horseshoes. **Guest Services:** gift shop, coin laundry. **Cards:** AX, DC, DS, MC, VI. **Special Amenities:** free local telephone calls and early check-in/late check-out.

SOME UNITS

FEE                      FEE

## WINDHAM

―――――― WHERE TO DINE ――――――

**CHARLIE BEIGGS**                 Lunch: $6-$10          Dinner: $14-$23          Phone: 207-892-8595

American  **Location:** On US 302; center. 754 Roosevelt Tr 04062. **Hours:** 11 am-9 pm, Fri & Sat-9:30 pm. Closed: 11/25, 12/25. **Reservations:** accepted. **Features:** This locally popular restaurant has a variety of seafood, steaks, pasta, and sandwiches. Outdoor dining is available seasonally. Casual dress; cocktails. **Parking:** on-site. **Cards:** AX, DC, DS, MC, VI.

**THE LANDING RESTAURANT**        Lunch: $5-$10          Dinner: $6-$14          Phone: 207/892-2299

Steak & Seafood  **Location:** US 302, just n of jct SR 35/115; center. 750 Roosevelt Tr 04062. **Hours:** 11 am-9 pm; hours vary seasonally. Closed: 11/25, 12/25. **Features:** The menu at the family restaurant emphasizes steak and seafood. A casual atmosphere prevails in the spacious dining room. Casual dress; cocktails. **Parking:** on-site. **Cards:** AX, DS, MC, VI.

# WISCASSET pop. 1,203

―――――― WHERE TO DINE ――――――

**LE GARAGE**
American
Lunch: $6-$18          Dinner: $10-$22          Phone: 207/882-5409
**Location:** Just e; downtown. 15 Water St 04578. **Hours:** Open 5/1-12/31 & 2/1-4/30; 11:30 am-2:30 & 5-8:30 pm, Fri & Sat-9 pm; 11:30 am-3 & 5-9 pm in summer. **Closed:** Mon 9/10-5/25. **Reservations:** accepted. **Features:** Le Garage features an excellent view of the Sheepscot River from its glassed-in porch. The exceptional menu offers finnan haddie, charbroiled lamb, seafood Newburg, steak and vegetarian dishes. Large, wrought-iron candelabra provide romantic lighting. Casual dress; cocktails. **Parking:** street. **Cards:** MC, VI.

**SARAH'S CAFE**
American
Lunch: $5-$16          Dinner: $5-$16          Phone: 207/882-7504
**Location:** On US 1; center. 45 Water St 04578. **Hours:** 11 am-9 pm, Sat & Sun also 6:30-10:30 am; hours vary off season. **Closed:** 3/27, 12/25. **Features:** Near the waterfront, the popular restaurant offers a beautiful river view and a varied menu of value-priced choices, including pizza, lobster, sandwiches, Mexican dishes and excellent desserts. Country breakfast is served on weekends. The deck is a nice seasonal retreat. Crayons are on the table for children. Cocktails. **Parking:** street. **Cards:** AX, DS, MC, VI.

**SEA BASKET RESTAURANT**
Seafood
Lunch: $6-$13          Dinner: $6-$13          Phone: 207/882-6581
**Location:** On US 1, 1.2 mi s of center. 303 Bath Rd 04578. **Hours:** Open 5/1-12/15 & 2/1-4/30; 11 am-8 pm. **Closed:** Sun; also Mon 2/1-6/30 & 9/1-12/15. **Features:** Colorful seaside murals decorate the walls of the traditional seafood restaurant. Fresh Maine seafood is cooked in a convection fryer for lighter and healthier fried seafood. Patrons can bring their own bottle. **Parking:** on-site. **Cards:** MC, VI.

# WOOLWICH pop. 2,810

―――――― WHERE TO DINE ――――――

**THE TASTE OF MAINE RESTAURANT**
Seafood
Lunch: $11-$18          Dinner: $11-$18          Phone: 207/443-4554
**Location:** 0.6 mi n of Bath Bridge. US Rt 1 04579. **Hours:** Open 5/1-12/31 & 3/1-4/30; 11 am-9 pm. **Closed:** 12/25. **Reservations:** suggested. **Features:** Lobster is the focus, but patrons also can select chicken, steak and a few vegetarian entrees. Fresh seafood arrives daily. The family-friendly restaurant provides an area where children can play while parents eat. Casual dress; cocktails. **Parking:** on-site. **Cards:** AX, DS, MC, VI.

# YARMOUTH pop. 3,560

―――――― WHERE TO STAY ――――――

**BROOKSIDE MOTEL**
Motel
Phone: 207/846-5512

| | | | |
|---|---|---|---|
| 7/18-10/15 | 1P: $95-$125 | 2P: $95-$125 | XP: $10 |
| 6/6-7/17 | 1P: $69-$95 | 2P: $69-$95 | XP: $10 |
| 5/1-6/5 & 10/16-4/30 | 1P: $49-$69 | 2P: $49-$69 | XP: $10 |

**Location:** I-295, exit 15, 0.3 mi n. 219 US Rt 1 04096. **Facility:** 12 one-bedroom standard units. 1 story, exterior corridors. *Bath:* shower only. **Parking:** on-site. **Terms:** office hours 7 am-midnight. **Amenities:** hair dryers. **Cards:** AX, DS, MC, VI.

SOME UNITS

**DOWN-EAST VILLAGE MOTEL**
SAVE
Small-scale Hotel
Phone: 207/846-5161

| | | | | |
|---|---|---|---|---|
| 6/25-10/16 | 1P: $99-$115 | 2P: $99-$115 | XP: $10 | F18 |
| 5/1-6/24 & 10/17-12/31 | 1P: $75-$85 | 2P: $75-$85 | XP: $10 | F18 |
| 1/1-4/30 | 1P: $65-$75 | 2P: $65-$75 | XP: $10 | F18 |

**Location:** I-295, exit 15 northbound; exit 17 southbound. 705 US Rt 1 04096-6927. **Fax:** 207/846-1078. **Facility:** Smoke free premises. 31 one-bedroom standard units. 1 story, exterior corridors. **Parking:** on-site. **Terms:** office hours 7 am-11 pm, pets ($8 extra charge). **Amenities:** *Some:* hair dryers. **Dining:** restaurant, see separate listing. **Pool(s):** outdoor. **Leisure Activities:** playground. **Business Services:** meeting rooms. **Cards:** AX, CB, DC, DS, MC, VI. **Special Amenities:** free local telephone calls and free newspaper. *(See color ad p 224)*

FEE

―――――― WHERE TO DINE ――――――

**DOWN-EAST VILLAGE RESTAURANT**
American
Lunch: $6-$12          Dinner: $10-$20          Phone: 207/846-5161
**Location:** I-295, exit 15 northbound; exit 17 southbound; in Down-East Village Motel. 705 US Rt 1 04096-6927. **Hours:** 7 am-2 & 5-9 pm, Sun 7 am-11 & noon-2 pm. **Closed:** 1/1, 11/25, 12/25; also for dinner 12/24. **Reservations:** accepted. **Features:** Close to the Royal River, the dining rooms have a rustic decor with a large stone fireplace and a casual atmosphere. The menu features a variety of well-prepared seafood, beef and chicken dishes. Light and full menus are available all day. Off season hours may vary. Casual dress; cocktails. **Parking:** on-site. **Cards:** AX, DS, MC, VI. *(See color ad p 224)*

**MUDDY RUDDER RESTAURANT**
American
Lunch: $6-$9          Dinner: $11-$18          Phone: 207/846-3082
**Location:** US 1, at north end of town limits. 1335 US Rt 1 04096. **Hours:** 11 am-midnight; closing hours may vary. **Closed:** 12/25. **Reservations:** accepted. **Features:** Soup, stew, salad, lobster pie, steak and seafood dinners are offered at this warm and inviting Muddy Rudder, which has good views of the wildlife on Cousins River. The downeast clambake is also popular here. Tables display area maps from the 1800s. Casual dress; cocktails; entertainment. **Parking:** on-site. **Cards:** AX, DC, DS, MC, VI. *(See color ad p 222)*

**ROYAL RIVER GRILLHOUSE**   **Lunch:** $8-$14      **Dinner:** $16-$32      **Phone:** 207/846-1226
▽▽ ▽▽      **Location:** I-295, exit 17, just s on US 1, then 1 mi s on SR 88, follow sign. 106 Lafayette St 04096. **Hours:** 11:30
American      am-2:30 & 5-9 pm; hours vary seasonally. **Closed:** 11/25, 12/25. **Features:** Overlooking the Royal River,
            this casual restaurant is on the site of a former seafood cannery. Large windows in the dining room give an
unrestricted view of the marine activity. The seasonally changing menu features native seafood, including
shellfish, as well as beef and poultry entrees. Outdoor dining on the deck is available seasonally. Cocktails. **Parking:** on-site.
**Cards:** AX, DS, MC, VI.

# YORK

―――― **WHERE TO STAY** ――――

**THE CAPE NEDDICK HOUSE**                                          **Phone:** (207)363-2500
▽▽▽▽      6/4-9/2 [BP]            1P: $115-$125      2P: $125-$145      XP: $20      D12
            9/3-10/31 [BP]         1P: $125-$135      2P: $125-$140      XP: $20      D12
Historic Bed   5/1-6/3 [BP]          1P: $110-$115      2P: $125-$130      XP: $20      D12
& Breakfast   11/1-4/30 [BP]         1P: $115-$125      2P: $120-$130      XP: $20      D12
            **Location:** I-95, exit 7 (York Ogunquit), 3.5 mi n. 1300 US 1 03902 (PO Box 70, CAPE NEDDICK). Fax: 207/363-4499.
**Facility:** A converted 1880s farmhouse, the inn has Victorian-style common areas and individually themed guest rooms. Smoke
free premises. 5 units. 4 one-bedroom standard units. 1 one-bedroom suite ($130-$175). 2 stories (no elevator), interior corridors. *Bath:* combo or shower only. **Parking:** on-site. **Terms:** 2 night minimum stay - weekends 6/1-10/31, age restrictions may
apply, 7 day cancellation notice, package plans - seasonal, no pets allowed (owner's pet on premises). **Amenities:** hair dryers.
**Leisure Activities:** cross country skiing, hiking trails. **Guest Services:** TV in common area.

**DOCKSIDE GUEST QUARTERS**                                        **Phone:** (207)363-2868
▽▽▽      5/1-12/18 & 2/11-4/30            2P: $85-$180      XP: $10      F12
            **Location:** Jct US 1A, just s on SR 103 to Harris Island Rd, then just s. Located in a rural area. (PO Box 205 Harris Is-
Country Inn   land). Fax: 207/363-1977. **Facility:** On a small private island, the property includes a main inn and cottages
            in a harbor setting; phone for seasonal availability. Designated smoking area. 25 units. 19 one-bedroom stan-
dard units. 6 one-bedroom suites ($120-$250) with efficiencies. 2 stories (no elevator), interior/exterior corridors. *Bath:* combo or
shower only. **Parking:** on-site. **Terms:** open 5/1-12/18 & 2/11-4/30, office hours 8 am-9 pm, 2 night minimum stay - weekends
& 7/1-8/31, 14 day cancellation notice-fee imposed, weekly rates available, package plans - off season, no pets allowed (owner's pet on premises). **Amenities:** irons. **Dining:** restaurant, see separate listing. **Leisure Activities:** canoeing, fishing, bicycles.
*Fee:* boats, marina. **Cards:** DS, MC, VI.
                                                                  SOME UNITS

―――― **WHERE TO DINE** ――――

**CAPE NEDDICK INN**          **Dinner:** $19-$29            **Phone:** 207/363-2899
▽▽▽▽      **Location:** I-95, exit 7 (York Ogunquit); US 1, 3.5 mi n. 1233 US Rt 1 03902. **Hours:** Open 5/1-2/28 & 4/1-4/30;
            5:30 pm-10 pm. **Closed:** 12/25; also Mon, Tues 4/1-4/30. **Reservations:** suggested. **Features:** The
American      restaurant's attractive dining room is also an art gallery with a quiet and informal, yet sophisticated,
            atmosphere. Well-prepared, French-influenced American cuisine makes use of fresh, local and seasonal
ingredients. The wine list is excellent. Casual dress; cocktails. **Parking:** on-site. **Cards:** AX, MC, VI.

**CLAY HILL FARM**            **Dinner:** $17-$28            **Phone:** 207/361-2272
▽▽▽▽      **Location:** 0.5 mi s on US 1, 2 mi w on Agamenticus Rd. 220 Clay Hill Rd 03909. **Hours:** 5:30 pm-9 pm; hours
            vary seasonally. **Closed:** Mon 11/1-3/15. **Reservations:** suggested. **Features:** The restaurant's gracious
American      dining rooms provide views of the peaceful country setting. Guests can enjoy the casual elegance while
            dining on beautifully prepared New England regional cuisine. Diners are soothed by a piano in season.
Cocktails. **Parking:** valet. **Cards:** AX, DS, MC, VI.

**DOCKSIDE RESTAURANT**      **Lunch:** $7-$11      **Dinner:** $11-$23      **Phone:** 207/363-2722
▽▽ ▽▽      **Location:** Jct US 1A, just s on SR 103 to Harris Island Rd; then just s; in Dockside Guest Quarters. **Hours:** Open
            5/26-10/14; 11:30 am-2 & 5:30-9 pm; hours may vary off season. **Closed:** Mon. **Reservations:** suggested.
American      **Features:** You'll enjoy Dockside's attractive and informal dining room and screened porch overlooking York
            Harbor and marina. The menu features a nice variety of seafood dishes as well as chicken and beef.
Lighter fare is available at lunch. This is a popular place. Casual dress; cocktails. **Parking:** on-site. **Cards:** DS, MC, VI.

**FAZIO'S**                  **Dinner:** $5-$18            **Phone:** 207/363-7019
▽▽ ▽▽      **Location:** I-95, exit 7 (York Ogunquit), 0.5 mi s on US 1, 1 mi n on US 1A, 0.3 mi nw on Long Sands Rd, then 0.3 mi
            e. 38 Woodbridge Rd 03909. **Hours:** 4 pm-9:30 pm; to 9 pm 10/1-5/15. **Closed:** 3/27, 11/25, 12/24, 12/25;
Italian      also Mon 10/18-4/30. **Features:** In a warm, casual dining room, Fazio's offers a wide variety of
            well-prepared Italian dishes. Menu items, including pasta, risotto, soup, sauce and dessert are made on
the premises. All offerings are reasonably priced. Don't miss the delicious cannoli. Casual dress; cocktails. **Parking:** on-site.
**Cards:** AX, DS, MC, VI.

**LOBSTER BARN**             **Lunch:** $6-$14      **Dinner:** $10-$22      **Phone:** 207/363-4721
▽▽ ▽▽      **Location:** I-95, exit 7 (York Ogunquit), 2.5 mi n. 1000 US Rt 1 03909. **Hours:** Open 5/1-11/15 & 4/15-4/30; 4
            pm-9 pm; hours may vary seasonally. **Closed:** Mon-Thurs 4/15-6/15 & 9/7-11/15. **Features:** The Lobster
Steak & Seafood   Barn is well named—it's in a real New England barn displaying many farm artifacts. The setting is warm
            and cozy, with lanterns and candles on the tables. Maine lobster is the specialty, but the menu also offers
steak and blueberry pie. Casual dress; cocktails. **Parking:** on-site. **Cards:** AX, MC, VI.

―――― *The following restaurant has not been evaluated by AAA*
*but is listed for your information only.* ――――

**WILD WILLY'S BURGERS**                                          **Phone:** 207/363-9924
fyi      **Not evaluated. Location:** 765 US Rt 1 03909. **Features:** Thick, juicy, Angus beef burgers are the trademark
            of the popular restaurant.

# YORK BEACH

## ———— WHERE TO STAY ————

**THE ANCHORAGE INN**

| | | | | Phone: 207/363-5112 |
|---|---|---|---|---|
| ◈◈◈ ◈◈◈ | 6/25-9/5 | 1P: $152-$200 | 2P: $152-$200 | |
| | 9/6-4/30 | 1P: $118-$148 | 2P: $118-$148 | |
| Small-scale Hotel | 5/21-6/24 | 1P: $117-$148 | 2P: $117-$148 | |
| | 5/1-5/20 | 1P: $95-$125 | 2P: $95-$125 | |

**Location:** 1.5 mi s on US 1A. 265 Long Beach Ave 03910 (PO Box 1329). Fax: 207/363-6753. **Facility:** Smoke free premises. 178 units. 172 one- and 5 two-bedroom standard units, some with efficiencies. 1 two-bedroom suite ($190-$360) with kitchen. 3 stories, interior/exterior corridors. *Bath:* combo or shower only. **Parking:** on-site. **Terms:** 15 day cancellation notice-fee imposed, package plans. **Amenities:** hair dryers. *Some:* irons. **Pool(s):** outdoor, 2 heated indoor. **Leisure Activities:** whirlpools, exercise room. **Business Services:** meeting rooms. **Cards:** MC, VI. *(See color ad below)*

SOME UNITS

🍴 🍸 🕸 ✕ 📶 / 💻 /

**LIGHTHOUSE INN & CARRIAGE HOUSE**

| | | | | Phone: 207/363-6072 |
|---|---|---|---|---|
| ◈◈◈ ◈◈◈ | 6/25-9/6 | 2P: $125-$175 | XP: $10 | F7 |
| | 5/21-6/24 | 2P: $85-$140 | XP: $10 | F7 |
| Motel | 5/1-5/20 & 9/7-10/31 | 2P: $75-$140 | XP: $10 | F7 |

**Location:** 0.5 mi s on US 1A, then just e. 18-20 Nubble Rd 03910 (PO Box 249). **Facility:** 30 units. 29 one- and 1 two-bedroom standard units. 2 stories (no elevator), interior/exterior corridors. *Bath:* combo or shower only. **Parking:** on-site. **Terms:** open 5/1-10/31, office hours 8 am-9 pm, 1-2 night minimum stay, 7 day cancellation notice-fee imposed, [CP] meal plan available, no pets allowed (owner's pet on premises). **Amenities:** *Some:* hair dryers. **Pool(s):** heated outdoor. **Leisure Activities:** whirlpool. **Cards:** AX, DS, MC, VI.

SOME UNITS

🕸 ✕ 📶 🛢 / VCR /

**SUNRISE MOTEL**                                                                                    Phone: (207)363-4542

♦♦ ♦♦  6/26-9/5                                              2P: $150-$210        XP: $20              D17
         9/6-10/12                                             2P: $95-$140         XP: $20              D17
Motel    5/1-6/35                                             2P: $90-$135         XP: $20              D17
         10/13-4/30                                            2P: $70-$120         XP: $20              D17
**Location:** 2 mi s on US 1A. 340 Long Sands Rd 03910 (PO Box 1044, YORK HARBOR, 03911). Fax: 207/363-1695. **Facility:** 25 units. 23 one- and 1 two-bedroom standard units, some with efficiencies and/or whirlpools. 1 one-bedroom suite ($110-$220). 3 stories (no elevator), exterior corridors. **Parking:** on-site. **Terms:** 2 night minimum stay - 7/1-8/31, 7 day cancellation notice-fee imposed, package plans - 11/1-5/10. **Amenities:** hair dryers. **Cards:** MC, VI. *(See color ad p 303)*

SOME UNITS

🔲 🖥 / ⊠ 📷 /

**THE UNION BLUFF HOTEL**                                                                              Phone: 207/363-1333

(AAA) (SAVE)  6/20-9/8                                        1P: $139-$289        2P: $139-$289       XP: $10      F3
              5/1-6/19 & 9/9-10/26                            1P: $69-$219         2P: $69-$219        XP: $10      F3
♦♦ ♦♦ ♦♦      10/27-4/30                                       1P: $59-$209         2P: $59-$209        XP: $10      F3
Small-scale Hotel  **Location:** Center. 8 Beach St 03910 (PO Box 1860). Fax: 207/363-1381. **Facility:** Smoke free premises. 62 one-
              bedroom standard units, some with whirlpools. 5 stories, interior/exterior corridors. **Parking:** on-site.
**Terms:** 2 night minimum stay - weekends & in summer, 14 day cancellation notice-fee imposed, [MAP] meal plan available, package plans. **Amenities:** voice mail, hair dryers. *Some:* irons. **Dining:** 7:30 am-11 & 11:30-10 pm, cocktails. **Leisure Activities:** golf privileges. **Guest Services:** valet laundry. **Cards:** AX, DS, MC, VI.

SOME UNITS

🍴 🍸 🔳 ⊠ 📹 [DATA PORT] 🔲 / (VCR) 📷 /

--------- **WHERE TO DINE** ---------

**CHEF MIMMO'S**                              **Dinner:** $14-$18                           Phone: 207/363-3807
♦♦ ♦♦       **Location:** 1.5 mi s on US 1A. **Hours:** 5 pm-10 pm. Closed: 11/25, 12/25; also Mon & Tues 10/1-6/30.
Italian      **Reservations:** suggested. **Features:** Chef Mimmo's features casual dining across the street from Long
             Sands Beach. They serve ample portions, a full breakfast menu and a good selection of Continental Italian
dishes and desserts. No alcohol is served; it's BYOB. The enclosed porch is nice. Casual dress. **Parking:** on-site. **Cards:** AX, DS, MC, VI.                                                                                    ⊠

**FOX'S LOBSTER HOUSE**          **Lunch:** $12-$25         **Dinner:** $12-$25          Phone: 207/363-2643
♦♦ ♦♦       **Location:** At Nobble Point. Sawyer Park Rd 03910. **Hours:** Open 5/1-10/17; 11:30 am-9 pm. **Features:** Lovely
Seafood      views of Nubble Lighthouse and the ocean enhance the dining experience. The menu lists not only
             traditional lobster dinners but also pasta, steak and other seafood. Guests can dine inside or order
take-out. Casual dress; cocktails. **Parking:** on-site. **Cards:** MC, VI.                                        ⊠

# YORK HARBOR pop. 3,321

———— **WHERE TO STAY** ————

**EDWARDS HARBORSIDE INN**
**Phone:** 207/363-3037

| | | | |
|---|---|---|---|
| 7/1-9/10 | 1P: $120-$270 | 2P: $120-$270 | XP: $25 |
| 5/1-6/30 & 9/11-10/31 | 1P: $70-$170 | 2P: $70-$170 | XP: $25 |
| 11/1-4/30 | 1P: $50-$130 | 2P: $50-$130 | XP: $25 |

Historic Bed & Breakfast

**Location:** Off US 1A, 2 mi n of jct US 1. 7 Stage Neck Rd 03911 (PO Box 866). Fax: 207/363-1544. **Facility:** A picturesque setting overlooking York Harbor enhances this handsomely decorated Victorian summer residence. Smoke free premises. 8 units. 6 one- and 1 two-bedroom standard units, some with whirlpools. 1 one-bedroom suite ($180-$270). 3 stories (no elevator), interior corridors. *Bath:* combo or shower only. **Parking:** on-site. **Terms:** 2 night minimum stay - weekends, 5 nights in summer, age restrictions may apply, 14 day cancellation notice-fee imposed, package plans - 11/1-4/30, 8% service charge. **Leisure Activities:** boat dock, fishing. **Cards:** MC, VI.

SOME UNITS
[fridge] [✕] / [VCR] [•] /

**INN AT HARMON PARK**
**Phone:** (207)363-2031

| | | | |
|---|---|---|---|
| 5/1-10/31 | 1P: $69-$129 | 2P: $79-$129 | XP: $15 |
| 11/1-4/30 | 1P: $49-$109 | 2P: $59-$109 | XP: $15 |

Bed & Breakfast

**Location:** I-95, exit 7 (York Ogunquit), 0.3 mi s on US 1, 1.5 mi n; thru York Village on US 1A. Located in a residential area. 415 York St 03911 (PO Box 495). **Facility:** An 1899 Victorian-style home, the inn offers charming decor and gracious hospitality. Smoke free premises. 5 units. 4 one-bedroom standard units. 1 one-bedroom suite. 2 stories (no elevator), interior corridors. *Bath:* combo or shower only. **Parking:** on-site. **Terms:** 2 night minimum stay - weekends, age restrictions may apply. 7 day cancellation notice-fee imposed, weekly rates available, no pets allowed (owner's pet on premises). **Amenities:** video library.

[✕] [AC] [VCR] [☎]

**STAGE NECK INN**
**Phone:** 207/363-3850

| | | | | |
|---|---|---|---|---|
| 5/17-8/31 | 1P: $235-$340 | 2P: $240-$345 | XP: $10 | F6 |
| 9/1-10/24 | 1P: $185-$250 | 2P: $190-$255 | XP: $10 | F6 |
| 5/1-5/16 | 1P: $165-$205 | 2P: $170-$210 | XP: $10 | F6 |
| 10/25-4/30 | 1P: $145-$190 | 2P: $150-$195 | XP: $10 | F6 |

Small-scale Hotel

**Location:** Off US 1A via Harbor Beach Rd. Stage Neck Rd 03911 (PO Box 70). Fax: 207/363-2221. **Facility:** A traditional New England-style oceanside inn, the property has good ocean and harbor views and well-tended landscaping; rooms are richly decorated. Smoke free premises. 60 one-bedroom standard units, some with whirlpools. 3 stories, interior corridors. **Parking:** on-site, winter plug-ins. **Terms:** 2 night minimum stay - weekends, 3 night minimum weekends 7/1-8/31, 14 day cancellation notice-fee imposed, [MAP] meal plan available, package plans, 18% service charge. **Amenities:** video library, CD players, voice mail, safes, irons, hair dryers. **Dining:** 7:30 am-10 & noon-9 pm, Fri & Sat-10 pm, cocktails. **Pool(s):** heated outdoor, heated indoor. **Leisure Activities:** sauna, whirlpool, 2 tennis courts, exercise room. *Fee:* massage. **Guest Services:** valet and coin laundry. **Business Services:** meeting rooms, fax. **Cards:** AX, DC, DS, MC, VI. *(See color ad below)*

[dining] [cocktails] [pool] [✕] [✕] [VCR] [DATA PORT] [•] [□]

## YORK HARBOR INN

| | | | Phone: (207)363-5119 |
|---|---|---|---|
| 6/20-9/1 | 1P: $132-$325 | 2P: $132-$325 | XP: $20    F12 |
| 5/1-6/19 & 9/2-10/26 | 1P: $122-$325 | 2P: $122-$325 | XP: $20    F12 |
| 10/27-4/30 | 1P: $99-$299 | 2P: $99-$299 | XP: $20    F12 |

**Location:** On US 1A; center. 480 York St 03911 (PO Box 573). Fax: 207/363-7151. **Facility:** Sections of this inn date from the 1600s, lending a feel of yesteryear combined with modern amenities; room size varies from compact to more spacious. Smoke free premises. 33 units. 32 one-bedroom standard units, some with whirlpools. 1 one-bedroom suite with whirlpool. 3 stories (no elevator); interior/exterior corridors. *Bath:* combo or shower only. **Parking:** on-site. **Terms:** 2 night minimum stay - weekends, 14 day cancellation notice-fee imposed, [MAP] meal plan available, package plans, $4 service charge. **Amenities:** voice mail, irons, hair dryers. **Dining:** dining room, see separate listing. **Leisure Activities:** whirlpool. **Guest Services:** gift shop. **Business Services:** meeting rooms. **Cards:** AX, CB, DC, MC, VI. **Special Amenities: free expanded continental breakfast and free newspaper.** *(See color ad p 305)*

SOME UNITS

[¶] [✕] [DATA PORT] / [🛏] /

─────── **WHERE TO DINE** ───────

### FOSTER'S DOWNEAST LOBSTER & CLAMBAKE

◈

Seafood

**Lunch:** $6-$25    **Dinner:** $8-$26    **Phone:** 207/363-3255

**Location:** Off US 1A. 1 Axholme Rd 03911. **Hours:** Open 5/1-10/31; 11:30 am-8 pm. **Reservations:** required, for clambake. **Features:** Two restaurants in one, there is a traditional New England clambake with all the fixings and an all day counter service operation with an emphasis on seafood. A large, pavilion with communal tables is the scene of the clambake. Casual dress; cocktails. **Parking:** on-site. **Cards:** MC, VI.

[✕]

### LOBSTER COVE

◈◈

American

**Lunch:** $6-$9    **Dinner:** $7-$15    **Phone:** 207/351-1100

**Location:** On US 1A. 756 York St 03910. **Hours:** 7:30 am-9 pm; hour vary seasonally. Closed: 11/25, 12/25. **Reservations:** accepted. **Features:** With lovely water views, the restaurant is open for breakfast, lunch and dinner. Eclectic menus emphasize fresh seafood. Deck seating is available seasonally. Casual dress; cocktails. **Parking:** on-site. **Cards:** AX, MC, VI.

[¶] [✕]

### THE YORK HARBOR INN   Country Inn

◈◈◈

Regional American

**Lunch:** $5-$13    **Dinner:** $19-$28    **Phone:** 207/363-5119

**Location:** On US 1A; center; in York Harbor Inn. **Hours:** 11:30 am-2:30 & 5:30-9:30 pm, Sun from 5:30 pm. Closed: 12/24, 12/25. **Reservations:** suggested. **Features:** Located in a true historic Colonial country inn, this restaurant showcases an elegant and upscale decor with wide windows offering a great view of the ocean. The menu reflects a regional cuisine featuring seafood prepared with international flavors. Casual dress; cocktails. **Parking:** on-site. **Cards:** AX, DC, MC, VI.

[¶] [✕]

# New Hampshire

Eaton Center
© F. Sieb
Robertstock

# AMHERST

### ——— WHERE TO DINE ———

**AMATO'S GOURMET**
Italian

Lunch: $5-$8    Dinner: $5-$8    Phone: 603/577-3875
**Location:** Everett Tpke (US 3), exit 8, 7 mi w. 109 SR 101A 03031. **Hours:** 9 am-7 pm, Sat-5 pm, Sun 11 am-3 pm. Closed major holidays. **Features:** Self-service is the mode at the New York-Italian delicatessen and pasta shop. Patrons can stop in for a sandwich, fresh pastry, pasta dish or bowl of homemade soup. A wide selection of pre-made, take-out entrees is available. **Parking:** on-site. **Cards:** AX, MC, VI.

**THE BLACK FOREST CAFE & BAKERY**
American
Casual dress; beer & wine only.

Lunch: $5-$10    Phone: 603/672-0500
**Location:** On SR 101. 212 SR 101 03031. **Hours:** 11 am-3:30 pm, Sun 8 am-2:30 pm. Closed major holidays. **Reservations:** accepted. **Features:** Representative of dishes that might grace the seasonally inspired menu are pear and goat cheese salad, Vermont cheddar and apple-smoked bacon sandwich and Black Forest meatloaf. Homemade pastries, pies, breads and cakes are delectable. Breakfast is served all day. **Parking:** on-site. **Cards:** DS, MC, VI.

**TIME-LESS DINER**
American
beer & wine only.

Lunch: $5-$16    Dinner: $5-$16    Phone: 603/577-8955
**Location:** Everett Tpke (US 3), exit 8, 6.5 mi w. 1 Craftsman Ln 03031. **Hours:** 6 am-9 pm, Fri & Sat-10 pm. Closed: 11/25, 12/25. **Features:** The newly built eatery was intended to replicate an old-fashioned diner, and it does via its long luncheon counter, chrome-edged Formica tables and sparkling vinyl booths. The menu lists fries with brown gravy, steak tips, a Monte Cristo sandwich and other classics. Casual dress; **Parking:** on-site. **Cards:** AX, DC, DS, MC, VI.

# ANDOVER

### ——— WHERE TO STAY ———

**HIGHLAND LAKE INN BED & BREAKFAST**
Historic Bed & Breakfast

Phone: 603/735-6426
All Year [BP]    1P: $90-$130    2P: $90-$130    XP: $30
**Location:** I-93, exit 17, 15.5 mi w on US 4, 3.6 mi ne on SR 11E, then 1.5 mi w. 32 Maple St 03231 (PO Box 164, EAST ANDOVER). Fax: 603/735-5355. **Facility:** This handsome Colonial farmhouse dating from 1760 is convenient to a lake for summer and winter recreation. Smoke free premises. 10 one-bedroom standard units. 3 stories (no elevator), interior corridors. *Bath:* shower only. **Parking:** on-site. **Terms:** office hours 9 am-8 pm, age restrictions may apply, 14 day cancellation notice-fee imposed. **Guest Services:** TV in common area. **Cards:** AX, DC, MC, VI. **Special Amenities:** free full breakfast and free local telephone calls.

SOME UNITS

# Know Your Future

--------- WHERE TO DINE ---------

**THE POTTER PLACE INN & RESTAURANT**  Historic          **Dinner:** $17-$28                    **Phone:** 603/735-5141

American

**Location:** I-93, exit 17, 18 mi w on US 4, then just s. 88 Depot St 03216. **Hours:** 5:30 pm-9 pm. Closed: 12/25; also Sun & Mon. **Reservations:** suggested. **Features:** Enjoy casually elegant dining in the historic Potter Place section of Andover. The ultimate dining experience awaits you, featuring uniquely prepared gourmet meats and seafood with an extensive wine list. Casual dress; cocktails. **Parking:** on-site. **Cards:** AX, DS, MC, VI.

# ANTRIM pop. 1,398

--------- WHERE TO DINE ---------

**THE MAPLEHURST INN & RESTAURANT**          **Lunch:** $5-$12          **Dinner:** $12-$22          **Phone:** 603/588-8000

American

**Location:** On SR 202; center; in The Maplehurst Inn. 67 Main St 03440. **Hours:** 5 pm-8 pm, Wed noon-2 pm; Sunday brunch 10 am-2 pm. Closed: 12/25; also Mon & Tues. **Reservations:** accepted. **Features:** In a 200-year-old building, the Victorian-style room coexists with The Tavern, a separate, comfortable lounge with a brick fireplace. Among restaurant specialties are prime rib, seafood specials, pasta, vegetarian fare, salads and homemade soups. Casual dress; cocktails. **Parking:** on-site. **Cards:** MC, VI.

# ASHLAND

--------- WHERE TO STAY ---------

**COMFORT INN**          *Book at aaa.com*                                        **Phone:** (603)968-7668

Small-scale Hotel

| | | | | |
|---|---|---|---|---|
| 7/1-10/31 [CP] | 1P: $69-$150 | 2P: $69-$150 | XP: $10 | F18 |
| 5/1-6/30 [CP] | 1P: $59-$99 | 2P: $59-$99 | XP: $10 | F18 |
| 11/1-4/30 [CP] | 1P: $49-$89 | 2P: $49-$89 | XP: $10 | F18 |

**Location:** I-93, exit 24 (SR 25 and US 3). 53 West St 03217. Fax: 603/968-9527. **Facility:** 40 one-bedroom standard units. 3 stories (no elevator), interior corridors. **Parking:** on-site. **Terms:** 2 night minimum stay - weekends in summer, 7 day cancellation notice, weekends in summer, [ECP] meal plan available. **Amenities:** high-speed Internet, irons, hair dryers. **Pool(s):** heated outdoor. **Business Services:** meeting rooms. **Cards:** AX, DC, DS, JC, MC, VI. *(See color ad below)*

SOME UNITS
ASK SD ⊞ ⊟ ⊟ / X ⊞ ⊟ /

**GLYNN HOUSE INN**                                                    **Phone:** (603)968-3775

Historic Bed & Breakfast

| | | | | |
|---|---|---|---|---|
| 5/28-10/24 | 1P: $119-$239 | 2P: $119-$239 | XP: $25 | D12 |
| 5/1-5/27 & 10/25-4/30 | 1P: $119-$209 | 2P: $119-$209 | XP: $25 | D12 |

**Location:** I-93, exit 24 (SR 25 and US 3), 0.8 mi e to flag pole in center of town (Highland), then 0.3 mi nw. Located in a quiet area. 59 Highland St 03217-0719 (PO Box 719, 03217). Fax: 603/968-9415. **Facility:** This attractive inn, which dates from 1895, features handsome furnishings and decor. Smoke free premises. 13 units. 7 one-bedroom standard units, some with whirlpools. 6 one-bedroom suites with whirlpools. 3 stories (no elevator), interior/exterior corridors. *Bath:* combo or shower only. **Parking:** on-site. **Terms:** 2 night minimum stay - weekends, age restrictions may apply, cancellation fee imposed, [BP] meal plan available, package plans - seasonal. **Amenities:** video library. *Some:* CD players, hair dryers. **Cards:** AX, CB, DC, MC, VI.

X VCR DATA PORT

------- *The following lodging was either not evaluated or did not* -------
*meet AAA rating requirements but is listed for your information only.*

**COLD SPRINGS RESORT**                                                    **Phone:** 603/536-4600

[fyi]

Not evaluated. **Location:** North Ashland Rd 03217. Facilities, services, and decor characterize a mid-range property.

--------- WHERE TO DINE ---------

**THE COMMON MAN**          **Lunch:** $5-$9          **Dinner:** $11-$19          **Phone:** 603/968-7030

American

**Location:** I-93, exit 24, 0.5 mi e on US 3. 24 S Main St 03217. **Hours:** 11:30 am-3 & 5-9 pm, Fri & Sat-9:30 pm. Closed: 11/25, 12/24, 12/25. **Features:** The restaurant features a charming decor and pleasant upstairs pub. On the menu are steak, seafood, chicken and vegetarian dishes served in generous portions. Lobster corn chowder is popular at lunch; white chocolate mousse is a specialty. Casual dress; cocktails. **Parking:** on-site. **Cards:** AX, DS, MC, VI.

# BARTLETT

─── **WHERE TO STAY** ───

**THE GRAND SUMMIT RESORT HOTEL CONFERENCE CENTER ATTITASH BEAR PEAK** *Book at aaa.com*

**Phone:** (603)374-1900

All Year        2P: $275-$415      XP: $20      F12

Resort
Small-scale Hotel

**Location:** 2.5 mi e. US 302 03812 (PO Box 308). Fax: 603/374-3040. **Facility:** Guests can ski to resort facilities from this modern hotel at the base of the Bear Peak ski area. Smoke free premises. 143 units. 131 one-bedroom standard units with kitchens. 10 two- and 2 three-bedroom suites ($475-$535) with kitchens, some with whirlpools. 4 stories, interior corridors. **Parking:** on-site. **Terms:** check-in 4:30 pm, 2 night minimum stay - weekends, cancellation fee imposed, [BP] meal plan available, package plans, 4% service charge. **Amenities:** video games (fee), voice mail, irons, hair dryers. *Some:* CD players. **Dining:** 2 restaurants, 7:30 am-9:30 pm; hours vary seasonally, cocktails. **Pool(s):** heated outdoor. **Leisure Activities:** sauna, whirlpools, steamroom, alpine & waterslide, golf driving range, recreation programs, BMX and skating parks, climbing wall, mountain boarding, trampoline, hiking trails, playground, horseshoes, volleyball. *Fee:* downhill & cross country skiing, bicycles, horseback riding, massage, game room. **Guest Services:** gift shop, coin laundry. **Business Services:** conference facilities, fax (fee). **Cards:** AX, DS, MC, VI. *(See color ad below)*

SOME UNITS

**NORTH COLONY MOTEL**

**Phone:** (603)374-6679

Motel

| | | | |
|---|---|---|---|
| 6/18-10/11 | 2P: $49-$149 | XP: $9 | F12 |
| 10/12-4/30 | 2P: $36-$99 | XP: $9 | F12 |
| 5/1-6/17 | 2P: $36-$79 | XP: $9 | F12 |

**Location:** 1.5 mi e on US 302, 1 mi w of Attitash Mountain. US 302 03812 (PO Box 1). Fax: 603/374-6216. **Facility:** 16 units. 14 one-bedroom standard units. 2 cottages ($69-$169), 1 story, exterior corridors. **Parking:** on-site. **Terms:** office hours 7 am-10 pm, 10 day cancellation notice-fee imposed. **Pool(s):** heated outdoor. **Leisure Activities:** cross country skiing, badminton, grills, picnic area, playground, basketball, volleyball. **Cards:** DC, MC, VI. **Special Amenities:** free local telephone calls and free room upgrade (subject to availability with advanced reservations). *(See color ad p 373)*

SOME UNITS

**THE VILLAGER MOTEL**
Phone: 603/374-2742

△△△ (SAVE)

▽▽▽ ▽▽▽
Motel

| | | | |
|---|---|---|---|
| 6/25-10/12 | 1P: $59-$99 | 2P: $89-$159 | XP: $10 F12 |
| 10/13-4/30 | 1P: $39-$99 | 2P: $49-$139 | XP: $10 F12 |
| 5/1-6/24 | 1P: $39-$89 | 2P: $49-$119 | XP: $10 F12 |

**Location:** 1 mi e on US 302; 1.3 mi w of Attitash Mountain. US 302 03812 (PO Box 427). Fax: 603/374-1965. **Facility:** 37 units. 33 one-bedroom standard units, some with efficiencies. 1 two-bedroom suite ($99-$169) with kitchen. 3 cabins ($69-$139). 1 story, exterior corridors. **Parking:** on-site. **Terms:** office hours 7:30 am-8 pm, 10 day cancellation notice-fee imposed, pets ($8 extra charge, with prior approval). **Pool(s):** heated outdoor. **Leisure Activities:** fishing, charcoal grills, picnic tables, hiking trails, playground, volleyball. **Guest Services:** coin laundry. **Cards:** AX, DS, MC, VI. **Special Amenities:** free local telephone calls and free newspaper. *(See color ad p 330)*

SOME UNITS

🐕 ⚓ 🚫 ⊗ 🗄 / 📺 /
FEE

---

*The following lodging was either not evaluated or did not meet AAA rating requirements but is listed for your information only.*

ATTITASH MOUNTAIN RESORT
Phone: 603/374-6500

[fyi]

Not evaluated. **Location:** Rt 302, Box 358 03812. Facilities, services, and decor characterize a mid-range property.

# BEDFORD

## ——— WHERE TO STAY ———

**BEDFORD VILLAGE INN**
Phone: (603)472-2001

△△△ (SAVE)

▽▽▽ ▽▽▽
Historic
Country Inn

| | | | |
|---|---|---|---|
| All Year | 1P: $205-$355 | 2P: $205-$355 | XP: $35 |

**Location:** On SR 101, 0.3 mi w of jct SR 114. Located in a rural area. 2 Village Inn Ln 03110. Fax: 603/472-2379. **Facility:** Housed.in a converted dairy barn dating from 1810, this country inn offers elegantly appointed guest rooms and common areas. 14 units. 8 one-bedroom standard units with whirlpools. 6 one-bedroom suites with whirlpools. 3 stories, interior/exterior corridors. **Parking:** on-site. **Terms:** 10 day cancellation notice, [BP], [CP] & [MAP] meal plans available. **Amenities:** voice mail, irons, hair dryers. **Dining:** restaurant, see separate listing. **Guest Services:** valet laundry. **Business Services:** meeting rooms. **Cards:** AX, DC, DS, MC, VI.

SOME UNITS

🍴 ♨️ 📺 DATA PORT 💻 / ⊗ 🗄 /

---

**HILL-BROOK MOTEL**
Phone: (603)472-3788

△△△ (SAVE)

▽▽▽
Motel

| | | | |
|---|---|---|---|
| All Year | 1P: $45-$70 | 2P: $60-$85 | XP: $10 F3 |

**Location:** On SR 101, 2.5 mi w of jct SR 114. 250 SR 101 03110. **Facility:** 18 units. 17 one-bedroom standard units, some with efficiencies or kitchens. 1 one-bedroom suite ($65-$95) with kitchen. 1 story, exterior corridors. **Parking:** on-site. **Terms:** office hours 7 am-10 pm, cancellation fee imposed, weekly rates available. **Cards:** AX, DS, MC, VI. **Special Amenities:** preferred room (subject to availability with advanced reservations).

SOME UNITS

DATA PORT / ⊗ 🗄 📺 💻 /

## ——— WHERE TO DINE ———

**BEDFORD VILLAGE INN RESTAURANT** Historic Lunch: $10-$20 Dinner: $18-$32 Phone: 603/472-2001

△△△

▽▽▽ ▽▽▽
Continental

**Location:** On SR 101, 0.3 mi w of jct SR 114; in Bedford Village Inn. 2 Village Inn Ln 03110. **Hours:** 7-10:30 am, 11:30-2 & 5:30-9:30 pm, Thurs & Fri-10 pm, Sat 8-10:30 am, 11:30-2 & 5:30-10 pm, Sun 8-10 am, 11-2 & 5:30-8 pm. **Closed:** 12/25. **Reservations:** suggested. **Features:** This 1810 farmhouse has been transformed into an elegant setting with authentic antiques and several intimate dining rooms. The menu is creative and offers a variety of dishes and one-of-a-kind dessert and pastry. Semi-formal attire; cocktails. **Parking:** on-site. **Cards:** AX, CB, DC, MC, VI.

🍸 ⊗

---

**CARRABBA'S ITALIAN GRILL**
Dinner: $8-$19
Phone: 603/641-0004

▽▽▽ ▽▽▽
Italian

**Location:** Jct US 3 and I-293. 2 Upjohn St 03110. **Hours:** 4 pm-10 pm, Fri-11 pm, Sat 3 pm-11 pm, Sun 3 pm-9 pm. **Closed:** 11/25, 12/25. **Features:** The trendy eatery serves terrific cuisine. Some upscale diner-style seating overlooks the activity in the open kitchen. Casual dress; cocktails. **Parking:** on-site. **Cards:** AX, DC, DS, MC, VI.

🅼 ⊗

---

**CHEN YANG LI CHINESE RESTAURANT**
Lunch: $6-$12
Dinner: $12-$22
Phone: 603/641-6922

▽▽▽ ▽▽▽
Chinese

**Location:** US 3, just n of jct I-293; in Woodbury Court Plaza. 124 S River Rd 03110. **Hours:** 11:30 am-10 pm, Fri & Sat-11 pm. **Reservations:** suggested. **Features:** The exceptional restaurant prepares many house specialties and standard favorites. The wonderfully descriptive menu also lists a nice selection of sushi items. An elegant atmosphere and helpful staff make for an enjoyable experience. Casual dress; cocktails. **Parking:** on-site. **Cards:** AX, DC, DS, MC, VI.

🅼 🍸 ⊗

---

**C R SPARKS RESTAURANT & BAR**
Lunch: $7-$12
Dinner: $14-$28
Phone: 603/647-7275

▽▽▽ ▽▽▽
American

**Location:** Jct I-293 and US 3, 0.5 mi n on US 3, then just w. 18 Kilton Rd 03110. **Hours:** 11:30 am-3 & 4-9:30 pm, Fri & Sat-10:30 pm, Sun 2 pm-8:30 pm. **Closed:** 1/1, 12/25. **Reservations:** suggested. **Features:** Fresh contemporary decor marks the dining room. On the menu are well-prepared and nicely presented American dishes with a Mediterranean accent. Meals include olive oil, herbed whipped butter and olive spread presented with warm bread. Creative first-course and main-dish items are prepared with fresh ingredients. Homemade desserts are displayed on a tiered tray presented by the server and described in detail. Dressy casual; cocktails. **Parking:** on-site. **Cards:** AX, DC, DS, MC, VI.

🍸 ⊗

---

**PANERA BREAD**
Lunch: $3-$8
Dinner: $3-$8
Phone: 603/641-0500

▽▽▽
Deli/Subs
Sandwiches

**Location:** SR 101, exit 3, 1 mi n. 7 Colby Ct 03110. **Hours:** 6:30 am-9 pm, Sun 7:30 am-7 pm. **Closed:** 11/25, 12/25. **Features:** The chain sets the standard for healthy quick-serve fare. Soups are fresh, bread is made daily, and the sandwiches are creative. Casual dress. **Parking:** on-site. **Cards:** AX, MC, VI.

⊗

**SHORTY'S MEXICAN ROADHOUSE**  **Lunch:** $5-$16  **Dinner:** $5-$16  **Phone:** 603/472-3656
Mexican
**Location:** 1.9 mi w on SR 101, jct SR 114. 230 Rt 101 W 03110. **Hours:** 11:30 am-10 pm, Fri & Sat-11 pm, Sun noon-10 pm. Closed: 3/27, 11/25, 12/25. **Features:** Well-prepared specialties include nachos, quesadillas, fajitas, chimichangas, burritos and enchiladas, as well as chili, soups and pasta. The colorful decor is casual, and the serving staff is attentive. Casual dress; cocktails. **Parking:** on-site. **Cards:** AX, DC, DS, MC, VI.

**TAIPEI & TOKYO CHINESE & JAPANESE RESTAURANT**  **Lunch:** $6-$22  **Dinner:** $10-$22  **Phone:** 603/622-2588
Japanese
**Location:** SR 101, exit 3, 1 mi n. 7 Colby Ct, Unit 6 03110. **Hours:** 11:30 am-10 pm, Fri & Sat-11 pm, Sun noon-10 pm. Closed major holidays. **Reservations:** accepted. **Features:** In Colby Court Plaza, the restaurant presents a lengthy menu of Japanese and Chinese cuisine. Patrons also can choose selections from the extensive sushi bar. Casual dress; cocktails. **Parking:** on-site. **Cards:** AX, MC, VI.

**T-BONES GREAT AMERICAN EATERY**  **Lunch:** $6-$17  **Dinner:** $6-$17  **Phone:** 603/641-6100
American
**Location:** Jct I-293 and US 3, 1 mi n on US 3. 25 S River Rd 03110. **Hours:** 11:30 am-10 pm, Fri & Sat-11 pm. Closed: 11/25, 12/25. **Features:** One of three locations, the local eatery prepares burgers, steaks, sandwiches and more. All menu items are made from scratch on the premises. Casual dress; cocktails. **Parking:** on-site. **Cards:** AX, DS, MC, VI.

**WEATHERVANE**  **Lunch:** $6-$10  **Dinner:** $7-$18  **Phone:** 603/472-2749
Seafood
**Location:** Jct SR 114, 3.7 mi w. 393 US 101 W 03102. **Hours:** 11 am-9 pm, Fri & Sat-9:30 pm. Closed: 11/25, 12/25; also for dinner 12/24. **Features:** The simple and casual family-friendly restaurant serves a wide variety of seafood, chicken, steak, burgers, pasta and chowder. Portions are ample, and service is pleasant. Casual dress; cocktails. **Parking:** on-site. **Cards:** AX, MC, VI.

**ZINGARELLA'S ITALIAN GRILL & CAFE**  **Lunch:** $6-$12  **Dinner:** $10-$23  **Phone:** 603/471-1888
Italian
**Location:** On SR 101, 2.5 mi w of jct SR 114; in The Bedford Village Shoppes. 170 SR 101 03110. **Hours:** 11 am-9 pm, Thurs & Fri-10 pm, Sat 4 pm-10 pm, Sun 3 pm-9 pm. Closed: 11/25, 12/25. **Features:** The bistro prepares wonderful homemade pasta, sauces and pastries. An accordion player strolls through the dining room each evening. Casual dress; cocktails. **Parking:** on-site. **Cards:** AX, DC, DS, MC, VI.

# BELMONT

### ——— WHERE TO DINE ———

**CHINA GARDEN**  **Lunch:** $6-$16  **Dinner:** $8-$16  **Phone:** 603/524-6340
Chinese
**Location:** On US 3; center. 200 Daniel Webster Hwy 03220. **Hours:** 11:30 am-8:30 pm. Closed: 11/25, 12/25; also Tues. **Features:** Representative of traditional fare are sweet and sour dishes, chop suey, chow mein and the pu pu platter. The casual setting is comfortable for families. Casual dress; cocktails. **Parking:** on-site. **Cards:** AX, DS, MC, VI.

**HICKORY STICK FARM**  Country Inn  **Dinner:** $13-$22  **Phone:** 603/524-3333
American
**Location:** I-93, exit 20 (US 3), 5 mi n, then right on Union Rd, follow signs. 66 Bean Hill Rd 03220. **Hours:** 5 pm-9 pm, Sun also 10 am-2 pm; Fri & Sat 5 pm-9 pm, Sun 10 am-2 pm 10/11-5/14. Closed: Mon; Tues 10/12-5/13. **Reservations:** suggested. **Features:** A delicious slow-roasted duckling with orange sherry sauce is the house specialty at the Hickory Stick, a family-owned restaurant serving guests since 1950. It's in a charming country farmhouse with antiques, pine floors and two beautiful fireplaces. Casual dress; cocktails. **Parking:** on-site. **Cards:** AX, DS, MC, VI.

# BETHLEHEM

### ——— WHERE TO STAY ———

**ADAIR COUNTRY INN**  **Phone:** (603)444-2600
Historic Country Inn

| |  |  |  |
|---|---|---|---|
| 10/24-4/30 [BP] | 1P: $180-$350 | 2P: $180-$350 | XP: $35 |
| 9/17-10/23 [BP] | 1P: $225-$345 | 2P: $225-$345 | XP: $35 |
| 5/1-9/16 [BP] | 1P: $175-$295 | 2P: $175-$295 | XP: $35 |

**Location:** I-93, exit 40, just e on US 302. Located in a quiet area. 80 Guider Ln 03574. Fax: 603/444-4823. **Facility:** Furnished with antiques and reproductions, this 1927 Georgian Colonial is on 200 wooded acres with ponds, hills, lawns and perennial gardens. Smoke free premises. 10 units. 9 one-bedroom standard units, some with whirlpools. 1 cottage ($355-$400). 3 stories (no elevator), interior corridors. **Parking:** on-site, winter plug-ins. **Terms:** 2 night minimum stay - weekends, 15 day cancellation notice-fee imposed, package plans - 11/1-5/31, no pets allowed (owner's cat on premises). **Amenities:** video library, CD players, hair dryers. Some: irons. Dining: 5:30 pm-9 pm; closed Mon, Tues, 11/1-12/10 & 4/1-5/25; dinner by reservation in season, wine/beer only. **Leisure Activities:** golf privileges, tennis court, snowshoes, recreation programs. **Business Services:** fax (fee). **Cards:** AX, MC, VI. **Special Amenities:** free full breakfast and free local telephone calls.

SOME UNITS

**THE GRANDE VICTORIAN COTTAGE**  **Phone:** 603/869-5755
Bed & Breakfast

| |  |  |  |
|---|---|---|---|
| 5/25-10/18 | 1P: $75-$125 | 2P: $75-$135 | XP: $25 |

**Location:** I-93, exit 40, 2.5 mi e on US 302. 53 Berkeley St 03574 (PO Box 426). **Facility:** Antique furnishings and a circular porch overlooking well-tended grounds set the tone at this restored turn-of-the-20th-century Victorian mansion. Smoke free premises. 8 one-bedroom standard units. 3 stories (no elevator), interior corridors. Bath: some shared or private, combo, shower or tub only. **Parking:** on-site. **Terms:** open 5/25-10/18, check-in 4 pm, age restrictions may apply, 14 day cancellation notice-fee imposed.

SOME UNITS

## THE MULBURN INN AT BETHLEHEM

**Phone:** (603)869-3389

| | | |
|---|---|---|
| 9/13-10/25 | 1P: $120-$175 | 2P: $125-$175 | XP: $45 | D18 |
| 5/1-9/12, 10/26-11/10 & 12/1-4/5 | 1P: $85-$135 | 2P: $90-$135 | XP: $25 | D18 |

**Historic Bed & Breakfast**

**Location:** I-93, exit 40, 3.5 mi e on US 302. 2370 Main St 03574. Fax: 603/869-5633. **Facility:** The large, elm-tree-shaded verandas at this Tudor-style 1908 summer estate overlook a sprawling lawn. Smoke free premises. 7 one-bedroom standard units. 3 stories (no elevator), interior corridors. *Bath:* combo or shower only. **Parking:** on-site, winter plug-ins. **Terms:** open 5/1-11/10 & 12/1-4/5, check-in 4 pm, 2 night minimum stay - weekends, 14 day cancellation notice-fee imposed, [BP] meal plan available, pets ($20 fee, with prior approval). **Amenities:** hair dryers. **Leisure Activities:** cross country skiing, snowmobiling, exercise room, volleyball. **Guest Services:** TV in common area, gift shop. **Business Services:** meeting rooms, PC, fax. **Cards:** MC, VI.

---

## THE NORTHERN STAR INN    *Book at aaa.com*

**Phone:** 603/869-4395

| | | |
|---|---|---|
| All Year [BP] | 1P: $60-$105 | 2P: $60-$105 | XP: $25 | D12 |

**Bed & Breakfast**

**Location:** On SR 142, just n of jct US 302. 157 Maple St 03574. Fax: 603/869-4351. **Facility:** Designated smoking area. 14 one-bedroom standard units. 2 stories (no elevator), interior corridors. *Bath:* combo or shower only. **Parking:** on-site. **Terms:** 7 day cancellation notice. **Leisure Activities:** snowmobiling, badminton, board games, horseshoes. **Business Services:** meeting rooms. **Cards:** DS, MC, VI.

---

## THE WAYSIDE INN

**Phone:** (603)869-3364

| | | |
|---|---|---|
| 5/14-10/17 & 12/3-3/20 [BP] | 1P: $88-$128 | 2P: $98-$138 | XP: $18 | D12 |

**Motel**

**Location:** I-93, exit 40, 6.3 mi e on US 302. 3738 Main St 03574 (PO Box 480). Fax: 603/869-5765. **Facility:** 26 one-bedroom standard units, some with whirlpools. 2 stories (no elevator), interior/exterior corridors. **Parking:** on-site, winter plug-ins. **Terms:** open 5/14-10/17 & 12/3-3/20, 10 day cancellation notice, [MAP] meal plan available, no pets allowed (owner's pets on premises). **Amenities:** *Some:* hair dryers. **Dining:** Riverview Restaurant at the Wayside Inn, see separate listing. **Leisure Activities:** fishing, cross country skiing, snowmobiling, horseshoes. **Fee:** massage. **Cards:** AX, DS, MC, VI.

---

### ———— WHERE TO DINE ————

## LLOYD HILL'S RESTAURANT

**Lunch:** $5-$9          **Dinner:** $8-$20          **Phone:** 603/869-2141

**American**

**Location:** On US 302; center. 2061 Main St 03574. **Hours:** 5 pm-9 pm, Fri from 11 am, Sat from 10 am, Sun from 8 am. Closed: 11/25, 12/25; also Mon. **Reservations:** suggested. **Features:** This restaurant offers well-prepared and imaginative dishes with freshly made soup and French bread, sandwiches, salads, seafood, steaks, and breakfast to 2 pm daily. Casual atmosphere, friendly service, ample portions, terrace dining in season are definite perks. Casual dress; cocktails. **Parking:** street. **Cards:** DS, MC, VI.

---

## RIVERVIEW RESTAURANT AT THE WAYSIDE INN    Country Inn

**Dinner:** $11-$20          **Phone:** 603/869-3364

**Continental**

**Location:** I-93, exit 40, 6.3 mi e on US 302; in The Wayside Inn. 3738 Main St (Rt 302) 03574. **Hours:** Open 5/15-10/15 & 12/26-3/31; 6 pm-8 pm, Fri & Sat-9 pm. Closed: Mon 5/15-10/15 & Sun-Thurs 12/26-3/31. **Reservations:** suggested. **Features:** The Riverview's menu features Swiss specialties such as Wiener schnitzel and browned shredded potatoes, as well as steak, salad and terrific dessert. The informal and comfortable dining room offers pleasant views of the river. Service is friendly. Casual dress; cocktails. **Parking:** on-site. **Cards:** AX, DS, MC, VI.

---

## ROSA FLAMINGO'S

**Lunch:** $5-$10          **Dinner:** $10-$20          **Phone:** 603/869-3111

**Italian**

**Location:** I-93, exit 40, 3 mi e on US 302; in village center. **Hours:** 4 pm-9 pm, Fri-Sun 11:30 am-10 pm. Closed: 3/27, 11/25, 12/25. **Reservations:** suggested. **Features:** This family-style restaurant features good food and friendly, attentive service. The varied menu offers pizza, pasta, pork tenderloin, beef, seafood and chicken dishes and fresh vegetables and salad. Lounge and smoking area are on the lower level. Casual dress; cocktails. **Parking:** on-site. **Cards:** AX, MC, VI.

---

# BRADFORD

### ———— WHERE TO STAY ————

## CANDLELITE INN BED & BREAKFAST

**Phone:** (603)938-5571

| | | |
|---|---|---|
| All Year [BP] | 1P: $95-$140 | 2P: $105-$145 |

**Bed & Breakfast**

**Location:** 0.3 mi n on SR 114, from SR 103. 5 Greenhouse Ln 03221. Fax: 603/938-2564. **Facility:** Smoke free premises. 6 one-bedroom standard units. 2 stories (no elevator), interior/exterior corridors. *Bath:* combo or shower only. **Parking:** on-site. **Terms:** office hours 8 am-10 pm, 2-3 night minimum stay - seasonal, 14 day cancellation notice-fee imposed. **Amenities:** hair dryers. **Cards:** AX, DC, DS, MC, VI.

---

## ROSEWOOD COUNTRY INN

**Phone:** 603/938-5253

| | | |
|---|---|---|
| All Year [BP] | 1P: $119-$279 | 2P: $119-$279 | XP: $25 |

**Historic Bed & Breakfast**

**Location:** US 89, exit 9, 7 mi sw on SR 103, 2.5 mi s on Main St, follow signs. 67 Pleasant View Rd 03221. **Facility:** Period oil paintings decorate this 1896 Victorian-style inn, which is on manicured grounds and offers many added amenities. Smoke free premises. 11 one-bedroom standard units, some with whirlpools. 3 stories (no elevator), interior corridors. *Bath:* combo or shower only. **Parking:** on-site. **Terms:** office hours 7 am-10 pm, 2 night minimum stay - weekends, age restrictions may apply, 14 day cancellation notice-fee imposed. **Amenities:** video library, hair dryers. **Cards:** AX, DC, DS, MC, VI.

## —— WHERE TO DINE ——

**BRADFORD JUNCTION RESTAURANT & BAKERY**        **Lunch:** $2-$7        **Phone:** 603/938-2424
▽
American
**Location:** On SR 114. 2370 SR 114 03221. **Hours:** 11:30 am-2:30 pm. Closed: 12/25. **Features:** The restaurant combines cheap eats and good comfort foods all in one. An attached caboose serves as one of the dining rooms. Casual dress. **Parking:** on-site.        ⊠

# BRETTON WOODS

## —— WHERE TO STAY ——

**ABOVE THE NOTCH MOTOR INN**        **Phone:** 603/846-5156
▽▽
Motel
All Year        1P: $63-$68        2P: $63-$78        XP: $7
**Location:** Jct US 3, 4 mi e. 2058 US 302 03595 (PO Box 429). **Fax:** 603/846-2183. **Facility:** 13 one-bedroom standard units. 1 story, exterior corridors. **Parking:** on-site, winter plug-ins. **Terms:** 5 day cancellation notice. **Leisure Activities:** snowmobiling, hiking trails, playground. **Guest Services:** area transportation.
**Cards:** DS, MC, VI.
SOME UNITS
🛎 ⊠ 🅰 📺 / ⊠ /

**THE BRETTON ARMS COUNTRY INN**        **Phone:** (603)278-1000
▽▽▽
Historic
Country Inn
All Year [BP]        1P: $100-$339        2P: $110-$349        XP: $20        F4
**Location:** Center. US 302 03575. **Fax:** 603/278-8868. **Facility:** This charming 1896 inn offers an intimate ambience. Designated smoking area. 33 units. 30 one-bedroom standard units. 3 one-bedroom suites ($178-$429). 3 stories, interior corridors. **Parking:** on-site, winter plug-ins. **Terms:** 2 night minimum stay - weekends, 15 day cancellation notice-fee imposed, package plans. **Amenities:** high-speed Internet (fee), voice mail, irons, hair dryers. **Leisure Activities:** racquetball courts, ice skating, recreation programs, hiking trails, jogging, playground, exercise room. **Fee:** golf-27 holes, 15 tennis courts, downhill & cross country skiing, bicycles, horseback riding, massage. **Guest Services:** valet laundry, area transportation. **Business Services:** meeting rooms. **Cards:** AX, DS, MC, VI.
*(See color ad p 353 & p 380)*
🛎 🍽 🅰 ⊠ ⊠ 🅰 DATA PORT

**THE LODGE AT BRETTON WOODS**        **Phone:** (603)278-1000
▽▽▽
Motel
All Year        1P: $79-$219        2P: $79-$219
**Location:** Center. 2652 US 302 03575. **Fax:** 603/278-8898. **Facility:** 50 one-bedroom standard units. 2 stories (no elevator), exterior corridors. **Parking:** on-site. **Terms:** 2 night minimum stay - weekends, 15 day cancellation notice-fee imposed, package plans. **Amenities:** high-speed Internet (fee), voice mail. **Pool(s):** heated indoor. **Leisure Activities:** sauna, whirlpool, racquetball courts, ice skating, bicycles, hiking trails, horseback riding. **Fee:** golf-27 holes, 15 tennis courts, downhill & cross country skiing, massage, game room. **Guest Services:** coin laundry, area transportation. **Business Services:** meeting rooms. **Cards:** AX, DS, MC, VI. *(See color ad p 353 & p 380)*
SOME UNITS
🛎 🍽 🅰 🏊 🏊 ⊠ DATA PORT / ⊠ VCR 🖥
FEE

**THE MOUNT WASHINGTON HOTEL & RESORT**        *Book at aaa.com*        **Phone:** (603)278-1000
▽▽▽
Classic Historic
Large-scale Hotel
All Year [MAP]        1P: $190-$959        2P: $230-$999        XP: $70        F4
**Location:** Center. US 302 03575. **Fax:** 603/278-8838. **Facility:** Built in 1902, this hotel is on expansive, manicured grounds and offers mountain views. Designated smoking area. 200 units. 195 one-bedroom standard units, some with whirlpools. 5 one-bedroom suites ($800-$1869). 5 stories, interior corridors. *Bath:* combo or shower only. **Parking:** on-site and valet. **Terms:** 2 night minimum stay - weekends, 15 day cancellation notice-fee imposed, package plans. **Amenities:** high-speed Internet, voice mail, irons, hair dryers. **Dining:** restaurant, see separate listing. **Pool(s):** heated outdoor, heated indoor. **Leisure Activities:** sauna, whirlpool, racquetball courts, ice skating, recreation programs, hiking trails, jogging, playground. **Fee:** golf-27 holes, 15 tennis courts, downhill & cross country skiing, bicycles, horseback riding, massage, game room. **Guest Services:** gift shop, valet and coin laundry, area transportation. **Business Services:** conference facilities, fax. **Cards:** AX, DS, MC, VI. *(See color ad p 353 & ad p 91 & color ad p 380)*
SOME UNITS
🛎 🍽 🅰 🏊 🏊 ⊠ ⊠ DATA PORT / 🅰 VCR 🖥 📺
FEE

**THE TOWNHOMES AT BRETTON WOODS**        **Phone:** (603)278-2000
▽▽▽
Resort
Condominium
All Year        1P: $149-$659        2P: $149-$659
**Location:** Center. Rt 302 03575. **Fax:** 603/278-8828. **Facility:** These accommodations are at the base of a ski hill; all have fireplaces and kitchens. 70 vacation homes, some with pools and some with whirlpools. 1-3 stories (no elevator), exterior corridors. **Parking:** on-site. **Terms:** check-in 4 pm, 2 night minimum stay, 15 day cancellation notice-fee imposed, weekly rates available, package plans. **Amenities:** video library (fee), voice mail, irons, hair dryers. *Some:* DVD players, CD players. **Leisure Activities:** sauna, whirlpool, steamrooms, racquetball courts, downhill skiing, snowmobiling, ice skating, horseback riding, exercise room. **Fee:** golf-27 holes, 15 tennis courts, cross country skiing, massage. **Guest Services:** gift shop, area transportation. **Business Services:** meeting rooms. **Cards:** AX, DS, MC, VI. *(See color ad p 353 & p 380)*
SOME UNITS
🛎 🅰 🏊 ⊠ VCR DATA PORT 🖥 🖨 / ⊠ 🅰

## —— WHERE TO DINE ——

**THE DINING ROOM AT THE MOUNT WASHINGTON**        **Dinner:** $60        **Phone:** 603/278-1000
▽▽▽ ▽▽▽
Continental
**Location:** Center. US 302 03575. **Hours:** 6 pm-9 pm. **Reservations:** suggested. **Features:** This elegant dining room has panoramic views of the mountains and the resort's lush grounds, which are breathtaking. Guests will appreciate that each dish is prepared with a creative flair and delectable flavor. Semi-formal attire; cocktails. **Parking:** on-site and valet. **Cards:** AX, DS, MC, VI.        🍸 ⊠

FABYAN'S STATION RESTAURANT & LOUNGE | **Lunch:** $6-$20 | **Dinner:** $6-$20 | **Phone:** 603/278-2222

American
DS, MC, VI.

**Location:** Jct of access road to Cog Railway. US 302 03575. **Hours:** 11:30 am-10 pm. **Reservations:** accepted. **Features:** This restaurant, located in a restored railroad station in the heart of the White Mountains, is well-known for its nachos, burgers, ribs and seafood dishes. The decor displays train memorabilia, original woodwork and stained-glass windows. Good service. Casual dress; cocktails. **Parking:** on-site. **Cards:** AX,

# BRIDGEWATER

## ———— WHERE TO STAY ————

THE INN ON NEWFOUND LAKE | | | **Phone:** (603)744-9111

| | 6/1-10/18 | 1P: $135-$150 | 2P: $135-$150 | XP: $30 |
| | 5/1-5/31 & 10/19-4/30 | 1P: $105-$135 | 2P: $105-$135 | XP: $30 |

Historic
Country Inn

**Location:** 5 mi n of Bristol on US 3A. 1030 Mayhew Tpke 03222. Fax: 603/744-3894. **Facility:** This large inn with an annex dating to 1840 offers good lake views. Designated smoking area. 28 units. 26 one-bedroom standard units. 2 one-bedroom suites ($295-$345). 4 stories (no elevator), interior corridors. *Bath:* some shared or private, combo or shower only. **Parking:** on-site. **Terms:** office hours 9 am-11 pm, 2 night minimum stay - weekends, age restrictions may apply, cancellation fee imposed. **Leisure Activities:** whirlpool, boat dock, exercise room. **Cards:** AX, DC, MC, VI.

# BRISTOL pop. 1,670

## ———— WHERE TO DINE ————

CU NA MARA IRISH RESTAURANT | **Lunch:** $7-$14 | **Dinner:** $7-$14 | **Phone:** 603/744-6336

Irish

**Location:** On US 3A. 11 Hobart Rd 03222. **Hours:** 11 am-9 pm. Closed: 12/25; also Tues. **Features:** An Irish pub is an unusual find along the busy state highway. The menu includes beer-battered fish and chips, shepherd's pie, Guinness beef stew and bangers and mash among the sampling of homemade items. Enjoy traditional Irish music on Sunday evening with no cover charge from 4 pm-8 pm. Casual dress; cocktails. **Parking:** on-site. **Cards:** AX, DC, DS, MC, VI.

# BROOKLINE

## ———— WHERE TO DINE ————

GRIFFING'S RIVERSIDE RESTAURANT | **Lunch:** $6-$15 | **Dinner:** $6-$15 | **Phone:** 603/673-4698

American

**Location:** 1 mi s on SR 13 from jct SR 130. 99 SR 13 S 03033. **Hours:** 11:30 am-8 pm, Sun from 9 am. Closed: 11/25, 12/25; also Mon. **Reservations:** accepted. **Features:** The restaurant features colorful, eclectic decor, with old signs, nostalgic items and country appointments. The varied menu offers well-prepared seafood platters of shrimp, haddock and scallops, as well as steak and chicken. A pub is on site. Casual dress; cocktails. **Parking:** on-site. **Cards:** AX, DS, MC, VI.

# CAMPTON

## ———— WHERE TO STAY ————

SUPER 8 MOTEL | *Book at aaa.com* | | **Phone:** 603/536-3520

Property failed to provide current rates

Small-scale Hotel

**Location:** I-93, exit 27, just ne. 1513 US 3 03223. Fax: 603/536-8114. **Facility:** 100 one-bedroom standard units. 2 stories (no elevator), interior corridors. **Parking:** on-site. **Terms:** office hours 6:30 am-midnight, pets ($10 extra charge). **Pool(s):** heated indoor. **Leisure Activities:** sauna, whirlpool. **Guest Services:** coin laundry. **Business Services:** meeting rooms. *(See color ad p 354)*

SOME UNITS
FEE

## ———— WHERE TO DINE ————

THE COUNTRY COW RESTUARANT & BAR | **Lunch:** $6-$9 | **Dinner:** $6-$20 | **Phone:** 603/536-1331

American

**Location:** I-93, exit 27, just ne. 57 Blair Rd 03223. **Hours:** 11:30 am-9 pm, Sun from 8:30 am. Closed: 12/25; also Tues. **Reservations:** accepted. **Features:** The casual eatery affords views of one of the state's historic covered bridges. Steak, chicken and seafood dishes are prepared traditionally. Casual dress; cocktails. **Parking:** on-site. **Cards:** MC, VI.

MAD RIVER TAVERN | **Lunch:** $5-$15 | **Dinner:** $5-$18 | **Phone:** 603/726-4290

American

**Location:** I-93, exit 28, 1 mi e. SR 49 03223. **Hours:** 11:30 am-10 pm, Fri & Sat-11 pm. Closed: 11/25, 12/25; also Tues. **Reservations:** accepted. **Features:** Diners can stop by for a bite of tasty homemade fare on their way to ski or hike the mountains. The pleasant atmosphere makes this a nice place to unwind. Casual dress; cocktails. **Parking:** on-site. **Cards:** AX, DS, MC, VI.

SUNSET GRILL | **Lunch:** $5-$18 | **Dinner:** $5-$18 | **Phone:** 603/726-3108

American

**Location:** I-93, exit 28, 1 mi w on SR 49. US 3 03223. **Hours:** 11:30 am-10 pm, Sun 9 am-9 pm. Closed major holidays; also Mon. **Features:** The traditional menu lists burgers, steaks, salads, pasta, seafood, chicken and more. The decor is accented with antique cameras throughout. Casual dress; cocktails. **Parking:** on-site. **Cards:** AX, DS, MC, VI.

## CANTERBURY CENTER

———— **WHERE TO DINE** ————

THE CREAMERY RESTAURANT **Lunch:** $7-$14 **Dinner:** $41 **Phone:** 603/783-9511
◆◆ ◆◆ **Location:** I-93, exit 18, 6 mi e, follow signs on SR 132, 1 mi n to Shaker Village. 288 Shaker Rd 03224.
**Hours:** Open 5/1-12/31 & 4/1-4/30; 11:30 am-2:30 pm, Fri & Sat candlelight dinner, seating at 6:45 pm by
Regional American reservation only; Sat-Sun only 4/1-4/31 & 11/1-12/31. Closed: 11/25, 12/24, 12/25. **Features:** The
restaurant's recipes, fresh herbs, organic vegetables, furniture and communal seating all are in keeping
with the Shaker tradition. Diners delight in shepherd's pie, chilled strawberry soup, smoked pork ribs and spiced grape drink.
Casual dress; beer & wine only. **Parking:** on-site. **Cards:** AX, MC, VI. ☒

## CENTER SANDWICH

———— **WHERE TO DINE** ————

CORNER HOUSE INN **Lunch:** $5-$10 **Dinner:** $12-$21 **Phone:** 603/284-6219
◆◆ ◆◆ **Location:** Jct SR 109 and 113; center. 22 Main St 03227. **Hours:** 11:30 am-2:30 & 5:30-9:30 pm; 4 pm-10 pm,
Sun 11:30 am-9 pm 11/1-5/31. Closed: 11/25, 12/24, 12/25. **Reservations:** suggested. **Features:** The
Regional American restaurant in a country inn and converted barn has a Colonial-tavern atmosphere and decor. Superb
cuisine focuses primarily on New England seafood; lobster and mushroom soup is a delicious specialty.
Creations by local artists are displayed. Casual dress; cocktails. **Parking:** on-site. **Cards:** AX, DS, MC, VI. ☒

## CHESTERFIELD

———— **WHERE TO STAY** ————

CHESTERFIELD INN **Phone:** 603/256-3211
◆◆◆◆ All Year [BP] 1P: $150-$250 2P: $150-$250 XP: $15 F7
**Location:** I-91, exit 3, 2 mi e on SR 9. 399 Cross Rd 03466 (PO Box 155, 03443). Fax: 603/256-6131. **Facility:** A
Historic farm in the late 18th-century, this restored country inn offers individually decorated guest rooms, many with
Country Inn fireplaces and balconies or patios. Smoke free premises. 15 units. 13 one-bedroom standard units, some
with whirlpools. 2 one-bedroom suites ($200-$225). 2 stories (no elevator), interior/exterior corridors.
**Parking:** on-site. **Terms:** 5 day cancellation notice, pets (with prior approval). **Amenities:** CD players, honor bars, irons, hair
dryers. **Dining:** dining room, see separate listing. **Guest Services:** valet laundry. **Business Services:** meeting rooms.
**Cards:** AX, DC, MC, VI.

SOME UNITS
⟨S⟩ 🐾 ⟨¶⟩ ☒ ⟨DATA PORT⟩ 🔲 🔳 / ⟨VCR⟩ /

———— **WHERE TO DINE** ————

CHESTERFIELD INN **Dinner:** $16-$27 **Phone:** 603/256-3211
◆◆◆◆ **Location:** I-91, exit 3, 2 mi e on SR 9; in Chesterfield Inn. 399 Cross Rd 03443. **Hours:** 5:30 pm-9 pm. Closed:
Sun. **Reservations:** suggested. **Features:** The candlelit restaurant in the elegant, romantic inn features a
American feast for the eyes and palate. Guests enjoy the beautiful view of rolling hills and gorgeous sunsets, as well
as crab cakes with remoulade and chocolate cake with creme anglaise. Dressy casual; cocktails. **Parking:**
on-site. **Cards:** AX, DC, DS, MC, VI. ☒

## CHICHESTER

———— **WHERE TO DINE** ————

WEATHERVANE **Lunch:** $5-$15 **Dinner:** $5-$15 **Phone:** 603/225-4044
◆ **Location:** I-93, exit 15E, on SR 4, 4.7 mi e on I-393, then 0.4 mi e. 379 Dover Rd 03301. **Hours:** 11 am-9 pm; to
9:30 pm in summer. Closed: 11/25, 12/25. **Features:** The popular family restaurant features a good menu
Seafood variety that includes lobster, fried clams and crisp Cape Cod apple-cranberry cobbler. Flavorful dishes are
served in large portions, and servers are friendly and attentive. Casual dress; cocktails. **Parking:** on-site.
**Cards:** AX, MC, VI. ⟨&M⟩ ⟨Y⟩ ☒

## CHOCORUA

———— **WHERE TO STAY** ————

MT CHOCORUA VIEW HOUSE **Phone:** (603)323-8350
◆◆◆ 9/1-10/31 1P: $80-$135 2P: $80-$135 XP: $20
5/1-8/31 & 11/1-3/31 1P: $70-$125 2P: $70-$125 XP: $20
Historic Bed **Location:** On SR 16, 2.8 mi n of jct SR 25. 201 White Mountain Hwy 03817 (PO Box 395). Fax: 603/323-3319.
& Breakfast **Facility:** This Victorian-era inn is furnished with antiques, reproductions and family heirlooms. Smoke free
premises. 7 units. 6 one- and 1 two-bedroom standard units. 3 stories (no elevator), interior corridors. *Bath:*
some shared or private, combo or shower only. **Parking:** on-site. **Terms:** open 5/1-3/31, office hours 8 am-9 pm, 2 night minimum
stay - weekends in summer & 9/15-10/15, age restrictions may apply, 14 day cancellation notice-fee imposed, weekly rates available, [BP] meal plan available, package plans. **Leisure Activities:** exercise room, horseshoes. **Guest Services:** TV in common
area. **Cards:** AX, DS, MC, VI. ☒ ⟨P⟩ ☒

# CLAREMONT pop. 13,151

### ——— WHERE TO STAY ———

**BEST BUDGET INN**
(AAA) [SAVE]
◆◆◆◆ ◆◆◆◆
Motel

All Year | 1P: $38-$52 | 2P: $53-$70 | XP: $8 | F9
**Phone:** 603/542-9567

**Location:** Just n of jct SR 11/12/103/120; center. 24 Sullivan St 03743-2521. Fax: 603/542-9568. **Facility:** 21 one-bedroom standard units, some with efficiencies. 1 story, exterior corridors. *Bath:* combo or shower only. **Parking:** on-site, winter plug-ins. **Terms:** 3 day cancellation notice, small pets only ($5-$10 extra charge). **Cards:** AX, DC, MC, VI.

SOME UNITS
[S🅳] [🛏] [🏄] FEE / [✕] [🛢] [🎞] /

# COLEBROOK

### ——— WHERE TO STAY ———

**NORTHERN COMFORT MOTEL**
(AAA) [SAVE]
◆◆◆◆ ◆◆◆◆
Motel

All Year | 1P: $58-$74 | 2P: $64-$74 | XP: $12 | D12
**Phone:** 603/237-4440

**Location:** 1.5 mi s. Rt 3 03576 (RR 1, Box 520). Fax: 603/237-4440. **Facility:** 19 units. 17 one- and 2 two-bedroom standard units, some with kitchens. 1 story, exterior corridors. *Bath:* combo or shower only. **Parking:** on-site. **Terms:** office hours 7 am-10 pm, 3 day cancellation notice, [CP] meal plan available, small pets only ($5 extra charge). **Pool(s):** heated outdoor. **Leisure Activities:** snowmobiling, playground, sports court, volleyball. **Cards:** AX, DS, MC, VI. **Special Amenities: free continental breakfast and free local telephone calls.**

SOME UNITS
[🛏] [🏊] [✕] [🏄] [DATA PORT] FEE [🛢] / [✕] [VCR] [🎞] /

# CONCORD pop. 40,687

### ——— WHERE TO STAY ———

**BEST WESTERN CONCORD INN & SUITES** *Book at aaa.com*
(AAA) [SAVE]
◆◆◆◆◆ ◆◆◆◆
Small-scale Hotel

| | | | | |
|---|---|---|---|---|
| 7/1-10/31 | 1P: $69-$199 | 2P: $69-$199 | XP: $10 | F16 |
| 5/1-6/30 | 1P: $59-$199 | 2P: $59-$199 | XP: $10 | F16 |
| 1/1-4/30 | 1P: $59-$179 | 2P: $59-$179 | | |
| 11/1-12/31 | 1P: $59-$149 | 2P: $59-$149 | XP: $10 | F16 |

**Phone:** (603)228-4300

**Location:** I-93, exit 13, just n on Main St, then 0.5 mi w. 97 Hall St 03301. Fax: 603/228-4301. **Facility:** 66 units. 62 one-bedroom standard units. 4 one-bedroom suites, some with whirlpools. 3 stories, interior corridors. **Parking:** on-site. **Terms:** [ECP] meal plan available, pets ($10 extra charge). **Amenities:** voice mail, irons, hair dryers. **Pool(s):** heated indoor. **Leisure Activities:** sauna, whirlpool, exercise room. **Guest Services:** valet and coin laundry. **Business Services:** meeting rooms. **Cards:** AX, CB, DC, DS, MC, VI. **Special Amenities: free continental breakfast and free newspaper.**
*(See color ad below)*

SOME UNITS
[S🅳] [🛏] [🏊] [✕] [🏄] [DATA PORT] FEE [🛢] [🎞] [📺] / [✕] /

**CAPITOL INN**
(AAA) [SAVE]
◆◆◆◆ ◆◆◆◆
Motel

| | | | | |
|---|---|---|---|---|
| 5/1-10/31 [CP] | 1P: $79-$175 | 2P: $79-$200 | XP: $25 | F12 |
| 11/1-4/30 [CP] | 1P: $79-$120 | 2P: $59-$175 | XP: $10 | F12 |

**Phone:** 603/224-2511

**Location:** I-93, exit 12S on SR 3A. 406 S Main St 03301. Fax: 603/224-6032. **Facility:** 40 one-bedroom standard units, some with whirlpools. 2 stories (no elevator), exterior corridors. **Amenities:** voice mail, irons, hair dryers. **Pool(s):** outdoor. **Cards:** AX, DC, DS, MC, VI. **Special Amenities: free continental breakfast and free local telephone calls.**

SOME UNITS
[S🅳] [🏊] [🏄] [DATA PORT] / [✕] [🛢] [🎞] /

CENTENNIAL INN    *Book at aaa.com*    Phone: (603)227-9000

| | | | |
|---|---|---|---|
| 5/1-10/31 | 1P: $139-$189 | 2P: $149-$199 | XP: $10    F12 |
| 11/1-4/30 | 1P: $109-$179 | 2P: $119-$189 | XP: $10    F12 |

Historic Country Inn

**Location:** I-93, exit 14, just w to Main St, just s to Pleasant St (SR 9), then 0.5 mi w. 96 Pleasant St 03301. Fax: 603/225-5031. **Facility:** Turrets, porches and handsomely furnished common areas enhance this brick Victorian mansion dating from 1892. 32 one-bedroom standard units, some with whirlpools. 3 stories, interior corridors. **Parking:** on-site. **Terms:** 3 day cancellation notice, [AP], [BP], [CP] & [MAP] meal plans available. **Amenities:** video library (fee), irons, hair dryers. *Some:* safes. **Dining:** Franklin Pierce Dining Room, see separate listing. **Guest Services:** valet laundry. **Business Services:** meeting rooms. **Cards:** AX, CB, DC, DS, MC, VI. *(See color ad below)*

SOME UNITS

ASK S_D ⑪ &M ⊘ VCR DATA PORT ▣ / ✕ 🖬 /

CONCORD COMFORT INN    *Book at aaa.com*    Phone: 603/226-4100

| | | | |
|---|---|---|---|
| 9/8-10/19 | 1P: $119 | 2P: $119 | XP: $10    F |
| 7/21-9/7 | 1P: $99 | 2P: $99 | XP: $10    F |
| 5/1-7/20 | 1P: $89 | 2P: $89 | XP: $10    F |
| 10/20-4/30 | 1P: $59 | 2P: $59 | XP: $10    F |

Small-scale Hotel

**Location:** I-93, exit 13, just n on Main St, then 0.3 mi w. Located in a residential area. 71 Hall St 03301. Fax: 603/228-2106. **Facility:** 100 one-bedroom standard units, some with whirlpools. 3 stories, interior corridors. **Bath:** combo or shower only. **Parking:** on-site. **Terms:** cancellation fee imposed, [ECP] meal plan available, pets ($10 extra charge). **Amenities:** voice mail, irons, hair dryers. *Fee:* video library, video games. **Pool(s):** heated indoor. **Leisure Activities:** sauna, whirlpool, exercise room. **Business Services:** meeting rooms. **Cards:** AX, DC, DS, MC, VI.

SOME UNITS

🛏 &M ⊡ ⊘ ➥ ✕ DATA PORT ▣ / ✕ VCR 🖬 /
FEE                                    FEE

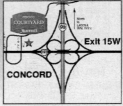

## COURTYARD BY MARRIOTT-CONCORD

**Book at aaa.com**  **Phone:** (603)225-0303

AAA SAVE

| |  |  |  |  |
|---|---|---|---|---|
| 6/1-10/31 | 1P: $119-$209 | 2P: $119-$209 | XP: $10 | F16 |
| 5/1-5/31 | 1P: $109-$119 | 2P: $109-$119 | XP: $10 | F16 |
| 11/1-4/30 | 1P: $99-$119 | 2P: $99-$119 | XP: $10 | F16 |

**Small-scale Hotel** **Location:** I-93, exit 15W. Located at Corporate Center at Horseshoe Pond. 70 Constitution Ave 03301. **Fax:** 603/225-0606. **Facility:** 90 units. 87 one-bedroom standard units, some with whirlpools. 3 one-bedroom suites ($139-$249). 3 stories, interior corridors. *Bath:* combo or shower only. **Parking:** on-site.
**Amenities:** dual phone lines, voice mail, irons, hair dryers. *Fee:* video library, video games. **Dining:** 6:30 am-10:30 & 5-9 pm, Sat 7 am-11 & 5-9 pm, Sun 7 am-noon & 5-9 pm, cocktails. **Pool(s):** heated indoor. **Leisure Activities:** whirlpool, exercise room. **Guest Services:** valet and coin laundry, airport transportation (fee)-Manchester International Airport. **Business Services:** meeting rooms, fax. **Cards:** AX, CB, DC, DS, JC, MC, VI. *(See ad p 318)*

SOME UNITS

---

## FAIRFIELD INN

**Book at aaa.com**  **Phone:** 603/224-4011

| 9/12-11/6 [ECP] | 1P: $119 |
|---|---|
| 5/1-9/11 [ECP] | 1P: $89 |
| 11/7-12/31 [ECP] | 1P: $74 |
| 1/1-4/30 [ECP] | 1P: $69 |

**Small-scale Hotel**

**Location:** I-93, exit 13 northbound, just n on Main St, immediate right turn. 4 Gulf St 03301. **Fax:** 603/228-3353. **Facility:** 105 one-bedroom standard units, some with whirlpools. 3 stories, interior corridors. *Bath:* combo or shower only. **Parking:** on-site.
**Terms:** cancellation fee imposed. **Amenities:** voice mail, irons, hair dryers. **Pool(s):** heated indoor. **Leisure Activities:** whirlpool, exercise room. **Guest Services:** valet and coin laundry. **Business Services:** meeting rooms. **Cards:** AX, DC, DS, MC, VI.

SOME UNITS

---

## HAMPTON INN

**Book at aaa.com**  **Phone:** (603)224-5322

| 6/11-10/17 [ECP] | 1P: $99-$139 | XP: $10 | F17 |
|---|---|---|---|
| 5/1-6/10 [ECP] | 1P: $79-$109 | XP: $10 | F17 |
| 10/18-4/30 [ECP] | 1P: $59-$79 | XP: $10 | F17 |

**Small-scale Hotel** **Location:** I-89, exit 1. 515 South St 03304. **Fax:** 603/224-4282. **Facility:** 145 one-bedroom standard units, some with whirlpools. 4 stories, interior corridors. *Bath:* combo or shower only. **Parking:** on-site. **Terms:** age restrictions may apply, cancellation fee imposed. **Amenities:** video library (fee), voice mail, irons, hair dryers. *Some:* dual phone lines. **Pool(s):** heated indoor. **Leisure Activities:** whirlpool. **Guest Services:** valet and coin laundry. **Cards:** AX, CB, DC, DS, MC, VI.
*(See ad below)*

SOME UNITS

FEE

---

## HOLIDAY INN

**Book at aaa.com**  **Phone:** (603)224-9534

| 10/31-4/30 | 1P: $129-$159 | 2P: $129-$159 |
|---|---|---|
| 5/1-10/30 | 1P: $119-$139 | 2P: $119-$139 |

**Small-scale Hotel** **Location:** I-93, exit 14, jct US 3 (Manchester St) and 4; downtown. 172 N Main St 03301. **Fax:** 603/224-8266. **Facility:** 122 units. 121 one-bedroom standard units. 1 one-bedroom suite with whirlpool. 4 stories, interior corridors. *Bath:* combo or shower only. **Parking:** on-site. **Terms:** 1-3 night minimum stay, [BP] meal plan available, package plans - in winter. **Amenities:** voice mail, irons, hair dryers. *Fee:* video library, video games. **Pool(s):** heated indoor. **Leisure Activities:** sauna, whirlpool, exercise room. **Guest Services:** valet laundry. **Business Services:** conference facilities, fax. **Cards:** AX, DC, DS, MC, VI.

SOME UNITS

—— **WHERE TO DINE** ——

**ANGELINA'S RISTORANTE ITALIANO**    **Lunch:** $8-$13    **Dinner:** $10-$18    **Phone:** 603/228-3313
▼▼▼   **Location:** Just off Main St; downtown. 11 Depot St 03301. **Hours:** 11:30 am-2 & 5-9 pm, Fri-10 pm, Sat 5 pm-10
Regional pm. Closed major holidays; also Sun. **Reservations:** accepted. **Features:** Veal piccata is wonderful at the
Italian attractive, intimate restaurant. Well-prepared cuisine is enhanced by an extensive wine list. Simple decor
lends to a casual setting; the entrance is at the building's rear corner. Casual dress; cocktails. **Parking:**
street. **Cards:** AX, CB, DC, DS, MC, VI. ✕

**THE BARLEY HOUSE RESTAURANT & TAVERN**    **Lunch:** $7-$9    **Dinner:** $7-$16    **Phone:** 603/228-6363
▼▼▼   **Location:** Center. 132 N Main St 03301. **Hours:** 11 am-1 am. Closed: 3/27, 11/25, 12/25; also Sun.
American **Features:** The casual downtown eatery presents entertainment on most evenings. Representative of menu
choices are traditional burgers, applewood-smoked pork chops and vegetable lasagna. Casual dress;
cocktails; entertainment. **Parking:** street. **Cards:** AX, DC, DS, MC, VI. ▼ ✕

**CAPITOL GRILLE**    **Lunch:** $5-$8    **Dinner:** $13-$20    **Phone:** 603/228-6608
▼▼▼   **Location:** Downtown. 1 Eagle Sq. (on Main St) 03301. **Hours:** 11 am-1 am. Closed: 12/25; also Mon.
American **Reservations:** accepted. **Features:** Located in downtown Concord near the Capital, this eatery offers a
casual menu of tasty sandwiches and soups; catering is available. Casual dress; cocktails. **Parking:** street.
**Cards:** AX, DC, DS, MC, VI. ▼ ✕

**THE CAT N' FIDDLE RESTAURANT**    **Lunch:** $8-$14    **Dinner:** $12-$22    **Phone:** 603/228-8911
▲▲▲   **Location:** I-93, exit 13, 1 mi e on US 3 (Manchester St). 118 Manchester St 03301. **Hours:** 11 am-9 pm, Fri &
Sat-10 pm. Closed: 12/25. **Reservations:** accepted. **Features:** The roadside restaurant has large dining
▼▼ rooms with murals of Greece on the walls and a good-size fireplace. Seniors favor the casual family
American atmosphere. Portions are large. The menu is expansive, with a variety of steak, chicken and fresh seafood
items. Some Greek and Italian entrees are featured. Cocktails. **Parking:** on-site. **Cards:** AX, DS, MC, VI.
▼ ✕

**CHEN YANG LI**    **Lunch:** $6-$18    **Dinner:** $11-$18    **Phone:** 603/228-8508
▼▼▼   **Location:** I-89, exit 1. 520 South St 03304. **Hours:** 11:30 am-10 pm. Closed: 11/25. **Reservations:** accepted.
Chinese **Features:** The restaurant's third location continues the tradition of offering exceptional Chinese cuisine,
serving many house specialties and standard favorites. Their wonderfully descriptive menu also has a nice
selection of sushi items. An elegant dining atmosphere and helpful staff make for a very enjoyable
experience. Dressy casual; cocktails. **Parking:** on-site. **Cards:** AX, DS, MC, VI. ✕

**THE COMMON MAN**    **Lunch:** $4-$8    **Dinner:** $11-$18    **Phone:** 603/228-3463
▼▼▼   **Location:** I-93, exit 13, just n. 25 Water St 03301. **Hours:** 11:30 am-9 pm. Closed: 11/25, 12/25. **Features:** The
decor is charming, both in the dining room and the pleasant upstairs pub. On the menu are steak, seafood,
American chicken and vegetarian dishes served in generous portions. Lobster corn chowder is popular at lunch. The
specialty white chocolate mousse is another favorite choice. Casual dress; cocktails. **Parking:** on-site.
**Cards:** AX, DS, MC, VI. ▼

**CORNER VIEW RESTAURANT**    **Lunch:** $6-$8    **Dinner:** $8-$12    **Phone:** 603/229-4554
▼▼▼   **Location:** I-93, exit 12N, 0.5 mi n, then 1.5 mi w on Broadway. 80 1/2 South St 03301. **Hours:** 7 am-9 pm. Closed:
7/4, 11/25, 12/25. **Reservations:** accepted. **Features:** This family owned restaurant is cozy and
American comfortable and serves tasty homemade dishes of fresh seafood, steaks, pasta and chicken. Casual
dress; cocktails. **Parking:** on-site. **Cards:** AX, MC, VI. ✕

**DON GIOVANNI'S**    **Lunch:** $7-$13    **Dinner:** $7-$13    **Phone:** 603/226-4723
▼▼▼   **Location:** Just e off US 3; downtown. 11 Depot St 03301. **Hours:** 11 am-9 pm, Sun 4 pm-9 pm. Closed major
holidays. **Features:** The casual eatery serves traditional homemade pasta dishes with sauces that are
Italian prepared daily. Casual dress; beer & wine only. **Parking:** street. **Cards:** AX, DS, MC, VI. ✕

**FRANKLIN PIERCE DINING ROOM**   Historic    **Lunch:** $7-$12    **Dinner:** $15-$27    **Phone:** 603/227-9000
▼▼▼   **Location:** I-93, exit 14, just w to Main St, just s to Pleasant St (SR 9), then 0.5 mi w; in Centennial Inn. 96 Pleasant St
03301. **Hours:** 11:30 am-2 & 5-9 pm; from 5 pm 5/16-9/14. **Reservations:** suggested. **Features:** The
American attractive and romantic dining room occupies a historic Victorian mansion. Healthful preparations and
eye-appealing presentations characterize specialties of New England cuisine. Smoking is permitted in the
lounge. Casual dress; cocktails. **Parking:** on-site. **Cards:** AX, CB, DC, DS, MC, VI. ▼ ✕

**HERMANOS COCINA MEXICANA**    **Lunch:** $5-$15    **Dinner:** $5-$15    **Phone:** 603/224-5669
▲▲▲   **Location:** Center. 11 Hills Ave 03301. **Hours:** 11:30 am-2:30 & 5-9 pm, Fri & Sat-10 pm, Sun 5 pm-9 pm.
Closed: 3/27, 11/25, 12/25. **Features:** The restaurant has simple decor with an Aztec flavor. The extensive
▼▼ menu includes traditional Mexican favorites, some with a slightly different twist. Live jazz is played five
Mexican nights a week in the lounge. Parking before 6 p.m. is metered. Don't miss the strawberry burrito for
dessert. Casual dress; cocktails. **Parking:** on-site. **Cards:** DS, MC, VI. ▼ ✕

**MAKRIS LOBSTER & STEAK HOUSE**    **Lunch:** $5-$10    **Dinner:** $8-$15    **Phone:** 603/225-7665
▲▲▲   **Location:** I-393, exit 3, 0.5 mi n on SR 106. 354 Sheep Davis Rd 03301. **Hours:** 11 am-9 pm. Closed major
holidays; also Mon 9/15-5/15. **Features:** The friendly, family-run restaurant serves fresh seafood and
▼ lobster in a casual, no-nonsense atmosphere. Casual dress; cocktails. **Parking:** on-site. **Cards:** AX, DS,
Steak & Seafood MC, VI. ✕

**SIAM ORCHID**
Thai

Lunch: $6-$10    Dinner: $8-$16    **Phone: 603/228-3633**

**Location:** Center. 158 N Main St 03301. **Hours:** 11:30 am-3 & 5-10 pm, Fri & Sat-10:30 pm, Sun 4 pm-9:30 pm. Closed major holidays. **Features:** The small storefront restaurant is downtown near the capitol building. The menu lists an extensive collection of delicious Thai cuisine, including seafood, chicken, beef, pork and vegetarian entrees. Noodles, fried rice, soup appetizers and curry selections are available as well. Don't miss the chicken satay and golden triangle appetizers. Casual dress; cocktails. **Parking:** street. **Cards:** AX, DC, DS, MC, VI.

**VEANO'S ITALIAN KITCHEN**
Italian

Lunch: $6-$14    Dinner: $6-$14    **Phone: 603/224-2400**

**Location:** On SR 9, just w of SR 132. 142 Loudon Rd 03301. **Hours:** 11 am-9 pm. Closed: 11/25, 12/25. **Features:** Family owned and operated since 1973, the restaurant serves families traditional favorites in a casual setting. Casual dress; beer & wine only. **Parking:** on-site. **Cards:** AX, MC, VI.

---

*The following restaurant has not been evaluated by AAA but is listed for your information only.*

---

**CONSTANTLY PIZZA**
[fyi]

**Phone: 603/224-9366**

Not evaluated. **Location:** 39 S Main St 03301. **Features:** Patrons can choose one of the restaurant's creative concoctions or create their own specialty pizza.

# CONWAY pop. 1,692—See also NORTH CONWAY.

--- WHERE TO STAY ---

**THE CONWAY VALLEY INN**
Motel

| | | | |
|---|---|---|---|
| 6/1-10/18 | 2P: $49-$199 | XP: $10 | D12 |
| 5/1-5/31 & 10/19-4/30 | 2P: $39-$99 | XP: $10 | D12 |

**Phone: 603/447-3858**

**Location:** Jct US 302, 1 mi s on SR 16; 1.5 mi n of village center. 850 White Mountain Hwy (SR 16) 03818 (PO Box 2005, NORTH CONWAY, 03860). **Facility:** 20 units. 13 one-bedroom standard units, some with efficiencies. 7 cottages. 1 story, exterior corridors. *Bath:* combo or shower only. **Parking:** on-site. **Terms:** office hours 9 am-10 pm, 7 day cancellation notice-fee imposed. **Pool(s):** heated outdoor. **Cards:** DS, MC, VI. *(See color ad p 373)*

SOME UNITS

**THE DARBY FIELD INN**    *Book at aaa.com*
(AAA) (SAVE)
Historic Country Inn

| | | |
|---|---|---|
| All Year [BP] | 1P: $80-$150 | 2P: $100-$170    XP: $40 |

**Phone: (603)447-2181**

**Location:** 1 mi s on SR 16, watch for Bald Hill Rd, 2 mi w, follow signs. Located in a secluded, rural area. 185 Chase Hill Rd 03818. Fax: 603/447-5726. **Facility:** In a secluded, rural area, this inn sits atop a small mountain offering gardens and commanding views of the surrounding mountains. Smoke free premises. 13 units. 7 one-bedroom standard units. 6 one-bedroom suites ($170-$280), some with whirlpools. 3 stories (no elevator), interior corridors. *Bath:* combo or shower only. **Parking:** on-site. **Terms:** office hours 9 am-8 pm, 2 night minimum stay - most weekends, age restrictions may apply, 14 day cancellation notice-fee imposed, [MAP] meal plan available. **Dining:** Fri & Sat 6 pm-8 pm; Sun-Thurs by reservation, cocktails. **Pool(s):** heated outdoor. **Leisure Activities:** cross country skiing, lawn games, bicycles, hiking trails. *Fee:* carriage & sleigh rides, snowshoeing. **Cards:** MC, VI. **Special Amenities: free full breakfast and free local telephone calls.**

SOME UNITS

**MERRILL FARM RESORT**
(AAA) (SAVE)
Motel

| | | | |
|---|---|---|---|
| 5/1-10/31 | 2P: $85-$155 | XP: $12 | F18 |
| 11/1-4/30 | 2P: $65-$155 | XP: $12 | F18 |

**Phone: (603)447-3866**

**Location:** Jct SR 16 and US 302, 1.5 mi s on SR 16; 0.5 mi n of village center on SR 16. 428 White Mountain Hwy 03860. Fax: 603/447-3867. **Facility:** 60 units. 59 one-bedroom standard units, some with whirlpools. 1 one-bedroom suite. 2 stories (no elevator), interior/exterior corridors. *Bath:* combo or shower only. **Parking:** on-site. **Terms:** office hours 7 am-10 pm, 7 day cancellation notice-fee imposed. **Pool(s):** outdoor. **Leisure Activities:** sauna, whirlpool, canoeing. *Fee:* hot tub. **Guest Services:** coin laundry. **Business Services:** meeting rooms. **Cards:** AX, DC, DS, MC, VI. **Special Amenities: free expanded continental breakfast and free local telephone calls.**

SOME UNITS

**MOUNTAIN VALLEY MANNER**
Historic Bed & Breakfast

| | | | |
|---|---|---|---|
| 9/24-10/23 [BP] | 1P: $109-$135 | 2P: $109-$135 | XP: $15 | F13 |
| 6/25-9/23 [BP] | 1P: $89-$125 | 2P: $89-$125 | XP: $15 | F13 |
| 10/24-4/30 [BP] | 1P: $79-$95 | 2P: $79-$95 | XP: $15 | F13 |
| 5/1-6/24 [BP] | 1P: $69-$85 | 2P: $69-$85 | XP: $15 | F13 |

**Phone: (603)447-3988**

**Location:** Jct SR 16 and 153, 0.5 mi w on Washington St/Westside Rd bearing left at fork by covered bridge. Located in a quiet area. 148 Washington St/Westside Rd 03818 (PO Box 1649). Fax: 603/447-3988. **Facility:** High ceilings, four-poster beds and Victorian-era antiques add appeal to this B&B, which is within a national forest. Smoke free premises. 3 units. 2 one-bedroom standard units. 1 two-bedroom suite ($85-$135). 2 stories (no elevator), interior corridors. *Bath:* combo or shower only. **Parking:** on-site. **Terms:** check-in 4:30 pm, 10 day cancellation notice. **Amenities:** hair dryers. **Pool(s):** outdoor. **Leisure Activities:** fishing. **Cards:** DC, MC, VI.

SOME UNITS

**WHITE DEER MOTEL**
Motel

| | | |
|---|---|---|
| All Year | 1P: $49-$149 | 2P: $49-$149    XP: $10    F17 |

**Phone: 603/447-5366**

**Location:** 2.1 mi s of jct US 302, 0.5 mi n of village center on SR 16. 379 White Mountain Hwy 03818. **Facility:** 14 one-bedroom standard units, some with whirlpools. 2 stories (no elevator), interior/exterior corridors. *Bath:* combo or shower only. **Parking:** on-site. **Terms:** office hours 7 am-10 pm, 3 day cancellation notice-fee imposed, pets ($35 deposit, $10 extra charge). **Amenities:** voice mail. **Cards:** MC, VI.

SOME UNITS

––––––– **WHERE TO DINE** –––––––

**CAFE NOCHE MEXICAN** — **Lunch:** $4-$8 — **Dinner:** $8-$15 — **Phone:** 603/447-5050

Mexican

**Location:** Center. 147 Main St 03818. **Hours:** 11:30 am-9 pm. **Closed:** 11/25, 12/24, 12/25; also 2 weeks in mid April and mid November. **Features:** Colorful Southwestern decor and a casual atmosphere welcome diners to the small restaurant. The menu features Mexican favorites made to order from fresh ingredients. More than 80 displayed hot sauces can be ordered to season meals. Everything can be prepared to accommodate vegetarian tastes. Prices are reasonable. Outdoor seating is available in the summer. Cocktails. **Parking:** on-site. **Cards:** AX, DS, MC, VI.

---

# CORNISH pop. 1,661

––––––– **WHERE TO STAY** –––––––

**THE CHASE HOUSE BED & BREAKFAST INN** — **Phone:** 603/675-5391

Bed & Breakfast

All Year — 2P: $150-$225 — XP: $35

**Location:** On SR 12A, 1.2 mi s of jct SR 44. 1001 SR 12A 03745. **Fax:** 603/675-5010. **Facility:** Restored Federal style birthplace of Salmon P. Chase, founder of Republican Party. Smoke free premises. 9 one-bedroom standard units. 2 stories (no elevator), interior corridors. *Bath:* combo or shower only. **Parking:** on-site. **Terms:** office hours 9 am-11 pm, check-in 4 pm, 2 night minimum stay - seasonal & weekends, age restrictions may apply, 14 day cancellation notice-fee imposed, [BP] meal plan available, package plans. **Leisure Activities:** sauna, exercise room, basketball, volleyball. **Guest Services:** gift shop. **Business Services:** meeting rooms. **Cards:** MC, VI.

SOME UNITS

---

# DERRY pop. 22,661

––––––– **WHERE TO DINE** –––––––

**MADDENS FAMILY RESTAURANT** — **Lunch:** $3-$14 — **Dinner:** $3-$14 — **Phone:** 603/432-8403

American

**Location:** 0.5 mi n of SR 102. 39 Crystal Ave 03038. **Hours:** 7 am-9 pm. **Closed:** 11/25, 12/25. **Features:** The casual restaurant is perfect for families and large groups. The menu centers on traditional preparations of steak, chicken and fish, often fried or broiled. Casual dress; beer & wine only. **Parking:** on-site. **Cards:** AX, DS, MC, VI.

---

––––––– *The following restaurant has not been evaluated by AAA* –––––––
*but is listed for your information only.*

**PINKERTON TAVERN** — **Phone:** 603/425-6665

[fyi]

Not evaluated. **Location:** 13 Manchester Rd 03038-3006. **Features:** The eatery prepares a terrific selection of unusual big game, including buffalo and boar.

---

# DIXVILLE NOTCH

––––––– **WHERE TO STAY** –––––––

––––––– *The following lodging was either not evaluated or did not* –––––––
*meet AAA rating requirements but is listed for your information only.*

**THE BALSAMS GRAND RESORT HOTEL** — **Phone:** 603/255-3400

[fyi]

Not evaluated. **Location:** Off SR 26 03576. Facilities, services, and decor characterize a mid-range property.

---

# DOVER pop. 26,884

––––––– **WHERE TO STAY** –––––––

**DAYS INN** — *Book at aaa.com* — **Phone:** (603)742-0400

Motel

All Year [ECP] — 1P: $80-$140 — 2P: $80-$140 — XP: $10 — F17

**Location:** Spaulding Tpke, exit 7, 2 mi n on SR 108; downtown. 481 Central Ave 03820. **Fax:** 603/742-7790. **Facility:** 63 units. 62 one-bedroom standard units, some with kitchens. 1 two-bedroom suite with kitchen. 2 stories, interior/exterior corridors. *Bath:* combo or shower only. **Parking:** on-site. **Terms:** pets ($50 extra charge). **Amenities:** video library (fee), voice mail, irons, hair dryers. **Pool(s):** heated indoor. **Leisure Activities:** whirlpool. **Cards:** AX, CB, DC, DS, JC, MC, VI.

SOME UNITS

(ASK) (S/D) FEE — FEE

---

––––––– **WHERE TO DINE** –––––––

**ALEXANDERS ITALIAN RESTAURANT** — **Lunch:** $6-$22 — **Dinner:** $6-$22 — **Phone:** 603/742-2650

Italian

**Location:** 1 mi e on SR 4. 489 Portland Ave 03820. **Hours:** 11:30 am-9 pm, Fri-10 pm, Sat 4 pm-10 pm, Sun noon-8 pm. Closed major holidays; also Mon. **Features:** Prime rib, veal parmigiana and chicken cacciatore with linguine are a few of the excellent offerings. A brick fireplace and chandeliers enhance the cozy and warm surroundings. The serving staff is friendly and attentive. Casual dress; cocktails. **Parking:** on-site.

**Cards:** AX, MC, VI.

## THE FISH SHANTY

▽▽ ▽▽

Seafood

**Lunch:** $6-$19          **Dinner:** $6-$19          **Phone:** 603/749-1001

**Location:** Spaulding Tpke, exit 7, 1 mi e on SR 108 to Central Ave; downtown. 471 Central Ave 03820. **Hours:** 11:30 am-8 pm; Fri & Sat-9 pm. Closed major holidays; also Sun & Mon. **Features:** In the heart of downtown, the popular, family-owned and managed restaurant has a bilevel dining room with clean, simple decor and a casual atmosphere. The menu features fresh seafood as well as steak and chicken entrees. Lots of sandwiches and well-prepared salads can be ordered all day. Don't pass up one of the delicious desserts. Cocktails. **Parking:** street. **Cards:** AX, DS, MC, VI.

⊠

## NEWICK'S LOBSTER HOUSE

Ⓐ

▽▽

Seafood

**Lunch:** $5-$20          **Dinner:** $5-$20          **Phone:** 603/742-3205

**Location:** SR 4, exit 6W, follow signs to Dover Point business district. 431 Dover Point Rd 03820. **Hours:** 11 am-8:30 pm, Fri & Sat-9 pm. Closed: 11/25, 12/25. **Features:** The menu incorporates a good selection of baked and broiled seafood, steamers and chowders. Guests appreciate the views of Great Bay and geese, eagles and seals. Save space for the heaping strawberry shortcake for dessert. Casual dress; cocktails. **Parking:** on-site. **Cards:** AX, DS, MC, VI.

Ⓜ ⊠

## WEATHERVANE

▽▽ ▽▽

Seafood

**Lunch:** $4-$10          **Dinner:** $5-$18          **Phone:** 603/749-2341

**Location:** Spaulding Tpke, exit 6N, 4 mi n on SR 16 (Dover Point Rd). 2 Dover Point Rd 03820. **Hours:** 11 am-9 pm; to 9:30 pm 5/27-10/14. Closed: 11/25, 12/25. **Features:** The popular, family-oriented restaurant features a good menu variety that includes lobster, fried clams and crisp Cape Cod apple-cranberry cobbler. Flavorful dishes are served in large portions, and there's a fish market on the premises. Casual dress; cocktails. **Parking:** on-site. **Cards:** AX, MC, VI.

Ⓜ ⊠

---
### The following restaurant has not been evaluated by AAA but is listed for your information only.
---

## CRESCENT CITY BISTRO

[fyi]

**Phone:** 603/742-1611

Not evaluated. **Location:** 83 Washington St 03820. **Features:** The owner-chef fuses Cajun and Creole influences into New England cuisine. The high-end-style bistro is modeled after the Palace Cafe in New Orleans.

# DUBLIN pop. 1,476

——— WHERE TO DINE ———

## AUDREY'S CAFE

▽▽

American

**Lunch:** $4-$9          **Dinner:** $6-$15          **Phone:** 603/876-3316

**Location:** Center. SR 101 03444. **Hours:** 7 am-3 pm, Thurs-Sat to 8 pm, Sun 8 am-3 pm. Closed: 12/25; also Mon. **Features:** Off a busy state route, the roadside location welcomes diners in for tasty traditional comfort foods. Casual dress; beer & wine only. **Parking:** on-site. **Cards:** AX, MC, VI.

🅐 ⊠

# DURHAM pop. 9,024

——— WHERE TO STAY ———

## HICKORY POND INN & GOLF COURSE

▽▽ ▽▽

Bed & Breakfast

**Phone:** 603/659-2227

| | | | |
|---|---|---|---|
| All Year | 1P: $69-$79 | 2P: $119-$139 | XP: $15   F12 |

**Location:** 2.8 mi s on SR 108. 1 Stagecoach Rd 03824. Fax: 603/659-7910. **Facility:** Designated smoking area. 18 one-bedroom standard units. 2 stories (no elevator), interior corridors. *Bath:* some shared or private. **Parking:** on-site. **Terms:** 3 day cancellation notice, [ECP] meal plan available, package plans - seasonal, pets ($10 extra charge, in limited units). **Amenities:** high-speed Internet. **Leisure Activities:** cross country skiing. *Fee:* golf-9 holes. **Business Services:** meeting rooms. **Cards:** AX, CB, DC, DS, MC, VI.

SOME UNITS
🅰ⓈⓀ Ⓢ 🛏 ⊠ /🆅🅲🆁/
FEE

## NEW ENGLAND CENTER HOTEL    *Book at aaa.com*

▽▽ ▽▽ ▽▽

Small-scale Hotel

**Phone:** (603)862-2801

| | | | |
|---|---|---|---|
| 5/1-10/31 | 1P: $107-$129 | | XP: $10   F12 |
| 11/1-4/30 | 1P: $97-$119 | | XP: $10   F12 |

**Location:** SR 4 to Madbury Rd (signs to New England Center), 1 mi s to Edgewood Rd, then 0.3 mi s. Located on the University of New Hampshire campus. 15 Strafford Ave/UNH 03824. Fax: 603/862-0692. **Facility:** 115 units. 111 one- and 2 two-bedroom standard units. 2 one-bedroom suites ($139-$159). 6-8 stories, interior corridors. **Parking:** on-site. **Terms:** check-in 4 pm, cancellation fee imposed, [AP] meal plan available, package plans. **Amenities:** voice mail, irons, hair dryers. **Dining:** Acorns Restaurant, Cafe & Lounge, see separate listing. **Pool(s):** outdoor. **Leisure Activities:** 10 lighted tennis courts, racquetball courts, basketball. **Guest Services:** valet and coin laundry. **Business Services:** conference facilities. **Cards:** AX, DC, DS, MC, VI.

SOME UNITS
🅰ⓈⓀ Ⓢ 🍽 Ⓜ 📷 🏊 🐾 ⊠ 🎥 🖧 💻 /⊠🖥/

## THREE CHIMNEYS INN    *Book at aaa.com*

Ⓐ [SAVE]

▽▽ ▽▽ ▽▽

Historic Country Inn

**Phone:** (603)868-7800

| | | | |
|---|---|---|---|
| 8/1-11/14 [BP] | 1P: $189-$219 | 2P: $189-$219 | XP: $25   D6 |
| 5/1-7/31 & 11/15-4/30 [BP] | 1P: $159-$189 | 2P: $159-$189 | XP: $25   D6 |

**Location:** On SR 108; center. 17 Newmarket Rd 03824. Fax: 603/868-2964. **Facility:** Antique artwork, Georgian-era mahogany furniture and four-poster beds with period drapery bring an elegant ambience to this hilltop hotel. Smoke free premises. 23 one-bedroom standard units, some with whirlpools. 4 stories (no elevator), interior/exterior corridors. *Bath:* combo or shower only. **Parking:** on-site. **Terms:** check-in 4 pm, age restrictions may apply, 7 day cancellation notice-fee imposed. **Amenities:** hair dryers. **Dining:** 8:30 am-9 & 11:30-9 pm, Sat 8 am-9:30 & 11:30-10 pm, Sun 8 am-9:30 & 3-9 pm, cocktails, also, Maples Diningroom and ffrost Sawyer Tavern, see separate listing. **Guest Services:** valet laundry. **Business Services:** meeting rooms. **Cards:** AX, DC, DS, MC, VI. **Special Amenities:** free full breakfast.

🍽 🅶 ⊠ 🖧

——— WHERE TO DINE ———

**ACORNS RESTAURANT, CAFE & LOUNGE**      **Lunch:** $6-$15      **Dinner:** $11-$27      **Phone:** 603/862-2815
▼▼▼     **Location:** SR 4 to Madbury Rd (signs to New England Center), 1 mi s to Edgewood Rd, then 0.3 mi s; in New
England Center Hotel. 15 Strafford Ave/UNH 03824. **Hours:** 7 am-9 pm. Closed: Christmas break.
American     **Reservations:** required. **Features:** Located at and operated by the University of New Hampshire and
students of its culinary and hospitality school, the restaurant seats guests in several dining rooms
overlooking the wooded campus. An art gallery is on the second level. The eclectic menu lists a variety of New England
seafood favorites, in addition to Italian and Oriental entrees. Casual dress; cocktails. **Parking:** on-site. **Cards:** AX, DC, DS,
MC, VI.

**MAPLES DININGROOM AND**
  **FFROST SAWYER TAVERN**   Country Inn      **Lunch:** $8-$13      **Dinner:** $17-$28      **Phone:** 603/868-7800
▼▼▼     **Location:** On SR 108; center; in Three Chimneys Inn. 17 Newmarket Rd 03824. **Hours:** 8:30 am-9 & 11:30-9 pm,
Sat 8 am-9:30 & 11:30-10 pm, Sun 8 am-9:30 & 3-9 pm. Closed: 12/24, 12/25. **Features:** In a beautifully
American     renovated 18th-century farmhouse, the restaurant sustains a casual pub atmosphere amid comfortable
surroundings. American cuisine emphasizes fresh local ingredients prepared with international influences.
Casual dress; cocktails. **Parking:** on-site. **Cards:** AX, DC, DS, MC, VI.

# EAST MADISON

——— WHERE TO STAY ———

**PURITY SPRING RESORT**                                                         **Phone:** (603)367-8896
▼▼▼     All Year                    1P: $51-$146         2P: $73-$262         XP: $48              D12
**Location:** SR 153, 9 mi s of jct SR 16; 5.5 mi n of jct SR 25. SR 153 03849 (HC 63, Box 40). Fax: 603/367-8664.
Resort     **Facility:** Sprawling grounds surround this family resort near mountains and woodlands. 48 units. 27 one- and
Small-scale Hotel  11 two-bedroom standard units, some with whirlpools. 3 two- and 1 three-bedroom suites ($222-$266), some
with whirlpools. 6 cabins. 1-3 stories (no elevator), interior/exterior corridors. **Bath:** combo or shower only.
**Parking:** on-site. **Terms:** office hours 8 am-10 pm, 2-3 night minimum stay - weekends, 14 day cancellation notice-fee imposed,
package plans - seasonal & weekends. **Amenities:** Some: irons. **Pool(s):** heated pool. **Leisure Activities:** whirlpool, boating,
canoeing, sailboats, waterskiing, fishing, 5 tennis courts (1 lighted), downhill & cross country skiing, ice skating, recreation programs, hiking trails, playground, exercise room, basketball, horseshoes, shuffleboard, volleyball. **Fee:** bicycles, game room.
**Guest Services:** gift shop, coin laundry. **Business Services:** meeting rooms. **Cards:** AX, DS, MC, VI.

SOME UNITS

# EATON CENTER

——— WHERE TO STAY ———

**INN AT CRYSTAL LAKE**                                                          **Phone:** 603/447-2120
⬡⬡⬡ [SAVE]   All Year                1P: $79-$229         2P: $89-$239         XP: $20
**Location:** On SR 153; center. 2356 Eaton Rd 03832 (PO Box 12). Fax: 603/447-3599. **Facility:** Guests can sit out-
▼▼▼     side on the patio to enjoy the perennial gardens or wander downstairs to their cozy bar to keep warm. The
guest rooms in this 1885 home are individually decorated with antiques and reproductions. Smoke free prem-
Historic    ises. 11 units. 10 one-bedroom standard units. 1 one-bedroom suite. 4 stories (no elevator), interior/exterior
Country Inn  corridors. **Bath:** combo or shower only. **Parking:** on-site. **Terms:** office hours 8 am-10 pm, 2-3 night minimum
stay - weekends, age restrictions may apply, 14 day cancellation notice-fee imposed, [BP] meal plan available, package plans, pets (in limited units). **Amenities:** video library, CD players. Some: hair dryers. **Dining:** light pub fare
Wed-Sun 5 pm-10 pm. **Cards:** MC, VI. **Special Amenities: free full breakfast and free room upgrade (subject to availability
with advanced reservations).**

SOME UNITS
🛏 ⊠ [VCR]  / ⯃ /

# EXETER pop. 9,759

## ──── WHERE TO STAY ────

**INN & CONFERENCE CENTER OF EXETER**   *Book at aaa.com*        **Phone:** (603)772-5901
All Year        1P: $89-$299      2P: $104-$299     XP: $15
Country Inn    **Location:** On SR 111; just w from village center. Located at the Phillips Exeter Academy. 90 Front St 03833.
Fax: 603/778-8757. **Facility:** The inn has a Georgian brick exterior and is elegantly decorated with period
antiques. 46 units. 43 one-bedroom standard units. 3 one-bedroom suites, some with whirlpools. 3 stories,
interior corridors. **Parking:** on-site. **Terms:** 3 day cancellation notice. **Amenities:** voice mail. *Some:* hair dryers. **Dining:** Terrace
Restaurant at the Inn of Exeter, see separate listing. **Guest Services:** valet laundry. **Business Services:** meeting rooms.
**Cards:** AX, DC, DS, MC, VI. *(See color ad below)*

SOME UNITS

**THE INN BY THE BANDSTAND**                             **Phone:** 603/772-6352
All Year        1P: $129-$165      2P: $129-$165     XP: $20
**Location:** Center; across from Bandstand. Front St 03833. **Facility:** "By the bandstand" best
describes the location of this Federal-style property in the village center; a short walk away is the Phillips Ex-
Bed & Breakfast   eter Academy. 9 units. 8 one- and 1 two-bedroom standard units, some with whirlpools. 3 stories (no elevator), interior corridors. *Bath:* combo or shower only. **Parking:** on-site. **Terms:** check-in 4 pm, 1-2 night
minimum stay - weekends 5/1-10/31, 10 day cancellation notice-fee imposed, [BP] meal plan available, no
pets allowed (owner's dog on premises). **Amenities:** voice mail, hair dryers. *Some:* irons. **Cards:** AX, DC, MC, VI.
**Special Amenities:** free full breakfast and free local telephone calls.

SOME UNITS

## ──── WHERE TO DINE ────

**TAVERN AT RIVER'S EDGE**            **Dinner:** $8-$22          **Phone:** 603/772-7393
**Location:** Center. 163 Water St 03833. **Hours:** 3 pm-10 pm. Closed major holidays; also Sun. **Features:** The
setting is comfortable in the Victorian-era room. The food includes upscale entrees, as well as lighter
Continental   tavern fare. Among specialties are New Zealand rack of lamb, filet mignon, fresh salmon and
sesame-encrusted tuna. The entrance is on the stoop's right side and downstairs. Cocktails. **Parking:**
street. **Cards:** AX, DS, MC, VI.

**TERRACE RESTAURANT AT THE INN OF EXETER**   Country Inn   **Lunch:** $7-$12 **Dinner:** $15-$26 **Phone:** 603/772-5901
**Location:** On SR 111; just w from village center; in Inn & Conference Center of Exeter. 90 Front St 03833.
**Hours:** 7-10:30 am, 11:30-2 & 5-9 pm, Fri & Sat 5:30 pm-10 pm, Sun 7-9 am, 10-2 & 5-9 pm.
Continental   **Reservations:** suggested. **Features:** In an upscale country inn near Phillips Exeter Academy, the
Colonial-style restaurant features creative Continental cuisine made with fresh local ingredients. Roast pork
tenderloin prepared Montreal-style is a superb choice. The wine list is good. Dressy casual; cocktails. **Parking:** on-site.
**Cards:** AX, DC, DS, MC, VI.

──── *The following restaurant has not been evaluated by AAA* ────
*but is listed for your information only.*

**LOAF & LADLE**                            **Phone:** 603/778-8955
Not evaluated. **Location:** 9 Water St 03833. **Features:** Self-described as a natural foods eatery, this place
serves a selection of nearly 50 soups and 60 bread varieties, all of which are homemade and prepared
daily.

# FRANCONIA

## ——— WHERE TO STAY ———

**FRANCONIA INN**
Phone: (603)823-5542
5/15-4/30    1P: $96-$116    2P: $106-$126    XP: $10    F5

Country Inn

**Location:** I-93, exit 38, 2.3 mi sw on SR 116. 1300 Easton Valley Rd 03580. Fax: 603/823-8078. **Facility:** A scenic mountain is the backdrop for this inn, which offers cozy common areas and varied-size rooms with some antique furnishings. Designated smoking area. 36 units. 33 one- and 2 two-bedroom standard units, some with whirlpools. 1 one-bedroom suite with efficiency. 3 stories (no elevator), interior corridors. **Bath:** combo or shower only. **Parking:** on-site, winter plug-ins. **Terms:** open 5/15-4/30, 5 day cancellation notice, [BP] & [MAP] meal plans available. **Dining:** dining room, see separate listing. **Pool(s):** heated outdoor. **Leisure Activities:** whirlpool, fishing, 4 tennis courts, cross country skiing, ice skating, bicycles. *Fee:* horseback riding, game room. **Business Services:** meeting rooms. **Cards:** AX, DC, MC, VI.
*(See color ad below)*

SOME UNITS

**FRANCONIA VILLAGE HOTEL RESORT & CONFERENCE CENTER**
Phone: (603)823-7422

| | | | | |
|---|---|---|---|---|
| 5/1-10/31 | 1P: $79-$119 | 2P: $79-$119 | XP: $10 | F12 |
| 1/16-3/31 | 1P: $79-$109 | 2P: $79-$109 | XP: $10 | F12 |
| 11/1-1/15 | 1P: $69-$99 | 2P: $69-$99 | XP: $10 | F12 |
| 4/1-4/30 | 1P: $59-$89 | 2P: $59-$89 | XP: $10 | F12 |

Small-scale Hotel **Location:** I-93, exit 38, just e. 87 Wallace Hill Rd 03580 (PO Box 724). Fax: 603/823-5638. **Facility:** 61 units. 60 one-bedroom standard units. 1 one-bedroom suite with kitchen. 2 stories (no elevator), interior corridors. **Parking:** on-site, winter plug-ins. **Terms:** 3 day cancellation notice-fee imposed, pets ($10 extra charge). **Amenities:** voice mail, irons, hair dryers. **Dining:** 6:30 am-10 & 5:30-9:30 pm, Sun 6:30 am-11 & 5:30-9:30 pm; hours vary in winter, cocktails. **Pool(s):** heated indoor. **Leisure Activities:** saunas, whirlpool, exercise room, horseshoes. *Fee:* game room. **Guest Services:** coin laundry. **Business Services:** meeting rooms, fax (fee). **Cards:** AX, DS, MC, VI. **Special Amenities:** free continental breakfast and free newspaper.** *(See color ad below)*

SOME UNITS

**GALE RIVER MOTEL**

AAA SAVE

Motel

| | | |
|---|---|---|
| 9/24-10/18 | 2P: $95-$105 | XP: $15  F15 |
| 5/1-9/23 | 2P: $75-$95 | XP: $10  F15 |

**Phone: 603/823-5655**

**Location:** I-93, exit 38, 0.8 mi n on SR 18. 1 Main St 03580. Fax: 603/823-5280. **Facility:** 12 units. 10 one-bedroom standard units. 2 cottages ($120-$130). 1 story, exterior corridors. *Bath:* combo or shower only. **Parking:** on-site. **Terms:** open 5/1-10/18, 7 day cancellation notice, pets ($15 extra charge, with prior approval). **Pool(s):** outdoor. **Leisure Activities:** whirlpools, barbecues, horseshoes, shuffleboard. **Guest Services:** coin laundry. **Cards:** DS, MC, VI. **Special Amenities:** free local telephone calls and early check-in/late check-out.

SOME UNITS

FEE

**LOVETTS INN BY LAFAYETTE BROOK**

Historic
Country Inn

| | | |
|---|---|---|
| All Year | 2P: $125-$250 | XP: $35  F5 |

**Phone: 603/823-7761**

**Location:** I-93, exit 38, 2.1 mi s on SR 18. 1474 Profile Rd 03580. Fax: 603/823-7130. **Facility:** This 1784 inn overlooks the mountains and offers guest rooms as well as cottages with fireplaces. Designated smoking area. 20 units. 19 one-bedroom standard units, some with whirlpools. 1 cottage with whirlpool. 1-2 stories (no elevator), interior/exterior corridors. **Parking:** on-site. **Terms:** 7 day cancellation notice, [BP] & [MAP] meal plans available. **Amenities:** video library, hair dryers. *Some:* CD players. **Dining:** dining room, see separate listing. **Pool(s):** outdoor. **Leisure Activities:** cross country skiing, ice skating, shuffleboard, volleyball. **Business Services:** meeting rooms. **Cards:** DS, MC, VI.

SOME UNITS

**STONYBROOK MOTEL & LODGE**

AAA SAVE

Motel

| | | |
|---|---|---|
| All Year | 2P: $65-$100 | XP: $10  F15 |

**Phone: 603/823-5800**

**Location:** I-93, exit 38, 1.5 mi s on SR 18. 1098 Profile Rd 03580. Fax: 603/823-5888. **Facility:** 23 one-bedroom standard units. 1-2 stories (no elevator), interior/exterior corridors. *Bath:* combo or shower only. **Parking:** on-site. **Terms:** 7 day cancellation notice. **Amenities:** *Some:* hair dryers. **Pool(s):** outdoor, heated indoor. **Leisure Activities:** Fee: game room. **Business Services:** meeting rooms. **Cards:** MC, VI.
*(See color ad below)*

SOME UNITS

## Savings at Your Fingertips

When you have a AAA TourBook® guide in your hand, you have a world of savings right at your fingertips. AAA Official Appointment lodgings that display the bright-red AAA logo, SAVE icon and Diamond rating in their listing want business from AAA Members, and many offer discounts and special amenities to them*.

So, when planning your next vacation, be sure to consult your AAA TourBook for the familiar red SAVE icon.

SAVE

*See TourBook Navigator, page 14, for details.*

## ──── WHERE TO DINE ────

**FRANCONIA INN** Country Inn      **Dinner:** $16-$27      **Phone:** 603/823-5542
**Location:** I-93, exit 38, 2.3 mi sw on SR 116; in Franconia Inn. 1300 Easton Valley Rd 03580. **Hours:** Open 5/18-3/26; 7:30 am-10 & 6-9 pm; 8 am-9:30 & 6-8:30 pm, Sun 7:30 am-10:30 & 6-9 pm 10/31-12/16.
Regional American    Closed: Mon-Thurs 11/3-11/27. **Reservations:** suggested. **Features:** The frequently updated menu here offers many meals with a Continental touch. Specialties include lamb and seasonal seafood, with a good selection of health-conscious items. The unpretentious elegance of the decor offers fine views of the White Mountains. Casual dress; cocktails. **Parking:** on-site. **Cards:** AX, MC, VI. *(See color ad p 326)*

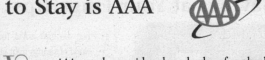

**FRANCONIA VILLAGE HOUSE RESTAURANT**    **Lunch:** $6-$10    **Dinner:** $9-$20    **Phone:** 603/823-5405
**Location:** I-93, exit 38, 0.5 mi s on SR 18. 651 Main St 03580. **Hours:** 5 pm-9 pm, Fri-10 pm, Sat 11:30 am-3 & 5-10 pm, Sun 11:30 am-3 & 5-9 pm. Closed: 12/25. **Reservations:** accepted. **Features:** You'll enjoy this
American    country atmosphere with a fireplace, friendly service and fine meals featuring Angus beef, fresh cod, salmon and tuna, Caesar salad, and dessert made on the premises. Prime rib is the specialty Saturday night. A lighter fare is offered in the lounge. Casual dress; cocktails. **Parking:** on-site. **Cards:** AX, DS, MC, VI.

**HUNT ROOM AT THE HORSE & HOUND** Country Inn    **Dinner:** $16-$26    **Phone:** 603/823-5501
**Location:** I-93, exit 38, 2.5 mi s on SR 18, then 0.5 mi w; in The Horse and Hound Inn. 205 Wells Rd 03580. **Hours:** Open 5/8-10/20 & 11/24-3/31; 6 pm-8 pm. Closed: Sun-Wed. **Reservations:** required.
American    **Features:** This inviting wood-pannelled candlelit dining room is located in a cozy country inn located in a quaint rural town. Casual dress; cocktails. **Parking:** on-site. **Cards:** AX, DC, DS, MC, VI.

**LOVETTS INN BY LAFAYETTE BROOK RESTAURANT** Country Inn    **Dinner:** $16-$22    **Phone:** 603/823-7761
**Location:** I-93, exit 38, 2.1 mi s on SR 18; in Lovetts Inn by Lafayette Brook. 1474 Profile Rd 03580. **Hours:** Open 5/1-3/31; 8 am-9:30 & 6-9 pm. Closed: 12/25; also Mon & Tues. **Reservations:** suggested. **Features:** This
Continental    informal dining room, located in an 18th-century inn, has elegant table tops, antique hard-wood chairs and quality wood trimmed walls. Guests may enjoy such entrees as pasta primavera, chicken forestiere, roast pork tenderloin, New York sirloin, roast duck, poached salmon and pan-fried boneless trout. Casual dress; cocktails. **Parking:** on-site. **Cards:** DS, MC, VI.

## FRANKLIN pop. 8,405

## ──── WHERE TO STAY ────

**ATWOOD INN**      **Phone:** (603)934-3666
All Year [BP]    1P: $65-$75    2P: $90-$100    XP: $25    F11
Historic Bed & Breakfast    **Location:** On SR 3A, 5 mi s on US 3, then 1.5 mi n. 71 Hill Rd (Rt 3A) 03235. **Facility:** This pleasant 1830 inn's landscaping is attractive and beautifully maintained; fireplaces are featured in four of their cozy guestrooms. Smoke free premises. 7 one-bedroom standard units. 3 stories (no elevator), interior corridors. **Bath:** combo or shower only. **Parking:** on-site. **Terms:** office hours 10 am-8 pm, 2 night minimum stay - weekends, 10 day cancellation notice-fee imposed. **Guest Services:** TV in common area. **Cards:** AX, DC, MC, VI.
SOME UNITS

## ──── WHERE TO DINE ────

**MR. D'S RESTAURANT**    **Lunch:** $7-$12    **Dinner:** $9-$18    **Phone:** 603/934-3142
**Location:** In West Franklin; jct SR 3A and 11. 428 N Main St 03235. **Hours:** 6 am-2 pm, Thurs-8 pm, Fri-9 pm, Sat-8:30 pm, Sun 8 am-2 pm, Mon 6 am-8 pm. Closed major holidays. **Features:** The restaurant specializes in seafood dishes, including fisherman's platters, clams, scallops, shrimp and chowders, as well
American    as steak, veal and lamb preparations. There are two main dining rooms, plus a full bar to complete the comfortable atmosphere. Casual dress; cocktails. **Parking:** on-site. **Cards:** AX, DC, DS, MC, VI.

# GILFORD

## ———— WHERE TO STAY ————

**BELKNAP POINT MOTEL**

Motel

| | | | |
|---|---|---|---|
| 6/11-9/6 | 1P: $100-$120 | 2P: $100-$120 | XP: $15   F16 |
| 5/1-6/10 & 9/7-10/11 | 1P: $87-$107 | 2P: $87-$107 | XP: $15   F16 |
| 10/12-4/30 | 1P: $72-$92 | 2P: $72-$92 | XP: $15   F16 |

Phone: 603/293-7511

**Location:** 3.5 mi e of ne jct US 3 and SR 11 N. 107 Belknap Point Rd 03249. Fax: 603/293-3552. **Facility:** 16 units. 13 one- and 1 two-bedroom standard units, some with efficiencies. 2 one-bedroom suites with efficiencies. 1-2 stories (no elevator), exterior corridors. *Bath:* combo or shower only. **Parking:** on-site. **Terms:** office hours 8:30 am-10 pm, 3 night minimum stay - 7/1-8/31, 14 day cancellation notice-fee imposed. **Amenities:** voice mail. **Leisure Activities:** boat dock, fishing. **Cards:** DS, MC, VI.

SOME UNITS

---

**B MAE'S RESORT INN & SUITES**

Small-scale Hotel

| | | |
|---|---|---|
| 5/20-8/31 [CP] | 2P: $116-$200 | XP: $15   F12 |
| 9/1-10/16 [CP] | 2P: $110-$200 | XP: $15   F12 |
| 5/1-5/19 [CP] | 2P: $80-$200 | XP: $15   F12 |
| 10/17-4/30 [CP] | 2P: $80-$150 | XP: $15   F12 |

Phone: (603)293-7526

**Location:** Jct SR 11 and 11B, 2.5 mi e of jct US 3 N. 17 Harris Shore Rd 03249. **Facility:** 83 units. 59 one-bedroom standard units. 24 one-bedroom suites with kitchens. 2 stories (no elevator), interior corridors. *Bath:* combo or shower only. **Parking:** on-site. **Terms:** 2-3 night minimum stay - weekends. **Amenities:** video library (fee), safes, irons, hair dryers. **Pool(s):** heated outdoor, heated indoor. **Leisure Activities:** whirlpool, exercise room. **Business Services:** meeting rooms. **Cards:** AX, CB, DC, DS, MC, VI. *(See color ad p 347 & below)*

SOME UNITS

---

**THE INN AT SMITH COVE**

Bed & Breakfast

| | | |
|---|---|---|
| All Year | 1P: $90-$170 | XP: $20   F11 |

Phone: 603/293-1111

**Location:** SR 11, 3 mi e of jct US 3 N. Roberts Rd 03249. Fax: 603/293-7660. **Facility:** Rooms are individually decorated and retain a cottage feel at this restored 1894 Victorian home; a dock and gazebo border the lake. Smoke free premises. 11 units. 10 one-bedroom standard units, some with whirlpools. 1 one-bedroom suite with whirlpool. 3 stories (no elevator), interior/exterior corridors. **Parking:** on-site. **Terms:** 2 night minimum stay - weekends, 7 day cancellation notice-fee imposed. **Leisure Activities:** boat dock. **Cards:** AX, DC, DS, MC, VI.

## ———— WHERE TO DINE ————

**PATRICK'S PUB & EATERY**

American

**Lunch:** $7-$17     **Dinner:** $7-$17     Phone: 603/293-0841
**Location:** Jct SR 11 and 11B; in Gilford Square. 18 Weirs Rd 03249. **Hours:** 11:30 am-10 pm. Closed: 11/25, 12/25. **Features:** The Irish-style pub has two sections: one with a lively bar atmosphere and a quieter area, which is appropriate for families. The large-portioned dishes are tasty. Casual dress; cocktails. **Parking:** on-site. **Cards:** MC, VI.

---

**VICTORIAN HOUSE**

French

**Dinner:** $17-$26     Phone: 603/293-8155
**Location:** Jct SR 11B, 3.3 mi se on SR 11. 2645 Lakeshore Rd 03249. **Hours:** 5 pm-9 pm. Closed: 11/25, 12/25. **Reservations:** suggested. **Features:** In an early 19th-century building that used to be an inn, the restaurant prepares such delicious country French specialties as roast rack of New Zealand lamb with fresh mint sauce and sauteed oysters with red peppers. The gardens are lovely. Dressy casual; cocktails. **Parking:** on-site. **Cards:** AX, DC, DS, MC, VI.

# GLEN

## —— WHERE TO STAY ——

### BERNERHOF INN
**Phone:** 603/383-9132

AAA SAVE
WWW
Country Inn

All Year [BP]          1P: $99-$199       2P: $99-$199      XP: $40      F12
**Location:** On US 302, 1.5 mi w of jct SR 16. US 302 03838 (PO Box 240). Fax: 603/383-0809. **Facility:** This small Victorian country inn features well-decorated guest rooms and is convenient to outlet stores. Smoke free premises. 9 units. 7 one-bedroom standard units, some with whirlpools. 2 one-bedroom suites with whirlpools. 3 stories (no elevator), interior corridors. *Bath:* combo or shower only. **Parking:** on-site. **Terms:** office hours 9 am-9 pm, 2-3 night minimum stay - seasonal, 14 day cancellation notice, [MAP] meal plan available, package plans - seasonal. **Amenities:** hair dryers. *Some:* CD players, irons. **Dining:** 6 pm-9 pm, cocktails. **Leisure Activities:** pool privileges. **Cards:** AX, DS, MC, VI. **Special Amenities: free full breakfast and preferred room (subject to availability with advanced reservations).**

SOME UNITS
[🍽] [🍷] [✖] / [VCR] /

### COVERED BRIDGE HOUSE
**Phone:** (603)383-9109

WWW
Historic Bed
& Breakfast

5/1-3/31 [BP]         1P: $64-$119       2P: $74-$119      XP: $15      D11
**Location:** On US 302, 1.9 mi w of jct SR 16. US 302 03838 (PO Box 989). Fax: 603/383-8089. **Facility:** A covered bridge built in 1850 houses a gift shop at this riverfront B&B, which offers well-appointed accommodations. Smoke free premises. 6 one-bedroom standard units. 2 stories (no elevator), interior corridors. *Bath:* some shared or private, combo or shower only. **Parking:** on-site. **Terms:** open 5/1-3/31, office hours 8 am-10 pm, 2 night minimum stay - seasonal & weekends, 14 day cancellation notice-fee imposed. **Guest Services:** TV in common area, gift shop. **Cards:** AX, DS, MC, VI.

[✖] [📺] [☎]

### THE RED APPLE INN
**Phone:** 603/383-9680

AAA SAVE
WWW
Motel

All Year [ECP]         1P: $49-$189       2P: $49-$189      XP: $10      F12
**Location:** On US 302, 1.5 mi w of jct SR 16. US 302 03838 (PO Box 103). Fax: 603/383-9680. **Facility:** Smoke free premises. 17 units. 16 one-bedroom standard units. 1 one-bedroom suite. 1-2 stories (no elevator), interior/exterior corridors. **Parking:** on-site. **Terms:** office hours 8 am-10 pm, 2 night minimum stay - seasonal, 14 day cancellation notice, package plans - seasonal. **Amenities:** *Some:* hair dryers. **Pool(s):** outdoor. **Leisure Activities:** picnic areas, barbecues, playground. *Fee:* game room. **Cards:** AX, DS, MC, VI. **Special Amenities: free expanded continental breakfast and preferred room (subject to availability with advanced reservations).**

SOME UNITS
[🍽] [🏊] [✖] [✖] [🛏] / [VCR] [📺] /

### WILL'S INN
**Phone:** 603/383-6757

AAA SAVE
WWW
Motel

All Year         1P: $45-$225       2P: $45-$225
**Location:** On US 302, 2 mi w of jct SR 16. US 302 03838 (PO Box 359, BARTLETT, 03812). Fax: 603/383-4552. **Facility:** Smoke free premises. 26 units. 16 one- and 1 two-bedroom standard units, some with efficiencies or kitchens. 4 one- and 1 two-bedroom suites ($119-$199), some with kitchens. 4 cabins. 2 stories (no elevator), exterior corridors. *Bath:* combo or shower only. **Parking:** on-site. **Terms:** office hours 8 am-7 pm, check-in 4 pm, 2-3 night minimum stay - seasonal & weekends, 14 day cancellation notice-fee imposed. **Pool(s):** heated outdoor. **Leisure Activities:** badminton, picnic area with barbecue grill, ping pong, playground, basketball, horseshoes, volleyball. *Fee:* game room. **Guest Services:** coin laundry. **Cards:** AX, DC, MC, VI.

SOME UNITS
[🆂] [🏊] [✖] [✖] [🛏] / [VCR] [📺] /

# GORHAM pop. 1,773

──────── **WHERE TO STAY** ────────

**COLONIAL COMFORT INN**

Motel

All Year      1P: $39-$85      2P: $48-$130     **Phone:** 603/466-2732   XP: $5    F12
**Location:** Jct US 2 and SR 16. 370 Main St 03581. **Facility:** 14 one-bedroom standard units. 1 story, exterior corridors. *Bath:* combo or shower only. **Parking:** on-site. **Terms:** 3 day cancellation notice. **Guest Services:** coin laundry. **Cards:** AX, DS, MC, VI.

SOME UNITS

FEE

**MOOSE BROOK MOTEL**

Motel

5/1-10/31      1P: $39-$79      2P: $39-$79     **Phone:** 603/466-5400   XP: $5    F17
**Location:** Jct SR 16, 0.5 mi w on US 2. 65 Lancaster Rd 03581. **Facility:** 13 units. 11 one- and 2 two-bedroom standard units, some with kitchens. 1 story, exterior corridors. *Bath:* combo or shower only. **Parking:** on-site. **Terms:** open 5/1-10/31, office hours 8 am-10 pm, 5 day cancellation notice, small pets only ($5 fee, in smoking units). **Pool(s):** outdoor. **Cards:** AX, DS, MC, VI.

SOME UNITS
FEE

**MT MADISON MOTEL**

Motel

5/15-10/31      1P: $37-$108      2P: $47-$124     **Phone:** (603)466-3622   XP: $10    F17
**Location:** 1.2 mi n on US 2 and SR 16. 365 Main St 03581. Fax: 603/466-3353. **Facility:** 32 units. 29 one- and 3 two-bedroom standard units. 1-2 stories (no elevator), exterior corridors. *Bath:* combo or shower only. **Parking:** on-site. **Terms:** open 5/15-10/31, office hours 7 am-10 pm, 3 day cancellation notice, weekly rates available, package plans - weekends, small pets only. **Pool(s):** heated outdoor. **Cards:** AX, DS, MC, VI. *(See color ad below)*

SOME UNITS

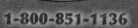

**ROYALTY INN**

Small-scale Hotel

| | | | |
|---|---|---|---|
| 7/1-10/16 | 1P: $64-$94 | 2P: $68-$102 | XP: $5    F3 |
| 12/27-4/30 | 1P: $51-$74 | 2P: $63-$79 | XP: $4    F3 |
| 5/1-6/30 | 1P: $50-$72 | 2P: $61-$79 | XP: $4    F3 |
| 10/17-12/26 | 1P: $51-$67 | 2P: $61-$74 | XP: $4    F3 |

Phone: (603)466-3312

**Location:** On US 2 and SR 16; center. 130 Main St 03581. Fax: 603/466-5802. **Facility:** 88 one-bedroom standard units, some with efficiencies. 1-2 stories (no elevator), interior/exterior corridors. **Parking:** on-site, winter plug-ins. **Terms:** pets ($5 extra charge). **Amenities:** voice mail. **Pool(s):** heated outdoor, heated indoor. **Leisure Activities:** sauna, whirlpool, racquetball courts, basketball. **Fee:** massage, game room. **Guest Services:** coin laundry. **Business Services:** meeting rooms, fax (fee). **Cards:** AX, CB, DC, DS, MC, VI. **(See color ad below)**

## TOP NOTCH INN

**Book at aaa.com**

Motel

| | | | |
|---|---|---|---|
| 7/2-10/16 | 1P: $65-$142 | 2P: $65-$142 | XP: $10 F12 |
| 6/12-7/1 | 1P: $54-$87 | 2P: $54-$87 | XP: $10 F12 |
| 5/8-6/11 | 1P: $44-$76 | 2P: $44-$76 | XP: $10 F12 |
| 10/17-10/30 | 1P: $44-$54 | 2P: $44-$54 | XP: $10 F12 |

**Phone:** (603)466-5496

**Location:** On US 2 and SR 16; center. 265 Main St 03581. **Facility:** 36 one-bedroom standard units. 1-2 stories (no elevator), interior/exterior corridors. *Bath:* combo or shower only. **Parking:** on-site. **Terms:** open 5/8-10/30, office hours 8 am-10 pm, cancellation fee imposed, pets (small dogs only). **Amenities:** *Some:* hair dryers. **Pool(s):** outdoor. **Leisure Activities:** whirlpool. **Guest Services:** coin laundry. **Cards:** AX, DS, MC, VI. **Special Amenities:** free local telephone calls and free newspaper. *(See color ad p 332)*

SOME UNITS

## TOWN & COUNTRY MOTOR INN

Small-scale Hotel

| | | | |
|---|---|---|---|
| 9/17-10/18 | 1P: $50-$86 | 2P: $68-$96 | XP: $6 F16 |
| 6/19-9/16 | 1P: $50-$76 | 2P: $58-$86 | XP: $6 F16 |
| 10/19-4/30 | 1P: $50-$72 | 2P: $62-$76 | XP: $6 F16 |
| 5/1-6/18 | 1P: $48-$72 | 2P: $62-$76 | XP: $6 F16 |

**Phone:** (603)466-3315

**Location:** 0.5 mi e of jct SR 16. US Rt 2 03581 (PO Box 220). **Fax:** 603/466-3316. **Facility:** 160 units. 157 one-bedroom standard units, some with whirlpools. 3 two-bedroom suites ($115). 2 stories (no elevator), interior/exterior corridors. **Parking:** on-site, winter plug-ins. **Terms:** package plans, pets ($6 extra charge). **Amenities:** hair dryers. **Dining:** dining room, see separate listing. **Pool(s):** heated indoor. **Leisure Activities:** saunas, whirlpool, steamroom, recreation programs, bicycles, hiking trails, jogging, exercise room. **Fee:** golf-18 holes, massage, game room. **Business Services:** meeting rooms. **Cards:** AX, CB, DC, DS, MC, VI. *(See color ad below)*

SOME UNITS

FEE FEE

---

## —— WHERE TO DINE ——

### MARY'S PIZZA & PASTA

Italian

**Lunch:** $5-$11    **Dinner:** $6-$14    **Phone:** 603/752-6150

**Location:** 2.7 mi n on SR 16 from jct US 2; 2 mi s on SR 16 from jct SR 110. 9 Cascade Flats 03581. **Hours:** 4 pm-9 pm, Wed-Sat from 11 am. Closed major holidays; also Sun. **Features:** This third-generation family diner established in 1947 specializes in pizza and homemade pasta. Small or large portions are available including fettuccini Alfredo, spaghetti with white clam sauce, linguini and manicotti. Casual dress; beer & wine only. **Parking:** on-site. **Cards:** AX, DS, MC, VI.

### TOWN & COUNTRY MOTOR INN

American

**Dinner:** $12-$19    **Phone:** 603/466-3315

**Location:** 0.5 mi e of jct SR 16; in Town & Country Motor Inn. US Rt 2 03581. **Hours:** 6 am-10:30 & 5:30-10 pm, Sun 6 am-10:30 & noon-9 pm. Closed: 12/25. **Reservations:** suggested. **Features:** The varied menu features New England prime beef, chops and fresh seafood. The dining room is informal and pleasantly decorated. Menu items include filet mignon, New York sirloin, lamb chops, pork chops, veal cutlets, Maine lobster, filet of haddock, cape scallops and vegetable linguini. Casual dress; cocktails. **Parking:** on-site. **Cards:** AX, DC, DS, MC, VI.

### WILFRED'S RESTAURANT

American

**Lunch:** $3-$8    **Dinner:** $8-$15    **Phone:** 603/466-2380

**Location:** On US 2; center. 117 Main St 03581. **Hours:** 11 am-9 pm. Closed: Wed. **Reservations:** accepted. **Features:** If you like turkey, you'll love Wilfred's! They know how to serve it properly and deliciously; it has been a specialty here for nearly 60 years. Hearty portions and a good dessert selection are also offered. Casual dress; cocktails. **Parking:** on-site. **Cards:** AX, DS, MC, VI.

### YOKOHAMA RESTAURANT

Japanese

**Lunch:** $4-$9    **Dinner:** $8-$18    **Phone:** 603/466-2501

**Location:** 0.8 mi n on US 2 and SR 16. 288 Main St 03581. **Hours:** 11 am-9 pm. Closed: 11/25, 12/24, 12/25; also Mon. **Reservations:** accepted. **Features:** The menu features a good selection of American dishes in addition to the well-prepared and nicely presented Japanese offerings. You'll find that the serving staff is home-style friendly and attentive. The traditional decor is comfortable. Casual dress; cocktails. **Parking:** on-site. **Cards:** AX, MC, VI.

**HAMPTON** pop. 9,162—*See also NORTH HAMPTON.*

### ———— WHERE TO STAY ————

**THE INN OF HAMPTON AND CONFERENCE CENTER**  *Book at aaa.com*  Phone: (603)926-6771

| | | |
|---|---|---|
| AAA SAVE | 5/1-9/30 [ECP] | 1P: $139-$195 | 2P: $139-$195 | XP: $10 | F12 |
| ▼▼▼ | 10/1-4/30 [ECP] | 1P: $105-$170 | 2P: $105-$170 | XP: $10 | F12 |

Small-scale Hotel  **Location:** 0.5 mi n on US 1. 815 Lafayette Rd 03842. Fax: 603/929-2160. **Facility:** 71 units. 69 one-bedroom standard units, some with kitchens. 2 two-bedroom suites. 2 stories, interior corridors. *Bath:* combo or shower only. **Parking:** on-site. **Terms:** 2 night minimum stay - weekends 6/4-9/4, 4 day cancellation notice-fee imposed. **Amenities:** voice mail, safes, irons, hair dryers. **Dining:** 6:30 am-9:30 & 5-9 pm, Fri-10 pm, Sat 8 am-11 & 5-10 pm; closed Sun, cocktails. **Pool(s):** heated indoor. **Leisure Activities:** whirlpool, exercise room. *Fee:* game room. **Guest Services:** valet and coin laundry. **Business Services:** conference facilities. **Cards:** AX, DC, DS, MC, VI. **Special Amenities:** free expanded continental breakfast and free local telephone calls.

SOME UNITS

⊙ 🅂ⅅ ❙❙ ⊡ Ⓜ 👍 🐕 ➳ ✕ 🔌 DATA PORT 📶 📷 💳 / ✕ VCR /

**LAMIE'S INN & TAVERN**  *Book at aaa.com*  Phone: (603)926-0330

| | | |
|---|---|---|
| ▼▼▼ | 5/1-10/31 [ECP] | 2P: $105-$145 | XP: $15 | F12 |
| ▼▼▼ | 11/1-4/30 [ECP] | 2P: $95-$115 | XP: $10 | F12 |

Country Inn  **Location:** Jct SR 27 on US 1. 490 Lafayette Rd 03842. Fax: 603/929-0017. **Facility:** This service-oriented country inn has a cozy atmosphere offering modern amenities and B&B hospitality. 32 one-bedroom standard units. 2 stories (no elevator), interior corridors. *Bath:* combo or shower only. **Parking:** on-site. **Terms:** 3 day cancellation notice, small pets only ($100 deposit, $10 extra charge). **Dining:** Old Salt Eating & Drinking Place, see separate listing. **Guest Services:** valet laundry. **Business Services:** meeting rooms. **Cards:** AX, DC, DS, MC, VI.

SOME UNITS

ASK 🅂ⅅ 🐕 ❙❙ 👍 👍 📷 DATA PORT / ✕ 📶 /
　　　FEE　　　　FEE

**THE SEASCAPE INN AT PLAICE COVE**  Phone: 603/926-1750

| | | |
|---|---|---|
| AAA SAVE | 6/23-9/4 [CP] | 1P: $105-$115 | 2P: $115-$130 | XP: $10 | F3 |
| ▼▼▼ | 9/5-10/31 [CP] | 1P: $70-$85 | 2P: $85-$95 | XP: $10 | F3 |
| | 5/1-6/22 [CP] | 1P: $70-$85 | 2P: $80-$95 | XP: $10 | F3 |

Motel  **Location:** SR 1A, 0.3 mi n of SR 27. 955 Ocean Blvd 03842-1435. **Facility:** Smoke free premises. 19 one-bedroom standard units. 2 stories (no elevator), exterior corridors. *Bath:* shower only. **Parking:** on-site. **Terms:** open 5/1-10/31, 2-3 night minimum stay - weekends 7/1-8/31, 7 day cancellation notice-fee imposed. **Cards:** AX, MC, VI. **Special Amenities:** free continental breakfast and free local telephone calls. *(See color ad below)*

🅂ⅅ ❙❙ ✕ 📶

**THE VICTORIA INN**  Phone: (603)929-1437

| | | |
|---|---|---|
| ▼▼▼ | 11/1-4/30 | 2P: $130-$260 | XP: $25 | F5 |
| | 5/1-10/31 | 2P: $120-$250 | XP: $20 | F5 |

Bed & Breakfast  **Location:** Jct US 1, 1.7 mi e on SR 27. 430 High St 03842. Fax: 603/929-0747. **Facility:** In summer, English-style gardens grace the grounds of this attractive inn, which dates from 1875. 6 units. 3 one-bedroom standard units. 2 one- and 1 two-bedroom suites. 3 stories (no elevator), interior corridors. *Bath:* combo or shower only. **Parking:** on-site. **Terms:** office hours 8 am-11 pm, 2 night minimum stay - weekends in season, age restrictions may apply, 14 day cancellation notice-fee imposed, [BP] meal plan available, package plans - seasonal. **Guest Services:** complimentary evening beverages. **Cards:** AX, MC, VI.

SOME UNITS

ASK 🅂ⅅ 📷 DATA PORT / ✕ /

### ———— WHERE TO DINE ————

**CRUST & CRUMB BAKERY & CAFE**  Lunch: $5-$7  Phone: 603/929-0700

▼▼▼  **Location:** Jct SR 27, 1 mi n on US 1. 881 Lafayette Rd 03842. **Hours:** 6:30 am-3 pm, Sun from 7 am. Closed: 1/1, 11/25, 12/25. **Features:** The vast breakfast menu of sweet and savory items is a terrific way to start the day. Delicatessen sandwiches and soups are available for lunch. Casual dress. **Parking:** on-site.
Bakery/Desserts  **Cards:** AX, MC, VI.

**THE GALLEY HATCH RESTAURANT & GOURMET BAKERY**   **Lunch:** $6-$22   **Dinner:** $6-$22   **Phone:** 603/926-6152
American
**Location:** On US 1, just s of jct SR 27. 325 Lafayette Rd (Rt 1) 03842. **Hours:** 11:30 am-9 pm. Closed: 11/25, 12/25. **Reservations:** accepted. **Features:** The freshly baked desserts, pastries and breads are themselves worth the trip. However, the main dishes are terrific as well, including fresh fish, roasted chicken, New York Sirloin and a variety of creative sandwiches. Casual dress; cocktails. **Parking:** on-site.
**Cards:** AX, DC, DS, MC, VI.

**OLD SALT EATING & DRINKING PLACE**   **Lunch:** $5-$15   **Dinner:** $5-$15   **Phone:** 603/926-8322
Seafood
**Location:** Jct SR 27 on US 1; in Lamie's Inn & Tavern. 490 Lafayette Rd (US 1) 03842. **Hours:** 11:30 am-10 pm, Fri & Sat-11 pm, Sun 10 am-10 pm. Closed: 12/25. **Reservations:** accepted. **Features:** In a pleasant country inn, the renovated dining room resembles an old barn with high, beamed ceilings and decor fitting a traditional New England theme. The menu features well-prepared steaks and seafood. Everything is made from scratch, including the salad dressing. Portions are huge. Casual dress; cocktails. **Parking:** on-site. **Cards:** AX, DS, MC, VI.

**RON'S LANDING AT ROCKY BEND**   **Dinner:** $18-$27   **Phone:** 603/929-2122
Seafood
**Location:** I-95, exit 2, just e on SR 101 to US 1A (Ocean Blvd), then 0.3 mi n. 379 Ocean Blvd 03842. **Hours:** 4 pm-10 pm, Sun 2 pm-8 pm; closing hours may vary off season. Closed: 1/1, 11/25, 12/25. **Reservations:** suggested. **Features:** The restaurant specializes in fresh seafood, but the menu also lists beef, veal, chicken and pasta dishes. Check out the dessert menu, too. The casually elegant dining room affords great views of the ocean. Casual dress; cocktails. **Parking:** on-site. **Cards:** AX, DC, DS, MC, VI.

**WIDOW FLETCHER'S TAVERN**   **Dinner:** $8-$20   **Phone:** 603/926-8800
American
**Location:** In center of Hampton Village on US 1, just s of jct SR 27. 401 Lafayette Rd (US 1) 03842. **Hours:** 4:30 pm-9 pm. Closed: 11/25, 12/25. **Reservations:** suggested. **Features:** The casual and classic English-style tavern derives character from its rustic decor. The menu features some traditional pub fare, such as bangers and mash, as well as seafood, pork, poultry, beef and sandwiches. A number of lighter meals are also offered. Vegetables are fresh, and salad dressings are made in house. Casual dress; cocktails. **Parking:** on-site. **Cards:** AX, DS, MC, VI.

----------- *The following restaurant has not been evaluated by AAA* -----------
*but is listed for your information only.*

**THE ATLANTIC GRILL**   **Phone:** 603/926-5668
[fyi]
Not evaluated. **Location:** 6 High St 03842. **Features:** In a convenient spot on the way to Hampton Beach, the grill provides parking in the back of the building.

# HAMPTON BEACH

----------- **WHERE TO STAY** -----------

**ASHWORTH BY THE SEA HOTEL**   **Phone:** (603)926-6762

| | | | | |
|---|---|---|---|---|
| 6/18-9/12 | 1P: $155-$235 | 2P: $165-$235 | XP: $20 | D18 |
| 9/13-10/17 | 1P: $125-$185 | 2P: $125-$185 | XP: $20 | D18 |
| 5/1-6/17 | 1P: $115-$185 | 2P: $115-$185 | XP: $20 | D18 |
| 10/18-4/30 | 1P: $95-$155 | 2P: $95-$155 | XP: $20 | D18 |

Small-scale Hotel **Location:** I-95, exit 2, 3 mi e on SR 101. 295 Ocean Blvd 03842. Fax: 603/926-2002. **Facility:** 105 one-bedroom standard units. 3-4 stories, interior corridors. *Bath:* combo or shower only. **Parking:** on-site. **Terms:** 2-3 night minimum stay - seasonal & some weekends, 7 day cancellation notice, package plans. **Amenities:** voice mail, hair dryers. *Some:* irons. **Dining:** 2 restaurants, 6:30 am-11 pm, cocktails, entertainment. **Pool(s):** heated indoor. **Guest Services:** valet laundry. **Business Services:** meeting rooms. **Cards:** AX, CB, DC, DS, MC, VI. **Special Amenities:** free local telephone calls.
*(See color ad below)*

SOME UNITS

**HAMPTON HARBOR MOTEL**

| | | | |
|---|---|---|---|
| | 6/19-9/12 | 1P: $99-$189 | 2P: $99-$189 | XP: $15 | F12 |
| | 5/1-6/18 | 1P: $59-$99 | 2P: $59-$99 | XP: $15 | F12 |
| Motel | 9/13-4/30 | 1P: $49-$89 | 2P: $49-$89 | XP: $15 | F12 |

Phone: 603/926-4432

**Location:** 0.5 mi s on US 1A (Ocean Blvd). 210 Ashworth Ave 03842. Fax: 603/929-0225. **Facility:** 22 one-bedroom standard units, some with efficiencies. 3 stories (no elevator), exterior corridors. **Parking:** on-site. **Terms:** office hours 8 am-10 pm, 2 night minimum stay, 7 day cancellation notice, weekly rates available. **Pool(s):** heated outdoor. **Cards:** DS, MC, VI.

SOME UNITS

## HAMPTON FALLS pop. 1,880

────── WHERE TO STAY ──────

**HAMPTON FALLS INN**

| | | | |
|---|---|---|---|
| | 6/16-8/31 | 1P: $109-$169 | 2P: $109-$169 | XP: $10 | F12 |
| | 9/1-10/31 | 1P: $89-$139 | 2P: $89-$139 | XP: $10 | F12 |
| Motel | 5/1-6/15 & 11/1-4/30 | 1P: $69-$139 | 2P: $69-$139 | XP: $10 | F12 |

Phone: (603)926-9545

**Location:** I-95, exit 1, 0.5 mi e on SR 107, 1 mi n on US 1. 11 Lafayette Rd 03844. Fax: 603/926-4155. **Facility:** 48 units. 45 one-bedroom standard units. 3 one-bedroom suites. 3 stories (no elevator), interior corridors. **Parking:** on-site. **Terms:** cancellation fee imposed, pets ($50 deposit, small dogs only, with prior approval). **Amenities:** video library (fee), voice mail, safes, irons, hair dryers. **Dining:** 7 am-noon; hours may vary seasonally. **Pool(s):** heated indoor. **Leisure Activities:** whirlpool. **Guest Services:** valet laundry. **Business Services:** meeting rooms. **Cards:** AX, CB, DC, DS, MC, VI. *(See color ad below)*

SOME UNITS

FEE                                          FEE

## HANCOCK

────── WHERE TO STAY ──────

**THE HANCOCK INN**

Country Inn

All Year [BP]     1P: $120-$270     2P: $120-$270     XP: $25     F12

Phone: 603/525-3318

**Location:** Jct of SR 123 and 137; center. 33 Main St 03449 (PO Box 96). Fax: 603/525-9301. **Facility:** Dating to 1789, this small-town property is one of the oldest continuously operating inns in New England. Smoke free premises. 15 one-bedroom standard units, some with whirlpools. 3 stories (no elevator), interior corridors. *Bath:* combo or shower only. **Parking:** on-site. **Terms:** office hours 7 am-10 pm, 2-3 night minimum stay - weekends, age restrictions may apply, 15 day cancellation notice-fee imposed. **Dining:** restaurant, see separate listing. **Business Services:** meeting rooms. **Cards:** AX, DC, DS, MC, VI.

────── WHERE TO DINE ──────

**HANCOCK INN**

American

DC, DS, MC, VI.

Dinner: $21-$29

Phone: 603/525-3318

**Location:** Jct SR 123 and 137; center; in The Hancock Inn. 33 Main St 03449. **Hours:** 6 pm-9 pm. Closed: 12/25. **Reservations:** suggested. **Features:** The restaurant's elegant surroundings and country-inn atmosphere blend to create a memorable experience. Menu selections are exquisitely prepared and attractively presented, and servers are vigilant to diners' needs. Casual dress; cocktails. **Parking:** on-site. **Cards:** AX,

**FIDDLEHEAD'S CAFE**                                                                    Phone: 603/525-4432
[fyi]   Not evaluated. **Location:** 28 Main St 03449. **Features:** A loyal local following patronizes the casual cafe, which is open for breakfast, lunch and dinner.

# HANOVER pop. 8,162

## ———— WHERE TO STAY ————

**CHIEFTAIN MOTOR INN**                                                                 Phone: 603/643-2550
AAA [SAVE]   All Year                    1P: $100-$150
WWW WW       **Location:** I-91, exit 13; SR 10, 2.5 mi n. 84 Lyme Rd 03755. Fax: 603/643-5265. **Facility:** 22 one-bedroom stan-
Motel        dard units. 1-2 stories (no elevator), exterior corridors. **Bath:** combo or shower only. **Parking:** on-site.
             **Terms:** office hours 7 am-9 pm, cancellation fee imposed, weekly rates available, package plans, pets ($20
             extra charge). **Amenities:** voice mail. **Pool(s):** heated outdoor. **Leisure Activities:** canoeing, boat dock, bar-
             becue grills. **Guest Services:** sundries. **Business Services:** fax (fee). **Cards:** AX, DC, MC, VI.
**Special Amenities: free expanded continental breakfast and free room upgrade (subject to availability with advanced reservations).**

SOME UNITS

**THE HANOVER INN AT DARTMOUTH COLLEGE**                                                Phone: 603/643-4300
[fyi]   Not evaluated. **Location:** Center. Main & Wheelocke St 03755 (PO Box 151). Facilities, services, and decor characterize an upscale property.

## ———— WHERE TO DINE ————

**JESSE'S**              **Lunch:** $7-$10       **Dinner:** $11-$20        Phone: 603/643-4111
AAA   **Location:** I-89, exit 18, 3 mi n. SR 120 03755. **Hours:** 11:30 am-3 & 5-9:30 pm, Fri-10:30 pm, Sat 5 pm-10:30
WW WW  pm, Sun 4:30 pm-9:30 pm; 5 pm-10 pm, Fri & Sat-10:30 pm, Sun 4:30 pm-9:30 pm 5/28-9/6. Closed:
American   11/25, 12/24, 12/25; also Super Bowl Sun. **Reservations:** accepted. **Features:** Jesse's is famous for prime
       rib and fresh Maine lobster dishes. They offer house specialties such as teriyaki sirloin, peppercorn steak
       and delectable desserts. The rustic log cabin has three distinct dining rooms: Victorian, Adirondack and
       Greenhouse. Casual dress; cocktails. **Parking:** on-site. **Cards:** AX, MC, VI.

**LOU'S RESTAURANT & BAKERY**         **Lunch:** $5-$8            Phone: 603/643-3321
WW    **Location:** Center. 30 S Main St 03755. **Hours:** 6 am-3 pm, Sat & Sun from 7 am. Closed: 11/25, 12/25.
American   **Features:** Breakfast served all day is the specialty. In 2000, Market Surveys of American named the
      restaurant the "best breakfast spot in the Upper Valley for the last five years." Don't miss the delicious
      pies, cakes and other goodies prepared daily in the on-site bakery. Casual dress. **Parking:** street.
**Cards:** AX, MC, VI.

**MOLLY'S RESTAURANT & BAR**          **Lunch:** $6-$10      **Dinner:** $10-$20     Phone: 603/643-2570
AAA   **Location:** Center. 43 S Main St 03755. **Hours:** 11:30 am-10 pm, Fri & Sat-11 pm. Closed: 11/25, 12/25; also
WW WW  Super Bowl Sun. **Reservations:** accepted. **Features:** Located on the campus of Dartmouth College,
American   Molly's Restaurant offers a casual, comfortable atmosphere, a friendly, attentive staff, and imaginative
      offerings of pizza, pasta, stew, soup, burgers, sandwiches, fish and full dinners, and patio dining. Casual
      dress; cocktails. **Parking:** on-site. **Cards:** AX, MC, VI.

**MURPHY'S ON THE GREEN**             **Lunch:** $6-$12     **Dinner:** $6-$20      Phone: 603/643-4075
WWW WWW   **Location:** Center. 11 S Main St 03755. **Hours:** 11 am-10 pm. Closed: 11/25, 12/25. **Reservations:** accepted.
American   **Features:** Locals consider the restaurant a great place to get together and enjoy a good variety of burgers,
      sandwiches, pasta dishes or the "legendary" prime rib. Order a pint from the extensive selection of
      domestic and imported beer and ale. Casual dress; cocktails. **Parking:** street. **Cards:** AX, DC, DS, MC, VI.

# HARTS LOCATION

## ———— WHERE TO STAY ————

**NOTCHLAND INN**                                                                       Phone: (603)374-6131
WWW WW   9/17-10/16 [BP]            1P: $210-$270       2P: $240-$300       XP: $25
Historic  5/1-9/16 & 10/17-4/30 [BP]  1P: $160-$220       2P: $190-$250       XP: $25
Country Inn   **Location:** From Bartlett, 6.4 mi w. US 302 03812. Fax: 603/374-6168. **Facility:** A granite mansion built in 1862 in
       the midst of the White Mountains, the inn offers elegant public areas. Smoke free premises. 14 units. 7 one-
       bedroom standard units. 6 one-bedroom suites, some with whirlpools. 1 cottage with whirlpool. 2 stories (no
elevator), interior corridors. **Bath:** combo or shower only. **Parking:** on-site. **Terms:** office hours 9 am-9 pm, check-in 4 pm, 2 night
minimum stay - with Saturday stayover, 14 day cancellation notice-fee imposed, [MAP] meal plan available, package plans -
seasonal midweek, pets ($10 extra charge, in limited units, owner's pet on premises). **Amenities:** CD players, irons, hair dryers.
**Leisure Activities:** whirlpool, cross country skiing, ice skating, hiking trails. **Guest Services:** gift shop. **Cards:** DS, MC, VI.

SOME UNITS

# HENNIKER pop. 1,627

——— WHERE TO STAY ———

**COLBY HILL INN**
▼▼▼
Historic
Country Inn

Phone: (603)428-3281
All Year [BP]　　　　1P: $105-$255　　2P: $115-$265　　XP: $20　　D12
**Location:** 0.5 mi s of US 202 and SR 9, via SR 114, 0.5 mi w on Western Ave. Located in a quiet area. 3 The Oaks 03242 (PO Box 779). Fax: 603/428-9218. **Facility:** Set in a quiet village, this 1800s farmhouse is furnished with many antiques and offers varied-size rooms. Designated smoking area. 16 one-bedroom standard units, some with whirlpools. 2 stories (no elevator), interior corridors. *Bath:* combo or shower only. **Parking:** on-site.
**Terms:** 2 night minimum stay - some weekends, age restrictions may apply, 7 day cancellation notice-fee imposed, package plans. **Amenities:** hair dryers. **Dining:** restaurant, see separate listing. **Pool(s):** outdoor. **Leisure Activities:** volleyball. **Guest Services:** TV in common area. **Business Services:** meeting rooms. **Cards:** AX, CB, DC, DS, MC, VI.

〔❙❙〕 〔⊃〕 ✕ 〔Ｗ〕 〔DATA PORT〕

**HENNIKER MOTEL**
▼▼
Motel

Phone: 603-428-3536
All Year　　　　　　1P: $68-$110　　2P: $68-$110　　XP: $15
**Location:** I-89, exit 5, 6.5 mi w on US 202 and SR 9, to jct SR 114, 3 mi s on SR 114 to Flanders Rd, then 0.5 mi w, follow signs. 21 one-bedroom standard units. 2 stories (no elevator), interior/exterior corridors. *Bath:* combo or shower only. **Parking:** on-site. **Terms:** office hours 7 am-9 pm, check-in 4 pm, 7 day cancellation notice-fee imposed. **Amenities:** voice mail. **Pool(s):** heated indoor. **Cards:** AX, MC, VI.

SOME UNITS
〔❙❙→〕 〔⊃〕 〔📷〕 〔DATA PORT〕 🔒 / ✕ /

**MEETING HOUSE INN**
🆎 (SAVE)
▼▼▼
Historic
Country Inn

Phone: 603-428-3228
All Year [BP]　　　　1P: $85-$105　　2P: $85-$105　　XP: $20　　D10
**Location:** I-89, exit 5, 6.5 mi w on US 202 and SR 9 to jct SR 114, 3 mi s on SR 114 to Flanders Rd, then 0.5 mi w, follow signs. Located adjacent to Pat's Peak ski area. 35 Flanders Rd 03242. Fax: 603/428-6334. **Facility:** This 18th-century house was rebuilt in 1840 and offers cozy guest rooms with modest decor; an attached barn houses a restaurant. Smoke free premises. 6 units. 4 one-bedroom standard units. 2 one-bedroom suites ($125), some with efficiencies. 2 stories (no elevator), interior corridors. *Bath:* combo, shower or tub only. **Parking:** on-site. **Terms:** office hours 8 am-10 pm, 3 day cancellation notice. **Dining:** restaurant, see separate listing. **Leisure Activities:** Fee: private whirlpool. **Guest Services:** TV in common area. **Cards:** AX, MC, VI. **Special Amenities:** free full breakfast.

SOME UNITS
〔❙❙〕 ✕ 〔Ｗ〕 〔📷〕 〔✉〕 / 🔒 〔▦〕 /

——— WHERE TO DINE ———

**COLBY HILL INN RESTAURANT**　Country Inn
▼▼▼
American

Dinner: $21-$31　　　　Phone: 603-428-3281
**Location:** 0.5 mi s of US 202 and SR 9, via SR 114, 0.5 mi w on Western Ave; in Colby Hill Inn. 3 The Oaks 03242. **Hours:** 5:30 pm-8:30 pm. Closed: 12/24, 12/25; also Mon 1/1-4/30. **Reservations:** suggested, weekends. **Features:** New England favorites are prepared with a Continental flair and served in candlelit dining rooms. Trained chefs make all foods strictly from scratch. Delightful perennial gardens and a gazebo surround the 1790 farmhouse. Children must be older than 7 to dine here. Casual dress; cocktails. **Parking:** on-site. **Cards:** AX, CB, DC, DS, MC, VI.

✕

**MEETING HOUSE INN RESTAURANT**　Historic
▼▼▼
Continental

Dinner: $15-$28　　　　Phone: 603-428-3228
**Location:** I-89, exit 5, 6.5 mi w on US 202 and SR 9, to jct SR 114, 3 mi s on SR 114 to Flanders Rd, then 0.5 mi w, follow signs; in The Meeting House Inn. 35 Flanders Rd 03242. **Hours:** 4 pm-11 pm. Closed: 1/1, 11/25, 12/25; also Mon. **Reservations:** suggested. **Features:** New owners have reinvented the Meeting House from New England cuisine to more Middle Eastern haute cuisine. Also on the menu are traditional favorites. Casual dress; cocktails. **Parking:** on-site. **Cards:** AX, MC, VI.

✕

# HOLDERNESS

——— WHERE TO STAY ———

**THE MANOR ON GOLDEN POND**
🆎 (SAVE)
▼▼▼ ▼▼▼
Historic
Country Inn

Phone: 603-968-3348
5/13-10/31 [BP]　　　　　　　2P: $225-$450　　XP: $35
5/1-5/12 & 11/1-4/30 [BP]　　　2P: $180-$450　　XP: $35
**Location:** I-93, exit 24, 5 mi e on US 3. Shepard Hill Rd 03245 (PO Box T). Fax: 603/968-2116. **Facility:** This English-style mansion situated atop a knoll overlooking Squam Lake and graced with lovely grounds and even some private cottages. Smoke free premises. 25 one-bedroom standard units, some with whirlpools. 1-2 stories (no elevator), interior/exterior corridors. *Bath:* combo or shower only. **Parking:** on-site. **Terms:** 2 night minimum stay - weekends in summer, age restrictions may apply, 30 day cancellation notice-fee imposed. **Amenities:** CD players, irons, hair dryers. **Dining:** The Manor Dining Room, see separate listing. **Pool(s):** outdoor. **Leisure Activities:** canoeing, paddleboats, boat dock, fishing, lighted tennis court, croquet, horseshoes, volleyball. *Fee:* massage. **Business Services:** meeting rooms. **Cards:** AX, DS, MC, VI. **Special Amenities:** free full breakfast and free newspaper.

SOME UNITS
〔❙❙〕 〔Ｙ〕 〔⊃〕 〔✕〕 ✕ 〔VCR〕 〔DATA PORT〕 / 🔒 〔▥〕

——— WHERE TO DINE ———

**THE MANOR DINING ROOM**　Historic
🆎
▼▼▼ ▼▼▼
American

Dinner: $25-$38　　　　Phone: 603-968-3348
**Location:** I-93, exit 24, 5 mi e on US 3; in The Manor on Golden Pond. Shepard Hill Rd 03245. **Hours:** 6 pm-8:30 pm; hours vary off season. Closed: Mon & Tues 11/1-5/15. **Reservations:** suggested. **Features:** The Manor's creative New American cuisine offers three- or five-course fixed-price dinners that are artistically presented and wonderfully flavorful, with a hint of French influence. The decor is elegant and relaxed; service is superb. Dressy casual; cocktails. **Parking:** on-site. **Cards:** AX, DS, MC, VI.

〔Ｙ〕 ✕

**WALTER'S BASIN**
American
**Lunch:** $6-$12   **Dinner:** $11-$22   **Phone:** 603/968-4412
**Location:** I-93, exit 24, 4 mi e. US 3 03245. **Hours:** 11:30 am-10 pm. Closed: 12/24, 12/25.
**Reservations:** accepted. **Features:** On Little Squam Lake, the restaurant serves lunch, dinner and Sunday brunch. Casual dress; cocktails. **Parking:** street. **Cards:** AX, MC, VI.

## HUDSON pop. 7,814

——— **WHERE TO DINE** ———

**STEVIE P'S YACHT CLUB**
Seafood
**Lunch:** $6-$14   **Dinner:** $6-$14   **Phone:** 603/886-5191
**Location:** On SR 3A; 0.8 mi s of jct SR 111. 49 Lowell Rd 03051. **Hours:** 11:30 am-8 pm, Thurs-Sat to 9 pm.
Closed: 12/25; also Mon. **Features:** The restaurant's setting looks like a boatyard, and the nautical theme is continued inside. The extensive menu features shrimp, haddock, scallops and clam dishes, as well as pasta, chicken, steak and burgers. A fixed-price menu for seniors is offered. Casual dress; cocktails.
**Parking:** on-site. **Cards:** AX, DS, MC, VI.

## INTERVALE

——— **WHERE TO STAY** ———

**THE FOREST, A COUNTRY INN**   **Phone:** (603)356-9772
Historic Bed & Breakfast
| 9/23-10/24 [BP] | 2P: $129-$179 |
| 7/1-9/22 & 10/25-3/31 [BP] | 2P: $89-$139 |
| 5/1-6/30 [BP] | 2P: $79-$129 |
**Location:** Jct US 302 and SR 16, southbound 1.5 mi ne; northbound 1 mi se; 2.5 mi n of village of N Conway. Located in a quiet area. SR 16A 03845 (PO Box 37). Fax: 603/356-5652. **Facility:** Nestled in a peaceful mountain setting, this 1890s Victorian inn is furnished with period antiques. Smoke free premises. 11 one-bedroom standard units, some with whirlpools. 3 stories (no elevator), interior corridors. *Bath:* combo or shower only. **Parking:** on-site. **Terms:** open 5/1-3/31, office hours 8 am-10 pm, 2 night minimum stay - weekends, age restrictions may apply, 14 day cancellation notice-fee imposed. **Pool(s):** outdoor. **Leisure Activities:** cross country skiing. **Guest Services:** TV in common area. **Cards:** AX, DS, MC, VI.

**THE NEW ENGLAND INN**   **Phone:** (603)356-5541
Country Inn
| 10/18-4/30 | 1P: $69-$105 | 2P: $104-$325 | XP: $28 | F12 |
| 9/17-10/17 | 1P: $80 | 2P: $95-$260 | XP: $35 | F12 |
| 6/22-9/16 | 1P: $69 | 2P: $104-$235 | XP: $28 | F12 |
| 5/1-6/21 | 1P: $52 | 2P: $69-$225 | XP: $20 | F12 |
**Location:** Jct US 302 and SR 16, 1.8 mi ne. SR 16A 03845 (PO Box 100). Fax: 603/356-2191. **Facility:** A ski lodge, cottages and a traditional country inn offer accommodations at this property. 42 units. 17 one-bedroom standard units. 16 one-bedroom suites ($110-$325), some with whirlpools. 6 cabins ($175-$250) and 3 cottages ($135-$185) with whirlpools. 2 stories (no elevator), interior/exterior corridors. *Bath:* combo or shower only. **Parking:** on-site. **Terms:** office hours 7:30 am-10:30 pm, 2 night minimum stay, 15 day cancellation notice-fee imposed, [MAP] meal plan available, package plans. **Amenities:** video library (fee). **Pool(s):** heated outdoor. **Leisure Activities:** cross country skiing, hiking trails. **Business Services:** meeting rooms. **Cards:** AX, DS, MC, VI. *(See color ad p 381)*
SOME UNITS

**OLD FIELD HOUSE COUNTRY LODGE**   **Phone:** (603)356-5478
Motel
| 9/24-10/16 [ECP] | 1P: $100-$160 | 2P: $100-$160 | XP: $10 |
| 6/25-9/23 [ECP] | 1P: $80-$150 | 2P: $80-$150 | XP: $10 |
| 10/17-4/30 [ECP] | 1P: $65-$150 | 2P: $65-$150 | XP: $10 |
| 5/1-6/24 [ECP] | 1P: $65-$100 | 2P: $65-$100 | XP: $10 |
**Location:** Jct US 302 and SR 16, 1.8 mi ne of SR 16A. SR 16A 03845 (PO Box 1). Fax: 603/356-7688. **Facility:** Smoke free premises. 20 one-bedroom standard units, some with whirlpools. 2 stories (no elevator), interior corridors. *Bath:* combo or shower only. **Parking:** on-site, winter plug-ins. **Terms:** office hours 8 am-9 pm, 2 night minimum stay, 14 day cancellation notice. **Amenities:** hair dryers. **Pool(s):** heated outdoor. **Leisure Activities:** whirlpool. *Fee:* game room. **Guest Services:** coin laundry. **Cards:** AX, DS, MC, VI. **Special Amenities: free expanded continental breakfast and free local telephone calls.** *(See color ad p 380)*
SOME UNITS

## JACKSON

——— **WHERE TO STAY** ———

**CARTER NOTCH INN**   **Phone:** (603)383-9630
Historic Bed & Breakfast
| 9/13-11/1 [BP] | 1P: $99-$189 | 2P: $109-$209 | XP: $25 |
| 12/26-4/1 [BP] | 1P: $79-$129 | 2P: $109-$209 | XP: $25 |
| 5/26-9/12 [BP] | 1P: $79-$149 | 2P: $89-$169 | XP: $25 |
**Location:** From village, 0.7 mi n on SR 16B. 163 Carter Notch Rd 03846 (PO Box 269). Fax: 603/383-9642. **Facility:** This late-19th-century cottage-style inn is on a mountain road near the village; it features a wraparound porch overlooking the valley. Smoke free premises. 7 units. 6 one- and 1 two-bedroom standard units, some with whirlpools. 3 stories (no elevator), interior corridors. *Bath:* combo or shower only. **Parking:** on-site. **Terms:** open 5/26-11/1 & 12/26-4/1, office hours 9 am-9 pm, 2 night minimum stay - weekends, age restrictions may apply, 14 day cancellation notice-fee imposed, package plans, no pets allowed (owner's pet on premises). **Leisure Activities:** whirlpool. **Cards:** AX, DS, MC, VI.
SOME UNITS

## CHRISTMAS FARM INN

AAA SAVE

| | | | | |
|---|---|---|---|---|
| 7/4-8/31 [MAP] | 1P: $99-$239 | 2P: $99-$239 | XP: $49 | D12 |
| 9/1-11/27 [MAP] | 1P: $85-$199 | 2P: $85-$199 | XP: $49 | D12 |
| 11/28-4/30 [MAP] | 1P: $69-$199 | 2P: $69-$199 | XP: $49 | D12 |
| 5/1-7/3 [MAP] | 1P: $69-$119 | 2P: $69-$119 | XP: $49 | D12 |

Phone: (603)383-4313

Historic Country Inn

**Location:** On SR 16B, 0.3 mi n. Rt 16B 03846 (PO Box CC). Fax: 603/383-6495. **Facility:** Accommodations at this property are offered in a main inn, converted outbuildings and duplex cottages. 41 units. 17 one- and 1 two-bedroom standard units, some with whirlpools. 14 one- and 2 two-bedroom suites ($129-$269), some with whirlpools. 7 cottages. 2 stories (no elevator), interior/exterior corridors. **Bath:** combo or shower only. **Parking:** on-site. **Terms:** 14 day cancellation notice-fee imposed, [BP] meal plan available, package plans - seasonal. **Amenities:** voice mail. *Some:* irons, hair dryers. **Dining:** 8 am-10 & 5:30-9 pm, Fri & Sat-9:30 pm; non smoking dining room, cocktails. **Pool(s):** heated outdoor. **Leisure Activities:** whirlpool, putting green, cross country skiing, playground, exercise room. **Guest Services:** gift shop, coin laundry. **Business Services:** meeting rooms. **Cards:** AX, DS, MC, VI. **Special Amenities:** free full breakfast and free local telephone calls.

SOME UNITS

## THE CROWES' NEST

AAA SAVE

| | | | |
|---|---|---|---|
| 5/1-10/25 [BP] | 1P: $135-$250 | 2P: $135-$250 | XP: $25 |
| 10/26-4/30 [BP] | 1P: $105-$205 | 2P: $105-$205 | XP: $25 |

Phone: 603/383-8913

Bed & Breakfast

**Location:** Off SR 16A, just e; center. Evergreen Trail 03846 (PO Box 427). Fax: 603/383-8241. **Facility:** This hilltop location offers spectacular mountain views with comfortable-contemporary guest rooms that maintain the integrity of this c.1922 home. Several guest rooms have a working fireplace. Smoke free premises. 7 units. 5 one-bedroom standard units, some with whirlpools. 2 one-bedroom suites. 2 stories (no elevator), interior corridors. **Bath:** combo or shower only. **Parking:** office hours 9 am-9 pm, 2 night minimum stay - seasonal & weekends, 15 day cancellation notice-fee imposed, package plans, no pets allowed (owner's dog on premises). **Amenities:** *Some:* CD players. **Guest Services:** TV in common area. **Cards:** AX, DS, MC, VI. **Special Amenities:** free full breakfast and free local telephone calls.

## THE EAGLE MOUNTAIN HOUSE    *Book at aaa.com*

AAA SAVE

| | | | |
|---|---|---|---|
| 9/21-10/16 | 1P: $129-$169 | 2P: $129-$169 | XP: $15 | F18 |
| 6/18-9/20 | 1P: $109-$159 | 2P: $109-$159 | XP: $15 | F18 |
| 10/17-4/30 | 1P: $89-$139 | 2P: $89-$139 | XP: $15 | F18 |
| 5/1-6/17 | 1P: $79-$119 | 2P: $79-$119 | XP: $15 | F18 |

Phone: (603)383-9111

Historic Small-scale Hotel

**Location:** SR 16B, from village center follow SR 16B across bridge to immediate right turn, 0.7 mi n. Carter Notch Rd 03846 (PO Box E). Fax: 603/383-0854. **Facility:** An Old World ambience enhances this restored hotel, which is in a picturesque mountain setting. 93 units. 69 one-bedroom standard units. 24 one-bedroom suites ($109-$199). 5 stories, interior corridors. **Bath:** combo or shower only. **Parking:** on-site. **Terms:** 2 night minimum stay - weekends, 5 day cancellation notice, [BP] & [MAP] meal plans available. **Dining:** Highfields, see separate listing. **Pool(s):** heated outdoor. **Leisure Activities:** saunas, whirlpool, lighted tennis court, cross country skiing, hiking trails, playground, exercise room. Fee: golf-9 holes, game room. **Guest Services:** gift shop, coin laundry. **Business Services:** meeting rooms. **Cards:** AX, CB, DC, DS, MC, VI. **Special Amenities:** free local telephone calls. *(See color ad p 374)*

SOME UNITS

## ELLIS RIVER HOUSE    *Book at aaa.com*

AAA SAVE

| | | | |
|---|---|---|---|
| 9/25-10/18 [BP] | 1P: $140-$285 | 2P: $150-$295 | XP: $25 |
| 12/26-4/30 [BP] | 1P: $115-$245 | 2P: $125-$255 | XP: $25 |
| 5/1-9/24 [BP] | 1P: $95-$225 | 2P: $105-$235 | XP: $25 |
| 10/19-12/23 [BP] | 1P: $85-$215 | 2P: $95-$225 | XP: $25 |

Phone: 603/383-9339

Bed & Breakfast

**Location:** SR 16 and 16A at Jackson covered bridge, 0.5 mi n. Located in a quiet area. Rt 16 03846 (PO Box 656). Fax: 603/383-4142. **Facility:** A quiet riverfront setting offers tastefully decorated guest rooms furnished with period antiques and equipped with modern amenities. Many rooms have a fireplace. Smoke free premises. 21 units. 18 one-bedroom standard units, some with whirlpools. 2 one-bedroom suites with whirlpools. 1 cottage with whirlpool. 3 stories (no elevator), interior corridors. **Bath:** combo or shower only. **Parking:** on-site. **Terms:** open 5/1-12/23 & 12/26-4/30, office hours 8 am-9 pm, 2 night minimum stay - weekends, age restrictions may apply, 14 day cancellation notice-fee imposed, package plans - seasonal. **Amenities:** video library. *Some:* CD players, irons. **Pool(s):** heated outdoor. **Leisure Activities:** sauna, whirlpool, canoeing, fishing, hot tub, kayaking, downhill & cross country skiing, game room. **Cards:** AX, DS, MC, VI. **Special Amenities:** free full breakfast and free local telephone calls. *(See color ad below)*

SOME UNITS

### THE INN AT JACKSON

Ⓐ Ⓐ Ⓐ (SAVE)
▽▽▽

Bed & Breakfast

| | |
|---|---|
| 9/17-10/17 [BP] | |
| 5/1-9/16 [BP] | |
| 10/18-4/30 [BP] | |

2P: $179-$199   XP: $20
2P: $99-$159    XP: $20
2P: $99-$139    XP: $20

**Phone:** (603)383-4321

**Location:** Off SR 16A; center. Thorn Hill Rd 03846 (PO Box 807). Fax: 603/383-4085. **Facility:** On a grassy knoll overlooking the village, this large, traditional-style inn features some guest rooms with four-poster beds. 14 one-bedroom standard units. 3 stories (no elevator), interior corridors. *Bath:* combo, shower or tub only. **Parking:** on-site. **Terms:** office hours 7 am-10 pm, 2 night minimum stay - weekends in winter, 14 day cancellation notice-fee imposed, package plans - seasonal. **Amenities:** *Some:* irons, hair dryers. **Leisure Activities:** whirlpool, cross country skiing. **Cards:** AX, CB, DC, DS, MC, VI. **Special Amenities:** free full breakfast and free newspaper.

SOME UNITS
Ⓢ🅳 ⓩ /✕/

### THE LODGE AT JACKSON VILLAGE

Ⓐ Ⓐ Ⓐ (SAVE)
▽▽▽

Small-scale Hotel

| | | | |
|---|---|---|---|
| 9/17-10/16 | 1P: $119-$189 | 2P: $129-$199 | XP: $15   F17 |
| 10/17-4/30 | 1P: $89-$169 | 2P: $99-$179 | XP: $15   F17 |
| 6/25-9/16 | 1P: $109-$159 | 2P: $119-$169 | XP: $15   F17 |
| 5/1-6/24 | 1P: $89-$139 | 2P: $99-$149 | XP: $15   F17 |

**Phone:** 603/383-0999

**Location:** Jct SR 16 and 16A at covered bridge, 0.5 mi n. SR 16 03846 (PO Box 593). Fax: 603/383-6104. **Facility:** Smoke free premises. 32 one-bedroom standard units, some with whirlpools. 2 stories, interior corridors. **Parking:** on-site. **Terms:** 2-3 night minimum stay - some weekends, 7 day cancellation notice. **Amenities:** hair dryers. **Pool(s):** outdoor. **Leisure Activities:** whirlpool, fishing, tennis court, cross country skiing. *Fee:* golf-18 holes. **Guest Services:** coin laundry. **Business Services:** meeting rooms. **Cards:** AX, DS, MC, VI. *(See color ad below)*

Ⓢ🅳 ⑪⁺ 🅛Ⓜ ➤ ✕ ✕ 📧

### LUXURY MOUNTAIN GETAWAYS

Ⓐ Ⓐ Ⓐ (SAVE)
▽▽▽

Resort
Condominium

| | |
|---|---|
| 7/12-9/1 | |
| 9/2-4/30 | |
| 5/1-7/11 | |

2P: $149-$1599
2P: $99-$1599
2P: $99-$1299

**Phone:** (603)383-9101

**Location:** 1 mi s of village. Rt 16 03846. Fax: 603/383-9823. **Facility:** Extensive grounds and enhanced luxury-level amenities add appeal to this mountainside property. 225 units. 45 one-bedroom standard units with whirlpools, some with efficiencies or kitchens. 64 one-, 100 two- and 16 three-bedroom suites with kitchens, some with whirlpools. 2-3 stories (no elevator), exterior corridors. **Parking:** on-site. **Terms:** office hours 8 am-10 pm, check-in 3:30 pm, 2 night minimum stay, age restrictions may apply, 7 day cancellation notice, package plans, 10% service charge. **Amenities:** *Some:* CD players. **Pool(s):** outdoor, 5 heated outdoor, heated indoor. **Leisure Activities:** saunas, whirlpools, steamroom, boating, tennis court, cross country skiing, ice skating, recreation programs, lawn games, nightly bonfires, hiking trails, playground, basketball, horseshoes, volleyball. *Fee:* sleigh rides, snowshoeing, exercise room, game room. **Cards:** DS, MC, VI. *(See color ad p 343)*

SOME UNITS
➤ ✕ Ⓥ🅒🅡 🎦 /✕ 🅐🅒 📧 🖥 🖵 /

**NESTLENOOK FARM RESORT** *Book at aaa.com*

Phone: 603/383-9443

All Year      2P: $135-$370

Historic Bed & Breakfast

**Location:** Jct SR 16 and 16A, just through covered bridge, 0.3 mi s. Dinsmore Rd 03846 (PO Box Q). Fax: 603/383-4515. **Facility:** Some of this Victorian-style resort's accommodations feature fireplaces or gas stoves, while others offer canopy beds. Smoke free premises. 7 units. 5 one-bedroom standard units with whirlpools. 2 one-bedroom suites with whirlpools. 3 stories (no elevator), interior corridors. **Parking:** on-site. **Terms:** office hours 7:30 am-10 pm, age restrictions may apply, 14 day cancellation notice, [BP] meal plan available, package plans, 15% service charge. **Amenities:** video library. *Some:* DVD players. **Leisure Activities:** boating, fishing, ice skating, bicycles, hiking trails. *Fee:* ice skates, snowshoeing, Austrian sleigh rides. **Guest Services:** TV in common area, complimentary evening beverages. **Cards:** DS, MC, VI. **Special Amenities:** free full breakfast. *(See color ad p 343)*

SOME UNITS

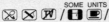

**SNOWFLAKE INN**

Phone: (603)383-8259

All Year [CP]      2P: $165-$350

Bed & Breakfast

**Location:** On SR 16A; center. 95 Main St (SR 16A) 03846 (PO Box 814). Fax: 603/383-6545. **Facility:** Smoke free premises. 20 one-bedroom standard units with whirlpools. 2 stories (no elevator), interior corridors. **Parking:** on-site. **Terms:** office hours 7 am-11 pm, off-site registration, 2 night minimum stay - weekends, age restrictions may apply, 14 day cancellation notice. **Amenities:** DVD players, CD players, high-speed Internet, hair dryers. **Pool(s):** heated indoor. **Cards:** AX, DS, MC, VI. *(See color ad below)*

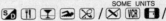

**WENTWORTH RESORT HOTEL**

Phone: (603)383-9700

| |  |  |  | |
|---|---|---|---|---|
| 9/17-10/14 [MAP] | 1P: $177-$187 | 2P: $215-$225 | XP: $48 | F12 |
| 1/2-4/30 [MAP] | 1P: $157-$167 | 2P: $195-$205 | XP: $48 | F12 |
| 5/1-9/16 & 10/15-1/1 [MAP] | 1P: $147-$157 | 2P: $185-$195 | XP: $48 | F12 |

Historic Small-scale Hotel

**Location:** Jct SR 16A and 16B; center. 16A Carter Notch Rd 03846 (PO Box M). Fax: 603/383-4265. **Facility:** The resort centers on a building dating from 1900; its annexes offer standard and luxury lodgings with upgrades such as whirlpools and fireplaces. 51 units. 44 one-bedroom standard units, some with whirlpools. 7 one-bedroom suites ($245-$345) with whirlpools. 3 stories (no elevator), interior/exterior corridors. **Parking:** on-site. **Terms:** 2-3 night minimum stay - weekends, 7 day cancellation notice-fee imposed. **Amenities:** video library, hair dryers. *Some:* DVD players, CD players. **Dining:** dining room, see separate listing. **Pool(s):** heated outdoor. **Leisure Activities:** tennis court, cross country skiing. *Fee:* golf-18 holes, snowshoes. **Business Services:** meeting rooms. **Cards:** AX, CB, DC, DS, JC, MC, VI. **Special Amenities:** free local telephone calls and free newspaper.

SOME UNITS

——— *The following lodging was either not evaluated or did not* ———
*meet AAA rating requirements but is listed for your information only.*

**THE INN AT THORN HILL**                                                                    Phone: 603/383-4242
[fyi]        9/17-10/18 [BP]                          2P: $175-$200      XP: $35
              5/1-9/16 & 10/19-4/30 [BP]             2P: $125-$150      XP: $35
Historic     Too new to rate. **Location:** Off SR 16A, watch for Thorn Hill Rd, just e; center. Thorn Hill Rd 03846 (PO Box A).
Country Inn   Fax: 603/383-8062. **Amenities:** 19 units, restaurant, coffeemakers, refrigerators, pool. **Terms:** 2 night
              minimum stay - weekends, age restrictions may apply, 14 day cancellation notice-fee imposed. **Cards:** AX,
DS, MC, VI.

——— **WHERE TO DINE** ———

**HIGHFIELDS**                        **Dinner:** $15-$24                   Phone: 603/383-9111
(AAA)         **Location:** SR 16B, from village center follow SR 16B across bridge to immediate right turn, 0.7 mi n; in The Eagle
▽▽▽▽         Mountain House. Carter Notch Rd 03846. **Hours:** 7:30 am-10 & 6-9 pm, Fri & Sat-10 pm.
              **Reservations:** accepted. **Features:** The vintage hotel's dining room is elegantly decorated, and the
American      service is attentive and friendly. On the varied menu is classic New England cuisine: fresh seafood, beef,
              poultry and some wild game selections. Casual dress; cocktails. **Parking:** on-site. **Cards:** AX, DC, MC, VI.

**THOMPSON HOUSE EATERY**          **Lunch:** $6-$15      **Dinner:** $12-$26      Phone: 603/383-9341
▽▽▽▽         **Location:** In village. SR 16A 03846. **Hours:** 11:30 am-3:30 & 5:30-10 pm. Closed: Tues, 4/1-5/15 &
              Mon-Thurs 11/1-11/30. **Reservations:** suggested. **Features:** In an early 1800s farmhouse, the restaurant
American      includes an ice cream fountain and farm stand. The casual atmosphere extends to a patio that is available
              for seasonal dining. The owner/chef creates distinctive contemporary dishes from fresh local ingredients,
many of which come from the restaurant's organic garden. The smoke-free bar presents a pub-style menu and exhibits a
collection of local artwork. The restaurant does not have high chairs or booster seats. Cocktails. **Parking:** on-site. **Cards:** DS,
MC, VI.

**WENTWORTH DINING ROOM**   Country Inn        **Dinner:** $21-$29      Phone: 603/383-9700
▽▽▽▽         **Location:** Jct SR 16A and 16B; center; in Wentworth Resort Hotel. 16 A Carter Notch Rd 03846. **Hours:** 7:30 am-10
              & 6-9 pm, Fri & Sat-10 pm. **Reservations:** suggested. **Features:** Although the Wentworth features intimate
Regional American dining in an elegant setting, the restaurant's atmosphere remains informal. Creative offerings are skillfully
              prepared with local produce, premium meat and seafood harvested from New England waters. Dressy
casual; cocktails. **Parking:** on-site. **Cards:** AX, DC, DS, MC, VI.

**THE WILDCAT INN & TAVERN**       **Lunch:** $6-$12      **Dinner:** $17-$25      Phone: 603/383-4245
▽▽▽▽         **Location:** Jct SR 16 and 16A, at covered bridge, then 0.5 mi ne on SR 16A. Main St 03846. **Hours:** 11:30 am-3 &
              6-9 pm, Fri & Sat-10 pm; call for seasonal lunch hours. Closed: 12/25. **Reservations:** suggested.
Nouvelle American **Features:** This 19th-century country inn is located in the center of the village and has a pleasant informal
              atmosphere. Garden dining is available in the summer. They describe the cuisine as country gourmet and
entrees are made to order. Ingredients are fresh as much as possible. A lighter menu is available in the tavern. Casual dress;
cocktails. **Parking:** on-site. **Cards:** AX, DC, MC, VI.

——— *The following restaurant has not been evaluated by AAA* ———
*but is listed for your information only.*

**AS YOU LIKE IT**                                                                       Phone: 603/383-6425
[fyi]        Not evaluated. **Location:** On SR 16B; center. Jackson Falls Marketplace 03846. **Features:** This local lunch spot
              is located in the central village of Jackson.

# JAFFREY pop. 2,802

——— **WHERE TO STAY** ———

**THE BENJAMIN PRESCOTT INN**                                                             Phone: (603)532-6637
▽▽▽▽         7/1-10/31 [BP]                         2P: $85-$160       XP: $15
              5/1-6/30 & 11/1-4/30 [BP]             2P: $75-$150       XP: $15
Historic Bed  **Location:** Jct SR 202, 2 mi e. 433 SR 124 E 03452. Fax: 603/532-6637. **Facility:** Each guest room at this classic
& Breakfast   Greek Revival-style inn is named for a family member of the colonel who had the home built in 1853. Smoke
              free premises. 10 units. 7 one-bedroom standard units. 3 one-bedroom suites ($105-$160). 3 stories (no el-
evator), interior/exterior corridors. *Bath:* combo or shower only. **Parking:** on-site. **Terms:** office hours 9 am-9 pm, age restrictions
may apply, 10 day cancellation notice, package plans. **Cards:** AX, MC, VI.

SOME UNITS
(ASK) (SD) (X) (🕾) / (K) (TV) (🔌) /

# JAFFREY CENTER

## ——— WHERE TO DINE ———

THE INN AT JAFFREY CENTER   Country Inn          **Lunch:** $7-$10          **Dinner:** $15-$22          **Phone:** 603/532-7800
▼▼◆▼   **Location:** Jct SR 202, 1.7 mi w on SR 124. 379 Main St 03052. **Hours:** 11:30 am-2 & 5:30-8 pm, Sat-9 pm, Sun
American   10 am-2 pm. **Reservations:** accepted. **Features:** Creative, home-cooked dishes are well-prepared. Diners
can enjoy their meals in the country cottage-style dining room. Casual dress; cocktails. **Parking:** on-site.
**Cards:** MC, VI.

# JEFFERSON

## ——— WHERE TO STAY ———

EVERGREEN MOTEL                                                                                    **Phone:** 603/586-4449
▼▼   All Year                          1P: $45-$65          2P: $50-$70          XP: $5
Motel   **Location:** 0.5 mi w. 537 Presidential Hwy 03583. Fax: 603/586-7016. **Facility:** 18 one-bedroom standard units. 1
story, exterior corridors. **Parking:** on-site. **Terms:** 2 night minimum stay - weekends, 3 day cancellation notice, [CP] meal plan available. **Amenities:** voice mail. **Pool(s):** outdoor. **Cards:** AX, MC, VI.

JEFFERSON INN                                                                                      **Phone:** (603)586-7998
▲▲▲ SAVE   9/14-10/28                     1P: $90-$120          2P: $100-$160          XP: $20          F3
5/1-9/13 & 10/29-4/30          1P: $80-$120          2P: $90-$140          XP: $20          F3
▼▼◆▼   **Location:** US 2, 0.5 mi e of SR 116. 6 Renaissance Ln 03583. Fax: 603/586-7808. **Facility:** Perched on a hilltop,
Historic Bed   the inn offers guest rooms and a veranda with good mountain views; it is furnished with many antiques.
& Breakfast   Smoke free premises. 11 units. 9 one- and 2 two-bedroom standard units. 3 stories (no elevator), interior
corridors. *Bath:* combo or shower only. **Parking:** on-site. **Terms:** office hours 8 am-9 pm, 14 day cancellation
notice-fee imposed. [BP] meal plan available. **Leisure Activities:** cross country skiing, snowmobiling, ice
skating, tobogganing, cycling trails, hiking trails. **Guest Services:** complimentary evening beverages. **Cards:** AX, DS, MC, VI.
SOME UNITS

THE LANTERN RESORT                                                                                **Phone:** 603/586-7151
▼▼ ▼▼   5/1-10/14                          2P: $45-$79          XP: $4
Motel   **Location:** On US 2, 0.5 mi w. Located across from Santa's Village. 571 Presidential Hwy 03583 (PO Box 97).
**Facility:** 30 one-bedroom standard units. 2 stories (no elevator), exterior corridors. **Parking:** on-site.
**Terms:** open 5/1-10/14, office hours 7 am-10 pm, 7 day cancellation notice-fee imposed. **Amenities:** hair
dryers. **Pool(s):** 2 heated outdoor, wading. **Leisure Activities:** whirlpools, recreation programs, hiking trails, playground, basket-
ball, horseshoes, volleyball. *Fee:* game room. **Guest Services:** coin laundry. **Cards:** DC, MC, VI.
SOME UNITS

# KEENE pop. 22,563

## ——— WHERE TO STAY ———

BEST WESTERN SOVEREIGN HOTEL   *Book at aaa.com*                                                   **Phone:** (603)357-3038
▼▼◆▼   7/2-10/30                     1P: $85-$195          2P: $85-$195          XP: $12          F18
5/1-7/1 & 10/31-4/30          1P: $69-$195          2P: $69-$195          XP: $12          F18
Small-scale Hotel   **Location:** SR 10, just s of jct SR 12 and 101. 401 Winchester St 03431. Fax: 603/357-4776. **Facility:** 131 one-
bedroom standard units. 2 stories (no elevator), interior corridors. **Parking:** on-site. **Terms:** [BP] meal plan
available, package plans, pets ($10 fee). **Amenities:** irons, hair dryers. *Fee:* video library, video games. **Pool(s):** heated indoor.
**Leisure Activities:** exercise room. **Guest Services:** valet laundry. **Business Services:** meeting rooms. **Cards:** AX, DC, DS,
MC, VI.
SOME UNITS

**EF LANE HOTEL** *Book at aaa.com*    Phone: (603)357-7070

| | | | | |
|---|---|---|---|---|
| 8/1-9/16 [ECP] | 1P: $159-$275 | 2P: $174-$290 | XP: $15 | F5 |
| 5/1-7/31 & 9/17-4/30 [ECP] | 1P: $129-$275 | 2P: $144-$290 | XP: $15 | F5 |

Small-scale Hotel    **Location:** Between Church and Roxbury sts; downtown. 30 Main St 03431. Fax: 603/357-7075. **Facility:** 40 units. 31 one-bedroom standard units. 9 one-bedroom suites ($225-$275), some with whirlpools. 4 stories, interior corridors. **Parking:** on-site. **Terms:** 2 night minimum stay - seasonal weekends, package plans. **Amenities:** high-speed Internet (fee), voice mail, irons, hair dryers. *Some:* DVD players. **Dining:** Salmon Chase American Bistro, see separate listing. **Guest Services:** valet laundry. **Business Services:** meeting rooms. **Cards:** AX, CB, DC, DS, MC, VI. *(See color ad p 345)*

SOME UNITS

(ASK) (S/D) (T1) (Y) (&M) (++) (P) (DATA PORT) (DP) / (X) (VCR) (B) /

FEE

---

**HOLIDAY INN EXPRESS**    *Book at aaa.com*    Phone: 603/352-7616

| | | | | |
|---|---|---|---|---|
| 9/22-10/31 [ECP] | 1P: $160-$180 | 2P: $160-$180 | XP: $10 | F18 |
| 7/1-9/21 [ECP] | 1P: $135-$165 | 2P: $135-$165 | XP: $10 | F18 |
| 5/1-6/30 [ECP] | 1P: $100-$165 | 2P: $100-$165 | XP: $10 | F18 |
| 11/1-4/30 [ECP] | 1P: $105-$120 | 2P: $105-$120 | XP: $10 | F18 |

Small-scale Hotel    **Location:** SR 101, just n, via Winchester St, then 0.3 mi w. Located in a business park. 175 Key Rd 03431. Fax: 603/357-3619. **Facility:** 80 one-bedroom standard units, some with whirlpools. 2 stories, interior corridors. *Bath:* combo or shower only. **Parking:** on-site. **Terms:** pets ($10 extra charge). **Amenities:** video games (fee), voice mail, irons, hair dryers. **Pool(s):** heated indoor. **Leisure Activities:** whirlpool, exercise room. **Guest Services:** valet laundry. **Cards:** AX, DC, DS, MC, VI.

SOME UNITS

(H) (&M) (E/) (Q) (R) (P) (DATA PORT) (DP) / (X) (B) (画) /

FEE

---

**SUPER 8 KEENE**    *Book at aaa.com*    Phone: (603)352-9780

(AAA) (SAVE)

| | | | | |
|---|---|---|---|---|
| 9/15-10/31 [CP] | 1P: $115-$145 | 2P: $120-$150 | XP: $5 | F17 |
| 5/1-5/31 [CP] | 1P: $75-$130 | 2P: $80-$140 | XP: $5 | F17 |
| 6/1-9/14 [CP] | 1P: $80-$115 | 2P: $85-$120 | XP: $5 | F17 |
| 11/1-4/30 [CP] | 1P: $65-$80 | 2P: $70-$85 | XP: $5 | F17 |

Motel    **Location:** Jct SR 9 and 12, just w. 3 Ashbrook Rd 03431. Fax: 603/357-5215. **Facility:** 61 one-bedroom standard units. 2 stories (no elevator), interior corridors. **Parking:** on-site. **Terms:** pets ($20 fee). **Amenities:** high-speed Internet. **Cards:** AX, CB, DC, DS, MC, VI. **Special Amenities:** free continental breakfast and free local telephone calls.

SOME UNITS

(S/D) (H) (&M) (R) (DATA PORT) / (X) (B) (画) /

FEE

---

——— **WHERE TO DINE** ———

**176 MAIN**    **Lunch:** $5-$8    **Dinner:** $9-$22    Phone: 603/357-3100

American    **Location:** Jct SR 101 and 12, 0.6 mi n; downtown. 176 Main St 03431. **Hours:** 11:30 am-9 pm, Wed & Thurs-10 pm, Fri & Sat-11 pm; Saturday & Sunday brunch. Closed major holidays. **Reservations:** accepted. **Features:** Across from Keene State College, the downtown restaurant is on the National Register of Historic Places. The rustic-casual decor includes local memorabilia on exposed brick walls and potted plants strategically placed throughout. The tavern-style eatery prepares seafood, beef and pasta specialties, which go well with an excellent selection of imported and domestic beer and ale. Locals and visitors alike enjoy this place. Casual dress; cocktails. **Parking:** on-site. **Cards:** AX, DC, DS, MC, VI.

(Y) (X)

---

**THE PUB RESTAURANT & CATERERS**    **Lunch:** $4-$8    **Dinner:** $7-$15    Phone: 603/352-3135

Greek    **Location:** Jct SR 9/10/101, 0.5 mi n. 131 Winchester St 03431. **Hours:** 7 am-9 pm. Closed: 12/25. **Reservations:** suggested. **Features:** The pub's atmosphere is laid-back, and the serving staff is friendly, prompt and courteous. The Greek and Italian flavors of the menu's offerings should please everyone in the family. Meals are hot, well-seasoned, plentiful and tasty. Casual dress; cocktails. **Parking:** on-site. **Cards:** AX, CB, DC, DS, MC, VI.

(Y) (X)

---

**SALMON CHASE AMERICAN BISTRO**    **Lunch:** $4-$12    **Dinner:** $8-$20    Phone: 603/357-7070

American    **Location:** Between Church and Roxbury sts; downtown; in EF Lane Hotel. 30 Main St 03431. **Hours:** 11:30 am-2 & 5:30-9 pm. **Reservations:** accepted. **Features:** Offering a terrific view of Main Street, the restaurant's comfortable and casual decor is overshadowed by the chef's creative menu selections. The dishes may include rack of lamb, grilled salmon, bouillabaisse, wild mushroom pasta and other delightful edibles. At lunchtime, diners may feast on smaller portioned dinner items or classic sandwiches. Casual dress; cocktails. **Parking:** on-site. **Cards:** AX, DC, DS, MC, VI.

(Y) (X)

---

# KINGSTON

——— **WHERE TO DINE** ———

**KINGSTON 1686 HOUSE**    Historic    **Dinner:** $17-$32    Phone: 603/642-3637

(AAA)

American    **Location:** Main St and Scotland Rd; in center of village. 127 Main St 03848. **Hours:** 5:30 pm-9 pm, Sun 2 pm-7 pm. Closed: 1/1, 12/25; also Mon, Tues & 6/28-7/14. **Reservations:** suggested, weekends. **Features:** For a historic 300-year-old house with original fireplaces, hand-cut beams and pine floors is the setting for a wonderful experience. Creative, flavorful New England fare reflects Greek influences. Service is good. The wine list is sensational. Dressy casual; cocktails. **Parking:** on-site. **Cards:** AX, DC, DS, MC, VI. (Y) (X)

# LACONIA pop. 16,411

## ——— WHERE TO STAY ———

**BARTON'S MOTEL**

| | | | **Phone:** 603/524-5674 | |
| 6/15-9/15 | 1P: $90-$100 | 2P: $90-$100 | XP: $15 | D15 |
| 5/1-6/14 & 9/16-10/31 | 1P: $70-$80 | 2P: $70-$80 | XP: $15 | D15 |

Motel **Location:** 0.8 mi n on old US 3 (Union Ave); center. 1330 Union Ave 03246. **Facility:** 40 units. 34 one-bedroom standard units. 2 two-bedroom suites with kitchens. 4 cottages ($165-$185). 1 story, exterior corridors. **Parking:** on-site. **Terms:** open 5/1-10/31, office hours 9 am-10 pm, 2 night minimum stay - seasonal weekends, 14 day cancellation notice. **Pool(s):** heated outdoor. **Leisure Activities:** boating, boat dock, fishing, shuffleboard. **Cards:** AX, MC, VI.

SOME UNITS

**BAY TOP**

| | | | **Phone:** 603/366-2225 | |
| 6/11-9/7 | 1P: $79-$119 | 2P: $79-$119 | XP: $10 | F12 |
| 5/1-6/10 & 9/8-4/30 | 1P: $55-$89 | 2P: $55-$89 | XP: $10 | F12 |

Motel **Location:** 0.5 mi s on US 3. 1025 Weirs Blvd 03246-1625. Fax: 603/366-2577. **Facility:** 12 one-bedroom standard units. 1 story, interior/exterior corridors. *Bath:* shower only. **Parking:** on-site. **Terms:** office hours 9 am-9 pm, 2 night minimum stay - weekends, 7 day cancellation notice-fee imposed. **Pool(s):** outdoor. **Leisure Activities:** whirlpool, horseshoes. **Cards:** AX, DS, MC, VI.

SOME UNITS

**BIRCH KNOLL MOTEL**

| | | | **Phone:** 603/366-4958 | |
| 6/24-9/1 | 1P: $85-$129 | 2P: $85-$129 | XP: $10 | F10 |
| 5/15-6/23 & 9/2-10/16 | 1P: $59-$89 | 2P: $59-$89 | XP: $10 | F10 |

Motel **Location:** 1 mi s of Weirs Beach on US 3. 867 Weirs Blvd 03247 (PO Box 5172). **Facility:** 24 one-bedroom standard units. 1-2 stories (no elevator), exterior corridors. *Bath:* shower only. **Parking:** on-site. **Terms:** open 5/15-10/16, office hours 7:30 am-9 pm, 2 night minimum stay - weekends in summer, 7 day cancellation notice. **Pool(s):** heated outdoor. **Leisure Activities:** fishing. *Fee:* game room. **Cards:** DS, MC, VI.

SOME UNITS

## FERRY POINT HOUSE

**Phone: 603/524-0087**

Historic Bed & Breakfast

| | | | |
|---|---|---|---|
| 9/15-10/31 [BP] | 1P: $110-$160 | 2P: $110-$160 | XP: $35 |
| 5/1-9/14 [BP] | 1P: $100-$150 | 2P: $100-$150 | XP: $35 |

**Location:** I-93, exit 20, 4.5 mi e on US 3, at light before bridge, 0.5 mi n on Bay Rd, then 0.5 mi. (100 Lower Bay Rd). **Fax:** 603/524-0959. **Facility:** This Victorian inn overlooking a lake features a wide front porch with hanging flowerpots and white wicker furniture. Smoke free premises. 7 one-bedroom standard units, some with whirl-pools. 2 stories (no elevator), interior corridors. *Bath:* combo or shower only. **Parking:** on-site. **Terms:** open 5/1-10/31, office hours 9 am-9 pm, 2 night minimum stay - 7/1-10/31 & weekends 5/1-6/30, age restrictions may apply, 14 day cancellation notice-fee imposed. **Amenities:** video library, hair dryers. **Leisure Activities:** boating, paddleboats, boat dock, fishing. **Guest Services:** TV in common area.

SOME UNITS

⊠ ⊠ (AC) (PW) ☎ / VCR /

## GRAND VIEW MOTEL & COTTAGE

**Phone: 603/366-4973**

Motel

| | | | |
|---|---|---|---|
| 5/28-9/6 | | 2P: $88 | XP: $8 | D10 |
| 5/1-5/27 & 9/7-11/1 | | 2P: $65 | XP: $8 | D10 |

**Location:** On US 3, 0.5 mi n. 291 Endicott St N (US 3) 03247 (PO Box 5051). **Facility:** 22 units. 12 one-bedroom standard units, some with kitchens. 10 cottages ($88-$104). 2 stories (no elevator), exterior corridors. *Bath:* combo or shower only. **Parking:** on-site. **Terms:** open 5/1-11/1, office hours 7 am-11 pm, 14 day cancellation notice. **Pool(s):** outdoor. **Cards:** AX, MC, VI.

SOME UNITS

🛏 ⊠ ☎ / 🖥 🖨 /

## THE MARGATE ON WINNIPESAUKEE

**Phone: (603)524-5210**

Small-scale Hotel

| | | | |
|---|---|---|---|
| 7/2-9/5 | | 2P: $129-$269 | XP: $15 | F18 |
| 5/1-7/1 & 9/6-10/16 | | 2P: $89-$149 | XP: $15 | F18 |
| 10/17-4/30 | | 2P: $89-$139 | XP: $15 | F18 |

**Location:** I-93, exit 20, 13 mi e on US 3. 76 Lake St 03246. **Fax:** 603/528-4485. **Facility:** 141 units. 134 one-bedroom standard units. 7 two-bedroom suites. 1-4 stories, interior/exterior corridors. *Bath:* combo or shower only. **Parking:** on-site. **Terms:** check-in 4 pm, 7 day cancellation notice, [MAP] meal plan available, package plans. **Amenities:** *Some:* hair dryers. **Pool(s):** outdoor, heated indoor. **Leisure Activities:** sauna, whirlpool, rental boats, fishing, playground, exercise room. *Fee:* boat dock, game room. **Guest Services:** gift shop, valet laundry, tanning facility. **Business Services:** meeting rooms. **Cards:** AX, DC, DS, MC, VI. *(See color ad p 347)*

SOME UNITS

(ASK) 🍴 🍸 📶 🖥 🏊 ⊠ ⊠ / 🖨 /
FEE

## ST. MORITZ TERRACE MOTEL & CHALETS RESORT

**Phone: 603/366-4482**

Property failed to provide current rates

Motel

**Location:** 1 mi s on US 3. 937 Weirs Blvd 03246. **Facility:** 17 units. 10 one-bedroom standard units. 7 cottages. 1 story, exterior corridors. *Bath:* combo or shower only. **Parking:** on-site. **Terms:** open 5/23-10/14, office hours 7 am-10 pm. **Pool(s):** outdoor. **Leisure Activities:** fishing, basketball, shuffleboard.

SOME UNITS

🛏 ⊠ ☎ / ⊠ 🖨 /

## ──── WHERE TO DINE ────

## FRATELLO'S RISTORANTE ITALIANO

**Lunch:** $6-$15   **Dinner:** $9-$20   **Phone: 603/528-2022**

Italian

**Location:** 1.5 mi n on Old US 3; center. 799 Union Ave 03246. **Hours:** 11:30 am-2 & 4:30-9:30 pm, Sat 4:30 pm-10 pm, Sun noon-9:30 pm. Closed: 11/25, 12/25. **Features:** This popular restaurant presents a menu of such varied Italian favorites as piccata, parmigiana, spaghetti, Caesar salad and terrific desserts, all served in a fun atmosphere. Casual dress; cocktails. **Parking:** on-site. **Cards:** AX, DS, MC, VI.   ⊠

# LANCASTER pop. 1,695

## ──── WHERE TO STAY ────

## CABOT MOTOR INN

**Phone: 603/788-3346**

Small-scale Hotel

| | | | |
|---|---|---|---|
| 6/18-10/17 | 1P: $74 | 2P: $79 | | |
| 5/1-6/17 & 10/18-4/30 | 1P: $60 | 2P: $65 | XP: $5 | D17 |

**Location:** 1.5 mi e of jct US 3, on US 2. 200 Portland St 03584. **Fax:** 603/788-3346. **Facility:** 54 units. 53 one- and 1 two-bedroom standard units, some with efficiencies or kitchens. 3 stories, interior corridors. *Bath:* combo or shower only. **Parking:** on-site, winter plug-ins. **Amenities:** video library. **Pool(s):** heated indoor, wading. **Leisure Activities:** saunas, whirlpool, snowmobiling, jogging, playground, exercise room, horseshoes. *Fee:* game room. **Guest Services:** coin laundry. **Business Services:** meeting rooms. **Cards:** AX, DC, DS, MC, VI.

SOME UNITS

🍴 🍸 📶 🏊 ⊠ / ⊠ VCR DATA PORT 🖨 🖨
FEE        FEE

## COOS MOTOR INN

**Phone: 603/788-3079**

Small-scale Hotel

| | | | |
|---|---|---|---|
| 6/18-10/13 | 1P: $64 | 2P: $69 | XP: $5 | D17 |
| 5/1-6/17 & 10/14-4/30 | 1P: $60 | 2P: $65 | XP: $5 | D17 |

**Location:** On US 2 and 3; center. 209 Main St 03584. **Fax:** 603/788-3079. **Facility:** 41 units. 40 one- and 1 two-bedroom standard units. 2 stories, interior corridors. *Bath:* combo or shower only. **Parking:** on-site, winter plug-ins. **Terms:** [CP] meal plan available. **Guest Services:** coin laundry. **Cards:** AX, DC, DS, MC, VI.

SOME UNITS

📶 DATA PORT / ⊠ VCR 🖨 /
FEE FEE

## ROGER'S MOTEL

**Phone: 603/788-4885**

Motel

| | | | |
|---|---|---|---|
| 5/1-10/15 | | 2P: $76 | XP: $5 | F3 |

**Location:** 2 mi e on US 2. 10 Roger's Campground Rd 03584. **Fax:** 603/788-3697. **Facility:** 52 one-bedroom standard units. 2 stories (no elevator), exterior corridors. **Parking:** on-site. **Terms:** open 5/1-10/15, office hours 8 am-10 pm, 14 day cancellation notice, weekly rates available. **Pool(s):** 2 outdoor, wading. **Leisure Activities:** whirlpool, tennis court, playground, basketball, horseshoes, shuffleboard, volleyball. *Fee:* waterslide, miniature golf, game room. **Guest Services:** coin laundry. **Cards:** AX, DS, MC, VI.

🍴 🏊 ⊠ ⊠

# LEBANON pop. 12,586—See also WEST LEBANON.

## ———— WHERE TO STAY ————

**DAYS INN**   *Book at aaa.com*   **Phone:** (603)448-5070

| | 9/5-10/31 | 1P: $129-$189 | 2P: $139-$189 | XP: $10 | F12 |
|---|---|---|---|---|---|
| | 5/1-9/4 | 1P: $99-$139 | 2P: $109-$189 | XP: $10 | F12 |
| Motel | 11/1-4/30 | 1P: $89-$99 | 2P: $89-$109 | XP: $10 | F12 |

**Location:** I-89, exit 18, 0.8 mi n. 135 SR 120 03766. Fax: 603/448-6127. **Facility:** 49 one-bedroom standard units. 2 stories (no elevator), interior/exterior corridors. **Parking:** on-site, winter plug-ins. **Terms:** [BP], [CP] & [ECP] meal plans available, pets ($20 fee, in smoking units). **Amenities:** video library (fee), irons, hair dryers. **Guest Services:** valet laundry. **Cards:** AX, DC, DS, MC, VI.

(ASK) (S🐕) (🛏) (DATA PORT/FEE) (🔌) (📺) / (✕) /   SOME UNITS

**RESIDENCE INN BY MARRIOTT-LEBANON**   *Book at aaa.com*   **Phone:** (603)643-4511

All Year [BP]   1P: $149-$299

Small-scale Hotel   **Location:** I-89, exit 18, 2.5 mi n on SR 120. 32 Centerra Pkwy 03766. Fax: 603/643-0546. **Facility:** 114 units. 66 one-bedroom standard units with kitchens. 30 one- and 18 two-bedroom suites with kitchens. 3 stories, interior corridors. *Bath:* combo or shower only. **Parking:** on-site. **Terms:** pets ($150 fee, $5 extra charge). **Amenities:** video library (fee), voice mail, irons, hair dryers. **Pool(s):** heated indoor. **Leisure Activities:** whirlpool, exercise room. **Guest Services:** complimentary evening beverages: Mon-Thurs, valet and coin laundry. **Business Services:** meeting rooms, fax (fee). **Cards:** AX, CB, DC, DS, JC, MC, VI.

(ASK) (S🐕) (🛏) (🍴) (🚶M) (🔥) (🏊) (📹) (DATA PORT/FEE) (🔌) (📺) (💻) / (✕) /   SOME UNITS

## ———— WHERE TO DINE ————

**GRENACHE**   **Lunch:** $7-$15   **Dinner:** $18-$25   **Phone:** 603/643-7728

French   **Location:** I-89, exit 18, 2.5 mi n on SR 120. 18 Centerra Pkwy 03766. **Hours:** 11:30 am-2 & 5:30-10 pm, Sat from 5:30 pm. Closed major holidays; also Sun. **Reservations:** accepted. **Features:** The cutting-edge chef prepares wonderfully creative dishes—such as cassoulet-duck confit, crispy roast duck with caramelized orange sauce and celery root puree—along with rotisserie items and homemade desserts. Dressy casual; cocktails. **Parking:** on-site. **Cards:** AX, MC, VI.

(🚶M) (🍸) (✕)

## Hungry? Look for the RED AAA Logo

*N*ext time you look through a AAA/CAA TourBook® guide in search of a place to dine, take note of the bright red AAA logo just under a select group of restaurant names! These Official Appointment restaurants place a high value on the business they receive from dedicated AAA/CAA travelers.

As a member, you already turn to TourBooks for quality travel information. Now look for restaurants that display the bright red AAA logo in their listing for dining experiences you'll long remember!

# LINCOLN

## WHERE TO STAY

**COMFORT INN & SUITES** *Book at aaa.com*
Phone: (603)745-6700

| | | |
|---|---|---|
| 6/17-10/23 & 12/25-4/30 [ECP] | 1P: $109-$199 | 2P: $109-$199 |
| 5/1-6/16 & 10/24-12/24 [ECP] | 1P: $99-$189 | 2P: $99-$189 |

XP: $10   F18
XP: $10   F18

Small-scale Hotel **Location:** I-93, exit 32. Rt 112 at Hobo Railroad 03251 (PO Box 519). Fax: 603/745-2131. **Facility:** 82 units. 71 one-bedroom standard units. 11 one-bedroom suites ($159-$279), some with whirlpools. 4 stories, interior corridors. **Bath:** combo or shower only. **Parking:** on-site. **Terms:** 7 day cancellation notice, weekly rates available. **Amenities:** voice mail, hair dryers. *Some:* irons. **Pool(s):** heated indoor. **Leisure Activities:** whirlpool, exercise room. *Fee:* game room. **Guest Services:** coin laundry. **Business Services:** meeting rooms. **Cards:** AX, CB, DC, DS, JC, MC, VI.

SOME UNITS

ASK SD &M (& ⊠ ⊠ ⊞ DATA PORT 🖭 / ⊠ ▣ 🖥 💻 /

### DRUMMER BOY MOTOR INN

[AAA] [SAVE]
▽▽▽▽ ▽▽▽▽
Motel

Phone: (603)745-3661

| | |
|---|---|
| 5/1-10/12 | 2P: $79-$99 |
| 12/25-4/1 | 2P: $59-$99 |
| 10/13-12/24 & 4/2-4/30 | 2P: $59-$79 |

**Location:** I-93, exit 33 (US 3), 0.3 mi ne. US 3 03251 (RR 118). **Fax:** 603/745-9829. **Facility:** 53 units. 49 one-bedroom standard units, some with efficiencies and/or whirlpools. 1 two-bedroom suite ($99-$139). 1 vacation home ($209-$259) and 2 cottages ($99-$139). 1-2 stories (no elevator), interior/exterior corridors. **Parking:** on-site, winter plug-ins. **Terms:** office hours 7 am-11 pm, 7 day cancellation notice. **Amenities:** irons, hair dryers. **Pool(s):** heated outdoor, heated indoor. **Leisure Activities:** sauna, whirlpool, playground, limited exercise equipment. *Fee:* game room. **Guest Services:** coin laundry. **Business Services:** meeting rooms. **Cards:** AX, DS, MC, VI. **Special Amenities: free continental breakfast.** *(See color ad p 350)*

SOME UNITS
[S℗] [↑↓] [⊘] [≈] [✕] / [✕] [📷] [💻] /

### FRANCONIA NOTCH MOTEL

[AAA] [SAVE]
▽▽▽▽ ▽▽▽▽
Motel

Phone: (603)745-2229

| | | | |
|---|---|---|---|
| 6/18-10/16 | 1P: $55-$70 | 2P: $60-$85 | XP: $6 | D18 |
| 12/24-4/30 | 1P: $35-$60 | 2P: $40-$80 | | |
| 5/1-6/17 | 1P: $40-$60 | 2P: $45-$65 | XP: $5 | D18 |
| 10/17-12/23 | 1P: $35-$50 | 2P: $40-$60 | XP: $5 | D18 |

**Location:** I-93, exit 33 (US 3), 1.3 mi ne. Located along the river. US 3 03251 (RFD 1, Box 98B). **Fax:** 603/745-8550. **Facility:** 18 units. 12 one-bedroom standard units. 6 cottages ($60-$85). 1 story, exterior corridors. *Bath:* combo or shower only. **Parking:** on-site. **Terms:** office hours 8 am-11 pm, 3 day cancellation notice, [MAP] meal plan available. **Leisure Activities:** fishing. **Cards:** AX, DS, MC, VI. **Special Amenities: free local telephone calls.**

SOME UNITS
[↑↓] [✕] / [VCR] [💻] /
FEE FEE

### INDIAN HEAD RESORT     *Book at aaa.com*

[AAA] [SAVE]
▽▽▽▽ ▽▽▽▽
Motel

Phone: (603)745-8000

| | | | |
|---|---|---|---|
| 7/1-10/16 | 1P: $135-$175 | 2P: $135-$175 | XP: $10 | F5 |
| 10/17-4/30 | 1P: $99-$139 | 2P: $99-$139 | XP: $10 | F5 |
| 5/1-6/30 | 1P: $89-$119 | 2P: $89-$119 | XP: $10 | F5 |

**Location:** I-93, exit 33 (US 3), 1.5 mi ne. Rt 3 03251 (RR 1, Box 99). **Fax:** 603/745-8414. **Facility:** 98 one-bedroom standard units, some with whirlpools. 2 stories (no elevator), exterior corridors. **Parking:** on-site. **Terms:** check-in 4 pm, 2 night minimum stay - weekends, 7 day cancellation notice, [MAP] meal plan available, package plans. **Amenities:** voice mail. **Dining:** Profile Room, see separate listing, entertainment. **Pool(s):** heated outdoor, heated indoor. **Leisure Activities:** saunas, whirlpools, paddleboats, fishing, 2 lighted tennis courts, cross country skiing, recreation programs. **Guest Services:** gift shop, coin laundry. **Business Services:** meeting rooms. **Cards:** AX, CB, DC, DS, MC, VI. *(See color ad p 350 & ad p 354)*

SOME UNITS
[🍴] [▽] [≈] [✕] [🎣] [DATA PORT] [💻] [💻] / [✕] /

### KANCAMAGUS MOTOR LODGE

▽▽▽▽ ▽▽▽▽
Motel

Phone: (603)745-3365

| | | | |
|---|---|---|---|
| 6/2-10/18 | 1P: $79-$119 | 2P: $79-$119 | XP: $10 | F12 |
| 12/19-4/30 | 1P: $69-$119 | 2P: $69-$119 | XP: $10 | F12 |
| 10/19-12/18 | 1P: $59-$109 | 2P: $59-$109 | XP: $10 | F12 |
| 5/1-6/1 | 1P: $59-$99 | 2P: $59-$99 | XP: $10 | F12 |

**Location:** I-93, exit 32, 1.6 mi e. SR 112 03251 (PO Box 505). **Fax:** 603/745-6691. **Facility:** 34 one-bedroom standard units. 2 stories (no elevator), exterior corridors. **Parking:** on-site. **Terms:** office hours 8 am-10 pm, 3 day cancellation notice, [MAP] meal plan available, package plans. **Pool(s):** heated indoor. **Leisure Activities:** playground. *Fee:* game room. **Guest Services:** coin laundry. **Cards:** AX, DC, DS, MC, VI.

SOME UNITS
[A$K] [S℗] [🍴] [≈] / [✕] [💻] /

### THE LODGE AT LINCOLN STATION

[AAA] [SAVE]
▽▽▽▽ ▽▽▽▽
Small-scale Hotel

Phone: (603)745-3441

| | | |
|---|---|---|
| 6/11-10/24 | 1P: $109-$219 | 2P: $109-$219 |
| 12/24-4/30 | 1P: $69-$219 | 2P: $69-$219 |
| 5/1-6/10 & 10/25-12/23 | 1P: $69-$129 | 2P: $69-$129 |

**Location:** I-93, exit 32, 1.4 mi e. SR 112 (Kancamagus Hwy) 03251 (PO Box 906). **Fax:** 603/745-3232. **Facility:** 95 units. 51 one-bedroom standard units with efficiencies. 44 one-bedroom suites with efficiencies, some with whirlpools. 3 stories, interior corridors. **Parking:** on-site. **Terms:** check-in 4 pm, 2 night minimum stay - some weekends, 7 day cancellation notice-fee imposed, weekly rates available, package plans - seasonal, 10% service charge. **Amenities:** irons, hair dryers. **Pool(s):** outdoor, heated indoor. **Leisure Activities:** sauna, whirlpool. *Fee:* game room. **Guest Services:** coin laundry, area transportation-Loon Mountain. **Business Services:** meeting rooms. **Cards:** AX, DS, MC, VI. *(See color ad p 352)*

SOME UNITS
[S℗] [↑↓] [≈] [✕] [🎣] [💻] [💻] [💻] / [✕] [AC] [VCR] /

**MILL HOUSE INN**　　　　　　　　　　　　　　　　　　　　　**Phone: (603)745-6261**

(AAA) (SAVE)

▽▽ ▽▽

Small-scale Hotel

| | 6/11-10/24 & 12/24-4/30 | 1P: $109-$199 | 2P: $109-$199 |
| | 5/1-6/10 & 10/25-12/23 | 1P: $59-$119 | 2P: $59-$119 |

**Location:** I-93, exit 32, 1 mi e. Located adjacent to a market. SR 112 (Kancamagus Hwy) 03251 (PO Box 696). Fax: 603/745-6896. **Facility:** 95 units. 91 one-bedroom standard units. 4 two-bedroom suites with kitchens. 4 stories, interior corridors. **Parking:** on-site. **Terms:** check-in 4 pm, 2 night minimum stay - weekends, package plans - seasonal, 10% service charge. **Amenities:** voice mail, hair dryers. **Pool(s):** heated outdoor, heated indoor. **Leisure Activities:** saunas, whirlpools, 3 tennis courts, horse drawn wagon rides in summer, exercise room. *Fee:* game room. **Guest Services:** area transportation-Loon Mountain. **Business Services:** meeting rooms. **Cards:** AX, DS, MC, VI. *(See color ad below)*

SOME UNITS

⊟ ⊞ ⊠ ⊠ / ⊠ 🄥 ⊟ ⊟ ⊟ /
FEE

---

**THE MOUNTAIN CLUB ON LOON**　　*Book at aaa.com*　　　　**Phone: (603)745-2244**

(AAA) (SAVE)

▽▽▽ ▽▽▽

Resort
Large-scale Hotel

| | 1/1-4/30 | 2P: $89-$254 |
| | 6/28-12/31 | 2P: $89-$230 |
| | 5/1-6/27 | 2P: $89-$109 |

**Location:** I-93, exit 32, 3 mi e. Located in Loon Mountain Ski and Recreation Area. SR 112 03251 (RR 1, Box 40). Fax: 603/745-2317. **Facility:** The resort, located on Loon Mountain within the national forest, offers ski-in/ski-out access. 238 one-bedroom standard units, some with kitchens and/or whirlpools. 3-4 stories, interior corridors. **Parking:** on-site. **Terms:** check-in 5 pm, 2 night minimum stay - weekends, 14 day cancellation notice-fee imposed, [MAP] meal plan available, package plans. **Amenities:** voice mail, hair dryers. *Some:* irons. **Dining:** 7 am-9 pm, cocktails. **Pool(s):** heated outdoor, heated indoor. **Leisure Activities:** saunas, whirlpools, steamrooms, 2 tennis courts, racquetball court, recreation programs, rental bicycles, hiking trails, playground, exercise room, spa, volleyball. *Fee:* downhill & cross country skiing, ice skating, ski lifts, instructions & equipment, gondola rides, inline skates, pony rides, squash court, horseback riding, game room. **Guest Services:** gift shop, coin laundry. *Fee:* tanning facility. **Business Services:** meeting rooms. **Cards:** AX, DC, DS, MC, VI. *(See color ad p 353)*

SOME UNITS

⊟ ⊞ ⊻ ⊟ ⊞ ⊘ ⊠ ⊠ 🄿 DATA/PORT ⊟ / ⊠ ⊟ ⊟ /

---

**MOUNT COOLIDGE MOTEL**　　　　　　　　　　　　　　　**Phone: (603)745-8052**

(AAA) (SAVE)

▽▽ ▽▽

Motel

| | 5/1-11/1 | 1P: $42-$72 | 2P: $49-$89 | XP: $8 | F15 |

**Location:** I-93, exit 33 (US 3), 0.3 mi n. Located along a mountain stream. US 3 03262 (PO Box 275, NORTH WOODSTOCK). **Facility:** 20 units. 18 one-bedroom standard units. 2 cottages ($59-$135). 1 story, exterior corridors. **Parking:** on-site. **Terms:** open 5/1-11/1, office hours 7 am-10 pm. **Pool(s):** heated outdoor. **Leisure Activities:** fishing. **Cards:** MC, VI. **Special Amenities:** early check-in/late check-out and free room upgrade (subject to availability with advanced reservations).

⊟ ⊞ ⊻ ⊠ ⊟

## PROFILE MOTEL & COTTAGES

**Phone: 603/745-2759**

| | | | |
|---|---|---|---|
| AAA SAVE | 5/1-10/31 | 1P: $42-$82 | 2P: $48-$89 | XP: $10 | F12 |
| | 11/1-4/30 | 1P: $32-$62 | 2P: $38-$68 | XP: $10 | F12 |

Motel

**Location:** I-93, exit 33 (US 3), 0.5 mi ne. Rt 3, Box 117 03251. Fax: 603/745-3518. **Facility:** Smoke free premises. 18 units. 10 one-bedroom standard units. 8 cottages. 1 story, exterior corridors. *Bath:* combo or shower only. **Parking:** on-site. **Terms:** office hours 7:30 am-11 pm, 2-3 night minimum stay - weekends, 3 day cancellation notice. **Pool(s):** heated outdoor. **Leisure Activities:** picnic area with grills, hiking trails, playground, basketball, horseshoes, volleyball. **Cards:** DS, MC, VI. **Special Amenities:** free local telephone calls and free room upgrade **(subject to availability with advanced reservations).**

SOME UNITS

## RED DOORS MOTEL

**Phone: 603/745-2267**

| | | | |
|---|---|---|---|
| AAA SAVE | All Year | 2P: $45-$89 | XP: $10 | F5 |

Motel

**Location:** I-93, exit 33 (US 3), 0.5 mi ne. US 3 03251 (RFD 1, Box 109A). Fax: 603/745-3646. **Facility:** 30 one-bedroom standard units. 2 stories (no elevator), exterior corridors. **Parking:** on-site. **Terms:** office hours 7 am-11 pm, 7 day cancellation notice. **Pool(s):** heated outdoor. **Leisure Activities:** barbecue grills in picnic area, playground, shuffleboard. *Fee:* game room. **Guest Services:** coin laundry. **Cards:** AX, MC, VI.

SOME UNITS
FEE

## RIVERGREEN RESORT HOTEL

**Phone: (603)745-2450**

| | | |
|---|---|---|
| AAA SAVE | 6/11-10/24 | 1P: $109-$309 |
| | 12/25-4/30 | 1P: $69-$309 |
| | 5/1-6/10 & 10/25-12/24 | 1P: $69-$139 |

Small-scale Hotel

**Location:** I-93, exit 32, 1 mi e. SR 112 (Kancamagus Hwy) 03251 (PO Box 1056). Fax: 603/745-6777. **Facility:** 120 units. 57 one-bedroom standard units with whirlpools. 43 one- and 20 two-bedroom suites with efficiencies, some with whirlpools. 4 stories, interior corridors. **Parking:** on-site. **Terms:** check-in 4 pm, 2 night minimum stay - some weekends, 7 day cancellation notice, 10% service charge. **Amenities:** voice mail, irons, hair dryers. **Leisure Activities:** recreational privileges at the Mill House Inn. **Guest Services:** coin laundry, area transportation-Loon Mountain. **Cards:** AX, DS, MC, VI. *(See color ad p 352)*

SOME UNITS

## WOODWARD'S RESORT

**Phone: (603)745-8141**

| | | | |
|---|---|---|---|
| AAA SAVE | 6/25-10/11 | 1P: $89-$125 | 2P: $89-$125 | XP: $5 | F12 |
| | 10/12-4/30 | 1P: $50-$125 | 2P: $50-$125 | XP: $5 | F12 |
| | 5/1-6/24 | 1P: $69-$89 | 2P: $69-$89 | XP: $5 | F12 |

Motel

**Location:** I-93, exit 33 (US 3), 1.4 mi ne. US 3 03251 (RFD 1, Box 107). Fax: 603/745-3408. **Facility:** 85 units. 78 one- and 7 two-bedroom standard units. 1-2 stories (no elevator), interior/exterior corridors. **Parking:** on-site, winter plug-ins. **Terms:** office hours 7 am-10 pm, 7 day cancellation notice, [MAP] meal plan available. **Amenities:** hair dryers. **Dining:** Woodward's Open Hearth Steak House, see separate listing. **Pool(s):** heated outdoor, heated indoor. **Leisure Activities:** sauna, whirlpool, tennis court, ice skating, badminton, playground, basketball, horseshoes, shuffleboard, volleyball. *Fee:* racquetball court, game room. **Guest Services:** coin laundry. **Business Services:** meeting rooms. **Cards:** AX, CB, DC, DS, MC, VI. *(See color ad p 354)*

SOME UNITS
FEE

---

## WHERE TO DINE

---

### CHIENG GARDENS

**Lunch:** $6-$18    **Dinner:** $8-$18    **Phone: 603/745-8612**

Chinese

**Location:** I-93, exit 32, 1.5 mi e; in Lincoln Square Mall. SR 112 03251. **Hours:** 11:30 am-10 pm, Fri & Sat-11 pm. Closed: 11/25, 12/25. **Reservations:** accepted. **Features:** Near Loon Mountain, the Asian-oriented restaurant serves traditional Chinese cuisine. This place is on the second floor of a small strip mall. Casual dress; cocktails. **Parking:** on-site. **Cards:** AX, DS, MC, VI.

### THE COMMON MAN

**Dinner:** $10-$20    **Phone: 603/745-3463**

American

**Location:** I-93, exit 32, 1.6 mi e. SR 112 03251. **Hours:** 5 pm-9 pm, Fri & Sat-9:30 pm. Closed: 11/25, 12/25. **Features:** The decor is charming and the cuisine tasty. A menu of original comfort foods includes the signature lobster and corn chowder, chicken Kiev, steaks and seafood. Diners should be sure to sample the white chocolate mousse served at the end of the meal. Casual dress; cocktails. **Parking:** on-site. **Cards:** AX, DS, MC, VI.

### GORDI'S FISH & STEAK HOUSE

**Lunch:** $7-$12    **Dinner:** $10-$19    **Phone: 603/745-6635**

Steak & Seafood

**Location:** I-93, exit 32, 1.5 mi e. SR 112 03251. **Hours:** 4:30 pm-9 pm, Fri & Sat-9:30 pm; also noon-3 pm 5/29-10/17. Closed: 11/25, 12/25. **Reservations:** accepted. **Features:** The owners, Gordi and Karen Eaton, were on the Olympic ski team spanning the 1960s and '70s, and ski memorabilia graces the walls. The menu lists a wide selection, from prime rib and fresh Maine lobster to sandwiches and Santa Fe chicken. Casual dress; cocktails. **Parking:** on-site. **Cards:** AX, DS, MC, VI.

### PROFILE ROOM

**Lunch:** $5-$14    **Dinner:** $11-$22    **Phone: 603/745-8000**

American

**Location:** I-93, exit 33 (US 3), 1.5 mi ne; in Indian Head Resort. **Hours:** 7 am-9:30 pm, to 8 pm 10/29-6/29. **Features:** New England favorites, such as Yankee pot roast and baked stuffed haddock, as well as innovative dishes including sauteed shrimp and feta and veggie medley are among menu choices. The decor has a Native American motif, and the dining room affords scenic views. Casual dress; cocktails; entertainment. **Parking:** on-site. **Cards:** AX, CB, DC, DS, MC, VI. *(See color ad p 350 & ad p 354)*

**WISE GUYS CAFE**

American

**Lunch:** $4-$7    **Dinner:** $4-$7    **Phone:** 603/745-8503
**Location:** I-93, exit 32, 1 mi e. SR 112 at the Mill 03251. **Hours:** noon-8 pm. Closed major holidays.
**Features:** In a small strip mall, the family-run cafe serves homemade soups, sandwiches and ice cream. Casual dress. **Parking:** on-site.

**WOODWARD'S OPEN HEARTH STEAK HOUSE**

American

**Dinner:** $14-$20    **Phone:** 603/745-8141
**Location:** I-93, exit 33 (US 3), 1.4 mi ne; in Woodward's Resort. **Hours:** 7:30 am-11 & 5-9 pm; 7:30 am-10 & 5-8:30 pm off season. Closed: 11/1-11/25. **Reservations:** suggested. **Features:** The focal point of the friendly, family-oriented steakhouse's dining room is its open-grill cooking area. The menu lists the house specialty prime rib among offerings of hand-cut steaks and fresh seafood. Also offered are stir-fry choices and such sauteed items as veal. Servers are prompt and friendly. Casual dress; cocktails. **Parking:** on-site. **Cards:** AX, CB, DC, DS, MC, VI.

——— *The following restaurant has not been evaluated by AAA* ———
*but is listed for your information only.*

**SEVEN SEAS SEAFOOD RESTAURANT**

(fyi)

**Phone:** 603/745-6536
Not evaluated. **Location:** I-93, exit 32, 0.5 mi e. SR 112 03251. **Features:** A good variety of fried seafoods and grill items are served each day in a friendly atmosphere.

# LISBON pop. 1,070

——— **WHERE TO STAY** ———

**AMMONOOSUC INN**

Historic
Country Inn

**Phone:** (603)838-6118

| | 1P | 2P | XP |
|---|---|---|---|
| 9/12-10/26 | 1P: $75-$115 | 2P: $90-$130 | XP: $15 |
| 5/23-9/11 | 1P: $65-$105 | 2P: $80-$120 | XP: $15 |
| 5/1-5/22 & 10/27-4/30 | 1P: $50-$90 | 2P: $65-$105 | XP: $15 |

**Location:** US 302 and SR 10, just nw on Lyman Rd, then 1 mi sw. 641 Bishop Rd 03585. Fax: 603/250-0049. **Facility:** This 1880s country inn is in a scenic wooded area overlooking a river and a golf course. Designated smoking area. 9 one-bedroom standard units. 3 stories (no elevator), interior corridors. *Bath:* combo or shower only. **Parking:** on-site. **Terms:** office hours 8 am-10 pm, age restrictions may apply, 14 day cancellation notice-fee imposed, [MAP] meal plan available, small pets only (in designated units). **Leisure Activities:** fishing, cross country skiing, hiking trails. **Guest Services:** TV in common area. **Business Services:** meeting rooms. **Cards:** MC, VI.

# LITTLETON pop. 4,431

——— **WHERE TO STAY** ———

**THE BEAL HOUSE INN**

Historic
Country Inn

**Phone:** (603)444-2661

| | 1P | 2P | XP | |
|---|---|---|---|---|
| 9/16-10/31 | 1P: $135-$225 | 2P: $135-$225 | XP: $35 | D12 |
| 5/1-9/15 | 1P: $125-$205 | 2P: $125-$205 | XP: $25 | D12 |
| 11/1-4/30 | 1P: $115-$195 | 2P: $115-$195 | XP: $25 | D12 |

**Location:** Jct US 302 and SR 18; center. 2 W Main St 03561. Fax: 603/444-6224. **Facility:** Built in 1833, this inn has attractive and comfortable guest rooms and many with a gas fireplace. Smoke free premises. 8 units. 3 one-bedroom and 1 two-bedroom suites, some with whirlpools. 3 stories (no elevator), interior corridors. **Parking:** on-site. **Terms:** 7 day cancellation notice-fee imposed, weekly rates available, [BP] meal plan available, package plans - seasonal, 5% service charge. **Amenities:** CD players, hair dryers. *Some:* irons. **Business Services:** meeting rooms, fax. **Cards:** AX, MC, VI.

SOME UNITS

**COUNTRY SQUIRE MOTEL**

Motel

**Phone:** 603/444-5610

| | 1P | 2P | XP | |
|---|---|---|---|---|
| 9/24-10/16 | 1P: $59-$64 | 2P: $64-$69 | XP: $7 | F12 |
| 6/25-9/23 | 1P: $49-$54 | 2P: $54-$59 | XP: $7 | F12 |
| 5/14-6/24 & 10/17-11/7 | 1P: $39-$49 | 2P: $44-$54 | XP: $7 | F12 |

**Location:** I-93, exit 43, 1.3 mi se on SR 18; 0.5 mi nw of jct US 302. Located in a quiet area. 172 W Main St, SR 18 03561. **Facility:** 8 one-bedroom standard units. 1 story, exterior corridors. *Bath:* shower only. **Parking:** on-site. **Terms:** open 5/14-11/7, 2 night minimum stay - weekends, 5 day cancellation notice-fee imposed. **Pool(s):** outdoor. **Cards:** AX, DS, MC, VI.

SOME UNITS

**EASTGATE MOTOR INN**

Motel

**Phone:** 603/444-3971

| | 1P | 2P | XP | |
|---|---|---|---|---|
| 9/27-10/31 [CP] | 1P: $83-$93 | 2P: $89-$99 | XP: $7 | F7 |
| 6/29-9/26 [CP] | 1P: $63-$73 | 2P: $69-$79 | XP: $7 | F7 |
| 11/1-4/30 [CP] | 1P: $53-$63 | 2P: $59-$69 | XP: $7 | F7 |
| 5/1-6/28 [CP] | 1P: $43-$53 | 2P: $49-$59 | XP: $7 | F7 |

**Location:** I-93, exit 41, just e. Located in a quiet area. 335 Cottage St 03561. Fax: 603/444-3971. **Facility:** 55 one-bedroom standard units. 1 story, interior/exterior corridors. *Bath:* combo or shower only. **Parking:** on-site, winter plug-ins. **Terms:** pets (with prior approval). **Dining:** dining room, see separate listing. **Pool(s):** outdoor, wading. **Leisure Activities:** snowmobiling, playground. **Business Services:** meeting rooms, fax (fee). **Cards:** AX, DS, MC, VI. **Special Amenities:** free continental breakfast and free local telephone calls.

SOME UNITS

## HISTORIC THAYERS INN

**Phone:** 603/444-6469

All Year        1P: $59-$99        2P: $59-$99

Historic Small-scale Hotel

**Location:** I-93, exit 42, 1.3 mi e on US 302 and SR 10; center. 111 Main St 03561. **Fax:** 603/444-6469. **Facility:** This 19th-century hotel in the town center features a model of an 1840s-era guest room. 36 units. 30 one- and 6 two-bedroom standard units, some with efficiencies. 4 stories (no elevator), interior corridors. *Bath:* some shared or private, combo-or shower only. **Parking:** on-site, winter plug-ins. **Terms:** cancellation fee imposed, [CP] meal plan available, pets (with prior approval). **Amenities:** video library. **Cards:** AX, CB, DC, DS, MC, VI.

SOME UNITS

🔊 🐾 🍴 / ✕ 📼 🅩 📞 /

## LITTLETON MOTEL

**Phone:** 603/444-5780

| | | | |
|---|---|---|---|
| 9/26-10/30 | 1P: $68-$71 | 2P: $78-$82 | XP: $8   F12 |
| 6/28-9/25 | 1P: $52 | 2P: $58-$64 | XP: $8   F12 |
| 5/15-6/27 | 1P: $48-$52 | 2P: $58-$62 | XP: $8   F12 |

Motel

**Location:** I-93, exit 42, 1.2 mi e on US 302 and SR 10; center. 166 Main St 03561. **Fax:** 603/444-0484. **Facility:** Smoke free premises. 19 units. 18 one-bedroom standard units. 1 one-bedroom suite. 1 story, exterior corridors. *Bath:* combo or shower only. **Parking:** on-site. **Terms:** open 5/15-10/30, small pets only. **Pool(s):** outdoor. **Cards:** AX, MC, VI.

🐾 🍴 ⇌ ✕ 📠 📞

## MAPLE LEAF MOTEL

**Phone:** 603/444-5105

| | | | |
|---|---|---|---|
| 9/17-10/10 | 1P: $59-$79 | 2P: $69-$89 | XP: $7   F12 |
| 6/18-9/16 | 1P: $49-$69 | 2P: $59-$79 | XP: $7   F12 |
| 10/11-3/28 | 1P: $49-$69 | 2P: $49-$69 | XP: $7   F12 |
| 5/1-6/17 | 1P: $47-$69 | 2P: $47-$69 | XP: $7   F12 |

Motel

**Location:** Jct US 302, 0.5 mi nw on SR 18. Located in a quiet area. 150 W Main St 03561. **Fax:** 603/444-0571. **Facility:** 13 units. 12 one-bedroom standard units, some with kitchens. 1 two-bedroom suite with kitchen. 1 story, exterior corridors. **Parking:** on-site, winter plug-ins. **Terms:** open 5/1-3/28, 3 day cancellation notice-fee imposed. **Pool(s):** heated outdoor. **Leisure Activities:** playground, horseshoes. **Cards:** AX, DC, DS, MC, VI.

SOME UNITS

(ASK) ⇌ 📠 📞 / ✕ 🖥 /

---

## —— WHERE TO DINE ——

### THE BEAL HOUSE INN RESTAURANT

**Dinner:** $15-$25      **Phone:** 603/444-2661

International

**Location:** Jct US 302 and SR 18; center. 2 W Main St 03561. **Hours:** Open 5/1-11/17 & 11/27-4/20; 5:30 pm-9 pm. Closed: 3/27, 11/25; also Mon, Tues & Super Bowl Sun. **Reservations:** suggested. **Features:** Elegant and intimate dining is enhanced with soft lighting, a long copper-lined bar, light jazz playing in the background, and pleasant servers. The dishes, described as global cuisine with an eclectic flair are thoughtfully prepared by the owner/chef. Dressy casual; cocktails. **Parking:** on-site. **Cards:** AX, MC, VI.

🍸 ✕

### THE CLAMSHELL RESTAURANT

**Lunch:** $5-$12      **Dinner:** $10-$18      **Phone:** 603/444-6445

Seafood

**Location:** I-93, exit 42 on US 302 and SR 10. 274 Dells Rd 03561. **Hours:** 11:30 am-4 & 5-9 pm, Fri & Sat-9:30 pm. Closed: 12/25. **Reservations:** suggested. **Features:** This popular family restaurant has a rustic New England decor and specializes in seafood. Menu highlights include Marine shrimps, haddock, clams and scallops. The service is friendly and attentive. Casual dress; cocktails. **Parking:** on-site. **Cards:** AX, DS, MC, VI.

🍸 ✕

### EASTGATE RESTAURANT

**Dinner:** $6-$19      **Phone:** 603/444-3971

American

**Location:** I-93, exit 41, just e; in Eastgate Motor Inn. 335 Cottage St 03561. **Hours:** 5 pm-9 pm, Fri & Sat-9:30 pm. Closed: 12/24. **Reservations:** suggested, weekends. **Features:** The inviting dining room has a relaxed atmosphere with a small water fountain and large picture windows overlooking the grounds. The well-prepared entrees include chicken, pasta, seafood and steak. Casual dress; cocktails. **Parking:** on-site. **Cards:** AX, CB, DC, DS, MC, VI.

🍸 ✕

### ITALIAN OASIS RESTAURANT & BREWERY

**Lunch:** $6-$12      **Dinner:** $6-$16      **Phone:** 603/444-6995

Italian

**Location:** US 302 and SR 10; center; in Parker's Marketplace. 106 Main St 03561. **Hours:** 11:30 am-10 pm, Fri & Sat-11 pm. Closed: 3/27, 11/25, 12/25. **Reservations:** suggested. **Features:** Good hearty food and friendly service are the attractions here. The fun menu features pizza, pasta and microbrews. The casual atmosphere includes an atrium and terrace, and there's live entertainment on Friday in the summer. The lounge is open to 12:30 am. Casual dress; cocktails. **Parking:** on-site. **Cards:** AX, DS, MC, VI.

🍸 ✕

# LONDONDERRY pop. 11,417

──────── WHERE TO STAY ────────

**SLEEP INN**   *Book at aaa.com*                                  **Phone: (603)425-2110**

(AAA) (SAVE)      5/1-10/31             1P: $79-$119       2P: $79-$119       XP: $5       F16

▼▼▼ ▼▼      11/1-4/30             1P: $59-$89        2P: $59-$89        XP: $5       F16

Small-scale Hotel    **Location:** I-93, exit 5. 72 Perkins Rd 03053. **Fax:** 603/425-2129. **Facility:** 100 one-bedroom standard units. 3 stories, interior corridors. *Bath:* shower only. **Parking:** on-site. **Terms:** [ECP] meal plan available. **Amenities:** voice mail, safes (fee), irons, hair dryers. **Pool(s):** heated indoor. **Leisure Activities:** whirlpool, exercise room. **Guest Services:** airport transportation-Manchester Airport. **Business Services:** meeting rooms. **Cards:** AX, DC, DS, MC, VI. **Special Amenities:** free continental breakfast and free local telephone calls.

SOME UNITS

(icons)

──────── WHERE TO DINE ────────

**THE HOMESTEAD RESTAURANT & LOUNGE**       **Dinner:** $14-$23       **Phone: 603/437-2022**

▼▼ ▼▼    **Location:** I-93, exit 4, 1.7 mi w on SR 102. SR 102 & Mammoth Rd 03053. **Hours:** 4:30 pm-9 pm; Sunday brunch

American    11 am-2 pm. **Closed:** 12/25. **Features:** There is something for everyone at this family run restaurant. Menu offerings include broiled Boston scrod, chicken parmesan, steak au poivre, and much more to choose from. Several dining rooms are throughout this restored farmhouse and the lounge is located on the second level. Casual dress; cocktails. **Parking:** on-site. **Cards:** AX, DS, MC, VI.

(icon)

# LOUDON

──────── WHERE TO STAY ────────

**LOVEJOY FARM BED & BREAKFAST**                            **Phone: 603/783-4007**

▼▼▼▼      5/1-1/5 [BP]           1P: $84          2P: $99-$109       XP: $30       F6

Historic Bed    **Location:** Jct SR 106 and 129, just w on SR 129, just nw on Village Rd, then 1.2 mi n. Located in a quiet, rural area.

& Breakfast    268 Lovejoy Rd 03307. **Fax:** 603/783-8389. **Facility:** This 1790 Georgian Colonial and carriage house are in a country setting surrounded by woods and fields. Smoke free premises. 8 one-bedroom standard units. 2 stories (no elevator), interior corridors. *Bath:* combo or shower only. **Parking:** on-site. **Terms:** open 5/1-1/5, 14 day cancellation notice, pets (with prior approval). **Leisure Activities:** cross country skiing, hiking trails. **Guest Services:** TV in common area. **Cards:** AX, MC, VI.

SOME UNITS

(icons)

# LYME

──────── WHERE TO DINE ────────

**ALDEN COUNTRY INN**    Country Inn       **Dinner:** $12-$26       **Phone: 603/795-2222**

▼▼ ▼▼    **Location:** Just off SR 10 on the common; center. 1 Market St 03768. **Hours:** 5:30 pm-9 pm.

American    **Reservations:** suggested. **Features:** The historic country inn's intimate dining room, with its cozy fireplace, is ideal for fine dining. Seating on the enclosed porch is often requested in summer. American cuisine, particularly New England specialties, uses local and international ingredients. Casual dress; cocktails.

**Parking:** on-site. **Cards:** AX, DC, DS, MC, VI.

(icons)

# MANCHESTER pop. 107,006

──────── WHERE TO STAY ────────

**BEST WESTERN EXECUTIVE COURT INN & CONFERENCE CENTER**    *Book at aaa.com*    **Phone: (603)627-2525**

(AAA) (SAVE)      5/1-10/31 [ECP]       1P: $129-$159       2P: $129-$159       XP: $10       F17

▼▼▼ ▼▼      11/1-4/30 [ECP]       1P: $119-$129       2P: $119-$129       XP: $10       F17

Small-scale Hotel    **Location:** I-293, exit 1, 0.5 mi s on SR 28, then 1 mi e. 13500 S Willow St 03109. **Fax:** 603/665-7090. **Facility:** 135 units. 123 one-bedroom standard units, some with whirlpools. 12 one-bedroom suites with whirlpools. 3 stories, interior corridors. *Bath:* combo or shower only. **Parking:** on-site. **Amenities:** dual phone lines, voice mail, irons, hair dryers. *Some:* safes. **Pool(s):** heated indoor. **Leisure Activities:** whirlpool, billiards, foosball, exercise room. *Fee:* game room. **Guest Services:** valet and coin laundry. **Business Services:** conference facilities, fax (fee). **Cards:** AX, DC, DS, MC, VI. **Special Amenities:** free expanded continental breakfast and preferred room (subject to availability with advanced reservations).

SOME UNITS

(icons)

**CENTER OF NEW HAMPSHIRE-HOLIDAY INN**    *Book at aaa.com*    **Phone: (603)625-1000**

▼▼▼ ▼▼▼      All Year       1P: $99-$169       2P: $109-$179       XP: $10       F18

Large-scale Hotel    **Location:** Jct Granite St; downtown. 700 Elm St 03101. **Fax:** 603/668-2948. **Facility:** 250 units. 242 one-bedroom standard units. 8 one-bedroom suites ($225-$500). 12 stories, interior corridors. *Bath:* combo or shower only. **Parking:** on-site (fee). **Terms:** pets ($50 fee). **Amenities:** dual phone lines, voice mail, irons, hair dryers. **Pool(s):** heated indoor. **Leisure Activities:** saunas, whirlpool. **Guest Services:** gift shop, valet laundry. **Business Services:** conference facilities, fax (fee). **Cards:** AX, CB, DC, DS, JC, MC, VI.

SOME UNITS

(icons)    FEE          FEE FEE

**FAIRFIELD INN BY MARRIOTT-MANCHESTER AIRPORT**    *Book at aaa.com*    **Phone: (603)625-2020**

▼▼ ▼▼      All Year [ECP]       1P: $84-$129       2P: $84-$129       XP: $10       F17

Small-scale Hotel    **Location:** I-293, exit 1, just ne on SR 28. 860 S Porter St 03103. **Fax:** 603/623-7562. **Facility:** 102 one-bedroom standard units. 4 stories, interior corridors. *Bath:* combo or shower only. **Parking:** on-site. **Amenities:** voice mail, irons, hair dryers. *Fee:* video library, video games. **Pool(s):** outdoor. **Leisure Activities:** limited exercise equipment. **Guest Services:** valet laundry. **Cards:** AX, CB, DC, DS, JC, MC, VI.

SOME UNITS

(icons)

**FOUR POINTS BY SHERATON MANCHESTER**    *Book at aaa.com*                    Phone: (603)668-6110

(AAA) (SAVE)    All Year                          1P: $140-$175        2P: $140-$175           XP: $10                    F17
            **Location:** I-293, exit 1, just nw on SR 28. 55 John E Devine Dr 03103. Fax: 603/668-0408. **Facility:** 120 one-
            bedroom standard units. 4 stories, interior corridors. **Parking:** on-site. **Terms:** 1-2 night minimum stay, can-
Small-scale Hotel  cellation fee imposed. **Amenities:** dual phone lines, voice mail, irons, hair dryers. *Fee:* video library, video
            games. *Some:* fax. **Dining:** 6 am-9 pm, cocktails. **Pool(s):** heated indoor. **Leisure Activities:** whirlpool.
            **Guest Services:** valet laundry, area transportation-health club. **Business Services:** meeting rooms.
**Cards:** AX, CB, DC, DS, JC, MC, VI. **Special Amenities:** free local telephone calls and free newspaper.
*(See color ad p 5)*

SOME UNITS
FEE FEE

---

**THE HIGHLANDER INN**    *Book at aaa.com*                                    Phone: (603)625-6426

            9/1-10/31                             1P: $119-$139                        XP: $10                    F18
            5/1-8/31 & 11/1-4/30                  1P: $129-$149                        XP: $10                    F18
Small-scale Hotel  **Location:** I-293, exit 2, 1.4 mi s on Brown Ave, then 0.3 mi e to airport. 2 Highlander Way 03103. Fax: 603/625-6466.
            **Facility:** 88 one-bedroom standard units, some with whirlpools. 3 stories, interior corridors. **Parking:** on-site.
**Terms:** cancellation fee imposed, [AP] meal plan available, $2 service charge. **Amenities:** voice mail, irons, hair dryers. **Pool(s):**
outdoor. **Leisure Activities:** whirlpool. **Guest Services:** valet laundry. **Business Services:** conference facilities, fax (fee).
**Cards:** AX, DC, DS, MC, VI.

SOME UNITS
FEE

---

**HOLIDAY INN EXPRESS HOTEL & SUITES - MANCHESTER AIRPORT**    *Book at aaa.com*    Phone: (603)669-6800

            5/1-10/31 [ECP]                       1P: $139-$159        2P: $139-$159
            11/1-4/30 [ECP]                       1P: $129-$149        2P: $129-$149
Small-scale Hotel  **Location:** I-293, exit 1. 1298 S Porter St 03103. Fax: 603/647-3197. **Facility:** 108 one-bedroom standard units,
            some with whirlpools. 3 stories, interior corridors. *Bath:* combo or shower only. **Parking:** on-site.
**Terms:** package plans - weekends, pets ($125 deposit, $10 extra charge). **Amenities:** video games (fee), high-speed Internet,
dual phone lines, voice mail, irons, hair dryers. **Pool(s):** heated indoor. **Leisure Activities:** whirlpool, exercise room. **Guest
Services:** sundries, valet and coin laundry, area transportation. **Business Services:** meeting rooms, fax (fee). **Cards:** AX, CB,
DC, DS, MC, VI.

SOME UNITS
FEE

---

**HOMEWOOD SUITES BY HILTON**    *Book at aaa.com*                            Phone: 603/668-2200

            All Year [BP]                         1P: $109-$169        2P: $129-$199           XP: $10                    F
            **Location:** I-293, exit 2 (Brown Ave), follow signs to Manchester airport. 1000 Perimeter Rd 03103. Fax: 603/668-2201.
Small-scale Hotel  **Facility:** 124 units. 46 one-bedroom standard units with kitchens. 58 one- and 20 two-bedroom suites with
            kitchens. 4 stories, interior corridors. *Bath:* combo or shower only. **Parking:** on-site. **Terms:** small pets only
($100 fee). **Amenities:** dual phone lines, voice mail, irons, hair dryers. *Fee:* video games, high-speed Internet. *Some:* DVD
players. **Pool(s):** small indoor. **Leisure Activities:** whirlpool, exercise room, sports court. **Guest Services:** sundries, valet and
coin laundry. **Business Services:** meeting rooms, business center. **Cards:** AX, CB.

SOME UNITS
FEE

---

**MANCHESTER COURTYARD BY MARRIOTT**    *Book at aaa.com*                     Phone: (603)641-4900

            9/16-10/31                            1P: $119-$189
            5/1-9/15                              1P: $109-$179
            11/1-4/30                             1P: $99-$169
Small-scale Hotel  **Location:** I-293, exit 1, 0.5 mi se on SR 28. 700 Huse Rd 03103. Fax: 603/641-0001. **Facility:** 90 units. 87 one-
            bedroom standard units, some with whirlpools. 3 one-bedroom suites. 3 stories, interior corridors. *Bath:* combo or shower only.
**Parking:** on-site. **Terms:** cancellation fee imposed, [BP] meal plan available. **Amenities:** video library (fee), voice mail, irons,
hair dryers. **Pool(s):** heated indoor. **Leisure Activities:** whirlpool, exercise room. **Guest Services:** valet and coin laundry. **Business Services:** meeting rooms. **Cards:** AX, DC, DS, JC, MC, VI.

SOME UNITS

**SPRINGHILL SUITES MARRIOTT-MANCHESTER AIRPORT**   *Book at aaa.com*   **Phone:** (603)668-9400

9/12-11/6 [ECP]             1P: $129-$179      2P: $129-$179
5/1-9/11 & 11/7-4/30 [ECP]  1P: $109-$169      2P: $109-$169

Small-scale Hotel   **Location:** I-293, exit 2, follow signs to Manchester Airport. 975 N Perimeter Rd 03103. Fax: 603/668-8200. **Facility:** 100 one-bedroom standard units, some with whirlpools. 3 stories, interior corridors. *Bath:* combo or shower only. **Parking:** on-site. **Amenities:** video library (fee), dual phone lines, voice mail, irons, hair dryers. **Pool(s):** heated indoor. **Leisure Activities:** whirlpool, exercise room. **Guest Services:** sundries, valet and coin laundry. **Business Services:** business center. **Cards:** AX, CB, DC, DS, MC, VI.

SOME UNITS

(ASK) (SD) (&M) [icons] (DATA PORT) [icons] / (X) /

---

**TAGE INN**   *Book at aaa.com*   **Phone:** (603)641-6466

All Year   1P: $110-$140   2P: $110-$140   XP: $8   F16

Small-scale Hotel   **Location:** I-293, exit 2, just s. 2280 Brown Ave 03103. Fax: 603/641-5655. **Facility:** 96 units. 92 one-bedroom standard units. 4 one-bedroom suites. 4 stories, interior corridors. *Bath:* combo or shower only. **Parking:** on-site. **Terms:** [ECP] meal plan available. **Amenities:** video games (fee), high-speed Internet, dual phone lines, voice mail, irons, hair dryers. **Pool(s):** heated indoor. **Leisure Activities:** whirlpool, exercise room. **Guest Services:** valet and coin laundry, area transportation. **Business Services:** meeting rooms, business center. **Cards:** AX, DC, DS, MC, VI.
*(See color ad p 359)*

SOME UNITS

(ASK) (SD) [icons] (DATA PORT) [icons] / (X) /

---

**TOWNEPLACE SUITES BY MARRIOTT**   *Book at aaa.com*   **Phone:** (603)641-2288

All Year   1P: $119-$139

Small-scale Hotel   **Location:** I-293, exit 1, 0.5 mi se on SR 28. 686 Huse Rd 03103. Fax: 603/641-2223. **Facility:** 77 units. 46 one-bedroom standard units with kitchens. 13 one- and 18 two-bedroom suites with kitchens. 3 stories, interior corridors. *Bath:* combo or shower only. **Parking:** on-site. **Terms:** pets ($175 fee). **Amenities:** video library (fee), voice mail, irons, hair dryers. **Pool(s):** heated indoor. **Leisure Activities:** exercise room. **Guest Services:** valet and coin laundry. **Cards:** AX, CB, DC, DS, JC, MC, VI.

SOME UNITS

(ASK) (SD) [icons] (FEE) [icons] (DATA PORT) [icons] / (X) (VCR) / FEE

---

## ——— WHERE TO DINE ———

**BALDWIN'S ON ELM**   **Dinner:** $13-$25   **Phone:** 603/622-5975

Continental   **Location:** Between Lowell and Bridge sts; downtown. 1105 Elm St 03103. **Hours:** 5 pm-9:30 pm, Fri & Sat-10 pm. Closed major holidays; also Sun. **Reservations:** required. **Features:** The chef-owned bistro offers extraordinary cuisine in a contemporary, sleek, yet cozy, atmosphere. High-back banquettes and soft lighting lend to an intimate atmosphere. Menu selections are "seasonally inspired" as quoted by Nathan Baldwin. Those with sensitive ears should be aware of increased noise during busy times—although ultimately this does not detract from the experience. Dressy casual; cocktails. **Parking:** street. **Cards:** AX, DS, MC, VI.

(X)

---

**BERNARDO'S-THE ITALIAN AMERICAN EXPERIENCE**   **Dinner:** $7-$16   **Phone:** 603/623-3838

Italian   **Location:** I-293, exit 1, 0.5 mi se on SR 28. 1707 S Willow St 03103. **Hours:** 4 pm-9 pm, Thurs-Sat to 10 pm. Closed: 11/25, 12/25; also Mon. **Reservations:** accepted. **Features:** This family owned Italian restaurant is very popular and reservations are strongly encouraged; the menu offers traditional Italian cuisine. Casual dress; cocktails. **Parking:** on-site. **Cards:** AX, DC, DS, MC, VI.

(X)

---

**BILLY'S SPORTS BAR & GRILL**   **Lunch:** $5-$12   **Dinner:** $5-$12   **Phone:** 603/625-6294

American   **Location:** 1.5 mi e of Elm St (SR 3). 34 Tarrytown Rd 03107. **Hours:** 11 am-midnight, Sat & Sun from 7:30 am. Closed: 11/25, 12/25. **Features:** Off the beaten track about three miles from the center of town, the lively and casual sports bar is decorated in the traditional style, with lots of sports memorabilia and TVs surrounding the perimeter. Typical American fare—burgers, soups, salads and sandwiches—makes up the menu. Casual dress; cocktails. **Parking:** on-site. **Cards:** AX, DC, DS, MC, VI.

---

**CJ'S CACTUS JACKS**   **Lunch:** $7-$16   **Dinner:** $7-$16   **Phone:** 603/627-8600

Mexican   **Location:** I-293, exit 1, 1 mi nw on SR 28. 782 S Willow St 03103. **Hours:** 11:30 am-10 pm, Fri & Sat-11 pm. Closed: 11/25, 12/25. **Features:** The popular, lively restaurant prepares from-scratch dishes ranging from soups and pasta to quesadillas and desserts. Calling ahead is encouraged. Casual dress; cocktails. **Parking:** on-site. **Cards:** AX, DS, MC, VI.

(Y) (X)

---

**COTTON**   **Lunch:** $5-$9   **Dinner:** $15-$20   **Phone:** 603/622-5488

Nouvelle American   **Location:** At Arms Park on the River, just off Commercial St; downtown. 75 Arms Park Dr 03101. **Hours:** 11:30 am-3 & 5-9 pm, Fri-10 pm, Sat 4 pm-10 pm, Sun 10 am-2 pm. Closed major holidays. **Reservations:** suggested. **Features:** In a restored textile mill overlooking the Merrimack River, the trendy bistro offers an incredible and memorable dining experience. The appealing, upscale decor is crisp and sleek. Highly trained servers are eager to share their knowledge of the menu and offer a wine suggestion. Casual dress; cocktails. **Parking:** on-site. **Cards:** AX, DC, DS, MC, VI.

(Y) (X)

---

**FRATELLO'S RISTORANTE ITALIANO**   **Lunch:** $8-$13   **Dinner:** $11-$18   **Phone:** 603/624-2022

Italian   **Location:** I-293, exit 6 (W Bridge St), 0.3 mi e, 0.3 mi n on Canal St, then just e. 155 Dow St 03101. **Hours:** 11:30 am-2:30 & 4:30-9 pm, Fri-10 pm, Sat 4:30 pm-10 pm, Sun noon-9 pm. Closed: 11/25, 12/25. **Features:** In a renovated turn-of-the-20th-century textile mill, the popular restaurant presents a menu of such varied Italian favorites as piccata, parmigiana and Caesar salad. The atmosphere is fun. Casual dress; cocktails. **Parking:** on-site. **Cards:** AX, DS, MC, VI.

(Y) (X)

**THE KOREAN PLACE RESTAURANT**
Korean
**Lunch:** $9-$13 **Dinner:** $15-$17 **Phone:** 603/622-9377
**Location:** Corner of Chestnut St; downtown. 110 Hanover St 03101. **Hours:** 11 am-2 & 5-9 pm, Sat from 5 pm, Wed 11 am-2 pm. Closed major holidays; also Sun-Tues. **Features:** Korean cuisine is terrifically crisp and highly fresh. Each creative dish is prepared to order. Representative of choices are pan-seared scallops on fiddlehead ferns, crispy beef and tofu in light garlic sauce. Casual dress. **Parking:** street.

**LA CARRETA**
Mexican
**Lunch:** $6-$13 **Dinner:** $8-$15 **Phone:** 603/628-6899
**Location:** I-93, exit 9S, 0.5 mi s; in the Maple Tree Mall. 545 Daniel Webster Hwy 03104. **Hours:** 11 am-2:30 & 5-10 pm, Fri-11 pm, Sat noon-11 pm. Closed major holidays. **Features:** In a small strip mall, the casual eatery prepares traditional Mexican fare. Casual dress; cocktails. **Parking:** on-site. **Cards:** AX, DC, DS, MC, VI.

**MILLY'S TAVERN**
American
**Lunch:** $5-$10 **Dinner:** $10-$20 **Phone:** 603/625-4444
**Location:** Jct of W Bridge St; downtown. 500 Commercial St 03101. **Hours:** 11 am-10:30 pm. Closed: 11/25, 12/25. **Features:** This eatery is a great spot for a quick bite in a casual and lively atmosphere, featuring live entertainment on weekends. Casual dress; cocktails. **Parking:** on-site (fee). **Cards:** AX, MC, VI.

**NUTFIELD ALE & STEAK HOUSE**
American
**Lunch:** $5-$25 **Dinner:** $14-$25 **Phone:** 603/666-3030
**Location:** I-293, exit 1, just w. 55 John E Devine Dr 03103. **Hours:** 6 am-10 & 11:30-10 pm, Sat 7 am-11 & 11:30-10 pm, Sun 7 am-9 pm. Closed: 11/25, 12/25. **Features:** The locally known Nutfield Ale Co. also has a restaurant. Guests can expect a casual atmosphere, friendly servers, good food and great beer. Casual dress; cocktails. **Parking:** on-site. **Cards:** AX, MC, VI.

**OLLIE'S FOOD & SPIRITS**
American
**Lunch:** $5-$14 **Dinner:** $5-$14 **Phone:** 603/626-3711
**Location:** On SR 114A. 761 Mast Rd 03102. **Hours:** 11 am-10 pm, Fri & Sat-11 pm. Closed: 3/27, 11/25, 12/25. **Features:** Local charm is found at the restaurant, where the menu consists mostly of traditional comfort foods. Among choices are fried chicken, barbecue lamb, fried haddock, burgers and delicatessen sandwiches. Casual dress; cocktails. **Parking:** on-site. **Cards:** MC, VI.

**PANERA BREAD**
Deli/Subs
Sandwiches
**Lunch:** $3-$8 **Dinner:** $3-$8 **Phone:** 603/627-2443
**Location:** I-293, exit 1, 0.5 mi n on SR 28; in the TJ Maxx Plaza. 52 March Ave 03103. **Hours:** 6:30 am-9 pm, Sun 7:30 am-7 pm. Closed: 11/25, 12/25. **Features:** The chain sets the standard for healthy quick-serve fare. Soups are fresh, bread is made daily, and the sandwiches are creative. Casual dress. **Parking:** on-site. **Cards:** MC, VI.

**PICCOLA RISTORANTE**
Italian
**Lunch:** $5-$12 **Dinner:** $8-$23 **Phone:** 603/606-5100
**Location:** Between Merrimack and Manchester sts; downtown. 827 Elm St 03101. **Hours:** 4 pm-11 pm, Fri-11:30 pm, Sat noon-11:30 pm, Sun noon-11 pm. Closed: 11/25. **Reservations:** suggested. **Features:** This is an attractive but small bistro with tightly spaced seating. Ultimately, the dishes are terrific with homemade pastas, sauces and desserts. Casual dress; cocktails. **Parking:** street. **Cards:** AX, DS, MC, VI.

**PURITAN BACKROOM**
American
**Lunch:** $4-$20 **Dinner:** $4-$20 **Phone:** 603/669-6890
**Location:** I-93, exit 9, 1 mi s. 245 Hooksett Rd 03104. **Hours:** 11 am-11 pm, Fri & Sat-midnight. Closed: 11/25, 12/25. **Features:** Established in 1917, the popular eatery is a local landmark. Favorite libations and edibles include mudslides, fried chicken tenders, the Texasburger and Greek special pizza. Casual dress; cocktails. **Parking:** on-site. **Cards:** AX, DC, DS, MC, VI.

**RICHARD'S BISTRO**
Continental
**Lunch:** $7-$13 **Dinner:** $20-$30 **Phone:** 603/644-1180
**Location:** Jct Elm St, just e; downtown. 36 Lowell St 03101. **Hours:** 11:30 am-2 & 4-10 pm, Sun 10 am-2 & 4-9 pm. Closed: 11/25, 12/25. **Reservations:** suggested. **Features:** The cozy downtown bistro displays attractive, trendy decor and features an open concept kitchen. Dishes on the creative, ever-changing menu surprise the palate. Among intriguing choices are spring roll drizzled with mustard sauce, crabmeat ravioli with cream sauce and creme brulee. All are prepared with the freshest of seasonal ingredients. Dressy casual; cocktails. **Parking:** street. **Cards:** AX, DS, MC, VI.

**SHORTY'S MEXICAN ROADHOUSE**
Mexican
**Lunch:** $6-$17 **Dinner:** $6-$17 **Phone:** 603/625-1730
**Location:** I-93, exit 9S; in Northside Plaza Shopping Center. 1050 Bicentennial Dr 03105. **Hours:** 11:30 am-10 pm, Wed & Thurs-11 pm, Fri & Sat-midnight, Sun noon-10 pm. Closed: 3/27, 11/25, 12/25. **Features:** Well-prepared specialties include nachos, quesadillas, fajitas, chimichangas, burritos and enchiladas, as well as chili, soups and salads. The colorful decor is casual and comfortable, and the serving staff is friendly and attentive. Casual dress; cocktails. **Parking:** on-site. **Cards:** AX, DC, DS, MC, VI.

**SIAM ORCHID**
Thai
**Lunch:** $6-$15 **Dinner:** $7-$15 **Phone:** 603/647-5547
**Location:** I-293, exit 4, just n. 581 Second St 03102. **Hours:** 11:30 am-3 & 5-10 pm, Fri & Sat-10:30 pm, Sun 4 pm-9:30 pm. Closed major holidays. **Reservations:** accepted. **Features:** The extensive collection of delicious food includes seafood, chicken, beef, pork and vegetarian entrees. Noodles, fried rice, soup appetizers and curry selections also are available. Chicken satay and golden triangle appetizers shouldn't be missed. The restaurant is in a small strip mall with ample parking. Casual dress; cocktails. **Parking:** on-site. **Cards:** AX, DS, MC, VI.

**SPATT'S**

American

**Dinner:** $12-$33

**Phone:** 603/627-9959

**Location:** SR 101, exit 1, just s on Londonderry Tpke (road), enter roundabout and take second exit. 2264 Candia Rd 03109. **Hours:** 4:30 pm-9 pm, Fri & Sat-10 pm, Sun 4 pm-8 pm. Closed major holidays. **Features:** They are well known for the prime rib preparations, but don't forget about their seafood specialties and pasta dishes. Casual dress; cocktails. **Parking:** on-site. **Cards:** DS, MC, VI.

**STARFISH GRILL**

Seafood

**Dinner:** $10-$18

**Phone:** 603/296-0706

**Location:** Commercial and Granite sts; downtown. 33 S Commerical St 03101. **Hours:** 4 pm-9 pm, Sun-8 pm. Closed major holidays. **Features:** In the city's restored mill district, the open-air restaurant serves fresh-off-the-boat fish and crustaceans that the chef will prepare in any number of ways—from poached to grilled to pan-seared. The food is terrific, and the service and atmosphere are bustling. Casual dress; cocktails. **Parking:** on-site. **Cards:** AX, DC, DS, MC, VI.

**TINKER'S SEAFOOD**

Seafood

**Lunch:** $5-$21          **Dinner:** $5-$21          **Phone:** 603/622-4272

**Location:** I-93, exit 95, 0.5 mi s on SR 28/US 3; in Maple Tree Mall. 545 Daniel Webster Hwy 03104. **Hours:** 11 am-9 pm, Sun & Mon-8 pm. Closed major holidays. **Features:** Fresh seafood is fried to order immediately after diners order at the counter and wait for a number. Take-out is popular, as is the adjacent seafood market. Casual dress; beer & wine only. **Parking:** on-site. **Cards:** DS, MC, VI.

## MELVIN VILLAGE

—— WHERE TO STAY ——

**PINE VIEW LODGE**

Motel

**Phone:** 603/544-3800

| | | |
|---|---|---|
| 6/2-11/1 | 2P: $69-$125 | XP: $10  F12 |
| 5/1-6/1 & 11/2-4/30 | 2P: $49-$89 | XP: $10  F12 |

**Location:** Jct SR 109 and 25, 7 mi s on SR 109. 427 Governor Wentworth Hwy 03850 (PO Box 207). **Facility:** Smoke free premises. 12 one-bedroom standard units. 1 story, exterior corridors. *Bath:* shower only. **Parking:** on-site. **Terms:** office hours 7 am-7 pm, 14 day cancellation notice-fee imposed. **Guest Services:** coin laundry. **Cards:** DC, MC, VI.

## MEREDITH pop. 1,739

—— WHERE TO STAY ——

**CHASE HOUSE AT MILL FALLS**

Small-scale Hotel

**Phone:** (603)279-7006

| | | |
|---|---|---|
| 5/1-10/24 [CP] | 1P: $169-$299 | 2P: $169-$299 | XP: $15  F12 |
| 10/25-4/30 [CP] | 1P: $139-$259 | 2P: $139-$259 | XP: $15  F12 |

**Location:** I-92, exit 23, 10 mi e of jct US 3 and SR 25; center. 312 Daniel Webster Hwy 03253. Fax: 603/279-6797. **Facility:** Smoke free premises. 23 units. 20 one-bedroom standard units, some with whirlpools. 3 one-bedroom suites ($209-$299) with whirlpools. 3 stories, interior corridors. *Bath:* combo or shower only. **Parking:** on-site. **Terms:** 2 night minimum stay - weekends in season, 3 day cancellation notice, [BP] & [MAP] meal plans available, package plans - seasonal & weekends, $2 service charge. **Amenities:** voice mail, irons, hair dryers. **Business Services:** conference facilities. **Cards:** AX, DC, DS, MC, VI. *(See color ad below)*

The Inns at Mill Falls:

Mill Falls

Bay Point

Chase House

Church Landing -
*Opening May 2004*

Breathtaking lake views

Designer decorated guestrooms

In-room fireplaces & lake views

Two indoor pools & a deluxe
health club

Quaint New England village

Six unique restaurants

*Four Charming Inns.*
*One Historic New Hampshire Village.*

THE INNS AT **Mill Falls**

On Lake Winnipesaukee ▪ Route 3 and 25 ▪ Meredith, NH 03253 ▪ millfalls.com ▪ 603.279.7006 ▪ 800.622.6455

## THE INN AT BAY POINT

▽▼▽▼ ▽▼▽▼

Small-scale Hotel

| | | | |
|---|---|---|---|
| 5/1-10/24 [CP] | 1P: $189-$299 | 2P: $189-$299 | XP: $15 F12 |
| 10/25-4/30 [CP] | 1P: $149-$259 | 2P: $149-$259 | XP: $15 F12 |

**Phone:** (603)279-7006

**Location:** Jct US 3 and SR 25; center. 1 Bay Pt 03253 (312 Daniel Webster Hwy, Suite 28). **Fax:** 603/279-7402. **Facility:** Smoke free premises. 24 one-bedroom standard units, some with whirlpools. 4 stories, interior corridors. **Parking:** on-site. **Terms:** office hours 7 am-11 pm, 2 night minimum stay - weekends in season, 3 day cancellation notice, [BP] meal plan available, package plans - seasonal & weekends, $2 service charge. **Amenities:** voice mail, irons, hair dryers. **Leisure Activities:** sauna, whirlpool, boat dock. **Cards:** AX, DC, DS, MC, VI. *(See color ad p 362)*

SOME UNITS

[S/D] [📶] [🛎] [⌨] [☒] [☒] [DATA PORT] [💻] / [VCR] [🔌] /

## THE INN AT MILL FALLS

▽▼▽▼ ▽▼▽▼

Small-scale Hotel

| | | | |
|---|---|---|---|
| 5/1-10/24 [CP] | 1P: $109-$249 | 2P: $109-$249 | XP: $15 F12 |
| 10/25-4/30 [CP] | 1P: $99-$189 | 2P: $99-$189 | XP: $15 F12 |

**Phone:** (603)279-7006

**Location:** Jct US 3 and SR 25; center. 312 Daniel Webster Hwy 03253. **Fax:** 603/279-6797. **Facility:** 54 one-bedroom standard units, some with whirlpools. 4 stories, interior corridors. **Parking:** on-site. **Terms:** 2 night minimum stay - weekends in season, 3 day cancellation notice, [BP] & [MAP] meal plans available, package plans - seasonal & weekends, $2 service charge. **Amenities:** voice mail, irons, hair dryers. **Pool(s):** heated indoor. **Leisure Activities:** sauna, whirlpool, exercise room. **Guest Services:** gift shop. **Business Services:** meeting rooms. **Cards:** AX, DC, DS, MC, VI. *(See color ad p 362)*

SOME UNITS

[S/D] [📶] [🏊] [☒] [DATA PORT] / [☒] [VCR] [🔌] [💻] /

## MEREDITH INN, B & B

▽▼▽▼ ▽▼▽▼

Bed & Breakfast

| | | | |
|---|---|---|---|
| 5/1-11/1 [BP] | 1P: $125-$175 | 2P: $125-$175 | XP: $25 |
| 11/2-4/30 [BP] | 1P: $105-$159 | 2P: $105-$159 | XP: $25 |

**Phone:** (603)279-0000

**Location:** Jct US 3 and SR 25, just sw on Main St. 2 Waukewan St 03253 (PO Box 115). **Fax:** 603/279-4017. **Facility:** A renovated Victorian "painted lady," the inn was built in 1897 and offers spacious rooms with many antique furnishings. Smoke free premises. 8 one-bedroom standard units, some with whirlpools. 2 stories (no elevator), interior corridors. *Bath:* combo or shower only. **Parking:** on-site. **Terms:** office hours 10 am-9 pm, 2-3 night minimum stay - seasonal, age restrictions may apply, 14 day cancellation notice-fee imposed, no pets allowed (owner's pet on premises). **Cards:** DS, MC, VI.

[☒] [DATA PORT]

------ **WHERE TO DINE** ------

## GIUSEPPE'S

▽▼▽ ▽▼▽

Italian

**Lunch:** $7-$19   **Dinner:** $7-$19   **Phone:** 603/279-3313

**Location:** Jct SR 25 and US 3; in Mill Falls Marketplace. 312 Daniel Webster Hwy 03253. **Hours:** 11 am-10:45 pm. Closed major holidays. **Reservations:** accepted. **Features:** In a bustling marketplace, the restaurant serves large portions of antipasti, gourmet pizza, scampi, parmigiana and more. Casual dress; cocktails. **Parking:** on-site. **Cards:** AX, DS, MC, VI.

[🛎] [☒]

## HART'S TURKEY FARM RESTAURANT

(AAA)

▽▼▽ ▽▼▽

American

**Lunch:** $5-$9   **Dinner:** $8-$19   **Phone:** 603/279-6212

**Location:** Jct US 3 and SR 104. 233 Daniel Webster Hwy 03253. **Hours:** 11:15 am-8:30 pm; closing hours vary seasonally. Closed: 12/25. **Features:** Operated by the Hart family since 1954, the popular family restaurant specializes in home-style cooking, particularly turkey preparations. Also on the menu are beef, pasta and seafood dishes. Almost everything is made on the premises. Contributing to the decor is an extensive collection of turkey plates. Casual dress; cocktails. **Parking:** on-site. **Cards:** AX, DC, DS, MC, VI.

[🛎] [☒]

## MAME'S RESTAURANT   Historic

▽▽▽▽ ▽▽▽▽

American

MC, VI.

**Lunch:** $6-$12   **Dinner:** $9-$23   **Phone:** 603/279-4631

**Location:** Just w of jct US 3 and SR 25; center. 8 Plymouth St 03253. **Hours:** 11:30 am-9 pm, Fri & Sat-9:30 pm. Closed: 12/25. **Features:** Close to shops and lodgings, the cozy, informal restaurant was converted from a private residence dating to 1825. The cuisine includes seafood, steak and pasta entrees; flavorful prime rib is a specialty. Lighter fare is served in the pub. Casual dress; cocktails. **Parking:** on-site. **Cards:** AX, DS,

[🛎] [☒]

# MERRIMACK

------ **WHERE TO STAY** ------

## DAYS INN MERRIMACK   *Book at aaa.com*

▽▽▽▽ ▽▽▽▽

Motel

| | | | |
|---|---|---|---|
| 8/1-10/30 | 1P: $70-$75 | 2P: $75-$80 | XP: $5 F16 |
| 5/1-7/31 & 10/31-12/31 | 1P: $65-$70 | 2P: $70-$75 | XP: $5 F16 |
| 1/1-4/30 | 1P: $55-$60 | 2P: $60-$65 | XP: $5 F16 |

**Phone:** (603)429-4600

**Location:** Everett Tpke, exit 11, just e, then 0.7 mi s on US 3. 242 Daniel Webster Hwy 03054. **Fax:** 603/424-3804. **Facility:** 69 one-bedroom standard units. 2 stories (no elevator), interior corridors. *Bath:* combo or shower only. **Parking:** on-site. **Terms:** cancellation fee imposed, $2 service charge, small pets only ($25 fee). **Amenities:** safes (fee), hair dryers. *Some:* irons. **Guest Services:** coin laundry. **Cards:** AX, CB, DC, DS, MC, VI.

SOME UNITS

[ASK] [S/D] [🐾] [&M] [📶] [🍴] [♿] [📷] [DATA PORT] [💻] / [☒] [🔌] [📠] /
FEE

**FAIRFIELD INN**
*Book at aaa.com*
Phone: 603/424-7500
5/28-10/29 [CP]  1P: $79-$109  2P: $79-$109
5/1-5/27 & 10/30-4/30 [CP]  1P: $59-$69  2P: $59-$69
Small-scale Hotel
**Location:** Everett Tpke, exit 11, just w. 4 Amherst Rd 03054. Fax: 603/424-7500. **Facility:** 116 one-bedroom standard units. 3 stories, interior corridors. *Bath:* combo or shower only. **Parking:** on-site. **Amenities:** video library (fee), irons. **Pool(s):** heated outdoor. **Guest Services:** valet laundry. **Business Services:** meeting rooms. **Cards:** AX, DC, DS, MC, VI.

SOME UNITS / FEE

**RADISSON HOTEL AND CONFERENCE CENTER**
*Book at aaa.com*
Phone: (603)424-8000
9/21-11/15  1P: $109  2P: $189  XP: $10
5/1-9/20  1P: $89  2P: $179  XP: $10
11/16-4/30  1P: $69  2P: $129  XP: $10
Small-scale Hotel
**Location:** Everett Tpke, exit 11, just w. 4 Executive Park Dr 03054. Fax: 603/423-8081. **Facility:** 203 one-bedroom standard units. 4 stories, interior corridors. *Bath:* combo or shower only. **Parking:** on-site. **Terms:** cancellation fee imposed. **Amenities:** dual phone lines, voice mail, irons, hair dryers. *Fee:* video library, video games. **Dining:** 6:30 am-11 pm, Sat & Sun from 7 am, cocktails. **Pool(s):** heated indoor. **Leisure Activities:** whirlpool, steamroom, basketball, volleyball. **Guest Services:** valet laundry. **Business Services:** conference facilities. **Cards:** AX, CB, DC, DS, JC, MC, VI. **Special Amenities:** free newspaper and free room upgrade (subject to availability with advanced reservations).
*(See color ads below)*

SOME UNITS / FEE FEE

**RESIDENCE INN BY MARRIOTT**
*Book at aaa.com*
Phone: (603)424-8100
7/5-11/19 [BP]  1P: $99-$159
5/28-7/4 & 11/20-4/30 [BP]  1P: $89-$149
5/1-5/27 [BP]  1P: $89-$139
Small-scale Hotel
**Location:** Everett Tpke, exit 11, just e, then 0.6 mi s on US 3. 246 Daniel Webster Hwy 03054. Fax: 603/424-3128. **Facility:** 129 units. 93 one-bedroom standard units with kitchens. 36 two-bedroom suites with kitchens. 2-3 stories, interior/exterior corridors. *Bath:* combo or shower only. **Parking:** on-site, winter plug-ins. **Terms:** pets ($50 fee, $5 extra charge). **Amenities:** video games (fee), high-speed Internet, voice mail, irons, hair dryers. **Pool(s):** outdoor. **Leisure Activities:** whirlpool, exercise room, sports court. **Guest Services:** complimentary evening beverages: Mon-Thurs, valet and coin laundry. **Business Services:** meeting rooms. **Cards:** AX, CB, DC, DS, JC, MC, VI.

SOME UNITS / FEE

──────── **WHERE TO DINE** ────────

**THE HANNAH JACK TAVERN**

American

▼▼ ▼▼

**Lunch:** $5-$10    **Dinner:** $12-$24    **Phone:** 603/424-4171
**Location:** Everett Tpke, exit 11, just e. US 3 03054. **Hours:** 11:30 am-2 & 5-8:30 pm, Fri-9 pm, Sat 4:30 pm-9:30 pm, Sun 4 pm-8:30 pm. Closed: 7/4, 12/25. **Reservations:** accepted. **Features:** Guests can create their favorite combination or choose from an excellent selection of beef, seafood and poultry entrees. Meals are served with eye-appealing presentation, and the comfortable surroundings have a country flair. Casual dress; cocktails. **Parking:** on-site. **Cards:** AX, DS, MC, VI.

**THE LOBSTER BOAT RESTAURANT**

Seafood

▼▼ ▼▼

**Lunch:** $5-$18    **Dinner:** $5-$18    **Phone:** 603/424-5221
**Location:** 1.5 mi n on US 3. 453 Daniel Webster Hwy 03054. **Hours:** 11:30 am-8 pm, Fri & Sat-8:30 pm, Sun-7:30 pm. Closed: 1/1. **Features:** The friendly staff at the highly casual local favorite serves fried seafood, burgers and more. Casual dress; cocktails. **Parking:** on-site. **Cards:** AX, DS, MC, VI.

**MADDEN'S CASUAL FAMILY DINING**

American

▼▼

**Lunch:** $3-$15    **Dinner:** $15    **Phone:** 603/424-4572
**Location:** 3 mi n on US 3. 583 Daniel Webster Hwy 03054. **Hours:** 7 am-9 pm. Closed major holidays. **Features:** The casual restaurant is perfect for families and large groups. The menu centers on traditional preparations of steak, chicken and fish. Casual dress; cocktails. **Parking:** on-site. **Cards:** AX, DS, MC, VI.

**MAGNOLIA RESTAURANT**

Cajun

▼▼ ▼▼▼

**Dinner:** $19-$24    **Phone:** 603/424-2755
**Location:** 1.7 mi n on SR 3. 438 Daniel Webster Hwy 03054. **Hours:** 5 pm-9 pm, Fri & Sat-10 pm, Mon-11 pm. Closed: 11/25, 12/25. **Reservations:** suggested. **Features:** In a Colonial-style home with attractive decor, the restaurant specializes in Cajun cuisine. Diners might enjoy delectable seafood crepes prepared with bay scallops, shrimp and crawfish; fried New England clam chowder; or this place's twist on seafood jambalaya. The separate lounge sustains a fun, lively atmosphere. Casual dress; cocktails; entertainment. **Parking:** on-site. **Cards:** AX, DC, DS, MC, VI.

**NEWICK'S SEAFOOD RESTAURANT**

AAA

▼▼

Seafood

**Lunch:** $6-$16    **Dinner:** $6-$16    **Phone:** 603/429-0262
**Location:** Jct US 3 and SR 101, 4.5 mi s on US 3; in Bedford. 696 Daniel Webster Hwy 03054. **Hours:** 11:30 am-8:30 pm, Fri & Sat-9 pm. Closed: 11/25, 12/25. **Features:** Fresh seafood is baked, broiled or fried at the popular restaurant, which also lists steaks and chicken dishes on its menu. The pleasant, informal atmosphere has a nautical feel. The fish market and lobster pound adds to the New England theme. Casual dress; cocktails. **Parking:** on-site. **Cards:** AX, DS, MC, VI.

# MILFORD pop. 8,293

──────── **WHERE TO DINE** ────────

**PASTA LOFT**

Italian

▼▼ ▼▼

**Lunch:** $7-$11    **Dinner:** $9-$20    **Phone:** 603/672-2270
**Location:** Center. 241 Union Square 03055. **Hours:** 11:30 am-9 pm, Fri & Sat-11 pm. Closed major holidays. **Reservations:** accepted. **Features:** This casual eatery is located in the main square of downtown Milford. The pasta and sauces are homemade daily and are particularly memorable. Casual dress; cocktails. **Parking:** street. **Cards:** AX, DS, MC, VI.

# MOULTONBOROUGH

──────── **WHERE TO STAY** ────────

**MATTERHORN MOTOR LODGE**

Motel

▼▼ ▼▼

**Phone:** 603/253-4314

| | 1P: $99-$125 | 2P: $109-$145 | XP: $20 | F12 |
| 5/1-10/18 | | | | |
| 10/19-4/30 | 1P: $79-$99 | 2P: $89-$109 | XP: $20 | F12 |

**Location:** On SR 25, 3 mi w. 340 SR 25 03254 (PO Box 366, 03254-0123). Fax: 603/253-4813. **Facility:** 28 one-bedroom standard units. 2 stories (no elevator), exterior corridors. **Parking:** on-site, winter plug-ins. **Terms:** 2-3 night minimum stay - weekends, 7 day cancellation notice-fee imposed, weekly rates available, [CP] meal plan available. **Pool(s):** heated outdoor. **Leisure Activities:** snowmobiling. **Cards:** AX, CB, DC, MC, VI.

SOME UNITS

**OLDE ORCHARD INN**

Historic Bed & Breakfast

▼▼ ▼▼▼

**Phone:** 603/476-5004

| 5/17-10/24 [BP] | 1P: $115-$185 | 2P: $115-$185 | XP: $25 |
| 10/25-4/30 [BP] | 1P: $85-$170 | 2P: $85-$170 | XP: $25 |
| 5/1-5/16 [BP] | 1P: $85-$150 | 2P: $85-$150 | XP: $25 |

**Location:** Jct SR 25 and Old SR 109, 0.5 mi s on Old SR 109 to Lee Rd, then 0.5 mi s. Located in a quiet area. 108 Lee Rd 03254 (RR 1, Box 256). Fax: 603/476-5419. **Facility:** Oriental rugs and antique furnishings decorate guest rooms at this early-1800s farmhouse overlooking a large apple orchard. Smoke free premises. 9 one-bedroom standard units, some with whirlpools. 2 stories (no elevator), interior corridors. *Bath:* combo or shower only. **Parking:** on-site. **Terms:** office hours 10 am-8 pm, 10 day cancellation notice-fee imposed, no pets allowed (owner's pet on premises). **Leisure Activities:** sauna, whirlpool, fishing, cross country skiing, ice skating, hiking trails. **Cards:** MC, VI.

──────── **WHERE TO DINE** ────────

**THE WOODSHED RESTAURANT**

American

▼▼ ▼▼▼

**Dinner:** $15-$25    **Phone:** 603/476-2311
**Location:** Jct SR 25 and Old SR 109 by airport, 1.1 mi s on SR 109, 0.7 mi w. 128 Lees Mill Rd 03254. **Hours:** 5 pm-9 pm; to 8:30 pm in winter. Closed: 11/25, 12/25; also for dinner 12/24 & Mon. **Reservations:** suggested. **Features:** The popular restaurant is in a 200-year-old farmhouse and barn. Handsome surroundings add to a pleasant, rustic dining experience. Among offerings are tasty prime rib, seafood and local vegetables. Smoking is permitted only in the lounge. Casual dress; cocktails. **Parking:** on-site. **Cards:** AX, DS, MC, VI.

# NASHUA pop. 86,605

## ——— WHERE TO STAY ———

**COMFORT INN**   *Book at aaa.com*            Phone: 603/883-7700

| | 7/23-10/24 | 1P: $89 | 2P: $89 | XP: $5 | F18 |
| | 5/1-7/22 & 10/25-4/30 | 1P: $69 | 2P: $69 | XP: $5 | F18 |

Small-scale Hotel  **Location:** US 3 (Everett Tpke), exit 7E, just e. 10 St. Laurent St 03060. Fax: 603/595-2107. **Facility:** 101 one-bedroom standard units. 2 stories (no elevator), interior corridors. **Parking:** on-site. **Terms:** 30 day cancellation notice, weekly rates available, [ECP] meal plan available. **Amenities:** high-speed Internet, irons, hair dryers. **Pool(s):** outdoor. **Guest Services:** valet and coin laundry. **Cards:** AX, CB, DC, DS, MC, VI. *(See color ad below)*

SOME UNITS

(ASK) 🏊 🐾 📺 (DATA PORT) 💻 / 🍽 (VCR) 📶 🖥 /
FEE

**CROWNE PLAZA HOTEL NASHUA**   *Book at aaa.com*        Phone: (603)886-1200

| | 9/7-11/13 & 3/1-4/30 | 1P: $139-$179 | 2P: $139-$179 | |
| | 5/1-9/6 | 1P: $129-$159 | 2P: $129-$159 | |
| | 11/14-2/28 | 1P: $119-$149 | 2P: $119-$149 | |

Large-scale Hotel  **Location:** US 3 (Everett Tpke), exit 8, just w. 2 Somerset Pkwy 03063. Fax: 603/595-4199. **Facility:** 230 units. 210 one-bedroom standard units, some with whirlpools. 18 one- and 2 two-bedroom suites with efficiencies. 8 stories, interior corridors. *Bath:* combo or shower only. **Parking:** on-site. **Amenities:** dual phone lines, voice mail, irons, hair dryers. *Fee:* video library, video games. *Some:* DVD players (fee). **Pool(s):** heated indoor. **Leisure Activities:** saunas, whirlpool. **Guest Services:** gift shop, valet laundry. **Business Services:** conference facilities. **Cards:** AX, CB, DC, DS, JC, MC, VI.

SOME UNITS

(ASK) (SD) 🍴 🍽 (&M) ♿ 🐾 🏊 🐾 📺 (DATA PORT) 💻 / 🍽 (VCR) 📶 🖥 /
FEE

**EXTENDED STAYAMERICA-NASHUA**   *Book at aaa.com*        Phone: (603)577-9900

| | All Year | 1P: $59-$79 | 2P: $64-$84 | |

Small-scale Hotel  **Location:** US 3 (Everett Tpke), exit 8, just w. 2000 Southwood Dr 03063. Fax: 603/886-1300. **Facility:** 101 one-bedroom standard units with efficiencies. 3 stories, interior corridors. *Bath:* combo or shower only. **Parking:** on-site. **Terms:** weekly rates available. **Amenities:** dual phone lines, voice mail. **Guest Services:** coin laundry. **Cards:** AX, CB, DC, DS, MC, VI.

SOME UNITS

(&M) ♿ 🐾 📺 (DATA PORT) 📶 🖥 💻 / 🍽 /

**HOLIDAY INN NASHUA**   *Book at aaa.com*        Phone: (603)888-1551

| | All Year | 1P: $75-$150 | 2P: $75-$150 | XP: $5 | F18 |

Small-scale Hotel  **Location:** US 3 (Everett Tpke), exit 4, just w, then 0.3 mi n. 9 Northeastern Blvd 03062. Fax: 603/888-7193. **Facility:** 208 one-bedroom standard units, some with kitchens. 4 stories, interior corridors. **Parking:** on-site. **Terms:** check-in 4 pm, weekly rates available, small pets only ($25 fee). **Amenities:** video library (fee), voice mail, irons, hair dryers. *Some:* dual phone lines. **Pool(s):** outdoor. **Leisure Activities:** exercise room. **Guest Services:** valet and coin laundry. **Business Services:** conference facilities. **Cards:** AX, CB, DC, DS, JC, MC, VI.

SOME UNITS

(ASK) (SD) 🐾 🐾 🍴 🍽 (&M) ♿ 🐾 📺 (DATA PORT) 💻 / 🍽 📶 🖥 /
FEE FEE

**NASHUA MARRIOTT**   *Book at aaa.com*        Phone: (603)880-9100

| | 9/12-11/13 | 1P: $99-$150 | |
| | 1/1-4/30 | 1P: $89-$145 | |
| | 5/1-9/11 & 11/14-12/31 | 1P: $89-$140 | |

Large-scale Hotel  **Location:** US 3 (Everett Tpke) exit 8, just w. Located in Southwood Corporate Park. 2200 Southwood Dr 03063. Fax: 603/886-9489. **Facility:** 245 units. 244 one-bedroom standard units. 1 one-bedroom suite. 4 stories, interior corridors. **Parking:** on-site. **Amenities:** voice mail, irons, hair dryers. *Fee:* video library, video games, high-speed Internet. **Pool(s):** heated indoor. **Leisure Activities:** whirlpool, playground, exercise room, basketball. **Guest Services:** gift shop, valet laundry. **Business Services:** meeting rooms, business center. **Cards:** AX, CB, DC, DS, JC, MC, VI.

SOME UNITS

(ASK) 🐾 🍴 🍽 (&M) ♿ 🐾 ✕ 📺 (DATA PORT) 💻 / 🍽 📶 /

## RED ROOF INN
**Book at aaa.com**

**Phone: (603)888-1893**

AAA SAVE

| | | | |
|---|---|---|---|
| 5/21-10/23 | 1P: $62-$84 | 2P: $68-$84 | XP: $6 | F18 |
| 5/1-5/20 | 1P: $54-$76 | 2P: $58-$76 | XP: $4 | F18 |
| 1/1-4/30 | 1P: $50-$76 | 2P: $54-$76 | XP: $4 | F18 |
| 10/24-12/31 | 1P: $52-$70 | 2P: $56-$70 | XP: $4 | F18 |

Motel
**Location:** US 3 (Everett Tpke), exit 1, just e. 77 Spitbrook Rd 03060. Fax: 603/888-5889. **Facility:** 115 one-bedroom standard units. 3 stories, exterior corridors. *Bath:* combo or shower only. **Parking:** on-site. **Amenities:** video games (fee), voice mail. **Guest Services:** valet and coin laundry. **Cards:** AX, CB, DC, DS, MC, VI. **Special Amenities:** free local telephone calls and free newspaper.

SOME UNITS

## SHERATON NASHUA HOTEL
**Book at aaa.com**

**Phone: (603)888-9970**

AAA SAVE

| | | | |
|---|---|---|---|
| All Year | 1P: $99-$189 | | XP: $10 | F12 |

Large-scale Hotel
**Location:** US 3 (Everett Tpke), exit 1, just w. 11 Tara Blvd 03062. Fax: 603/888-4112. **Facility:** 336 one-bedroom standard units, some with whirlpools. 7 stories, interior corridors. *Bath:* combo or shower only. **Parking:** on-site. **Terms:** cancellation fee imposed. **Amenities:** dual phone lines, voice mail, irons, hair dryers. *Fee:* video library, video games. *Some:* high-speed Internet. **Dining:** 6:30 am-11 pm, cocktails. **Pool(s):** outdoor, heated indoor. **Leisure Activities:** sauna, whirlpool, steamrooms, jogging. *Fee:* massage. **Guest Services:** gift shop, valet laundry. **Business Services:** conference facilities, business center. **Cards:** AX, CB, DC, MC, VI. **Special Amenities:** free newspaper and preferred room (subject to availability with advanced reservations). *(See color ad p 5)*

SOME UNITS

---

## WHERE TO DINE

### BERTUCCI'S BRICK OVEN PIZZERIA
**Lunch: $8-$18   Dinner: $10-$18   Phone: 603/595-7244**

Pizza
**Location:** US 3 (Everett Tpke), exit 8 at SR 101A. 406 Amherst St 03063. **Hours:** 11 am-10 pm, Fri & Sat-11 pm. Closed: 11/25, 12/25. **Features:** Pizza cooked in a brick oven is the specialty at the New England-based chain. Pizzas are imaginative and delicious, as are pasta and chicken dishes. Casual dress; cocktails. **Parking:** on-site. **Cards:** AX, DS, MC, VI.

### CHARMAN'S
**Lunch: $5-$14   Dinner: $9-$22   Phone: 603/883-4052**

American
**Location:** US 3 (Everett Tpke), exit 1 just w on SR 101A. 537 Amherst St 03063. **Hours:** 6 am-9:30 pm, Sun 6:30 am-1 pm. Closed: 3/27, 11/25, 12/25. **Features:** This family run restaurant is strictly casual and serves up homemade dishes of pasta, steak, salads and more. Their large fish tank is a diversion for the kids. Casual dress; cocktails. **Parking:** on-site. **Cards:** AX, DS, MC, VI.

### CHEN YANG LI
**Lunch: $6-$9   Dinner: $10-$17   Phone: 603/883-6800**

Chinese
**Location:** US 3 (Everett Tpke), exit 7, 2 mi w on SR 101A. 337 Amherst St 03063. **Hours:** 11:30 am-10 pm, Fri & Sat-11 pm. Closed: 11/25. **Reservations:** accepted. **Features:** The exceptional restaurant prepares many house specialties and standard favorites. The wonderfully descriptive menu also lists an extensive selection of sushi items. A comfortable atmosphere and helpful staff make for an enjoyable experience. Casual dress; cocktails. **Parking:** on-site. **Cards:** AX, DS, MC, VI.

### THE COUNTRY TAVERN
**Lunch: $6-$8   Dinner: $15-$21   Phone: 603/889-5871**

Steak & Seafood
**Location:** US 3 (Everett Tpke), exit 8, 1 mi w on SR 101A. 452 Amherst St 03063. **Hours:** 11:30 am-9 pm, Sat 4 pm-9:30 pm, Sun 10 am-9 pm. Closed: 12/25. **Reservations:** accepted. **Features:** Some diners may feel the presence of Elizabeth the "friendly ghost." The menu lists a vast selection of comfort foods. Casual dress; cocktails. **Parking:** on-site. **Cards:** AX, DC, DS, MC, VI.

### JOE'S AMERICAN BAR & GRILL
**Lunch: $8-$14   Dinner: $8-$20   Phone: 603/891-2060**

American
**Location:** In Pheasant Lane Mall. 310 Daniel Webster Hwy 03060. **Hours:** 11 am-10 pm, Fri & Sat-11 pm. Closed: 11/25, 12/25. **Features:** The New England chain's wide selection is sure to satisfy almost everyone. Preparations include prime rib, meatloaf, soups, salads and fresh fish entrees. Casual dress; cocktails. **Parking:** on-site. **Cards:** AX, CB, DC, DS, JC, MC, VI.

### LA CARRETA RESTAURANTE MEXICANO
**Lunch: $5-$14   Dinner: $8-$14   Phone: 603/891-0055**

Mexican
**Location:** US 3 (Everett Tpke), exit 1, just n. 139 Daniel Webster Hwy 03060. **Hours:** 11 am-2:30 & 5-10 pm, Fri-11 pm, Sat 11 am-11 pm, Sun noon-midnight. Closed major holidays. **Features:** In a small strip mall, the Mexican bistro offers colorful decor, a friendly staff and a wide selection of favorites. Casual dress; cocktails. **Parking:** on-site. **Cards:** MC, VI.

### LILAC BLOSSOM
**Lunch: $7-$19   Dinner: $9-$19   Phone: 603/886-8420**

Chinese
**Location:** 3 mi w of US 3 (Everett Tpke) on SR 101 A; in Greystone Plaza. 650 Amherst St 03063. **Hours:** 11:30 am-10 pm, Fri & Sat-11 pm, Sun noon-10 pm. Closed major holidays. **Features:** The restaurant serves Asian cuisine in a casual atmosphere and is very popular among the locals. Casual dress; cocktails. **Parking:** on-site. **Cards:** MC, VI.

### MARTHA'S EXCHANGE RESTAURANT & BREWING CO
**Lunch: $6-$16   Dinner: $6-$16   Phone: 603/883-8781**

American
**Location:** Between High and Garden sts; downtown. 185 Main St 03060. **Hours:** 11 am-9 pm, Sat & Sun from 8:30 am. Closed major holidays. **Reservations:** accepted. **Features:** The friendly neighborhood pub serves a good variety of comfort foods and an extensive selection of homemade specialty brews. Casual dress; cocktails. **Parking:** street. **Cards:** AX, MC, VI.

**MICHAEL TIMOTHY'S**   **Lunch:** $8-$20   **Dinner:** $16-$28   **Phone:** 603/595-9334
▽▼▽▼▽▼   **Location:** US 3 (Everett Tpke), 1.5 mi se on SR 101A, 0.5 mi s. 212 Main St 03060. **Hours:** 11:30 am-2 & 5:30-9
American   pm, Sat 5 pm-9:30 pm, Sun 10 am-2 & 5-9 pm. Closed major holidays. **Reservations:** suggested.
**Features:** This chef-owned bistro provides a memorable dining experience with a strong creative flair,
romantic dining and exceptional service. Their jazz bar has live entertainment Thursday-Sunday. Dressy
casual; cocktails. **Parking:** street. **Cards:** AX, DS, MC, VI.   🍸 ✖

**SKOL RESTAURANT & LOUNGE**   **Lunch:** $6-$10   **Dinner:** $17-$23   **Phone:** 603/598-8007
▽▼▽ ▽▼▽   **Location:** US 3 (Everett Tpke), exit 7E, 1.5 mi se on SR 101A, 0.5 mi s, then just w. 112 W Pearl St 03060.
Continental   **Hours:** 11:30 am-11 pm, Fri-midnight, Sat noon-midnight. Closed: 11/25, 12/25; also Sun.
**Reservations:** suggested, dinner. **Features:** The chef-owned downtown restaurant serves continental
cuisine, such as marinated New Zealand venison roasted with apple-raisin chutney, roasted rack of lamb
and Alaskan halibut. Servers are friendly and competent. Modest decor surrounds the spacious but comfortable dining room.
Dressy casual; cocktails. **Parking:** street. **Cards:** AX, DC, DS, MC, VI.   🍸 ✖

**VILLA BANCA**   **Lunch:** $6-$12   **Dinner:** $12-$22   **Phone:** 603/598-0500
▽▼▽▼▽▼   **Location:** US 3 (Everett Tpke), 1.5 mi se on SR 101A, then 0.4 mi s. 194 Main St 03060. **Hours:** 11:30 am-9 pm,
Italian   Fri-10 pm, Sat 4 pm-10 pm, Sun 4 pm-9 pm. Closed major holidays. **Reservations:** suggested.
**Features:** The chef-owned downtown restaurant provides fantastic Italian fare, with homemade pasta and
trendy and tasteful   other creatively prepared traditional dishes. Intimate dining is enhanced with muted background music,
decor and thoughtful service. Casual dress; cocktails. **Parking:** on-site (fee) and street. **Cards:** AX, DC,
DS, MC, VI.   🍸 ✖

# NEWBURY

———— **WHERE TO STAY** ————

**BEST WESTERN SUNAPEE LAKE LODGE**   *Book at aaa.com*   **Phone:** (603)763-2010
(AAA) (SAVE)   All Year [CP]   1P: $99-$289   2P: $99-$289   XP: $8   F17
▽▼▽ ▽▼▽   **Location:** Jct SR 103B, just e. 1403 Rt 103 03255. **Fax:** 603/763-3314. **Facility:** 55 one-bedroom standard units,
Small-scale Hotel   some with whirlpools. 3 stories, interior corridors. *Bath:* combo or shower only. **Parking:** on-site. **Terms:** 2
with prior approval). **Amenities:** voice mail, irons, hair dryers. *Some:* fax. **Pool(s):** heated indoor. **Leisure**
night minimum stay - weekends, 14 day cancellation notice-fee imposed, small pets only ($8 extra charge,
**Activities:** ice skating, sledding, exercise room, volleyball. *Fee:* game room. **Guest Services:** coin laundry.
*Fee:* tanning facility. **Business Services:** meeting rooms. **Cards:** AX, CB, DC, DS, JC, MC, VI. **Special Amenities:** free continental breakfast and free local telephone calls.   SOME UNITS
[icons: 🅢/🄳 🛏 🍴 🚿♿ 📶 🐾 ✖ 🐕 DATA/PORT 💻 / ✖ VCR 🔌 📷]
FEE

**LAKEVIEW MOTOR LODGE AT MT. SUNAPEE**   **Phone:** 603/763-2701
(AAA) (SAVE)   All Year   1P: $59-$99   2P: $79-$119   XP: $10
▽▼▽ ▽▼▽   **Location:** Jct SR 103B, 0.3 mi s on SR 103; near Mount Sunapee. 1349 Rt 103 03255 (PO Box 61).
Motel   **Fax:** 603/763-2992. **Facility:** 12 one-bedroom standard units. 1-2 stories (no elevator), exterior corridors.
**Parking:** on-site. **Terms:** office hours 8:30 am-9:30 pm, 7 day cancellation notice-fee imposed.
**Amenities:** hair dryers. **Cards:** DS, MC, VI. **Special Amenities:** free expanded continental breakfast.
SOME UNITS
[icons: ✖ VCR 🔌 💻 / 🎬 /]

———— **WHERE TO DINE** ————

**MURPHY'S GRILL**   **Lunch:** $7-$17   **Dinner:** $7-$17   **Phone:** 603/763-3113
▽▼▽   **Location:** Jct SR 103B, 0.3 mi s. 1407 SR 103 03255. **Hours:** 11:30 am-9 pm, Fri & Sat-10 pm.
American   **Features:** Convenient to the Mount Sunapee ski area, the grill features a good menu variety, including
soup, salad, burgers, steak, seafood, pasta, desserts and a full bar selection. The informal dining room
offers nice views. Casual dress; cocktails. **Parking:** on-site. **Cards:** AX, DS, MC, VI.   ✖

# NEW CASTLE pop. 1,010

———— **WHERE TO STAY** ————

**WENTWORTH BY THE SEA MARRIOTT HOTEL & SPA**   **Phone:** 603/422-7322
(AAA) (SAVE)   5/1-9/30   1P: $199-$369   2P: $199-$369
10/1-4/30   1P: $159-$329   2P: $159-$329
▽▼▽ ▽▼▽   **Location:** On SR 1B, 2 mi e of SR 1A. 588 Wentworth Rd 03854. **Fax:** 603/422-7329. **Facility:** A grand and his-
Large-scale Hotel   toric oceanside hotel, once host to many dignitaries, the property is luxuriously restored yet retains an ambience of bygone times. 161 units. 143 one-bedroom standard units. 7 one- and 11 two-bedroom suites
($319-$479) with kitchens, some with efficiencies and/or whirlpools. 4 stories, interior/exterior corridors. *Bath:*
combo or shower only. **Parking:** valet. **Terms:** check-in 4 pm, 3 day cancellation notice, [BP] & [MAP] meal plans available,
package plans, small pets only. **Amenities:** video games (fee), CD players, high-speed Internet, dual phone lines, voice mail,
safes, honor bars, irons, hair dryers. **Dining:** 2 restaurants, 6:30 am-10 pm, cocktails. **Pool(s):** 2 heated outdoor, heated indoor.
**Leisure Activities:** whirlpools, steamrooms, lighted tennis court, exercise room, spa. *Fee:* golf-18 holes. **Guest Services:** gift
shop, valet laundry. **Business Services:** conference facilities, business center. **Cards:** AX, DC, DS, MC, VI. **Special Amenities:**
free newspaper. *(See color ad p 391)*   SOME UNITS
[icons: 🛏 🍴 ✖ 🐕 DATA/PORT 💻 / ✖ 📷]

# NEWFIELDS

——— **WHERE TO DINE** ———

**SHIP TO SHORE FOOD & SPIRITS**          **Dinner:** $17-$26          **Phone:** 603/778-7898
▼▼ ▼▼          **Location:** On SR 108, 0.5 mi n of SR 85. SR 108 03856. **Hours:** 5 pm-9 pm. Closed: 11/25, 12/25; also Sun &
          Mon. **Reservations:** suggested. **Features:** Ship to Shore's lively setting is in a 1793 New England barn. It
Regional American          was built by a master shipbuilder who formed the beams of the attic as though for a mast of a ship. The
          unusual atmosphere features a quaint decor and menu offerings of chargrilled steak, homemade pasta and
fresh seafood. The serving staff is prompt, friendly and knowledgeable. Casual dress; cocktails. **Parking:** on-site. **Cards:** AX,
DS, MC, VI.

# NEW LONDON

——— **WHERE TO STAY** ———

**FAIRWAY MOTEL AT LAKE SUNAPEE COUNTRY CLUB**                    **Phone:** 603/526-6040
ⓐⓐⓐ (SAVE)          All Year          1P: $65-$80          2P: $79-$89          XP: $8          F12
▼▼ ▼▼          **Location:** I-89, exit 11, 3 mi e on SR 11. N Andover Rd 03257 (PO Box 2460). Fax: 603/526-0220. **Facility:** 12 one-
          bedroom standard units. 2 stories (no elevator), exterior corridors. **Parking:** on-site. **Terms:** office hours 8
Motel          am-4 pm, 2 night minimum stay - weekends 5/30-10/15, 14 day cancellation notice, package plans. **Pool(s):**
          outdoor. **Cards:** DS, MC, VI.
                                                    SOME UNITS

**THE INN AT PLEASANT LAKE**                    **Phone:** (603)526-6271
▼▼ ▼▼ ▼▼          5/1-11/3 & 11/17-4/1          1P: $120-$185          2P: $120-$185          XP: $25          D
          **Location:** 1.5 mi n; center. 853 Pleasant St 03257 (PO Box 1030). Fax: 603/526-4111. **Facility:** This attractive 1790
Country Inn          farmhouse overlooks a lake; five-course dinners are offered on Wednesday through Sunday in season.
          Smoke free premises. 10 units. 5 one-bedroom standard units. 5 one-bedroom suites, some with whirlpools.
3 stories (no elevator), interior corridors. *Bath:* combo or shower only. **Parking:** on-site. **Terms:** open 5/1-11/3 & 11/17-4/1, office hours 7:30 am-10 pm, 2-3 night minimum stay - weekends, cancellation fee imposed, [BP] meal plan available. **Leisure Activities:** fishing, exercise room. **Cards:** AX, DS, MC, VI.

**NEW LONDON INN**                    **Phone:** 603/526-2791
▼▼ ▼▼          All Year          1P: $100-$109          2P: $109-$140          XP: $5          F12
          **Location:** Center. Located adjacent to Colby-Sawyer College. 353 Main St 03257 (PO Box 8). Fax: 603/843-0500.
Historic          **Facility:** Antiques and reproductions are among the furnishings at this inn dating from 1792. Smoke free
Country Inn          premises. 23 units. 21 one-bedroom standard units. 2 one-bedroom suites. 3 stories (no elevator), interior
          corridors. *Bath:* combo or shower only. **Parking:** on-site. **Terms:** office hours 9 am-10 pm, 2 night minimum
stay - 5/1-10/31, 7 day cancellation notice-fee imposed, [BP] meal plan available. **Amenities:** voice mail. **Cards:** AX, MC, VI.
                                                    SOME UNITS

——— **WHERE TO DINE** ———

**FOUR CORNERS GRILLE & FLYING GOOSE BREW PUB**     **Lunch:** $7-$12     **Dinner:** $7-$18     **Phone:** 603/526-6899
▼▼ ▼▼ ▼▼          **Location:** I-89, exit 11, 1 mi e to jct SR 11 and 114. Rt 11 03257. **Hours:** 11:30 am-9 pm. Closed: 11/25, 12/25.
          **Reservations:** suggested, weekends. **Features:** Well-prepared American cuisine is served in an informal
American          setting. The microbrewery serves Flying Goose and 16 house brews in a rustic pub-style atmosphere. Try
          the chocolate hazelnut porter cake while admiring views of Mount Kearsarge. Casual dress; cocktails.
**Parking:** on-site. **Cards:** AX, CB, DS, MC, VI.

**MILLSTONE RESTAURANT**          **Lunch:** $6-$25          **Dinner:** $10-$25          **Phone:** 603/526-4201
ⓐⓐⓐ          **Location:** I-89, exit 12, 2.2 mi e. Newport Rd 03257. **Hours:** 11:30 am-2:30 & 5-9 pm. Closed: 12/25.
          **Reservations:** suggested. **Features:** The light, airy setting has a casual elegance that fits perfectly with
▼▼ ▼▼ ▼▼          the cuisine of well-prepared seafood, wild game, pasta, vegetarian dishes and desserts. A full wine list is
          presented. Servers are knowledgeable. Casual dress; cocktails. **Parking:** on-site. **Cards:** AX, DS, MC, VI.
American

**PETER CHRISTIAN'S**          **Lunch:** $4-$12          **Dinner:** $7-$12          **Phone:** 603/526-4042
▼▼ ▼▼          **Location:** Center. 186 Main St 03257. **Hours:** 11 am-9:30 pm. Closed: 3/27, 11/25, 12/25. **Features:** The
          restaurant's tavern-like dining room has exposed beams and a rustic feel. The menu includes a good
American          selection of sandwiches, quiche and lighter fare, as well as creative homemade soups, entrees, desserts
          and root beer. Casual dress; cocktails. **Parking:** on-site. **Cards:** DS, MC, VI.

# NORTH CONWAY pop. 2,069—*See also CONWAY.*

——— **WHERE TO STAY** ———

**THE 1785 INN**                    **Phone:** (603)356-9025
▼▼ ▼▼          9/17-10/23 [BP]          1P: $79-$199          2P: $99-$219          XP: $20
          5/1-9/16 & 10/24-4/30 [BP]          1P: $49-$119          2P: $69-$139          XP: $20
Historic          **Location:** 2 mi n on US 302 and SR 16; village center. 3582 N White Mountain Hwy 03860-1785 (PO Box 1785).
Country Inn          Fax: 603/356-6081. **Facility:** Mountain views enhance some guest rooms at the inn, which is furnished with
          antiques and reproductions. Smoke free premises. 17 units. 16 one-bedroom standard units. 1 one-bedroom
suite ($149-$259) with kitchen. 3 stories (no elevator), interior corridors. *Bath:* some shared or private, combo or shower only.
**Parking:** on-site, winter plug-ins. **Terms:** office hours 7 am-11 pm, 7 day cancellation notice-fee imposed, [MAP] meal plan available, package plans. **Dining:** restaurant, see separate listing. **Pool(s):** outdoor. **Leisure Activities:** cross country skiing, hiking
trails, jogging. **Cards:** AX, CB, DC, DS, JC, MC, VI.
                                                    SOME UNITS

**BEST WESTERN RED JACKET MOUNTAIN VIEW** *Book at aaa.com*　　Phone: (603)356-5411

All Year　　　　　1P: $119-$379
**Location:** 1 mi s on US 302 and SR 16. 2251 White Mountain Hwy 03860 (PO Box 2000). Fax: 603/356-3842. **Facility:** Guest rooms at this property have either mountain or garden views, and many of the rooms have balconies. 163 units. 151 one-bedroom standard units, some with whirlpools. 12 two-bedroom suites. 3 stories, interior/exterior corridors. **Parking:** on-site. **Terms:** 1-3 night minimum stay - weekends, 7 day cancellation notice-fee imposed, [BP] & [MAP] meal plans available, package plans. **Amenities:** voice mail, irons, hair dryers. **Dining:** 7:30 am-10:30 & noon-9 pm, cocktails. **Pool(s):** outdoor, heated indoor. **Leisure Activities:** saunas, whirlpool, 2 lighted tennis courts, cross country skiing, snowmobiling, tobogganing, recreation programs, extensive lawn sports, playground, exercise room. *Fee:* game room. **Guest Services:** valet and coin laundry. **Business Services:** conference facilities. **Cards:** AX, DC, DS, MC, VI. *(See color ad p 377)*

Resort
Large-scale Hotel

SOME UNITS

## BRIARCLIFF MOTEL

Phone: 603-356-5584

All Year    2P: $59-$150

**Location:** 0.5 mi s on SR 16; village center. 2304 White Mountain Hwy 03860 (PO Box 504). Fax: 603/356-4165. **Facility:** 31 one-bedroom standard units. 1 story, exterior corridors. **Parking:** on-site. **Terms:** office hours 8 am-10 pm, 4 night minimum stay - some weekends, 5 day cancellation notice-fee imposed, package plans - seasonal. **Amenities:** voice mail. **Pool(s):** heated outdoor. **Leisure Activities:** ski lockers, shuffleboard. **Cards:** AX, DS, MC, VI. **Special Amenities:** free local telephone calls and free newspaper.

Motel

*(See color ad p 372)*

SOME UNITS

## THE BUTTONWOOD INN

Phone: 603-356-2625

All Year [BP]    2P: $95-$240    XP: $25

Historic Bed & Breakfast

**Location:** Jct US 302 and Kearsarge St, 1.5 mi e, n on Kearsarge St, at stop sign continue straight ahead, then 0.5 mi n. Located in a quiet area. Mt Surprise Rd 03860 (PO Box 1817). Fax: 603/356-3140. **Facility:** A charming, country-style ambience characterizes this B&B on wooded grounds; phone for seasonal availability. Smoke free premises. 10 one-bedroom standard units, some with whirlpools. 2 stories (no elevator), interior/exterior corridors. *Bath:* combo or shower only. **Parking:** on-site. **Terms:** office hours 7 am-10 pm, age restrictions may apply, 14 day cancellation notice-fee imposed. **Pool(s):** outdoor. **Leisure Activities:** cross country skiing. **Cards:** AX, DS, MC, VI.

SOME UNITS

**CABERNET INN**

All Year — Phone: 603/356-4704

▼▼▼▼ All Year | 1P: $90-$225 | 2P: $90-$225 | XP: $20

**Location:** 1.5 mi on SR 16 and US 302; village center. 3552 White Mountain Hwy 03860 (PO Box 489). Bed & Breakfast — Fax: 603/356-5399. **Facility:** On grounds highlighted by picturesque gardens, this 1842 property features some guest rooms with fireplaces. Smoke free premises. 11 one-bedroom standard units, some with whirlpools. 3 stories (no elevator), interior/exterior corridors. *Bath:* combo or shower only. **Parking:** on-site. **Terms:** office hours 9 am-8 pm, 2 night minimum stay - seasonal weekends, age restrictions may apply, 15 day cancellation notice-fee imposed, [BP] meal plan available. **Amenities:** hair dryers. *Some:* CD players. **Leisure Activities:** cross country skiing. **Guest Services:** TV in common area. **Cards:** AX, DS, MC, VI.

**CLARENDON MOTEL**

▼▼▼ All Year | 1P: $45-$125 | 2P: $45-$135 | XP: $10 | F12

Phone: (603)356-3551

**Location:** 1.5 mi n on US 302 and SR 16; village center. 3537 White Mountain Hwy (Rt 16) 03860 (PO Box 241, INTERVALE, 03845). **Facility:** 17 one-bedroom standard units, some with kitchens. 1 story, exterior corridors. *Bath:* Motel — combo or shower only. **Parking:** on-site. **Terms:** office hours 8 am-10 pm, 7 day cancellation notice-fee imposed. **Cards:** MC, VI.

SOME UNITS

*It's more than a room. It's Comfort.*℠

The Comfort Inn and Suites at Pirate's Cove Marketplace has been recognized as the perfect hotel in North Conway for the active family. There's a heated indoor pool and exercise room, while restaurants and shops are a short walk away.

The hotel offers 59 comfortable suites that feature large, oversized rooms with partially divided sitting and sleeping areas. Each suite includes:
• sleeping area with 1 king-size or 2 queen-size beds
• sitting area with a queen-size sofa bed
• a wet bar with microwave, refrigerator, coffee maker
• 25-inch television with HBO
• iron and ironing board
• hair dryer

Each morning you'll be treated to a complimentary deluxe continental breakfast; it's the ideal way to start your day.

## COMFORT INN & SUITES    *Book at aaa.com*

**AAA SAVE**

**Small-scale Hotel**

All Year [ECP]    1P: $99-$184    2P: $99-$184    XP: $10    F18
**Phone:** (603)356-8811
**Location:** 1.4 mi s on US 302 and SR 16. 2001 White Mountain Hwy 03860 (PO Box 1486). Fax: 603/356-7770. **Facility:** 59 units. 54 one-bedroom standard units. 5 one-bedroom suites ($199-$299), some with whirlpools. 3 stories, interior corridors. *Bath:* combo or shower only. **Parking:** on-site. **Terms:** check-in 4 pm. **Amenities:** irons, hair dryers. **Pool(s):** heated indoor. **Leisure Activities:** exercise room. **Guest Services:** coin laundry. **Business Services:** meeting rooms. **Cards:** AX, DC, DS, JC, MC, VI. **Special Amenities:** free expanded continental breakfast and free local telephone calls. *(See color ad p 372)*

SOME UNITS

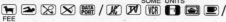

## CRANMORE MT LODGE

**AAA SAVE**

**Historic Bed & Breakfast**

9/20-10/31 [BP]    2P: $110-$350    XP: $15    F6
6/17-9/19 & 11/1-4/30 [BP]    2P: $110-$260    XP: $15    F6
5/1-6/16 [BP]    2P: $60-$260    XP: $15    F6
**Phone:** 603/356-2044
**Location:** On US 302, e at traffic light, then 1.3 mi, follow signs; from n, 1.2 mi e on Hurricane Mountain Rd, follow signs; village center. Located in a quiet area. 859 Kearsarge Rd 03860 (PO Box 1194). Fax: 603/356-4498. **Facility:** Woods, a mountain stream and a pond beautify the sprawling grounds of this 19th-century farmhouse; some farm animals are kept on the site. Smoke free premises. 22 units. 16 one-bedroom standard units, some with whirlpools. 6 one-bedroom suites, some with efficiencies or kitchens. 3 stories (no elevator), interior/exterior corridors. *Bath:* combo or shower only. **Parking:** on-site. **Terms:** 14 day cancellation notice-fee imposed, pets ($10 extra charge, with prior approval). **Pool(s):** heated outdoor. **Leisure Activities:** whirlpool, lighted tennis court, cross country skiing, ice skating, tobogganing, recreation programs, petting barn, hiking trails, basketball, volleyball. **Cards:** AX, MC, VI. **Special Amenities:** free full breakfast and free local telephone calls. *(See color ad below)*

SOME UNITS

FEE

## EASTERN INNS

AAA SAVE
♦♦♦♦

Small-scale Hotel

All Year        1P: $55-$65       2P: $65-$121      **Phone:** 603/356-5447
XP: $10              F12
**Location:** 0.5 mi n on US 302 and SR 16; village center. 2955 White Mountain Hwy 03860 (PO Box 775).
Fax: 603/356-8936. **Facility:** Smoke free premises. 56 one-bedroom standard units. 2 stories (no elevator), interior/exterior corridors. **Parking:** on-site. **Terms:** 3 day cancellation notice-fee imposed, [ECP] meal plan available. **Pool(s):** heated indoor. **Leisure Activities:** whirlpool, cross country skiing, playground, exercise room, basketball, game room. **Guest Services:** coin laundry. **Cards:** AX, DS, MC, VI. **Special Amenities:** free expanded continental breakfast. *(See color ad below)*

SOME UNITS
🏊 ✕ ✕ / VCR 📶 🖥 /
FEE

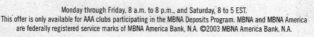

**EASTMAN INN**

Phone: 603/356-6707

▽▽▽▽

Historic Bed & Breakfast

9/19-10/19    1P: $130-$220    2P: $150-$240
5/1-9/18 & 10/20-4/30    1P: $80-$150    2P: $100-$170

**Location:** 0.5 mi s on US 302 and SR 16; village center. 2331 White Mountain Hwy 03860 (PO Box 882) **Fax:** 603/356-7708. **Facility:** A wraparound porch offers outdoor lounging space at this inn built in 1777 guest rooms are in the main house and in an annex. Smoke free premises. 13 units. 12 one- and 1 two bedroom standard units, some with whirlpools. 3 stories (no elevator), interior/exterior corridors. *Bath:* combo or shower only **Parking:** on-site. **Terms:** 2 night minimum stay - weekends, age restrictions may apply, 14 day cancellation notice-fee imposed [BP] meal plan available. **Amenities:** *Some:* hair dryers. **Cards:** AX, DS, MC, VI.

---

**THE FARM BY THE RIVER BED & BREAKFAST**

Phone: 603/356-269

(AAA) (SAVE)

▽▽▽▽

Historic Bed & Breakfast

9/19-10/26 [BP]    1P: $110-$225    2P: $130-$230    XP: $30   F
12/21-4/30 [BP]    1P: $85-$160    2P: $125-$185    XP: $25   F
5/1-9/18 [BP]    1P: $80    2P: $125-$185    XP: $25   F
10/27-12/20 [BP]    1P: $85-$155    2P: $120-$175    XP: $25   F

**Location:** Jct SR 16/113/153 at Conway traffic light, turn onto Washington St to West Side Rd, then 5 mi on right. Lo cated in a quiet, rural area. 2555 West Side Rd 03860. **Fax:** 603/356-2694. **Facility:** Covering 70-acres, this is a former working farm with pastures and sugar maple orchards; guided trail rides originate from a stable on the property. Some rooms with fireplace. Smoke free premises. 9 one-bedroom standard units, some with whirlpools. 2 stories (no elevator), interior corridors. *Bath:* combo or shower only. **Parking:** on-site. **Terms:** office hours 5:30 am-8:30 pm, check-in 4 pm 14 day cancellation notice-fee imposed, package plans - seasonal, no pets allowed (owner's pet on premises). **Leisure Activities:** fishing, cross country skiing, snowshoeing, walking trails, fall foliage wagon ride, bird-watching walks in spring. *Fee:* horse drawn winter sleigh rides, horseback riding. **Guest Services:** TV in common area, complimentary evening beverages **Cards:** MC, VI. **Special Amenities:** free full breakfast and free local telephone calls. *(See color ad below)*

SOME UNITS

---

**FOX RIDGE RESORT**    *Book at aaa.com*

Phone: (603)356-315

(AAA) (SAVE)

▽▽▽▽

Small-scale Hotel

9/24-11/13    1P: $89-$185    2P: $89-$185    XP: $10   F1
6/18-9/5    1P: $109-$175    2P: $109-$175    XP: $10   F1
9/6-9/23    1P: $75-$150    2P: $75-$150    XP: $10   F1
5/21-6/17    1P: $75-$149    2P: $75-$149    XP: $10   F1

**Location:** On US 302 and SR 16, 1.5 mi s. Located in a quiet, secluded area. 1979 White Mountain Hwy (SR 16) 03860 (PO Box 990). **Fax:** 603/356-0096. **Facility:** Smoke free premises. 136 one-bedroom standard units, some with whirlpools. 2 stories (no elevator), interior corridors. **Parking:** on-site. **Terms:** open 5/21-11/13, 2 night minimum stay - with some Saturday stayover, cancellation fee imposed, [BP] meal plan available. **Amenities:** voice mail, hair dryers. **Dining:** 7:30-1 am. **Pool(s):** heated outdoor, heated indoor. **Leisure Activities:** whirlpool, miniature golf, 3 tennis courts, hiking trails, play ground, basketball, shuffleboard. *Fee:* game room. **Guest Services:** coin laundry. **Business Services:** meeting rooms **Cards:** AX, MC, VI. *(See color ad p 377)*

SOME UNITS

---

**GOLDEN GABLES INN**

Phone: (603)356-287

(AAA) (SAVE)

▽▽▽ ▽▽

Motel

6/20-10/23    1P: $65-$169    2P: $69-$169    XP: $6   F1
5/1-6/19    1P: $55-$99    2P: $59-$99    XP: $6   F1
10/24-4/30    1P: $55-$85    2P: $59-$95    XP: $6   F1

**Location:** Jct US 302 and SR 16, 1 mi n. 1860 White Mountain Hwy 03860 (PO Box 626). **Fax:** 603/356-9094 **Facility:** 40 one-bedroom standard units. 1-2 stories (no elevator), exterior corridors. **Parking:** on-site. **Terms:** office hours 7 am-10 pm, cancellation fee imposed. **Amenities:** hair dryers. **Pool(s):** heated outdoor **Leisure Activities:** whirlpool. **Guest Services:** coin laundry. **Cards:** AX, DS, MC, VI. **Special Amenities:** free local telephone calls and early check-in/late check-out.

SOME UNITS

## GREEN GRANITE INN AND CONFERENCE CENTER

| | | | Phone: (603)356-6901 |
|---|---|---|---|
| 8/29-10/10 [ECP] | 1P: $80-$195 | 2P: $80-$195 | XP: $20    F15 |
| 6/25-8/28 [ECP] | 1P: $115-$165 | 2P: $115-$165 | XP: $20    F15 |
| 5/1-6/24 & 10/11-4/30 [ECP] | 1P: $70-$165 | 2P: $70-$165 | XP: $20    F15 |

**Location:** 2.3 mi s on US 302 and SR 16; village center. 1515 White Mountain Hwy (Rt 16) 03860 (PO Box 3127).
**Small-scale Hotel** Fax: 603/356-6980. **Facility:** 91 units. 80 one-bedroom standard units. 4 one- and 7 two-bedroom suites ($130-$260), some with kitchens and/or whirlpools. 2 stories (no elevator), interior/exterior corridors.
**Parking:** on-site. **Terms:** 2 night minimum stay - seasonal, cancellation fee imposed, [CP] meal plan available, package plans - seasonal. **Amenities:** *Some:* irons, hair dryers. **Pool(s):** heated outdoor, heated indoor. **Leisure Activities:** whirlpool, exercise room. *Fee:* game room. **Guest Services:** valet and coin laundry. **Business Services:** meeting rooms. **Cards:** AX, DS, MC, VI.
**Special Amenities:** free expanded continental breakfast and free newspaper. *(See color ad p 378)*

SOME UNITS

# TWO PREMIER RESORTS, ONE GREAT LOCATION.

### ASK ABOUT OUR SPECIAL MID-WEEK RATES

Both Fox Ridge and The Mountain View are part of the Red Jacket Resort family. So the quality of the hotel is excellent and the list of enjoyable amenities is long. Plus, both have great views and are right in North Conway near outlet shopping, Story Land, scenic drives and many fine restaurants.

Rt. 16, North Conway, NH • Tel: 800-RJACKET, 800-752-2538 • RedJacketResorts.com

**HOLIDAY INN EXPRESS HOTEL & SUITES**  *Book at aaa.com*  Phone: (603)356-2551

AAA SAVE

| | | | |
|---|---|---|---|
| 6/20-10/16 | 1P: $100-$190 | 2P: $100-$190 | XP: $10  F19 |
| 12/19-4/30 | 1P: $80-$170 | 2P: $80-$170 | XP: $10  F19 |
| 5/1-6/19 & 10/17-12/18 | 1P: $80-$140 | 2P: $80-$140 | XP: $10  F19 |

Small-scale Hotel **Location:** 2 mi s on US 302 and SR 16; village center. 1732 White Mountain Hwy 03860 (PO Box 3367). Fax: 603/356-7569. **Facility:** 78 units. 76 one-bedroom standard units, some with whirlpools. 2 one-bedroom suites ($140-$260) with whirlpools. 3 stories, interior corridors. *Bath:* combo or shower only. **Parking:** on-site. **Terms:** 2 night minimum stay - weekends, [ECP] meal plan available. **Amenities:** dual phone lines, voice mail, irons, hair dryers. **Pool(s):** heated indoor. **Leisure Activities:** whirlpool. *Fee:* game room. **Guest Services:** valet and coin laundry. **Cards:** AX, DC, DS, MC, VI. **Special Amenities:** free continental breakfast and free local telephone calls.

SOME UNITS

🛎🗗 📶 🍸 👫Ⓜ 🛋 🐾 🛥 🏊 📷 DATA PORT 💻 / 🗙 📞 🖨 /

**NORTH CONWAY GRAND HOTEL**  *Book at aaa.com*  Phone: (603)356-9300

AAA SAVE

| | | | |
|---|---|---|---|
| 7/1-10/31 | 1P: $89-$199 | 2P: $89-$199 | XP: $10  F17 |
| 11/1-4/30 | 1P: $69-$189 | 2P: $69-$189 | XP: $10  F17 |
| 5/1-6/30 | 1P: $69-$139 | 2P: $69-$139 | XP: $10  F17 |

Large-scale Hotel **Location:** 0.5 mi n of southern jct SR 16 and US 302, 0.3 mi e at sign. Located at Settlers Green. SR 16 at Settlers Green 03860 (PO Box 3189). Fax: 603/356-6028. **Facility:** 200 units. 189 one-bedroom standard units, some with whirlpools. 11 one-bedroom suites ($189-$329), some with whirlpools. 4 stories, interior corridors. *Bath:* combo or shower only. **Parking:** on-site. **Terms:** 3 day cancellation notice, [BP] & [MAP] meal plans available, package plans - seasonal. **Amenities:** voice mail, irons, hair dryers. *Fee:* video library, video games. **Dining:** 7 am-10 pm, cocktails. **Pool(s):** heated indoor. **Leisure Activities:** saunas, whirlpool, cross country skiing, ice skating, hiking trails, exercise room. **Guest Services:** valet and coin laundry. **Business Services:** conference facilities, fax (fee). **Cards:** AX, DC, DS, MC, VI. *(See color ad p 379)*

SOME UNITS

🛎🗗 📶 🍸 👫Ⓜ 🛋 🐾 🛥 🗙 📷 DATA PORT / 🗙 📞 💻 /

North Conway's Premier Hotel in the Perfect Location!
NORTH CONWAY
GRAND HOTEL
Located at Outlet Village Plus with over 50 Shops Directly On Site
2 Pools, Jacuzzi, Saunas, Fitness Center Playground, Tennis Courts, Game Room
Mountainside Tavern & Restaurant with Free Kids' Breakfast
Beautifully-renovated oversized rooms feature marble bathrooms, 27" Television, DVD player with free DVD library, Nintendo and refrigerator. Family suites and jacuzzi suites also available. Great Story Land and ski packages.
AAA
Approved
888-522-1793
Route 16 at Settlers' Green O.V.P. North Conway, NH 03860 • www.northconwaygrand.com

**NORTH CONWAY MOUNTAIN INN**

Phone: 603/356-2803

AAA [SAVE]

| | | |
|---|---|---|
| 6/15-10/31 | | 2P: $69-$169 |
| 5/1-6/14 | | 2P: $69-$125 |
| 11/1-4/30 | | 2P: $59-$125 |

Motel

**Location:** 1 mi s on US 302 and SR 16; village center. 2114 White Mountain Hwy 03860 (PO Box 3175). Fax: 603/356-3228. **Facility:** Smoke free premises. 32 one-bedroom standard units. 2 stories (no elevator), exterior corridors. **Parking:** on-site. **Terms:** office hours 9 am-11 pm, 3 day cancellation notice, pets (in limited units). **Cards:** AX, DC, MC, VI. **Special Amenities:** free local telephone calls and early check-in/late check-out.

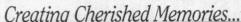

**SPRUCE MOOSE LODGE AND COTTAGES**

Historic Bed & Breakfast

9/21-10/25 [BP]
5/1-9/20 & 10/26-4/30 [BP]

2P: $89-$149
2P: $49-$109

**Phone:** 603/356-6239

**Location:** US 302 and SR 16, 0.5 mi e; village center. 207 Seavey St 03860 (PO Box 557). **Facility:** Individual decor gives the cozy guest rooms at this B&B a country charm. Smoke free premises. 12 units. 9 one-bedroom standard units, some with whirlpools. 3 cottages ($109-$235). 2 stories (no elevator), interior/exterior corridors. *Bath:* combo or shower only. **Parking:** on-site. **Terms:** office hours 9 am-9 pm, 2 night minimum stay - weekends, 21 day cancellation notice, pets ($100 deposit, $10 extra charge, in cottages). **Amenities:** *Some:* CD players. **Cards:** AX, MC, VI.

SOME UNITS

FEE

**VICTORIAN HARVEST INN**

Bed & Breakfast

All Year

2P: $100-$240

XP: $30

**Phone:** 603/356-3548

**Location:** South jct US 302 and SR 16, 2 mi n on SR 16 to Locust Ln, then just e; from village center, 0.5 mi s on SR 16 and US 302. Located in a quiet area. 28 Locust Ln 03860 (PO Box 1763). Fax: 603/356-8430. **Facility:** The inn offers well-appointed guest rooms, including one with a fireplace. Smoke free premises. 8 one-bedroom standard units, some with whirlpools. 2 stories (no elevator), interior corridors. *Bath:* combo or shower only. **Parking:** on-site. **Terms:** office hours 7 am-10 pm, age restrictions may apply, 14 day cancellation notice-fee imposed, [BP] meal plan available. **Amenities:** hair dryers. *Some:* irons. **Pool(s):** outdoor. **Leisure Activities:** cross country skiing. **Cards:** AX, MC, VI.

SOME UNITS

## WHITE MOUNTAIN HOTEL & RESORT

**Phone: (603)356-7100**

AAA SAVE

| | | | | |
|---|---|---|---|---|
| 9/24-10/10 | 1P: $179-$209 | 2P: $179-$209 | XP: $14 | F18 |
| 6/18-9/23 | 1P: $149-$199 | 2P: $149-$199 | XP: $14 | F18 |
| 10/11-4/30 | 1P: $109-$179 | 2P: $109-$179 | XP: $14 | F18 |
| 5/1-6/17 | 1P: $89-$139 | 2P: $89-$139 | XP: $14 | F18 |

Small-scale Hotel **Location:** Jct SR 16/113/153 at Conway traffic light, turn onto Washington St to West Side Rd (do not cross covered bridge), then 5 mi on left. West Side Rd 03860 (PO Box 1828). Fax: 603/356-7100. **Facility:** 80 one-bedroom standard units, some with whirlpools. 3 stories, interior corridors. **Parking:** on-site. **Terms:** 2 night minimum stay - weekends, 5 day cancellation notice, [BP] & [MAP] meal plans available. **Amenities:** voice mail, irons, hair dryers. **Dining:** 7-10 am, 11:30-2 & 5:30-9 pm; 7 am-10 & 5:30-9 pm 4-30, also, Ledges Dining Room, see separate listing. **Pool(s):** heated outdoor. **Leisure Activities:** saunas, whirlpool, tennis court, cross country skiing, exercise room. *Fee:* golf-9 holes, game room. **Guest Services:** gift shop, coin laundry. **Business Services:** meeting rooms. **Cards:** AX, DS, MC, VI. *(See color ad p 381)*

SOME UNITS

## WHITE TRELLIS MOTEL

**Phone: 603/356-2492**

Motel

| | | |
|---|---|---|
| All Year | 2P: $45-$145 | XP: $10 |

**Location:** 0.8 mi n on US 302 and SR 16; village center. 3245 White Mountain Hwy 03860 (PO Box 441). **Facility:** 22 units. 21 one- and 1 two-bedroom standard units. 1 story, exterior corridors. *Bath:* combo or shower only. **Parking:** on-site. **Terms:** office hours 8 am-10 pm, 7 day cancellation notice-fee imposed. **Cards:** DS, MC, VI.

SOME UNITS

## WYATT HOUSE COUNTRY INN

**Phone: (603)356-7977**

| | | | |
|---|---|---|---|
| 9/16-10/15 [BP] | 1P: $149-$229 | 2P: $149-$229 | XP: $25 |
| 12/16-4/30 [BP] | 1P: $99-$179 | 2P: $109-$199 | XP: $25 |
| 5/1-9/15 [BP] | 1P: $89-$169 | 2P: $109-$189 | XP: $25 |
| 10/16-12/15 [BP] | 1P: $89-$149 | 2P: $99-$169 | XP: $25 |

Bed & Breakfast **Location:** 0.5 mi n on US 302 and SR 16; village center. 3046 White Mountain Hwy 03860 (PO Box 777). Fax: 603/356-2183. **Facility:** This inn is decorated with a decidedly Victorian influence. Smoke free premises. 9 units. 6 one-bedroom standard units, some with whirlpools. 3 one-bedroom suites. 3 stories (no elevator), interior/exterior corridors. *Bath:* combo, shower or tub only. **Parking:** on-site. **Terms:** 2 night minimum stay - weekends, age restrictions may apply, 14 day cancellation notice-fee imposed. **Amenities:** hair dryers. **Cards:** AX, DS, MC, VI.

---

*The following lodgings were either not evaluated or did not meet AAA rating requirements but are listed for your information only.*

---

## CROWN RIDGE RESORT

**Phone: 603/356-5088**

fyi  Not evaluated. **Location:** Crown Ridge Rd 03860. Facilities, services, and decor characterize a mid-range property.

## THE EASTERN SLOPE INN RESORT

**Phone: 603/356-6321**

fyi  Not evaluated. **Location:** 2760 Main St 03860. Facilities, services, and decor characterize a mid-range property.

--- **WHERE TO DINE** ---

**THE 1785 INN RESTAURANT**  Country Inn  **Dinner:** $16-$28  **Phone:** 603/356-9025

**Location:** 2 mi n on US 302 and SR 16; village center, in The 1785 Inn. 3582 N White Mountain Hwy 03860-1785. **Hours:** 8 am-9:30 & 5-9 pm, Fri & Sat-10 pm. Closed: 12/25. **Reservations:** suggested. **Features:** In the original section of a Colonial inn, the restaurant overlooks a scenic vista. Entrees made to order with fresh ingredients include duckling, rabbit, veal, lamb, chicken, beef and seafood preparations. Desserts are made on the premises. The wine list is award-winning. Diners seeking a romantic atmosphere should request a table near the fireplace. Casual dress; cocktails. **Parking:** on-site. **Cards:** AX, CB, DC, DS, MC, VI.

**BELLINI'S**  **Dinner:** $12-$25  **Phone:** 603/356-7000

Italian  **Location:** Just e; village center. 33 Seavey St 03860. **Hours:** 5 pm-10 pm, Fri & Sat-11 pm, Sun 4 pm-9 pm. Closed major holidays; also Mon & Tues. **Features:** Among offerings of Northern and Southern Italian cuisine are eggplant parmigiana, veal Marsala and Caesar salad prepared with fresh Parmesan cheese sprinkled over crisp romaine. Fresh pasta benefits from richly flavored sauces, and homemade breads and soups are tempting accompaniments. Alfresco dining is a nice seasonal option. The staff is friendly and knowledgeable. Casual dress; cocktails. **Parking:** on-site. **Cards:** AX, CB, DC, DS, MC, VI.

**THE BLUEBERRY MUFFIN**  **Lunch:** $3-$8  **Phone:** 603/356-2811

American  **Location:** 1.3 mi s on SR 16 and US 302; center. 1769 White Mountain Hwy 03860. **Hours:** 8 am-2 pm. Closed major holidays. **Features:** Casual, diner-style atmosphere and fare are popular with locals. Service is swift, and portions are large. Casual dress. **Parking:** on-site. **Cards:** MC, VI.

**DELANEY'S HOLE IN THE WALL**  **Lunch:** $5-$18  **Dinner:** $5-$18  **Phone:** 603/356-7776

American  **Location:** 1 mi n on US 302 and SR 16. 2942 White Mountain Hwy 03860. **Hours:** 11:30 am-11 pm. Closed: 3/27, 11/25, 12/25. **Features:** In the heart of town, the restaurant was named after a member of the infamous Hole in the Wall Gang of Butch Cassidy and the Sundance Kid. Decor is reminiscent of the period, and the atmosphere is casual and family-focused. On the menu are seafood, steaks, pasta, burgers, soup and salads. Made-from-scratch dishes employ fresh ingredients, whenever possible, and are served in large portions. Casual dress; cocktails. **Parking:** on-site. **Cards:** AX, DS, MC, VI.

**FANDANGLE'S**

American

**Lunch:** $6-$17    **Dinner:** $8-$20    **Phone:** 603/356-2741
**Location:** Jct US 302 S and SR 16. 1439 White Mountain Hwy 03860. **Hours:** 11 am-10 pm; to 9:30 pm 11/1-6/1. Closed: 11/25, 12/25. **Features:** Service is prompt and friendly, and the menu offers good variety. Attractively presented dishes are served in ample portions and include fried seafood selections and vegetables. Casual dress; cocktails. **Parking:** on-site. **Cards:** AX, DS, MC, VI.

**HOOLIGAN'S FOOD AND DRINK**

AAA

American

**Lunch:** $5-$9    **Dinner:** $8-$15    **Phone:** 603/356-6110
**Location:** Just e of SR 16; village center. 21 Kearsarge Rd 03860. **Hours:** 11 am-11 pm. Closed: 1/1, 11/25, 12/25. **Features:** Popular with the locals, the rustic, pub-style restaurant has planked walls and beamed ceilings. On the menu is a good selection of meat and seafood entrees, as well as basic comfort foods. Casual dress; cocktails. **Parking:** street. **Cards:** DC, MC, VI.

**LEDGES DINING ROOM**

American

**Lunch:** $5-$15    **Dinner:** $17-$25    **Phone:** 603/356-7100
**Location:** Jct SR 16/113/153 at Conway traffic light, turn onto Washington St to West Side Rd (do not cross covered bridge), then 5 mi on left; in White Mountain Hotel & Resort. At Hales Location West Side Rd 03860. **Hours:** 7 am-10 & 5:30-9 pm; also 11:30 am-2 pm 11/1-4/30. **Reservations:** suggested. **Features:** In a beautiful mountain setting, the elegant dining room affords great views of the colorful gardens. Representative of creative cuisine is a casserole with couscous, shrimp, scallops, mussels and haddock. A pianist performs nightly in season, weekends in the off-season. Dressy casual; cocktails; entertainment. **Parking:** on-site. **Cards:** AX, DS, MC, VI. *(See color ad p 381)*

**MOAT MT SMOKEHOUSE**

Barbecue

**Lunch:** $4-$10    **Dinner:** $13-$20    **Phone:** 603/356-6381
**Location:** 1.5 mi n on US 302 and SR 16. 3378 White Mountain Hwy 03860. **Hours:** 11:30 am-9 pm. Closed: 12/25; also for dinner 12/24 & Mon; closed 1 week in May. **Features:** Specializing in barbecue items, the restaurant serves richly flavored ribs and chicken, homemade soups and other traditional favorites. The casual dining room, with paneled walls and diner-styled tables, offers a great atmosphere for families and the after-skiing crowd. Casual dress; cocktails. **Parking:** on-site. **Cards:** AX, MC, VI.

**MUDDY MOOSE RESTAURANT & PUB**

American

**Lunch:** $6-$17    **Dinner:** $6-$17    **Phone:** 603/356-7696
**Location:** On US 302 and SR 16, 1 mi s. 2344 White Mountain Hwy 03860. **Hours:** 11:30 am-9 pm. Closed: 11/25, 12/25. **Features:** In a convenient site on a busy highway, the fun and upbeat restaurant serves traditional American fare. Casual dress; cocktails. **Parking:** on-site. **Cards:** AX, DS, MC, VI.

**THE SPICY LIME**

Thai

**Lunch:** $6-$10    **Dinner:** $10-$16    **Phone:** 603/356-9466
**Location:** 1.2 mi s on US 302 and SR 16. 2115 White Mountain Hwy 03860. **Hours:** 11 am-11 pm. Closed: 11/25, 12/25. **Reservations:** accepted. **Features:** The casual family-oriented restaurant delivers flavorful Thai dishes ranging from spicy to mild. Guests can sample a selection of fresh seafood, curry and stir-fried noodles. Casual dress; cocktails. **Parking:** on-site. **Cards:** AX, MC, VI.

# NORTH HAMPTON —See also HAMPTON.

## ———— WHERE TO DINE ————

**ABERCROMBIE & FINCH**

Steak & Seafood

**Lunch:** $7-$19    **Dinner:** $7-$19    **Phone:** 603/964-9774
**Location:** Jct SR 101D, 0.2 mi n on US 1. 219 Lafayette Rd 03862. **Hours:** 11:30 am-9 pm. Closed: 9/6, 11/25. **Reservations:** accepted. **Features:** The popular restaurant serves traditional British pub fare along the lines of olde beer-battered fish and chips, Buckingham's steak sandwich and Aber's chips. Casual dress; cocktails. **Parking:** on-site. **Cards:** AX, DS, MC, VI.

**THE COPPER LANTERN**

American

**Lunch:** $5-$16    **Dinner:** $5-$16    **Phone:** 603/964-5008
**Location:** On US 1, 0.5 mi s of SR 101D. 54 Lafayette Rd 03862. **Hours:** 7-11 am, 11:30-2 & 5-8 pm, Sun 8 am-noon. Closed major holidays; also Mon & Tues. **Features:** In a convenient location, the cozy little restaurant serves good homemade comfort foods. Menu items include deep-fried and baked seafood, burgers and sirloin steak. Casual dress; cocktails. **Parking:** on-site. **Cards:** MC, VI.

**SPUD'S RESTAURANT & PUB**

American

**Lunch:** $6-$10    **Dinner:** $8-$16    **Phone:** 603/964-5497
**Location:** Jct SR 111, 2.5 mi n on US 1. 215 Lafayette Rd, Rt 1 03862. **Hours:** 11 am-9 pm, Fri & Sat-10 pm. Closed: 7/4, 11/25, 12/25. **Features:** The casual family restaurant's affordable American home-style cuisine is popular with locals and tourists alike. Among menu items are soup, salad, chicken, beef, seafood, pasta, burgers and sandwiches. A few low-calorie, low-cholesterol dishes also are prepared. Dessert is made on the premises. Try the baked seafood casserole. Casual dress; cocktails. **Parking:** on-site. **Cards:** AX, DS, MC, VI.

## ———— *The following restaurant has not been evaluated by AAA* ———— *but is listed for your information only.*

**RINALDO'S ITALIAN RESTAURANT**    **Phone:** 603/964-5064

fyl    Not evaluated. **Location:** 69 Lafayette Rd 03862. **Features:** The popular bistro is situated in a small strip mall off the northbound stretch of US 1.

# NORTH SUTTON

## ———— WHERE TO STAY ————

**FOLLANSBEE INN ON KEZAR LAKE**
All Year [BP]    1P: $110-$175    2P: $110-$175    **Phone:** 603/927-4221
XP: $30
▼▼▼▼
**Location:** I-89, exit 10, SR 114; follow signs to North Sutton, 4 mi s of New London on Kezar Lake. Keyser St 03260
Historic Bed    (PO Box 92). Fax: 603/927-6307. **Facility:** This charming 1840s country inn overlooks a lake. Smoke free
& Breakfast     premises. 18 units. 16 one-bedroom standard units. 2 one-bedroom suites ($175) with whirlpools. 3 stories
(no elevator), interior corridors. *Bath:* combo or shower only. **Parking:** on-site. **Terms:** office hours 8 am-8
pm, 2 night minimum stay - in summer, age restrictions may apply, 10 day cancellation notice-fee imposed, package plans.
**Leisure Activities:** boating, canoeing, paddleboats, boat dock, cross country skiing, bicycles. **Business Services:** meeting
rooms. **Cards:** MC, VI.

# NORTHWOOD pop. 3,640

## ———— WHERE TO DINE ————

**CHADBOURN'S**    Lunch: $3-$14    **Dinner:** $14    **Phone:** 603/942-5992
▼▼
**Location:** Located on "Antiques Alley" (US 4). 261 First NH Tpke 03261. **Hours:** 8 am-8 pm, Thurs-Sat from 6:30
American    am, Sun 6:30 am-2 pm. Closed major holidays; also Mon. **Features:** The restaurant offers reasonably
priced New England comfort food. Casual dress. **Parking:** on-site. **Cards:** MC, VI.

**JOHNSON'S STEAK & SEAFOOD**    Lunch: $5-$10    **Dinner:** $8-$17    **Phone:** 603/942-7300
▼▼
**Location:** On US 4/202. 1334 First NH Tpke 03261. **Hours:** 11 am-9 pm. Closed: 11/25, 12/24, 12/25.
Seafood    **Features:** Diners can choose to sit down and order inside or, during the summer months, order at the
outdoor counter before plunking down on a picnic bench. The seafood is fresh and tasty. Dishes are
primarily fried. Casual dress; cocktails. **Parking:** on-site. **Cards:** AX, MC, VI.

# NORTH WOODSTOCK

## ———— WHERE TO STAY ————

**THREE RIVERS HOUSE**    **Phone:** (603)745-2711
(AAA) (SAVE)    5/1-10/31    1P: $65-$115    2P: $75-$125    XP: $25
12/26-4/2    1P: $65-$115    2P: $75-$125    XP: $35
▼▼▼▼ ▼▼
**Location:** Jct SR 112, just s on US 3. 19 S Main St 03262 (RR 1, Box 72). Fax: 603/745-2773. **Facility:** Rooms vary
Historic Bed    in size and decor at this 1875 inn just south of downtown; the property is recognizable by the large moose
& Breakfast     statue on its front lawn. Smoke free premises. 19 units. 12 one-bedroom standard units, some with whirlpools. 7 one-bedroom suites ($95-$145), some with kitchens and/or whirlpools. 4 stories (no elevator), interior corridors. *Bath:* combo or shower only. **Parking:** on-site. **Terms:** open 5/1-10/31 & 12/26-4/2, office hours
8 am-10 pm, 2 night minimum stay - weekends in season, 7 day cancellation notice-fee imposed, weekly rates available, package
plans, $3 service charge. **Cards:** AX, DS, MC, VI. **Special Amenities: free full breakfast and preferred room (subject to
availability with advanced reservations).**

SOME UNITS

**WILDERNESS INN BED & BREAKFAST**    **Phone:** (603)745-3890
▼▼▼    9/17-10/23    1P: $90-$160    2P: $95-$165    XP: $10    F6
10/24-4/30    1P: $60-$160    2P: $65-$165    XP: $10    F6
5/1-9/16    1P: $60-$115    2P: $65-$115    XP: $10    F6
Bed & Breakfast    **Location:** On US 3, just s of SR 112. 57 Main St (SR 3) 03262 (RFD 1, Box 69). **Facility:** Near downtown, the inn
is convenient to year-round activities. Smoke free premises. 8 units. 5 one- and 1 two-bedroom standard units, some with whirlpools. 1 two-bedroom suite with whirlpool. 1 cottage with whirlpool. 2 stories (no elevator), interior corridors. *Bath:* combo or
shower only. **Parking:** on-site. **Terms:** office hours 7 am-10 pm, 2 night minimum stay - weekends in season, 15 day cancellation notice, [BP] meal plan available, package plans - seasonal. **Cards:** AX, MC, VI.

SOME UNITS

**WOODSTOCK INN**    **Phone:** 603/745-3951
(AAA) (SAVE)    9/17-10/17 [BP]    2P: $99-$230    XP: $15    F12
6/11-9/16 [BP]    2P: $94-$182    XP: $15    F12
▼▼▼▼    5/1-6/10 [BP]    2P: $65-$182    XP: $15    F12
10/18-4/30 [BP]    2P: $65-$172    XP: $15    F12
Historic    **Location:** On US 3, 0.3 mi n of SR 112. 135 Main St 03262 (PO Box 118). Fax: 603/745-3701. **Facility:** In the center
Country Inn    of town, the inn is close to mountain recreation areas; the building, decorated in a Victorian style, is more
than a hundred years old. 24 units. 22 one-bedroom standard units, some with whirlpools. 2 one-bedroom
suites with whirlpools. 2-3 stories (no elevator), interior corridors. *Bath:* some shared or private, combo or shower only. **Parking:**
on-site. **Terms:** office hours 8 am-11 pm, 2 night minimum stay - seasonal & weekends, 7 day cancellation notice-fee imposed,
[MAP] meal plan available, package plans. **Amenities:** hair dryers. **Dining:** Woodstock Station, Clement Room, see separate
listings. **Leisure Activities:** whirlpool. **Guest Services:** gift shop, complimentary evening beverages. **Cards:** AX, DS, MC, VI.
**Special Amenities: free full breakfast.**

SOME UNITS

## ———— WHERE TO DINE ————

**CHALET RESTAURANT**    Lunch: $4-$12    **Dinner:** $12-$22    **Phone:** 603/745-2256
▼▼ ▼▼
**Location:** On US 3, just n of jct SR 112 and US 3. 93 Main St 03262. **Hours:** 11:30 am-9 pm. Closed: 11/25,
American    12/25. **Reservations:** accepted. **Features:** The family restaurant is located on the main street area of town
and features a menu that is varied and sure to please everyone; kids love the mini ice cream bar. Casual
dress; cocktails. **Parking:** on-site. **Cards:** AX, DS, MC, VI.

**CLEMENT ROOM**

◈◈◈◈

▼▼◈▼▼

American

**Dinner:** $12-$24                    **Phone:** 603/745-3951
**Location:** On US 3, 0.3 mi n of SR 112; in Woodstock Inn. 135 Main St 03262. **Hours:** 7:30 am-11 & 5:30-8:30 pm; to 9:30 pm 7/1-10/31; Sunday brunch 10 am-2 pm. Closed: 12/25; also after 3 pm 12/24. **Reservations:** accepted. **Features:** The attractive dining room features Victorian decor, intriguing cuisine and a pleasant, well-informed staff. Flavorful broiled salmon has an appealing presentation. Servers are professional and friendly. Casual dress; cocktails. **Parking:** on-site. **Cards:** AX, DS, MC, VI.

🍸 ✕

**WOODSTOCK STATION**

▼▼◈▼▼

American

DS, MC, VI.

**Lunch:** $6-$18                **Dinner:** $6-$18                **Phone:** 603/745-3951
**Location:** On US 3, 0.3 mi n of SR 112; in Woodstock Inn. 135 Main St 03262. **Hours:** 11:30 am-9 pm. Closed: 12/25; also after 3 pm 12/24. **Features:** An old railroad station is the setting for relaxed dining. Among lunch and dinner offerings are chimichangas, homemade root beer and salads. Servers are prompt, friendly and attentive. The patio is open seasonally. Casual dress; cocktails. **Parking:** on-site. **Cards:** AX,

🍸 ✕

——————  *The following restaurant has not been evaluated by AAA*  ——————
*but is listed for your information only.*

**CAFE LAFAYETTE DINNER TRAIN**

(fyi)

Not evaluated. **Location:** I-93, exit 32, just w. 3 Crossing @ Riverplace 03262. **Features:** Preparations of "area-friendly contemporary" cuisine center around fresh regional ingredients.                    **Phone:** 603/745-3500

# PETERBOROUGH pop. 2,944

——————  **WHERE TO DINE**  ——————

——————  *The following restaurant has not been evaluated by AAA*  ——————
*but is listed for your information only.*

**THE CAFE AT NOONE FALLS**

(fyi)

Not evaluated. **Location:** On US 202. 50 Jaffrey Rd 03458. **Features:** An area favorite, the quaint eatery focuses on homemade soups and sandwiches.                    **Phone:** 603/924-6818

# PITTSBURG

------ WHERE TO STAY ------

THE GLEN
**Phone:** 603/538-6500

Cabin

5/16-10/15                1P: $90-$110          2P: $180-$220
**Location:** 8.1 mi n on US 3, then 0.7 mi se via Varney Rd, follow signs. Located in a rustic area. 118 Glen Rd 03592.
**Fax:** 603/538-7121. **Facility:** 16 units. 6 one-bedroom standard units. 10 cabins. 1-2 stories (no elevator),
interior/exterior corridors. *Bath:* combo or shower only. **Parking:** on-site. **Terms:** open 5/16-10/15, office
hours 7 am-8 pm, 7 day cancellation notice, weekly rates available, [AP] meal plan available, package plans, pets (in cabins).
**Leisure Activities:** rental boats, boat dock, fishing, hiking trails, horseshoes.

SOME UNITS

# PLAINFIELD

------ WHERE TO STAY ------

HOME HILL FRENCH INN     *Book at aaa.com*
**Phone:** 603/675-6165
XP: $30

Historic
Country Inn

5/1-1/1 & 1/31-4/30 [ECP]                      2P: $235-$425
**Location:** I-89, exit 20, 3 mi s via SR 12A, then 3 mi w. 703 River Rd 03781. **Fax:** 603/675-5220. **Facility:** Guests
will find this beautiful French country themed inn set back on attractive gated grounds. The guest rooms are
lovely and generally quite spacious, decorated using upscale fabrics and fine antiques. Smoke free premises.
11 units. 9 one-bedroom standard units. 2 one-bedroom suites. 2 stories (no elevator), interior corridors.
*Bath:* combo or shower only. **Parking:** on-site. **Terms:** open 5/1-1/1 & 1/31-4/30, age restrictions may apply, 30 day cancellation
notice-fee imposed, 15% service charge. **Amenities:** hair dryers. **Dining:** restaurant, see separate listing. **Pool(s):** outdoor.
**Leisure Activities:** tennis court, cross country skiing, bicycles, exercise room. *Fee:* massage. **Cards:** AX, CB, DC, DS, JC,
MC, VI.

------ WHERE TO DINE ------

HOME HILL FRENCH INN & RESTAURANT   Country Inn          **Dinner:** $28-$89      **Phone:** 603/675-6165

French

**Location:** I-89, exit 20, 3 mi s via SR 12A, then 3 mi w; in Home Hill French Inn. 703 River Rd 03781. **Hours:** 6
pm-9 pm. Closed: 12/24, 12/25; also Mon & Tues; may be closed 2 weeks in Jan.
**Reservations:** suggested. **Features:** Situated on 25 beautifully landscaped acres is this 1813 Federal
House now elegant French restaurant featuring smoked salmon with a delicately flavored lemon coulis,
rabbit pate en terrine with fresh mixed greens, perfectly seasoned and prepared rack of lamb served with
julienne vegetables. Complete your meal with a delectable trio of creme brulee. This is a glimpse of their
creative menu — bon appetit. The cozy atmosphere is romantic and intimate. Terrace dining is available in season. Dressy
casual; cocktails. **Parking:** on-site. **Cards:** AX, CB, DC, DS, JC, MC, VI.

# PLYMOUTH pop. 3,528

------ WHERE TO STAY ------

THE COMMON MAN INN & SPA
**Phone:** (603)536-2200
F12

Small-scale Hotel

All Year [ECP]            1P: $69-$189          2P: $69-$189          XP: $15
**Location:** I-93, exit 26, on US 3. 231 Main St 03264. **Fax:** 603/536-7773. **Facility:** Smoke free premises. 37 units.
36 one-bedroom standard units, some with whirlpools. 1 two-bedroom suite. 2-3 stories, interior corridors.
**Parking:** on-site. **Terms:** 3 day cancellation notice-fee imposed, package plans - seasonal. **Amenities:** high-
speed Internet (fee), voice mail, hair dryers. *Some:* DVD players. **Pool(s):** heated indoor. **Leisure Activities:** saunas, whirlpools,
exercise room, spa. **Guest Services:** gift shop, valet and coin laundry. **Business Services:** conference facilities, fax (fee).
**Cards:** AX, DS, MC, VI. *(See ad below)*

SOME UNITS

# PORTSMOUTH pop. 20,784

──── WHERE TO STAY ────

## ANCHORAGE INN & SUITES

Phone: (603)431-8111

(AAA) (SAVE)
▼▼▼

Motel

| | | | |
|---|---|---|---|
| 7/1-10/31 [ECP] | 1P: $89-$159 | 2P: $89-$159 | XP: $10 | F17 |
| 5/1-6/30 & 11/1-4/30 [ECP] | 1P: $69-$129 | 2P: $69-$129 | XP: $10 | F17 |

**Location:** Jct US 1 and I-95; at Portsmouth Traffic Circle. 417 Woodbury Ave 03801. Fax: 603/431-4443. **Facility:** 93 units. 89 one-bedroom standard units. 4 one-bedroom suites ($109-$229) with whirlpools. 3 stories, interior corridors. **Parking:** on-site. **Terms:** cancellation fee imposed, package plans - seasonal & weekends. **Amenities:** voice mail. *Some:* irons, hair dryers. **Pool(s):** heated indoor. **Leisure Activities:** sauna, whirlpool. **Guest Services:** valet laundry. **Business Services:** meeting rooms. **Cards:** AX, CB, DC, DS, MC, VI. **Special Amenities: free expanded continental breakfast and free local telephone calls.** *(See color ad below)*

SOME UNITS

FEE

## BEST INN  *Book at aaa.com*

Phone: (603)431-4400

▼▼ ▼▼

Motel

| | | | |
|---|---|---|---|
| 7/1-8/31 [ECP] | 1P: $109-$129 | 2P: $109-$129 | XP: $10 | F17 |
| 9/1-10/31 [ECP] | 1P: $89-$109 | 2P: $89-$109 | XP: $10 | F17 |
| 5/1-6/30 [ECP] | 1P: $69-$89 | 2P: $69-$89 | XP: $10 | F17 |
| 11/1-4/30 [ECP] | 1P: $59 | 2P: $59 | XP: $10 | F17 |

**Location:** I-95, exit 5 at Portsmouth Traffic Circle. 383 Woodbury Ave 03801. Fax: 603/431-4845. **Facility:** 61 one-bedroom standard units. 4 stories, interior corridors. **Parking:** on-site. **Terms:** [CP] meal plan available. **Cards:** AX, DC, DS, MC, VI.

SOME UNITS
(ASK) (SD) ⊞ ⊡ / ⊠ ⊟ ⊡ /

## THE BEST WESTERN WYNWOOD HOTEL & SUITES  *Book at aaa.com*

Phone: (603)436-7600

(AAA) (SAVE)
▼▼▼▼

Large-scale Hotel

| | | | |
|---|---|---|---|
| 7/1-10/31 | 1P: $90-$350 | 2P: $90-$350 | XP: $10 | F17 |
| 5/1-6/30 | 1P: $70-$199 | 2P: $75-$199 | XP: $5 | F17 |
| 11/1-4/30 | 1P: $70-$185 | 2P: $70-$185 | XP: $5 | F17 |

**Location:** I-95, exit 5 at Portsmouth Traffic Circle and jct US 1. 580 US Hwy 1 Bypass 03801. Fax: 603/436-7600. **Facility:** 169 units. 137 one-bedroom standard units, some with whirlpools. 32 one-bedroom suites ($115-$375) with efficiencies and whirlpools. 2-6 stories, interior/exterior corridors. *Bath:* combo or shower only. **Parking:** on-site. **Terms:** 2 night minimum stay - with Saturday stayover 7/1-10/31. **Amenities:** voice mail, irons, hair dryers. **Dining:** 24 hours, cocktails. **Pool(s):** outdoor, heated indoor. **Leisure Activities:** whirlpool, exercise room. **Guest Services:** gift shop, valet and coin laundry. **Business Services:** meeting rooms. **Cards:** AX, CB, DC, DS, JC, MC, VI. **Special Amenities: free local telephone calls.**

SOME UNITS
(SD) ⊟ ⊔ ⊠ ⊡ / ⊠ ⊡ /

## BOW STREET INN

Phone: 603/431-7760

▼▼▼

Historic Bed
& Breakfast

| | | |
|---|---|---|
| All Year | 1P: $120-$175 | 2P: $120-$175 | XP: $10 |

**Location:** Center. Located in the Seacoast Repertory Theatre Building. 121 Bow St 03801. Fax: 603/433-1680. **Facility:** Occupying a 19th-century brewery storage building, this distinctive B&B offers several rooms with a view of the river. Smoke free premises. 10 one-bedroom standard units. 3 stories, interior corridors. **Parking:** street. **Terms:** office hours 8 am-7 pm, 7 day cancellation notice-fee imposed, [ECP] meal plan available, package plans - seasonal. **Amenities:** hair dryers. *Some:* voice mail, irons. **Guest Services:** valet laundry. **Cards:** AX, DS, MC, VI.

SOME UNITS
⊠ ⊟ / ⊟ /

**COMFORT INN AT YOKEN'S**     *Book at aaa.com*                    **Phone:** (603)433-3338
6/11-11/6 [ECP]              1P: $110-$140        2P: $110-$140
5/11-6/10 & 11/7-4/30 [ECP]  1P: $70-$100         2P: $80-$100
**Small-scale Hotel**   **Location:** I-95, exit 5 at Portsmouth Traffic Circle, 1.5 mi s on US 1. 1390 Lafayette Rd (US 1) 03801.
Fax: 603/431-1639. **Facility:** 121 one-bedroom standard units. 6 stories, interior corridors. **Parking:** on-site.
**Amenities:** irons, hair dryers. **Fee:** video library, video games. **Pool(s):** small heated indoor. **Leisure Activities:** whirlpool, exercise room. **Guest Services:** coin laundry. **Business Services:** conference facilities. **Cards:** AX, CB, DC, DS, JC, MC, VI.

SOME UNITS
(ASK) (S/D) (TI+) (⌐) (≈) (⌐) (DATA PORT) / (X) (VCR) (🗖) (🖭) (🖭) /
FEE

**COURTYARD BY MARRIOTT**     *Book at aaa.com*                    **Phone:** (603)436-2121
All Year                     1P: $179-$209
**Location:** I-95, exit 7. 1000 Market St 03801. Fax: 603/430-7666. **Facility:** 133 units. 129 one-bedroom standard
units. 4 one-bedroom suites ($199-$299). 4 stories, interior corridors. *Bath:* combo or shower only. **Parking:**
**Small-scale Hotel**   on-site. **Terms:** [AP], [BP] & [CP] meal plans available. **Amenities:** dual phone lines, voice mail, irons, hair
dryers. **Pool(s):** heated indoor. **Leisure Activities:** whirlpool, 2 lighted tennis courts, exercise room. **Guest Services:** valet and
coin laundry. **Business Services:** meeting rooms, fax (fee). **Cards:** AX, CB, DC, DS, JC, MC, VI.

SOME UNITS
(ASK) (S/D) (TI) (Y) (⌐) (L/M) (⌐) (⌐) (≈) (X) (⌐) (DATA PORT) / (X) (VCR) (🗖) (🖭) /
FEE

**FAIRFIELD INN BY MARRIOTT-PORTSMOUTH SEACOAST**     *Book at aaa.com*                    **Phone:** (603)436-6363
All Year [ECP]               1P: $89-$149         2P: $89-$149         XP: $10         F17
**Location:** I-95, exit 5; jct US 1 Bypass and Portsmouth Traffic Circle. 650 Borthwick Ave 03801. Fax: 603/436-1621.
**Facility:** 105 one-bedroom standard units. 4 stories, interior corridors. *Bath:* combo or shower only. **Parking:**
**Small-scale Hotel**   on-site. **Amenities:** voice mail, irons. **Fee:** video library, video games. **Pool(s):** outdoor. **Guest Services:**
valet and coin laundry. **Cards:** AX, CB, DC, DS, JC, MC, VI.

SOME UNITS
(ASK) (S/D) (L/M) (⌐) (⌐) (≈) (⌐) (DATA PORT) / (X) /

**THE GOVERNOR'S HOUSE**                        **Phone:** 603/427-5140
Property failed to provide current rates
**Location:** I-95, exit 3, 2 mi e on SR 33, 0.5 mi on US 1 N, then 0.5 mi e. 32 Miller Ave 03801. Fax: 603/427-5145.
**Facility:** The innkeeper's at the Governor's House have thought of everything to from comfort to amenities
**Historic Bed**   to make each visit memorable. Smoke free premises. 4 one-bedroom standard units, some with whirlpools.
**& Breakfast**   3 stories (no elevator), interior corridors. *Bath:* combo or shower only. **Parking:** on-site. **Terms:** no pets allowed (owner's dog on premises). **Amenities:** video library, DVD players, CD players, voice mail, irons, hair dryers. **Leisure Activities:** lighted tennis court, bicycles. **Business Services:** meeting rooms, PC.

(X) (DATA PORT)

**HAMPTON INN-PORTSMOUTH**     *Book at aaa.com*                    **Phone:** (603)431-6111
5/1-10/30 [ECP]              1P: $139-$269        2P: $139-$269        XP: $10         F18
10/31-4/30 [ECP]            1P: $119-$199        2P: $119-$199        XP: $10         F18
**Small-scale Hotel**   **Location:** I-95, exit 7, 1 mi w via Market St and Woodbury Ave to Durgin Ln, then 0.3 mi s. 99 Durgin Ln 03801.
Fax: 603/431-6222. **Facility:** 123 one-bedroom standard units, some with whirlpools. 5 stories, interior corridors. *Bath:* combo or shower only. **Parking:** on-site. **Terms:** 3 day cancellation notice-fee imposed. **Amenities:** dual phone lines, voice mail, irons, hair dryers. **Fee:** video library, video games. **Pool(s):** heated indoor. **Leisure Activities:** whirlpool, exercise room. **Guest Services:** complimentary evening beverages, valet laundry, area transportation. **Business Services:** meeting rooms. **Cards:** AX, CB, DC, DS, JC, MC, VI. *(See color ad p 389)*

SOME UNITS
(ASK) (S/D) (✈) (L/M) (⌐) (⌐) (≈) (⌐) (DATA PORT) (🖭) / (X) (🗖) (🖭) /

**HOLIDAY INN PORTSMOUTH**
**Phone: (603)431-8000**

| | | | |
|---|---|---|---|
| 7/1-8/31 | 1P: $170 | 2P: $170 | XP: $10 F17 |
| 5/1-6/30 & 9/1-10/31 | 1P: $140 | 2P: $140 | XP: $10 F17 |
| 11/1-4/30 | 1P: $89 | 2P: $89 | XP: $10 F17 |

Large-scale Hotel **Location:** I-95, exit 5 at Portsmouth Traffic Circle, jct US 1, (300 Woodbury Ave). Fax: 603/431-2065. **Facility:** 130 one-bedroom standard units. 6 stories, interior corridors. **Parking:** on-site. **Terms:** [MAP] meal plan available. **Amenities:** voice mail, irons, hair dryers. *Fee:* video library, video games. *Some:* dual phone lines. **Pool(s):** heated indoor. **Leisure Activities:** exercise room. **Guest Services:** valet laundry. **Business Services:** meeting rooms. **Cards:** AX, DC, DS, MC, VI.

SOME UNITS
(ASK) (S_D) (Y1) (Y) (≈) (R) (DATA PORT) (D) / (X) (◻) (▤) /

**THE INN AT CHRISTIAN SHORE**
**Phone: 603/431-6770**

| | | |
|---|---|---|
| 6/1-10/31 | | 2P: $100-$120 |
| 5/1-5/31 & 11/1-4/30 | | 2P: $95-$100 |

Historic Bed & Breakfast **Location:** I-95, exit 5 at Portsmouth Traffic Circle; US 1 N, exit Maplewood Ave, then e. 335 Maplewood Ave 03801. Fax: 603/431-7743. **Facility:** Period antiques, art objects and an eclectic mix of Colonial-style furnishings decorate this restored 1800s Federal-style building. Smoke free premises. 5 one-bedroom standard units. 2 stories (no elevator), interior corridors. *Bath:* combo or shower only. **Parking:** on-site. **Terms:** age restrictions may apply, 10 day cancellation notice, weekly rates available. **Cards:** MC, VI.

(X) (☎)

**THE INN AT STRAWBERY BANKE**
**Phone: 603/436-7242**

| | | | |
|---|---|---|---|
| 5/15-10/31 [BP] | 1P: $120-$125 | 2P: $135-$140 | XP: $20 |
| 5/1-5/14 & 11/1-4/30 [BP] | 1P: $85-$90 | 2P: $100-$105 | XP: $20 |

Historic Bed & Breakfast **Location:** Between Pleasant and Washington sts; center. Located in the Strawbery Banke Historic District. 314 Court St 03801. **Facility:** This early-19th-century sea captain's house is a short walk from downtown and the waterfront. Smoke free premises. 7 one-bedroom standard units. 3 stories (no elevator), interior corridors. *Bath:* combo or shower only. **Parking:** on-site. **Terms:** office hours 9 am-9 pm, 2 night minimum stay - weekends 5/15-10/31, age restrictions may apply, 14 day cancellation notice-fee imposed. **Guest Services:** TV in common area. **Cards:** AX, DS, MC, VI.

(X) (W) (☎)

**MARTIN HILL INN**
**Phone: 603/436-2287**

(AAA) (SAVE)

| | | |
|---|---|---|
| 6/16-10/31 [BP] | 1P: $125-$145 | 2P: $125-$145 |
| 5/1-6/15 & 11/1-4/30 [BP] | 1P: $98-$115 | 2P: $98-$115 |

Historic Bed & Breakfast **Location:** I-95 to Portsmouth Traffic Circle, follow signs to Woodbury Ave, 0.3 mi e on Woodbury to Bartlett, e on Bartlett to Islington St, then just n. 404 Islington St 03801. **Facility:** Convenient to downtown, this early-19th-century inn is furnished with antiques and offers colorful perennial gardens in season. Smoke free premises. 7 units. 4 one-bedroom standard units. 3 one-bedroom suites. 2 stories (no elevator), interior corridors. *Bath:* combo or shower only. **Parking:** on-site. **Terms:** office hours 8 am-10 pm, check-in 4 pm, age restrictions may apply, 14 day cancellation notice-fee imposed. **Amenities:** hair dryers. **Cards:** MC, VI. **Special Amenities:** free full breakfast and free local telephone calls.

(X) (W) (☎)

**MEADOWBROOK INN**

Motel

**Phone:** (603)436-2700

| | 6/20-10/30 [ECP] | 1P: $89-$109 | 2P: $99-$129 | XP: $10 | F18 |
| | 5/1-6/19 [ECP] | 1P: $69-$79 | 2P: $79-$89 | XP: $10 | F18 |
| | 10/31-4/30 [ECP] | 1P: $59-$79 | 2P: $69-$89 | XP: $10 | F18 |

**Location:** I-95, exit 5; jct US 1 Bypass and Portsmouth Traffic Circle. 549 US Hwy 1 Bypass 03801. **Fax:** 603/433-2700. **Facility:** 123 one-bedroom standard units. 1-3 stories (no elevator), interior/exterior corridors. **Parking:** on-site. **Terms:** weekly rates available, pets ($50 deposit). **Pool(s):** outdoor. **Guest Services:** coin laundry. **Cards:** AX, DC, DS, MC, VI.

SOME UNITS

**THE PORT INN**

*Book at aaa.com*

Motel

**Phone:** (603)436-4378

| | 6/26-8/31 [CP] | 1P: $139-$159 | 2P: $149-$169 | XP: $6 | F12 |
| | 9/1-10/23 [CP] | 1P: $99-$149 | 2P: $109-$159 | XP: $6 | F12 |
| | 5/1-6/25 [CP] | 1P: $89-$139 | 2P: $99-$149 | XP: $6 | F12 |
| | 10/24-4/30 [CP] | 1P: $79-$99 | 2P: $89-$109 | XP: $6 | F12 |

**Location:** I-95, exit 5; jct US 1 Bypass S and Portsmouth Traffic Circle. 505 US 1 Bypass 03801. Fax: 603/436-4378. **Facility:** 57 units. 54 one-bedroom standard units. 2 one- and 1 two-bedroom suites ($109-$259). 2 stories (no elevator), exterior corridors. **Parking:** on-site. **Amenities:** voice mail. **Pool(s):** heated outdoor. **Guest Services:** valet and coin laundry. **Cards:** AX, CB, DC, DS, MC, VI. **Special Amenities:** free continental breakfast. *(See color ad below)*

SOME UNITS

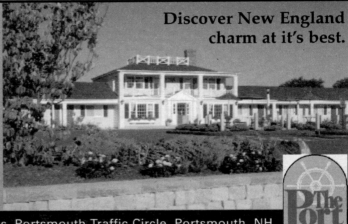

## RESIDENCE INN BY MARRIOTT

*Book at aaa.com*

**Phone:** (603)436-8880

▼◇◇◇▼ Small-scale Hotel

| | |
|---|---|
| 7/4-10/31 | 1P: $229-$289    2P: $229-$289 |
| 5/1-7/3 | 1P: $189-$239    2P: $189-$239 |
| 11/1-1/31 | 1P: $179-$219    2P: $179-$219 |
| 2/1-4/30 | 1P: $159-$219    2P: $159-$219 |

**Location:** SR 4/16, exit 1, just s. 1 International Dr 03801. Fax: 603/422-0888. **Facility:** 90 units. 36 one-bedroom standard units with kitchens. 36 one- and 18 two-bedroom suites, some with kitchens. 3 stories, interior corridors. *Bath:* combo or shower only. **Parking:** on-site. **Terms:** cancellation fee imposed, package plans, pets ($250 fee). **Amenities:** dual phone lines, voice mail, irons, hair dryers. **Pool(s):** heated indoor. **Leisure Activities:** whirlpool, exercise room, sports court. **Guest Services:** complimentary evening beverages: Mon-Thurs, valet and coin laundry. **Business Services:** meeting rooms. **Cards:** AX, DC, DS, MC, VI.

SOME UNITS

ASK S☐ 🐾 ♿M 🛗 📷 🏊 ✕ 🐕 DATA PORT 🔌 📷 💻 / ✕ /
FEE

## SHERATON HARBORSIDE PORTSMOUTH HOTEL & CONFERENCE CENTER    *Book at aaa.com*

**Phone:** (603)431-2300

▼◇◇◇▼ Large-scale Hotel

| | |
|---|---|
| All Year | 1P: $99-$269    2P: $99-$269    XP: $10    F18 |

**Location:** Downtown. 250 Market St 03801. Fax: 603/431-7805. **Facility:** 202 units. 185 one-bedroom standard units. 6 one- and 11 two-bedroom suites with kitchens. 4 stories, interior corridors. **Parking:** on-site. **Terms:** [AP] meal plan available. **Amenities:** dual phone lines, voice mail, honor bars, irons, hair dryers. *Fee:* video library, video games. *Some:* CD players, fax. **Dining:** Harbor's Edge Restaurant, see separate listing. **Pool(s):** heated indoor. **Leisure Activities:** sauna, exercise room. **Guest Services:** valet laundry. **Business Services:** conference facilities, business center. **Cards:** AX, CB, DC, DS, MC, VI. *(See color ad p 5)*

SOME UNITS

ASK S☐ 🍽 🍸 ♿M 📷 🏊 🐕 DATA PORT 💻 / ✕ VCR 🔌 📷 /

## SISE INN    *Book at aaa.com*

**Phone:** (603)433-1200

AAA SAVE
▼◇◇▼ Historic
Small-scale Hotel

| | |
|---|---|
| 5/14-10/30 [ECP] | 1P: $189-$269    2P: $189-$269    XP: $15    F17 |
| 5/1-5/13 & 10/31-4/30 [ECP] | 1P: $129-$199    2P: $129-$199    XP: $15    F17 |

**Location:** At Middle St; downtown. Located in historic district. 40 Court St 03801. Fax: 603/431-0200. **Facility:** Notable for its fine interior woodwork, the inn dates from 1881 and offers attractively decorated guest rooms. 34 units. 25 one-bedroom standard units, some with whirlpools. 9 one-bedroom suites ($159-$269), some with efficiencies and/or whirlpools. 4 stories, interior/exterior corridors. **Parking:** on-site. **Terms:** check-in 4 pm. **Amenities:** irons. **Guest Services:** valet laundry. **Business Services:** meeting rooms. **Cards:** AX, DC, DS, MC, VI. **Special Amenities:** free expanded continental breakfast and free local telephone calls. *(See color ad p 390)*

SOME UNITS

S☐ VCR DATA PORT / ✕ 🔌 📷 💻 /

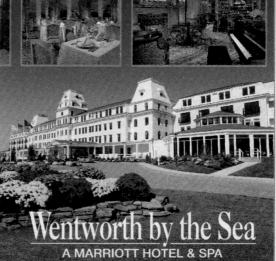

**WREN'S NEST VILLAGE INN**     *Book at aaa.com*                                                      **Phone:** 603/436-2481
▼▼▼     6/25-10/31                    1P: $99-$129          2P: $99-$129          XP: $20                                F
            5/1-6/24                                              2P: $79-$109          XP: $20                                F
            11/1-4/30                                             2P: $69-$109          XP: $20                                F
Small-scale Hotel   **Location:** I-95, exit 5 at Portsmouth Traffic Circle, 4 mi s. 3548 Lafayette Rd (US 1) 03801. Fax: 603/436-6782.
**Facility:** 33 units. 22 one-bedroom standard units, some with efficiencies and/or whirlpools. 7 one-bedroom suites ($169-$259)
with kitchens, some with whirlpools. 4 cottages ($129-$159). 2 stories (no elevator), interior/exterior corridors. **Parking:** on-site.
**Terms:** office hours 7 am-11 pm, 7 day cancellation notice-fee imposed, [ECP] meal plan available. **Amenities:** video library
(fee), voice mail, irons, hair dryers. *Some:* CD players. **Pool(s):** heated indoor. **Leisure Activities:** whirlpool, rental bicycles,
horseshoes, volleyball. **Guest Services:** coin laundry. **Cards:** AX, DS, MC, VI.

SOME UNITS

------- **WHERE TO DINE** -------

**ANTHONY ALBERTO'S RISTORANTE ITALIANO**              **Dinner:** $18-$30              **Phone:** 603/436-4000
▼▼▼     **Location:** Downtown. 59 Penhallow St 03801. **Hours:** 5 pm-9:30 pm, Fri & Sat-10:30 pm. Closed major
            holidays; also Sun. **Reservations:** suggested. **Features:** Dishes are prepared to order and paired nicely
Italian       with popular Italian wines that match them well. Dressy casual; cocktails. **Parking:** street. **Cards:** AX,
            MC, VI.

**BANANAS BAR & GRILL**              **Lunch:** $7-$21              **Dinner:** $7-$21              **Phone:** 603/431-5795
▼▼▼     **Location:** Downtown; adjacent to Parade Mall (east side). 172 Hanover St 03801. **Hours:** 11:15 am-9 pm, Sun 9
            am-9 pm. Closed: 11/25, 12/25; also Mon. **Reservations:** accepted. **Features:** A tropical theme—complete
American   with a glass-enclosed patio, papier-mache giraffes and paintings of birds—dominates the scenery. Two
            popular dishes are the barbecue and boneless buffalo chicken. Couples and college students frequent this
place. Casual dress; cocktails. **Parking:** street. **Cards:** AX, DC, DS, MC, VI.

**BLUE MERMAID WORLD GRILL**              **Lunch:** $7-$14              **Dinner:** $14-$20              **Phone:** 603/427-2583
▼▼     **Location:** Corner of Hanover and High sts; downtown. 409 The Hill 03801. **Hours:** 11:30 am-9 pm, Sat noon-10
            pm, Sun noon-9 pm. Closed major holidays. **Features:** The restaurant's eclectic menu offers Asian,
Seafood   Moroccan, Jamaican and Caribbean cuisine. The dishes are creatively prepared, including calypso
            seasoned hanger steak, plantain encrusted grouper, island rubbed grilled porch chops and much more.
Casual dress; cocktails. **Parking:** on-site. **Cards:** AX, DS, MC, VI.

**CAFE' MEDITTERRANEO**              **Lunch:** $6-$13              **Dinner:** $8-$20              **Phone:** 603/427-5563
▼▼     **Location:** Downtown; just off Market Square. 152 Fleet St 03801. **Hours:** 11:30 am-2:30 & 5-10 pm; closing
            hours may vary. Closed: 11/25, 12/25. **Reservations:** suggested, weekends. **Features:** Well-prepared,
Mediterranean   traditional Mediterranean dishes are on the bistro-style eatery's menu. Among favorites are baked salmon,
            lobster ravioli and tiramisu. Service is friendly, and the European-style decor is casual. A municipal parking
lot is adjacent. Casual dress; cocktails. **Parking:** street. **Cards:** AX, DS, MC, VI.

**CAFE MIRABELLE**              **Dinner:** $14-$27              **Phone:** 603/430-9301
▼▼▼     **Location:** Corner of Hanover and Bridge sts; downtown. 64 Bridge St 03801. **Hours:** 5:15 pm-9 pm. Closed major
            holidays; also Mon & Tues. **Reservations:** suggested. **Features:** American cuisine reflects a distinct
French       French accent. The menu features nicely prepared bouillabaisse, beef Alexander and profiterole. Two
            levels of dining space provide seating for 60 people. The atmosphere is warm, cozy and casually elegant.
Casual dress; cocktails. **Parking:** street. **Cards:** MC, VI.

**CATAQUA PUBLIC HOUSE AT REDHOOK BREWERY**              **Lunch:** $6-$11    **Dinner:** $6-$11    **Phone:** 603/430-8600
▼▼     **Location:** At Pease International Tradeport. 35 Corporate Dr 03801. **Hours:** 11:30 am-9 pm, Sun noon-6 pm.
            Closed: 1/1, 11/25, 12/25. **Features:** Traditional pub fare is on the menu at the popular restaurant attached
American   to Redhook Brewery. In season, patrons can enjoy lunch or dinner in the beer garden or take a tour of the
            brewery. Beer & wine only. **Parking:** on-site. **Cards:** AX, MC, VI.

**COAT OF ARMS**              **Lunch:** $6-$17              **Dinner:** $5-$16              **Phone:** 603/431-0407
▼▼▼     **Location:** Corner of Fleet and Hanover sts; downtown. 174 Fleet St 03801. **Hours:** 4 pm-10 pm, Fri-Sun from
            11:30 am. Closed: 11/25, 12/25. **Reservations:** accepted. **Features:** The lively British-style pub includes
British       fish and chips, beef Wellington, steak and kidney pie, chicken curry, bangers and mash, shepherd's pie
            and a good selection of beers and ales. The bar area has dartboards, snooker tables and live music on
Thursday. Casual dress; cocktails. **Parking:** street. **Cards:** AX, DC, DS, MC, VI.

**CURRENTS BISTRO**              **Lunch:** $6-$14              **Dinner:** $12-$20              **Phone:** 603/427-5427
▼▼▼     **Location:** Between Hanover and Congress/Daniel sts; downtown. 23 Market St 03801. **Hours:** 11 am-3 & 5-9 pm,
            Sat 8 am-3 & 5-9:30 pm, Sun 8 am-2 pm, Mon & Tues 11 am-3 pm. Closed major holidays. **Reservations:** accepted. **Features:** The cozy bistro's owner-chef prepares Mediterranean-inspired dishes
Mediterranean   that exude eclectic flavors. Casual dress; beer & wine only. **Parking:** street. **Cards:** AX, DS, MC, VI.

**DINNERHORN RESTAURANT**              **Lunch:** $5-$10              **Dinner:** $10-$20              **Phone:** 603/436-0717
AAA     **Location:** I-95, exit 5, 1.3 mi s on US 1. 980 Lafayette Rd 03801. **Hours:** 11:30 am-9 pm, Fri & Sat-10 pm.
▼▼     Closed: 11/25, 12/25. **Reservations:** accepted. **Features:** Convenient to businesses south of downtown,
            the casual restaurant displays pleasant contemporary decor. The menu focuses primarily on seafood,
Seafood     including raw bar items, but also includes steak, chicken, pizza and pasta entrees. Smaller portions are
            available at lunch. Cocktails. **Parking:** on-site. **Cards:** AX, DC, DS, MC, VI.

**DOLPHIN STRIKER**  Historic      **Lunch:** $8-$17      **Dinner:** $14-$27      **Phone:** 603/431-5222
Seafood
**Location:** Corner of Bow and Ceres sts; downtown. 15 Bow St 03801. **Hours:** 11:30 am-2 & 5-9 pm, Mon-Wed from 5 pm. Closed: 11/25, 12/25. **Reservations:** accepted. **Features:** In a restored 18th-century waterfront warehouse, the restaurant's lower level contains a spring-fed well that once was used to replenish sailing ships. Representative of New American cuisine are tasty seafood, chicken, pork, beef and pasta dishes. Service is good. Smoking is permitted only in the lounge. Casual dress; cocktails; entertainment. **Parking:** street. **Cards:** AX, DC, DS, MC, VI.

**HARBOR'S EDGE RESTAURANT**      **Lunch:** $8-$16      **Dinner:** $17-$29      **Phone:** 603/559-2626
American
**Location:** Downtown; in Sheraton Harborside Portsmouth Hotel & Conference Center. 250 Market St 03801. **Hours:** 6:30 am-10:30 pm, Sat & Sun from 7 am. **Reservations:** suggested. **Features:** Superb lobster chowder and rack of lamb are two flavorful choices at the pleasant restaurant, which overlooks historic Portsmouth Harbor. The menu also lists a variety of seafood, beef, chicken and pasta entrees, as well as mouthwatering local desserts. Casual dress; cocktails. **Parking:** on-site. **Cards:** AX, DC, DS, MC, VI.

**THE LIBRARY RESTAURANT**      **Lunch:** $9-$13      **Dinner:** $18-$30      **Phone:** 603/431-5202
American
**Location:** State and Chestnut sts; downtown; at the Rockingham House. 401 State St 03801. **Hours:** 11:30 am-3 & 5-9:30 pm, Fri & Sat-10 pm. Closed: 12/25. **Reservations:** suggested. **Features:** The popular restaurant lives up to its name. The warm, cozy decor features bookcases, stone fireplaces and lighting fixtures from 1785. The creative menu lists delicious rack of lamb, salmon with barbecue sauce and eggplant parmigiana. Casual dress; cocktails. **Parking:** street. **Cards:** AX, DC, DS, MC, VI.

**LINBERGH'S CROSSING BISTRO & WINE BAR**      **Dinner:** $16-$26      **Phone:** 603/431-0887
Regional French
**Location:** On the waterfront, just below corner of Bow and Ceres sts; downtown. 29 Ceres St 03801. **Hours:** 5:30 pm-10 pm, Fri & Sat-10:30 pm; to 9:30 pm Sun-Thurs 10/1-4/30. Closed major holidays. **Reservations:** suggested. **Features:** In the historic docks area, the restaurant occupies a 1797 setting. New England influences are evident in country French dishes. Walls and beams reflect the sailing commerce of the 18th century. Casual dress; cocktails. **Parking:** street. **Cards:** AX, DC, MC, VI.

**MARGARITAS**      **Lunch:** $9-$17      **Dinner:** $9-$17      **Phone:** 603/431-5828
Mexican
**Location:** I-95, exit 5 at Portsmouth Traffic Circle, 2 mi s on US 1. 775 Lafayette Rd 03801. **Hours:** 11:30 am-10 pm, Mon-Wed from 4 pm. Closed major holidays. **Features:** Traditional Southwestern preparations are served in a colorful, lively dining room. Casual dress; cocktails. **Parking:** on-site. **Cards:** AX, DS, MC, VI.

**THE METRO, AN AMERICAN BISTRO**      **Lunch:** $8-$12      **Dinner:** $12-$26      **Phone:** 603/436-0521
American
**Location:** Downtown. 20 High St 03801. **Hours:** 11:30 am-2:30 & 5:30-9:30 pm, Fri & Sat-10 pm. Closed: 1/1, 11/25, 12/25; also Sun. **Reservations:** suggested. **Features:** The eatery evokes the mood of a turn-of-the-20th-century art nouveau bistro, with lovely paneling and stained glass. Changing twice a year, the menu features contemporary American compilations of fresh seafood, poultry, beef and veal. Breads and desserts are made on the premises. Selections from the award-winning wine list are designed to complement any meal. Cocktails; entertainment. **Parking:** on-site. **Cards:** AX, DC, MC, VI.

**MOLLY MALONE'S**      **Lunch:** $8-$12      **Dinner:** $12-$26      **Phone:** 603/433-7233
American
**Location:** Corner of State and Penhallow sts; downtown. 177 State St 03801. **Hours:** 11:30 am-9:30 pm, Fri & Sat-10:30 pm, Sun 10:30 am-3:30 & 4-10 pm. Closed: 12/24, 12/25; also Mon except holidays. **Reservations:** suggested. **Features:** In the downtown area, the converted brick home houses an Irish pub on the second floor. The room is charmingly decorated in kelly green and has Irish prints and books on Ireland available at each table and booth. The atmosphere is pleasant and informal. The steakhouse prepares both Irish specialties and American favorites. Casual dress; cocktails. **Parking:** on-site (fee). **Cards:** AX, DS, MC, VI.

**MUDDY RIVER SMOKEHOUSE**      **Lunch:** $6-$20      **Dinner:** $6-$20      **Phone:** 603/430-9582
Barbecue
**Location:** Between Fleet and High sts; downtown. 21 Congress St 03801. **Hours:** 11 am-9 pm, Fri & Sat-10:30 pm. Closed: 11/25, 12/25. **Features:** A fun atmosphere with lively diners, newspaper style menus and delicious barbeque and smokehouse-style cuisine. This restaurant features live music in their Newberry Room Wednesday-Saturday. Casual dress; cocktails. **Parking:** street. **Cards:** AX, MC, VI.

**THE OAR HOUSE RESTAURANT**  Historic      **Lunch:** $7-$13      **Dinner:** $18-$30      **Phone:** 603/436-4025
American
**Location:** Downtown; on waterfront. 55 Ceres St 03801. **Hours:** 11:30 am-3 & 5-9:30 pm, Fri & Sat-10 pm, Sun 11:30 am-9 pm; to 10:30 pm in summer. Closed: 11/25, 12/25; also for dinner 12/24. **Reservations:** suggested. **Features:** Beautifully located on the water in a circa-1800 warehouse, the restaurant displays memorabilia of ships built in Portsmouth. The menu lists seafood casseroles, baked haddock, pan-seared salmon and chocolate raspberry Bavarian cake. Deck seating can be requested in summer. Casual dress; cocktails. **Parking:** on-site. **Cards:** AX, DC, DS, MC, VI.

**OLD FERRY LANDING**      **Lunch:** $7-$20      **Dinner:** $7-$20      **Phone:** 603/431-5510
Seafood
**Location:** Along the waterfront just n of Bow St; downtown. 10 Ceres St 03801. **Hours:** Open 5/1-9/10 & 4/15-4/30; 11:30 am-9 pm. **Features:** Most of the off-the-boat-fresh seafood is fried, but broiled selections also are an option. Casual dress; cocktails. **Parking:** street. **Cards:** AX, DS, MC, VI.

**PESCE BLUE**

Seafood

**Lunch:** $9-$18     **Dinner:** $16-$27     **Phone:** 603/430-7766
**Location:** Corner of Congress St and Vaughan Mall; downtown. 103 Congress St 03801. **Hours:** 11:45 am-2 & 5:30-10 pm, Sat 5:30 pm-10:30 pm, Sun 5:30 pm-10 pm; to 9 pm, Fri & Sat-10 pm 10/15-4/15. Closed major holidays. **Reservations:** suggested. **Features:** A new addition to Portsmouth's restaurant scene, Pesce Blue has a sleek, sophistcated look. The menu which changes seasonally, features contemporary Italian cuisine with an emphasis on the freshest of seafood. Casual dress; cocktails. **Parking:** street. **Cards:** AX, MC, VI.

**THE PORTSMOUTH BREWERY**

American

**Lunch:** $7-$9     **Dinner:** $7-$20     **Phone:** 603/431-1115
**Location:** Downtown. 56 Market St 03801. **Hours:** 11:30 am-11 pm, Fri & Sat-midnight. **Closed:** 11/25, 12/25. **Features:** The downtown restaurant gives diners an occasional glimpse of the brew masters at work. Menu favorites include burgers, sandwiches and fresh fish. Casual dress; cocktails. **Parking:** street. **Cards:** AX, DC, DS, MC, VI.

**PORTSMOUTH GAS LIGHT CO**

American

**Lunch:** $5-$17     **Dinner:** $5-$17     **Phone:** 603/430-9122
**Location:** Center. 64 Market St 03801. **Hours:** 11:30 am-10 pm, Fri & Sat-11 pm. **Closed:** 3/27, 11/25, 12/25. **Features:** In historic downtown, the restaurant is the site of the city's former gaslight utility company. The main dining room is at street level, while the pizza parlor, where pies are made in a wood-fired brick oven, is downstairs. Outdoor seating can be requested in the summer months, with live entertainment Thursday through Saturday. The menu lists sandwiches and burgers, as well as pasta, chicken, seafood and steak. While no reservations are accepted, a call-ahead program is offered. Casual dress; cocktails. **Parking:** street. **Cards:** AX, DS, MC, VI.

**THE ROSA RESTAURANT**

Italian

**Lunch:** $6-$12     **Dinner:** $9-$20     **Phone:** 603/436-9715
**Location:** Downtown; 1 blk from old bridge to Kittery; adjacent to Strawbery Banke Historic District. 80 State St 03801. **Hours:** 11:30 am-9:30 pm, Fri & Sat-10:30 pm, Sun 2 pm-9:30 pm. **Closed:** 11/25, 12/25. **Reservations:** suggested. **Features:** At the edge of Strawbery Banke, the popular restaurant has served guests since 1927. The pleasant, informal setting invites guests to relax over a plate of fresh seafood and grilled chicken pizza. Chocolate desserts are mouthwatering. Each room has a different feel. Casual dress; cocktails. **Parking:** on-site (fee) and street. **Cards:** AX, CB, DC, DS, MC, VI.

**SAKE JAPANESE RESTAURANT**

Japanese

**Lunch:** $7-$19     **Dinner:** $10-$27     **Phone:** 603/431-1822
**Location:** Between Maplewood Ave and Fleet St; downtown. 141 Congress St 03801. **Hours:** 11:30 am-10 pm, Fri & Sat-11 pm, Sun 12:30 pm-10 pm. Closed major holidays. **Features:** Traditional decor fills the restaurant, which offers Japanese cuisine and a full sushi bar. Casual dress; cocktails. **Parking:** on-site. **Cards:** AX, MC, VI.

**STOCKPOT**

American

**Lunch:** $5-$12     **Dinner:** $8-$20     **Phone:** 603/431-1851
**Location:** Downtown. 53 Bow St 03801. **Hours:** 11 am-10:30 pm; to 11:30 pm in summer. **Closed:** 11/25, 12/25. **Features:** Lovely views of the Piscataqua River and Portsmouth Seaport distinguish the casual restaurant. The tavern is at street level, and the dining room is a level below. The menu—which includes seafood, steak, salads, sandwiches and burgers—change seasonally. Seating on the deck is an option during the summer season. Cocktails. **Parking:** street. **Cards:** AX, DC, DS, MC, VI.

**TAIPEI & TOKYO CHINESE & JAPANESE RESTAURANT**

Chinese

**Lunch:** $6-$14     **Dinner:** $8-$17     **Phone:** 603/431-3668
**Location:** I-95, exit 7, 1.5 mi w at Marshall Mall. 1465 Woodbury Ave 03801. **Hours:** 11:30 am-10 pm, Fri & Sat-11 pm, Sun 12:30 pm-10 pm. Closed major holidays. **Features:** The sushi bar lines up an extensive selection, as does the regular menu. The restaurant is in Marshall Mall. Casual dress; cocktails. **Parking:** on-site. **Cards:** AX, MC, VI.

**THAI PARADISE**

Thai

**Lunch:** $7-$13     **Dinner:** $10-$18     **Phone:** 603/431-9193
**Location:** Corner of Hanover St; downtown. 96 Bridge St 03801. **Hours:** 11:30 am-2 & 5-9:30 pm. Closed major holidays; also Mon. **Features:** Tasty Thai cuisine is prepared to order. The atmosphere is cozy and the decor eclectic. Casual dress; beer & wine only. **Parking:** street. **Cards:** AX, MC, VI.

**THE WELLINGTON ROOM**

Italian

**Dinner:** $14-$23     **Phone:** 603/431-2989
**Location:** Downtown; overlooking the river. 67 Bow St 03801. **Hours:** 5:30 pm-9:30 pm. **Closed:** 1/1, 11/25, 12/24, 12/25; also Mon & Tues. **Reservations:** suggested. **Features:** The small, intimate dining room affords a great river view. Traditional Southern Italian cuisine uses authentic recipes, superb preparation methods and attractive presentations. The serving staff is pleasant and knowledgeable. Casual dress; cocktails. **Parking:** street. **Cards:** AX, MC, VI.

**YOKEN'S 'THAR SHE BLOWS'**

Seafood

**Lunch:** $5-$17     **Dinner:** $9-$17     **Phone:** 603/436-8224
**Location:** I-95, exit 5, 2.5 mi s of Portsmouth Traffic Circle on US 1. 1390 Lafayette Rd 03801. **Hours:** 11 am-8 pm, Sat-9 pm; to 9 pm 7/1-9/3. **Closed:** 11/25, 12/25. **Features:** A distinctive whale sign has helped make the relaxed restaurant a local landmark since its 1947 opening. Contributing to the rustic decor are wood-planked walls, nautical appointments and large, saltwater aquariums. Basic, reasonably priced seafood is prepared a variety of ways. Families and senior citizens are a big part of the clientele. Casual dress; cocktails. **Parking:** on-site. **Cards:** AX, DS, MC, VI.

---

**The following restaurants have not been evaluated by AAA but are listed for your information only.**

---

**43 NORTH**

[fyi]

Phone: 603/430-0225

Not evaluated. **Location:** 75 Pleasant St 03801. **Features:** This popular bistro is located in downtown Portsmouth.

**CAFE BRIOCHE**

[fyi]

Phone: 603/430-9225

Not evaluated. **Location:** Center of downtown. 14 Market Square 03801. **Features:** A favorite eatery located in the center of downtown Portsmouth. Nearly everything is homemade and includes: pastries, cakes, cookies. Also serves sandwiches, soups, and salads.

**CHESTNUTS AT THE NEST**

[fyi]

Phone: 603/373-6515

Not evaluated. **Location:** I-95, exit 5 at Portsmouth Traffic Circle, 4 mi s on US 1. 3548 Lafayette Rd 03801. **Features:** The intimate setting is nestled behind the Wren's Nest. The chef presents a creative menu.

**FRIENDLY TOAST**

[fyi]

Phone: 603/430-2154

Not evaluated. **Location:** 121 Congress St 03801. **Features:** Open 24 hours on weekends and regular hours on weekdays, the restaurant tempts customers with such breakfast favorites as Almond Joy pancakes and green eggs and ham.

**GILLEY'S**

[fyi]

Phone: 603/431-6343

Not evaluated. **Location:** 175 Fleet St 03801. **Features:** Since 1912, the hamburger and hot dog joint has offered animated counter service and good food. Seating is limited to 10 people.

**KING TIKI**

[fyi]

Phone: 603/430-5227

Not evaluated. **Location:** 2 Bow St 03801. **Features:** The restaurant shows a Polynesian flair in both the dining room, which is accented with Hawaiian art, and on the menu of Caribbean cuisine.

**PADDY'S AN AMERICAN GRILLE**

[fyi]

Phone: 603/430-9450

Not evaluated. **Location:** SR 4/16, exit 1, just s. 27 International Dr 03801. **Features:** On what was the former Pease Air Force Base campus, the popular restaurant resides amid many thriving businesses.

# ROCHESTER pop. 28,461

--------- **WHERE TO STAY** ---------

**ANCHORAGE INN**

[AAA] [SAVE]
▽▽ ▽▽
Motel

Phone: (603)332-3350

| | | | |
|---|---|---|---|
| 7/1-10/31 [CP] | 1P: $79-$129 | 2P: $79-$129 | XP: $10    F16 |
| 5/1-6/30 [CP] | 1P: $59-$119 | 2P: $59-$119 | XP: $10    F16 |
| 11/1-4/30 [CP] | 1P: $49-$99 | 2P: $49-$99 | XP: $10    F16 |

**Location:** Jct Spaulding Tpke and SR 125, exit 12. 13 Wadleigh Rd 03867 (80 Main, 03839). Fax: 603/332-3350. **Facility:** 31 one-bedroom standard units. 1 story, exterior corridors. *Bath:* combo or shower only. **Parking:** on-site. **Terms:** office hours 7 am-10 pm, cancellation fee imposed, pets ($10 extra charge). **Pool(s):** outdoor. **Leisure Activities:** picnic area with grills, horseshoes. **Cards:** AX, DC, DS, MC, VI. **Special Amenities: free continental breakfast and free local telephone calls.**

SOME UNITS

[S/D] [🛏] [🛎] [📺] [🔌] / [✕] [🖼] /
FEE

**THE GOVERNOR'S INN**

▽▽▽▽
Historic
Country Inn

Phone: (603)332-0107

| | | | |
|---|---|---|---|
| 5/1-10/31 [CP] | 1P: $88-$158 | 2P: $88-$158 | XP: $15    F12 |
| 11/1-4/30 [CP] | 1P: $88-$138 | 2P: $88-$138 | XP: $15    F12 |

**Location:** On SR 125 and 108, just n of monument; center. 78 Wakefield St 03867. Fax: 603/335-1984. **Facility:** A Georgian Colonial built in 1920, the inn features fine woodwork, marble fireplaces and attractive grounds. Smoke free premises. 19 units. 17 one-bedroom standard units. 2 one-bedroom suites with efficiencies. 3 stories (no elevator), interior corridors. *Bath:* combo or shower only. **Parking:** on-site. **Terms:** office hours 7 am-midnight, 14 day cancellation notice, on weekends-fee imposed. **Amenities:** voice mail, irons, hair dryers. **Dining:** dining room, see separate listing. **Business Services:** conference facilities. **Cards:** AX, DS, MC, VI.

SOME UNITS

[ASK] [🍽] [Y] [✕] [DATA PORT] / [VCR] [🔌] [🖼] [💲] /

--------- **WHERE TO DINE** ---------

**GOVERNOR'S INN DINING ROOM**   Historic

▽▽▽
American

**Dinner:** $15-$24          Phone: 603/332-0107

**Location:** On SR 125 and 108, just n of monument; center; in The Governor's Inn. 78 Wakefield St 03867. **Hours:** 5 pm-9 pm. Closed major holidays; also Mon. **Reservations:** suggested. **Features:** Diners appreciate a pleasant dining experience in the traditional New England country inn. The menu features regional cuisine, with an emphasis on seafood. Lighter fare is available at lunch. Courtyard seating is an option from May through October. Dressy casual; cocktails. **Parking:** on-site. **Cards:** AX, DS, MC, VI.

[Y] [✕]

---

**The following restaurant has not been evaluated by AAA but is listed for your information only.**

---

**SLIM'S TEX-MEX**

[fyi]

Phone: 603/332-0107

Not evaluated. **Location:** 45 N Main St 03867. **Features:** Traditional dishes are served in a lively setting. Guests can enjoy entertainment on the weekends.

# RUMNEY pop. 1,480

## ——— WHERE TO DINE ———

**STEVE'S RESTAURANT**
American
**Lunch:** $5-$19   **Dinner:** $5-$19   **Phone:** 603/786-9788
**Location:** Just e of SR 25. 27 Main St 03266. **Hours:** 11 am-9 pm, Fri & Sat-9:30 pm, Sun 10 am-8 pm. Closed: 1/1, 11/25, 12/25; also Mon. **Features:** The good family restaurant prepares many house specialties, such as seafood tortellini Alfredo, chicken cordon bleu, buffalo chicken salad and burgers. Casual dress; cocktails. **Parking:** on-site. **Cards:** DS, MC, VI.

# RYE

## ——— WHERE TO STAY ———

*——— The following lodgings were either not evaluated or did not ———*
*meet AAA rating requirements but are listed for your information only.*

**ATLANTIC FOUR WINDS COTTAGES**
[fyi]
**Phone:** 603/436-5140
Not evaluated. **Location:** On US 1A. 1215 Ocean Blvd 03870. Facilities, services, and decor characterize a basic property.

**CROWN COLONY COTTAGES**
[fyi]
**Phone:** 603/436-8923
Not evaluated. **Location:** On US 1A. 1381 Ocean Blvd 03870. Facilities, services, and decor characterize a basic property.

**HOYT'S LODGES...COTTAGES BY THE SEA**
[fyi]
**Phone:** 603/436-5350
Not evaluated. **Location:** On US 1A. 891 Ocean Blvd 03870. Facilities, services, and decor characterize a basic property.

**PEBBLE COVE MOTEL**
[fyi]
**Phone:** 603/436-8108
Not evaluated. **Location:** On US 1A. 741 Ocean Blvd 03870. Facilities, services, and decor characterize a basic property.

## ——— WHERE TO DINE ———

**THE CARRIAGE HOUSE**
American
**Dinner:** $14-$27   **Phone:** 603/964-8251
**Location:** Jct US 1A and SR 11, 2.4 mi n on US 1A. 2263 Ocean Blvd 03870. **Hours:** 5 pm-9 pm, Fri & Sat-10 pm; hours may vary in summer. Closed major holidays; also 12/24. **Reservations:** suggested. **Features:** Representative of the close-to-the-beach restaurant's Mediterranean cuisine are excellent seafood and veal specialties. Meals, including heart-healthy entrees, are nicely prepared and served in generous portions. Cocktails. **Parking:** on-site. **Cards:** AX, MC, VI.

**PETEY'S SUMMERTIME SEAFOOD & BAR**
Seafood
**Lunch:** $6-$21   **Dinner:** $6-$21   **Phone:** 603/433-1937
**Location:** On US 1A. 1323 Ocean Blvd 03870. **Hours:** Open 5/1-11/15 & 3/20-4/30; 11:30 am-10 pm. Closed: Mon. **Features:** The super-casual spot prepares super-good seafood. Homemade chowders are made daily. Steamed lobster and fried clams are among dishes worth the wait. Casual dress; cocktails. **Parking:** on-site. **Cards:** AX, MC, VI.

**SAUNDERS AT RYE HARBOR**
Seafood
**Lunch:** $8-$21   **Dinner:** $8-$21   **Phone:** 603/964-6466
**Location:** At Rye Harbor; just off of US 1A. Rye Harbor 03870. **Hours:** noon-9 pm, Sun-8 pm. Closed: 12/24, 12/25. **Features:** On the harbor, the restaurant affords views of the marina and the water life. The award-winning seafood chowder alone is worth the trip. Casual dress; cocktails. **Parking:** on-site. **Cards:** AX, DS, MC, VI.

*——— The following restaurant has not been evaluated by AAA ———*
*but is listed for your information only.*

**POCKET FULL OF RYE CAFE**
[fyi]
**Phone:** 603/436-5453
Not evaluated. **Location:** 25 Sagamore Rd 03870. **Features:** This casual deli offers homemade soups and breads.

# SALEM

## ——— WHERE TO STAY ———

**FAIRFIELD INN BY MARRIOTT-SALEM**   *Book at aaa.com*
Motel
All Year [ECP]   1P: $59-$109   2P: $59-$109   XP: $10   F17
**Phone:** (603)893-4722
**Location:** I-93, exit 2, just sw. Located in a quiet area. 8 Keewaydin Dr 03079. Fax: 603/893-2898. **Facility:** 105 one-bedroom standard units. 4 stories, interior corridors. *Bath:* combo or shower only. **Parking:** on-site. **Amenities:** voice mail, irons. *Fee:* video library, video games. **Pool(s):** outdoor. **Guest Services:** valet and coin laundry. **Cards:** AX, CB, DC, DS, JC, MC, VI.

SOME UNITS

FEE

**HOLIDAY INN-SALEM NEW HAMPSHIRE**   *Book at aaa.com*         **Phone:** (603)893-5511

| | | |
|---|---|---|
| 6/20-10/12 | 1P: $95-$159 | XP: $10   F |
| 5/1-6/19 | 1P: $83-$139 | XP: $10   F |
| 10/13-12/31 | 1P: $74-$134 | XP: $10   F |
| 1/1-4/30 | 1P: $77-$129 | XP: $10   F |

Small-scale Hotel

**Location:** I-93, exit 2, just sw. 1 Keewaydin Dr 03079. Fax: 603/894-6728. **Facility:** 85 units. 84 one-bedroom standard units. 1 one-bedroom suite ($153-$279) with whirlpool. 6 stories, interior corridors. *Bath:* combo or shower only. **Parking:** on-site. **Terms:** cancellation fee imposed. **Amenities:** video games (fee), voice mail, irons, hair dryers. **Pool(s):** outdoor. **Leisure Activities:** exercise room. **Guest Services:** valet laundry. **Business Services:** meeting rooms. **Cards:** AX, CB, DC, DS, MC, VI.

SOME UNITS

**PARK VIEW INN**                         **Phone:** (603)898-5632

Motel

All Year       1P: $59-$83       2P: $59-$83

**Location:** I-93, exit 1, 1 mi e, then just n on SR 28. 109 S Broadway 03079. Fax: 603/894-6579. **Facility:** 58 one-bedroom standard units, some with efficiencies. 1 story, exterior corridors. **Terms:** weekly rates available, [CP] meal plan available. **Amenities:** voice mail, hair dryers. **Guest Services:** coin laundry. **Cards:** AX, CB, DC, DS, JC, MC, VI.

SOME UNITS

**RED ROOF INN**   *Book at aaa.com*            **Phone:** (603)898-6422

| | | |
|---|---|---|
| 6/25-9/4 | 1P: $72 | 2P: $72 |
| 5/1-6/24 | 1P: $61 | 2P: $61 |
| 9/5-10/23 | 1P: $55 | 2P: $55 |
| 10/24-4/30 | 1P: $51 | 2P: $51 |

Motel

**Location:** I-93, exit 2, just se. 15 Red Roof Ln 03079. Fax: 603/898-6497. **Facility:** 108 one-bedroom standard units. 2 stories (no elevator), exterior corridors. **Parking:** on-site. **Terms:** small pets only. **Amenities:** voice mail. *Fee:* video library, video games. **Guest Services:** coin laundry. **Cards:** AX, CB, DC, DS, MC, VI. **Special Amenities:** free local telephone calls and free newspaper.

SOME UNITS

------- **WHERE TO DINE** -------

**THE COLOSSEUM**       **Lunch:** $7-$13       **Dinner:** $8-$25       **Phone:** 603/898-1190

Italian

**Location:** I-93, exit 1, 1 mi w to SR 28, then 2.3 mi n on SR 28; in Breckenridge Mall. 264 N Broadway 03079. **Hours:** 11:30 am-3 & 4-9:45 pm, Fri-10:45 pm, Sat noon-10:45 pm, Sun noon-9:45 pm. Closed major holidays; also Mon. **Reservations:** accepted. **Features:** The family-owned and operated eatery serves homemade traditional delights. The casual atmosphere is welcoming to families and friends. Casual dress; cocktails. **Parking:** on-site. **Cards:** AX, MC, VI.

**LINDY'S GOURMET DELI**            **Lunch:** $5-$7       **Phone:** 603/890-1133

Deli/Subs
Sandwiches

**Location:** Jct SR 111 and 28. 1 Range Rd #2 03079. **Hours:** 10 am-3 pm. Closed major holidays; also Sun. **Features:** Made-to-order delicatessen sandwiches are created on the spot. Sandwiches are named after movie stars. Casual dress. **Parking:** on-site. **Cards:** MC, VI.

**LOAFER'S AMERICAN RESTAURANT**       **Lunch:** $6-$13       **Dinner:** $15-$26       **Phone:** 603/890-6363

American

**Location:** I-93, exit 2, just e. 43 Pelham Rd 03079. **Hours:** 11:30 am-2:30 & 5-9 pm, Fri & Sat from 5 pm. Closed: 12/25; also Sun. **Reservations:** suggested. **Features:** Located off the interstate and features a whimsical decor of dog and puppy motifs. Their menu offers a varied selection of American cuisine that is sure to appeal to everyone. Dressy casual; cocktails. **Parking:** on-site. **Cards:** AX, DS, MC, VI.

**T-BONES GREAT AMERICAN EATERY**       **Lunch:** $5-$12       **Dinner:** $10-$16       **Phone:** 603/893-3444

American

**Location:** 1 mi s of Rockingham Pk on US 28. 311 S Broadway 03079. **Hours:** 11:30 am-10 pm, Fri & Sat-11 pm. Closed: 11/25, 12/25. **Features:** One of three locations, the local eatery prepares burgers, steaks, sandwiches and more. All menu items are made from scratch on the premises. Casual dress; cocktails. **Parking:** on-site. **Cards:** MC, VI.

**WEATHERVANE**       **Lunch:** $6-$10       **Dinner:** $7-$16       **Phone:** 603/893-6269

Seafood

**Location:** I-93, exit 1, 1 mi n on SR 28. 41 S Broadway 03079. **Hours:** 11 am-9 pm. Closed: 11/25, 12/25. **Features:** The simple, casual family restaurant prepares a wide variety of seafood, chicken, steak, burgers, pasta and chowder. Portions are ample, and the service is pleasant. Casual dress; cocktails. **Parking:** on-site. **Cards:** AX, MC, VI.

------- *The following restaurant has not been evaluated by AAA* -------
*but is listed for your information only.*

**CHATILA'S BAKERY**                         **Phone:** 603/898-5459

[fyi]

Not evaluated. **Location:** In Breckenridge Plaza. 254 N Broadway 03079. **Features:** The bakery is dedicated to preparing low-fat and sugar-free pastries, muffins, cheesecake and more.

# SEABROOK

### ——— WHERE TO STAY ———

**BEST WESTERN SEABROOK INN** *Book at aaa.com*       **Phone:** (603)474-3078

| | | | |
|---|---|---|---|
| (AAA) (SAVE) | 6/11-10/31 [ECP] | 1P: $84-$94 | 2P: $84-$94 | XP: $6 | F12 |
| ▼▼▼▼ | 5/1-6/10 & 11/1-4/30 [ECP] | 1P: $59-$69 | 2P: $59-$69 | XP: $6 | F12 |

Motel     **Location:** I-95, exit 1, just w on SR 107. 9 Stard Rd 03874 (PO Box 1209). Fax: 603/474-9055. **Facility:** 192 one-bedroom standard units. 2 stories (no elevator), exterior corridors. *Bath:* combo or shower only. **Parking:** on-site. **Terms:** check-in 4 pm, package plans - seasonal. **Pool(s):** heated outdoor. **Leisure Activities:** waterslide, playground. **Guest Services:** coin laundry. **Cards:** AX, CB, DC, DS, MC, VI.
**Special Amenities:** free expanded continental breakfast and free newspaper. *(See color ad p 388)*

SOME UNITS
(S)(D) (T+) (≋) (🖬) (DATA PORT) / (X) (🖬) /

**HAMPSHIRE INN**       **Phone:** (603)474-5700

| | | | |
|---|---|---|---|
| (AAA) (SAVE) | 6/1-10/31 [ECP] | 1P: $103-$163 | 2P: $103-$163 | XP: $10 | F5 |
| ▼▼▼▼ | 5/1-5/31 & 4/1-4/30 [ECP] | 1P: $93-$143 | 2P: $93-$143 | XP: $10 | F5 |
| Motel | 11/1-3/31 [ECP] | 1P: $83-$133 | 2P: $83-$133 | XP: $10 | F5 |

**Location:** I-95, exit 1 on SR 107. 20 Spur Rd 03874 (PO Box 2480). Fax: 603/474-2886. **Facility:** 35 units. 23 one-bedroom standard units, some with whirlpools. 12 one-bedroom suites. 3 stories, interior corridors. *Bath:* combo or shower only. **Parking:** on-site. **Terms:** 2 night minimum stay - 6/1-10/31, package plans - seasonal. **Pool(s):** heated indoor. **Leisure Activities:** whirlpool, exercise room. **Guest Services:** valet and coin laundry. **Business Services:** meeting rooms. **Cards:** AX, CB, DC, MC, VI. *(See color ad p 389)*

SOME UNITS
(S)(D) (🗗) (≋) (🖬) (DATA PORT) (🖬) (🖃) / (X) (VCR) /
FEE

# SNOWVILLE

### ——— WHERE TO STAY ———

**SNOWVILLAGE INN**       **Phone:** 603/447-2818

| | | | |
|---|---|---|---|
| ▼▼▼ | All Year | 1P: $99-$214 | 2P: $129-$249 | XP: $25 | D12 |

Country Inn    **Location:** Jct SR 16, 5 mi s on SR 153, turn at Crystal Lake, then 1.5 mi s, follow signs. Located in a quiet, secluded area. 146 Stewart Rd 03832 (PO Box 68). Fax: 603/447-5268. **Facility:** Set in a tranquil area of scenic mountain views, this inn has rooms of varying size with decor ranging from turn-of-the-century to modern. Smoke free premises. 18 one-bedroom standard units. 2 stories (no elevator), interior/exterior corridors. *Bath:* combo or shower only. **Parking:** on-site. **Terms:** office hours 9 am-9 pm, 2 night minimum stay - weekends, age restrictions may apply, 14 day cancellation notice-fee imposed, [BP] & [MAP] meal plans available, package plans - weekends, 5% service charge, no pets allowed (owner's pet on premises). **Leisure Activities:** sauna, fishing, cross country skiing, hiking trails. **Cards:** AX, DC, DS, MC, VI.

SOME UNITS
(ASK) (TI) (X) (X) (📺) / (🍴) /

# SUGAR HILL

### ——— WHERE TO STAY ———

**THE HILLTOP INN**       **Phone:** 603/823-5695

| | | | |
|---|---|---|---|
| ▼▼▼ | 9/24-10/12 [BP] | 1P: $115-$185 | 2P: $125-$195 | XP: $50 | |
| | 5/1-9/23 & 10/13-4/30 [BP] | 1P: $80-$110 | 2P: $90-$120 | XP: $35 | |

Historic Bed & Breakfast    **Location:** I-93, exit 38, 0.5 mi n on SR 18, then 2.8 mi w on SR 117. 1348 Main St 03585. Fax: 603/823-5518. **Facility:** This attractive turn-of-the-20th-century home is in the village center and features cable television in the common area. Smoke free premises. 6 units. 5 one-bedroom standard units. 1 one-bedroom suite. 2 stories (no elevator), interior corridors. **Parking:** on-site. **Terms:** 2 night minimum stay - seasonal & weekends, 8 day cancellation notice-fee imposed, pets ($10 extra charge, dogs only). **Leisure Activities:** cross country skiing, hiking trails. **Business Services:** meeting rooms, fax (fee). **Cards:** MC, VI.

SOME UNITS
(🐾) (X) (🍴) (📺) / (🖬) /
FEE

**SUGAR HILL INN**       **Phone:** 603/823-5621

| | | | |
|---|---|---|---|
| ▼▼▼ | 9/18-10/19 [MAP] | | 2P: $255-$380 | XP: $75 | |
| | 5/1-9/17 & 10/20-3/31 [BP] | 1P: $100-$225 | 2P: $100-$225 | XP: $35 | |

Historic Country Inn    **Location:** I-93, exit 38, 0.5 mi n on SR 18, then 0.4 mi w. Located in a quiet area. 116 SR 117 03585 (PO Box 954, FRANCONIA, 03580). Fax: 603/823-5639. **Facility:** Converted to an inn in 1929, this property originated as a farmhouse in 1789; in a country setting, it includes both guest rooms and cottages. Smoke free premises. 16 units. 10 one-bedroom standard units, some with whirlpools. 6 cottages. 1-2 stories (no elevator), interior/exterior corridors. *Bath:* combo or shower only. **Parking:** on-site. **Terms:** open 5/1-3/31, 2 night minimum stay - weekends, cancellation fee imposed. **Amenities:** hair dryers. **Leisure Activities:** Fee: massage. **Cards:** AX, MC, VI.

SOME UNITS
(TI) (Y) (X) (🗗) / (🍴) (📺) (🖃) /

**SUNSET HILL HOUSE - A GRAND INN** *Book at aaa.com*       **Phone:** (603)823-5522

| | | | |
|---|---|---|---|
| ▼▼▼ | 9/16-10/20 [BP] | 1P: $100-$495 | 2P: $100-$495 | XP: $30 | F3 |
| | 5/1-9/15 & 10/21-4/30 [BP] | 1P: $100-$395 | 2P: $100-$395 | XP: $30 | F3 |

Historic Country Inn    **Location:** I-93, exit 38, 0.5 mi n on SR 18, 2.2 mi w on SR 117, then 0.5 mi s. 231 Sunset Hill Rd 03585. Fax: 603/823-5738. **Facility:** Perched on a 1,700-foot-high ridge, this turn-of-the-20th-century inn is elegantly and comfortably restored and offers commanding mountain views. Smoke free premises. 28 units. 26 one-bedroom standard units, some with whirlpools. 2 one-bedroom suites ($295-$595) with whirlpools. 3 stories (no elevator), interior corridors. *Bath:* combo or shower only. **Parking:** on-site. **Terms:** 14 day cancellation notice-fee imposed, [MAP] meal plan available, package plans - seasonal. **Dining:** restaurant, see separate listing. **Pool(s):** heated outdoor. **Leisure Activities:** cross country skiing, recreation programs, hiking trails. *Fee:* golf-9 holes. **Business Services:** meeting rooms, fax. **Cards:** AX, DS, MC, VI.

SOME UNITS
(TI) (⛷) (≋) (X) (X) / (📺) (DATA PORT) (🖬) (🖃) /

## ———— WHERE TO DINE ————

**POLLY'S PANCAKE PARLOUR**
*American*
MC, VI.

**Lunch:** $5-$15      **Phone:** 603/823-5575
**Location:** I-93, exit 38, 0.5 mi n on SR 18, then 1.4 mi w. 672 Rt 117 03585. **Hours:** Open 5/15-10/15; 7 am-2 pm, Sat & Sun-3 pm. **Features:** Patrons come from far and near to feast upon the family's own pancake recipe that they have been grilling up for generations. The eatery, set on a working maple sugar farm, the rustic charm, even lures the occasional moose to stop by. Casual dress. **Parking:** on-site. **Cards:** AX, DS,

---

**SUNSET HILL HOUSE RESTAURANT**   Country Inn
*Continental*

**Dinner:** $21-$35      **Phone:** 603/823-5522
**Location:** I-93, exit 38, 0.5 mi n on SR 18, 2.2 mi w on SR 117, then 0.5 mi s; in Sunset Hill House-A Grand Inn. 231 Sunset Hill Rd 03585. **Hours:** 5:30 pm-9 pm. Closed: Mon-Wed 11/1-5/1, except holiday periods. **Reservations:** required. **Features:** You'll appreciate the views of gorgeous mountains and dramatic sunsets from this elegant restaurant's huge picture windows. The seasonal menu highlights innovative preparation including house-smoked fish, herbed lamb, and grilled seafood soup. Casual dress; cocktails. **Parking:** on-site. **Cards:** AX, DS, MC, VI.

# SUNAPEE

## ———— WHERE TO STAY ————

**DEXTER'S INN**
*Historic Bed & Breakfast*

All Year [BP]    1P: $100-$150    2P: $125-$175    XP: $25    D18
**Phone:** (603)763-5571
**Location:** Jct SR 103B and 11, 0.4 mi w on SR 11, 1.75 mi s (Winn Hill Rd). Located in a quiet area. 258 Stagecoach Rd 03782 (PO Box 703). **Facility:** A main inn and a converted barn annex both offer accommodations at this inn set on sprawling grounds in a scenic area. Smoke free premises. 19 units. 17 one-bedroom standard units. 1 two-bedroom suite ($200-$300). 1 cottage ($300-$400). 2 stories (no elevator), interior/exterior corridors. *Bath:* combo or shower only. **Parking:** on-site. **Terms:** office hours 8 am-10 pm, 14 day cancellation notice-fee imposed, pets ($10 extra charge, in limited units). **Amenities:** hair dryers. **Pool(s):** outdoor. **Leisure Activities:** 3 tennis courts, horseshoes, shuffleboard, volleyball, game room. **Guest Services:** TV in common area. **Business Services:** meeting rooms. **Cards:** AX, DS, MC, VI.

# SWANZEY

## ———— WHERE TO STAY ————

**THE BRIDGES INN AT WHITCOMB HOUSE**
*Historic Bed & Breakfast*

All Year [BP]    1P: $95-$125    2P: $95-$125    XP: $20    F12
**Phone:** 603/357-6624
**Location:** 4 mi s of Keene on SR 10, then 0.5 mi e through the single lane covered bridge. 27 Main St 03446. Fax: 530/389-8810. **Facility:** New owners now welcome guests to this historic B&B, dating back two centuries. Charlotte creates a wonderful breakfast each morning and sends each guest home with one of her homemade tea breads. Smoke free premises. 6 one-bedroom standard units. 3 stories (no elevator), interior corridors. *Bath:* combo or shower only. **Parking:** on-site. **Terms:** office hours 7 am-10 pm, 2 night minimum stay - seasonal, 7 day cancellation notice-fee imposed, weekly rates available, package plans - Sun-Thurs, no pets allowed (owner's pet on premises). **Guest Services:** TV in common area, gift shop. **Cards:** MC, VI.

# TAMWORTH

## ———— WHERE TO STAY ————

**TAMWORTH INN**
*Historic Country Inn*

| | | | | |
|---|---|---|---|---|
| 9/1-10/31 [BP] | 1P: $105-$260 | 2P: $115-$280 | XP: $50 | F3 |
| 5/1-6/30 & 11/1-4/1 [BP] | 1P: $105-$240 | 2P: $115-$250 | XP: $35 | F3 |
| 7/1-8/31 [BP] | 1P: $115-$235 | 2P: $125-$235 | XP: $50 | F3 |

**Phone:** 603/323-7721
**Location:** Jct SR 16 and 113, 3 mi w on SR 113; center. 15 Cleveland Hill Rd 03886. **Facility:** Dating from 1830, the inn is set in a historic village and many of its guest rooms feature fireplaces. Designated smoking area. 16 units. 12 one- and 1 two-bedroom standard units. 3 one-bedroom suites, some with whirlpools. 3 stories (no elevator), interior corridors. *Bath:* combo or shower only. **Parking:** on-site. **Terms:** open 5/1-4/1, office hours 9 am-8 pm, 2 night minimum stay - in summer, cancellation fee imposed, package plans - seasonal, pets ($10 extra charge, dogs only, owner's pet on premises). **Amenities:** video library. *Some:* CD players. **Dining:** restaurant, see separate listing. **Pool(s):** heated outdoor. **Leisure Activities:** fishing, cross country skiing, hiking trails. **Guest Services:** TV in common area. **Business Services:** meeting rooms. **Cards:** AX, MC, VI.

## ———— WHERE TO DINE ————

**TAMWORTH INN**   Country Inn
*American*

**Dinner:** $12-$23      **Phone:** 603/323-7721
**Location:** Jct SR 16 and 113, 3 mi w on SR 113; center; in The Tamworth Inn. 15 Cleveland Hill Rd 03886. **Hours:** Open 5/1-11/1 & 11/15-3/31; 5:30 pm-9 pm; hours may vary in winter. Closed: Sun & Mon, also Tues & Wed 11/1-6/14. **Reservations:** required. **Features:** The house salad of wild field greens, roasted corn, peppers, pecans, Parmesan, garlic and tomato vinaigrette combines interesting textures and flavors. Sauteed seafood with linguine, spinach and pine nuts is a specialty of creative American cuisine. Casual dress; cocktails. **Parking:** on-site. **Cards:** AX, MC, VI.

# TEMPLE

## ────── WHERE TO STAY ──────

**BIRCHWOOD INN**
Phone: 603/878-3285

*Historic Country Inn*

All Year      1P: $74-$84      2P: $79-$89

**Location:** 1.6 mi s of jct SR 101. Located in a quiet, rural area. 340 SR 45 03084 (PO Box 197). Fax: 603/878-2159. **Facility:** The inn was established in 1775. Designated smoking area. 7 one-bedroom standard units. 2 stories (no elevator), interior corridors. *Bath:* some shared or private, combo or shower only. **Parking:** on-site. **Terms:** office hours 7 am-11 pm, 2 night minimum stay - seasonal weekends, age restrictions may apply, 14 day cancellation notice, [MAP] meal plan available. **Guest Services:** TV in common area.

# THORNTON

## ────── WHERE TO STAY ──────

**SHAMROCK MOTEL**
Phone: 603/726-3534

*Motel*

| | | | |
|---|---|---|---|
| 6/8-10/19 | 1P: $45-$50 | 2P: $55-$60 | XP: $8   F16 |
| 12/20-4/30 | 1P: $40-$45 | 2P: $50-$55 | XP: $8   F16 |
| 5/1-6/7 & 10/20-12/19 | 1P: $35-$40 | 2P: $40-$45 | XP: $8   F16 |

**Location:** I-93, exit 29, 2.3 mi n. 2913 US 3 03223. Fax: 603/726-7298. **Facility:** 8 units. 4 one-bedroom standard units, some with efficiencies. 4 cottages ($58-$75). 1 story, exterior corridors. *Bath:* combo or shower only. **Parking:** on-site. **Terms:** office hours 8 am-9 pm, 7 day cancellation notice. **Pool(s):** outdoor. **Leisure Activities:** game room. **Guest Services:** gift shop. **Cards:** AX, DS, MC, VI.

SOME UNITS

## ────── WHERE TO DINE ──────

**THE WILLIAM TELL**
**Dinner:** $11-$23
Phone: 603/726-3618

*German*

**Location:** I-93, exit 28, 3.1 mi on SR 49; 9 mi w of Waterville Valley on SR 49. Waterville Valley Rd 03223. **Hours:** Open 5/1-10/31 & 12/1-4/30; 5 pm-10 pm, Sun from noon. Closed: Wed 5/1-10/31. **Reservations:** suggested. **Features:** The William Tell offers a comfortable, Swiss-chalet decor, inviting ambience and well-prepared cuisine with Italian, French and German influences. This place is popular with local residents and visitors alike. Patio dining is available in season. Cocktails. **Parking:** on-site. **Cards:** AX, DS, MC, VI.

# TILTON

## ────── WHERE TO STAY ──────

**THE 1875 INN AT TILTON**
Phone: (603)286-7774

*Country Inn*

All Year [BP]      2P: $86-$216      XP: $25   F5

**Location:** I-93, exit 20, 1 mi w on US 3. 255 Main St 03276. Fax: 603/286-8340. **Facility:** Smoke free premises. 11 one-bedroom standard units. 3 stories (no elevator), interior corridors. *Bath:* combo or shower only. **Parking:** street. **Terms:** office hours 9 am-9 pm, 14 day cancellation notice, weekly rates available, package plans. **Business Services:** meeting rooms. **Cards:** MC, VI.

**BLACK SWAN INN**
Phone: (603)286-4524

(AAA) [SAVE]

*Historic Bed & Breakfast*

All Year [BP]      1P: $95-$140      2P: $99-$145      XP: $25

**Location:** I-93, exit 19 northbound, 1 mi n on SR 132, 0.3 mi w on SR 3 and 11; exit 20 southbound, 1.5 mi w on SR 3 and 11. 354 W Main St 03276. Fax: 603/286-8260. **Facility:** A hand-carved carousel horse accents the gathering room of this 1880s home; stained-glass leaded windows distinguish the dining room. Smoke free premises. 9 units. 7 one-bedroom standard units. 2 one-bedroom suites. 3 stories (no elevator), interior corridors. *Bath:* some shared or private, combo or shower only. **Parking:** on-site. **Terms:** office hours 8 am-9 pm, age restrictions may apply, 14 day cancellation notice. **Guest Services:** TV in common area. **Cards:** AX, CB, DC, DS, JC, MC, VI.

SOME UNITS

**SUPER 8 MOTEL OF TILTON**    *Book at aaa.com*
Phone: 603/286-8882

*Motel*

| | | | |
|---|---|---|---|
| 6/1-10/16 | 1P: $70-$99 | 2P: $79-$109 | XP: $10   F12 |
| 5/1-5/31 | 1P: $60-$99 | 2P: $69-$109 | XP: $10   F12 |
| 10/17-4/30 | 1P: $49-$69 | 2P: $59-$89 | XP: $10   F12 |

**Location:** I-93, exit 20. 7 Tilton Rd 03276. Fax: 603/286-8788. **Facility:** 63 one-bedroom standard units. 2 stories (no elevator), interior corridors. **Parking:** on-site. **Amenities:** hair dryers. **Cards:** AX, DC, DS, MC, VI.

SOME UNITS

FEE

## ────── WHERE TO DINE ──────

**OLIVER'S RESTAURANT & PUB**
**Lunch:** $5-$15     **Dinner:** $11-$22
Phone: 603/286-7379

*American*

**Location:** I-93, exit 20 on US 3. 4 Sanborn Rd 03276. **Hours:** 11 am-9 pm, Fri & Sat-11 pm. Closed: 12/25. **Reservations:** accepted. **Features:** Serving traditional New England fare and convenient to the interstate and outlet shopping mall. Casual dress; cocktails. **Parking:** on-site. **Cards:** AX, DS, MC, VI.

**THE PATRIOTS TAVERN**
**Lunch:** $6-$8     **Dinner:** $7-$15
Phone: 603/286-7774

*American*

**Location:** I-93, exit 20, 1.5 mi w on US 3. 255 Main St 03276. **Hours:** 9 am-3 pm, Fri & Sat-8 pm. Closed major holidays. **Reservations:** accepted. **Features:** This eatery is located within the 1875 Inn at Tilton. Casual dress; cocktails. **Parking:** street. **Cards:** MC, VI.

**TILT'N DINER**
American

**Lunch:** $4-$15    **Dinner:** $4-$15    **Phone:** 603/286-2204
**Location:** I-93, exit 20, just n on US 3. 61 Laconia Rd 03276. **Hours:** 6 am-9 pm, Fri & Sat-10 pm. Closed: 12/24, 12/25. **Features:** The "old-time" traditional diner specializes in the expected burgers, cheese fries, hot dogs, salads and sandwiches. Casual dress; cocktails. **Parking:** on-site.

# TWIN MOUNTAIN

——— WHERE TO STAY ———

**CARLSON'S LODGE**
AAA SAVE
Small-scale Hotel

**Phone:** 603/846-5501
| | | | |
|---|---|---|---|
| 5/1-10/23 & 11/27-4/10 | 1P: $64-$95 | 2P: $64-$95 | XP: $7    F15 |

**Location:** US 302, 0.5 mi w of jct US 3. US 302 03595 (PO Box 350). **Facility:** Smoke free premises. 27 units. 25 one- and 2 two-bedroom standard units, some with efficiencies. 2 stories (no elevator), interior corridors. **Parking:** on-site. **Terms:** open 5/1-10/23 & 11/27-4/10, office hours 8 am-11 pm, 2-3 night minimum stay - seasonal with Saturday stayover, 14 day cancellation notice-fee imposed. **Pool(s):** outdoor. **Leisure Activities:** cross country skiing, snowmobiling, hiking trails, playground. **Fee:** game room. **Cards:** AX, DS, MC, VI. **Special Amenities:** free local telephone calls.

SOME UNITS

**SEVEN DWARFS MOTEL**
AAA SAVE
Motel

**Phone:** (603)846-5535
| | | | |
|---|---|---|---|
| 5/1-10/25 | 1P: $48-$56 | 2P: $62-$135 | XP: $15 |

**Location:** Jct US 302, 1 mi e at sign, 1 mi s on US 3. Located in a quiet area. 528 Little River Rd 03595 (PO Box 118). Fax: 603/846-5089. **Facility:** 14 units. 7 one-bedroom standard units, some with kitchens. 3 one-, 2 two- and 2 three-bedroom suites, some with kitchens and/or whirlpools. 1 story, exterior corridors. **Parking:** on-site. **Terms:** open 5/1-10/25, office hours 8 am-10 pm, 7 day cancellation notice-fee imposed, [MAP] meal plan available. **Amenities:** Some: hair dryers. **Dining:** 8 am-10 & 4-9 pm. **Leisure Activities:** fishing, bike trails, picnic area by stream, hiking trails, playground, basketball, horseshoes, volleyball. **Guest Services:** gift shop. **Cards:** DC, MC, VI. **Special Amenities:** free local telephone calls and preferred room (subject to availability with advanced reservations).

SOME UNITS

**SHAKESPEARE'S INN**
AAA SAVE
Motel

**Phone:** 603/846-5562
| | | | |
|---|---|---|---|
| 6/1-10/31 & 12/26-4/30 | 1P: $65-$85 | 2P: $65-$85 | XP: $15    F12 |
| 5/1-5/31 & 11/1-12/25 | 1P: $60-$80 | 2P: $60-$80 | XP: $15    F12 |

**Location:** Jct US 302, 1.3 mi s. 675 US 3 03595 (PO Box 305). Fax: 603/846-5782. **Facility:** 33 units. 32 one-bedroom standard units. 1 one-bedroom suite ($155-$215). 1-2 stories (no elevator), interior/exterior corridors. **Parking:** on-site. **Terms:** office hours 6 am-11 pm, 2 night minimum stay - weekends, 7 day cancellation notice-fee imposed. **Amenities:** voice mail. **Dining:** Shakespeare's Table, see separate listing. **Pool(s):** outdoor. **Leisure Activities:** tennis court, snowmobiling. **Cards:** AX, DS, MC, VI.

SOME UNITS

——— WHERE TO DINE ———

**SHAKESPEARE'S TABLE**
American

**Dinner:** $9-$15    **Phone:** 603/846-5562
**Location:** Jct US 302, 1.3 mi s; in Shakespeare's Inn. 675 Rt 3 03595. **Hours:** Open 5/1-10/31 & 2/1-4/1; 7 am-10 & 5-9 pm. Closed: Mon-Wed 11/1-1/31. **Reservations:** accepted. **Features:** This menu features traditional American fare and delicious seafood served in a casual, family-style dining atmosphere. A stone fireplace and antique kitchen stove help to create the comfortable and cozy surroundings with a good view of White Mountains. Casual dress; cocktails. **Parking:** on-site. **Cards:** AX, DS, MC, VI.

# WAKEFIELD

——— WHERE TO STAY ———

**LAKE IVANHOE INN**
Bed & Breakfast

**Phone:** (603)522-8824
| | | | |
|---|---|---|---|
| 5/1-12/15 [CP] | 1P: $85-$125 | 2P: $85-$125 | XP: $15    D |

**Location:** N on SR 16 to jct Wakefield Rd, 0.5 mi e to jct SR 153, 2.5 mi n to Acton Ridge Rd, then 1.3 mi e. Co-located with an RV resort. 631 Acton Ridge Rd 03830. Fax: 603/522-9235. **Facility:** Smoke free premises. 6 one-bedroom standard units, some with efficiencies. 2 stories (no elevator), interior corridors. **Bath:** some shared or private, combo or shower only. **Parking:** on-site. **Terms:** open 5/1-12/15, 2 night minimum stay - weekends, 14 day cancellation notice. **Leisure Activities:** rental canoes, rental paddleboats, fishing, recreation programs, playground, basketball, horseshoes, shuffleboard, volleyball. **Fee:** game room. **Cards:** MC, VI.

SOME UNITS

**WAKEFIELD INN BED & BREAKFAST**
Historic Bed & Breakfast

**Phone:** 603/522-8272
| | | | |
|---|---|---|---|
| All Year [BP] | | 2P: $75-$90 | XP: $20    D |

**Location:** SR 16, 0.5 mi e. Located in a historic district. 2723 Wakefield Rd 03872. **Facility:** This 19th-century inn features a spiral staircase in the entryway and an original stone fireplace in the breakfast area. Designated smoking area. 7 units. 5 one- and 2 two-bedroom units. 3 stories (no elevator), interior corridors. **Bath:** combo or shower only. **Parking:** on-site. **Terms:** office hours 9 am-10 pm, 2 night minimum stay - weekends 6/1-8/31, age restrictions may apply, 7 day cancellation notice-fee imposed, $20 service charge, no pets allowed (owner's cat on premises). **Amenities:** hair dryers. **Guest Services:** TV in common area. **Cards:** DS, MC, VI.

SOME UNITS

## ———— WHERE TO DINE ————

**PINE RIVER STEAKHOUSE**

Steak & Seafood

**Lunch:** $5-$10   **Dinner:** $8-$18   **Phone:** 603/522-3417

**Location:** 0.5 mi e of jct SR 16. Pine River Rd 03872. **Hours:** 11:30 am-9 pm; Mon & Tues from 4 pm. Closed: 3/27, 11/25, 12/25; also Mon & Tues 10/1-5/31. **Features:** The family-friendly restaurant prepares a fine selection of steak, seafood and chicken dishes. Casual dress; cocktails. **Parking:** on-site. **Cards:** MC, VI.

———— *The following restaurant has not been evaluated by AAA but is listed for your information only.* ————

**POOR PEOPLE'S PUB**
[fyi]
**Phone:** 603/522-8681

Not evaluated. **Location:** Meadow St 03830. **Features:** This casual restaurant is a favorite among the locals.

# WATERVILLE VALLEY

## ———— WHERE TO STAY ————

**BEST WESTERN SILVER FOX INN**

*Book at aaa.com*
**Phone:** (603)236-3699

Small-scale Hotel

All Year   1P: $79-$119   2P: $79-$119

**Location:** I-93, exit 28, 11 mi e on SR 49, then just n. 14 Snowsbrook Rd 03215 (PO Box 379). **Fax:** 603/236-4128. **Facility:** Smoke free premises. 32 one-bedroom standard units. 3 stories, interior corridors. **Parking:** on-site. **Terms:** office hours 7:30 am-9 pm, check-in 4 pm, cancellation fee imposed, [CP] meal plan available. **Amenities:** irons, hair dryers. **Leisure Activities:** sports center privileges. **Guest Services:** coin laundry, area transportation-ski area. **Business Services:** meeting rooms. **Cards:** AX, CB, DC, DS, MC, VI.
**Special Amenities:** free continental breakfast and free newspaper.

**BLACK BEAR LODGE**

Large-scale Hotel

| | |
|---|---|
| 12/24-4/30 | 1P: $130-$250 |
| 6/19-10/16 | 1P: $130-$240 |
| 10/17-12/23 | 1P: $110-$185 |
| 5/1-6/18 | 1P: $99-$170 |

**Phone:** (603)236-4501

**Location:** I-93, exit 28, 11 mi e on SR 49, then just n. 3 Village Rd 03215 (PO Box 357). **Fax:** 603/236-4114. **Facility:** 102 one-bedroom standard units with kitchens. 6 stories, interior corridors. **Parking:** on-site. **Terms:** check-in 4 pm, 15 day cancellation notice, package plans - seasonal. **Amenities:** voice mail, hair dryers. **Pool(s):** heated indoor/outdoor. **Leisure Activities:** whirlpool, steamroom, exercise room. **Guest Services:** coin laundry, area transportation-ski area. **Business Services:** meeting rooms. **Cards:** AX, DS, MC, VI.

SOME UNITS

**SNOWY OWL INN**

Small-scale Hotel

| | |
|---|---|
| 12/13-1/1 | 2P: $199-$309   XP: $10   F12 |
| 1/2-4/30 | 2P: $89-$249   XP: $10   F12 |
| 6/20-12/12 | 2P: $89-$219   XP: $10   F12 |
| 5/1-6/19 | 2P: $89-$169   XP: $10   F12 |

**Phone:** (603)236-8383

**Location:** I-93, exit 28, 11 mi e on SR 49. Located in a commerical area. 4 Village Rd 03215 (PO Box 407). **Fax:** 603/236-4890. **Facility:** Smoke free premises. 85 units. 82 one-bedroom standard units, some with kitchens and/or whirlpools. 2 one- and 1 two-bedroom suites with kitchens, some with whirlpools. 4 stories, interior corridors. **Parking:** on-site. **Terms:** check-in 4 pm, 15 day cancellation notice. **Amenities:** voice mail, irons, hair dryers. **Pool(s):** heated outdoor, heated indoor. **Leisure Activities:** saunas, whirlpools, bicycles, exercise room, horseshoes, volleyball. *Fee:* golf-9 holes, tennis court, racquetball court. **Guest Services:** complimentary evening beverages, coin laundry, area transportation. **Business Services:** meeting rooms. **Cards:** AX, DC, DS, MC, VI.

SOME UNITS

**THE VALLEY INN**

Small-scale Hotel

| | |
|---|---|
| 1/1-4/30 [ECP] | 2P: $104-$293   XP: $10   F5 |
| 6/17-12/31 [ECP] | 2P: $75-$240   XP: $10   F5 |
| 5/1-6/16 [ECP] | 2P: $64-$185   XP: $10   F5 |

**Phone:** (603)236-8336

**Location:** I-93, exit 28, just n on SR 49. 17 Tecumseh Rd 03215 (PO Box 1). **Fax:** 603/236-4294. **Facility:** Smoke free premises. 50 one-bedroom standard units, some with whirlpools. 4 stories, interior corridors. **Parking:** on-site. **Terms:** check-in 4 pm, 2 night minimum stay - weekends, 14 day cancellation notice-fee imposed, no pets allowed (owner's pet on premises). **Amenities:** *Some:* irons, hair dryers. **Dining:** Red Fox Dining Room, see separate listing. **Pool(s):** heated indoor/outdoor. **Leisure Activities:** saunas, whirlpool. **Guest Services:** coin laundry, area transportation. **Business Services:** meeting rooms. **Cards:** AX, CB, DC, DS, MC, VI.

SOME UNITS

———— *The following lodging was either not evaluated or did not meet AAA rating requirements but is listed for your information only.* ————

**INNS OF WATERVILLE VALLEY-THE BIRCHES**
[fyi]
**Phone:** 603/236-8366

Not evaluated. **Location:** Snows Brook Rd 03215. Facilities, services, and decor characterize a mid-range property.

─────── **WHERE TO DINE** ───────

**LATITUDE'S CAFE**          **Lunch:** $7-$13          **Dinner:** $7-$21          **Phone:** 603/236-4646
American          **Location:** I-93, exit 28, 11 mi e on SR 49. Town Center 03215. **Hours:** 11:30 am-4:30 & 5-9 pm. Closed major holidays. **Features:** On the lower level at Village Square Shops, the cafe is a good spot for lighter fare in a casual setting. Casual dress; cocktails. **Parking:** on-site. **Cards:** AX, DS, MC, VI.

**RED FOX DINING ROOM**          **Dinner:** $12-$20          **Phone:** 603/236-8336
American          **Location:** I-93, exit 28, just n on SR 49; in The Valley Inn. 17 Tecumseh Rd 03215. **Hours:** 5:30 pm-9 pm. **Reservations:** suggested. **Features:** The restaurant has a casual ambience and a Colonial-style decor. The menu includes salad, duck, chicken, seafood, steak, pork chops and veal. Don't miss the prime rib. Casual dress; cocktails. **Parking:** on-site. **Cards:** AX, CB, DC, DS, MC, VI.

# WEST LEBANON —See also LEBANON.

─────── **WHERE TO STAY** ───────

**AIRPORT ECONOMY INN**          **Phone:** (603)298-8888
 SAVE          5/1-11/1          1P: $55-$105          2P: $65-$115          XP: $10          F12
          11/2-4/30          1P: $53-$60          2P: $63-$70          XP: $10          F12
Motel          **Location:** I-89, exit 20 (SR 12A), just s, then just e. 45 Airport Rd 03784. Fax: 603/298-5473. **Facility:** 56 one-bedroom standard units. 4 stories, interior corridors. **Parking:** on-site, winter plug-ins. **Terms:** cancellation fee imposed, pets ($10 extra charge). **Amenities:** hair dryers. **Pool(s):** outdoor. **Leisure Activities:** Fee: game room. **Guest Services:** coin laundry. **Cards:** AX, DC, DS, MC, VI. **Special Amenities:** free continental breakfast and free local telephone calls.

SOME UNITS

**FIRESIDE INN AND SUITES**          **Phone:** (603)298-5906
          All Year          1P: $99-$149          2P: $99-$149          XP: $10          F17
Small-scale Hotel          **Location:** I-89, exit 20 (SR 12A), just s. 25 Airport Rd 03784. Fax: 603/298-0340. **Facility:** 126 one-bedroom standard units. 2 stories (no elevator), interior corridors. **Parking:** on-site. **Terms:** [MAP] meal plan available, package plans, small pets only ($10 extra charge). **Amenities:** irons, hair dryers. **Pool(s):** heated indoor. **Leisure Activities:** whirlpool, exercise room. **Guest Services:** gift shop, coin laundry. **Business Services:** meeting rooms. **Cards:** AX, DC, DS, MC, VI. *(See color ad p 349 & p 490)*

SOME UNITS

**SUNSET MOTOR INN**          **Phone:** (603)298-8721
          9/12-11/1          1P: $68-$92          2P: $68-$92
          5/21-9/11          1P: $58-$85          2P: $58-$85
Motel          5/1-5/20 & 11/2-4/30          1P: $46-$85          2P: $46-$85
          **Location:** SR 10, 2 mi s of Dartmouth College. 305 N Main St 03784. **Facility:** Smoke free premises. 18 one-bedroom standard units. 1 story, exterior corridors. *Bath:* combo or shower only. **Parking:** on-site. **Terms:** office hours 8 am-11 pm, 3 day cancellation notice, [CP] meal plan available. **Cards:** AX, DS, MC, VI.

SOME UNITS

─────── **WHERE TO DINE** ───────

**WEATHERVANE**          **Lunch:** $5-$14          **Dinner:** $5-$14          **Phone:** 603/298-7805
Seafood          **Location:** I-89, exit 20, 0.3 mi s. Rt 12A 03874. **Hours:** 11 am-9 pm. Closed: 11/25, 12/25. **Features:** The family restaurant specializes in excellent seafood, particularly its signature dish: delicious, creamy New England clam chowder. The atmosphere is casual and relaxed. Casual dress; cocktails. **Parking:** on-site. **Cards:** AX, MC, VI.

# WEST OSSIPEE

## ——— WHERE TO DINE ———

**WHITTIER HOUSE RESTAURANT & TAVERN**     **Lunch:** $7-$16     **Dinner:** $7-$16     **Phone:** 603/539-4513
**Location:** Jct of SR 16 and 25 W. Rt 16 03890. **Hours:** 11:30 am-9 pm, Sun from 7:30 am. Closed: 12/24, 12/25. **Features:** Traditional American fare is at the heart of the busy eatery's menu. Good food, reasonable prices and the casual atmosphere are what attract the local clientele. This restaurant also serves sushi every other Thursday evening from 6 pm-9 pm. Casual dress; cocktails. **Parking:** on-site.
American
**Cards:** AX, DS, MC, VI.

**THE YANKEE SMOKEHOUSE**     **Lunch:** $4-$17     **Dinner:** $4-$17     **Phone:** 603/539-7427
**Location:** Jct SR 16 and 25. Rt 16/25 03890. **Hours:** 11:30 am-9 pm. Closed: 3/27, 11/25, 12/25.
**Features:** Patrons should ask for extra napkins to prepare for the terrific barbecue ribs, chicken and more. Casual dress; beer & wine only. **Parking:** on-site. **Cards:** MC, VI.
Barbecue

# WHITEFIELD pop. 1,089

## ——— WHERE TO STAY ———

**MOUNTAIN VIEW GRAND HOTEL**     **Phone:** 603/837-2100

| | |  | |  |
|---|---|---|---|---|
| 6/18-10/24 | 1P: $239-$489 | 2P: $239-$489 | XP: $15 | F12 |
| 5/1-6/17 & 10/25-4/30 | 1P: $139-$399 | 2P: $139-$399 | XP: $15 | F12 |

**Location:** 2.5 mi n on US 3, then just e. Mountain View Rd 03598. Fax: 603/837-8720. **Facility:** Outfitted with many luxury touches, this stately hotel offers sweeping views and an ambience of yesteryear. 145 units. 133 one-bedroom standard units. 12 one-bedroom suites ($399-$800), some with whirlpools. 4 stories, interior corridors. *Bath:* combo or shower only. **Parking:** on-site and valet. **Terms:** 2 night minimum stay - weekends, 14 day cancellation notice, [BP] & [MAP] meal plans available, package plans, $3 service charge.
Classic Historic
Large-scale Hotel
**Amenities:** voice mail, hair dryers. **Dining:** 7:30-10:30 am, 11:30-2 & 5:30-9 pm, Fri & Sat-10 pm, cocktails, also, Juliet's, see separate listing. **Pool(s):** heated outdoor, heated indoor. **Leisure Activities:** whirlpools, steamroom, 2 lighted tennis courts, cross country skiing, snowshoeing, snow tubing, badminton, croquet, hiking trails, playground, exercise room, spa, basketball, horseshoes, shuffleboard, volleyball. **Fee:** golf-9 holes, horseback riding, game room. **Guest Services:** gift shop. **Business Services:** conference facilities, business center. **Cards:** AX, DC, DS, MC, VI. *(See color ad p 380)*

## ——— WHERE TO DINE ———

**INN AT WHITEFIELD**     **Lunch:** $8-$12     **Dinner:** $9-$20     **Phone:** 603/837-2760
**Location:** Jct SR 116, 2.5 mi n. US 3 N 03598. **Hours:** 11:30 am-11:30 pm; Tues-Sat 5 pm-9 pm 10/15-5/31. Closed: 12/19-12/26. **Reservations:** suggested. **Features:** This pleasant informal dining room is located in a country inn next to a popular summer theater. The varied menu of regional and continental cuisine includes specialties like stuffed sole, steak au poivre, portabello ravioli in a pesto sauce, haddock and salmon. Casual dress; cocktails; entertainment. **Parking:** on-site. **Cards:** AX, DS, MC, VI.
Continental

**JULIET'S**     **Dinner:** $14-$34     **Phone:** 603/837-2100
**Location:** 2.5 mi n on US 3, then just e; in Mountain View Grand Hotel. Mountain View Rd 03598. **Hours:** 7 am-10:30 & 5:30-9 pm. **Reservations:** accepted. **Features:** Located within the newly restored historic Mountain View Grand Hotel. The panoramic views of the Presidential Range and highly trained chef offer a memorable dining experience. Dressy casual; cocktails. **Parking:** on-site and valet. **Cards:** AX, DS,
Continental
MC, VI.

# WINNISQUAM

## ——— WHERE TO STAY ———

**LORD HAMPSHIRE MOTEL & COTTAGES**     **Phone:** 603/524-4331

| | |  |  | |
|---|---|---|---|---|
| 6/1-8/31 [ECP] | | 2P: $95-$195 | XP: $20 | F11 |
| 5/1-5/31 & 9/1-4/30 [ECP] | | 2P: $55-$105 | XP: $20 | F11 |

**Location:** I-93, exit 20 (Laconia Rd), 4 mi n on US 3. 885 Laconia Rd 03289 (PO Box 455). Fax: 603/524-1897.
**Facility:** 20 units. 8 one-bedroom standard units, some with efficiencies. 12 cottages ($580-$1295). 1 story, exterior corridors. *Bath:* shower only. **Parking:** on-site. **Terms:** office hours 8 am-10 pm, 7 day cancellation notice, to 30 day seasonal-fee imposed, weekly rates available, package plans, 8% service charge.
Cottage
**Amenities:** *Some:* hair dryers. **Leisure Activities:** rental boats, rental canoes, fishing, horseshoes, shuffleboard, volleyball. **Fee:** boat dock, game room. **Guest Services:** gift shop. **Cards:** AX, DS, MC, VI.
SOME UNITS

**LYNNMERE MOTEL**     **Phone:** (603)524-0912

| |  |  |  |
|---|---|---|---|
| 6/1-10/31 | 1P: $55-$75 | 2P: $65-$85 | |
| 5/1-5/31 & 4/1-4/30 | 1P: $45-$65 | 2P: $55-$75 | XP: $15 |

**Location:** I-93, exit 20 (Laconia Rd), 3 mi n on US 3. 850 Laconia Rd 03289. Fax: 603/527-2533. **Facility:** Smoke free premises. 8 one-bedroom standard units, some with efficiencies. 1 story, exterior corridors. *Bath:* combo or shower only. **Parking:** on-site. **Terms:** open 5/1-10/31 & 4/1-4/30, office hours 8 am-11 pm, 2 night minimum stay, 14 day cancellation notice-fee imposed. **Leisure Activities:** rental boats, canoeing, paddleboats, boat dock, fishing. **Fee:** charter fishing, waverunners. **Special Amenities:** free local telephone calls.
Motel

# WOLFEBORO pop. 2,979

─────── **WHERE TO STAY** ───────

**THE LAKE MOTEL**
**Phone: 603/569-1100**

◆◇◆◇ ◆◇◆◇
Motel

5/1-10/31 — 2P: $119-$139 — XP: $10 — F6
**Location:** 0.5 mi se on SR 28. 280 S Main St 03894 (PO Box 887). Fax: 603/569-1258. **Facility:** 35 units. 30 one-bedroom standard units. 5 one-bedroom suites ($119-$139) with kitchens. 1 story, interior/exterior corridors. **Parking:** on-site. **Terms:** open 5/1-10/31, office hours 8 am-10 pm, 2 night minimum stay - weekends, 14 day cancellation notice, weekly rates available, small pets only (with prior approval). **Leisure Activities:** rental boats, rental canoes, boat dock, fishing, tennis court, playground. **Cards:** AX, DC, MC, VI.

SOME UNITS
🛏 🕻 ⊠ / 🔒 🖥 /

**LAKEVIEW INN & MOTOR LODGE**
**Phone: 603/569-1335**

(AAA) [SAVE]
◆◇◆◇ ◆◇◆◇
Motel

7/1-10/31 — 2P: $90-$100 — XP: $10 — F10
5/1-6/30 — 2P: $80-$90 — XP: $10 — F10
11/1-4/30 — 2P: $60 — XP: $10 — F10
**Location:** 0.5 mi n on SR 109. 200 N Main St 03894 (PO Box 713). Fax: 603/569-9426. **Facility:** 17 one-bedroom standard units, some with kitchens. 2 stories (no elevator), interior/exterior corridors. **Bath:** combo or shower only. **Parking:** on-site. **Terms:** office hours 8 am-8:30 pm, 2 night minimum stay - weekends, 10 day cancellation notice. **Dining:** restaurant, see separate listing. **Cards:** AX, MC, VI.

SOME UNITS
🕻 🖥 / ⊠ 🔒 /

**PIPING ROCK RESORT**
**Phone: 603/569-1915**

(AAA) [SAVE]
◆◇◆◇ ◆◇◆◇
Motel

6/25-9/4 — 1P: $99-$170 — 2P: $99-$170
9/5-10/17 — 1P: $89-$109 — 2P: $89-$109
5/1-6/24 — 1P: $79-$89 — 2P: $79-$89
10/18-4/30 — 1P: $59-$89 — 2P: $59-$89
**Location:** 3.1 mi n on SR 109 N. 680 N Main St 03894. Fax: 603/569-1915. **Facility:** 17 units. 6 one- and 1 two-bedroom standard units with efficiencies. 1 three-bedroom suite ($555-$1190) with kitchen. 9 cottages. 2 stories (no elevator), exterior corridors. **Bath:** combo or shower only. **Parking:** on-site. **Terms:** office hours 9 am-5 pm, 2 night minimum stay - weekends in summer, 7 nights in cottages in summer, 60 day cancellation notice-fee imposed. **Leisure Activities:** canoeing, fishing, barbecue grills, lawn games. **Fee:** boat dock. **Cards:** AX, DS. **Special Amenities:** free local telephone calls.

SOME UNITS
⊠ [VCR] 🔒 🖥 / ⊠ [AC] /

**THE WOLFEBORO INN**
**Phone: 603/569-3016**

◆◇◆◇ ◆◇◆◇
Small-scale Hotel

7/1-8/31 [ECP] — 1P: $180-$325 — 2P: $180-$325 — XP: $15
9/1-10/31 [ECP] — 1P: $140-$325 — 2P: $140-$325 — XP: $15
5/1-6/30 [ECP] — 1P: $135-$275 — 2P: $135-$275 — XP: $15
11/1-4/30 [ECP] — 1P: $95-$225 — 2P: $95-$225 — XP: $15
**Location:** On SR 109, 0.5 mi n of jct SR 28; center. 90 N Main St 03894 (PO Box 1270). Fax: 603/569-5375. **Facility:** 44 one-bedroom standard units, some with kitchens. 3 stories, interior corridors. **Bath:** combo or shower only. **Parking:** on-site. **Terms:** 2-3 night minimum stay - weekends, 10 day cancellation notice-fee imposed, [BP] & [MAP] meal plans available, package plans, $2 service charge. **Amenities:** irons, hair dryers. **Dining:** 1812 Steakhouse, see separate listing. **Leisure Activities:** boating, boat dock, fishing, cross country skiing, ice skating. **Fee:** massage. **Guest Services:** area transportation. **Business Services:** meeting rooms. **Cards:** AX, DS, MC, VI. *(See color ad below)*

SOME UNITS
🕻 🍸 ⊠ 🖥 / ⊠ [VCR] 🔒 /
FEE

─────── **WHERE TO DINE** ───────

**1812 STEAKHOUSE**
**Dinner:** $16-$22
**Phone: 603/569-3016**

◆◇◆◇ ◆◇
American

**Location:** On SR 109, 0.5 mi n of jct SR 28; center; in The Wolfeboro Inn. 90 N Main St 03894. **Hours:** Open 5/1-10/15; 5 pm-9 pm; hours vary off - season. Closed: Sun-Thurs. **Reservations:** suggested. **Features:** The restaurant builds its menu on regional cuisine of seafood and aged Angus beef. Prime rib with popovers is superb. Large windows in the elegant, Colonial dining room overlook the colorful perennial gardens. Casual dress; cocktails. **Parking:** on-site. **Cards:** AX, DS, MC, VI.

🍸 ⊠

## THE CIDER PRESS

AAA

American

**Dinner:** $13-$20

**Phone:** 603/569-2028

**Location:** 2.8 mi s on SR 28, just s. 30 Middleton Rd 03894. **Hours:** 5 pm-9 pm; hours may vary in winter. Closed: 11/25, 12/24, 12/25; also Mon. **Reservations:** suggested. **Features:** Several dining rooms feature country decor, with a fireplace and raised hearth. The casual, family-friendly restaurant specializes in delicious grilled ribs and chops and flavorful seafood dishes. Prompt, friendly service is the norm. Casual dress; cocktails. **Parking:** on-site. **Cards:** MC, VI.

## LAKEVIEW INN RESTAURANT

Continental

cocktails.

**Dinner:** $9-$23

**Phone:** 603/569-1335

**Location:** 0.5 mi n on SR 109; in Lakeview Inn & Motor Lodge. 200 N Main St 03894. **Hours:** 5 pm-9 pm. Closed: 12/24, 12/25; also Sun & Mon 11/1-6/11. **Reservations:** suggested. **Features:** In a quaint country inn, the restaurant offers good seafood dishes, such as shrimp scampi, as well as veal, lamb, chicken and venison meals. A fine selection of desserts, wine and a full-service bar complete the experience. Casual dress; **Parking:** on-site. **Cards:** AX, MC, VI.

## LOVES' QUAY

Continental

**Lunch:** $6-$12          **Dinner:** $12-$28          **Phone:** 603/569-3303

**Location:** Just e of SR 109. 51 Mill St 03894. **Hours:** 11:30 am-2 & 5-9 pm, Fri & Sat-10 pm; to 10 pm 7/1-8/30. Closed: 12/25. **Reservations:** suggested, for dinner. **Features:** In the heart of town, the restaurant overlooks the water, and boaters often dock nearby to dine inside. All entrees are made to order and the chef is willing to adjust items to individual tastes. The eclectic menu, which emphasizes seafood, blends Portuguese, Northern Italian and French influences. Dessert and the delicious butter is made on the premises. Casual dress; cocktails. **Parking:** on-site. **Cards:** AX, MC, VI.

## STRAWBERRY PATCH

American

**Lunch:** $6-$10

**Phone:** 603/569-5523

**Location:** Center. 50 N Main St 03894. **Hours:** Open 5/1-11/1; 7:30 am-2 pm, Sun-1 pm. **Features:** Hearty breakfasts and lunches are served at the country-style, smoke-free restaurant, where everything is homemade and fresh. Diners seated at tables set with berry-pattern plates and antique milk-glass vases filled with fresh flowers can gaze outside through bay windows. Casual dress. **Parking:** on-site.

# WOODSVILLE pop. 1,100

## ——— WHERE TO STAY ———

### ALL SEASONS MOTEL

AAA SAVE

Motel

**Phone:** (603)747-2157

| | | | |
|---|---|---|---|
| 9/24-10/17 | 1P: $55-$70 | 2P: $70-$75 | XP: $5 | D18 |
| 5/1-9/23 | 1P: $45-$65 | 2P: $55-$75 | XP: $5 | D18 |
| 10/18-4/30 | 1P: $40-$60 | 2P: $50-$70 | XP: $5 | D18 |

**Location:** Jct SR 10, 0.4 mi w on US 302, then 0.3 mi se. 36 Smith St 03785. Fax: 603/747-4068. **Facility:** 14 units. 11 one-bedroom standard units, some with efficiencies. 3 one-bedroom suites with efficiencies. 1 story, exterior corridors. *Bath:* combo or shower only. **Parking:** on-site. **Terms:** pets (in limited units). **Pool(s):** outdoor. **Leisure Activities:** barbecue facility, picnic area, playground, sports court. **Cards:** AX, DC, DS, MC, VI. **Special Amenities:** free local telephone calls and preferred room (subject to availability with advanced reservations).

SOME UNITS

### NOOTKA LODGE

AAA SAVE

Motel

**Phone:** (603)747-2418

| | | | |
|---|---|---|---|
| 9/24-10/17 | 1P: $65-$114 | 2P: $75-$140 | XP: $10 | F18 |
| 5/1-9/23 | 1P: $55-$99 | 2P: $60-$125 | XP: $10 | F18 |
| 10/18-4/30 | 1P: $50-$85 | 2P: $55-$115 | XP: $10 | F18 |

**Location:** Jct SR 10 and US 302. Jct 10 & 302 03785. Fax: 603/747-4068. **Facility:** 33 units. 32 one- and 1 two-bedroom standard units, some with efficiencies, kitchens and/or whirlpools. 2 stories (no elevator), exterior corridors. *Bath:* combo or shower only. **Parking:** on-site. **Terms:** small pets only (in limited units). **Amenities:** voice mail. **Pool(s):** outdoor. **Leisure Activities:** whirlpool, snowmobiling, ATV & walking trails, barbecue facility, picnic area, exercise room, horseshoes, volleyball, game room. **Business Services:** meeting rooms, fax (fee). **Cards:** AX, DC, DS, MC, VI.

SOME UNITS

# Vermont

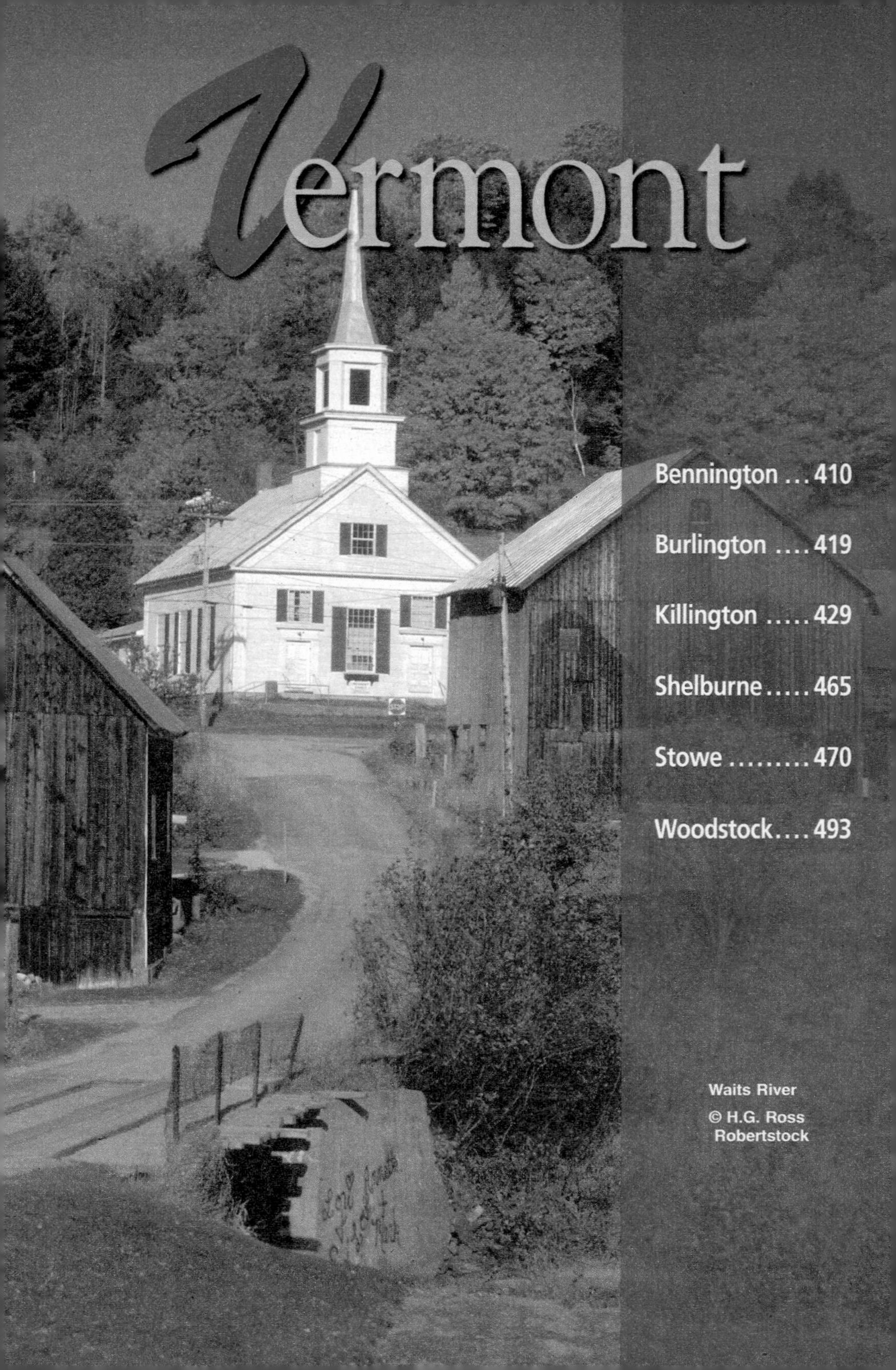

Waits River
© H.G. Ross
Robertstock

# ALBURG pop. 488

───── **WHERE TO STAY** ─────

**RANSOM BAY INN**                                                                      **Phone:** 802/796-3399
◆◆◆◆                   All Year                    1P: $60           2P: $75           XP: $15              F12
Historic Bed          **Location:** 0.5 mi s on US 2, from jct SR 78. 4 Center Bay Rd 05440. **Fax:** 802/796-3399. **Facility:** Spacious, taste-
& Breakfast           fully decorated guest rooms with modest baths are offered at this long-established inn. Smoke free premises.
                      4 one-bedroom standard units. 2 stories (no elevator), interior corridors. *Bath:* combo or shower only.
                      **Parking:** on-site. **Terms:** weekly rates available, [BP] meal plan available, small pets only (owner's cat on
premises). **Amenities:** hair dryers. **Guest Services:** area transportation. **Cards:** AX, DS, MC, VI.    🛏 ✕ 🅦 ☎

# ARLINGTON pop. 1,199

───── **WHERE TO STAY** ─────

**THE ARLINGTON INN**                                                                   **Phone:** (802)375-6532
AAA SAVE               All Year [BP]                                 2P: $125-$350      XP: $20              F6
◆◆◆◆                   **Location:** Center. 3904 Historic SR 7A 05250 (PO Box 369). **Fax:** 802/375-6534. **Facility:** Consisting of an 1848
Historic              Greek Revival mansion and three annexes, this country inn is rich with local history and handsome antiques.
Country Inn           Smoke free premises. 18 units. 17 one-bedroom standard units, some with whirlpools. 1 one-bedroom suite
                      ($200-$350). 2 stories (no elevator), interior/exterior corridors. *Bath:* combo or shower only. **Parking:** on-site.
                      **Terms:** 1-3 night minimum stay - in season, 14 day cancellation notice-fee imposed, [MAP] meal plan avail-
                      able, package plans - seasonal & midweek. **Dining:** dining room, see separate listing. **Guest Services:** gift
shop, complimentary evening beverages. **Cards:** AX, DS, MC, VI. **Special Amenities:** free full breakfast and free room upgrade (subject to availability with advanced reservations).                          🆂 🍽 ✕ 📷 DATA
                                                                                                           PORT

**CANDLELIGHT MOTEL**                                                                   **Phone:** 802/375-6647
AAA SAVE               All Year [CP]                 1P: $52-$115      2P: $52-$115      XP: $10              F8
◆◆◆                    **Location:** 1 mi n on Historic SR 7A. 4893 SR 7A 05250 (PO Box 97). **Fax:** 802/375-2566. **Facility:** 17 one-bedroom
Motel                 standard units. 1 story, exterior corridors. **Parking:** on-site. **Terms:** office hours 7:30 am-10 pm, 2-3 night
                      minimum stay - seasonal & weekends, 14 day cancellation notice-fee imposed. **Amenities:** hair dryers.
                      **Pool(s):** outdoor. **Cards:** AX, MC, VI. **Special Amenities:** free continental breakfast and free local tele-
phone calls.
                                                                                              SOME UNITS
                                                                                       ⌨ 🔋 / ✕ VCR /

───── **WHERE TO DINE** ─────

**ARLINGTON INN**                         **Dinner:** $20-$29                            **Phone:** 802/375-6532
◆◆◆                    **Location:** Center; in The Arlington Inn. 3904 Historic SR 7A 05250. **Hours:** 5:30 pm-9 pm; hours may vary
American              seasonally. **Closed:** Sun & Mon. **Reservations:** suggested. **Features:** In a quiet Vermont village, the lovely
                      1840s Greek Revival inn is known for creative dishes prepared with fresh, local ingredients. Menu
                      highlights include sirloin steak, roasted salmon, lobster ravioli, hazelnut-encrusted chicken and veal
medallions. Dressy casual; cocktails. **Parking:** on-site. **Cards:** AX, DC, DS, MC, VI.                   🍸 ✕

**ARLINGTON'S SOUTHSIDE CAFE & RESTAURANT**         **Lunch:** $6-$8    **Dinner:** $6-$9    **Phone:** 802/375-9900
◆◆                     **Location:** In Arlington Plaza. Historic SR 7A 05250. **Hours:** 11 am-2 & 5-9 pm. **Closed:** 11/25, 12/25; also Sun
American              & Mon. **Reservations:** accepted. **Features:** The simple, casual restaurant offers friendly service and their
                      New England clam chowder is a must-try if you enjoy it thick and creamy. Casual dress; cocktails.
                      **Parking:** on-site. **Cards:** AX, MC, VI.                                            ✕

# ASCUTNEY

───── **WHERE TO DINE** ─────

**MR G'S RESTAURANT**                     **Lunch:** $5-$8     **Dinner:** $10-$14       **Phone:** 802/674-2486
◆◆                     **Location:** I-91, exit 8, just e. SR 131 05030. **Hours:** 6 am-8 pm, Fri & Sat-9 pm, Sun 6:30 am-9 pm. **Closed:**
American              11/25, 12/25. **Reservations:** accepted. **Features:** The restaurant is a local favorite, offering good food in a
                      simple, casual atmosphere. Casual dress; beer & wine only. **Parking:** on-site. **Cards:** MC, VI.           ✕

# BARNARD

───── **WHERE TO STAY** ─────

**THE MAPLE LEAF INN**                                                                  **Phone:** 802/234-5342
AAA SAVE               All Year                    1P: $130-$260      2P: $130-$260
◆◆◆◆                   **Location:** Just s on SR 12 from center. Located in a quiet, rural area. Rt 12 05031 (PO Box 273). **Facility:** A newly
                      constructed Victorian-style farmhouse, this property near picturesque Silver Lake offers well-furnished guest
Bed & Breakfast       rooms with fireplaces. Smoke free premises. 7 one-bedroom standard units, some with whirlpools. 3 stories
                      (no elevator), interior corridors. *Bath:* combo or shower only. **Parking:** on-site. **Terms:** 2 night minimum stay
                      - most weekends, age restrictions may apply, 14 day cancellation notice-fee imposed, [BP] meal plan avail-
able. **Amenities:** video library, hair dryers. **Leisure Activities:** cross country skiing, snowshoe trails, badminton, croquet. **Guest
Services:** gift shop, complimentary evening beverages. **Business Services:** fax. **Cards:** AX, CB, DC, DS, JC, MC, VI.
**Special Amenities:** free full breakfast and free local telephone calls.                    ✕ ✕ VCR 📷

---

**The following lodging was either not evaluated or did not meet AAA rating requirements but is listed for your information only.**

TWIN FARMS

[fyi]

Phone: 802/234-9999

Not evaluated. **Location:** 1.5 mi e of SR 12. Stage Rd 05031. Facilities, services, and decor characterize an upscale property.

--- **WHERE TO DINE** ---

BARNARD INN RESTAURANT & TAVERN

▼▼▼▼

French

**Dinner:** $40                                    **Phone:** 802/234-9961

**Location:** I-89, exit 3, just s on SR 12. 5518 Vermont Rt 12 05031. **Hours:** 6 pm-9 pm; hours may vary. Closed major holidays; also Sun-Tues. **Reservations:** required. **Features:** The restaurant offers intimate dining in one of four elegant dining rooms. The chef-owners specialize in preparing Provencal cuisine. The extensive wine list offers a choice of more than 300 selections. Off the beaten path, this place occupies a lovely inn near beautiful Silver Lake in the quaint, picturesque town. Meals are memorable. Dressy casual; cocktails. **Parking:** on-site. **Cards:** AX, MC, VI.

Ⓨ Ⓧ

# BARRE pop. 9,291

--- **WHERE TO STAY** ---

DAYS INN-BARRE      *Book at aaa.com*
AAA [SAVE]
▼▼▼▼
Motel

Phone: (802)476-6678

| | | | |
|---|---|---|---|
| All Year | 1P: $39-$109 | 2P: $39-$109 | XP: $10      F12 |

**Location:** I-89, exit 6, 1 mi n on SR 14. 173 S Main St 05641. **Fax:** 802/476-6678. **Facility:** 42 one-bedroom standard units, some with efficiencies. 2 stories (no elevator), exterior corridors. **Parking:** on-site, winter plug-ins. **Terms:** cancellation fee imposed, [MAP] meal plan available, package plans. **Amenities:** hair dryers. **Dining:** 7-10 am, Sat & Sun 7 am-11 & 5-9 pm; closed Sun for dinner & Mon for breakfast 10/15-6/15, cocktails. **Pool(s):** heated indoor. **Leisure Activities:** whirlpool, basketball. **Guest Services:** sundries. **Business Services:** meeting rooms. **Cards:** AX, CB, DC, DS, MC, VI. **Special Amenities:** free newspaper and preferred room (subject to availability with advanced reservations).

SOME UNITS
Ⓢⓓ 🍽 🛏 📺 [DATA PORT] / Ⓧ 🛢 🖼 /

THE HOLLOW INN & MOTEL
AAA [SAVE]
▼▼▼▼
Motel

Phone: 802/479-9313

| | | | |
|---|---|---|---|
| 9/15-10/20 | 1P: $115-$125 | 2P: $115-$135 | XP: $10      D8 |
| 6/15-9/14 | 1P: $95-$105 | 2P: $110-$115 | XP: $10      D8 |
| 5/1-6/14 & 10/21-4/30 | 1P: $80-$90 | 2P: $90-$100 | XP: $10      D8 |

**Location:** Jct US 302, 1 mi s on SR 14; I-89, exit 6, 4.3 mi e on SR 63, 0.7 mi n on SR 14. 278 S Main St 05641. **Fax:** 802/476-5242. **Facility:** 41 units. 38 one-bedroom standard units, some with efficiencies. 3 one-bedroom suites. 2 stories (no elevator), interior/exterior corridors. **Parking:** on-site. **Terms:** 3 day cancellation notice, [AP] & [CP] meal plans available, small pets only ($10 extra charge). **Amenities:** video library (fee), irons, hair dryers. **Pool(s):** heated outdoor. **Leisure Activities:** sauna, whirlpools, snowmobiling, exercise room. **Guest Services:** coin laundry. **Business Services:** meeting rooms, fax. **Cards:** AX, CB, DC, DS, MC, VI.

Ⓢⓓ 🛏 Ⓧ [VCR] [DATA PORT] 🛢 🖼 🖥
FEE

PIERRE MOTEL
AAA [SAVE]
▼▼
Motel

Phone: 802/476-3188

| | | | |
|---|---|---|---|
| 9/22-10/22 | 1P: $69-$89 | 2P: $89-$99 | XP: $10 |
| 5/1-9/21 | 1P: $47-$59 | 2P: $59-$79 | XP: $6 |
| 10/23-12/31 | 1P: $45-$59 | 2P: $59-$69 | XP: $6 |
| 1/1-4/30 | 1P: $42-$59 | 2P: $59-$69 | XP: $6 |

**Location:** I-89, exit 7, 4 mi e on SR 62; jct US 302. 362 N Main St 05641. **Fax:** 802/476-3189. **Facility:** 20 one-bedroom standard units. 2 stories (no elevator), exterior corridors. **Bath:** combo or shower only. **Parking:** on-site, winter plug-ins. **Terms:** 3 day cancellation notice-fee imposed, [ECP] meal plan available. **Pool(s):** outdoor. **Cards:** AX, DS, MC, VI. **Special Amenities:** free continental breakfast and free local telephone calls.

SOME UNITS
Ⓢⓓ 🛏 📺 🛢 / Ⓧ /

--- **WHERE TO DINE** ---

THE FARMERS DINER
▼▼
American

**Lunch:** $3-$8          **Dinner:** $3-$8          **Phone:** 802/476-7623

**Location:** Center. 240 Main St 05641. **Hours:** 6 am-9 pm, Sat from 7 am, Sun 7 am-4 pm. Closed: 12/25. **Features:** The unique diner features all local Vermont-grown products; the food is delicious and the service is friendly. Casual dress; beer & wine only. **Parking:** street. **Cards:** AX, DS, MC, VI.

Ⓧ

MR. Z'S
▼▼
Italian

**Lunch:** $4-$9          **Dinner:** $4-$9          **Phone:** 802/479-3259

**Location:** Jct SR 14/US 302. 379 N Main St 05641. **Hours:** 11 am-9 pm. Closed major holidays. **Features:** The cute Italian bistro-themed restaurant offers a variety of burgers, grinders, pizza and pasta dishes. Casual dress; beer & wine only. **Parking:** on-site. **Cards:** AX, DC, DS, MC, VI.

Ⓧ

THE STEAK HOUSE RESTAURANT
▼▼
Steak & Seafood

**Dinner:** $10-$18          **Phone:** 802/479-9181

**Location:** 3 mi w on US 302, from jct SR 14 N. 1239 US Rt 302 05641. **Hours:** 4 pm-10 pm, Sun noon-9 pm. Closed: 11/25, 12/25. **Reservations:** suggested, weekends. **Features:** The dining room has a comfortable, rustic-style consisting of timbers from old barns that were knocked down and reassembled. The menu features teriyaki steak, baked haddock, chicken and pasta dishes, and salad and dessert bar. Enjoy the prompt, friendly service. Casual dress; cocktails. **Parking:** on-site. **Cards:** AX, MC, VI.

Ⓨ Ⓧ

---

**The following restaurant has not been evaluated by AAA but is listed for your information only.**

JACK'S BACKYARD

[fyi]

Phone: 802/479-9134

Not evaluated. **Location:** Just n of jct US 302/SR 14. 9 Maple Ave 05641. **Features:** The casual eatery is open from lunch until about midnight and is a good spot for light fare.

# BENNINGTON pop. 9,168

―――― **WHERE TO STAY** ――――

### ALEXANDRA BED & BREAKFAST INN
Phone: 802/442-5619

AAA SAVE All Year [BP] 1P: $85-$135 2P: $100-$165 XP: $15

**Location:** 1 mi n on Historic SR 7A. 916 Orchard Rd (SR 7A) 05201. Fax: 802/442-5592. **Facility:** This farmhouse-style B&B built in 1859 is on a knoll, offering good views of the surrounding countryside and distant mountains. Smoke free premises. 12 one-bedroom standard units, some with whirlpools. 2 stories (no elevator),

Bed & Breakfast interior/exterior corridors. **Parking:** on-site, winter plug-ins. **Terms:** office hours 7 am-9:30 pm, 1-2 night minimum stay - weekends, 12 day cancellation notice, package plans. **Amenities:** high-speed Internet, hair dryers. **Business Services:** fax. **Cards:** AX, DS, MC, VI. **Special Amenities:** free full breakfast and free local telephone calls.

SOME UNITS
⊠ / VCR DATA PORT /

### APPLE VALLEY INN & CAFE
Phone: (802)442-6588

AAA SAVE 9/11-10/26 1P: $59-$89 2P: $69-$94 XP: $8 F16
5/1-9/10 1P: $49-$65 2P: $49-$75 F16
10/27-4/30 1P: $45-$59 2P: $45-$59 XP: $6 F16

**Location:** Jct SR 9, 1.8 mi s. 979 US Hwy 7 S 05201. Fax: 802/447-1078. **Facility:** 18 one-bedroom standard

Motel units. 2 stories (no elevator), interior/exterior corridors. *Bath:* combo or shower only. **Parking:** on-site. **Terms:** cancellation fee imposed, [BP] meal plan available. **Dining:** 7-11 am. **Pool(s):** outdoor. **Leisure Activities:** croquet, shuffleboard. **Business Services:** meeting rooms. **Cards:** AX, DS, MC, VI. **Special Amenities:** free local telephone calls and free newspaper.

SOME UNITS
SD ⊶ ⊤↑ ⊇ ⊛ DATA PORT / ⊠ VCR ▤ ▣ /

### BENNINGTON MOTOR INN
Phone: 802/442-5479

AAA SAVE 9/16-10/17 2P: $99-$108 XP: $10 D12
5/28-9/15 & 10/18-4/30 2P: $79-$85 XP: $10 D12
5/1-5/27 2P: $73-$78 XP: $10 D12

**Location:** Jct US 7, 0.4 mi w on SR 9. 143 W Main St 05201. **Facility:** 16 units. 15 one- and 1 two-bedroom stan-

Motel dard units. 2 stories (no elevator), exterior corridors. *Bath:* combo or shower only. **Parking:** on-site, winter plug-ins. **Terms:** 2 night minimum stay - weekends 9/16-10/17, 10 day cancellation notice, 9/16-10/17-fee imposed, pets ($20 extra charge, in limited units). **Guest Services:** sundries. **Cards:** AX, DS, MC, VI. **Special Amenities:** free local telephone calls and preferred room (subject to availability with advanced reservations). *(See color ad below)*

SOME UNITS
⊶ ⊛ DATA PORT ▭ / ⊠ ▣ /
FEE

**BEST WESTERN-NEW ENGLANDER** Book at aaa.com **Phone:** (802)442-6311

SAVE

Motel

All Year 1P: $59-$92 2P: $59-$92 XP: $7 F12

**Location:** Jct SR 9, 1.2 mi n on US 7, then 0.7 mi n on Historic SR 7A. 220 Northside Dr 05201. Fax: 802/442-5885. **Facility:** 58 units. 56 one-bedroom standard units, some with whirlpools. 2 one-bedroom suites. 1-2 stories (no elevator), interior/exterior corridors. *Bath:* combo or shower only. **Parking:** on-site, winter plug-ins. **Terms:** cancellation fee imposed. **Amenities:** high-speed Internet, voice mail, irons, hair dryers. **Dining:** 11:30 am-10 pm, Fri & Sat-11 pm, Sun noon-10 pm. **Pool(s):** outdoor. **Guest Services:** gift shop. **Business Services:** meeting rooms, fax. **Cards:** AX, DC, DS, MC, VI. **Special Amenities: free continental breakfast and free local telephone calls.** *(See color ad p 410)*

SOME UNITS

**CATAMOUNT MOTEL** **Phone:** 802/442-5977

SAVE

Motel

| | | |
|---|---|---|
| 9/15-10/17 | 2P: $82-$103 | XP: $10 F10 |
| 5/1-9/14 | 2P: $59-$88 | XP: $10 F10 |
| 10/18-4/30 | 2P: $52-$75 | XP: $8 F10 |

**Location:** Jct SR 9, 0.4 mi s on US 7. 500 South St 05201. Fax: 802/447-8765. **Facility:** 17 one-bedroom standard units, some with kitchens (no utensils). 1 story, exterior corridors. *Bath:* shower only. **Parking:** on-site. **Terms:** 3 day cancellation notice-fee imposed. **Pool(s):** outdoor. **Leisure Activities:** barbecue grills, picnic area. **Cards:** AX, DS, MC, VI. **Special Amenities: early check-in/late check-out and preferred room (subject to availability with advanced reservations).** *(See color ad below)*

SOME UNITS

**DARLING KELLY'S MOTEL** **Phone:** (802)442-2322

SAVE

Motel

| | | | |
|---|---|---|---|
| 9/10-10/24 | 1P: $82-$105 | 2P: $82-$105 | XP: $7 |
| 5/1-9/9 | 1P: $58-$81 | 2P: $58-$81 | XP: $5 |
| 10/25-4/30 | 1P: $43-$73 | 2P: $43-$73 | XP: $5 |

**Location:** Jct SR 9 and US 7, 1.2 mi s. 357 US 7 S 05201. Fax: 802/442-2322. **Facility:** 21 one-bedroom standard units. 1 story, exterior corridors. *Bath:* combo or shower only. **Parking:** on-site, winter plug-ins. **Terms:** 3 day cancellation notice, [ECP] meal plan available, pets ($5 extra charge, in designated units). **Pool(s):** outdoor. **Guest Services:** gift shop. **Cards:** AX, DS, MC, VI. **Special Amenities: free local telephone calls.** *(See color ad below)*

SOME UNITS

FEE

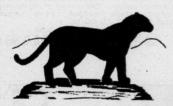

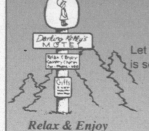

**FIFE 'N DRUM MOTEL**

**Phone: 802/442-4074**

AAA (SAVE)
▽▽▽▽ Motel

| | | | |
|---|---|---|---|
| 9/17-10/16 | | 2P: $69-$112 | XP: $10 |
| 5/21-9/16 | | 2P: $55-$84 | XP: $8 |
| 10/17-1/2 | | 2P: $49-$79 | XP: $8 |
| 5/1-5/20 | | 2P: $47-$65 | XP: $7 |

**Location:** Jct SR 9 and US 7, 1.6 mi s. 693 US Rt 7 S 05201. Fax: 802/442-8471. **Facility:** 18 one-bedroom standard units, some with kitchens. 1-2 stories (no elevator), exterior corridors. *Bath:* combo or shower only. **Parking:** on-site. **Terms:** open 5/1-1/2, 3 day cancellation notice, small pets only ($6 fee, in designated units). **Pool(s):** heated outdoor. **Leisure Activities:** whirlpool, picnic area with grills, badminton, croquet, tetherball, basketball, horseshoes, shuffleboard. **Guest Services:** gift shop. **Cards:** AX, DS, MC, VI. **Special Amenities:** free local telephone calls and free newspaper. *(See color ad below)*

SOME UNITS

🆂🅳 🐕 🛏 ⊠ 🎥 DATA⁄PORT 🔌 💻 / ⊠ VCR 🖥 /
FEE                                    FEE

**HARWOOD HILL MOTEL**

**Phone: 802/442-6278**

AAA (SAVE)
▽▽▽ Motel

| | | | |
|---|---|---|---|
| 9/10-10/23 | 1P: $51-$74 | 2P: $51-$74 | XP: $8 |
| 5/15-9/9 | 1P: $45-$68 | 2P: $45-$68 | XP: $8 |
| 5/1-5/14 & 12/5-4/30 | 1P: $38-$48 | 2P: $38-$48 | XP: $8 |

**Location:** Jct SR 9, 1.2 mi n on US 7, then 1.7 mi n on Historic SR 7A. 898 Harwood Hill Rd (Historic Rt 7A) 05201. Fax: 802/442-6278. **Facility:** 19 units. 16 one-bedroom standard units. 3 cottages. 1 story, exterior corridors. *Bath:* combo or shower only. **Parking:** on-site. **Terms:** open 5/1-10/23 & 12/5-4/30, office hours 8 am-10 pm, 3 day cancellation notice, no pets allowed (owner's dog on premises). **Leisure Activities:** barbecue grills, picnic tables. **Business Services:** fax. **Cards:** CB, DC, DS, MC, VI. **Special Amenities:** free local telephone calls.

SOME UNITS

📶 / ⊠ 🅩 🔌 /

**KNOTTY PINE MOTEL**

**Phone: 802/442-5487**

▽▽▽▽ ▽▽▽▽
Motel

| | | | |
|---|---|---|---|
| 9/16-10/31 | 1P: $79-$95 | 2P: $79-$95 | XP: $8 |
| 5/1-9/15 | 1P: $63-$77 | 2P: $63-$77 | XP: $8 |
| 11/1-4/30 | 1P: $51-$65 | 2P: $51-$65 | XP: $8 |

**Location:** Jct SR 9, 1.2 mi n on US 7, then just n on Historic SR 7A. 130 Northside Dr (SR 7A) 05201. Fax: 802/442-2231. **Facility:** 19 one-bedroom standard units, some with kitchens. 1 story, exterior corridors. *Bath:* combo or shower only. **Parking:** on-site, winter plug-ins. **Terms:** office hours 7:30 am-10 pm, weekly rates available. **Amenities:** *Some:* irons, hair dryers. **Pool(s):** outdoor. **Cards:** AX, CB, DC, DS, JC, MC, VI.

SOME UNITS

🐕 📶 🛏 🔌 💻 / ⊠ 🖥 /

**VERMONTER MOTOR LODGE**

**Phone: (802)442-2529**

AAA (SAVE)
▽▽▽▽ ▽▽▽▽
Motel

| | | | | |
|---|---|---|---|---|
| 3/28-4/30 | 1P: $95-$129 | 2P: $95-$129 | XP: $10 | F12 |
| 10/29-3/27 | 1P: $85-$109 | 2P: $85-$109 | XP: $10 | F12 |
| 5/1-10/28 | 1P: $66-$90 | 2P: $80-$90 | XP: $10 | F12 |

**Location:** 3.9 mi w on SR 9, from jct US 7. 2968 West Rd 05201. Fax: 802/442-0444. **Facility:** 28 units. 18 one-bedroom standard units. 10 cabins ($70-$75). 1 story, exterior corridors. *Bath:* combo or shower only. **Parking:** on-site. **Terms:** cancellation fee imposed, weekly rates available. **Amenities:** voice mail. **Leisure Activities:** paddleboats, sailboats, fishing, badminton, croquet, soccer, volleyball. **Cards:** AX, CB, DC, MC, VI.

SOME UNITS

🆂🅳 🐕 📶 ⊠ DATA⁄PORT / ⊠ 🔌 🖥 /

—— **WHERE TO DINE** ——

**BENNINGTON STATION**  Historic
American
**Lunch:** $6-$10   **Dinner:** $11-$20   **Phone:** 802/447-1080
**Location:** At River St. 150 Depot St 05201. **Hours:** 11:30 am-9 pm, Fri & Sat-10 pm, Sun 10:30 am-9 pm. **Closed:** 12/25. **Reservations:** suggested. **Features:** In a beautifully restored 1897 railroad station, the casual downtown eatery serves attractively garnished American cuisine, including lots of fresh seafood and steak. Portions are generous. Casual dress; cocktails. **Parking:** on-site. **Cards:** AX, DC, DS, MC, VI.

**CARMODY'S**
American
**Lunch:** $6-$15   **Dinner:** $6-$15   **Phone:** 802/447-5748
**Location:** Center. 421 Main St 05201. **Hours:** 11 am-10 pm, Fri & Sat-11 pm. **Closed:** 7/4, 12/25. **Features:** Patrons can enjoy a variety of American dishes served up in this inviting tavern. Casual dress; cocktails. **Parking:** street. **Cards:** AX, MC, VI.

**FOUR CHIMNEY'S RESTAURANT**  Country Inn
American
**Dinner:** $20-$30   **Phone:** 802/447-3500
**Location:** On SR 9, 1.3 mi w of jct US 7; in The Four Chimney's Inn. 21 West Rd 05201. **Hours:** 6 pm-8:30 pm, Sun 5 pm-8 pm. **Closed:** Mon & Tues. **Reservations:** suggested. **Features:** In a former private mansion, the charming country inn combines American and Continental-style dishes on its menu. Local ingredients are used in such menu highlights as seafood pasta, filet mignon, crab cakes, New York strip steak, New Zealand lamb, salmon and chicken Florentine. Casual dress; cocktails. **Parking:** on-site. **Cards:** AX, DC, DS, MC, VI.

**MADISON BREWING CO. PUB & RESTAURANT**
American
**Lunch:** $5-$10   **Dinner:** $7-$18   **Phone:** 802/442-7397
**Location:** On SR 9; center. 428 Main St 05201. **Hours:** 11:30 am-10 pm, Fri & Sat-10:30 pm, Sun noon-9:30 pm. **Closed:** 3/27, 11/25, 12/25. **Features:** The relaxed brewpub serves traditional pub fare, along the lines of tasty sandwiches and burgers, as well as chicken, seafood, pasta and beef dishes. Among yummy desserts are chocolate mousse pie with a ladyfinger crust. Casual dress; cocktails. **Parking:** on-site. **Cards:** AX, MC, VI.

**MCMORLAND'S**
Steak & Seafood
**Dinner:** $14-$26   **Phone:** 802/442-7500
**Location:** Jct SR 9/US 7, 1.2 mi n on US 7, then 1.8 mi n. 782 Harwood Hill (Historic Rt 7A) 05201. **Hours:** 4:30 pm-9 pm, Fri & Sat-10 pm; Sunday brunch 11 am-2:30 pm; hours may vary. **Closed:** 12/25. **Reservations:** accepted. **Features:** The restaurant features a variety of steaks, lamb, pork, chicken and seafood served up in a warm rustic atmosphere; check out the animal heads and variety of cow hides. Casual dress; cocktails. **Parking:** on-site. **Cards:** AX, MC, VI.

**MT ANTHONY COUNTRY CLUB**
American
**Lunch:** $5-$11   **Dinner:** $13-$25   **Phone:** 802/442-2617
**Location:** Jct US 7, 0.5 mi w on SR 9, 0.5 mi n on Convent Ave. 180 Country Club Dr 05251. **Hours:** 11 am-3 & 5-8:30 pm, Fri & Sat-9:30 pm, Sun noon-3 & 5-8 pm. **Closed:** 1/1, 11/25; also Sun & Mon 11/1-3/27. **Reservations:** accepted. **Features:** A laid back, no-frills atmosphere awaits at this country club eatery, in a quiet residential area. The menu lists a varied selection of well-prepared American cuisine served in large portions. Casual dress; cocktails. **Parking:** on-site. **Cards:** AX, DS, MC, VI.

**RATTLESNAKE CAFE**
Mexican
**Dinner:** $6-$17   **Phone:** 802/447-7018
**Location:** Just n of jct US 7/SR 9. 230 North St 05201. **Hours:** 4:30 pm-9 pm. **Closed:** 1/1, 11/25, 12/25; also Mon. **Features:** Serving huge portions of traditional Mexican dishes and the chef's own daily creative selections, the restaurant features selections for all appetites and palates. Among choices are veggie nachos, prepared with a medley of steamed vegetables, and tomato cream soup with a Mexican flair. Casual dress; cocktails. **Parking:** on-site. **Cards:** AX, DS, MC, VI.

**SUGAR MAPLE INNE**
Continental
**Lunch:** $5-$9   **Dinner:** $13-$19   **Phone:** 802/447-7003
**Location:** 3.9 mi w on SR 9 from jct US 7. 2377 West Rd 05201. **Hours:** 7:30-11 am, Fri & Sat 5 pm-8 pm, Sun 7:30 am-noon. **Reservations:** suggested. **Features:** Contributing to the motel dining room's country-cottage decor are assorted crafts displayed on the walls. Fresh seafood, veal, chicken and steak dishes blend Continental, American and Mediterranean influences. Casual dress; cocktails. **Parking:** on-site. **Cards:** AX, DS, MC, VI.

# BERLIN

—— **WHERE TO STAY** ——

**COMFORT INN AT MAPLEWOOD LTD**   *Book at aaa.com*   **Phone:** (802)229-2222

Small-scale Hotel

| |  |  |  | |
|---|---|---|---|---|
| 9/1-11/1 | 1P: $95 | 2P: $105 | XP: $10 | F18 |
| 5/1-8/31 | 1P: $85 | 2P: $95 | XP: $10 | F18 |
| 11/2-4/30 | 1P: $75 | 2P: $85 | XP: $10 | F18 |

**Location:** I-89, exit 7 (SR 62), 0.3 mi e. 213 Paine Tpke N (213 Paine Tpke N, MONTPELIER, 05602). **Fax:** 802/229-2222. **Facility:** 89 units. 70 one-bedroom standard units. 19 one-bedroom suites ($105-$235), some with efficiencies and/or whirlpools. 3 stories (no elevator), interior corridors. **Parking:** on-site, winter plug-ins. **Terms:** 2 night minimum stay - seasonal, cancellation fee imposed, [CP] meal plan available. **Amenities:** video library. *Some:* irons, hair dryers. **Guest Services:** coin laundry. **Business Services:** meeting rooms, fax. **Cards:** AX, CB, DC, DS, MC, VI.

SOME UNITS
FEE

**LA GUE INNS**
*Book at aaa.com*
Small-scale Hotel

| | | | Phone: (802)229-5766 |
|---|---|---|---|
| 9/22-10/12 | 1P: $85-$95 | 2P: $110-$125 | XP: $10  F11 |
| 5/1-9/21 & 10/13-4/30 | 1P: $55-$65 | 2P: $75-$80 | XP: $10  F11 |

**Location:** I-89, exit 7 (SR 62), 1.3 mi e. 3472 Airport Rd 05602 (PO Box 573, BARRE, 05641). Fax: 802/229-5766. **Facility:** 80 one-bedroom standard units. 2 stories, interior corridors. *Bath:* combo or shower only. **Parking:** on-site, winter plug-ins. **Amenities:** *Some:* hair dryers. **Pool(s):** heated indoor. **Leisure Activities:** snowmobiling. **Guest Services:** coin laundry, area transportation. **Business Services:** meeting rooms, fax. **Cards:** AX, CB, DC, MC, VI.

SOME UNITS

(ASK) (S⒟) (✈) (¶) (Y) (⊅) (✇) / (⊠) (VCR) (🖥) (📠) /
FEE

--------- WHERE TO DINE ---------

**WAYSIDE RESTAURANT & BAKERY**  Historic
American

| | Lunch: $4-$6 | Dinner: $6-$12 | Phone: 802-223-6611 |
|---|---|---|---|

**Location:** I-89, exit 7 (SR 62), 0.3 mi w. 1873 US Rt 302 05602. **Hours:** 6:30 am-9:30 pm. Closed major holidays. **Features:** The popular family restaurant and bakery has been a local favorite for breakfast lunch and dinner since 1918. The menu features familiar New England dishes, including fried clams, fried tripe, scallops and haddock, as well as pasta, burgers, steak, chicken, meatloaf, roast beef, ham, sandwiches, daily specials and freshly made pies. Casual dress; cocktails. **Parking:** on-site. **Cards:** AX, DS, MC, VI.

(⊠)

# BETHEL pop. 1,968

--------- WHERE TO DINE ---------

**WILSONS RESTAURANT**
American

| | Lunch: $3-$6 | Dinner: $6-$12 | Phone: 802/234-9680 |
|---|---|---|---|

**Location:** Corner of SR 107 and 12. Rts 12 & 107. **Hours:** 7 am-2 pm, Fri & Sat-8 pm. Closed: 11/25, 12/25. **Reservations:** accepted. **Features:** The locally-popular diner-style restaurant has been a favorite in the area for over 47 years; the road it is situated on is known as "Wilson Flats". Casual dress. **Parking:** on-site. **Cards:** DS, MC, VI.

(M⒞) (⊠)

# BOLTON VALLEY

--------- WHERE TO STAY ---------

**BLACK BEAR INN**
Country Inn

| | | | Phone: 802/434-2126 |
|---|---|---|---|
| 9/21-10/21 [BP] | | 2P: $140-$275 | XP: $15  D11 |
| 12/21-4/30 [BP] | | 2P: $105-$255 | XP: $15  D11 |
| 5/1-9/20 & 10/22-12/20 [BP] | | 2P: $99-$250 | XP: $15  D11 |

**Location:** I-89, exit 10 northbound, 6.2 mi w on US 2, then 4 mi n; exit 11 southbound, 8.4 mi w on US 2, then 4 mi n. 4010 Bolton Access Rd 05477. Fax: 802/434-5161. **Facility:** Offering accommodations ranging from standard rooms to suites, this inn is also home to Oscar, a friendly basset hound. Smoke free premises. 25 units. 22 one- and 2 two-bedroom standard units. 1 one-bedroom suite with efficiency. 2 stories (no elevator), interior/exterior corridors. **Parking:** on-site, winter plug-ins. **Terms:** 21 day cancellation notice-fee imposed, [MAP] meal plan available, pets ($10 extra charge, in kennel only, owner's pet on premises). **Amenities:** voice mail, hair dryers. *Some:* DVD players, CD players. **Pool(s):** heated outdoor. **Leisure Activities:** whirlpool. **Guest Services:** gift shop. **Business Services:** meeting rooms. **Cards:** MC, VI. *(See color ad p 419)*

SOME UNITS

(🛏) (¶) (Y) (⊅) (⊠) (M⒞) / (VCR) (🖥) (📠) /
FEE

# BONDVILLE

--------- WHERE TO DINE ---------

**THE FOGGY GROGGLE STEAKHOUSE**
Steak & Seafood

| | Dinner: $16-$28 | Phone: 802/297-1300 |
|---|---|---|

**Location:** Center. 1 River Rd 05340. **Hours:** 5 pm-10 pm; hours may vary. Closed: Mon-Wed. **Reservations:** suggested. **Features:** The popular family restaurant features a pub atmosphere where folks like to kick back and enjoy the live bands. Casual dress; cocktails. **Parking:** on-site. **Cards:** AX, MC, VI.

(⊠)

**OUT BACK AT WINHALL RIVER**
American

| | Dinner: $16-$22 | Phone: 802/297-3663 |
|---|---|---|

**Location:** Center. **Hours:** Open 5/1-11/1 & 11/15-4/15; 5 pm-9 pm, Sat & Sun from 11:30 am. **Reservations:** accepted. **Features:** A variety of dishes are served up by a friendly staff at this former yacht club, which features a separate casual pub downstairs. Casual dress; cocktails. **Parking:** on-site. **Cards:** MC, VI.

(Y) (⊠)

# BRADFORD pop. 815

--------- WHERE TO DINE ---------

**COLATINA**
Italian

| | Dinner: $8-$19 | Phone: 802/222-9008 |
|---|---|---|

**Location:** Center. 164 Main St 05033. **Hours:** 5 pm-9 pm. Closed: 3/27, 11/25, 12/25. **Features:** The restaurant has an Italian bistro atmosphere with rough hewn walls and a painted tin ceiling where patrons will find fresh food and friendly, casual service. Casual dress; cocktails. **Parking:** street. **Cards:** AX, MC, VI.

(⊠)

**THE PERFECT PEAR CAFE**    **Lunch:** $4-$7    **Dinner:** $9-$20    **Phone:** 802/222-5912

American

**Location:** Just s of center. 48 Main St 05033. **Hours:** 11:30 am-2:30 & 5-9 pm, Tues & Wed-2:30 pm; hours may vary seasonally. **Closed:** 1/1, 11/25, 12/25; also Sun & Mon. **Features:** The restaurant is a charming eatery offering patrons a definite twist when it comes to comfort foods; "creative and delicious" is the the best way to describe them. Casual dress; cocktails. **Parking:** on-site. **Cards:** AX, DS, MC, VI.

## BRANDON pop. 1,684

------- WHERE TO STAY -------

**BRANDON MOTOR LODGE**    **Phone:** 802/247-9594

| | | |
|---|---|---|
| 9/22-10/21 [CP] | 1P: $65-$75 | 2P: $65-$95 |
| 5/1-9/21 [CP] | 1P: $55-$65 | 2P: $55-$85 |
| 10/22-4/30 [CP] | 1P: $55-$65 | 2P: $55-$75 |

Motel

**Location:** 2 mi s on US 7. 2095 Franklin St 05733. **Facility:** 25 one-bedroom standard units. 1 story, exterior corridors. *Bath:* combo or shower only. **Parking:** on-site. **Terms:** weekly rates available, pets ($5 extra charge, in designated units). **Amenities:** *Some:* voice mail, irons. **Leisure Activities:** whirlpool, picnic table, croquet, bocci, horseshoes. **Business Services:** meeting rooms. **Cards:** AX, DS, MC, VI. **Special Amenities: free continental breakfast and free local telephone calls.**

SOME UNITS

FEE

**THE LILAC INN**    **Phone:** (802)247-5463

| | | | |
|---|---|---|---|
| 9/10-10/11 | 1P: $250 | 2P: $325 | XP: $30    F12 |
| 5/1-9/9 & 10/12-4/30 | 1P: $140-$230 | 2P: $140-$230 | XP: $30    F12 |

Historic Country Inn

**Location:** Just e on SR 73. Located in a historic district. 53 Park St 05733. Fax: 802/247-5499. **Facility:** A restored 1909 mansion offering spacious guest rooms furnished with antiques and reproductions, the property is in a quiet historic village. Smoke free premises. 9 one-bedroom standard units, some with whirlpools. 2 stories (no elevator), interior corridors. *Bath:* combo or tub only. **Parking:** on-site. **Terms:** 2 night minimum stay - weekends, age restrictions may apply, 30 day cancellation notice-fee imposed, [BP] meal plan available, package plans - weekends, pets ($30 extra charge). **Amenities:** irons, hair dryers. *Some:* DVD players. **Business Services:** meeting rooms. **Cards:** AX, MC, VI.

FEE

------- WHERE TO DINE -------

**PATRICIA'S RESTAURANT AKA SULLY'S PLACE**    **Lunch:** $5-$7    **Dinner:** $12-$22    **Phone:** 802/247-3223

American

**Location:** Center. 18-20 Center St 05733. **Hours:** 11 am-9 pm, Sun from 9 am. **Closed:** 1/1, 12/25. **Reservations:** accepted. **Features:** Casual dining in an atmosphere featuring Vermont wildlife, antique creels, rods and wildlife prints adorns the walls. Diners can also enjoy the outdoor deck and umbrella tables in the summer, as well as a fine brunch on Sunday. Cocktails. **Parking:** street. **Cards:** DS, MC, VI.

## BRATTLEBORO pop. 8,289—*See also WEST BRATTLEBORO.*

------- WHERE TO STAY -------

**COLONIAL MOTEL & SPA**    **Phone:** 802/257-7733

| | | | |
|---|---|---|---|
| All Year | 1P: $50 | 2P: $130 | XP: $10    F12 |

Small-scale Hotel

**Location:** I-91, exit 3, just e on SR 9, then 0.5 mi s on US 5. 889 Putney Rd 05301. Fax: 802/257-7733. **Facility:** 68 units. 61 one-bedroom standard units. 7 one-bedroom suites, some with kitchens. 1-2 stories (no elevator), exterior corridors. *Bath:* combo or shower only. **Parking:** on-site, winter plug-ins. **Terms:** [CP] meal plan available, pets ($10 fee). **Amenities:** voice mail, irons, hair dryers. **Dining:** Michele's Ristorante, see separate listing. **Pool(s):** small outdoor, heated indoor. **Leisure Activities:** saunas, whirlpool, steamrooms. *Fee:* massage. **Guest Services:** valet laundry. **Business Services:** meeting rooms. **Cards:** AX, DS, MC, VI. **Special Amenities: free continental breakfast and free local telephone calls.**

SOME UNITS

FEE

**ECONO LODGE** *Book at aaa.com*

Phone: (802)254-2360

| | | | | |
|---|---|---|---|---|
| 10/1-10/31 | 1P: $60-$130 | 2P: $60-$130 | XP: $10 | F18 |
| 5/1-9/30 | 1P: $49-$119 | 2P: $49-$119 | XP: $5 | F18 |
| 11/1-4/30 | 1P: $40-$80 | 2P: $40-$80 | XP: $5 | F18 |

Motel **Location:** I-91, exit 1, 0.3 mi n on US 5. 515 Canal St 05301. Fax: 802/251-0910. **Facility:** 40 one-bedroom standard units. 1-2 stories (no elevator), exterior corridors. *Bath:* combo or shower only. **Parking:** on-site, winter plug-ins. **Terms:** [ECP] meal plan available, pets ($15 extra charge). **Amenities:** high-speed Internet, hair dryers. **Pool(s):** outdoor. **Cards:** AX, CB, DC, DS, JC, MC, VI. *(See color ad p 415)*

SOME UNITS

FEE

---

**HOLIDAY INN EXPRESS HOTEL & SUITES** *Book at aaa.com*

Phone: (802)257-2400

All Year [ECP]     1P: $99-$179     2P: $99-$179
**Location:** I-91, exit 3, just e on SR 9, then 0.5 mi s on US 5. 100 Chickering Dr 05301. Fax: 802/257-8616.
**Facility:** 86 units. 84 one-bedroom standard units, some with whirlpools. 2 two-bedroom suites ($129-$209).
3 stories, interior corridors. *Bath:* combo or shower only. **Parking:** on-site. **Amenities:** video games, dual
Small-scale Hotel phone lines, voice mail, irons, hair dryers. **Pool(s):** heated indoor. **Leisure Activities:** whirlpool, exercise
room. **Guest Services:** valet and coin laundry. **Business Services:** meeting rooms, business center.
**Cards:** AX, CB, DC, DS, MC, VI. **Special Amenities:** free expanded continental breakfast and free local telephone calls.
*(See color ad below)*

SOME UNITS

---

---

**MEADOWLARK INN**
Historic Bed & Breakfast

9/15-4/30 [BP]
5/1-9/14 [BP]

1P: $125-$180
1P: $115-$170

2P: $125-$180
2P: $115-$170

Phone: 802/257-4582
XP: $35
XP: $25

**Location:** I-91, exit 2, just w on SR 9, then 1.5 mi n on Orchard St. Located in a quiet area. 13 Gibson Rd 05301 (PO Box 2048, WEST BRATTLEBORO, 05303). Fax: 802/257-4582. **Facility:** The B&B in a tranquil setting includes an old farmhouse and renovated outbuilding and offers distant hillside views. Smoke free premises. 8 one-bedroom standard units, some with whirlpools. 1-2 stories (no elevator), interior corridors. *Bath:* combo or shower only. **Parking:** on-site. **Terms:** 2 night minimum stay - weekends in fall & summer, 7 day cancellation notice, no pets allowed (owner's dog on premises). **Amenities:** video library, hair dryers. *Some:* CD players. **Guest Services:** complimentary evening beverages. **Cards:** AX, MC, VI.

SOME UNITS
ASK S🚭 ✕ / 🅰🄲 📵 VCR 📶 /

**QUALITY INN & SUITES**      *Book at aaa.com*
Small-scale Hotel

All Year

1P: $79-$169

2P: $79-$169

Phone: (802)254-8701
XP: $10          F18

**Location:** I-91, exit 3, 0.6 mi n on US 5. 1380 Putney Rd 05301. Fax: 802/257-4727. **Facility:** 107 units. 98 one-bedroom standard units. 6 one- and 3 two-bedroom suites ($110-$189) with kitchens. 2 stories (no elevator), interior corridors. **Parking:** on-site, winter plug-ins. **Terms:** [BP] & [ECP] meal plans available, pets ($50 fee in designated suites). **Amenities:** voice mail, irons, hair dryers. *Some:* high-speed Internet. **Pool(s):** outdoor, heated indoor. **Leisure Activities:** sauna, whirlpool, exercise room. *Fee:* game room. **Guest Services:** valet and coin laundry. **Business Services:** meeting rooms, PC (fee). **Cards:** AX, DC, DS, MC, VI. *(See color ad below)*

SOME UNITS
ASK S🚭 🛏 🍴 🍽 🛁 🛬 ✕ 🎮 DATA PORT 📶 💻 / ✕ VCR 📶 /
FEE                                                                    FEE

---

---

**SUPER 8 MOTEL**     *Book at aaa.com*                                                    Phone: 802/254-8889

(AAA) (SAVE)      10/1-10/31 [CP]              1P: $85-$110        2P: $90-$115        XP: $5                    F
                  8/1-9/30 [CP]               1P: $75-$85         2P: $80-$90         XP: $5                    F
▼▼▼ ▼▼▼           5/1-7/31 [CP]               1P: $46-$75         2P: $50-$80         XP: $5                    F
                  11/1-4/30 [CP]              1P: $46-$55         2P: $50-$60         XP: $5                    F
Motel        **Location:** I-91, exit 3, just e on SR 9, then just s on US 5. 1043 Putney Rd 05301. Fax: 802/254-8323. **Facility:** 63
             one-bedroom standard units. 2 stories (no elevator), interior corridors. **Parking:** on-site, winter plug-ins.
**Terms:** pets ($20 fee). **Amenities:** high-speed Internet. **Cards:** AX, DC, DS, MC, VI. **Special Amenities:** free continental
breakfast and free local telephone calls.

SOME UNITS

🛏️ 🍴➕ 🚿Ⓜ️ 📷 📠DATA/PORT / ✕ 🛗 🖥️ / 
FEE

──────── **WHERE TO DINE** ────────

**BRATTLEBORO FOOD CO-OP, MARKET, DELI, & CAFE**     **Lunch:** $5-$15     **Dinner:** $5-$15     **Phone:** 802/257-0236
▼▼▼          **Location:** Center; in Brookside Plaza. 2 Main St 05301. **Hours:** 8 am-9 pm, Sun 9 am-8 pm. Closed major
             holidays. **Features:** The deli at this community-owned market attracts hard-core vegetarians as well as
Natural/Organic   non-vegetarians just looking for a healthy break. It offers a wide variety of vegetarian and organic foods
             including comforting soups, fresh salads and a good selection of hot entrees. A limited choice of fish and
meat dishes are also available. Opt to eat in or take out and let yourself be tempted by a delicious concoction from the juice
bar. Casual dress. **Parking:** on-site. **Cards:** MC, VI.                                                     ✕

**LUCCA BISTRO & BREWERY**                          **Dinner:** $12-$22                        **Phone:** 802/254-4747
(AAA)        **Location:** I-91, exit 3, 2.5 mi s on US 5, then just w. 6 Flat St 05301. **Hours:** 5:30 pm-9:30 pm, Fri & Sat-10 pm.
▼▼▼ ▼▼▼       Closed: Tues. **Reservations:** suggested. **Features:** Tuscan-style Italian cuisine is served in a casual yet
             elegant environment. Among menu selections are potato gnocchi with English peas and prosciutto and an
Italian      appetizer of roasted shrimp over Tuscan-style canellini beans. Dressy casual; cocktails. **Parking:** street.
             **Cards:** AX, MC, VI.                                                            🍸 ✕

**THE MARINA RESTAURANT**                 **Lunch:** $5-$12        **Dinner:** $7-$15          **Phone:** 802/257-7563
▼▼▼ ▼▼        **Location:** I-91, exit 3, 1.3 mi s on US 5, then just w. 28 Springtree Rd 05301. **Hours:** 11:30 am-10 pm, Sun 11
             am-9 pm. Closed: 11/25, 12/24, 12/25. **Reservations:** accepted. **Features:** On the West River, the
American     restaurant serves casual fare in an open-air setting. Lending to the relaxed mood are reggae music and
             Caribbean decor. Casual dress; cocktails. **Parking:** on-site. **Cards:** MC, VI.            🍸 ✕

**MICHELE'S RISTORANTE**                            **Dinner:** $11-$20                        **Phone:** 802/254-5267
▼▼▼ ▼▼▼       **Location:** I-91, exit 3, just e on SR 9, then 0.5 mi s on US 5; in Colonial Motel & Spa. 889 Putney Rd 05301.
             **Hours:** 5:30 pm-9 pm, Fri & Sat-10 pm. Closed: 11/25, 12/24, 12/25; also Sun. **Reservations:** suggested.
Nouvelle Italian   **Features:** Classic, Italian dishes such as veal saltin bocca, braciolone and salsiccia, expertly prepared and
             served in a warm and intimate setting are the hallmark of Michele's. Dressy casual; cocktails. **Parking:**
on-site. **Cards:** MC, VI.                                                                     ✕

**PANDA NORTH CHINESE RESTAURANT**            **Lunch:** $5-$6      **Dinner:** $6-$15         **Phone:** 802/257-4578
▼▼▼ ▼▼▼       **Location:** I-91, exit 3, 0.4 mi n on US 5. 1332 Putney Rd 05301. **Hours:** 11:30 am-9:30 pm, Fri & Sat-10:30 pm,
             Sun noon-9:30 pm. Closed: 11/25. **Reservations:** accepted. **Features:** Panda North features Szechuan,
Chinese      Hunan, Shanghai, Peking and Cantonese cuisine offering seafood, chicken, pork, beef and vegetarian
             entrees. General Tso's chicken is superb! Lunch specials include soup and rice. The prompt, friendly
service and casual atmosphere are delightful. Casual dress; cocktails. **Parking:** on-site. **Cards:** AX, DS, MC, VI.   ✕

# BRIDGEWATER

──────── **WHERE TO DINE** ────────

**1920'S PIZZA & PASTA HOUSE**                      **Dinner:** $4-$15                        **Phone:** 802/672-5120
▼▼▼ ▼▼        **Location:** 7 mi w of Woodstock Center. US Rt 4 05034. **Hours:** 3 pm-midnight. Closed: 11/25, 12/25; also Tues.
             **Features:** The family-style restaurant is decorated in a well coordinated 1920s theme and features a
Italian      variety of pizzas and pasta dishes. Casual dress; cocktails. **Parking:** on-site. **Cards:** MC, VI.    🎱 ✕

# BRIDGEWATER CORNERS

──────── **WHERE TO DINE** ────────

──── *The following restaurant has not been evaluated by AAA* ────
*but is listed for your information only.*

**LONG TRAIL BREWING COMPANY**                                                                **Phone:** 802/672-5011
(fyi)        Not evaluated. **Location:** Jct US 4 and SR 100A. Jct US Rt 4 & SR 100A 05035. **Features:** Open for lunch and
             dinner, the microbrewery offers diners a simple, casual meal.

# BRISTOL

## ─────── WHERE TO DINE ───────

**INN AT BALDWIN CREEK-MARY'S RESTAURANT**   Historic          **Dinner:** $16-$22          **Phone:** 802/453-2432

ⒶⒶⒶ
▼▼◆▼▼

Regional
American

**Location:** Jct SR 17 and 116, just n, then 3 mi n. 1868 N SR 116 05443. **Hours:** 5:30 pm-9:30 pm. Closed: 12/25; also Mon & Tues, 1st week in April & 1st week in Nov. **Reservations:** suggested. **Features:** Famous for its cream of garlic soup, Mary's uses fresh products from local farms. The menu is changed seasonally and supplemented with daily specials to take advantage of the freshest ingredients. The 1790 farmhouse setting at foot of Green Mountains is warm and cozy. Dressy casual; cocktails. **Parking:** on-site. **Cards:** MC, VI.

ⓨ ⓧ

# BROOKFIELD pop. 1,222

## ─────── WHERE TO DINE ───────

**ARIEL'S RESTAURANT**                              **Dinner:** $19-$25                              **Phone:** 802/276-3939

▼▼◆▼▼

American

**Location:** Center. 29 Stone Rd 05036. **Hours:** Open 5/1-10/31 & 12/1-4/30; 5:30 pm-9:30 pm. Closed: 1/1, 11/25; also Sun-Thurs. **Reservations:** suggested. **Features:** The restaurant is in Pond Village, aptly named for beautiful Sunset Lake, which is known for its floating bridge. On weekends, patrons can sample exceptionally prepared cuisine in the dining room. Offerings include butternut squash soup with hazelnuts, locally raised grilled quail and such international favorites as traditional Pad Thai. Dressy casual; cocktails. **Parking:** on-site. **Cards:** DS, MC, VI.

ⓨ Ⓚ ⓧ

# BURLINGTON pop. 38,889—See also SOUTH BURLINGTON.

## ─────── WHERE TO STAY ───────

**TOWN & COUNTRY MOTEL**                                                                      **Phone:** 802/862-5786

ⒶⒶⒶ ⓢⒶⓥⒺ
▼▼ ◆▼

Motel

All Year                        1P: $59-$109          2P: $59-$109          XP: $5          F12
**Location:** I-89, exit 13, just n on US 7 N. 490 Shelburne Rd 05401 (PO Box 64678, 05406-4678). **Facility:** 12 one-bedroom standard units. 1 story, exterior corridors. **Parking:** on-site. **Terms:** 3 day cancellation notice-fee imposed, pets ($10 extra charge, dogs only). **Cards:** AX, CB, DC, DS, MC, VI.

SOME UNITS

I want to take
a break from all
the stresses of
kindergarten

**WYNDHAM BURLINGTON**
*Book at aaa.com*
Phone: (802)658-6500

| | 5/1-10/31 | 1P: $159-$289 | 2P: $159-$289 | XP: $20 | F17 |
| | 11/1-4/30 | 1P: $159-$219 | 2P: $159-$219 | XP: $20 | F17 |

Large-scale Hotel **Location:** At Battery and College sts; just n of ferry terminal; center. 60 Battery St 05401. **Fax:** 802/658-4659. **Facility:** 256 units. 249 one-bedroom standard units, some with whirlpools. 6 one- and 1 two-bedroom suites. 8 stories, interior corridors. *Bath:* combo or shower only. **Parking:** on-site (fee). **Terms:** [AP], [BP], [CP] & [MAP] meal plans available. **Amenities:** dual phone lines, voice mail, safes, irons, hair dryers. *Fee:* video games, high-speed Internet. **Pool(s):** heated indoor. **Leisure Activities:** whirlpool, exercise room. **Guest Services:** gift shop, valet laundry. **Business Services:** conference facilities, business center. **Cards:** AX, DC, DS, MC, VI. *(See color ad p 419)* SOME UNITS

Reservations: **800-336-1869**
Information: 802-863-7000

**www.vtanchorageinn.com**

*One of Burlington's Best Lodging Values!*

# Anchorage Inn

- *Indoor Pool*
- *Sauna and Whirlpool*
- *Free Continental Breakfast*
- *60-Channel Cable TV including HBO*
- *Discount Ski Packages with all northern Vermont Resorts*

**SEE LISTING IN SO. BURLINGTON**

108 Dorset Street, South Burlington VT 05403 • Exit 14E off I-89

**The Bridges®**
FAMILY RESORT & TENNIS CLUB

- 4-SEASON CONDOMINIUM RESORT
- FIREPLACES
- 3 POOLS
- 12 TENNIS COURTS
- FITNESS CENTER, HOT TUB, SAUNA AND GAME ROOM

202 BRIDGES CIRCLE
WARREN, VERMONT 05674
1-800-453-2922
WWW.BRIDGESRESORT.COM

## Burlington's only Clarion is pure Vermont.

- 15% AAA Discount*
- 160 rooms including 33 2-room luxury suites
- Indoor pool, spa & fitness center
- Outdoor courtyard
- Signature award-winning restaurant & lounge
- Across from Vermont's largest mall
- Minutes from downtown, waterfront, UVM

PLATINUM HOSPITALITY AWARD

**Clarion Hotel**
I-89 & U.S. 2, Exit 14E
1117 Williston Road
Burlington, VT 05403-5717
www.clarionvermont.com
1.800.CLARION or
802.658.0250

**800.228.1AAA**
choicehotels.com

We'll see you there.™

**Clarion**
Hotel & Suites

© 2003 Choice Hotels International, Inc.

* Off published rates. Subject to availability.

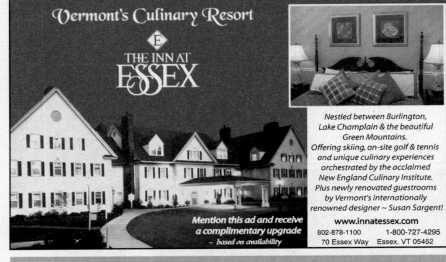
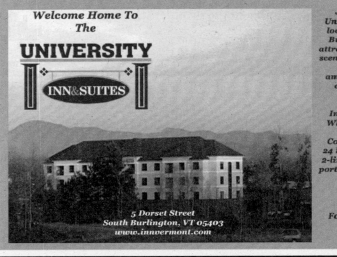

——— WHERE TO DINE ———

**FIVE SPICE CAFE**

Asian

Lunch: $7-$9   Dinner: $13-$17   Phone: 802/864-4045
**Location:** Corner Main St; downtown. 175 Church St 05401. **Hours:** 11:30 am-3 & 5-9:30 pm, Fri & Sat-10 pm, Sun 11 am-2:30 & 3-9 pm. Closed: 11/25, 12/25. **Reservations:** suggested. **Features:** Drawing inspiration from a side variety of Asian cultures, Five Spice Cafe describes its menu as "multi-Asian cuisine". The atmosphere is decidedly casual and almost Bohemian in this little restaurant just off of Main St in downtown Burlington. Casual dress; cocktails. **Parking:** street. **Cards:** AX, DC, DS, MC, VI.

**THE ICE HOUSE**
Steak & Seafood

Lunch: $6-$12   Dinner: $15-$25   Phone: 802/864-1800
**Location:** Lakeside; at ferry entrance. 171 Battery St 05401. **Hours:** 11:30 am-10 pm; hours may vary in winter. Closed: 1/1, 11/25, 12/25. **Reservations:** suggested. **Features:** A lovely view of Lake Champlain awaits visitors to the converted, turn-of-the-20th-century, former icehouse. On the menu are seafood, steaks and delicatessen and grilled sandwiches. Brunch is served Sundays, except during winter. Smoking is allowed on the deck, which is open seasonally. Casual dress; cocktails. **Parking:** on-site. **Cards:** AX, DC, DS, MC, VI.

**RI RA**
Irish

Lunch: $6-$12   Dinner: $6-$12   Phone: 802/860-9401
**Location:** Between College and Main sts; downtown. 123 Church St 05401. **Hours:** 11:30 am-10 pm. **Features:** Traditional Irish and American meals are served with many imported beers, ales and lagers. Casual dress; cocktails. **Parking:** street. **Cards:** AX, DC, MC, VI.

**SAKURA JAPANESE RESTAURANT**
Japanese

Lunch: $5-$12   Dinner: $9-$20   Phone: 802/863-1988
**Location:** Center; in the Church St Market Place. 2 Church St 05401. **Hours:** 11:30 am-2 & 5-9:30 pm, Fri & Sat-10:30 pm, Sun-9 pm. Closed major holidays; also for lunch Sun. **Reservations:** suggested. **Features:** You'll enjoy this popular restaurant offering a softly lit, bustling atmosphere and fresh flowers in the comfortable decor. The traditional offerings include eye-appealing sashimi, noodles, nabe and tempura choices as well as sushi bar temptations. Casual dress; cocktails. **Parking:** street. **Cards:** AX, DC, DS, MC, VI.

**SWEETWATERS**
American

Lunch: $5-$10   Dinner: $11-$15   Phone: 802/864-9800
**Location:** Corner of Church and College sts; downtown. 120 Church St 05401. **Hours:** 11:30 am-midnight, Sat-1 am, Sun-11:30 pm. Closed: 11/25, 12/25. **Reservations:** suggested, weekends. **Features:** This popular restaurant located in a former bank building has a Southwestern theme. The varied menu offers unusual variations of traditional dishes and includes wood-grilled specialties, pasta, seafood and chicken offerings. Seasonal patio dining. Casual dress; cocktails. **Parking:** street. **Cards:** AX, CB, DC, DS, MC, VI.

# CAVENDISH

——— WHERE TO STAY ———

**CLARION HOTEL AT CAVENDISH POINTE**
Small-scale Hotel

*Book at aaa.com*

| |  |  |  | |
|---|---|---|---|---|
| 12/19-4/2 | 1P: $99-$289 | 2P: $99-$289 | XP: $15 | F17 |
| 5/1-12/18 & 4/3-4/30 | 1P: $89-$179 | 2P: $89-$179 | XP: $15 | F17 |

Phone: (802)226-7688
**Location:** On SR 103, just n of jct SR 131. 2940 SR 103 05142 (PO Box 525, LUDLOW, 05149). Fax: 802/226-7689. **Facility:** 70 one-bedroom standard units, some with whirlpools. 2 stories, interior corridors. **Parking:** on-site, winter plug-ins. **Terms:** 1-3 night minimum stay - weekends, 14 day cancellation notice, package plans, small pets only ($20 extra charge). **Amenities:** voice mail, irons, hair dryers. *Some:* dual phone lines. **Dining:** 7 am-10 & 5:30-9 pm, cocktails. **Pool(s):** heated indoor. **Leisure Activities:** whirlpool, spa. *Fee:* game room. **Business Services:** meeting rooms, PC, fax. **Cards:** AX, CB, DC, DS, JC, MC, VI. **Special Amenities:** free local telephone calls.

SOME UNITS

——— WHERE TO DINE ———

**THE CASTLE**
Continental

Dinner: $21-$29   Phone: 802/226-7361
**Location:** Next to the Clarion Hotel at Cavendish Pointe. 2910 Rt 103 05149. **Hours:** 5:30 pm-9 pm; call for availability. Closed: Mon; Sun 5/31-12/20. **Reservations:** suggested. **Features:** Truly an architectural gem, this former Governor's mansion built by European craftsmen at the turn of the century features elaborate, drawn plaster ceilings, paneled reception rooms and an extremely rich, yet romantic interior; the staff is just as gracious as its surroundings. Casual dress; cocktails. **Parking:** on-site. **Cards:** AX, DS, MC, VI.

# CHESTER

——— WHERE TO STAY ———

**THE STONE HEARTH INN**
Historic Country Inn

*Book at aaa.com*

| |  |  |  | |
|---|---|---|---|---|
| 9/16-10/31 [BP] | 1P: $99-$149 | 2P: $109-$159 | XP: $15 | D17 |
| 12/16-4/30 [BP] | 1P: $79-$149 | 2P: $79-$159 | XP: $15 | D17 |
| 5/1-9/15 [BP] | 1P: $69-$139 | 2P: $79-$149 | XP: $15 | D17 |
| 11/1-12/15 [BP] | 1P: $69-$139 | 2P: $79-$139 | XP: $15 | D17 |

Phone: (802)875-2525
**Location:** 1.5 mi w. 698 Rt 11 W 05143. Fax: 802/875-1588. **Facility:** This rambling farmhouse, which dates from 1810, has country charm but is close to downtown. Smoke free premises. 10 one-bedroom standard units. 2 stories (no elevator), interior corridors. *Bath:* combo or shower only. **Parking:** on-site. **Terms:** check-in 4 pm, 2-3 night minimum stay, age restrictions may apply, 14 day cancellation notice, pets ($30 fee). **Cards:** AX, DS, MC, VI.

SOME UNITS

──────── **WHERE TO DINE** ────────

**CITY SLICKERS**
American
**Lunch:** $3-$6 **Dinner:** $6-$8 **Phone:** 802/875-1062
**Location:** 0.5 mi s of jct SR 103S/11E. SR 103 05143. **Hours:** 6 am-8 pm, Fri-9 pm. Closed: 11/25, 12/25.
**Features:** The restaurant is an old-time dining car decorated with a variety of antiques and bric-a-brac, offering basic diner fare served up with casual pleasant service. Casual dress. **Parking:** on-site.

**THE COUNTRY GIRL DINER**
American
**Lunch:** $4-$6 **Dinner:** $7-$9 **Phone:** 802/875-2650
**Location:** Just e of jct SR 103/11 W. S Main St 05143. **Hours:** 6 am-8 pm, Sun from 7 am. Closed: 3/27, 11/25, 12/25. **Features:** Located in an authentic Silk City Diner car, the restaurant offers a simple atmosphere, pleasant service and good food; especially their signature corn-tomato chowder. Casual dress. **Parking:** on-site.

**RASPBERRIES AND TYME**
American
**Lunch:** $7-$12 **Dinner:** $17-$25 **Phone:** 802/875-4486
**Location:** On the town common. 90 The Common 05143. **Hours:** 8 am-9 pm; hours may vary. Closed: 12/25. **Features:** The restaurant is located in a turn-of-the-century Victorian house; join them for a hearty breakfast or stop by for a lovely lunch or dinner. Casual dress; cocktails. **Parking:** street. **Cards:** AX, DC, DS, MC, VI.

# CHITTENDEN

──────── **WHERE TO STAY** ────────

**THE MOUNTAIN TOP INN & RESORT** *Book at aaa.com* **Phone:** (802)483-2311
Country Inn

| |  |  |  | |
|---|---|---|---|---|
| 9/24-10/17 | 1P: $195-$415 | 2P: $195-$415 | XP: $45 | F5 |
| 5/1-9/23 & 12/18-4/30 | 1P: $155-$365 | 2P: $155-$365 | XP: $45 | F5 |
| 10/18-12/17 | 1P: $115-$265 | 2P: $115-$265 | XP: $45 | F5 |

**Location:** Jct US 4, 1.8 mi n on Meadowlake Dr, 2.8 mi e on Chittenden Rd, then 2 mi n. Located in a secluded area, near the monument. 195 Mountain Top Rd 05737. **Fax:** 802/483-6373. **Facility:** The inn, on 1,000 acres, features a lodge and cottages with sweeping views of a scenic lake and mountains. Smoke free premises. 45 units. 34 one-bedroom standard units. 5 cabins ($175-$450) and 6 cottages ($175-$450). 1-3 stories (no elevator), interior/exterior corridors. **Parking:** on-site. **Terms:** 2 night minimum stay - weekends in season, 21 day cancellation notice-fee imposed, [AP], [BP] & [MAP] meal plans available, package plans - seasonal, 15% service charge, pets ($25 extra charge, in cottages). **Amenities:** voice mail. *Some:* CD players, irons, hair dryers. **Pool(s):** outdoor. **Leisure Activities:** sauna, boating, canoeing, fishing, tennis court, cross country skiing, ice skating, tobogganing, recreation programs in season, hiking trails, limited exercise equipment, horseshoes, shuffleboard. *Fee:* horseback riding, massage. **Guest Services:** gift shop, valet laundry. **Business Services:** meeting rooms, PC. **Cards:** AX, MC, VI.

SOME UNITS

# COLCHESTER

──────── **WHERE TO STAY** ────────

**DAYS INN** *Book at aaa.com* **Phone:** (802)655-0900
Small-scale Hotel

| |  |  |  | |
|---|---|---|---|---|
| 8/1-10/31 [ECP] | 1P: $75-$165 | 2P: $85-$175 | XP: $10 | F16 |
| 5/1-7/31 [ECP] | 1P: $65-$125 | 2P: $70-$130 | XP: $10 | F16 |
| 11/1-4/30 [ECP] | 1P: $40-$90 | 2P: $50-$95 | XP: $10 | F16 |

**Location:** I-89, exit 15 northbound, just e on SR 15; exit 16 southbound, 1.1 mi s on US 7, then 1 mi e on SR 15. 23 College Pkwy 05446. **Fax:** 802/655-6851. **Facility:** 73 one-bedroom standard units, some with efficiencies (no utensils) and/or whirlpools. 4 stories, interior corridors. *Bath:* combo or shower only. **Parking:** on-site. **Terms:** pets ($50 deposit, $10 extra charge, in smoking units). **Amenities:** safes, hair dryers. **Pool(s):** heated indoor. **Guest Services:** coin laundry. **Business Services:** meeting rooms. **Cards:** AX, CB, DC, DS, JC, MC, VI.

SOME UNITS

**FAIRFIELD INN BY MARRIOTT** *Book at aaa.com* **Phone:** 802/655-1400
Small-scale Hotel

| |  |  |
|---|---|---|
| 7/2-10/17 | 1P: $89-$109 | 2P: $89-$109 |
| 6/2-7/1 | 1P: $79-$89 | 2P: $79-$89 |
| 5/1-6/1 | 1P: $69-$79 | 2P: $69-$79 |
| 10/18-4/30 | 1P: $54-$69 | 2P: $54-$69 |

**Location:** I-89, exit 16, just s on US 7. 84 S Park Dr 05446. **Fax:** 802/338-9158. **Facility:** 117 one-bedroom standard units. 3 stories, interior/exterior corridors. *Bath:* combo or shower only. **Parking:** on-site, winter plug-ins. **Terms:** [CP] meal plan available. **Amenities:** irons, hair dryers. **Pool(s):** heated outdoor. **Guest Services:** valet laundry. **Cards:** AX, DC, DS, MC, VI.

SOME UNITS

**HAMPTON INN & CONFERENCE CENTER** *Book at aaa.com* **Phone:** (802)655-6177
Small-scale Hotel

| |  |  |
|---|---|---|
| All Year [ECP] | 1P: $89-$149 | 2P: $99-$159 |

**Location:** I-89, exit 16, just n on US 7. 42 Lower Mountain View Dr 05446. **Fax:** 802/655-4962. **Facility:** 188 units. 186 one-bedroom standard units, some with efficiencies or kitchens. 2 one-bedroom suites ($129-$209) with kitchens. 4 stories, interior corridors. *Bath:* combo or shower only. **Parking:** on-site, winter plug-ins. **Terms:** weekly rates available, small pets only. **Amenities:** video games (fee), voice mail, irons, hair dryers. **Pool(s):** heated indoor. **Leisure Activities:** whirlpool, exercise room. **Guest Services:** valet and coin laundry. **Business Services:** conference facilities, PC. **Cards:** AX, DC, DS, MC, VI.

SOME UNITS

**MOTEL 6**  *Book at aaa.com*  **Phone: 802/654-6860**

WWW WWW (Small-scale Hotel)

| | | | | |
|---|---|---|---|---|
| 9/7-10/23 | 1P: $49-$85 | 2P: $55-$91 | XP: $3 | F17 |
| 7/8-9/6 | 1P: $52-$70 | 2P: $58-$76 | XP: $3 | F17 |
| 5/1-7/7 | 1P: $41-$66 | 2P: $47-$72 | XP: $3 | F17 |
| 10/24-4/30 | 1P: $39-$49 | 2P: $45-$55 | XP: $3 | F17 |

**Location:** I-89, exit 16, just s on US 7. 74 S Park Dr 05446. **Fax:** 802/655-3515. **Facility:** 106 one-bedroom standard units. 3 stories, interior corridors. *Bath:* combo or shower only. **Parking:** on-site, winter plug-ins. **Pool(s):** heated outdoor. **Guest Services:** coin laundry. **Cards:** AX, CB, DC, DS, MC, VI.

SOME UNITS

—————— WHERE TO DINE ——————

**LIBBY'S DINER**  **Lunch:** $5-$7  **Dinner:** $8-$10  **Phone: 802/655-0343**

WWW (American)

**Location:** I-89, exit 16, just sw. 46 High Point Center 05446. **Hours:** 6 am-9 pm, Sat from 7 am, Sun 7 am-2 pm. **Closed:** 7/4, 11/25, 12/25; also Mon. **Features:** A virtual Vermont icon for the last 12 years, the diner prepares traditional comfort foods in one of the last-produced, original Worcester Lunch dining cars. Casual dress; beer & wine only. **Parking:** on-site. **Cards:** AX, MC, VI.

# COVENTRY

—————— WHERE TO DINE ——————

**HEERMANSMITH FARM INN**  Country Inn  **Dinner:** $18-$25  **Phone: 802/754-8866**

WWW WWW (Nouvelle American)

**Location:** From Main St, 0.5 mi nw up steep hill on to dirt road. 550 Heermanville Rd 05825. **Hours:** 5:30 pm-9 pm. **Closed:** Mon & Tues. **Reservations:** suggested. **Features:** You're sure to enjoy this 1860s farmhouse offering a warm, candlelit atmosphere as well as fresh homegrown berries and vegetables. The roast duck specialty is delicious, and so are the steaks, baked stuffed prawns, shrimp Louise, Peking Nantucket quail. Casual dress; cocktails. **Parking:** on-site. **Cards:** AX, DS, MC, VI.

# CRAFTSBURY COMMON

—————— WHERE TO STAY ——————

**INN ON THE COMMON**  **Phone: (802)586-9619**

WWW WWW (Historic Country Inn)

| 5/1-3/31 [BP] | | 2P: $109-$239 | XP: $25 | F9 |
|---|---|---|---|---|

**Location:** Center. 1162 N Craftsbury Rd 05827 (PO Box 75). **Fax:** 802/586-2249. **Facility:** This village-like complex on manicured grounds includes three restored lodging buildings furnished with fine antiques. Smoke free premises. 16 units. 15 one- and 1 two-bedroom standard units, some with kitchens. 2 stories (no elevator), interior/exterior corridors. *Bath:* combo or shower only. **Parking:** on-site. **Terms:** open 5/1-3/31, 30 day cancellation notice-fee imposed, [MAP] meal plan available, package plans - seasonal, pets ($25 fee, in designated units). **Amenities:** hair dryers. **Pool(s):** outdoor. **Leisure Activities:** cross country skiing, hiking trails. **Guest Services:** gift shop, complimentary laundry. **Cards:** AX, MC, VI.

SOME UNITS

FEE

# DANVILLE

—————— WHERE TO STAY ——————

**DANVILLE INN**  **Phone: (802)684-3484**

WWW WW (Historic Country Inn)

| All Year [BP] | 1P: $58 | 2P: $68 | XP: $10 | D10 |
|---|---|---|---|---|

**Location:** Center. 86 US 2 W 05828 (PO Box 201). **Facility:** Guest rooms at this Victorian-style farmhouse have shared bathrooms. Smoke free premises. 4 one-bedroom standard units. 2 stories (no elevator), interior corridors. *Bath:* some shared, combo or shower only. **Parking:** on-site. **Terms:** 7 day cancellation notice. **Amenities:** *Some:* hair dryers. **Guest Services:** gift shop. **Cards:** MC, VI.

SOME UNITS

—————— WHERE TO DINE ——————

**THE CREAMERY**  **Lunch:** $6-$12  **Dinner:** $15-$17  **Phone: 802/684-3616**

WWW WWW (American)

**Location:** I-91, exit 21, 6.8 mi w on US 2, then just n; center. 44 Hill St 05828. **Hours:** 11:30 am-2 & 5-8 pm, Sat from 5 pm. **Closed:** Sun & Mon. **Reservations:** suggested. **Features:** This country-style restaurant features very nicely prepared dishes. Soup, sandwiches and pasta are offered for lunch, with more elaborate choices including fresh seafood, beef and chicken for dinner. Pub fare is available in the lounge starting at 4 pm. Casual dress; cocktails. **Parking:** on-site. **Cards:** AX, MC, VI.

# DERBY

—————— WHERE TO STAY ——————

**DERBY SUPER 8 MOTEL**  **Phone: 802/334-1775**

WWW WW (Motel)

| 10/26-4/30 [CP] | 1P: $55-$75 | 2P: $63-$85 | XP: $6 | F12 |
|---|---|---|---|---|
| 5/1-8/31 [CP] | 1P: $54-$75 | 2P: $62-$85 | XP: $6 | F12 |
| 9/1-10/25 [CP] | 1P: $62-$75 | 2P: $69-$84 | XP: $6 | F12 |

**Location:** I-91, exit 28, just w of US 5/SR 105. Located next to a truck stop. 4412 US Rt 5 05855 (444 E Main St, NEWPORT). **Fax:** 802/334-1994. **Facility:** 52 one-bedroom standard units. 2 stories (no elevator), interior corridors. **Parking:** on-site, winter plug-ins. **Terms:** 30 day cancellation notice. **Amenities:** hair dryers. **Cards:** AX, DC, DS, MC, VI.

SOME UNITS

## DORSET —See also EAST DORSET.

——— WHERE TO STAY ———

**INN AT WEST VIEW FARM**
▽▽▽▽

Historic
Country Inn

**Phone:** (802)867-5715

| | | | |
|---|---|---|---|
| 9/24-10/31 [BP] | 1P: $140-$215 | 2P: $150-$225 | XP: $20 |
| 5/1-9/23 [BP] | 1P: $115-$165 | 2P: $125-$175 | XP: $20 |
| 11/1-4/30 [BP] | 1P: $90-$165 | 2P: $100-$175 | XP: $20 |

**Location:** On SR 30, 0.5 mi s. 2928 Rt 30 05251. Fax: 802/867-0468. **Facility:** This attractive inn, which was once a farmhouse, offers modern rooms and spacious, comfortable common areas. Smoke free premises. 10 units. 9 one-bedroom standard units. 1 one-bedroom suite. 2 stories (no elevator), interior corridors. *Bath:* combo or shower only. **Parking:** on-site. **Terms:** 2 night minimum stay - seasonal, age restrictions may apply, 14 day cancellation notice-fee imposed. **Amenities:** video library, CD players. **Cards:** AX, MC, VI.

SOME UNITS
(A$K) (YI) (Y) (X) (🐾) (📞) / (📺) (VCR)

——— WHERE TO DINE ———

**BARROWS HOUSE**　Country Inn
▽▽▽▽

Regional American

**Dinner:** $14-$29　　**Phone:** 802/867-4455

**Location:** Center. 3156 Rt 30 05251. **Hours:** 6 pm-9 pm; from 5:30 pm 6/1-9/30. **Reservations:** suggested. **Features:** Market-fresh ingredients and artistic presentations make the dishes stand out at the pleasant, comfortable restaurant. Seating can be requested in the main dining room, the atrium or a small tavern area. Casual dress; cocktails. **Parking:** on-site. **Cards:** AX, DS, MC, VI.

(Y) (X)

## EAST DORSET —See also DORSET.

——— WHERE TO STAY ———

**EYRIE MOTEL**
▽▽▽

Motel

**Phone:** (802)362-1208

| | | |
|---|---|---|
| All Year [CP] | 1P: $64-$115 | 2P: $64-$115 | XP: $15 |

**Location:** On US 7, 7 mi n of jct SR 11, then just e. 158 Bowen Hill Rd 05253. Fax: 802/362-2948. **Facility:** 12 one-bedroom standard units. 1 story, exterior corridors. **Parking:** on-site. **Terms:** 2-3 night minimum stay - seasonal weekends, 14 day cancellation notice-fee imposed. **Amenities:** video library, hair dryers. **Pool(s):** outdoor. **Leisure Activities:** shuffleboard, volleyball. **Cards:** AX, DS, MC, VI.

SOME UNITS
(🛎) (X) (🐾) (DATA PORT) (📞) / (VCR) /

**MARBLEDGE MOTOR INN**
▽▽▽ ▽▽▽

Motel

**Phone:** 802/362-1418

| | | | |
|---|---|---|---|
| 7/1-10/20 | 1P: $58-$88 | 2P: $68-$98 | XP: $15 | F12 |
| 10/21-2/28 | 1P: $52-$85 | 2P: $62-$95 | XP: $15 | F12 |
| 5/1-6/30 | 1P: $52-$62 | 2P: $58-$78 | XP: $15 | F12 |
| 3/1-4/30 | 1P: $52-$62 | 2P: $58-$72 | XP: $15 | F12 |

**Location:** On US 7, 0.6 mi n of jct Historic SR 7A. 2123 US 7 05253 (PO Box 505). **Facility:** Smoke free premises. 17 units. 10 one-bedroom standard units. 7 cabins. 2 stories (no elevator), exterior corridors. **Parking:** on-site, winter plug-ins. **Terms:** 2-3 night minimum stay - some weekends, 14 day cancellation notice. **Leisure Activities:** hiking trails, basketball. **Cards:** AX, DC, MC, VI.

SOME UNITS
(YI) (X) (🐾) / (VCR) (📞) (📷) (💻) /

——— WHERE TO DINE ———

**CHANTECLEER**
(AAA)
▽▽▽ ▽▽▽

Continental

**Dinner:** $28-$35　　**Phone:** 802/362-1616

**Location:** Jct SR 11/30 N, 3.5 mi n on Historic SR 7A. 8 Read Farm Rd (Historic SR 7A) 05253. **Hours:** Open 5/15-4/15; 6 pm-9 pm. Closed: 11/25, 12/25; also Tues, Mon 5/16-10/1. **Reservations:** suggested. **Features:** Ensconced in the beautiful countryside, the converted dairy barn features provincial, decorative accents and intriguing French and European dishes that incorporate fresh, high-quality ingredients. Renowned among local residents, the restaurant is well worth a drive. Dressy casual; cocktails. **Parking:** on-site. **Cards:** AX, DS, MC, VI.

(X)

## EAST MIDDLEBURY —See also MIDDLEBURY.

——— WHERE TO DINE ———

**WAYBURY INN DINING ROOM**　Country Inn
▽▽▽▽

American

**Dinner:** $13-$27　　**Phone:** 802/388-4015

**Location:** On SR 125; 1.3 mi e of jct US 7. 457 Main St (SR 125) 05740. **Hours:** 5 pm-9 pm, Sun 11 am-2 & 5-9 pm. **Reservations:** suggested. **Features:** Traditional Vermont cooking in comfortable dining room. Homemade muffins, bread, and relish. A cheerful pub is located below the dining room. Overall atmosphere is graced with a roaring gas fireplace and soft music. Casual dress; cocktails. **Parking:** on-site. **Cards:** AX, DC, DS, MC, VI.

(Y) (X)

# ESSEX JUNCTION pop. 8,591

## ———— WHERE TO STAY ————

**THE INN AT ESSEX**  *Book at aaa.com*  Phone: 802/878-1100

AAA SAVE

| | | | | |
|---|---|---|---|---|
| 8/1-10/31 [CP] | 1P: $179-$399 | 2P: $189-$499 | XP: $10 | F12 |
| 5/1-7/31 & 11/1-4/30 [CP] | 1P: $159-$399 | 2P: $169-$499 | XP: $10 | F12 |

Small-scale Hotel   **Location:** SR 289, exit 10, then 0.3 mi s. 70 Essex Way 05452. Fax: 802/878-0063. **Facility:** 119 units. 97 one-bedroom standard units, some with kitchens and/or whirlpools. 20 one- and 2 two-bedroom suites with kitchens, some with whirlpools. 3 stories, interior corridors. *Bath:* combo or shower only. **Parking:** on-site. **Terms:** 7 day cancellation notice-fee imposed, pets ($25 extra charge). **Amenities:** voice mail, irons, hair dryers. *Some:* CD players, high-speed Internet. **Dining:** 2 restaurants, also, Butler's Restaurant, see separate listing. **Pool(s):** heated outdoor. **Leisure Activities:** 6 tennis courts, garden checker board, garden tours, lawn games, hiking trails, exercise room, volleyball. *Fee:* massage. **Guest Services:** gift shop, valet and coin laundry, airport transportation-Burlington International Airport, area transportation (fee)-local businesses. **Business Services:** conference facilities, PC. **Cards:** AX, CB, DC, DS, JC, MC, VI. **Special Amenities:** free continental breakfast and free newspaper. *(See color ad p 422)*

SOME UNITS

**THE WILSON INN**  Phone: 802/879-1515

| | | | | |
|---|---|---|---|---|
| 9/17-10/18 [ECP] | 1P: $99-$239 | 2P: $99-$239 | XP: $10 | F12 |
| 5/1-9/16 & 10/19-4/30 [ECP] | 1P: $65-$189 | 2P: $65-$189 | XP: $10 | F12 |

Small-scale Hotel   **Location:** I-89, exit 15 northbound, 2.1 mi e on SR 15, then 0.5 mi n on Susie Wilson Rd; exit 16 southbound, 1 mi s on US 7, 2.8 mi e on SR 15, then 0.5 mi n on Susie Wilson Rd. 10 Kellogg Rd 05452. Fax: 802/764-5149. **Facility:** 42 units. 2 one-bedroom standard units with kitchens. 28 one- and 12 two-bedroom suites with kitchens, some with whirlpools. 3 stories, interior corridors. *Bath:* combo or shower only. **Parking:** on-site, winter plug-ins. **Terms:** pets ($10 extra charge). **Amenities:** voice mail, irons, hair dryers. **Pool(s):** heated outdoor. **Leisure Activities:** playground, exercise room, basketball. **Guest Services:** valet and coin laundry. **Cards:** AX, DC, DS, MC, VI.

SOME UNITS

## ———— WHERE TO DINE ————

**BUTLER'S RESTAURANT**  **Lunch:** $7-$9  **Dinner:** $28-$44  **Phone:** 802/764-1413

**Location:** SR 289, exit 10, then 0.3 mi s; in The Inn at Essex. 70 Essex Way 05452. **Hours:** 6:30-10:30 am, 11:30-2 & 6-9:45 pm, Fri-10 pm, Sat 7 am-10 pm, Sun 8 am-9:30 & 10-2 pm. Closed: Sun 1/1-4/30.

Nouvelle American   **Reservations:** suggested. **Features:** Butler's is operated by the New England Culinary Institute and offers a fine-dining experience. The fixed-price menu changes nightly and features classic cooking and new interpretations of seafood, chicken, filet mignon and duck dishes. Decadent desserts abound. Dressy casual; cocktails. **Parking:** on-site. **Cards:** AX, DC, DS, MC, VI.

# FAIRFAX

## ———— WHERE TO STAY ————

**THE INN AT BUCK HOLLOW FARM**  *Book at aaa.com*  Phone: (802)849-2400

| | | | | |
|---|---|---|---|---|
| All Year [BP] | 1P: $63-$93 | 2P: $73-$93 | XP: $10 | F5 |

Historic Bed & Breakfast   **Location:** 6.4 mi n of jct SR 104 via Buck Hollow Rd. Located in a rural area. 2150 Buck Hollow Rd 05454 (2150 Buck Hollow Rd). Fax: 802/849-9744. **Facility:** This 1790 carriage house is on 400 acres and features themed rooms; an antiques shop is on the grounds. Smoke free premises. 4 one-bedroom standard units. 2 stories (no elevator), interior corridors. *Bath:* shared. **Parking:** on-site. **Terms:** 14 day cancellation notice, pets (with prior approval, owner's pets on premises). **Amenities:** CD players, irons, hair dryers. **Pool(s):** heated outdoor. **Leisure Activities:** whirlpool, cross country skiing, hiking trails, playground. **Cards:** AX, DS, MC, VI.

# FAIRLEE

## ———— WHERE TO STAY ————

**SILVER MAPLE LODGE & COTTAGES**  Phone: (802)333-4326

AAA SAVE

| | | | | |
|---|---|---|---|---|
| All Year [CP] | 1P: $60-$85 | 2P: $64-$89 | XP: $6 | D18 |

Historic Bed & Breakfast   **Location:** I-91, exit 15, 0.5 mi s. 520 US 5 S 05045. **Facility:** Pleasant cottages and late 1700s country inn. 15 units. 8 one-bedroom standard units. 7 cottages ($79-$98). 2 stories (no elevator), interior/exterior corridors. *Bath:* some shared or private, combo or shower only. **Parking:** on-site. **Terms:** office hours 7 am-10 pm, 14 day cancellation notice, weekly rates available, small pets only (in cottages, owner's cat on premises). **Leisure Activities:** rental bicycles. **Cards:** AX, DS, MC, VI. **Special Amenities:** free continental breakfast and preferred room (subject to availability with advanced reservations).

SOME UNITS

# FERRISBURG

## ———— WHERE TO STAY ————

**SKYVIEW MOTEL**  Phone: 802/877-3410

AAA SAVE

| | | | | |
|---|---|---|---|---|
| 9/15-10/31 | 1P: $65-$85 | 2P: $75-$95 | XP: $10 | F12 |
| 5/1-9/14 | 1P: $55-$75 | 2P: $65-$85 | XP: $10 | F12 |
| 11/1-4/30 | 1P: $40-$55 | 2P: $50-$65 | XP: $10 | F12 |

Motel   **Location:** On US 7, 0.3 mi s. 2956 US Rt 7 05456. **Facility:** 15 one-bedroom standard units. 1 story, exterior corridors. *Bath:* combo or shower only. **Parking:** on-site, winter plug-ins. **Terms:** 3 day cancellation notice, pets ($10 fee). **Leisure Activities:** volleyball. **Cards:** AX, DC, DS, MC, VI. **Special Amenities:** free local telephone calls and early check-in/late check-out.

SOME UNITS

# GRAFTON

## —— WHERE TO DINE ——

**THE OLD TAVERN AT GRAFTON**  Country Inn
**Dinner:** $25-$33
**Phone:** 802/843-2231

(AAA)
**Location:** On SR 121; center. 92 Main St 05146. **Hours:** Open 5/1-3/31; 8 am-10 & 6-9 pm. **Reservations:** suggested. **Features:** The Old Tavern serves an excellent and attractively presented turkey breast and mashed potatoes with gravy dinner. The grilled salmon, roasted rack of lamb and beef tenderloin meals are also good choices. A beautifully restored 1801 inn with a full bar. Dressy casual; cocktails. **Parking:** on-site. **Cards:** AX, MC, VI.

Regional
American

# GREENSBORO

## —— WHERE TO STAY ——

**HIGHLAND LODGE**
**Phone:** (802)533-2647

| | | | | |
|---|---|---|---|---|
| 7/1-10/14 & 12/17-1/1 [MAP] | 1P: $125-$170 | 2P: $240-$300 | XP: $115 | D20 |
| 5/21-6/30 & 1/2-3/13 [MAP] | 1P: $125 | 2P: $240 | XP: $110 | D20 |

Cabin
**Location:** 1.8 mi n. 1608 Craftsbury Rd 05841. Fax: 802/533-7494. **Facility:** Smoke free premises. 22 units. 11 one-bedroom standard units. 11 cabins. 1-2 stories (no elevator); interior/exterior corridors. *Bath:* combo, shower or tub only. **Parking:** on-site, winter plug-ins. **Terms:** open 5/21-10/14 & 12/17-3/13, 14 day cancellation notice, 90 days 7/1-8/31-fee imposed, package plans. **Leisure Activities:** boating, canoeing, paddleboats, boat dock, fishing, tennis court, cross country skiing, tobogganing, recreation programs, hiking trails, volleyball, game room. *Fee:* sailboats, bicycles, massage. **Guest Services:** gift shop. **Business Services:** meeting rooms. **Cards:** DC, MC, VI.

SOME UNITS

# HANCOCK

## —— WHERE TO DINE ——

—— *The following restaurant has not been evaluated by AAA* ——
*but is listed for your information only.*

**VERMONT HOME BAKERY**
**Phone:** 802/767-4976

[fyi]
Not evaluated. **Location:** In the Old Hancock Hotel. Jct SR 100/125 05748. **Features:** The simple bakery is open for breakfast, lunch and dinner and has limited seating as most of their business is take-out only.

# HARTLAND  pop. 3,223

## —— WHERE TO DINE ——

**SKUNK HOLLOW TAVERN**
**Dinner:** $10-$24
**Phone:** 802/436-2139

**Location:** I-91, exit 9 (Hartland/Windsor); at Hartland 4 Corners. Hartland 4 Corners 05049. **Hours:** 5 pm-9 pm. Closed: 11/25, 12/24, 12/25; also Mon & Tues; first week of Dec. **Reservations:** suggested. **Features:** Enjoy a casual or intimate dinner in an authentic 18th-century country tavern. Casual dress; cocktails. **Parking:** on-site. **Cards:** AX, DS, MC, VI.

American

# HYDE PARK  pop. 415

## —— WHERE TO STAY ——

**FITCH HILL INN**
**Phone:** (802)888-3834

(AAA) [SAVE]

| | | | | |
|---|---|---|---|---|
| 9/24-10/16 [BP] | 1P: $135-$155 | 2P: $135-$155 | XP: $20 | F6 |
| 5/1-9/23 & 10/17-4/30 [BP] | 1P: $85-$135 | 2P: $85-$135 | XP: $20 | F6 |

Historic Bed
& Breakfast
**Location:** 1.8 mi w on SR 15, from jct SR 100, then 0.3 mi n. 258 Fitch Hill Rd 05655. Fax: 802/888-7789. **Facility:** Set on spacious landscaped grounds, this restored 1797 home is furnished with antiques and has several rooms with a small bathroom or fireplace. Smoke free premises. 6 one-bedroom standard units, some with whirlpools. 2 stories (no elevator); interior/exterior corridors. *Bath:* combo or shower only. **Parking:** on-site. **Terms:** 2 night minimum stay - most weekends, age restrictions may apply, 15 day cancellation notice-fee imposed. **Amenities:** video library, hair dryers. *Some:* irons. **Leisure Activities:** whirlpool. **Guest Services:** complimentary evening beverages. **Cards:** AX, DS, MC, VI. **Special Amenities:** free full breakfast and free local telephone calls.

SOME UNITS

# JAMAICA

## —— WHERE TO STAY ——

**THREE MOUNTAIN INN**
**Phone:** (802)874-4140

(AAA) [SAVE]

| | | | |
|---|---|---|---|
| All Year [BP] | | 2P: $145-$345 | XP: $25 | D18 |

Historic
Country Inn
**Location:** On SR 30; center. 3732 Main St 05343 (PO Box 180). Fax: 802/874-4745. **Facility:** In the village center, this 1790s inn has a rustic ambience with fireplaces, original wood-plank floors and antique furnishings. Smoke free premises. 15 units. 13 one-bedroom standard units, some with whirlpools. 1 one-bedroom suite with whirlpool. 1 cottage with whirlpool. 3 stories (no elevator); interior/exterior corridors. *Bath:* combo or shower only. **Parking:** on-site, winter plug-ins. **Terms:** 2-3 night minimum stay - weekends, age restrictions may apply, 10 day cancellation notice-fee imposed, pets ($25 fee, $75 deposit, with prior approval, in designated units). **Amenities:** video library, CD players, hair dryers. **Dining:** dining room, see separate listing. **Pool(s):** outdoor. **Leisure Activities:** snowshoes, bicycles, hiking trails, jogging. *Fee:* massage. **Guest Services:** complimentary evening beverages. **Business Services:** meeting rooms. **Cards:** AX, DS, MC, VI. **Special Amenities:** free full breakfast and free room upgrade (subject to availability with advanced reservations).

SOME UNITS

FEE

——— **WHERE TO DINE** ———

### THREE MOUNTAIN INN DINING ROOM

Continental

**Dinner:** $27-$38

**Phone:** 802/874-4140

**Location:** On SR 30; center; in Three Mountain Inn. 3732 Main St 05343. **Hours:** 6 pm-8 pm. Closed: Mon & Tues off season. **Reservations:** suggested. **Features:** Set in a lovely old inn, the intimate dining rooms, which are adult oriented, are a perfect setting to enjoy attentive service and carefully prepared and artistically presented dishes that are created from market fresh products. Dressy casual; cocktails. **Parking:** on-site. **Cards:** AX, DS, MC, VI.

⏹️ ❎

## JEFFERSONVILLE pop. 568

——— **WHERE TO STAY** ———

### DEER RUN MOTOR INN

♦

Motel
($10 extra charge).

**All Year**

1P: $70                 2P: $85

**Phone:** 802/644-8866

XP: $10                 F10

**Location:** 0.7 mi e on SR 15. Located in a rural area. 80 Deer Run Loop 05464. **Facility:** 26 one-bedroom standard units. 2 stories (no elevator), interior/exterior corridors. *Bath:* combo or shower only. **Parking:** on-site, winter plug-ins. **Terms:** 2 night minimum stay - weekends, 15 day cancellation notice, weekly rates available, pets **Pool(s):** outdoor. **Leisure Activities:** basketball. **Cards:** AX, DS, MC, VI.

SOME UNITS

🐾 🌊 🛢 🖨 🖵 /❎/
FEE

## KILLINGTON —See also MENDON.

——— **WHERE TO STAY** ———

### BIRCH RIDGE INN

AAA SAVE

Country Inn

| | | |
|---|---|---|
| 9/20-3/28 | 1P: $120-$300 | 2P: $120-$300 |
| 3/29-4/30 | 1P: $100-$200 | 2P: $100-$200 |
| 5/1-9/19 | 1P: $80-$200 | 2P: $80-$200 |

**Phone:** (802)422-4293

**Location:** 2.2 mi s on Killington Rd, from jct SR 100/US 4, then just w. 37 Butler Rd 05751. Fax: 802/422-3406. **Facility:** Fine dining is offered at this modern, well-furnished inn perched on the slopes of the Killington ski area. Smoke free premises. 10 one-bedroom standard units, some with whirlpools. 2 stories (no elevator), interior corridors. *Bath:* combo or shower only. **Parking:** on-site. **Terms:** 2 night minimum stay - weekends, age restrictions may apply, 14 day cancellation notice-fee imposed, [BP] meal plan available. **Amenities:** hair dryers. **Dining:** restaurant, see separate listing. **Cards:** AX, DS, MC, VI. **Special Amenities: free full breakfast and preferred room (subject to availability with advanced reservations).**

SOME UNITS

🍽️ 📶 ❎ 📠 /❌/

### BUTTERNUT ON THE MOUNTAIN

AAA SAVE

Small-scale Hotel

| | | | |
|---|---|---|---|
| 11/23-4/18 [BP] | 1P: $78-$200 | 2P: $89-$205 | XP: $35 | F3 |
| 9/20-10/20 [BP] | 1P: $56-$110 | 2P: $72-$112 | XP: $25 | F3 |
| 7/1-9/19 [CP] | 1P: $52-$72 | 2P: $58-$78 | XP: $25 | F3 |

**Phone:** (802)422-2000

**Location:** Jct SR 100/US 4, 1.1 mi s on Killington Rd, then just e. 63 Weathervane Rd 05751 (PO Box 306). Fax: 802/422-3937. **Facility:** Smoke free premises. 18 one-bedroom standard units. 2 stories (no elevator), interior/exterior corridors. *Bath:* combo or shower only. **Parking:** on-site, winter plug-ins. **Terms:** open 7/1-10/20 & 11/23-4/18, check-in 4 pm, 2-7 night minimum stay - seasonal, 30 day cancellation notice-fee imposed, [BP] meal plan available, package plans - seasonal, 15% service charge, pets (with prior approval, in summer only, owner's dog on premises). **Amenities:** video library. **Dining:** 5 pm-10 pm; closed Mon-Thurs 4/1-11/27, cocktails. **Pool(s):** heated indoor. **Leisure Activities:** whirlpool. *Fee:* game room. **Guest Services:** coin laundry, airport transportation (fee)-Rutland Airport. **Cards:** AX, DS, MC, VI. **Special Amenities: free full breakfast and free local telephone calls.**

SOME UNITS

🍴 🛏️ 🍽️ ⏹️ 🌊 ❎ /❌/ VCR 📠 🛢 🖨 🖵 /
FEE                                    FEE  FEE

**THE CASCADES LODGE** *Book at aaa.com*
Phone: (802)422-3731

| | | | |
|---|---|---|---|
| 12/17-3/31 [BP] | 1P: $99-$189 | 2P: $119-$229 | XP: $35 | D12 |
| 9/17-12/16 [BP] | 1P: $69-$169 | 2P: $79-$199 | XP: $25 | D12 |
| 5/1-9/16 & 4/1-4/30 [BP] | 1P: $81-$119 | 2P: $89-$139 | XP: $10 | D12 |

**Location:** 3.6 mi s on Killington Rd, from jct SR 100/US 4, then just e. 58 Old Mill Rd 05751. Fax: 802/422-3351. Small-scale Hotel **Facility:** 47 units. 41 one-bedroom standard units. 6 one-bedroom suites ($128-$308). 2-3 stories (no elevator), interior corridors. **Parking:** on-site, winter plug-ins. **Terms:** 21 day cancellation notice, [MAP] meal plan available, 9% service charge, pets ($25 extra charge). **Amenities:** video library, voice mail, hair dryers. *Some:* video games. **Dining:** restaurant, see separate listing. **Pool(s):** heated indoor. **Leisure Activities:** sauna, whirlpool, reading room, hiking trails, exercise room. *Fee:* massage. **Guest Services:** valet laundry. **Business Services:** meeting rooms. **Cards:** AX, DS, JC, MC, VI. **Special Amenities:** free full breakfast and free local telephone calls. *(See color ad below)*

SOME UNITS

**COMFORT INN KILLINGTON CENTER** *Book at aaa.com*
Phone: (802)422-4222

| | | |
|---|---|---|
| 11/23-4/30 | 1P: $86-$224 | 2P: $86-$224 |
| 5/1-11/22 | 1P: $70-$128 | 2P: $70-$128 |

**Location:** 1 mi s of jct US 4. 905 Killington Rd 05751 (PO Box 493). Fax: 802/422-4226. **Facility:** 66 one-bedroom standard units, some with efficiencies and/or whirlpools. 2 stories (no elevator), exterior corridors. **Parking:** Small-scale Hotel on-site. **Terms:** check-in 4 pm, 14 day cancellation notice-fee imposed, [CP] meal plan available. **Amenities:** irons, hair dryers. **Pool(s):** heated outdoor. **Leisure Activities:** picnic tables, playground. **Guest Services:** coin laundry. **Cards:** AX, CB, DC, DS, MC, VI. **Special Amenities:** free continental breakfast and free local telephone calls. *(See color ad below)*

SOME UNITS

# The Cascades Lodge

- Award-winning cuisine
- 46 spacious rooms & suites
- Situated at 2200 foot elevation
- Spectacular mountain views
- Walk to golf, biking & skiing
- Under 18 stay free summer & fall
- Closest full-service lodge to the slopes
- Indoor heated pool, sauna, whirlpool & lounge

*The MacKenzie Family - Innkeepers*

Killington Village • 58 Old Mill Road
Killington, VT 05751
800-578-9665 • Fax 802-422-3351
www.cascadeslodge.com • info@cascadeslodge.com

## Located in the Heart of the Green Mountains

- Fully Air Conditioned
- Outdoor Heated Pool
- 95% Non Smoking
- Free Continental Breakfast
- Adjacent to Killington Four Season Resort
- Quiet Townhouse Setting

**Comfort Inn**
905 Killington Rd.,
P.O. 493
Killington, VT 05751

**800.257.8664**
**www.comfortK1.com**

© 2002 Choice Hotels International, Inc.

The Power of Being There. **GO**

**Comfort Inn**

BY CHOICE HOTELS

## GREENBRIER INN

Motel

All Year [CP]   1P: $60-$225   2P: $60-$225   XP: $10   F12
**Phone:** (802)775-1575

**Location:** 0.4 mi w of jct SR 100 N. US 4 05751 (PO Box 286). **Facility:** Smoke free premises. 21 one-bedroom standard units. 2 stories (no elevator), interior corridors. **Parking:** on-site, winter plug-ins. **Terms:** office hours 7 am-11 pm, 7 day cancellation notice, no pets allowed (owner's dog on premises). **Pool(s):** outdoor. **Leisure Activities:** nature trail, hiking trails. **Business Services:** meeting rooms. **Cards:** AX, MC, VI. **Special Amenities: free continental breakfast and free local telephone calls.**

## GREY BONNET INN

Small-scale Hotel

| | | | |
|---|---|---|---|
| 11/24-4/30 | 1P: $79-$185 | 2P: $79-$185 | XP: $30   D6 |
| 6/1-10/30 | 1P: $75-$145 | 2P: $75-$145 | XP: $30   D6 |

**Phone:** (802)775-2537

**Location:** Jct US 4, 0.8 mi n. Located in a quiet area. 831 Rt 100 05751. Fax: 802/775-3371. **Facility:** Smoke free premises. 41 one-bedroom standard units. 3 stories (no elevator), interior corridors. **Parking:** on-site, winter plug-ins. **Terms:** open 6/1-10/30 & 11/24-4/30, 2 night minimum stay - weekends, 14 day cancellation notice-fee imposed. [BP] & [MAP] meal plans available, package plans - seasonal. **Dining:** Olivia's, see separate listing. **Pool(s):** outdoor, heated indoor. **Leisure Activities:** sauna, hot tub, tennis court, toboganing, hiking trails, exercise room, horseshoes. *Fee:* cross country skiing, massage, game room. **Business Services:** meeting rooms. **Cards:** DC, MC, VI.

SOME UNITS

## THE INN OF THE SIX MOUNTAINS   *Book at aaa.com*

Large-scale Hotel

| | | | |
|---|---|---|---|
| 12/20-4/30 [CP] | 1P: $149-$309 | 2P: $149-$309 | XP: $17   F12 |
| 9/15-10/15 [CP] | 1P: $159-$209 | 2P: $159-$209 | XP: $17   F12 |
| 5/1-9/14 & 10/16-12/19 [CP] | 1P: $99-$169 | 2P: $99-$169 | XP: $17   F12 |

**Phone:** (802)422-4302

**Location:** 2.7 mi s on Killington Rd, from jct SR 100/US 4. 2617 Killington Rd 05751. Fax: 802/422-4321. **Facility:** 103 units. 99 one-bedroom standard units. 4 one-bedroom suites with kitchens. 4 stories, interior corridors. **Parking:** on-site. **Terms:** check-in 4 pm, 8 day cancellation notice-fee imposed. **Amenities:** voice mail, safes, hair dryers. *Some:* irons. **Dining:** 7 am-10 & 5:30-9 pm; seasonal hours may vary, cocktails. **Pool(s):** heated outdoor, heated indoor. **Leisure Activities:** whirlpools, tennis court, hiking trails, jogging, exercise room. *Fee:* massage, game room. **Guest Services:** valet laundry, area transportation-ski area. **Business Services:** meeting rooms. **Cards:** AX, CB, DC, DS, MC, VI. *(See color ad below)*

SOME UNITS

**KILLINGTON GRAND RESORT HOTEL** *Book at aaa.com* **Phone:** (802)422-5001

▼▼▼▼ 12/17-3/31 1P: $305-$385 2P: $305-$385
10/29-12/16 & 4/1-4/30 1P: $154-$190 2P: $154-$190
Resort 5/1-10/28 1P: $103-$141 2P: $103-$141
Large-scale Hotel **Location:** 3.6 mi s on Killington Rd, from jct SR 100/US 4, then just e. 228 E Mountain Rd 05751. **Fax:** 802/422-6881. **Facility:** The property's attractive and spacious guest rooms are designed to combine all the conveniences of home with the luxuries of a resort hotel. 200 units. 148 one-bedroom standard units, some with kitchens. 41 one-, 6 two- and 5 three-bedroom suites with kitchens. 4 stories, interior corridors. *Bath:* combo or shower only. **Parking:** on-site. **Terms:** check-in 4:30 pm, 2 night minimum stay - weekends in winter, 21 day cancellation notice-fee imposed, weekly rates available, [BP] & [MAP] meal plans available. **Amenities:** video games, CD players, high-speed Internet, voice mail, irons, hair dryers. **Pool(s):** heated outdoor. **Leisure Activities:** sauna, whirlpools, steamroom, 2 tennis courts, downhill skiing, recreation programs, hiking trails, jogging, playground. *Fee:* golf-18 holes, bicycles, massage, game room. **Guest Services:** gift shop, valet and coin laundry. **Business Services:** conference facilities, business center. **Cards:** AX, DS, MC, VI.

SOME UNITS

(ASK) (S/D) (TI) (T) (A) (⌂) (⇌) (✦) (⊠) (VCR) (⚡) (DATA PORT) (💻) / (⊠) (🔒) (🏠) /

**MOUNTAIN GREEN SKI & GOLF RESORT** **Phone:** (802)422-3000

(AAA) (SAVE) 12/17-4/30 1P: $126-$963 2P: $126-$963
11/1-12/16 1P: $126-$468 2P: $126-$468
▼▼▼▼ 9/17-10/31 1P: $98-$326 2P: $98-$326
5/1-9/16 1P: $74-$242 2P: $74-$242
Resort **Location:** 3.7 mi s on Killington Rd, from jct US 4. 133 E Mountain Rd 05751. **Fax:** 802/422-2328. **Facility:** 190
Condominium units. 17 one-bedroom standard units with kitchens. 80 one-, 74 two- and 19 three-bedroom suites with kitchens. 7 stories, interior corridors. **Parking:** on-site, winter plug-ins. **Terms:** check-in 6 pm, 2 night minimum stay, 21 day cancellation notice-fee imposed, package plans - seasonal, 4% service charge. **Amenities:** DVD players, hair dryers. *Some:* CD players, safes, irons. **Pool(s):** heated outdoor, heated indoor. **Leisure Activities:** sauna, whirlpools, steamroom, spa. *Fee:* game room. **Guest Services:** coin laundry. **Cards:** AX, DC, DS, MC, VI. **Special Amenities:** free local telephone calls. *(See color ad below)*

(TI) (T) (⇌) (✦) (⊠) (K) (VCR) (🔒) (🏠) (💻)

**THE MOUNTAIN INN** **Phone:** (802)422-3595

(AAA) (SAVE) 11/1-3/31 [ECP] 1P: $79-$210 2P: $79-$210 XP: $30 D4
9/3-10/31 [ECP] 1P: $79-$169 2P: $79-$169 XP: $20 D4
▼▼▼▼ 5/1-9/2 & 4/1-4/30 [ECP] 1P: $69-$119 2P: $69-$119 XP: $20 D4
Small-scale Hotel **Location:** 3.6 mi s on Killington Rd, from jct SR 100/US 4, then just e. 47 Old Mill Rd 05751. **Fax:** 802/422-4599. **Facility:** Designated smoking area. 51 units. 49 one-bedroom standard units. 1 one- and 1 two-bedroom suites, some with whirlpools. 3 stories (no elevator), interior corridors. **Parking:** on-site, winter plug-ins. **Terms:** 2 night minimum stay - weekends 12/1-3/31, 21 day cancellation notice-fee imposed, package plans, 10% service charge. **Amenities:** video library, hair dryers. **Dining:** 7 am-10 & 5-10 pm; seasonal hours may vary, cocktails. **Pool(s):** heated outdoor. **Leisure Activities:** sauna, whirlpool. *Fee:* game room. **Guest Services:** coin laundry. **Business Services:** meeting rooms. **Cards:** AX, CB, DC, DS, MC, VI. **Special Amenities:** free expanded continental breakfast and free local telephone calls.

SOME UNITS

(S/D) (TI) (T) (⇌) (⊠) (⊠) (K) / (VCR) (🔒) /

## MOUNTAIN MEADOWS LODGE

Phone: 802/775-1010

▼▼▼ ▼▼▼

| | | |
|---|---|---|
| 11/15-4/30 [BP] | 1P: $85-$360 | 2P: $85-$360 | XP: $38 | D11 |
| 6/1-10/30 [BP] | 1P: $85-$200 | 2P: $85-$200 | XP: $20 | D11 |

Fax: 802/773-4459.

Small-scale Hotel **Location:** 0.3 mi e on US 4, from jct SR 100 N; then 0.5 mi n. 285 Thundering Brook Rd 05751. **Facility:** Smoke free premises. 20 one-bedroom standard units. 2-3 stories (no elevator), interior corridors. *Bath:* combo or shower only. **Parking:** on-site. **Terms:** open 6/1-10/30 & 11/15-4/30, 21 day cancellation notice-fee imposed, no pets allowed (owner's pot belly pig on premises). **Amenities:** video library. **Pool(s):** outdoor. **Leisure Activities:** sauna, whirlpool, boating, canoeing, boat dock, fishing, cross country skiing, tobogganing, hiking trails, playground, horseshoes, volleyball. *Fee:* massage, game room. **Guest Services:** complimentary evening beverages, area transportation. **Business Services:** meeting rooms. **Cards:** AX, DS, MC, VI.

SOME UNITS

⊞ ⑪ ⊻ ⌂ ⌦ ⊠ ⊗ ⓐ / ⓦ ⓥⓒⓡ /

## MOUNTAIN SPORTS INN

Phone: (802)422-3315

▼▼▼ ▼▼▼

| | | |
|---|---|---|
| 10/17-4/30 [CP] | 1P: $48-$150 | 2P: $54-$150 | XP: $15 | F6 |
| 9/24-10/16 [CP] | 1P: $54-$98 | 2P: $66-$105 | XP: $7 | F6 |
| 8/1-9/23 | 1P: $45-$50 | 2P: $55-$60 | XP: $5 | F6 |

Small-scale Hotel **Location:** 0.8 mi s, from jct US 4. 813 Killington Rd 05751. Fax: 802/422-5126. **Facility:** 30 units. 29 one-bedroom standard units. 1 two-bedroom unit (no elevator), interior corridors. *Bath:* combo or shower only. **Parking:** on-site, winter plug-ins. **Terms:** open 8/1-4/30, check-in 4 pm, 14 day cancellation notice-fee imposed, package plans. **Amenities:** video library, voice mail. **Leisure Activities:** sauna, exercise room. **Cards:** AX, DS, MC, VI.

SOME UNITS

ⒶⓈⓀ Ⓢ▼ ⓐ ⓐ / ⊗ ⓥⓒⓡ ⓓⓐⓣⓐⓟⓞⓡⓣ /

## THE PEAK CHALET

Phone: (802)422-4278

▼▼▼ ▼▼▼

| | | |
|---|---|---|
| 12/24-3/26 [CP] | 1P: $115-$127 | 2P: $115-$127 | XP: $30 | |
| 5/1-12/23 [CP] | 1P: $95-$110 | 2P: $95-$110 | XP: $25 | |
| 3/27-4/30 | 1P: $95 | 2P: $95 | XP: $25 | |

Bed & Breakfast **Location:** 1.3 mi s on Killington Rd, from jct US 4, then just e. 184 S View Path 05751 (PO Box 511). **Facility:** Well-suited for skiers, this modern home features a sitting room which overlooks Killington Mountain. Smoke free premises. 5 units. 4 one-bedroom standard units. 1 one-bedroom suite ($95-$185) with kitchen. 2 stories (no elevator), interior/exterior corridors. *Bath:* shower only. **Parking:** on-site. **Terms:** check-in 4 pm, 2 night minimum stay - seasonal weekends, age restrictions may apply, 30 day cancellation notice-fee imposed. **Amenities:** *Some:* irons, hair dryers. **Cards:** MC, VI.

SOME UNITS

⊗ ⓐ / ⓦ ⓥⓒⓡ ⓓⓐⓣⓐⓟⓞⓡⓣ ☎ 🖥 ▣ ▣ /

## SHERBURNE-KILLINGTON MOTEL

**Phone: (802)773-9535**

| | | | |
|---|---|---|---|
| 9/19-10/10 [CP] | 1P: $88-$125 | 2P: $88-$125 | XP: $8 F12 |
| 12/19-4/30 [CP] | 1P: $79-$125 | 2P: $79-$125 | XP: $16 F12 |
| 5/1-9/18 [CP] | 1P: $54-$65 | 2P: $54-$65 | XP: $8 F12 |
| 10/11-12/18 [CP] | 1P: $62 | 2P: $62 | XP: $8 F12 |

Motel **Location:** Jct SR 100 N, 0.3 mi w. 1946 Rt 4 05751. Fax: 802/773-0011. **Facility:** 20 one-bedroom standard units. 1 story, exterior corridors. **Parking:** on-site. **Terms:** office hours 7:30 am-11 pm, 2 night minimum stay - weekends 12/17-4/1 with Friday/Saturday stayover, 7 day cancellation notice-fee imposed. **Amenities:** video library. **Pool(s):** heated outdoor. **Leisure Activities:** picnic table, playground, basketball, volleyball. **Guest Services:** complimentary evening beverages. **Cards:** AX, DS, MC, VI. **Special Amenities:** free continental breakfast. *(See color ad below)*

SOME UNITS

## SNOWED INN

**Phone: (802)422-3407**

| | | | |
|---|---|---|---|
| 9/20-10/17 & 12/20-4/18 [ECP] | 1P: $70-$162 | 2P: $99-$162 | XP: $20 D12 |
| 11/5-12/19 [ECP] | 1P: $65-$109 | 2P: $75-$109 | XP: $20 D12 |
| 6/18-9/19 [ECP] | 1P: $70-$90 | 2P: $80-$90 | XP: $20 D12 |

Bed & Breakfast **Location:** 2 mi s on Killington Rd, from jct SR 100/US 4, then just w. 104 Miller Brook Rd 05751. Fax: 802/422-8126. **Facility:** Contemporary country accommodations are offered at this inn set on the slopes of the Killington ski resort. Smoke free premises. 20 units. 19 one-bedroom standard units, some with efficiencies and/or whirl-pools. 1 one-bedroom suite ($100-$245) with kitchen and whirlpool. 2-3 stories (no elevator), interior/exterior corridors. *Bath:* combo or shower only. **Parking:** on-site. **Terms:** open 6/18-10/17 & 11/5-4/18, 14 day cancellation notice-fee imposed, package plans - seasonal, 10% service charge, no pets allowed (owner's dog on premises). **Leisure Activities:** ski tuning room, game room. **Cards:** AX, DS, MC, VI. **Special Amenities:** free expanded continental breakfast and free local telephone calls.

SOME UNITS

## THE SUMMIT LODGE

**Phone: (802)422-3535**

| | | | |
|---|---|---|---|
| 11/26-4/30 [BP] | 1P: $88-$410 | 2P: $101-$410 | XP: $45 F3 |
| 9/13-10/17 | 1P: $85-$153 | 2P: $99-$196 | XP: $15 F3 |
| 5/1-9/12 | 1P: $51-$87 | 2P: $66-$101 | XP: $15 F3 |
| 10/18-11/25 | 1P: $60-$66 | 2P: $74-$80 | XP: $15 F3 |

Small-scale Hotel **Location:** 1.3 mi s on Killington Rd, from jct SR 100/US 4. 200 Summit Rd 05751 (PO Box 119). Fax: 802/422-3536. **Facility:** 45 units. 43 one-bedroom standard units. 2 one-bedroom suites. 3 stories (no elevator), interior cor-ridors. *Bath:* combo or shower only. **Parking:** on-site. **Terms:** 30 day cancellation notice-fee imposed, weekly rates available, [BP] & [MAP] meal plans available, no pets allowed (owner's pets on premises). **Amenities:** *Some:* hair dryers. **Dining:** 2 res-taurants, 7 am-9:30 & 5-9 pm; hours may vary seasonally, cocktails. **Pool(s):** outdoor, heated outdoor. **Leisure Activi-ties:** saunas, whirlpool, fishing, 5 tennis courts, tennis instruction 7/1-8/31, ice skating, bocci, nature trail, horseshoes, shuffleboard, game room. *Fee:* racquetball courts, massage. **Guest Services:** gift shop, coin laundry, airport transportation (fee)-Rutland Airport, area transportation-ski area. **Business Services:** meeting rooms, fax (fee). **Cards:** AX, DC, MC, VI.

SOME UNITS

FEE

## VAL ROC MOTEL

**Phone: (802)422-3881**

| | | | |
|---|---|---|---|
| 11/23-4/30 | 1P: $64-$120 | 2P: $64-$120 | XP: $10 F10 |
| 5/1-11/22 | 1P: $49-$65 | 2P: $59-$75 | XP: $10 F10 |

Motel **Location:** 5.9 mi e on US 4, from jct SR 100 N. 8006 US 4 05751. Fax: 802/422-6601. **Facility:** 24 units. 23 one-bedroom standard units. 1 one-bedroom suite with efficiency. 1-2 stories (no elevator), interior/exterior corri-dors. **Parking:** on-site. **Terms:** 2 night minimum stay - weekends in winter, 14 day cancellation notice-fee imposed, weekly rates available, [CP] meal plan available, package plans - in winter, pets ($5 extra charge). **Amenities:** voice mail. **Pool(s):** heated outdoor. **Leisure Activities:** whirlpool, tennis court, sled hill, playground, basketball, vol-leyball, game room. **Cards:** AX, CB, DC, DS, MC, VI. **Special Amenities:** free continental breakfast and free local telephone calls. *(See color ad p 435)*

SOME UNITS

FEE

## ——— WHERE TO DINE ———

**BACK BEHIND SALOON RESTAURANT**      **Dinner:** $13-$23      **Phone: 802/422-9907**

▼▼ ▼▼    **Location:** Jct SR 100 S and US 4. **Hours:** Open 6/1-4/5; 4 pm-10 pm. Closed: 11/25, 12/25; also Tues &
Wed. **Features:** Originally constructed in the early 1900s, the laid-back "saloon" has been a local favorite
American    since it opened its doors as an eatery in 1974. Featuring a 1946 Wurlitzer juke box and a distinctive
fireplace built from collected stones, fossils and petrified wood, the restaurant is a great place to enjoy a
relaxing meal, either inside or out on the deck. For delicious after-dinner ice cream treats during summer, visit the 100-year-old
on-site caboose. Casual dress; cocktails. **Parking:** on-site. **Cards:** AX, DS, MC, VI.

**BIRCH RIDGE INN**      **Dinner:** $19-$29      **Phone: 802/422-4293**

▼▼ ▼▼ ▼▼    **Location:** 2.2 mi s on Killington Rd, from jct SR 100/US 4, then just w; in Birch Ridge Inn. 37 Butler Rd 05751.
**Hours:** 6 pm-9:30 pm. Closed: 11/25, 12/25; also Mon, Tues & 3 weeks in May. **Reservations:** suggested.
American    **Features:** This pleasant little dining room is one of the jewels of Killington's dining establishments. Its
somewhat limited but inspired menu is sure to please the more refined palate with such creations as
pistachio encrusted rack of New Zealand lamb served with fresh mint pesto or the pan-seared diver scallops served with
shellfish risotto and braised fennel cream. The atmosphere is intimate and relaxed, and service very capable. Enjoy a cocktail
or an after-dinner drink in the lounge. Casual dress; cocktails. **Parking:** on-site. **Cards:** AX, DS, MC, VI.

**THE CASCADES RESTAURANT**      **Dinner:** $10-$25      **Phone: 802/422-3731**

▼▼ ▼▼    **Location:** 3.5 mi off US 4 on Killington Rd; in The Cascades Lodge. 58 Old Mill Rd 05751. **Hours:** Open 7/1-10/20
& 11/20-4/15; 7:30 am-10 & 5-9 pm. **Reservations:** suggested. **Features:** Featuring a country decor with
American    striking views of the mountains. The menu has a wide variety and offers large portions of the freshest
ingredients. Try the flavorful gazpacho or swordfish with fresh sea scallops. Sensational! Casual dress;
cocktails. **Parking:** on-site. **Cards:** AX, DS, JC, MC, VI.

**GRIST MILL RESTAURANT**      **Lunch:** $5-$7      **Dinner:** $13-$19      **Phone: 802/422-3970**

▼▼ ▼▼    **Location:** Jct US 4, 1.2 mi s. Killington Mountain Rd 05751. **Hours:** 11 am-11 pm. **Features:** A recipient of the
prestigious Roger Brown Memorial award for architectural design, the grist mill sits on the edge of Summit
American    Pond and offers spectacular views of Killington Mountain. Among extensive menu offerings are steaks,
seafood, chicken and pasta. Snow Country Magazine named this place one of the top five restaurant
lounges in North American ski country. Casual dress; cocktails. **Parking:** on-site. **Cards:** AX, MC, VI.

**HEMINGWAY'S RESTAURANT**   Historic      **Dinner:** $55-$65      **Phone: 802/422-3886**

ΑΑΑ    **Location:** On US 4, 2.5 mi e of Killington Summit Basin Rd. 4988 US Rt 4 05751. **Hours:** 6 pm-9 pm, Sat-10 pm;
hours/days may vary seasonally. Closed: 1/1, 12/25; also Mon, Tues & 10/26-11/19.
▼▼ ▼▼ ▼▼    **Reservations:** suggested. **Features:** Hemingway's is a charming restored 1860 home offering elegant
Nouvelle    dining in Vermont's mountainous region. Interesting and creative dishes are offered on their three- or
American    four-course tasting menu including vegetarian selections. Dressy casual; cocktails. **Parking:** on-site.
**Cards:** AX, CB, DC, DS, MC, VI.

**OLIVIA'S**      **Dinner:** $13-$20      **Phone: 802/775-2537**

▼▼ ▼▼    **Location:** Jct US 4, 0.8 mi n; in Grey Bonnet Inn. 831 SR 100 N 05751. **Hours:** Open 6/1-10/31 & 11/22-4/15;
7:30 am-9:30 & 5:30-9 pm. Closed: 5/31; also Tues & Wed. **Reservations:** suggested. **Features:** The
American    country-style dining room overlooks mountains and a lovely landscaped area. A roaring fireplace is fed in
the winter. The often-changing menu offers a nice selection of fresh fish, fowl and homemade pasta, all
creatively prepared with flavor in mind. Casual dress; cocktails. **Parking:** on-site. **Cards:** AX, DS, MC, VI.

**PEPPINO'S**      **Dinner:** $10-$19      **Phone: 802/422-3293**

▼▼ ▼▼    **Location:** 0.7 mi n from jct US 4/Killington Mountain Rd. Killington Mountain Rd 05751. **Hours:** 5 pm-9 pm. Closed
major holidays. **Reservations:** accepted. **Features:** The restaurant offers diners plentiful, hearty Italian
Italian    dishes in a casual yet intimate setting. Casual dress; cocktails. **Parking:** on-site. **Cards:** MC, VI.

**PIZZA JERKS**      **Lunch:** $5-$18      **Dinner:** $5-$18      **Phone: 802/422-4111**

▼▼    **Location:** Jct US 4/Killington Rd, 1.3 mi n. 1307 Killington Rd 05751. **Hours:** 11 am-10 pm, Fri & Sat-11 pm.
**Features:** The basic, functional restaurant offers walk-up counter service and the food is fresh and tasty,
Pizza    especially the calzones. Casual dress; beer & wine only. **Parking:** on-site. **Cards:** AX, DS, MC, VI.

**RED CLOVER INN DINING ROOM**   Country Inn      **Dinner:** $18-$30      **Phone: 802/775-2290**

▼▼ ▼▼ ▼▼    **Location:** 0.5 mi s of US 4, 5.3 mi e of jct US 7; in Red Clover Inn. 7 Woodward Rd 05701. **Hours:** Open
5/29-10/31 & 11/25-4/1; 6 pm-8 pm. Closed: Sun. **Reservations:** suggested. **Features:** Tucked away on a
American    country road, this is a diner's delight featuring a beautiful decor, sparkling stemware, fresh flowers and a
3,000-bottle wine cellar with many by-the-glass choices. The duck breast glazed with ginger and maple
sauce is mouthwatering. Casual dress; cocktails. **Parking:** on-site. **Cards:** AX, DS, MC, VI.

**THE WOBBLY BARN**      **Dinner:** $10-$23      **Phone: 802/422-3392**

▼▼ ▼▼    **Location:** Jct US 4/ Killington Rd, 1.3 mi n. 2229 Killington Rd 05751. **Hours:** 4:30 pm-10 pm, Fri & Sat-11 pm.
**Features:** The restaurant is a seasonal eatery which has been locally popular for over 35 years now.
Steak & Seafood    Casual dress; cocktails; entertainment. **Parking:** on-site. **Cards:** AX, CB, DC, DS, MC, VI.

# LONDONDERRY

## ——— WHERE TO STAY ———

**MAGIC VIEW MOTEL**
**Phone: (802)824-3793**

| | | |
|---|---|---|
| 9/24-10/17 [BP] | 1P: $60-$65 | 2P: $79-$85 | XP: $17 | F3 |
| 12/17-4/28 [BP] | 1P: $43-$60 | 2P: $59-$85 | XP: $17 | F3 |
| 6/25-9/23 & 10/18-12/16 | 1P: $37-$40 | 2P: $50-$55 | XP: $12 | F3 |

Motel   **Location:** 1.6 mi e on SR 11, from jct SR 100. 3806 VT Rt 11 05148. Fax: 802/824-3794. **Facility:** 19 units. 18 one-bedroom standard units. 1 one-bedroom suite ($130-$180) with kitchen. 1-2 stories (no elevator), interior/exterior corridors. *Bath:* combo or shower only. **Parking:** on-site, winter plug-ins. **Terms:** open 6/25-4/28, 2-5 night minimum stay - seasonal, 10 day cancellation notice-fee imposed, weekly rates available, package plans. **Leisure Activities:** Fee: game room. **Cards:** MC, VI.

SOME UNITS
(ASK) (SD) (K) (E) (B) / (X) (B) /

**SNOWDON MOTEL**
**Phone: 802/824-6047**

All Year   1P: $45-$55   2P: $60-$90   XP: $15

Motel   **Location:** 2 mi e on SR 11, from jct SR 100. 4071 VT Rt 11 05148 (PO Box 137). Fax: 802/824-6047. **Facility:** 12 one-bedroom standard units. 1-2 stories (no elevator), exterior corridors. *Bath:* combo or shower only. **Parking:** on-site, winter plug-ins. **Terms:** 2-3 night minimum stay - weekends, 14 day cancellation notice, [BP] meal plan available.

SOME UNITS
(X) (K) / (B) /

## ——— WHERE TO DINE ———

**THE GARDEN CAFE & GALLERY**
**Lunch: $4-$14**   **Dinner: $8-$12**   **Phone: 802/824-9574**

Continental   **Location:** Center. SR 11/30 05148. **Hours:** 11:30 am-9 pm; Sunday brunch. Closed: 11/25, 12/25; also Tues. **Reservations:** suggested. **Features:** The restaurant offers patrons a relaxing atmosphere to enjoy deliciously prepared foods. Casual dress; cocktails. **Parking:** on-site. **Cards:** MC, VI.

(K) (X)

**JAKE'S CAFE**
**Lunch: $7-$10**   **Dinner: $12-$20**   **Phone: 802/824-6614**

American   **Location:** In the Mountain Marketplace. Mountain Marketplace 05148. **Hours:** noon-9 pm. Closed: 11/25, 12/25. **Features:** The eatery has a fun chili-pepper theme, casual friendly service and good food, especially the soup. Casual dress; cocktails. **Parking:** on-site. **Cards:** MC, VI.

(Y) (X)

**THE MILL TAVERN**
**Dinner: $19-$23**   **Phone: 802/824-3247**

American   **Location:** Jct SR 11/100. 2118 N Main St 05359. **Hours:** Open 12/15-3/31; 5 pm-9:30 pm. Closed: 12/25. **Features:** The restaurant is in a historic mill dating back to the 1800s and over 10,000 antique handmade tools hang from the ceilings; the cozy wood-burning fireplace is sure to keep patrons warm. Casual dress; cocktails. **Parking:** on-site. **Cards:** MC, VI.

(K) (X)

**SWISS INN DINING ROOM**
**Dinner: $13-$23**   **Phone: 802/824-3442**

Continental   **Location:** Jct SR 100, 1.5 mi w; in the Swiss Inn. 249 Rt 11 05148. **Hours:** 5 pm-8:30 pm. **Reservations:** suggested. **Features:** The friendly, knowledgeable service and the excellent, flavorful food will have you yodeling praise for this Swiss/German food. The fondues won't disappoint you, and the veal in a white wine cream sauce will delight you. Casual dress; cocktails. **Parking:** on-site. **Cards:** MC, VI.

(Y) (X)

# LOWER WATERFORD

## ——— WHERE TO STAY ———

**RABBIT HILL INN**
**Phone: 802/748-5168**

(AAA) (SAVE)

| | | |
|---|---|---|
| 9/1-10/31 [MAP] | 1P: $315-$355 | 2P: $365-$405 | XP: $75 |
| 5/1-8/31 & 11/19-4/3 [MAP] | 1P: $275-$315 | 2P: $325-$365 | XP: $75 |

Historic
Country Inn   **Location:** I-93, exit 44 northbound, 2.6 mi n on SR 18; exit 1 southbound, 6.3 mi s on SR 18. 48 Lower Waterford Rd 05848. Fax: 802/748-8342. **Facility:** This handsome 200-year-old inn sits prominently in the center of a sleepy little town and offers individually decorated guest rooms. Smoke free premises. 19 one-bedroom standard units, some with whirlpools. 2-3 stories (no elevator), interior/exterior corridors. *Bath:* combo or shower only. **Parking:** on-site. **Terms:** open 5/1-10/31 & 11/19-4/3, 2 night minimum stay - weekends, age restrictions may apply, 30 day cancellation notice-fee imposed, no pets allowed (owner's cat on premises). **Amenities:** video library, CD players, irons, hair dryers. **Dining:** dining room, see separate listing. **Leisure Activities:** fishing, golf privileges, cross country skiing, video room, lawn games, hiking trails. *Fee:* massage. **Guest Services:** gift shop. **Cards:** AX, MC, VI. **Special Amenities: free full breakfast and free local telephone calls.**

SOME UNITS
(¶) (&) (X) (X) (W) (E) (B) / (K) /

## ——— WHERE TO DINE ———

**RABBIT HILL INN DINING ROOM**   Country Inn   **Dinner: $50**   **Phone: 802/748-5168**

Regional American   **Location:** I-93, exit 44 northbound, 2.6 mi n on SR 18; exit 1 southbound, 6.3 mi s on SR 18; in Rabbit Hill Inn. 48 Lower Waterford Rd 05848. **Hours:** 6 pm-8:30 pm. Closed: first two weeks of April & Nov. **Reservations:** required. **Features:** You'll appreciate this candlelit experience in a charming inn. The seasonally changed prix fixe menu offers many exciting food combinations featuring beef, chicken, vegetarian, fresh seafood, pasta, wild-game and local ingredients. Dressy casual; cocktails. **Parking:** on-site. **Cards:** AX, MC, VI.

(Y) (X)

## LUDLOW pop. 958

—————— WHERE TO STAY ——————

**ALL SEASONS MOTEL**                                          Phone: (802)228-8100
(AAA) (SAVE)   10/17-3/26        1P: $90-$140      2P: $100-$150    XP: $20         F16
              9/17-10/16        1P: $90-$130      2P: $110-$140    XP: $20         F16
▽▽ ▽▽        5/1-9/16 & 3/27-4/30  1P: $70-$100   2P: $80-$110     XP: $20         F16
              **Location:** On SR 103; center. 112 Main St 05149. **Fax:** 802/228-4915. **Facility:** 17 units. 16 one-bedroom stan-
Small-scale Hotel  dard units, some with efficiencies. 1 one-bedroom suite ($120-$250) with efficiency. 2 stories (no elevator),
              interior/exterior corridors. *Bath:* combo or shower only. **Parking:** on-site. **Terms:** office hours 7:30 am-10 pm,
2 night minimum stay - weekends, 14 day cancellation notice, 12/17-3/20-fee imposed, package plans - midweek.
**Amenities:** voice mail, hair dryers. **Pool(s):** outdoor. **Business Services:** fax (fee). **Cards:** AX, DS, MC, VI. **Special Amenities:**
free local telephone calls and free room upgrade (subject to availability with advanced reservations).

SOME UNITS
[S/D] [⊷] [✕] [DATA PORT] [▯] / [✗] [▭]

**THE ANDRIE ROSE INN**                                        Phone: 802/228-4846
(AAA) (SAVE)   9/16-4/30        1P: $120-$330     2P: $120-$330
              5/1-9/15        1P: $100-$240     2P: $100-$240
▽▽▽▽        **Location:** Corner of Depot St; center. 13 Pleasant St 05149. **Fax:** 802/228-7910. **Facility:** Attractive furnishings
              and gas fireplaces add charm to guest rooms at this fully restored 1829 house located in the heart of Ludlow.
Historic Bed   Smoke free premises. 20 units. 17 one-bedroom standard units, some with whirlpools. 1 one- and 2 two-
& Breakfast   bedroom suites with whirlpools, some with kitchens. 2-3 stories (no elevator), interior corridors. *Bath:* combo
              or shower only. **Parking:** on-site, winter plug-ins. **Terms:** 2 night minimum stay - weekends, age restrictions
may apply, 20 day cancellation notice-fee imposed. **Amenities:** video library, hair dryers. *Some:* CD players, irons. **Dining:** Fri
& Sat 6 pm-8:30 pm; by reservation only. **Leisure Activities:** bicycles, croquet. **Guest Services:** gift shop, valet laundry.
**Cards:** AX, MC, VI.

SOME UNITS
[❙❙] [✕] [⊷] / [✗] [▯] [VCR] [⊠] [▯] [▭] [▭] /

**BEST WESTERN LUDLOW COLONIAL MOTEL**  *Book at aaa.com*      Phone: (802)228-8188
(AAA) (SAVE)   10/17-3/26        1P: $100-$150     2P: $110-$160    XP: $20         F16
              9/17-10/16        1P: $100-$140     2P: $110-$150    XP: $20         F16
▽▽▽▽        5/1-9/16 & 3/27-4/30  1P: $80-$100   2P: $90-$120     XP: $20         F16
              **Location:** On SR 103; center. 93 Main St 05149. **Fax:** 802/228-7731. **Facility:** 48 units. 38 one-bedroom stan-
Small-scale Hotel  dard units. 8 one- and 2 two-bedroom suites ($150-$300), some with efficiencies, kitchens and/or whirlpools.
              2-3 stories (no elevator), interior/exterior corridors. *Bath:* combo or shower only. **Parking:** on-site, winter
plug-ins. **Terms:** 2 night minimum stay - weekends, 14 day cancellation notice, 12/17-3/20-fee imposed, [CP] meal plan avail-
able, package plans - midweek. **Amenities:** voice mail, irons, hair dryers. **Pool(s):** outdoor. **Leisure Activities:** exercise room.
**Guest Services:** complimentary laundry. **Business Services:** meeting rooms. **Cards:** AX, CB, DC, DS, JC, MC, VI.
**Special Amenities:** free continental breakfast and early check-in/late check-out. *(See color ad below)*

SOME UNITS
[S/D] [❙❙] [⊷] [✕] [DATA PORT] [▯] [▭] [▭] / [✕] [VCR] /

## HAPPY TRAILS MOTEL

**Phone: 802/228-8888**

AAA SAVE ◇◇ ◇◇

| |  |  | |
|---|---|---|---|
| 1/1-3/31 | 2P: $80-$150 | XP: $10 | F12 |
| 5/1-10/16 | 2P: $70-$125 | XP: $10 | F12 |
| 4/1-4/30 | 2P: $70-$105 | XP: $10 | F12 |
| 10/17-12/31 | 2P: $65-$105 | XP: $10 | F12 |

Small-scale Hotel **Location:** Jct SR 100, 1.6 mi e. 321 Rt 103 S 05149. Fax: 802/228-8287. **Facility:** 28 units. 25 one-bedroom standard units, some with kitchens. 2 one-bedroom suites ($110-$185) with kitchens. 1 cottage ($140-$275). 2 stories (no elevator), interior/exterior corridors. *Bath:* combo or shower only. **Parking:** on-site, winter plug-ins. **Terms:** office hours 8 am-10 pm, 1-3 night minimum stay - some weekends, 7 day cancellation notice-fee imposed. **Amenities:** voice mail. **Leisure Activities:** fishing, winter hot tub, hiking trails. **Cards:** AX, DS, MC, VI. **Special Amenities:** free local telephone calls and preferred room (subject to availability with advanced reservations).

SOME UNITS

🖅 ✕ 📺 DATA/PORT 🔌 💻 / VCR 📷 /

## TIMBER INN MOTEL

**Phone: (802)228-8666**

AAA SAVE ◇◇ ◇◇
Motel

| |  |  | |
|---|---|---|---|
| 12/17-3/19 | 2P: $84-$179 | XP: $15 | F6 |
| 9/17-12/16 | 2P: $84-$149 | XP: $15 | F6 |
| 3/20-4/30 | 2P: $69-$149 | XP: $15 | F6 |
| 5/1-9/16 | 2P: $69-$119 | XP: $15 | F6 |

**Location:** On SR 103 S, 1 mi e. 112 Rt 103 S 05149. Fax: 802/228-8703. **Facility:** 18 one-bedroom standard units, some with kitchens. 2 stories (no elevator), exterior corridors. *Bath:* combo or shower only. **Parking:** on-site. **Terms:** 2 night minimum stay - weekends in winter, 14 day cancellation notice-fee imposed, package plans, pets ($10 extra charge 4/15-9/15, dogs only). **Amenities:** video library. **Pool(s):** outdoor. **Leisure Activities:** sauna, whirlpool, fishing, playground. **Cards:** AX, DS, MC, VI. *(See color ad below)*

SOME UNITS

S D 🐾 ⛵ 🖅 📺 / ✕ VCR DATA/PORT 🔌 💻 /
FEE

## WHERE TO DINE

**ARCHIE'S PRIME TIME STEAK HOUSE**
Steak House
**Dinner:** $11-$23
**Phone:** 802/228-3003
**Location:** In the Okemo Marketplace. 57 Pond St (SR 103) 05149. **Hours:** 4:30 pm-10 pm, Fri & Sat-11 pm; hours may vary off season. Closed: 11/25. **Features:** The restaurant has a pub/steakhouse atmosphere and serves up large portions of well prepared foods. Casual dress; cocktails. **Parking:** on-site. **Cards:** AX, MC, VI.

**NIKKI'S RESTAURANT**
Regional American
**Dinner:** $14-$32
**Phone:** 802/228-7797
**Location:** On SR 103, n of town center. 44 Pond St 05149. **Hours:** Open 5/15-4/15; 5:30 pm-9 pm. Closed: 11/25; also Sun & Mon from mid-May to mid-Dec. **Features:** Ludlow's finest restaurant offers a casual-sophisticated atmosphere, capable and attentive service, fine creative cuisine and a lovely selection of wines. Casual dress; cocktails. **Parking:** on-site. **Cards:** AX, DC, DS, MC, VI.

**WICKED GOOD PIZZA**
Pizza
**Lunch:** $5-$20
**Dinner:** $5-$20
**Phone:** 802/228-4131
**Location:** On SR 103; center. 117 Main St 05149. **Hours:** 11:30 am-9 pm, Fri & Sat-9:30 pm, Sun noon-8 pm. Closed: 3/27, 11/25, 12/25. **Features:** What makes this place so popular that owners have had to move to a larger location? The answer is, the wicked New York-style pizzas. Among the most popular is the Tuscan with pesto, olive oil, garlic, artichoke hearts, roasted peppers, Kalamata olives and mozzarella. Also on the menu you'll find calzones, salads, pasta and subs. Heed the sign at the entrance that reads, "no dough, no pizza..." — cash-only transactions, please! Casual dress; beer & wine only. **Parking:** on-site.

---

### The following restaurants have not been evaluated by AAA but are listed for your information only.

**JAVA BABA'S SLOW FOOD CAFE**
[fyi]
**Phone:** 802/228-2326
Not evaluated. **Location:** In Okemo Marketplace. 57 Pond St 05149. **Features:** The simple, quick-serve facility is open for breakfast, lunch and dinner.

**THE SITTING BULL**
[fyi]
**Phone:** 802/228-4041
Not evaluated. **Location:** At Okemo Mountain base lodge. Okemo Mountain Access Rd 05148. **Features:** The Sitting Bull offers light fare in a casual setting. Perfect for that afternoon pre-ski meal.

# LYNDON

## WHERE TO STAY

**BRANCH BROOK BED & BREAKFAST**
Historic Bed
& Breakfast
All Year [BP]    1P: $72-$94    2P: $77-$100    XP: $15    F10
**Phone:** (802)626-8316
**Location:** I-91, exit 23, just s on US 5, then 0.3 mi w on S Wheelock Rd. Located in a quiet area. 36 Branch Brook Ln 05849 (PO Box 217). Fax: 802/626-5772. **Facility:** Set in a quiet village some call the covered bridge capital of Vermont, this restored 1830s house has a quaint ambience. Smoke free premises. 5 one-bedroom standard units. 2 stories (no elevator), interior corridors. *Bath:* some shared or private, combo, shower or tub only. **Parking:** on-site, winter plug-ins. **Terms:** 2 night minimum stay - 9/15-10/15, 14 day cancellation notice-fee imposed. **Cards:** MC, VI. **Special Amenities:** free full breakfast and free local telephone calls.
SOME UNITS

# LYNDONVILLE pop. 1,227

## WHERE TO STAY

**COLONNADE INN**
Motel
9/15-10/15    1P: $60-$65    2P: $65-$85    XP: $5    F12
5/1-9/14 & 10/16-4/30    1P: $50-$55    2P: $65-$70    XP: $5    F12
**Phone:** 802/626-9316
**Location:** I-91, exit 23, just n on US 5. 28 Back Center Rd 05851. Fax: 802/626-1023. **Facility:** 40 one-bedroom standard units. 2 stories (no elevator), exterior corridors. **Parking:** on-site, winter plug-ins. **Terms:** [CP] meal plan available. **Amenities:** irons. **Cards:** AX, CB, DC, DS, JC, MC, VI. **Special Amenities:** free continental breakfast and free local telephone calls.
SOME UNITS

## WHERE TO DINE

**ASIA**
Chinese
**Lunch:** $4-$8
**Dinner:** $6-$9
**Phone:** 802/626-3368
**Location:** I-91, exit 23, 1.4 mi n on US 5; center. 17 Depot St 05850. **Hours:** 11 am-9 pm, Fri & Sat-10 pm, Sun noon-9 pm. Closed: 11/25. **Reservations:** suggested, weekends. **Features:** The restaurant prepares a nice selection of Mandarin, Szechuan and Cantonese dishes for both lunch and dinner. Casual dress; cocktails. **Parking:** on-site. **Cards:** AX, DS, MC, VI.

**MISS LYNDONVILLE DINER**
American
**Lunch:** $5-$6
**Dinner:** $6-$7
**Phone:** 802/626-9890
**Location:** I-91, exit 23, 1.1 mi n. US Rt 5 N 05851. **Hours:** 6 am-8 pm, Fri & Sat-9 pm. Closed: 11/25, 12/25. **Features:** A veritable Vermont icon for nearly a quarter of a century, the restaurant keeps folks coming back for its memorable breakfasts served all day, as well as its fresh fruit pies and delicious burgers prepared on homemade bread with Vermont cheese. Casual dress. **Parking:** on-site. **Cards:** MC, VI.

# MANCHESTER pop. 602

### ———— WHERE TO STAY ————

**BRITTANY INN MOTEL**
Phone: 802/362-1033
▼▼▼
All Year · 1P: $65-$115 · 2P: $65-$115 · XP: $10 · F5
Motel
**Location:** Jct SR 11/30, 3.8 mi s on Historic SR 7A. 1056 Main St (Historic SR 7A) 05254 (PO Box 359). **Fax:** 802/362-0551. **Facility:** Designated smoking area. 12 one-bedroom standard units. 1 story, exterior corridors. **Parking:** on-site. **Terms:** office hours 8 am-10 pm, 2 night minimum stay - weekends 6/1-10/31, 14 day cancellation notice, small pets only ($20 deposit). **Cards:** MC, VI.

**THE INN AT ORMSBY HILL**
Phone: 802/362-1163
(AAA) [SAVE]
All Year · 1P: $165-$400 · 2P: $187-$420
▼▼▼▼
**Location:** On Historic SR 7A, 3 mi s of jct SR 11/30. 1842 Main St 05255. Fax: 802/362-5176. **Facility:** A hot breakfast, complete with the inn's house granola and a breakfast dessert, is the specialty at this historic B&B built in 1764. Smoke free premises. 10 one-bedroom standard units with whirlpools. 2 stories (no elevator),
Bed & Breakfast
interior/exterior corridors. **Parking:** on-site, winter plug-ins. **Terms:** age restrictions may apply, cancellation fee imposed, no pets allowed (owner's pet on premises). **Amenities:** CD players, hair dryers. **Leisure Activities:** croquet, hiking trails. **Guest Services:** gift shop. **Cards:** MC, VI. **Special Amenities:** free full breakfast and free local telephone calls.

**NORTH SHIRE MOTEL**
Phone: (802)362-2336
(AAA) [SAVE]
All Year [ECP] · 1P: $74-$130 · 2P: $74-$130 · XP: $10
▼▼▼▼
**Location:** 4.5 mi s on Historic SR 7A, from jct SR 11/30. 97 Main St 05254 (PO Box 413). **Facility:** 14 one-bedroom standard units. 1 story, exterior corridors. **Parking:** on-site. **Terms:** 2 night minimum stay - weekends in season, 14 day cancellation notice-fee imposed, no pets allowed (owner's pet on premises).
Motel
**Amenities:** video library, irons, hair dryers. **Pool(s):** outdoor. **Cards:** AX, DS, MC, VI. **Special Amenities:** free expanded continental breakfast and free local telephone calls.

**WEATHERVANE MOTEL**
Phone: 802/362-2444
▼▼▼
All Year · 2P: $65-$150 · XP: $10
Motel
**Location:** Jct SR 11/30, 2.3 mi s. 2212 Main St, Historic SR 7A 05254 (PO Box 378). Fax: 802/362-4616. **Facility:** 22 one-bedroom standard units. 1 story, exterior corridors. *Bath:* combo or shower only. **Parking:** on-site. **Terms:** 2 night minimum stay - weekends, 10 day cancellation notice-fee imposed, [CP] meal plan available. **Amenities:** *Some:* hair dryers. **Pool(s):** heated outdoor. **Leisure Activities:** putting green. **Cards:** AX, DS, MC, VI.

SOME UNITS

### ———— WHERE TO DINE ————

**ANGEL'S RESTAURANT** Historic
**Dinner:** $18-$32
Phone: 802/362-1792
▼▼▼
**Location:** On Historic SR 7A, 1 mi s of jct SR 11/30; in The Village Country Inn. 3835 Main St (Rt 7A) 05254. **Hours:** 8 am-10 & 5:30-9 pm. **Reservations:** suggested. **Features:** Angel's is set in a lovely, romantic
American
country inn atmosphere in the heart of the village. The menu features excellently prepared and presented Continental cuisine served in an atmosphere of European elegance with crisp, cloth-covered tables and vine-covered white lattice screens. Casual dress; cocktails. **Parking:** on-site. **Cards:** AX, DS, MC, VI.

**THE BUTTERY**
**Lunch:** $4-$9
Phone: 802/362-3544
▼▼
**Location:** In the Jelly Mill. Historic SR 7A S 05254. **Hours:** 9:30 am-3 pm. Closed: 3/27, 11/25, 12/25.
**Reservations:** accepted. **Features:** The restaurant is a simple family-style dining facility with friendly but
American
casual service. Casual dress; cocktails. **Parking:** on-site. **Cards:** AX, DS, MC, VI.

# MANCHESTER CENTER pop. 2,065

### ———— WHERE TO STAY ————

**ASPEN MOTEL**
Phone: 802/362-2450
▼▼▼
9/17-10/17 · 1P: $85-$125 · 2P: $85-$125 · XP: $10
10/18-4/30 · 1P: $65-$125 · 2P: $65-$125 · XP: $10
Motel
5/1-9/16 · 1P: $75-$115 · 2P: $75-$115 · XP: $10
**Location:** Jct SR 11/30, 0.9 mi n on Historic SR 7A. Located in a quiet area. 5669 Main St (Rt 7A) 05255 (PO Box 548). Fax: 802/362-1348. **Facility:** Smoke free premises. 25 units. 24 one-bedroom standard units. 1 two-bedroom suite with efficiency. 1 story, exterior corridors. *Bath:* combo or shower only. **Parking:** on-site, winter plug-ins. **Terms:** office hours 8 am-10 pm, 2-3 night minimum stay - in season & weekends, 14 day cancellation notice-fee imposed. **Amenities:** *Some:* hair dryers. **Pool(s):** outdoor. **Leisure Activities:** horseshoes, shuffleboard. **Cards:** AX, DS, MC, VI.

SOME UNITS

**CASABLANCA MOTEL**
Phone: 802/362-2145
▼▼▼
9/24-10/23 · 1P: $84-$148 · 2P: $84-$148 · XP: $10 · F12
10/24-4/30 · 1P: $54-$148 · 2P: $54-$148 · XP: $10 · F12
6/11-9/23 · 1P: $74-$128 · 2P: $74-$128 · XP: $10 · F12
Cottage
5/1-6/10 · 1P: $52-$118 · 2P: $54-$128 · XP: $10 · F12
**Location:** Jct SR 11/30 N, 1 mi n on Historic SR 7A. 5927 Main St (Rt 7A) 05255. Fax: 802/362-0190. **Facility:** 12 units. 1 one-bedroom suite. 11 cottages. 1 story, exterior corridors. *Bath:* combo or shower only. **Parking:** on-site, winter plug-ins. **Terms:** office hours 8 am-10 pm, 14 day cancellation notice-fee imposed, no pets allowed (owner's cat on premises). **Amenities:** hair dryers. **Pool(s):** heated outdoor. **Cards:** AX, DS, MC, VI.

SOME UNITS

## CHALET MOTEL

**Phone:** (802)362-1622

| | | | |
|---|---|---|---|
| 7/9-10/16 | 1P: $90-$150 | 2P: $100-$160 | XP: $10 F18 |
| 10/17-3/19 | 1P: $70-$110 | 2P: $85-$150 | XP: $10 F18 |
| 5/1-7/8 | 1P: $60-$90 | 2P: $80-$110 | XP: $10 F18 |
| 3/20-4/30 | 1P: $65-$75 | 2P: $75-$85 | XP: $10 F18 |

Motel

**Location:** On SR 11/30, 0.3 mi e of jct US 7. 1875 Depot St (SR 11/30) 05255. Fax: 802/362-1753. **Facility:** 43 one-bedroom standard units. 1 story, exterior corridors. *Bath:* combo or shower only. **Parking:** on-site, winter plug-ins. **Terms:** office hours 8:30 am-11 pm, 30 day cancellation notice-fee imposed, package plans - in summer & winter. **Amenities:** hair dryers. **Dining:** Bistro Henry's, see separate listing. **Pool(s):** heated outdoor. **Leisure Activities:** sauna, whirlpool, golf & tennis privileges. **Guest Services:** sundries. **Cards:** AX, CB, DC, DS, MC, VI.

SOME UNITS

## FOUR WINDS COUNTRY MOTEL

**Phone:** 802/362-1105

| | |
|---|---|
| 10/1-4/30 [ECP] | 1P: $85-$120 |
| 7/1-9/30 [ECP] | 1P: $78-$109 |
| 6/1-6/30 [ECP] | 1P: $74-$104 |
| 5/1-5/31 [ECP] | 1P: $66-$95 |

Motel

**Location:** Jct SR 11/30, 2.5 mi n on Historic SR 7A. Located in a rural area. 7379 Main St (Rt 7A) 05255. Fax: 802/362-0905. **Facility:** Smoke free premises. 18 units. 17 one- and 1 two-bedroom standard units. 1 story, exterior corridors. *Bath:* combo or shower only. **Parking:** on-site, winter plug-ins. **Terms:** office hours 7:30 am-11 pm, 3 day cancellation notice, no pets allowed (owner's dog on premises). **Amenities:** irons, hair dryers. **Pool(s):** outdoor. **Leisure Activities:** picnic tables, ping pong, basketball, horseshoes. **Cards:** AX, DS, MC, VI.

SOME UNITS

## THE MANCHESTER VIEW
▼▽▼▽ ▼▽ 
5/1-11/30    2P: $105-$230    XP: $15
12/1-4/30    2P: $85-$230    XP: $15

**Phone:** 802/362-2739

Small-scale Hotel **Location:** On Historic SR 7A, 2 mi n of jct SR 11/30 N, then just e. High Meadow Way 05255 (PO Box 1268). Fax: 802/362-2199. **Facility:** Smoke free premises. 35 units. 27 one-bedroom standard units, some with whirlpools. 5 one- and 3 two-bedroom suites ($185-$270), some with whirlpools. 1-2 stories (no elevator), interior/exterior corridors. *Bath:* combo or shower only. **Parking:** on-site. **Terms:** office hours 8 am-9 pm, 2-3 night minimum stay - weekends, 14 day cancellation notice-fee imposed, [CP] meal plan available. **Amenities:** voice mail, hair dryers. *Some:* irons. **Pool(s):** heated outdoor. **Cards:** AX, CB, DC, DS, MC, VI. *(See color ad p 442)*

## OLYMPIA MOTOR LODGE
▼▽▼▽ ▼▽▼▽
All Year    2P: $62-$120    XP: $15

**Phone:** (802)362-1700    F5

Motel **Location:** Jct SR 11/30, 2.5 mi n on Historic SR 7A. 7259 Main St 05255 (PO Box 606). Fax: 802/362-1705. **Facility:** Smoke free premises. 24 one-bedroom standard units. 1-2 stories (no elevator), interior/exterior corridors. **Parking:** on-site. **Terms:** office hours 7:30 am-9:30 pm, 2 night minimum stay - seasonal weekends, 14 day cancellation notice, no pets allowed (owner's dog on premises). **Pool(s):** heated outdoor. **Leisure Activities:** tennis court, basketball, volleyball. **Business Services:** meeting rooms. **Cards:** AX, DS, MC, VI.

SOME UNITS

## PALMER HOUSE RESORT MOTEL
AAA SAVE 
▼▽▼▽ ▼▽▼▽
9/24-10/23    2P: $150-$320
10/24-4/30    2P: $90-$275
6/18-9/23    2P: $120-$250
5/1-6/17    2P: $90-$120    XP: $20

**Phone:** 802/362-3600

Small-scale Hotel **Location:** Jct SR 11/30 N, 0.5 mi n on Historic SR 7A. 121 Main St (Rt 7A N) 05255 (PO Box 1964). Fax: 802/362-3600. **Facility:** 50 units. 39 one-bedroom standard units. 8 one- and 3 two-bedroom suites ($180-$320) with whirlpools. 1-2 stories (no elevator), interior/exterior corridors. **Parking:** on-site, winter plug-ins. **Terms:** office hours 7 am-10 pm, 2-3 night minimum stay - weekends, age restrictions may apply, 15 day cancellation notice-fee imposed, [ECP] meal plan available. **Amenities:** voice mail, hair dryers. **Pool(s):** heated outdoor, heated indoor. **Leisure Activities:** sauna, whirlpool, boating, fishing, 9-hole pitch & putt golf course, 2 tennis courts, recreation programs, antique doll display, country club privileges. **Business Services:** meeting rooms. **Cards:** AX, DS, MC, VI. **Special Amenities:** free local telephone calls and free newspaper. *(See color ad p 442)*

SOME UNITS

## STAMFORD MOTEL
AAA SAVE 
▼▽▼▽ ▼▽▼▽
5/1-10/27    1P: $65-$80    2P: $68-$90    XP: $10    D16
10/28-4/30    1P: $60-$75    2P: $68-$80    XP: $10    D16

**Phone:** (802)362-2342

Motel **Location:** Jct SR 11/30, 1.5 mi n on Historic SR 7A. 6458 Main St (SR 7A N) 05255. Fax: 802/362-1935. **Facility:** 14 one-bedroom standard units. 1-2 stories (no elevator), interior/exterior corridors. *Bath:* combo or shower only. **Parking:** on-site, winter plug-ins. **Terms:** office hours 7 am-11 pm, 3 day cancellation notice. **Pool(s):** small heated outdoor. **Leisure Activities:** golf & tennis privileges at Manchester Country Club. **Cards:** AX, CB, DC, DS, MC, VI. **Special Amenities:** free local telephone calls and preferred room (subject to availability with advanced reservations).

SOME UNITS

## TOLL ROAD MOTOR INN
▼▽▼▽ ▼▽
All Year    2P: $69-$129    XP: $15

**Phone:** 802/362-1711    F12

Motel **Location:** On SR 11/30, 0.8 mi e of jct US 7, exit 4. 2220 Depot St 05255 (PO Box 813). Fax: 802/362-1715. **Facility:** Smoke free premises. 16 one-bedroom standard units. 2 stories (no elevator), interior corridors. **Parking:** on-site. **Terms:** office hours 8:30 am-10 pm, 2-3 night minimum stay - seasonal, 14 day cancellation notice, package plans. **Pool(s):** outdoor. **Cards:** AX, DC, MC, VI.

---

## ─── WHERE TO DINE ───

## BISTRO HENRY'S
AAA
▼▽▼▽ ▼▽
Mediterranean

**Dinner:** $18-$24    **Phone:** 802/362-4982

**Location:** On SR 11/30, 0.3 mi e of jct US 7; in Chalet Motel. 1778 SR 11/30 05255. **Hours:** Open 5/16-12/1 & 12/16-4/15; 5 pm-9 pm, Fri & Sat-10 pm. Closed major holidays; also Mon, Sun 11/1-4/14. **Reservations:** suggested. **Features:** Bistro Henry features a Mediterranean cuisine with a touch of fun! The contemporary menu offers pasta, seafood, chicken, certified Angus beef dishes and a terrific selection of wine. The ambience is open, airy and relaxed. Casual dress; cocktails. **Parking:** on-site. **Cards:** AX, CB, DC, DS, MC, VI.

## CHINA CITY
▼▽▼▽
Chinese

**Lunch:** $4-$14    **Dinner:** $4-$14    **Phone:** 802/366-8281

**Location:** In Manchester Shopping Center. 263-3 Depot St (SR 11/30) 05255. **Hours:** 11 am-10:30 pm, Fri & Sat-11 pm, Sun 11:30 am-10:30 pm. **Features:** The basic restaurant offers mostly deep-fried or stir-fried foods via walk-up counter service. Casual dress. **Parking:** on-site.

## CHRISTOS PIZZA & PASTA
▼▽▼▽
Greek

**Lunch:** $5-$21    **Dinner:** $5-$21    **Phone:** 802/362-2408

**Location:** Just n of jct SR 11/30/7A. 4931 Historic 7A 05255. **Hours:** 11 am-10 pm, Fri & Sat-11 pm, Sun noon-10 pm. Closed: 3/27, 11/25, 12/25. **Features:** The eatery is a basic, functional dining facility with walk-up counter service offering tasty entrees and salads. Casual dress; beer & wine only. **Parking:** street.

## FORTY NINE FORTY
▼▽▼▽ ▼▽
American

**Lunch:** $7-$9    **Dinner:** $13-$19    **Phone:** 802/362-0699

**Location:** Center. 4940 Main St 05255. **Hours:** 11 am-9 pm, Mon & Tues-5 pm; hours may vary. Closed: 11/25, 12/25. **Reservations:** accepted. **Features:** The eatery offers a casual atmosphere and very friendly service; be sure to try the wings. Casual dress; cocktails. **Parking:** street. **Cards:** AX, MC, VI.

**GARLIC JOHN'S**

Italian

**Dinner: $6-$24**

**Phone: 802-362-9843**

**Location:** US 7, exit 4, just e. SR 11 and 30 05255. **Hours:** 4 pm-9 pm, Fri & Sat-10 pm. Closed: 11/25, 12/24, 12/25. **Features:** The restaurant serves plentiful, well-prepared portions of both Southern and Northern Italian cuisine in a rustic, casual atmosphere. Hundreds of Chianti bottles hang from the wood-beamed ceiling. Dinner can be enjoyed both inside, as well as outside on the deck, where views of the mountains are stunning. Casual dress; cocktails. **Parking:** on-site. **Cards:** AX, MC, VI.

**THE GOURMET DELI & CAFE**

American

**Lunch: $3-$9**

**Phone: 802/362-1254**

**Location:** In Green Mountain Village Shoppes. 4961 Main St, Suite #2 05255. **Hours:** 7:30 am-3:30 pm. Closed: 11/25, 12/25. **Features:** The restaurant offers patrons fresh delicious foods in a quaint cafe atmosphere. If you like beans, don't miss the 15 bean soup. Casual dress; beer & wine only. **Parking:** on-site. **Cards:** MC, VI.

**LANEY'S RESTAURANT**

American

**Dinner: $12-$19**

**Phone: 802/362-4456**

**Location:** Jct US 7, just e on SR 11/30. Rt 11/30 05255. **Hours:** 4:30 pm-9 pm, Fri & Sat-10 pm. Closed: Mon & Tues 4/1-5/31. **Reservations:** suggested. **Features:** Barbecue baby back ribs and chicken, brick-oven pizza, fresh seafood specials and hand-cut steaks are among choices at the family-friendly eatery. The comfortable dining room is casual and festive. Guests can choose from a good representation of microbrewed beers. Casual dress; cocktails. **Parking:** on-site. **Cards:** AX, DC, MC, VI.

**MANCHESTER PIZZA HOUSE**

Pizza

**Lunch: $4-$8**

**Dinner: $6-$8**

**Phone: 802/362-3338**

**Location:** In Manchester Shopping Center. SR 11/30 05255. **Hours:** 11 am-10 pm, Fri & Sat-11 pm. Closed: 11/25, 12/25. **Features:** The simple restaurant offers limited facilities with walk-up counter service. Casual dress; beer & wine only. **Parking:** on-site.

**MIKA'S**

Pacific Rim

**Lunch: $6-$24**

**Dinner: $6-$24**

**Phone: 802/362-8100**

**Location:** 0.8 mi e of jct SR 11/30 N; at Avalanche Motel. SR 11/30 N 05255. **Hours:** 11:30 am-10 pm, Fri & Sat-11 pm. Closed: 11/25. **Reservations:** accepted. **Features:** The lovely atmosphere makes guests feel as though they just entered a Japanese pagoda; the staff really know how to prepare sushi and the service is very friendly. Casual dress; cocktails. **Parking:** on-site. **Cards:** AX, DS, MC, VI.

**MISTRAL'S AT TOLL GATE**

French

**Dinner: $24-$33**

**Phone: 802/362-1779**

**Location:** US 7, exit 4, 2 mi e on SR 11. 10 Toll Gate Rd 05255. **Hours:** Open 5/1-3/31; 6 pm-9 pm. Closed: 1/1, 11/25, 12/24, 12/25; also Wed & Tues 11/1-6/30. **Reservations:** suggested. **Features:** The restaurant presents a sophisticated yet intimate atmosphere offering guests fresh, delightful dishes. Dressy casual; cocktails. **Parking:** on-site. **Cards:** AX, MC, VI.

**MOOSE CROSSING**

American

**Lunch: $8-$13**

**Dinner: $13-$30**

**Phone: 802/362-5220**

**Location:** 1 mi e of jct SR 11/30. 1844 Depot St (SR 11) 05255. **Hours:** 5 pm-10 pm. Closed: 12/24 & Tues. **Reservations:** suggested. **Features:** The restaurant features a well coordinated, attractive moose theme throughout. A gift shop is located downstairs. Dressy casual; cocktails. **Parking:** on-site. **Cards:** AX, MC, VI.

**MULLIGAN'S OF MANCHESTER**

American

**Lunch: $7-$12**

**Dinner: $10-$21**

**Phone: 802/362-3663**

**Location:** SR 7A. SR 11/30 05255. **Hours:** 11:30 am-10 pm, Fri & Sat-11 pm, Sun-9 pm. Closed: 11/25, 12/25. **Features:** The casual restaurant serves a wide variety of dishes to please nearly everyone—from creative pasta to burgers and deli sandwiches. Specialties include traditional New England clam chowder and New York strip cooked to the diner's specifications. Casual dress; cocktails. **Parking:** on-site. **Cards:** AX, MC, VI.

**PANDA GARDEN**

Chinese

**Lunch: $5-$7**

**Dinner: $12-$26**

**Phone: 802/362-9175**

**Location:** In Highridge Plaza. 4519 Main St 05255. **Hours:** 11:30 am-10 pm, Fri & Sat-11 pm. Closed: 11/25; also Mon. **Reservations:** accepted. **Features:** The restaurant has a upscale, modern decor and offers well prepared, tasty food. Casual dress; cocktails. **Parking:** on-site. **Cards:** AX, DS, MC, VI.

**THE PERFECT WIFE**

American

**Dinner: $14-$26**

**Phone: 802/362-2817**

**Location:** US 7, exit 4, 3.9 mi e on SR 11/30. 2594 Depot St (SR 11 E) 05255. **Hours:** 5 pm-10 pm. Closed major holidays; also Mon. **Reservations:** suggested. **Features:** The restaurant's noticeably distinct interior features a solarium ceiling and stained glass panels hanging, while the second dining room has unusual stone walls and a knotty pine vaulted ceiling. The food is fresh, innovative and tasty. Dressy casual; cocktails. **Parking:** on-site. **Cards:** AX, DC, MC, VI.

**THE RESTAURANT AT WILLOW POND**

Italian

**Dinner: $13-$25**

**Phone: 802/362-4733**

**Location:** 2.9 mi n of jct SR 30/11. Historic Rt 7A 05255. **Hours:** 5:30 pm-9 pm. Closed: 12/25. **Reservations:** suggested. **Features:** The rich, warm interior in this fully restored 18th-century farmhouse is complete with a 300-year-old, three-sided wood-burning fireplace. Dressy casual; cocktails. **Parking:** on-site. **Cards:** AX, CB, DC, DS, MC, VI.

**SHERRIE'S CAFE**

American

**Lunch: $5-$8**

**Phone: 802/362-3468**

**Location:** 0.7 mi e of jct SR 11/30. 709A Depot St 05255. **Hours:** 8 am-3 pm. Closed: 3/27, 11/25, 12/25. **Reservations:** accepted. **Features:** The restaurant offers a bistro-style atmosphere with casual service and delicious foods. Casual dress; cocktails. **Parking:** on-site. **Cards:** MC, VI.

**SIRLOIN SALOON**

American

**Dinner: $15-$25**  **Phone: 802/362-2600**
**Location:** Jct US 7, just e on SR 11/30. 135 Depot St 05255. **Hours:** 4:30 pm-10 pm, Fri & Sat-11 pm. Closed: 11/25. **Reservations:** accepted. **Features:** Paintings and American Indian artifacts are part of the decor at this restaurant, which serves home-baked bread with meals. The menu offers grilled chicken and grain-fed, aged beef, locally grown organic vegetables, wines and microbrews. Servers are friendly and efficient. Casual dress; cocktails. **Parking:** on-site. **Cards:** AX, CB, DC, DS, MC, VI.

**ZOEY'S DELI & BAKERY**
American

**Lunch: $4-$10**  **Phone: 802/362-0005**
**Location:** On SR 11/30; center. **Hours:** 10 am-3 pm. Closed: 3/27, 11/25, 12/25. **Features:** Popular among the locals as well as tourists, don't be surprised to find a line out the door, as the food is well worth waiting for! Go with an appetite, as their sandwiches are huge and served on their house baked breads and rolls for which they are famous for. Casual dress. **Parking:** on-site. **Cards:** AX, MC, VI.

**ZOEY'S DOUBLE HEX RESTAURANT**
American

**Lunch: $6-$12**  **Dinner: $9-$17**  **Phone: 802/362-4600**
**Location:** Jct US 7 and SR 11/30. SR 11/30 05255. **Hours:** 11 am-9 pm. Closed: 3/27, 11/25, 12/25; also Tues. **Features:** The sister to "Zoey's Deli & Bakery" the Double Hex features a vaulted, hexagonal shape ceiling for which it bears its name and features the same great fare as their deli location. An extra treat is large deck with spectacular mountain views, available for dining in warm weather. Casual dress; cocktails. **Parking:** on-site. **Cards:** AX, MC, VI.

─────── *The following restaurant has not been evaluated by AAA* ───────
*but is listed for your information only.*

**VP FOR BREAKFAST**
[fyi]

**Phone: 802/362-4204**
Not evaluated. **Location:** Center. 4935 Main St 05255. **Features:** The local favorite for breakfast offers patrons creative choices made from Vermont products.

# MANCHESTER VILLAGE

─────── **WHERE TO STAY** ───────

**THE EQUINOX RESORT & SPA**  *Book at aaa.com*  **Phone: (802)362-4700**

Resort
Large-scale Hotel

| | | | | |
|---|---|---|---|---|
| 5/1-10/31 | 1P: $229-$429 | 2P: $239-$459 | XP: $50 | F12 |
| 11/1-4/30 | 1P: $159-$429 | 2P: $169-$459 | XP: $50 | F12 |

**Location:** 1.3 mi s on Historic SR 7A, from jct SR 11/30. 3567 Main St 05254 (PO Box 46). Fax: 802/362-4861. **Facility:** This restored 1769 hotel, in the center of a pretty village, features upscale-country decor and offers a variety of luxurious guest rooms and suites. 183 units. 170 one-bedroom standard units, some with whirlpools. 13 one-bedroom suites ($399-$1209), some with kitchens and/or whirlpools. 3-4 stories, interior corridors. **Parking:** on-site. **Terms:** check-in 4 pm, 2 night minimum stay - weekends, 21 day cancellation notice-fee imposed, [AP], [BP] & [MAP] meal plans available, $5 service charge. **Amenities:** video games, high-speed Internet, voice mail, irons, hair dryers. *Some:* CD players. **Dining:** 2 restaurants, 7 am-10:30 pm, cocktails, also, The Marsh Tavern at The Equinox, see separate listing, entertainment. **Pool(s):** heated indoor. **Leisure Activities:** saunas, whirlpool, steamrooms, Orvis School of Fly Fishing, cross country skiing, ice skating, recreation programs, British School of Falconry, archery school, off-road driving school, croquet, hiking trails, spa. *Fee:* golf-18 holes, 3 indoor tennis courts, bicycles, horseback riding. **Guest Services:** gift shop, valet laundry, airport transportation (fee)-Albany International Airport, area transportation-within 2 mi. **Business Services:** conference facilities, business center. **Cards:** AX, CB, DC, DS, MC, VI.

**THE VILLAGE COUNTRY INN**  **Phone: 802/362-1792**

Historic
Country Inn

All Year  2P: $129-$345
**Location:** On Historic SR 7A, 1 mi s of jct SR 11/30. 3835 Main St 05254 (PO Box 408). Fax: 802/362-7238. **Facility:** Country French decor accents this turn-of-the-20th-century inn which is furnished with some antique pieces. Smoke free premises. 32 units. 22 one-bedroom standard units, some with whirlpools. 10 one-bedroom suites. 3 stories (no elevator), interior/exterior corridors. *Bath:* combo or shower only. **Parking:** on-site, winter plug-ins. **Terms:** 2-3 night minimum stay - weekends, age restrictions may apply, 7 day cancellation notice, [BP] meal plan available. **Amenities:** hair dryers. *Some:* CD players, irons. **Dining:** Angel's Restaurant, see separate listing. **Pool(s):** outdoor. **Guest Services:** gift shop. **Cards:** AX, DS, MC, VI.

─────── **WHERE TO DINE** ───────

**THE BLACK SWAN**  Historic
Continental

**Dinner: $16-$24**  **Phone: 802/362-3807**
**Location:** 0.4 mi s on Historic SR 7A, from jct SR 11/30. 4384 Main St 05254. **Hours:** 5:30 pm-8:30 pm, Fri & Sat-9:30 pm. Closed: 11/25, 12/25; also 2 weeks in April & Nov. **Reservations:** suggested. **Features:** In a converted 19th-century brick farmhouse located in a charming and bustling New England village, it presents excellently prepared Continental cuisine. The white cloth covered tables, fine flower patterned china, decorative sconce lighting and cozy fireplace make for a comfortable fine dining experience. Restaurant hours may vary, call ahead. Dressy casual; cocktails. **Parking:** on-site. **Cards:** AX, MC, VI.

**THE MARSH TAVERN AT THE EQUINOX**     **Lunch:** $8-$15     **Dinner:** $16-$28     **Phone:** 802/362-7833
▼▼▼     **Location:** 1.3 mi s on Historic SR 7A, from jct SR 11/30; in The Equinox Resort & Spa. 3567 Main St 05254.
**Hours:** noon-2:30 & 6-9:30 pm. **Reservations:** required. **Features:** In addition to offering a comfortable,
American     upscale tavern atmosphere, the eatery also offers creative American cuisine with traditional New England
flair. The menu makes use of authentic Vermont ingredients whenever possible and always incorporates
the freshest in local produce. The main dining room closes between lunch and dinner but light fare is always available in the
tavern portion. Dressy casual; cocktails. **Parking:** on-site. **Cards:** AX, DC, DS, MC, VI.     ⓨ ⓧ

**RELUCTANT PANTHER INN RESTAURANT**   Country Inn     **Dinner:** $23-$33     **Phone:** 802/362-2568
▼▼▼     **Location:** Historic SR 7A, 1.1 mi s of SR 11/30; in Reluctant Panther Inn. 39 West Rd 05254. **Hours:** 6 pm-9 pm.
Closed major holidays; also Sun & Mon-Thurs 11/1-5/31. **Reservations:** suggested. **Features:** Located in
American     a charming country inn, the inn features a lovely romantic European-style ambience with decorative sconce
lights, flowing drapes, white linen tabletops and exquisite paintings. The cuisine is excellently prepared
American with some European influences with all dishes beautifully presented. An attractive Terrace room is also available for
dining and adjoins the main dining area, is more casual and overlooks a garden. Dressy casual; cocktails. **Parking:** on-site.
**Cards:** AX, DS, MC, VI.     ⓨ ⓧ

# MENDON —See also KILLINGTON.

## ────── WHERE TO STAY ──────

**CORTINA INN AND RESORT**   *Book at aaa.com*     **Phone:** (802)773-3333
▼▼▼     1/1-4/30 [BP]     1P: $109-$209     2P: $139-$229     XP: $29     F14
5/1-12/31 [BP]     1P: $99-$129     2P: $119-$179     XP: $29     F14
Resort     **Location:** Jct SR 100 N, 3 mi w. 103 US 4 05751-9460 (103 US Rt 4, KILLINGTON). Fax: 802/775-6948.
Small-scale Hotel     **Facility:** Ample activities are offered at this resort nestled among pine trees. 96 units. 89 one-bedroom standard units, some with whirlpools. 3 one- and 4 two-bedroom suites ($85-$120), some with kitchens. 2 sto-
ries, interior corridors. **Parking:** on-site, winter plug-ins. **Terms:** cancellation fee imposed, package plans, pets ($10 extra
charge). **Amenities:** voice mail, irons, hair dryers. *Some:* DVD players. **Dining:** Zola's Grille, see separate listing. **Pool(s):**
heated indoor. **Leisure Activities:** saunas, fishing, 8 tennis courts, snowmobiling, ice skating, hiking trails, playground, horseshoes, shuffleboard, game room. **Fee:** bicycles, massage. **Guest Services:** gift shop, valet laundry, area transportation. **Business Services:** meeting rooms, fax. **Cards:** AX, CB, DC, DS, JC, MC, VI.     SOME UNITS
ⒶⓈⓀ ⓈⒹ ⊁ ⊬ ⑪ ⌖ ⌂ ⊹ ⓧ 〔DATA PORT〕 / ⓧ ⓋⒸⓇ ▤ ▥ ▯ /

**ECONO LODGE-KILLINGTON AREA**   *Book at aaa.com*     **Phone:** (802)773-6644
ⒶⒶⒶ ⓈⒶⓋⒺ     12/26-4/18 [CP]     1P: $49-$100     2P: $55-$135     XP: $10     F17
▼▼     9/21-10/20 [CP]     1P: $45-$90     2P: $50-$100     XP: $10     F17
10/21-12/25 [CP]     1P: $40-$50     2P: $45-$65     XP: $10     F17
5/21-9/20 [CP]     1P: $45-$50     2P: $50-$60     XP: $10     F17
Small-scale Hotel     **Location:** Jct US 7, 5.3 mi e. 51 US 4 05701. Fax: 802/773-2193. **Facility:** 30 one-bedroom standard units, some
with kitchens. 2 stories (no elevator), interior corridors. **Parking:** on-site, winter plug-ins. **Terms:** open 5/21-
4/18, office hours 7 am-11 pm, check-in 4 pm, 2-5 night minimum stay - weekends, 7 day cancellation notice-fee imposed, pets
($10 fee). **Amenities:** safes (fee). **Pool(s):** outdoor. **Leisure Activities:** whirlpool, library. **Fee:** game room. **Guest Services:** gift
shop. **Business Services:** meeting rooms. **Cards:** AX, DS, MC, VI. **Special Amenities:** free continental breakfast and free
local telephone calls.     SOME UNITS
ⓈⒹ ⊬ ⌂ ⓧ 〔DATA PORT〕 / ⓧ ▤ ▥ ▯ /

**KILLINGTON-PICO MOTOR INN**     **Phone:** (802)773-4088
▼▼▼     9/16-4/30 [CP]     1P: $45-$130     2P: $45-$130     XP: $10     F6
5/1-9/15 [CP]     1P: $45     2P: $45     XP: $5     F6
Motel     **Location:** 6 mi e of US 7. 64 US Rt 4 05751 (64 US Rt 4, KILLINGTON). Fax: 802/775-9705. **Facility:** 28 one-
bedroom standard units. 1 story, exterior corridors. *Bath:* combo or shower only. **Parking:** on-site, winter
plug-ins. **Terms:** 14 day cancellation notice. **Amenities:** video library. **Pool(s):** outdoor. **Leisure Activities:** basketball, game
room. **Business Services:** PC. **Cards:** AX, DC, DS, MC, VI. *(See color ad p 432)*     SOME UNITS
ⒶⓈⓀ ⓈⒹ ⊁ ⑪ ⓨ ⌂ ⊹ ▤ / ⓧ ⓋⒸⓇ

**MENDON MOUNTAINVIEW RESORT LODGE**     **Phone:** (802)773-4311
ⒶⒶⒶ ⓈⒶⓋⒺ     11/24-3/31 [BP]     2P: $59-$169     XP: $20
9/24-11/23 [BP]     2P: $59-$109     XP: $20
▼▼▼     5/1-9/23 [BP]     2P: $59-$99     XP: $20
4/1-4/30 [BP]     2P: $59-$89     XP: $20
Small-scale Hotel     **Location:** On US 4, 6 mi e of jct US 7. 78 US 4 05751 (78 US 4, KILLINGTON). Fax: 802/773-4071. **Facility:** 40
one-bedroom standard units, some with whirlpools. 3 stories, interior corridors. **Parking:** on-site, winter plug-
ins. **Terms:** 2 night minimum stay - weekends, 7 day cancellation notice-fee imposed, small pets only ($50 deposit).
**Amenities:** video library. *Some:* hair dryers. **Pool(s):** heated outdoor. **Leisure Activities:** saunas, whirlpool, hiking trails, basketball, horseshoes, volleyball, game room. **Business Services:** meeting rooms. **Cards:** DS, MC, VI. **Special Amenities:** free
full breakfast and early check-in/late check-out. *(See color ad p 433)*     SOME UNITS
ⓈⒹ ⊬ ⓨ ⌂ ⓧ 〔DATA PORT〕 / ⓧ Ⓚ ⓋⒸⓇ ▯ /

**RED CARPET INN**   *Book at aaa.com*     **Phone:** (802)775-5577
ⒶⒶⒶ ⓈⒶⓋⒺ     All Year     1P: $42-$115     2P: $54-$135     XP: $15     F10
Location: Jct SR 100 N, 3 mi w. 119 Rt 4 05701. Fax: 802/773-4178. **Facility:** 37 one-bedroom standard units.
▼▼▼     1 story, exterior corridors. *Bath:* combo or shower only. **Parking:** on-site, winter plug-ins. **Terms:** office hours
Motel     7:30 am-11 pm, 14 day cancellation notice-fee imposed, pets ($5 extra charge, in limited units). **Pool(s):** out-
door. **Leisure Activities:** sauna, hot tub, horseback riding, playground, basketball, volleyball, game room.
**Cards:** AX, DC, MC, VI. **Special Amenities:** free continental breakfast and early check-in/late check-
out. *(See color ad p 433)*     SOME UNITS
ⓈⒹ ⊬ ⌂ ⓧ 〔DATA PORT〕 / ⓧ ▤ ▥ ▯ /

**THE VERMONT INN**

AAA SAVE     9/26-10/23 & 12/21-4/8 [BP]     1P: $80-$225     2P: $80-$225     XP: $30     Phone: (802)775-0708

◆◆◆     5/20-9/25 & 10/24-12/20 [BP]     1P: $50-$135     2P: $50-$135     XP: $30

**Historic Country Inn**

**Location:** US 7, 6 mi e. 69 US 4 05701. Fax: 802/773-5810. **Facility:** Built in 1840, this former dairy-farm residence features a restaurant and offers two guest rooms with fireplaces. Smoke free premises. 18 one-bedroom standard units, some with whirlpools. 2 stories (no elevator), interior corridors. *Bath:* combo or shower only. **Parking:** on-site. **Terms:** open 5/20-4/8, office hours 7 am-11 pm, 2 night minimum stay - weekends, 14 day cancellation notice, [MAP] meal plan available, package plans, no pets allowed (owner's cats on premises). **Dining:** restaurant, see separate listing. **Pool(s):** outdoor. **Leisure Activities:** sauna, whirlpool, tennis court, basketball, shuffleboard. **Business Services:** fax (fee). **Cards:** AX, DC, DS, MC, VI. **Special Amenities: free full breakfast and free local telephone calls.** *(See ad p 435)*

SOME UNITS

⬛ 🍽 🏊 ⊠ ⊠ 📺 🎱 / 🐾 /

---

## ——— WHERE TO DINE ———

**BJARNS**

◆◆◆     **Dinner:** $11-$25     Phone: 802/775-2000

**American**

**Location:** Jct US 4 and 7 in Rutland, 3 mi e. 27 US Rt 4 E 05701. **Hours:** 5 pm-9 pm. Closed: 12/25; also Mon. **Reservations:** accepted. **Features:** Family-oriented dining famous for its mouth watering prime rib, Bjarn's is just minutes away from the many specialty shops in historic, downtown Rutland. Diners will also enjoy the "Coaches Lounge" upstairs. Casual dress; cocktails. **Parking:** on-site. **Cards:** AX, CB, DC, DS, MC, VI.

🍸 ⊠

---

**SHARKEY'S GRILL & CANTINA**

◆◆◆     **Dinner:** $7-$25     Phone: 802/742-4400

**Mexican**

**Location:** 6.7 mi e of jct US 4 and 7. 74 US Rt 4 05701. **Hours:** 4 pm-9 pm, Fri & Sat-10 pm. **Reservations:** accepted. **Features:** The restaurant offers tasty foods and very casual service in a casual sealife atmosphere with large shells, stuffed sharks and aquariums. Casual dress; cocktails. **Parking:** on-site. **Cards:** AX, DS, MC, VI.

⊠

---

**THE VERMONT INN**   Country Inn     **Dinner:** $12-$22     Phone: 802/775-0708

◆◆◆

**Continental**

**Location:** US 7, 6 mi e; in The Vermont Inn. 69 US 4 05701. **Hours:** Open 5/21-4/12; 5:30 pm-9:30 pm. **Reservations:** suggested. **Features:** Guests appreciate New England cuisine, including preparations of veal, lamb and fresh seafood. Apple-crisp bread pudding is a favorite at the friendly country inn, which offers fireside seating in the winter. The wine list is extensive. Don't miss the full country breakfast. Casual dress; cocktails. **Parking:** on-site. **Cards:** AX, DC, DS, MC, VI.

🍸 ⊠

---

**ZOLA'S GRILLE**

◆◆◆     **Dinner:** $16-$30     Phone: 802/773-3333

**American**

**Location:** Jct SR 100 N, 3 mi w; in Cortina Inn and Resort. 103 US 4 05751. **Hours:** 7 am-10 & 6-9 pm, Sunday brunch 11 am-1:30 pm. **Reservations:** suggested. **Features:** An elegant country atmosphere characterizes a sophisticated restaurant. The creative menu lists dishes ranging from homemade pasta to grilled fish. Comfortable seating is offered at well-appointed tables. Staff members are courteous. Casual dress; cocktails. **Parking:** on-site. **Cards:** AX, CB, DC, DS, JC, MC, VI.

🍸 ⊠

---

**MIDDLEBURY** pop. 6,252—*See also EAST MIDDLEBURY.*

─────── WHERE TO STAY ───────

**GREYSTONE MOTEL**

| | | | Phone: 802/388-4935 |
|---|---|---|---|
| 5/1-10/31 | 1P: $75-$95 | 2P: $75-$125 | XP: $10    F10 |
| 11/1-4/30 | 1P: $55-$70 | 2P: $65-$95 | XP: $10    F10 |

⬥⬥⬥ (AAA) (SAVE)

⬥⬥ Motel

**Location:** On US 7, 1.5 mi s. 1395 US 7 S 05753. Fax: 802/388-7810. **Facility:** 10 one-bedroom standard units. 1 story, exterior corridors. *Bath:* shower only. **Parking:** on-site, winter plug-ins. **Terms:** 7 day cancellation notice-fee imposed, [CP] meal plan available. **Cards:** AX, DS, MC, VI.

✉ ▮

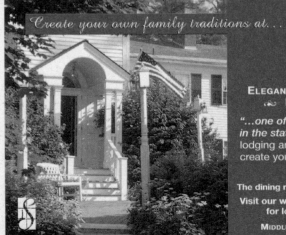

**THE MIDDLEBURY INN**  *Book at aaa.com*  Phone: (802)388-4961
(AAA) (SAVE) All Year [ECP] 1P: $78-$335 2P: $88-$395 XP: $10 F18
▽▽▽▽ **Location:** On US 7; center. 14 Court Square 05753 (PO Box 631). Fax: 802/388-4563. **Facility:** Built in 1827, this
Historic imposing red-brick Georgian inn offers rooms in a range of sizes; to the rear of the property is a section of
Small-scale Hotel motel rooms. 75 units. 72 one- and 2 two-bedroom standard units, some with efficiencies and/or whirlpools.
1 two-bedroom suite ($165-$395). 1-4 stories, interior/exterior corridors. **Parking:** on-site, winter plug-ins.
**Terms:** 2 night minimum stay - seasonal, 3 day cancellation notice-fee imposed, [MAP] meal plan available,
small pets only (with prior approval). **Amenities:** voice mail, irons, hair dryers. **Dining:** 2 restaurants, 7-10
am, 11:30-2 & 5-9 pm; dinner reservations are suggested. **Guest Services:** gift shop, valet laundry. **Business Services:** meeting
rooms. **Cards:** AX, DC, DS, MC, VI. **Special Amenities:** free expanded continental breakfast and free local telephone
calls. *(See color ad p 448)*

SOME UNITS
[icons]

**SWIFT HOUSE INN**  Phone: 802-388-9925
(AAA) (SAVE) 9/17-10/17 [ECP] 1P: $115-$255 2P: $115-$255 XP: $20
▽▽▽▽ 5/1-9/16 & 10/18-4/30 [ECP] 1P: $100-$235 2P: $100-$235 XP: $20
**Location:** 0.3 mi n on US 7 from jct SR 125 W. 25 Stewart Ln 05753. Fax: 802/388-9927. **Facility:** Set on spacious,
Historic well-manicured grounds, this Federal-style 1815 home features individually decorated rooms (some with fire-
Country Inn places). 21 one-bedroom standard units, some with whirlpools. 2 stories (no elevator), interior/exterior corridors. *Bath:* combo or shower only. **Parking:** on-site, winter plug-ins. **Terms:** 14 day cancellation notice-fee
imposed, package plans, $6 service charge. **Amenities:** voice mail, irons, hair dryers. **Dining:** 8 am-10 &
6-9 pm, Tues & Wed-10 am. **Leisure Activities:** sauna, steamroom, lawn games, hiking trails, jogging. **Business Services:** complimentary evening beverages. **Business Services:** meeting rooms. **Cards:** AX, CB, DC, DS, MC, VI. **Special Amenities:** free
expanded continental breakfast and preferred room (subject to availability with advanced reservations).
*(See color ad p 448)*

SOME UNITS
[icons]

──────── *The following lodging was either not evaluated or did not* ────────
*meet AAA rating requirements but is listed for your information only.*

**COURTYARD BY MARRIOTT**  Phone: 802-388-7600
[fyi] All Year 1P: $89-$339 2P: $89-$339 XP: $10 F18
Small-scale Hotel Too new to rate. **Location:** 1 mi s on US 7. 309 Court St 05753. Fax: 802/388-7602. **Amenities:** 89 units, coffeemakers, pool. **Terms:** 2-3 night minimum stay - seasonal weekends. **Cards:** AX, CB, DC, DS, JC, MC, VI.

──────── **WHERE TO DINE** ────────

**FIRE & ICE RESTAURANT**  **Lunch:** $7-$12 **Dinner:** $15-$25 Phone: 802-388-7166
(AAA) **Location:** Jct SR 125 W and US 7, just w. 26 Seymour St 05753. **Hours:** 11:30 am-8:15 pm, Fri & Sat-8:30 pm,
▽▽ ▽▽ Sun 1 pm-8:15 pm. Closed: 12/25. **Reservations:** suggested. **Features:** A city landmark for more than a
quarter of a century, the restaurant features hand-cut steaks, prime rib, fresh seafood and its own
homemade mashed potatoes, as well as an impressive 55-item salad bar. Informal dining rooms display an
Steak & Seafood eclectic collection of World War I wooden airplane propellers, a 1921 Hacker Craft motorboat, 50 model
boats and 200 antique skis. Casual dress; cocktails. **Parking:** on-site. **Cards:** AX, CB, DC, DS, MC, VI.

[icons]

**ROSIE'S**  **Lunch:** $3-$14 **Dinner:** $3-$14 Phone: 802-388-7052
(AAA) **Location:** 1.3 mi s on US 7, on west side. 886 US 7 05753. **Hours:** 6 am-9 pm, Fri & Sat-10 pm; to 10 pm
▽▽ ▽▽ 7/1-10/31. Closed: 11/25, 12/25. **Features:** Rosie's is a popular, cheerful, family-style roadside restaurant
offering table and counter service. The diverse menu features a great selection of appetizers, sandwiches,
pasta dishes, beef plates and side dishes. Casual dress; cocktails. **Parking:** on-site. **Cards:** AX, DS,
American MC, VI.

[icon]

# MIDDLESEX

──────── **WHERE TO STAY** ────────

**CAMP MEADE MOTOR COURT**  Phone: (802)223-5537
(AAA) (SAVE) 9/20-10/17 [ECP] 1P: $73 2P: $73-$83
▽▽ ▽▽ 5/1-9/19 [ECP] 1P: $63 2P: $63-$73
**Location:** I-89, exit 9 to US 2, just e. 961 US Rt 2 05602. **Facility:** 19 cabins. 1 story, exterior corridors. *Bath:*
Cabin combo or shower only. **Parking:** on-site. **Terms:** open 5/1-10/17. **Pool(s):** outdoor. **Leisure Activities:** croquet, ping pong, pool table, horseshoes. **Guest Services:** gift shop. **Cards:** MC, VI. **Special Amenities:** free
expanded continental breakfast and free local telephone calls.

SOME UNITS
[icons]

# MONTGOMERY CENTER

──────── **WHERE TO STAY** ────────

**THE INN ON TROUT RIVER**  Phone: 802-326-4391
▽▽ ▽▽ 12/20-1/5 1P: $80 2P: $118-$145 XP: $65 F4
9/15-12/19 & 1/6-4/30 1P: $73 2P: $108-$135 XP: $60 F4
Historic 5/1-9/14 1P: $64 2P: $103-$115 XP: $58 F4
Country Inn **Location:** On SR 118; center. 241 Main St 05471 (PO Box 76). Fax: 802/326-3194. **Facility:** A trout stream runs
behind this attractively restored Victorian home. Smoke free premises. 10 units. 9 one- and 1 two-bedroom
standard units. 2 stories (no elevator), interior corridors. *Bath:* combo or shower only. **Parking:** on-site, winter plug-ins.
**Terms:** 2-3 night minimum stay - weekends, 14 day cancellation notice-fee imposed, [MAP] meal plan available, 10% service
charge. **Dining:** Lemoine's-A Restaurant & Pub, see separate listing. **Leisure Activities:** fishing, cross country skiing, snowmobiling. **Cards:** AX, DS, MC, VI.

[icons]

## —— WHERE TO DINE ——

**LEMOINE'S-A RESTAURANT & PUB**  Country Inn          **Dinner:** $14-$20          **Phone:** 802-326-4391
(AAA)
◆◆◆◆
International
**Location:** On SR 118; center; in The Inn on Trout River. 241 Main St 05471. **Hours:** 6 pm-9 pm. **Closed:** 12/24. **Reservations:** suggested. **Features:** The owner/chef features a specialty of Vermont banana butterscotch pie that is very popular with guests. The century-old Victorian inn is warm, intimate and cozy. The delicious entrees come in hearty portions with local seasonal ingredients. Casual dress; cocktails. **Parking:** on-site. **Cards:** AX, DS, MC, VI.

# MONTPELIER pop. 8,035

## —— WHERE TO STAY ——

**BETSY'S B&B**                                                                              **Phone:** (802)229-0466
◆◆◆◆

| | | | |
|---|---|---|---|
| 9/22-10/21 | 1P: $80-$100 | 2P: $90-$110 | XP: $10 |
| 5/1-9/21 | 1P: $70-$90 | 2P: $80-$100 | XP: $10 |
| 10/22-4/30 | 1P: $60-$90 | 2P: $70-$100 | XP: $10 |

Bed & Breakfast  **Location:** 0.3 mi e of Main St; center. Located in a residential area. 74 E State St 05602. Fax: 802/229-5412. **Facility:** Two picturesque Victorian homes make up this quaint B&B, which is on a quiet street within walking distance of the city. Smoke free premises. 12 units. 11 one-bedroom standard units, some with kitchens. 1 two-bedroom suite ($110-$220) with kitchen. 2 stories (no elevator), interior corridors. *Bath:* combo or shower only. **Parking:** on-site. **Terms:** check-in 4 pm, 3 day cancellation notice, [BP] meal plan available, no pets allowed (owner's pets on premises). **Amenities:** dual phone lines, voice mail. **Business Services:** PC, fax. **Cards:** AX, DS, MC, VI.

SOME UNITS

**CAPITOL PLAZA HOTEL & CONFERENCE CENTER**                                **Phone:** (802)223-5252
(AAA) (SAVE)

| | | | |
|---|---|---|---|
| 9/17-10/21 | 1P: $116-$196 | 2P: $126-$196 | XP: $10    F16 |
| 10/22-4/30 | 1P: $96-$174 | 2P: $106-$176 | XP: $10    F16 |
| 5/1-9/16 | 1P: $96-$174 | 2P: $106-$174 | XP: $10    F16 |

Large-scale Hotel  **Location:** Center; 1 blk from the state capitol building. 100 State St 05602. Fax: 802/229-5427. **Facility:** 56 units. 53 one-bedroom standard units. 3 one-bedroom suites with whirlpools. 4 stories, interior corridors. *Some:* high-speed Internet, dual phone lines. **Dining:** 7 am-9 pm, Fri & Sat-10 pm; hours may vary, cocktails. **Guest Services:** gift shop, valet laundry. **Business Services:** conference facilities, fax. **Cards:** AX, DS, MC, VI.
**Parking:** on-site. **Terms:** cancellation fee imposed. **Amenities:** voice mail, irons, hair dryers.
*(See color ad.below)*

SOME UNITS

**ECONO LODGE**      *Book at aaa.com*                                       **Phone:** 802/223-5258
(AAA) (SAVE)

| | | | |
|---|---|---|---|
| 10/1-12/31 | 1P: $50-$60 | 2P: $65-$75 | XP: $4    F15 |
| 7/6-9/30 | 1P: $48-$58 | 2P: $60-$65 | XP: $4    F15 |
| 5/1-7/5 | 1P: $45-$55 | 2P: $55-$65 | XP: $4    F15 |
| 1/1-4/30 | 1P: $45-$55 | 2P: $55-$62 | XP: $4    F15 |

Motel  **Location:** Just s of jct US 302/SR 12. 101 Northfield St 05602. Fax: 802/223-0716. **Facility:** 54 units. 53 one- and 1 two-bedroom standard units. 2 stories (no elevator), exterior corridors. **Parking:** on-site. **Terms:** package plans, pets ($5 extra charge). **Amenities:** voice mail. *Some:* hair dryers. **Dining:** 11 am-2 & 5:30-9:30 pm. **Guest Services:** area transportation-Amtrak Station. **Cards:** AX, CB, DC, DS, MC, VI. **Special Amenities:** free continental breakfast and free local telephone calls.

SOME UNITS

## THE INN AT MONTPELIER

**Phone:** 802/223-2727

[AAA] [SAVE]

| | 1P: $126-$184 | 2P: $136-$194 | XP: $15 | F6 |
|---|---|---|---|---|
| 9/15-10/21 [ECP] | 1P: $104-$169 | 2P: $114-$179 | XP: $15 | F6 |
| 5/21-9/14 [ECP] | 1P: $99-$162 | 2P: $109-$172 | XP: $15 | F6 |
| 5/1-5/20 & 10/22-4/30 [ECP] | | | | |

*Bed & Breakfast*

**Location:** Just e of State St; center. 147 Main St 05602. Fax: 802/223-0722. **Facility:** This inn, consisting of two adjacent 19th-century homes, features typical New England architecture and antique and reproduction furnishings. Smoke free premises. 19 one-bedroom standard units. 2 stories (no elevator), interior corridors. *Bath:* combo or shower only. **Parking:** on-site. **Terms:** office hours 7 am-9 pm, 14 day cancellation notice-fee imposed. **Guest Services:** sundries, valet laundry. **Business Services:** meeting rooms. **Cards:** AX, DC, DS, MC, VI.

SOME UNITS

[S/D] [X] [DATA PORT] / [VCR] /

––––––– **WHERE TO DINE** –––––––

## ANGELENO'S

**Lunch:** $4-$20    **Dinner:** $4-$20    **Phone:** 802/229-5721

*Italian*

**Location:** Just e of jct Main and Barre sts. 15 Barre St 05602. **Hours:** 11 am-9:30 pm, Fri & Sat-10 pm, Sun-9 pm. Closed: 3/27, 11/25, 12/25. **Reservations:** accepted. **Features:** The casual Italian-themed restaurant offers a variety of Italian and American dishes. Casual dress; beer & wine only. **Parking:** on-site. **Cards:** AX, DS, MC, VI.

[X]

## CAPITOL GROUNDS

**Lunch:** $3-$7    **Dinner:** $3-$7    **Phone:** 802/223-7800

*American*

**Location:** Center. 45 State St 05602. **Hours:** 6:15 am-7 pm, Fri-9 pm, Sat 7 am-9 pm, Sun 8 am-5 pm. Closed: 12/25. **Features:** The restaurant is a pleasant coffeehouse with great fresh-brewed coffee and delicious desserts served via walk-up counter service. Casual dress. **Parking:** street.

[X]

## CHEF'S TABLE

**Lunch:** $6-$8    **Dinner:** $14-$22    **Phone:** 802/229-9202

[AAA]

*American*

**Location:** Between School and State sts; center. 118 Main St 05602. **Hours:** 11:30 am-2 & 5:30-9:30 pm, Sat from 5:30 pm. Closed: 11/25, 12/25; also Sun. **Reservations:** suggested. **Features:** Operated by students of the New England Culinary Institute. Imaginative dishes and artistic presentations including beef tenderloin, duck confit salad, venison, fowl and pasta. Sophisticated atmosphere. Casual dress; cocktails. **Parking:** street. **Cards:** AX, DC, DS, MC, VI.

[Y] [X]

## CONOSCENTI

**Dinner:** $13-$19    **Phone:** 802/262-3500

*Italian*

**Location:** Center. 52 State St 05602. **Hours:** 5 pm-11 pm. Closed major holidays; also Sun 1/1-5/1. **Reservations:** suggested. **Features:** The restaurant's upscale, elegant atmosphere includes a personable touch as guests can view the owner's family through the lovely black and white photographs that line the walls; the food is wonderfully creative and delicious. Casual dress; cocktails. **Parking:** street. **Cards:** AX, CB, DC, DS, MC, VI.

[X]

## ISABELLA'S BISTRO

**Dinner:** $14-$20    **Phone:** 802/223-6695

*Mediterranean*

**Location:** Center; across from state capitol. 440-42 State St 05602. **Hours:** 5 pm-9 pm, Fri & Sat-10 pm. Closed major holidays. **Reservations:** suggested. **Features:** The restaurant features a simple, elegant atmosphere with a light jazz background, and the menu changes often in order to offer patrons fresh, seasonal foods. Dressy casual; cocktails. **Parking:** street. **Cards:** AX, MC, VI.

[AC] [X]

## LA BRIOCHE BAKERY & CAFE

**Lunch:** $5-$6    **Dinner:** $5-$6    **Phone:** 802/229-0443

*American*

**Location:** I-89, exit 8, center. 89 Main St 05602. **Hours:** 6:30 am-7 pm, Sat 7 am-5 pm, Sun 8 am-5 pm. **Features:** The eatery is simple and basic overall but offers tasty food and walk-up counter service. Casual dress. **Parking:** street. **Cards:** MC, VI.

[X]

## MAIN STREET GRILL & BAR

**Lunch:** $5-$8    **Dinner:** $9-$14    **Phone:** 802/223-3188

*American*

**Location:** Between School and State sts; center. 118 Main St 05602. **Hours:** 11:30 am-2 & 5:30-9 pm, Sat 8 am-11 & 5:30-9:30 pm, Sun 10 am-9 pm. Closed: 11/25, 12/25. **Reservations:** suggested. **Features:** Operated by students of the New England Culinary Institute. Pleasant, informal cafe atmosphere offering creative and internationally influenced American cuisine. Specialties include grilled meats, seafood, salmon and vegetarian dishes. Pub menu available from 2 pm. Casual dress; cocktails. **Parking:** street. **Cards:** AX, DC, DS, MC, VI.

[Y] [X]

## MCGILLICUDDY'S IRISH PUB

**Lunch:** $3-$7    **Dinner:** $3-$7    **Phone:** 802/223-2721

*American*

**Location:** Center. 14 Langdon St 05602. **Hours:** 11 am-10:30 pm, Fri & Sat-11 pm. Closed: 11/25, 12/25. **Reservations:** accepted. **Features:** The restaurant offers mostly fried or grilled menu items in a simple, casual atmosphere; be sure to try the beer cheddar soup. Casual dress; cocktails. **Parking:** street. **Cards:** MC, VI.

## SARDUCCI'S RESTAURANT AND BAR

**Lunch:** $5-$7    **Dinner:** $7-$15    **Phone:** 802/223-0229

*Italian*

**Location:** Just n of US 2; center. 3 Main St 05602. **Hours:** 11:30 am-9 pm, Fri & Sat-9:30 pm, Sun 4:30 pm-9 pm. Closed: 11/25, 12/25. **Features:** The casual family restaurant specializes in Northern Italian dishes, many of which are prepared in the wood-burning oven. Casual dress; cocktails. **Parking:** on-site. **Cards:** AX, DC, DS, MC, VI.

[X]

# MORRISVILLE pop. 2,009

## ——— WHERE TO STAY ———

**PLAZA HOTEL**
▽▽▽
Small-scale Hotel

| | 1P: $80-$125 | 2P: $100-$150 | XP: $10 | F12 |
| 9/11-11/1 | 1P: $65-$110 | 2P: $80-$130 | XP: $10 | F12 |
| 5/1-9/10 & 11/2-4/30 | | | | |

Phone: (802)888-7761

**Location:** On SR 100, 0.3 mi s of jct SR 15. Located in Northgate Shopping Plaza. 120 Northgate Plaza 05661. Fax: 802/888-2842. **Facility:** 21 one-bedroom standard units, some with kitchens. 2 stories, interior corridors. **Parking:** on-site. **Amenities:** hair dryers. **Business Services:** meeting rooms. **Cards:** AX, DS, MC, VI.

SOME UNITS
(ASK) (SD) (T+) (VCR) (▯) / (✕) (🖬) /

**SUNSET MOTOR INN** *Book at aaa.com*
(AAA) (SAVE)
▽▽ ▽▽
Motel

| 9/17-10/10 [CP] | 2P: $85-$135 | XP: $10 | F12 |
| 5/1-9/16 [CP] | 2P: $68-$102 | XP: $10 | F12 |
| 10/11-4/30 [CP] | 2P: $58-$92 | XP: $10 | F12 |

Phone: (802)888-4956

**Location:** On SR 15, just w of jct SR 100. 160 VT Rt 15 W 05661. Fax: 802/888-3698. **Facility:** 55 one-bedroom standard units, some with whirlpools. 2 stories (no elevator), interior/exterior corridors. **Parking:** on-site, winter plug-ins. **Terms:** 2-3 night minimum stay - weekends, 7 day cancellation notice-fee imposed, weekly rates available, package plans - seasonal. **Amenities:** irons, hair dryers. **Pool(s):** outdoor. **Leisure Activities:** snowmobile trails, playground. **Cards:** AX, DC, DS, MC, VI. **Special Amenities:** free continental breakfast and free newspaper. *(See color ad p 480)*

SOME UNITS
(SD) (T+) (&M) (≈) (✱) / (✕) (VCR) (DATA PORT) (🖬) (🖵) /

**VILLAGE VICTORIAN BED & BREAKFAST**
▽▽▽
Bed & Breakfast

| 9/23-10/16 [BP] | 1P: $110-$140 | 2P: $120-$150 | XP: $20 | D6 |
| 5/1-9/22 & 10/17-4/30 [BP] | 1P: $80-$110 | 2P: $90-$120 | XP: $20 | D6 |

Phone: (802)888-8850

**Location:** From center, just e, then just n. 107 Union St 05661. **Facility:** The B&B is a charming, quaint, 1890s Victorian inn that offers guests great service and many personal touches. 4 one-bedroom standard units. 2 stories (no elevator), interior corridors. **Parking:** on-site. **Terms:** check-in 4 pm, cancellation fee imposed, package plans. **Amenities:** video library, hair dryers. **Leisure Activities:** playground, basketball. **Guest Services:** sundries. **Cards:** AX, MC, VI.

(ASK) (SD) (✕) (VCR) (☎)

# MOUNT HOLLY pop. 1,241

## ——— WHERE TO DINE ———

**HARRY'S**
▽▽ ▽▽
International

**Dinner:** $7-$18

Phone: 802/259-2996

**Location:** Jct SR 103 S/155 in E Wallingford, 6.2 mi s. SR 103 05758. **Hours:** 5 pm-9 pm. Closed major holidays. **Reservations:** accepted. **Features:** The eatery has a funky, fun, Carribean-style atmosphere along with casual service and tasty food. Casual dress; cocktails. **Parking:** on-site. **Cards:** MC, VI.          (✕)

# NEWFANE pop. 116

## ——— WHERE TO STAY ———

**FOUR COLUMNS INN**
▽▽▽
Historic
Country Inn

All Year [ECP]          1P: $125-$340          2P: $125-$340          XP: $35

Phone: (802)365-7713

**Location:** Just w of SR 30; center. 21 West St 05345 (PO Box 278). Fax: 802/365-0022. **Facility:** A prominent part of the village, this 1832 Greek Revival-style house offers manicured gardens, upscale common areas and beautifully appointed rooms. Smoke free premises. 16 one-bedroom standard units, some with whirlpools. 2-3 stories (no elevator), interior corridors. *Bath:* combo or shower only. **Parking:** on-site. **Terms:** 2 night minimum stay - weekends, 14 day cancellation notice, package plans - seasonal, pets ($10 extra charge). **Amenities:** hair dryers. *Some:* CD players. **Dining:** dining room, see separate listing. **Pool(s):** outdoor. **Leisure Activities:** hiking trails. *Fee:* massage. **Guest Services:** complimentary evening beverages. **Cards:** AX, CB, DC, DS, MC, VI.

SOME UNITS
(🛏) (T|) (≈) (✕) / (🅿) (VCR)
FEE

## ——— WHERE TO DINE ———

**THE FOUR COLUMNS INN DINING ROOM** Historic
▽▽▽
Continental

**Dinner:** $22-$32

Phone: 802/365-7713

**Location:** Just w of SR 30; center; in Four Columns Inn. 21 West St 05345. **Hours:** 5:30 pm-9 pm. Closed: 12/24, 12/25. **Reservations:** suggested. **Features:** In a charming country inn, the fine dining room exudes a refined ambience and follows a rustic, French country theme in its design. Internationally influenced cuisine includes fresh Vermont produce whenever possible. Dressy casual; cocktails. **Parking:** on-site. **Cards:** AX, CB, DC, DS, MC, VI.          (✕)

**THE OLD NEWFANE INN** Country Inn
▽▽▽
Continental

**Dinner:** $21-$28

Phone: 802/365-4427

**Location:** Center. SR 30 05345. **Hours:** Open 5/1-10/31 & 12/16-3/31; 6 pm-9 pm. Closed: Mon. **Reservations:** suggested. **Features:** Located in a Colonial-style country inn, this dining room's decor is true to the period. The menu features European influences including items such as a tasty Hungarian goulash. The upscale atmosphere and semi-formal attire is complemented by knowledgeable servers. Dressy casual; cocktails. **Parking:** on-site.          (🍸) (✕)

**RICK'S TAVERN**
▽
American

**Lunch:** $5-$7          **Dinner:** $8-$14

Phone: 802/365-4310

**Location:** From town green, 0.8 mi s. 386 VT Rt 30 05345. **Hours:** 11 am-9 pm, Fri & Sat-10 pm. Closed: 12/25; also Tues. **Features:** Originally a tool shed adjacent to a 1956 sawmill, the pub offers a casual, relaxed, rustic atmosphere. Casual dress; cocktails. **Parking:** on-site. **Cards:** MC, VI.          (✕)

## NEWPORT pop. 5,005

### ———— WHERE TO STAY ————

**NEWPORT CITY MOTEL**

(AAA) (SAVE)

Motel

| | | | | |
|---|---|---|---|---|
| 9/1-10/25 | 1P: $69-$83 | 2P: $83-$95 | XP: $6 | F6 |
| 5/1-8/31 & 10/26-4/30 | 1P: $59-$70 | 2P: $63-$82 | XP: $6 | F6 |

**Phone: 802/334-6558**

**Location:** I-91, exit 27, 1.8 mi n on SR 191, 0.5 mi e on Sias Ave, then just n. 444 E Main St 05855. Fax: 802/334-6557. **Facility:** 64 units. 63 one- and 1 two-bedroom standard units, some with whirlpools. 2 stories (no elevator), exterior corridors. *Bath:* combo or shower only. **Parking:** on-site, winter plug-ins (fee). **Terms:** 30 day cancellation notice. **Amenities:** *Some:* hair dryers. **Pool(s):** heated indoor. **Leisure Activities:** hot tub, exercise room. **Guest Services:** coin laundry. **Business Services:** meeting rooms. **Cards:** AX, DC, DS, MC, VI.

SOME UNITS

[🍴] [🛝] [DATA PORT] [▭] / [✕] [VCR] [🔌] /
FEE

### ———— WHERE TO DINE ————

**THE EASTSIDE RESTAURANT & PUB**       **Lunch:** $4-$8       **Dinner:** $8-$15       **Phone:** 802/334-2340

American

**Location:** Jct SR 191, just n via US 5, SR 105 and Union St, entrance under railway bridge. 47 Landing St 05855. **Hours:** 11 am-9 pm, Sat & Sun from 7 am. Closed: 12/25. **Reservations:** accepted, Sun-Thurs. **Features:** The locally popular Eastside is a bustling restaurant offering great views of mountains and lakes. Hearty portions of dishes such as chicken and biscuits and fried scallops are featured, and the pub has a cozy fireplace. There's terrace dining too. Casual dress; cocktails. **Parking:** on-site. **Cards:** AX, DS, MC, VI.

[♿M] [Y] [✕]

## NORTH BENNINGTON pop. 1,428

### ———— WHERE TO DINE ————

**PANGAEA**       **Dinner:** $22-$32       **Phone:** 802/442-7171

American

**Location:** Jct US 7/SR 67A to SR 67; center. 1 Prospect St 05257. **Hours:** Open 5/1-2/28 & 4/1-4/30; 5 pm-9 pm. Closed: 12/25. **Reservations:** suggested. **Features:** Exceptionally prepared, beautifully presented dishes are served in a quaint dining room appointed with original, eclectic paintings by a local artist. The restaurant is near the famous Park-McCullough House. Dressy casual; cocktails. **Parking:** on-site. **Cards:** AX, DS, MC, VI.

[✕]

## NORTH HERO

### ———— WHERE TO STAY ————

**NORTH HERO HOUSE**

(AAA) (SAVE)

Historic Country Inn

| | | | | |
|---|---|---|---|---|
| 5/1-10/19 [BP] | 1P: $125-$295 | 2P: $125-$295 | XP: $30 | |
| 10/20-4/30 [BP] | 1P: $85-$255 | 2P: $85-$255 | XP: $30 | |

**Phone: (802)372-4732**

**Location:** Center. 3643 Rt 2 05474 (PO Box 207). Fax: 802/372-3218. **Facility:** Part of a village on a Lake Champlain island, this property dating from 1891 is a rambling complex of four buildings and offers varied rooms. Smoke free premises. 26 units. 23 one-bedroom standard units, some with whirlpools. 3 one-bedroom suites ($225-$295), some with whirlpools. 2-3 stories (no elevator), interior/exterior corridors. *Bath:* combo or shower only. **Parking:** on-site. **Terms:** 2 night minimum stay - weekends in summer, 15 day cancellation notice-fee imposed, package plans - seasonal, no pets allowed (owner's dog on premises). **Amenities:** hair dryers. **Dining:** dining room, see separate listing. **Leisure Activities:** whirlpool, rental boats, rental canoes, kayak, massage. **Business Services:** meeting rooms. **Cards:** AX, MC, VI. **Special Amenities:** free expanded continental breakfast.

SOME UNITS

[🍴] [✕] [✕] [📹] [DATA PORT] / [🔌] [▭] /

**SHORE ACRES INN**

(AAA) (SAVE)

Small-scale Hotel

| | | | | |
|---|---|---|---|---|
| 5/1-10/31 | 1P: $105-$195 | 2P: $105-$195 | XP: $15 | F |
| 11/1-4/30 | 1P: $85 | 2P: $85 | | |

**Phone: 802/372-8722**

**Location:** 1 mi s on US 2. 237 Shore Acres Dr 05474. **Facility:** Smoke free premises. 23 one-bedroom standard units. 1-2 stories (no elevator), interior/exterior corridors. *Bath:* combo or shower only. **Parking:** on-site. **Terms:** 2 night minimum stay - some weekends, 10 day cancellation notice-fee imposed, pets ($10 fee, $5 extra charge). **Dining:** restaurant, see separate listing. **Leisure Activities:** boat dock, fishing, target golf course, 2 tennis courts, croquet, lawn games, shuffleboard. **Cards:** MC, VI.

SOME UNITS

[🐾] [🍴] [✕] [✕] [🚭] [🔌] / [📺] [🖨] /
FEE

### ———— WHERE TO DINE ————

**NORTH HERO HOUSE DINING ROOM**   Country Inn       **Dinner:** $13-$30       **Phone:** 802/372-4732

American

**Location:** Center; in North Hero House. 3643 Rt 2 05474. **Hours:** 8 am-10 & 5-9 pm, Sun 8 am-2 & 5-8:30 pm. Closed: Sun-Tues 11/20-5/1. **Reservations:** suggested. **Features:** The comfortable and relaxing country inn and restaurant offers a good selection of beer, wine and cocktails with its a la carte menu. A Friday night lobster buffet lure patrons in July and August. Casual dress; cocktails. **Parking:** on-site. **Cards:** AX, MC, VI.

[Y] [✕]

**SHORE ACRES RESTAURANT**       **Dinner:** $14-$25       **Phone:** 802/372-8722

Regional American

**Location:** 0.5 mi s on US 2; in Shore Acres Inn. 237 Shore Acres Dr 05474. **Hours:** Open 5/1-11/1; 5 pm-9 pm; also 7:30-9:30 am 7/1-8/31; hours may vary. **Reservations:** suggested. **Features:** Shore Acres specializes in fresh grilled fish, steak and chops, homemade bread, pastry and dessert, nightly specials and health-conscious appetizers. The decor is cozy New England and the site overlooks Lake Champlain. Casual dress; cocktails. **Parking:** on-site. **Cards:** MC, VI.

[✕]

## NORWICH

─────── WHERE TO DINE ───────

**THE NORWICH INN**
▼▼▼
International

**Lunch:** $4-$9          **Dinner:** $16-$22          **Phone:** 802/649-1143
**Location:** I-91, exit 13, 0.4 mi w; center. 325 Main St 05055. **Hours:** 11:30 am-2 & 5:30-9 pm. Closed: 12/25; also Mon. **Reservations:** suggested. **Features:** The restaurant offers patrons creative, wonderful foods in a lovely historic setting. Dressy casual; cocktails. **Parking:** on-site. **Cards:** AX, CB, DC, DS, MC, VI.

## PERKINSVILLE pop. 142

─────── WHERE TO STAY ───────

**THE INN AT WEATHERSFIELD**
▼▼▼
Historic
Country Inn

**Phone:** 802/263-9217
All Year                    2P: $130-$210          XP: $25
**Location:** On SR 106, 2 mi n of jct SR 10. 1342 Rt 106 05151. Fax: 802/263-9219. **Facility:** This farmhouse, set well back from the road, dates from 1792; guest rooms feature country-style decor and many have gas or wood-burning fireplaces. Smoke free premises. 12 units. 9 one-bedroom standard units. 3 one-bedroom suites, some with whirlpools. 3 stories (no elevator), interior corridors. *Bath:* combo or shower only. **Parking:** on-site. **Terms:** age restrictions may apply, 14 day cancellation notice-fee imposed, [BP] meal plan available. **Amenities:** video library, voice mail, hair dryers. *Some:* DVD players, CD players. **Dining:** restaurant, see separate listing. **Leisure Activities:** ice skating, hiking trails. **Guest Services:** gift shop, complimentary evening beverages. **Business Services:** meeting rooms, PC. **Cards:** AX, DS, MC, VI.

SOME UNITS

─────── WHERE TO DINE ───────

**THE INN AT WEATHERSFIELD**   Country Inn
▼▼▼
International

**Dinner:** $18-$26          **Phone:** 802/263-9217
**Location:** On SR 106, 2 mi n of jct SR 10; in The Inn at Weathersfield. 1342 VT Rt 106 05151. **Hours:** 5:30 pm-8:30 pm. Closed: Sun-Wed. **Reservations:** suggested. **Features:** This romantic room in a rustic inn features a regional cuisine that's sensational! The fixed-price dinner offers five courses and selections are changed daily. Fresh local, seasonal ingredients are used, and the desserts are delightful. Dressy casual; cocktails. **Parking:** on-site. **Cards:** AX, DS, MC, VI.

## PERU

─────── WHERE TO STAY ───────

**JOHNNY SEESAW'S**
▼▼ ▼▼
Country Inn

**Phone:** 802/824-5533
| | | |
|---|---|---|
| 11/25-3/31 [BP] | 1P: $102-$150 | XP: $20 | D6 |
| 9/19-11/24 [BP] | 1P: $100-$140 | XP: $15 | D6 |
| 5/28-9/18 [BP] | 1P: $80-$100 | XP: $12 | D6 |

**Location:** 2.1 mi e on SR 11, from jct SR 30 S. 3574 Vt Rt 11 05152 (PO Box 68). Fax: 802/824-5533. **Facility:** 19 units. 11 one- and 4 two-bedroom standard units. 4 cottages ($110-$180). 1-2 stories (no elevator), interior/exterior corridors. *Bath:* combo or shower only. **Parking:** on-site, winter plug-ins. **Terms:** open 5/28-3/31, 14 day cancellation notice-fee imposed, [MAP] meal plan available, package plans, 15% service charge, pets ($10 extra charge, with prior approval). **Amenities:** video library. **Pool(s):** outdoor. **Leisure Activities:** tennis court. *Fee:* game room. **Business Services:** meeting rooms. **Cards:** DS, MC, VI.

SOME UNITS

FEE

─────── WHERE TO DINE ───────

**JOHNNY SEESAW'S**
▼▼
American

**Dinner:** $15-$30          **Phone:** 802/824-5533
**Location:** Jct SR 30/11, 2.5 mi e on SR 11. 3574 VT Rt 11 05152. **Hours:** Open 5/15-4/1; 5:30 pm-9 pm; weekends only 11/1-11/30. **Reservations:** suggested. **Features:** Originally built in 1920, by a Russian logger who, legend has it, has a penchant for wild women and song, Johnny Seesaw's has become one of the area's favorite restaurants for both locals and travelers alike. Famous for its prime rib, large portions, extensive wine list and large, circular fireplace, it has retained much of its original charm and lively, yet warm atmosphere. Casual dress; cocktails. **Parking:** on-site. **Cards:** DS, MC, VI.

## PLYMOUTH

─────── WHERE TO STAY ───────

**FARMBROOK MOTEL**
▼▼ ▼▼
Motel

**Phone:** 802/672-3621
5/28-10/18          1P: $50-$60          2P: $55-$75          XP: $10          F12
**Location:** 4 mi n on SR 100A, from jct SR 100; 3 mi s of jct US 4. Located in a quiet, secluded area. 706 SR 100A 05056 (PO Box 320). **Facility:** 12 units. 11 one-bedroom standard units, some with efficiencies. 1 one-bedroom suite. 1-2 stories, interior/exterior corridors. *Bath:* combo or shower only. **Parking:** on-site. **Terms:** open 5/28-10/18, 7 day cancellation notice. **Leisure Activities:** fishing.

SOME UNITS

**INN AT WATER'S EDGE**                                                           Phone: 802/228-8143

△△△ SAVE   All Year [MAP]                    1P: $125-$225          2P: $175-$300
▽▽▽ ▽▽▽   **Location:** On SR 100, 3.6 mi n of jct SR 103. 45 Kingdom Rd 05149 (45 Kingdom Rd, LUDLOW). Fax: 802/228-8443.
Historic   **Facility:** Beautifully restored, this 1878 Victorian farmhouse sits on the edge of Black River and Echo Lake
Country Inn   and features its own small beach. Smoke free premises. 11 units. 9 one- and 1 two-bedroom standard units,
some with whirlpools. 1 one-bedroom suite with whirlpool. 2 stories (no elevator); interior corridors. *Bath:*
combo or shower only. **Parking:** on-site, winter plug-ins. **Terms:** 2 night minimum stay, age restrictions may
apply, 14 day cancellation notice, [BP] meal plan available, package plans. **Amenities:** video library, hair
dryers. **Dining:** 7:30 pm seating, by reservation only, cocktails. **Leisure Activities:** boating, canoeing, fishing, hot tub, cross
country skiing, bicycles, hiking trails, snowshoes, bocci, croquet, billiards, horseshoes. *Fee:* massage. **Guest Services:** complimentary evening beverages, airport transportation-Rutland Airport, area transportation-bus station. **Business Services:** meeting
rooms, business center. **Cards:** AX, MC, VI. **Special Amenities: free local telephone calls and free room upgrade (subject
to availability with advanced reservations).** *(See color ad p 439)*

SOME UNITS

⊞ ⑪ ☂ 🐾 ⊠ ⊠ ☎ / 🅦 /

─────────────── **WHERE TO DINE** ───────────────

**ECHO LAKE INN DINING ROOM**   Country Inn      **Dinner:** $17-$25          Phone: 802/228-8602
▽▽▽   **Location:** On SR 100; in Tyson Village. 2 Dublin Rd 05056. **Hours:** Open 5/1-10/19 & 11/25-3/31; 8 am-9 &
6-8:30 pm, Fri & Sat-9 pm. **Reservations:** suggested. **Features:** Located in a Victorian-era hotel, this
Regional American   restaurant in the lakes region features a sumptuous, New England cuisine that includes rainbow trout in
Chablis sauce, wild rice, local vegetables and Creole seafood soup. Locals and visitors alike enjoy Echo.
Casual dress; cocktails. **Parking:** on-site. **Cards:** AX, MC, VI.

☂ ⊠

**RIVER TAVERN**                       **Dinner:** $14-$23          Phone: 802/672-3811
▽▽▽   **Location:** 2 mi s on SR 100; in Hawk Inn & Mountain Resort. **Hours:** 6 pm-9 pm, Sat also 7:30-9:30 am, Sun
7:30-9:30 am. **Reservations:** suggested. **Features:** You'll enjoy this upscale resort's restaurant and its
American   well-prepared cuisine with an emphasis on New England favorites. The decor is formal, but the
atmosphere is casual and comfortable. Cocktails. **Parking:** on-site. **Cards:** AX, CB, DC, DS, MC, VI.

& M ⊠

# PROCTORSVILLE

─────────────── **WHERE TO DINE** ───────────────

**BLACK RIVER BREWING CO**            **Lunch:** $6-$9          **Dinner:** $9-$16          Phone: 802/228-3100
▽▽   **Location:** Just s of jct SR 103/131. 2588 Rt 103 05153. **Hours:** Open 5/24-4/20; 3 pm-9 pm, Fri-11 pm, Sat
noon-11 pm, Sun noon-9 pm; hours may vary. **Features:** The casual pub environment offers friendly
American   service and good food; a cozy wood-burning fireplace will keep you warm and patrons can watch TV or
MC, VI.   play some pool while waiting for their food. Casual dress; cocktails. **Parking:** on-site. **Cards:** AX, DS,

⊠

# PUTNEY

─────────────── **WHERE TO STAY** ───────────────

**THE PUTNEY INN**                                                           Phone: (802)387-5517
▽▽▽   All Year                    1P: $78-$158          2P: $78-$158          XP: $20          F14
**Location:** I-91, exit 4, just e. 57 Putney Landing Rd 05346 (PO Box 181). Fax: 802/387-5211. **Facility:** 25 one-
Small-scale Hotel   bedroom standard units. 2 stories (no elevator), exterior corridors. **Parking:** on-site, winter plug-ins.
**Terms:** [BP] meal plan available, small pets only ($10 extra charge, with prior approval). **Amenities:** irons,
hair dryers. **Dining:** restaurant, see separate listing. **Business Services:** meeting rooms. **Cards:** AX, DS, MC, VI.
*(See color ad p 417)*

SOME UNITS

ASK S🄳 🐾 ⑪ DATA PORT ☕ / ⊠ /
                    FEE

─────────────── **WHERE TO DINE** ───────────────

**PUTNEY INN**                       **Lunch:** $8-$13          **Dinner:** $13-$22          Phone: 802/387-5517
▽▽▽   **Location:** I-91, exit 4; in Putney Inn. 57 Putney Landing Rd 05346. **Hours:** 8-10:30 am, 11:30-2:30 & 5-8 pm, Fri
& Sat-8:30 pm, Sun 8 am-11 & noon-8 pm. **Reservations:** suggested. **Features:** Hand-hewn beams
Regional American   highlight this restaurant featuring New England country decor in a comfortable and relaxing atmosphere.
The creative New England menu offers all fresh, local and regional ingredients. Their new wine cellar
offers an expanded and diverse wine selection. Dressy casual; cocktails. **Parking:** on-site. **Cards:** AX, DS, MC, VI.

☂ ⊠

# QUECHEE

─────────────── **WHERE TO STAY** ───────────────

**THE QUECHEE INN AT MARSHLAND FARM**                                        Phone: (802)295-3133
△△△ SAVE   5/28-10/30 [BP]        1P: $110-$215        2P: $110-$215        XP: $25        D12
▽▽▽ ▽▽▽   10/31-12/31 [BP]       1P: $90-$215         2P: $90-$215         XP: $25        D12
5/1-5/27 [BP]          1P: $110-$175        2P: $110-$175        XP: $25        D12
Historic   1/1-4/30 [BP]          1P: $90-$175         2P: $90-$175         XP: $25        D12
Country Inn   **Location:** 1 mi n of US 4. Located in a quiet area. 1119 Quechee Main St 05059 (PO Box 747). Fax: 802/295-6587.
**Facility:** Dating from the 18th century, this Colonial-style farmhouse is in a tranquil setting; a restaurant is on
site. Smoke free premises. 25 units. 23 one-bedroom standard units. 2 one-bedroom suites ($135-$245). 2
stories (no elevator), interior corridors. *Bath:* combo or shower only. **Parking:** on-site. **Terms:** office hours 8 am-9 pm, 2-3 night
minimum stay - weekends, 14 day cancellation notice-fee imposed. **Amenities:** voice mail, irons, hair dryers. **Dining:** The Dining
Room at The Quechee Inn, see separate listing. **Leisure Activities:** rental canoes, fishing, kayaking, golf & country club privileges, cross country skiing, showshoeing, mountain biking. *Fee:* fly-fishing instructions, snowshoes, bicycles. **Business Services:** meeting rooms. **Cards:** AX, CB, DC, DS, MC, VI. **Special Amenities: free full breakfast.**

SOME UNITS

S🄳 ⑪ 🐾 ⊠ ⊠ DATA PORT 🖥 / VCR 🖥 /
                    FEE                                    FEE

——— **WHERE TO DINE** ———

**BOSTOCK'S BLACK ANGUS CAFE & MEETING PLACE**   Lunch: $6-$16   Dinner: $11-$18   Phone: 802/295-1151
▼▼▼▼   **Location:** I-89, exit 1 (Woodstock), 4 mi w. US Rt 4. **Hours:** 11:30 am-9:30 pm, Fri & Sat-10 pm. Closed: 12/25.
**Reservations:** accepted. **Features:** Just outside the resort town of Woodstock and close to the famous
Steak House   Quechee Gorge, the casual eatery serves traditional steak, chicken and pasta dishes. Casual dress;
cocktails. **Parking:** on-site. **Cards:** MC, VI.

**THE DINING ROOM AT THE QUECHEE INN**   Country Inn   Dinner: $17-$25   Phone: 802/295-3133
▼▼▼▼   **Location:** 1 mi n of US 4; in The Quechee Inn at Marshland Farm. Quechee Main St 05059. **Hours:** 6 pm-9 pm.
**Reservations:** suggested. **Features:** The restaurant occupies the beautiful, historic 1793 former home and
American   farm of Col. John Marsh, Vermont's first lieutenant governor, and is recorded on the National Register of
Historic Places. Innovative chefs prepare a variety of complex recipes with fresh ingredients, resulting in
excellent flavors. Dishes are presented with careful attention to colors and textures. The experience is wonderful. Casual
dress; cocktails. **Parking:** on-site. **Cards:** AX, DC, DS, MC, VI.

**THE FARINA FAMILY DINER & RESTAURANT**   Lunch: $4-$10   Phone: 802/295-8955
▼   **Location:** In Quechee Gorge Village Shopping Center. US Rt 4 E 05059. **Hours:** 7 am-3 pm. Closed: 1/1, 11/25,
12/24, 12/25. **Features:** Set in a 1946 Worester Semi Streamliner dining car - #787, this unique setting
American   offers "comfort foods" reminiscent of a 1950s style diner, such as good old fashioned meatloaf and baked
ham. The interior is a step back in time and features a life size statue of James Dean, a Wurlitzer juke box
and original advertising and movie posters. Casual dress. **Parking:** on-site. **Cards:** AX, DS, MC, VI.

**FIRESTONES**   Lunch: $8-$17   Dinner: $8-$22   Phone: 802/295-1600
▼▼▼   **Location:** I-89, exit 1 (Woodstock); at Waterman Place. Waterman Place, US Rt 4 E 05059. **Hours:** 11:30 am-9:30
pm, Fri & Sat-10 pm, Sun 11 am-4 pm; Sunday brunch. Closed: 11/25, 12/25. **Reservations:** suggested.
American   **Features:** The restaurant offers patrons a coordinated, fun, rustic atmosphere featuring a large,
wood-burning oven in which many dishes are prepared. Casual dress; cocktails. **Parking:** on-site.
**Cards:** AX, DC, DS, MC, VI.

**PARKER HOUSE INN**   Historic   Dinner: $17-$24   Phone: 802/295-6077
▼▼▼▼   **Location:** 0.3 mi n on Waterman Hill Place from flashing light on US 4. 1792 Quechee Main St 05059. **Hours:** 5:30
pm-9 pm. Closed: 12/24, Mon-Fri 11/1-5/31. **Reservations:** suggested. **Features:** Along the Ottauquechee
Regional American   River, the restored 1857 Victorian-style inn is on the National Register of Historic Places. The chef-owner
prepares innovative beef, lamb, pork and seafood dishes using only the freshest, locally grown produce.
Summer guests can enjoy a relaxing yet elegant dinner on the outside patio, with a beautiful view of the sun setting over the
river. Dressy casual; cocktails. **Parking:** on-site. **Cards:** AX, MC, VI.

**SIMON PEARCE RESTAURANT**   Lunch: $9-$14   Dinner: $18-$29   Phone: 802/295-1470
▼▼▼▼   **Location:** 0.3 mi n on Waterman Hill Place from flashing light on US 4. The Mill 05059. **Hours:** 11:30 am-2:45 &
6-9 pm. Closed: 11/25, 12/25. **Reservations:** accepted, for dinner. **Features:** In a restored mill where
Regional American   hand-blown glass and pottery demonstrations are given, the restaurant features good views, Irish and
Continental dishes and place settings with its own glassware and pottery. It's well worth the usual wait at
the popular establishment. Semi-formal attire; cocktails. **Parking:** on-site. **Cards:** AX, CB, DC, DS, MC, VI.

# RANDOLPH

——— **WHERE TO STAY** ———

**SWEETSERENITY B&B**   Phone: (802)728-9590
▼▼▼   All Year [BP]   1P: $75-$95   2P: $90-$110   XP: $25   F4
**Location:** I-89, exit 4, 2.6 mi w on SR 66, 0.4 mi s on SR 12, then 0.3 mi e on Merchants Row. Located adjacent to
Historic Bed   Montague Golf Course. 40 Randolph Ave 05060. Fax: 775/414-9487. **Facility:** Golf packages are offered at this
& Breakfast   historic B&B set at the end of a quiet street next to the 18-hole Montague Golf Course. Smoke free prem-
ises. 3 one-bedroom standard units. 2 stories (no elevator), interior corridors. *Bath:* some shared or private,
combo or shower only. **Parking:** on-site. **Terms:** 14 day cancellation notice-fee imposed. **Leisure Activities:** Fee: massage.
**Cards:** AX, DS, MC, VI.

——— **WHERE TO DINE** ———

**DEBBIE'S CORNER CAFE**   Lunch: $3-$7   Phone: 802/728-6062
▼▼▼   **Location:** I-89, exit 4, 3 mi w on SR 66. 2 Merchants Row 05060. **Hours:** 7 am-3 pm, Sun 8 am-1 pm. Closed
major holidays; also Mon. **Reservations:** accepted. **Features:** The busy, popular restaurant serves
American   home-style dishes made from the owner's own recipes. Food is prepared fresh daily in a casual, country
atmosphere. Among favorites are Debbie's own Belgian waffles, muffins, cinnamon French toast and other
freshly baked goodies. Casual dress; beer & wine only. **Parking:** on-site. **Cards:** MC, VI.

**LIPPITT'S RESTAURANT**   Dinner: $15-$25   Phone: 802/728-5575
▼▼▼▼   **Location:** I-89, exit 4 (SR 66), 1.8 mi w on Stock Farm Rd 05060. **Hours:** 5 pm-9 pm, Sun-8 pm. Closed: 12/25;
also Mon; first week in April. **Reservations:** suggested. **Features:** Nestled in the foothills of the Green
American   Mountains and bordering the White River, the restaurant is in the charming Three Stallion Inn, originally the
farm house on a working horse farm, and situated on 1,300 pastoral acres. The chefs delight with offerings
of contemporary American cuisine, as well as creative entrees of ethnic cuisine. All dishes are prepared using farm-fresh
Vermont products. Casual dress; cocktails. **Parking:** on-site. **Cards:** AX, DS, MC, VI.

**MORGAN'S PUB**

▽▽▽▽

American

**Dinner:** $15-$25    **Phone:** 802/728-5575
**Location:** I-89, exit 4 (SR 66), 1.9 mi w. Stock Farm Rd 05060. **Hours:** 5 pm-9 pm, Sun-8 pm. Closed: 12/25; also Mon. **Reservations:** suggested. **Features:** The restaurant features a casual pub atmosphere and offers an excellent selection of charcouterie plate items. Casual dress; cocktails. **Parking:** on-site. **Cards:** AX, DS, MC, VI.

(Y) (X)

**RANDOLPH VILLAGE PIZZA**

▽▽▽

Pizza

**Lunch:** $3-$14    **Dinner:** $3-$14    **Phone:** 802/728-9677
**Location:** Center; just over railroad tracks. 1 S Main St 05060. **Hours:** 11 am-9 pm. Closed: 3/27, 11/25, 12/25. **Features:** The very simple, basic operation offers good food and self-service at the walk-up counter. Casual dress. **Parking:** street.

(X)

# RAWSONVILLE

──── **WHERE TO STAY** ────

**INN AT BEAR CREEK**

▽▽▽▽

Motel

**Phone:** 802/297-1700
10/1-4/30    1P: $69-$149    2P: $69-$149
**Location:** Just s of center, then just w. 81 Upper Bear Ln 05340 (PO Box 191, BONDVILLE). **Facility:** 12 one-bedroom standard units. 3 stories (no elevator), interior/exterior corridors. **Parking:** on-site. **Terms:** open 10/1-4/30, check-in 4 pm, 30 day cancellation notice-fee imposed. **Pool(s):** heated outdoor. **Leisure Activities:** 5 tennis courts (3 lighted). **Guest Services:** area transportation. **Cards:** AX, CB, DC, DS, MC, VI.

SOME UNITS

(▥) (⇝) (Ⓚ) (❀) (☎) / (X) /

# RIPTON pop. 566

──── **WHERE TO STAY** ────

**THE CHIPMAN INN**

▽▽  ▽▽

Historic Bed
& Breakfast

**Phone:** 802/388-2390
All Year [BP]    1P: $75-$105    2P: $115-$155    XP: $20
**Location:** 4.4 mi e on SR 125, from jct US 7. 1233 Ripton Rt 125 05766 (PO Box 115). **Facility:** 8 units. 7 one-bedroom standard units. 1 one-bedroom suite ($115-$155). 2 stories (no elevator). **Bath:** combo or shower only. **Parking:** on-site. **Terms:** age restrictions may apply, 14 day cancellation notice-fee imposed. **Amenities:** hair dryers. **Cards:** DS, MC, VI.

SOME UNITS

(Y) / (X) (Ⓚ) /

# ROCKINGHAM

──── **WHERE TO STAY** ────

**THE INN AT CRANBERRY FARM**

▽▽▽  ▽▽▽

Bed & Breakfast

**Phone:** (802)463-1339
All Year [BP]    1P: $149-$159    2P: $149-$159    XP: $25
**Location:** I-91, exit 6, 3.4 mi n on SR 103 to Brockway Mills Rd, 0.4 mi e, then just n. (61 Williams River Rd, CHESTER, 05143). Fax: 802/463-8169. **Facility:** This contemporary inn located on 60 acres of mountain meadow land offers lovely guest rooms and public areas accented with wood beams and fireplaces. Smoke free premises. 14 units. 10 one- and 1 two-bedroom standard units. 3 one-bedroom suites ($239-$249) with whirlpools. 3 stories (no elevator), interior/exterior corridors. **Parking:** on-site. **Terms:** age restrictions may apply, 10 day cancellation notice. **Amenities:** video library, hair dryers. **Leisure Activities:** fishing, ice skating, tobogganing, hiking trails, volleyball. **Guest Services:** gift shop, complimentary evening beverages. **Business Services:** meeting rooms. **Cards:** AX, DS, MC, VI.

SOME UNITS

(ASK) (S🄳) (X) (X) (☎) / (𝒲) /

# ROYALTON

──── **WHERE TO DINE** ────

**EATON'S SUGARHOUSE RESTAURANT & COUNTRY STORE**

▽▽

American

**Lunch:** $3-$9    **Phone:** 802/763-8809
**Location:** I-89, exit 3 (SR 107). Jct SR 14 & 107 05068. **Hours:** 7 am-3 pm. Closed: 11/25, 12/25. **Features:** Satisfying customers since 1963, the restaurant is more than just a great place to eat breakfast. Guests can experience the Vermont tradition of maple-syrup making—watching as maple sap is boiled to create delicious maple-sugar candy and maple cream—or browse the antiques and collectibles on the front porch. Casual dress. **Parking:** on-site. **Cards:** AX, DS, MC, VI.

(X)

**THE FOX STAND INN**   Historic

▽▽  ▽▽

American

**Dinner:** $7-$22    **Phone:** 802/763-8437
**Location:** I-89, exit 3 (SR 107), 0.3 mi e to SR 14, then 0.3 mi s. 5615 Rt 14 05068. **Hours:** 5 pm-9 pm. Closed: Sun & Mon. **Reservations:** suggested, weekends. **Features:** This quaint country inn dating back to the early 1800s is off the beaten path. The creative entrees of beef, fish, chicken and quail are prepared fresh and listed nightly on an old-fashioned chalkboard. The decor is rustic and inviting. Casual dress; cocktails. **Parking:** on-site. **Cards:** MC, VI.

(Y) (Ⓚ) (X)

# RUTLAND pop. 17,292

## ———— WHERE TO STAY ————

**BEST WESTERN INN & SUITES**    *Book at aaa.com*    Phone: (802)773-3200

| | | | |
|---|---|---|---|
| 9/17-10/17 [ECP] | 1P: $169-$209 | 2P: $179-$219 | XP: $10   F12 |
| 5/1-9/16 & 1/29-4/30 [ECP] | 1P: $103-$139 | 2P: $103-$139 | XP: $10   F12 |
| 10/18-1/28 [ECP] | 1P: $93-$129 | 2P: $103-$139 | XP: $10   F12 |

Small-scale Hotel    **Location:** 2.6 mi e on US 4, from jct US 7. 1 US 4 E 05701. **Fax:** 802/773-6615. **Facility:** 112 units. 56 one-bedroom standard units. 56 one-bedroom suites ($109-$539) with kitchens. 2 stories (no elevator), exterior corridors. **Parking:** on-site, winter plug-ins. **Terms:** check-in 4 pm, 14 day cancellation notice, package plans. **Amenities:** video games (fee), voice mail, irons, hair dryers. **Pool(s):** heated outdoor. **Leisure Activities:** 2 tennis courts, playground, exercise room, basketball, volleyball. **Guest Services:** valet and coin laundry. **Business Services:** meeting rooms, fax. **Cards:** AX, CB, DC, DS, MC, VI. *(See color ad p 429)*

SOME UNITS

ASK SD 📶 🌐 🗙 📺 DATA PORT 💻 / 🗙 🔒 📧 /

**ECONO LODGE**    *Book at aaa.com*    Phone: (802)773-2784

| | | | |
|---|---|---|---|
| All Year | 1P: $39-$129 | 2P: $44-$159 | XP: $10   F18 |

Motel    **Location:** On US 7, 1.3 mi s of jct US 4 E. 238 S Main St (Rt 7 S) 05701. **Fax:** 803/775-2787. **Facility:** 54 one-bedroom standard units. 2 stories (no elevator), exterior corridors. *Bath:* combo or shower only. **Parking:** on-site, winter plug-ins. **Terms:** [CP] meal plan available. **Amenities:** video library. **Guest Services:** sundries. **Business Services:** fax. **Cards:** AX, CB, DC, DS, MC, VI.

SOME UNITS

ASK SD DATA PORT 💻 / 🗙 VCR

**HOLIDAY INN RUTLAND/KILLINGTON**    *Book at aaa.com*    Phone: (802)775-1911

AAA SAVE

| | |
|---|---|
| 9/17-10/16 & 12/26-4/30 | 1P: $139-$299 |
| 5/1-9/16 & 10/17-12/25 | 1P: $139-$179 |

Large-scale Hotel    **Location:** 2.4 mi s on US 7, from US 4 W; 0.4 mi n, US 7 from US 4 E. Located in a commercial area. 476 US Rt 7 S 05701. **Fax:** 802/775-0113. **Facility:** 150 one-bedroom standard units. 2 stories (no elevator), interior corridors. **Parking:** on-site, winter plug-ins. **Terms:** [AP], [BP], [CP] & [ECP] meal plans available, package plans, pets ($10 extra charge). **Amenities:** high-speed Internet, voice mail, honor bars, irons, hair dryers. **Dining:** 6:30 am-10 pm, cocktails. **Pool(s):** heated indoor. **Leisure Activities:** sauna, whirlpools, exercise room. **Guest Services:** valet and coin laundry, airport transportation-Vermont State Airport, area transportation-train & bus depot. **Business Services:** conference facilities, business center. **Cards:** AX, CB, DC, DS, JC, MC, VI. **Special Amenities:** early check-in/late check-out and free room upgrade (subject to availability with advanced reservations). *(See color ad below)*

SOME UNITS

SD 🦽 🐕 🍴 &M 🚫 🏊 🗙 📺 DATA PORT 🔒 📧 💻 / 🗙 /
FEE

**THE INN AT RUTLAND**    *Book at aaa.com*    Phone: (802)773-0575

| | | | |
|---|---|---|---|
| 9/17-10/24 & 12/24-4/30 [BP] | 1P: $150-$230 | 2P: $150-$230 | XP: $25 |
| 5/1-9/16 & 10/25-12/23 [BP] | 1P: $100-$190 | 2P: $100-$190 | XP: $25 |

Historic Bed & Breakfast    **Location:** Just n on US 7, from US 4 E. 70 N Main St 05701. **Fax:** 802/775-3506. **Facility:** An 1890s Victorian mansion with many distinctive architectural features, this downtown property near several restaurants offers well-appointed rooms. Smoke free premises. 11 one-bedroom standard units. 3 stories (no elevator), interior corridors. *Bath:* combo or shower only. **Parking:** on-site. **Terms:** 2 night minimum stay - seasonal, cancellation fee imposed, no pets allowed (owner's cats on premises). **Amenities:** hair dryers. **Cards:** AX, DS, MC, VI.

🦽 🗙 DATA PORT

**RAMADA LIMITED OF RUTLAND**  *Book at aaa.com*  Phone: (802)773-3361

| | | | |
|---|---|---|---|
| 10/16-4/30 [ECP] | 1P: $49-$179 | 2P: $49-$179 | XP: $10 | F17 |
| 7/1-10/15 [ECP] | 1P: $69-$169 | 2P: $69-$169 | XP: $10 | F17 |
| 5/1-6/30 [ECP] | 1P: $69-$99 | 2P: $69-$99 | XP: $10 | F17 |

**Location:** 1.3 mi s on US 7, from US 4 W; 1.5 mi n US 7, from US 4 E. 253 S Main St, US 7 05701. Fax: 802/773-4892. **Facility:** 75 units. 73 one-bedroom standard units. 2 one-bedroom suites with kitchens. 2 stories (no elevator), interior corridors. **Parking:** on-site. **Terms:** pets ($25 fee). **Amenities:** voice mail, irons, hair dryers. **Pool(s):** heated indoor. **Guest Services:** valet laundry. **Business Services:** meeting rooms, fax (fee). **Cards:** AX, CB, DC, DS, MC, VI. **Special Amenities:** free expanded continental breakfast and free local telephone calls. *(See ad below)*

Small-scale Hotel

SOME UNITS

---

**RED ROOF INN RUTLAND-KILLINGTON**  *Book at aaa.com*  Phone: (802)775-4303

| | | | |
|---|---|---|---|
| 9/15-10/19 | 1P: $79-$169 | 2P: $89-$179 | XP: $10 | F17 |
| 10/20-4/30 | 1P: $69-$159 | 2P: $79-$169 | XP: $10 | F17 |
| 7/1-9/14 | 1P: $69-$109 | 2P: $79-$119 | XP: $10 | F17 |
| 5/1-6/30 | 1P: $59-$99 | 2P: $69-$109 | XP: $10 | F17 |

Small-scale Hotel

**Location:** On US 7/4, 1 US Hwy 7 S 05701. Fax: 802/775-6840. **Facility:** 101 one-bedroom standard units, some with whirlpools. 2 stories (no elevator), interior corridors. *Bath:* combo or shower only. **Parking:** on-site, winter plug-ins. **Terms:** 14 day cancellation notice, [CP] meal plan available. **Amenities:** video games, irons, hair dryers. **Pool(s):** heated indoor. **Leisure Activities:** sauna. *Fee:* game room. **Guest Services:** coin laundry. **Business Services:** PC. **Cards:** AX, CB, DC, DS, MC, VI.

SOME UNITS

---

**RODEWAY INN**  *Book at aaa.com*  Phone: (802)775-2575

| | | | |
|---|---|---|---|
| 9/16-10/25 | 1P: $79-$129 | 2P: $79-$165 | XP: $5 | F12 |
| 10/26-4/30 | 1P: $44-$79 | 2P: $79-$129 | XP: $5 | F12 |
| 7/1-9/15 | 1P: $44-$79 | 2P: $44-$99 | XP: $5 | F12 |
| 5/1-6/30 | 1P: $39-$49 | 2P: $39-$49 | XP: $5 | F12 |

Motel

**Location:** US 7, 0.5 mi n of jct US 4 E. 138 N Main St 05701. Fax: 802/773-6392. **Facility:** 29 units. 28 one-bedroom standard units. 1 two-bedroom suite. 2 stories (no elevator), exterior corridors. *Bath:* combo or shower only. **Parking:** on-site, winter plug-ins. **Terms:** 5 day cancellation notice-fee imposed, pets ($5 fee). **Pool(s):** outdoor. **Business Services:** fax (fee). **Cards:** AX, DC, MC, VI. **Special Amenities:** free room upgrade and preferred room (each subject to availability with advanced reservations). *(See color ad below)*

SOME UNITS

**ROYAL MOTEL**

Motel

**Phone:** (802)773-9176

All Year        1P: $42-$99        2P: $52-$109        XP: $10        F
**Location:** Jct US 7, 0.5 mi e on US 4 (Woodstock Ave). 115 Woodstock Ave 05701. **Fax:** 802/775-3654. **Facility:** 18 one-bedroom standard units. 1-2 stories (no elevator), interior/exterior corridors. **Parking:** on-site, winter plug-ins. **Terms:** office hours 7:30 am-10 pm, 2-3 night minimum stay - in fall, 7 day cancellation notice-fee imposed, [CP] meal plan available, package plans, pets ($10 extra charge). **Pool(s):** outdoor. **Guest Services:** coin laundry. **Business Services:** fax. **Cards:** AX, DC, DS, MC, VI.

SOME UNITS

---

## ──── WHERE TO DINE ────

**BACK HOME AGAIN**

Vegetarian

**Lunch:** $5-$10        **Dinner:** $5-$10        **Phone:** 802/775-9800
**Location:** Just n of Merchants Row; downtown. 23 Center St 05701. **Hours:** 11 am-9 pm, Fri-3 pm, Sun 9-9 pm. Closed: Sun. **Features:** The health-conscious spot is decorated to resemble a forest, with a tangle of branches overhead, plank tables and log benches. Fresh soups, salads and wrap sandwiches are favorites, but many patrons stop in just for such desserts as maple cream cookies and such teas as mate, a coffee alternative. Casual dress. **Parking:** street. **Cards:** AX, DC, DS, MC, VI.

**CANDELERO'S**

Southwestern

**Lunch:** $5-$16        **Dinner:** $10-$16        **Phone:** 802/775-9730
**Location:** Just n of Merchants Row; between Center and West sts; downtown. 24 Wales St 05701. **Hours:** 11:30 am-9 pm, Thurs-Sat to 10 pm. **Features:** Patrons leave Vermont behind when they step into the authentically decorated Southwest haven, complete with plank flooring. Guacamole prepared tableside and the house special margaritas are a great way to start any meal. Entrees range from steaks to chicken mole, but perhaps the easiest choice is to order the sampler platter, which includes chiles rellenos. Casual dress; cocktails. **Parking:** street. **Cards:** DC, DS, MC, VI.

**THE COUNTRYMAN'S PLEASURE RESTAURANT**  Historic

Continental

**Dinner:** $13-$26        **Phone:** 802/773-7141
**Location:** Jct US 7, 2.5 mi e on US 4, then just s. 3 Town Line Rd 05701. **Hours:** 5 pm-9 pm. Closed: 12/24, 12/25. **Reservations:** suggested. **Features:** The charming, 19th-century, farmhouse-style restaurant specializes in a nice selection of Austrian-German-American dishes. Preparations of seafood, venison, duck, veal, vegetarian fare and sauerbraten go well with a good selection of German wines and beers. Desserts are excellent. Casual dress; cocktails. **Parking:** on-site. **Cards:** AX, DC, DS, MC, VI.

**LITTLE HARRY'S**

International

**Dinner:** $11-$18        **Phone:** 802/747-4848
**Location:** Center of downtown. 121 West St 05701. **Hours:** 5 pm-10 pm. Closed major holidays. **Reservations:** accepted. **Features:** The eatery is a funky, fun yet intimate atmosphere offering guests good food and casual service; the spicy cornbread is delicious. Casual dress; cocktails. **Parking:** street. **Cards:** MC, VI.

**ROYAL'S 121 HEARTHSIDE RESTAURANT**

American

**Lunch:** $8-$15        **Dinner:** $17-$27        **Phone:** 802/775-0856
**Location:** On US 7 at jct US 4. 37 N Main St 05701. **Hours:** 11 am-3 & 5-9:30 pm, Sun noon-9 pm. Closed: 12/24, 12/25. **Reservations:** suggested. **Features:** Serving diners since 1962, the restaurant sets itself apart by offering noteworthy complimentary accompaniments before the meal: fresh crudites, whipped cheese and crackers, baked popovers and fresh bread. The staff butchers the meats, filets the fresh fish and prepares all the dressings and sauces to create delicious meals. Service is casual and friendly in an intimate setting. Diners don't leave hungry. Casual dress; cocktails. **Parking:** on-site. **Cards:** AX, MC, VI.

**SAL'S**

Italian

**Lunch:** $5-$17        **Dinner:** $7-$20        **Phone:** 802/775-3360
**Location:** Downtown. 148 West St 05751. **Hours:** 11:30 am-9 pm, Fri & Sat-9:30 pm, Sun 3 pm-9 pm. Closed: 3/27, 11/25, 12/25. **Reservations:** accepted. **Features:** The coordinated, Italian-themed restaurant offers simple fare and casual service. Casual dress; beer & wine only. **Cards:** MC, VI.

**SIRLOIN SALOON**

Steak & Seafood

**Dinner:** $10-$22        **Phone:** 802/773-7900
**Location:** 0.5 mi s on US 7. 200 S Main St 05701. **Hours:** 4:30 pm-10 pm, Fri & Sat-11 pm. Closed: 11/25. **Reservations:** suggested. **Features:** Native American decorations and belt-and-pulley ceiling fans help to create a turn-of-the-century atmosphere in this restaurant. A salad bar with organic vegetables is offered in season. The fresh, flavorful scrod is made with maple and garlic seasoning. Casual dress; cocktails. **Parking:** on-site. **Cards:** AX, DC, DS, MC, VI.

**SOUTH STATION**

American

**Lunch:** $6-$10        **Dinner:** $9-$19        **Phone:** 802/775-1736
**Location:** 0.8 mi s on US 7; in Trolley Barn Center. 170 S Main St 05701. **Hours:** 11:30 am-3 & 5-9:30 pm, Sun 10 am-2 & 3-9 pm; Sunday brunch. **Reservations:** suggested. **Features:** South Station features a salad bar with 35 offerings and a potato salad that is worth writing home about! The modern and stylish restaurant also features a display tank with live lobsters. Casual dress; cocktails. **Parking:** on-site. **Cards:** AX, CB, DS, MC, VI.

**TAPAS RESTAURANT & TAVERN**

American

**Lunch:** $6-$10        **Dinner:** $6-$13        **Phone:** 802/775-1550
**Location:** Downtown; across from shopping center. 128 Merchants Row 05701. **Hours:** 11:30 am-9 pm, Fri & Sat-10 pm, Mon-2:30 pm. Closed major holidays; also Sun. **Reservations:** accepted. **Features:** Tapas features a nice selection of full dinners and light fare offerings that include beef, chicken, fish, vegetarian and pasta dishes. There's outdoor deck dining in season. Casual dress; cocktails. **Parking:** on-site. **Cards:** AX, DC, MC, VI.

**THREE TOMATOES TRATTOR..**
♦♦♦ Italian
MC, VI.
**Dinner:** $11-$20     **Phone:** 802/747-7747
**Location:** Between ___ __ __ __t sts; downtown. 88 Merchants Row 05701. **Hours:** 5 pm-9 pm, Fri & Sat-10 pm. Closed major holiu__. ___res: Traditional Italian-American entrees and pasta are served in the modern spot, which has an op__ __ __hen in the rear. This place is a local favorite for Italian wines, which are served in Tuscan ceram__. Casual dress; cocktails. **Parking:** street. **Cards:** AX,

**TOKYO HOUSE**
♦♦♦ Japanese
**Lunch:** $6-$9     **Dinner**     **Phone:** 802/786-8080
**Location:** In the Grand Theatre Building. 106 West St 05701. **Hours:** __ 4:30-10:30 pm, Sun noon-3 & 4:30-10 pm. Closed: 11/25. **Reservations:** accepted. **Features:** All y__ __vorites, including sushi, are available at this casual Japanese restaurant. Casual dress; beer & wine oniy. **Parking:** street. **Cards:** AX, DS, MC, VI.

**WEATHERVANE SEAFOOD RESTAURANT**
♦♦ Seafood
**Lunch:** $4-$10     **Dinner:** $7-$20     **Phone:** 802/773-0382
**Location:** Jct US 7, 0.5 mi e on US 4. 124 Woodstock Ave 05701. **Hours:** 11 am-9 pm. Closed: 11/25, 12/25. **Features:** The family restaurant specializes in excellent seafood, particularly its signature dish: delicious and creamy New England style clam chowder. The atmosphere is casual and relaxed. Casual dress; cocktails. **Parking:** on-site. **Cards:** MC, VI.

## ST. ALBANS pop. 7,650

———— **WHERE TO STAY** ————

**COMFORT INN & SUITES** _Book at aaa.com_

♦♦♦ Small-scale Hotel

**Phone:** (802)524-3300

| |  |  |  | |
|---|---|---|---|---|
| 6/30-10/12 | 1P: $90 | 2P: $140 | XP: $10 | F18 |
| 5/1-6/29 | 1P: $80 | 2P: $130 | XP: $10 | F18 |
| 10/13-4/30 | 1P: $70 | 2P: $120 | XP: $10 | F18 |

**Location:** I-89, exit 19, just w, then just s on SR 104. 813 Fairfax Rd 05478 (PO Box 847). Fax: 802/524-3300. **Facility:** 63 one-bedroom standard units, some with whirlpools. 3 stories, interior corridors. *Bath:* combo or shower only. **Parking:** on-site, winter plug-ins. **Terms:** 2-4 night minimum stay - seasonal, [ECP] meal plan available, small pets only ($100 deposit, $10 extra charge). **Amenities:** dual phone lines, voice mail, irons, hair dryers. **Pool(s):** heated indoor. **Leisure Activities:** exercise room. *Fee:* game room. **Guest Services:** coin laundry. **Business Services:** meeting rooms. **Cards:** AX, CB, DC, DS, MC, VI. *(See color ad p 421)*

SOME UNITS
(ASK) (S/D) 🛏 (&M) 🏊 📷 (DATA PORT) 🖥 / ✕ (VCR) 🧳 🍴 /
     FEE                 FEE

**ECONO LODGE** _Book at aaa.com_

(AAA) (SAVE)
♦♦♦ Motel

**Phone:** (802)524-5956

| |  |  |  | |
|---|---|---|---|---|
| 9/16-10/15 [CP] | 1P: $79-$89 | 2P: $90-$109 | XP: $10 | F17 |
| 6/1-9/15 [CP] | 1P: $55-$69 | 2P: $65-$79 | XP: $10 | F17 |
| 10/16-4/30 [CP] | 1P: $50-$65 | 2P: $59-$75 | XP: $10 | F17 |
| 5/1-5/31 [CP] | 1P: $50-$69 | 2P: $55-$74 | XP: $10 | F17 |

**Location:** I-89, exit 19, 1 mi w to US 7, then 0.5 mi s. 287 S Main St 05478. Fax: 802/524-5956. **Facility:** 29 one-bedroom standard units. 1-2 stories (no elevator), interior/exterior corridors. *Bath:* combo or shower only. **Parking:** on-site, winter plug-ins. **Terms:** pets ($10 fee, in smoking units). **Amenities:** hair dryers. **Cards:** AX, DC, DS, MC, VI. **Special Amenities:** free continental breakfast and free local telephone calls. *(See color ad below)*

SOME UNITS
(S/D) 🛏 📷 (DATA PORT) 🧳 / ✕ 🍴 🖥 /
     FEE

———— **WHERE TO DINE** ————

**CHOW! BELLA CAFE & WINE BAR**
♦♦♦ Mediterranean
**Lunch:** $5-$10     **Dinner:** $9-$18     **Phone:** 802/524-1405
**Location:** Between Lake and Kingman sts; downtown. 28 N Main St 05478. **Hours:** 11 am-9:30 pm, Mon & Tues from 5 pm. Closed major holidays; also Sun. **Reservations:** suggested. **Features:** Delicious, distinctive flatbreads and pasta dishes are favorites at the casual cafe. Casual dress; cocktails. **Parking:** street. **Cards:** AX, CB, DC, DS, MC, VI.

(&M) ✕

**DIAMOND JIM'S GRILLE**
♦♦♦ ♦♦♦
Steak & Seafood

**Dinner:** $10-$20        **Phone:** 802/524-9280
**Location:** I-89, exit 20 (US 7/SR 207), just w, then just s. Highgate Commons Shopping Plaza 05478. **Hours:** 4:30 pm-9 pm. Closed major holidays; also Mon & Tues. **Reservations:** suggested. **Features:** Decadent desserts, which are baked fresh daily, top off meals of hearty Southwestern fare. Casual dress; cocktails. **Parking:** on-site. **Cards:** DS, MC, VI.

**JEFF'S MAINE SEAFOOD**
♦♦♦ ♦♦♦
Seafood

**Lunch:** $4-$11     **Dinner:** $13-$19     **Phone:** 802/524-6135
**Location:** On US 7, corner of Bank St; center. 65 N Main St 05478. **Hours:** 11:30 am-3 & 5-9 pm. Closed: 1/1, 11/25, 12/25; also Sun & for dinner Mon. **Reservations:** suggested. **Features:** The easily accessible, downtown full-service restaurant also offers options other than seafood including chicken and prime rib. Casual dress; cocktails. **Parking:** street. **Cards:** AX, DC, MC, VI.

# ST. JOHNSBURY pop. 6,319

-------- WHERE TO STAY --------

**COMFORT INN & SUITES**    *Book at aaa.com*
♦♦♦ ♦♦♦
Small-scale Hotel

**Phone:** (802)748-1500

| |  |  |  | |
|---|---|---|---|---|
| 9/17-10/16 | 1P: $169-$399 | 2P: $169-$399 | XP: $10 | F18 |
| 6/1-9/16 | 1P: $129-$399 | 2P: $129-$399 | XP: $10 | F18 |
| 5/1-5/31 & 10/17-4/30 | 1P: $109-$359 | 2P: $109-$359 | XP: $10 | F18 |

**Location:** I-91, exit 20, just s. 703 US Rt 5 S 05819. Fax: 802/748-1243. **Facility:** 107 units. 104 one-bedroom standard units, some with whirlpools. 3 one-bedroom suites ($189-$399). 4 stories, interior corridors. *Bath:* combo or shower only. **Parking:** on-site. **Terms:** [ECP] meal plan available, package plans. **Amenities:** video games (fee), voice mail, irons, hair dryers. **Pool(s):** heated indoor. **Leisure Activities:** sauna, whirlpool, snowmobiling, exercise room. *Fee:* game room. **Guest Services:** valet and coin laundry. **Business Services:** meeting rooms, fax. **Cards:** AX, CB, DC, DS, MC, VI.
*(See color ad below)*

SOME UNITS

(ASK) (S/D) (GM) (icons) (DATA PORT) / (icons) /

# The One For All

*Y*ou know how AAA can simplify your life. Now make the lives of those you love the most a little easier–give them AAA associate memberships.

Associate members are eligible for the same security, services, and savings as primary members–emergency road service, valuable savings, access to travel services, and more. And all this protection is available for a reduced enrollment fee.

*Help your family members simplify their lives with AAA associate memberships. Call or stop by your nearest AAA office today. And make AAA the one for you.*

**FAIRBANKS INN**

| | | | | | |
|---|---|---|---|---|---|
| Motel | 9/19-10/18 | 1P: $99-$169 | 2P: $99-$169 | XP: $10 | F18 |
| | 6/27-9/18 | 1P: $79-$139 | 2P: $79-$139 | XP: $10 | F18 |
| | 5/1-6/26 | 1P: $79-$129 | 2P: $79-$129 | XP: $10 | F18 |
| | 10/19-4/30 | 1P: $69-$99 | 2P: $69-$99 | XP: $10 | F18 |

**Phone:** (802)748-5666

**Location:** I-91, exit 21, 1 mi e on US 2. 401 Western Ave 05819. Fax: 802/748-1242. **Facility:** 46 units. 45 one-bedroom standard units, some with efficiencies and/or whirlpools. 1 one-bedroom suite ($159-$279) with whirlpool. 3 stories (no elevator), exterior corridors. **Parking:** on-site. **Terms:** cancellation fee imposed, [CP] meal plan available, pets ($5 extra charge, dogs only). **Pool(s):** heated outdoor. **Guest Services:** valet laundry. **Cards:** AX, DS, MC, VI. *(See color ad below)*

SOME UNITS

ASK S D 📞 🍳 📶 DATA PORT / ✕ VCR 🔲 🔲 🔲 /

## HOLIDAY MOTEL & ANNEX

**Phone:** 802/748-8192

| | | | |
|---|---|---|---|
| 9/19-10/21 | 1P: $79-$139 | 2P: $79-$139 | XP: $10 | D17 |
| 6/27-9/18 | 1P: $59-$109 | 2P: $59-$109 | XP: $10 | D17 |
| 5/1-6/26 | 1P: $59-$99 | 2P: $59-$99 | XP: $10 | D17 |
| 10/22-4/30 | 1P: $49-$79 | 2P: $49-$79 | XP: $10 | D17 |

Motel

**Location:** Jct US 5 and Alternate 5. 222 Hastings St 05819. Fax: 802/748-1244. **Facility:** 66 units. 65 one-bedroom standard units. 1 one-bedroom suite. 1-2 stories (no elevator), interior/exterior corridors. **Parking:** on-site. **Terms:** [CP] meal plan available, small pets only ($10 extra charge, in designated units, no cats). **Amenities:** voice mail. **Pool(s):** heated outdoor. **Guest Services:** valet laundry. **Cards:** AX, DS, MC, VI. *(See color ad p 463)*

SOME UNITS

(ASK) (S) [icons] / [icons]
FEE

## YANKEE TRAVELER MOTEL

**Phone:** 802/748-3156

| | | | |
|---|---|---|---|
| 9/19-10/21 | 1P: $79-$139 | 2P: $79-$139 | XP: $10 | F17 |
| 6/27-9/18 | 1P: $59-$109 | 2P: $59-$109 | XP: $10 | F17 |
| 5/1-6/26 | 1P: $59-$99 | 2P: $59-$99 | XP: $10 | F17 |
| 10/22-4/30 | 1P: $49-$79 | 2P: $49-$79 | XP: $10 | F17 |

Motel

**Location:** On US 2 E, 0.4 mi e of jct US 5; center. 342 Portland St 05819. Fax: 802/748-1247. **Facility:** 32 one-bedroom standard units. 1 story, exterior corridors. **Terms:** office hours 7:30 am-11 pm, [CP] meal plan available. **Pool(s):** heated outdoor. **Guest Services:** valet laundry. **Cards:** AX, DS, MC, VI. *(See color ad p 463)*

SOME UNITS

(ASK) (S) [icons] / [icons]
FEE   FEE

### ——— WHERE TO DINE ———

## CUCINA DI GERARDO

**Dinner:** $12-$25                **Phone:** 802/748-6772

Italian

**Location:** I-91, exit 20, 0.5 mi s on US 5. 1216 Railroad St 05819. **Hours:** 5 pm-9 pm; to 10 pm. Closed major holidays; also Mon & Tues. **Reservations:** suggested. **Features:** The intimate, family-owned and operated restaurant specializes in Southern Italian cuisine. Portions are plentiful. Dressy casual; cocktails. **Parking:** on-site. **Cards:** AX, DS, MC, VI.

[icon]

# SHAFTSBURY

### ——— WHERE TO STAY ———

## GOVERNOR'S ROCK MOTEL

**Phone:** 802/442-4734

| | | | |
|---|---|---|---|
| 9/16-11/1 [CP] | | 2P: $59-$84 | XP: $7 | F10 |
| 5/1-9/15 & 11/21-3/15 [CP] | | 2P: $49-$69 | XP: $7 | F10 |

Motel

**Location:** 3.3 mi n on Historic SR 7A, from jct SR 67. 4325 Rt 7A 05262. Fax: 802/442-9692. **Facility:** 10 one-bedroom standard units. 1 story, exterior corridors. *Bath:* shower only. **Parking:** on-site. **Terms:** open 5/1-11/1 & 11/21-3/15, 5 day cancellation notice. **Cards:** AX, DS, MC, VI.

SOME UNITS

(ASK) (S) [icons] / [icons]

## IRON KETTLE MOTEL

**Phone:** 802/442-4316

Property failed to provide current rates

Motel

**Location:** 0.6 mi n of jct SR 7A/67 W. 1838 Historic Rt 7A 05262 (PO Box 195). Fax: 802/442-4316. **Facility:** 20 one-bedroom standard units. 1 story, exterior corridors. **Parking:** on-site. **Pool(s):** outdoor. **Leisure Activities:** fishing, putting green. **Guest Services:** coin laundry. **Business Services:** meeting rooms, fax.

SOME UNITS

[icons] / [icons]

## SERENITY MOTEL

**Phone:** 802/442-6490

| | | | |
|---|---|---|---|
| 10/1-10/31 | 1P: $65-$75 | 2P: $70-$80 | XP: $5 | F12 |
| 5/1-9/30 | 1P: $60-$70 | 2P: $65-$75 | XP: $5 | F12 |

Cottage

**Location:** 3.3 mi n on Historic SR 7A, from jct SR 67. 4379 Rt 7A 05262. Fax: 802/442-6490. **Facility:** 8 cottages. 1 story, exterior corridors. *Bath:* shower only. **Parking:** on-site. **Terms:** open 5/1-10/31, weekly rates available. **Cards:** AX, DS, MC, VI.

[icons]

# SHELBURNE

## ———— WHERE TO STAY ————

### COUNTRYSIDE MOTEL

Phone: (802)985-2839

| | | | | |
|---|---|---|---|---|
| AAA SAVE | 9/17-10/17 [CP] | 1P: $92 | 2P: $142 | XP: $10 | D12 |
| ▼▼ ▼▼ | 7/1-9/16 [CP] | 1P: $78 | 2P: $102 | XP: $10 | D12 |
| | 5/1-6/30 [CP] | 1P: $62 | 2P: $92 | XP: $8 | D12 |
| Motel | 10/18-4/30 | 1P: $58 | 2P: $92 | XP: $8 | D12 |

**Location:** I-89, exit 13, w on I-189 to US 7, then 6 mi s. Located in a rural area. 6475 Shelburne Rd 05482 (PO Box 277). Fax: 802/985-8526. **Facility:** Smoke free premises. 12 one-bedroom standard units, some with kitchens (no utensils). 1-2 stories (no elevator), exterior corridors. **Parking:** on-site, winter plug-ins. **Terms:** 7 day cancellation notice. **Amenities:** voice mail. **Pool(s):** outdoor. **Leisure Activities:** picnic tables. **Cards:** AX, DS, MC, VI. **Special Amenities:** free continental breakfast and free local telephone calls. *(See color ad below)*

SOME UNITS

### T-BIRD MOTOR INN

Phone: (802)985-3663

| | | | |
|---|---|---|---|
| AAA SAVE | 9/17-10/24 | 1P: $78-$148 | 2P: $78-$148 | XP: $10 |
| ▼▼▼ | 6/25-9/16 | 1P: $68-$128 | 2P: $68-$128 | XP: $10 |
| Motel | 5/14-6/24 | 1P: $64-$118 | 2P: $64-$118 | XP: $10 |

**Location:** I-89, exit 13 to US 7, then 4 mi s. 4405 Shelburne Rd 05482. Fax: 802/985-9942. **Facility:** 24 one-bedroom standard units. 1 story, exterior corridors. **Parking:** on-site. **Terms:** open 5/14-10/24, 7 day cancellation notice, [CP] meal plan available. **Amenities:** hair dryers. **Pool(s):** outdoor. **Cards:** AX, MC, VI. **Special Amenities: free continental breakfast and free newspaper.** *(See color ad below)*

SOME UNITS

## ——— WHERE TO DINE ———

**CAFE SHELBURNE**
▼▼▼
French
Casual dress; cocktails.

**Dinner:** $19-$24

**Phone:** 802/985-3939

**Location:** On US 7; opposite Shelburne Museum. 5573 US 7 05482. **Hours:** 5:30 pm-9 pm. Closed: 12/25; also Sun & Mon (except holidays). **Reservations:** suggested. **Features:** The unadorned exterior and unpretentious dining room give patrons no hint of the delights that await. Owner/chef Patrick Grangien prepares classic French cuisine to perfection. Dishes are as much a delight to the eye as to the palate. **Parking:** on-site. **Cards:** AX, MC, VI.

**CHEF LEU'S HOUSE**
AAA
▼▼▼
Chinese

**Lunch:** $5-$15

**Dinner:** $5-$15

**Phone:** 802/985-5258

**Location:** 1.7 mi n on US 7. 3761 Shelburne Rd 05482-6516. **Hours:** 11:30 am-9:30 pm, Fri & Sat-10:30 pm, Sun noon-9:30 pm. Closed: 11/25. **Reservations:** accepted. **Features:** A large selection of Szechuan, Hunan, Mandarin and Vietnamese specialties are prepared in moo shu, kung pao, yu hsiang and chang liu styles. The Leu family makes a concerted effort to please all customers. Casual dress; cocktails. **Parking:** on-site. **Cards:** AX, DC, DS, MC, VI.

**THE INN AT SHELBURNE FARMS**   Historic
▼▼▼
American
**Cards:** AX, DC, DS, MC, VI.

**Dinner:** $18-$29

**Phone:** 802/985-8498

**Location:** 3.6 mi w of US 7; at Shelburne Farms. 1611 Harbor Rd 05482. **Hours:** Open 5/13-10/22; 7:30 am-11:30 & 5:30-9:30 pm, Sun 8 am-1 & 5:30-9:30 pm. **Reservations:** required. **Features:** You will dine in a stately 1886 Vanderbilt mansion with dramatic views of Lake Champlain and New York's Adirondack Mountains beyond. Marble-tiled floors, fabric-covered walls and candlelight illumination set an elegant mood. The food is locally grown produce, much of it raised on this very farm using environmentally-friendly agriculture methods. As only the freshest local produce is used, the menu changes daily. Dressy casual; cocktails. **Parking:** on-site.

**SIRLOIN SALOON**
AAA
▼▼▼
Steak & Seafood

**Dinner:** $12-$24

**Phone:** 802/985-2200

**Location:** 3 mi n on US 7. 1912 Shelburne Rd 05482. **Hours:** 4:30 pm-10 pm, Fri-11 pm, Sat 4 pm-11 pm, Sun 4 pm-10 pm. Closed: 11/25, 12/25. **Reservations:** suggested, weekends. **Features:** Prime, grain-fed beef is served in a Southwestern setting accented with museum-quality American Indian artifacts. The salad bar selections are numerous, and entree and dessert portions are generous. Service is with a smile. Casual dress; cocktails. **Parking:** on-site. **Cards:** AX, CB, DC, DS, JC, MC, VI.

## SOUTH BURLINGTON pop. 15,814—*See also BURLINGTON.*

## ——— WHERE TO STAY ———

**ANCHORAGE INN**
▼▼▼
Small-scale Hotel

**Phone:** (802)863-7000

| | | | |
|---|---|---|---|
| 7/29-10/20 [CP] | 1P: $65-$100 | 2P: $75-$110 | XP: $5 | F17 |
| 10/21-4/30 [CP] | 1P: $50-$90 | 2P: $60-$110 | XP: $5 | F17 |
| 5/1-7/28 [CP] | 1P: $58-$85 | 2P: $68-$95 | XP: $5 | F17 |

**Location:** I-89, exit 14E, just e on US 2 to Dorset St, then 0.3 mi s. Located across from University Mall. 108 Dorset St 05403. Fax: 802/658-3351. **Facility:** 89 one-bedroom standard units. 3 stories (no elevator), interior corridors. **Parking:** on-site, winter plug-ins. **Terms:** pets ($50 deposit, dogs only, must be attended). **Amenities:** *Some:* hair dryers. **Pool(s):** heated indoor. **Leisure Activities:** whirlpool. **Cards:** AX, CB, DC, DS, MC, VI, JC. *(See color ad p 420)*

SOME UNITS

**BEST WESTERN WINDJAMMER INN & CONFERENCE CENTER**   *Book at aaa.com*
▼▼▼
Small-scale Hotel

**Phone:** (802)863-1125

| | | | |
|---|---|---|---|
| 9/6-10/24 | 1P: $125-$154 | 2P: $124-$154 | XP: $10 | F18 |
| 6/21-9/5 | 1P: $104-$134 | 2P: $104-$134 | XP: $10 | F18 |
| 5/1-6/20 & 10/25-4/30 | 1P: $89-$119 | 2P: $89-$119 | XP: $10 | F18 |

**Location:** I-89, exit 14E, 0.3 mi e on US 2. 1076 Williston Rd 05403. Fax: 802/658-1296. **Facility:** 171 units. 167 one-bedroom standard units. 4 one-bedroom suites. 2 stories, interior corridors. **Bath:** combo or shower only. **Parking:** on-site, winter plug-ins. **Terms:** cancellation fee imposed, package plans, pets ($5 extra charge). **Amenities:** video games, irons, hair dryers. **Dining:** Windjammer, see separate listing. **Pool(s):** outdoor, heated indoor. **Leisure Activities:** sauna, whirlpool, exercise room. **Guest Services:** valet and coin laundry. **Business Services:** meeting rooms, fax. **Cards:** AX, CB, DC, DS, MC, VI.

SOME UNITS

**CLARION HOTEL AND SUITES**   *Book at aaa.com*
AAA SAVE
▼▼▼
Small-scale Hotel

**Phone:** (802)658-0250

| | | | |
|---|---|---|---|
| 8/1-10/31 | 1P: $139-$199 | 2P: $139-$199 | XP: $10 | F18 |
| 5/1-7/31 | 1P: $109-$159 | 2P: $109-$159 | XP: $10 | F18 |
| 11/1-4/30 | 1P: $109-$149 | 2P: $109-$159 | XP: $10 | F18 |

**Location:** I-89, exit 14E, just e on US 2. 1285 Williston Rd 05403. Fax: 802/660-7516. **Facility:** 161 units. 128 one-bedroom standard units. 33 one-bedroom suites ($129-$219) with efficiencies, some with whirlpools. 2 stories, interior corridors. **Bath:** combo or shower only. **Parking:** on-site, winter plug-ins. **Terms:** pets ($50 deposit). **Amenities:** video games, voice mail, irons, hair dryers. *Some:* high-speed Internet. **Dining:** 6:30 am-9 pm, Fri-10 pm, Sat 7 am-10 pm, Sun 7 am-9 pm. **Pool(s):** heated indoor. **Leisure Activities:** whirlpool, exercise room. **Guest Services:** gift shop, valet laundry, airport transportation-Burlington International Airport. **Business Services:** conference facilities, PC, fax. **Cards:** AX, CB, DC, DS, JC, MC, VI. **Special Amenities:** free newspaper. *(See color ad p 420)*

SOME UNITS

**COMFORT INN**   *Book at aaa.com*
▼▼▼
Small-scale Hotel

**Phone:** (802)865-3400

| | | | |
|---|---|---|---|
| All Year [CP] | 1P: $69-$159 | 2P: $69-$159 | XP: $10 | F |

**Location:** I-89, exit 14E, 0.5 mi e on US 2. 1285 Williston Rd 05403. Fax: 802/846-3411. **Facility:** 105 units. 104 one-bedroom standard units. 1 one-bedroom suite with efficiency. 3 stories, interior corridors. **Parking:** on-site, winter plug-ins. **Terms:** 2 night minimum stay - seasonal, pets ($10 extra charge). **Amenities:** dual phone lines, voice mail, irons, hair dryers. **Pool(s):** heated outdoor. **Leisure Activities:** exercise room. **Guest Services:** valet and coin laundry. **Business Services:** meeting rooms. **Cards:** AX, DC, DS, JC, MC, VI. *(See color ad p 421)*

SOME UNITS

## HAWTHORN SUITES HOTEL   Book at aaa.com
Phone: (802)860-1212

AAA SAVE

Small-scale Hotel

| | | |
|---|---|---|
| 7/1-10/24 [BP] | 1P: $150-$190 | 2P: $150-$190 |
| 5/1-6/30 [BP] | 1P: $125-$150 | 2P: $125-$150 |
| 10/25-4/30 [BP] | 1P: $105-$125 | 2P: $105-$125 |

**Location:** I-89, exit 14E, just e on US 2, then 0.8 mi s. 401 Dorset St 05403. Fax: 802/860-1800. **Facility:** 104 units. 96 one- and 8 two-bedroom suites with kitchens, some with whirlpools. 3 stories, interior corridors. *Bath:* combo or shower only. **Parking:** on-site. **Terms:** 7 day cancellation notice, pets ($5 extra charge). **Amenities:** video games, high-speed Internet, dual phone lines, voice mail, irons, hair dryers. **Pool(s):** heated indoor. **Leisure Activities:** whirlpool, library, exercise room. **Guest Services:** sundries, complimentary evening beverages: Mon-Thurs, valet and coin laundry, airport transportation-Burlington International Airport. **Business Services:** meeting rooms. **Cards:** AX, CB, DC, DS, JC, MC, VI. **Special Amenities:** free full breakfast and free newspaper. *(See color ad p 421)*

SOME UNITS

---

## HOLIDAY INN BURLINGTON   Book at aaa.com
Phone: (802)863-6363

AAA SAVE

Large-scale Hotel

| | | |
|---|---|---|
| All Year | 1P: $84-$188 | 2P: $84-$188 |

**Location:** I-89, exit 14E, just e on US 2. 1068 Williston Rd 05403. Fax: 802/863-3061. **Facility:** 173 one-bedroom standard units. 4 stories, interior corridors. **Parking:** on-site, winter plug-ins. **Terms:** cancellation fee imposed, package plans - seasonal, small pets only ($10 extra charge). **Amenities:** dual phone lines, voice mail, irons, hair dryers. **Dining:** 6 am-2 & 5-10 pm, cocktails, entertainment. **Pool(s):** heated outdoor, heated indoor. **Leisure Activities:** sauna, exercise room. **Guest Services:** valet and coin laundry, airport transportation-Burlington International Aiport, area transportation-within 1 mi. **Business Services:** conference facilities, business center. **Cards:** AX, DC, DS, MC, VI. **Special Amenities:** early check-in/late check-out and free room upgrade (subject to availability with advanced reservations).** *(See color ad p 421)*

SOME UNITS

---

## HOLIDAY INN EXPRESS HOTEL & SUITES   Book at aaa.com
Phone: (802)860-1112

Small-scale Hotel

| | | | |
|---|---|---|---|
| 9/3-10/18 | 1P: $132-$156 | 2P: $132-$156 | XP: $10 | F18 |
| 5/1-9/2 | 1P: $103-$129 | 2P: $103-$129 | XP: $10 | F18 |
| 10/19-4/30 | 1P: $103 | 2P: $103 | XP: $10 | F18 |

**Location:** I-89, exit 13, w on I-189 to US 7, then 1.5 mi s. 1712 Shelburne Rd 05403. Fax: 802/846-1926. **Facility:** 84 units. 66 one-bedroom standard units, some with whirlpools. 18 one-bedroom suites with kitchens (no utensils). 4 stories, interior corridors. **Parking:** on-site, winter plug-ins. **Terms:** [ECP] meal plan available. **Amenities:** dual phone lines, voice mail, irons, hair dryers. *Some:* high-speed Internet. **Guest Services:** valet and coin laundry. **Business Services:** conference facilities, business center. **Cards:** AX, DC, DS, MC, VI.

SOME UNITS

---

## HOWARD JOHNSON HOTEL   Book at aaa.com
Phone: 802/860-6000

Small-scale Hotel

Property failed to provide current rates

**Location:** I-89, exit 13 to US 7, then 1.5 mi s. 1720 Shelburne Rd 05403. Fax: 802/864-9919. **Facility:** 121 units. 120 one-bedroom standard units, some with whirlpools. 1 one-bedroom suite. 4-5 stories, interior corridors. **Parking:** on-site, winter plug-ins. **Amenities:** video games (fee), high-speed Internet, voice mail, irons, hair dryers. **Pool(s):** heated indoor. **Leisure Activities:** saunas, whirlpool, exercise room. **Guest Services:** valet and coin laundry. **Business Services:** meeting rooms, PC. *(See color ad below)*

SOME UNITS

---

## MAINSTAY SUITES   Book at aaa.com
Phone: (802)860-1986

Small-scale Hotel

| | | | |
|---|---|---|---|
| 8/1-10/31 [ECP] | 1P: $129-$199 | 2P: $129-$199 | XP: $10 | F18 |
| 5/1-7/31 [ECP] | 1P: $109-$169 | 2P: $109-$169 | XP: $10 | F18 |
| 11/1-4/30 [ECP] | 1P: $109-$149 | 2P: $109-$149 | XP: $10 | F18 |

**Location:** I-89, exit 13 to US 7, then 1.5 mi s. 1702 Shelburne Rd 05403. Fax: 802/846-1987. **Facility:** 74 units. 32 one-bedroom standard units with efficiencies. 38 one- and 4 two-bedroom suites with kitchens, some with whirlpools. 4 stories, interior corridors. **Parking:** on-site, winter plug-ins. **Terms:** small pets only ($50 fee, in designated units). **Amenities:** high-speed Internet, dual phone lines, voice mail, irons, hair dryers. **Leisure Activities:** limited exercise equipment. **Guest Services:** valet and coin laundry. **Business Services:** business center. **Cards:** AX, CB, DC, DS, JC, MC, VI.

SOME UNITS

## RODEWAY INN

**Phone:** 802/862-0230

Motel

| | | | |
|---|---|---|---|
| 10/1-10/31 | 1P: $99-$149 | 2P: $99-$149 | XP: $10 F18 |
| 9/1-9/30 | 1P: $79-$99 | 2P: $79-$99 | XP: $10 F18 |
| 5/1-8/31 | 1P: $75-$89 | 2P: $75-$89 | XP: $10 F18 |
| 11/1-4/30 | 1P: $49-$59 | 2P: $49-$59 | XP: $10 F18 |

**Location:** I-89, exit 13 to US 7, then 1.9 mi s. 1860 Shelburne Rd 05403. Fax: 802/862-6204. **Facility:** 22 one-bedroom standard units, some with efficiencies. 2 stories (no elevator), interior corridors. **Bath:** combo or shower only. **Parking:** on-site. **Terms:** 4 day cancellation notice, [CP], meal plan available. **Amenities:** voice mail. **Pool(s):** outdoor. **Leisure Activities:** playground. **Cards:** AX, DC, DS, MC, VI.

SOME UNITS

ASK ⊗ ⊗ ⊗ ⊗ ⊗ ⊗ ⊗ / ⊗ /

## SHERATON BURLINGTON HOTEL & CONFERENCE CENTER   *Book at aaa.com*

**Phone:** (802)865-6600

Large-scale Hotel

All Year                1P: $159-$249        2P: $159-$249        XP: $10 F18
**Location:** I-89, exit 14W, just w on US 2. 870 Williston Rd 05403. Fax: 802/865-6670. **Facility:** 309 one-bedroom standard units, some with efficiencies. 2-4 stories, interior corridors. **Parking:** on-site, winter plug-ins. **Terms:** cancellation fee imposed. **Amenities:** video games (fee), high-speed Internet, voice mail, irons, hair dryers. **Dining:** 6:30 am-11 pm, cocktails. **Pool(s):** heated indoor. **Leisure Activities:** whirlpools, sun deck, exercise room. **Guest Services:** gift shop, valet laundry, airport transportation-Burlington International Airport. **Business Services:** conference facilities, business center. **Cards:** AX, CB, DC, MC, VI. *(See color ad p 5)*

SOME UNITS

⊗ ⊗ ⊗ ⊗ ⊗ ⊗ ⊗ ⊗ ⊗ ⊗ / ⊗ VCR ⊗
                                                      FEE   FEE

## SMART SUITES   *Book at aaa.com*

**Phone:** (802)860-9900

Small-scale Hotel

| | | | |
|---|---|---|---|
| 8/1-10/31 | 1P: $129-$199 | 2P: $129-$199 | XP: $10 F18 |
| 5/1-7/31 | 1P: $109-$169 | 2P: $109-$169 | XP: $10 F18 |
| 11/1-4/30 | 1P: $99-$149 | 2P: $99-$149 | XP: $10 F18 |

**Location:** I-89, exit 13 to US 7, then 1.5 mi s. 1700 Shelburne Rd 05403. Fax: 802/846-1996. **Facility:** 81 units. 27 one-bedroom standard units with efficiencies, some with whirlpools. 53 one- and 1 two-bedroom suites with kitchens. 3-4 stories, interior corridors. **Parking:** on-site, winter plug-ins. **Terms:** [ECP] meal plan available, small pets only ($50 fee, in designated units). **Amenities:** high-speed Internet, dual phone lines, voice mail, irons, hair dryers. **Leisure Activities:** pool, sauna and whirlpool privileges, exercise room. **Guest Services:** valet and coin laundry, airport transportation-Burlington International Airport. **Business Services:** meeting rooms, business center. **Cards:** AX, CB, DC, DS, MC, VI. **Special Amenities:** free expanded continental breakfast and free local telephone calls. *(See ad p 421)*

SOME UNITS

SD ⊗ ⊗ ⊗ ⊗ DATA PORT ⊗ ⊗ ⊗ / ⊗ /
        FEE

## UNIVERSITY INN & SUITES   *Book at aaa.com*

**Phone:** (802)863-5541

Small-scale Hotel

5/1-10/29              1P: $89-$149         2P: $89-$149
10/30-4/30             1P: $69-$99          2P: $69-$99
**Location:** I-89, exit 14E, just e on US 2, then just s. 5 Dorset St 05403. Fax: 802/862-2755. **Facility:** 175 units. 166 one-bedroom standard units, some with efficiencies and/or whirlpools. 9 one-bedroom suites ($109-$199) with efficiencies, some with whirlpools. 2-4 stories, interior corridors. **Parking:** on-site, winter plug-ins. **Terms:** 1-2 night minimum stay - seasonal, cancellation fee imposed. **Amenities:** video games, voice mail, irons, hair dryers. *Some:* high-speed Internet, dual phone lines. **Pool(s):** heated outdoor, heated indoor. **Leisure Activities:** saunas, whirlpool, exercise room. **Fee:** game room. **Guest Services:** sundries, complimentary evening beverages, valet and coin laundry, airport transportation-Burlington International Airport. **Business Services:** meeting rooms, business center. **Cards:** AX, DC, DS, MC, VI. **Special Amenities:** free local telephone calls and free newspaper. *(See color ad p 422)*

SOME UNITS

SD ⊗ ⊗ ⊗ ⊗ ⊗ ⊗ ⊗ DATA PORT ⊗ / ⊗ ⊗ ⊗ /

---

### WHERE TO DINE

---

## AL'S FRENCH FRIES

**Lunch:** $2-$5          **Dinner:** $2-$5          **Phone:** 802/863-6511

American

**Location:** I-89, exit 14E (US 2), 0.5 mi e. 1251 Williston Rd 05403-5719. **Hours:** 10:30 am-11 pm, Fri & Sat-midnight. Closed major holidays. **Features:** Selected by Yankee Magazine's 1999 Travel Guide to New England as "one of the outstanding reasons to visit New England," the restaurant is known for its great French fries. Long, yet quickly moving, lines are worth the wait for Al's chili dogs, burgers, fries and other old-time favorites. The atmosphere evokes the feel of a '50s-style malt shop. This place has been a Vermont landmark since 1948. Casual dress. **Parking:** on-site.

⊗ ⊗

## CACTUS PETE'S STEAK HOUSE & SALOON

**Lunch:** $7-$11          **Dinner:** $11-$20          **Phone:** 802/863-1138

Steak House

**Location:** Jct I-89, 0.6 mi s; in small shopping plaza. 7 Fayette Rd 05403. **Hours:** 11 am-9 pm, Fri & Sat-10 pm, Sun noon-8:30 pm. Closed: 11/25, 12/25. **Features:** Punctuated by a Western theme, the restaurant features a chuckwagon, all-you-can-eat salad bar and substantial portions of American beef steaks, ribs, chicken and seafood. A Southwestern kick jazzes up many dishes. Casual dress; cocktails. **Parking:** on-site. **Cards:** AX, CB, DC, DS, JC, MC, VI.

⊗

## LAKE VIEW BAR & GRILLE

**Lunch:** $6-$12          **Dinner:** $9-$25          **Phone:** 802/865-3200

American

**Location:** I-89, exit 13 (I-189/US 7), 1.5 mi s on US 7. 1710 Shelburne Rd 05403. **Hours:** 11:30 am-10 pm; to 9:30 pm 11/30-5/31. Closed major holidays; also Sun. **Reservations:** accepted. **Features:** The casual eatery occupies a restored Victorian mansion built in the mid-1800s on land that was originally part of the Lake View Farm. Away from the hustle and bustle of the city, this place is a welcoming respite for travelers. On the menu are traditional chicken, fish, pasta and beef dishes. Casual dress; cocktails. **Parking:** on-site. **Cards:** AX, DS, MC, VI.

⊗ ⊗

**PAULINE'S**

Nouvelle
American

**Lunch:** $7-$12          **Dinner:** $15-$24          **Phone:** 802/862-1081
**Location:** I-89, exit 13 (I-189/US 7), 4 mi s. 1834 Shelburne Rd 05403. **Hours:** 11:30 am-2 & 5-9:30 pm, Fri & Sat-10 pm, Sun 11 am-2:30 & 5-9:30 pm. Closed: 7/4, 12/24, 12/25. **Reservations:** suggested. **Features:** The restaurant has come a long way from the early days when this was a truck stop serving comfort foods. The fine-dining establishment features innovative, nouvelle, regional cuisine. Diners can choose seating in either the casual ground-floor dining room, the more intimate upstairs dining room or the enclosed seasonal patio. Dressy casual; cocktails. **Parking:** on-site. **Cards:** AX, CB, DS, MC, VI.

**PERRY'S FISH HOUSE**
Seafood

**Dinner:** $11-$17          **Phone:** 802/862-1300
**Location:** I-89, exit 13 (I-189/US 7), 1 mi s on US 7. 1080 Shelburne Rd 05403. **Hours:** 5 pm-10 pm, Fri & Sat 4:30 pm-10:30 pm, Sun 10 am-2 & 4-9 pm; Mon-Thurs 4:30 pm-9:30 pm in winter. Closed: 11/25, 12/25. **Reservations:** suggested, weekends. **Features:** The fishing skiff, lobster traps and buoy landscaping—along with the cawing of the gulls—beckon the casual diner to enter the "fish market" for fresh offerings of native fish and East Coast seafood. Casual dress; cocktails. **Parking:** on-site. **Cards:** AX, CB, DC, DS, MC, VI.

**WINDJAMMER**
American

**Lunch:** $7-$11          **Dinner:** $14-$21          **Phone:** 802/862-6585
**Location:** I-89, exit 14E, 0.3 mi e on US 2; in Best Western Windjammer Inn & Conference Center. 1076 Williston Rd 05403. **Hours:** 11:30 am-2:30 & 5-10 pm, Sun 5 pm-9 pm. Closed: 11/25, 12/25. **Reservations:** suggested, dinner & wknds. **Features:** You're sure to enjoy Windjammer's specialties of fresh seafood from New England ports and flavorful prime rib. The restaurant also offers nightly specials, a salad bar with 40 choices and local seasonal produce, a popular pub menu and pleasant service. Casual dress; cocktails. **Parking:** on-site. **Cards:** AX, CB, DC, DS, MC, VI.

# SOUTH ROYALTON

## ——— WHERE TO DINE ———

SOUTH ROYALTON HOUSE RESTAURANT & PUB          **Dinner:** $7-$16          **Phone:** 802-763-8315
American

**Location:** On the village green. 53 N Park St 05068. **Hours:** 5:30 pm-9 pm. Closed major holidays; also Sat-Mon. **Reservations:** accepted. **Features:** The restaurant's coordinated pub decor features the original interior stone walls of this 1800s historic building; patrons will find simple foods and casual service. Casual dress; cocktails. **Parking:** on-site. **Cards:** AX, DS, MC, VI.

# SOUTH WOODSTOCK

## ——— WHERE TO STAY ———

**KEDRON VALLEY INN**
Historic
Country Inn

|  |  | **Phone:** (802)457-1473 |
| --- | --- | --- |
| 9/25-10/19 [BP] | 1P: $154-$319 | 2P: $163-$327 | XP: $10 | F |
| 11/24-4/1 [BP] | 1P: $122-$289 | 2P: $131-$297 | XP: $10 | F |
| 5/1-9/24 & 10/20-11/14 [BP] | 1P: $99-$264 | 2P: $109-$272 | XP: $10 | F |

**Location:** Jct US 4, 5 mi s. Rt 106 05071 (PO Box 145, Rt 106). Fax: 802/457-4469. **Facility:** Located minutes from historic Woodstock, this country inn features spacious grounds and a private beach; many rooms offer a fireplace. 28 units. 25 one-bedroom standard units, some with whirlpools. 3 one-bedroom suites with whirlpools, some with kitchens. 1-3 stories (no elevator). *Bath:* combo or shower only. **Parking:** on-site. **Terms:** open 5/1-11/14 & 11/24-4/1, check-in 3:30 pm, 2 night minimum stay - most weekends, 7 day cancellation notice, [MAP] meal plan available, package plans - seasonal. **Amenities:** hair dryers. *Some:* DVD players, CD players, irons. **Dining:** restaurant, see separate listing. **Leisure Activities:** catch & release fish pond, cross country skiing, snowmobiling, hiking trails, volleyball. **Business Services:** meeting rooms. **Cards:** AX, MC, VI. *(See color ad p 493)*

SOME UNITS

## ——— WHERE TO DINE ———

KEDRON VALLEY INN   Country Inn          **Dinner:** $17-$28          **Phone:** 802/457-1473
American

**Location:** Jct US 4, 5 mi s; in Kedron Valley Inn. Rt 106 05071. **Hours:** Open 5/1-3/31; 6 pm-9 pm; seating on the half-hour; hours may vary off season. **Reservations:** suggested. **Features:** Off the beaten track in the scenic countryside, the picturesque inn is the site of the famous Anheuser-Busch commercial. The experience here is relaxing yet elegant. Casual dress; cocktails. **Parking:** on-site. **Cards:** AX, MC, VI.

# SPRINGFIELD pop. 3,938

## ——— WHERE TO STAY ———

THE HARTNESS HOUSE   *Book at aaa.com*          **Phone:** (802)885-2115
Country Inn

All Year [BP]          1P: $90-$185          2P: $99-$220          XP: $20          F6

**Location:** 0.4 mi n on Summer St, bear left at old cemetery. 30 Orchard St 05156. Fax: 802/885-2207. **Facility:** This 1903, Victorian, mansion has been the resting place of such notables as Charles Lindbergh, and houses its own historic observatory. 41 one-bedroom standard units. 3 stories (no elevator), interior corridors. *Bath:* combo or shower only. **Parking:** on-site, winter plug-ins. **Terms:** office hours 6:30 am-10 pm, 7 day cancellation notice-fee imposed, [MAP] meal plan available. **Amenities:** voice mail. **Dining:** restaurant, see separate listing. **Pool(s):** outdoor. **Leisure Activities:** boating, canoeing, hiking trails, jogging. *Fee:* massage. **Guest Services:** gift shop, valet laundry. **Business Services:** meeting rooms, fax (fee). **Cards:** AX, DS, MC, VI.

SOME UNITS

**HOLIDAY INN EXPRESS** *Book at aaa.com*

Phone: (802)885-4516

| | | | |
|---|---|---|---|
| 9/18-10/24 & 12/25-4/30 | 1P: $169 | 2P: $169 | XP: $10 F18 |
| 5/1-9/17 | 1P: $129-$159 | 2P: $129-$159 | XP: $10 F18 |
| 10/25-12/24 | 1P: $109-$129 | 2P: $109-$129 | XP: $10 F18 |

Small-scale Hotel **Location:** I-91, exit 7. 818 Charlestown Rd 05156. Fax: 802/885-4595. **Facility:** 88 one-bedroom standard units, some with whirlpools. 2 stories (no elevator), interior corridors. *Bath:* combo or shower only. **Parking:** on-site. **Terms:** [ECP] meal plan available, pets (in smoking units). **Amenities:** video games, voice mail, irons, hair dryers. **Pool(s):** heated indoor. **Leisure Activities:** exercise room, game room. **Guest Services:** valet and coin laundry. **Business Services:** meeting rooms, PC, fax. **Cards:** AX, CB, DC, DS, JC, MC, VI.

SOME UNITS

---

### WHERE TO DINE

**THE HARTNESS HOUSE RESTAURANT** Historic    **Lunch:** $6-$8    **Dinner:** $14-$23    Phone: 802/885-2115

**Location:** 0.4 mi n on Summer St, bear left at old cemetery; in The Hartness House. 30 Orchard St 05156. **Hours:** 7-9 am, 11:30-2 & 5-8 pm, Sat 8 am-10 & 5-9 pm, Sun 8-10 am, Mon 7-9 am. Closed: 12/25.

American **Reservations:** suggested. **Features:** Located in a comfortable country inn that's on the National Register of Historic Places, this locally popular dining room features a New England cuisine, fresh ingredients and a good value for your dollar. They have the Hartness 1910 telescope on-site. Casual dress; cocktails. **Parking:** on-site. **Cards:** AX, DS, MC, VI.

**MORNING STAR CAFE**    **Lunch:** $5-$7    **Dinner:** $12-$19    Phone: 802/885-6987

**Location:** Center. 56 Main St 05156. **Hours:** 7 am-5 pm, Wed & Thurs-9 pm, Fri-9:30 pm, Sat 8 am-9:30 pm. Closed: 7/4, 11/25, 12/25; also Sun. **Features:** This funky, community-oriented cafe offers a healthy American alternative for the more health-conscious diner and is a wonderful place to come just to read a paper and sip a cup of freshly brewed coffee or to chat with friends. Described as "free style cuisine" by the owners, the light luncheon menu is a wonderful mix of creative salads, soups and sandwiches, all ordered at the counter. Dinner, served four nights a week, is a chance for guests to try more eclectic and international foods. Casual dress; beer & wine only. **Parking:** on-site. **Cards:** MC, VI.

**PENELOPES**    **Lunch:** $4-$12    **Dinner:** $12-$25    Phone: 802/885-9186

**Location:** Center. 30 Main St 05156. **Hours:** 11:30 am-9 pm, Fri-10 pm, Sat 5 pm-10 pm. Closed major holidays; also Sun. **Reservations:** accepted. **Features:** Famous for their French onion soup gratinee, American fresh ocean fish and homemade desserts, Penelope's offers a diverse menu in a casual, relaxed atmosphere. All items are available for take-out, including those from their Wednesday night Mexican menu. Casual dress; cocktails. **Parking:** street. **Cards:** DS, MC, VI.

**SHANGHAI GARDEN**    **Lunch:** $5-$6    **Dinner:** $8-$14    Phone: 802/885-5555

**Location:** I-91, exit 7, 3 mi w on SR 11. 129 Clinton St 05156. **Hours:** 11 am-9:30 pm. Closed: 11/25, 12/25. Chinese **Features:** The old-time yellow dining car is hard to miss; the restaurant provides a simple atmosphere with casual friendly service. Casual dress. **Parking:** on-site. **Cards:** MC, VI.

---

## STOCKBRIDGE pop. 674

### WHERE TO DINE

**PEAVINE RESTAURANT & THE THIRSTY BULL BREW PUB**    **Dinner:** $6-$17    Phone: 802/234-9434

**Location:** Jct SR 107/12, 4.7 mi w. 3657 Rt 107 05772. **Hours:** 4 pm-10 pm. Closed: 11/25, 12/25; also Sun. American **Features:** The decor is interesting with a wildlife motif and vaulted ceilings with a large electric train running along the edges. The restaurant offers typical American fare served up pub-style. Casual dress; cocktails. **Parking:** on-site. **Cards:** AX, MC, VI.

---

## STOWE

### WHERE TO STAY

**1066 YE OLDE ENGLAND INNE**

Phone: 802/253-7558

| | | |
|---|---|---|
| 9/17-10/20 [BP] | 2P: $169-$359 | XP: $55 |
| 7/2-9/16 & 10/21-4/30 [BP] | 2P: $139-$269 | XP: $35 |
| 5/1-7/1 [BP] | 2P: $119-$239 | XP: $35 |

Country Inn **Location:** 0.4 mi w on SR 108, from jct SR 100. 433 Mountain Rd 05672. Fax: 802/253-8944. **Facility:** The main inn, a reproduction of an Old English inn, offers smaller units while the rear unit situated on a bluff offers spacious, modern guest rooms. Smoke free premises. 30 units. 17 one-bedroom standard units, some with whirlpools. 10 one-bedroom suites ($189-$359) with whirlpools. 3 cottages ($199-$359) with whirlpools. 3-4 stories (no elevator), interior/exterior corridors. *Bath:* combo or shower only. **Parking:** on-site. **Terms:** 2 night minimum stay - weekends, 15 day cancellation notice-fee imposed, weekly rates available, [MAP] meal plan available, 7% service charge, pets (in cottages only). **Amenities:** irons, hair dryers. **Dining:** Mr. Pickwick's, see separate listing. **Pool(s):** heated outdoor. **Leisure Activities:** whirlpool. *Fee:* massage. **Guest Services:** valet laundry. **Business Services:** meeting rooms. **Cards:** AX, MC, VI.

SOME UNITS

## ANDERSEN LODGE-AN AUSTRIAN INN

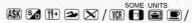

| | | | | Phone: (802)253-7336 |
|---|---|---|---|---|
| | 12/23-4/15 [BP] | 1P: $78-$168 | 2P: $108-$198 | XP: $20 | F12 |
| | 7/1-10/25 [BP] | 1P: $88-$158 | 2P: $98-$168 | XP: $20 | F12 |
| | 12/15-12/22 [BP] | 1P: $78-$88 | 2P: $98-$118 | XP: $20 | F12 |
| Country Inn | 6/1-6/30 [BP] | 1P: $58-$88 | 2P: $68-$98 | XP: $20 | F12 |

**Location:** 3.5 mi w on SR 108, from jct SR 100. 3430 Mountain Rd 05672. Fax: 802/253-4715. **Facility:** 18 one-bedroom standard units. 2 stories (no elevator), interior corridors. *Bath:* combo or shower only. **Parking:** on-site, winter plug-ins. **Terms:** open 6/1-10/25 & 12/15-4/15, 4 day cancellation notice, weekly rates available, [MAP] meal plan available, small pets only. **Amenities:** *Some:* hair dryers. **Dining:** 8-9:30 am, dinner seating at 6:45 pm only; open to public by reservation in winter. **Pool(s):** heated outdoor. **Leisure Activities:** sauna, whirlpool, tennis court, bumper pool, ping pong, hiking trails, limited exercise equipment, basketball. *Fee:* game room. **Guest Services:** complimentary evening beverages. **Cards:** AX, DS, MC, VI. **Special Amenities:** free full breakfast and free local telephone calls.

SOME UNITS

## ARBOR INN

| | | | | Phone: 802/253-4772 |
|---|---|---|---|---|
| | 10/1-10/31 | 1P: $109-$129 | 2P: $109-$129 | XP: $20 | D |
| | 7/1-9/30 & 11/1-4/30 | 1P: $89-$99 | 2P: $89-$99 | XP: $20 | D |
| Bed & Breakfast | 5/1-6/30 | 1P: $79-$89 | 2P: $79-$89 | XP: $20 | D |

**Location:** 3.3 mi w on SR 108, from jct SR 100. 3214 Mountain Rd 05672. Fax: 802/253-9486. **Facility:** This pleasant property located west of the town center offers attractive grounds and a range of guest rooms. Smoke free premises. 12 units. 10 one- and 1 two-bedroom standard units, some with kitchens and/or whirlpools. 1 one-bedroom suite ($189-$329) with kitchen. 2 stories (no elevator), exterior corridors. **Parking:** on-site. **Terms:** 2 night minimum stay, 15 day cancellation notice-fee imposed, [AP] meal plan available, package plans, no pets allowed (owner's pet on premises). **Amenities:** video library, hair dryers. *Some:* CD players. **Pool(s):** heated outdoor. **Leisure Activities:** whirlpool. **Cards:** AX, DS, MC, VI.

SOME UNITS

## AUBERGE DE STOWE BED & BREAKFAST

| | | | Phone: 802/253-7787 |
|---|---|---|---|
| | All Year [CP] | 2P: $58-$98 | |

Bed & Breakfast

**Location:** 0.5 mi s of jct SR 100/108. 692 S Main St 05672. **Facility:** 6 units. 4 one- and 2 two-bedroom standard units. 2 stories (no elevator), interior corridors. *Bath:* combo or shower only. **Parking:** on-site. **Terms:** check-in 3:30 pm, 2 night minimum stay - in season, 14 day cancellation notice, package plans. **Pool(s):** outdoor. **Leisure Activities:** fishing, limited exercise equipment, volleyball. **Cards:** AX, MC, VI.

**BRASS LANTERN INN** *Book at aaa.com*

**Phone:** (802)253-2229

AAA SAVE 9/17-10/16 [BP] 2P: $115-$225 XP: $25
5/1-9/16 & 10/17-4/30 [BP] 2P: $95-$175 XP: $25

Historic Bed & Breakfast

**Location:** 0.8 mi n on SR 100, from jct SR 108. 717 Maple St 05672. Fax: 802/253-7425. **Facility:** A converted 1800 farmhouse and carriage barn, this inn overlooks Mount Mansfield; guest rooms are attractively appointed and furnished with antiques. Smoke free premises. 9 one-bedroom standard units, some with whirlpools. 2 stories (no elevator), interior corridors. *Bath:* combo or shower only. **Parking:** on-site, winter plug-ins. **Terms:** 2 night minimum stay - most weekends, 15 day cancellation notice-fee imposed, package plans. **Amenities:** hair dryers. **Guest Services:** complimentary evening beverages. **Business Services:** meeting rooms. **Cards:** AX, MC, VI. **Special Amenities:** free full breakfast and free local telephone calls. *(See color ad below)*

SOME UNITS

**BUTTERNUT ON THE RIVER**

**Phone:** (802)253-4277

AAA SAVE All Year 2P: $60-$260 XP: $15 F18

Bed & Breakfast

**Location:** 2.2 mi w on SR 108, from jct SR 100. 2309 Mountain Rd 05672. Fax: 802/253-5263. **Facility:** Smoke free premises. 18 one-bedroom standard units, some with whirlpools. 3 stories (no elevator), interior corridors. *Bath:* some shared or private, combo or shower only. **Parking:** on-site. **Terms:** check-in 4 pm, 2-4 night minimum stay - seasonal, age restrictions may apply, 14 day cancellation notice-fee imposed, [BP] & [MAP] meal plans available, package plans, 5% service charge. **Amenities:** video library. **Pool(s):** outdoor. **Leisure Activities:** fishing, hot tubs, swimming holes, croquet, adjacent to recreation path, gas grills, picnic tables. **Cards:** AX, DC, MC, VI.

SOME UNITS

## COMMODORES INN
*Book at aaa.com*

| | | Phone: (802)253-7131 |
|---|---|---|
| 10/19-12/31 [BP] | 1P: $78-$138 | 2P: $98-$198 |
| 9/25-10/18 [BP] | 1P: $118 | 2P: $168 |
| 1/1-4/30 [BP] | 1P: $88-$108 | 2P: $108-$158 |
| 5/1-9/24 [BP] | 1P: $78-$98 | 2P: $98-$138 |

**Large-scale Hotel** **Location:** Jct SR 108, 0.8 mi s on SR 100. 823 S Main St 05672 (PO Box 970). Fax: 802/253-2360. **Facility:** 72 one-bedroom standard units. 3 stories, interior corridors. *Bath:* some combo or shower only. **Parking:** on-site, winter plug-ins. **Terms:** 7 day cancellation notice, [MAP] meal plan available, package plans - seasonal. **Dining:** 7:30 am-10:30 & 5:30-9 pm, cocktails. **Pool(s):** heated outdoor, heated indoor. **Leisure Activities:** saunas, whirlpools, canoeing, paddleboats, boat ramp, fishing, radio-controlled model sailboat races on pond, ice skating, exercise room. **Business Services:** meeting rooms, fax (fee). **Cards:** AX, CB, DC, DS, JC, MC, VI. **Special Amenities:** free local telephone calls and preferred room **(subject to availability with advanced reservations).** *(See color ad p 472)*

SOME UNITS

---

## EDSON HILL MANOR

| | | Phone: (802)253-7371 |
|---|---|---|
| 5/21-10/30 & 12/10-4/30 [BP] | 1P: $119-$179 | 2P: $139-$199 | XP: $30 | F4 |
| 5/1-5/20 & 10/31-12/9 [BP] | 1P: $89-$119 | 2P: $99-$139 | XP: $30 | F4 |

**Country Inn** **Location:** Jct SR 100, 3.5 mi w on SR 108, then 1.3 mi n. Located in a quiet area. 1500 Edson Hill Rd 05672. Fax: 802/253-4036. **Facility:** Nestled on 60 acres of rolling countryside, this inn offers accommodations in a restored manor and in separate carriage houses. 25 one-bedroom standard units. 1-2 stories (no elevator), interior/exterior corridors. *Bath:* combo or shower only. **Parking:** on-site, winter plug-ins. **Terms:** 15 day cancellation notice-fee imposed, [CP] & [MAP] meal plans available, package plans, 15% service charge, pets (in designated units). **Dining:** dining room, see separate listing. **Pool(s):** outdoor. **Leisure Activities:** cross country skiing, hiking trails. *Fee:* horseback riding, massage. **Guest Services:** complimentary evening beverages. **Cards:** DS, MC, VI.

SOME UNITS

---

## GOLDEN EAGLE RESORT
*Book at aaa.com*

| | | Phone: (802)253-4811 |
|---|---|---|
| 12/17-4/30 | 1P: $89-$189 | 2P: $99-$199 | XP: $10 | F12 |
| 6/11-10/16 | 1P: $89-$179 | 2P: $99-$189 | XP: $10 | F12 |
| 5/1-6/10 & 10/17-12/16 | 1P: $79-$144 | 2P: $89-$154 | XP: $10 | F12 |

**Motel** **Location:** 0.5 mi w on SR 108, from jct SR 100. 511 Mountain Rd 05672 (PO Box 1090). Fax: 802/253-2561. **Facility:** Smoke free premises. 94 units. 89 one-bedroom standard units, some with efficiencies and/or whirlpools. 5 one-bedroom suites ($189-$279) with kitchens. 1-2 stories (no elevator), exterior corridors. **Parking:** on-site, winter plug-ins. **Terms:** 2 night minimum stay - some weekends, 5 day cancellation notice-fee imposed, weekly rates available, [BP] meal plan available, package plans. **Amenities:** video library, voice mail, hair dryers. *Some:* irons. **Dining:** 7-11 am. **Pool(s):** heated outdoor. **Leisure Activities:** sauna, whirlpool, fishing, tennis court, cross country skiing, ice skating, recreation programs, hiking trails, playground, exercise room, horseshoes, shuffleboard. *Fee:* massage, game room. **Guest Services:** gift shop, valet and coin laundry, area transportation-within 5 mi, Amtrack & bus stations. **Business Services:** meeting rooms, PC. **Cards:** AX, DS, MC, VI. *(See color ad below)*

SOME UNITS

FEE

## GREEN MOUNTAIN INN

Book at aaa.com

Phone: (802)253-7301

| |  |  |  | |
|---|---|---|---|---|
| 12/23-4/30 | 1P: $105-$215 | 2P: $115-$225 | XP: $20 | F12 |
| 9/24-10/16 | 1P: $145-$155 | 2P: $155-$165 | XP: $20 | F12 |
| 5/1-9/23 | 1P: $95-$125 | 2P: $105-$135 | XP: $20 | F12 |
| 10/17-12/22 | 1P: $105-$115 | 2P: $115-$125 | XP: $20 | F12 |

Historic Country Inn

**Location:** Jct SR 108 on SR 100; center. 18 S Main St 05672 (PO Box 60). Fax: 802/253-5096. **Facility:** This restored 1833 inn in the village center reflects the ambience of the era and offers tastefully decorated rooms and suites. 105 units. 81 one-bedroom standard units, some with whirlpools. 18 one- and 2 two-bedroom suites ($135-$635), some with kitchens and/or whirlpools. 4 vacation homes ($275-$695), some with whirlpools. 3 stories (no elevator), interior/exterior corridors. **Bath:** combo or shower only. **Parking:** on-site, winter plug-ins. **Terms:** 2 night minimum stay - seasonal weekends, 14 day cancellation notice-fee imposed, [BP] & [CP] meal plans available, package plans - seasonal, 5% service charge, small pets only ($20 extra charge, in designated units). **Amenities:** video library (fee), voice mail, hair dryers. *Some:* DVD players, CD players, high-speed Internet, safes, honor bars, irons. **Dining:** 7:30 am-10 & 11:30-9:30 pm; hours may vary, also, The Whip Bar & Grill, see separate listing. **Pool(s):** heated outdoor. **Leisure Activities:** sauna, whirlpool, steamroom, lawn games. *Fee:* massage, game room. **Guest Services:** gift shop, valet laundry. **Business Services:** meeting rooms, fax (fee). **Cards:** AX, DS, MC, VI. *(See color ad below)*

SOME UNITS

**GREY FOX INN & RESORT**   *Book at aaa.com*

Phone: (802)253-8921

| | | | |
|---|---|---|---|
| 12/17-4/30 [BP] | 1P: $86-$213 | 2P: $96-$223 | XP: $20 | F12 |
| 6/18-10/11 [BP] | 1P: $84-$181 | 2P: $94-$191 | XP: $20 | F12 |
| 5/1-6/17 & 10/12-12/16 [BP] | 1P: $70-$157 | 2P: $80-$167 | XP: $20 | F12 |

Motel

**Location:** Jct SR 100, 1 mi w on SR 108. 990 Mountain Rd 05672. Fax: 802/253-8344. **Facility:** Smoke free premises. 42 units. 33 one-bedroom standard units. 6 one- and 3 two-bedroom suites ($103-$371), some with kitchens and/or whirlpools. 1-3 stories (no elevator), interior/exterior corridors. **Parking:** on-site. **Terms:** office hours 7 am-10 pm, 2 night minimum stay - some weekends, 15 day cancellation notice-fee imposed, 10% service charge. **Amenities:** voice mail, hair dryers. *Some:* DVD players, irons. **Dining:** 7:30 am-11 & 5:30-8:30 pm 12/23-3/18; 8-11 am 3/19-4/20, 5/21-10/29 & 11/23-12/22; hours may vary, wine/beer only. **Pool(s):** heated indoor. **Leisure Activities:** sauna, whirlpool, outdoor pool privileges, rental bicycles, exercise room, sports court. **Guest Services:** sundries, coin laundry. **Business Services:** meeting rooms, fax (fee). **Cards:** AX, DS, MC, VI. **Special Amenities:** free full breakfast and early check-in/late check-out. *(See color ad below)*

SOME UNITS

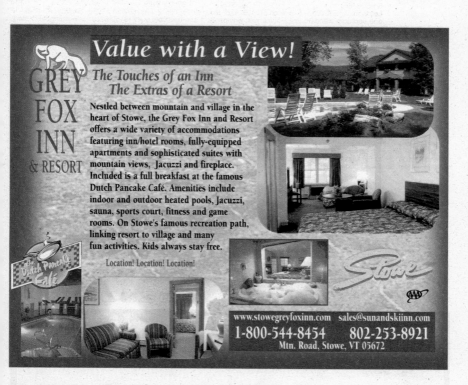

Value with a View!

The Touches of an Inn
The Extras of a Resort

Nestled between mountain and village in the heart of Stowe, the Grey Fox Inn and Resort offers a wide variety of accommodations featuring inn/hotel rooms, fully-equipped apartments and sophisticated suites with mountain views, Jacuzzi and fireplace. Included is a full breakfast at the famous Dutch Pancake Café. Amenities include indoor and outdoor heated pools, Jacuzzi, sauna, sports court, fitness and game rooms. On Stowe's famous recreation path, linking resort to village and many fun activities. Kids always stay free.

Location! Location! Location!

www.stowegreyfoxinn.com   sales@sunandskiinn.com
1-800-544-8454   802-253-8921
Mtn. Road, Stowe, VT 05672

At The Top of Vermont!

*Streamside resort, beneath Vermont's highest peak.*

*Fireside Cafe for breakfast, afternoon teas & ales.*

*Heated pool, health spa, spa services.*

*Biking, x-c skiing, skating, paddle tennis.*

800-225-8582
802-253-8582
www.innsbruckinn.com

## HOB KNOB INN & RESTAURANT
**Phone:** (802)253-8549

(AAA) (SAVE)

| | | | |
|---|---|---|---|
| 12/12-4/30 [BP] | 1P: $95-$210 | 2P: $95-$210 | XP: $15 F6 |
| 6/20-10/19 [CP] | 1P: $95-$165 | 2P: $95-$165 | XP: $15 F6 |
| 5/1-6/19 & 10/20-12/11 | 1P: $75-$135 | 2P: $75-$135 | XP: $15 F6 |

Motel

**Location:** Jct SR 100, 2.5 mi w on SR 108. 2364 Mountain Rd 05672. Fax: 802/253-7621. **Facility:** 21 units. 19 one-bedroom standard units, some with efficiencies. 1 one-bedroom suite ($125-$210) with kitchen and whirlpool. 1 cottage. 2 stories (no elevator), interior/exterior corridors. *Bath:* combo or shower only. **Parking:** onsite, winter plug-ins. **Terms:** office hours 8 am-10 pm, 14 day cancellation notice, [ECP] meal plan available, package plans, pets ($10 fee). **Amenities:** hair dryers. **Dining:** 6 pm-9 pm; closed Tues, also 4/1-5/18 & 10/21-12/14. **Pool(s):** outdoor. **Business Services:** fax. **Cards:** AX, DC, DS, MC, VI. *(See color ad p 472)*

SOME UNITS

## HONEYWOOD COUNTRY LODGE
**Phone:** (802)253-4124

(AAA) (SAVE)

| | | | |
|---|---|---|---|
| 9/19-10/20 [BP] | 1P: $119-$179 | 2P: $139-$179 | XP: $25 F10 |
| 10/21-4/30 [BP] | 1P: $79-$139 | 2P: $89-$149 | XP: $20 F10 |
| 6/27-9/18 [BP] | 1P: $79-$129 | 2P: $89-$139 | XP: $15 F10 |
| 5/1-6/26 [BP] | 1P: $65-$129 | 2P: $65-$129 | XP: $15 F10 |

Motel

**Location:** Jct SR 100, 4.5 mi w on SR 100. 4527 Mountain Rd 05672. Fax: 802/253-7050. **Facility:** 13 units. 12 one-bedroom standard units, some with whirlpools. 1 one-bedroom suite ($159-$229) with whirlpool. 1 story, exterior corridors. **Parking:** on-site, winter plug-ins. **Terms:** office hours 8 am-10 pm, 2 night minimum stay - seasonal weekends & in season, 15 day cancellation notice, 30 day notice in season-fee imposed, weekly rates available, package plans - midweek, 10% service charge, pets ($10 extra charge, in designated units). **Amenities:** voice mail. **Leisure Activities:** whirlpools, fishing, cross country skiing, picnic area, hiking trails. **Business Services:** fax (fee). **Cards:** AX, DS, MC, VI. *(See color ad below)*

SOME UNITS

## HONEYWOOD INN
**Phone:** (802)253-4846

| | | | |
|---|---|---|---|
| 9/19-10/20 [BP] | 1P: $109-$179 | 2P: $139-$179 | XP: $25 |
| 10/21-4/30 [BP] | 1P: $79-$119 | 2P: $89-$119 | XP: $20 |
| 6/27-9/18 [BP] | 1P: $79-$109 | 2P: $89-$109 | XP: $15 |
| 5/1-6/26 [BP] | 1P: $65-$99 | 2P: $65-$99 | XP: $15 |

Bed & Breakfast

**Location:** On SR 108, 4.7 mi w of jct SR 100. 4583 Mountain Rd 05672 (4527 Mountain Rd). Fax: 802/253-7050. **Facility:** This Swiss-style ski lodge offers pleasant and individually decorated guest rooms furnished with some fine antiques. Smoke free premises. 10 units. 8 one-bedroom standard units. 2 one-bedroom suites ($159-$229), some with whirlpools. 2 stories (no elevator), interior corridors. **Parking:** on-site. **Terms:** 1-4 night minimum stay - weekends & seasonal, age restrictions may apply, 15 day cancellation notice, 30 day in season-fee imposed, weekly rates available, package plans. **Amenities:** video library. **Pool(s):** heated outdoor. **Guest Services:** complimentary evening beverages: in winter. **Cards:** AX, DS, MC, VI. *(See color ad below)*

SOME UNITS

## INN AT THE MOUNTAIN
**Phone:** (802)253-3656

(AAA) (SAVE)

Resort
Small-scale Hotel

| | | | |
|---|---|---|---|
| All Year | 1P: $99-$599 | 2P: $99-$599 | XP: $15 F18 |

**Location:** Jct SR 100, 6 mi w on SR 108. Located at Stowe Mountain Resort. 5781 Mountain Rd 05672. Fax: 802/253-3659. **Facility:** All rooms have private balconies and mountain views at this country-style inn located at the base of Mount Mansfield. 33 units. 26 one-bedroom standard units. 7 one-bedroom suites, some with whirlpools. 2-3 stories (no elevator), interior corridors. **Parking:** on-site. **Terms:** check-in 4 pm, 15 day cancellation notice-fee imposed. **Dining:** 7-10 am Sat & Sun; also 5:30 pm-9 pm 9/15-10/15; closed 10/16-5/31, cocktails. **Pool(s):** 3 heated outdoor. **Leisure Activities:** sauna, whirlpool, 6 tennis courts, picnic tables, hiking trails, exercise room, basketball. *Fee:* golf school, tennis instruction, downhill & cross country skiing, alpine slide, ski instruction & equipment, gondola rides, in-line skate park, massage, game room. **Guest Services:** valet laundry, area transportation-within resort complex. **Business Services:** conference facilities. **Cards:** AX, DC, DS, MC, VI.

SOME UNITS

## INNSBRUCK INN AT STOWE

**Book at aaa.com**

**Phone:** (802)253-8582

| | | | |
|---|---|---|---|
| 12/17-4/30 [BP] | 1P: $59-$159 | 2P: $69-$169 | XP: $18 | F12 |
| 6/18-10/16 [ECP] | 1P: $59-$154 | 2P: $69-$159 | XP: $15 | F12 |
| 10/17-12/16 [ECP] | 1P: $59-$124 | 2P: $69-$129 | XP: $15 | F12 |
| 5/1-6/17 [ECP] | 1P: $59-$119 | 2P: $69-$124 | XP: $10 | F12 |

Motel

**Location:** 4.5 mi w on SR 108, from jct SR 100. 4361 Mountain Rd 05672. Fax: 802/253-2260. **Facility:** Smoke free premises. 26 units. 25 one-bedroom standard units, some with efficiencies and/or whirlpools. 1 cabin. 1-2 stories (no elevator), interior/exterior corridors. **Parking:** on-site, winter plug-ins. **Terms:** 14 day cancellation notice-fee imposed, weekly rates available, [MAP] meal plan available, package plans, small pets only ($10 extra charge). **Amenities:** CD players, voice mail, hair dryers. *Some:* video games (fee). **Pool(s):** heated outdoor. **Leisure Activities:** sauna, whirlpool, lighted tennis court, ice skating, rental bicycles, limited exercise equipment, basketball, horseshoes. *Fee:* game room. **Guest Services:** complimentary evening beverages. **Business Services:** PC. **Cards:** AX, DC, DS, MC, VI. *(See color ad p 475)*

SOME UNITS

## THE MOUNTAIN ROAD RESORT AT STOWE

**Book at aaa.com**

**Phone:** (802)253-4566

| | | | |
|---|---|---|---|
| All Year | 1P: $115-$260 | 2P: $115-$260 | XP: $25 | D12 |

Motel

**Location:** 1 mi w on SR 108, from jct SR 100. 1007 Mountain Rd 05672 (PO Box 8). Fax: 802/253-7397. **Facility:** Smoke free premises. 30 units. 24 one-bedroom standard units, some with efficiencies (no utensils) and/or whirlpools. 6 one-bedroom suites ($215-$560) with whirlpools, some with efficiencies or kitchens (no utensils). 1-2 stories, exterior corridors. **Parking:** on-site, winter plug-ins. **Terms:** 15 day cancellation notice-fee imposed, [BP], [ECP] & [MAP] meal plans available, pets ($15-$25 fee). **Amenities:** voice mail, irons, hair dryers. *Some:* DVD players, CD players, high-speed Internet. **Pool(s):** heated outdoor, heated indoor. **Leisure Activities:** sauna, whirlpools, French petanque court, bicycles, playground, exercise room. *Fee:* clay tennis court. **Guest Services:** valet and coin laundry, area transportation (fee)-ski area. **Business Services:** meeting rooms. **Cards:** AX, CB, DC, DS, MC, VI. **Special Amenities:** free local telephone calls and free newspaper. *(See color ad below)*

SOME UNITS

## MOUNTAIN WOOD INN

**Phone:** (802)253-9080

| | | | |
|---|---|---|---|
| All Year [BP] | 1P: $95-$195 | 2P: $95-$195 | | F16 |

Bed & Breakfast

**Location:** SR 108, 4.5 mi w of jct SR 100. 4492 Mountain Rd 05672 (PO Box 816). Fax: 802/253-7873. **Facility:** Smoke free premises. 9 one-bedroom standard units. 2 stories (no elevator), interior corridors. *Bath:* some shared or private, combo or shower only. **Parking:** on-site. **Terms:** office hours 7 am-10 pm, 14 day cancellation notice. **Amenities:** video library, high-speed Internet. **Leisure Activities:** horseshoes, volleyball. **Cards:** AX, DS, MC, VI.

SOME UNITS

## NOTCH BROOK CONDOMINIUMS

**Phone:** (802)253-4882

| | | |
|---|---|---|
| All Year | 1P: $51-$107 | 2P: $51-$107 |

Condominium

**Location:** 5.1 mi w on SR 108, from jct SR 100, then 1.3 mi n, 1229 Notch Brook Rd 05672. Fax: 802/253-4882. **Facility:** 39 units. 23 one-, 13 two- and 3 three-bedroom suites ($83-$485), some with kitchens. 3 stories (no elevator), exterior corridors. **Parking:** on-site, winter plug-ins. **Terms:** check-in 4 pm, 15 day cancellation notice-fee imposed, weekly rates available, pets ($10 fee). **Amenities:** voice mail, cooking. **Pool(s):** heated outdoor. **Leisure Activities:** saunas, 2 tennis courts, playground. **Guest Services:** coin laundry. **Cards:** AX, MC, VI.

SOME UNITS

## SEASON'S PASS INN

**Phone: 802/253-7244**

| | | | |
|---|---|---|---|
| 12/10-4/30 [ECP] | 1P: $75-$110 | 2P: $75-$130 | XP: $10 · F12 |
| 9/17-10/31 [ECP] | 1P: $78-$100 | 2P: $78-$115 | XP: $10 · F12 |
| 5/1-9/16 [ECP] | 1P: $60-$90 | 2P: $60-$105 | XP: $10 · F12 |
| 11/1-12/9 [CP] | 1P: $60-$85 | 2P: $60-$95 | XP: $10 · F12 |

Motel

**Location:** 0.6 mi s on SR 100, from jct SR 108. 613 S Main St 05672 (PO Box 896). Fax: 802/253-6836. **Facility:** Smoke free premises. 14 one-bedroom standard units, some with efficiencies. 2 stories (no elevator), interior/exterior corridors. *Bath:* combo or shower only. **Parking:** on-site, winter plug-ins. **Terms:** 15 day cancellation notice-fee imposed. **Amenities:** video library. **Pool(s):** heated indoor. **Leisure Activities:** barbecue grill, picnic tables. **Guest Services:** complimentary evening beverages. **Business Services:** meeting rooms. **Cards:** DS, MC, VI. **Special Amenities: free expanded continental breakfast and free local telephone calls.**

SOME UNITS

## THE SNOWDRIFT MOTEL

**Phone: 802/253-7305**

| | | | |
|---|---|---|---|
| 9/30-10/16 [ECP] | 1P: $110-$125 | 2P: $110-$125 | XP: $10 |
| 6/18-9/29 [ECP] | 1P: $78-$94 | 2P: $84-$104 | XP: $10 |
| 10/17-4/30 [ECP] | 1P: $64-$94 | 2P: $72-$104 | XP: $10 |
| 5/1-6/17 [ECP] | 1P: $62-$68 | 2P: $66-$76 | XP: $10 |

Motel

**Location:** Jct SR 100, 2.1 mi w on SR 108. 2135 Mountain Rd 05672 (2043 Mountain Rd). Fax: 802/253-9971. **Facility:** 40 units. 38 one-bedroom standard units, some with efficiencies. 2 one-bedroom suites with kitchens. 1-2 stories, interior/exterior corridors. **Parking:** on-site. **Terms:** check-in 4 pm, 2 night minimum stay - seasonal weekends, 15 day cancellation notice. **Amenities:** voice mail, hair dryers. **Pool(s):** heated outdoor. **Leisure Activities:** whirlpool, tennis court, bicycles. *Fee:* game room. **Business Services:** PC. **Cards:** AX, DS, MC, VI.

SOME UNITS

## STOWEFLAKE MOUNTAIN RESORT & SPA

*Book at aaa.com*

**Phone: (802)253-7355**

| | | | |
|---|---|---|---|
| 1/1-4/30 | 1P: $180-$300 | 2P: $180-$300 | XP: $20 · F12 |
| 10/25-12/31 | 1P: $160-$280 | 2P: $180-$300 | XP: $20 · F12 |
| 7/2-10/24 | 1P: $170-$300 | 2P: $170-$300 | XP: $20 · F12 |
| 5/1-7/1 | 1P: $150-$280 | 2P: $150-$280 | XP: $20 · F12 |

Resort
Small-scale Hotel

**Location:** Jct SR 100, 1.5 mi w on SR 108. 1746 Mountain Rd 05672 (PO Box 369). Fax: 802/253-6858. **Facility:** Located near Mount Mansfield and the village center, this resort on 60 acres of manicured lawns and gardens offers many rooms with mountain views. 118 units. 108 one-bedroom standard units, some with whirlpools. 10 one-bedroom suites ($320-$450) with whirlpools. 2 stories, interior/exterior corridors. *Bath:* combo or shower only. **Parking:** on-site, winter plug-ins. **Terms:** 1-7 night minimum stay - weekends, 14 day cancellation notice, weekly rates available, [BP] & [MAP] meal plans available, package plans. **Amenities:** voice mail, irons, hair dryers. *Some:* DVD players, CD players, high-speed Internet, dual phone lines. **Dining:** 2 restaurants, 7:30 am-10:30 & noon-10 pm, cocktails, also, Winfield's Bistro, see separate listing. **Pool(s):** heated outdoor, heated indoor. **Leisure Activities:** sauna, whirlpool, steamroom, putting green, 2 tennis courts, ice skating, snowshoe center, recreation programs, hiking trails, jogging, playground, spa, sports court. *Fee:* driving range, squash/racquetball court, bicycles, game room. **Guest Services:** gift shop, valet laundry. **Business Services:** conference facilities, business center. **Cards:** AX, DC, DS, MC, VI. *(See color ad below)*

SOME UNITS

FEE

# DESERVED INDULGENCE.

Our luxury accommodations and brand new, world-class spa, are dedicated to soaking, massaging and indulging your every comfort. Special baths, gentle buffs, and premium fare at our award-winning restaurants are just a few of the treats we have on hand to make you look and feel like new again.

**Stoweflake**
*Mountain Resort & Spa*

Stowe, Vermont
**800-253-2232**
info@stoweflake.com   www.stoweflake.com/aaa

**STOWEHOF INN**

Country Inn

All Year        1P: $70-$292      2P: $83-$305     XP: $25     F3

Phone: 802/253-9722

**Location:** 3.4 mi w on SR 108, from jct SR 100, then 0.5 mi n. Located in a rustic area. 434 Edson Hill Rd 05672. Fax: 802/253-7513. **Facility:** Thirty acres of forested and landscaped grounds surround this property; rooms come in a variety of shapes and sizes, all individually decorated. 45 units. 44 one-bedroom standard units, some with efficiencies. 1 one-bedroom suite. 2-3 stories, interior corridors. **Parking:** on-site. **Terms:** 15 day cancellation notice-fee imposed, [BP] & [MAP] meal plans available. **Amenities:** video library. *Some:* hair dryers. **Dining:** Emily's, see separate listing. **Pool(s):** heated outdoor, heated indoor. **Leisure Activities:** sauna, whirlpool, fishing, 4 tennis courts, cross country skiing, tobogganing, hiking trails, exercise room, horseshoes, shuffleboard, volleyball. *Fee:* massage. **Guest Services:** complimentary evening beverages, area transportation. **Business Services:** meeting rooms. **Cards:** DC, DS, MC, VI.

SOME UNITS

(ASK) [TI] [≈] [✕] [✕] [VCR] [DATA PORT] / [AC] [📷] [💻] /

---

**STOWE MOTEL**     *Book at aaa.com*

Motel

| | | | |
|---|---|---|---|
| 9/30-10/16 | 1P: $120-$130 | 2P: $120-$130 | XP: $10   F6 |
| 6/18-9/29 | 1P: $89-$99 | 2P: $99-$110 | XP: $10   F6 |
| 10/17-4/30 | 1P: $70-$99 | 2P: $78-$110 | XP: $10   F6 |
| 5/1-6/17 | 1P: $70-$78 | 2P: $76-$84 | XP: $10   F6 |

Phone: (802)253-7629

**Location:** Jct SR 100, 2.1 mi w on SR 108. 2043 Mountain Rd 05672. Fax: 802/253-9971. **Facility:** Smoke free premises. 21 units. 12 one-bedroom standard units with efficiencies. 4 two-bedroom suites ($140-$300) with kitchens. 5 vacation homes ($180-$900), some with whirlpools. 1-2 stories, exterior corridors. *Bath:* combo or shower only. **Parking:** on-site, winter plug-ins. **Terms:** check-in 4 pm, 2 night minimum stay - seasonal weekends, 15 day cancellation notice, package plans. **Amenities:** irons, hair dryers. *Some:* voice mail. **Pool(s):** heated outdoor. **Leisure Activities:** whirlpool, tennis court, bicycles. *Fee:* game room. **Business Services:** PC. **Cards:** AX, DS, MC, VI. *(See color ad below)*

SOME UNITS

[TI] [≈] [✕] [✕] [DATA PORT] [📷] [💻] / [VCR] [📷] /

## SUN & SKI INN AND SUITES   *Book at aaa.com*

**Phone:** (802)253-7159

AAA [SAVE]

| | | | |
|---|---|---|---|
| 6/18-10/11 [ECP] | 1P: $85-$106 | 2P: $93-$116 | XP: $20  F12 |
| 12/17-4/30 [ECP] | 1P: $65-$102 | 2P: $75-$112 | XP: $20  F12 |
| 5/1-6/17 & 10/12-12/16 [ECP] | 1P: $63-$82 | 2P: $73-$92 | XP: $20  F12 |

Motel

**Location:** SR 108, 1.7 mi w of jct SR 100. 1613 Mountain Rd 05672 (990 Mountain Rd). **Fax:** 802/253-7150. **Facility:** 25 one-bedroom standard units, some with kitchens. 1 story, exterior corridors. *Bath:* combo or shower only. **Parking:** on-site, winter plug-ins. **Terms:** 2 night minimum stay - some weekends, 15 day cancellation notice-fee imposed, 5% service charge. **Pool(s):** heated outdoor. **Leisure Activities:** sauna, fishing, grill, picnic tables, bicycles. **Fee:** 19-hole miniature golf putting course. **Guest Services:** complimentary evening beverages. **Cards:** AX, DS, MC, VI. **Special Amenities:** free expanded continental breakfast and early check-in/late check-out. *(See color ad p 479)*

SOME UNITS

[S⊘] [▮¹⁺] [⇌] [⊠] [🔒] [▭] / [⊠] /

## TEN ACRES LODGE

**Phone:** 802/253-7638

| | | | |
|---|---|---|---|
| All Year [BP] | 1P: $149-$550 | 2P: $149-$600 | XP: $50 |

Country Inn

**Location:** Jct SR 100, 2.1 mi w on SR 108, then 0.5 mi s on Luce Hill Rd. 14 Barrows Rd 05672. **Fax:** 802/253-6589. **Facility:** In addition to inn rooms, this restored 1830 farmhouse offers detached cottages, all tastefully furnished with contemporary and antique furnishings. Smoke free premises. 18 units. 16 one-bedroom standard units. 2 cottages ($450-$600). 1-2 stories (no elevator), interior/exterior corridors. **Parking:** on-site, winter plug-ins. **Terms:** 30 day cancellation notice-fee imposed, pets ($50 fee, in cottages). **Amenities:** video library, hair dryers. *Some:* CD players, irons. **Pool(s):** heated outdoor. **Leisure Activities:** lighted tennis court, cross country skiing, bicycles, basketball. **Guest Services:** complimentary evening beverages. **Cards:** AX, DS, MC, VI.

SOME UNITS

[A$K] [S⊘] [🐾] [▮¹] [▾] [⇌] [⊠] [⊠] [🎥] / [VCR] [🔒] [▭] [▭] /
FEE

## TOPNOTCH AT STOWE RESORT & SPA   *Book at aaa.com*

**Phone:** (802)253-8585

AAA [SAVE]

| | | | |
|---|---|---|---|
| 6/20-10/19 & 12/20-4/30 | 1P: $235-$355 | 2P: $235-$355 | XP: $45  F12 |
| 5/1-6/19 & 10/20-12/19 | 1P: $175-$290 | 2P: $175-$290 | XP: $45  F12 |

Resort
Large-scale Hotel

**Location:** 4.2 mi w on SR 108, from jct SR 100. 4000 Mountain Rd 05672. **Fax:** 802/253-9263. **Facility:** Aside from the main hotel, this property also offers lovely townhouses; the resort offers extensive recreational and spa facilities. 121 units. 77 one-bedroom standard units. 6 one- and 7 two-bedroom suites ($325-$850), some with efficiencies. 31 vacation homes ($510-$1200), some with whirlpools. 3 stories, interior/exterior corridors. **Parking:** on-site, winter plug-ins. **Terms:** check-in 3:30 pm, 2-3 night minimum stay - weekends, 14 day cancellation notice-fee imposed, [AP], [BP], [CP] & [MAP] meal plans available, package plans - seasonal weekends, small pets only. **Amenities:** video games, high-speed Internet, voice mail, safes, irons, hair dryers. *Some:* DVD players, CD players. **Dining:** 2 restaurants, 7 am-10 pm, also, Maxwell's at Topnotch, see separate listing. **Pool(s):** heated outdoor, heated indoor. **Leisure Activities:** saunas, whirlpools, steamrooms, cross country skiing, ski center, instruction, sleigh rides, snowshoeing, rental bicycles, hiking trails, jogging. **Fee:** 14 tennis courts (4 indoor, 4 lighted), tennis instruction, in-line skates, horseback riding, massage, game room. **Guest Services:** gift shop, complimentary evening beverages, valet laundry, airport transportation (fee)-Burlington International Airport, area transportation-ski slopes. **Business Services:** conference facilities, business center. **Cards:** AX, DC, DS, MC, VI. **Special Amenities:** free local telephone calls and free newspaper.

SOME UNITS

[⊞] [🐾] [▮¹] [▾] [♠] [⇌] [♨] [⊠] [VCR] [🎥] [DATA PORT] [🔒] [▭] / [⊠] [▭] /
FEE

## TOWN & COUNTRY RESORT MOTOR INN

**Book at aaa.com**

[AAA] [SAVE]

| | | | Phone: (802)253-7595 |
|---|---|---|---|
| 12/10-4/30 [BP] | 1P: $80-$140 | 2P: $93-$155 | XP: $19 — D13 |
| 6/11-10/23 [BP] | 1P: $82-$140 | 2P: $91-$155 | XP: $18 — D13 |
| 10/24-12/9 | 1P: $59-$84 | 2P: $66-$94 | XP: $12 — D13 |
| 5/1-6/10 | 1P: $57-$82 | 2P: $65-$94 | XP: $12 — D13 |

Motel

**Location:** 0.9 mi w on SR 108, from jct SR 100. 876 Mountain Rd 05672 (PO Box 1497). Fax: 802/253-4764. **Facility:** Smoke free premises. 46 units. 45 one-bedroom standard units. 1 vacation home. 1-2 stories (no elevator), exterior corridors. *Bath:* combo or shower only. **Parking:** on-site, winter plug-ins. **Terms:** 2 night minimum stay - weekends in season, 7 day cancellation notice, in summer, 14 day in winter-fee imposed, [MAP] meal plan available, package plans - seasonal. **Amenities:** hair dryers. **Dining:** 7:30 am-9:30 & 5:30-9 pm; hours vary in season, cocktails. **Pool(s):** outdoor, heated indoor, wading. **Leisure Activities:** sauna, whirlpool, fishing, tennis court, barbecue grill, picnic table, jogging, volleyball. **Business Services:** meeting rooms. **Cards:** AX, CB, DC, DS, MC, VI.

SOME UNITS

## TRAPP FAMILY LODGE

**Book at aaa.com**

| | | | Phone: (802)253-8511 |
|---|---|---|---|
| 12/23-4/30 | 1P: $200-$505 | 2P: $200-$505 | XP: $25 — F12 |
| 9/24-10/16 | 1P: $270 | 2P: $270 | XP: $25 — F12 |
| 5/1-9/23 | 1P: $198-$260 | 2P: $198-$260 | XP: $25 — F12 |
| 10/17-12/22 | 1P: $198 | 2P: $198 | XP: $25 — F12 |

Large-scale Hotel

**Location:** Jct SR 100, 2.1 mi w on SR 108, 1.4 mi s on Luce Hill Rd, follow signs. 700 Trapp Hill Rd 05672 (PO Box 1428). Fax: 802/253-5740. **Facility:** Smoke free premises. 96 units. 88 one-bedroom standard units, some with whirlpools. 7 one- and 1 two-bedroom suites ($278-$830), some with efficiencies and/or whirlpools. 2-4 stories, interior/exterior corridors. **Parking:** on-site, winter plug-ins. **Terms:** 14 day cancellation notice-fee imposed, [BP] & [MAP] meal plans available, package plans - seasonal, $5 service charge. **Amenities:** voice mail, hair dryers. *Some:* CD players, high-speed Internet, dual phone lines, irons. **Pool(s):** 2 heated outdoor, heated indoor. **Leisure Activities:** sauna, 4 tennis courts, cross country skiing, ice skating, recreation programs, hiking trails, playground, exercise room, volleyball. *Fee:* massage. **Guest Services:** gift shop, valet and coin laundry. **Business Services:** conference facilities, business center. **Cards:** AX, DC, DS, MC, VI.

SOME UNITS

---

*The following lodging was either not evaluated or did not meet AAA rating requirements but is listed for your information only.*

## THE VILLAGE GREEN AT STOWE

[fyi]

Phone: 802/253-9705

Not evaluated. **Location:** 1003 Cape Cod Rd 05672. Facilities, services, and decor characterize a mid-range property.

---

## ─── WHERE TO DINE ───

## THE CACTUS CAFE

**Dinner:** $9-$17    Phone: 802/253-7770

Mexican

**Location:** I-89, exit 10, jct SR 100, 2.1 mi w on SR 108. 2160 Mountain Rd 05672. **Hours:** 5 pm-10 pm. Closed: 11/25, 12/25. **Reservations:** suggested. **Features:** Featuring traditional Mexican entrees and appetizers with a Vermont flair, such as buffalo-style wings served with a Vermont-produced, spicy, honey sauce. Casual dress; cocktails. **Parking:** on-site. **Cards:** MC, VI.

## THE CHELSEA GRILL

**Dinner:** $16-$28    Phone: 802/253-3075

American

**Location:** Jct SR 108/100, 3.5 mi w on SR 108. 18 Edson Hill Rd 05672. **Hours:** 5:30 pm-9:30 pm. Closed: 11/25, 12/25. **Reservations:** suggested. **Features:** The restaurant has an interesting modern atmosphere and serves up creative dishes using fresh ingredients. Casual dress; cocktails. **Parking:** on-site. **Cards:** AX, DS, MC, VI.

## DEPOT STREET MALT SHOP

**Lunch:** $4-$7    **Dinner:** $4-$7    Phone: 802/253-4269

American

**Location:** Center. 57 Depot St 05672. **Hours:** 11:30 am-8 pm, Fri-Sun to 9 pm. Closed: 3/27, 11/25, 12/25. **Features:** The coordinated 1950s malt shop offers casual service and mostly fried or grilled menu items. Casual dress. **Parking:** street.

## EDSON HILL MANOR DINING ROOM

**Dinner:** $17-$23    Phone: 802/253-7371

American California cuisine.

**Location:** 3.5 mi w on SR 108 from jct SR 100, then 1.3 mi n; in Edson Hill Manor. 1500 Edson Hill Rd 05672. **Hours:** 6 pm-9 pm. Closed: Mon-Thurs 11/1-12/15 & 4/1-5/31. **Reservations:** suggested. **Features:** In the resort area of Sugarbush Mountain, the intimate Vermont country estate offers a pleasant respite tucked away on a hilltop with lovely views. Innovative meat and seafood dishes are influenced by flavorful California cuisine. The wine list includes a nice selection. Casual dress; cocktails. **Parking:** on-site. **Cards:** DS, MC, VI.

## EMILY'S

**Dinner:** $18-$28    Phone: 802/253-9722

American glace.

**Location:** 3.4 mi w on SR 108, from jct SR 100, then 0.5 mi n; in Stowehof Inn. 434 Edson Hill Rd 05672. **Hours:** 8 am-10 & 5:30-9:30 pm. Closed: Sun-Thurs 4/1-11/30. **Reservations:** suggested. **Features:** The dining room offers beautiful views and exceptionally prepared dishes; such as a western rack of lamb, Muscovy breast of duck, and their house specialty, Steak Diane, prepared with brandy and a Morel mushroom demi glace. Dressy casual; cocktails. **Parking:** on-site. **Cards:** DC, DS, MC, VI.

## FOXFIRE INN

**Country Inn**    **Dinner:** $11-$20    Phone: 802/253-4887

Italian

**Location:** Jct SR 108, 1.6 mi n on SR 100. 1606 Pucker St 05672. **Hours:** 5:30 pm-9:30 pm. Closed: 11/25. **Reservations:** suggested. **Features:** In a circa 1850s country farmhouse, the restaurant specializes in Northern and Southern Italian cuisine. On the menu are excellent steak, veal, chicken, seafood and pasta dishes. Casual dress; cocktails. **Parking:** on-site. **Cards:** AX, DS, MC, VI.

## GRACIE'S RESTAURANT

**Lunch:** $6-$12   **Dinner:** $6-$19   **Phone:** 802/253-8741

*American*

**Location:** Jct SR 108, just n on SR 100. 20 Main St 05672. **Hours:** 11:30 am-11 pm. Closed: 11/25, 12/25. **Features:** Cozy neighborhood bar and restaurant decorated with dozens of framed photos of dogs. Located on sub-level with fine gift shop upstairs. Specialties include prime rib (Friday and Saturday evenings), wide selection of burgers, steak and seafood. Fresh baked bread. Locally brewed beer on tap. Casual dress; cocktails. **Parking:** on-site. **Cards:** AX, DS, MC, VI.

## GRILL 108

**Dinner:** $9-$30   **Phone:** 802/253-5276

*Steak House*

**Location:** On SR 108, 2 mi w of jct SR 100. 1899 Mountain Rd 05672. **Hours:** 5 pm-10 pm. Closed: 11/25, 12/24, 12/25. **Reservations:** suggested. **Features:** In a busy resort area, the casual eatery specializes in steaks and creative appetizers, such as crawfish cakes, ginger-marinated duck drumettes, whole-wheat crepes and Vermont cheddar cheese puffs. Casual dress; cocktails. **Parking:** on-site. **Cards:** AX, DC, DS, MC, VI.

## MAXWELL'S AT TOPNOTCH

**Dinner:** $17-$39   **Phone:** 802/253-8585

*American*

**Location:** 4.2 mi w on SR 108, from jct SR 100; in Topnotch at Stowe Resort & Spa. 4000 Mountain Rd 05672. **Hours:** 7 am-11 & 6-10 pm. **Reservations:** suggested. **Features:** The spectacular mountain view alone is worth the visit to the restaurant's dining room. Guests can enjoy the scenery while dining on American cuisine prepared with classical, regional and seasonal influences. Among offerings are prime aged meat, fresh seafood and local game and produce. Dressy casual; cocktails. **Parking:** on-site. **Cards:** AX, DC, DS, MC, VI.

## MES AMIS RESTAURANT-BISTROT

**Dinner:** $17-$20   **Phone:** 802/253-8669

*French*

**Location:** On SR 108. 311 Mountain Rd 05672. **Hours:** 5:30 pm-10 pm. Closed: Mon. **Features:** The chef/owner of this fine-dining restaurant prepares an excellent cuisine that displays her ten years of experience in French cooking. The creative menu features Vermont influences in the swordfish au poivre, filet mignon, poached salmon, roasted duck. Casual dress; cocktails. **Parking:** on-site. **Cards:** DS, MC, VI.

## MR. PICKWICK'S

**Lunch:** $7-$13   **Dinner:** $18-$28   **Phone:** 802/253-7558

*American*

**Location:** 0.4 mi w on SR 108, from jct SR 100; in 1066 Ye Olde England Inne. 433 Mountain Rd 05672. **Hours:** 11:30 am-10 pm. **Reservations:** suggested. **Features:** Patrons shouldn't let the casual, pub atmosphere fool them. The British brew pub specializes in the preparation of Old English specialty dishes, as well as interesting, creative wild game selections. The impressive "connoisseur's collection" includes an extensive selection of fine, rare ales, wines, cordials, vintage ports and single malts. Casual dress; cocktails. **Parking:** on-site. **Cards:** AX, DS, MC, VI.

## THE OLD VIENNA TEA ROOM

**Lunch:** $12-$18   **Dinner:** $19-$28   **Phone:** 802/253-9500

*Austrian*

**Location:** Jct SR 100/108, 2.1 mi n on SR 108. 2038 Mountain Rd 05672. **Hours:** 11:30 am-3 & 6-9 pm. Closed: 11/25, 12/25. **Reservations:** suggested. **Features:** The restaurant offers patrons delightful, creative dishes served up in a refined, Austrian themed atmosphere. The staff offers personable and friendly service and dessert is a must, so save room. Dressy casual. **Parking:** on-site. **Cards:** AX, MC, VI.

## OLIVE'S BISTRO

**Dinner:** $11-$18   **Phone:** 802/253-2033

*Mediterranean*

**Location:** Jct SR 100, 1.2 mi w on SR 108. 1056 Mountain Rd 05672. **Hours:** 5 pm-9 pm; hours vary seasonally. Closed: 11/25, 12/24, 12/25; also Sun. **Reservations:** suggested. **Features:** The restaurant offers good food and casual, pleasant service; patrons almost feel as though they are in a garden with all the live plants. Casual dress; cocktails. **Parking:** on-site. **Cards:** AX, MC, VI.

## PARTRIDGE INN

**Dinner:** $15-$20   **Phone:** 802/253-8000

*Steak & Seafood*

**Location:** On SR 108; 0.5 mi nw of jct SR 100. 504 Mountain Rd 05672. **Hours:** 5:30 pm-9:30 pm. Closed: 4/15-4/30 & 11/5-11/24. **Reservations:** suggested. **Features:** Located in an old farmhouse with a comfortable country inn atmosphere, this restaurant offers a good selection of market fresh seafood. Also featured are steak and some pasta. The service provided is casual, yet knowledgeable and friendly. This popular restaurant can be busy at peak times. Casual dress; cocktails. **Parking:** on-site. **Cards:** AX, DC, MC, VI.

## RED BASIL THAI SUSHI & MARTINI BAR

**Dinner:** $13-$20   **Phone:** 802/253-4478

*Thai*

**Location:** Jct SR 100/108, 0.5 mi n on SR 108. 294 Mountain Rd 05672. **Hours:** 11:30 am-3 & 4:30-10 pm, Fri-11 pm, Sat 2 pm-11 pm, Sun 2 pm-10 pm. **Reservations:** suggested. **Features:** Trendy interior design with unique lighting lends the feel of being in a NYC jazz cafe; patrons will enjoy good food and casual service. Casual dress; cocktails. **Parking:** on-site. **Cards:** MC, VI.

## RESTAURANT SWISSPOT

**Lunch:** $3-$10   **Dinner:** $11-$17   **Phone:** 802/253-4622

*Swiss*

**Location:** Jct SR 108, just n on SR 100; center; opposite community church. 128 Main St 05672. **Hours:** Open 6/25-10/15 & 12/15-4/1; 4 pm-10 pm, Sat & Sun from 11:30 am; from 11:30 am on holidays. **Features:** Originally a showpiece of the Swiss government at the Montreal World Expo, the restaurant showcases Swiss cuisine. Among offerings are many imported cheeses, chocolates and other specialties. Favorites include beef fondue cooked tableside and hand-rolled quiche pies baked to order. Casual dress; cocktails. **Parking:** on-site. **Cards:** AX, DC, DS, MC, VI.

## THE SHED RESTAURANT & BREWERY

**Lunch:** $7-$11   **Dinner:** $10-$20   **Phone:** 802/253-4364

*American*

**Location:** I-89, exit 10, jct SR 100, 4 mi w on SR 108. 1859 Mountain Rd 05672. **Hours:** 11:30 am-10 pm. Closed: 11/25. **Reservations:** suggested. **Features:** Open for both lunch and dinner, this casual eatery, famous for its signature burger, "The Shed Burger," serves a traditional, pub menu, as well as popular, American fare. Casual dress; cocktails. **Parking:** on-site. **Cards:** AX, CB, DC, DS, MC, VI.

**SUNSET GRILL & TAP ROOM**
American
**Lunch:** $5-$8    **Dinner:** $10-$15    **Phone:** 802/253-9281
**Location:** 2.2 mi n of jct SR 100/108, then just e. 140 Cottage Club Rd 05672. **Hours:** 11:30 am-4 & 4:30-10 pm. **Closed:** 3/27, 11/25, 12/25. **Reservations:** accepted. **Features:** The restaurant offers simple foods and laid-back service in a sports bar atmosphere. Casual dress; cocktails. **Parking:** on-site. **Cards:** DS, MC, VI.

**TEN ACRES LODGE DINING ROOM**   Country Inn
American
**Dinner:** $20-$36    **Phone:** 802/253-7638
**Location:** Jct SR 100, 2.1 mi nw on SR 108, 0.5 mi w on Luce Hill Rd; in Ten Acres Lodge. 14 Barrows Rd 05672. **Hours:** 6 pm-9 pm. **Closed:** Tues & Wed. **Reservations:** suggested. **Features:** The Ten Acres serves an innovative American cuisine offering fine preparation and presentation methods, creative and flavorful dishes and a wonderful wine list. The candlelit dining room creates an intimate atmosphere. The service is friendly and good. Dressy casual; cocktails. **Parking:** on-site. **Cards:** AX, DS, MC, VI.

**THE WHIP BAR & GRILL**
Regional American
**Lunch:** $6-$13    **Dinner:** $8-$21    **Phone:** 802/253-7301
**Location:** Jct SR 108 on SR 100; center; in Green Mountain Inn. 18 S Main St 05672. **Hours:** 11:30 am-9:30 pm, Fri & Sat-10 pm. **Reservations:** accepted, for guests only. **Features:** The warm, inviting dining room displays plenty of wood and brass, as well as an interesting collection of old buggy whips. On the varied menu are fresh seafood, hand-cut steaks, vegetarian dishes, daily specials, homemade desserts and bread and a good selection of wines. The patio is a nice dining spot in warm weather. Casual dress; cocktails. **Parking:** on-site. **Cards:** AX, DS, MC, VI. *(See color ad p 474)*

**WINFIELD'S BISTRO**
Nouvelle American
**Dinner:** $17-$29    **Phone:** 802/253-7355
**Location:** Jct SR 100, 1.5 mi w on SR 108; in Stoweflake Mountain Resort & Spa. 1746 Mountain Rd 05672. **Hours:** 6 pm-9:30 pm. **Reservations:** suggested. **Features:** This bistro offers casual, elegant surroundings and professional, unpretentious service. The menu evolves with the seasons and takes advantage of local Vermont produce. Nightly chef tasting menus list such intriguing entrees as peppered scallops with saffron potato, baby leeks and beurre rouge and five-spice duck breast with sweet-potato puree, plantains and Tasmanian honey glaze. Dressy casual; cocktails. **Parking:** on-site. **Cards:** AX, DC, DS, MC, VI.

# STRATTON pop. 136

## ──── WHERE TO DINE ────

**MULLIGAN'S TAVERN**
American
**Lunch:** $9-$15    **Dinner:** $9-$25    **Phone:** 802/297-9293
**Location:** In The Village Square at Stratton Mountain. Stratton Mountain Rd 05155. **Hours:** 11:30 am-10 pm, Fri & Sat-11 pm, Sun-9 pm. **Closed:** 11/25, 12/25. **Features:** The eatery offers steaks, chicken, seafood, burgers and a variety of appetizers in a sports pub atmosphere. Casual dress; cocktails. **Parking:** on-site. **Cards:** AX, MC, VI.

**VERDE MEDITERRANEAN GRILLE**
Mediterranean
**Dinner:** $22-$34    **Phone:** 802/297-9200
**Location:** In The Village Square at Stratton Mountain. 19 Village Lodge Rd 05155. **Hours:** Open 6/1-4/15; 7 am-11 & 5:30-9 pm; hours may vary seasonally. **Closed:** Tues. **Reservations:** suggested. **Features:** The eatery features wonderfully creative and delicious Mediterranean dishes served up in a sophisticated atmosphere. Casual dress; cocktails. **Parking:** on-site. **Cards:** AX, DC, DS, MC, VI.

# STRATTON MOUNTAIN

## ──── WHERE TO STAY ────

**STRATTON MOUNTAIN INN**   *Book at aaa.com*
Resort
Large-scale Hotel

**Phone:** (802)297-2500

| |  |  |  | |
|---|---|---|---|---|
| 11/16-4/30 | 1P: $229-$289 | 2P: $229-$289 | XP: $20 | F17 |
| 5/1-11/15 | 1P: $69-$99 | 2P: $69-$99 | XP: $20 | F17 |

**Location:** Jct SR 30, 4 mi s on Stratton Mountain Rd, then just e. 61 Middle Ridge Rd 05155. Fax: 802/297-3539. **Facility:** This manageable-sized resort is located at the base of Stratton Mountain in a European-style village. 121 one-bedroom standard units. 3 stories (no elevator), interior corridors. **Parking:** on-site, winter plug-ins. **Terms:** check-in 4 pm, 2 night minimum stay - weekends in winter, 14 day cancellation notice-fee imposed, package plans, pets ($50 deposit). **Amenities:** voice mail, safes, hair dryers. **Pool(s):** heated outdoor. **Leisure Activities:** sauna, whirlpool, tennis court, ice skating, hiking trails, jogging, exercise room, basketball, horseshoes, shuffleboard, volleyball. **Fee:** golf-27 holes, downhill & cross country skiing, game room. **Guest Services:** area transportation. **Business Services:** meeting rooms. **Cards:** AX, CB, DC, DS, MC, VI.

SOME UNITS

# SWANTON pop. 2,548

## ──── WHERE TO STAY ────

**SWANTON MOTEL**
Motel
**All Year**    1P: $50-$89    2P: $59-$99    XP: $10    F14
**Phone:** (802)868-4284
**Location:** I-89, exit 21, 1 mi w on SR 78, then 0.5 mi s on US 7. 112 Grand Ave 05488. Fax: 802/868-3155. **Facility:** 12 units. 11 one- and 1 two-bedroom standard units. 1 story, exterior corridors. *Bath:* combo or shower only. **Parking:** on-site, winter plug-ins. **Terms:** cancellation fee imposed, package plans. **Pool(s):** outdoor. **Cards:** AX, DC, DS, MC, VI. **Special Amenities:** free local telephone calls and preferred room (subject to availability with advanced reservations).

SOME UNITS

## ———— WHERE TO DINE ————

———— *The following restaurant has not been evaluated by AAA* ————
*but is listed for your information only.*

**LAVENDER MOON**
[fyi]
**Phone:** 802/868-5700
Not evaluated. **Location:** 7 Merchants Row 05488. **Features:** Open only for dinner, this American grill is popular with the locals.

# VERGENNES pop. 2,741

## ———— WHERE TO STAY ————

**STRONG HOUSE INN**   *Book at aaa.com*
AAA [SAVE]
▼▼▼▼
Historic
Country Inn
**Phone:** (802)877-3337
9/16-10/31 [BP]          1P: $125-$305        2P: $125-$305      XP: $30
5/1-9/15 & 11/1-4/30 [BP]  1P: $95-$275        2P: $95-$275       XP: $30
**Location:** 0.3 mi s on SR 22 A. 94 W Main St 05491. Fax: 802/877-2599. **Facility:** The lovely 1834 country inn and newer Rabbit Ridge Country House with seven working fireplaces are set on six acres of beautifully maintained grounds. Smoke free premises. 13 units. 12 one-bedroom standard units, some with whirlpools. 1 one-bedroom suite. 2 stories (no elevator), interior corridors. *Bath:* combo or shower only. **Parking:** on-site. **Terms:** 2 night minimum stay - some weekends, age restrictions may apply, 14 day cancellation notice-fee imposed. **Amenities:** video library, voice mail, hair dryers. *Some:* CD players, irons. **Dining:** 6:30 pm seating; reservations required; call for dates opened, cocktails. **Leisure Activities:** ice skating, snowshoeing, sledding, hiking trails, game room. *Fee:* massage. **Guest Services:** gift shop, complimentary evening beverages, valet laundry. **Business Services:** meeting rooms. **Cards:** AX, DC, MC, VI. **Special Amenities:** free full breakfast and free local telephone calls.   SOME UNITS

[⊞] [🍷] [👤M] [⊠] [✕] [📷] [DATA PORT] / [VCR] [🔌] [▣] /

# WAITSFIELD

## ———— WHERE TO STAY ————

**1824 HOUSE INN**
▼▼▼
Historic Bed
& Breakfast
**Phone:** (802)496-7555
All Year [BP]                    2P: $99-$148        XP: $35
**Location:** 2 mi n on SR 100; center. 2150 Main St 05673. Fax: 802/496-7559. **Facility:** This restored 1824 farmhouse is on 15 wooded acres next to the Mad River. Smoke free premises. 8 one-bedroom standard units. 2 stories (no elevator), interior corridors. *Bath:* combo or shower only. **Parking:** on-site. **Terms:** office hours 8 am-10 pm, check-in 4 pm, 2 night minimum stay - weekends, age restrictions may apply, 30 day cancellation notice-fee imposed, package plans, no pets allowed (owner's dogs on premises). **Amenities:** video library, hair dryers. **Leisure Activities:** whirlpool, fishing, tobogganing. **Business Services:** fax (fee). **Cards:** AX, MC, VI.

[ASK] [S🔌] [⊠] [✕] [🄺] [🄿] [ℤ]

**THE INN AT ROUND BARN FARM**   *Book at aaa.com*
▼▼▼
Historic Bed
& Breakfast
**Phone:** (802)496-2276
5/1-11/12 & 12/3-4/15 [BP]        2P: $140-$280      XP: $25
**Location:** Jct SR 100, 1.8 mi e on E Warren Rd, over covered bridge. Located in a quiet, rural area. 1661 E Warren Rd 05673. **Facility:** Set on 245 acres, this lovely inn functioned as a dairy farm up until 1969; rooms are elegant with a mix of contemporary and antique furnishings. Smoke free premises. 12 units. 11 one-bedroom standard units, some with whirlpools. 1 one-bedroom suite with whirlpool. 2-3 stories (no elevator), interior corridors. *Bath:* combo or shower only. **Parking:** on-site. **Terms:** open 5/1-11/12 & 12/3-4/15, 2 night minimum stay - weekends, age restrictions may apply, 21 day cancellation notice-fee imposed, package plans - in winter, 4% service charge. **Amenities:** hair dryers. *Some:* CD players. **Leisure Activities:** cross country skiing, tobogganing, hiking trails, exercise room. **Guest Services:** gift shop. **Business Services:** meeting rooms. **Cards:** AX, DS, MC, VI.   SOME UNITS

[⊠] [✕] / [🄺] [🄿] [ℤ] /

**TUCKER HILL INN**   *Book at aaa.com*
AAA [SAVE]
▼▼▼
Country Inn
**Phone:** (802)496-3983
All Year [ECP]              1P: $79-$199        2P: $79-$199
**Location:** On SR 17, 1.5 mi w of SR 100. 65 Marble Hill Rd 05673 (PO Box 707). **Facility:** Landscaped lawns bordered by woods accent this renovated Colonial inn offering attractively decorated guest rooms of varying sizes. 18 units. 16 one-bedroom standard units, some with whirlpools. 2 one-bedroom suites. 3 stories (no elevator), interior/exterior corridors. *Bath:* combo or shower only. **Parking:** on-site. **Terms:** 14 day cancellation notice-fee imposed. **Amenities:** video library. *Some:* hair dryers. **Dining:** The Steak Place at Tucker Hill, see separate listing. **Pool(s):** outdoor. **Leisure Activities:** 2 tennis courts, hiking trails. **Business Services:** meeting rooms. **Cards:** AX, MC, VI. **Special Amenities:** free expanded continental breakfast and free local telephone calls.   SOME UNITS

[S🔌] [⊞] [🏊] [✕] [VCR] [DATA PORT] / [🄺] /

## ———— WHERE TO DINE ————

**THE DEN**
▼▼
Steak & Seafood
**Lunch:** $3-$9          **Dinner:** $3-$16        **Phone:** 802/496-8800
**Location:** Jct SR 100/17. 5351 Main St 05673. **Hours:** 11:30 am-10 pm, Fri & Sat-11 pm. Closed: 11/25, 12/25. **Features:** The cute, coordinated pub theme features various antique bric-a-brac and old black and white train photographs. The restaurant offers friendly, casual service and tasty food; definitely try the creamy garlic soup. Casual dress; cocktails. **Parking:** on-site. **Cards:** MC, VI.

[✕]

**JAY'S RESTAURANT**
▼▼▼
American
**Lunch:** $4-$7          **Dinner:** $5-$15        **Phone:** 802/496-8282
**Location:** SR 100, 0.8 mi s of center; in Mad River Green Shopping Center. 114 Rt 100 05673. **Hours:** 8 am-10 pm. **Features:** Jay's is a family restaurant with a lounge area separated from the main room. Meals are very satisfying. The menu offers Italian dishes, steak, chicken, chops, pizza and dessert such as the chocolate cappuccino pie. Casual dress; cocktails. **Parking:** on-site. **Cards:** DS, MC, VI.

[🍷] [✕]

**THE SPOTTED COW**
Continental

**Lunch:** $6-$14    **Dinner:** $9-$26    **Phone:** 802/496-5151
**Location:** In Bridge Street Marketplace. Bridge St 05673. **Hours:** 11:30 am-3 & 5:30-9 pm. Closed: 11/25, 12/25; also Mon. **Reservations:** suggested. **Features:** The restaurant is a local favorite, offering creative dishes and a comfortable atmosphere with a light piano jazz background; be sure to try the Bermuda fish chowder. Dressy casual; cocktails. **Parking:** street. **Cards:** MC, VI.

**THE STEAK PLACE AT TUCKER HILL**   Country Inn
Steak & Seafood

**Dinner:** $13-$33    **Phone:** 802/496-3025
**Location:** SR 17, 1.5 mi w of SR 100; in Tucker Hill Inn. 65 Marble Hill Rd 05673. **Hours:** Open 6/16-3/31; 5:30 pm-9:30 pm. Closed: 12/25; also Tues-Thurs. **Reservations:** suggested. **Features:** This restaurant's specialty is tasty smoked baby back ribs. They're wonderful! Also offered are certified Angus beef steaks and prime rib, chicken, pork, seafood and pasta specials. The warm and inviting room is freshly renovated with a lovely fireplace. Casual dress; cocktails. **Parking:** on-site. **Cards:** AX, MC, VI.

# WALLINGFORD pop. 948

## ——— WHERE TO STAY ———

**I B MUNSON HOUSE BED & BREAKFAST INN**
Historic Bed & Breakfast

**Phone:** 802/446-2860
All Year    1P: $120-$215    2P: $120-$215    XP: $35
**Location:** On SR 7; center. 37 S Main St 05773 (PO Box 427). **Facility:** Centered in a historic village, this B&B is a classic 19th-century mansion with a Victorian ambience. Smoke free premises. 7 one-bedroom standard units. 2 stories (no elevator), interior corridors. *Bath:* combo or shower only. **Parking:** on-site. **Terms:** age restrictions may apply, 14 day cancellation notice-fee imposed. **Amenities:** *Some:* CD players. **Guest Services:** complimentary evening beverages. **Cards:** AX, MC, VI.

SOME UNITS

## ——— WHERE TO DINE ———

**MOM'S COUNTRY KITCHEN**
American

**Lunch:** $4-$6    **Phone:** 802/446-2606
**Location:** Center. 5 N Main St 05773. **Hours:** 6:30 am-2 pm, Tues-11 am, Sun 7 am-1 pm; hours may vary. Closed major holidays; also Mon 3/1-4/7. **Features:** Located in a circa-1824 historic house (the first house in town with electricity), the restaurant offers mostly short-order items and the service is casual but friendly. Casual dress. **Parking:** on-site.

**SAL'S SOUTH**
Italian

**Lunch:** $5-$17    **Dinner:** $7-$20    **Phone:** 802/446-2935
**Location:** Jct of SR 140/US 7; center. 15 S Main St 05773. **Hours:** 11:30 am-9 pm, Fri & Sat-9:30 pm, Sun 3 pm-9 pm. Closed: 3/27, 11/25, 12/25; also Mon. **Reservations:** accepted. **Features:** Coordinated Italian theme with Frank Sinatra playing in the background. Very casual atmosphere, friendly service. Casual dress; beer & wine only. **Parking:** street. **Cards:** MC, VI.

# WARDSBORO

## ——— WHERE TO DINE ———

**CINDY'S A LITTLE EATING PLACE & BAKERY**
American

**Lunch:** $3-$7    **Phone:** 802/896-9464
**Location:** Center. Rt 100 05355. **Hours:** 6 am-2 pm, Sun from 7 am; hours vary in winter. Closed: 12/25; also Thurs. **Features:** Off the beaten path in a charming New England village, the terrific little bakery/delicatessen is worth the trip. Among its breakfast and lunch offerings are aromatic homemade bread and baked goods, sandwiches and soups. Credit cards are not accepted. Casual dress. **Parking:** on-site.

# WARREN

## ——— WHERE TO STAY ———

**THE BRIDGES FAMILY RESORT & TENNIS CLUB**
Resort Condominium

**Phone:** (802)583-2922
11/5-4/30    1P: $136-$615    2P: $136-$615
5/1-11/4     1P: $125-$245    2P: $125-$245
**Location:** 2.6 mi w on Sugarbush Access Rd, from jct SR 100. 202 Bridges Cir 05674. Fax: 802/583-1018. **Facility:** Fireplaces are featured in all of these condominium-style apartments; a shared base lodge is half a mile away. 64 units. 10 one-, 44 two- and 10 three-bedroom suites with kitchens. 1-3 stories (no elevator), exterior corridors. *Bath:* combo or shower only. **Parking:** on-site, winter plug-ins. **Terms:** check-in 6 pm, 2 night minimum stay - weekends, 21 day cancellation notice-fee imposed, package plans, 3% service charge. **Amenities:** video library, voice mail, irons, hair dryers. *Some:* DVD players, CD players. **Dining:** 11 am-3 pm end of June to the end of Aug; Fri & Sat 4 pm-10 pm end of Dec to end of March. **Pool(s):** 2 heated outdoor, heated indoor. **Leisure Activities:** saunas, whirlpool, 12 tennis courts (2 indoor), recreation programs in summer, playground, aerobic & aqua aerobic instruction, kick boxing, tai-chi, yoga, sports court, basketball, horseshoes, volleyball, game room. **Fee:** tennis instruction. **Guest Services:** area transportation-base lodge. **Business Services:** meeting rooms. **Cards:** AX, MC, VI. *(See color ad p 420)*

SOME UNITS

**THE PITCHER INN**
Country Inn

**Phone:** 802/496-6350
All Year    2P: $330-$600    XP: $75
**Location:** Center. 275 Main St 05674 (PO Box 347). Fax: 802/496-6354. **Facility:** Smoke free premises. 11 units. 9 one-bedroom standard units with whirlpools, some with kitchens. 2 two-bedroom suites ($660) with efficiencies and whirlpools. 3 stories, interior corridors. **Parking:** on-site. **Terms:** 2 night minimum stay - weekends, age restrictions may apply, 30 day cancellation notice-fee imposed, [BP] meal plan available. **Amenities:** video library, CD players, dual phone lines, fax, hair dryers. **Dining:** dining room, see separate listing. **Leisure Activities:** spa privileges, shuffleboard, game room. **Fee:** massage. **Guest Services:** gift shop. **Business Services:** meeting rooms. **Cards:** AX, MC, VI.

SOME UNITS

### POWDERHOUND INN & CONDOMINIUMS
**Phone: 802/496-5100**

AAA SAVE

Condominium

| | | | | |
|---|---|---|---|---|
| 12/1-3/31 | 1P: $84-$159 | 2P: $84-$129 | XP: $10 | F6 |
| 5/1-11/30 | 1P: $84-$109 | 2P: $84-$109 | XP: $10 | F6 |
| 4/1-4/30 | 1P: $84-$99 | 2P: $84-$99 | XP: $10 | F6 |

**Location:** On SR 100, 0.3 mi s of jct Sugarbush Access Rd. Located in a rural area. 203 Powderhound Rd 05674 (Box 369, 05674-0369). Fax: 802/496-5163. **Facility:** 46 units. 2 one-bedroom standard units. 44 one-bedroom suites with efficiencies. 2 stories (no elevator); exterior corridors. *Bath:* combo or shower only. **Parking:** on-site. **Terms:** 2 night minimum stay - weekends, 14 day cancellation notice-fee imposed, weekly rates available, package plans, 3% service charge, pets ($5 extra charge). **Amenities:** voice mail. **Dining:** 5:30 pm-9 pm; closed Mon-Wed, also mid-April to mid-June & mid-October to mid-December. **Pool(s):** outdoor. **Leisure Activities:** hot tub. **Cards:** AX, DS, MC, VI. **Special Amenities: free local telephone calls and early check-in/late check-out.**

SOME UNITS
[icons] FEE

### THE SUGAR LODGE  *Book at aaa.com*
**Phone: 802/583-3300**

Small-scale Hotel

| | | |
|---|---|---|
| All Year | 1P: $75-$115 | 2P: $75-$115 |

**Location:** 1.7 mi n on SR 100, 2.2 mi w. 2197 Sugarbush Access Rd 05674. Fax: 802/583-1148. **Facility:** Smoke free premises. 23 units. 22 one-bedroom standard units. 1 one-bedroom suite with efficiency. 2 stories (no elevator); interior corridors. **Parking:** on-site. **Terms:** office hours 7 am-10 pm, check-in 4 pm, 2-3 night minimum stay - weekends, 14 day cancellation notice, [ECP] meal plan available, package plans. **Pool(s):** outdoor. **Guest Services:** coin laundry, area transportation. **Cards:** AX, MC, VI.

[icons]

### THE SUGARTREE  *Book at aaa.com*
**Phone: (802)583-3211**

AAA SAVE

Bed & Breakfast

| | | | |
|---|---|---|---|
| 9/17-10/24 [BP] | 1P: $150-$195 | 2P: $150-$195 | XP: $30 |
| 12/17-4/30 [BP] | 1P: $119-$175 | 2P: $119-$195 | XP: $30 |
| 5/1-9/16 & 10/25-12/16 [BP] | 1P: $99-$150 | 2P: $119-$150 | XP: $30 |

**Location:** 1.7 mi n on SR 100, 2.5 mi w. 2440 Sugarbush Access Rd 05674. Fax: 802/583-3203. **Facility:** Half a mile from its base lodge, this inn offers a variety of individually decorated guest rooms, one with a fireplace. Smoke free premises. 9 units. 8 one-bedroom standard units. 1 two-bedroom suite. 3 stories (no elevator); interior corridors. *Bath:* combo or shower only. **Parking:** on-site, winter plug-ins. **Terms:** office hours 8 am-10 pm, age restrictions may apply, 21 day cancellation notice-fee imposed. **Amenities:** hair dryers. **Cards:** AX, DS, MC, VI. **Special Amenities: free full breakfast and free room upgrade (subject to availability with advanced reservations).**

SOME UNITS
[icons] DATA PORT

--------- **WHERE TO DINE** ---------

### CHEZ HENRI
**Lunch: $7-$15**   **Dinner: $17-$27**   **Phone: 802/583-2600**

French

**Location:** 1.4 mi n on SR 100, 3 mi w, on Sugarbush Access Rd, then just n on Village Rd to parking area, cross foot bridge; in Sugarbush Village. 80 Sugarbush Village 05674. **Hours:** Open 6/21-4/30; 11:30 am-9 pm; from 5:30 pm 6/21-11/30. **Reservations:** suggested. **Features:** This bistro restaurant features a classic cuisine including dinner and lighter fare. There's a fireplace in the dining room, and the summer terrace overlooks a small brook. The location allows you to ski in and ski out. Casual dress; cocktails. **Parking:** on-site. **Cards:** AX, MC, VI.

[icons]

### THE COMMON MAN
**Dinner: $13-$26**   **Phone: 802/583-2800**

International

**Location:** 1.7 mi n on SR 100, 1.8 mi w, then just n. 3209 German Flats Rd 05674. **Hours:** 6 pm-9 pm, Sat 5:30 pm-9:30 pm; hours may vary. Closed: 11/25, 12/25. **Reservations:** suggested. **Features:** The restaurant has a coordinated Italian theme with Frank Sinatra playing in the background; expect a very casual atmosphere and friendly service. Casual dress; cocktails. **Parking:** on-site. **Cards:** AX, DS, MC, VI.

[icon]

### THE DINING ROOM AT THE PITCHER INN
**Dinner: $22-$32**   **Phone: 802/496-6350**

International

**Location:** Center; in The Pitcher Inn. 275 Main St 05674. **Hours:** 6 pm-9:30 pm. Closed major holidays; also Tues. **Reservations:** suggested. **Features:** The restaurant features a refined, sophisticated atmosphere with a warm, inviting wood-burning fireplace, service that is gracious and attentive, and delightful and deliciously creative dishes that continually change with the market and season. Dressy casual; cocktails. **Parking:** on-site. **Cards:** AX, MC, VI.

[icons]

### THE WARREN HOUSE RESTAURANT
**Dinner: $14-$21**   **Phone: 802/583-2421**

Regional American

**Location:** Jct SR 100, 2.6 mi w. 2585 Sugarbush Access Rd 05674. **Hours:** 5:30 pm-9 pm, Fri & Sat-9:30 pm. Closed: Tues in summer. **Reservations:** suggested. **Features:** In the heart of the Sugarbush Mountain resort area, the unassuming, rustic restaurant serves excellent appetizers and superb entrees, such as Long Island duck marinated in molasses. The wine selection is terrific, as are the mouthwatering desserts. Casual dress; cocktails. **Parking:** on-site. **Cards:** AX, MC, VI.

[icons]

## WATERBURY pop. 1,706

--------- **WHERE TO STAY** ---------

### THE BEST WESTERN INN OF WATERBURY-STOWE  *Book at aaa.com*
**Phone: (802)244-7822**

AAA SAVE

Small-scale Hotel

| | | | | |
|---|---|---|---|---|
| 9/17-10/16 [ECP] | 1P: $109-$199 | 2P: $109-$199 | XP: $10 | F19 |
| 10/17-12/31 [ECP] | 1P: $59-$179 | 2P: $59-$179 | XP: $10 | F19 |
| 5/1-9/16 & 1/1-4/30 [ECP] | 1P: $69-$169 | 2P: $69-$169 | XP: $10 | F19 |

**Location:** I-89, exit 10, just nw on SR 100. 45 Blush Hill Rd 05676 (PO Box 149). Fax: 802/244-6395. **Facility:** 83 units. 79 one-bedroom standard units. 4 one-bedroom suites ($149-$399) with whirlpools. 2 stories (no elevator); interior corridors. **Parking:** on-site, winter plug-ins. **Terms:** 3 day cancellation notice. **Amenities:** voice mail, irons, hair dryers. *Some:* safes. **Dining:** 6:30 am-10:30 & 5-9 pm; closed Sun, cocktails. **Pool(s):** heated indoor. **Leisure Activities:** saunas, whirlpool, tennis court, snowmobiling, snowshoes, snowshoe trails, snowmobile trails. *Fee:* game room. **Guest Services:** valet and coin laundry. **Business Services:** meeting rooms. **Cards:** AX, CB, DC, DS, MC, VI. **Special Amenities: free expanded continental breakfast and free local telephone calls.**

SOME UNITS
[icons] FEE FEE FEE

## THE OLD STAGECOACH INN

(AAA) (SAVE)

Historic Bed & Breakfast

MC, VI.

| | | | |
|---|---|---|---|
| 9/24-4/30 [BP] | 1P: $75-$180 | 2P: $75-$180 | XP: $20 | F10 |
| 5/1-9/23 [BP] | 1P: $60-$120 | 2P: $60-$120 | XP: $10 | F10 |

**Phone:** 802/244-5056

**Location:** I-89, exit 10, 0.5 mi s on SR 100. 18 N Main St 05676. Fax: 802/244-6956. **Facility:** A former stagecoach stop, this restored property is within walking distance of restaurants and shops. Smoke free premises. 11 units. 10 one-bedroom standard units, some with kitchens. 1 two-bedroom suite with kitchen. 2-3 stories (no elevator), interior/exterior corridors. *Bath:* some shared or private, combo or shower only. **Parking:** on-site. **Terms:** 14 day cancellation notice, package plans. **Dining:** 7:30-9 am, Sat & Sun-11 am. **Cards:** AX, DS,

SOME UNITS

[symbols]

## THATCHER BROOK INN

Country Inn

All Year [BP]    1P: $80-$205    2P: $80-$205    XP: $25

**Phone:** (802)244-5911

**Location:** I-89, exit 10, 0.5 mi n on SR 100. 1017 Waterbury-Stowe Rd (SR 100) 05676 (PO Box 490). Fax: 802/244-1294. A renovated 1899 Victorian home with newer wings, this inn offers large rooms, many accented by hardwood trim. Smoke free premises. 22 units. 21 one-bedroom standard units, some with whirlpools. 1 one-bedroom suite. 2 stories (no elevator), interior/exterior corridors. *Bath:* combo or shower only. **Parking:** on-site. **Terms:** office hours 7:30 am-10 pm, 2-3 night minimum stay - seasonal, 14 day cancellation notice-fee imposed, package plans - seasonal, $5 service charge. **Dining:** dining room, see separate listing. **Business Services:** meeting rooms, fax. **Cards:** AX, DC, DS, MC, VI.

SOME UNITS

[symbols]

——— WHERE TO DINE ———

## ARVAD'S GRILL & PUB

American

cocktails.

**Lunch:** $5-$8    **Dinner:** $6-$18    **Phone:** 802/244-8973

**Location:** I-89, exit 10, just s on SR 100. 3 S Main St 05676. **Hours:** 11:30 am-11:30 pm. Closed: 11/25, 12/25. **Features:** The casual, pub-like eatery serves more than 10 Vermont brews with a large selection of sandwiches, salads, burgers, seafood, meat and pasta preparations. Dishes are prepared with Vermont-made products and seasonal produce. Smoking is allowed on the outdoor patio. Casual dress; **Parking:** street. **Cards:** AX, DC, DS, MC, VI.

[symbols]

## MARSALA SALSA

Caribbean

**Dinner:** $5-$14    **Phone:** 802/244-1150

**Location:** Center. 13-15 Stowe St 05671. **Hours:** 5 pm-9:30 pm. Closed: 11/25, 12/25; also Sun. **Reservations:** suggested. **Features:** The restaurant features an interesting Indian and Caribbean theme throughout; the walls are filled with Indian tapestries and rugs which have been hand painted in a variety of colors and patterns. Casual dress; cocktails. **Parking:** street. **Cards:** MC, VI.

[symbol]

## THE MIST GRILL

American

**Lunch:** $7-$13    **Dinner:** $16-$24    **Phone:** 802/244-8522

**Location:** I-89, exit 10; center. 92 Stowe St 05676. **Hours:** 11:30 am-2:30 pm, Thurs & Fri also 5:30-9 pm, Sat & Sun from 5:30 pm. Closed: 1/1, 11/25, 12/25. **Reservations:** suggested. **Features:** The former grist mill still has the orginial 1807 stone walls; the service is casual but friendly and the menu is made up of a variety of regional and specialty dishes. Dressy casual; cocktails. **Parking:** on-site. **Cards:** AX, MC, VI.

[symbols]

# WATERBURY CENTER

——— WHERE TO STAY ———

## THE BLACK LOCUST INN

(AAA) (SAVE)

Historic Bed & Breakfast

**Phone:** 802/244-7490

5/13-10/29 & 12/27-3/28    1P: $135-$225    2P: $135-$225

**Location:** I-89, exit 10, 4.8 mi n on SR 100. 5088 Waterbury-Stowe Rd 05677. Fax: 802/244-8473. **Facility:** Rooms and common areas in this restored 1832 farmhouse are decorated with hand-crafted art; beds are plush and nightly turndown service is offered. Smoke free premises. 6 one-bedroom standard units. 2 stories (no elevator), interior corridors. *Bath:* shower only. **Parking:** on-site. **Terms:** open 5/13-10/29 & 12/27-3/28, check-in 4 pm, 2 night minimum stay, age restrictions may apply, 14 day cancellation notice-fee imposed, [BP] meal plan available, package plans - seasonal. **Amenities:** hair dryers. **Leisure Activities:** snowshoes, barbecue facilities. **Guest Services:** complimentary evening beverages. **Cards:** DS, MC, VI. **Special Amenities:** free full breakfast and free local telephone calls.

[symbols]

——— WHERE TO DINE ———

## MICHAEL'S ON THE HILL

Continental

**Dinner:** $15-$29    **Phone:** 802/244-7476

**Location:** I-89, exit 10, 4.2 mi n of jct SR 100/2. 4182 Stowe-Waterbury Rd (SR 100) 05677. **Hours:** 5:30 pm-9 pm. Closed: Tues. **Reservations:** suggested. **Features:** Located in a 1820 farmhouse, the restaurant offers guests an intimate and delightful dining experience. Dressy casual; cocktails. **Parking:** on-site. **Cards:** AX, DS, MC, VI.

[symbols]

## TANGLEWOODS

American

**Dinner:** $12-$22    **Phone:** 802/244-7855

**Location:** I-89, exit 10, 1.5 mi n on SR 100, then just e. 179 Guptil Rd 05672. **Hours:** 5:30 pm-9 pm; hours may vary. Closed: 11/25, 12/24, 12/25; also Mon. **Reservations:** accepted. **Features:** This restaurant's noticeably distinct yet charmingly rustic interior features a wood-burning fireplace, exposed beams and knotty pine walls. Casual dress; cocktails. **Parking:** on-site. **Cards:** AX, MC, VI.

[symbol]

# WELLS RIVER pop. 325

## ——— WHERE TO STAY ———

**THE WHIPPLE-TREE B&B**                                    Phone: (802)429-2076
 All Year [BP]          1P: $140-$190        2P: $140-$190        XP: $15
**Bed & Breakfast**  **Location:** I-91, exit 17, just e on US 302, 1.9 mi w on Leighton Hill Rd, 0.6 mi nw on Fish Pond Rd, then just n on Stevens Pl; last mile on dirt packed road. Located in a quiet area. 487 Stevens Pl 05081. Fax: 802/429-2858. **Facility:** Scenic mountain vistas greet guests as they travel the long meandering road leading to this charming B&B. Smoke free premises. 6 one-bedroom standard units. 2 stories (no elevator), interior corridors. *Bath:* combo or shower only. **Parking:** on-site. **Terms:** 14 day cancellation notice-fee imposed. **Amenities:** video library, voice mail, hair dryers. **Leisure Activities:** whirlpool, paddleboats, cross country skiing, snowmobiling, hiking trails, jogging, exercise room. *Fee:* game room. **Cards:** AX, DS, MC, VI.

SOME UNITS

## ——— WHERE TO DINE ———

**P & H TRUCK STOP**            **Lunch:** $3-$6          **Dinner:** $4-$8          Phone: 802/429-2141
**Location:** I-91, exit 17, just w. 2886 US Rt 302 05081. **Hours:** 24 hours. **Reservations:** accepted.
**American**   **Features:** The basic eatery offers pleasant service and mostly short-order menu items. Casual dress. **Parking:** on-site. **Cards:** AX, DS, MC, VI.

# WEST BRATTLEBORO pop. 3,222—See also BRATTLEBORO.

## ——— WHERE TO STAY ———

**DALEM'S CHALET**                                      Phone: (802)254-4323
(AAA) (SAVE)  9/24-10/30      1P: $74-$115      2P: $74-$115      XP: $8      F12
              5/1-9/23        1P: $68-$110      2P: $68-$110      XP: $8      F12
              10/31-4/30      1P: $58-$95       2P: $58-$95       XP: $8      F12
**Motel**  **Location:** I-91, exit 2, 1.1 mi w on SR 9, then just s. 78 South St 05301. Fax: 802/254-3883. **Facility:** 27 one-bedroom standard units, some with efficiencies. 2 stories (no elevator), interior/exterior corridors. *Bath:* combo or shower only. **Parking:** on-site. **Terms:** weekly rates available, [MAP] meal plan available. **Amenities:** voice mail, hair dryers. **Dining:** restaurant, see separate listing. **Pool(s):** small outdoor, small heated indoor. **Cards:** AX, DC, MC, VI. **Special Amenities:** free continental breakfast and preferred room (subject to availability with advanced reservations).** *(See color ad p 416)*

SOME UNITS

**MOLLY STARK MOTEL**                                    Phone: (802)254-2440
  9/20-10/25       1P: $50-$80       2P: $50-$80       XP: $8      F12
              5/1-9/19 & 10/26-4/30   1P: $40-$70    2P: $45-$70       XP: $8      F12
**Motel**  **Location:** I-91, exit 2, 3.3 mi w on SR 9. 829 Marlboro Rd 05301. Fax: 802/254-7646. **Facility:** 14 units. 13 one- and 1 two-bedroom standard units. 1 story, exterior corridors. *Bath:* shower only. **Parking:** on-site. **Terms:** weekly rates available, pets ($8 extra charge). **Cards:** AX, DS, MC, VI.

SOME UNITS
FEE

## ——— WHERE TO DINE ———

**DALEM'S CHALET**                **Dinner:** $13-$20         Phone: 802/254-4323
(AAA)  **Location:** I-91, exit 2, 1.1 mi w on SR 9, then just s; in Dalem's Chalet. 78 South St 05301. **Hours:** Open 5/1-10/31 & 12/1-3/31; 8 am-9:30 & 5:30-9 pm, Sun 5 pm-8:30 pm. Closed: 12/25; also for dinner 12/24, Mon & Tues. **Reservations:** suggested. **Features:** Dalem's features an inviting Bavarian atmosphere with a dining room that overlooks mountains and a pond with swans. The menu offers Swiss, German, Austrian and American dishes with lighter fare offerings as well. The Wiener schnitzel is flavorful. Casual dress; cocktails. **Parking:** on-site. **Cards:** AX, DS, MC, VI. *(See color ad p 416)*
**Continental**

**ZITER'S PUTNEY INN BAKERY & CAFE**         **Lunch:** $4-$14         Phone: 802/257-4994
**Location:** I-91, exit 2, 0.9 mi w. 849 Western Ave 05301. **Hours:** 7 am-4 pm. Closed major holidays.
**Deli/Subs**  **Features:** This popular cafe and bakery is the source for the wonderful breads and baked goods featured
**Sandwiches**  at their more formal restaurant, The Putney Inn a few miles north off the interstate, as well as here at their more casual eatery. Save room for dessert for they are not only extraordinary, but almost a meal unto themselves! Casual dress; beer & wine only. **Parking:** street. **Cards:** AX, MC, VI.

# WEST BRIDGEWATER —See KILLINGTON.

# WEST DOVER

## ——— WHERE TO STAY ———

**BIG BEAR'S LODGE**                                    Phone: 802/464-5591
(AAA) (SAVE)  All Year           2P: $70-$140          XP: $25          F12
**Location:** 8.7 mi n on SR 100, from jct SR 9. 344 Rt 100 N 05356. Fax: 802/464-7163. **Facility:** Smoke free premises. 24 one-bedroom standard units. 2 stories (no elevator), interior/exterior corridors. *Bath:* combo or shower only. **Parking:** on-site. **Terms:** 7 day cancellation notice-fee imposed. **Amenities:** video library.
**Motel**  **Pool(s):** heated outdoor. **Leisure Activities:** hot tub, billiards, barbecue grill, play area for toddlers, hiking trails, volleyball. **Cards:** AX, DC, MC, VI. **Special Amenities:** early check-in/late check-out.

## GRAND SUMMIT RESORT HOTEL & CONFERENCE CENTER

*Book at aaa.com*   **Phone:** (802)464-6600

▼▼▼▼
Resort
Large-scale Hotel

| | | |
|---|---|---|
| 12/22-3/31 | 1P: $220-$382 | 2P: $220-$650 |
| 11/1-12/21 | 1P: $118-$292 | 2P: $118-$497 |
| 5/1-10/31 & 4/1-4/30 | 1P: $70-$157 | 2P: $70-$268 |

**Location:** 9 mi n on SR 100 from jct SR 9, then w on Mountain Rd, follow signs. 89 Mountain Rd 05356 (Rt 100, Grand Summit at Mount Snow). Fax: 802/464-6610. **Facility:** Located slopeside to Mount Snow, this attractive resort offers tastefully decorated guest rooms, many with full kitchens and some with fireplaces. Smoke free premises. 197 units. 130 one-bedroom standard units, some with kitchens. 54 one-, 11 two- and 2 three-bedroom suites with kitchens, some with whirlpools. 3 stories, interior corridors. **Parking:** on-site. **Terms:** check-in 4 pm, 2 night minimum stay - weekends, 21 day cancellation notice-fee imposed, package plans, 8% service charge. **Amenities:** high-speed Internet, voice mail, irons, hair dryers. *Fee:* video library, video games. *Some:* CD players. **Pool(s):** heated outdoor. **Leisure Activities:** sauna, whirlpools, steamroom, snowmobiling, recreation programs, hiking trails, playground, exercise room, spa, volleyball. *Fee:* golf-18 holes, downhill & cross country skiing, bicycles, game room. **Guest Services:** gift shop, complimentary evening beverages, coin laundry. **Business Services:** conference facilities, administrative services (fee). **Cards:** AX, DS, MC, VI. *(See color ad below)*

SOME UNITS

(ASK) (🍴) (🍸) (📶) (🔥M) (🏃) (🏊) (✖) (✖) (VCR) (🎥) (DATA PORT) (💻) / (🔔) (📷) /

## THE GRAY GHOST INN

**Phone:** (802)464-2474

(AAA) (SAVE)
▼▼ ▼▼
Small-scale Hotel

| | | | | |
|---|---|---|---|---|
| 9/12-10/24 [BP] | 1P: $57 | 2P: $84 | XP: $12 | F3 |
| 10/25-4/1 [BP] | 1P: $50 | 2P: $83 | XP: $12 | F3 |
| 5/15-9/11 [BP] | 1P: $52 | 2P: $77 | XP: $12 | F3 |

**Location:** 7.8 mi n on SR 100, from jct SR 9. 290 Rt 100 N 05356. Fax: 802/464-5236. **Facility:** Smoke free premises. 27 units. 26 one-bedroom standard units. 1 three-bedroom suite ($250) with whirlpool. 3 stories (no elevator), interior corridors. *Bath:* combo or shower only. **Parking:** on-site, winter plug-ins. **Terms:** open 5/15-4/1, 2-3 night minimum stay - weekends in winter, 14 day cancellation notice-fee imposed, pets (in summer and fall only). **Amenities:** video library. *Some:* DVD players. **Dining:** 5:30 pm-8 pm in winter; guest only. **Leisure Activities:** sauna, hot tub, billiards, foosball, game table, ping pong, playground. **Guest Services:** complimentary evening beverages. **Cards:** AX, MC, VI.

SOME UNITS

(S/D) (🛏) (✖) (✖) (🎥) (📞) / (📺) (VCR) /

## SNOW GOOSE INN

**Phone:** 802/464-3984

(AAA) (SAVE)
▼▼ ▼▼
Bed & Breakfast

| | | | |
|---|---|---|---|
| All Year [BP] | 1P: $95-$360 | 2P: $95-$360 | XP: $50   F5 |

**Location:** 7.5 mi n on SR 100, from jct SR 9. 259 Rt 100 05356 (PO Box 366). Fax: 802/464-5322. **Facility:** Attractive grounds surround this pleasant B&B; guest rooms are individually decorated and several feature whirlpools and wood fireplaces. Smoke free premises. 13 units. 11 one-bedroom standard units, some with whirlpools. 1 one- and 1 two-bedroom suites ($195-$395) with whirlpools. 4 stories (no elevator), interior corridors. *Bath:* combo or shower only. **Parking:** on-site. **Terms:** 2 night minimum stay - weekends, 14 day cancellation notice-fee imposed, 15% service charge, pets ($25 extra charge). **Amenities:** high-speed Internet. *Some:* CD players, hair dryers. **Guest Services:** complimentary evening beverages. **Cards:** AX, CB, DS, JC, MC, VI. **Special Amenities:** free full breakfast and free local telephone calls.

SOME UNITS

(S/D) (🛏) (✖) (VCR) (🎥) (📞) / (🎥) (🔔) /
FEE

---

### ──── WHERE TO DINE ────

## FIRST WOK

**Lunch:** $5-$6   **Dinner:** $9-$15   **Phone:** 802/464-5861

▼▼ ▼▼
Chinese
MC, VI.

**Location:** 1 mi n on SR 100. Mountain Park Shopping Plaza 05356. **Hours:** 11:30 am-9 pm, Fri & Sat-10:30 pm, Sun noon-9:30 pm. Closed: 11/25. **Features:** Located near Mount Snow Village, this restaurant serves Szechuan, Hunan and Cantonese cuisine. The menu offers a nice selection of house specialties including chicken, beef, shrimp and vegetable dishes. Casual dress; cocktails. **Parking:** on-site. **Cards:** AX, DS,

(✖)

## SILO FAMILY RESTAURANT

**Lunch:** $5-$7   **Dinner:** $11-$25   **Phone:** 802/464-2553

▼▼ ▼▼
American

**Location:** 7.8 mi n of jct SR 9 and 100 N. 324 SR 100 05356. **Hours:** 11 am-2 pm; to 10 pm 11/26-3/27. Closed: Tues & Wed 5/31-11/25. **Features:** The restaurant's well-coordinated rustic interior includes vaulted ceilings and intricate beams from which large hanging plants drift down. Casual dress; cocktails. **Parking:** on-site. **Cards:** AX, DS, MC, VI.

(🍸) (✖)

---

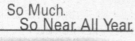

# WESTMORE

------ WHERE TO STAY ------

**WILLOUGHVALE INN ON LAKE WILLOUGHBY**
**Phone:** (802)525-4123

<AAA> <SAVE>
5/1-10/18 [CP]    1P: $119-$209    2P: $129-$219    XP: $20   F12
10/19-4/30 [CP]    1P: $79-$195    2P: $79-$195    XP: $20   F12

▽▽▽▽
Country Inn
**Location:** Just s on SR 5A, from jct SR 16. 793 VT Rt 5A 05860. Fax: 802/525-4514. **Facility:** The rooms at this contemporary country inn overlook beautiful Lake Willoughby; each lakefront cottage offers fireplace, screened porch and deck. Smoke free premises. 14 units. 9 one-bedroom standard units, some with whirlpools. 1 one-bedroom suite with whirlpool. 4 cottages ($149-$249). 2 stories (no elevator), interior/exterior corridors. **Bath:** combo or shower only. **Parking:** on-site. **Terms:** 7 night minimum stay - seasonal, 14 day cancellation notice-fee imposed, 5% service charge, small pets only ($20 fee, in designated units). **Amenities:** hair dryers. *Some:* DVD players, CD players, irons. **Dining:** 5:30 pm-9 pm; hours may vary in season. **Leisure Activities:** boating, canoeing, fishing, badminton, hiking trails, horseshoes. *Fee:* kayaks, snowshoes, bicycles. **Cards:** AX, MC, VI.

SOME UNITS
🛏️(FEE) 🍴 🍷 ✕ ✕ / VCR ▯ 🖼️ 🖥️ /

# WESTON

------ WHERE TO STAY ------

**BRANDMEYER'S MOUNTAINSIDE LODGE**
**Phone:** 802/824-5851

◆◆
1/1-4/30 [BP]    2P: $109-$170    XP: $35   F11
5/1-12/31 [BP]    2P: $99-$160    XP: $35   F11

Small-scale Hotel
**Location:** On SR 100, 1.7 mi n. 913 Rt 100 05161. **Facility:** Smoke free premises, 10 one-bedroom standard units. 1-3 stories (no elevator), interior/exterior corridors. **Bath:** combo or shower only. **Parking:** on-site. **Terms:** 2 night minimum stay - weekends, 10 day cancellation notice-fee imposed, no pets allowed (owner's dog on premises). **Amenities:** safes, hair dryers. **Cards:** AX, MC, VI.

SOME UNITS
ASK 🍴 🍷 ✕ ☎ ▯ / ✕ /

# WHITE RIVER JUNCTION pop. 2,569

------ WHERE TO STAY ------

**BEST WESTERN AT THE JUNCTION**    *Book at aaa.com*
**Phone:** 802/295-3015

<AAA> <SAVE>
9/17-10/31    1P: $109-$149    2P: $119-$159    XP: $10   F18
5/1-9/16 & 11/1-4/30    1P: $69-$109    2P: $79-$119    XP: $10   F18

▽▽▽▽
Small-scale Hotel
**Location:** Jct I-89 and 91. 306 N Harland Rd (US 5) 05001. Fax: 802/296-2581. **Facility:** 112 one-bedroom standard units. 2 stories (no elevator), interior corridors. **Parking:** on-site, winter plug-ins. **Terms:** [CP] meal plan available, pets ($10 fee). **Amenities:** voice mail, irons, hair dryers. **Pool(s):** heated indoor, wading. **Leisure Activities:** sauna, whirlpool, picnic tables, playground, exercise room. **Guest Services:** sundries, coin laundry. **Cards:** AX, CB, DC, DS, JC, MC, VI. **Special Amenities:** free continental breakfast and free newspaper.

SOME UNITS
S/D 🛏️(FEE) 🏊 ✕ 📺 DATA PORT ▯ / ✕ ▯ 🖼️(FEE) (FEE) /

**COMFORT INN**    *Book at aaa.com*
**Phone:** (802)295-3051

▽▽ ▽▽▽
9/10-10/23 [ECP]    1P: $89-$199    2P: $99-$209    XP: $5   F18
5/1-9/9 [ECP]    1P: $82-$139    2P: $85-$149    XP: $5   F18
10/24-4/30 [ECP]    1P: $82-$109    2P: $85-$119    XP: $5   F18

Small-scale Hotel
**Location:** I-91, exit 11, just e. 8 Sykes Mountain Ave 05001. Fax: 802/295-5990. **Facility:** 94 one-bedroom standard units. 4 stories, interior corridors. **Parking:** on-site, winter plug-ins. **Amenities:** irons, hair dryers. **Pool(s):** outdoor. **Guest Services:** sundries, coin laundry. **Business Services:** meeting rooms, fax. **Cards:** AX, DC, DS, MC, VI.

SOME UNITS
ASK S/D 🍴 ⓜ 🏊 🛏️ 🔧 📺 DATA PORT ▯ / ✕ ▯ 🖼️ /

## HAMPTON INN WHITE RIVER JUNCTION   Book at aaa.com

Phone: 802/296-2800

All Year | 1P: $79-$250 | 2P: $89-$250 | XP: $10 | F18

Small-scale Hotel

**Location:** On US 5, just s of jct I-89 and 91. 104 Ballardvale Dr 05001. Fax: 802/296-2884. **Facility:** 96 one-bedroom standard units. 3 stories, interior corridors. *Bath:* combo or shower only. **Parking:** on-site, winter plug-ins. **Terms:** [ECP] meal plan available. **Amenities:** voice mail, irons, hair dryers. **Pool(s):** heated indoor. **Leisure Activities:** exercise room. **Guest Services:** sundries, coin laundry. **Business Services:** meeting rooms, fax. **Cards:** AX, DC, DS, MC, VI.

SOME UNITS
FEE   FEE

--- WHERE TO DINE ---

## AJ'S RESTAURANT

**Dinner:** $8-$17

Phone: 802/295-3071

Steak & Seafood

German shepherd

**Location:** I-91, exit 11, 0.5 mi e on Sykes Ave. 40 Bowling Ln 05001. **Hours:** 5 pm-9:30 pm, Sun 4 pm-8:30 pm. **Closed:** 11/25, 12/24, 12/25. **Reservations:** accepted. **Features:** The busy and popular restaurant serves large portions of prime rib, as well as seafood dishes. Also available are a nicely stocked salad bar, terrific desserts and a good selection of beer and wine. Guests shouldn't be surprised to see the friendly resident lounging with guests near the wood stove in the rustic waiting area. Casual dress; cocktails. **Parking:** on-site. **Cards:** AX, DC, DS, MC, VI.

# WILLIAMSTOWN

--- WHERE TO STAY ---

## AUTUMN HARVEST INN

Phone: (802)433-1355

All Year | 1P: $79-$139 | | XP: $10

Country Inn

**Location:** I-89, exit 5, 2.1 mi e on SR 64; in Autumn Harvest Inn. 118 Clark Rd 05679. Fax: 802/433-5501. **Facility:** Smoke free premises. 18 one-bedroom standard units. 2 stories (no elevator), interior corridors. *Bath:* combo or shower only. **Parking:** on-site, winter plug-ins. **Terms:** 14 day cancellation notice. **Amenities:** video library. **Dining:** restaurant, see separate listing. **Leisure Activities:** fishing, cross country skiing, snowmobiling, hiking trails, horseback riding, basketball, volleyball. **Cards:** AX, MC, VI.

--- WHERE TO DINE ---

## AUTUMN HARVEST INN RESTAURANT

**Dinner:** $8-$18

Phone: 802/433-1355

American

**Location:** I-89, exit 5, 2.1 mi e on SR 64; in Autumn Harvest Inn. 118 Clark Rd 05679. **Hours:** 5:30 pm-9 pm. **Closed:** Sun-Tues. **Reservations:** suggested. **Features:** This casual restaurant is located in what was once a working dairy farm. This lovely inn offers majestic views of the surrounding area. Cocktails. **Parking:** on-site. **Cards:** AX, MC, VI.

# WILLISTON

--- WHERE TO STAY ---

## COURTYARD BY MARRIOTT   Book at aaa.com

Phone: (802)879-0100

5/1-10/31 | 1P: $99-$149 | 2P: $99-$149
11/1-4/30 | 1P: $79-$99 | 2P: $79-$99

Small-scale Hotel

**Location:** I-89, exit 12, just s on SR 2A, then just e. 177 Hurricane Ln 05495. Fax: 802/879-0101. **Facility:** 90 units. 87 one-bedroom standard units, some with whirlpools. 3 one-bedroom suites. 3 stories, interior corridors. *Bath:* combo or shower only. **Parking:** on-site, winter plug-ins. **Amenities:** high-speed Internet, dual phone lines, voice mail, irons, hair dryers. **Pool(s):** heated indoor. **Leisure Activities:** whirlpool, exercise room. **Guest Services:** valet and coin laundry. **Business Services:** meeting rooms, business center. **Cards:** AX, CB, DC, DS, JC, MC, VI.

SOME UNITS

## FAIRFIELD INN BY MARRIOTT   Book at aaa.com

Phone: 802/879-8999

All Year [CP] | 1P: $79-$129 | 2P: $79-$129

Small-scale Hotel

**Location:** I-89, exit 12, just n on SR 2A. 2488 St George Rd 05495. Fax: 802/879-2735. **Facility:** 105 one-bedroom standard units. 3 stories, interior corridors. *Bath:* combo or shower only. **Parking:** on-site. **Terms:** cancellation fee imposed. **Amenities:** video games (fee), voice mail, irons, hair dryers. **Pool(s):** outdoor. **Guest Services:** valet and coin laundry. **Cards:** AX, CB, DC, DS, MC, VI.

SOME UNITS
FEE

## TOWNEPLACE SUITES BY MARRIOTT   Book at aaa.com

Phone: 802/872-5900

8/1-10/15 | 1P: $129-$149 | 2P: $149-$189
5/1-7/31 | 1P: $99-$119 | 2P: $119-$179
10/16-4/30 | 1P: $79-$99 | 2P: $109-$159

Small-scale Hotel

**Location:** I-89, exit 12, 1.1 mi n on SR 2A. 66 Zephyr Rd 05495. Fax: 802/878-0422. **Facility:** 95 units. 69 one-bedroom standard units with kitchens. 4 one- and 22 two-bedroom suites with kitchens. 3 stories, interior corridors. *Bath:* combo or shower only. **Parking:** on-site, winter plug-ins. **Terms:** cancellation fee imposed, pets ($10 extra charge). **Amenities:** high-speed Internet, dual phone lines, voice mail, irons, hair dryers. **Pool(s):** heated indoor. **Leisure Activities:** playground, exercise room. **Guest Services:** valet and coin laundry. **Business Services:** business center. **Cards:** AX, CB, DC, DS, JC, MC, VI.

SOME UNITS
FEE   FEE

——— WHERE TO DINE ———

**CHEF'S CORNER CAFE & BAKERY**
American
**Lunch:** $7-$11     **Phone:** 802/878-5524
**Location:** I-89, exit 12, 1 mi n on SR 2A. 2121 Essex Rd 05495. **Hours:** 7 am-3 pm, Mon from 7:30 am, Sat from 8 am, Sun 8 am-2:30 pm. Closed major holidays. **Features:** Since opening its doors in 1997, this trendy bakery-cafe continues to delight both locals and visitors alike with its selection of sweet treats and entrees. Open for breakfast and lunch, this cafe offers a healthier alternative for the more health-conscious. Menu offerings include sandwiches, soups, quiche and traditional house items like blackened chicken panini or the corner veggie burger. A full weekend brunch is available, as is outdoor seating. Casual dress; beer & wine only. **Parking:** on-site. **Cards:** AX, MC, VI.

**EVERGREEN EDDY'S WILDERNESS BAR & GRILL**
American
**Lunch:** $6-$9    **Dinner:** $8-$15    **Phone:** 802/879-7060
**Location:** I-89, exit 12, just n on SR 2A. 2 Marshall Rd 05495. **Hours:** 11 am-9:30 pm, Fri & Sat-10 pm, Sun-9 pm. Closed: 3/27, 11/25, 12/25. **Features:** The pleasant family-style establishment serves pasta, sandwiches, burgers, seafood and beef and chicken dishes. Casual dress; cocktails. **Parking:** on-site. **Cards:** AX, DS, MC, VI.

# WILMINGTON

——— WHERE TO STAY ———

**HORIZON INN**
AAA SAVE
Small-scale Hotel
**Phone:** 802/464-2131
All Year    1P: $75-$155    2P: $75-$155    XP: $10    F6
**Location:** On SR 9, 4 mi e. Located in a rural area. 861 SR 9 E 05363 (PO Box 817). Fax: 802/464-8302. **Facility:** 28 units. 27 one-bedroom standard units. 1 one-bedroom suite ($150-$300). 2 stories (no elevator), interior/exterior corridors. *Bath:* combo or shower only. **Parking:** on-site, winter plug-ins. **Terms:** 14 day cancellation notice. **Amenities:** hair dryers. **Dining:** Fri & Sat 7 am-10 & 5-8:30 pm; closed 4/1-4/30 & 11/1-11/30, cocktails. **Pool(s):** heated indoor. **Leisure Activities:** sauna, whirlpool, tobogganing, billiards, ping pong, exercise room, shuffleboard. *Fee:* game room. **Guest Services:** gift shop. **Business Services:** meeting rooms. **Cards:** DS, MC, VI. **Special Amenities:** free local telephone calls and preferred room (subject to availability with advanced reservations).
SOME UNITS

**NORDIC HILLS LODGE**
Small-scale Hotel
**Phone:** (802)464-5130
11/26-3/23    2P: $90-$135    XP: $20    F10
5/14-10/30    2P: $75-$90    XP: $10    F10
**Location:** 2.5 mi n on SR 100, from jct SR 9, then 0.6 mi w on Colbrook Rd. 34 Look Rd 05363. Fax: 802/464-8248. **Facility:** Smoke free premises. 25 one-bedroom standard units. 3 stories (no elevator), interior corridors. *Bath:* combo or shower only. **Parking:** on-site, winter plug-ins. **Terms:** open 5/14-10/30 & 11/26-3/23, check-in 4 pm, 2 night minimum stay - weekends in winter, 15 day cancellation notice-fee imposed, [BP] & [MAP] meal plans available, package plans - weekends 1/2-3/14, 3% service charge. **Amenities:** hair dryers. **Pool(s):** heated outdoor. **Leisure Activities:** whirlpool, basketball, horseshoes, shuffleboard. *Fee:* game room. **Guest Services:** gift shop, complimentary evening beverages. **Cards:** AX, DC, MC, VI.
SOME UNITS

**NUTMEG COUNTRY INN**
Historic Bed & Breakfast
**Phone:** (802)464-7400
12/15-4/30 [BP]    1P: $109-$199    2P: $109-$199
9/21-10/21 [BP]    1P: $119-$189    2P: $119-$189
10/22-12/14 [BP]    1P: $109-$169    2P: $109-$169
5/1-9/20 [BP]    1P: $99-$149    2P: $99-$149
**Location:** 0.8 mi w. 153 Rt 9 W 05363 (PO Box 1899). Fax: 802/464-7331. **Facility:** Located on the fringes of town, this charming 1777 farmhouse offers a comfortable blend of antiques and modern furnishings. Smoke free premises. 14 units. 10 one-bedroom standard units, some with whirlpools. 3 one- and 1 two-bedroom suites ($169-$209), some with whirlpools. 2 stories (no elevator), interior corridors. *Bath:* combo or shower only. **Parking:** on-site. **Terms:** age restrictions may apply, 14 day cancellation notice-fee imposed, package plans - seasonal. **Amenities:** video library. **Leisure Activities:** cross country skiing, snowmobiling, hiking trails. **Guest Services:** complimentary evening beverages. **Cards:** AX, CB, DC, DS, MC, VI.
SOME UNITS

——— WHERE TO DINE ———

**LE PETIT CHEF** Historic
French
**Dinner:** $20-$34     **Phone:** 802/464-8437
**Location:** 4 mi n on SR 100, from jct SR 9. 840 Rt 100 05363. **Hours:** 6 pm-9 pm, Fri & Sat-10 pm. Closed: Tues, mid-April to Memorial Day & end of Oct to Thanksgiving. **Reservations:** suggested. **Features:** This chef-owned bistro serves excellent French cuisine in a lovely restored 1789 farmhouse. Dining is leisurely paced and elegant with a warm country atmosphere. Soft jazz plays in the background; candlelit tables, and knowledgeable staff make for very enjoyable dining. Dressy casual; cocktails. **Parking:** on-site. **Cards:** AX, MC, VI.

**THE WHITE HOUSE OF WILMINGTON** Country Inn
Continental
**Dinner:** $18-$27     **Phone:** 802/464-2135
**Location:** On SR 9, 0.5 mi e. 178 Rt 9 E 05363. **Hours:** 5:30 pm-9 pm, Sat-9:30 pm, Sun 11 am-2:30 & 5:30-9 pm. Closed: Mon & first 3 weeks of Nov. **Reservations:** suggested. **Features:** The White House is an elegant English-style dining room in a country inn high on a hill. The setting offers lovely views. Its cuisine reveals hints of French influences. This restaurant is closed during part of November, so call ahead for reservations. Dressy casual; cocktails. **Parking:** on-site. **Cards:** AX, DS, MC, VI.

# WINDSOR

## ——— WHERE TO STAY ———

**JUNIPER HILL INN**
▼▼▼▼▼
**Phone: 802/674-5273**
Historic
Country Inn
5/1-10/31 & 11/12-3/27   1P: $105-$215   2P: $105-$215   XP: $25
**Location:** I-91, exit 9, 2.9 mi s on US 5 to Juniper Hill Rd, then 0.5 mi w. 153 Pembroke Rd 05089. Fax: 802/674-2041. **Facility:** This stately turn-of-the-20th-century Colonial Revival mansion offers spacious guest rooms (many with fireplaces) and a picturesque hilltop setting. Smoke free premises. 16 one-bedroom standard units. 3 stories (no elevator), interior corridors. *Bath:* combo or shower only. **Parking:** on-site. **Terms:** open 5/1-10/31 & 11/12-3/27, age restrictions may apply, 15 day cancellation notice-fee imposed, [BP] meal plan available, no pets allowed (owner's dogs on premises). **Amenities:** CD players, hair dryers. **Pool(s):** outdoor. **Leisure Activities:** hiking trails. **Guest Services:** complimentary evening beverages. **Business Services:** meeting rooms. **Cards:** DS, MC, VI.

🍽 🛶 ✕ 🅦 ☎

## ——— WHERE TO DINE ———

**WINDSOR STATION RESTAURANT**   Historic
ⒶⒶⒶ
▼▼▼▼▼
American
**Dinner:** $13-$23   **Phone: 802/674-2052**
**Location:** Just e of Main St. Depot Ave 05089. **Hours:** 5:30 pm-9 pm. Closed major holidays; also Mon 10/11-6/30. **Reservations:** suggested. **Features:** In a turn-of-the-20th-century train depot, the restaurant prepares entrees of seafood, steak, veal, chicken and pasta. Homemade desserts are fresh. The fine restaurant is a good spot for families. Casual dress; cocktails. **Parking:** on-site. **Cards:** AX, DS, MC, VI.

✕

# WOODSTOCK pop. 977

## ——— WHERE TO STAY ———

**BRAESIDE MOTEL**
ⒶⒶⒶ Ⓢ🅐🅥🅔
▼▼▼▼▼
Motel
**Phone: 802/457-1366**
9/1-10/31   1P: $88-$108   2P: $88-$108
5/1-8/31   1P: $78-$108   2P: $78-$108
11/1-4/30   1P: $68-$108   2P: $68-$108
**Location:** 1 mi e. 432 US 4 E (Woodstock Rd) 05091 (PO Box 411). Fax: 802/457-9892. **Facility:** Smoke free premises. 12 one-bedroom standard units. 1 story, exterior corridors. **Parking:** on-site. **Terms:** 2 night minimum stay - weekends, 15 day cancellation notice-fee imposed, pets ($10 extra charge, in limited units). **Pool(s):** outdoor. **Leisure Activities:** basketball. *Fee:* sports center privileges at Woodstock Inn & Resort. **Business Services:** fax. **Cards:** AX, DC, MC, VI. **Special Amenities:** free local telephone calls and preferred room (subject to availability with advanced reservations).

SOME UNITS
🛏 🛶 ✕ 🅳🅰🆃🅰 PORT 🕮 / 🆅🅲🆁 /
FEE

**DEER BROOK INN**
▼▼▼▼▼
Historic Bed
& Breakfast
**Phone: 802/672-3713**
All Year [BP]   1P: $75-$110   2P: $95-$150   XP: $20
D12
**Location:** I-89, exit 1 (Woodstock), 4.5 mi w of Village Green. 535 US Rt 4 05091. **Facility:** Guest rooms at this early-1800s farmhouse are large and well maintained. Smoke free premises. 5 units. 4 one-bedroom standard units. 1 one-bedroom suite. 2 stories (no elevator), interior corridors. **Parking:** on-site. **Terms:** 1-2 night minimum stay - some weekends, 14 day cancellation notice, no pets allowed (owner's dog on premises). **Cards:** AX, MC, VI.

SOME UNITS
✕ ☎ / 🅦 🆅🅲🆁 /

**THE JACKSON HOUSE INN & RESTAURANT**
▼▼▼▼▼
Country Inn
**Phone: 802/457-2065**
9/16-10/17   1P: $230-$395   2P: $230-$395
5/1-9/15 & 10/18-4/30   1P: $195-$340   2P: $195-$340
**Location:** 1.5 mi w of Village Green on US 4. 114-3 Senior Ln 05091. Fax: 802/457-9290. **Facility:** This service-oriented inn is found on scenic grounds not far from a main street of galleries and shops. Smoke free premises. 15 one-bedroom standard units, some with whirlpools. 3 stories (no elevator), interior corridors. *Bath:* combo or shower only. **Parking:** on-site. **Terms:** 2 night minimum stay - weekends, age restrictions may apply, 16 day cancellation notice-fee imposed, [BP] meal plan available, package plans - seasonal, 10% service charge. **Amenities:** high-speed Internet, hair dryers. *Some:* CD players. **Dining:** restaurant, see separate listing. **Guest Services:** complimentary evening beverages. **Cards:** AX, MC, VI.

SOME UNITS
🆂🅓 🍽 ✕ 🐾 🅳🅰🆃🅰 PORT / 🅦 /

**OTTAUQUECHEE MOTOR LODGE**
All Year
Motel

Phone: 802/672-3404

| | | XP: $10 |
| 1P: $59-$130 | 2P: $59-$130 | |

**Location:** US 4, 4.5 mi w. 529 US Rt 4 05091 (PO Box 418). **Facility:** Smoke free premises. 15 one-bedroom standard units. 1-2 stories, interior/exterior corridors. **Parking:** on-site, winter plug-ins. **Terms:** 2-14 night minimum stay - weekends, 14 day cancellation notice-fee imposed. **Cards:** MC, VI.

---

**POND RIDGE MOTEL**
Motel

Phone: 802-457-1667

| | | | |
| 9/6-10/26 | 1P: $99-$125 | 2P: $99-$150 | XP: $10 | F7 |
| 10/27-4/30 | 1P: $69-$99 | 2P: $79-$125 | XP: $10 | F7 |
| 5/1-9/5 | 1P: $69-$99 | 2P: $69-$125 | XP: $10 | F7 |

**Location:** 1.8 mi w. 506 US Rt 4 W 05091. Fax: 802/457-1667. **Facility:** 19 units. 18 one- and 1 two-bedroom standard units, some with kitchens. 1-2 stories (no elevator), exterior corridors. *Bath:* combo or shower only. **Parking:** on-site. **Terms:** 2-3 night minimum stay - seasonal, 7 day cancellation notice-fee imposed. **Leisure Activities:** fishing. **Cards:** AX, MC, VI. **Special Amenities:** free local telephone calls and preferred room (subject to availability with advanced reservations).

SOME UNITS

---

**THE SHIRE RIVERVIEW MOTEL**
Motel

Phone: 802/457-2211

| | | | |
| 9/17-10/24 | 1P: $158-$318 | 2P: $158-$318 | XP: $10 | F14 |
| 5/27-9/16 | 1P: $128-$318 | 2P: $128-$318 | XP: $10 | F14 |
| 5/1-5/26 & 10/25-4/30 | 1P: $78-$228 | 2P: $78-$228 | XP: $10 | F14 |

**Location:** Just e on US 4; downtown. 46 Pleasant St 05091. Fax: 802/457-5836. **Facility:** Smoke free premises. 33 one-bedroom standard units. 2 stories (no elevator), interior/exterior corridors. **Parking:** on-site. **Terms:** 2 night minimum stay - weekends, 14 day cancellation notice-fee imposed. **Amenities:** voice mail. **Cards:** AX, DS, MC, VI. *(See color ad below)*

---

**THE VILLAGE INN OF WOODSTOCK**
Historic Country Inn

Phone: 802/457-1255

| | | |
| 9/24-10/23 | 1P: $115-$240 | 2P: $115-$240 |
| 10/24-4/30 | 1P: $90-$185 | 2P: $90-$185 |
| 5/1-9/23 | 1P: $90-$175 | 2P: $90-$175 |

**Location:** On US 4, 0.3 mi e. 41 Pleasant St (US 4) 05091. Fax: 802/457-3109. **Facility:** Common areas in this 1899 house feature original woodwork, ornate tin ceilings and stained-glass windows. Smoke free premises. 7 one-bedroom standard units, some with whirlpools. 3 stories (no elevator), interior corridors. *Bath:* combo or shower only. **Parking:** on-site. **Terms:** 2 night minimum stay - weekends in summer, age restrictions may apply, 14 day cancellation notice-fee imposed, [BP] meal plan available, 5% service charge, no pets allowed (owner's dog on premises). **Cards:** MC, VI.

---

**THE WINSLOW HOUSE**
Historic Bed & Breakfast

Phone: 802/457-1820

| | | | |
| 9/21-10/23 [BP] | 1P: $125-$165 | 2P: $125-$165 | XP: $15 | D7 |
| 6/2-9/20 [BP] | 1P: $110-$140 | 2P: $110-$140 | XP: $15 | D7 |
| 10/24-4/30 [BP] | 1P: $110-$135 | 2P: $110-$135 | XP: $15 | D7 |
| 5/1-6/1 [BP] | 1P: $100-$125 | 2P: $100-$125 | XP: $15 | D7 |

**Location:** 1.3 mi w on US 4. 492 Woodstock Rd 05091. Fax: 802/457-9195. **Facility:** This 1872 farmhouse is furnished with antiques; seasonal gardens produce fresh herbs and vegetables which are included in the breakfast fare. Smoke free premises. 5 units. 2 one-bedroom standard units. 3 one-bedroom suites. 2 stories (no elevator), interior corridors. *Bath:* combo or shower only. **Parking:** on-site. **Terms:** 2 night minimum stay - 9/21-10/26, age restrictions may apply, 14 day cancellation notice-fee imposed, pets ($10 deposit). **Amenities:** video library. **Leisure Activities:** exercise room. **Guest Services:** complimentary evening beverages. **Cards:** AX, MC, VI. **Special Amenities:** free full breakfast and free local telephone calls.

SOME UNITS

FEE

## THE WOODSTOCKER BED & BREAKFAST

All Year [BP]      1P: $85-$175      2P: $85-$175      XP: $20      F12

Phone: (802)457-3896

Historic Bed & Breakfast

**Location:** 0.5 mi w on US 4. Located in a residential area. 61 River St 05091. Fax: 802/457-3897. **Facility:** An 1830 Cape Cod-style house, the B&B is in a picturesque area within walking distance of the Village Green. Smoke free premises. 9 units. 7 one-bedroom standard units. 2 one-bedroom suites ($115-$205) with kitchens. 2 stories (no elevator), interior corridors. **Parking:** on-site, winter plug-ins. **Terms:** 2-3 night minimum stay - seasonal, 14 day cancellation notice. **Amenities:** video library. **Leisure Activities:** hiking trails. **Guest Services:** gift shop. **Cards:** AX, DC, MC, VI.

SOME UNITS

(ASK) (S/D) ⊗ ☎ / ⊗ 🅦 🍴 🖥 📺 /

## WOODSTOCK INN & RESORT    *Book at aaa.com*

All Year      1P: $209-$609      2P: $209-$609      XP: $30      F14

Phone: (802)457-1100

Resort Large-scale Hotel

**Location:** On US 4; center. Located on the Village Green. 14 The Green 05091. Fax: 802/457-6699. **Facility:** Spacious public areas, large guest rooms and manicured grounds characterize this traditional in-town resort. 142 units. 133 one-bedroom standard units. 9 one-bedroom suites. 4 stories, interior corridors. **Parking:** on-site. **Terms:** 2 night minimum stay - weekends, 14 day cancellation notice-fee imposed, [MAP] meal plan available, package plans - seasonal. **Amenities:** video games (fee), voice mail, irons, hair dryers. *Some:* CD players, safes. **Dining:** 3 restaurants, 7 am-9 pm, dining room, see separate listing. **Pool(s):** heated outdoor, heated indoor. **Leisure Activities:** saunas, whirlpool, steamroom, spa. *Fee:* golf-18 holes, 12 tennis courts (2 indoor), racquetball courts, racquet sport equipment & instruction, squash, downhill & cross country skiing, bicycles, game room. **Guest Services:** gift shop, valet laundry, area transportation-local recreation facility. **Business Services:** conference facilities, business center. **Cards:** AX, DC, MC, VI.

SOME UNITS

(S/D) 🍴 ⊃ 📶 ⊗ 📹 📠 📺 / ⊗ 🍴 /

---

## ———— WHERE TO DINE ————

### BENTLEY'S

Lunch: $6-$11      Dinner: $7-$22      Phone: 802/457-3232

American

**Location:** Center (US 4). 3 Elm St 05091. **Hours:** 11 am-9:30 pm, Fri & Sat-10 pm. Closed: 11/25, 12/25. **Features:** This is a favorite spot for locals and tourists alike, located near the Village Green. They serve traditional New England fare with the freshest of ingredients and home-style cooking. The casual decor has a hodgepodge of wall hangings and a complementary mismatch of hanging lights, charming darkwood floors and antique style lamps. Diners may have the option to sit at an antique love seat or a traditonal table and chair. Casual dress; cocktails. **Parking:** street. **Cards:** AX, DC, DS, MC, VI.

⊗

### THE JACKSON HOUSE INN & RESTAURANT   Country Inn

Dinner: $55      Phone: 802/457-2065

Continental

**Location:** 1.5 mi w of Village Green on US 4; in The Jackson House Inn & Restaurant. 114-3 Senior Ln 05091. **Hours:** 6 pm-9 pm. Closed: 1/1, 12/25; also Mon & Tues 11/1-5/31 & 1st two weeks in April. **Reservations:** suggested. **Features:** The window-filled dining room offers a serene view of the grounds that enhance the elegant and tasteful decor inside. Located near the village of Woodstock, this restaurant features exceptional dining in a lovely setting. Their Old World approach to dining combines artfully prepared food with excellent and elegant table service. Dishes are fresh, creative and flavorful. Dressy casual; cocktails. **Parking:** on-site. **Cards:** AX, MC, VI.

🍷 ⊗

### MANGOWOOD RESTAURANT   Historic

Dinner: $13-$25      Phone: 802/457-3312

Continental

**Location:** 3 mi w on US 4 from Village Green; in The Lincoln Inn at The Covered Bridge. US 4 W, 530 Woodstock Rd 05091. **Hours:** Open 5/1-4/1; 6 pm-9:30 pm. Closed: Sun & Mon. **Reservations:** suggested. **Features:** Classically trained European chefs emphasize food quality and flavor in wonderful food. The Victorian farmhouse features outstanding filet mignon, lamb chops, duck and trout entrees, as well as homemade desserts. Casual dress; cocktails. **Parking:** on-site. **Cards:** AX, DS, MC, VI.

🍷 ⊗

### MOUNTAIN CREAMERY

Lunch: $4-$7      Phone: 802/457-1715

American

**Location:** Center. 33 Center St 05091. **Hours:** 7 am-3 pm; in season take-out window open until 5 pm. Closed: 11/25, 12/25. **Features:** For those with fond memories of a soda fountain, this eatery offers a nice nostalgic retreat. Patrons can sample hand-made ice cream and homemade pastries and pies. Also on a menu of "from-scratch" items are traditional breakfast dishes and deli sandwiches. Casual dress. **Parking:** street.

⊗

**NEW ENGLAND STEAKHOUSE (FORMERLY SPOONERS)**     **Dinner:** $9-$28     **Phone:** 802/457-4022
**Location:** Just e of village center. Sunset Farm US Rt 4 E 05091. **Hours:** 5 pm-9:30 pm, Fri & Sat-10 pm. Closed: 11/25, 12/25. **Reservations:** accepted. **Features:** Located in the former Spooner Barn at Sunset Farm and built nearly a century ago, the New England Steakhouse is known for its fresh seafood which is delivered daily from the coast of New England, along with certified Angus beef dishes. Casual dress; cocktails. **Parking:** on-site. **Cards:** MC, VI.

Steak House

**THE PRINCE & THE PAUPER**     **Dinner:** $26-$33     **Phone:** 802/457-1818
**Location:** Just e of the Green; in town. 24 Elm St 05091. **Hours:** 6 pm-9 pm, Fri & Sat-9:30 pm. Closed: 11/25, 12/25. **Reservations:** suggested. **Features:** This restaurant, located just off Woodstock's main street, features very creative and flavorful entrees prepared with a local flair. The comfortable rustic atmosphere offers outdoor dining as the weather permits. This is an exceptional dining experience. Dressy casual; cocktails. **Parking:** street. **Cards:** AX, DS, MC, VI.

Continental

**WILD GRASS RESTAURANT**     **Dinner:** $13-$18     **Phone:** 802/457-1917
**Location:** On US 4, 1 mi s. Rt 4 E 05091. **Hours:** 6 pm-9 pm, Fri & Sat-9:30 pm. Closed: 11/25, 12/25. **Reservations:** suggested. **Features:** As stated on their menu, a dinner at "Wild Grass" is a "true dining experience," from the subdued lighting and ecclectic decor, to their unique presentations of classic meat and seafood dishes superbly prepared with Asian, as well as Meditterranean influences. Casual dress; cocktails. **Parking:** on-site. **Cards:** DC, DS, MC, VI.

American

**WOODSTOCK FARMERS MARKET**     **Lunch:** $4-$6     **Dinner:** $4-$6     **Phone:** 802/457-3658
**Location:** 5.6 mi w of Town Green. 468 Woodstock Rd (US Rt 4 W) 05091. **Hours:** 7:30 am-6 pm, Fri & Sat-7 pm, Sun 9 am-5 pm. Closed: 1/1, 11/25, 12/25; also Mon. **Features:** Locally popular for their wide selection of locally grown produce, fresh meats and imported wines and confections. Casual dress. **Parking:** on-site. **Cards:** AX, DS, MC, VI.

American

**WOODSTOCK INN MAIN DINING ROOM**     **Dinner:** $19-$32     **Phone:** 802/457-1100
**Location:** US 4; on the Village Green; in Woodstock Inn & Resort. 14 The Green 05091. **Hours:** 6 pm-9 pm, Sun also 10 am-1 pm. **Reservations:** suggested. **Features:** An elegant dining experience is found inside this semi-circular and window-filled room; feeling as though you have stepped back in time. Small white lights are threaded through vines and shimmer against the glass. The chef is creative and serves flavorful dishes, prepared with fresh ingredients and presented with imagination. Service is warm, professional and friendly. Dressy casual; cocktails. **Parking:** on-site. **Cards:** AX, MC, VI.

Continental

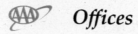 *Offices*

Cities with main offices are listed in **BOLD TYPE** and toll-free member service numbers in *ITALIC TYPE*.
All are closed Saturdays, Sundays and holidays unless otherwise indicated.

The type of service provided is designated below the name of the city where the office is located:

✦ Auto travel services, including books/maps, marked maps and on-demand Triptik maps
● Auto travel services, including books/maps, marked maps but no on-demand Triptik maps
■ Provides books/maps only. No marked maps or on-demand Triptik maps available
▲ Travel agency services

**NATIONAL OFFICE:** 1000 AAA DRIVE, HEATHROW, FLORIDA 32746-5063, (407) 444-7000

## MAINE

**AUBURN**—AAA NORTHERN NEW ENGLAND, 670 TURNER ST, 04210. MON-FRI 8:30-5, SAT 9-1. (207) 786-0664, *(800) 310-1222.*●▲

**AUGUSTA**—AAA NORTHERN NEW ENGLAND, 12 SHUMAN AVE STE 6, 04330. MON-FRI 8:30-5, SAT 9-1. (207) 622-2221, *(800) 640-5608.*●▲

**BANGOR**—AAA NORTHERN NEW ENGLAND, 339 GRIFFIN RD, 04401. MON-FRI 8:30-5, SAT 9-1. (207) 942-8287, *(800) 223-3700.*●▲

**BRUNSWICK**—AAA NORTHERN NEW ENGLAND, 147 BATH RD, 04011. MON-FRI 8:30-5, SAT 9-1. (207) 729-3300, *(800) 499-3111.*●▲

**KENNEBUNK**—AAA NORTHERN NEW ENGLAND, 169 PORT RD, 04043. MON-FRI 8:30-5, SAT 9-1. (207) 967-0222, *(800) 974-2222.*●▲

**PORTLAND**—**AAA NORTHERN NEW ENGLAND,** 68 MARGINAL WAY, 04101. MON-FRI 8:30-5, SAT 9-1. (207) 780-6800, *(800) 222-3612.*●▲

**SOUTH PORTLAND**—AAA NORTHERN NEW ENGLAND, 443 WESTERN AVE, 04106. MON-FRI 8:30-5, SAT 9-1. (207) 775-6211, *(800) 336-6211.*●▲

## NEW HAMPSHIRE

**CONCORD**—AAA NORTHERN NEW ENGLAND, TWO CAPITAL PLZ/MAIN ST, 03301. MON-FRI 8:30-5, SAT 9-1. (603) 228-0301, *(800) 222-3422.*✦▲

**KEENE**—AAA NORTHERN NEW ENGLAND, 351 WINCHESTER ST, 03431. MON-FRI 8:30-5, SAT 9-1. (603) 358-0460, *(800) 222-3407.*●▲

**MANCHESTER**—AAA NORTHERN NEW ENGLAND, 89 MARCH AVE, 03103. MON-FRI 8:30-5, SAT 9-1. (603) 669-0101.✦▲

**NASHUA**—AAA NORTHERN NEW ENGLAND, ONE TRAFALGAR SQ, 03063. MON-FRI 8:30-5, SAT 9-1. (603) 889-0165, *(800) 222-3750.*✦▲

**PORTSMOUTH**—AAA NORTHERN NEW ENGLAND, PARADE MALL, 03801. MON-FRI 8:30-5, SAT 9-1. (603) 436-8610, *(800) 222-3420.*✦▲

## VERMONT

**MONTPELIER**—AAA NORTHERN NEW ENGLAND, 317 RIVER ST, 05602. MON-FRI 8:30-5, SAT 9-1. (802) 229-0505, *(800) 717-0222.*●▲

**RUTLAND**—AAA NORTHERN NEW ENGLAND, 31 N MAIN ST, 05701. MON-FRI 8:30-5, SAT 9-1. (802) 775-1558, *(800) 388-1558.*●▲

**SOUTH BURLINGTON**—AAA NORTHERN NEW ENGLAND, 1 TAFT CORNERS SHPPNG CTR, 05495. MON-FRI 8:30-5, SAT 9-1. (802) 878-8233, *(800) 477-1323.*●▲

# Look For Savings

When you pick up a AAA TourBook® guide, look for establishments that display a bright red AAA logo, SAVE icon, and Diamond rating in their listing. These AAA Official Appointment establishments place a high value on the patronage they receive from AAA members. And, by offering members great room rates*, they are willing to go the extra mile to get your business.

So, when you turn to the AAA TourBook guide to make your travel plans, look for the establishments that will give you the special treatment you deserve.

*\* See TourBook Navigator section, page 14, for complete details.*

# GOLDEN PASSPORTS

Golden Passports, available in three types, offer benefits and significant savings to individuals who plan to visit federal recreation sites.

*The Golden Eagle Passport*, available for a **$65** annual fee, is valid for entrance only to all federal recreation areas that have an entrance fee. Sites include those operated by the National Forest Service, National Park Service, Bureau of Land Management and the U.S. Fish and Wildlife Service. The passport admits all occupants of a private vehicle at locations where entrance is on a per vehicle basis. At locations where a per person fee is charged, the pass covers the pass holder, spouse, parents and children.

Citizens or permanent residents of the United States who are 62 and older can obtain *Golden Age Passports* for a one-time **$10** fee. Proof of age is required.

*Golden Access Passports* are free to citizens or permanent residents of the United States (regardless of age) who are medically blind or permanently disabled.

Both *Golden Age* and *Golden Access passports* cover entrance fees for the holder and accompanying private party to all national parks and sites managed by the U.S. Fish and Wildlife Service, the U.S. Forest Service and the Bureau of Land Management, plus half off camping and other fees. When a per person fee is imposed, the pass covers the pass holder, spouse and children. Apply in person at a federally operated area where an entrance fee is charged.

# NATIONAL PARKS PASS

The *National Parks Pass*, valid for 1 year from its first use in a park, allows unlimited admissions to all U.S. national parks. The **$50** pass covers all occupants of a private vehicle at parks where the entrance fee is per vehicle. At parks with individual entry fees, the pass covers the pass holder, spouse, parents and children.

As a result of a partnership with the National Park Foundation, AAA members may purchase the pass for **$48**, either through AAA's internet site (www.aaa.com) or by visiting a participating AAA office. Members may also phone the National Park Foundation at **(888) 467-2757** or purchase the pass online at www.nationalparks.org. Non-members may purchase the pass through participating AAA offices for the full **$50** price or online at www.nationalparks.org.

For an upgrade fee of **$15**, a Golden Eagle hologram sticker can be added to a *National Parks Pass*. The hologram covers entrance fees not just at national parks, but at any federal recreation area that has an admission fee. Valid for the duration of the *National Parks Pass* to which it is affixed, the Golden Eagle hologram is available at National Park Service, Fish and Wildlife Service and Bureau of Land Management fee stations.

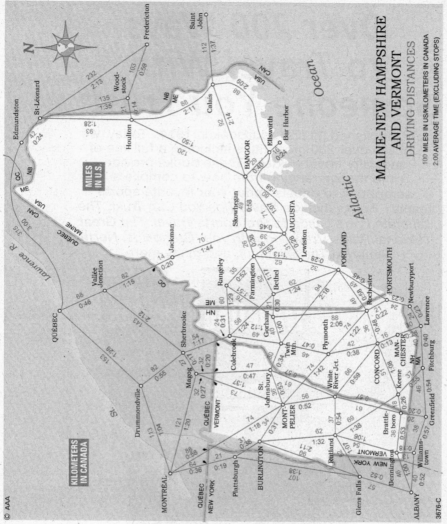

# Know Your Future

# SAVE *Attraction Admission Discount Index*

# AMERICA ON THE MOVE
## A NEW EXHIBITION ON TRANSPORTATION IN AMERICAN HISTORY

Smithsonian
*National Museum of American History*
*Behring Center*

# Points of Interest Index

## Index Legend

| | |
|---|---|
| NB. | national battlefield |
| NBP. | national battlefield park |
| NC. | national cemetery |
| NF. | national forest |
| NHM. | national historic(al) monument |
| NHP. | national historic(al) park |
| NHS. | national historic(al) site |
| NL. | national lakeshore |
| NME. | national memorial |
| NMO. | national monument |
| NMP. | national military park |
| NP. | national park |
| NRA. | national recreation area |
| NR. | national river |
| NS. | national seashore |
| NWR. | national wildlife refuge |
| PHP. | provincial historic(al) park |
| PHS. | provincial historic(al) site |
| PP. | provincial park |
| SF. | state forest |
| SHM. | state historic(al) monument |
| SHP. | state historic(al) park |
| SHS. | state historic(al) site |
| SME. | state memorial |
| SP. | state park |
| SRA. | state recreation area |

▽ GEM: Points of Interest Offering a *Great Experience for Members*®

## MUSIC HALLS & OPERA HOUSES

## NATURAL PHENOMENA

## NATURE CENTERS

## NATURE TRAILS

## OBSERVATORIES

## PAINTINGS

## PARKS, CITY; STATE; PROVINCIAL

## PARKS, NATIONAL

## PLANETARIUMS

## RACETRACKS-AUTO

## RACETRACKS-HORSE

## RAILROADS

## RAILROADS-LOCOMOTIVES & CARS

## RAILROADS & SKI LIFTS, CABLE; COG; INCLINE;

## NARROW GAUGE

## RANCHES

## RECREATION-SUMMER ACTIVITIES

## RECREATION-WINTER ACTIVITIES

## RELIGIOUS COLONIES

## RESEARCH ORGANIZATIONS

## RESTORED VILLAGES & SETTLEMENTS

## RIVERS

## ROCKS

## SCENIC DRIVES

## SCHOOL BUILDINGS

## SCHOOLS

## SCHOOLS-ACADEMIES

## WALKING TOURS

## WATERFALLS

## WATER PARKS

## WILDERNESS AREAS

## WILDLIFE SANCTUARIES

## WINERIES

## ZOOLOGICAL PARKS & EXHIBITS

## ZOOLOGICAL PARKS & EXHIBITS-CHILDREN'S ZOOS

# Border Information

## FOR CANADIAN RESIDENTS ENTERING THE UNITED STATES

**PASSPORTS** to enter the United States or return to Canada are not required for native-born citizens of either country. However, **a Canadian passport remains the best internationally accepted evidence of Canadian citizenship and its use is strongly suggested.** Proof of citizenship must be carried; a certified birth certificate, accompanied by a photo ID will usually suffice. Proof of residence also may be required. Unmarried parents who share custody of children should carry copies of the legal custody documents.

**UNITED STATES CUSTOMS** permits you to bring, free of duty, for personal use and not intended for sale: clothing, personal effects and equipment appropriate to the trip. Personal effects may include 200 cigarettes *or* 50 cigars *or* 4.4 pounds (2 kgs) of smoking tobacco *or* proportionate amounts of each, and 1 litre of alcoholic beverage. **Cuban cigars are denied entry.**

If you are planning to be in the United States **at least 72 hours,** you may bring gifts up to a fair retail value of $100 (U.S.), provided you have not claimed this exemption within the preceding 6 months. Family members may not combine their gift exemptions. Perfume containing alcohol and valued at more than $5 retail, tobacco products (except for 100 cigars) and alcoholic beverages are excluded from the gift provision.

**RADIO COMMUNICATION EQUIPMENT:** You may use your Family Radio Service (FRS) radio and cellular phone in the United States without any restrictions.

## RETURNING TO CANADA

**CANADIAN CUSTOMS** allows you to bring, free of duty and taxes, goods valued up to $200 (Canadian) any number of times per year, provided you have been in the United States **48 hours or more.** All goods must accompany you; a written declaration may be required.

You may claim a $50 (Canadian) exemption on goods, excluding alcoholic beverages and tobacco products, if you are returning after an absence of **24 hours or more** and are not using any other exemption. If more than $50 worth of goods are brought back, the regular rate of duty and taxes will be levied on the entire value. This exemption may apply any number of times in a year.

If you are returning after **7 days or more** in the United States (not counting the day of departure from Canada), you may claim an exemption on goods valued up to $750 (Canadian). Goods, other than alcohol and tobacco products, are not required to accompany you; a written declaration may be required.

Permitted within the $200 and $750 exemptions are up to 50 cigars, 200 cigarettes, 200 tobacco sticks and 7 ounces (200 gm) of tobacco and up to 40 ounces (1.14 L) of liquor *or* 1.6 quarts (1.5 L) of wine *or* 9 quarts (8.5 L) of beer and/or ale (or its equivalent of 24 twelve-ounce bottles or cans). You must meet the minimum age requirement of the province entered to claim alcohol or tobacco products. Northwest Territories and Nunavut do not allow you to bring in more than the duty-free allowance of alcohol.

There is nothing to prevent you from importing any quantity of goods, even if you do not qualify for any kind of personal exemption, provided the goods you are importing are not restricted and you pay the full rate of duty and taxes

**Special Tariff:** When you exceed your $200 or $750 exemptions, a special rate of 7 percent combined duty and taxes is levied on the next $300 value in goods (except tobacco and alcohol) in excess of maximum exemptible amounts, provided the goods are of U.S. origin. Regular duties apply on any amount over that. For detailed information concerning specific duty rates, consult Canadian Customs before leaving on your trip.

All exemptions are individual and may not be combined with those of another person. You may be asked to verify the length of your visit; dated receipts normally constitute proof.

**GIFTS** to the value of $60 (Canadian) may be sent from abroad, free of duty or taxes. These may not include alcoholic beverages, tobacco products or advertising matter. Gifts valued at over $60 (Canadian) are subject to duty and taxes on the amount in excess of $60. Gifts sent from abroad do not count against your personal exemption, but gifts brought back must be included as part of your exemption.

# Bed & Breakfast Lodgings Index

Some bed and breakfasts listed below might have historical significance. Those properties are also referenced in the Historical index. The indication that continental [CP] or full breakfast [BP] is included in the room rate reflects whether a property is a Bed-and-Breakfast facility.

## BED & BREAKFAST LODGINGS (CONT'D)

### VERMONT

#### ACCOMMODATIONS

# Country Inns Index

Some of the following country inns can also be considered as bed-and-breakfast operations. The indication that continental [CP] or full breakfast [BP] is included in the room rate reflects whether a property is a Bed-and-Breakfast facility.

### MAINE

#### ACCOMMODATIONS

#### RESTAURANTS

### NEW HAMPSHIRE

#### ACCOMMODATIONS

# Historical Lodgings & Restaurants Index

Some of the following historical lodgings can also be considered as bed-and-breakfast operations. The indication that continental [CP] or full breakfast [BP] is included in the room rate reflects whether a property is a Bed-and-Breakfast facility.

## MAINE

## Resorts Index

Many establishments are located in resort areas; however, the following places have extensive on-premises recreational facilities:

# Look For Savings

When you pick up a AAA TourBook® guide, look for establishments that display a bright red AAA logo, 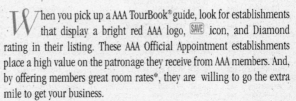 icon, and Diamond rating in their listing. These AAA Official Appointment establishments place a high value on the patronage they receive from AAA members. And, by offering members great room rates*, they are willing to go the extra mile to get your business.

So, when you turn to the AAA TourBook guide to make your travel plans, look for the establishments that will give you the special treatment you deserve.

*See TourBook Navigator section, page 14, for complete details.*

# Comprehensive City Index

Here is an alphabetical list of all cities appearing in this TourBook® guide. Cities are presented by state/province. Page numbers under the POI column indicate where points of interest text begins. Page numbers under the L&R column indicate where lodging and restaurant listings begin.

## Comprehensive City Index (cont'd)

# COMPREHENSIVE CITY INDEX (CONT'D)

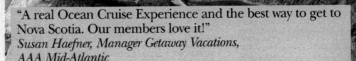